D1179471

Russian-English Translator's Dictionary

A Guide to Scientific and Technical Usage

Third Edition

Русско–английский научно–технический словарь переводчика

Михаил Циммерман
Клавдия Веденеева

Russian-English Translator's Dictionary

A Guide to Scientific and Technical Usage

Third Edition

Mikhail Zimmerman
Claudia Vedeneeva

NAUKA PUBLISHERS
Moscow

JOHN WILEY & SONS
Chichester · New York · Brisbane
Toronto · Singapore

Second English edition published by John Wiley & Sons Ltd., 1984.

First English edition published by Plenum Press, a division of Plenum Publishing Corporation, New York, by arrangement with Mezhdunarodnaya Kniga 1967.

Other Wiley Editorial Offices

John Wiley & Sons, Inc., 605 Third Avenue,
New York, NY 10158-0012, USA

Jacaranda Wiley Ltd, G.P.O. Box 859, Brisbane,
Queensland 4001, Australia

John Wiley & Sons (Canada) Ltd, 22 Worcester Road,
Rexdale, Ontario M9W 1L1, Canada

John Wiley & Sons (SEA) Pte Ltd, 37 Jalan Pemimpin #05-04,
Block B, Union Industrial Building, Singapore 2057

Library of Congress Cataloging-in-Publication Data

Zimmerman, Mikhail.
Russian–English translator's dictionary : a guide to scientific and technical usage / Mikhail Zimmerman, Claudia Vedeneeva.—3rd ed.
p. cm.
Title on added t.p.: Russko-angliĭskiĭ nauchno-tekhnicheskiĭ slovar ' perevodchika.
ISBN 0 471 93316 3
1. Science—Dictionaries—Russian. 2. Engineering—Dictionaries–Russian. 3. Russian language—Dictionaries—English.
I. Vedeneeva, Claudia. II. Title. III. Title: Russko-angliĭskiĭ nauchno-tekhnicheskiĭ slovar ' perevodchika.
Q123.Z55 1992
503—dc20 92-319
CIP

British Library Cataloguing in Publication Data

A catalogue record for this book is available from the British Library

ISBN 0 471 93316 3

Typeset in the USSR by Nauka Publishers
Printed and bound in Great Britain by Biddles Ltd, Guildford, Surrey

To the undying memory of Milla Callaham,
our dear teacher and beloved friend,
queen of Russian-English lexicology

PREFACE TO THE FIRST EDITION

When a translator of scientific and technical literature from Russian into English seeks the counterpart of some specialized term he turns to a dictionary or an original source in English. But terms are not the whole problem. They must be couched in the language of the particular branch of science or technology. A translation should be free of unidiomatic or amateurish passages. "The right word in the right place" is the translators' motto.

The present dictionary is an attempt to supply word combinations and expressions that may be of help in achieving this aim. It is not a dictionary of terms or idioms, but a collection of typical examples from scientific and technical sources. The words that make up the combinations are usually common to a number of branches of science and technology. The remaining words of illustrative context are not so important since they are only meant as "fillers" to link the combination elements together. The user's attention should be focussed on the words in bold type.

The system of arrangement is strictly alphabetical (hyphenated combinations are considered as one word), but there are many cross-references to assist the user. These are given merely for general guidance and the translator should not confine himself to the item referred to, but should examine carefully the entry in question and several adjacent entries. Synonymous words or expressions are given in brackets.

Whenever you fail to find the Russian combination you need, think of possible synonyms. Practical experience has demonstrated the expediency of this method.

The compilation of the dictionary took seven years. Since this was the first experiment of its kind numerous difficulties arose and quite a few questions remained unanswered. I realised that many more years would be needed to bring the job to a state anywhere near completion, and in a moment of weakness I was on the verge of dropping it altogether. It was L.E. Levant, head of the English Department of Mir Publishers, who persuaded me to have the book published there and then and took the job into his own hands. For this I will always be grateful to him.

I wish to express my deep appreciation to my conscientious and strict editor G. Yankovsky, who possesses a perfect command of his native English, has for many years been working in Russian-English lexicography, and is an experienced scientific and technical translator. Thanks are also due to my friends and colleagues at the English Department of Mir Publishers who supplied me with some useful expressions. Most helpful and enthusiastic assistance was given by N. Weinstein, our top translator in the field of mechanical engineering.

M.G. Zimmerman

PREFACE TO THE SECOND EDITION

After the first edition of the Dictionary was published in 1966 I devoted another 15 years to scrutinizing the latest English and American scientific and technical books and magazines, enlarging and updating the text. Seeking out new phrases became more difficult each year, because the old ones repeated with astounding regularity. Finally I had twice as many items as before, and a second edition became a matter of urgency. Numerous requests from translators added coals to the fire, and I got down to putting the book in shape.

In all my work I was guided by the shining example of Mrs. Ludmilla Ignatiev Callaham, author of the world-famous Russian-English Chemical and Polytechnical Dictionary, who constantly encouraged me by letter and by word. With her book (which our translators tenderly refer to as Ludmilla) always on my desk I never failed to make a good living by translation. My friends and fellow translators Nick Weinstein and Valeri Agranat have made important contributions to my card file, and George Koval supplied me lavishly with invaluable literature. I am deeply grateful to them. The Wiley team have been extremely cooperative and made every possible effort at improving, promoting and publishing the Dictionary up to the best modern standards.

I hope this edition will prove more effective in helping the translator to surmount the numerous difficulties facing him in his arduous work.

M.G. Zimmerman, Moscow, USSR

PREFACE TO THE THIRD EDITION

No dictionary can catch up with the rapid development of science and technology, particularly in the computer area. In an attempt to fill the gap, at least partly, this third and final edition was conceived.

Considering my age, I found the job difficult and therefore invited my wife, Claudia Vedeneeva, to cooperate. I knew that with her knowledge and thorough approach we could pull the job successfully.

We wish to thank Svetlana Osipova and Dmitri Zaidin, who gave us a helping hand with some of the latest English and American scientific and technical books.

M. G. Zimmerman

РУССКИЙ АЛФАВИТ			АНГЛИЙСКИЙ АЛФАВИТ		
А а	К к	Х х	A a	J j	S s
Б б	Л л	Ц ц	B b	K k	T t
В в	М м	Ч ч	C c	L l	U u
Г г	Н н	Ш ш	D d	M m	V v
Д д	О о	Щ щ	E e	N n	W w
Е е	П п	Ъ ъ	F f	O o	X x
Ё ё	Р р	Ы ы	G g	P p	Y y
Ж ж	С с	Ь ь	H h	Q q	Z z
З з	Т т	Э э	I i	R r	
И и	У у	Ю ю			
Й й	Ф ф	Я я			

СПИСОК СОКРАЩЕНИЙ

авиа.	авиация	Aviation
автотр.	автотранспорт	Motor transport
анат.	анатомия	Anatomy
антон.	антоним	Antonym
астр.	астрономия	Astronomy
биол.	биология	Biology
геол.	геология	Geology
крист.	кристаллография	Crystallography
матем.	математика	Mathematics
машстр.	машиностроение	Mechanical engineering
опт.	оптика	Optics
син.	синоним	Synonym
см.	смотри	See
см. тж.	смотри также	See also
с. х.	сельское хозяйство	Agriculture
физ.	физика	Physics
хим.	химия	Chemistry
эл.	электротехника	Electrical engineering

А

А [*см. тж.* **В то время как**]
Note that Condition (1) is equivalent to stability, **whereas** (*or* **while**) Condition (2) can always be satisfied by scaling.

А вместе с ним и
The positive charge will be reduced, **and with it** the coulombic attraction for the ligand.

А именно
The movement itself gives rise to a second field, **namely,** the magnetic field.

А как насчёт
What of the vast masses of granite now between the remnants? How and when did they originate?

А может быть и [*см. тж.* **Если не**]
In such circumstances collaborative tests become very important **if not** essential.
The only explanation is that some variable components of a quasar, **if not** the entire quasar, may be not much larger than the solar system.

А на самом деле это не так
The alternating double and single bonds should be of different lengths, **which they are not.**

А не
These deviations may be manifested in the form of an accelerating **instead of** a decelerating wave.
Under such circumstances, the two donor atoms on the same chelate molecule coordinate with different metal atoms **rather than** with one; thus, a polymeric chain may result **rather than** [*or* (**and**) **not**] a ring structure.
Since the various types of microscope supply different kinds of information, they complement each other **rather than** competing.
That means that the laser beam is elliptical **instead of** round.
The resulting *F*-band is dependent upon the particular alkali halide used, **not** upon the alkali metal vapour.

А не на
Most of the energy goes into heating the bulk gas **instead of** (*or* **and not**) into promoting the desired reactions.

А не наоборот
It is much more likely that the motion of the lithospheric plate governs the flow of convection currents in the asthenosphere, **rather than** (*or* **and not**) **the reverse** (*geol.*).

А не только
All air must be heated, **and not just** the small fraction that contributes to the formation of the product.

А пока
We shall revert to this subject in a later paragraph; **for the moment** we assume that ...
We will learn how to develop such equations in the next chapter; **for now,** we may rely on a set of tabulated equations given in Appendix *D*.
The *rms* speed is different from ...; **for the present,** the value of $\sqrt{\bar{u}}$ will be taken as indicative of ...

For the time being, draw all plate boundaries as single lines, without any distinction as to the type of boundary each represents.

А потому и [*см.* **И, следовательно**].

А, следовательно, и [*см. тж.* **И, следовательно**]
Supercharging increases cylinder weight charge **and consequently** (*or* **thus,** *or* **hence**) power output.

А также [*см. тж.* **Вместе с; Как и; Так же, как и**]
This detector is highly selective **as well as** sensitive.
Absorption bands arise in the ultraviolet **as well as in** the visible portion of the spectrum when ...
Ethanol and sulphuric acid always react to yield a mixture of ethylene, ethyl hydrogen sulphate, and diethyl ether, **along with** a few minor by-products.
Cadmium-coated articles should not be used in contact with food, **nor** should cadmium-plated articles be welded or used in ovens.
Aluminium hydroxide can react with a strong base **as well as with** acids (*or* **and also with** acids, *or* **and with** acids **too**).
This fact **combined** (*or* **coupled,** *or* **together**) **with** the absence of ... led to some confusion.
The collenchyma cell wall is composed of cellulose and pectic compounds **plus** a very high proportion of water.
These are chiefly nickel and arsenic, **together with** smaller amounts of other elements.

А также не
The structure is not reciprocal, **nor (is it)** anti-reciprocal.
The rocks were not hydrated, **nor was there** any retention of CO_2.
As a rule, microspheres do not show a capacity for concentrating materials, **nor do** they possess the ability to ...

Абсолютно [*см. тж.* **Вообще, Совершенно**]
The comet tail is almost **perfectly** (*or* **absolutely**) transparent.
These techniques were **totally** unknown at the time.

Абсолютно все [*см.* **Все без исключения**].

Абсолютно не встречая сопротивления
The free electrons are able to move through the crystal lattice **without any resistance whatsoever.**

Абсолютно не соответствовать
Then anxiety assumes a significance which **is out of all proportion to** the actual size of the problem.

Абсолютно отличаться от [*см. тж.* **В корне отличаться от**]
Totally different from the conventional machine is the Photon typesetter.
The truth was **vastly different** and more complex than the dreams of the science-fiction writers.

Абсолютно ясно
One thing **is abundantly** (*or* **quite,** *or* **absolutely**) **clear:** we do not know how to predict ...

Абсолютный [*см.* **В полной темноте**].

Абсорбировать
Because of their tendency to **take up** (*or* **absorb**) oxygen, solutions of sulphurous acid almost invariably contain sulphate ions.

Абсорбироваться
The nitrate **is taken up** (*or* **absorbed**) **by** the plants.

Аварийная остановка
There must be provision for **emergency stopping** of the machine.

Аварийная ситуация
To shut a reactor down in **an emergency,** ...

Аварийный [*см.* **Запасной**].

Аварийный ремонт
Both periodic and **casualty** (*or* **emergency**) **repairs** ...

Авария [*см.* **Безаварийный**].

Автоматизированный
Automated inspection ...

Автоматический
An **automatic(ally operated)** direction finder ...

Автоматическое (*или* **Автоматизированное) оборудование**
Automated equipment.

Автомобилестроение [*см.* **В области автомобилестроения**].

Автомобильный
Automotive fuel (pumps, etc.).

Авторитет
Professor B. is **an authority on** radiobiology.

Авторитетный
Expert (*or* **Authoritative**) information ...

Автором которого является [*см.* **Выведенный**].

Автором является [*см.* **Выведенный, Принадлежать**].

Адсорбироваться на
The molecules **are adsorbed on** (*or* **by**) the catalyst.

Ажиотаж [*см.* **Вызывать значительный ажиотаж**].

Азот воздуха
Nitrogen oxides result from the reaction of **atmospheric nitrogen** (*or* **nitrogen of the air**) with oxygen.

Активно заниматься
Many geologists **have been deeply involved in** this research.

Активно участвовать в
We were too busy **to take an active part in** the new venture.

Актуальнейший
The study of this aspect is one of **the "hottest"** (*sl.*) areas in current research.

Актуальный
The above account outlines the **topical** (*or* **urgent,** *or* **currently central,** *or* **pressing,** *or* **burning**) problems.

Алгебраические выкладки
To avoid much **algebraic manipulation,** we used a simple shortcut method.

Алгебраическое действие над
Algebraic operations on numbers of ...

Алфавитный порядок [*см.* **В алфавитном порядке**].

Амбулаторные условия [*см.* **В амбулаторных условиях**].

Амортизировать удар [*см.* **Воспринимать удар, Предохранять от ударов**].

Анализ
Satisfactory **analysis** (*or* **assay**) can be performed (*or* **made,** *or* **done**) on these samples.
Blood **examination.**
This may be determined from an **analysis** of moonrock.
Test (*or* **Analysis**) **for** alkalinity (*or* **for** beryllium) ...
Medical **tests** (*such as* **specimen analyses**) ...
Urinalysis (***an*** **analysis of urine**) ...

Анализ на присутствие
This compound is used **to test for the presence of** glucosamine.

Анализировать
To analyze the blood **for** malaria, ...
The samples **were analyzed for** lactic acid.
Mouse interferon mRNA **was assayed** biologically.

Анализируемый [*см. тж.* **Подлежащий анализу**]
The substance (**to be,** *or* **being**) **analyzed** ...

Аналогичен [*см. тж.* **Весьма аналогичен**]
This multiplier **is identical in** design **to** (*or* **with**) the first.
The shock waves **are analogous to** the surface waves.
This equation **is similar** (*or* **akin**) **to** Eq. 3.

Аналогичен по конструкции
The apparatus **is similar in design to** that described elsewhere.

Аналогичен по (своему)
Comparators that depend on contact **are similar** (*or* **analogous**) **in** physical arrangement.

Аналогично [*см. тж.* **Совершенно аналогично**]
In a similar (*or* **like**) **manner** (*or* **Along similar lines**), design equations may be derived from the general formula.
This type of door can be folded **in a manner like** the operation of the camera bellows.
The device would operate **in much the same way** (*or* **manner,** *or* **fashion**) **as** (*or* **similarly,** *or* **analogously, to**) a core array.

The retina cells transform the light image into a spatial pattern of electrical signals, **much as** a television camera does.
Gases behave **similarly** (*or* **in a similar way**) in all directions.
The components of strain are specified **in a similar way to** the stresses.

Аналогично тому, как
The lines of force represent the strength of the field, **much as** the lines on a geologist's map represent the height of the land.

Аналогично этому
In a like (*or* **similar**) **manner** (*or* **Similarly**), the length of a crossed belt is cut down accordingly.

Аналогичного размера
We have found **similar-sized** intermediates for both ribosomal particles.

Аналогичного характера
Proteins **of a similar nature** have now been isolated.

Аналогичные [*см.* **Близкие (друг к другу)**].

Аналогичные рассуждения приводят к выводу о том, что
Similar reasoning shows that ...

Аналогичный
This is something **akin to** the previously described model.
To have analogy to (*or* **with**) ...
Kindred pumping services are grouped together wherever possible with a common driving unit.
The carrier and the cruiser will be powered by **like** plants.
Like atoms are at minimum separations.
Later trials subjected glucose to **like** temperatures.
Related work on two-photon ionization of NA_2 and BaCl beams was carried out by...
Related bimolecular reactions show the same result.
A **related** explanation has been advanced for ...
Elements with **similar** (*or* **analogous**) properties...
Another suggestion **along similar lines** is that ...

Аналогичный по химическому составу
A **chemically similar** body of water would appear to be a likely environment.

Аналогичным образом [*см. тж.* **Точно так же**]
Micelles also have been explored **along comparable** (*or* **similar**) **lines.**
In an analogous way [*or* **Analogously,** *or* **Likewise,** *or* **In a similar way** (*or* **manner,** *or* **fashion**), *or* **Similarly**] it is sometimes useful to consider alternatives.
Aliphatic hydrocarbons containing a large number of double bonds are named **in analogous** (*or* **similar**) **fashion.**
In a similar spirit it is easy to prove that ...
Gases behave approximately **in a like manner.**

Аналогия [*см. тж.* **По аналогии**]
A common **analogy to** the above-mentioned effect is given by ...
The analogy with (*or* **The similarity to**) helium is fairly close.
The **parallels between** electrical and magnetic phenomena ...

Аннулировать
We compute rotation matrices that approximately **undo** the effect of the sensor position.

Анод [*см.* **На катоде**].

Апогей [*см.* В **апогее**].

Аппаратура
Temperatures in electrical **apparatus ...**

Аргумент [*см.* **Приводить аргумент**].

Арифметическое действие
This requires thousands of **arithmetic operations.**

Армированный стекловолокном
Fiberglass-reinforced polyester (*or* Polyester **reinforced with fiberglass**) withstands years of use.

Аспект
The laboratory workers revealed another interesting **facet** (*or* **aspect**) of this reaction.

Ассортимент [*см. тж.* **Большой выбор**]
Ferric oxides are available in a broad **range of** particle sizes and shapes.
We have a wide **variety** (*or* **assortment,** *or* **choice,** *or* **selection**) **of** standard packages.
The physiotherapist can try out the full **range of** aids and appliances.

Атмосфера [*см. тж.* **В верхних слоях атмосферы, Верхние слои атмосферы, Выбрасывать в атмосферу**]
World-wide pollution of **the atmosphere** is a threat to life.

Атмосферное влияние [*см.* **Воздействие атмосферы**].

Атмосферное давление [*см.* **Находиться под атмосферным давлением**].

Атмосферные условия [*см.* **Находиться под действием атмосферных условий**].

Атомы, расположенные в узлах
The atoms embedded at specific **sites** in the lattice of a crystal.

Б

База [*см.* **Подводить базу под теорию**].

Балл [*см.* **Землетрясение в 8 баллов**].

Баллистическая траектория
Nonpowered phase (*or* **Coasting**).
Ballistic trajectory [*or* **flight path** (*or* **course**)].

Баллистический полёт [*см.* **Свободный полет**].

Барботировать
To bubble the gas **through** the solution, ...

Барьер для
There is an energy **barrier to** rotation.

Батарея
An **array of** photomultiplier tubes is directed at the night sky.
A **bank of** capacitors (*or* counters, etc.) ...

Беглое ознакомление
Even a **cursory examination** showed that the samples were of histological thinness.

Беден [*см. тж.* **Богат**]
The sample **was lean** (*or* **low,** *or* **poor,** *or* **deficient) in** carbon 13.
The Moon **is low in** sodium and potassium.

Беден кобальтом
In these countries **a cobalt deficiency exists** in the soil and natural vegetation.

Беден электронами
Carbonium ions **are electron deficient.**

Бедная растительность
The area is characterized by **scanty vegetation.**

Бедный [*см. тж.* **Богатый**]
Metal-**poor** clusters ...

Бедный кислородом
An **oxygen-poor** (*or* **-deficient**) environment was a major obstacle in the path of...

Без [*см. тж.* **Минус, Не содержащий**]
Figure 10 shows the energy level diagram for a semiconductor *p-n* junction **with no** applied potential.
Transmission yielding excellent quality television pictures was also made **with** the transmitter lens **removed.**
Now, **with** both the zeroth- and first order terms **missing,** the control system is unstable.
The drag **exclusive of** (*or* **minus,** *or* **less**) the induced drag of the aircraft can now be estimated.
The shank must be **free of** burrs (*or* must **be** burr **free**).
A rubber sheet **free of** pinholes is required.
The lapping tool, **minus** the handle, is inserted into the opening.

Без аварий [*см.* **Безаварийный**].

Без видимой причины
Such attacks occur in older people and occasionally **for no apparent reason.**

Без вреда для [*см. тж.* **Без ущерба для**]
This part can be omitted **without damage to** the study of plate tectonics.
This compound can be added **without destroying** the superb qualities of this glass.
The gas can be breathed for a short time **without ill** (*or* **adverse**) **effects to** man.

Без герметической оболочки
Never take a **naked** light into a fuel-oil tank.

Без движения
Fouling arises when the propeller **is stationary** (*or* **idle**) for long periods.

Без дефектов
The objective glass must **be flawless.**

Без доказательства
If this simplification is accepted **without proof, ...**

Без допплеровского смещения (уширения)
Doppler-free techniques have been developed for ...

Без доступа солнечного света
H_2O_2 must be stored **away from sunlight.**

Без единого
The atom crosses the chamber **without a single** collision.

Без затрат
Both raw materials can be conveniently obtained directly from the atmosphere **without cost.**

Без затруднений
The mean orbital velocity can be calculated **without trouble** (*or* **difficulty**) by taking...

Без изменения [*см. тж.* **Не меняя, Оставаться без изменений**]
These molecules are not utilized and pass through the body essentially **intact.**
Doubling the volume **with** (*or* **for**) **no change of** mass...
Nearly all the photons pass through **unaffected** (*or* **unaltered**, *or* **unchanged**).

Без искажения
In that case the angle of ninety degrees is projected **in its true value** on the corresponding plane.

Без искажения размеров и формы
The resolved **true size and shape** quadrilaterals can be constructed by the above method.

Без исключения
For Σ to be true it must hold **without exception** for all points s belonging to the set S.

Без использования [*см. тж.* **Не прибегая к**]
The engine is run at its optimum speed **without recourse** (*or* **resort**) **to** variable blading.

Без колебания
I recommend this book **without reservation.**

Без конца [*см. тж.* **Безгранично, Бесконечно**]
We can start the series 3, 4, 5, and so on **endlessly.**

Без нагрузки
The discharge pressure varies from a maximum **at no load** to ...
Starting a motor **under no-load conditions** ...

Без нарушения допусков [*см.* **Деталь, изготовленная без нарушения допусков**].

Без необходимости
This **needlessly** restricts the maximum allowable sample-cell length.

Без облицовки
Unlined ducts...
Ducts **unlined with** insulating materials ...

Без обработки
Much of the gravel is used **"as is"** (*col.*) for building roads.

Без обслуживающего персонала
An **unmanned** factory ...
The installation can be operated **without attention** (*or* **unattended**).

Без оптического прибора [*см.* **Видимый невооружённым глазом**].

Без помех из-за
This permits most metals to be deposited **without interference from** hydrogen evolution.

Без последствий [*см.* **Безболезненно**].

Без потери общности
Coulomb friction can be considered as an extended load **without (the) loss of** (*or* **in**) **generality.**

Без примеси [*см.* **Беспримесный**].

Без проскальзывания [*см.* **Без скольжения**].

Без разрушения образца
Nondestructive testing...

Без риска
When the shield is raised, the operator can **safely** remove and load work.

Без скольжения
This motion can be represented as two circular cones rolling on each other **without slip(ping)**.

Без смазки [*см. тж.* **Всухую, Обрабатывать всухую**]

The disk clutch may be operated **dry** or wet.

Без сомнения [*см.* **Наверняка**].

Без соприкосновения с воздухом
The purpose of the process is to melt, cast, and tap the metal **out of contact with air.**

Без трещин
A new group of **crack-free** coatings is on the way.

Без указания
Surface resistivity is expressed in ... **without specifying** the dimensions of ...

Без учёта [*см. тж.* **Учёт, Учитывать**]
It is difficult to estimate the water solubilities **without considering** additional factors.
An electronic circuit is assembled on a board **without regard for** final locations of components.

Без ущерба для [*см. тж.* **Без вреда для**]
The mandrel's light weight was achieved **without sacrifice of** precision.
These advantages of the sealant are obtained **without sacrificing** its valuable properties.

Без царапин
A scratch-free (*or* **An unscratched**) surface is obtained.

Безаварийная работа
Trouble-free service (*or* **operation**).

Безаварийно
To fly an airplane **safely** (*or* **trouble free**), ...

Безаварийный
These nuclear installations are **accident proof** (*or* **trouble free**).

Безболезненно
Such final control elements cannot be ignored **without serious consequences.**

Безграничен
There is no limit to the number of bosons that can occupy a single state.

Безгранично [*см. тж.* **Бесконечно, Неограниченно**]
The density cannot increase **without limit** (*or* **unboundedly**).

Безгранично расширять знания о
These data **have added immeasurably to knowledge of** star birth.

Безграничные возможности
Boundless opportunities.

Безграничный
Then the technological potential of superconductivity would be almost **unbounded.**

Безопасное обращение с
The safe handling of fluorine ...

Безопасное расстояние от [*см.* **На безопасном расстоянии от**].

Безопасный [*см.* **Безаварийный**].

Безопасный уровень [*см.* **Снижаться до безопасного уровня**].

Безотказный
Modern material(s) handling devices must be more **trouble free** (*or* **reliable**) than ever before.

Безразлично [*см. тж.* **Не иметь значения**]
It does not matter whether we are cooling or heating.

Безрезультатно
Helmholtz had tried a different experiment **with null** (*or* **without**) **results.**

Безрезультатный [*см.* **Оставаться безрезультатным**].

Безрельсовый
The automobile is a four-wheeled, **trackless** self-propelled vehicle.

Безрессорный
Unsprung (*or* **Without springs**).

Безупречный [*см.* **Без дефектов**].

Безусловно [*см.* **Бесспорно самый лучший, Бесспорно самый распространённый**].

Безуспешный [*см.* **Не увенчаться успехом, Не удаваться**].

Берег [*см.* **Вблизи берега, На берегу, Недалеко от побережья**].

Берег, изрезанный фьордами
A fiorded coast.

Береговой
Shore-side supervisory engineers ...
Coastal weather stations ...
Onshore drilling rigs ...

Бесконечно [*см. тж.* **Безгранично**]
Dissolved solids can travel downstream **indefinitely** and may reach the ocean.
Chain reactions do not continue **indefinitely.**

Бесконечно велик
The energy of the particle would be **infinitely high.**

Бесконечно далёкий
An **infinitely distant** object ...

Бесконечно малая величина
An **infinitesimal** (*or* **infinitesimally small**) **quantity.**

Бесконечно малый
An **infinitesimal** (*or* **infinitely small**) change in ...

Бесконечно разбавленный раствор
An **infinitely dilute solution.**

Бесконечное число членов
A set with an **infinity** (*or* **infinitely large number**) **of members ...**

Бесконечной протяжённости
A magnetic field **of infinite extent ...**

Бесконечность [*см. тж.* **До бесконечности, На бесконечности, Стремиться к бесконечности**]
The potential energy is taken as zero **for** (*or* **as,** *or* **with,** *or* **when**) $a \to \infty$ ...

Бесконечный
There are an **infinite** number of equations that would ...

Бесконечных размеров
The wave is **infinite in size** (*or* **of infinite size**).

Бесперебойно
The machine operates **trouble free.**
The battery can deliver enormous surges of power **without fail.**

Беспокойство [*см. тж.* **Вызывать беспокойство, Выражать беспокойство относительно**]
One cannot take the global view of pollutants without feeling some **concern about** the rate of use of natural resources.

Беспокойство населения по поводу загрязнения окружающей среды
The act reflects **the** growing **public concern over the environment.**

Бесполезен для
Until this transition occurred, such an enzyme would be **useless to** the organism.
Otherwise the pigment will be **of no use for** getting spectral data.

Бесполезная трата
This will be **a waste of** laser power.

Бесполезно [*см. тж.* **Не иметь смысла, Не приводить ни к чему**]
It is (of) no use (*or* **It serves no purpose,** *or* **It is useless**) **to** install a highly efficient pump if...

Беспорядочно
A second possibility is that newly made proteins are simply inserted **at random** into a pre-existing membrane.
Randomly packed beds of uniform spheres are used.
The errors fluctuate **in a random manner.**

Беспорядочно двигающийся
Randomly moving particles...

Беспорядочно расположенные
An ensemble of 50 **randomly positioned** (*or* **arranged**) bodies ...

Беспорядочно расположены
The molecules in liquid water **are** quite **randomly arranged.**

Беспорядочное движение
The molecules move around in constant, **erratic** (*or* **chaotic**, *or* **random**) **movement** (*or* **motion**).

Беспрепятственно
The particles so vapourized fly **unimpeded** (*or* **unhindered**, *or* **unobstructed**) to the walls of the chamber.

Беспрепятственное наблюдение над
The absence of any physical barriers ensured an **unobstructed view of** the working area.

Беспрепятственное прохождение
These sections of the dam may be lowered to permit **unobstructed passage of** boats and barges.

Беспримесный
An **undoped** material ...

Бессилен [*см.* **Не удаваться**].

Бессмысленно [*см.* **Не иметь смысла**].

Бесспорно самый лучший
This is **far and away** (*or* **by far,** *or* **undeniably**) your **best** buy in a centreless grinder.

Бесспорно самый распространённый
The Scotch boiler is **by far the most common(ly used)** firetube boiler in marine work.

Бесстолкновительный
A **collision-free** beam ...

Бесценная помощь [*см.* **Оказывать бесценную помощь при**].

Бесчисленное множество
There are **infinitely many** different ellipses with the same major diameter.

Биение
There is an arrangement to compensate for spindle **run-out.**

Биологическое разложение отходов
The **biological degradation of wastes.**

Битком набит (*разг.*)
The spacecraft **was crammed with** instruments.

Благодарен за
We **are indebted** (*or* **grateful,** *or* **thankful**) **to** Dr. T. **for** helpful discussion.

Благодарный
The ease of cultivation makes this leech a **favourable** material for development studies.
A very interesting and **rewarding** field of research is open for this young technique.

Благодаря
A is chosen **for** consistency with ...
Thanks (*or* **Owing**) **to** computer work, eight such stars have been located.
Illumination periods are increased **through** the presence of an atmosphere.
Hydrogen iodide, **by virtue of** (*or* **because of**, *or* **owing to**) its capacity to reduce ... always adds in the normal manner.
These materials are used mainly **for** their refractive properties.

Благодаря которому происходит
The orbital transitions of the formaldehyde molecule **that are responsible for** absorptions in the ultraviolet regions ...

Благодаря ... можно
This arrangement **ensured that** radiation **can be** detected when ...

Благодаря ... можно успешно применять
The ease of the addition of bromine to ... **makes** this element **a useful tool** in organic synthesis.

Благодаря... стало возможно получить
The introduction of the laser as a spectroscopic tool **has made it possible** (*or* **feasible**) **to produce** extremely narrow "resonances" in ...

Благодатная почва для [*см. тж.* **Представлять благодатную почву для**]
The hunt for monopoles **has been a fertile field** (*or* **ground**) for theoretical speculation.

Благоприятен для
The load and speed of operation **are favourable to** (*or* **favour**) the generation of a complete fluid film.

Благоприятное влияние на
Tin has **a beneficial effect on** cast iron.

Благоприятствовать
The addition of ... **is favoured** (*or* **promoted**) **by** low temperature.
Warm temperatures **are favourable for** the precipitation of ...

Благоразумно
It would be **sound practice** (*or* **reasonable,** *or* **wise**) **to** establish ...

Блеск
The crystals are colourless with **a** vitreous **lustre**.
Metallic **lustre ...**

Блестящий I
The fibre (*волокно*) **is lustrous.**
Protactinium metal **is shiny** (*or* **lustrous**, *or* **bright**) (**in appearance**).

Блестящий II [*см. тж.* **Яркий**]
These observations were a **dramatic** demonstration of ion acceleration to useful energies.
Huygens' most **startling** (*or* **dramatic**) astronomic discovery involved Saturn.

Ближайшая задача
The immediate task.

Ближайшее большее число
The transcendental numbers belong to **the next higher** transfinite **number.**

Ближайшее будущее [*см.* **В ближайшем будущем**].

Ближайшие годы [*см.* **В течение ближайших нескольких лет, На ближайшие годы**].

Ближайшие и долгосрочные перспективы
The immediate and long-term prospects of the fusion-power program were discussed.

Ближайшие несколько лет [*см.* **В течение ближайших нескольких лет**].

Ближайший к
That part of the shaft **nearest** (*or* **closest**) **to** the propeller twists the least.
The layer of air **next to** the water surface ...

Ближайший сосед (*матем.*)
The sum of the terms for all **nearest neighbours ...**

Ближе всего
The planet would be at that point which was **nearest** the Sun.

Ближе (п)ознакомиться с
In this section we **shall take a closer look at** the case with the general first-order control system.

Ближе приближаться к
The more terms you use, **the closer you get to** 1 ...

Ближний конец
The Earth will attract **the near end of** the vehicle more strongly than it will attract the far end.

Ближняя сторона Луны
The lunar nearside [*or* **The nearside** (*or* **The near,** *or* **The front side**) **of the Moon**].

Близки [*см.* **Весьма близки (друг к другу)**].

Близкие (друг к другу)
Analogous colours are **closely related** colours, e.g. red—orange, and yellow—orange, etc.

Близкий к
Barreters must have resistance **approximating** (*or* **approaching**) the impedance of ...
The phase-angles **were close to** 90 deg.
We produced temperatures **near** the absolute zero.
To maintain **near-**saturation conditions, ...
Hailstones have **near-**spherical shape.

Близкий к действительности
A more **realistic** description of the interaction between molecules can be given by...

Близкий по составу [*см.* **Приблизительно совпадать с ... по составу**].

Близко друг к другу
The two strips are mounted **close together** (*or* **close to each other**).

Близко знако́м с
They **were closely acquainted with** the subject.

Близко напоминать
Electronic telephone switching systems **closely resemble** large digital computers.

Близко приближающийся к
A comet **making a close approach to** Jupiter may undergo severe changes.
Terms **closely approximating** those of hydrogen ...

Близко расположенные [*см. тж.* **Расположенные близко друг к другу**]
Lines **close together** indicate the strongest regions of the field.
Another important application of laser spectroscopy is the study of **closely-spaced** atomic and molecular energy levels.
Simultaneous condensation of matter around two **nearby** (*or* **adjacent,** *or* **neighbouring**) centres...
Closely-pitched ribs can be provided to ensure ample cooling area.
With the unit particles **in close proximity,** this effect may extend throughout ...

Близко расположенный [*см. тж.* **Близлежащий**]
Radiation from **nearby** stars ...

Близко совпадать
The results obtained by the two methods **are in close agreement.**

Близко совпадать с
The constants **agree closely with** the expected values.
The rate of sediment accumulation **closely matched** the rate of crustal sinking.
The geomagnetic axis **coincides very closely with** the axis of rotation.
The phase of the locally produced subcarrier must **correspond closely with** the phase of the original subcarrier vector (*mathem.*).

Близлежащий
There is a **nearby** source of limestone.

Близок [*см.* **Приближаться к**].

Близок к
This speed **approaches** the speed of light.

Близок к действительности
These data **are close to the truth.**

Близок по возрасту к
These mountains **are much of an age with** the peaks of New Jersey.

Близок по химическому составу к
Fluids of plants and animals **are chemically close to** seawater.

Близость [*см. тж.* **В непосредственной близости от**]
The **proximity of** a neighbouring level ... (*phys.*).

Блокирован
The entire control cycle of the machine **is interlocked**, and an emergency stop button is provided.

Блокировать [*см.* **Сблокирован с**].

Блокировка
An electrical **interlock with** the selector switch precludes...

Блуждать по
These electrons are not bound to any particular atom and can **wander throughout** the metal.

Богат
The country **is (very) favourably endowed with** coal.
The semiconducting material **is rich in** electrons.
The fluid was then found **to be richly supplied with** microspheres.

Богат железом
The ore **is rich in iron** (*or* **is iron rich**, *or* **has a high iron content**).

Богатство
No section of the earth is exactly like any other in resource **endowment** (*or* **abundance**).

Богатый
Metal-**rich** clusters...

Богатый опыт
In most of the Third World there was no such **pool of experience.**
An engineer with **wide experience** (*or* **a wealth of experience**) **in** telemetry operation is wanted.

Богатый органическими веществами
Organic-rich clays ...

Богатый электронами
Electron rich (*or* **Rich in electrons**).

Богатый энергией
Energy rich.

Боковой люфт
Spring washers eliminate **side play** in assemblies.

Более [*см. тж.* **Всё более и более, И более, Свыше**]
He obtained boron of **better than** 98% purity.
In excess of one in ten elderly people suffer with this problem at some stage.
The compound forms complexes with **over** (*or* **more than**) ten elements.

Более близок к
These processes **more closely paralleled** contemporary biological mechanisms than most others did.

Более быстрый из двух
The second reaction **is the faster of the two.**

Более важно [*см.* **Что более важно**].

Более внимательное рассмотрение
Closer inspection will show that...

Более выносливый
This factor should permit development of **longer-lasting** natural rubber tires.

Более выпуклый
The earth **bulges** at the equator.

Более высокого порядка
The **higher-order** modes have larger diffraction losses.

Более высококипящий, чем
This compound is **higher boiling than ...**

Более детально [*см. тж.* **Более подробно**]
This theory has been published **in more** (*or* **greater**) **detail** elsewhere.

Более доступен
When the alkene **is more readily available, ...**

Более или менее
Such, **more or less,** was the condition of the North American prairie before the advent of Europeans.

Более или менее определённо указывать на то, что
The absence of absorption in this region **is fair indication that** the compound is not a benzene derivative.

Более или менее точно
A series of elements whose atomic weights were known **with some degree of certainty** had an interesting relationship.

Более или менее часто
We should expect floods **every so often.**

Более интенсивный, чем
Precipitation from shower clouds **is of greater intensity than** that from layer clouds.

Более легкоразрешимый
Equation (3.15) can be reduced to **the more readily solved** Laplace equation by a simple solution.

Более мелкозернистый, чем
Usually ball clays **are finer grained than** china clays.

Более не [*см.* **Больше не**].

Более не равен[*см. тж.* **Уже не равен**]
However, on another fibre with the same profile it **is no longer** zero.

Более низкокипящий, чем
Acetylene **is lower boiling than** ethylene.

Более подробно
Let us consider **in greater** (*or* **more**) **detail** the flow of energy through the earth's surface environment.
This point will be discussed **at greater length** (*or* **more elaborately,** *or* **more comprehensively,** *or* **more fully**) in the next section.

Более подробно ознакомиться с
For those who wish **to read more widely in** particular subjects ...

Более подробное изучение (*или* **рассмотрение**)
Closer examination of the table ...

Более подробный
For an **extended** discussion see the next chapter.

Более поздний
The method has been used by **subsequent** investigators.
A **more recent** development is the application of similar genetic principles to ...

Более похож на [*см.* **Больше напоминать**].

Более продолжительный срок службы [*см.* **Иметь более продолжительный срок службы, чем**].

Более ранней конструкции
These workers made their measurements with **an earlier** detector based on ...

Более серьёзные трудности, чем
The problem here **is worse than** it was with homostructure lasers.

Более того
Spectroscopic studies confirm this pattern and **furthermore** (*or* **moreover**, *or* **in addition**) provide values for ...
What's more (*or* **Further still**) our wide variety of alloys assures you of efficient performance.

Более точно называется
The discussion deals with the prokaryotic structure, which **is more appropriately known as** the nucleoid (*biol.*).
In such cases, the attractive forces at these boundaries **are more properly referred to as** adhesive.

Более точное приближение
We have arrived at **a higher** (*or* **closer**) **approximation to** the Boltzmann equation.

Более тщательно изучать
For more extensive data **a closer look into** the arrangement of outer electrons **must be taken.**
It is necessary **to look more closely at** the results.

Более тщательное изучение
Closer examination (*or* **inspection**) of the earth's crust shows that ...

Более чем
This effect **more than** compensates for the increase in kinetic energy.

Более чем достаточно
Indications of surface volcanic activity on the Moon **are by no means lacking.**
Fewer than 40 tRNAs per organism should **be more than sufficient** (*biol.*).

Более эффективный
Other codes **do better:** they require fewer reversals.

Болезнь [*см.* **Бороться с болезнями, Вызывать заболевание, Переносить болезни**].

Болезнь наступает [*см.* **Наступление болезни**].

Болеутоляющее [*см.* **Ослабление боли**].

Болт [*см.* **Прикреплять болтами, Скреплять болтами**].

Болтово́е соединение
A **bolted joint.**

Боль [*см.* **Не испытывать боли, Ослабление боли**].

Больша́я вероятность
A **high probability.**

Больша́я заслуга принадлежит
A lot of the credit must go to this research group.

Больша́я масса [*см.* **Обладать большей массой**].

Больша́я нагрузка [*см.* **Для большой нагрузки**].

Больша́я перегрузка
Heavy (*or* **Great**) **overload.**

Больша́я планета
A **major** (*or* **large,** *or* **great**) **planet.**

Больша́я потеря
A **severe sacrifice in** sensitivity ...

Больша́я продолжительность
The long persistence of the vibrations caused by moon quakes can be explained by ...

Бо́льшая точность
The components can be positioned with **an accuracy better than** 0.010 in.

Больша́я трудность
A **severe** experimental **difficulty** is the low intensity of the scattering spectrum.

Больша́я утечка
Some dosimeters **leak badly.**

Бо́льшая часть
For the most part these theories can be tested by ...
Semiconductors will occupy our attention in **the bulk of** this work.
Most of the power is lost by radiation.
During **most of** the Precambrian period ...

Больша́я часть [*см. тж.* **Значительная часть**]
Some hyperiids spend **a large share of** their lives encased within medusas.

Больша́я экономия [*см.* **Добиваться большой экономии**].

Больше [*см. тж.* **Значительно больше, Свыше**]
This was 0.1% **above** the true value.
Saturated hydrocarbons absorb only very high energy radiation, usually **beyond** 160 nm.
Over (*or* **In excess of,** *or* **More than**) 50 kilos ...

Больше в ... раз, чем [*см.* **Меньше в ... раз, чем**].

Больше во много раз [*см.* **Во много раз больше**].

Больше всего [*см. тж.* **Наибольшее количество**]
That part of the propeller twists **the most.**

Больше (меньше) всего
The rays with ... are attenuated **most** and the rays with ... are attenuated **least.**

Больше всего подходить для
These methods **are best suited to** the determination of...

Больше или меньше, чем
One volume **is greater or less than** another.

Больше напоминать
The opaque ringlets of Saturn **more closely resemble** the *A* and *B* rings in their composition.

Больше не
The Curie temperature is that temperature above which a substance **is no longer** magnetic.
As a result the components **are no longer** equal.

Больше не играет никакой роли
The diatomic hydrogen sticks permanently to the cold walls and **is of no further consequence.**

Больше среднего
A droplet appreciably **larger than average** will fall faster than ...

Больше чем достаточно [*см.* **Нет недостатка в**].

Больше чем необходимо
More coke is produced in the reactor **than is required** (*or* **needed,** *or* **necessary**) for heat balance.

Бо́льшие возможности [*см.* **Иметь бо́льшие возможности**].

Бо́льшие изменения
The **wide variations of** D_{AB} with pressure ...

Бо́льшие трудности
Severe (*or* **Great**) **difficulties.**

Бо́льшие усилия [*см.* **Прилагать бо́льшие усилия к**].

Бо́льший
RAT was cancelled in 1958 because *ASROC*, a weapon of **superior** (*or* **greater,** *or* **larger**) range was under development.

Бо́льший или ме́ньший [*см.* **В бо́льшей или ме́ньшей степени**].

Бо́льший или равный
This is a positive integer **greater than, or equal to,** *m*.

Большинство [*см. тж.* **В большинстве случаев, Подавляющее большинство**]
For the most part the machines employed for this work are fully automatic.
The majority (*or* **Most**) **of** these units will be small.
In **most** (*or* **the majority of**) cases ...

Большинство, а может быть и все [*см.* **Большинство, если не все**].

Большинство, если не все
Most if not all of the computation is done by purely electronic means.

Большое влияние
Heat may have **a dramatic effect on** the rate of reaction.
The amount of water present on the surface has **a profound effect on** activity.

Большое внимание уделено
Other methods of ventilation **have received much consideration** (*or* **attention**) (*or* **Much attention is given to**).

Большое движение [*см.* **Дороги с большим движением**].

Большое достижение
The shock tube investigation of the hydrogen-oxygen reaction presents **a major breakthrough** (*or* **achievement**) **in** the understanding of this reaction.

Большое значение [*см.* **Важное значение**].

Большое количество [*см. тж.* **Водиться в больших количествах, Иметься в изобилии, Много, Присутствовать в большом количестве в**]
A rich variety of schemes has been suggested.
The shale contains **abundant** (*or* **a great quantity of**) fossil organisms.
A great deal of energy might be stored in ...
Small black holes were created **in great numbers** in the early universe.

Большое количество данных
Ample (*or* **Considerable,** *or* **Abundant**) geological **evidence** shows that climate has changed greatly during ...
A great body of information (*or* **data**).

Большое преувеличение
This **is a gross overestimate** (*or* **overstatement,** *or* **exaggeration**).

Большое разбавление
High dilution.

Большое разнообразие [*см. тж.* **Ввиду широкого разнообразия**]
A wide variety of (different) products are formed.

Большое увеличение [*см. тж.* **При большом увеличении**]
Because of the **high magnification** the tiniest details are clearly seen.

Большое число
Once these variables have been calculated **a wealth of** (*or* **a great many**) dependent quantities can be derived.
A wide range of metals could be mined here.

Большой [*см. тж.* **Значительный**]
Amply-dimensional flywheels ...
This small grader is built to handle those jobs for which **a full-size** grader would be an extravagance.
A major installation such as our laboratory ...
Profound (*or* **Gross**) changes occur in the physical and chemical properties of the substance.
The cells draw current from the battery at **a very significant** (*or* **substantial**) rate.
A **sizable** arc forms between the contacts.
The solar system may remain in existence without **major** changes for ... additional years.
Metal is not believed to make **much (of a)** contribution to the interior material of the mantle.

"Большой взрыв" (*в теории происхождения вселенной*)
The "Big Bang".

Большой вклад в
The book is **a major contribution to** the current literature.

Большой выбор
You have **a wide selection (to pick from).**

Большой допуск
Generous allowance must be made **for** unscheduled changes in ...

Большой износ
Heavy wear(-and-tear) is produced by violent pressure changes.

Большой процент брака
Rejects were high.

Большой разброс
The wide scatter of the published data is illustrated in the following graph.

Большой спрос [*см.* **В большом спросе**].

Большой шаг вперёд
This steel is **a leap** [*or* **a (great) stride**] **forward in** metal working.

Большой шаг на пути к
A major step (*or* **A great stride**) **toward** our present concept of covalent bonding...

Бóльшую часть времени
Many channels of desert streams are dry **most of the time.**

Бороться с
Galvanic action **is combatted** (*or* **controlled,** *or* **prevented**) in either of two ways.

Бороться с болезнями
There are three ways in which viral **diseases** can **be controlled** in man.

Бортовое оборудование
Shipborne equipment.
Airborne equipment.
Spaceborne equipment.

Бортовой
In-flight measurements are currently being made.
An **onboard** sensor ...

Борьба с
Methods for **combatting** corrosion (*or* corrosion **control**) ...

Борьба с болезнями
Disease control.

Борьба с загрязнением среды [*см.* **Организация по борьбе с загрязнением среды**].

Борьба с пожарами
Fire control (*or* **fighting**).

Брак [*см. тж.* **Большой процент брака**]
Unsoundness occurs more frequently in the middle cavities.
There are no **scrapped parts** [*or* **rejects,** *or* **reject(ed) parts**] now, **scrappage** (*or* **rejection**) has been completely eliminated.

Браковать [*см.* **Забраковать, Отбраковывать дефектные детали**].

Брать I [*см. тж.* **Взять на себя**]
These data **are borrowed** (*or* **taken**) **from ...**

Брать II
Often the tool in such an operation is a costly diamond wheel, since nothing else **will attack** the hard material.

Брать в скобки
To bracket (*or* **enclose in brackets,** *or* **put in parentheses**).

Брать интеграл
The **integral is taken along** the magnetic lines of force.

Брать крутые повороты
Sharp bends are more easily **negotiated** with leaning front wheels.

Брать на себя задачу
They **undertook to** identify these particles.

Брать на себя функции управления
Once the workpiece has been loaded and the computer has been informed that it is ready to enter the system, the computer **takes over.**

Брать начало в
The ray **originates at** *P*.

Брать начало в ... и впадать в
The Rio Grande **rises in** Colorado **and empties into** the Gulf of Mexico.

Брать образцы [*см. тж.* **Отбирать образцы**]
Samples were withdrawn (*or* **taken,** *or* **obtained**) **from** an artery (*or* **from** a fermentor, etc.).
Oceanographers **have been sampling** the sediments of the ocean floor.
Gas analyzers **sampled** the Martian soil for signs of life.

Брать предел [*см.* **В пределе**].

Брать пример из
The **example is drawn from** my own laboratory experience.

Брать пробу [*см.* **Брать образцы**].

Брать производную по
Take the derivatives of these expressions **with respect to** time.

Брать свое название от
The Mississippian system **takes its name from** the river along which strata of this age are exposed.

Бремя [*см.* **Ложиться бременем на**].

Бросать в
If a filter paper **is dropped into** chlorine, ...

Бросать монетку (*теория вероятности*)
To flip a coin.

Бросаться в глаза [*см. тж.* **Сразу обнаруживается**]
The Spodosol profile has strongly developed horizons that **catch the eye** (*geol.*).
If one looks at a map of the world ocean, several features **stand out.**
In the study of the nuclei of atoms and the nuclei of comets two similarities **stand out:** invisibility and relative size.

Будем считать, что
A laser **will be considered to** have three subunits: ...

Будет [*см.* **Должен быть**].

Будучи
Deprived of (*будучи лишенным*) a continuing energy source, the star collapses and then explodes as a supernova.
The condensed water, **once** convert**ed** into snow crystals, has a much greater opportunity of ...
When dissolv**ed** in water, the molecules are delivered to biochemical sites for various processes.

Будущее [*см.* **В ближайшем будущем, В весьма отдалённом будущем, В далёком будущем, В не столь отдалённом будущем, В обозримом будущем, В перспективе имеется, Дело далёкого будущего**].

Будущее принадлежит
The future of high-speed ground transportation **may (well) lie with** vehicles that “fly” a foot above...

Будь он ... или нет
All molecules, **symmetric or not,** are polarizable.

Будь то [*см. тж.* **Независимо от того**]
Zinc atoms can move into the gallium arse-

nide lattice from an external source, **be it** vapour, liquid or solid.
In this way, the desirable properties of each of the coals, **whether it be** in impurity content or in its contribution to the character of the coke, are utilized.

Будь то ... или какой-либо другой
The method was independent of quasar colour, ultraviolet **or otherwise.**

Буква или цифра в кружке
A circled (*or* **An encircled**) **letter or figure.**

Буквально [*см.* **В буквальном смысле слова**].

Буквенная часть
In the term $4x^2y$ the known multiplier of **the literal part** is the coefficient.

Бурная реакция
If fluorine gas is introduced into a vessel containing some metallic lithium, a **violent reaction** occurs.

Бурно [*см.* **Весьма бурно**].

Бурно гореть
Magnesium **burns with vigour** (*or* **vigorously**) if heated in steam.

Бурно реагировать с
Sodium **attacks** cold water **vigorously.**
Sodium **reacts violently** (*or* **vigorously**) **with** other elements.

Бурный протест [*см.* **Вызывать бурный протест**].

Бурный рост населения
Population explosion.

Бывает [*см.* **Как часто случается**].

Бывает вызван
Seal failure after operation at high temperatures **is** often **associated with** some change in operating conditions.

Бывает и наоборот
The female adrenal is usually larger, **but the reverse may be true.**

Бывает разного цвета от ... до
Brick **ranges in colour from** a burned black **to** nearly white cream.

Бывают
The reluctance motors **come in** various sizes.

Бывают двух видов
Busways **are made in two (general) types.**

Бывают разных размеров
The conveyor buckets **vary in size.**

Был(о) упомянут(о)
Mention was made of the practice adopted by that firm.

Быстрая реакция I
The device **is fast in its response.**

Быстрая реакция II
A high-rate (*or* **fast**) chemical **reaction** took place.

Быстрая смена резцов
A **quick-change tooling** system for large lathes and the vertical boring mills was introduced.

Быстро
This probability declines **rapidly** (*or* **steeply,** *or* **fast**).

Быстро осознать, что
He **was quick to realize that** the new findings favoured his hypothesis.

Быстро шагать вперёд
The power industry **makes rapid strides.**

Быстродействующий
Anodic compounds are **fast acting** and do not attack the base metal.
The mathematical intricacies require a **fast** (*or* **high-speed**) computer.

Быстрое завершение
The speedy completion of the project improved the situation.

Быстрый [*см. тж.* **Более быстрый из двух**]
The **high-velocity** ions were deflected the least.
A **rapid** (*or* **steep,** *or* **fast**) decline in the probability of ...

Бытовой [*см. тж.* **Домашний**]
The butanes are components of the **domestic** fuel, liquefied petroleum gas.
Household ammonia ...

Бытовые потребности [*см. тж.* **Потребление в домашнем хозяйстве**]
Domestic demand for water, etc.

Быть [*см.* **Находиться, Представлять собой, Являться**].

Быть абсолютно уверенным в том, что
We **have great confidence** [*or* We **are quite confident** (*or* **certain**, *or* **sure**)] **that ...**

Быть аналогичным
This law **bears a close analogy** (*or* **an analogy**) (*or* **is similar**) (*or* **analogous**) **to** the one discussed previously.

Быть безуспешным [*см.* **Не удаваться**].

Быть в курсе дела
One should **bring oneself** (*or* **keep**) **abreast of** the trends in ...

Быть в курсе новейших достижений
This requires a major effort **to keep abreast of new** (*or* **the latest**) **developments.**

Быть в состоянии
Now we **are in a position to** deduce the rotation period of Jupiter.
Inside the red cell the molecules of water are physically close to the hemoglobin molecules and should **be in a position to** react readily with hemoglobin.

Быть весьма перспективным
This process **has** always **had great potential** (*or* **has been very promising**).

Быть весьма популярным
The hypothesis **holds much favour** (*or* **is very popular**).

Быть вызванным
Machine-tool applications of the cone clutch **arose from** the requirements for reversing the spindle on ...

Быть действительным для
This expression **holds (good) for** two different gases.

Быть достигнутым благодаря
The advances **have come about through** the adaptation of ...

Быть знакомым с
The "material working" engineer should **have an acquaintance** [*or* **be familiar** (*or* **acquainted**)] **with** the various plastics.

Быть известным под названием
This relation **is known as** the Biot-Savart law.

Быть известным *чем-л.*
The tiger beetles **are (well) known for** their bright colours.

Быть на правильном пути
In so doing he **was on the right track.**

Быть наготове
An expert is not required to remain on the site but he must **be on call** to report within an hour.

Быть направленным вниз или вверх
The spin vector can **point either up or down.**

Быть неподвижным по отношению к
One major plate **has no motion** [*or* **is fixed** (*or* **stationary**)] **with respect** (*or* **reference**) **to** the lower mantle.

Быть непосредственно связанным с [*см.* **Иметь непосредственное отношение к**].

Быть обычным делом
In installations made twenty years ago **it was not unusual** (*or* **it was usual**) **to** see two or even three central processing units tied together to ensure reliable operation.

Быть обычным явлением
Volcanism **was common** (*or* **usual**) in the Northern Rockies until about 40 million years ago.

Быть обязанным своим происхождением
The base 10 **has its origin in the fact that** man has a total of 10 digits on both hands.

Быть опасным
Hydrogen may **present a safety problem** [*or* **be hazardous** (*or* **dangerous**)] if ...

Быть основанным на
Kepler's vicarious theory **rested** (*or* **was based**) **on** two assumptions.

Быть перспективным
Liquids that sustain laser action **hold promise** (*or* **are promising**) in high-power pulsed applications.

Быть полезным
These observations **will be of use** (*or* **useful**) to you.

Быть причиной [*см. тж.* **Вызывать**]
Contact electrification **accounts for** (*or*

causes) many nuisances and hazards of electrostatics.

Быть связанным с
These experiments **were concerned with** (*or* **involved**) the irradiation of ...

Быть справедливым для
That ratio **would hold for** all circles.

Быть хорошо (*или* **плотно**) **подогнанными (друг к другу)**
The parts should **fit closely** when assembled.

В

В [*см. тж.* **Выражать в, Направлять в**]
The number of collisions **per** second ...
To obtain the dipole moment **in** (units of) Debyes, ...

В алфавитном порядке
The ligands are named **in alphabetical order.**

В амбулаторных условиях
Barium tests can be arranged **on an outpatient basis.**

В апогее
The Moon **is at apogee.**

В ассоциации (*геол.*)
Arsenopyrite **is associated with** ores of tin, tungsten, and ...

В безопасное место
The fuse (*шнур*) burns at a slow rate towards the charge permitting the workman to move away **to safety** (*or* **to a safe place**).

В беспорядке [*см.* **Беспорядочно**].

В ближайшее десятилетие
In the coming (*or* **the next**) **decade ...**

В ближайшем будущем
In the immediate future there will be ample opportunities for increasing productivity.

В ближайшем будущем появится
The coming years will witness the appearance in print **of** a still greater body of literature.

В ближайшие месяцы
In the months ahead (*or* **In the coming months**), much more attention will be paid to ...

В близком будущем
We shall obtain newer information **in the near future.**

В более общем виде
More generally we can write this law as: ...

В более общих выражениях
$x^S = \lambda(s/p)$ is characteristic at P if $\Delta_p = 0$. **More generally,** a manifold is characteristic at P if its tangent hyperplane at P is characteristic.

В более узких пределах
With the aim of checking over great distances and **to closer limits,** optical equipment was introduced.

В более широком смысле
In a more comprehensive (*or* **wider**) **sense,** photogrammetry means the process of ...

В больничных условиях
The other neurological abnormalities are best investigated **in a hospital setting** (*or* **in the hospital environment**).

В большей или меньшей степени
These reactions may affect the overall process **to a greater or lesser extent** (*or* **degree**).

В большей степени, чем
This expansion drops the pressure **to a greater extent than** the isothermal processes would do.

В большинстве случаев
The bushings are beautifully simple and **for the most part** quite inexpensive.
For the most part the expectation is borne out by experiment.
More often than not the application of these agents causes ...
In most (*or* **In the majority of**) **cases** (*or* **instances**) ...

В больших масштабах
This process is employed **on a large scale.**

В большой степени [*см.* **В значительной степени, Значительная часть**].

В большом избытке
If one of the reactants is present **in large excess, ...**

В большом количестве [*см. тж.* **В изобилии, Встречаться в большом количестве, Иметься в изобилии, С большим выходом**]
Gluonium is produced **abundantly.**
Sediment rich in calcium carbonate accumulates **in abundance.**
Such computers now reach the market **in volume.**
The production of an antibiotic **in quantity** (*or* **in large quantities**) by fermentation often requires long periods of time.
Low-carbon ferrochromium is also produced **in quantity** by the reduction of ...

В большом спросе
Coke **is in large demand** for industrial smelting operations.
Marble **is much in demand** as a construction stone.

В будущем [*см. тж.* **В дальнейшем**]
Copper and cobalt may be extracted profitably from nodules **at some future date** (*or* **in the future**).

В буквальном смысле слова
In a literal sense, almost all real control systems are cascade systems.

В быту [*см.* **В домашнем хозяйстве**].

В вакууме [*см. тж.* **Плавиться под вакуумом, Под вакуумом**]
The melt was placed **in (a) vacuum.**
The velocity of light **in vacuo ...**

В вертикальном или наклонном положении
Lubrication is provided with the press **in either an upright or inclined position.**

В верхних слоях атмосферы
In the upper atmosphere.

В весьма значительной степени
Our environment consists **very largely** (*or* **to a great extent**) of inorganic materials.

В весьма отдалённом будущем
In the very long run (*or* **In the very distant future**) we shall need energy that is absolutely pollution free.

В весьма хорошем приближении
To a quite good approximation, the constant p can be taken to be the same for all ...

В виде [*см. тж.* **В форме, Выражать в виде, Следующим образом**]
The normal audibility curve is represented **as** a straight line.
A portion of the absorbed energy remains **as** heat in the absorbing material.
Hydrogen enters the solvent **as** hydrogen ions.
This equation can be written **as** $E = mc^2$.
The chart is prepared **in** booklet **form.**
The units are available **in** cabinets and consoles.
The new system is sold **in** standardized models.
The samples are usually **in the form of** films.
Scintillators are prepared **in the form of** filaments.
These concepts are formulated **in terms of** integrals.
The molecule is projected **in the shape of** a cross.

В ... виде
Sodium acetylides cannot be kept safely **when** dry.

В виде варианта [*см.* **В качестве варианта**].

В виде дроби
Write the operation **in fractional form** (*or* **in the form of a fraction**).

В виде книги
The paper was reprinted **in book form.**

В виде кристаллов
Calcite **in** transparent **crystals** is used in certain optical instruments.

В виде соединения
Nitrogen occurs **combined** in Chile saltpetre and in all living organisms.

В виде столбца
A chronologic arrangement of rock units **in columnar form ...**

В виде таблицы
The cam profile can be shown **in tabulated form.**

В виде формулы это выражается следующим образом
Symbolically,
$A^* + B \to A + B^+ + e^-$.

В воздухе I [*см.. тж.* **Полёт в воздухе**]

The motion of the projectile **through the air ...**
A discontinuity in layering means that the hailstone has broken **in midair.**
The size distribution of raindrops **aloft ...**

В воздухе II [*см. тж.* **Взвешенный в воздухе**]
Airborne pollutants ...

В восточном направлении [*см.* **В западном направлении**].

В глобальном масштабе
We give the most important relationships **on a global scale.**

В глубине I [*см. тж.* **В толще**]
We find these minerals exposed as surface rocks only in extremely dry climates; but **at depth** these rocks are common.

В глубине II
These elements are produced by nuclear fusion **deep inside** stars.
These electric currents are generated **deep in the interior of** the Moon.
Plutonic igneous rocks are formed **deep within** the earth's crust.

В глубине земли
The quantity of methane still **deep in the earth** would be enormous.

В горячем виде
Most alloys are **hot** extruded (*or* extruded **hot**).
Wax seals are poured **while hot.**

В готовом для использования виде
The mandrels are brought to the worktable **in readiness for use** by the die casting machine operators.

В граммах на моль
To calculate the molecular weight **in grammes per mole, ...**

В грубом приближении
As a rough approximation, such nonpolar regions are sufficient to reduce the solubility of ...

В далёком (*или* **отдалённом) будущем**
If, **in the (far) distant future,** mankind should attempt travel to distant stars, ...

В дальнейшем [*см. тж.* **В последующем изложении, Для использования позже**]
A permanent record of ... may thus be obtained for examination **at a later time** (*or* **date**) (*or* **later on**).
From this point on (*or* **Hereafter,** *or* **Hereinafter,** *or* **Henceforward,** *or* **From here on**) we shall use the term "control system" to mean "automatic control system".
In the subsequent discussion we assume that ...
In what follows the value of any quantity ... will be specified by...
This rule was **thereafter** generally adopted.

В данной области
The first announcement was greeted by workers **in the field** because the new lasers could be made very small and ...
That was an innovation **in this line.**

В данной ситуации I
The strong virtue of the engine **in the present state of affairs** is its cleanness of operation.

В данной ситуации II
The quarks are bound together by the strong force, but **in this context** the force has a form quite different from the one observed between protons and neutrons.

В данном виде
For many purposes, equation (14) is useful **as it stands.** It may, however, be rearranged **to read:** ...

В данном случае
The limiting resource is, **in this instance** (*or* **case**), a sufficient explanation for ...

В данном контексте означает, что
Plane symmetry **as used here signifies that ...**

В данный момент [*см. тж.* **В настоящее время, На этой стадии**]
At this junction (*or* **At the moment**) we cannot say for certain ...

В данных условиях
In (*or* **Under**) **these circumstances** (*or* **conditions**) the jump relations describe a shock wave.
In the present context (*or* **Under the circumstances**) this process signifies that ...

В два раза [*см.* **Уменьшать вдвое**].

В два раза более растворим, чем
Calcium hydroxide **is twice as soluble** at 20°C **as** at 100°C.

В два раза больше, чем
The bond energy for H_2 **is** nearly **twice as large as** that for H^+ or He_2^+.
The double-acting compressor discharges **twice as much** fluid per cylinder **as** the single-acting.
The distance between the objectives **is twice** (*or* **double**) **that** between the eye-pieces.
The length of the geosyncline should be more that **twice its** width.
The total capacity of these steam fields **is** only about **twice what** a single nuclear power plant develops.

В два раза больший
This activity proceeded **at a twofold rate.**

В два раза быстрее
Loading trucks **in double-quick time** (*or* **in half the time**) ...

В два раза выше, чем
The tubing will withstand temperatures up to 600°F—**twice its** shrinking temperature.

В два раза меньше, чем
At this density there are **half as many** atoms **as** there are sites.

В действительности [*см. тж.* **В практической работе, Фактически**]
This deviation is often negligible **in practical situations.**
In actuality (*or* **In actual fact,** *or* **Actually**) the engineer is concerned with other problems.
In (actual) practice (*or* **conditions**) (*or* **In reality,** *or* **In practical work**) complete equilibrium can never be attained.
In actual truth, no satellite planet has been located for Mercury.
This is a simplified representation; **in real situations** many different spots are formed.

В день
The output is 500 tonnes of iron **daily** (*or* **per day**) (*or* **The daily** output is 500 tonnes of iron).

В десятичных дробях [*см.* **Выраженный в десятичных дробях**].

В диаметре
These pipes are 15 metres long and 0.5 cm **across** (*or* **in diameter**).

В диапазоне [*см. тж.* **Лежать в диапазоне**]
Such lasers generate continuous radiation **over a** wide **range** (**of wavelengths**).

В диапазоне от ... до
In experiments *n* typically lies **(in the range) between** 10 **and** 100 (*or* **from** 10 **to** 100).

В длину
Acoeles seldom exceed 1 cm **in length.**

В домашнем хозяйстве
Dilute aqueous solution of ammonia finds use **as a domestic** (*or* **household**) cleansing agent.
Many of the products used **in the home** and in industry may be potentially dangerous to man.

В дополнение к [*см. тж.* **Кроме, Наряду с, Помимо**]
Molecular-orbital calculations provide detailed orbital shapes and orbital energies **in addition to** [*or* (**to go**) **along with**] the qualitative results from symmetry considerations.
This technique is used **as an adjunct to** other spectrometric methods in the identification of...
In addition to ... the tank contains 15 litres of water.

В достаточной степени
The reactions of coal with ... have not yet been **adequately** (*or* **sufficiently**) explored.

В достаточной степени соответствовать
An adequate mathematical model must **give a reasonable fit to** existing data.

В других местах
Such events have been detected **elsewhere** in the world.

В других отношениях
Effects of nutritional, toxic or **otherwise** active substances...
The burner jet is fitted with ...; **otherwise** the construction is identical to ...

В других случаях
This system of equations is hyperbolic in case (f), **otherwise** it is elliptic.

В других условиях
Under (a) different (set of) conditions, precipitation of mineral matter is carried out by circulating ground water.

В другое место
The melt can move **elsewhere** to form an igneous rock.

В другом месте
A complete series of such relations has been listed **elsewhere.**

В другом отношении
This radiation would differ from ordinary light **in another respect.**

В единицах [*см. тж.* **Выражать в единицах**]
Aircraft engine performance is evaluated **in terms** (*or* **units**) **of** horsepower output.
Fermentation efficiency is expressed **in terms of** lactic acid yields.

В единицу времени
The quantity of water that percolates **in a unit (of) time** across a unit area ...

В естественных условиях
This system appears to be feasible **under** such **natural situations** (*or* **conditions**) as deserts or warm beaches.

В жёстких условиях
In (*or* **Under**) **drastic** (*or* **arduous,** *or* **violent,** *or* **severe**) **conditions ...**
This alloy has been used **for severe service** at high temperatures.

В зависимости от I [*см. тж.* **В соответствии с**]
The critical temperature varies **with** (*or* **according to**) the carbon content of the steel.
Speeds up to 100 rpm are used **in accordance with** the size of pump.
Different approaches are used **depending (up)on** the number of variables.
The capacity may be varied **to suit** changing needs.
The ratio of hydrogen varies **with** the manufacturing process.

В зависимости от II [*см. тж.* **Отложен на графике в зависимости от, По**]
Roll load **against** (*or* **versus,** *or* **vs.,** *or* **as a function of**) strip thickness ...
The pressure-**versus**-flowrate curve ...
To describe the distribution of organisms **in relation to** their physical and biotic environments ...
The plot shows the energy **in relation to** the distance between the molecules.

В зависимости от времени года
Rivers vary greatly, both **seasonally** and from year to year, in the amount of water they carry.

В зависимости от желания
The jacket may be filled with water, glycerine, or air **depending on the** manufacturer's **preference.**

В зависимости от обстоятельств
Those substances are able to rotate the plane of polarized light to the left or to the right, **as the case may be.**
Definitions may be altered **as dictated by the convenience of the situation.**
The molten metal is charged into alloying furnaces, or cast into pigs, **as (may be) required.**
The temperature of the solution is controlled by introducing hot or cold solution, **as the situation requires.**

В зависимости от положения
The stresses vary **with position.**

В зависимости от потребностей
The bunsen ice calorimeter can receive or give up heat, **as the case requires.**

В зависимости от применения
The heating elements are enclosed in shielded cages or within conveyorized ovens, **as required by the application.**

В зависимости от того ...
The atoms either emit or absorb radiation **depending on** (*or* **according to**) **whether** (*or* **according as**) the temperature of the gas is higher or lower than that of the source.

В зависимости от того, который из
The difference in products between the two types of reactions arises **according to which** element, hydrogen or bromine, adds first.

В зависимости от того, который из них
The tie-line construction should be based on the composition corresponding to the average value of m or L_M/Ge_M, **whichever** appears to vary more over the tower.

В заводских условиях
The preparation of colloidal dispersions in the laboratory or **in industrial situations** (*or* **conditions**) ...

В заключение
In summary (*or* **In conclusion,** *or* **In closing**) it may be said that ...

В закрытом помещении
Nonferrous scrap is stored **indoors.**

В замедленном темпе
Chemists would like to observe such a reaction **in slow motion.**

В западном направлении
Plate *A* is moving **in a westward direction.**

В зачаточном состоянии
The technique of roof bolting **is** still **in its infancy.**

В защиту
In defense of the thermal approach he pointed out that ...
The evidence presented **in support of** the proposal was as follows.

В земных условиях
These compounds would be gases **under earthly** (*or* **terrestrial**) **conditions.**

В значительной мере [*см.* **В значительной степени**].

В значительной мере подтверждать
The results of a recent investigation **add considerable support for** the foregoing deduction.

В значительной степени
Only the ground state **is appreciably** (*or* **substantially**) populated.
The aircraft's altitude exceeded the desired angle of attack **by a large** (*or* **considerable**) **margin.**
The fidelity of the amplifier depends **to a large measure** [*or* **in large measure,** *or* **to a large extent** (*or* **degree**), *or* **largely,** *or* **to a great** (*or* **marked**) **extent,** *or* **in great** (*or* **large**) **part**] on its ability to ...
The heading remains **much** as in the previous version.
The waxes are the cause of **much of** the trouble in the dyeing of cotton goods.
The longer domain is still **largely** unknown.
Much of the importance of the glass electrode stems from ...
These properties vary **significantly** with time.
The ventilation passages are (**very**) **materially** obstructed.

В значительной части I
Many models are useful **well into** the radio-frequency range.

В значительной части II
The pebbles are transported **in large part** by turbidity currents.

В значительных масштабах
The Oxo reaction is now used **on a substantial scale.**

В зоне видимости
The satellite **has** at least one of the ground stations **in view** when it receives the emergency transmission.
The satellite passes **within view** of a system ground station.

В... и из него
The flux of molecules **in and out of** the two regions may be the same.
Pumping air **in and out of** the ballonets ...
To transfer electrons **to and from** the solution, ...

В идеале
For observation and experiment, a population should **ideally** consist of a group of ...
Ideally, the concentration of a solute should remain Gaussian.

В идеальном случае [*см.* **В идеале**].

В избытке I [*см. тж.* **В большом избытке**]
The acid is added **in excess.**
Hydrogen is present **in excess.**

В избытке II
The hydroxides redissolve **in excess of** the alkali.

В изобилии [*см. тж.* **Содержать большое количество**]
This substance is produced **in abundance.**

В... или вокруг него
A large concentration of mass **in or around** the central object ...

В ... или около него
It is unlikely that the Moon originated **in or near** the asteroid belt.

В ином случае
This explains the difference in N_{OG} values, which **otherwise** would agree.
The availability of ... is reduced to half what it **otherwise** would be.

В интервале
This function satisfies the equation identically **on** some **interval** $a < x < b$.
Over this **interval** the smooth wave remains smooth.

В интервале от ... до
In the range from (*or* **of**) 6 **to** 12 ...

В интересах
In the interests of speed, a higher temperature may be considered desirable, but ...

В исключительно тяжёлых условиях
Under the most exacting (*or* **severe**) **conditions ...**

В исключительных случаях
This effect may **in exceptional cases** persist for months.

В истекшем году
In the year just ended ...

В историческом плане
Historically, most of the work in optical competing has been in the analogue, continuous domain.

В каждодневной практике
The processor **routinely** performs feats of analysis.

В каждый момент времени
At each instant of time.
At every instant.

В какой бы форме ... ни встречался
The heats of formation refer to the net enthalpy change for the process of formation of a compound from its component elements **in whatever form** these elements **occur** naturally.

В какой-то момент
At some time in the amplification process the photon density is sufficiently large so that ...

В какой-то период
Rock that formed **at one time or another** during some 550 million years ...

В какой-то степени [*см.* **В некоторой степени**].

В какой-то точке
The intensity of the electric field **at a** (*or* **some**) **point** is defined as ...

В каком-либо направлении
First we investigate the distribution **along a particular direction.**

В качестве [*см. тж.* **Вводить (в выражение) в качестве, Действовать в качестве, Использоваться в качестве пищи**]
For a lamp he used an automobile light bulb.
He served **as** chief engineer.
Water was selected **for** (*or* **as**) the heat-transfer medium.

В качестве варианта
Alternatively, the dependence of internal energy on volume can be obtained.
As an alternative to this principle the company has introduced ...

В качестве дополнительной меры предосторожности
As a further precaution, the protective devices are designed to divert ...

В качестве заменителя
Sodium sulphate can be used **as an alternative to** anhydrous sodium carbonate in the manufacture of ...

В качестве иллюстрации
By way of illustration (*or* **As an illustration**) let us consider ...

В качестве основы для
Equation (23) is often used **as a basis for** the calculation of ...

В качестве отправного пункта
We take, **as the starting point,** the following equation: ...

В качестве приближения [*см. тж.* **В первом приближении, В хорошем приближении**]
As an approximation, C may be neglected in comparison with A.

В качестве приближения к
The dipole moment of a polyatomic molecule can **be approximated by** the vector sum of ...

В качестве примера [*см. тж.* **Для примера**]
In this chapter we attempt such an assessment, taking, **as a case in point,** the rapidly evolving technology of ...
By way of example (*or* **illustration**) let us consider ...
As an example (*or* **illustration**) we refer to ...

В качестве примера можно указать на
Examples are found in such diverse cells as ...
An example is hydrochloric acid.

В качестве реакции на
The rate of release of insulin is accelerated **in response to** high glucose concentrations in the blood.

В качестве справочного пособия [*см.* **Для справок**].

В количестве
The uranium, thorium, and potassium together supply heat **at a rate of** 3×10^{-9} W/ton.
The events take place **at a rate of** only a few per day.
Benzaldehyde is produced **at the rate of** about 2,000,000 lb annually.
Barium is found **to the extent of** 0.04% in the earth's crust.
Lactose is present in milk **to the extent of** about 4 percent.
Iron may be added for particular purposes **in amounts of** 1% or more.

В количественном (качественном) отношении
In a quantitative (qualitative) sense.

В комплекте с [*см. тж.* **Вместе с**]
The missile weighs 28 pounds **complete with** its launcher.

В конечном счёте (*или* итоге) [*см. тж.* **В конце концов**]
That proved to be a perfectly soluble problem **in the end.**
The acid decomposes **finally** (*or* **ultimately**) to sulphuric acid and hydrogen peroxide.
In the final (*or* **last**) **analysis** (*or* **In the long run**) the performance characteristics will be limited by ...
The solution we **eventually** adopted was to devise ...
The total number of factors in protein synthesis may **eventually** be reduced.
The value of the electric field at any point is determined **ultimately** by ...
Eventually [*or* **Ultimately,** *or* **In** (*or* **Over**) **the long run**] the ellipse becomes a parabola.
In the end the efficiency of marine propellers is usually about 70 percent.
The chemical identity of an atom **ultimately** depends on ...
Whatever the mechanism may **ultimately** prove to be, these processes are certainly far from simple.

В конечном счёте будет иметь
Such a star **will end up with** 2 percent of neon 22 in its core.

В конце
At the end of the catalogue ...
He began his career **in late** 1954.
The fuel is injected **late in** the cycle.
The liquid can be filtered **at the close of** the preparation.

В конце века
The first model was developed **in the latter part** (*or* **at the end of,** *or* **late in**) the 19th **century.**
Better pumps became available **at the turn of the century.**

В конце концов [*см. тж.* **В конечном счёте** (*или* **итоге**)]
Eventually (*or* **In the long run**) the material reaches an ignition point and bursts into flame.

В конце 1970-х годов
Late in the (19)70s.
In the late (19)70s.

В корне [*см. тж.* **Изменять в корне**]
These changes **profoundly** (*or* **radically**) alter the nature of ...

В корне отличаться от
Such a computer **constitutes a radical departure** (*or* **differs radically**) **from** those designed so far.

В короткий срок
We shall arrange the demonstration of spacesuits **on short notice.**

В космических масштабах
Evidence of resonance radiation pressure **on a cosmic scale** has been discovered in astronomy.

В космосе
In (outer) space.

В котором
A gas welding process **wherein** (*or* **in which**) the welding heat is obtained from ...

В котором используется
Any device **that uses** copper wire ...

В котором поддерживается температура
The mixture was heated in an oven **held at a temperature of** 170°C (*or* where **a temperature of** 170°C **was maintained**).

В котором размещён
An angle-iron frame, **which accommodates** (*or* **encloses**) the capacitance loop, is bolted to ...

В котором участвует [*см. тж.* **С участием**]
In extraction procedures **involving** metal chelates ...
For reactions **involving** (*or* **that involve**) solid or liquid reactants ...

В крайнем случае
As a last resort, the entire runner system can be welded up and re-cut.

В краткой форме
The solution can be obtained **in a concise form** (*math.*).
These larvae are heterogeneous and are therefore undefinable **in brief terms.**

В ... -кратном размере
This amount of water is enough to fill the Mediterranean **ten times over.**

В кратчайшее время
In the shortest possible time.

В кубе (*матем.*)
The load **cubed ...**

В курсе [*см.* **Быть в курсе новейших достижений**].

В курсе дела [*см.* **Быть в курсе дела**].

В лабораторных масштабах
Both processes have been demonstrated **on a** (*or* **the**) **laboratory scale,** and full-scale plant tests are under way.

В левой (правой) части уравнения
On (*or* **In**) **the left- (right-)(hand) side of the equation ...**
In the left (right) member of the equation ...

В литературе
Additional data can be found **in the literature.**
Literature values vary considerably.

В лучшем случае [*см. тж.* **Самое бóльшее**]
Distillation at atmospheric pressure can yield, **at best,** a distillate of 95 percent ethanol.
Because such measurements are made with pure minerals they can **at best** only approximate the Moon's actual composition.
If the area of the junction plane of the laser diode were a square centimetre, the current would, **in the best case,** be 25,000 amperes.
At most, the wind is only strong enough to move material of sand size.
At its best, the rub wheel reached an efficiency of 20 percent.

В любой момент [*см. тж.* **Всегда**]
At every instant all electron-pair waves are at the same stage in their cycle.
The hydraulic overload protection facilities enable the machine to be stopped **at all times.**
This implies that $\nabla = B$ **for all time.**
Since molecules vibrate, **at any instant** there will be molecules with a range of internuclear distances.

В любом отношении
At these jobs, horses can compete successfully with tractors **on** almost **any count.**

В любом случае [*см. тж.* **И в том, и в другом случае**]
In any event (*or* **case**) the gate valves must be provided with ...

В любом случае из двух [*см. тж.* **В обоих случаях**]
In either case, a simple messenger was present (*biol.*).

В любом соотношении
Methyl alcohol mixes with water **in all proportions.**

В любую погоду [*см.* **Кабина для работы в любую погоду**].

В максимуме
This is the transition state *A—B—C* where the potential energy is **at a maximum** (*or* **maximal**).

At the maximum of the curve.

В малом (*матем.*)
The existence of solutions **in the small** has been established.
The non-tangency condition can be asserted **in the small.**

В масштабе
The individual beds of sandstone are too thin to be mapped **at the** usual **scale.**
The master form is drawn **to a scale** corresponding to the magnification of the optical system.
Antennas are often constructed **to scale** in miniature.
Draw a picture of the orbits of the Earth and Moon about the Sun exactly **to scale.**

В масштабе 1:5
A **one-fifth scale** model.

В математическом выражении
These slopes are, **in calculus notation,** $(\partial V/\partial n_A)_{n_B}$ and $(\partial V/\partial n_B)_{n_A}$.
Expressed mathematically, Ohm's law is $V = IR$.

В медицинских целях
Mercurous chloride is still used **medicinally.**

В международном масштабе
Internationally (*or* **On an international scale**), there are five distinct systems in use for the telegraphic sending of time signals.

В меньшей степени
To a lesser (*or* **smaller**) **degree** (*or* **extent**) this dependence refers to different vibrational levels.

В меру своих возможностей
The operator can only establish this condition **to the best of his ability** by the "feel" of the assembly.

В месте
The ultrasonic softening concentrates **at the** deformation **site.**
Interaction **at** different **sites** on the surface ...

В месте назначения
The pieces are assembled **at their destination.**

В месте происхождения
Controls should be applied to stop the discharge of harmful mercury wastes **at the point of origin.**

В месте соединения
Figure 5 shows an element **at the juncture of** two strips.

В микроскоп [*см. тж.* **Виден в микроскоп, Если рассматривать ... в микроскоп**]
These cracks can be seen **with** (*or* **in,** *or* **under**) **a microscope.**

В миллион раз
The luminosity of the intersecting storage rings is about **a million times** smaller.

В мире I
This forest formation produces **the world's** most important commercial softwood lumber.

В мире II
In the realm of sound ...
In the animal (plant) **kingdom ...**

В мировом масштабе [*см. тж.* **В глобальном масштабе, Во всём мире**]
On a global scale, ...

В... можно вставить
The holder **takes** standard inserts.

В момент [*см.* **В тот момент когда**].

В момент вылета из
At the instant the projectile **leaves** the gun barrel ...

В момент написания этой книги
As this book is being prepared (*or* **At this writing**), tests are being run.

В надежде на то, что
The new synchrotron was being built **in the hope** (*or* **expectation**) **that ...**

В направлении [*см. тж.* **Идти по направлению**]
t **is directed in the sense of** increasing y.
Sunlight **is reflected from** the Moon **toward** the Earth.

В направлении вниз
In a downward direction.

В направлении вперёд
In a forward direction.

В направлении от центра [*см.* **С удалением от центра**].

В направлении, противоположном
The buoyant force acts **in opposition** (*or* **in a direction opposite**) **to** the gravitation force.

В направлении увеличения времени
The normal is oriented **in the direction of increasing time.**

В настоящее время [*см. тж.* **Имеющийся в настоящее время**]
As of now, these molecules have been identified.
The engine will operate on **currently** available fuels.
At the moment it is not clear how these standards might be arrived at.
This kind of switch is **currently** (*or* **presently**) constructed of silicon.
The mechanism of this reaction is **presently** unknown.
At present (*or* **At the present time,** *or* **Nowadays**) there is a strong trend towards ...
The **now** popular electronic calculators...

В натуральную величину [*см. тж.* **Натуральных размеров**]
The pivot section **is full scale** (*or* **full size**).
A complete **full-scale** engine will be ready for testing within a year.
A **full-size** image ...

В натянутом состоянии
Both parts of the belt must **be in tension** to maintain contact between the belt and the pulleys.
The thread **is taut.**

В начале [*см. тж.* **На раннем этапе развития**]
In the early nineteenth century (*or* **Early in** the 19th century) ...
Early in the crystallization of a melt ...
Dropping of the leaves occurs **at the inception** (*or* **beginning**) of an unfavourable season.
He began his career **in early** 1954.

В начале координат
The slope of the curve **at the origin (of the coordinates)** is ...

В начале развития [*см. тж.* **На раннем этапе развития**]
Early in the history (*or* **At the beginning**) of steam navigation ...

В начальной стадии развития [*см. тж.* **На раннем этапе развития, Находиться в эмбриональном состоянии**]
In the early days (*or* **stage**) of nuclear power ...

В наше время
In modern times (*or* **Presently**) this definition usually includes ...

В наши дни
Our compasses **today** depend upon the same forces.

В не столь отдалённом будущем
In the not (too) distant future these substances will be used in farming.

В неблагоприятных атмосферных условиях
During inclement weather ...

В небольшом избытке
The calcium carbonate **is in slight excess.**

В невыгодном положении
The surface ship **is at a (great) disadvantage.**

В недостатке
If mixed with **insufficient** oxygen, nitrogen causes death by suffocation.

В недрах земли
These materials could have been incorporated **in the (deep) interior of the earth.**
Hot molten rock reservoirs situated **deep in the earth ...**

В незначительной степени [*см.* **Лишь в незначительной степени**].

В незначительном количестве
Unsubstituted furanose sugars have never been isolated, although they do exist **in small proportion** (*or* **to a small extent**) in solution.

В некоторой степени [*см. тж.* **В некотором смысле, Несколько**]
Picornaviruses appear to be **somewhat** allied to the *RNA* bacteriophages.
The existence of a definite half-life has been confirmed **to a degree** (*or* **to some extent,** *or* **to an extent**).

В некотором смысле [*см. тж.* **Несколько**]
The solutions satisfy the original equations **in some** (*or* **a**) **sense.**

In a sense the photon is a vector meson, a tiny fraction of the time.
In a way this represents increasing convenience.

В некоторых местах
In places, all weathered rock was removed.

В некоторых отношениях [*см. тж.* **Несколько**]
Elements that are close to one another or alike **in some** (*or* **certain**) **respects** tend to be grouped together.
Removal of these irregularities resembles **in some ways** removal of rapids by a stream.

В некоторых случаях [*см.* **В отдельных случаях**].

В необработанном виде [*см.* **Без обработки**].

В непосредственной близости
When holes are drilled in boiler plate, the metal **in the immediate vicinity** develops tiny cracks.

В непосредственной близости от [*см. тж.* **Непосредственно прилегающий к**]
A concentration gradient of oxygen exists in air **in the immediate vicinity** (*or* **neighbourhood**) **of** a hot radiator.

В несколько этапов
The isotope of carbon decays **in several steps** to ^{12}C.

В... нет ни(какого) намёка на то, что
The marine rocks provided **not so much as a hint that** they were actually from the continental shelf.

В нетронутом виде [*см.* **Без изменения**].

В нижнем положении
In the down position, the guard is 1/4 in. above the work material.

В нижнем (*антон.* **верхнем**) **течении реки**
In the lower (*anton.* **upper**) **reaches of the river ...**

В области I
In the field (*or* **area**) **of** organic chemistry it is often helpful to ...
The latest development **in this line** is ...

В области II
Not much has been done **in the way of** actually assessing a technology.

В области III
The flux is uniform **over the** whole **area** (*or* **region**).

В области автомобилестроения
These clutches are capable of wide application **in the automotive field.**

В области ... произошёл поворот
Laser technology **has taken a (new) turn** that may speed up ...

В области теоретических исследований
On the theoretical side much work remains.

В область
Physicists have extrapolated this notion **to the realm of** elementary particles.

В обозримом будущем [*см. тж.* **В предвидимом будущем**]
For (*or* **In**) **the foreseeable future** this appears to belong to the realm of science fiction.

В обоих случаях [*см. тж.* **В любом случае из двух**]
The coefficient γ is found either by averaging ..., or by summing ...; **either way** we have $\gamma = T/Z_p = NT$.
In either case (*or* **In both cases**) ...

В ... образовалась течь
The primary system of the reactor now **had a leak.**

В ... образуется
This clay **shows** wide, deep cracks in dry seasons.

В обратном направлении
The ions were moving **in the opposite direction.**
This reaction goes **the other way** during the deposition stage.

В обратном порядке
The same transformations were applied to the same hadron, but **in the reverse sequence** (*or* **order**).

В общей сложности [*см. тж.* **В сумме**]
We drilled **an aggregate** (*or* **a total**) **of** 4000 inches [*or* 4000 inches **(all) in all**].

В общем (и целом) [*см. тж.* **В целом, Всего**]
(All) in all, the observations and experiments tended to support this hypothesis.
In sum (*or* **Overall**) there was no clinical symptom that placed a limit on the doses we administered.
All told, the emissions have contributed 27% of ...
On the whole, these results support the findings of ...

В общем напоминать
The chloride **shows** (*or* **bears**) **a general resemblance to** $SiCl_4$.

В общем случае
In the general case (*or* **Generally**) the directions of the tensors will not coincide.
In a general way, the higher the boiling point of the gas, the more readily it is adsorbed.

В общем смысле
We might think of "saturated" **in a general sense** as "being as full as possible".

В общем соответствовать
These figures **are in general agreement with** the model.

В общем сходиться во мнении, что
Geologists are **in general agreement that** petroleum originated from...

В общих чертах [*см. тж.* **Описывать в общих чертах**]
The period distribution of the observed pulsars can be **roughly** understood on the basis of ...
In general terms, the block diagram for the controller can be drawn as in Fig. 2.23.
The following notes are only intended to show **in outline** just what factors have to be considered.

В обычном смысле слова
Hydrochloric acid is not a reducing agent **in the ordinary sense.**

В ограниченном количестве [*см. тж.* **Иметься в ограниченном количестве**]
This cereal is grown only **in limited amounts.**
Coal is also found in Jurassic strata, but **to a limited extent.**

В ограниченных масштабах
On a limited scale, ultrafiltration may remove colloidal particles.

В огромном большинстве случаев
In the vast (*or* **overwhelming**) **majority of cases ...**

В огромных количествах
Such "alpha-particle nuclei" are **copiously** manufactured in stellar processes.

В одинаковой степени
The pigment accumulation is not always present **to the same extent** in the same organs in different individuals.

В одних случаях ..., а в других случаях [*см.* **Иногда ..., а иногда**].

В однозначном соответствии с
These curves can be matched **one-to-one with** the points in a line.

В одном и другом отношении
The theory succeeded **in one way and** failed **in another.**

В одном из следующих разделов
I will discuss the details of the model **in a later section.**

В одном лишь
The number of binary star systems **in** our own Galaxy **alone** is probably several hundred millions.

В одном направлении
Component *A* diffuses **unidirectionally** (*or* **in one direction**).

В окрестности
In the neighbourhood (*or* **vicinity**) **of** a point *P* ...
These regions are **on the outskirts of** the Solar System.

В определённом порядке
These minerals weather chemically **in a certain order.**

В определённых пределах
The growth response of the organism is a function, **within (certain) limits,** of the amount of ...

В основе ... лежит [*см. тж.* **Лежащий в основе**]
The basis for (*or* **The foundation of**) this theory **is** the Pauli exclusion principle.

Electromagnetic radiation **has its origins in** atomic and molecular processes.
For every pathology **there is an underlying** biochemical effect.

В основном [*см. тж.* **Большинство, Главным образом, По существу**]
The earth's atmosphere is **largely** composed of nitrogen and oxygen.
Concretions are composed **(pre)dominantly** of calcium carbonate.
This chapter **principally** compares the characteristics of...
Nitric acid is **significantly** natural in its occurrence.
Most of the theory is **basically** the same as that of sound waves in air.
Basically, these variations result from ...
Bone ash gives **essentially** the same counting efficiency as ...
The instrument consists **essentially** of a prism, a pan of mercury, ...
For the most (*or* **major,** *or* **greater**) **part,** the subjects are covered adequately.
The shield has been designed **for the most part** from common materials.
The region for linear operation will be determined **fundamentally** by the maximum width of ...
The heading remains **much as in** the previous version.
Axial transport in unpacked tubes **is predominantly** (*or* **principally,** *or* **chiefly,** *or* **mainly,** *or* **in the main**) by conversion.
The article is **primarily** concerned with ...
Some types of sedimentary rocks are **substantially** of the same composition as clay.
The corpuscular radiation from the Sun, **mostly** electrons and protons, is an efficient source of ...
This fuel resists combustion knock **principally** because it has ...
Typically the canopy is closed and the forest is dark, although ...
The colour force is **overwhelmingly** employed in the service sector.
When the process is **substantially** complete, ...

В основном принято использовать
The most commonly used convention employs the delta scale.

В основном разумный
His ideas were **basically sound.**

В основном состоять в
Essentially, the discharge **involves** the passage of electrons from the cathode to the anode.

В основном тот же
This model employs **the same basic** (*or* **basically the same**) approach.

В особенности [*см. тж.* **Особенно**]
Some metals, **notably** (*or* **particularly**) iron and steel, are capable of being magnetized.
The same cannot be said of certain other particles, **most notably** the electrons.
The results of this study relate **specifically** to the matched filter optical processors.

В особых случаях
In special situations (*or* **cases**), the right-hand side of Eq. (11-8) vanishes.

В остальном
Otherwise the main differences between ... are their forging speed and the way they store energy.

В остатке
131 divided by 3 is 43 with **a remainder of** 2.

В ответ на
In (*or* **As a**) **response** (*or* **In answer**) **to** stresses the body of a mammal mobilizes a system of defensive reaction.

В отдельности
It is not necessary to know **the individual** values of l, m and n but only the combinations $\zeta = 18l + 4m + 2n$.

В отдельности и вместе [*см.* **Как в отдельности, так и вместе**].

В отдельных случаях
In specific (*or* **individual**) **cases** excess ammonium hydroxide dissolves copper as a complex ion.
In some instances one can use pulsed laser to permit ...
This material may, **on occasion,** be seen to leave the comet's nucleus.

В отличие от [*см. тж.* **В противоположность**]
Active current: in alternating current that part in the phase with the voltage or the effective energy, **as differentiated** (*or* **distinguished,** *or* **distinct**) **from** the wattless or useless energy.

The transistor is a current-controlled device **as opposed to** [*or* **as distinct from,** *or* **in distinction to**, *or* **in contradistinction to,** *or* **in contrast to** (*or* **with**), *or* **as contrasted to,** *or* **unlike**) the vacuum tube, which is a voltage-controlled device.
The company has achieved a 200% increase in productivity by using the robot **as opposed to** manual servicing.
The ultrasonic welding machine is semi-portable. **By contrast,** the resistance welder is a relatively cumbersome unit to move to a new location.
Unlike copper windings, permanent magnets never wear out.
These reactors are called light-water reactors **to distinguish them from** the type that uses heavy water.
Contrary to the usual practice of ...
Sediments deposited by contour currents are called contourites, **to set them apart from** turbidites.

В отличие от этого
For liquids and solids, **contrastingly,** no simple relation exists.

В отличном состоянии
Now you can keep your indicators **in top** (*or* **first-class**) **condition.**

В отношении I
The dimethyl-amine group and the aldehyde group **are in the 1.4 relationship to each other.**
Jupiter's atmosphere is hydrogen and helium **in a three-to-one ratio.**

В отношении II
There are differences **as to** (*or* **concerning,** *or* **regarding,** *or* **as regards**) the time of drying (*or* **as far as** the time of drying **is concerned**).
The term binding energy is sometimes used **to describe** the energy which must be ...
The conditions for measurement must be optimized **with reference** (*or* **in respect,** *or* **with respect,** *or* **in regard,** *or* **with regard**) **to** (*or* **in respect of**) the choice of ...
Now we can do the same **for** the set of even integers.

В отношении... к
Isostatic restoration occurs **in the ratio (of)** 4:5.

В отношении 3:2
The triplet and quartet have areas **in the ratio (of) 3:2.**

В отрыве от
The origin and density of the energy in the universe cannot be completely understood **in isolation from** the phenomena of life and consciousness.

В отсутствие [*см. тж.* **При отсутствии**]
In the absence of samples from the planets, the meteorites were studied by chemists...

В очень редких случаях
Very occasionally 0.3 mg of thyroxine is necessary.

В первом приближении
As a first approximation, assume that ...
To a first approximation, the energies of all orbits of the same n are equal.
The first approximation composition **of** the mantle **may be taken as** that of chondrites (*geol.*).

В первом случае из двух
In the former case ...

В первую очередь
Scattering by crystalline materials will be studied **first.**
The new engineer should **make it his first business to** trace ... (*or* **should first of all** trace ...)
The magnitude of the thermal current is **primarily** a function of temperature.
The company has introduced the constant-pressure system **primarily** to meet demand in ...

В переднем (*антон.* **заднем**) **конце**
These glands concentrate **posteriorly** (*anton.* **anteriorly**) (*biol.*).

В перигелии
Mercury's orbit **at its perihelion ...**

В период
In that case many of the stable or long-lived atoms present would have been produced **at a period when** the meteorite was ...

В период наибольшей яркости
The star was extraordinarily luminous **at its brightest.**

В перспективе имеется
Many opportunities for commercial applications at higher temperatures **are in sight.**

В печати
In the press.

В плане [*см.. тж.* **Если смотреть сверху**]
In plan delta wings are somewhat triangular resembling the Greek letter Δ.

В плоскости
This perpendicular lies **in the plane of** the orbit.

В ... подаётся
The tube **is fed (with)** 28.5 cm^3/s pure water.

В ... поддерживаются условия
The cell **is maintained under** isothermal **conditions.**

В поддержку [*см.* **В защиту**].

В поднятом положении
The pawls of both motors **are in the raised position.**

В подтверждение
In support of this interpretation one can argue that ...

В подтверждение этого предположения
In support of this conjecture it was noted that ...

В поисках
In search(ing) for better logic devices ...
To waste energy and effort **in the search for** (*or* **of**) nonexistent deposits ...
The boreholes drilled **in search of** oil ...

В покое [*см.* **В состоянии покоя**].

В полевых условиях
These units are immediately available for **in-the-field** replacement.

В полёте [*см. тж.* **Бортовой**]
In-flight vibration of the aircraft ...

В полной мере
These vacancies do not contribute **in full measure** to the resistivity.

В полной темноте
The experiments were conducted **in total darkness.**

В полной уверенности, что
Man has polluted the atmosphere **in the certainty that** the waste gases would be diluted past harm.

В полном смысле слова
The asthenosphere is not a **true** liquid.

В половинной степени
In this formula the oxygen concentration occurs only **to the one-half power.**

В положении
Substitution occurs **at the meta-position** (*chem.*).

В положении "включено"
The switch **is in the "on" position.**

В положении "пара" по отношению к (*хим.*)
The amino group **is located para (p) to** the hydroxyl group.

В полтора раза больше
That distance **is half (as much) again** the width of the Moon.

В полузаводском масштабе
Preparation of 2,3-butanediol has been by fermentation **on a pilot plant basis** (*or* **on a pilot scale**).

В пользу [*см.* **Всё говорит в пользу, Говорить в пользу, Данные в пользу, Довод в пользу**].

В пользу ... говорит
The difference **is supported** (*or* **corroborated,** *or* **confirmed**) **by** comparable tests.
It counts in favour of this hypothesis **that** it covers.

В помощь
Here, it will be useful to outline some basic concepts of the physics of metals **for the benefit of** readers who may not be familiar with ...

В поперечнике [*см. тж.* **В диаметре**]
One might start with an electron beam a few centimetres **across** (*or* **in diameter**).
Craterlike basins tens of kilometres **across ...**

В попытках
In an effort to form curved microchannels we use ...

В попытке
Investigators have determined exponent *n* **in an attempt to** specify ...

В порошкообразной форме
When **in the powdered form,** dolomite effervesces with ...

В ... порядке
Uniform doping is, **to first order,** a sufficient condition to assure that ...

В порядке возрастания длины
The wires are grouped **in ascending order of length** (*or* **in order of increasing length**).

В порядке возрастания энергии
Orbitals are filled **in order of increasing energy.**

В порядке живой очереди
Prospective users apply for licences **on the first-come, first-served basis.**

В порядке, обратном
These minerals tend to weather **in inverse order to** their sequence of crystallization.

В порядке подготовки к
Preparatory to solving this equation, we first discuss ...
In preparation for this work ...

В порядке проведения программы
UN began a systematic search for mineral brines **as part of its program of** geothermal investigation.

В порядке убывающей твёрдости
The chief natural abrasives, **in order of decreasing hardness,** are diamond, corundum, emery ...

В порядке увеличения
The variety of magnetic "bottles" designed for this purpose over the years can be arranged **in order of increasing** plasma density.
The characteristic speeds are indexed **in increasing** (*or* **ascending**) **order (of magnitude).**

В порядке увеличения размера
The various transfinities can be listed **in increasing size.**

В порядке уменьшения
The next category of uranium ore **in descending** (*or* **decreasing**) **order of** uranium content consists of ...

В последнее время
Considerable **recent** attention has been focussed on ...
Currently some evidence has been advanced which ...
No improvements have been noted **recently** (*or* **in recent years,** *or* **in the last few years**).

В последнее время предпочитают пользоваться
Recent trends are toward increased use of electronic components.

В последнем случае (из двух)
If the latter is the case, the lamp pattern indicates ...
In the latter case *n* is some whole number of ...

В последовательном порядке
You will find the explanations arranged **consecutively.**
The photographs are taken **in an orderly sequence.**

В последующем изложении
The point of view to be discussed **from here on** (*or* **in the subsequent text,** *or* **in what follows**) is one that has been ...
In the following, we will expand upon these problems.

В последующие годы
In succeeding years rocket flights confirmed our initial results.
These devices, manufactured since 1915, have undergone many changes **during the ensuing years** (*or* **during the years which followed**).

В последующих главах
These principles are discussed **in the chapters that follow** [*or* **in the following** (*or* **subsequent**) **chapters**].

В ... поступает
The blood vessels **receive** hormonal secretions.

В правой верхней части
This is the condition existing **at the upper right of** Fig. 8.1.

В правой части уравнения
If SI units are used for the quantities **on the right** (*or* **in the right-hand side,** *or* **in the right member**) **of** Eq. (2-36) ...

В практической работе
In practice, we almost always deal with systems for which ...

В предвидимом будущем [*см. тж.* **В обозримом будущем**]
This type of machine will continue most effectively to meet the needs of large-scale production **in the foreseeable future.**
There will be no shortage of communication channels **as far ahead as anyone can see.**

В пределах [*см. тж.* **Надёжный в пределах**]
The uncertainty with respect to the depth of the hypocentres remains **a matter of** kilometres.
The width of the buildings **is in the range from** 14 **to** 20 metres.
Each pin is adjustable **over a** one-inch **range.**
Area is a measure of the amount of space contained **within the boundaries** (*or* **limits**) **of** a plane figure.
To stop the aircraft **within the confines of** the airfield ...
Different functional groups **within** the same molecule may react with each other.
Coastal marshes lie **within** the tidal zone.
The temperature is held **to within** 0.5K.

В пределах видимости
Take bearings from a known position, or **within sight of** the transmitter.

В пределах возможностей
A fast for 40 days **is (well) within the capability of** a healthy adult.

В пределах диапазона [*см.* **В диапазоне**].

В пределах досягаемости
Loaded mandrels are pushed to a position **within reach of** the casting machine operator.
The layer holds capillary water **within reach of** plant roots.

В пределах досягаемости на данном уровне развития науки
Signal gains of this order **are within the grasp of the present state of the art.**

В пределах нормы
The T4 level **is within the normal range.**

В пределах ... миль от
The greatest portion of the atmosphere lies **within** a few **miles of** the earth's surface.

В пределах ошибки эксперимента
The results agree with values predicted from the shock velocity, **to within (the) experimental error of** the velocity measurement.
Within the limits of experimental error, $n = 2$.

В пределах точности анализа
The discrepancy **is within the accuracy of the analysis.**

В пределе
Excessive heads involve excessive velocities and consequently low absolute pressures which, **in the limit,** involve cavitation and loss of efficiency.
In the limit of an infinitely closely spaced grid ...
Maxwell's equations lead to the results of Part I **in the limit of** small wavelengths.
Raoult's law is followed by the solvent **in the** dilute-solution **limit.**

В пределе, взятом по
In the limit $t \to 0$ **taken in** L these quantities still have to be subject to the same relation.

В пределе сильного поля
In the strong-field limit ...

В предельном случае
In the limiting case ...

В предположении, что [*см. тж.* **Исходя из предположения, что; Предположив, что; При предположении**]
Air-speed sensing equipment is generally designed **on the assumption that** flow is subsonic.
Most of the investigators have analyzed their data **under the assumption** (*or* **assuming) that** plug flow prevailed.

В ... приближении
In this **approximation,** the number of molecules per unit volume is ...
(With)in the weak-guidance **approximation,** Eq. (35) gives: ...

В приведённом порядке
All chapters need not be read **sequentially.**

В ... приводится обзор
The final chapter **reviews** the geology of ...

В ... приёмов
The part is machined **in** two **steps.**

В приложении к
(When) applied to one-dimensional flow, these equations take the form: ...

В применении к
This equation, **as applied to** semiconductors, takes the form: ...

В принципе
Fundamentally, the giant planets differ from the Earth chiefly in that ...
The artificially induced mutations are **in principle** (*or* **basically**) of the same kind as the spontaneous ones.
In principle, the capacitance of the reference condenser can be deduced from its geometry.
This mechanism is simple **in concept** (*or* **conceptually**).
The treatment of alluvial tin is not **essentially** different, though varying in detail.

В природных условиях
Phosphate is present **naturally** in water and soil in sufficient amounts to ...

В присутствии
The same estimation can be used **with** the reaction **present** (*or* **in the presence of** the reaction).
Protein loss from the renal tract will lead to a degree of hypoalbuminaemia, especially **if there is** a nephrotic syndrome.

В присутствии и в отсутствие
Rate coefficients of packed columns used for gas absorption and solvent extraction, **with and without** simultaneous chemical reaction, ...

В продолжение [*см.* **В процессе, В течение**].

В продольном направлении
The block is perforated **lengthwise.**

В ... происходит
This material **exhibits** a phase transition of a different kind.

В промежутке [*см.* **В интервале**].

В промежуточный период
Many important things happened **in the intervening period.**

В промышленности [*см. тж.* **Использоваться в промышленности**]
The same method is used **industrially** for a continuous indication of liquid density.

В промышленных масштабах
A new capacitor is now manufactured **in production quantities** [*or* **on an** (*or* **the**) **industrial** (*or* **commercial**) **scale**].

В промышленных условиях
Acetic anhydride is prepared **industrially** from acetic acid.

В пропорции
In the proportion 1 part coal **to** 4 parts barite ...
Mix chlorite with hypochlorite **in the ratio of** 1 chlorite to 1.5 hypochlorite.

В пространстве и времени [*см.* **Во времени и пространстве**].

В... протекает ток
An external circuit connected to the diode **experiences a current flow.**

В противном случае [*см.* **Который иначе оставался бы неиспользованным**].

В противоположном направлении [*см. тж.* **В том же или в противоположном направлении**]
If the laser frequency is lower than the centre frequency, the molecules selected will be moving **in the opposite direction.**

В противоположном случае
The potential must be designated positive if ...; **otherwise** it is negative.

В противоположность [*см. тж.* **В отличие от**]
The helium-neon and argon-ion lasers provided a continuous output of laser light, **as opposed to** the pulsed output of the metal vapours.
The metal-oxide-semiconductors technology produces transistors of the unipolar type **in contradistinction** (*or* **in contrast**) **to** the earlier junction transistors, which are bipolar.

Contrary to upsetting, extrusion reduces the diameter of ...
Contrary to popular belief, not all mixtures of hydrogen and oxygen are dangerous.
In contrast to most metals, the conductivity of semiconductors increases with temperature.

В противоположность ему
Histone H1 is the largest of them; **contrastingly,** H4 is the smallest.

В противоположность общепринятому представлению
Gout is commoner in women, **contrary to popular opinion** (*or* **belief**).

В противоположность ожиданиям [*см.* **Вопреки ожиданиям**].

В противоположность тому, чего можно было бы ожидать исходя из ... соображений
Contrary to what might be expected from physicochemical **considerations, ...**

В противоположность этому [*см. тж.* **Наоборот**]
By contrast, the corresponding ratios for liquid metals are greater than unity.
In contrast (to this), alkyl substitution results in ...

В противоположные стороны [*см.* **Действовать в противоположные стороны, Направлены в противоположные стороны**].

В противоположных направлениях
The oscillating electric field of the laser light accelerates the plasma electrons **in opposite directions.**

В процентах [*см. тж.* **Измеряться в процентах, Определяться в процентах**]
The galvanometer is calibrated **in percent of** carbon dioxide.
The quantity of each element is expressed **on a percentage basis.**
Coke-oven byproducts, **in percentage of** the coal used, are gas 18.5, light oil 1.0, and tar 3.5.
This ratio is expressed **as a percentage of** the power output to the power input.

В процентном отношении
In percentage terms (*or* **Percentagewise**), the greatest variability is in the driest areas.

В процессе
In the course of [*or* **During the process of** (*or* **During**)] the test the downstream pressure never reached 2.0 Torr.
During the progress of the job ...

В процессе образования
The eddy was recorded **in the act of forming.**

В процессе производства
The coating protects gears **while in production** or on the shelf.

В процессе работы
In operation we stop the lathe and advance the bar in the turret.

В процессе развития
As development progresses (*or* **continues**) [*or* **In the course** (*or* **process**) **of development**] the *acanthella* becomes elongate.
This proportion gradually increased **with development.**

В процессе сборки
The product is transferred manually between operators **as it is assembled.**

В процессе формирования
Two potential ore deposits **in the act of being formed** may have been discovered at ...

В прошлом
In the past (*or* **Previously**) this asymmetry has been interpreted in terms of ...

В рабочее положение
The machine elements move rapidly **into position.**

В рабочем состоянии [*см.* **Исправный**].

В рабочих условиях
It is essential to have data on the height of the theoretical unit to be expected **under the running** (*or* **the operating**) **conditions.**
In service, pores may develop by enlargement of ...

В равновесии
Because nitrogen gas **is at equilibrium**

free energy must be supplied in order to form nitrogen compounds.
When two dissimilar solids **are at equilibrium ...**
When the system **is at** (*or* **in**) **equilibrium, ...**

В равновесии с
The magnetization of the sample **is in balance with** the field.
The liquid **is in equilibrium with** the vapour.

В равной мере относиться к
The previous comments regarding the aldoses **pertain** (*or* **refer**) **equally to** the ketoses.

В ... раз
The flux detectors increase magnetic-flux density **a hundred times.**
One can say that the universe has expanded **by a factor of three** since the radiation left the emitter.
The potassium ratio is changed **tenfold.**
The particle can be cooler **by the factor** $1/\sqrt{2}$.

В ... раз более
Phenol **is a** million **times more** reactive than benzene in most substitution reactions.

В ... раз больше
The resultant enhancement of intensity may be **as great as 100-fold.**
The nucleus of a uranium atom **is six times larger.**
The titrant **is twenty times as** concentrated **as** the analyte solution.

В ... раз больше по массе *и т.п.,* **чем**
The Earth **is 81 times as massive as** the Moon.

В ... раз больше своего объёма
The solution liberates **20 times its own volume of** oxygen when heated.

В ... раз больше, чем
This thickness **is four times greater** than platform strata laid down in the same time period (*geol.*).
The exponential factor **is** $\mathbf{1.2 \times 10^4}$ **times as large** for the 610.4 nm transition **as** for the 670.8 one.
Thus the efficiency **is three times as great as** (*or* **greater than**) before.
The laser spectral bandwidth **is 5-10 times larger than** the atom profile.
There is approximately **10-50 times more** potassium inside the cell **than** outside (*or* **10-50 times as much ... as** outside).
The oxygen atoms have about **ten times** the efficiency of the molecules.
The mass of the Earth **is 81 times that of** the Moon.
The incidence of the disease in patients who received this material **is six-fold higher than** expected.
These fields have **eight times as many** components **as** the electromagnetic field has.

В ... раз короче
The molecule **is a tenth as long as** one would expect.

В ... раз менее тяжёлый, чем
The electron **is 100,000 times less massive than ...**

В ... раз меньше, чем
The anomaly frequency **is smaller than ... by a factor of 1,000.**
Neutron stars **are 1,000,000 times smaller than** ordinary stars.
The rate **is one-tenth that** for the larger K°_{L}.
Sodium compounds are to be preferred over calcium compounds because the former cost **one-sixth as much.**
The cost per electron volt **was 10 times less than** it was at the *SLAC* accelerator.
This momentum **would be a factor of 10 short of** the momentum needed to explain ...
The field of view of the camera covers an area of the sky about **a fifth as large as** it does in the wide-field mode.

В ... раз ниже, чем
This temperature **was ten times lower than** (*or* **ten times as low as**) anyone had achieved before.

В ... раз шире, чем
The central maximum **is twice as wide as** the subsidiary one.

В разгаре [*см. тж.* **В самом разгаре**]
The spaceship **is in the midst of** the test.

В разделе о
These methods are described **under** synthesis.
This can be caused by the conditions described **under the heading of** acute confusional states.

В различной степени
Bisphenols are counteracted **to a variable degree** (*or* **extent**) by organic matter.
The energy is distributed **in** (*or* **to**) **varying** (*or* **to variable**) **degrees** among four forms of excitation.

В различных местах
These rocks vary in composition **from place to place.**

В различных направлениях
Attempts at solving the problem have been made **along diversity of avenues** (*or* **in different directions**).

В различных отношениях
Our existence depends on communication **in more ways than one.**

В разное время
The various spectrometric techniques developed **at different times ...**

В разобранном виде
The vibration damping control system, shown **exploded** above, is ...

В разрезе
The pressure governor is shown **in section** in Fig. 74.
The unit body is of square shape **in section.**

В районе [*см.* **Вблизи**].

В рамках
The weak force and electromagnetism can now be understood **in the context of** a single theory.
The mass of the electron cannot be calculated **(with)in the framework** (*or* **context**) of quantum electrodynamics.
Within the limits of ideal gas behaviour, this equation provides ...

В ранний период [*см.* **В начале развития**].

В ... расположен
The narrow ocean basin **was the site of** thick salt deposits.

В распоряжении [*см.* **Иметь в распоряжении (*или* в наличии)**].

В рассматриваемом случае
In the case being considered (*or* **under consideration,** *or* **under review,** *or* **under study,** *or* **at (in) hand,** *or* **in question**) there is an inertia term and ...

В рассматриваемый период
Stock markets were active **during the period under review.**

В растворе
The acyclic aldehyde form exists **in solution** to a very small extent.
Chemical colorimeters measure the concentration of a known constituent **in solution.**

В реальных условиях [*см. тж.* **В действительности**]
In actual practice this may not be true.

В редких случаях
In rare instances (*or* **cases**) there may be ...

В резком противоречии с [*см.* **Находиться в резком противоречии с**].

В результате [*см. тж.* **Вследствие**]
The hypothesis assumes that the genetic code was universal **in** (*or* **as a**) **consequence of** its being established in the ancestral stock.
The internal energy increases **as a result of** the reaction.
In this zone, mixing occurs **as the result of** convection.
In response to the increase of pressure the emergency system went into action.
The changes in band intensity **associated with** changes in pH ...
A hydrogen atom is first formed **by** collision.
The work is done **by virtue of** the volume change.
The first term is the energy contribution **due to** the translational motion of ...
The possible carbonium ions that can form **from** the addition of ...
With the single-heterostructure laser some of the light is still lost **owing to** its penetration across ...
The external springs are less likely to deteriorate **through** heating.
Contamination of condensate may occur **from** leakage of ...
The pulse shapes were derived **from** scanning different types of particles.

This work **has resulted in** two waveguides.
Bentonite shrinks **upon** drying.

В результате действия на
City smogs are produced **by the action of** sunlight **on** oxides of nitrogen from automobiles.

В результате ... остаётся мало [*см. тж.* **После ... остаётся**]
Ionizations, which require a large energy, **leave** the expelled electrons **with little** kinetic energy.

В результате происходит
An explosion **results.**

В результате реакции образуется
The reaction of ketones with alcohols **forms** (or **produces**) hemiketals and ketals.

В результате рекомбинации
One percent of the ejected electrons is lost in the base **by recombination.**

В результате употребления
Changes in the external gel surface **with use** (*or* **because**) **of** contamination occur ...

В результате чего
The temperature is increased, **causing** the gas to expand.
Several types of electronic multipliers develop an output of the form v_1v_2/v_3, **with the result that** (*or* **as a result of which**) either multiplication or division is impossible.

В результате чего (*или* **которого**) **образуется** [*см. тж.* **Что даёт**]
The addition of an electron to a neutral atom **with the resulting formation of** a negative ion ...

В результате чего получаем
We can apply this equation **to give: ...**

В результате чего получается
The derivative is integrated *n* times **to yield** (*or* **give**) *y*.

В результате чего ... становится
The new Hamiltonian can be made to vanish, **rendering** the equation of motion **trivial.**

В результате этого
As a consequence [*or* **In consequence (of this)**, *or* **As a result**] the reflected shock is bifurcated.
This **has the effect of** diminishing the second electron yield.

В ряд [*см.* **Выстраивать в ряд**].

В самое последнее время
This term has been introduced **most recently.**
Only **in the very recent past** has enough information become available.

В са́мом начале [*см. тж.* **В начале, Вначале**]
In was apparent **very early in** the study of crystals that ...
Very early in the earth's history ...
To estimate **at the outset** what a patient's initial treatment should be, ...

В са́мом разгаре
At the height of a violent dust storm ...

В са́мом широком смысле
In the widest sense the term neutralization refers to ...

В свете
A large number of attenuation measurements have been surveyed **in (the) light of** the various theoretical and empirical relations.
In the light of the new methods of synthesis this objection may no longer be valid.

В свободном состоянии
Benzoic acid is found **free** (*or* **in the free state**) and combined in nature.

В своё время
One might think that the entire surface of Venus could be mapped **in due course.**
In due time (*or* **course**) such work should yield a general theory of star formation.

В свою очередь
The outer spindle only is driven, and **in (its) turn** drives the inner spindle.

В связи с
The rules are worked out **in connection with** the multiplication of negative numbers.
It is important to consider these findings **in the context of** the evolutionary relationship of life on our planet to the presence of mercury.

These factors will now be discussed **in the context** of paramagnetic resonance.
In relation to this topic, it is pertinent to note that...

В связи с этим [*см. тж.* **В этой связи**]
In this connection it should be noted that ...

В связи с этим возникает вопрос
This brings up another point.
This raises the question of (*or* **as to**) **whether** the supply is likely to run out.

В северном направлении [*см.* **В западном направлении**].

В середине... века
In the mid-nineteenth **century ...**

В середине 80-х годов
In the mid-(19)80s (*or* **In the middle 80s**) ...

В середине июня *и т.п.*
In mid-June ...

В сечении А–А
At section A–A the bending moment is ...

В силу [*см. тж.* **Ввиду**]
In view of (*or* **On the strength of,** *or* **By virtue of**) Eq. (8.2) flow is governed by ...
The molecule has kinetic energy **by virtue of** its motion through space.

В силу геометрических соображений
This perimeter has to be less than that of the circle by elementary **geometrical reasoning.**

В силу необходимости
Gravity tanks must **of necessity** be located on deck.
The existing correlations of data on transport rates are **of necessity** (*or* **necessarily,** *or* **inevitably**) largely empirical.

В силу различных обстоятельств [*см.* **По разным причинам**].

В силу само́й своей природы
By its very nature, a model is temporary.

В силу симметрии
By symmetry, the midpoint touches ...

В силу ... соображений
From gravitational **considerations,** Saturn's rings could not be one piece of material.

В силу того, что
The detached electron will conduct electricity **by virtue of the fact that** it carries a negative charge.

В скобках
In this case, the **bracketed** (*or* **parenthetical**) expression must be zero.
The term **in brackets** (*or* **in parentheses**) stands for ...

В скором времени [*см. тж.* **В ближайшем будущем**]
In the short run (*or* **Before long**) we shall need energy that is readily usable and abundant.

В следующем десятилетии
In the decade that followed (*or* **In the following decade**) new rules were introduced.

В следующем порядке
Reactivity decreases **in the order:** $3° > 2° > 1° > CH_3 - Z$.
The slopes of the curves decrease **in the (following) order:** $M^{3+} > M^{2+} > M^{+}$.

В следующем разделе
In the succeeding (*or* **next,** *or* **following**) **section ...**

В случае I
Assuming a diffuse source, the powers of ... are equal.

В случае II [*см. тж.* **Как и в случае**]
For (*or* **In the case of**) real gases, the internal energy does not depend on ...
A more complex pattern can arise, as **in the example of** calcium oxalate.
This is not the case **for** any component of ...
In the event of faulty functioning of the press ...

В случае аварии
A handwheel must be provided so that supply of fuel may be shut off from deck **in** [(*or* **in case,** *or* **in the event**) **of**] **an emergency.**

В случае когда
In the special **case that** the system is linear ...

В случае малейшего сомнения относительно
If you are the least bit doubtful of (*col.*) what you should use ...

В случае необходимости [*см. тж.* **По мере необходимости, При необходимости**]
The negative is then combined, **when the occasion requires,** with other line negatives.

В случае неполадки
Safety devices stop the presses **if malfunctions occur.**

В случае обесточивания
The spring provides braking action **if the power fails.**

В случае чрезвычайных обстоятельств
Six push buttons, for stopping the machine **in an emergency,** are placed at convenient points.

В смеси с [*см. тж.* **Смешанный с**]
The leaves of coca, either alone or **mixed with** lime and ... are chewed by the natives.

В смысле
It is easy to find out what the user of a building wants **in terms of** light and heat.
Boron carbide is less important **from the point of view** (*or* **from the viewpoint,** *or* **from the standpoint**) **of ...**
In a mechanical **sense ...**

В современной практике
In modern practice ...

В современном виде
The Moon's surface **as we see it today** is an accumulation surface.

В современном языке принято называть ископаемым *и т.п.*
In modern usage the term fossil denotes any evidence of former life.

В соединении с [*см. тж.* **В сочетании с**]
Silica may form adherent scale, especially **in combination with** unreacted calcium or magnesium.
These compounds contain carbon **combined with** hydrogen, ...

В соединениях
Benzoic acid is found free and **combined** in nature.
Cobalt is similar to iron and nickel in both its free and **combined states.**

В сокращённом виде
The hydronium ion is usually represented **in shorthand form** by the symbol H^+.
The hydrogen-oxygen group is referred to **in abbreviated** (*or* **concise**) **form** as a "hydroxyl group".

В... сообщается о
That communication **reports** the fragmentation pattern of...

В соответствии с [*см. тж.* **В зависимости от, Изменяться в соответствии с кривой, Классификация по, Находиться в соответствии с, Согласно, Соответствие**]
In line with this assumption, we have devised a model of ...
To modify the beach profile **in response to** changing wave conditions ...
Evaporators for marine use are classed as horizontal or vertical **by** (*or* **according to,** *or* **depending on**) the position of their tubes.
The test report is performed **in accord (ance)** (*or* **conformity,** *or* **compliance**) **with** the specifications.
In keeping with the limitation of only four orbitals, the formation of double or triple bonds between atoms of these elements reduces the coordination number of the central atom.
The machine is designed and built **to** higher standards of accuracy.
The sketch can be interpreted **in terms of** either system.
The console pressure can be regulated **to match** the individual gauge range.
In the reactors designed **around** this approach the energy-carrying neutrons released by thermonuclear reactions will be absorbed in a lithium blanket.
These techniques must be selected **in relation to** the properties of the substances being separated.

В соответствии с индивидуальными потребностями
Special tooling can be designed and built **to individual requirements.**

В соответствии с которым
A simplified procedure has been developed, **whereby** fixed values have been allocated to certain variables.

В соответствии с механизмом [*см.* **По механизму**].

В соответствии с программой [*см.* **Действовать в соответствии с программой**].

В соответствии с техническими требованиями
Washer manufacturers will produce washers **to fit** your **specifications.**
The system was built **to** our **specifications.**

В соответствии с традицией
Following a common practice for appraising the potential usefulness of a drug, we established a "model system" in mice.

В соответствии с требованиями
Special machines are built from standard units **to suit** customer's **requirements.**

В соответствии с формой
The plates are curved **to fit** the plate cylinder of a rotary press.

В соответствующей пропорции
When added together **in the proper proportions, ...**

В соответствующих местах
This property is further discussed **where appropriate** in later chapters.

В соотношении [*см.* **В пропорции, Находиться в соотношении**].

В состоянии [*см.* **Быть в состоянии**].

В ... состоянии
These steels are difficult to machine **in the** hardened **condition.**
Minerals must be **in the** solid **state.**

В состоянии готовности к
Conveyor section *L* descends automatically, **in readiness to** receive the next tray.

В состоянии покоя [*см. тж.* **Пребывание в состоянии покоя**]
At time $t = 0$, the mass **is at rest.**
These ion movements are largely prevented **during rest.**

В состоянии равновесия [*см. тж.* **При равновесии**]
At the state of equilibrium (*or* **At the equilibrium state**) ...

В сотрудничестве с
A larger accelerator ring was built **in collaboration** (*or* **cooperation**) **with** the Lawrence Berkeley Laboratory.

В сочетании с [*см. тж.* **В соединении с, Совместно с**]
Hydrazine hydrate can be used as a rocket fuel **in association with** nitric acid.
Coupled (*or* **In combination,** *or* **Together**) **with** a recording system, these devices are used to measure ...
The system can be used **in conjunction with** a computer to perform diagnostic programming and checking industrial processes.
A neoplasm can often be suspected on the basis of the findings from the history and the examination **in conjunction with** a routine blood count (*med.*).
The value of the curvature, **together with** the magnitude of the field, gives the momentum.
When coupled with solubility information on common salts this will allow us to develop quite a variety of "predictable" processes.

В сочетании с тем, что
This resistance to combustion, **coupled with the fact that ...** suggested that this substance might be ideal for ...

В спокойном состоянии
These volcanoes **are in a** relatively **quiescent phase** (*or* **state**).

В сравнении с [*см.* **По сравнению с**].

В среднем
Estimates indicate that **an average of** 23,000 gallons per month would be discharged.
In the average this must be ...
They cost, **on (the) average,** £750.
In the mean, both circulations transfer energy from lower to higher latitudes.
On (the) average, about 43% of the solar radiation reaches the surface of the earth.

В среднем положении
At mid-position, both studs are in engagement.

В среднем составлять [*см.* **Составлять в среднем**].

В срок
The computer people often tend to promise results that cannot be delivered **on time.**

В стадии проектирования
More powerful telescopes **are** already **on the drawing boards** (*or* **in the design stage,** *or* **being designed**).

В стадии развития
This science **is** still **in its developmental stage.**

В стадии разработки
The engine **is in development stage.**

В стадии строительства
The tunnel **is under construction.**

В стационарном случае
The existence of the spatial discontinuity **in the steady case** implies that ...

В стационарном состоянии
The output power **at steady state** can then be determined by ...

В степени
Coordinates of the chart are temperature and pressure **to the power 2/7.**
The volume **to the 2/3 power** ($V^{2/3}$) is used as the area term.
Tidal action is proportional **to the** inverse **sixth power of** the distance Earth-Moon.
This figure is multiplied by 10 **to the ninth power.**

В степени 1/2 [*см.* **В половинной степени**].

В степени 4/3
This number is proportional **to the four-thirds power of** *Z*.

В стороне
Overburden is removed from a trench and piled **to one side.**

В стороне от
The drainage structure discharges the water **clear of** the landing area.

В сторону
The larger fragments tend to be moved **sideways** as well as upward.

В сторону моря
Storm waves tend to cause a sand movement **in the seaward direction.**

В сторону, противоположную [*см.* **Направлен в сторону, противоположную Солнцу**].

В стороны
In a vacuum the electrostatic forces tend to make the beam grow **laterally.**

В стране и вне её [*см.* **Внутри страны и вне её**].

В стратосфере
Freons are decomposed by ultraviolet light **in the stratosphere.**

В стремлении
Water species move downward **in an attempt** to stay in their preferred environment.
In an attempt to produce more effective medicines ...
Sometimes surface integrity is overlooked **in the attempt to** achieve high production rates.
In his quest to design beautiful objects, man has copied nature's symmetry.
They produced more sulphur trioxide **in the effort to** reduce ...

В строгом смысле слова
In the strict sense (of the word), an admixture is a material added to ...

В стройном порядке
The molecules arrange themselves **in an orderly fashion.**

В структурном отношении [*см. тж.* **С точки зрения структуры**]
Borazene is **structurally** very similar to benzene.
Structurally related sample constituents ...

В сумме [*см. тж.* **Давать в сумме**]
The rock samples weighed **in (the) aggregate** 99 kilograms.

В существующем виде [*см. тж.* **Без обработки**]
The device **as it stands** constitutes a promising new particle transport system.
I am solely responsible for the text **as it stands.**
The tracks **as they exist** may withstand the weight of ...

В сущности
Group technology is **in effect** an electronic card file ...

В таблице перечислены
The table gives (*or* **lists**) the percentage content of ...

In Table 26 are listed (*or* **tabulated,** *or* **given,** *or* **enumerated**) the various ...
The etching treatments that were used in the present investigation **are listed in the table.**

В такой же мере [*см.* **Ничуть не менее**].

В такой же степени как и
Accuracy of delivery **is as much** an element of effectiveness **as** the destructive power of the bomb itself.

В такой степени
Physical events in other parts of the continent are not **as well** known.

В такой степени, что [*см.тж.* **До такой степени, когда**]
If the seating surface is damaged **to the extent that** it must be renewed, ...
Only in recent years has the state of knowledge improved **to the point where** it is possible to obtain generally good results.

В таком случае
In such an event, the hypothesis is abandoned.
In such a situation, the untrue hypothesis would not be rejected.

В темноте
The halogens react very slowly with alkanes **in the dark.**

В тех случаях, когда
This is an important consideration **where** (*or* **when**) stepped pulleys are to be used.

В течение [*см. тж.* **В процессе, Во врéмя, На протяжении**]
Stirring is continued **during (the course of)** the reaction.
The decrease in neutral atom concentration **during the course of** the pulse ...
Many thousands of major earthquakes are likely to occur **in the course of** a few million years.
The outflow of Gulf Stream water **over the course of** a year ...
This holds the swept signal constant **throughout** each sweep period.
Most valves are assembled and shipped **within** two to four weeks.
The light output of some quasars has been observed to change significantly **in a matter of** days.

Over (*or* **During**) **a period of** several decades the group experimented with the infusion of fats.

В течение ближайших нескольких лет
A considerable amount of research is expected **within the next few years.**

В течение времени
Amplification takes place **for a time** $T_2 - T_1$.
The paper traces the role of continental drift **through** geological **time.**

В течение всего
The drops rise and fall **through(out)** the second phase.

В течение всего года
In the equatorial areas, the rainfall is fairly well distributed **throughout the year.**

В течение всего существования
Throughout the (whole) lifetime of the solar system ...

В течение всей истории человечества
All through (*or* **Throughout**) **history,** man has freely poured gaseous wastes into our atmosphere.

В течение длительного времени I
The transform boundary will not remain **for long** in its original location.
The pressure increase acts **over a long period (of time).**

В течение длительного времени II
There is no prospect of exhaustion of this metal **for a long time to come.**
An open vessel filled with a superfluid will not stay filled **for long.**
The neutrino was **long** thought to be massless.

В течение значительной части века
Systematic observations continued **well into the** first **century** A.D.

В течение значительной части года
This keeps the ground frozen **for much of the year.**

В течение короткого периода
The rings will be operated **briefly** as a synchrotron.

В течение многих лет [*см. тж.* **Издавна**]
Many of these techniques have been used **for years** (*or* **over many years**).

В течение некоторого времени
For a (*or* **some**) **time,** we thought that ...
The heart will beat normally **for a** (*or* **some**) **time.**
This machine will remain **for some time** (**to come**) the most powerful electron accelerator in the world.
Field measurements may be made continuously **over a period of time.**

В течение неопределённого времени
The particles remain **indefinitely** suspended in a mixture with water.
Many alloys remain in the glassy state **indefinitely** at room temperature.

В течение нескольких ближайших лет
It is likely that these materials will dominate the field of high-performance composites **for some years to come.**

В течение ночи
A thermal storage battery can be charged **overnight** and discharged during the day.

В течение продолжительного времени (*или* **периода**)
It is unlikely that anyone would be irradiated by a single beam **for any length of time.**
A child who has suffered undernourishment very early and **for an appreciable length of time** will never reach normal size for his age.
The text was developed **over a protracted period of** the last 10 years.
The screens are designed to give maximum output **over prolonged** (*or* **extended**) **periods.**

В течение ряда лет
Over a period of years several such devices were developed.

В течение следующих ... лет
Over the next 20 years they kept trying to find ...

В течение следующих нескольких недель
In the weeks that followed several lesser explosions occurred.

В течение такого длительного времени, что
Many names of organic compounds have been accepted **for so long that** they have become permanent parts of the language of chemistry.

В то время
At the (*or* **that**) **time,** however, that discovery was met with disbelief.

В то время как I
As the capacitor charges, the grid and cathode voltages of the output tube rise simultaneously with respect to earth.

В то время как II [*см. тж.* **А, Тогда как, Хотя**]
Whereas (*or* **While**) pillow lavas dominate the Middle Atlantic rift floor, smooth-faced sheet lavas are extensive in the Eastern Pacific rift floors.
Whereas there is just one kind of electric charge, there are three kinds of colour charge.
Meridional rays have the same transit times, **whereas** transit times for skew rays depend on ...

В то же время
Certain problems not directly connected with ancient objects and **yet** important to the archaeologist, ...
The alloy has high strength for rough service, **yet** has sufficient machinability ...
It was difficult to imagine a kind of water that would rigidly exclude ions such as potassium **while** (*or* **at the same time**) readily dissolving glucose and ethyl alcohol.

В то же время не
These states will influence the minority-carrier mobility **while not** influencing the majority-carrier transport.

В то или иное время
Some 10 percent of us suffer migraine headaches **at one time or another** during out lifetime.

В толще
The relaxation process occurs **within the thickness of** the shock front.

В том виде, в каком они встречаются
The isotopic composition of all elements **as they occur** in nature is constant.

В том же или в противоположном направлении
The drying gases may flow **cocurrent with or countercurrent to** the spray.

В том или ином виде
This type of control has been on the welding scene for a number of years, **in one form or another.**

В том или ином отношении
These satellites have dynamics that are unusual **in one way or another.**
Almost every element is chemically useful **in some way or another.**

В том отношении [*см.* **В том смысле, что**].

В том случае, если
In the event that $X = Y$, the bilinear form becomes the quadratic form.
Churn drills are sometimes used for prospecting **where** analysis of the cuttings gives sufficient information.

В том смысле, в каком он употребляется в физике *и т.п.*
The term collision, **as used in physics,** does not necessarily imply actual contact.

В том смысле, что [*см. тж.* **Важен в том смысле, что**]
This test is ideal **in that** full-scale components can be tested at flight air speeds.
As a family these bacteria are aerobic **in (the sense) that** elemental oxygen participates in cellular respiration.

В тот момент когда
At the instant a field is applied to a flame, ...

В точке поверхности
The pressure **at a point on the surface** may change from day to day.

В точности как
m varies with time **exactly as does** *c*.

В точности как указано выше
Aluminium oxide cannot be prepared **quite as above,** because nitric acid does not attack aluminium.

В тяжёлых условиях
The valve must operate **under rugged** (*or* **severe**) **conditions.**

В увеличенном масштабе
Make a master drawing **on an enlarged scale.**

В углах
In silicates, four oxygens arranged **at the corners of** a tetrahedron surround ...

В ... уделяется большое внимание
This design **places high emphasis on** the safety of ...

В удобной для использования форме
We offer this information **in an easy-to-use form.**

В узких пределах
The output of the process remains constant **within narrow limits.**

В узком смысле
In its most limited (*or* **restricted**) **sense** (*or* **In a narrow sense**), analytical chemistry is that branch of chemistry which ...

В указанной форме
Newton's law **as stated** implies that ...

В указанном порядке
The rest of the ground water has been used for municipal water supply, rural use, and industry, **in that order.**
Equation (5) gives these three factors **in the order named.**

В указанных пределах
The proportions of two or more elements may be variable **within stated** (*or* **indicated**) **limits** in a single compound.

В уменьшенном масштабе
The drawing is then photographed **on a reduced scale.**

В условиях
During (*or* **Under,** *or* **In**) windy **conditions** such measurements are not representative of ...
In terms of this coordinate system the differentiation becomes simplified.
It is often necessary to control the pH of a solution **in circumstances where** hydrogen ions are being generated.
These quantities are conserved **in** certain **contexts.**

В условиях Земли [*см. тж.* **В земных условиях**]
The diatomic gas is the equilibrium state of nitrogen **under terrestrial conditions.**

В условиях окружающей среды
Nitrogen fixation **under ambient conditions** is not novel.

В условиях практической работы [*см.* **В действительности**].

В условиях эксперимента
Experimentally, the dielectric constant is determined by the ratio of ...

В условиях эксплуатации
Under operating conditions, steam would be formed at this lift.

В ... устранен
The new types of computer architectures **avoid** some processing bottlenecks.

В ... участвует
The reaction **involves** a carbonium ion.

В фазе
The emitted waves **are in phase.**

В форме [*см.* **В виде, Выражать в виде, Располагаться в форме шестиугольника**].

В форме графиков
Published data have been summarized **in graphical form.**

В форме таблицы
Arrange the computations **in tabular** (*or* **tabulated**) **form.**

В функции
Load **against** (*or* **versus,** *or* **vs.**) strip thickness (*in a graph*).
Figure 2 shows the maximum rates of lactic acid production **as a function of ...**
The pressure drop **versus** flowrate curve ...
The transmission of the probe radiation was studied **as a function of** the laser frequency.

В функциональном отношении
Functionally, the various enzymes appear to be similar to those of prokaryotes.

В фунтах ... в час
Estimate the absorption rate **as pounds** CO_2 **per hour.**

В химическом *и т.п.* **отношении**
Minerals of this group are similar **chemically** to ...

В химическом *и т.п.* **смысле слова**
Chemically, isotopes of the same element are nearly identical.

В ходе [*см.* **В процессе**].

В ходе выполнения программы
As part of an exploration **program** for new gypsum deposits, it was necessary to sink a shaft.

В ходе реакции
In (*or* **During**) **the course of the reaction ...**

В холодном виде
Copper must be worked **cold.**

В хорошем приближении
To a good approximation the scattering from deuterium nuclei is simply the sum of the scattering from neutrons and protons.
A result identical with Eq. (8.45) can be obtained **as a good approximation** even when $D_B = D_A$.
This eddy-current loss may be expressed **to close** (*or* **in good**) **approximation** by the relation ...

В целом I
By and large they seem to be incidental.
The disk of interstellar gas occupies a small volume compared with the volume of the galaxy **as a whole.**
The molecule **as a whole** is nonpolar.

В целом II [*см.* **В сумме**].

В целом составлять [*см.* **Составлять в сумме**].

В целях [*см. тж.* **Исследования с целью**]
In an effort to test this hypothesis we repeated the original experiment.

В центре
The lake is 135 ft deep **at its centre.**
At the centre of the lens ...

В центре внимания [*см. тж.* **Находиться в центре внимания**]
Benzene **has been the focus** (*or* **centre**) **of attention** of those who ...

В центре которого расположен
The hydroxyl ions are arranged in the form of a tetrahedron **with** the silicon atom **at the centre.**

В центре слева
This system can be seen **at left-centre** in Fig. 4.

В цеховых условиях
The device has been found to operate satisfactorily **under shop conditions.**

В частности
The amount of work needed to achieve that temperature is determined, **among other factors,** by ...
Volcanic activity, glaciation, and sedimentation, **among other processes,** have varied greatly throughout geologic history.
In particular, $\log_e x = \ln x$.
Among other things the system gave us a measure of the degree of homogeneity of the pressure within the sample.
This is due **in part** (*or* **in particular**) to ...
This task is complicated by many things, **among them** the difficulty of ...
This theory is peculiar to the analytical flame, and to the experimental configuration in Fig. 3 **in particular**.
Secular changes in the orbits, **specifically** of the semimajor axis, are well known.
Specifically, the atmosphere of Titan has carbon, nitrogen, and hydrogen.

В честь [*см. тж.* **Назван в честь**]
The unit torr was selected **to honour** (*or* **in honour of**) Evangelista Torricelli.

В число ... входит
Increased horse power and faster travel speeds **are among** several improvements recently announced.
Among the acids produced were alamine, glycine, cysteine, ...
Included in such movements **are** continental drift and seafloor spreading.
The list of elements present in sea water **includes** most of those known.

В число которых входит
Most stars, the sun **among them,** are less brilliant.

В чистом виде
In the uncombined (*or* **pure**) **state,** deuterium finds use as a research tool.
This salt has never been obtained **pure.**

В широких пределах
The solute concentration may be varied **over wide limits** (*or* **over a wide range**).

В широкой области [*см.* **В широком диапазоне**].

В широком диапазоне
Variable-pitch propellers can operate **over a wide range of** powers and at any one speed.

В широком смысле слова
In a broad sense, there is only one completely discrete animal community, the entire fauna of the earth.
The process of evaporation **in the broad sense** is quite simple.

В ... широтах
At (*or* **In**) middle **latitudes ...**

В эмбриональном состоянии [*см. тж.* **В зачаточном состоянии**]
When geology was **in its infancy, ...**

В ... этапов [*см. тж.* **В ... приёмов**]
The reaction occurs **in** two **stages.**

В этих условиях [*см. тж.* **В данных условиях**]
Under (*or* **In**) **these conditions** (*or* **circumstances**), neighbouring particles can acquire large individual charges.

В этих целях
In pursuing these aims (*or* **For this purpose,** *or* **To this end**), the company has investigated numerous alternatives.

В это время [*см.* **При этом**].

В этой области проводятся интенсивные исследования
This is an active area of research.

В этой связи [*см. тж.* **В связи с этим**]
It is interesting to note **in this connection** (*or* **in connection with this**) that ...

В этой статье обсуждается
This article discusses true clovers, sweet clover, and clover diseases.

В этом заключается
Therein lies a difficulty which to this time has appeared insurmountable.

В этом заключается ответ на вопрос о
Therein lies the answer to the sorting of sediment by streams.

В этом направлении

A research program is being developed **along these** lines.
Evolutionary progress **along this line** is poorly represented.

В этом отношении
In this regard (*or* **respect**) the scanning microscope should be an improvement on the transmission instrument.
Although there is some uncertainty **on this point, ...**

В этом случае
Reflection **in this situation** (*or* **case,** *or* **instance**) is governed by Snell's law.
Here, a single coacervate is produced.
In that event (*or* **case,** *or* **instance**) part of the radioactivity could be released.
Then different expressions must be developed.
Liver disease is also a cause of a low serum albumin and **if so** there will often be other stigmata of hepatic pathology.

В этом ... что-то есть.
There is something to this viewpoint.

В этот момент
At this point (*or* **At that instant**) the diode begins to conduct.

В эту рубрику входят
Under this head(ing) come meat, fish, etc.

В южном направлении [*см.* **В западном направлении**].

В явном виде
The reciprocal relation between the ray and the normal velocity is given **in an explicit form.**

Важен [*см. тж.* **Особенно важен**]
This calculation **is of importance.**

Важен в том смысле, что
This revision **is important in** allowing us to relate ...

Важен для
The above experimental results **hold significance in** understanding the activities of living creatures.
This consideration **is of importance to** the study of ...

Важен для объяснения
These forces **are** also **of importance in explaining ...**

Важен для понимания
Interparticle forces **are essential to the understanding of ...**

Важная проблема
Detecting the output correlation peak **is a vital issue in** missile guidance.

Важная роль
This hormone **plays a key** (*or* **vital,** *or* **prominent,** *or* **important**) **part** (*or* **role**) **in** the transmission of nerve impulses in the sympathetic nervous system.

Важная услуга [*см.* **Оказывать важную услугу**].

Важнее [*см.* **Ещё важнее то, что**].

Важнее всего то, что
Most important of all, we don't really know ...

Важнее то, что [*см.* **Что более важно**].

Важнейший [*см. тж.* **Исключительно важный, Основной**]
Table 4.4 includes some of **the more** (*or* **most**) **important** chelated systems.

Важнейший пример
Sulphate, nitrate, phosphate and aluminate are **notable examples** whose effects have been well studied.

Важно [*см. тж.* **Необходимо**]
It is of value (*or* **important**) **to** have diagrams showing not only ...
What counts is the precision in relative angle and relative energy between the incident and the scattered electrons.
It is vital to note that ...

Важно иметь в виду, что
It is important to keep in mind (*or* **remember**) **that** *w* will vary as the dye laser beam passes through the sample cell.

Важно отметить, что
It is significant that ...

Важно то, что
An important point is that titanium is one of the group of elements called the transition metals.

Важно только знать расположение *и т.п.*
What mattered was only the placement of the equant point, which Tycho had determined with fair precision.

Важное [*см.* **Главное**].

Важное значение
Of fundamental (*or* **great,** *or* **vital) importance is** the polar sequence ...

Важное место [*см.* **Занимать важное место в**].

Важность для
The importance of research **to** the country's economy ...

Важный [*см. тж.* **Жизненно важен для, Играть важную роль, Исключительно важный**]
This inertness is **the** most **salient** characteristic of the DNA molecule.
A **critical** question ...
The spectrophotometer is a **key** element in the process.
Whenever dyeing is a **paramount** requirement ...
An **essential** (*or* **important**) feature of the device is ...
A **major** application of the high vacuum environment is in the design of vacuum tubes.
A **vital** part of the magnetron is the permanent magnet.
This approach **is of significance** despite the complexity of ...

Важный для
The principal quantum number **is of (considerable) importance** (*or* **significance**) **in** defining ...
Hydroxylating reactions **are important** (*or* **essential**) **for** the biosynthesis of corticoids.
Each of these factors **is important** (*or* **essential**) **to** the end results.
The bibliographies supplied **will be valuable to** workers in the field.
This circumstance may **have been of consequence for** the origin of life.

Важный для медицины
Mycobacterium species include such **medically important** bacteria as the agents of tuberculosis ...

Важный для промышленности [*см.* **Представляющий важность для промышленности**].

Вакуум [*см. тж.* **В вакууме, Под вакуумом**]
In this respect gaseous plasma is superior to **a vacuum**.

Валентность ... равна
The **valence** of carbon in methane **is** four (*or* Carbon **has a valence** of four in methane).

Вариант [*см. тж.* **В качестве варианта, Видоизменение, Разновидность, Способ**]
Once several **alternative** syntheses have been outlined in this way, the most promising approach can be selected.
TF 791C/1 is **an alternative to** (*or* a **variant of**) the existing TF 79/C.
The actual method employed was **a variation of** this method.
Two **versions of** the machine are available, the F12-l for turning only, and the F12-111 for turning and second operations including cross-drilling, slotting, etc.
A **variation of** the previous electrode is one in which ...
Another **version** of the theory ...

Варьировать I
The engineer can **tailor** (*or* **vary**) the structure to meet the stress pattern of the application.

Варьировать II [*см. тж.* **Изменяться, Колебаться**]
The means of transmission **extend** (*or* **vary**) **from** broad-band microwave radio circuits down **to** standard telephone message channels.

Вблизи [*см. тж.* **В непосредственной близости от, В окрестности**]
Sedimentation is especially rapid **adjacent to** volcanic islands.
In the vicinity of the Sun ...
The charge grows larger at long range than it is **close by** (*or* **at close range**).
This movement of the electrons, **in proximity** to the sensing electrodes ...
In the vicinity (*or* **neighbourhood**) **of** a Mach number of unity ...
Close to, Nearby ...
The sediment was deposited **in the vicinity** (*or* **neighbourhood**) **of** the island.
In the neighbourhood of room temperature ...

Вблизи берега
Oceanic trenches lie **offshore.**

Вблизи побережья [*см. тж.* **Недалеко от побережья**]
On the shelf **off the** Atlantic **coast ...**

Введение I [*см. тж.* **Включение**]
Administration of the medicine **to** patients.
Incorporation (*or* **Introduction**) **of** heavy elements **into** plastic scintillators.
Injection of the tracer **into** a vein.
The introduction of an opaque substance **into** the blood.
Hydrogen removal or oxygen **insertion ...**

Введение II
Introduction to *Printed Circuits (название книги).*

Введение III
The advent of broadcasting ...

Введение ... в уравнение
This can be done by **entering** (*or* **introducing,** *or* **inserting**) the function **into** the Schrödinger **equation.**
Substitution of these expressions **in(to) Eq.** (3-16) leads to ...

Введение через рот
When **administered by mouth ...**
Amphotericin B is usually non-toxic **by oral administration.**

Введён [*см. тж.* **Вводить**]
The Law **was enacted** in 1989.

Введён в строй
A new electroplating section **has been commissioned.**

Вверх [*см. тж.* **Направленный влево (вправо, вверх, вниз)**]
The molecules move **up** from the lower layer.
The **upward** tilt of the liquid surface curve ...

Вверх по течению
Turbulence generators were placed **upstream of** (*or* **from**) the cylinder.

Вверху справа
At the top right of the diagram ...

Ввёртывать до отказа
The regulator must **be screwed full in** (*or* **as far as it goes,** *or* **hard up,** *or* **to the limit**).
The screw was then only half-a-turn from **fully home**.

Ввиду [*см. тж.* **Благодаря, Вследствие, Из-за**]
The indicated horse power is less than the thermal horse power **by virtue of** (*or* **owing to**) radiation losses.
The water moderator was adopted **for reasons of** expediency.
In view of (*or* **Because of**) the presence of hydrogen ...
On account of the small magnitude ... the observation of these effects presents many difficulties.
Through its inertness the DNA molecule remains stable ...

Ввиду ... авторы предположили, что
Such discrepancies **led the authors to suggest that ...**

Ввиду нехватки места
It is impossible to give a complete account of these processes **for reasons of space.**

Ввиду отсутствия [*см. тж.* **За неимением, За отсутствием**]
For lack of understanding of the biological processes involved in mutation, the first efforts of inducing mutations to improve plants were not successful.
In default (*or* **For lack**) **of** any other adequate explanation, the nontidal tendency towards a shorter day length may be attributable to ...

Ввиду того, что [*см. тж.* **Поскольку**]
Since (*or* **Because,** *or* **Considering that,** *or* **In view of the fact that**) the heat of a reaction depends on ...
Because (*or* **Since**) normal stars could not be detected as sources of radio emission with the equipment then available, ...

Ввиду широкого разнообразия ... рискованно делать обобщения
The wide diversity of molecular substances **makes generalization** somewhat **risky.**

Ввинчивать [*см.* **Ввёртывать до отказа, Завинчивать**].

Ввинчиваться в
The bolt passes through one member and **threads into** the other.

Ввод
Inputing (*or* **Entering**) the data **into** the processor ...

Ввод в эксплуатацию
Before **commissioning** (*or* **putting into service,** *or* **putting into operation**) the sphere will be pressure tested.

Вводить [*см. тж.* **Которому ввели**]
The medicine **is administered to** the patients (*or* **into** the organism).
Gadolinium **is incorporated in** plastic scintillators.
The tracer **is injected into** a vein.
We **insert** information **into** the wire.
The probe can easily **be inserted into** the body.
The gas could **be introduced into** the system.
Slip the instrument **into** the cylinder.
The fuel **is injected into** the chamber.
All materials affect a magnetic field **in(to)** which they **are inserted.**
A group of volunteers **received injections of** the labelled morphine.
The tracer **is infused** intravenously.
We **insert** (*or* **introduce**) an arbitrary scale factor **in(to)** T_1^3.

Вводить в
In order to make nitrogen combine with other substances an irreducible quantity of energy must **be added to** the system.
Gases can **be admitted into** the evacuated ionization chamber.
Any of these procedures may **be built into** a process control system.
These coordinates can now **be entered into** Eq. (5-10).
The protons **are injected** (*or* **inserted**) **into** the synchrotron.
The teloblast cell **was injected with** the rhodaminepolypeptide complex (*biol.*).
Information **is entered into** the computer by means of ...

Вводить в действие
An auxiliary steam valve is provided by which additional steam nozzles can **be brought** (*or* **put**) **into use** when required.
A failure of a hydraulic system for lowering the gear might **call into play** a substitute electrical system for lowering it.
The station will **be commissioned** [*or* **put into operation,** *or* **brought into** (*or* **placed in**) **service**] next year.

Вводить (в выражение) в качестве
The reduced mass of μ **is inserted for** the mass term.

Вводить в курс
We **bring you up to date on** all of the new developments.

Вводить в промышленную эксплуатацию
The units **were placed in commercial operation.**

Вводить в режим
When the laser **is forced into the** Gaussian **mode, ...**

Вводить в строй [*см. тж.* **Вводить в действие**]
Additional plants **were brought into use.**

Вводить в уравнение
The ratio of lead to uranium **is** then **entered into the** following **equation.**

Вводить в эксплуатацию
The refinery **will come on stream** next year.
The computer **was placed** (*or* **brought**) **in(to) operation** in 1982.
The machine **has been brought into service.**
Other installations have been "automated" by introducing this type of control some time after they **were commissioned for service.**

Вводить поправку на
To **correct for** the difference, ...

Вводить термин [*см.* **Создавать термин**].

Вводиться
The restriction **enters** only when the like nuclei are truly identical.

Вводиться в
Helium **is injected** (*or* **introduced**) **into** flowing nitrogen.

Вворачивать [*см.* **Ввёртывать до отказа**].

Вдаваться в
It is not the intent of this chapter **to go into** technical theories.

Вдавливаться
The work blank **is forced down into** the cavity.

Вдали от [*см. тж.* **На большом расстоянии от**]

Away from the coastal areas the salinity of the ocean varies from 32 to 37 grams of dissolved solid per kilogram of seawater.

Вдвигать
If the atomizer **is in** far enough, ...
If the atomizer **is shoved** (*or* **pushed**) **in** too far, ...

Вдвое [*см.* **Складывать вдвое, Увеличивать вдвое (втрое), Уменьшать вдвое**].

Вдвое больше
Twice as many rods were used.
Twice as much (*or* **A double amount of**) beryllium will be required.

Вдвое лучше
The quality was **twice as good.**

Вдвое меньше [*см.* **В два раза меньше, чем**].

Вдвойне
This purity is achieved **in double measure** if ...

Вдоль [*см. тж.* **Направлен вдоль или против**]
The heat from the armature teeth can flow **lengthwise of** the laminations to the end of the tooth.

Вдоль всего
Along the length of the pipe ...
A rigid keel-like structure runs **the (whole) length of** the hull and bottom.

Вдоль всей длины [*см.* **По всей длине**].

Вдоль направления
Along the pressure **direction ...**

Вдоль оси [*см.* **Направленный вдоль оси**].

Вдумываться глубже [*см. тж.* **Если вдуматься глубже, то**]
Let us **look more closely into** the meaning of ...

Ведётся большая работа по
Much work is in progress on the conversion of saline water.

Ведётся работа
Work is underway on tool monitoring systems, but these are not yet in production.

Ведётся работа по созданию
Work is now underway toward the construction of a new theory.

Ведётся регистрация [*см.* **Постоянно ведётся регистрация**].

Ведутся исследования с целью
Efforts are underway to find commercial uses for the metal.

Ведутся поиски
The search is on for the rock in which ...

Ведущее положение [*см. тж.* **Занимать ведущее положение**]
This firm's **leadership** (*or* **leading position**) **in** klystrons...

Ведущий [*см. тж.* **Играть основную роль в**]
Some of our **foremost** (*or* **top-level,** *or* **leading**) scientists ...
Leading (*or* **Key**) industries ...

Везде [*см. тж.* **Всюду, Повсеместно использоваться, Повсюду**]
The triplet—CCA is omitted from the chart, because it is **universally** present (*biol.*).

Везде в этой книге
Throughout this book ...

Везде равен нулю
The flux *B* **is everywhere zero.**

Вездесущий [*см. тж.* **Встречаться повсеместно** (*или* **повсюду**)]
The **ubiquitous** cloud cover on Venus is so reflective that ...

Везти [*см.* **Нам повезло**].

Века́ми
Down the centuries many different systems of measurement have been devised and abandoned.
Through (*or* **over**) **the ages** (*or* **centuries**) science has often given inspiration to musical composers.

Величайший ... в истории человечества
He was the **greatest** physicist **who ever lived.**

Величина I
This causes the receiving cylinder to move by a corresponding **amount.**

If **the magnitude of** the refraction is known ...
The magnitude of *e* varies from 0 to 1.

Величина II [*см. тж.* **Бесконечно малая величина, Обратная величина, Постоянная (величина), Пренебрежимо малая величина**].
Bessel functions are used to represent such **quantities** as the temperature, ... as functions of space coordinates.
The quantity *m* is called the effective mass of electrons at K_0.

Величина III [*см.* **В натуральную величину, Второй по величине**].

Величина наклона
Planes with various **amounts of tilt ...**

Величина, обратная
The conductivity **is the reciprocal** (*or* **the inverse**) **of** the resistivity.
$A_{2,1}$ must be equal to **the reciprocal of** τ_2^0.

Величиной с [*см. тж.* **Размером с**]
Objects of considerable size, some **as large as** the Moon ...

Величиной с молекулу
If cells **the size of a molecule** are chosen, ...

Величины́
Centaurus contains two **first-magnitude** stars.

Венера
The **Venusian** surface temperature ...

Вера
His **faith in** his scheme remained strong.

Вероятнее всего [*см. тж.* **По всей вероятности**]
Differentiation **will most likely** (*or* **most probably**) **be** accomplished electronically.
Metal-nonmetal combinations **are most likely to be** ionic.
The chances are better than even that the photon will scatter out of the central crystal.

Вероятно [*см. тж.* **По-видимому**]
Traces of hydrogen **are apt** (*or* **likely**) **to be** present in the coolant.
The errors so obtained **are apt to be** unduly pessimistic.
Pressure drop across bubble-cap trays **is likely to be** greater than for sieve trays handling the same vapour flows.
It is likely (*or* **probable**) **that** this range extends considerably.
Ganymede, Jupiter's largest satellite, **probably** (*or* **presumably,** *or* **apparently,** *or* **evidently**) has a surface of crust ice, perhaps mixed with ...

Вероятно не произойдёт
If the acid and base are strong, **no** further reaction **is likely.**

Вероятность [*см. тж.* **Больша́я вероятность**]
The likelihood (*or* **probability**) **of** local buckling can be predicted by the theory of flat plates.

Вероятность ... велика
The chances that a few particles of some other species will be incorporated in crystalline "salt" **are good.**

Вероятность перехода (*физ.*)
The probability of the $E_1 \leftarrow E_2$ **transition (occurring)** is high.

Вероятность того, что
The presence of integration in the control logarithm greatly increases **the likelihood** (*or* **probability**) **of** the system becom**ing** unstable when overdriven.
This function expresses **the probability that** a molecule of salt or water will appear in the effluent at a time *t* after the step change.
The greater the complexity of the compound, the greater is **the chance that** other absorptions may obscure the 900-670 cm^{-1} region.
The likelihood that this collision will result in ... depends on ...

Вероятность того, что ... входит в
The probability of any configuration's **appearing in** the sequence is high.

Вероятный
This is a **likely** route (*or* pathway) for the reaction.
If neither the earth nor an asteroidal body is a **credible** source of such meteorites ...
The selection of **likely** (*or* **probable**) molecular formulas ...

Вертикаль
The cylinders are at a 45° angle with **the vertical.**

Вертикальный [*см. тж.* **В вертикальном или наклонном положении**]
The structure was raised to **an upright** (*or* **a vertical**) position.

Вертолёт [*см.* **Доставлять на самолёте (вертолёте)**].

Верхние слои атмосферы [*см. тж.* **В верхних слоях атмосферы**]
Ozone is produced **in the upper atmosphere** and carried downward toward the Earth's surface, where it is destroyed.

Верхние слои земной коры
The upper crust is less dense than the lower crust.

Верхний
See **top** photo.
The **upper** row of the matrix ...
The **uppermost** (*or* **topmost**) layer of the soil ...

Вес [*см.* **Отгрузочный вес, Под действием собственного веса, Потеря в весе**].

Вес без груза
Unladen weight.

Вес с грузом
Laden weight.

Весовой процент
It contains **26 wt %** UO_2 (*or* **26%** UO_2 **by weight**).
This component constitutes 41 **percent (by weight) of** the bulk.
The composition is usually expressed as **weight percent of ...**

Весом до
Workpieces **weighing as much as** 400 tons can be handled on the machine floorplates.

Вести́ записи [*или* **регистрацию**]
Keep a record of the variation of the room temperature.
To **record.** To **note.**

Вести́ исследования
One can use computers for **making** (*or* **conducting,** *or* **carrying out**) such **investigations.**
The laboratory is equipped to **perform** (*or* **carry on**) **research on** foamed plastics.
We **are** actively **pursuing investigations into ...**

Вести́ к [*см.* **Приводить к**].

Вести́ начало от
This simple proof **goes back to** the ancient Greeks.

Вести́ переговоры
To **carry on** (*or* **conduct**) **negotiations.**

Вести́ процесс
The process is conducted in two stages.

Вести́ работу [*см. тж.* **Ведётся большая работа по**]
To be engaged in (*or* **To do,** *or* **To carry on**) scientific **work.**

Вести́ реакцию [*см.* **Проводить реакцию**].

Вести́ регистрацию [*см.* **Вести́ записи**].

Вести́ свое начало от
This tradition **dates back** to antiquity.
All of Modern Chemistry **traces back** to that experiment.

Вести́ свое происхождение от
The sediments **from** which these shales **were derived...**
The term "fatty acids" **has its origin in** the fact that most fats are ...
The standard machines **trace their origin to** the rubber extruder.
Many meteors **have their origin(s) in** comets.

Вести́ себя нормально
Over the islands and the volcanoes gravity **is well behaved** (*or* **behaves well**), but over the associated deep-sea trenches gravity measurements are less than the calculated gravity.

Вести́ точный учёт [*см.* **Точно учитывать**].

Вести́ учет
The Property Control System **keeps track of** all capital equipment items.
Keep a record (*or* **an account**) **of** the quantity of oil added.

Вести́сь [*см. тж.* **Ведётся работа**]
The process **is conducted** (*or* **performed**) in a vacuum chamber.
Studies **are** now **in progress** on this model.
Diamond drilling **is proceeding.**
This work **is underway.**
The search for such deposits **is** actively **pursued.**

Весь [*см. тж.* **В течение всего, Во всём**]
Should the wear exceed this, **the complete** pump barrel should be bored out.
It was necessary to replace **the entire** bottom of the tank.
Throughout *(в течение всей)* history ...
There are a large number of reactions which may affect **the overall** process.
Cracks which have not crossed **the whole of** the specimen usually stop at ...
This provides smaller slenderness in the flange elements than in **the overall** column.
This system is chemically and physically uniform **throughout.**

Весь мир [*см.* **Во всём мире, Всемирно известный**].

Весь накопленный опыт
We take **the totality of experience** and call some parts of it "science".

Весьма [*см. тж.* **Очень, Сильно**]
Interferometry has been **notably** (*or* **very,** *or* **highly**) successfull in probing ...

Весьма аналогичен [*см. тж.* **Иметь много общего с**]
The equations **are closely analogous** (*or* **similar**) **to** (4.3).
For fast waves the situation **closely parallels** (*or* **is closely similar to,** *or* **is much the same as**) that in gas dynamics.
The theory of magnetic studies **parallels** that of electrical studies **so closely that** a detailed treatment need not be given.
The approaches employed in syntheses of polynucleotides **bear close similarity to** those used in the formation of polyamino acids.

Весьма аналогично
The asthenosphere behaves **(very) much like** a true fluid.

Весьма аналогичный
Conditions **closely approximating** ideal gas behaviour ...
Alkyl fluorides have physical properties **much like** those of ...

Весьма близки (друг к другу)
All these polymerases appeared **to be closely allied** structurally.

Весьма близкий
Vermiculites **are closely related to** the micas.

Весьма большой
Fused salts have **quite** (*or* **very**) **large** conductances.

Весьма бурно
When heated, magnesium combines with several non-metals–often **extremely violently** (*or* **with great violence**).

Весьма важная роль [*см.* **Играть весьма важную роль**].

Весьма важный [*см.* **Исключительно важный**].

Весьма вероятно, что
If only one bond breaks, **there is a good probability that** the broken bond will reform before the second bond is ruptured.
Something illuminating will **in all likelihood** occur.
This enzyme could **very likely** have been a derivative of ...

Весьма возможно, что
It is highly plausible (*or* **probable**) **that** superfluid helium is ...

Весьма значительно
The technology of data storage has advanced **dramatically.**

Весьма значительный
These deposits cannot be mined economically so far, but their quantity **is impressive** (*or* **quite considerable**).

Весьма маловероятен
Such an occurrence **is highly unlikely** (*or* **highly improbable**).

Весьма маловероятно, что
It is extremely (*or* **highly**) **unlikely that** a single molecule will retain any given velocity very long.

Весьма напоминать ... по
Venus **is a close match to** (*or* **closely resembles**) Earth **in** size and density.

Весьма незначительный [*см.* **Лишь незначительный**].

Весьма необходимый [*см.* **Остро необходимый**].

Весьма ограниченный [*см. тж.* **Сильно ограничен**]
Severely (*or* **Very**) **limited.**

Весьма осторожно [*см.* **С большой осторожностью**].

Весьма отдалённое будущее [*см.* **В весьма отдалённом будущем**].

Весьма перспективный
Poly I:C **shows considerable promise** as a means for exploiting the interferon mechanism.

Весьма перспективый в области
A method **of considerable promise for** the production of "superheavy" elements has been devised.

Весьма подвержен
The hot vapour **is highly susceptible to** excitation and ionization.

Весьма подробно
They discuss **at great length** the arguments for ...
The following sections examine a chemical transformation **in close detail.**

Весьма полезен
The orbital model **has considerable utility in** helping us to ...

Весьма пригодный для
This bridge circuit **is most useful for** the measurement of ...

Весьма разбавленный [*см.* **Сильно разбавленный чем-л.**].

Весьма различны [*см. тж.* **Сильно отличаться по**]
The dichroic spectra of the two structures **are significantly distinct.**
The colours of the anhydrous compounds **vary widely.**

Весьма различные
Vastly (*or* **Drastically,** *or* **Markedly**) **different** species ...

Весьма разнообразны
Such membranes **are of a great variety.**
These sequences **are highly** (*or* **widely**) **diversified.**

Весьма разнообразные формы
Calcite may exhibit **a wide variety of forms.**

Весьма родственны друг другу
All the calf histones **show close kinship** [*or* **are closely related (to each other)**] (*biol.*).

Весьма сомнителен
This statement **is subject to serious question** (*or* **is highly questionable**).

Весьма сходный с
The situation **closely parallels** (*or* **resembles) that in ...**

Весьма точный
This definition **is highly accurate.**

Весьма трудный
The task **was a considerable challenge** (*or* **extremely complicated**).

Весьма тщательно
The specimens are being studied **with great thoroughness** (*or* **very thoroughly**).

Весьма удобен
Conventional optical techniques **are a great convenience.**

Весьма усложнять эксперимент [*см.* **Больша́я трудность**].

Весьма успешно [*см. тж.* **С большим успехом**]
This principle has been applied **with much success** to the restoration of ...
This type of plant **is most advantageously** employed on welding work.

Весьма хорошее приближение [*см.* **В весьма хорошем приближении**].

Весьма ценно для
Of considerable value to industry **is** that all the motors can ...

Весьма чувствителен к
Pulse shape **is acutely sensitive to** deviations from ...

Весьма эффективен
The theory **works very well** (*or* **is highly efficient**).

Весьма ядовит для
Hydrogen sulphide **is highly toxic to** fishes.

Весьма яркий
The star **is highly luminous.**

Ветвь I [*см.* **Восходящий** (*антон.* **Нисходящий**)].

Ветвь II
The **arms** (*or* **branches**) **of** a Wheatstone bridge (*el.*).

Ветер [*см. тж.* **Слабый ветер**]
The **north-easterly** trade **winds** flow from the northern Hemisphere towards the Equator.
Westerly (Southerly, Easterly, Northerly) wind.

Веха
The next **milestone** in the development of the high-speed digital computer is ...

Веха в истории
This proof constitutes an important **milestone in the history of** mathematics.

Вешать [*см.* **Подвешен**].

Вещественная и мнимая части
E_r — **real part of** the classic modulus.
E_i — **imaginary part of** the elastic modulus.

Вещество [*см.* **Материал**].

Взад и вперёд
Solute molecules are continually moving **back and forth.**

Взаимная дополняемость
The complementarity of the base pairs (*chem.*) ...

Взаимная зависимость [*см.* **Взаимосвязь**].

Взаимная связь [*см.* **Взаимосвязь**].

Взаимно дополнять друг друга
The screens are said **to be complementary** when the opaque parts of one correspond to the transparent parts of the other.
Geology and palaeontology **complement each other.**

Взаимно заменять друг друга
The terms "mixing" and "stirring" **are** often **used interchangeably** in ordinary speech.

Взаимно исключать друг друга
The two processes **are mutually exclusive.**

Взаимно обратные величины
The conductance and resistance **are reciprocally related.**

Взаимно превращаться друг в друга
Ascorbic acid and dehydroascorbic acid **are** readily **interconverted** in plant and animal tissue.

Взаимно противоречивы
The two explanations **are mutually contradictory.**

Взаимно связанные I
Streams perform three **interrelated** forms of geologic work.

Взаимно связанные II
A system of **interconnecting** (*or* **interconnected**) channels ...

Взаимно связаны
The two phenomena **are interrelated.**

Взаимно уничтожаться
The opposite charges **cancel out.**
Equal vectors of opposite direction **cancel (each other).**
When a quark and an antiquark collide, they **annihilate each other.**

Взаимное отталкивание электронов [*см.* **Отталкивание электронов** *(взаимное)*].

Взаимное расположение [*см. тж.* **Относительное положение**]
To predict **the relative positions** (*or* **mutual arrangement**) **of** the two planets ...

Взаимодействие
Interaction between neighbouring elements of antenna array ...
Interaction of rotation **and** electronic motion ...
Interaction of acetyl chloride **with** sodium acetate ...
Let us consider **the interaction of** a plane wave of coherent laser light **with** a Doppler-broadened spectral line.
The **interplay of** physical processes in atmospheric clouds is very complicated.
Random **interplay of** longer **and** shorter wavelengths ...

Взаимодействие ... с
The interaction of graphite **with** concentrated nitric acid appears variable.

Взаимодействовать

The particles **interact (with each other).**
In this reaction the potassium chloride and the sulphate of potash-magnesia **will react** to yield potassium sulphate and magnesium chloride.
These factors **interplay** in an intricate fashion.
Optical signals can **interact** on a subpicosecond time scale.

Взаимодействовать с
The U-centres **interact with** other defects.

Взаимозависимость [*см.* **Взаимосвязь**].

Взаимозависимы
The two types of equipment **are interdependent.**

Взаимозаменяемые
Interchangeable parts ...

Взаимозаменяемый с
The tooling on the A-9 machine **is interchangeable with** that of the A-10 machine.

Взаимосвязь [*см. тж.* **Соотношение, Устанавливать взаимосвязь между**]
The interplay of physical processes in atmospheric clouds is very complicated.
Bioclimatology emphasizes **the interplay between** disciplines such as meteorology and physiology.
The interrelation between the location **and** strength of the start-up source ...
Interrelation of successive observations ...
The process engineer brings into focus **the interrelationship of** chemical **and** mechanical engineering.
The data show direct **relationship between** CO content **and** pH.
Interconnection. Mutual relations.
The figure shows **the input-output relationship.**

Взаимосвязь между ... и
There is **a** striking **correlation between** the major oil and gas regions **and** the principal zones of seismic activity.

Взаимосвязь между объёмом и температурой
The volume-temperature behaviour of ideal gases ...

Взамен [*см.* **Вместо**].

Взвешенное состояние [*см.* **Во взвешенном состоянии**].

Взвешенный
A filter is a device for separating liquids from **suspended** solids.

Взвешенный в воздухе
Airborne pollutants ...

Взвешенный по скорости
He obtained **velocity-weighted** average stream potentials.

Взвешивание на весах
Five **weighings on an** analytical **balance** showed ...

Взгляд [*см.* **На первый взгляд, С первого взгляда**].

Взгляды
According to the new **mode of thought** (*or* **views,** *or* **concepts**), knowledge of the electron is best expressed in terms of ...

Взорвать [*см.* **Взрывать**].

Взрыв [*см.* **Заглушать взрыв**].

Взрыв звезды
A **stellar explosion.**

Взрывать
Explosive charges of 30 lb will **be fired** (*or* **set off,** *or* **exploded**).

Взрываться
The mine (*мина*) **is set off by** the noise emitted by its intended target.

Взят из
The terms **are borrowed** (*or* **taken**) **from** the theory of groups.

Взят у
These data **are borrowed from** D.
The diffusion data for the system nickel-gold **were taken from** Reynolds et al.

Взятое вместе [*см.* **Всё это, вместе взятое, является**].

Взять на себя
Microcomputers **have taken up** many new functions.

Взять на себя задачу
A second network **would take over the task of** distributing information in bulk from central facilities to offices and homes.

Взять предел [*см.* **В пределе, взятом по**].

Взять среднее по
An **average of** the results must **be taken over** a long enough interval.

Взяться за
To check for taper, **grasp** the handle and traverse the gauge from one end of the cylinder to the other.

Взятые вместе [*см. тж.* **Вместе взятые**]
All these satellites, **lumped** (*or* **put**) **together,** have one-sixth the volume of the Moon.
(Taken) together, these results suggest that ...
All these differences **combined** should account for ...

Взятые по два *и т.п.*
There are only four possible sums of digits **taken two at a time:** 0 plus 0, 1 plus 0, 0 plus 1, and 1 + 1.

Вибрация [*см.* **Вызывать вибрацию, Для устранения вибрации, Под действием вибрации**].

Вид I [*см.* **Внешний вид, Внутренний вид, Общий вид**].

Вид II [*см. тж.* **В виде, В существующем виде, В том виде, в каком они встречаются; В том или ином виде, Выражающийся в виде, Иметь вид, По внешнему виду, Поставлять в собранном виде, Приобретать вид**]
The structure of a euctoid steel **in** the annealed **condition** (*or* **state**) is 100% pearlite.
All manner [*or* **kind(s)**] **of** attachments may be mounted on this tractor.
A new **type of** drill is used.

Вид III [*см. тж.* **Тип**]
Such a process involves division of the molecule into two **species.**

Вид крупным планом
The figure gives **a close-up view of** the working area.

Вид с воздуха
An aerial view of the factory is given in the heading illustration.

Вид сбоку
Side view.

Вид сбоку и сверху
The silicon-oxygen tetrahedron **viewed from the side and from above** (*or* **from the top**) ...

Вид сверху
Top view.

Вид сзади
Back view (*or* **Rear view**).

Вид снизу
Figure 2 is **an underside** (*or* **bottom**) **view of** the track.

Вид спереди
Front (*or* **Head-on**) **view.**

Вида [*см. тж.* **Типа**]
It is advisable to use an equation **of the form** (*or* **type**): ...

Виден I [*см. тж.* **На ... виден**]
These lines do not **show on** the diagram.
Several of these features **are visible** (*or* **seen**) **in** Fig. 18.3.
Another smoke ring **is evident** near the galactic centre.

Виден II
The secondary radiation emitted **is viewed through** a collimator at an angle of 90° to the incident beam.

Виден в микроскоп
Only the larger colloidal particles **can be seen through an** ordinary **microscope.**

Виден из
This effect **is seen from** [*or* **by considering** (*or* **referring to**)] the diagram of Fig. 7-2.

Видеть [*см.. тж.* **Легко видеть, что**]
From (A2) we **observe** (*or* **see**) **that ...**

Видеть ... под углом
The solar observer would find himself **viewing** the planet **from a** different **angle.**

Видимость [*см.* **В пределах видимости, При хорошей видимости**].

Видимый [*см. тж.* **Без видимой причины**]
Such tubes must withstand five quenches without **visible** damage.

Видимый глазом
The neodymium glass used in high-power

lasers **is** not directly **visible to the human eye.**

Видимый невооружённым глазом
One very large cell **visible to the unaided** (*or* **naked**) **eye** could always be found on the surface of the right pleural ganglion.
Naked-eye stars ...

Видимый спектр
The visual (*or* **visible**) **spectrum of** the Sun ...

Видно [*см. тж.* **Из... видно, что; Как видно из, Явствовать из**]
From this figure we **notice that ...**

Видный [*см.* **Выдающийся**].

Видоизменение
Depending on the accuracy desired, various **modifications of** the simple calorimeter may be required.
This was an **adaptation of** the iodometric method.
This is **a** slight **modification of** the method outlined above.

Видоизменён
The chamber cover **was modified by** the addition of ...

Видоизменённый
By the use of **modified** pitot tubes ...

Видоизменять [*см. тж.* **Изменять, Менять**]
This expression (*or* design, etc.) must **be modified.**
The instrument can **be modified** according to the experimenter's needs.

Видоизменять ... так, чтобы он
A drainage system gradually **evolves** its configuration **in such a way as to** carry out its work most efficiently.

Видоизменять ... так, чтобы он включал
We **modify** Eq. (38.34) **to incorporate** (*or* **include**) this function.

Визуальный осмотр
A **visual inspection of** the engine should be made.

Виновен в этом
One must try to elucidate the cause of hypocalcaemia; among those most likely **to be at fault** are anticonvulsants and carbenoxolone.

Виновником этого является
There are several drugs which will lead to potassium loss, diuretics being **the** chief **offender** (*med.*).

Винт [*см.* **Вывинчивать, Завинчивать, Освобождать винт, Поджимать винт, Туго поджимать винт**].

Висеть в воздухе
The Rotodyne airplane has a rotor for taking off, landing and **hovering;** propellers for faster cruising.

Висеть на ... с
Fuel tubes **are suspended by** rods **from** a top tube sheet.

Вклад [*см. тж.* **Большой вклад в, Вносить вклад в**]
The contributions of (*or* **from**) the higher terms are small.
Higher coefficients show **the contribution of** (*or* **from**) more complex interactions.

Вклад в
The contribution of (*or* **from**) each component **to** some property of the mixture ...

Вкладываемый
The thermal energy **contributed by** a vibrational mode ...

Включать I [*см. тж.* **Запускать**]
This switch **brings into operation** (*or* **actuates**) the printing mechanism.
To open or **close** the switch the spring is charged by means of ...
To **throw on** the X-rays, ...
Turn on the furnace (gas, magnet, etc.).
Each neuron is labelled according to the feature that **triggers** its activities.
When you **turn** (*or* **flip** — *col.*) **on** a light switch, ...

Включать II [*см. тж.* **Видоизменять ... так, чтобы он включал**]
The set **comprises** (*or* **contains,** *or* **includes**) a noise generator and a receiver.
The glossary **covers** 160 items.
Among such substances **are (included)** water, alcohol, etc.
The manufacture of a fountain pen **incorporates** most of the finishing steps mentioned in this Chapter.

Equation 8 **incorporates** the normal losses.
These sets **incorporate** a crystal filter.
The equation **involves** a series of volume terms.
The system **involves** (*or* **includes**) water as the principal solvent.
Among these considerations **are** comparisons of ...
This reaction **involves** a change at the asymmetric centre.

Включать III [*см. тж.* **Подсоединять к**]
To **incorporate** lasers **into** spectroscopic systems, ...
A high-speed computer can **be inserted in** the feedback path in place of human beings.
Both sections are so designed that more machines can **be integrated in** the system if required.

Включать в список почтовых отправлений
Ask **to be put on our mailing list.**

Включать двигатель
Before **switching on** (*or* **turning on,** *or* **cutting in,** *or* **energizing,** *or* **putting power into**) **the motor** for the first time it is advisable to ...

Включать и выключать
The alteration in shape under the influence of metabolites and hormones provides a mechanism for **turning** these enzymes **on and off** under different external conditions.
When loads **are thrown on and off ...**

Включать параллельно
Each of the bobbins **is put** (*or* **placed**) **in parallel with** a neon tube.

Включать ток
Power is turned on, and the shaft starts spinning.

Включать тормоз
This permits a flow of air **to set** (*or* **apply**) **the brake.**

Включаться
After that the lever **is engaged.**
The stand-by transmitter **is** quickly **switched on** (*or* **turned on,** *or* **brought into use**) should a failure occur in the unit.
The gas and water supply **are turned on by** depressing the push button.
The brake **is applied** automatically.
When the motor **turns on, ...**

Включающий
Equipment **incorporating** (*or* **which includes**) wetted-wall tubes is particularly advantageous for this purpose.
Consider a system of equations **involving** n independent variables.

Включая
Whatever the agents of biological stress were, disturbances of food chains **included**, the ability of ...
Various catalysts have been tried, **among them** (*or* **including**) tin ethanediocite.

Включение I [*см. тж.* **Введение**]
Such switches are used for **turning** (*or* **putting) on** lights and the heating system.

Включение II
The incorporation of carbon dioxide **in(to)** organic compounds ...
Inserting an amplifier **between ... and ...**

Включение и выключение электрической цепи
When the circuit **is made and** then **broken ...**

Включён I
When the controller **was energized ...**
The alarm **is set off.**
The light **was switched on.**
After this, power **can be switched** (*or* **turned**) **on.**
The two knife switches **were thrown in** simultaneously.
The air supply **can** now **be turned on.**
The gas **is turned on.**
During the time the laser **is on ...**

Включен II
These effects **are built into** the wave vector equation.
A full-flow filter **is** now **incorporated in** the hydraulic system.

Включённый I
Control of the welding current is by a trip-switch **connected in** the primary circuit of ...
The capacitor **connected into** the second stage of the amplifier ...
A relay **included in** the lamp circuit ...
High-value resistors **incorporated in** the grid connections ...

Включённый II
The circuit **in the "on" condition ...**

The chart-drive motor which **is on** when the switch toggle is in the down position ...

Включённый параллельно
The coils **placed in parallel ...**
The rectified outputs from each half of the **paralleled** secondaries are filtered.

Включённый последовательно
This arrangement uses a thermostat **connected** (*or* **placed**) **in series with** the solar cells.
A constant current is passed through the specimen by means of a battery and **series** resistor.
Two **series-connected** coils ...

Включительно [*см. тж.* **Вплоть до ..., включительно; До ..., включительно**]
All the integers from ... to 535 **inclusive ...**

Включиться в работу
During this phase all manufacturing personnel **got into the act,** helping to devise less costly ways of producing the mill.

Вкраплён между
Accessory substances containing ... **are interspersed between** the respiratory enzymes.

Вкрапленный в
When the geologist finds oolites **embedded in** rock, ...

Вкратце рассматривать
In this section, **we briefly review** multilevel optical computing.

Влагонепроницаемый
The housing **is moisture proof** (*or* **moisture tight,** *or* **moisture resistant,** *or* **damp proof**).

Влажный [*см.* **Поддерживать во влажном состоянии путём смачивания водой**].

Влажный воздух
Moist (*or* **Humid**) **air.**

Влажный климат
A moist climate.

Влево [*см.* **Вправо или влево, Направленный влево**].

Влечь за собой [*см. тж.* **Связан с**]
A decrease in E_g **implies** an increase in ...
This operation **entails** (*or* **involves,** *or* **results in,** *or* **leads to**) a waste of current.

Влияние [*см. тж.* **Благоприятное влияние на, Большое влияние, Влиять на, Вредное влияние** (*или* **действие**)**, Действие, Находиться под действием, Не влиять на, Не оказывать влияния на, Не поддаваться (воз)действию, Оказывать действие на, Оказывать главное влияние на, Отрицательно влиять на, Отрицательное влияние** (*или* **действие**) **на, Плохое влияние** (*или* **действие**) **на, Под действием, Подвергаться воздействию**]
The charge-coupling concept in semiconductor electronics may someday **have an impact on** our lives as dramatic as that of the transistor.
The impact of Avogadro's Law **upon** the development of chemistry ...
The action of temperature **on** the composition of ...
The effect (*or* **influence**) **of** strain-ageing **on** the temperature dependence of the yield stress is great.
We shall consider **the repercussions of** short slugs **on** the final stage of an extrusion operation.

Влияние внешней среды на
The enzyme is highly sensitive to **environmental influences on** the ATP molecule.

Влияние ... на
Oxygen had **a** dramatic **impact on** the traffic of carbon in the chloroplast.

Влияние на состояние здоровья
The health consequences of a reactor accident were studied.

Влияние человеческой деятельности на окружающую среду
The human impact on the environment ...

Влиять на [*см. тж.* **Отрицательно влиять на, Отрицательное влияние** (*или* **действие**) **на**]
The particle size of the oxidizer **affects** (*or* **influences**) the burning rate of the propellant.
Background noise **has** (*or* **exerts**) no **effect** (*or* **influence**) **on** the accuracy of calibration.

Вмерзать в
In that case the magnetic lines of force **would be frozen into** the highly conducting stellar material.

Вместе [*см. тж.* **А вместе с ним и, В сумме, Взятые вместе, Отдельно или вместе**].
Epinephrine and norepinephrine are referred to **collectively** as catecholamines.
When the ion is moved, the ionic atmosphere will move **with** it.

Вместе взятое [*см.* **Все это, вместе взятое, является**].

Вместе взятые
The two volume elements **(taken) together** contain ...

Вместе с [*см. тж.* **А также, В сочетании с, Заодно с корпусом, Совместно с**]
Many ions act **in concert with** enzyme systems necessary to the complex chemical processes in living organisms.
Once a frit has been selected it is charged into a mill, **along** (*or* **together**) **with** water, clay, and electrolytes.
The instrument reading is then recorded, **along with** the date.
This effect, **combined** (*or* **coupled**) **with** the magnetic storm, results in ...
Hand in hand with the development of higher-pressure steam turbines has come improvement in boiler design.
An additional resistor should be used **in conjunction with** a single capacitor.
Cast **integral with** the bed at each end are aprons to collect the oil from the sideways.

Вместе с ним
We saw no way of removing ash from the bed without removing a large amount of carbon **along with it.**

Вместо [*см. тж.* **А не, Подстановка** *N* **вместо** *M*]
Mount a piece of translucent paper **in place of** the film.
It is customary to use molality **rather than** mole fraction of the solute.
The use of this term **rather than** ΔG is usually preferable.
Aluminium alloys have been used **as alternatives to** copper for overhead lines.
In place (*or* **In lieu,** *or* **Instead**) **of** the usual fuse, a bimetallic circuit breaker is used.
The flame-arc lamp radiates light from the arc **instead of from** the electrode.

Вместо него
This variety, while lacking the σ subunit, had a much heavier one named *y* **in its stead.**
Table salt is the most common source, but other compounds may serve **instead.**

Вместо того, чтобы
Rather than wait for years for an appropriate earthquake, the petroleum prospectors generate their own sound waves.

Вместо этого [*см. тж.* **Или же**]
A given boundary segment need not consist of only one boundary type; **instead,** the segment may be made up of ...

Вмещать
This length **accommodates** ten nucleotide pairs.
The cavity **will house** a large detector.
The car **holds** 20 tons of material.
This automobile **accommodates** five passengers.
The plant has been designed **to accommodate** four additional furnaces at a later date.
The auditorium **holds** (*or* **seats**) 50 people.

Вмещать неограниченное количество
There is no limit to the volume of new plutonic rock **that can be accommodated in** the crust.

Вмещающий их
Concretions are distinguished from the sedimentary matrix **enclosing them by** ...
A container **holding** the equivalent amount of gasoline ...

Вмонтированный
The amplifier has **built-in** power supplies.
The motor **built into** the driving drum ...
Special devices **built into** the tank ...
Figure 2 shows the instrument **fitted into** a pipeline.
The transfer pot **incorporated in** the top section of the mould ...
The indexing unit **incorporated into** a machine tool ...
The by-pass capacitors **mounted** (or **incorporated**) **in** the unit ...

Вначале [*см. тж.* **Первоначально, Сначала**]

On the far side of the Moon a similar powder will remain fixed at the place where it **originally** (*or* **initially**) fell upon the surface.
Chemists **originally** believed that ...
At first (*or* **In the beginning,** *or* **Initially**) the machine operated trouble free.
At the outset (*or* **From the start**) it seemed possible that ...
The plant will operate at lower power **to start** (*or* **begin**) **with.**
Early in the game we built a sled on which we mounted the exposure chamber.

Вне [*см. тж.* **За пределами**]
These points lie **exterior to** the curve.
Outside (of) the sheath, the electron and ion densities are unperturbed.
Beyond the Earth's atmosphere ...
The set of points **exterior to** the circle ...
All points **external to** the profile ...
An **off**-axis point ...
The points which lie **off** these lines ...
Outside the building ...

Вне власти
These errors **are beyond the control** of the analyst.
This **is beyond the power of** scientists.

Вне всякого сомнения
Those meteorites that were actually seen to fall established **beyond question** (*or* **a doubt) that** extraterrestrial rocks were arriving from space.
The tests confirm **beyond any reasonable** (*or* **possible**) **doubt** that the dipolarionic formulation is the best description.

Вне клетки
The resulting compounds may accumulate **extracellularly.**

Вне помещения [*см.* **Внутри и вне помещений, На открытом воздухе**].

Вне пределов
Activation energy and the paths of chemical reactions **are outside the province** (*or* **domain,** *or* **realm**) **of** thermodynamics.

Вне пределов досягаемости
This would require a tower with a thermal efficiency of 10 percent, which in practice **is beyond reach.**

Вне страны [*см.* **Внутри страны и вне её**].

Внедрять
Our interest in **promoting** (*or* **introducing**) efficient methods of roadway maintenance ...

Внеземного происхождения
It is certain that much of the organic material in carbonaceous chondrites **is of extraterrestrial origin.**

Внесение поправки
After **applying the corrections for** self-induction of instruments ...

Внести поправку на
It is important **to correct** (*or* **introduce a correction**) **for** the deceleration of the wave.
This result **has to be corrected for** the factor ... in Eq. (9.86), which has been neglected thus far.

Внешне
The organometallic process is at least **superficially** similar to biological fixation.

Внешне напоминать
Fired enamels **resemble** organic coating **in appearance** (*or* **outwardly resemble ...**).
Sorocarps **superficially** (*or* **outwardly**) **resemble** simple plants.
The spectra of the known extragalactic point sources such as quasars often **bear a superficial resemblance to** the spectrum of the Crab Nebula.
These dryers **are similar in appearance to ...**

Внешне напоминать друг друга
These animals **are similar in appearance.**

Внешнее и внутреннее освещение
Outdoor and interior lighting.

Внешнее оформление [*см.* **Красивое внешнее оформление**].

Внешнее покрытие
A new **outer coating for** ships ...

Внешнее поле
Any magnetic system with an appreciable **external field ...**

Внешнее проявление
External manifestations are the emission of light and a hissing sound.

Внешние стенки
Exterior (*or* **Outer**) **walls.**

Внешний [*см. тж.* **Наружный**]
The laser is the **external** light source whose radiation ...

Внешний вид [*см. тж.* **Для красоты, По внешнему виду**]
Igneous rocks were named for their **visual appearance.**
Etching changes **the appearance** of the finish.
Drawing of **the** interior layout and **exterior appearance** (*of a building*) ...
Fig. 13. **Exterior view of** a modern substation.
The general **external** (*or* **outward**) **appearance of** this machine is...
An external view of the plant is shown in Fig. 5.

Внешний вид кристалла
The crystal habit.

Внешний мир
To transfer heat from the reactor core to **the outside world, ...**

Внешний слой [*см. тж.* **Внутренние и наружные слои**]
The weave consists of an inner layer of ... and **an outer layer of ...**

Внешняя граница
The outer boundary of the region surrounding the collector contact ...

Внешняя коррозия
External corrosion.

Внешняя поверхность [*см. тж.* **Наружная поверхность**]
This colloid was adsorbed on **the outer surfaces of** the pellets.

Внешняя сила
X_i is **the outside force** per unit mass at cell i.

Внешняя среда [*см.* **Влияние внешней среды на**].

Внешняя сторона [*см.* **С внешней стороны**].

Вниз [*см. тж.* **Направленный влево (вправо, вверх, вниз)**]
The molecules move **down** from the upper layer.
The arc is deflected **downwards** magnetically.
As the car rolls **downhill** its potential energy decreases and is converted to kinetic energy.

Вниз по склону
The geologists moved **downhill.**

Вниз и вверх по течению от
Temporary cofferdams are built both **downstream and upstream of** (*or* **from**) the site.

Вниз фланцем
Place the mercury level gauge, **flange downwards,** in the upstream chamber.

Внизу
The colder, denser air lies **at the bottom.**

Внизу и наверху
The layers change in texture from coarse **at the bottom** to fine **at the top.**

Внизу посредине
See Fig. 2, **bottom centre.**

Внизу слева
The crater **on the lower left** has ...

Внизу страницы
The lamp is illustrated **at the bottom of the page.**

Внизу таблицы
The electrodes **low down in** (*or* **at the bottom of**) **the table** have a tendency to ...

Вникать глубже в
To obtain further insight into the problem, ...

Внимание [*см.* **Большое внимание уделено, В центре внимания, Занимать** *чье-л.* **внимание, Заслуживать внимания, Не обращать внимания, Не принимать во внимание, Не учитывать, Обращать внимание на, Относиться с должным вниманием к, Предлагать вниманию, Пренебрегать, Привлекать внимание, Принимать во внимание, Уделять внимание**].

Внимание концентрируется на
Attention now **focusses on** the possible pathways for ...

Внимательное рассмотрение [*см. тж.* **Из внимательного рассмотрения ... видно, что**]

Close inspection of these data shows that ...
A close look at the map will show that ...

Внимательный [*см.* **Более внимательное рассмотрение**].

Внимательный наблюдатель
To **the careful observer,** the evidence of this slow movement of the soil may be seen in ...

Вновь
A **newly** (*or* **freshly**) plastered house ...
A **newly** synthesized material ...

Вновь введённый (в строй)
The **newly commissioned** wind tunnel ...

Вновь загруженный
The arm can be swung down to form a stop for locating a **freshly-loaded** blank.

Вновь образовавшийся
Lavas were erupted along the **newly formed** continental margins.
A **newborn** star ...

Вновь открытый (*или* **обнаруженный**)
A **newly discovered** deposit ...

Вновь приобретать [*см. тж.* **Возвращаться к**]
The water **returns to** (*or* **regains,** *or* **again takes on**) its normal colour.
Then the gel **resumes** its original form.

Вновь пробуждать интерес к
The introduction of the laser to spectroscopy **is causing a rebirth of interest in** the spectroscopic study of atoms and molecules.
Recent investigations of ... **have rekindled interest in** the origin of the Earth-Moon system.

Вновь разработанный
Newly developed techniques ...

Вновь сконструированный
Newly designed systems.

Вносимая ошибка
The error incurred in (*or* **introduced by**) assuming that ...

Вносимый
The free energy **contributed by** the components of ...

Вносить [*см.* **Вводить**].

Вносить в
This kind of proof **injects** (*or* **introduces**) an empirical element **into** mathematics.

Вносить в гранки
Corrections and changes by the author **are entered on the galley proofs.**

Вносить в список
To enter in the list.
I **put** his address **on my list** for a visit tomorrow.

Вносить вклад в
Once trapped, the carrier will be unable **to contribute** (*or* **make a contribution**) **to** (*or* **increase**) the conductivity of the material.
Thus the width of the region **contributing to** lasing is uncontrolled.

Вносить вклад в ... размере
Each methylene group **contributes 156.5 cal/mol to** the heat of combustion.

Вносить значительный вклад в
These rays **contribute significantly to** the total ray power.

Вносить изменения
Use of scraper units **has brought about a change in** the stripping procedures.
To make (*or* **introduce**) **alterations** (*or* **changes**) **in ...**
The firm can easily **make** (*or* **incorporate**) **modifications.**
The stratification **produces a change in** the source strength.

Вносить ошибку (*или* **погрешность**) **в**
Neglect of this may **introduce** large **errors into** the measurements.

Вносить поправку на [*см. тж.* **Внесение поправки**]
Barometer readings **must be corrected for** elevation of ...
To introduce a correction for the effect of pressure drop on gas velocity ...
A calibrating adjustment **corrects for** screw pitch error to make reading accurate to one digit.

Вносить предложение
To make (*or* **put forward**) **a suggestion.**

Вносить удобрения
To apply (*or* **introduce**) **fertilizers.**

Вносить усовершенствование (*или* **улучшение**)
An improvement may **be made** (*or* **introduced**).

Вносить ясность в
Further research **will** surely **clarify** the situation.

Внутреннее давление
Internal pressure.

Внутреннее и наружное освещение
Interior and outdoor lighting.

Внутренние и наружные слои
The bursting causes a strong interaction between **the inner and outer layers.**

Внутренние ресурсы
Internal resources.

Внутренние частицы
The ratio of surface particles to **interior particles ...**

Внутренний
At some **interior** point of the disturbed region ...

Внутренний вид
Inside (*or* **Internal**) **view.**

Внутренний диаметр
The bore [*or* **The inner** (*or* **inside**) **diameter**].

Внутренний осмотр
The inspector enters the boiler and **inspects** it **internally.**

Внутренний слой
The wave consists of **an inner layer of ...** and outer layer of ...

Внутренняя обшивка
Interior cladding (*or* **lining**) is of 5 mm plywood.

Внутренняя поверхность
The inner surface of the cup ...
A mandrel forms **the inside of** the tube, while a die forms the outside.

Внутренняя сторона [*см.* **На внутренней стороне, С внутренней стороны**].

Внутренняя точка
We consider **an interior point of** the disturbed region.

Внутренняя часть
Both **the interior** and exterior are coated with enamel.
The **interiors of** the cell are subject to visual inspection.
To continental **interiors** (*or* **The interior of** continents, *or* **The interior part of** continents).

Внутри [*см. тж.* **В пределах, В толще**]
Phenomena occurring **in** and outside the rocket ...
The core was placed **inside (of)** the tube.
The tubes will be insulated **on the inside.**
In the interior of the dielectric material between the condenser plates, such charges cancel out.
Temporary shutoff of equipment **within** the plant ...
If z_0 lies **interior to** the regular Jordan curve, ...
Within the carbon nucleus there are forces holding the positive protons together.
The rocks present **within** the earth are subject to ...
There is a shielding **within** the cone.
Nuclear fusion **in the interior of** stars ...

Внутри и вне помещения
Indoor and outdoor dusts are almost invariably charged.
Unit substations are used **indoors and outdoors.**

Внутри клетки
The resulting compounds may accumulate **intracellularly.**

Внутри плазмы
The density of electrons and ions increases rapidly from zero at the outer surface to a maximum **in the bulk of the plasma.**

Внутри страны и вне её
At home and abroad.

Внутризаводской
These bins are used for **inplant** storage of borax and soda ash.

Внутрь [*см. тж.* **В ... и из него, Направленный внутрь**]
The reaction proceeds **inward** from the surface of the alloy.
The electron starts moving **inward.**

Внутрь или наружу
To move the airship **in or out of** its hangar, ...

Внушать сомнение относительно
This **casts (some) doubt on** the validity of ...

Во взвешенном состоянии [*см. тж.* **Удерживать во взвешенном состоянии**]
A solid catalyst is provided in the form of fine particles maintained **in suspension** in the liquid.
Particles of clay, silt, and sometimes, fine sand are transported **in suspension.**

Во внутренней части
The troughs are similar to geosynclines but are located **within,** rather than at the margins of a plate.

Во времени [*см. тж.* **Изменяться во времени, Необратимый во времени**]
To understand how this reaction proceeds **in time, ...**
The decrease in oxygen **with time ...**

Во времени и пространстве
The fair-weather field at the Earth's surface is observed to fluctuate **with space and time.**

Во врéмя [*см. тж.* **В процессе, В течение, До или во время, При**]
Some die casting machines are here seen **in the process** (*or* **course**) **of** assembly.

Во врéмя вращения
As the disk rotates, the blades block.

Во врéмя его образования
In the atmosphere surrounding the earth **at its formation ...**

Во врéмя испытаний
On (*or* **During the**) **trials** the tug achieved a speed of 12 knots.

Во врéмя наблюдений
In the course of (*or* **During**) **observations ...**

Во врéмя опытов
In the course of their **experiments** they worked out ...

Во врéмя перевозки
Formaldehyde in water solutions should be kept warm **in** (*or* **during**) **transit** (*or* **transportation**).

Во врéмя работы
In (the course of) operation there will be a constant expansion of gas into the vacuum chamber.
In operation one side of the junction is connected to ...
In the operation of the water softener, the binding sites are originally occupied by unipositive ions.
The adjustment can be made **while** the machine **is running.**
Changes of feed can be made **whilst** the machine **is operating.**

Во всей области
The value of k is constant **everywhere over the region.**

Во всей шахте
This may affect the ventilation **throughout the mine.**

Во всех направлениях
The roads run **every which way** (*col.*) like shatter lines in glass.

Во всех остальных отношениях
Other than that the models disagreed disturbingly.

Во всех отношениях
This machine gives you more for your money **in every way** (*or* **respect**).
Phenomena identical **in every particular** (*or* **respect**) to those mentioned above were observed.

Во всех подробностях [*см.* **Напоминать во всех подробностях (деталях)**]
In the design of a control system, the control engineer will have considered **in depth** the controlled system and ...

Во всех случаях
In all instances (*or* **cases**) the halfwave potential of the anomalous wave was ...

Во всех случаях, когда это возможно
Wherever (*or* **Whenever**) **possible,** specify a chamfered undercut.

Во всём
The flow is completely hyperbolic **over all** space.
The basic structure of legs is the same **throughout the entire** class of insects.
Throughout the visible spectrum ...

Во всём мире [*см. тж.* **В мире I, Известен во всём мире**]
It has been agreed **internationally** that the terms disability and handicap should be used to denote different conditions.
That country is **the world's** largest consumer of cobalt.
Considerable evidence points toward a **world-wide** warming during the last 70-85 years.
Structures much larger than that have been transported **worldwide.**
These buckets are sold **all over the world** (*or* **the world over,** *or* **(a)round the world**).
The Fire Fighter is in use **throughout the world.**
World-wide repercussions of ...
It has been estimated that, **world-wide,** about 63,000 chemicals are in common use.

Во всяком случае [*см.* **В любом случае**].

Во второй половине века
In the latter half (*or* **the second part**) **of the** 19th **century ...**

Во втором случае (из двух) [*см. тж.* **В последнем случае (из двух)**]
In the latter case, ...

Во избежание [*см.* **Чтобы не**].

Во избежание ошибок
To ensure against error (*or* **To avoid errors**) there is a TV camera at ...

Во избежание путаницы
To avoid confusion, ...

Во избежание чрезмерного усложнения
Various simplifying assumptions will be made **to keep** the derivation **from becoming too involved.**

Во многих отношениях
Living organisms are dependent upon water **in a multitude of ways** (*or* **in many respects**).
Division **is in many ways** similar to multiplication.

Во многих случаях
Animals communicate without knowing how they communicate; **by and large,** so do we.
In many instances (*or* **cases**) ...
On numerous occasions ...

Во много десятков раз меньше
The smallest eddies **are many factors of ten smaller than** the large eddies.

Во много раз
This has increased **many-fold** (*or* **many times over**) the supply of ...

Во много раз больше
The width of the two-photon vibronic transition band **was many times the** dye laser linewidth.
The rate of dissolution of a solid sphere **is many times (higher than) that** predicted by Eq. (6.16).

Во много раз больше в длину, чем в ширину
The trough **was many times longer than it was wide.**

Во много раз лучше, чем
Helium conducts heat **many times better than ...**

Во́время
If ever an energy source can be said to have arrived **in (the nick of) time,** it is nuclear energy.
All operations will be performed **on time.**

Во-вторы́х [*см. тж.* **Во-пе́рвых, во-вторы́х, в-третьих ...**]
Second(ly) (*or* **In the second place**) ...

Вогнутый вниз, вверх
The line **is concave down(ward), up(ward).**
Downwardly (*or* **Upwardly**) **concave ...**

Вогнутый по отношению к
The Moon's orbit **is** everywhere **concave toward** the Sun.

Вода [*см.* **Водопроводная вода, Под водой, Растворимый в воде**].

Водиться в больших количествах
These fishes **abound** in the tidal waters along the coast.

Водное пространство
Steam-driven electric-power stations must be located near large **bodies** (or **stretches**) **of water** where ample cooling is available.

Водоём
Large **bodies of water** (*or* **water bodies**), such as the Great Lakes, ...

Водонепроницаемый
A **watertight** seal ...

Водоочистка [*см.* **Обработка воды**].

Водопроводная вода
Tap water.

Водорастворимый [*см.* **Растворимый в воде**].

Возбуждаемый лазером
Laser-excited atomic fluorescence ...

Возбуждать интерес [*см. тж.* **Вызывать интерес**]
These models **have aroused** considerable **interest in** many fields of manufacturing.
This **has awakened** fresh **interest in** celestial mechanics.
We are taking steps to **generate interest among** high school students **in** the career of mining and metallurgy.

Возбуждать любопытство
This question **aroused the curiosity of** a Canadian geologist.

Возбуждать на ... состояние (*физ.*)
The first two pulses **excite** the electron **to** an intermediate **state.**

Возведéние в степень
The tedious operations of **computing powers** and roots ...
This may be proved by **cubing** *(возведением в третью степень).*
Powering both sides of the equation ...
Raising to a power...

Возведённый в степень
The force is proportional to the pressure times *(умноженному на)* the opening **to the three halves power** *(в степени три вторых).*

Возводить в квадрат
To (take the) square (of) the value of ...

Возводить в степень
F **is raised to the** third **power.**

Возвратно-поступательное движение [*см.* **Совершать возвратно-поступательное движение**].

Возвращать в атмосферу
The movements of air **restore to the atmosphere** the heat lost by radiation into space.

Возвращать в первоначальное положение
On completion of this check the resistance thermometer connections must **be replaced in their original position.**
This automatically **restores** the pump unit **to its position** ready for the next power stroke.

Возвращаться в
The tar **is recycled to** the gas generator so as to achieve complete gasification.
Virtually all organic nitrogen **is recycled (back) to** the atmosphere.

Возвращаться в первоначальное положение
When the welding has been completed the table **returns to** (*or* **regains**) **its original position** for unloading.

Возвращаться в ... положение
As a result, the control valve **is reset to the** central **position.**

Возвращаться в седло (*о клапане*)
The valve **will reseat** quickly at a higher pressure.

Возвращаться в ... состояние
The electron **reverts to the** original **state.**

Возвращаться к [*см. тж.* **Вновь приобретать**]
We **revert** (*or* **return**) **to** our previous analogy.
β-sulphur **turns back to** its α-form if sublimed at abt. 320 K.
Then the material **reverts to** the metallic state.
The plant **is** now **back to** normal operation.
The crystal **regains** its original dimensions.
Each of these molecules **is restored to** its original form.
We **revert to** the ideal-gas expression.

Возвращаться к первоначальной форме
Then the material **recovered** (*or* **regained**) **its original shape.**

Возвращаться к первоначальному состоянию
This **brings** the voltage **back to its original state.**

Возвращающийся в земную атмосферу [*или* **в атмосферу Земли**]
This is the same process that cools the heat shield of a space vehicle **reentering the atmosphere.**

Возвращаясь к
Turning back (*or* **Reverting,** *or* **Returning**) **to** Fig. 5, we see that ...

Возвращение [*см. тж.* **На обратном пути**]
From the crushers, the stone is fed back to the bucket elevator for **recirculation to** the screen.
The recovery of equipment **from** orbit ...

Возвращение в атмосферу Земли [*или* **в земную атмосферу**]
Reentry (into the Earth's atmosphere).

Возвышаться на
Several mountain peaks **rise to heights of** 4 to 5 km.

Возвышаться над
Turtle Mountain **looms** 1,000 m **above** the valley.

Возвышающийся над
A mountain mass **rising above** the adjacent lowlands ...

Возглавить
He **took charge of** the project.

Возгораться [*см. тж.* **Загораться**]
Graphite **ignites** at red heat.
The mixture **will inflame** if slightly damped with water ...

Возгораться в воздухе
Magnesium **takes fire in air** if ...

Возгораться самопроизвольно[*см.* **Самопроизвольно возгораться**].

Воздвигать
The protective framework **is erected** (*or* **put up**).

Воздействие [*см. тж.* **Действие, Испытывать воздействие, Коррозионное воздействие, Под действием, Подвергаться воздействию**]
Acetylides are prepared **by the action of** acetylene on ...
The effect (*or* **influence**) **of** the environment **(up)on** animals ...
Failures after **exposure to** elevated temperatures have become more evident.
The action of zinc is the most convenient for laboratory preparations of hydrogen.
The alloy is resistant **to attack by** fluorine.
The effect is achieved by a 10-minute **exposure to** gamma rays.

Воздействие атмосферы
Exposure to the atmosphere.

Воздействие загрязнений на человека
The continuous **exposure of man to** many natural **pollutants** is great enough.

Воздействие микробов
Methane may be able to polymerize into crude oil under catalytic action, including **microbial action.**

Воздействие на
Subjection of rocks **to** (*or* **Action on** rocks **by**) alternate heating and cooling has produced significant results.

Воздействовать [*см.* **На ... действует**].

Воздействовать *чем-л.* **на** *ч.-л.*
We **react** atmospheric nitrogen **with** hydrogen *(воздействуем водородом на атмосферный азот).*

Воздействовать на I [*см. тж.* **Действовать на, Не воздействовать на, Обрабатывать, Оказывать действие на**]
The acid **attacks** the hydrogen carbonate.
The magnetic oscillations in the waves **act on** charged particles, causing them to vibrate.
Dichlorohydrins **may be reacted with** lime to produce epichlorohydrin.
Sodium hydroxide yields ... when **acted upon by** cold water.
We **react** ammonia **with** various acids.
A variety of bacteria in the soil can **operate on** these compounds and convert them to nitrates.

Воздействовать на II
We **exposed** the nervous system of embryos **to** glyoxylic acid.
He permitted sunlight to **act upon** paraldehyde solutions.

Воздействовать пáром на уголь

Liquid hydrocarbons can be produced **by reacting coal with steam.**

Воздух [*см.* **Азот воздуха, Вид с воздуха, Висеть в воздухе, Кондиционирование воздуха, На открытом воздухе, Распространяющийся в воздухе, Столб воздуха**].

Воздухонепроницаемый
An **airtight** seal ...

Воздушная подушка
The material rode along on **a cushion of air** (*or* **an air cushion**).

Воздушной закалки
The workpiece is made from **airhardened** steel.

Воздушный поток
An airflow.

Воззрения [*см.* **Взгляды**].

Возлагать надежды на
Steel mills **are counting on** stepped-up demand for rolled steel.
The oil industry **looks to** computers.
We **are pinning our hopes on** the new method.

Возмещать [*см.* **Компенсировать**].

Возмещать потерю
More heat was required **to make up** (*or* **to recompense,** *or* **to compensate**) **for** the heat lost under compression.

Возможен
Although seeding of the catheter by microorganisms circulating in the blood **is a possibility,** it has not been a significant problem.
This increase **is made possible by** a miraculous development in technology.

Возможно [*см. тж.* **Вполне возможно**]
It is conceivable (*or* **possible,** *or* **not improbable**) **that** the observed results are also consistent with some other hypothesis.

Возможно будет осуществить только через много лет
Any large-scale use of this energy **is many years in the future.**

Возможно, что
Conceivably the flows **might** represent ...

Возможности
The new methods can utilize the unique **capabilities** (*or* **potentials**) of modern laser sources.
He brought to public notice **the potential(itie)s of** the engine.

Возможности не безграничны
There is a limit to what can be done in this area.

Возможность [*см. тж.* **В меру своих возможностей, Вероятность, Давать возможность, Допускать возможность, Есть возможность, Имеется возможность, Иметь большие возможности, Иметь возможность, Исчерпывать возможности, Не иметь возможности, Обеспечивать возможность, По возможности, Позволять, Практическая возможность, Предусматривать возможность, При наличии возможности, Производственные возможности**]
Six compounds were investigated for **feasibility of** analysis by laser-induced fluorescence.
The clock effect provides **a possibility to** distinguish between ...
The possibilities for surface adsorption are fantastically increased.
It seems timely to consider **the potentialities** (*or* **possibilities**) **of** these methods.

Возможность длительного хранения
Long shelf-life.

Возможности для [*см.* **Обеспечивать большие возможности для**].

Возможность того, что
The possibility of this process occurring spontaneously can be deduced by ...

Возможный [*см. тж.* **Практически возможный** (*или* **осуществимый**)]
Printed transformer coils, made **feasible** (*or* **practicable,** *or* **possible**) **by** superconductive metals, could replace ...
The resulting equation represents **a plausible** reaction.
Suggest **plausible** electron configurations for ...
One **conceivable** reason for the existence of modified bases is ...

Вознаграждать усилия
There is no assurance from theory that **the effort will be rewarding.**

Возник очень давно
This concept **goes back a long way (in history).**

Возник спор относительно (*или* **по**)
An argument broke out over (the problem of) ...

Возникает вопрос [*см. тж.* **В связи с этим возникает вопрос о**]
But here another **point arises.**
This brings up the question: What is the overall length of the X-chromosome?
The question (now) arises of whether there are significant differences in ...

Возникает вопрос о том
The question arises as to whether there is an ultimate limit to the improvement possible.

Возникать I [*см. тж.* **Создавать волну, Создаваться**]
The repulsion between two electrons **comes about from** the exchange of photons.
An earthquake **is generated** (*or* **develops,** *or* **occurs**) when two blocks ...
The potential **appearing** across the output terminal is ...
These forces **arise from** the displacement of the aileron.
The methylamines are widely distributed in nature where they **arise** probably as the result of decompositon of ...
The strains that **are brought about** in steel during the hardening process ...
Planets may **come into being** (*or* **existence,** *or* may **result**) when small planetesimals fall together.
Above 1000°F another process **is coming into play.**
The pipe **developed** a leak (*в трубе возникла течь*).
Under such conditions, it is possible that a crack may **develop** in a furnace.
All tools **develop** (*во всех инструментах возникают*) residual internal stresses.
Under these conditions a bias **will be developed** because of the flow of electrons from grid to ground.
If a leak **occurs ...**
Problems invariably **occur** which call for ...
When life first **originated ...**
A wave **originating** at point *S* can reach any of the several detectors.
No known meteorites seem **to have originated** on the Moon.
A model of this type can be changed many times during the construction as new problems **present themselves.**
The temperature at which the disorder **sets in** is a function of ...
Chemistry **grew out of** the black magic of the dark ages and the alchemy of the middle ages.
New methods for seeking out genetic loci **are emerging.**
This definition **came about** because it simplified the study of control systems.
A dispute which **ensued** between the two groups ...
These forces **are generated** in the earth's interior.
Shear **is produced** in columns by (1) variation in ...

Возникать II [*см. тж.* **Появляться**]
Ultimately, a molecule similar to modern catalase **came into existence.**
Brain tumours are not likely **to arise** from a mature neuron.
Planets may **result** [*or* **come into being** (*or* **existence**)] when small planetesimals fall together.
As a result **there occurs** what is known as the Cerenkov effect.
These craters **date back to** a period of ...
Planets may **evolve into existence** when ...
Interest in developing... **goes back to** the 1950s.

Возникать III [*см. тж.* **В связи с этим возникает вопрос**]
Such forces **occur** when ...
In our galaxy, supernovae **occur** once every 30 years or so.
A complication **has cropped up.**
Three questions might **come to mind** about the properties of ...

Возникать в результате [*см. тж.* **Быть вызванным, В результате, Вызван, Являться результатом** (*или* **следствием**)]
The forces between quarks and antiquarks **come about from** an exchange of gluons.
Transitions **are caused by** radiation of ...

Errors that may **arise** (*or* **ensue**) **from** such disturbances ...
Gamma photons **arising from** capture in ^{15}N ...
The interplanetary navigator's most difficult problems **derive from** the fact that...
When combustion **originates from** a local exposure ...
These problems **spring** (*or* **stem**) **from** a number of different demands.
This disease **is acquired by** injury to the skin.
The first organic superconductors **have been an outgrowth of** attempts to build ...
The concept of actively "dumping" radiation from a laser cavity **grew out of** the pulse-width limitations of Q-switched laser systems.
The term electron optics **derives** (*or* **is derived**) **from** the fact that ...
This distortion **results from** a quadratic nonlinearity.
The felsic and intermediate magmas **come** largely **from** the melting of preexisting rock of the continental crust.
The theory of determinants **had its origin in** the solution of linear systems of equations.
Stress incontinence often **dates back to** pelvic floor damage **occurring** during child birth.
These devices **evolved from** a thorough study of ...

Возникать в результате этого
The structure that **results** is chemically stable.

Возникать из
The concept of symmetry **had its origin in** geometry.

Возникать на основе
The Periodic table **evolved from** careful observations of physical and chemical properties.

Возникать при
The idea of introducing substances directly into the bloodstream **goes back to** the discovery of the circulation of the blood.
The discontinuity **appears in** crossing the wave front.

Возникают затруднения
Difficulties ensue (*or* **emerge**) when the time has come to discontinue the treatment.

Возникают сомненения относительно
(Some) doubts are cast upon the involvement of ...
Now even the mass of the Galaxy **has come into question.**

Возникают трудности
Difficulties emerge when we consider the relation of ...
Problems **arise** if there is serious competition for the metal needed.

Возникающий в результате
Spectra **due to** transitions between ... are called electronic spectra.

Возникающий в результате этого
The resulting forces are repulsive.

Возникла мысль [*см.* **Зародилась мысль**].

Возникла неисправность
If the machine should **develop a fault** (*or* **trouble**) ...

Возникла потребность
In the latter half of the 19th century **a demand arose** (*or* **was created**) **for** a more efficient drive.

Возникновение
Delay lines are also used for establishing a time sequence for **the occurrence of** events.
Long before **the rise of** copper metallurgy ...

Возникновение дуги
The metal evaporates, creating conditions for **initiation of a** plasma **arc.**

Возникновение жизни
The synthesis of ... was a prelude to **the advent of life.**

Возникновение потока
Initiation of the flow.

Возникновение потребностей
The origination of demands by communications customers frequently displays a random character.

Возникший
Electrical impulses **originated** at one place are to be reproduced at a distant point.

Возобновлять операцию (*машстр.*)
The operation can be stopped and **restarted** (*or* **resumed**) anywhere in the automatic cycle without having to return to the starting position.

Возобновлять работу
The plant **resumed operation** after a shutdown in 1981.

Возобновляться
When work **is recommenced** (*or* **resumed**), ...
The deposition of sediments **resumed.**

Возражать, что
His opponents **argued that** the matching of these features was merely coincidence.

Возражение [*см.* **Вызыващий возражения**].

Возражение против
The third **objection to** the impurity atmosphere hypothesis is that ...
The objection against the theories presented above ...

Возраст, определённый методом K-Ar
Potassium-argon dates are regarded as minimum ages for a rock.

Возраст ... определяется
These rocks **can be dated** only **by** the ^{14}C **method.**

Возраст ... определяется в ... лет
Granitic rocks from Rainy Lake **are dated at** between 2.75 and 2.72 billion **years.**
These tools **are** usually **reckoned to be between** 10,000 **and** 11,000 **years old.**

Возрастает значение
Spectrographic analysis **is growing in importance** for identifying ...

Возрастание [*см.* **В порядке возрастания**].

Возрастать [*см.* **Расти, Увеличиваться**].

Возрождать интерес к
These findings **have inspired a renewed interest** (*or* **have regenerated interest**) **in** the organic constituents of meteorites.

Возрождаться
Enthusiasm for the World Accelerator **surfaced again** in 1975.
At first the "interlock" model **was revived,** but this was soon abandoned in favour of ...

Возьмем, например
Take for example the uranium-lead series.

Война умов
Electronic warfare is **a battle** (*or* **war**) **of wits.**

Вокруг
An astronaut in orbit **about** (*or* **around**) the Earth is virtually a surface satellite.
A coordinated polyhedron of anions is formed **about** each cation.

Вокруг Земли
Such a space station would continually travel in an orbit **about** (*or* **around,** *or* **round**) **the Earth.**

Вокруг оси [*см.* **Вращаться вокруг оси, Вращение вокруг оси**].

Волна [*см.* **На волне, На всех волнах, Настраивать на волну, Распространение**].

Волновать
These questions **have agitated** scientists for thousands of years.

Волновая природа частиц
The wave nature of particles provides calculation procedures that are ...

Волнообразно [*см.* **Распространяться волнообразно**].

Воображаемый
For any planet, real or **imaginary, ...**

Воображать [*см. тж.* **Представить себе**]
The beam **is imagined to** provide a forward flow of energy.
Let us **visualize** a point in space...

Вообще [*см. тж.* **Если вообще, Мало ..., если вообще имеет их; Не имеющий ... вообще**]
In certain cases we cannot observe the addition product **at all.**
If the condensation is to be observed **at all, ...**
The object of this is refining of the grain size, producing a more uniform structure and **generally** (*or* **in general**) improving the mechanical properties.
Where accuracy is **at all** important, ...
One of the greatest puzzles in particle physics is explaining nature's need for both muons and electrons **in the first place.**
In many cases it is unnecessary to have any wires **whatsoever.**

Вообще говоря [*см. тж.* **В общем (и целом)**]
Broadly speaking, any of the three designs might have been adapted to ...
These defects produce optical absorption bands in **otherwise** transparent crystal.
Generally speaking (*or* **In general**), corrosion is slower in coarse-grained material.
By and large all the divergence regions over the oceans are associated with high salinity.
In general terms a metric theory of gravity is one in which gravitation can be treated as being synonymous with the curvature of space and time.

Вообще и в частности
Calorimetric methods **generally** and bolometric methods **specifically** (*or* **in particular**) are almost universally used.

Вообще не иметь
Adenine **lacks** a third active site **of any sort** (*or* **altogether**).

Во-первых
In the first place, we can take it for granted that ...
Geologic study of deformed rocks requires **first** that we have some means of ...

Во-первых, во-вторых, в-третьих ...
Three features must be pointed out. **First(ly),** we must recognize ... **Second(ly),** ... **Third(ly),** ...
For one thing (*or* **On the one hand**), the susceptibility is low after cooling; **for another** [*or* **on the other (hand)**], this cooling rate seems too high to permit ...
In the first place, two major types exist; **second,** closer examination discloses that ...

Воплощать в
A similar concept (*идея*) **has been embodied in** a transonic aircraft.
We have made an outstanding record of **translating** research **into** new products.

Вопреки
In the lowest vibrational state, **contrary to** classical ideas, the most probable internuclear distance is ...

Вопреки ожиданиям
Contrary to the expectations the temperature did not fall to the initial value.
The studies of young animals showed, **contrary to the expectations,** that some degree of stress in infancy is necessary for the development of normal, adaptive behaviour.
However, **contrary to what you might expect,** the erosion velocity is quite high.

Вопреки рекомендациям
Less than a month later, **against the advice** of a select panel of scientists, Hiroshima and Nagasaki were obliterated.

Вопрос [*см. тж.* **В связи с этим возникает вопрос, Возникает вопрос, Выдвигать вопрос, Выяснять, Ещё вопрос, Обсуждаемый вопрос, По вопросу о, Под вопросом, Проблема**]
The major practical **issue is** how to detect ...
We must find the answer to **the question of** how such reactions occur.
This investigation serves to clarify **the issue** (*or* **matter,** *or* **question**).
Points (*or* **Questions,** *or* **Items**) on the agenda of the Conference ...
This **point** should be given more attention.

Вопрос времени
This is only **a matter of time.**

Вопрос, давно ожидающий ответа
The Space Telescope may finally resolve **the long-standing question of whether** there are planetary systems similar to the Solar system.

Вопрос о том
A question was raised as to whether turbulence can alter ...

Вопрос остается открытым
The issue remains open.
The question of life on Mars **is still an open question.**

Вопрос стоит остро
The problem is especially **acute** near the continental margins.

Воспламенять
The reaction with potassium is violent enough **to inflame** the hydrogen.

Воспламеняться
The injected fuel **ignites from** contact with the hot cylinder air.
If heated in air or oxygen, sulphur melts and **takes fire.**

Воспламеняться в результате
A stream of hydrogen sulphate **is ignited by** contact with ...

Воспламеняющийся со взрывом
The new gas **was explosively inflammable.**

Восполнение
If potassium **replacement** (*or* **replenishment**) is necessary it is best to use a preparation containing potassium chloride.

Восполнять [*см.* **Компенсировать**].

Восполнять недостаток
Blending sand had to be added **to make up** (*or* **compensate**) **for a deficiency in** fines.

Восполнять потерю
This **loss is made good from** a pot of nitric acid.
More heat was required **to make up** (*or* **compensate**) **for** the heat lost under compression.

Восполняться
In this way the supply of soil nutrients **is replenished**.
The lost liquid **is replenished from** the reservoir.

Воспользоваться [*см. тж.* **Использовать**]
In order to explain ..., one must **draw on** the principles of quantum mechanics.
The designer must **fall back on** semiempirical numerical methods of analysis.
Pascal **invoked** the principle of indifference by referring to a coin flip in his famous wager.
Recourse was made (*or* **We resorted**) **to** a propulsion unit incorporating ...
To take advantage of the higher potential, ...

Воспринимать
The clearness with which sounds **are perceived by** the hearers ...

Воспринимать ... как
The eye **perceives** the combination of colours **as** white.

Воспринимать удар
The shocks are taken (*or* **absorbed**) **by** coil springs.

Восприниматься как
Light passing through an emerald acquires a different distribution of wavelengths, which **are perceived as** green.

Воспроизведение [*см. тж.* **Повторение**]
Fossils are an aid in **the reconstruction of** ancient geography, environments, and climates.
Geologists began to make detailed **restoration of** earth history.

Воспроизводимость
The reproducibility of response ...

Воспроизводимый
Repeatable (*or* **Reproducible**) diagnostic results ...

Воспроизводить I
The electrical impulse from the cell **is displayed** (*or* **reproduced**) on an oscilloscope.

Воспроизводить II
It is easy **to duplicate** (*or* **reproduce**) this process in the laboratory.

Воспроизводить III
The astronomer may be able **to piece together** the evolution of the universe back to the moment of creation.
In order **to restore** (*or* **reconstruct**) the earth history ...

Воспроизводить магнитную запись
The tape record **is played back** on the ground after the aircraft has completed its tests.

Воспроизводить по данным
The damping curve **was reproduced from data** reported by ...

Воспроизводиться [*см.* **Лучше воспроизводиться**].

Восстанавливать
Some manufacturers **have reclaimed** cylinder liners by turning or boring them oversize and then plating the inside walls with chrome.
Remagnetization after high-temperature exposure does not **restore** the original properties of ...
A great variety of broken or worn tools **can be restored by** this process.
The initial state of the device **can be regained** if the traps are discharged by a reverse-voltage pulse.
To recapture (*or* **reconstruct**) the full history of the earth, ...

Восстанавливать до первоначального вида
Each of these molecules **is restored to its original form.**

Восстанавливать перпендикуляр к линии ... в точке
Erect a perpendicular to line *AB* at point *C*.

Восстанавливать равновесие
It is impossible **to redress** (*or* **restore**) **the balance** completely.
To re-establish equilibrium, ...

Восстанавливать свою первоначальную форму
The material **resumes** (*or* **recovers,** *or* **regains,** *or* **returns to**) **its original shape** when the stress is removed.

Восстанавливаться
When the double bonds **are re-established** (*or* **restored,** *or* **remade**), ...
One screw is adjusted relative to the other until perfect cross-slide alignment **is regained.**

Восстанавливаться до прежнего уровня
The OH emission decreases in intensity during morning twilight and then **regains its** night-time **value** during the day.

Восстановленный до первоначального состояния
The press **was restored to its original condition.**

Восточный конец стрелки компаса [*см.* **Северный конец стрелки компаса**].

Восходить к
The methods **go** (*or* **date**) **back to** Lavoisier's introduction of the analytical balance and gas burette.

Восходящая кривая
An ascending (*or* **A rising**) **curve.**

Восходящий (*антон.* **Нисходящий**)
The rising (*or* **ascending**) [*anton.* **dropping** (*or* **descending**)] branch of a curve ...

Восьмичасовой рабочий день
Most gas-chromatography labs operate **on an eight-hour day.**

Вот как
Here is how the computer would support the operator in a switching operation.

Вот почему
That is the reason that (*or* **why**) (*or* **That is why**) we use...

Впадать в [*см.* **Брать начало в ... и впадать в**].

Впадать в зимнюю спячку
As the days become shorter, hibernating animals **go into their winter sleep** (*or* **hibernation**).

Впадать в крайность
There is no need **to go into this extreme** (*or* **to go into extremes**).

Впадать в океан
These rivers **drain** (*or* **flow**) **into the** Arctic **Ocean.**

Впадина волны [*см.* **Гребень и впадина волны**].

Впадины и выступы (на поверхности)
Valleys and ridges.

Впервые [*см. тж.* **Первый**]
Saturn's rings **were first** (*or* **originally**) discovered by Huyghens.
We define each term when it is **first** used.
D. **was the first to** establish this fact.
The first experiment **to be** carried out with this apparatus took place in Prague.
By effectively eliminating Doppler broadening this laser technique enables one **for the first time to** resolve the fine structure of these spectral lines.

Впервые использовать
They **pioneered the use of** such beams.

Впервые применить
Our group **pioneered in applying** these operational techniques to the above-discussed process.
He **pioneered the application of** computer models for ...

Впереди [*см. тж.* **Непосредственно перед**]
If the radio station **is directly ahead, ...**
The box **is located immediately ahead of** the drive head.
Some atoms move **ahead of** others.
The numbers are written **in front of** symbols.

Впереди слева
The crushing house is shown **in the left foreground.**

Вперёд [*см. тж.* **В направлении вперёд**]
Enter the instrument into the panel aperture hinged side **first.**

Вперёд и назад [*см. тж.* **Двигаться вперёд и назад**]
As the droplets pass through two pairs of charged plates they are successively deflected **back and forth** and up and down.
The pilot shifts his body **fore and aft** (*av., mar.*).

Впечатляющий [*см. тж.* **Грандиозный**]
This remarkable result provided one of the most **dramatic** triumphs of the kinetic-molecular theory.
The most **dramatic** of these eddies are closed rings that break off from currents such as the Gulf Stream, etc.
These achievements are **impressive.**

Вписываться в [*см. тж.* **Естественно вписываться в**]
Nickel **fits** less well **into** the structure of silicate minerals.
This gas outflow did not **fit in with** the accepted picture of the formation of ...

Вписываться в схему
Genes do not always **fall into** this **pattern.**

Вписываться друг в друга наилучшим образом
They found that **the best fit between** the two continents could be obtained if ...

Впитывание [*см.* **Поглощение**].

Впитывать [*см. тж.* **Абсорбировать**]
Table salt **takes on** (*or* **takes up,** *or* **absorbs**) moisture from the air.
The plants **take up** nutrients from the soil.

Вплотную к [*см. тж.* **Помещать**]
The new plant stands **immediately adjacent to** No.1 shaft.
Screw nuts *A* **up against** spindle *C*.
The flexible tubes should be pushed **right up to** the shoulder of each elbow.

Вплоть до [*см. тж.* **До**]
The Mid-Atlantic Ridge continues **as far as** the tip of Baja California.
This equation is applicable to the behaviour of objects **down to** molecular and atomic dimensions.
At absolute zero all states are occupied **(right) up to** the Fermi energy.
Improvements in sensitivity **of up to** tenfold over conventional spectrophotometry ...
Tetracyclines can raise the blood urea **(even) to the extent of** producing severe renal failure.
The new detectors have a quantum efficiency **that goes as high as** 70 percent.
Protenoid microspheres tend to display certain similarities to living cells, **(even) to the point of** possessing a surface membrane.
Accuracy is maintained **down to** the lowest setting.
Specimens are hydrolized for various periods **ranging up to** 60 days.

Вплоть до ..., включительно
$n(x)$ takes values **down to and including** β.
Using these numbers, you can express any other number **up to and including** 1023 (*or* **up to** 1023, **inclusive**).

Вплоть до (полного) исчезновения
A single formation usually shows thickening in the seaward direction, while in the landward direction it may thin **to the point of disappearance.**

Вплоть до того, что
Amino acids possess inherent sequence-directing abilities **to the extent that** orderly peptide chains can be synthesized even in the absence of nucleic acids of any sort.

Вплоть до уровня, на котором
We increase the flexibility of optical processors **to the point of** being able to perform any operation that ...

Вполне
Machinability is very important and could **easily** be the topic of a separate chapter.
These differences can be **reasonably** expected.

Вполне возможен
The interaction of these nucleosides **is a distinct possibility** (*or* **is quite possible**).

Вполне возможно
This seemed **entirely** (*or* **quite**) **possible** at the time.

Вполне возможно, что
It seems plausible that the earth acquired much of its carbon in the form of ...

It is entirely (*or* **quite**) **possible that** the first polymers were comprised of ...
It is a distinct possibility that some of this condition might be attributable to ...
Such asteroids **stand a good chance of** orbital changes.
It is not unlikely that controlled fusion will some day help relieve the world's energy crisis.
It may well be that further knowledge of cloud behaviour will suggest new possibilities.
It is not inconceivable that further investigators may find ways to ...
It is not unlikely (*or* **is not improbable**) **that** this "powder laser" opens up new possibilities in display technology.
It is conceivable (*or* **is not improbable**) **that** most of the published data are in error.
What took place on the Earth more than three billion years ago **may well** take place on innumerable planets in the universe.

Вполне достаточно
Nine or ten decimal places **would be ample** (*or* **quite sufficient**).

Вполне достаточно пространства для
Each of these planets has **ample room for** large satellite systems.

Вполне естественно, что
It is reasonable that alkenes do not undergo nucleophilic addition unless the negative charge can be stabilized by ...

Вполне может
The activity-coefficient term **may well** change if ...

Вполне может конкурировать с
This process **is quite competitive with** chain propagation.

Вполне можно
These parameters can **be safely** ignored.

Вполне можно ожидать, что
On the basis of the foregoing discussion, **it is reasonable to expect that ...**

Вполне обоснован
This view **is well founded** (*or* **substantiated**).

Вполне пригоден для
These instruments **are well** (*or* **fully**) **suited for** such measurement.

Вполне резонно
It is not unreasonable to ask why ...

Вполне сравним с
The method is satisfactory, and the results **compare well with** those obtained by the previously described technique.

Вполне удовлетворительный
No **wholly satisfactory** theory is yet available.

Вполне укладываться в допустимые пределы
This **is well within the permissible limits.**

Вполовину [*см.* **Меньше вполовину, Наполовину, Уменьшать вдвое**].

Вполовину меньше [*см.* **В два раза меньше, чем**].

Впоследствии [*см. тж.* **В дальнейшем, Затем, Как мы увидим дальше**]
The Moon first formed outside of the Earth's orbit and was **subsequently** captured by the Earth.

Впоследствии стал известен как
The Brookhaven synchrotron **came to be known as** the Alternating Gradient Synchrotron.

Впотай [*см.* **Заподлицо**].

Вправо [*см.* **Направленный влево (вправо, вверх, вниз)**].

Вправо или влево
This chute can be directed **to(wards) the right or the left of** the separator.

Впредь [*см. тж.* **И впредь будет**]
The original matrix (*матрица–матем.*) **will henceforth** (*or* **henceforward,** *or* **from now on**) **be** referred to as the "cost-weight" matrix.
The Director of the Office [**here(in)after** in this section referred to as "Director"] shall ...

Впредь до
This was a temporary measure **pending** completion of the launch pads.

Впредь до подтверждения дальнейшими исследованиями
This structure is presumed to be correct, **subject to further confirmatory investigation.**

Впуск
The automatic water valves open for **the admission of** (*or* **to let in**) water during the cooling cycle.
To preheat the gas before **admission to** the burners ...
Valves for **admitting** and releasing air ...

Впускать в
A small amount of gas **is drawn** (*or* **admitted**) **into** the mass spectrometer and analyzed.

Впускаться
The air **is admitted (in)to** the shell by opening a shooting valve.
Some hot condensate **is let into** the purifier.

Впускаться через
The oil under pressure **is admitted by way of** a radial port.

Вращательное движение
Rotary motion.

Вращать [*см.* **Поворачивать**].

Вращать вокруг
We **rotate** the profile shape **about** (*or* **around**) the fibre axis.

Вращать на угол
Such an object **can be rotated through** (*or* **by**) 180°.

Вращаться [*см. тж.* **Заставлять вращаться**]
The rear turret **is indexed about** a vertical axis and serves for drilling, boring and other end-working operations.
The assembly **moves** (*or* **rotates**) **about** (*or* **on,** *or* **around**) its axis.
The electron and nucleus **revolve about** their common centre of gravity.
To revolve about (*or* **around,** *or* **round**) the Sun ...
The planetary electrons **revolve in** their orbits.
The Earth **rotates** daily (*on its axis*) and **revolves** annually (*about the Sun*).
Individually driven tandem wheels **pivot around** the main axle.

Вращаться в противоположные стороны
Adjacent rolls **have an opposite sense of rotation.**

Вращаться вокруг оси
Like an airplane, an insect can **roll around its longitudinal axis, pitch around a horizontal axis** perpendicular to its direction of flight or **yaw around a vertical axis.**
Because of the motion of the liquid, the ball **rotates on** (*or* **about,** *or* **around**) **an axis.**
The molecule **turns** (*or* **rotates,** *or* **spins**) **about** (*or* **around,** *or* **on**) **its axis.**

Вращаться вокруг Солнца по эллиптической орбите
Kepler's first law states that a planet **orbits** (*or* **circles**) **the Sun in an elliptical path** with the Sun at one focus of the ellipse.

Вращаться на ... градусов
The mirror **can be rotated by** (*or* **through**) 45 **degrees.**

Вращаться по орбите вокруг
The two stars **rotate in** elliptical **orbits about** a common centre of gravity.
The Moon **orbits** (*or* **circles**) the Earth.

Вращаться по часовой стрелке, против часовой стрелки
The cylinder **rotates clockwise, anti**(*or* **counter**)**clockwise.**

Вращаться со скоростью ... об/мин.
The disk **spins at 3,000 revolutions per minute.**

Вращающийся I
Some micrometers have a **rotatable** sleeve on the barrel.

Вращающийся II
The **spinning** (*or* **rotating**) Earth acts as a giant gyroscope.

Вращающийся в противоположную сторону
An **oppositely turning** propeller ...

Вращение
The rotation of the Sun.
This set of nozzles imparts **spin** to the missile.

Вращение вокруг Земли
The revolution of a body **about** (*or* **around,** *or* **round**) **the Earth.**

Вращение вокруг оси
Pouring is accomplished by **rotating** the furnace **about** (*or* **around**) a horizontal **axis.**

Вращение планет
The planetary rotations (*or* **The rotations of the planets**).

Вред [*см.* **Без вреда для**].

Вредить [*см. тж.* **Повреждён**]
Leaks in the casting of a boiler **are detrimental to** efficient operation (*or* **impair** operation).

Вредно влиять на [*см.* **Неблагоприятно влиять на, Оказывать вредное влияние на**].

Вредно отражаться на
Phosphorus is **detrimental to** the quality of the iron produced.

Вредное влияние (*или* **действие**)
It is suspected that these **deleterious** (*or* **adverse,** *or* **detrimental,** *or* **harmful,** *or* **unfavourable,** *or* **untoward**) **effects** result from overheating.
They are particularly resistant to **the ill effects of** abrasive erosion.

Вредное влияние... на
The injurious effects of some combustion products **on** the environment and human health ...

Вредный [*см. тж.* **Неблагоприятно влиять на**]
To kill the **objectionable** organisms that may be present in the milk, ...
The chief **deleterious** (*or* **harmful,** *or* **untoward**) constituents proved to be argillaceous limestone, clay and shale.
Iron carbonyl is not now used commercially because of its **deleterious** (*or* **ill**) effects on the engine.
Pressure fluctuations may be **injurious** (*or* **detrimental**) **to** (*or* **tough on**) the engine.

Вредный для здоровья
Noxious dusts, gases, fumes, mists...
Wet grinding is not so **unhealthy** [*or* **bad for the health,** *or* **harmful (to the health)**].
Unhealthy conditions of work ...

Вре́менно [*см.* **На некоторое время**].

Временно́й
The output has a quasi-random **temporal** distribution of intensity.

Временны́е изменения
Temporal changes in the solar-wind field ...

Время [*см.* **В кратчайшее время, В настоящее время, В наше время, В период, В последнее время, В самое последнее время, В своё время, В скором времени, В срок, В течение, В то время, В то же время, В то или иное время, Во времени, Во время, Всё время, Дать время, До настоящего времени, До последнего времени, До сих пор, За время, За период, Зависящий от времени, Изменяться во времени, Используемый в настоящее время, К настоящему времени, К тому времени когда, На всё время, Настало время, Необратимый во времени, Примерно в то время, когда; С момента, С течением времени, Со временем, Требовать много времени, Через некоторые промежутки времени, Через равные промежутки времени**].

Время, в течение которого
The value of τ **is the time it takes for** the concentration to fall to ...

Время года [*см.* **В зависимости от времени года**].

Время жизни
Positronium is a "non-nuclear" element with **an** average **existence** of less than 10^{-7} s.
Life time.
Relatively short **life spans** of some species ...

Время, за которое [*см.* **Время, необходимое для**].

Время истекло
Before **the** critical **time has elapsed,** *U* may cease to be Lipshitz continuous.

Время, истекшее (прошедшее) с
The instrument measures **the elapsed time from** the start of ...

Время между столкновениями
We must expect some **intercollision(al) times** to be greater and some to be less than τ.

Время, необходимое для
The time it takes for a given volume of the gas **to** be driven through ...

The time a ray **takes to** propagate distance *z* ...

Время от времени [*см. тж.* **От времени до времени**]
Today we see weather balloons **on occasion,** but passenger balloons are very rare.
Every now and then, the blade may strike a bump, breaking loose fragments of ...
The computer itself blunders **(every) now and then.**
For 600,000 years rhyolitic lava erupted on the Yellowstone Plateau **intermittently.**
At times (*or* **From time to time**), the basin water is shock treated.
Evaporate to dryness, turning the granules **occasionally** to insure uniform coverage.

Время, отведённое на
The time allotted for any one job is limited.

Время пребывания
The duration of stay at altitude ...
The average **residence time of** strontium-90 in the atmosphere ...

Время существования
During **the lifetime of** the catalyst each platinum atom leads to the reaction of some 20 million molecules of gasoline.

Время, требуемое для
This can have a dramatic effect on **the time taken to** complete an analysis.

Время установки
With this machine, **setting-up time** is significantly reduced.

Вроде [*см.* **Нечто вроде**].

Вручную [*см. тж.* **С ручным управлением, Сваренный вручную**]
The lorry was loaded **by hand**.
The injection pressure is gained **by manually** turning a large wheel.

Вряд ли [*см. тж.* **Едва ли**]
It is unlikely (*or* **hardly probable**) **that** any future accident will result in ...

Всас [*см.* **На всасе (насоса)**].

Всасываемый [*см.* **Втягиваемый**].

Все, без исключения
The term "nebula" formerly was applied **indiscriminately** to distant celestial objects of diffuse appearance.
The total quantity of water on earth exceeds **all conceivable** needs of the human population.

Все возможные меры [*см.* **Принимать все возможные меры к тому, чтобы**].

Все, за исключением нескольких
These stipulations rule out **all but a few** types of reactions.
All except a few diamonds are nonconductors of electricity.

Все, к кому это относится [*см.* **Все, кого это касается**].

Все, кого это касается
A more constant water supply is supposed to be better for **all concerned,** but ...

Все, кроме
In **all but** relatively simple cases, one must make use of ...

Все, кроме одного
All but one (*or* **except one**) **of** the spectra contained the minimum of two lines needed for establishing a red shift.
The filter eliminates **all but one** colour.

Все они
Point-to-point services, microwave repeaters, radio telescopes, **all** have characteristic types of antennas.

Все эти ..., вместе взятые
These combined effects rapidly heat the surface under treatment.
(Taken) together these observations point to a deep source for the gas.

Всевозможные
This film can be applied to photographs and printing **of every description** (*or* **to all kind(s) of** printing).

Всегда [*см. тж.* **В любой момент, Неизменно, Постоянно**]
All along, there have been some reasons for suspecting that convection might exist in the earth.
The disturbance retains its initial value **forever** (*or* **for all time**).
Direct viewing of the writing trace is possible **at all times.**
The expansion valves are **invariably** (*or* **universally,** *or* **always**) hand operated.

Всегда присутствовать
The satellite DNA of repetitive sequences **is universally present** adjacent to the centromeres (*biol.*).

Всего [*см. тж.* **В сумме**]
All told (*or* **Altogether**) there are more than 20,000 items distributed by the firm.
(All) in all, the program board carries 75 red and 75 black sockets.
A total of eight holes is drilled at the first working station.

Всего лишь [*см. тж.* **Лишь, Не более, чем; Только**]
While the life of components in orbit may be **as low as** a few days, quick passage through the radiation belt has little effect.
The orbital periods of these stars can be **as short as** a few years.
In this case a total of 200 shots **is all that** can be expected.
Ethane theoretically possesses an indefinite number of conformations; however if ..., there are **but** two significant conformations.
Other embryonic movements **are no more than** (*or* **are mere**) preludes to adult behaviour.
The factor *s* leads to **nothing more than** a decrease in scattering and therefore is generally ignored.
The innermost portion of the ring **is a mere** 7,000 miles above Saturn's face.
A stationary electron in a uniform magnetic field has **just** two distinct energy levels.
Tool-changing time can be **as little as** two seconds.
Such a backup system can operate for weeks on **as few as** three or four "penlight" batteries.
Scale differences **of only** 1-2% can cause a loss of ...

Всего лишь ... лет назад
As recently as 15 years ago ...

Всего лишь через
He found that **as soon as 20 minutes later** the level had fallen greatly.

Всего лишь через ... минут после
Early proteins appeared **as soon as 1 minute after** infection.

Вселять доверие к
This information **lends credence** (*or* **credibility**) **to** the concept of sidedness in membranes.

Вселять сомнение
Sometimes the decision must be reconsidered when new evidence **puts** the safety of an old food additive **in doubt.**
The estimates of zero-pressure properties **are open to question.**

Вселять уверенность в
These devices **instill confidence in** (*or* **give confidence to**) the operator.

Всеми признано, что
It is (now) generally accepted (*or* **recognized**) **that** deposition of a shallow sea floor is a discontinuous process.

Всемирно известный [*см. тж.* **Известен во всём мире**]
An **internationally known** expert in optics ...
The **world-renowned** method for ...
The **world-famous** manufacturer of photo cameras ...

Всемирного значения
Of world-wide significance (*or* **importance**).

Всемирный
The Mid-Atlantic Ridge is part of a **world-wide** system of oceanic ridges.
A **worldwide** system of seismic stations was established.
Worldwide glaciation ...

Всему виной [*см.* **Причина**].

Всеобъемлющий [*см. тж.* **Подробный**]
That was the most **comprehensive** (*or* **detailed,** *or* **thorough**) investigation of mass transfer from rotating cylinders.
There is no **all-inclusive** definition of composite materials.

Всеподчиняющий фактор
Since the filling time varies from cavity to cavity, the order in which the cavities fill becomes **a factor of overriding importance.**

Всерьёз
These investigations were not to begin **in earnest** until after World War II.

Всесторонний [*см. тж.* **Исчерпывающий**]
A **comprehensive** review of ... has recently been written.

Всех профилей
He was soon joined in his efforts by scientists **of every description.**

Всё более (и более) [*см. тж.* **Находить всё более широкое применение**]
Secondary reactions become **increasingly** (*or* **more and more**) important in determining gaseous product distribution.
The boiling of liquid in the main condenser leaves the liquid **progressively** richer in oxygen.
The **successively** higher energy levels ...

Всё больше (и больше)
The rocks of the core occupy **increasingly more** (*or* **more and more**) space (*geol.*).
Such data are being **increasingly** used for this purpose.
Ice crystals appear **in increasing numbers**.
The size of blastomeres diminishes **progressively** during cleavage (*biol.*).
Carbides **are finding** (*or* **coming into**) **ever increasing use.**
More and more [*or* **A constantly** (*or* **An ever**)] **increasing number of** highly efficient plants are coming into service.
This equipment is being used **to an increasing extent.**

Всё возрастающий [*см.* **Всё больше (и больше)**].

Всё время [*см. тж.* **На всё время, Постоянно**]
The material is kept under pressure **at all times** (*or* **constantly,** *or* **all the time,** *or* **the whole time**).

Все вышеуказанное
Most book manufacturers provide a complete service covering **all the above** (*or* **foregoing,** *or* **aforesaid**), together with ...

Всё говорит в пользу
There is evidently **a strong case for** radial vent ducts.

Всё ещё
The **as yet** unidentified product of ...

Всё ещё остаётся неотвеченным (*или* невыясненным)
Many questions **still remain to be answered.**

Всё ещё существует
A number of uncertainties **still persists** at the molecular level of life's origin.
The rim of that crater **persists** today.

Всё же
When symptoms **do** occur, they are usually mild.
Although ... is still in its infancy, it **does** have exciting analytical potential for ...

(Всё) менее и менее
Disturbances become **progressively less** severe (*or* **less and less** severe).

(Всё) меньше и меньше [*см. тж.* **Становиться всё меньше и меньше**]
This fraction becomes **progressively smaller.**

Всё равно [*см.* **Безразлично**].

Всё труднее и труднее
The dissolved material has **an increasingly difficult** (*or* **hard**) **time** working its way out of ...

Всё увеличивающийся
Successively (*or* **Progressively**) **higher** laser intensities ...

Всё чаще и чаще
We will find **in increasing frequency** articles on such processes.

Всё, что встречается на его (их) пути
The growing clouds destroy **everything in their path.**

Всё шире и шире использовать
The metallurgical industry **is finding increasing use for** spark-source mass spectrometry.

Всё это
The use of safety screens, trap doors, safety devices on the hoist and adequate ventilation **all** contribute to safety and efficiency.

Всё это, вместе взятое, является
New wheels, higher wheel speeds, faster feeds, more power, better control, and improved methods of handling materials **all add up to** a giant step forward for abrasive cutting technology.

Вскоре [*см. тж.* **В ближайшем будущем**]
We hope that this will enable us to answer these questions **before long.**

Before long, realization by production personnel of the potentialities of video tape created a demand for greater operational flexibility.

Вскоре после
Linear programming was developed **shortly after** World War II.

Вскоре после того как
The emergency system went into action **shortly after** a pressure-relief valve had opened.

Вскоре после этого
A short time later, a new pulse of volcanic activity occurred above the hot spot.
Shortly thereafter they identified this particle.
He found **soon afterwards** that ...

Вслед за [*см. тж.* **После**]
In the wake of the successful space mission the Agency is planning a new venture.
A high transverse momentum was detected **in the wake of** a proton-proton collision.
The process of multiple-star formation must have been terminated **following** the dispersion of the original association.
Subsequent to exposure at the desired temperature, the specimens were baked at 400°F.

Вслед за ним
The holes near an exposed face detonate first, **followed by** progressive detonation of adjacent holes.
The shear waves should arrive **next.**

Вслед за этим
Shaft sinking was commenced and, **subsequently,** an appreciable amount of development was conducted.

Вследствие [*см. тж.* **Благодаря, В результате, Ввиду, Из-за**]
In consequence of these features the axial pump has a distinct advantage for variable-speed services.
The spark was preferred to the arc **on account of** (*or* **because of,** *or* **owing to**) its ease of control.
As a consequence (*or* **result**) **of** its change in speed, a light ray passing obliquely from a vacuum to a material medium is refracted.
The body loses heat **by** radiation.
The hole density fluctuation is small **by virtue of** the condition $\beta(\psi - \psi_{ol} >> 1)$.

Вследствие того, что
Some black shales have been termed graptolite shales **from the fact that** (*or* **because**) bedding planes are covered by ...

Вследствие этого [*см. тж.* **Тем самым**]
As a consequence (*or* **Hence,** *or* **As a result**) heat is exchanged by ...
The deck of the triple-hull submarine is situated much lower and **in consequence** (*or* **therefore**) better utilization of space is possible.
Owing to (*or* **Because of**) this the deposit developed cracks.

Вспоминать
It is essential **to bring to mind** the fundamental function of ... and then deduce the minimal structural features needed for carrying it out.
If we **recall** (*or* If **it is recalled**) **that ...**
If you **think back to** (*col.*) the introductory discussion, it was stated that ...

Вспоминаться
Some familiar mechanical devices **come to mind** in visualizing this model.

Вспомним [*см. тж.* **Напомним, что**]
(Let us) recall the two peaks in that curve.

Вспомогательный
Controlling such a complicated device requires three large digital computers and many smaller **satellite** computers.
Certain **ancillary** (*or* **auxiliary**) circuits would also have to be included on the chip.

Вспыхивать
The lithium **bursts into flame.**

Вспышка света
As each drop of bromine touches the damp red phosphorus, there is **a flash of light.**

Вставка (*в рисунке*)
The upper **inset** at the right of the illustration ...

Вставлять [*см. тж.* **В ... можно вставить, Вводить**]
Engage the screwdriver end **in** the notch.
Enter the instrument **into** the panel aperture.
Taper shank drills **are** directly **fitted into** tapered holes in drilling machine spindles.
Insert (*or* **Put,** *or* **Place**) the free end of the excess tubing **into** the air hose.

A portion of ... is cut away and the release mechanism **is interposed.**

Вставляться в панель
The vacuum tube base **is plugged into a socket.**

Встраивать [*см. тж.* **Включать III**]
Today, the trend is **to integrate** small digital computers **into** the outlying parts of power control systems, such as telemetering systems.

Встраиваться в [*см. тж.* **Вписываться в**]
Gluconium does not **fit into** any of the established families of mesons.
Hydrogen atoms can **fit into** the crystal structure of a metal.

Встреча в космосе
Rendezvous in space.

Встречать [*см. тж.* **Можно встретить**]
You may **run across** (*or* **encounter**) other synonyms.
The calculus of infinitesimals **was received** with profound skepticism **by** many philosophers.
Thus, the current **encounters** (*or* **meets with**) less resistance.

Встречать препятствие
The water **encounters** (*or* **meets with,** *or* **comes up against**) some **obstacle.**

Встречать сопротивление
The gas **would meet** (*or* **encounter**) less **resistance.**

Встречаться [*см. тж.* **В какой бы форме ... ни встречался, Нередко встречается, Часто встречаться**]
Such oxidation states **are** most often **met with.**
This problem **crops up** (*or* **is encountered**) frequently in shock tube reactions.
Aragonite **is found** (*or* **occurs,** *or* **is encountered**) **in** many localities.
Plastic materials **are** not **found in** their natural form.
The temperature likely **to be met with** in practice ...
These absorption bands do not **occur** in the vapour phase.
A nonlinear equation that **occurs** frequently **in** scientific work ...
These features **are** not **encountered in** studies of ...
This forest formation **is** seldom **seen in** mature form.
Tall trees **are** sometimes **present** along the streams.
Occasionally, one **comes across** a patient with Milroy's disease.
Such situations often **occur in** practice.

Встречаться в большом количестве
Sulphur **is abundant** in the earth's crust.
Cobras **abound in** India and the Malay area.

Встречаться в виде
Apatite **occurs as** cryptocrystalline grains.

Встречаться в космосе
To rendezvous in space.

Встречаться в ограниченном количестве [*см.* **Иметься в ограниченном количестве**].

Встречаться в природе
Graphite **is found naturally** (*or* **occurs in nature**) in Siberia, Ceylon, ...
Ferroso ferric oxide **occurs naturally** as magnetite.

Встречаться и за пределами
Loess **is not restricted to** the Midwest.

Встречаться исключительно на континентах
High-silicon rocks **are** almost **exclusively confined to the continents.**

Встречаться очень редко
Positrons, on this planet at least, **are few and far between.**

Встречаться повсеместно (*или* **повсюду**)
Traces of lead **are** almost **ubiquitous** in nature.
This tripeptide **occurs universally in (all)** living matter.
These amino acids **are universal in occurrence.**

Встречаться с
He **encountered** (*or* **came across**) this phenomenon for the first time.

Встречаться с трудностями
We have run into (*or* **encountered**, *or* **met with**) **difficulties** with corrosion.

Встречаться только в
Such dunes **are restricted** (*or* **limited**) **to** deserts.

Встречающийся
Hand tools usually **found in** machine shops are ...
It is important to know the common oxidation states of **the** more frequently **met with** (*or* **occurring,** *or* **encountered**) elements.

Встречающийся в природе
Naturally occurring antioxidants are listed below.
Calcite is one of the most perfect crystals **occurring in nature.**

Встречающийся при
Some of the difficulties **involved in** (*or* **encountered when,** *or* **met with in**) applying transistors to line transmission can be seen from ...

Встречен враждебно [*см.* **Относиться враждебно к**].

Встречен доброжелательно
Our suggestion **was well received.**

Встроенный [*см. тж.* **Вмонтированный, Заложенный в**]
The device has a **built-in** laser amplifier.
The bottom electrode **is built into** (*or* **embedded in**) the refractory lining.
The measuring components **are built into** the microscope.
The machine has a **built-in** memory.

Встряхивать с
When this solution **is shaken with** finely divided silver, ...

Вступать в действие
To come into force (*or* **effect**) (*or* **To become valid**).

Вступать в контакт [*см. тж.* **Вступать в соприкосновение**]
This kept the solution from **coming in(to) contact with** air.
It has been proposed that the symmetrical precursor in an enzymatic reaction **makes contact with** the enzyme at three specific points.
A set of electrodes is arranged to move vertically and **make** electrical **contact with** the burden (*шихтой*).

Вступать в лобовое столкновение
In this mode of operation protons and antiprotons **collide head on.**
Protons **collide head on with** other protons.

Вступать в новую фазу
The debate **entered a new phase.**

Вступать в переговоры
To enter into negotiations.

Вступать в период
The country **is going into a period of** economic rise.

Вступать в противоречие с
The public's desire to have new generating stations located well outside populous areas **comes into conflict with** the desire not to disfigure the countryside with overhead transmission lines.

Вступать в реакцию [*см. тж.* **Реагировать**]
Water **enters into** innumerable **reactions.**
When gases **react** they do so in proportions by volume that ...

Вступать в свои права [*см. тж.* **Наступать**]
With the invention of the vacuum triode the age of electronics **was ushered in.**

Вступать в силу
The Act **came into force** [*or* **became effective** (*or* **valid**)] January 1, 1959.
At even higher fields a second limiting mechanism **sets in** (*or* **comes into play**), causing a complete saturation of velocity.

Вступать в соединение [*см. тж.* **Легко вступать в соединение с ...**]
Elements always **combine** in the same ratio by weight to form a given compound.
Excited molecules readily **enter into** many chemical combinations.
These compounds **combine** readily **with** basic oxides.

Вступать в соприкосновение с [*см. тж.* **Вступать в контакт, При соприкосновении, Соприкасаться**]
When the sea water **comes in(to) contact with** the clay particles ...
This prevents the foil from **making contact with** the wall surface.

Вступать в строй [*см. тж.* **Вступать в эксплуатацию**]
The first units are unlikely **to become operational** until early next year.

The refinery **will come** (*or* **go**) **on stream** in 1995.
A new haulage system **will** soon **go into operation.**
The new plant **will go into production** next year.
The unit **goes on line** in December.
A new particle accelerator **has been commissioned.**
The fighter plane **will** soon **enter** (*or* **come into**) **service.**
Efforts are being made to modify the fertilizer manufacturing process so that phosphate deposits of lower grade can **come into play.**

Вступать в эксплуатацию [*см. тж.* **Вступать в строй**]
More and more high-efficiency plants **are coming into service.**
The system **was put into service** (*or* **operation**) in 1981.
Mechanical-draft cooling towers first **came into use** about 55 years ago.
During the year five new nuclear power plants **went into operation.**

Вступление
Man's **entry into** the space age ...

Всухую [*см. тж.* **Обрабатывать всухую**]
Drilling is done **dry.**

Всюду [*см.* **Везде**].

Всякого рода
This simplifies **all sorts of** computation.
This film can be applied to photographs and printing **of every description** (*or* **of all kinds**).

Вторая половина
In **the latter part of** the sixteenth century ...

Вторгаться в
Ocean water **invades** the widening rift.
If such a rock **is invaded by** oil ...

Вторгаться в область
Then the coal paleobotanist begins **to encroach on the province of** the coal chemist.

Вторжение
Parts of the rift may remain blocked off from **the ingress of** ocean water.

Вторично
When you encounter this term **a second time, ...**

Второй по величине
Africa is **the second largest** continent, exceeded in size only by Eurasia.
The electric force is **the second strongest** force in nature.

Второй по значению
Ten years later oxygen steelmaking became **the second most important** method in this country.

Второй по распространённости [*см. тж.* **На втором месте по распространённости**]
Silicon is **the second most abundant** element in the rocks.

Второй по твёрдости
Boron nitride is **the second hardest** material known.

Второстепенное значение [*см.* **Иметь второстепенное значение**].

Второстепенной важности
A subplate is a plate **of secondary importance** set apart from ...

Вторым по значению после ... является
Second in importance to the Carboniferous coals **are** those deposited in ...

В-третьих [*см. тж.* **Во-первых**]
In the third place (*or* **Thirdly**).

Втыкать в
The inventor **pushed** the glass cylinders **into** a mass of wet clay.

Втягиваемый
The room is ventilated and cooled by the circulation of air **drawn in** from the outside.

Втягиваться [*см.* **Выпускаться и втягиваться** (*о щупальцах*)].

Вход I [*см. тж.* **Давление на входе (выходе), Место входа в, На входе**]
The inlet to the reactor tube ...
The entrance to the chamber ...

Вход II
The entry of the particles **into** the cell ...

Вход в ... и выход из него
This permits **entrance into and egress from** the nucleus.

Вход и выход газа *(на схеме)*
Gas in. Gas out.

Входить в I
The laser beam **enters** the sample.

Входить в II
Included in this group **are** structures of organic origin.
The Bessel function **enters into** (*or* **appears in**) all these problems.

Входить в выражение
This symbol **appears in the expression** for ...

Входить в обычай
It is (a) common practice to carry out a numerical analysis before entering upon an experimental investigation.
It has become customary to use overall coefficients.

Входить в подробности [*см. тж.* **Не вдаваясь в подробности**]
We shall not **go into details of** (*or* **delve into**) these differences.

Входить в практику
This method **has become the practice** (*or* **has become usual**).

Входить в рубрику
These improvements **come under the heading of** designing such radio systems.

Входить в силу [*см.* **Вступать в силу**].

Входить в соединение
The elements of this family also **enter into compounds** corresponding to higher oxidation states.

Входить в состав
Other cyclic hydrocarbons **are constituents of** plants and fruits.
Arginine was found **to be incorporated into** proteins.
These silicates **enter into the composition of** granite.
Our department **forms** (*or* **is**) **(a) part of** the above-mentioned organization.
He **is a member of** the Committee.

Входить в употребление
Larger laboratory compression presses **have come** (*or* **have been brought**) **into use.**
The term astronautic **was** then **coming into (general) use.**
This term **has come into common** (*or* **wide**) **use.**
The name broad-band communication network **is coming** increasingly **into play.**

Входить в уравнение
This term **appears in the equation.**
The total energy of an electron **enters into the** Boltzmann **equation.**
Catalysts **are** not **involved** as reactants or products **in the** net stoichiometric **equations.**

Входить в число [*см. тж.* **В число ... входит**]
Native gold and platinum **are among** the minerals extensively extracted from such deposits.
These universities **rank among** the best in the world.

Входить туго в
The pipe is machined **to fit tightly in** the solenoid.

Входить через
The air **enters by** the ducts ...

Входной
Inlet temperature ...

Входящие в него [*см. тж.* **Составляющие его**]
Differential equations are divided into ordinary and partial equations according to the number of independent variables **involved.**

Входящий луч
The incoming beam.

Вхождение в атмосферу Земли
To alter the angle of **re-entry, ...**

Вхолостую [*см.* **Работать вхолостую**].

Выбивать I
Drive out the remaining part of the rivet **with** a pin punch.

Выбивать II
The pressure rating must **be stamped on** the valve body.

Выбивать пробку
The pressure may **force the plug out.**

Выбивать электрон(ы) из
The free electrons are accelerated to velocities large enough **to knock** fixed **electrons from** (*or* **out of**) their parent atoms.
This radiation **expels** one **electron from** a pair of electrons.

Выбирать
This line **was adopted** (*or* **selected,** *or* **chosen**) because of the higher rotations.
To obtain values for the individual atoms, it is necessary **to pick** an arbitrary reference point.

Выбирать из
Out of these weights you may **choose ...**

Выбор [*см.* **Большой выбор, Использовать либо ..., либо... по желанию; Отдавать предпочтение, При выборе, Широкий ассортимент**]
By **picking** (*or* **choosing**) a large enough number *n* one can ...

Выбор одного из двух
The symmetry of these models can be an important factor in **deciding** (*or* **choosing**) **between them.**

Выборочно
Atoms in the flame are **selectively** excited to higher energy levels.

Выборочные данные
Selected performance **data** are given in Table I.

Выбрав
Once you **have decided upon** the right type of grinder for your jobs, you have to choose the most appropriate machine for you.

Выбран неудачно
This term **is an unfortunate choice.**

Выбрасываемые газы
Vent (*or* **Exhaust**) **gases**.

Выбрасывание
Geyser action consists of **the emission** (*or* **ejection**) **of** a column of steam and water droplets under high pressure **from** a small vent.

Выбрасывать I
Geysers **emit** (*or* **eject**) steam and hot water.
The gas bubbles may expand violently enough **to fling** the lava **into** the air.

Выбрасывать II
The salt fraction **is discarded** in the refining process in the form of tailings.

Выбрасывать в атмосферу
The gas **was vented** (*or* **discharged**) **to the atmosphere.**

Выбрасывать на рынок
These companies want to buy new products that they can **bring to market.**

Выбрасываться
The material **is ejected from** the comet at velocities of ...
The heat, in the form of hot water, **is rejected into** a nearby lake.

Выбрасываться в атмосферу
The hot combustion products **escape** (*or* **pass,** *or* **are discharged,** *or* **are exhausted**) **into the atmosphere.**
A cloud of steam **is propelled** high **into the atmosphere.**

Выбрасываться из
The welded component **is** automatically **ejected from** the machine **onto** the main line conveyor.

Выбрать одно из двух
To decide between the two versions, ...

Выброшен
The magma **was flung outward** by the explosion.

Выброшенный
Fallout of radioactive particles **released into** the atmosphere by nuclear explosions ...

Выведен из орбиты
Otherwise the satellites would **have been forced out of their orbits.**

Выведен из строя
The communications equipment can **be knocked out** or the control system can be damaged by discharges.

Выведенный
These **deduced** relations ...
An expression **due to** (*or* **derived by**) Poisson ...

Вывинчивать [*см. тж.* **Отвинчивать**]
Remove (*or* **Unscrew,** *or* **Take out**) the four

screws **from** the back of the meter and use them to secure the adaptor plate to the meter.

Вывод I [*см. тж.* **Делать вывод, Заключение, Из этого вытекает** (*или* **следует**), **что; Приходить к выводу**]
This **deduction** (*or* **conclusion,** *or* **inference**) is confirmed by results of catalytic hydrogenation.

Вывод II
The withdrawal of a rod ...

Вывод из
The implication of this analysis **is that** convection should be observed whenever ...

Вывод из эксплуатации
This permits the application of such coating to existing piping without its **removal from service.**

Вывод на орбиту
Orbital injection came 6 min 6 sec after launch.

Вывод относительно
Then it would be difficult to make any **inferences about** Archean climates.

Вывод уравнения
The deduction (*or* **derivation,** *or* **development**) **of an equation.**

Выводить I
The inlet pipes **are brought out** through holes.

Выводить II
To withdraw a rod.

Выводить III
To derive (*or* **deduce,** *or* **develop,** *or* **set up**) an equation.
For a nonabsorbing waveguide we **deduce:...**

Выводить выражение
To derive the expression for ...
He **inferred** the velocity of the particles **from** Doppler shifts.

Выводить доказательство
Exactly this kind of **proof was developed** by the ancient Greeks.

Выводить заключение [*см. тж.* **Делать вывод, Приходить к выводу**]
The following **conclusions** can be **reached:...**
He **concluded** (*or* **inferred,** *or* **deduced**) **from** this **that ...**

Выводить закон
Kepler's three **laws** could **be deduced from** Newton's theory of gravitation.
Rutherford **worked out the** mathematical **law** describing how one point of electric charge would be scattered by another point charge.

Выводить из I
The author **deduced** (*or* **concluded,** *or* **inferred**) **from** his investigations **that** the prostaglandins are fatty acids.
Configurations of other kinds may **be derived from** these.
From the temperature variation of *k*, the frequency variation of *l* may **be deduced.**

Выводить из II
This acid **is expelled** as a gas **from** the reaction mixture.

Выводить из зацепления
Both steam engine and hand gear should **be disengaged.**
The pawl of the opposed motor **is** lifted and **disengaged from** the toothend wheel.
The clutch **is thrown out** when the engine is idling.

Выводить из орбиты
The satellite **has been forced out of its orbit.**
The atmospheric drag **will take** the satellite **out of orbit.**

Выводить из равновесия
To disturb the equilibrium.
The airplane **is disturbed from an equilibrium condition.**
A push tends to tilt a standing person forward and thus **move** him **off balance.**

Выводить из состояния
The energy required **to remove** the electron **from the** ground **state** of ...

Выводить из строя
The filling fluid will leak out **making** the system **inoperative.**
To put out of action.
The high temperature **knocked out** (*sl.*) the transmitter before the spacecraft reached the surface.

A special control cock, by means of which the air pump can **be rendered inoperative ...**
This change **rendered unfit (for use)** a system of gravity-flow irrigation that had previously been installed.
The fire **disabled** one part of the pipeline.

Выводить из эксплуатации
The shells **were removed from** (*or* **taken out of**) **service.**

Выводить концы
The leads were brought out to the collector rings.

Выводить на орбиту
To place the vehicle **in orbit** around the planet ...
To put (*or* **inject,** *or* **insert**) a satellite **into orbit ...**

Выводить на орбиту вокруг Луны
In April, 1966, Luna 10 **was** successfully **placed in a lunar orbit** that came within 220 miles of the Moon.

Выводить на орбиту вокруг планеты
The spacecraft **was placed in orbit around the planet.**

Выводить на панели
25 contacts of the Uniselector **are brought out to sockets.**

Выводить обобщение из
One can **draw** some **generalizations from** these data.

Выводить породу (*с.х.*)
To raise (*or* **breed**) **the** best **strains** of cattle.

Выводить правило
The selection **rules have been derived** (*or* **deduced**).

Выводить решение
The corresponding **solution for** finite radius can **be deduced** (*or* **derived,** *or* **obtained**) **from** the work of ...

Выводить ряд
He **derived a series** which can be expressed as ...

Выводить соотношение между
With this information, **the relation between** E_{MG} **and** E_{OG} can **be developed.**

Выводить уравнение
Maxwell **produced** a set of **equations** that described ...
These **equations were derived** (*or* **deduced,** *or* **set up,** *or* **developed**) recently.

Выводиться из организма
Most immune complexes **are cleared from the body.**

Вывозить
One can mine the coal and **haul** (*or* **transport,** *or* **ship**) it **away to** some distant point where it will be burned.

Выглядеть I
The map gives the outlines of the continents as they **occur** today.
A surface with this property of absorbing colours might be expected **to appear** black, but ...

Выглядеть II
In the light of the new experimental information, how do the old theories about physiological tremor **stand up?**

Выглядеть как
The comet tail may **appear as** an extension of the coma.
Asteroids move against the background of the stars and so they **show up as** streaks of light.

Выгода [*см.* **Извлекать выгоду** (*или* **пользу**) **из**].

Выгодный [*см.* **Полезный**].

Выгорать
As the carbon **burns away,** the arc gap must be adjusted for efficient operation.

Выгравированный
A disk **engraved with** parallel lines is mounted on ...

Выгружать в
The ripping head **discharges** coal **onto** an intermediate conveyor.
The rock **is dumped into** a crusher.
The ore **is released through** a chute **into** the skip.
Raw materials **are emptied into** a bin.

Выгружаться из
Iron oxide **is discharged from** the kiln.

Выдавать I
A patent **has been issued for** a television set.
The process **was granted** a patent in 1981.

Выдавать II
The pit **is turning out** (*or* **producing,** *or* **yielding**) 800 tons of sand a day.

Выдавать данные
The new detectors **generate** enormous amounts of **data.**

Выдавать максимальную продукцию
The plant **is working at peak production.**

Выдавать разрешение [*см.* **Предоставлять разрешение**].

Выдавать патент
To grant a patent on a motor, etc.

Выдавать свое присутствие
The cometary planetoids **will reveal themselves** neither **by** luminosity nor by blocking the light of the stars.

Выдаваться
Information **is displayed** on the panel.

Выдающийся I
Among these features the most **outstanding** is the extreme constancy of length.

Выдающийся II
Outstanding (or **Distinguished,** *or* **Eminent,** *or* **Prominent**) scientists will be invited to the discussion.

Выдвигать аргумент (доказательство)
To adduce an argument (a proof).

Выдвигать вопрос
Interstellar matter **poses** a number of fascinating **problems.**
We should **raise** this **problem.**

Выдвигать гипотезу [*см. тж.* **Высказывать гипотезу о том, что**]
To determine if ..., one **sets up** (*or* **offers,** *or* **advances**) **the hypothesis that ...**
A new **hypothesis has** recently **been put forward** (*or* **proposed**) by a team of seismic investigators.

Выдвигать гипотезу о
Mantle convection was suggested in 1933.

Выдвигать гипотезу о том, что
He **proposed that** all the continents had formed ...

Выдвигать закон
Newton **advanced the law of** universal gravitation.

Выдвигать на первый план
To put in the forefront.
This discovery **brought to the fore** the age-old question of ...

Выдвигать план
Several **schemes have been proposed** (*or* **advanced,** *or* **suggested,** *or* **put up,** *or* **brought forward**).

Выдвигать предложение
They **came up with a proposal for** detecting neutrinos by ...

Выдвигать проблему
The extent of the drilling operations **brought forth** (*or* **posed**) many tough **problems.**

Выдвигать теорию
The author **puts forward** (*or* **forth**) (*or* **advances,** *or* **proposes**) **the** alternative **theory that ...**

Выдвигать условия
To lay down conditions.

Выдвинут
This hypothesis **was put forward** (*or* **advanced,** *or* **proposed**) **by** Einstein.

Выделение I
Emission of heat and light...
Beetles regulate their osmotic pressure through **the release of** amino acids.

Выделение II
The isolation of organometallic substances having the necessary characteristics ...

Выделение тепла
The production of this compound is attended with **the** maximum **heat evolution** (*or* **release,** *or* **liberation**).

Выделение энергии
The generation of energy by nuclear processes stopped the shrinkage of the primordial Sun.

Выделенный для [*см.* **Отведённый**].

Выделяемая энергия
The radiant **energy given out** (*or* **liberated,** *or* **released**) per second ...

Выделяемый
The shell matter **secreted by** animals is a crystalline inorganic substance.

Выделять I
The acid **evolves** hydrogen.
Materials which **give off** (*or* **release,** *or* **liberate**) corrosive products during a temperature rise ...
The hypothalamus **secretes** (*or* **puts out**) a substance called the cotropin-releasing factor.

Выделять II [*см. тж.* **Вылавливать сигнал**]
Several hundred chemical compounds **have been isolated from** coal tar.

Выделять III
Let us now rewrite this expression **separating out** the derivative normal to φ.

Выделять IV [*см.* **Различать**].

Выделять V
The regulatory authority used **to set aside** a region of the radio spectrum for a service.

Выделять газ
Halogenated polymers can **give off** (*or* **liberate,** *or* **release,** *or* **evolve**) corrosive **gases** under irradiation.

Выделять из
The cyclomatic manganese compound may **be separated** (*or* **isolated**) **from** the reaction mixture.
The most important feature which **sets apart** the kaolin group **from** the other two groups is ...

Выделять среди
The vastness of time is one of the most fascinating aspects of geology, it **sets off** both geology and astronomy **from** other physical and natural sciences.

Выделять тепло
To give off (*or* **release,** *or* **generate,** *or* **evolve,** *or* **liberate**) **heat.**
If a substance is compressed it **gives up** enough **heat** to maintain a constant temperature.

Выделять энергию
The heavier elements **give out** (*or* **release,** *or* **liberate**) **energy** on disintegrating.

Выделяться I
The combustible gases **are** continuously **evolved** (*or* **emitted**) **from** the surface.
Turpentine, the volatile portion of the gum that **exudes from** incisions in trunks of living pine trees ...
An exothermic reaction is a reaction of transformation during which heat **is liberated.**
Considerable heat **is released** (*or* **evolved**) during the fermentation.
Adding benzene to such a mixture raises the freezing point and ice **separates out.**
These enzymes **are secreted by** the labial glands.

Выделяться II
$N = O$ stretching bands **are prominent** at 1475 cm^{-1}.
Of the known separation methods, gas chromatography **stands out** as the most mature in development.
Certain of these groups of compounds **stand out** as being much more active than others.
Two other bright features **stand out** on the surface of Venus.

Выделяться на катоде (аноде)
Iodine **is liberated at the cathode** and chlorine **at the anode.**

Выделяться резко на фоне [*см.* **Ярко выделяться на фоне**].

Выделяться среди других
Although a number of oil shale deposits are known around the world, one **stands out** because of its very large size.

Выделяющийся в
The heat **given out** (*or* **released,** *or* **liberated**) **in** chemical reactions ...

Выдержать шторм
All the floating rigs are designed with the expectation that their crews **will ride out the** severest **storms, ...**

Выдерживание [*см. тж.* **При длительном выдерживании**]
After 6 hr of **exposure** at 80°C the samples were removed from the solutions.

Выдерживать I [*см. тж.* **Выносить, Лучше выдерживать**]
This material will **stand** the operating conditions.
The metal forming the hydride should **hold up** under many cycles of charging and discharging.
Pure quicklime **sustains** a temperature of about 2900 K without decomposition.
These objects must **stand up to** tremendous impact forces.
These materials can **tolerate** (*or* **endure,** *or* **stand up to**) high heat and rough handling.
Joints made with these electrodes **will withstand** bending and stretching operations satisfactorily.
The material **withstands** temperatures up to 1260°C without loss of properties.
Weights up to 500 lb can **be supported** on the worktable.
In an automotive environment, semiconductor chips **have to contend with** temperatures from -40° to 125°C, high humidity, salt and oil sprays, and vibration.
Titanium carbide will **tolerate** (*or* **withstand**) wide variations in cutting speed.
The amplifiers **survived** the shock very well.

Выдерживать II
The solution **was allowed** (*or* **left**) **to stand for** 9 hours.
The catalyst **was conditioned for** 16 hours under a high vacuum.
The solution **was "aged"** for 24hr by **standing** at room temperature.
The furnace temperature was lowered and the specimens **were held at** 850°C **for** three days for the terminal etching of the grain boundaries.
The process is accomplished by heating the metal to a high temperature, **holding** it **at** this temperature until ...
To season wood ...

Выдерживать вес человека
The material is hard enough **to support a man.**

Выдерживать допуски [*см. тж.* **Жёсткий допуск**]
Tolerances of ± 0.001 inch **can be** easily **maintained** during grinding.
The gyros **are held to** close **tolerances.**
Conversion to... permitted strict **tolerances to be held**.

Выдерживать жёсткое испытание
These resistors have **to satisfy** (*or* **withstand**) **severe** moisture-resistance **tests.**

Выдерживать интервал
The need **to maintain a** 500-ft **interval between** locomotives ...

Выдерживать испытание
To satisfy (*or* **stand up to,** *or* **withstand**) **a test.**

Выдерживать испытание временем
Adequately formulated standards **withstand the test of time.**

Выдерживать на воздухе.
These surfaces **have been allowed to stand in air** [*or* **have been kept** (*or* **held**) **in air**] **for** half an hour after polishing.

Выдерживать нагрузку
The bearing can **endure** (*or* **stand up to,** *or* **withstand**) such **a load.**

Выдерживать напряжение
Probes are made from titanium **to withstand** (*or* **sustain**) **stresses** caused by changes in velocity amplitude.

Выдерживать перегрузку
The fabric pressure-type airship can **accept an overload (condition)**, which in a nonpressurized airship would result in a structural failure.
Selenium's ability **to withstand overload ...**

Выдерживать расстояние [*см.* **Выдерживать интервал**].

Выдерживать сильные удары
The bolts **withstand severe shocks** in service.

Выдерживать сравнение с [*см. тж.* **Успешно выдерживать сравнение с**]
Beryllium is an excellent moderator for neutrons and **compares favourably with** hydrogen, deuterium, helium, carbon, and oxygen.

Выдерживать температуру
Viton **withstands temperatures of** 400°C and up.

Выдерживать тяжёлую нагрузку
These machines are built to **stand up to** (*or* **withstand**) **heavy duty.**

Выдерживаться
The glass **was held** (*or* **kept**) **at** the melting temperature for six hours.

Выдерживаться с точностью до
Roundness and straightness of the hole **is held to within** 0.0003 inch.

Выдувать в форму
This glass in its semi-solid state can **be blown in a mould.**

Выезд на объект [*см.* **Посещение объекта**].

Выждать несколько минут пока не
After the core has been driven into the sediment, **a few minutes are allowed for** the thermisters **to** respond to the temperature of ...

Выживать
Typical arctic species will be unable to **survive** the higher temperatures of the tropics.

Выжидать
A period of 300 millisec. **is allowed to elapse,** and a series of actions is then initiated.

Выжимать
The pressure of the overlying rock tends to **squeeze** the liquid **out.**

Вызвавший
The bacteria **responsible for** the disease produce a toxin.
The stress **responsible for** the initial rifting ...

Вызван [*см. тж.* **Быть вызванным, Возникать в результате, Объясняться, Относить за счёт, Являться результатом (*или* следствием)**]
The unstable slope conditions **were brought on by** the permafrost.
The phase difference **is accountable** (*or* **chargeable**) **to** gravity.
The high levels of alkaline phosphatase may **be associated with** a tumor of ...
Laser-excited molecular fluorescence can **be caused by** species present in the flame gases.
The fire **was set by** lightning.
The ionization **was produced by** the charged particle.
Such spectra are not sufficiently well resolved, which **owes to** the broad fluorescent vibronic bands.
The strain **is brought about** (*or* **caused**) **by** pressure.
Errors that may **arise** (*or* **stem**) **from** such disturbances ...
The production of foam **is associated with** a decrease in surface tension.
These faults **are attributable** (*or* **may be attributed**) **to** the video head assembly.
The fluctuations **are due to** roll eccentricity.
The fire **was induced by** lightning.
When combustion **originates from** local exposure ...
This increase **results from** (*or* **is caused by,** *or* **stems from,** *or* **arises from,** *or* **is due to,** *or* **is brought about by**) ...
These problems **spring** (*or* **derive**) **from** a number of different demands.
This effect **stems** (*or* **derives**) **from** (*or* **is due to,** *or* **is caused by**) reduced blood circulation.
Acute insufficiency may **be triggered** (*or* **caused,** *or* **occasioned**) **by** a generalized infection or massive stress.
A major earthquake **has** never **been triggered by** a nuclear test explosion.

Вызван тем, что [*см.* **Необходимость ... вызвана тем, что**].

Вызванный войной
The labour shortage **brought on by the war ...**

Вызванный гормонами
Hormonally related tumours ...

Вызванный облучением
Irradiation-produced (*or* **induced**) defects were revealed.

Вызываемый
There is very little combustion **attributable to** direct reaction between the molecules.
Cosmic Rays: extremely high-frequency radiation **set up** (*or* **caused,** *or* **produced,** *or* **induced**) **by** the bombardment of subatomic particles.

Вызывать [*см. тж.* **Благодаря которому происходит, Влечь за собой, Возбуж–**

дать, Заставлять, Не вызывать изменений, Создавать]
The X-rays can also **bring about** (*or* **cause,** *or* **elicit**) chemical changes in the environment of the chromosomes.
Bimolecular processes may **be responsible for** (*or* **cause,** *or* **trigger**) reactions at such low temperatures.
Use of scraper units **has brought about** (*or* **led to,** *or* **resulted in,** *or* **produced**) a change in the stripping procedures.
Exposure **will cause** the tubes **to** swell.
The unbalance voltage **causes** a galvanometer **to** deflect.
The use of a driving belt could **give rise to** vibrations.
The homogeneous para- to orthohydrogen conversion **is induced by** paramagnetic molecules.
Certain fungi **are responsible for** histoplasmosis, a lung infection.
It is important to know the conditions that **bring on** a spin (*av.*).
Resonance destabilization **will effect** a greater decrease in ...
Fertilization of the eggs **elicited** a pronounced increase of poly(A).
The detonator is a device used to **initiate** the explosion of a high explosive.
It is not certain what process **triggered** the initial collapse of the solar nebula.
Only a little heating above the glass temperature is needed **to provoke** crystallization.
Viscosity **sets up** (*or* **gives rise to**) tangential stress at the body surface.

Вызывать беспокойство
The incidents **give us** justifiable **concern about** the potential hazards of mercury.

Вызывать боль
This disease **is responsible for** back **pain.**

Вызывать бурный протест
A great hue and cry has been raised against (*col.*) any electric wires being used above ground.

Вызывать вибрацию
Other parts of the detector would be displaced slightly with respect to the centre of mass, **setting off** internal **vibrations** in the solid.
The energy of the field-accelerated carrier is large enough to **set** the semiconductor crystal **into vibration.**
Such a propeller might **set up** undesirable **vibrations.**

Вызывать возражение
The presence of gluons in the theory **provokes objections** (*nucl. phys.*).

Вызывать заболевание
The virus **will** not **produce** (*or* **cause**) **disease** in any known laboratory animal.

Вызывать загрязнение
The hot water released into a river may **create (a) pollution (problem).**

Вызывать затруднения
This calculation **presents** (*or* **involves**) **difficulties** [*or* **offers** (*or* **leads to**) **problems**].
The mathematical applications of chemical principles **are** often **troublesome.**

Вызывать значительный ажиотаж
A dozen years ago **considerable public excitement was generated by** the reported discovery of "RNA-dependent DNA polymerases" in human tumour cells.

Вызывать значительный интерес [*см.* **Привлекать к себе значительное внимание**].

Вызывать извержение
What **triggers** such a large **eruption?**

Вызывать изменение
High temperatures **produce** three types of **change** in permanent magnets.

Вызывать износ
The misalignment of the belt can **give rise to** (*or* **result in,** *or* **bring about**) rapid wear of ...

Вызывать интерес [*см. тж.* **Возбуждать интерес**]
These models **have aroused** considerable **interest in** many fields of manufacturing.
This oil well **attracted** particular **interest** because of its proximity to ...
We are taking steps **to generate interest among** high-school students **in** mining and metallurgy.
To provoke interest.

Вызывать меньше затруднений, чем
Although this requirement is severe, **it is less of a problem than** that encountered in optical pumping.

Вызывать много споров
The structure of this reagent **has been the subject of much controversy.**

Вызывать необходимость
Increasing demands of the industry **generate a need for ...**
This amount of leakage might **necessitate** large volumes in reserve.

Вызывать ожесточённые споры
This hypothesis **raised heated debate.**

Вызывать озабоченность населения
Many ionic compounds **have** recently **become of public concern.**

Вызывать опасения
To cause alarm (*or* **anxiety**).

Вызывать опасные последствия
Pollutant gases **pose threats,** ranging from lung damage to destruction of the ozone layer.

Вызывать оппозицию
His ideas **were met with** considerable **resistance.**

Вызывать осложнения
The necessary refrigeration **will create** (*or* **cause,** *or* **pose**) no serious **complications**.

Вызывать появление [*см. тж.* **Приводить к появлению**]
The drilling of the holes had **initiated** very fine cracks.

Вызывать путаницу
This name may **lead to** (*or* **cause**) **confusion.**

Вызывать реакцию
This heat is used to **produce** (*or* **induce,** *or* **trigger,** *or* **start,** *or* **initiate**) a chemical **reaction.**
These findings **touched off a** hysterical **reaction** in the scientific community.

Вызывать смерть через полчаса
0.13 percent of carbon monoxide **is fatal** to the average adult **in** about **half an hour.**

Вызывать сомнение относительно
The existence of double-stranded replicative forms **was doubted** for a time (*biol.*).
This **casts some doubt upon** the usefulness of ...
When atomic species identification **is in doubt, ...**

Вызывать трудности [*см.* **Вызывать затруднения**].

Вызывать упорное сопротивление
The project **has run into heavy opposition from** environmentalists.

Вызывать чрезмерное напряжение
Such practice **will put unnecessary strain on** the instrument and cause excessive wear on the threads.

Вызываться
Crevice corrosion **is** usually **associated with** stagnant conditions.

Вызывающий
Some of the components **responsible for** the allergic reaction to bee sting have been identified.
The forces **responsible for** the cohesion of solids ...

Вызывающий возражения
One of the **objectionable** features of the Bohr model of the atom was the assumption of quantized energy states for the electron.

Выигрывать
You **benefit** (*or* **profit**) **from** lower ultimate costs.
Such devices might **benefit from** new techniques.

Выигрыш
A considerable **gain** (*or* **increase**) **in** shock strength can be obtained by using a tube which converges at the diaphragm.

Выйти [*см.* **Выходить**].

Выйти из I
To allow time for unmetabolized traces to **clear from** the blood, ...

Выйти из II
It is not always possible to **recover from** a spin (*av.*).

Выкипать
As boiling continues, the liquid volume decreases until all the liquid **has boiled away.**
Carbon dioxide is moderately soluble in cold water, but is completely **boiled out** if the water is boiled.

Выкладки [*см.* **Алгебраические выкладки, Математические выкладки**].

Выклиниваться
The ore **thins** (*or* **tapers,** *or* **wedges,** *or* **pinches,** *or* **peters**) **out.**

Выключатель [*см.* **Замкнутый выключатель**].

Выключать [*см. тж.* **Включать и выключать, Выводить из зацепления, Выводить из эксплуатации**]
The air supply **is cut** (*or* **shut**) **off** immediately.
In the event of overheating this switch **cuts off** the welding current.
Cut the burner **out.**
An auxiliary circuit **de-energized** the controller.
The air blows to atmosphere until **it is shut down.**
To **shut off** the engine.
Shut (*or* **Turn**) **off** the hydrogen.
Switch (*or* **Turn**) **off** the light.
Turn off the nitrogen (flow).
The radiation source **is turned off.**
To shut the reactor **down, ...**

Выключаться
The motor **will be shut down** automatically.
The equipment **shuts off** when drilling has been completed.
The first stage of the Titan operated for 155 sec and then **shut down.**
When the control current **is withdrawn, ...**

Выключение
The **shutdown of** a reactor...

Выковывать [*см.* **Ковать в горячем состоянии**].

Выколачивать
Drive (*or* **Knock**) **out** the remaining part of the rivet.

Выкрашенный в ... цвет
The ammeters **are coloured green** up to full load and **red** beyond.
The pump **is finished in black** (*or* **is painted black**).

Выкрашивание
The through-type holes are more difficult to drill because of the possibility of **chipping** around the back of the hole.
A flat crest thread is recommended to prevent **chipping of** the thread.

Выкристаллизовываться из раствора
The liquid is cooled and any solid which **crystallizes out** is filtered off.

Вылавливать сигнал
An air-traffic controller needs a device that can swiftly and accurately **pick out the** unique identification **signal** assigned to each aircraft.

Вылет [*см.* **В момент вылета из**].

Вымачивание в
This is achieved by **soaking** the electrode **in** water for two hours.

Вымирать
The *chondrosteidae* **became extinct** in the Mesozoic.
The land animals **died out** first.

Вымывать
Rainwater **washes away** (*or* **out**) part of the soil.

Вымываться
These impurities do not readily **wash out.**

Вымываться из
Large particles with radii of 10 micrometres or more can **be washed out of** the air by raindrops or fall out directly.
Calcium **is washed out of** the soil by rainwater.

Вынимать
Parts must **be removed from** (*or* **taken out of**) the bath at frequent intervals.
The vane must **be** completely **withdrawn from** between the nozzles.
The bolt **may be withdrawn.**

Вынимать сверло
When cutting deep holes it is advisable **to back the drill out** frequently to prevent scorching.
After **the drill is withdrawn...**

Выниматься
The rotating chill core **is** progressively **withdrawn** (*or* **pulled out**) as the casting process continues.

Выносить
Such severe conditions **are tolerated** well **by** a number of grasses.

The ability **to withstand** severe oxygen deficiency...

Выносить за скобки
It is convenient **to factor out** the term for this degree of freedom **from** the partition function.

Выносить нагрузку [*см.* **Выдерживать нагрузку**].

Выносить решение
Decisions made by the authorities...

Выносить решение о
When **deciding on** (*or* **taking decisions on**) the choice of a material for...

Выносливый [*см.* **Более выносливый**].

Вынуждать [*см.* **Заставлять, Что заставит нас искать**].

Вынужден
Such a civilization **would be forced** (*or* **would have**) **to** use the metals in the ratios that...

Выпадает некоторое количество осадков
Even the driest deserts **receive some rainfall.**

Выпадает осадок
A white **precipitate occurs** if a sulphate is present.

Выпадать I
Undissolved material **settles out.**

Выпадать II
The logarithmic term **drops out.**

Выпадать в виде
The accumulated mass of water **falls out as** a heavy shower.

Выпадать из I
The tetrafluoroborate **will precipitate from** the aqueous solution.

Выпадать из II
The mass **drops out of** the problem (*math.*).

Выпадать из раствора
Most of the particles **precipitate from solution.**

Выпадать на долю
The role of expediter usually **falls to** the shop foreman.

Выпадение осадков из
Precipitation from shower clouds...

Выпаривать до малого объёма
Evaporate the solution **to small bulk.**

Выпаривать досуха
The ether solution **was evaporated to dryness.**

Выписывать полностью
If the largest Mersenne number **is written out in full, ...**

Выполнен
The bearings **are of** white metal.
The machine **is built of** standardized components.
The connectors **are constructed of** Neoprene.
The box was **made from** (*or* **of**) plywood.
The roof bolting **is executed** properly.

Выполнен заодно с [*см. тж.* **Неотъемлемая часть**]
An indicator may **be an integral part of** the measuring head or a separate unit.

Выполнение [*см.* **Осуществление**].

Выполнение операции (*произв.*)
The execution of the operation.

Выполнение условия
The fulfilment of this **condition** means that...

Выполненный по (индивидуальному) заказу
There is a wide variety of enclosure sized both standard and **custom built** (*or* **made to order**).

Выполненный согласно спецификации (*или* **техническим условиям) на**
This type has a strong body **built to the specifications of** earth-moving equipment tyres.

Выполненный целиком из алюминия
An **all-aluminium** exchanger.

Выполнять [*см. тж.* **Изготавливать, Осуществлять, Производить**]
Chlorination **is accomplished by** one chlorinator.
The firm **has completed** the design of this plant.
Design and construction of the furnaces **has been executed by** the same group.

Brackets **were made from** (*or* **of**) these materials.

Выполнять анализ
Satisfactory **analysis** can **be performed** (*or* **carried out**) on samples having...

Выполнять вычисления
The calculations were performed (*or* **done,** *or* **made,** *or* **carried out**) **by** our team.

Выполнять двойную функцию
The discharge **serves the dual function of** sputtering atoms from the cathode into the vapour phase and supplying the collisional environment required for the *OGE*.

Выполнять дифференцирование по [*см.* **Проводить дифференцирование по**].

Выполнять договорные обязательства
To meet treaty (*or* **contractual**) **obligations, ...**

Выполнять задачу
He **accomplished this task** in 1988.
This motor **will do the job** efficiently.

Выполнять заказ
How does our company **fill orders for** oversized workpieces?

Выполнять измерения
Measurements were taken (*or* **made**).

Выполнять инструкцию
To carry out instructions.

Выполнять на заказ
The unit can **be made to order** (*or* **custom made**) in a wide range of wood finishes.

Выполнять обязательства
To meet one's engagements (*or* **commitments**).

Выполнять операцию (*произв.*)
These **operations** can **be done** (*or* **performed,** *or* **carried out,** *or* **executed**) under pressure.
The computer routes the workpieces to the necessary machines, selects the proper tools, **executes the** proper **operations,** and when the part is finished returns it to the operator for unloading.
The spectrophotometer **does the job** in a fraction of a second.
Large radial drilling machines **handle** special **jobs.**

Выполнять план
To fulfil the plan.
To complete the plan ahead of schedule...

Выполнять по заказу [*см.* **Выполнять на заказ**].

Выполнять программу
An extensive **program** for... **is** at present **being implemented.**

Выполнять работу
The machine can **do the job** in one year.
Chemical energy can be utilized to **do** (*or* **perform**) **work.**
Gases in the process of expanding **do** no interior **work.**
The entire **job was completed** in five days.

Выполнять расчёты
The calculations are performed (*or* **carried out,** *or* **done,** *or* **made**) as shown in parts *a* and *b*.

Выполнять самые разнообразные функции
Peptides and proteins **play a broad spectrum of roles** in living systems.

Выполнять согласно техническим условиям
Die-cut shapes **are made to** (*or* **in accordance with,** *or* **in compliance with**) your **specifications.**

Выполнять ту же функцию [*см.* **Заменять его**].

Выполнять указания
The operator did not **follow** precisely **the directions** (*or* **instructions**) **of** his supervisor.

Выполнять условие
This **condition** should **be met** (*or* **fulfilled,** *or* **complied with**).

Выполнять функцию
The transistors **are acting** (*or* **serving,** *or* **functioning,** *or* **operating**) **as** switches.
To perform one's functions.
This simple charge-coupled device **fulfils the function of** an eight-bit shift register.
The function of load-frequency control **in discharged** automatically.
The sodium iodide **serves** three important **functions:...**

Выполняться I [*см. тж.* **Действителен для**]
Thus the familiar theorem of Green **asserts.**

Выполняться II
Raoult's law **is obeyed by** the solvent.

Выполняться с точностью до
The correlation **is good** (*or* **accurate**) **to** ±20 percent for a wide variety of systems, packings, and flow rates.

Выполняющий
All those **engaged in** (*or* **performing**) these operations should ...

Выпрямлять
This enables kinks in the pipeline to **be straightened out.**

Выпуклость изотермы
The northward **bulge of the isotherms** in the Iceland-Spitsbergen-Norway area ...

Выпуклый книзу (*антон.* **кверху**)
The curve **is convex down(wards)** [*anton.* **up(wards)**].

Выпуск в свет
The issuance of standards ...

Выпуск газа
The airship envelope contains one or more air cells which are used to maintain the required pressure in the envelope without adding or **valving** (*or* **release**) **of** gas as the airship ascends or descends.

Выпуск газа из
Sweeping out the gas from the apparatus...

Выпускать I
Being air-powered the loader **emits** no diesel exhaust fumes.
To **exhaust** the air (*or* to **let** the air **out**) ...
The gas is **vented** (*or* **liberated,** *or* **discharged**) **to** atmosphere.

Выпускать II
Each week the plant **turns out** (*or* **produces,** *or* **manufactures**) thousands of such units.
Some manufacturers **brought out** multichip microprocessors.

Выпускать III [*см.* **Издавать**].

Выпускать в атмосферу [*см.* **Выбрасывать в атмосферу**].

Выпускать дым
The technique is **to release a smoke from** the ground and ...

Выпускаться
Compressed air is allowed **to escape from** a selected pair of holes.
Sulphur **is released to** the atmosphere by sea spray.
The hot water **is released into** surface stream flow.

Выпускаться и втягиваться (*о щупальцах*)
Tentacles **are extruded and withdrawn** through the orifice.

Выпускаться наружу
The moist air **is discharged to** the outside.

Вырабатывать
The adrenal cortex **elaborates** many steroid hormones.
To work out (*or* **elaborate,** *or* **draw up**) proposals ...
To generate electricity ...
To draw up (*or* **elaborate,** *or* **map out**) a plan ...

Вырабатывать тепло
The reaction **generates** enough **heat** to maintain itself.

Выравнивание
Equalization of the population ...
A tendency toward **equalizing** the flow rates of the different parts of the gas ...

Выравниваться
These forces **level off** at a high temperature.
The current increases with applied potential, until **it levels off** at a limiting value.

Выражать [*см.* **Можно выразить в виде**].

Выражать беспокойство относительно
They **expressed concern over** shortages of petroleum fuel.

Выражать в
Rates of lactic acid formation **are expressed** (*or* **given**) **as** grams of lactic acid formed per 100 ml of mash per hour.
The Verdet constant **is** usually **expressed in** minutes per gauss centimetre.

These properties can **be expressed in terms of** two variables.
Pressure measurements **are reported as** atmospheres.

Выражать в виде
The effect of these forces can **be expressed in terms of** an experimental parameter known as...

Выражать в единицах
The energy is usually **expressed in terms of** a temperature, the Debye temperature θ_D.

Выражать в процентах
This fraction **is expressed as a percentage** (*or* **in percent**).

Выражать символом
We **have symbolized** it as *C*.

Выражать через
The number of moles *n* can **be expressed as** *in*/*M*.
The solutions (*решение*) can **be expressed in terms of** a single space coordinate *x*.

Выражаться [*см. тж.* **Даваться**]
The orientation of the molecule **is expressed by** the polar angular coordinates.
The rate of effusion **is expressed in terms of** molecules per unit time per unit effusion hole area.

Выражаться в единицах
The angular momentum of atomic nuclei is quantized and **comes in units of** $h/2\pi$.

Выражаться уравнением
This equilibrium **is expressed by Eq.** (20).

Выражающийся в виде
These metals are susceptible to permanent embrittlement **manifested as** intergranular fractures.

Выражен
If the real-gas behaviour **is expressed by** any other equation of state, ...

Выражен в
The current density **is written** (*or* **expressed**) **in terms of** drift.

Выражен в процентах
This value **is expressed as a percentage** (*or* **in percent**) **of**...

Выражен через
In the formula $C=E/I$ the impedance **is represented by** I.

Выражение [*см. тж.* **Входить в выражение, Выводить выражение, Соотношение**]
Some mathematical **relations** (*or* **expressions**) are helpful.

Выраженный [*см. тж.* **Чётко выраженный**]
These copolymers have a less **pronounced** (*or* **distinct,** *or* **marked**) block structure.

Выраженный в десятичных дробях
Decimally 22/7 is equal, roughly, to 3.142857.

Выраженный через
The location of the centre of gravity of ... **in terms of** the *x* and *y* coordinates of its atoms is...

Выращенный в темноте
Photochlorophyll has been found in **dark-grown** barley leaves and other plants in minute amounts.

Вырез в
Enter the instrument into **the cut-out from** the panel front.

Вырезан из
The can **is cut from** 3/32-inch sheet brass.

Вырисовывается картина [*см.* **Начинает вырисовываться картина**].

Вырисовываться на фоне
To an observer looking up from below, the fish **is silhouetted against** its bright **background**.

Вырожденный [*см. тж.* **Дважды вырожденный**]
Some of these equations may **be degenerate.**

Высасываться
The dust **is sucked off** and discharged.

Высверливать
Drilling out broken screws, bolts and studs...

Высвобождать I [*см. тж.* **Освобождать**]
The operator **releases** the mandrel and places it on the table.

Высвобождать II
There is much evidence indicating that earthquakes **release** gases from deep in the earth's mantle.

Высвобождаться I [*см. тж.* **Поглощаться и высвобождаться**]
As the energy **is liberated** (*or* **released,** *or* **generated**) in the oxidation reaction...
Electrons can **be knocked free** by an incoming electron.

Высвобождаться II
Calcium **is set free** by weathering and transported to the sea by rivers.

Высвобождаться из
In the oxidation process, ferrous iron **is released from** its place in the parent mineral and is oxidized.

Высказывать [*см.* **Выдвигать**].

Высказывать возражения против
They **raised objections against** the new theory.

Высказывать гипотезу о том, что [*см. тж.* **Выдвигать гипотезу о том, что**]
Kepler **hypothesized that** the Sun...

Высказывать замечание
The **remarks advanced** in the preceding section...

Высказывать мнение о том, что
Johannes Kepler **stated** his **belief that** the Moon influenced the tides.

Высказывать мысль
They **came up with an** alternative **idea.**

Высказывать опасения
Just a few years ago these **concerns were voiced** only by a handful of environmentalists.

Высказывать предположение о том, что
Kekule **made** his classical **proposal that** the six carbon atoms of benzene were arranged in a hexagon.
It has been proposed (*or* **speculated,** *or* **suggested**) **that** a series of reactions is involved.
He **suggested that** there should be two gas diffusion terms.
Goldbach **conjectured that** every even number...
He **proposed that** both attractive and repulsive forces could exist between atoms.
It is speculated that the oxygen resulted from the bombardment of the seas by certain wavelengths of ultraviolet light.
Scientists **theorize that** the planets in our solar system formed at...
It was conjectured that the eukaryotes had eliminated the need for... (*biol.*).
The suggestion has been made that the underlying asthenosphere has an undulating upper surface.
He **reasoned** (*or* **argued,** *or* **hypothesized**) **that** erosion must be burying layers of sediment under...

Высказывать сомнение относительно
Several reporters **have cast doubt on** the cerebral origin of...

Высказывать сомнения относительно того
It has been questioned whether or not it is meaningful to divide...

Высказывать соображения относительно
Similar **considerations can be applied to** the drift and diffusion of holes in and out of the *p*-type material.

Высказываться в пользу
A number of investigators **favoured** (*or* **advocated,** *or* **supported**) the use of...
He **argued for** the hot origin of the earth.

Высказываться в том же духе (*или* **аналогичным образом**)
He **argued along similar lines.**

Выскальзывать из-под
Take care that the airship envelope does not **slip out from under** the net.

Высокая степень развития
One form of fiber materials has already reached **an advanced stage of development.**

Высокая степень совершенства
These investigations have been developed to a **high degree of sophistication** (*or* **perfection**).

Высокая температура
At sufficiently **elevated temperatures...**

Высокая точность
Pinpoint accuracy (*or* **High precision**).

Высокая энергия [*см.* **Обладать большой энергией**].

Высокие требования к [*см. тж.* **Предъявлять высокие требования к**]
If we are to meet **the exacting needs** [*or* **high** (*or* **stringent**) **requirements**] **of** industry...

Высокий класс отделки поверхности
It is also possible with these tools to obtain **a high surface finish.**

Высокое содержание [*см.* **Богат, С высоким содержанием**].

Высокой чистоты
High-purity elements...
Hyperpure silicon...
Ultrapure titanium...

Высокой энергии
Even **energetic** (*or* **high-energy**) protons could be guided by such a field.

Высококачественный [*см. тж.* **Качественный, Самый высококачественный**]
High-performance (*or* **High-quality**) materials...
Quality binoculars...
Top-quality products...

Высококвалифицированный
Highly trained (*or* **Highly skilled**) personnel...

Высококипящий
A **high-boiling** compound...

Высоколегированная сталь
High-alloy steel.

Высокомолекулярный
High molecular (weight) amines...

Высокопроизводительный
A **high-efficiency** (*or* **highly efficient**) plant...

Высокопрочный
High-strength steels...

Высокоразвитый
The more complex, **highly evolved** (*or* **advanced,** *or* **developed**) species are found in rocks overlying those containing simpler, less advanced species.

Высокосортный
High-grade ore...

Высокосортный продукт
A **product of superior quality** (*or* A **(high-)quality product**).

Высокоточный
This process requires **highly accurate** (*or* **high-accuracy**) dies.

Высокоупорядоченный
Diamond and quartz may be thought of as **highly ordered** space network polymers.

Высокоустойчивый к
Strawberry clover is **highly tolerant of** (*or* **to**) wet soil.

Высокоэффективный [*см. тж.* **Эффективный**]
The **highly efficient** screening surface of...
High-performance (*or* **-efficiency**) memories...

Высота [*см. тж.* **На высоту, Набирать высоту, По высоте**]
Clouds have been occasionally observed near 23 km **altitude** over Scandinavia.
A person flying **at an elevation of** 5000 ft above the ground...
Winds blowing violently **at heights up to** seven or eight miles...

Высота заполнения колонки
The average height equivalent to a theoretical plate is obtained by dividing **the packed height** by the number of theoretical plates.

Высота... составляет от ... до [*см.* **Ширина ... составляет от ... до**].

Высотой [*см..* **Длиной, Толщиной**]

Выставлен
More than 2000 products **were on view** (*or* **on display,** *or* **on show**).

Выставлять
This loader **was displayed** (*or* **exhibited,** *or* **shown,** *or* **on exhibit**) at the recent mining machinery exhibition.

Выстраивать в ряд
The flip-flops can **be aligned in a row.**

Выстраиваться
The internal fields make it "easier" for the magnetic moments **to line up** in preferred directions.

Выстроенные
The casting contains fibres **aligned** in the longitudinal directions.

Выстроившиеся в ряд
Small craters **strung out along a line** can be identified.

Выступ [*см.* **Впадины и выступы (***на поверхности***)**].

Выступать I
This causes drops of blood **to ooze out at** the knees.

Выступать II
The ends of the main valve **project beyond** the port face.
One thread of the segment should **show** (*or* **extend,** *or* **protrude**) **below** the outer end of the nut.

Выступать в виде [*см.* **Проявляться**].

Выступать за
Physicists have long **advocated** international collaboration.

Выступать на
The length of the tube is such that it **extends** about **3/16 in. beyond** the tube sheet.
When riveted, the end of the stay before riveting should **extend** not less than **1/4 in. from** the surface of the plate.

Выступающий наружу
The upper portion of each valve disk is provided with **outward-projecting** lips [*or* lips **projecting** (*or* **extending,** *or* **protruding**) **outward**].

Выступы и впадины на поверхности
In the dissolution of benzoic acid from the inner cylinder, **peaks and valleys** developed **on** the acid **surface**, corresponding to the location of the vertices.

Высушивать
The borax obtained **is** washed with water, and **allowed to dry** (*or* **is dried**).
To dry the surface...

Высушивать без подогрева
The precipitate **is dried without heat.**

Высшего качества
This tube **is second to none** (*or* **of highest quality**).
This gives a **top quality** material (*or* material **of top quality**).

Высшего класса
The extreme requirements of a modern aircraft call for design **of the highest order.**

Высшие растения, животные
Higher plants, animals.

Высыпа́ться
Ore **pours into** the skip.
Some of the ore **spills to** the bottom of the shaft.

Выталкивать
The pressure of the gas **forces out** a stream of liquid.

Выталкивать вверх
The pressure would **force** the lighter fractions **upward.**

Вытекать [*см. тж.* **Следовать**]
The fluid **is exhausted** (*or* **flows,** *or* **pours**) **into** a chamber.

Вытекать из I [*см. тж.* **Из этого вытекает (***или* **следует), что; Объясняться**]
The mass ratio **follows from** the amplitudes of both velocity curves.
The term R/n^2 **results from** the simple Bohr theory.
Much of the utility of the binomial theorem **stems from** the properties of the coefficients.
The most important conclusion to **emerge from** such a model is that...
The above advantages **result from** the high spectral irradiances of lasers.

Вытекать из II
Lava flows **emerge from** fissures on the flanks of the dome.
Turbid water which **issues from** the mouths of streams inhibits reef development.

Вытекать со всей очевидностью из
This property **is readily apparent from** the molecular formula.

Вытекающий из I
The most obvious opportunity **afforded by** laser excitation of cryogenic samples is the increased ease of...

Вытекающий из II
A cylindrical liquid **issuing from** (*or* **flowing out of**) a sharp-edged orifice is the equivalent of a solid rod.

Вытеснен
Platinum and osmium have been used for making filaments, but they **have been superseded** (*or* **supplanted,** *or* **replaced**) **by** tungsten and tantalum.

Вытеснение
Compaction of clay sediments into rock is largely a process of **exclusion of** water under the pressure of the overlying sediments.

Вытеснять [*см. тж.* **Заменять, Практически вытеснивший**]
The liquid **is expelled** (*or* **displaced,** *or* **driven out**) **by** the admitted air.
The transistor **ousted** the thermionic valve **from** its place in electronics.
Better preparations **have supplanted** (*or* **displaced**) these drugs.
The myeloblasts **crowd out** other blood-forming elements.

Вытесняться из
As the confining pressure increases, water **is driven out of** the sediment, and the mineral particles become more closely packed.
Air **is displaced from** the bulb **by** oxygen.
Air **is forced out of** the bottle **by** a stream of water.

Вытирать [*см.* **Протирать**].

Вытирать дочиста
Wipe the shank **clean.**

Выточенный на токарном станке
The fixture consists of a **turned** wooden stand and...

Вытравливать
The oxide between the electrodes **is etched off.**

Вытягивать
An exhaust fan **to draw off** (*or* **exhaust**) the dry dust should be applied to...

Вытянутый
The polymer chains become slightly **extended.**

Выхлоп
The **escape** (*or* **exhaust,** *or* **discharge**) **of** the hot combustion products into the atmosphere...

Выхлопной газ [*см.* **Отработанный газ**].

Выход I [*см. тж.* **Вход в ... и выход из него, Давление на входе (выходе), Мощность на выходе, На выходе**]
After **leaving** the crushers, the ore passes to the wagons...
Gas **outlet...**
The **egress** of tracer from the organ...

Выход II
The **yield** of pig iron...

Выход III
The oil possibilities of Hungary were recognized because of the numerous **seeps.**
An oil or gas **show** in a nonproductive well...

Выход IV [*см.* **При входе и выходе**].

Выход в космос из космического корабля
Extra-vehicular excursion (*or* **activity**).
Walking in space.

Выход газа [*см.* **Вход и выход газа** (*на схеме*)].

Выход из положения
The theory's supporters could only hope that some **way out** would be found.

Выход из строя
The reliability of a valve can be defined as the probability of its **failure** after a certain length of time.

Выход на поверхность
The (surface) exposure of strata of Palaeozoic age...
Outcrops (*or* **Outcroppings**) **of** bituminous sand...

Выходить I [*см. тж.* **Выйти, Срок выходит**]
The sulphur is oxidized to SO_2 and **passes off** in the gases.
The nozzle from which the gas **issues** (*or* **emanates**)...
The air **leaves** through the duct.
The combustion gases **exit** at almost 200 mpf.

Выходить II [*см.* **У нас вышла вся бумага**].

Выходить в атмосферу
The air **passes to (the) atmosphere.**

Выходить в космос из космического корабля
To walk in space.

Выходить в свет
The book **has been published** (*or* **issued,** *or* **has appeared,** *or* **has come out,** *or* **is out**).

Выходить далеко за рамки
The importance of complex numbers **goes far beyond** their properties as roots of algebraic equations.

Выходить за пределы
This **is beyond** the scope of our present work.
Once the projectile **is clear of** the muzzle of the gun...

Выходить за пределы познаний
The requirements for structural stability **are** usually **outside the** user's **field of knowledge**.

Выходить за рамки
This **is beyond the scope** (*or* **purpose**) **of** our report.
Such discussions **do not enter into the scope of** the present book.
Certain factors **fall outside the scope of** a building code.
For a variety of reasons, which **do not come within the province of** this paper...
It is beyond the scope of this article **to** review these mechanisms (*рассмотрение этих механизмов выходит за рамки данной статьи*).

Выходить из [*см. тж.* **Покидать**]
No gas **came out from** the cylinder.
Once the laser pulse **emerges from** the laser, it is directed into a string of laser amplifiers.
The line **issues out of** the points $x = a$ and $x = -a$.
The liquid refrigerant *leaves* the condenser at a temperature of...
Only pure carrier gas **emerges from** the column.
The reflected ray **leaves** the interface at the same angle.
The gas **escapes from** the balloon.

Выходить из берегов
Streams **top** (*or* **overflow**) their **banks** from time to time.

Выходить из затруднения
To get out of (*or* **obviate**) **a difficulty.**

Выходить из равновесия
The tensile forces **are** then **out of balance.**

Выходить из строя [*см. тж.* **Приходить в нерабочее состояние**]
The press continually **breaks down** because of stress and strain on its steel die springs.
If one transformer **becomes disabled** [*or* **goes out of repair** (*or* **commission**)], ...
The transistor **failed** after two months of service.
If the rods **fail to operate...**
If a part **goes bad** (*or* **is in disrepair**), ...
The instrument **is made inoperative** by...
Both pipelines **have been put out of operation.**
The bearing became overheated and **gave out.**
The machine may **get out of order.**

Выходить из употребления
To fall into disuse.
To go out of use.
This type of car **has passed out of existence.**

Выходить из-под контроля
The reaction **got out of hand.**
The reactor **ran away.**

Выходить на орбиту
The satellite **has gone into orbit** (*or* **has been orbited,** *or* **has settled into orbit**).

Выходить на орбиту вокруг планеты
The spacecraft **went into orbit around the planet.**

Выходить на плато [*см. тж.* **Становиться горизонтальным**]
The curve **flattens out** at high Mach numbers.

Выходить на поверхность
The Precambrian rocks **crop out (at the surface).**
Coal seams **outcrop** (*or* **are exposed**) along the contour of the mountainsides.
If we can establish that molten rock **has** not **emerged** from the interior of the Moon, ...

Выходить через
The scattered beam **emerged through** a celluloid window.

Выходной
Outlet pressure ...

Выходной конец
The **exit end** of the furnace ...

Выходящий
The **exit** gas and entering fluid are dilute.
The difference between the compositions of the **emergent** (*or* **emerging,** *or* **issuing,** *or* **exit**) vapour and liquid streams is small.
The smoke particles are carried along by the **outward-moving** (*or* **outgoing**) gases.

Выходящий дым
The **smoke leaving** [*or* **issuing** (*or* **emerging) from**] a chimney forms a plume.

Выходящий из
This light is added to the light **coming from** lens 9.
The ion beam **emerging from** the accelerating tube consists of high-velocity hydrogen nuclei.
The jet **issuing from** the nozzle ...
The smoke **issuing from** (*or* **leaving**) the stack is clean.
The light **leaving** the specimen is measured separately.

Выходящий луч
The outgoing beam.

Выходящий на поверхность
The mine drifts are driven directly into the **exposed** coal seams.

Выходящий поток
The **outgoing stream** (*or* **flow**).

Выходящий снизу (сверху)
The countercurrent action permits the condensate **leaving** (*or* **issuing,** *or* **emerging**) **at the bottom** of the condenser to be much richer in the high-boiling component than the vapour **leaving at the top.**

Вычерчивание на графике
A traditional way of **graphing** a parabola...

Вычерчивать [*см. тж.* **Чертить**]
Using the above data, we **plot** (*or* **draw,** *or* **trace**) sensitivity curves.

Вычет [*см.* **За вычетом**].

Вычёркивать
We **cross out** every other number.

Вычисление [*см.* **Выполнять вычисления**].

Вычисления, связанные с
The arithmetic of X-ray diffraction...

Вычислительное устройство [*см.* **С помощью вычислительных устройств**].

Вычислять
Geologists **have figured out** just when the pole reversals occurred.
Halley began **to work out** the orbits of various comets.
Then the derivatives of the other functions **are worked out** (*or* **calculated,** *or* **found,** *or* **deduced**).

Вычислять по [*см.. тж.* **Подсчитывать по**]
The shear strength **was calculated** (*or* **computed**) **from** the data shown in Fig. 1.

Вычитать [*см.* **Прибавлять и вычитать, Складывать или вычитать**].

Вычищать из
Carbon deposits should **be cleaned out of** the grooves.

Выше I [*см. тж.* **Вверх по течению, Значительно выше, чем; И выше, Свыше**]
Efficiency is **better than** 96% at full load.
If the pressure is **above** (*or* **higher than,** *or* **over**) 3 mm, ...
When heating is continued **beyond** 1403°C the gamma iron changes to delta iron.
The thermocouple head should not be subject to temperatures **in excess** of 50°C.
The average Reynold's number was **over** 2300.
A wind tunnel which produces airflows to Mach 20 **plus...**
Temperatures **upwards of** 50 million degrees are required.

Выше II [*см. тж.* **Как отмечено выше, Смотри выше**]
In the reactions described **above** (or in the **above**-described reactions)...
The coefficients D_{AB} and D_{AM} employed **in the foregoing** (*or* **above,** *or* **previously**) are the common mutual diffusion coefficients.

Выше III
Water production **above** a given point on the river...

Выше на
The temperature **is higher by 4°C** (*or* **4°C higher**).

Выше нуля
Above zero.

Выше обычного
A slightly **higher-than-normal** voltage is required to start...

Выше ожидаемого
A **higher-than-expected** incidence of lymphomas has been observed in...

Выше среднего
How do the high-energy molecules accumulate their **greater-than-average** thermal energy?

Выше уровня моря
Above sea level.

Выше, чем у
The dielectric strength of a high vacuum **is superior to** gases at atmospheric pressure.

Вышеизложенный [*см. тж.* **Указанный**]
All of **the preceding** is intended to illustrate...
The above(-enumerated) objects of our invention are accomplished by...
The foregoing proves that...

Вышел срок [*см.* **Срок вышел**].

Вышеперечисленные
The four solutions of $x^4 - 1 = 0$ are all four complex numbers **just listed.**
The above-listed (*or* **-enumerated**) criteria...

Вышеприведённый [*см. тж.* **Из вышесказанного следует, что**]
It is evident from **the foregoing** equation that...
The foregoing shows that...
From **the above** discussion it is clear that...
We ignore refracting rays for reasons **given above** (*or* **for the above(-stated)** reasons).

Вышесказанное
From **the preceding** (*or* **aforesaid**), it may be seen that...

Вышесказанный [*см.* **Из вышесказанного** (*или* **вышеприведённого**) **следует, что**].

Вышеуказанный [*см.* **Вышеизложенный, Указанный**].

Вышеупомянутый
The above-mentioned (*or* **aforementioned**) resistance [*or* **The resistance mentioned earlier** (*or* **above**)]...
The ore deposit types **previously named** could have become involved in...

Вышла вся бумага
Our **paper has run out.**

Выщелачиваться из
These ions **are leached from** mineral deposits in the earth.

Выявилась закономерность в характере землетрясений
A regularity emerged in the earthquake pattern.

Выявление
Aqua regia is used for **revealing** the structure of stainless steel.

Выявление неисправностей (*или* **неполадок**)
Trouble-shooting.

Выявлять [*см. тж.* **Выяснять**]
Infrared observations **have revealed** a cluster of recently born stars.
Photographs **have revealed** the presence of such organisms on the ocean floor.

Выявлять причины
Careful investigations **have established the reasons for** the "unexpected" solubility of formaldehyde in benzene.

Выявляться [*см. тж.* **Сразу обнаруживаться**]
On closer examination, certain common features **emerged.**
A simple relationship of discharge to basin area **is revealed.**

Выявляться в результате
A second trend **has emerged from** the observation.

Выявляться наиболее ярко
It is here that the advantage of a grating instrument **is most noticeable.**

Выяснение
The goal of these studies **is the elucidation of** the mechanism of the reaction.

Выяснено, что
It has been found (*or* **established,** *or* **ascertained) that...**
It turns out (*or* **It appears) that** in a wave guide the group velocity is equal to...

Выяснять [*см. тж.* **Ещё вопрос, Определять, Остаётся выяснить, Устанавливать**]
Let us **find out** how fast the planet is moving.
We tried **to elucidate** the cause of hypocalcaemia (*med.*).
The processes by means of which each particular sequence of amino acids is specified **have been clarified** to a large degree.
A number of equations were introduced in order **to clarify** (*or* **elucidate,** *or* **clear up**) the behaviour of shock waves.

Выяснять вопрос
To clear up (*or* **elucidate,** *or* **clarify**) **a question.**

Выяснять структуру
The structure of morphine **was** not **elucidated** until 1925.

Выясняться
It emerges (*or* **transpires**) **that** Saturn is not unique in having rings.
In a series of experiments, a number of instructive details **were brought to light.**

Г

Габариты
The overall dimensions of the reflector...

Габариты увеличиваются
Gas turbines **are growing** steadily **in size.**

Газ [*см.* **Выбрасываемые газы, Выделять газ, Испускаемый газ, Неочищенный газ, Отапливаемый газом**].

Газонепроницаемый
A **gas-tight** seal...

Газообразное состояние
The gaseous state.

Газообразный
Gaseous hydrogen (*or* Hydrogen **gas**).

Гайка [*см.* **Ослаблять гайку, Отвинчивать гайку, Подтягивать гайку (винт), Туго затягивать гайку**].

Гарантирован от
The instrument **is safe against** self-destruction.

Гарантировать
Hydraulic design **assures** (*or* **ensures,** *or* **insures**) long, trouble-free life.

Гарантия
Have we any **assurance that** the values will be the same?

Гасить дугу
The gas and water flow will continue until **the arc is broken.**
To quench (*or* **extinguish,** *or* **snuff out**) **an arc.**

Гасить колебания
To quench oscillations.

Гауссовой формы
Gaussian shaped beams...

Гвоздь [*см.* **Забивать гвоздь**].

Где произошло короткое замыкание
A system **that suffers a short circuit...**

Генерировать пар
To produce (*or* **generate**) **steam.**

Генерируемый взрывом
Explosion-generated strain pulses...

Генерируемый солнцем
Solar-generated electricity...

Географическое распространение
Geographical distribution.

Геолог, изучающий Луну
A **lunar geologist.**

Геометрическим путём
Newton showed **by geometry** (*or* **geometrically**) that...

Геофизическая ракета
A **sounding rocket** (*or* **probe**).

Герметизирован
The unit **is hermetically sealed** (*or* **encapsulated**).

Герметизировать
The minicomponent assembly machine automatically assembles and **hermetically seals** cases for diodes, resistors and similar small components.

Гибкий
These are extremely **adaptable** (*or* **versatile**) power units.

Гигантский
A **gigantic** effect (*but* **A giant** molecule).

Гигантский труд
Our firm took on **the mammoth job** of rough and finish machining of these huge units.

Гидравлический привод [*см.* **С гидравлическим приводом**].

Гипотеза [*см.* **На основе гипотезы**].

Гипотеза о
Alternate **proposals** (*or* **hypotheses**) **for** the structure of benzene were made by Dewar.

Главная роль [*см.* **Играть главную роль**].

Главное
The first consideration in the design of such an anemometer is the selection of...

Главный [*см. тж.* **Один из главных, Основной**]
The key (*or* **main,** *or* **chief,** *or* **principal,** *or* **major**) advantages of the process are...
The major (*or* **main,** *or* **chief,** *or* **principal**) criterion is the minimum signal that can be detected.

Главный источник неполадок
The peripheral equipment, such as servo valves, pumps, filters, etc., **is the primary source of trouble.**

Главный элемент телескопа
The heart of the telescope is the objective.

Главным образом [*см. тж.* **В основном, В первую очередь**]
The attachment consists **essentially** (*or* **chiefly,** *or* **mainly,** *or* **in the main**) **of** a cable drum and...
The shield has been designed **for the most part** from common materials.
The greater (*or* **major**) **part of** our work was carried out indoors.
The foam consists **predominantly** of closed cells.
This element is composed **principally** (*or* **chiefly,** *or* **mainly,** *or* **primarily**) of Zircaloy-2.
This compound is presently used **primarily** as ...

Гладкая поверхность [*см.* **Иметь гладкую поверхность**].

Глаз [*см.* **Бросаться в глаза, Видимый глазом, Видимый невооружённым глазом, На глаз, На уровне глаз, Насколько видит глаз, Невидимый для глаза, У нас на глазах**].

Гласить
The principle of mathematical induction **says:** "If *P* is true ..."
The second law **states** (*or* **reads**): "If the same current flows ..."
This theory **holds** (*or* **asserts,** *or* **maintains**) **that** the atom ...

Глубже вникать [*см.* **Вникать глубже в**].

Глубина [*см.* **В глубине, До глубины, Из глубины земли, На глубине, С глубины**].

Глубина резания
Recommended **depth of cut** varies from 0.002 to 0.25 in.

Глубина ... составляет от .... до [*см.* **Ширина ... составляет от ... до**].

Глубинный
The presence of **deep-earth** (*or* **deep-seated**) gas ...
A **deep-seated** thermal process ...

Глубиной [*см.* **Длиной**].

Глубокие изменения
Profound alterations (*or* **changes**) in the structure of ...

Глубокий анализ
An **in-depth analysis** cannot be provided here for the lack of published data.
In some cases more **sophisticated** (*or* **thorough**) **analyses,** based on complicated equations of state, may be required.

Глубоко войти в нашу жизнь [*см..* **Настолько глубоко войти в нашу жизнь, что**].

Глубокое знание [*см. тж.* **Обладать глубокими познаниями в области**]
The author has **intimate knowledge of** his subject.

A **detailed knowledge of** the chemistry of ... is not necessary at this level.

Глубокое изучение
A development of such mechanisms requires more **in-depth study** than...

Глубокое понимание
This information is needed for **a fundamental understanding** [*or* **a deep** (*or* **keen**) **insight into**] the properties of ...
Such systems **provide insight into** cellular mechanisms.
This required **a sophisticated understanding of...**

Гнуть [*см.* **Изгибаться**].

Говорилось в [*см.* **О котором говорилось в**].

Говорит сам за себя
The diagram **is self-explanatory.**
The work done by the team **speaks for itself.**

Говорить в пользу [*см.* **В пользу ... говорит**]
This **argues for** making the devices large so that the control currents can be reduced to a minimum.
The evidence **favours** the entrapment hypothesis.
The wide distribution of this flora **strengthens the case for** a single continent.
This fact **counts in favour of** the hypothesis.

Говорить многое о
Both processes **tell a good deal about** the structure of the target particle.

Говорить о том, что
These results **indicate that ...**
The experimental evidence **points to the fact that ...**
This **suggests that** friction can considerably alter the flow forces.

Говорить против [*см.* **Опровергать**].

Говоря о
While on the subject of volcanoes formed of basaltic magma, we turn from the largest volcanoes to the smallest.

Говорят, что [*см. тж.* **Считается, что**]
The molecule **is said to** have six degrees of freedom.
A set of logic functions **is said to** be complete if ...

Говорят, что они
Such electrons **are referred to as being** (*or* **are said to be**) in metastable states.

Год [*см. тж.* **За последние годы, Из года в год, На ближайшие годы**]
By **the year** 2000...

Год спокойного солнца
The Quiescent Sun Year.

Годиться [*см.* **Подходить, Пригодный**].

Годный для полета
Flyable.

Годовой
The mill will have an **annual** (*or* **yearly**) capacity of 120,000 tons of ... [*or* a capacity of ... **per year** (*or* **per annum**, *or* **annually**)].

Головка [*см.* **С круглой головкой**].

Головной процесс
Head end process.

Гомолог элемента
The following five elements should be chemical **homologues to** the known **elements: ...**

Гореть пламенем
Free arsenic **burns with** a bluish coloured **flame.**

Горизонт [*см.* **На ... горизонте**].

Городское хозяйство [*см.* **Нужды городского хозяйства**].

Горький [*см.* **Обладать горьким вкусом**].

Горький на вкус
Bases **taste bitter** or brackish.

Горячо дискутироваться
Fifty years ago an origin for these valleys **was hotly** (*or* **furiously**) **debated.**

Готов [*см.* **Полностью подготовлен к**].

Готов для использования [*см. тж.* **В готовом для использования виде**]
Many parts **are** complete and **ready to use** as they come from the machine.

Готов явиться по вызову
Each expert must **be on call** to report within an hour.

Готовая деталь
Economic production quantities start at approximately 5000 **off** (*or* **finished parts**).

Готовить почву для
This development **is paving the way for** unusual optical shutters, digital displays and protective glasses.
This **will pave the way to** new achievements.

Готовиться к изданию
A tenth book **is in preparation** (*or* **in the works**—*col.*).

Готовность [*см.* **В состоянии готовности к**].

Готовое изделие
A finished product.

Готовый
The **completed** (*or* **finished**) coils are held in place by ...

Гравитационное притяжение
The gravitational pull of Jupiter ...

Градуировать [*см.* **Отградуированный в делениях величиной**].

Градус I
The temperature is measured **in degrees Celsius.**

Градус II [*см.* **Изгибаться на ... градусов, Изменяться на ... градусов, Наклоняться на ... градусов**].

Граммовые количества
This method makes it feasible to produce **gramme** and larger **amounts** (*or* **quantities**) of ^{231}Pa.

Грандиозный [*см. тж.* **Впечатляющий**]
In a spiral galaxy these **dramatic** explosions come about once every 100 years.

Граница [*см. тж.* **Внешняя граница, На границе**]
We should establish a strict **line of demarcation** (*or* **dividing line**) **between** mechanics' work and the work of mechanics' helpers.
The dashed line indicates **the demarcation** (*or* **boundary**) **between** these two regions.

Граница раздела [*см.* **Линия раздела**].

Граница раздела между
The tin/steel interface of tin-plate ...

Граничащий с
Flat regions **bordering** an ocean ...

Граничить на востоке (западе, севере, юге) с
This land mass **is bordered on east (west, north, south) by** highlands.

Граничить с
Laos **borders** Vietnam.
The park **borders on** the shores of the lake.
Wherever high mountains **border** deep seas there are earthquakes.
The continental nuclei are surrounded by or **are contiguous with** larger areas of shield rock.

Граничный
Another **borderline** group is slime moulds; these organisms exhibit both plant and animal characteristics during their life history.
Borderline sciences, such as chemical physics, ...

Грань [*см.* **На грани**].

График [*см. тж.* **В форме графиков, Нанесённый на график, Наносить на график, Отражаться на графике в виде**]
On **plots of** P versus V, curves for ... are steeper than...

Графическое изображение
These relationships may be determined from **graphical displays** (*or* **representations**) **of** experimental data.

Гребень и впадина волны
At other points **the crest of a wave** in one beam coincides with **the trough of a wave** in the other beam.

Греться
Graphite is useful for lubricating parts of machinery which may **run hot.**

Грозящая опасность
The instrument warns aircraft crews of **impending danger.**

Громоздкий [*см. тж.* **Сложный**]
This method **is too cumbersome** (*or* **unwieldy**) for everyday use.
This would lead to rather **cumbersome** (*or* **unwieldy**) expressions.

Грохот взрыва [*см.* **Гул взрыва**].

Грубая и чистовая обработка
The operations include **roughing and finishing of** the flanges.

Грубая модель
A crude model.

Грубая оценка [*см.* **Приближённая оценка**].

Грубо
Foodstuffs may be **broadly** (*or* **roughly**) divided into two classes.
This effect can be estimated **crudely** from ...

Грубо говоря
The absorption coefficient for gamma rays passing through a metal is **roughly** (*or* **approximately**) proportional to the density of the material.
Broadly (*or* **Roughly**) **speaking,** the world's consumption of energy for industrial purposes is now doubling approximately once per decade.
Loosely, ecology can be described as scientific natural history.
As a rough guide weak acids may be regarded as ...

Грубо обтачивать
The first operation **rough turns** the knuckle flange down to the spindle area.

Грубое приближение [*см. тж.* **В грубом приближении**]
The first maps are no more than **rough** (*or* **crude**) **approximations.**

Груз [*см. тж.* **Вес без груза, Вес с грузом**]
The first **shipload** (*or* **cargo**) **of** Russian coking coal reached Japan on October 12.

Груз в контейнерах
The plane takes 29 tonnes of **containerized cargo.**

Грузовое пространство
The ship's **cargo space** is divided into 36 tanks.

Грузоподъёмность
The second crane **is rated at** 5 tons.

Группа [*см. тж.* **Делиться на категории**]
Two research **teams** (*or* **groups**) photographed impacts in metals.

Группами
Sunspots usually appear **in groups** or pairs.
The feeders can be used singly or **grouped.**

Группировать [*см. тж.* **Сгруппировывать**]
All controls are conveniently **grouped together** on this truck.
He **grouped** these minerals **together.**

Группироваться
Human settlements **have been clustered** in the major river basins.

Гул взрыва
The boom from an explosion.

Гусеничный ход [*см.* **На гусеничном ходу**].

Густо окрашиваться
Telomeres **stained** especially **heavily** in these species (*biol.*).

Густо покрыт кратерами
The entire polar region of Mars **is heavily** (*or* **densely**) **cratered.**

Густо усыпанный
A zone **thickly strewn with** asteroids ...

Густонаселённый [*см.* **Наиболее густонаселённый**].

Густонаселённый район
A heavily populated area.

Д

Давать [*см. тж.* **В результате реакции образуется, Из ... получают, Обеспечивать**]
The integration **produced** Eq. (5-16).
This treatment **produces** a paper more suitable for ...
The theory **provides** a great deal of information on ...
Data for other isotopic forms of the molecule **provide** additional relations.
Petroleum **supplies** the hydrocarbon compounds for synthesizing ...
Oxidation of ... **yields** (*or* **gives**) a mixture of aromatic carboxylic acids.
The transistor **delivered** 15 watts.
Sources which have a large extension in the image plane **exhibit** a narrow spectrum in ...
The acid reacts with bases **to form** (*or* **yield,** *or* **give,** *or* **produce**) arsenates.
Slow distillation of ammonium acetate **furnishes** acetamide.
Transistors **gave** improved results.
This method **offers** minimum losses.

This company **is responsible for** over half of Canadian iron ore output.
The pit **is turning out** 800 tons of sand a day.
A 50-50 solder **yields** joints with higher tensiles.
One ton of bauxite **yields** about one ounce of gallium.
The integration **yields** (*or* **gives**) $T_2 = 61.3$.

Давать в сумме
The numbers 1, 2, and 3 **add up to** 6.
All the probabilities taken together must **add up** to 1.

Давать возможность [*см. тж.* **Обеспечивать возможность, Позволять**]
The effect of Venus on artificial probes **has given** astronomers **the chance to** calculate ...
These vectorlike properties **let us** derive an expression that ...
This relation **provides** (*or* **presents**) **a way** (*or* **a possibility,** *or* **a means**) **of** estimating the actual savings.
This **enables** the operator **to** detect changes in amine concentrations.
This method **enables one** (*or* **us**) **to** solve the Hitchcock problem.
The testing machine **makes possible testing** (*or* **makes it possible to test**) large components.
Knowledge of the numerical values of *a* and *c* **offers** (*or* **furnishes**) **a means** (*or* **a way**) **of** determining ...
These curves **permit** the life of bearings **to** be accurately specified.
A sharp peak due to stretching of the aldehydic C-H **serves to** differentiate it from other types of carbonyl compound.
Alpha emission **provides a way for** an unstable nucleus **to** lose two protons and two neutrons simultaneously.
These criteria **provide the means of** classifying (*or* **furnish an opportunity to** classify) the coal by rank.

Давать возможность понять
Analysis of these terms **provides insight into** the nature of the bond itself.

Давать достаточные основания для
This possibility **provides reason enough to** investigate ...

Давать изображение на экране радара
The ultralight airplane **presents** no **radar image.**

Давать информацию
Spectral studies **provide** such **data.**

Давать искру
Steel tools **spark** (*or* **give off sparks**) in certain conditions.

Давать ключ к
This **opens** (*or* **gives,** *or* **offers,** *or* **furnishes**) **a clue to** the individual masses of the two stars.

Давать лишь приблизительное представление о
The total surface of the dry packing **is but a rough index** (*or* **gives but a rough idea**) **of** the surface available for mass transfer.

Давать лучшие показатели (*или* **результаты**), **чем**
The Ejector drill **outperforms** twist, spade, and gun drills.

Давать многое
Thermodynamics **has much to offer** in this respect.

Давать наибольший эффект
It is in analysis of ... that infrared spectrometry **has had its greatest impact.**

Давать направление в работе
The programs are used to **provide guidelines for** the laser designers.

Давать напряжение
The sections can be connected in series **to furnish** (*or* **supply**) **240,000 volts.**

Давать некоторое представление о
To give the flavour of this research I shall describe three experiments.

Давать некоторое представление о том, как
This example **gives** you **some insight into** the way in which climate influences...

Давать необходимый эффект [*см. тж.* **Обеспечивать необходимый эффект**]
Then it was discovered that charge transfer can be achieved without rubbing—that mere contact between unlike surfaces **would do the job.**

Давать нефть
The smallest well **flowed 155 bbl of oil** per day.
These wells **produce oil** from a depth of ...

Давать общее направление
At least, these assumptions **gave** astronomers **a lead.**

Давать объяснение
No theory **offers** a satisfactory **explanation of** the observed facts.
Explanations are offered in a few instances.
This telescope **has supplied a** possible **explanation for** the ultraviolet "clouds".

Давать объяснение тому, что
No **explanation was provided for the fact that** atoms combine to form molecules.

Давать осадок
To leave (*or* **produce**) **a sediment.**

Давать осесть
The precipitates **were allowed to settle.**

Давать основание
Such a wavelength **leads one** (*or* **gives grounds**) **to** expect that ...

Давать основание надеяться, что
This **gives promise that** high power levels may be attained.

Давать основание ожидать, что
This **causes us to anticipate that** the importance of the laser will continue to escalate.

Давать основание полагать, что
This **suggests that** it might be convenient to introduce ...

Давать ответ на
Top-hat furnaces can often **provide** (*or* **supply,** *or* **give**) **the answer to ...**

Давать ответ на вопрос
This concept did not **provide answers to** such problems as the origin of mountain ranges, ...

Давать побочные явления
Cocaine **produces** undesirable **side effects** in the patient.

Давать показания
This flowmeter can be directly calibrated **to read** [*or* **to give** (*or* **provide**) **readings**] in units of flow.

Давать представление о
The difference in... **gives an estimate of** the resonance energy.
The last three chapters **have given** us **an insight into** the workings of the fluvial denudation process.
The foregoing discussion **gives an idea of** the error that would...
Figure 6 **gives an indication of** the variation of specific weight with engine size.
The respiratory quotient **provides a rough idea of** the chemical nature of a material being oxidized.

Давать представление о том ...
To give you an idea how good an approximation this is, ...

Давать преимущества
Since this function can be performed by other technologies also, one must ask what charge-coupling **has to offer.**

Давать разрешение
The name of the agency **granting permission** to make repairs ...

Давать реакцию
Solutions of salts formed from a weak base and a strong acid **show** (*or* **give**) **an** acidic **reaction.**

Давать результаты
Greases and solids **perform** less satisfactorily at lower temperatures.
This method **produces** (*or* **yields,** *or* **gives**) better **results.**
This approach **has some success.**

Давать сведения
Nuclear physics **furnishes** (*or* **supplies,** *or* **provides**) **information** on problems of ...
The analysis **revealed** little **information about ...**

Давать теоретическую основу
We will attempt **to provide some grounding in theory.**

Давать течь
The pipe **developed a leak.**

Давать ток
The generator is capable of **delivering a** welding **current of** 300 amps at 300 volts.
A transformer **supplies** (*or* **provides,** *or* **delivers**) **the current.**

Давать толчок [*см. тж.* **Стимулировать**]
The discovery of acetylcholine **gave impetus to** research concerning ...

Давать точную картину
The isotherms **give an accurate account of** the balance of pressures.

Давать хорошее представление о
The tables **give a good indication** (*or* **idea**) **of** the scope of gravimetry.

Давать хорошие результаты [*см. тж.* **Эффективен**]
The method **works well** only if ...

Давать щелочную реакцию
The solution **reacts alkaline.**

Давать экономию
These factors **effect a saving** (*or* **economy**) **in** operating costs.

Даваться I [*см. тж.* **Приводиться**]
These compounds have the special nomenclature that **appears** in Fig. 5.2.

Даваться II (*матем.*.) [*см. тж.* **Задавать**]
The negative resistance **is given by** $R = R/(A-1)$.

Давая
The potassium chloride and the sulphate of potash-magnesia will react **to yield** (*or* **to form**) potassium sulphate and magnesium chloride.
Only a thousandth of the pellet would burn, **yielding** a third of the laser's output.

Давить на
The surface elements of the clutch **apply pressure to** the rim.

Давление [*см.* **Внутреннее давление, Избыточное давление, Испытывать давление, Находиться под давлением, Оказываемое давление, Перепад давления на, Повышенное давление, Под давлением, Рабочее давление, Сбрасывать давление, Создавать давление**].

Давление на входе (выходе)
Inlet (outlet) pressure.

Давно
This classification **has long been** in use.
The use of such pigments **has long (since) been** abandoned.

Давно известно, что
Geologists **have long been aware that** the organic matter required for petroleum to be formed has accumulated in ...
It has long been known that sunspots usually appear in pairs or groups.

Давно исследованный
The **long-explored** areas ...

Даётся I
A complete review **is available in** a paper published in ...

Даётся II
The absorption flux **is given by** the following equation ...

Даже если
We shall be justified in using a planar geometry, **even though** the system as a whole may be of radial type.

Даже при
Even with such defects single-heterostructure lasers with a room-temperature threshold as low as about 8000 amperes per square centimetre have been made.

Даже при этом
Even so, the interaction rate of the eight intersection regions is more than 100,000 events per second.

Далее I [*см. тж.* **Затем**]
Furthermore, let k_1 be the rate constant for ...
Next (*or* **Further**) is was assumed that ...
In what follows we define ...
Let us **next** consider ...

Далее II
These bands may be **further** resolved into components due to ...

Далее именуемый
The Director of the Office (**here(in)after referred to as** "Director") shall ...
This block, **subsequently referred to as** Sec. 1, serves to ...

Далее посмотрим
Consider next a simple reaction of ...

Далекó [*см.* **Находиться далекó друг от друга, От ... ещё далекó до**].

Далекó друг от друга [*см. тж.* **На большом расстоянии друг от друга**]

Stars **are** so **far apart** (*or* so **distant from each other**) that their encounters must be extremely rare.

Далекó за пределами
This **was much outside** possible experimental error.
Ice once existed **far beyond** its present limits.
This **is well out of** the Stokes flow region.

Далекó за пределы
Very large fragments may roll **well beyond** the base of the cone.

Далекó идущие последствия
The far-reaching consequences of the wave nature of the interacting hadrons can best be appreciated by ...
The fact that our planet rotates has **far-reaching implications.**

Далекó идущий
It appears that there may be **far-ranging** new applications for acoustic surface waves.
This statement is a **far-reaching** and important guide in the studies of ...

Далекó не
The theory of solutions **is** still **far from** accurate.
Interplanetary space **is far from** empty.
The sensitivity for rubidium **is not nearly** so high as for sodium.
Although the new laser **is by no means** tiny, it is unusually compact for a carbon dioxide laser.

Далекó не достаточно
These techniques **are not nearly** sensitive **enough to** demonstrate ...

Далекó не достигать
This laser **does not even approach** the limiting power.

Далекó не оптимальный
The equipment **is far short of optimum.**

Далекó не просто
Finding a larger number **is by no means easy.**

Далекó не так
Other lubricants **were not nearly so** efficient.

Далекó не удаётся
The transition-state theory **falls far short of** the goal of a completely theoretical prediction of rate constants.

Далекó не является
Thus R^S **falls far short of being** a model for the real-number line.

Далекó от [*см. тж.* **Вдали от, На большом расстоянии от берега**]
In regions of nuclei **far removed from** closed shells ...
New towns **(well) apart from** the existing urban districts ...
We shall not perhaps **be** very **wide of** the truth if we say that ...
Away from ...
Remote from ...

Далекó отклоняться от
The frequency of occurrence of ... **departed** (*or* **deviated**) **widely from** the random frequencies expected.

Далекó отстоять друг от друга
The storage facilities **are widely spaced** (*or* **separated**) (*or* **are far apart**).

Далекó расположенные друг от друга [*см. тж.* **Расположенные далеко друг от друга**]
At seven points **widely distributed,** the ground plates are supplemented with iron pipes.

Далекó расположенный
A spinning star can be seen by a **distant** observer to vary regularly if its surface is not uniformly bright.
A signal can be conducted in this fashion between the central nervous system and a **distant** organ.

Далекó расположены друг от друга [*см..* **Далекó отстоять друг от друга, Расположены близко или далекó друг от друга**].

Далёкая галактика
A distant galaxy.

Далёкие друг от друга I
Such **widely separated** places as the Persian Gulf area and Japan ...

Далёкие друг от друга II
Rabbit globin *mRNA* was bound and translated by ribosomes from such **distantly related** forms as trout and kidney bean (*biol.*).

Далёкий [*см. тж.* **На значительном расстоянии от**]
To detect **distant** targets, ...

Далёкий остров
A **remote** (*or* **far-away**) **island.**

Далёкое будущее [*см.* **В далёком** (*или* **отдалённом**) **будущем, Дело далёкого будущего**].

Дальнейшие перспективы
Future trends: the following developments can be expected at some future time.

Дальнейший I [*см. тж.* **В последующих главах**]
In the discussion **that follows,** the properties of semiconductor diode lasers are described.
Such systems will be utilized in **the following** (*or* **subsequent**) discussion.
To obtain **further** information, ...
In **later** chapters electrochemical cells will be treated.

Дальнейший II
The acetone solvent protects the reaction products from **further** oxidation.
Such extracts require **further** purification.

Дальнейший текст
Much of **what follows** (*or* **the following**) is adapted from that article.

Дальний [*см. тж.* **Ближайшие и долгосрочные перспективы**]
It was necessary to start caving from **the far** limits.

Дальний конец
The Earth will attract the near end of the vehicle more strongly than it will attract **the far end.**

Дальняя связь
Long-range communications.

Дальше [*см. тж.* **Значительно дальше, Как мы увидим дальше**]
If the skip is accidentally lowered **beyond** the lowest point of the chute's travel ...
The **farther** the solution has travelled from the mixing chamber, the **further** the reaction will have gone.

Дальше расположенные друг от друга
Lines **farther apart** indicate the weaker regions of the field.

Данные [*см. тж.* **Большое количество данных, Выборочные данные, Детальные данные, Значительное количество сведений о, Из ... можно извлечь некоторые сведения о том, как; Информация, Комплект данных, Косвенные данные, Набор данных, Обработка данных, Подробные сведения о, Результаты, Снимать показания**]
The data on (*or* **for**) heating time ...
There is little **evidence for** the existence of antimonous acid.
These **findings** are in line with recent **results.**
To gather **information** (*or* **data**) **on** performance ...
Knowing the performance **particulars of** the vessel concerned (power, speed, and revolutions) ...
With this apparatus we obtained further **light on ...**

Данные в пользу
There is considerable **evidence for** (*or* **in favour of**) this mechanism.

Данные наблюдений
Observational data.

Данные о
Some **evidence from** sea urchin eggs has indicated ....
Some **data for** the critical points **are** shown in Table 1-3.
These sediments provide **evidence on** the environment of ...
Thus, **the record of** the strata over these positive belts tends to be incomplete.

Данные, полученные в результате измерений ..., указывающие на то, что
They have reported **evidence from** *NMR* **measurements that** growth of ... is accompanied by ...

Данные, приводимые в пользу
We do not believe that any of **the evidence** usually **invoked in favour of** an exclusively biological origin for petroleum is convincing.

Данные рентгеновских исследований
X-ray data were used to determine ...

Данные, указывающие на
There is **evidence for** some specialization of secretion in the various zones.

Данные, указывающие на существование
No **evidence** was found **for the existence of ...**

Данный [*см. тж.* **В данных условиях, Интересующий нас, Рассматриваемый, Тот или иной**]
The reaction **in question** (*or* **under discussion,** *or* **under review,** *or* **of interest**) is stoichiometric.
In the range **covered** the curves are in good agreement with experiment.
Figure 3 shows the result of raising the temperature on **a given** column.
For **a given** forward resistance, silicon diodes have greater capacitance than germanium ones.
This method is well suited for the purpose **in** (*or* **at**) **hand.**
This quantity can be obtained from the phase diagram of the system **involved** (*or* **in question,** *or* **of interest**).
The maximum rate of change of **a particular** characteristic of the orbit ...
This term is used to indicate that the material **referred to** consists of thin, separable lamellae or leaves.
In the **specific** case of 25-percent dehydration ...
Response to a **specified** output is of prime importance.

Дано
The problem is: **Given that** *a* and *b* are even numbers, prove that $a + b$ is even.

Дано ... Найти
Given: The engine consumes 27.5 gallons per hour.
Required: Amounts of gasoline consumed.

Дарвинистский
They were not ready to accept the **Darwinian** mechanisms.

Дать время
To allow time for unmetabolized tracer **to** clear from the blood ...

Дать необходимый эффект
Mere contact between unlike surfaces **will do the job.**

Дать ответ на этот вопрос
How does oxygen evolved by plants regulate photosynthesis? The isolated chloroplast might **provide an answer.**

Дать толчок
This work **has given impetus to** a large number of investigations.

Два или более
When **more than one** product is possible ...

Дважды вырожденный
The Alfvenic mode **is doubly degenerate.**

Две цели [*см.* **Двойная цель** (*или* **назначение**)].

Двигатель мощностью меньше 1 л.с.
A fractional horse power motor.

Двигаться [*см. тж.* **Находиться в движении, Передвигаться**]
When the charges **are in motion ...**
The molecules **move about** in a random way.
The milling heads **travel** in the same direction.

Двигаться в направлении
The vehicle **was headed in the direction of ...**
The Pacific plate **had a** northwesterly **motion** with respect to ... (*geol.*).
The Pacific plate **proceeded on a course** roughly **toward** the northeast.

Двигаться в пространстве
In the course of a single rotation the Earth **would have moved** an appreciable distance **through space.**

Двигаться вниз по склону
Every object has some tendency **to move downhill.**

Двигаться вокруг [*см. тж.* **Облетать ... за ... дней**]
The satellite **circles** the Earth.

Двигаться вперёд и назад
The molecules of the sample can **move** freely **back and forth** along a length of 10 cm.

Двигаться на юг *и т.п.*
Suppose that an air parcel **moves south.**

Двигаться относительно
The plates **move relative to** each other.

Двигаться перпендикулярно
If the electron **is moving perpendicularly** (*or* **normally**) **to** the field, ...

Двигаться по
A pointer **moves across** (*or* **over**) (*or* **traverses**) a scale at the bottom of the assembly.
Some of the electrons can escape from their parent atoms for a short time and **travel** freely **about** the crystal.
Relatively free electrons **move through** the crystal lattice.
Wood was incorporated in the sediment when the glacier **overrode** a forest.

Двигаться по кругу (эллипсу)
A planet **orbits** the Sun not **in a circle** but **in an ellipse.**

Двигаться по орбите
The planet **follows** (*or* **goes around**) **its orbit** of radius *R*.
This rocket **will orbit** [*or* **move** (*or* **travel**) **in its orbit**] in the same direction as the Earth.

Двигаться по поверхности
The initial point **moves over** (*or* **across**) **the surface.**

Двигаться по прямой
The inertia of the metal stream keeps it **moving in** (*or* **along**) **a straight line.**

Двигаться по спирали
The first sphere will **spiral** toward the second sphere.

Двигаться по траектории
The atoms **follow** a parabolic **path.**
The loss of mechanical energy of the body as it **proceeds along** its **trajectory** may be disregarded.
The atom can **take the path** requiring the least climbing.

Двигаться по эллипсу [*см.* **По эллипсу**].

Двигаться под действием
The electron **is propelled by** the applied potential.

Двигаться при помощи
The missile **is powered by** a ramjet engine.

Двигаться самотёком
Coal **gravitates** downwards against a rising flow of air and steam.

Двигаться со скоростью
The Earth's equatorial surface **moves at a rate of** 1,000 miles an hour.

Движение [*см. тж.* **Вращательное движение, Круговое движение, При движении, Приводить в движение, Сообщать движение**]
The direction of the belt **travel ...**
To reverse the direction of **motion of** the gases, ...
The particles continue their **journey.**

Движение воздуха
Air motion.

Движение от
The movement of the central ion **away from** the centre of the oppositely charged sphere ...

Движение транспорта и пешеходов
The bridge has an upper level for **vehicular and pedestrian traffic.**

Дви́жимый желанием
Spurred (on) by the desire for improved aircraft performance,metallurgists have formulated a series of materials able to withstand even higher temperatures.

Движущая сила
The atmosphere is **a driving** (*or* **motive**) **force for** geological processes.
Propelling force.
Motive power here is electric locomotives ...

Движущийся
Traces left by raindrops on the side windows of a car **in motion** (*or* a **moving** car) ...
Charged particles **in motion** produce a magnetic field.
Heat conduction by **mobile** charged particles ...

Двойная стенка [*см.* **С двойными стенками**].

Двойная функция [*см.* **Выполнять двойную функцию**].

Двойная цель (*или* **назначение**)
This shaft has **the dual purpose of** secondary surge shaft and intake shaft.
Disinfectant standardization has **a twofold purpose.**

Двойное преимущество
Twofold benefits are achieved.
The benefits are twofold: 1 ...

Двойной
These advances had a **twofold** effect: the

performance of minicomputers improved, and the size of the systems decreased.
Therefore **double the** quantity of air is required for cooling.

Двоякий
The benefits of ... are **twofold:** 1. ...

Двуслойный
A **two-layer(ed)** structure ...

Двустадийный
A **two-step** (*or* **two-stage**) mechanism ...

Двусторонняя связь
Two-way communication.

Двухкомпонентная смесь
A binary mixture.

Двухступенчатый процесс
A two-step (*or* **two-stage**) **process.**

Двухцелевой
A **dual-purpose** machine ...

Дежурный [*см.* **Для замены в случае необходимости**].

Действие I [*см. тж.* **Арифметическое действие, В результате действия на, Вводить в действие, Влияние, Воздействие, Вредное влияние (*или* действие), Находиться под действием, Не влиять на, Не подвергать действию, Оказывать действие на, Плохое влияние (*или* действие), Под действием, Подвергаться действию, Приводить в действие, Приходить в действие, Радиус действия**]
The action (*or* **function**) **of** the plate modulator ...
Such reagents have **an** oxidizing **action** (*or* **effect**).

Действие II
The algebraic **operations** are performed according to ...

Действие атмосферы
Aluminium is resistant to **atmospheric attack.**

Действие начинается через ... часов [*см.* **Начинать действовать через ... часов**].

Действие ... основано на
The instrument **depends for its action on** the differences in heat conduction from ...

Действителен
The equation **applies** at a low pressure.

Действителен для
This relation **holds** (**good,** *or* **true**) (*or* **is valid**) **for ...**

Действительная часть [*см.* **Вещественная и мнимая части**].

Действительно
For nonideal gases these interactions **do** occur.
To determine if a substance is **truly** (*or* **actually,** *or* **genuinely,** *or* **really**) homogeneous, ...

Действительность [*см.* **В действительности, Не соответствовать действительности**].

Действительный [*см. тж.* **Быть действительным для, Оставаться в силе**]
This assumption **is** still **valid** [*or* **holds true** (*or* **good**)].
The same laws **apply to ...**
The same relationship **holds** (*or* **is valid**) **for** other fuels.

Действительный и мнимый
A complex number has both a **real** part and an **imaginary** part.

Действовать [*см. тж.* **На ... действует, Не действовать**]
The pickup **acts** (*or* **functions,** *or* **operates**) **as** a miniature generator.
The acoustic mechanisms **operate** (*or* **are operative**) whenever ...
Diverse mechanisms **may be at work** in different places on the satellite.
This suggests that such forces **are in operation.**
Oxygen **operates as** an electron acceptor.
Both changes **operate** in the same direction.
Here again some common mechanism **is operating.**
This agreement indicates that no other large force **is operative.**

Действовать быстро [*см.* **Быстродействующий**].

Действовать в качестве
The multivibrator **acts as** a comparator.

Действовать в противоположные стороны
The two forces **act in opposition** (*or* **in opposite directions**).

Действовать в соответствии с программой
Magnetic-tape systems **operate under a program.**

Действовать как
These materials **act as** accelerators.

Действовать на расстоянии
The distance through which this force **acts ...**

Действовать разрушительно на
By its oxidizing action, ozone **is destructive of** many kinds of organic matter.

Действует сила
Where lateral **forces are involved** (*or* **operate**) the resultant moment requires anchor bolts.

Действуют факторы, изменяющие
A number of **factors are operating to affect** the length of the bond.

Действующий в противоположных направлениях
The result from **the opposing forces ...**

Действующие силы
The forces involved (*or* **The operating forces**) are greater than...

Действующий I [*см. тж.* **Силы, действующие между**]
The forces **exerted** (*or* **acting**) **on** a body in motion through the air ...

Действующий II
The system **now in force** may not be the best.
Accelerators **in service today** (*or* **now in operation**) are ...

Действующий вверх
An **upward** force ...

Действующий закон
The dynamic **laws** that **prevail in** mechanics ...

Действующий на
The force **(acting) on** a unit charge ...
The total force **experienced by** an electron ...

Действующий на него
The energy of interaction between a nucleus and the magnetic field **it experiences ...**

Делается попытка
This article **attempts to** offer a perspective on the past history and ...

Делать [*см. тж.* **Выполнять, Как это делается, Превращать в, Производить**]
This method **renders** (*or* **makes**) the material completely impervious to liquids.

Делать анализ
To analyze the blood **for** malaria ...
Satisfactory **analysis** can **be performed** (*or* **carried out**) on these samples.

Делать большие успехи
X-ray research **has advanced** (*or* **come**) **a long way** (*or* **has made great advances**) since the first application to simple crystal structures.

Делать вклад в
Maxwell's greatest **contribution to** astronomy **came** (*or* **was made**) in 1857.
Each molecule **makes a contribution to** the pressure ...

Делать возможным
Our discovery **has made possible** a new method of ...
The low flow rate **permits (of)** stable operation.

Делать возможным создание
These characteristics **make possible** microwave devices that ...

Делать всё возможное
The astronomers **do the best (they can)** (*or* **do their best**) with the tools they have at hand.

Делать вывод (*или* **заключение**) [*см. тж.* **Из этого вытекает** (*или* **следует**), **что; Приходить к выводу**]
Several **conclusions were reached** (*or* **made,** *or* **drawn**).
From these experiments **it was concluded** (*or* **inferred**) **that** in order to ...
To draw a conclusion (*or* **inference**).

Делать вывод о
We can only **infer** a reaction mechanism from indirect experimental evidence.

Thus one can **draw inferences about** the materials on the asteroids' surface.

Делать вывод о том, что
From the estimated rates the scientists **inferred** (*or* **concluded**) **that ...**
The geologist **inferred that** the deformed strata were originally in a soft condition.
From this fact, we **might reason that** the heating of rock will cause expansion of...
We can **make the inference** (*or* **draw the conclusion**) **that** in the early aeons of earth history ...

Делать вывод относительно
From this discussion we can **infer** certain properties of ....
From these experiments some general **conclusions can be drawn** regarding ...

Делать вычисления
The machine **performs** (*or* **carries out,** *or* **does**) **computations for** navigation.

Делать заключение из [*см.* **Выводить заключение**].

Делать замечание
Two general **points** (*or* **remarks**) need **to be made.**

Делать измерения
To take (*or* **make**) **measurements.**

Делать краткий обзор
I **will briefly review** the work which is being done on ...

Делать крупные капиталовложения в
The industry **is investing heavily in** this equipment.

Делать логический вывод
From these statements **logical deductions are drawn that ...**

Делать на заказ
The unit can **be made to order** (*or* **custom made**) in a wide range of wood finishes.

Делать невозможным
This **renders** detection of the equivalence point **impossible.**

Делать непригодным для
The technical difficulties **render** the method **impractical** (*or* **unsuitable**) **for** many applications.

Делать оборот вокруг
The body of the molecule must **make one turn about** (*or* **around**) its axis.

Делать обоснованную догадку о
Then one can **make an informed guess about** the mineralogy of the parent material.

Делать основной упор на
This statement **places primary emphasis upon** physical conditions.

Делать поправку на [*см.* **Вносить поправку на**].

Делать попытку
An attempt will be made to answer these questions.

Делать предположение о том, что
In was assumed that this transport process was fast with respect to ...

Делать приближение
To make an approximation.

Делать расчёты [*см.* **Выполнять расчёты**].

Делать упор на
It is better **to put** more **emphasis on** factors that determine ...
The reader may wonder why such **a** great **stress is being given to** a detailed understanding of the Crab Nebula.
The emphasis in this chapter **has been on** molecular diffusion.
Now and in the future **there must be emphasis on** reliability.
Emphasis is placed (*or* **made**) on the dye laser because ...

Делать фотоснимок
He **makes photographs,** collects rock samples ...
The **photographs were taken** through a glass.
This **picture was made** on Kodachrome film.

Делать целесообразным его применение для
What are the properties of the computer that **recommend it for** power-cont-44 rol.applications?

Делать чудеса
Modern science **has accomplished** (*or* **done**) **wonders**.

Делать экскурс в историю
We **shall make a (retrospective) journey into** the history of science to review ...

Деление I [*см. тж.* **Отградуированный в делениях величиной, С мелкими делениями**]
Graduations on the main scale are 0.020 in. apart.
The dial had **markings** numbered from 55 to 160.

Деление II
Division of the first expression **by** the second gives ...

Деление на I
In this form **the breakdown of** the enthalpy **into** a lowest-level energy and a thermal-energy component is more apparent.

Деление на II
Division of 20 **by** 5 yields 4.

Делить на I [*см. тж.* **Разделять**]
Divide *D* **into** 18.5.
M **should be divided by** *i*.
Ten **divided by** two **equals** five.

Делить на II
The machines to be served **should be broken down into** three groups.
Evaporators for marine use **are classed** (*or* **classified**) **as** horizontal or vertical.
Abrasive materials may **be classified in** two groups.
Hydroxyl compounds which are soluble in water may **be classified into** two main groups.
Such methods may **be divided into** four groups.
The power supply **is divided into** two sections.

Делить на III
The beam of the scale **is graduated into** milligramme divisions.
The range between these two points **is marked off into** 100 equal divisions.

Делить на категории [*см. тж.* **Разбивать на**]
The basically viable theories of gravity can **be** further **separated into** two types: metric theories and non-metric theories.
These crystals can **be classed into** three sections.
Vibrations can **be classified in** three categories: free, forced and self-excited.

Делить на части
This work may **be classified under three heads** [*or* **(sub)divided into three parts**]:
1. Preparation of abstracts;
2. ...
3. ...

Делить пополам
Bisect the side *AB* (*or* the angle *BAC*).
The great circle **bisects** the celestial sphere.
Divide the arc **in two.**

Делиться на I [*см. тж.* **Делить на**]
In the metric system all units **are** exactly **divisible** by 10 or 100.

Делиться на II
Tile **is classified as** load-bearing and non-load-bearing.
Steering-gear **comes under the** following groups: ...
Marine pumping equipment **falls into** two broad classes.
The elements **are classified in(to)** families or groups.

Делиться на категории
These hormones **fall** (*or* **are classified**) **into** four **categories.**

Делиться поровну между
The remaining underground water **is** about evenly **divided between** reservoirs deeper than 800 metres **and** reservoirs shallower than that level.

Дело [*см.* **Иметь дело с, Иначе обстоит дело с**].

Дело в том, что
The point (*or* **matter,** *or* **fact**) **is that** loads are not inputs the system is supposed to follow.

Дело далёкого будущего
The large-scale use of whiskers in composite materials **is** still **a good distance in the future.**
A complete description of the biochemistry of even the simplest cell **is** still **a long way** (*or* **many years**) **in the future.**

Дело касается [*см.* **Если идёт речь о**].

Дело обстоит иначе [*см. тж.* **Это не так**]
The situation is different now.

Дело обстоит иначе когда
The situation is reversed if the gas is highly soluble.

Дело обстоит совсем иначе
In the second case **we have a completely different situation.**

Дело усложняется тем, что
The added complication is that we must include ...

Делящийся на
We would have a series **divisible by** 4.

Демонстрирование
The detected output is suitable for **presentation** on the screen.

Демонстрировать [*см. тж.* **Показано**]
I will now proceed **to show** how this result was obtained.

Демонстрироваться [*см. тж.* **Выдаваться, Выставлен**]
This **is depicted** (*or* **shown,** *or* **exhibited,** *or* **displayed,** *or* **pictured,** *or* **illustrated**) in Fig. 3.
The electrical impulse from the cell **is displayed on** an oscilloscope.
This loader **was displayed** (*or* **shown,** *or* **exhibited,** *or* **on exhibit**) at the recent mining machinery exhibition.
Also **on display** (*or* **on show,** *or* **on view,** *or* **on exhibit**) **were** a range of pump units.
New technical developments in processes and materials **are featured in** a number of exhibits.

Демонстрироваться на экране
The output **is displayed on the** oscilloscope **screen.**

День за днём
Operating **day after day** at low efficiency makes the machine more expensive the more you use it.

Держать в запасе [*см.* **Иметь в запасе**].

Держать в поле зрения
The ground stations are so positioned that the satellite **has** at least one of them **in view.**

Держать в резерве
One of the pumps **is held** (*or* **kept**) **in reserve.**

Держать на вытянутой руке
To hold at arm's length.

Держать штат [*см.* **Иметь штат**].

Держаться на безопасном расстоянии от
All personnel should **keep clear of** (*or* **away from**) high-voltage equipment.

Десятичный знак [*см. тж.* **До ... десятичного знака**]
In division one can obtain as many **decimal places** as necessary.

Десятичный логарифм
The logarithm to the base 10 of ...

Десяток [*см. тж.* **Много десятков километров, Несколько десятков**]
The duration of these currents varies from millimicroseconds to **tens of** microseconds.

Деталь
Wire, bands, and similar **articles** are drawn continuously through the bath.
The welded **component** (*or* **part**) is automatically ejected from the machine.
The work (*or* **workpiece,** *or* **piece**) is set upon the worktable.

Деталь, изготовленная без нарушения допусков
A within-tolerance part.

Деталь, изготовленная с нарушением допусков
An out-of-tolerance part.

Детально [*см. тж.* **Более подробно, Во всех подробностях, Достаточно детально, Подробно**]
Let us investigate these movements **in great depth** (*or* **in detail**).
Six crystals were examined **in detail** (*or* **thoroughly**).
It is necessary to consider this problem **in some detail.**
The theory has been **extensively** investigated by many authors.

Детальные данные
That rocket has provided the first **comprehensive data** on ...

Детальный [*см. тж.* **Всеобъемлющий, Подробный**]
A new **comprehensive** catalogue has been issued.

A picture **with full details** is presented.
For an **extended** discussion of this subject see Chap. 3.

Детальный анализ
These sublevels permit a more **sophisticated treatment** of atomic spectra.

Дефект [*см. тж.* **Без дефектов, Брак, Обнаружение дефектов, Устранять дефект**]
A dangerous **flaw** in design ...
Streaks and other **flaws** causing rejection of moulded items often result from improper storage.
Defect, Blemish, Imperfection.

Дефектный
If no difference in performance occurs the gland is not **at fault** (*or* **faulty**).
The service man can check out the receiver and locate the **offending** component.

Дефекты обработки
The connecting rods had **machining errors** in the bores.

Дефицитен
In South America and Africa, coal **is scarce** (*or* **is in short supply**).

Дефицитный материал
A critical (*or* **scarce,** *or* **hard-to-get**) **material.**

Дешевле
These amplifiers **are lower in cost** (*or* **cheaper,** *or* **less expensive**).
This machine can do the job **at less cost.**

Дешёвый
This equipment **is low in cost.**
Low-priced (*or* **Low-cost,** *or* **Inexpensive**) parts ...

Деятельность
To investigate brain **function, ...**

Деятельность распространяется на
Thomas Edison's **activities extended into** chemistry, sound recording, ...

Диаграмма
The boiling-point **diagram** for the system ...

Диаметр [*см. тж.* **В диаметре, В поперечнике, Внутренний диаметр, По всему диаметру колонки, По диаметру**]
The largest raindrops **are** about 6 mm **across.**
The tubing **is 2 in. in diameter.**
Generating tubes, **of two-inch diameter** seamless steel ...

Диаметр молекулы
The molecular diameter.

Диаметр ... составляет от ... до
Small domestic wells **range in diameter from 5 to 10 cm.**

Диаметрально противоположный I
I pierced the ball at two **diametrically opposite** points.
Collisions will be observed at two points **diametrically opposed.**

Диаметрально противоположный II [*см. тж.* **Прямо противоположный**]
The situation is just **the opposite** here.
Exactly **the converse** situation will prevail if ...

Диаметром
The cell consists of a cylindrical glass vessel 3 mm **in diameter** (*or* **of diameter** 3 mm).
The particle is a few microns **across.**
The alloy is available in bar stock **in diameters up to** 2 in.
A molecule **with diameter** *d* ...
Craters **with diameters of** 100 m and larger ...

Диапазон [*см. тж.* **В диапазоне, В широком диапазоне, Изменяться в диапазоне, Лежать в диапазоне, Рабочий диапазон**]
The range of accuracy of pneumatic gauges ...
A wide **assortment** (*or* **variety,** *or* **range**) **of** shapes ...
Polymers with a broad **spectrum of** use ...
Grey iron is an iron-base material **within** broad composition **limits.**
Potential applications of belt conveyors cover the whole **gamut of** industrial operations.
Focal-plane shutters may have **a range of** speeds from several seconds to 1/1250 sec.

Диапазон температур
It maintains a tight seal over **a temperature span** (*or* **range,** *or* **interval**) stretching from -310 to 500°F.

Диета [*см.* **Лечение диетой**].

Дизельный привод [*см.* **С дизельным приводом**].

Дилетант
For both the physicist and **the layman** the principal interest is in ...

Дискуссия
Speculation (*or* **Discussion**) **about** the possible existence of magnetic monopoles has persisted for centuries.

Дискутироваться [*см.* **Горячо дискутироваться**].

Дискутируемый предмет
The origin of dolostones is a widely **debated topic** among geologists.

Дистанционно [*см.* **На расстоянии**].

Дистанционно управляемый
Azimuth-reference devices for **remotely operating** (*or* **controlled**) oceanographic instruments ...

Дифференциация
Our model is reliable in **differentiating among** relatively similar species.

Дифференцирование по [*см. тж.* **Проводить дифференцирование по**].
Differentiation with respect to time ...

Дифференцировать по
Differentiate the payload **with respect to** specific impulses.

Длина [*см. тж.* **В длину, По всей длине, По длине**]
The total **run** (*or* **length**) **of** pipe is divided into independent circuits.

Длина волны [*см.* **На волне**].

Длина ... составляет от ... до [*см.* **Ширина ... составляет от ... до**]

Длиной [*см. тж.* **Толщиной**]
The apparatus consists of a capillary tube 5 in. **in length** (*or* **long**).
A straight line **of length** l =41 in. ...

Длительная операция
Long-run jobs are obvious candidates for automatics.

Длительная перегрузка
Prolonged overload (conditions).

Длительное воздействие
This film is capable of resisting **prolonged exposure to** the atmosphere.

Длительное время [*см.* **В течение длительного времени, Продолжительное время**].

Длительное хранение [*см. тж.* **Возможность длительного хранения, При длительном хранении**]
Long-term (*or* **Prolonged**) **storage.**

Длительность [*см.* **Большая продолжительность**].

Длительные испытания
Prolonged service **testing** has proved that ...

Длительный [*см.* **Продолжительный**].

Длительный период [*см.* **В течение продолжительного времени** (*или* **периода**)].

Длиться [*см. тж.* **Продолжаться I**]
An epileptic seizure may **last** only a few minutes.

Для [*см. тж.* **Важность для, Важный для, Весьма ценно для, Вредный для здоровья, Использовать для, Непрозрачный для, Общий для, Подходить для, Предназначаться для, Прозрачный для, Проницаемый для, С целью, Типичный для, Характерный для**]
For (the purpose of) calculating the rotation of mixtures ...
In an effort to determine (*or* **With the aim of** determin**ing**) the principal corroding acid ...

Для большой нагрузки
The power saw is **a heavy-** (*or* **high-**)**duty** unit able to take deep cuts.

Для воротка [*см.* **Под вороток**].

Для выяснения возможности его использования в
The gas was studied **as a possibility for** refrigeration systems.

Для ... данного размера
For a given size crater ...

Для декоративных целей
Anodized aluminium is used **for ornamental purposes.**

Для достижения этой цели
To attain (*or* **accomplish**) **these ends** (*or* **With this aim in mind**) accuracy of classification has been subordinated to ...

Для замены в случае необходимости
This power supply is **for standby use** (*or* **duty**).

Для иллюстрации
As an illustration, Fig. 3 shows streak camera photographs of emergent waves.
By way of (*or* **For the purposes of**) **illustration** we shall treat the following equation ...

Для информации
For reference we have included definitions of all quantities relevant to ...

Для использования
These storage batteries have been developed **for** submarine **duty.**
The tester is designed **for** laboratory **use.**
Tools have been developed **for use** (*or* **to be used**) **in** a small-diameter tube.

Для использования в домашнем хозяйстве
A bleaching agent **for household use ...**

Для использования позже
This frees the symbol *m* **for later use** as a quantum number.

Для конкретности
To be specific, let us assume that the resonant molecules are in the absorbing phase.

Для которого характерно
The principal forms of anemia **marked** (*or* **characterized**) **by** a decrease in red cell formation are iron deficiency and pernicious anemia.

Для красоты
A stone facing may be added **for appearance.**

Для краткости
For brevity (sake), this process will be referred to as "eddy diffusion".
This interference is usually termed the "alkali metal interference" **for short** [*or* **for brevity (sake)**].

Для лёгких грузов
A flow rack **for light-duty applications** comes in a wide choice of shapes.

Для лучшего использования
In order to make the best use of the equipment ...
To make the most use of the cranes ...

Для лучшего понимания
To gain a better understanding of (*or* **a better insight into**) this mechanism, ...

Для малой нагрузки
A **light-duty** motor ...

Для научных исследований в области монокристаллов
Single-crystal research metals like iridium, osmium, ...

Для начала
As a preliminary we briefly review the diffraction of ...
The core will operate at low power **to start** (*or* **begin**) **with.**

Для наших целей
Brief summaries of several major categories will suffice **for present** (*or* **our**) **purposes.**

Для него
Mining apparatus and automatic feed control **therefore ...**
A series of experiments was conducted **for the benefit of** our company.

Для ... необходимо сделать следующее
To remove a control unit, **proceed as follows: ...**

Для ... нет готовых рецептов
The application of stainless steel for corrosion resistance **is never a "cut and dried" matter.**

Для нужд потребления
The Colorado River supplies more water **for consumptive use** than any other river in the U.S.

Для нужд человека
To supply fresh water **for human needs, ...**

Для обеспечения
Carbamite is added **to bring about** (*or* **ensure**) gelatinization of the nitrocellulose.
The end flanges are welded together **for** greater rigidity.

Для обеспечения безопасности

For safety (sake) it is essential to have some purge system.
The electrode is enclosed in a special housing **for reasons of safety.**

Для облегчения
To ease the task of transport, ...
To facilitate further observations, ...
For ease of winding, the conductor ends are allowed to overhang the core.

Для обозначения [*см. тж.* **В отношении**]
The term "hot tearing" is used **in reference to** the rupture of a casting owing to ...
The term "hydride" is used **to describe** a compound of an element with hydrogen.
To denote, To designate.

Для общности
This term has been retained here **for generality.**

Для объяснения
To account for such facts as these, the concept of resonance must be introduced.

Для определённости
For (the sake of) definiteness (*or* **For definiteness sake),** we shall say that the tortoise travels at one mile per hour.

Для подготовки к
This is a mechanical finishing process for polishing zinc-base die-castings **preparatory to** (*or* **to prepare them for**) plating.
The heat sink cools the fluid to its original temperature **in preparation for** another cycle.

Для полного понимания
Gaining a complete understanding of how the earth formed will require learning how ...

Для полноты
For completeness (sake) the basic ideas are outlined in Appendix F.

Для получения
Oxidation can be carried out **to give** (*or* **yield,** *or* **produce**) nitroamino compounds.
The evidence is still insufficient **to provide** a clear picture.

Для ... понадобится несколько лет
The synthetic production of a living system **is several years away.**

Для понимания
The textural aspect of coal is of importance **for an understanding of** the behaviour of ...
This analogy is sometimes useful **in understanding** the chemistry of various nitrogen compounds.

Для предотвращения [*см. тж.* **Во избежание**]
The turntable is heavy, **to ensure against** spurious rotational motions.
Measures **to avoid** (*or* **prevent,** *or* **preclude**) accidents have been taken.

Для примера [*см. тж.* **Например**]
By way of example (*or* **illustration**), assume that the water rate will be 20 percent greater than the theoretical minimum.
As an example, ...

Для примера берём
We take **as our example** the bedding plane of a sedimentary rock.

Для проверки
As a check on (*or* **To check**) the reading just obtained the mechanism is reset to zero.

Для простоты
A momentary on-off switch is recommended **for ease of** instrument use.
For (the sake of) simplicity (*or* **For simplicity sake**) assume that ...
Normalized ordinates are avoided **for (the sake of) simplicity.**
For simplicity's sake.

Для работы
The mechanical energy necessary **to run** (*or* **operate**) the generator ...

Для размещения
A terminal box is provided **to accommodate** the necessary busbar connections, etc.

Для сдачи "под ключ"
The press system was designed and built **on a turnkey basis.**

Для справок [*см. тж.* **Для информации**]
Use Table II **as a reference source.**
Chromatograms are stored **for** future **reference.**

Для сравнения
The results of our calculations are added **for comparison.**
For comparison (purposes) I include the Sun.
For reference, two other relations derived from earlier theories are also plotted in the same figure.

Для сравнения отметим, что
By comparison, the aircraft engines, powered with atomic fuel, will ...
For comparison (purposes), water has a density of ...

Для того времени
It was Arrhenius who made **the then** bold postulate that ...

Для того, чтобы [*см. тж.* **С целью, Чтобы убедиться в том, что**]
More extensive research is necessary **before** the significance of these findings can be understood.
Something more is needed **if we are to** understand how the Earth came to possess its core of iron.
A population inversion must be produced **if** laser action **is to** occur.
For energy **to be** absorbed radiation of a frequency ... must be supplied.
To ensure that ... remain constant, the electrode solution is usually a buffer.
Careful maintenance is essential **if** the machine **is to** give service and reliability of which it is capable.
All components must be accurately aligned **in order that** the pellet **(should) be** impacted symmetrically.
In order that *g* falls to 0.99 *g*, *y* must be 20 miles.
So that the worm and roller **will** continue to mesh, the contour of the underside of the worm gear is an arc with...
The rod should be made of mild steel **so that** it **will** bend easily.
For the laser approach **to** succeed the fuel must be compressed to 10,000 times normal liquid density.
In order for the switching system **to** work properly, the operations of the system must be synchronized.

Для того, чтобы ... был
If the isolation process **is to be** inexpensive, ...

Для того, чтобы выполнять
In order for such measurements **to be made, ...**

Для того, чтобы добиться хорошего согласия
For good agreement with the observed diamagnetic susceptibilities it is necessary to include ...

Для того, чтобы его рассматривать как
The properties of ... are sufficiently different from ... **for it to be treated as** a new kind of particle.

Для того, чтобы лучше представить себе
For better visualization of these ideas, we shall consider ...

Для того, чтобы отнести ... к категории
For a structure **to be classified as** a chargecoupled device it must possess ...

Для того, чтобы получить
Such extracts require further separation **before** the desired product **can be obtained** in reasonable purity.

Для того, чтобы это произошло
(In order) for this to happen, the tube must have a bias equal to ...

Для ... требуется
Making ... **requires** five kilograms of corn.

Для уверенности в
As an assurance of (*or* **To ensure**) complete decomposition of the nitrate, heat the oxide to constant mass.

Для удобства
Many of the trivial terms are still used **as (a matter of) convenience** [*or* **for convenience (sake)** (*or* **for the sake of convenience**)].

Для упрощения [*см.* **Для простоты**].

Для устранения вибрации
Where chatter is a problem (*or* **To eliminate chatter**) use ...

Для уточнения разъясняем, что
We have used the term sediment under the simplified definition given in Chapter 1; **to be more specific,** *sediment* is fragmented mineral and organic matter derived from ...

Для учёта
The analysis must be modified **to accommodate** the fact that ...
Formulas were developed **to account for** the effect of external pressure.
To correct for the effect of pressure drop on gas velocity ...
A simple modification is necessary **to take account of** non-equilibrium conditions.
To take into account (*or* **To allow for**) magnetic deflection ...
Corrections should be made **to account for** the distortion of ...

Для ... характерно [*см. тж.* **Характеризоваться**]
Typical of this method **is** the use of stereoscopic plotting instruments.
These regions **are typified by** the presence of volcanoes and ...

Для целей
Coke **for** metallurgical **uses** (*or* **purposes**) ...
For the purpose of design, consider ...

Для целей вычисления
For purposes of formula weight **calculation,** it is convenient to ...

Для чего
Potentiometry involves the measurement of the potential of a galvanic cell, **for which purpose** potentiometers are used.

Для экономии места
We will not dwell on this point **to save room.**

Для этого [*см. тж.* **С этой целью**]
It is possible to separate the hysteresis and eddy current losses; **to do this** (*or* **to accomplish this,** *or* **to this end,** *or* **for this purpose,** *or* **with this aim in view**), the total losses are plotted against ...
Nickel and chromium are applied to automobile parts to preserve a good appearance, but **to do so** they must also prevent corrosion.

Для этого необходим
To do this requires high voltage.

Для этого необходимо сделать следующее
To assemble the overload check valves, the chart plate must be removed. **Proceed as follows: ...**

Для этого нужно только
All one has to do is to transfer the system to ...

Для этого требуется
To do this would require a fixed-frequency laser.

Для этой цели [*см. тж.* **С этой целью**]
The camera was built specially **for the job** (*or* **for this purpose**).

Для ясности
For (purposes of) clarity (*or* **For clarity sake**), Fig. 2 illustrates a typical element.

Днём и ночью
In the upper layers of the atmosphere atoms and molecules emit light **both by day and at night.**

Дно [*см. тж.* **На дно, Осаждаться на дне**]
The floor of the truck body ...
A thin layer of dirt has accumulated on **the floor** (*or* **bottom**) **of** the tank.
The ocean **floor** (*or* **The floor of** the ocean).

До I [*см. тж.* **Доводить до**]
The lake is **up to** 600 m deep.
The total number of asteroids is estimated to be **as high as** 100,000.
As many as 50 individual reaction steps might be necessary for complete synthesis.
If the region of accumulation is extended **as far as** the emitter ...
These losses may be **as much as** 1.5% of the silver present.
Barretters can measure powers **as small as** 10^{-8} watt.
We have made wire in sizes **down to** 0.005 in diameter.
The heater will heat the gas **to** the desired temperature.
This will heat the thermistor enough to lower the resistance **to** 200 ohms.
Pieces weighing **up to** (*or* **not over**) three kilograms may be used for the test.

До II [*см. тж.* **Впредь до, За (один) год до, Иметь толщину до**]
The group I *tRNAs* arose **prior to** the others (*biol.*).
Prior to the seventeenth century ...
Until the Three Mile Island accident the most widely discussed type of reactor malfunction was ...

Prior to testing, all specimens were dried.
This decreases time **to** rupture.

До III
Paste adhesives are knife-coated **to** uniform thickness.

До IV [*см. тж.* **Перед**]
A globe valve is installed in the supply air line, **upstream from** (*or* **of**) the reducer, so that the air may be shut off by hand.

До V [*см.* **С точностью до**].

До абсурда
His goals as a geologist were ambitious **to the point of irrationality.**

До бесконечности
Thus, a constant becomes a pseudo first derivative and a first derivative becomes a pseudo second derivative, and so on **to infinity** (*or* **ad infinitum**).
The ray can propagate **indefinitely** without any loss of power.

До ..., включительно
Diameters range from 1/4 in. to **2 in. inclusive.**
Sizes **through 4 in.** can be used.
Data available **through 1983** (*or* **up to 1983 inclusive**) are published in our recent paper.
The individual particles of radiation emerge with a spectrum of energies and a wide range of velocities, **up to and including** the velocities of light.

До глубины
The parts are carburized **to a depth of 0.020 in.**
The hole was drilled **to a depth of 14,054 ft.**
Wells must be drilled **as deep as 1 mile** to obtain brines of bromine.

До ... десятичного знака
The temperature values have been calculated **to the third (decimal) place.**
Evaluate $1/\sqrt{2}$ **to three decimal places.**

До ... значащей цифры
This magnitude is known **to 6 significant figures** (*or* **to the sixth significant digit**).

До и после обработки
Both **pre- and post-machining** inspection operations are performed.

До и после рождения
Prenatal and postnatal irradiation ...

До или во врéмя
This is done **either in advance of** excavation **or as it proceeds.**

До конца [*см.* **Доводить реакцию до конца, Идти до конца**].

До краёв
Fill the bowl **(up) to the brim.**

До максимума
The planet's distance from the Sun has increased **to a maximum.**

До мельчайших деталей (*или* **подробностей**)
The microscope reveals the structure of material **to the last detail.**

До минимума [*см. тж.* **Сводить к минимуму**]
The planet's orbital velocity has slowed **to a minimum.**

До настоящего времени [*см. тж.* **До сих пор**]
The laser used **to date** has required ...
The gap between the two portions of Saturn's ring is called "Cassini's division" **to this** (*or* **the present**) **day**.
The switch makes possible **heretofore** impractical applications of ...
Huge reserves of ore, **hitherto** virtually untouched, will become available.
To date our highest emitter power has been ... wt/cm^2.
This movement is observed **to the present** (*or* **this**) **day.**
Until the present time few investigations have been conducted of ...
Up to now, there has been no detailed work done to find ...

До настоящей стадии
Up to this point in biological progress, all recognized living things have proven to consist of one or more cells.

До некоторой степени
The moisture content of the film has affected **to some degree** (*or* **extent**) the quality of the film.
The positions of these bands depend **to some extent** on ...
Fired enamels **somewhat** resemble organic coatings.

До неузнаваемости [*см.* **Изменяться до неузнаваемости**].

До нуля [*см.* **Падать до нуля**].

До определённой (*или* **некоторой) глубины**
Counterboring to enlarge the diameter of the hole **over part of the depth ...**

До отказа
Push the valves up **as far as they will go.**
Resetting occurs even with the reset valve turned **fully** clockwise.
Screw the nut **tight.**
Press the button **well home.**
Pressing the accelerator pedal **all the way down** will open ...

До пересечения с
These projections are extended **until they intersect** the projection of ...
Extend one of the sides of the *H* projection **to intersect** two of the lines of ...

До последнего времени
Until (very) recently, most porcelain enamels possessed limited alkali resistance.
Until (very) recent times the Nile valley was not really irrigated.

До последних лет
Until recent years (*or* **Until recently**) there was little direct evidence on this point.

До предела
Extend the line in either direction **as far as it will go.**

До разрушения [*см.* **Испытывать до разрушения**].

До сáмого [*см. тж.* **Вплоть до**]
The atom need not climb **all the way to** an energy peak.

До середины
The scale extends only to 4 million years, which is about **halfway into** the Pliocene Epoch.

До сих пор [*см. тж.* **До настоящего времени**]
This technique is one of the most effective separation methods **yet** devised.
Atomic hydrogen remains a gas at the lowest temperature we have **yet** investigated.
So far it has been assumed that the field applied to the gas is uniform.
The designs discussed **thus** (*or* **so**) **far** provide examples of ...
To this point the assumption has been made that ...
The discussion **up till** (*or* **to**) **now** (*or* **up to the present**) has been based upon ...
This can be done more rapidly and accurately than has **hitherto** been possible.
Up to this point it has been possible to work entirely with the concept of ...
The applications **heretofore** have tended towards special purpose machines.
The other investigations mentioned **up until this point** can be arranged without sending the patient to hospital.

До совпадения с
Rotate the inner disk **until** -10°C on the scale *A* **is opposite** the figure representing 6500 feet on the scale *B*.
This is accomplished through the revolution of the *H* and *P* planes **into coincidence with** *V*.
Rotate the micrometer sleeve **into alignment with** the zero mark on the thimble.

До срока
Several months **ahead of schedule ...**

До такого уровня, что
Charge may accumulate **to the point where** an industrial process will have to shut down temporarily.
This solution is concentrated **to the point where** (*or* **to such a degree that**) it will solidify immediately when cooled ...

До такой степени, когда
Few small *RNA* viral types have been studied **to the point where** a satisfactory picture of the replicatory processes can be presented (*biol.*).
We hope the instrument sensitivity will be improved **to the point where** galaxy clustering can be detected.

До температуры, превышающей... на несколько градусов
Cooling the tube **to within a few degrees of** absolute zero.

До тех пор пока [*см. тж.* **Пока**]

As long as there is enough positive electrical charge on ..., any chemical composition can exist.

This relationship will be maintained **for as long as** the proto-solar system remains within the cloud.

So long as there is a significant disparity between the grade of the ore being currently mined and the grade of the total ore reserves, an unbalanced condition exists.

These systems work only **so long as** they are intact.

До тех пор пока не

The nucleus continues to lose energy **until** it stops.

До того

Until (*or* **Up to**) **then** theoretical hydrodynamics had been largely an academic discipline.

До того как

Till (*or* **Until,** *or* **Before**) this gear was developed the chain steering-gear was the only type ...

The older strata were deformed and eroded **prior to being** covered by the later sediment.

До упора

The connector is inserted **up to the stop** at the rear.

Добавление [*см.* **При добавлении ... к**].

Добавлением

The intermediate precipitate is converted to lead (II) sulphide **by more** hydrogen sulphide.

Добавлять [*см. тж.* **К ... следует добавить**]

Each layer of semiconducting material **is doped with** a small amount of impurity.

The solution **was added to** the bottle with the carrier.

To our oil in water emulsion mentioned above **we add** a little soap.

The Bohr orbit and the angular momentum can be specified **by appending** the appropriate letter **to** the principal quantum number.

Добавлять каплями

500 g of this solution **was added dropwise to** the mixture.

Добавлять примесные элементы

The *n*-type semiconductor **is doped with elements** having an excess of electrons compared to the host material.

Добавлять частями

380 g of $KMnO_4$ **was added portionwise to** a solution of ...

Добиваться

To gain (*or* **attain,** *or* **achieve**) the flexibility needed for ...

The reason for this construction is **to get** the tube **to** withstand a high voltage.

To make 440 stainless-steel bearings work at high speed, ...

To obtain correct filter operation ...

To strive for higher productivity ...

Добиваться более ясного понимания

The information supplied by Mössbauer spectroscopy has been helpful to chemical theoreticians in their effort **to gain a clearer understanding of** (*or* **a better insight into**) bonding interactions in complex molecules.

Добиваться большой экономии

Engine repair depots can **gain important savings** by overhauling worn valve stems, connecting rods and other engine parts.

Добиваться многократного увеличения

It will thus be possible **to gain a large factor** in target volume.

Добиваться преимущества

Advantages can **be gained from** such effects as ...

Добиваться того, чтобы

The period can **be made** dependent upon the input light intensity.

Добиваться точности

He has refined the technique **to obtain an accuracy of** 10 decimal places.

Доброжелательно [*см.* **Встречен доброжелательно**].

Доброкачественный

In this manner a maximum amount of **sound** (*or* **quality**) steel is produced.

Добывать

These metals can **be extracted** (*or* **mined**) in useful quantities.

Добывать карьерным способом
The limestone **is quarried from** natural deposits.

Добывать рентабельно
Conglomerates **have been profitably mined.**

Добыча
The extraction (*or* **mining,** *or* **winning**) **of** ore ...
Rates of **extraction of** these non-renewable fossil fuels ...
Principal oil **production** is **from** the Devonian formation.

Добыча полезных ископаемых
Extraction (*or* **Mining**) **of** useful minerals.

Доверие [*см.* **Вселять доверие к, Не внушать доверия**].

Довод
We use physical **arguments** based on ...

Довод в пользу [*см. тж.* **Ещё один довод в пользу**]
There is another **point** (*or* **argument**) **in favour** (*or* **in support**) **of** the indirect method.

Довод против
This is **a** serious **argument against** the existence of the monopole.

Доводить до I
Huygens **brought** the total number of satellites **to** six.

Доводить до II
The atoms **had been brought to** an accurately known speed.
The concentration **was brought up to** the desired level.
Start the compressor slowly and gradually **work up to** the required speed.

Доводить до заданного размера
The pivot hole **is finished to size** after the hardening operation.

Доводить до заданных размера и формы
The material can **be brought to size and shape** by conventional methods.

Доводить до кипения
The author **brought** the mixture **to the boiling point.**

Доводить до меньшего размера
Copper rods are subsequently **worked down to smaller size** by rolling.

Доводить до минимума [*см.* **Сводить к минимуму**].

Доводить до сведения общественности
The purpose of the paper was **to bring to public notice** the potential of the steam engine for improving ...

Доводить до совершенства
To bring to perfection.

Доводить до современного уровня
Engineering societies develop standards and **bring them up to date.**
For this edition the original text **has been brought up to date** (*or* **updated**), and some new material added.

Доводить до уровня
Many years will elapse before the theory **is developed to the point** (*or* **brought to the level**) where it is useful in engineering design.

Доводить реакцию до конца
Sulphuric acid may be added **to drive** (*or* **bring**) **the reaction to completion.**

Довольно [*см. тж.* **Достаточно, Сравнительно**]
These variations can be predicted **reasonably** well.
The burning rate is **fairly** (*or* **rather**) high.

Довольно большой
Hydrogen sulphide must have formed a **reasonable** portion of the primitive atmosphere.

Довольно легко
It is a relatively simple matter to correct for ...

Довольно обычный метод
Reverse zoning **is not uncommon.**

Довольно плохо согласуется с
These results **are in rather poor agreement with** the observed binding energy.

Довольно подробно [*см. тж.* **Рассматривать довольно подробно**]
The method enabled us to investigate **in considerable detail** how ...

Довольно твёрдый
Moderately hard deposits are obtained.

Довольно хороший [*см.* **Находиться в довольно хорошем согласии с**].

Довольно часто [*см. тж.* **Более или менее часто**]
Meteorites **every so often** impact the earth.
This **not infrequently** introduces an error.

Догадка [*см. тж.* **Лишь догадка, Предположение**]
All this is not merely **guesswork.**

Догадываться [*см. тж.* **Предполагать**]
The nature of this star can only **be inferred,** since it has not been observed directly.

Догонять
The reflected rarefaction wave will always **catch up with** (*or* **overtake**) the incident shock.
Jupiter **catches up with** (*or* **on**) these particles in their orbits (*or* Jupiter **catches them up**).

Дойти до нас
Two different types of observations **have come down to us** from the Islamic world.

Доказательство [*см. тж.* **Косвенное доказательство того, что; Указывать**]
The evidence for the presence of ... is not fully convincing.
This is sufficient **demonstration** (*or* **proof**) **of** the efficacy of the device.

Доказательство обратного
However, **evidence to the contrary** exists.

Доказательство от обратного (*матем.*)
Poisson demolished the wave theory of light by **reductio ad absurdum.**

Доказывать [*см. тж.* **Указывать**]
This **establishes that** x_n is a Cauchy sequence.

Доказывать или опровергать
More data are needed **to prove or disprove** this suggestion.

Доказывать обратное [*см.* **Пока не доказано обратное**].

Доказывать справедливость
These results seemed **to give proof to** the idea of appreciable dissociation of ...

Доказывать теорему
This establishes (*or* **proves**) **the theorem.**
By purely mathematical reasoning it is possible **to demonstrate** (*or* **prove**) **a theorem** which ...
Thus the theorem is proved.

Доказывать утверждение
Thus we have established our claim (*or* **assertion**) concerning ...

Доказывать, что
This is proof (*or* **evidence**) (*or* **This proves**) **that** the magnetic field is enormous.

Документально доказано, что
It has been well documented that the nucleus plays the principal role in ...

Долго [*см.* **В течение длительного времени, В течение многих лет**].

Долго не заживать
Such sores **take a long time to heal.**

Долговечность [*см. тж.* **Испытание на долговечность**]
Ageing (quality) (*or* **Longevity**) **of** paper, etc.,
Durability.
Life of a machine ...
Useful life.
Longevity depends primarily on nutrition.

Долговечный [*см.* **Существовать долго**].

Долговременный
Good **long-term** stability is a major factor.

Долгоживущий (*антон.* **Короткоживущий**)
To obtain temporal resolution of a **long-lived** emission from a **short-lived** one, ...

Долгосрочный [*см.* **Ближайшие и долгосрочные перспективы**].

Должен [*см. тж.* **Вынужден**]
The energy requirement per individual **is bound to** increase.
The loads a building **is called upon to** support are dead load and live load.
The control engineer **is faced with** determining the optimum value of K_p.

A mechanical breakdown of the material **is liable to** cause trouble.

Должен быть
There are bound to be smaller orbiting objects in greater profusion.
A number of problems still **remain to be** solved.

Должен быть запущен
The satellite **is (due) to be** launched next year.

Должен быть таким, при котором
It is required of g **that** its domain **shall** contain numbers x as close to ...

Должен оказаться
Such schemes **are bound to be** disastrous in the long run.

Должное направление
This moves the threshold of sensitivity **in the proper direction.**

Должность [*см.* **В качестве**].

Должным образом [*см. тж.* **Правильно, Удовлетворительно, Учтён должным образом**]
This type of spectrum can be expected for most ... with **appropriately** chosen excitation energy.
One of the pictorial structures is inadequate **properly** to describe the substance.
The arc should be **properly** aligned.
To modify the input signal **in the required way, ...**

Дольше всего
Of all the igneous rock-forming minerals quartz survives **the longest** in the weathering zone.

Доля
The telemeter has an output of **a fraction of** a watt.
Shales make up **the** largest **proportion of** all sedimentary rocks in terms of volume.
The largest **share of** the water supply goes to agriculture.

Доля в
The contribution of these occupationally related cancers **to** the total incidence of cancer is small.

Доля секунды [*см.* **Через какую-то долю секунды после**].

Домашнее хозяйство [*см. тж.* **Бытовые потребности, В домашнем хозяйстве, Потребление в домашнем хозяйстве**]
Single-phase induction motors are widely used in fractional horsepower sizes, especially **in homes.**

Домашний
Such water softeners are installed in **household** water systems.

Дополнен
Today, these techniques **are supplemented by** various geophysical techniques.

Дополнение к [*см. тж.* **В дополнение к**]
Ultraviolet spectrometry is sometimes useful **as an adjunct to** other spectrometric methods for ...
The optical method **is complementary to** the method based on ...

Дополнительная плата [*см.* **За небольшую дополнительную плату**].

Дополнительно
The wave manages to oscillate as many as 100 times **extra** because of gravity.
The gasoline is of poor quality and must be **further** treated before use.
These tests are used **as supplementary** (*or* **additional,** *or* **in addition**) **to** the usual chemical tests.
In addition to ...

Дополнительное оборудование
We can supply, as **extra** (*or* **optional**) **equipment,** an intermediate platen.

Дополнительное преимущество
A side benefit (*or* **An added bonus**) has been the reduction of cycle times.

Дополнительное приспособление
Automatic wheel wear adjustment is **an optional extra.**

Дополнительное чтение
Supplementary reading.

Дополнительные детали
A wide selection of **options** [*or* **optional** (*or* **additional**) **parts**] is available.

Дополнительные комментарии [*см.* **Нуждаться в дополнительных комментариях**].

Дополнительный [*см.*. *тж.* **В качестве дополнительной меры предосторожности**]
Some **further** examples are given in Sec. 5.
Part III offers **supplementary** sections on mathematical methods.
As a **further** precaution the ground wire is connected to ...
This provides an **added** source of excitation to the machine.
Laser cutting machines will be a **complementary** tool to electron-beam machines.
Such ligands give **extra** stability to the complexes.

Дополнять
It has been necessary to **amplify** the wave theory of radiation **by** the quantum theory.
When molasses is used, it must **be supplemented with** nitrogen and phosphorus.
Supervisory control **supplements,** rather than replaces, fully automatic control.

Дополнять друг друга [*см. тж.* **Взаимно дополнять друг друга**]
The two types of data **complement each other** nicely.

Дополняться
The equipment **is complemented by** auxiliary engines.
Visual observations **were supplemented by** photographs.
The practical work **is supplemented with** a lecture course.

Допуск [*см.* **Выдерживать допуски, Деталь, изготовленная без нарушения допусков; Деталь, изготовленная с нарушением допусков; Если допуск в ... превышен, Изготавливать с нормальными допусками, С допуском, Устанавливать допуск на**].

Допускать [*см. тж.* **Давать возможность, Не следует допускать, Нельзя допускать, Позволять**]
The spectroscopic selection rule **allows** any change in the value of V.
One must know the greatest length of work the machine **will accept.**
Crystals **admit** only a very limited degree of variation in composition.
The equation **admits of** some real roots.
A certain amount of porosity may often **be tolerated** because it will be closed up during working.

Допускать возможность
The current view **leaves room for** a wide range of reflex behaviour.

Допускать образование
We also have models that **allow for the creation of** new plates of oceanic lithosphere where none previously existed.

Допуская
Allowing for occasional duplicate solution, we can say that ...

Допустим, что
(Let us) assume that ...

Допустимая нагрузка
These materials have specific **allowable** (*or* **permissible**) **loads** which they can carry.

Допустимый
Operating temperatures up to 350° **are allowable** (*or* **allowed,** *or* **permissible,** *or* **admissible,** *or* **acceptable**).
In this case carbon contents up to 0.04% **are tolerable** (*or* **may be tolerated**).

Допущение
These are rough estimates and as such serve as initial **assumptions** for solving Eqs. (6), (7), and (8).

Дороги с большим движением
This does not affect elevated levels of carbon monoxide in such places as **heavily travelled highways.**

Дорогостоящий
Such studies are too **costly** to be carried out in ...

Дорожные испытания [*см.* **Испытывать на дорогах, Проходить дорожные испытания**].

Досрочно выполнять план
To complete (*or* **fulfil**) **the plan ahead of schedule.**

Доставать
The unit can be steered into the aisles of the material storage racks, and can be elevated **to retrieve** material **from** the highest shelves of the latter.

Доставка [*см. тж.* **Стоимость с доставкой**]
Hauling in material from less populated areas is effected by ...

Доставленный с Луны
Samples **brought back** (*or* **returned**) **from the Moon ...**

Доставлять
Conveyors have been erected **to convey** (*or* **deliver,** *or* **transport,** *or* **carry**) coal **to** a convenient site.
The pipe-line **conveys** the water **down** the hillside.
Components **are** installed on the cylinder assembly and **forwarded** to the tractor assembly area.
An electrostatic discharge **delivers** the message **to** a muscle fiber.

Доставлять на баржах
The goods **will be barged to** the site.

Доставлять на самолёте (вертолёте)
Experts from Britain **were** specially **flown out** to advise on drilling methods.

Доставлять по жёлобу
Stampings **are delivered by shute.**

Достаточно I [*см. тж.* **Более чем достаточно, В достаточной степени**]
Heat from the rest of the rail **suffices** (*or* **is sufficient**) **to** temper the quenched portion.
One need look **only** in the vicinity of each point to tell whether ...
It will suffice to estimate the average composition ratios.
For complete adsorption in a dense plasma at thermonuclear temperatures this layer **need be only** 0.005 in. thick.

Достаточно II [*см. тж.* **Довольно, Относительно, Сравнительно**]
A **reasonably** concentrated solution ...
The temperatures will be constant over a **fairly** (*or* **rather,** *or* **sufficiently**) wide (*or* wide **enough**) range of ...

Достаточно III
When the fibre has such nonuniformities, we **need only** have knowledge of ...

Достаточно большой
As long as **reasonably** (*or* **sufficiently**) **large** samples could be obtained, ...

Достаточно далеко от
This may occur (**at distances**) **well away from** the source.

Достаточно детально
The distribution of energy is known **in sufficient detail.**

Достаточно для
Equation (26) **would suffice to** describe the expected radiation gain.

Достаточно ... для того, чтобы
Water movement in coastal marshes is **sufficiently** restricted **that** marsh plants may become established there (*or* **for** marsh plants **to** become ...).
The source is **sufficiently** large **that** it fully illuminates ...
When the pinhole **is large enough for** the molecules to pass through, ...

Достаточно иметь
A simple voltmeter **will suffice for** this purpose.

Достаточно легко
Water both donates and accepts protons **with reasonable facility.**

Достаточно мощный
The shock is **reasonably** (*or* **rather,** *or* **sufficiently,** *or* **comparatively,** *or* **relatively**) **strong.**

Достаточно определённо [*см.* **Более или менее определённо**].

Достаточно полно
These methods are covered (*освещены*) **adequately.**

Достаточно сказать, что
Suffice it to say that the yield of the individual fragment ions varies with laser power.

Достаточно точная картина
The figure provides **a reasonably** (*or* **rather,** *or* **sufficiently,** *or* **comparatively,** *or* **relatively**) **fair** (*or* **accurate**) **picture.**

Достаточно упомянуть, что
It will suffice to mention that ...

Достаточно ..., чтобы не оставалось сомнения в
Most of the complexes are **sufficiently** stable **to leave no doubt of** their nature.

Достаточное число
A piping system should have **sufficient** (*or* **a sufficient number of,** *or* **enough**) valves to ensure complete control of flow.

Достаточные основания (*или* **причины**)
An extensive hunt for a primary malignancy should not be undertaken in an older patient unless there is **a good cause** (*or* **reason**).

Достаточный [*см. тж.* **Удовлетворительный**]
The isolation of these compounds in **reasonable** quantity ...
The metal removed during cutting leaves **adequate** clearance.
The solution is calibrated with **fair** (*or* **sufficient**) accuracy.
The total radiation of a black body at the temperature chosen can be determined with **reasonable** accuracy.
The passage of the current **suffices** to melt the mixture.

Достигаемый
The accuracy **achievable** (*or* **obtainable,** *or* **attainable**) with these computing elements ...

Достигать I
At room temperature the electron's average diffusion distance for the *p-n* junction after injection may **be as much as** several microns.
This type of potential **ranges up to** about 100 millivolts.
The cadmium content of zinc concentrates may **run to** 1-2 percent.
The amount of mercury here may **run as high as** two parts per billion.
The permeability of iron may **be as great as** 2000.
After the orbit **has attained** its desired altitude ...
This **amounts up to** one third of the velocity of light.
The output **reaches** its peak.
The number of formulations (*составов*) **runs** (*or* **ranges**) **into** the thousands.
In metazoans, this may **amount to as much as** 11% of the deoxycytidines.
The pressure can be raised **to get to** point 3.
When equilibrium **is attained** (*or* **established**), ...

Достигать II [*см. тж.* **Многого можно достигнуть, Осуществлять**]
Almost complete conversion can **be obtained** at ordinary pressure.
Maximum efficiency **is accomplished** when ...
No improvement **was brought about** (*or* **attained,** *or* **achieved**) by applying this method.
A reduction in metal thickness can **be realized.**
This realignment of the molecules can **be brought about** in several ways.

Достигать III [*см. тж.* **Вне пределов досягаемости**]
These bodies of magma do not **make it to** the surface and solidify at depth ...
Almost all the heat generated in the earth's mantle **finds its way to** the ocean floor.

Достигать больших успехов в
Radio astronomers **have made great strides toward** (*or* **achieved much success in**) elucidating ...

Достигать максимума
The Parkinson tremor **peaks** at about five cycles per second.
Activity **peaked** at a concentration of 6 mM of enzyme.

Достигать наивысшего расцвета
Mass production **reached its fullest flower** with this model.

Достигать равновесия
Dilute the protein until **equilibrium is reached** (*or* **attained,** *or* **established**).

Достигать результата [*см.* **Получать результат**].

Достигать результатов, равных полученным
The high-powered laser system was capable of **matching the results obtained by** spectrofluorometry.

Достигать стадии
Interchangeability **has reached a point** where any fixture set can be broken or combined with another set.

Достигать ступени, на которой
Testing of ... **has progressed to the point where** we feel that ...

Достигать улучшений
A number of **advantages have been gained** by producing the casting by the lost-wax technique.

Достигать успехов
Considerable **advances have been made** in the area of preventing water contamination.
Progress was made towards the solution of this problem.
Success has finally **been achieved.**

Достигать цели
These **ends** may **be accomplished** (*or* **achieved**) by passing the tubing through a circular cooling die.
This **objective** (*or* **goal**) **is accomplished** (*or* **This aim is attained,** *or* **This purpose is served**) by reducing ...
The purposes of descriptive geometry **are accomplished through** the employment of ...
To achieve this **objective** one has to ...
The object has been attained by placing ...

Достигаться
This **is accomplished** (*or* **achieved**) by the use of mirrors on both ends of the laser medium.
Only six to eight percent saturation **is attained** (*or* **achieved**) under similar conditions.
A further considerable reduction in current thresholds **results** if an additional heterojunction is located at the *p-n* junction.

Достигнут
When a sufficiently large pressure **is built up** (*or* **attained**), ...

Достигнут благодаря [*см.* **Быть достигнутым благодаря**].

Достигнуть совершенно неожиданного успеха
They **succeeded beyond their fondest** (*or* **wildest**) **dreams.**

Достигнуть такого уровня, при котором
Research in water desalinization **has progressed to the stage where** it is often cheaper to prepare fresh water from sea water than to remove the contaminants.

Достигнуты значительные успехи в этом направлении
In the past few years **considerable progress has been made towards that goal.**

Достигнутый
The refinement may **be brought about** (*or* **achieved,** *or* **attained,** *or* **realized**) by suitable heat treatment.

Достижение I [*см. тж.* **Большое достижение**]
Such machines represent **a** considerable **step forward** [*or* **an achievement,** *or* **an accomplishment,** *or* **an advance(ment),** *or* **a breakthrough**] in a-c motor design.

Достижение II
Today the objective of the chemist is to aid in the interpretation of the universe; he has made much progress toward **meeting** this objective.

Достижение стационарного состояния
The contact times are too short to permit **the attainment of a steady state.**

Достижение цели [*см.* **Для достижения этой цели**].

Достижения техники
Now, because of **technological advances,** ten times that energy can be achieved.

Достоверно
By these procedures, the elastic response of the material is **reliably** established for several decades of frequencies.
The origin of these systems is not yet known **with assurance** (*or* **certainty**).

Достоверный
Our determinations of the star's mass have made possible some **plausible** guesses about its nature.

Достоин внимания [*см. тж.* **Заслуживать внимания**]
The interconnections between subunits **are noteworthy.**

Достоин доверия
The dual interacting system version **holds** more **credibility** than the one of the self-replicating single molecule.

Достоин изучения
A technique that can aid in ... may **be (well) worth examining.**

Достоин особого внимания
This **is especially noteworthy.**
One art in particular **is worthy of special attention.**

Достоин рассмотрения
Matrix isolation **deserves consideration** as a sampling technique.

Достоин упоминания
There is one more area of optical analogue computing which **deserves mention** (*or* **is worth mentioning,** *or* **is worthy of notice,** *or* **is noteworthy**).

Достоинства и недостатки
To evaluate the technical and economic **pros and cons** (*or* **merits and demerits,** *or* **advantages and disadvantages,** *or* **strengths and weaknesses**) **of** modernizing ...

Достоинство [*см. тж.* **Преимущество**]
The merits (*or* **advantages**) **of** plastic propellants are their unequalled chemical stability and good storage properties.
The virtues (*or* **assets**) **of** ammonium nitrate are its cheapness and the low toxicity of the gases produced.
The chief **value of** the RNAs is in a mechanical capacity as a carrier of ... (*biol.*).

Достойный упоминания
Histone *Hl* has a special property **deserving of mention.**
Another issue **worth mentioning** (*or* **noting**) is the problem of ...

Доступ [*см. тж.* **Иметь доступ к, Обеспечивать доступ к**]
Most amphibians have **access to** water or die of dehydration in a short time.

Доступен [*см.* **Легко доступен**].

Доступен для
More and more energy levels become **accessible to** the molecules.
Only this part **is available** (*or* **accessible**) **for** direct chemical analysis.
This book **is accessible to** undergraduates.
This rate **can be handled by** vacuum pumps.

Доступен для исследования
The Milky Way **is** less **open to inspection** because dust clouds cover its structure.

Доступен широким кругáм населения
Such computers **are widely available.**

Доступность
Because of **(ready) availability of** polyI:C we centred on this substance.

Доступный [*см.* **Легко доступный для**].

Доступный для
The front compartment **is** easily **accessible for** inspection and service.

Доступный для наблюдения
This part of our galactic system **is accessible to observation.**
This photometer is capable of detecting the smallest objects **observable with** such instruments.

Доступный для судоходства
To keep the existing Mississippi channel **open to shipping, ...**

Дóсуха [*см.* **Выпаривать досуха, Упаривать досуха**].

Досягаемость [*см.* **В пределах досягаемости**].

Дробить до
The ore **is crushed to** 6 in.

Дробить на
Mechanical weathering **breaks down** material **into** smaller and smaller pieces.

Дробиться в порошóк [*см.* **Размельчáть в порошóк**].

Дробление
The mechanical **breakdown of** rocks takes place in a number of ways.
Breakage of rock by explosives ...
Crushing of ores ...
The degree of **fragmentation** resulting from a given blast depends on ...

Дробь [*см. тж.* **В виде дроби**]
This is **a tenth (of)** the cost of the 600-ft structure.
Fractions less than **a thirty-second (1/32) in.** are disregarded.
The value of K_y was only about **one-third (of)** that in the annealed condition.
Jupiter has **1/1000 the** mass of the Sun.

Дрожание [*см.* **Для устранения вибрации**].

Друг друга [*см.* **Дополнять друг друга**].

Друг другу [*см.* **Противодействовать, Противоположны(е) друг другу**].

Друг к другу [*см.* **Подгонять друг к другу**].

Друг на друга [*см.* **Налагаться (друг на друга)**].

Друг от друга [*см.* **Далеко друг от друга, На расстоянии ... друг от друга, Независимо друг от друга, Отличаться друг от друга**].

Друг с другом
The relation of species **to one another ...**

Другая планета [*см.* **Жизнь на других планетах**].

Другие условия [*см.* **В других условиях**].

Другими словами [*см. тж.* **Иначе говоря, Иными словами**]
Another way of putting it is that matter can neither be created nor destroyed.
In other words (*or* **To put it differently**), rock is composed of inorganic matter.
To put this another way, the solution can tolerate ...

Другими способами
These values must be obtained by **other means.**

Другое дело [*см. тж.* **Одно дело ... Другое дело**]
But transverse waves **were another matter.**
Sulphuric acid **is a different matter** (*or* **something else again**).

Другое место [*см.* **В других местах**].

Другое решение (проблемы)
The alternative is to use a number of relatively small vessels operated in parallel.

Другой [*см. тж.* **В другом месте, Иной, Отличный от**]
Additional applications of laser-induced luminescence include ...
An **alternate** (*or* **alternative**) procedure consists of changing ...
Further (*or* **Other**) advantages of lasers are their monochromaticity, narrow spectral bandwidth, and collimation.
The cascade particle is an **alternative** name for the negatively charged hyperon.

Другой крайностью является
At the other extreme is the model proposed by ...

Другой метод
An alternative method of providing mass-transfer surface is to allow the liquid to flow over ...

Другой подход к
Another way of looking at this data **is to** imagine that ...

Другой подход состоит в
Another way of looking at it is to consider a possible net equation ...

Другой чем
Variations in V in directions **other than** x are ignored.

Дуга I [*см.* **Возникновение дуги, Гасить дугу, Зажигать дугу, Сваривать в дуге, Тушить дугу**].

Дуга II [*см.* **Описывать дугу**].

Дуга зажигается
The power voltage and the H.F. pilot voltage are switched on and **the arc strikes.**

Дуговая сварка [*см.* **Сваривать в дуге**].

Дурно пахнущий
The bacterial decomposition of protein often yields **foul-smelling** amines.
The acid **is a pungent,** corrosive liquid.

Дымиться
Aluminium chloride **fumes** in air by hydrolysis.

Дымящийся
Perchloric acid is a **fuming** liquid.

Дюжина
Opium contains about two **dozen** different alkaloids.

Е

Его [*см. тж.* **Их**]
This apparatus, or some modification **thereof, ...**

Его поверхность обрабатывается
Before the rod is drawn through the die, **it is surface treated** by pickling to remove scale.

Едва
Some of these markings were **barely** (*or* **hardly,** *or* **scarcely**) visible.

Едва виден
Alcor, a companion star, **is faintly visible to** someone with excellent eyesight.

Едва ли [*см. тж.* **Вряд ли; Маловероятно, что**]
It is not likely (*or* **It is unlikely**) **that** laser-based detectors can compete with ...
The electrode **is unlikely to** have a reproducible response.

Едва ли вероятен
Simultaneous rupture of both bonds holding the ligand to the metal **is highly improbable.**

Едва ли имеет смысл
There is little point (*or* **sense**) **in** listing all of the known amino acids.

Едва ли можно радоваться
This finding **is hardly a matter of rejoicing.**

Едва ли можно сомневаться в
There appears to be little doubt about the engineering feasibility of fast breeder reactors.

Едва ли можно сомневаться в том, что
There is little doubt (*or* **question**) **that** this will lead to great improvements.

Едва ли нужен
A fluid seal **is unlikely to be needed** here.

Едва ли нужно говорить, что
It hardly needs saying that a locust deprived of a rich sensory inflow would have difficulty foraging and migrating.

Едва ли произойдёт [*см.* **Вероятно не произойдёт**].

Едва ли следует сомневаться в том, что
There is little doubt that the rate can be accelerated.
We can have little doubt that something has happened since the rock was first formed.

Едва ли следует удивляться тому, что
It is hardly surprising that the problem of describing the rotation of the Earth accurately has intrigued physicists for more than two centuries.

Едва ли спросит *и т.п.*
Any reader who has come this far **will know better than to ask** the meaningless question: "Are reactors safe?"

Едва ли целесообразен для
Tuberculin test **is of doubtful value in** the elderly since its interpretation is very difficult.

Едва ли целесообразно
There is little point in developing the proposed power plant.
We see little reason for preserving a distinction in nomenclature.

Едва различим
The acoustic interactions we managed to observe **were barely perceptible.**

Единая теория
A unified theory.

Единица [*см. тж.* **В единицах, Выражать в единицах, На единицу времени**]
The thrust to local weight ratio **is** approximately **one** (*or* **unity**).

Единица измерения
The ampere is **the unit of measurement of** electric current strength.

Единица объёма
The mass of absorbing material **per unit volume ...**

Единичная поверхность
The force required to make a layer of **unit area** move with a unit velocity ...

Единичный
To produce a deuteron spin **of unity, ...**
The nitrogen nucleus has **one unit of** spin.
A **unit** circle ...

Единодушно сходиться во мнении относительно
A (good) consensus exists among the geologists **as to** ...

Единое мнение [*см.* **Нет согласия между ... относительно**].

Единое мнение относительно того
There is no **consensus (of opinion) on** how cosmic jets are produced.

Единственный [*см. тж.* **Один-единственный**]
An improved yield **is** not **the only** (*or* **the sole**) factor of importance.
Their **only** application is in rocket engines.
Every point on the square has **unique** *x* and *y* coordinates.
The sole (*or* **The only**) difference between them is ...

Единственный в своём роде
Chemical pumping **is unique in that** the first component of a laser intrinsically supplies the second.

Единственный важный элемент
Sometimes direction **is all that is important.**

Единственный путь
There is no way in which the two geometrical isomers can be interconverted **except by** the breaking of a carbon-carbon bond.

Единый
These are merely different manifestations of a **single** underlying force.
At the time Yukawa was seeking a **unified** explanation of the two nuclear forces: the strong and the weak.
A **unified** theory of ...
There is no entirely adequate **single** (*or* **unified,** *or* **unitary**) system for classifying adhesives.

Ежедневно [*см. тж.* **День за днём**]
These engineers deal **routinely** with plasmas and their useful properties.

Ежедневный [*см. тж.* **Каждодневный**]
These radio sources show **day-to-day** changes in their optical flux.
Day-to-day (*or* **Daily**) contact with animals ...
The catalyst circulation **on a daily basis** amounts to eight million tons.

Еле виден [*см.* **Едва виден**].

Еле видный
The gases are invisible and the cracks in the brickwork are **just** (*or* **hardly,** *or* **scarcely**) **visible.**

Если [*см. тж.* **Данó; При условии, что**]
This term is useful, however, **as long as** the complexities involved are kept in mind.
Once the surface of normal velocity has been obtained, the wave front may be easily constructed.
The exact structure, **providing** (*or* **provided**) it is known, is given in a schematic representation.
The coke recovered in this operation is of electrode grade **if** produce**d** from low-ash content feedstock.
All these jugs are housed in wooden boxes to catch fragments **in the event that** atmospheric pressure shatters the glass.
Such materials are satisfactory **provided (that) they** do not form corrosive chlorides.
Should the presence of cast iron escape the first examination it may then be detected and any adjustment necessary can be made on the spot.

Если бы не
A steam engine could not be made to produce work **but for** the high pressure ...
Were it not (*or* **If it were not**) **for** the radio there would be little point in sending satellites into space.

Если бы это было так
If this were the case (*or* **If this were so**), gases would diffuse at a fantastic rate.

Если вдуматься глубже, то
But **on second thought,** this conclusion appears false.

Если вообще
Certain agglutinating systems agglutinate weekly, **if at all.**

Если вообще встречается
This relationship seldom **if ever occurs** in the actual atmosphere.

Если вообще отличается
The wiring of the nervous system in these animals **varies** little, **if at all,** from animal to animal.

Если вообще содержит
The rock contains little, **if any,** ground water.

Если да, то
Can the equilibrium state be determined by ...? **If so,** can this function be understood as ...?

Если дан
Given *n* cubes, is there a formula for calculating the number of distinct polycubes of order *n*?

Если допуск в ... превышен
If the valve seat **is out of tolerance,** a red warning button comes into view in the little window on the gauge.

Если допустить, что
Even **if it is granted that** the entire process is feasible outside of a cell, there appears to be no means by which identical molecules can be produced.

Если его не учитывать
The high thermal expansion of fluorocarbon can cause machining problems **if not taken into consideration** (*or* **account**).

Если желательно
If desired, this value can be approximated by graphical integration of Eq. (4).

Если задан
Given the name of an element ..., write electron configurations for ...

Если, и только если
A stable $H(z)$ is bounded **if, and only if** the corresponding ...

Если идёт речь о
The trigonometric calculation could greatly magnify initial errors, particularly **where** small angles **were involved** (*or* **concerned**).

Если известен
Given the time of origin of the earthquake one can determine ...

Если иметь это в виду, то
With this in mind it becomes easier to understand why ...

Если исходить из
Based on the tetrahedral model of the carbon valences, the nominal angle subtended between two of the four valences of the carbon would be 109°28'.

Если исходить из гипотезы о том, что
On the hypothesis that the jet is 1.5 billion light years from our galaxy ...

Если исходить из предположения о
On the assumption of the area law the right orbit can differ only negligibly from the intermediate ellipse.

Если ... начался
In principle the chemical reactions, **once initiated,** could proceed without an outside source of power.

Если не
Colloids "protected" by such detergents are electrically neutral **unless** ions are adsorbed from dispersing solutions.
The space between steel and rock is filled with wood lagging and packing, **unless** steel lagging is used.

Если не считать [*см. тж.* **За исключением, Не считая**]
Other than hydrogen, helium is the least dense element known.
But for (*or* **With the exception of,** *or* **Except for**) a few substances, the state of the art has not advanced sufficiently to permit ...

Если не ..., то это приводит к
Failure to maintain a sufficient thiamine level in the diet **results in** the malfunction of these enzyme systems.

Если не указано иначе
The analysis presented here pertains to the operation of a single 6697A triode, **unless otherwise specified** (*or* **stated,** *or* **indicated**) (*or* **except as otherwise noted**).

Если не учитывать
Not counting conventional metal shrinkages, moulding accuracy is high.

Если нужно
If an insoluble starting material **is to be** converted into an insoluble product, ...

Если нужно получить
If the normal carbonate **is wanted,** sodium hydrogencarbonate is used as ...

Если он вообще возможен
The operation of differentiation is to be avoided **if at all possible.**

Если он есть
The fourth tube of the pump, **when present,** is used to carry extra water.

Если он существует
The magnetic-moment term, **if any** (*or* **if it exists**), is much larger than ...

There are few, **if any,** boundaries absolutely separating one animal community from another.

Если он является
The controller, particularly **if** electronic, can be designed to have ...

Если отвлечься от технической стороны вопроса
Technology apart, what are the limits on beam performance imposed by the laws of physics?

Если позволяют условия
If circumstances allow, advance the net toward the fire.

Если потребуется [*см. тж.* **При необходимости**]
The table shaft is hollow so that **if required** (*or* **if needed,** *or* **if necessary**), hydraulic lines can be ...

Если принять во внимание, что
The need for such fine oscillator tuning is apparent **when it is considered** (*or* **when taken into account) that ...**

Если принять за
Setting the world's production of phosphate **at** 100, salt was 80 and lime 106.

Если принять ... равным нулю *и т.п.*
This, **with** $V^{\circ}_{H_2}$ **taken as zero,** yields ...

Если рассматривать ... в микроскоп
When observed under (*or* **with**) **the microscope,** they show ...

Если речь идёт о [*см.* **Если идёт речь о**].

Если смотреть
The sense of the lines is clockwise **when looking** in the direction of the current.

Если смотреть из
Viewed from space, one of the most striking features of the earth's surface is ...

Если смотреть на
When facing the drum, the right-hand elbow is the upstream one.

Если смотреть сверху
(As) viewed from the top (*or* **from above**) the insect's abdomen swings to the top as if it were a rudder.

Если таковой имеется
The natural rotation of these carbons, **if any,** was not much larger than ...

Если ..., то и
If the bond energy changes, **so will** the linear susceptibility.

Если только не [*см.* **Если не**].

Если учесть
The advantage of this method becomes even greater **when** fixture costs **are** also **considered.**

Если учесть все обстоятельства
All things (*or* **Everything**) **considered,** some transplanted hearts behave remarkably well.

Если учесть, что
The need for such fine oscillator tuning is apparent **when it is considered** (*or* **if it is remembered**) **that ...**

Если это возможно
Whenever practicable (*or* **feasible,** *or* **possible**), belts should be installed so that ...

Если это вообще произойдёт
We shall rediscover this comet, **if at all,** only by accident.

Если это имеет место [*см.* **Если это так**].

Если это не будет сделано
Neglecting (*or* **Failure**) **to do this** will cause confusion.

Если это не так
If this is not the case, the curve is called time like.

Если это невозможно
It is preferable that both of the above safety devices should be used wherever possible, but **failing this** either one or the other should be incorporated.

Если это необходимо [*см. тж.* **По мере необходимости, При необходимости**]
These (and higher orbitals **if necessary**) provide a basis for ...
If need be, the angular momentum could rise to a very large value.

Если это потребуется [*см. тж.* **По мере необходимости**]
The reader is referred to the need of specialist advice **should the situation warrant it** (*or* **if required**).

Если это произойдёт [*см.* **В этом случае**].

Если это так
Active slip movement must be limited to the fault line between the offset ends; **if so,** seismic maps should show that ... (*geol.*).
If this is the case (*or* **When such is the case**) the valve will fail within a short period.
Should this be the case (then) the preferred treatment would be to ...

Естественно вписываться в
The positron **fits naturally into** this scheme.

Естественно предположить, что
It would appear reasonable (*or* **natural**) **that** the repulsions would increase with ...

Естественно, что [*см. тж.* **Вполне естественно, что**]
Clearly the most feasible approach was again to use radar.

Естественное освещение
Natural illumination in an industrial building ...

Есть [*см.* **Иметься**].

Есть возможность
You **stand a good chance of** getting the right gauge for your particular job.

Есть все основания полагать, что
There is good reason to believe (*or* **think**) **that** the sediments were deposited somewhat earlier.
There are strong grounds for believing (*or* **to believe**) **that ...**

Есть основания надеяться на то, что
There is reason to hope that this analysis will recover ...

Есть основания полагать (*или* **считать**, *или* **думать**), **что**
There is reason to think (*or* **believe**) **that** the stars ...
It is reasonable to suppose that the value of the integral depends only on ...
There are (good) grounds to believe (*or* **for believing**) **that** the *Sarcosporidia* may be fungi rather than protozoa.

Есть признаки того, что
Indications are that actinium is more basic in character.

Есть указания на
There is some evidence for deformation and intrusion ...

Есть указания на то, что
Evidence indicates (*or* **suggests**) **that** most carbohydrates exist principally in this form.
The largest pollutant by mass is carbon dioxide, and **there is (some) evidence that** man's activities are altering the concentrations formerly controlled by nature.
Carbonaceous chondrites **show evidence of** hav**ing** been formed from ...

Ещё [*см. тж.* **Пока ещё**]
An additional 254,000 words can be added.

Ещё более
In the light of these conclusions the need for conservation of mineral resources becomes **all the more** evident.
These figures could be **further** improved (*уточнены*) by the inclusion of additional data in the computation.

Ещё более важно то, что
Of even greater importance is the fact that the Bohr model could not be extended to ...

Ещё больше
The low pH **further** enhances the germicidal activity of iodine.
In order to increase **still further** the versatility of the machine ...

Ещё большую озабоченность вызывает
Of even greater concern are the water supplies for major urban centres.

Ещё будет рассматриваться
The lowest-energy term **has yet to be dealt with.**

Ещё в ... веке
This anomaly was measured **even in** (*or* **as early as**) **the** 19th **century,** long before there was any theory to explain it.

Ещё в ... году
As early (*or* **As far back,** *or* **As long ago**) **as** 1925, 300 models of such engines had been or were being developed.
This was accomplished **back in** 1770.

Ещё в течение многих лет

Overhead transmission lines will probably be tolerated in remote areas **for many years to come.**

Ещё важнее то, что [*см. тж.* **Что более важно**]
More important(ly) (*or* **What is more important**), the magnitude of the exponent for the second term becomes ...

Ещё вопрос
It remains to be seen whether the unit will operate efficiently.

Ещё далеко до [*см.* **От ... ещё далеко до**].

Ещё и [*см.* **Кроме того**].

Ещё лучше
Materials might be found that become superconductive at the higher temperatures of liquid hydrogen or, **better still** (*or* **what is still better**), of liquid nitrogen.

Ещё много десятилетий
Fossil-fuel-burning plants must be built **for many decades to come** in order to meet the nation's needs.

Ещё много лет
For many years to come, the practice of chemical engineering will remain both an art and a science.

Ещё многое можно сделать в области
Considerable room remains (*or* **There is still much room**) **for** improvement in employing the technique.
There is ample room for further research on the formation of ...

Ещё многое нужно сделать, чтобы
A great deal needs to be done before interfacial turbulence becomes well understood.

Ещё многое нужно узнать о
Much has yet to be learned about the problem.
There is much still to be learned (*or* **that we need to learn**) **about** superconductivity in organic materials.

Ещё многое остаётся неизвестным в области
There is still a great deal to learn about the chemistry of bee venom.

Ещё многое остаётся узнать о ...
Much remains to be learned about the nature of ...

Ещё не выяснено [*см.* **Пока не выяснено**].

Ещё не известный
The answer depends on the **as yet unknown** quantity *d*.

Ещё не проанализирован
A small fraction of the mixture **has yet to be analyzed.**

Ещё не скоро
We have a long way to go before we attain such a high yield.
We have still a long way to go toward understand**ing** how the planets came into being.

Ещё не скоро удастся
Scientists **are still a long way from** creat**ing** living molecules in the laboratory.

Ещё несколько лет
The experiments will have to be continued **for several more years.**

Ещё нужно
The products concerned **remain to be** identified.

Ещё нужно доказать
The utility of the theory **has yet to be demonstrated.**

Ещё один
A further difficulty is that ...
The common ion effect is **a further** (*or* **another,** *or* **one more**) important factor affecting solubilities.
One further (*or* **Yet another**) peculiarity of .. can be demonstrated.

Ещё один довод в пользу
The fact that beneficial secondary effects may also occur **is an added reason for** uti**lizing** polynucleotides.

Ещё одно доказательство
This was **further proof of** the galaxy's great distance.

Ещё остаётся выяснить
The influence of changes in hydrogen pressure on this value **is still to be determined.**
It remains to be seen whether the range achieved so far is small enough to be described by the theory.

Ещё раз [*см. тж.* **Снова**]
Our results show **once again** that scientists must always keep an open mind.

Ещё хуже то, что
To make matters worse [*or* **To complicate** (*or* **aggravate**) **matters** (*or* **the situation**)], the edges of both lens elements must be ground.

Ж

Желаемая цель
Screens may be of various shapes depending on **the purpose to be achieved.**

Желаемый
When the motor reaches **the desired** (*or* **wanted**) speed ...
The purity **sought** will depend on ...

Желание [*см.* **В зависимости от желания, По желанию**].

Желательно [*см. тж.* **Если желательно**]
It is desirable to use the maximum possible voltage.

Желательность
This indicates **the desirability of** operating an engine with ...

Желательный
The characteristics of a dye laser make it very **desirable** as an excitation source for ...
The two sidebands, one **wanted** and the other unwanted, can be separated.

Желеобразный [*см.* **Студенистый**].

Желтеть
The solution **turns yellow.**

Жертва [*см.* **Небольшая жертва, принесённая ради**].

Жертвовать [*см.* **За счёт**].

Жёсткие требования
We have to meet **exacting** (*or* **stringent,** *or* **rigid**) **requirements.**

Жёсткий допуск [*см. тж.* **Выдерживать допуски, Иметь жёсткий допуск**]
Close tolerances on tray levelness ...
The valve seat is machined **to close** (*or* **tight**) **tolerances.**

Жёсткий режим
Arduous (*or* **Severe,** *or* **Tough,** *or* **Rigorous,** *or* **Drastic**) **conditions.**

Жёстко закреплён
The position of the tube **is rigidly fixed.**

Жёстко закреплён на
The loop antenna **is mounted rigidly to** the aircraft.

Жёстко связан
Neighbouring atoms **were rigidly bound.**

Жёсткое испытание [*см. тж.* **Выдерживать жёсткое испытание**]
Arduous trials.
A stringent (*or* **strenuous**) **test.**

Жёсткость упругой системы станок-деталь-инструмент
Rigidity of the machine-tool-workpiece complex.

Живая материя
Living matter is characterized by ...

Живая очередь [*см.* **Обслуживание в порядке живой очереди**].

Живая ткань
Living tissue.

Живо интересоваться
Astronomers began **to take an active** (*or* **keen**) **interest in ...**

Живое существо
Phosphorylated compounds are abundant in **living things** (*or* **beings,** *or* **creatures**).

Живой интерес к
The keen (*or* **lively,** *or* **animated**) **interest of** this firm **in** research ...

Животный и растительный мир [*см.* **Растительный и животный мир**].

Живущий [*см.* **Обитающий на дне**].

Жизненно важен для
These hormones **are vitally important in** the regulation of many phases of metabolism.
These networks **are vital to** the city as a nerve system **is vital to** the body.
There are two points which **are of vital importance in** the design of a workhead spindle.

Жизнь I [*см.* **Время жизни, Средняя продолжительность жизни**].

Жизнь II [*см.* **Претворять в жизнь, Проводить в жизнь**].

Жизнь на других планетах
The possibility of **extraterrestrial life** has been widely discussed.

Жирный на ощупь
Brown clay is a soft plastic material **with a greasy feel** (*or* **greasy to the touch**).

Жирорастворимый
Fat-soluble constituents ...

Жить [*см.* **Обитающий на дне**].

З

За [*см. тж.* **Вслед за, Наблюдать за, После**]
The pickle plant handles 1000 tons of pickles **a** (*or* **per**) **season.**
The exhaust fan should be located **downstream** (*anton.* **upstream**) **from** (*or* **of**) the spray chamber.

За время
An electronic configuration will change **in a time** so short that ...
A detector may indicate the total amount of radiation incident **in a** definite **time.**

За всё время
The amount of oil and gas in the new fields was the lowest **on record.**

За вычетом
Upon reaching the point D the full battery voltage **less** (*or* **minus**) some small transistor drop is applied to ...

За ... говорит [*см.* **В пользу ... говорит**].

За год до
This Proton Synchrotron was completed about **a year ahead of** the Brookhaven AGS.

За данный период
To give an adequate yield of ... **in a given time,** ...

За единицу времени
The work done **in a unit time ...**

За исключением [*см. тж.* **Все, за исключением нескольких; Исключая, Кроме, Не считая, Помимо**]
All these compounds **except** the monomethylnaphthalenes are of some commercial importance.
Linear molecules, **other than** diatomics, can be treated similarly.
The machine requires practically no maintenance **apart from** electrode dressing.
But for a few substances, the state of the art has not advanced sufficiently to permit ...
These miniatures compare in every way **except** size with the larger connectors.
Except for the bubble caps, the plant was constructed entirely of carbon steel.
These particles are identical **except for** the sight of their charge.
Except in a few special cases, very little visible or radar energy is emitted.
Excepting the test pieces used for the experiment described in Sect. 7, all the specimens were heated at 200°C for 2000 min.
The total cost of the part, **exclusive of** (*or* **excluding,** *or* **with the exception of**) material costs, would be ...
The media used for assay of amino acids contain a complete mixture of pure amino acids, **save for** the one to be determined.
With the exception of some one-coat enamels, most porcelain enamels are applied in two or more coats.
The weight of the press, **less** the hydraulic equipment, is 37 tons.

За исключением одного
Considerable difficulty has been encountered with the various pumps, **with one exception** (*or* **save one**).

За исключением случаев, когда
Nitrogen content of flue gas is of little significance **except insofar as it might be** in combination with large amounts of excess air.
Except when the disks were completely wetted, the liquor rate did not affect the rate of absorption.
The right-hand side will give zero contributions **except when** $j = i$.

За исключением случаев, когда он находится
Except very close to the source, total light power in the core is the sum of ...

За исключением того, что [*см. тж.* **Если не считать**]
The assembly resembles a squirrel cage, **except that** the disks are tilted with respect to each other at an angle of eight degrees.
The salt solutions described by Kemp were employed, **except that** ammonium dibasic phosphate was substituted for the sodium hexametaphosphate.

За какие-то несколько часов
You swing from the saltiest to the most dilute waters on the planet **in a matter of hours.**

За какие-то секунды
In a matter of seconds a complex pattern develops.

За которым последует
First products to be offered will be a high-speed computer transistor **to be followed by** transistors which will serve ...

За которым следует
Glutamic acid constituted the greatest proportion (46%), **with** asparic acid **ranking next** (*or* **followed by** asparic acid) (18%).
Addition of water to this complex, **followed by** proton displacement of ...

За ... лет
The rate of subsidence of platforms is 12 **per** million **years.**

За ... лет до
Three **years prior to** our testing, ...

За ... лет до того, как
Jupiter's satellites had been discovered nine **years before** Kepler had announced his harmonic law.

За малыми исключениями
With few exceptions, all of the components in an alloy are metallic elements.

За небольшими исключениями
With (only) a few exceptions, the entropies of vaporization lie around ...

За небольшую дополнительную плату
The condenser can be supplied as a separate unit or, **for a small extra charge,** can be combined with the welding transformer.

За неимением
For want (*or* **lack**) **of** a better term we refer to the basic patterns as fracture zones.

За ... непосредственно следует
The emission of a high-energy particle **is closely followed by** the emission of γ-rays.

За несколькими исключениями [*см.* **За небольшими исключениями**].

За несколько дней
Nucleosides became phosphorylated **in a period of a few days.**

За несколько секунд
Plug sizes from 1/8 to 11 in. in diameter are interchangeable **in a matter of seconds.**

За ним следует
A shock advances first, **followed by** a constant discontinuity, and finally by a centred rarefaction wave.
Olivine and calcic feldspar are most easily affected, **followed by** the pyroxenes, amphiboles, biotite, ...
Metals re-use is highest for silver; lead **is next.**

За (один) год до
One year prior to (*or* **before**) the discovery of ...

За один оборот
Figure 38 shows the variation in flow from the pump **in one revolution.**

За один проход
This type of reamer will remove considerable metal **in one cut.**
Vertical seams are welded **in a single pass** without need for elaborate edge preparation.

За одним исключением [*см. тж.* **За исключением одного**]
With one exception, all the mechanisms have an element in common.

За одну операцию
Adhesive bonding both seals and joins **in one operation.**

За одну установку детали
This enables milling to be carried out over areas up to 16 by 20 in. **at one setting** (*or* **set-up**) **of** the work.

За отсутствием

Lacking a satisfactory theory of the phenomenon, the first questions to be answered are necessarily very simple ones.

За период
The increase in the carbon dioxide was 43 parts per million **over the** same **period.**
Within the span of fourteen years, scientists have studied many samples of this rock.

За пол-оборота
In one-half revolution ...

За последнее время [*см.* **В последнее время**].

За последнее столетие
Over the course of the past century science has progressed from ... to ...

За последние годы
There has been a trend **(with)in recent years** (*or* **recently**) to develop devices which employ moving parts.

За последние несколько десятилетий
In the last (*or* **past**) **few decades** great progress has been made in generating and measuring extremely narrow resonance lines ...

За последние несколько десятков тысяч лет
Changes of climate that may have occurred **throughout the past few tens of thousands of years ...**

За последние несколько лет
We have been supplying mining equipment **for the last** (*or* **past**) **few years.**
Over (*or* **During,** *or* **Within**) **the past few years** many other applications have been developed.
It has only been **(with)in the last few years,** however, that it has been possible to obtain ...

За ... последовал
This suggestion **was followed by** the microscopic theory of superconductivity.

За пределами [*см. тж.* **Вне пределов, Далеко за пределами**]
A shell of planetoids which surround the Sun, far **beyond** Pluto's orbit ...
The Moon formed **outside of** the Earth's orbit and ...
Eta Carinae is the brightest star **outside** the solar system.
Beyond (*or* **Outside**) this range it is necessary to use inorganic materials.
It would be difficult to maintain radio contact with a rocket much **beyond** the boundaries of the solar system.
Galaxies **external to** our own ...
These elements have a single electron **outside of** closed shells.
Outside the confines of our solar system ...
Beyond the loading point, K_G tends to increase rapidly with increasing G.

За пределами видимости
Such planes fly at altitudes and slant ranges **beyond the sight of** the controller.

За пределами страны [*см.* **Внутри страны и вне её**].

За пределы [*см. тж.* **Выходить за пределы, Не распространяться за пределы**]
If the skip is accidentally lowered **beyond** the lowest point of the chute's travel, ...

За ... принимается
For an airfoil, the cord length **is** usually **taken as** the characteristic length.
The jet velocity **is taken to be** the expanded velocity in supersonic flight.

За рамки [*см.* **Выходить за рамки**].

За редкими исключениями
With rare exception, only two general types are now built.

За ... секунд (часов *и т.п.***)**
Neutral pions break down **in a matter of ... fenitosecond**(s).

За ... следует
This initial etch **is followed by** a second or fine etch.
The original ruby laser **was succeeded by** other solid-state lasers.

За счёт [*см. тж.* **Относить за счёт**]
This multiplexing provides more input channels but **at a sacrifice in** (*or* **at the sacrifice of**) frequency response of each channel.

The thrust is increased **at the cost** (*or* **penalty**) **of** an increase in specific fuel consumption.
Ethylene production increases **at the expense of** the higher molecular weight olefins.
Such power has not been obtained **at the expense** (*or* **sacrifice**) **of** reliability.
Losses **through** evaporation are regarded as trifling.
Increasing the chromium content results in improved corrosion resistance to scaling, but **with** some **sacrifice in** other properties.

За цикл
In one (complete) cycle the current goes through ...

За этим последовал
What followed was development of a completely new technology of ...

За этим следует
Then comes a 4- to 8-hour drying period.

За это время
The angular distance traversed **in this (interval of) time** (*or* **in this period,** *or* **in this time interval**) is ...

Забивать [*см. тж.* **Закупоривать, Засорять**]
Organic slimes tend **to plug** (*or* **clog**) the filters.

Забивать гвоздь
To knock in (*or* **drive in,** *or* **hammer in**) a nail.

Забивать заклёпку [*см.* **Загонять заклёпку**].

Забивать сваю
Nine **piles will be driven** at each corner.

Забиваться
The filter should not tend **to clog.**
Asphalt content should be low, otherwise the heaters **will clog up** when the oil is heated.
Coarse files are recommended for thermoplastics since they do not **load up** as readily as the finer types.

Забирать I
From here the coal **is picked up by** the rear conveyor.

Забирать II
Centrifugal compressors **take in** fluid at the impeller eye.

Забирать слабину
A tension unit **takes up the sag from** the strips (*or* **the slack from** a rope).

Забитый грязью
The impellers **have become choked** (*or* **clogged,** *or* **plugged up**) **with dirt.**

Заболевание [*см.* **Вызывать заболевание**].

Заботиться [*см.* **Позаботиться о том, чтобы**].

Заботиться о том, чтобы [*см.* **Следить за тем, чтобы**].

Забраковать
We can **rule out** many of the possible molecular formulas.
Half of the parts **were rejected.**

Забывать о том, что [*см.* **Не следует забывать, что**].

Заваривать
It is possible **to weld up** cracks in cast iron.

Завернуть [*см.* **Заворачивать в**].

Завершать [*см.* **Выполнять, Осуществлять**]
This function **completes** the list of ...
This distance is required for the ray path **to complete** a full period.
Ammonia solution is then added **to complete** the reprecipitation .

Завершать цикл
The moving point **completes** one **cycle of** its motion in time $2\pi/\omega$.
The *M* phase **terminates** (*or* **completes**) **the cycle.**

Завершаться [*см. тж.* **Прекращаться**]
The setting of the casing **was accomplished** (*or* **brought to completion**) **in** 24 hours.
The entire job **was complete(d)** (*or* **accomplished,** *or* **finished**) **in** 5 days.
This research **has culminated in** the discovery of ...
The new series **would conclude with** a decreasing geometric progression.

The final splashdown (*приводнение*) of Apollo 17 **brought to a close** (*завершило*) the first exploration of the Moon's surface.
This work **culminated in** the Nobel Prize for the investigators.
Erosion must always **end in** deposition.

Завершаться успехом
The search **met with success.**

Завершающая стадия [*см.* **На завершающем этапе**].

Завершение [*см. тж.* **Окончание, Приближаться к завершению**]
The completion of the reaction ...
In order to expedite **completion** (*завершение строительства*) **of** the building ...

Завершён
To determine when the reaction **is complete(d), ...**

Завёрнут в
Each cup **is wrapped in** paper.

Завинчивание
Driving (*or* **Screwing in**) screws and studs ...

Завинчивать [*см. тж.* **Туго завинчивать**]
The cutters are clamped up by **screwing in** screws *B*.
The base of the trap can **be screwed on** by hand.

Зависеть от [*см. тж.* **Значительно зависеть от, Не зависеть от, Обусловливаться, От которого зависит**]
An understanding of ... **is contingent on** a knowledge of ...
The choice of buffer **is dictated by** the values of the various dissociation constants.
Such methods must **rely on** the development of techniques that ...
The length and weight of the drag rope **are functions of** the size of the balloon.
The location of the base line **is counting-rate dependent** (*зависит от скорости учёта*).
The length of the casing **is dependent** (*or* **depends**) **(up)on** the delay factor.
The plasma volume **is determined by** this equilibrium.
The material of the electrode **is governed by** the nature of the material to be separated.
The vigour of the reaction **is governed by** the proportion of chromic acid.
The decision **lies with** the management.
The monomeric frequency **is** strongly **solvent dependent** (*зависит от растворителя*).
Here h_0 **is temperature dependent.**
The direction of motion of these molecules **depends on** the sign of the detuning of the laser frequency.
The properties of clay materials **are controlled by** at least five major factors.
The understanding of the structures of chemical compounds **hinges on** the understanding of the electronic configuration of the elements.

Зависеть от давления
The permeability of a vapour **is pressure dependent** (*or* **depends on pressure**).

Зависеть от ... в отношении
These schemes **depend for** their success **on** the proper choice of certain parameters.
All of these new methods **depend on** the properties of gases **for** their operation.

Зависеть от температуры
The virial coefficients **are temperature dependent.**

Зависеть от того, как
The manner in which the load is deposited **depends (up)on how** the inflow decelerates.

Зависеть от того, является ли он
Many properties of molecules **depend on whether they are** polar or nonpolar.

Зависимость [*см.* **В зависимости от, Изменяться в зависимости от, Соотношение**].

Зависимость между [*см. тж.* **Взаимосвязь**]
The conductivity-concentration relationship of a DNA sample ...
Test data show **a direct relationship between** CO_2 content **and** pH.

Зависимость от давления
The pressure dependence of the boiling point is given by the Clapeyron equation.

Зависимость от *z и т.п.*
The *z*-**dependence of** the field amplitudes ...

Зависящий от
This is a complicated property **dependent** (*or* **depending**) **on** many factors.

Зависящий от времени
Integration is a **time-dependent** operation.

Зависящий от погоды
Infrared transmission may **be weather dependent.**

Зависящий от температуры
The number of such reactions is strongly **temperature dependent.**

Заводские условия [*см.* **В заводских условиях**].

Завоёвывать всеобщее признание
Dalton's atomic theory **won** (*or* **gained**) **general acceptance** (*or* **recognition**).

Завоёвывать всё большую популярность по сравнению с
The molecular-orbital approach **has** steadily **gained favour over** the valence-bond treatment.

Завоёвывать мировую славу
He **had won international recognition for** his system of ...

Завоёвывать популярность
These devices **are** rapidly **gaining (in) popularity.**

Завоёвывать права гражданства
In 1949 giant computers **were coming into their own.**
Structural bonding **is** rapidly **taking its place** along with bolting, rivetting, welding, and brazing as a method of fastening.
Another on-the-horizon development that **is gaining ground** is the laser.

Завоёвывать признание
These tanks **are gaining acceptance for** in-plant storage.
This design **has gained** (*or* **won**) **recognition.**

Завоёвывать принадлежащее ему по праву место
The furnace **is assuming its right place in** the production line.

Завоёвывать прочное положение
These starters **have become firmly established as** the most advanced ...

Завоёвывать широкое признание
This idea **gained wide (spread) acceptance** (*or* **recognition**).

Заворачивать в
Wrap the part **with** (*or* **in**) asbestos cloth.

Загадочный
The **puzzling** longevity of giant molecular clouds could be attributed to ...

Загибать по радиусу
The metal strip **is bent round a** small **radius.**

Загибаться кверху
The curves **bend upwards.**

Заглатывать или вдыхать
This amount of plutonium is considered hazardous for **ingestion or inhalation.**

Заглушать взрыв
Underground explosions can **be muffled.**

Заглядывать в
If you **consider** (*or* **consult**) Table 6, ...
Let us **look into** the history of ...
If you **refer to** a chart, you will notice that ...
Before you can proceed with ... blueprints must **be consulted.**

Заглядывать в будущее
In closing let me **look to the future.**

Заглядывать глубже в
Ample references have been provided for those interested **to delve deeper into** the mathematics of shock wave behaviour.

Загнут вниз
The equilibrium line **is curved downwards.**

Загнуть [*см.* **Загибать по радиусу**].

Загонять заклёпку
Driving rivets in sheet metal ...

Загораться [*см. тж.* **Воспламеняться**]
Eventually the material reaches an ignition point and **bursts into flame** (*or* **ignites**).
The oil well **caught fire** recently.

Загораться ... пламенем
Each drop **will burst into a** greenish **flame.**

Заготовка из чистого материала

Since filled and pigmented fluorocarbon can be more abrasive than **virgin stock,** longer tool life will result if ...

Загружать печь рудой
The furnace is charged with ore.

Загружаться в
In this process molten metal **is charged into** an open-hearth furnace.

Загруженный [*см.* **Вновь загруженный**].

Загрязнение [*см. тж.* **Воздействие загрязнений на человека, Вызывать загрязнение, Не допускать загрязнения**]
This water is chlorinated to prevent slimes from **fouling** plant units.
Fouling may be severe.
Industrial **pollution of** our environment by nonradioactive but toxic substances ...

Загрязнение атмосферы
Atmospheric contamination (*or* **pollution) from** surrounding industrial plants ...

Загрязнение, вызванное человеком
Then we shall be better able to understand how **man-made pollutants** are distributed in the ocean.

Загрязнение окружающей среды [*см. тж.* **Организация по борьбе с загрязнением окружающей среды**]
Pollution (*or* **Contamination) of the environment.**
Environmental pollution is reduced by economical spraying of plants (*растений*).

Загрязнение от автомобильных газов
Automobile(-exhaust) pollution.

Загрязнённый
The surface will become **contaminated by** this material.
The highly **polluted** air of an industrial city ...

Загрязнитель от автомашин
NO_x is one of the most difficult **automotive pollutants** to control.

Загрязнять [*см. тж.* **Не загрязнять окружающую среду**]
Glue used in bonding the pattern has a low ash content so that it **won't foul** metal in the mould.

Загрязняться
This water **is now being contaminated** (*or* **polluted) by** the addition of human and industrial waste products.

Загрязняющий газ
Pollutant gases pose threats.

Загущать
When necessary, the solution **is thickened with** gelatine.

Задаваемая задача [*см.* **Задача, задаваемая компьютеру**].

Задавать
The upper limit may **be preset** (*or* **specified,** *or* **preassigned,** *or* **prescribed**) according to the requirements.
This line **is given by** two simultaneous equations.
The diagonal points **are given by**
$\rho = (\alpha_a + \beta_b) / (\alpha + \beta)$.

Задавать значение
It will be desirable to **set the** limit **values** without measurement.

Задаваться
The vector field **is given by** the following expression: ...

Задан
ψ = constant may **be specified by** a straight line.
Any point on the plane can **be specified by** a pair of coordinates (*A*, *B*).

Задан произвольно
This value may **be prescribed** (*or* **assigned) arbitrarily.**

Заданная величина
A prescribed (*or* **predetermined,** *or* **preassigned,** *or* **preset,** *or* **specified**) **value.**

Заданный [*см. тж.* **Данный, Заранее установленный, При заданном**]
At **designated** pressure and temperature conditions ...
The *yw*-plane in which *z* is less than **a given** number ...
These systems are designed to meet certain specifications under **given** conditions.
The book is trimmed to **prearranged** size.
Prearranged schedule.
A relief valve, set at a **predetermined** (*or* **preassigned**) working pressure, spills the excess back to the reservoir.

If wear exceeds **prescribed** (*or* **preset,** *or* **preselected**) limits, the camshaft should be replaced.
Torpedoes can travel on **a preset** course.
The conveyor feeds **a specified** amount of coal into ...
When a rocket passes within **a specified** distance of the target, ...

Задача [*см. тж.* **Взять на себя задачу**]
Problem 1. To determine the projections of a line which ...
The challenge has been in design**ing** the turbine to direct this additional cooling air where it is really needed.
The challenge now **is to** explain why the atmosphere of Venus ...
It is the concern of the analyst **to** seek ...

Задача, задаваемая компьютеру
Typical linear-programming **problems presented to computers** involve hundreds or even thousands of variables.

Задача на пропорцию
A problem in proportion.

Задача о
Thus **the problem on** compact linear operators was solved.

Задача по акустике
In solving **problems in** room **acoustics,** the characteristics of the boundaries are usually expressed in terms of impedances.

Задача состоит в том, чтобы
Alcohol vapour **is to be** recovered from a hot gas stream.
It is desired to recover alcohol vapour from an air stream.
The challenge was to increase the sensitivity of ...

Задача, стоящая перед
The first major **problem facing** the control engineer is: ...

Задействовать
This energy goes into **setting in motion** the system made up of the two particles.

Заделан в
Coils **are encapsulated** (*or* **incorporated**) **in** a hollow, cylindrical shell.
The superconducting wire can be made of thin niobium-titanium filaments that **are embedded in** copper.
The wire **is embedded in** the floor.

Заделанный [*см.* **Встроенный**].

Задерживать [*см. тж.* **Замедлять, Мешать, Предотвращать, Препятствовать**]
Surfactants are known to **inhibit** (*or* **retard,** *or* **slow down**) crystal growth from supersaturated solutions.
This operation **was holding up** the entire assembly line.
These oil pockets **impede** the flow of air.
Sodium nitrate **inhibits** corrosion of underwater structures.
Some bacteria have clogged the flow of oil in the sands and **retarded** production.
The deficiency of rainfall **hampers** (*or* **stunts**) the growth of farm crops or other vegetation.

Задерживать развитие
Glass lenses have threatened **to block the development of** higher powered lasers.

Задерживать рост
This concentration of sugar is sufficient **to inhibit** (*or* **impede,** *or* **stunt,** *or* **delay,** *or* **retard**) **the growth of** most microorganisms.

Задерживаться [*см. тж.* **Проскакивать и задерживаться**]
Metalworking production operations **are** often **halted by** inefficiency in the materials-handling system.

Задний план [*см.* **На заднем плане, Отодвигать на задний план**].

Задолго до
An increase in deep-earth gas pressure **well before** (*or* **well in advance of**) an earthquake ...

Задолго до начала 20-го века
Long before the 20th century dawned (*or* **began**) (*or* **Long before the dawn of the 20th century**) ...

Задолго до того, как
This was **well** (*or* **long**) **before** the cells began to develop transformed appearance.

Задумайтесь на секунду (минуту) о том
Consider for a moment what would happen if shear stresses could exist parallel to the earth's surface.

Задуман как
The present article **is designed as** a tutorial on how best to expoit ...
This text **is** not **intended as** mathematical theory, but rather ...

Задумывать
The designer **conceived** the idea of a submarine with three pressure hulls.

Заедание
To avoid **binding between** parts, a minimum clearance is critical for a running fit.
Sticking of the valve stem ...
The jamming of the wheel shaft ...
A compensation cone prevents **seizures** from expansion due to moisture or heat.

Зажат между
The diaphragm **is clamped** (*or* **sandwiched**) **between** metal plates.

Зажигать дугу [*см. тж.* **Дуга зажигается**]
A pair of electrodes touch and **draw an arc.**
To initiate an arc.
To start (*or* **strike**) **an arc.**

Зажигать топливо
The heat of compression **ignites the fuel.**

Зажигаться I
The thyratron **will fire.**
The arc **is struck** between the electrode and the charge.
The electric arc **is drawn** between two electrodes.

Зажигаться II
The sample **is** placed in the combustion crucible of the calorimeter and **ignited by** electric connections.
The primary explosive detonates readily when **set afire by** the primer.

Зажигаться III
The light **blinks on** as the movement starts.

Зажимать в
Hold the tubing **in** a lathe collet.

Зажимать деталь
The part may be clamped in any position.

Зажимать между центрами
Parts up to 4 in. in length can **be held between centres.**

Зажимное приспособление
A **clamping device.**

Заземлённый на корпус
One wire **is earthed** (*or* **grounded**) **to the frame of** the instrument.

Заземляться
The case **is earthed** (*or* **grounded**) by one core of the connecting cable.

Зазор между
A tilted coupling allows tool removal with as little as 1/2-in. **clearance between** tool point and workpiece.
Piston-to-head clearance.

Заинтересоваться
They **have taken an interest in** the concept of ...

Займёмся
Here **we shall be concerned with** the systems in which ...
We **shall take up** this subject now.

Заказ [*см.* **Выполненный по (индивидуальному) заказу, Выполнять заказ, По заказу, Повторный заказ, Поставлять по заказу**].

Заказан
A new air-cooled transformer **is on order** (*or* **has been ordered**).

Закалённый на воздухе (в воде)
Air (Water) hardened.

Закалка [*см.* **Воздушной закалки**].

Закалка в воде
Water quenching.

Закалка в масле
Oil quenching.

Заканчивать [*см. тж.* **Завершать**]
The entire job **was completed** (*or* **accomplished,** *or* **finished**) in 5 days.

Заканчиваться [*см. тж.* **Завершаться, Прекращаться**]
The changes **come to a close** when the sediments become a solid sedimentary rock.
When the reaction **is complete(d), ...**
When the period of crustal stretching **is over** (*or* **ends**), ...
The Period **ends with** a noble gas (in the Mendeleyev Table).
Conductors **terminate** (*or* **end**) **in** space lugs for connection to ...

Закладывать [*см.* **Заложен, Заложить основу для**].

Закладывать в
Steel bars **are embedded in** the concrete if the structure involves tensile stresses.

Закладывать в компьютер
Data from the acquisition system can **be fed into a computer.**

Закладывать основу [*см. тж.* **Заложить основу для**]
The book **lays the groundwork for** the important area of solid state physics and ...
He **laid the groundwork** (*or* **foundation**) **for** the discipline of ethology.
The work of these pioneers **was** primarily **responsible for the development of** the theory.

Заклёпка [*см.* **Загонять заклёпку**].

Заключать [*см.* **Из этого вытекает** (*или* **следует**), **что**].

Заключать в
When such species **are confined in** a closed jar, they will die in a few hours.
To encase (*or* **enclose**) the crystal **in** a glass envelope ...

Заключать в оболочку
Such transducers are constructed by **placing a case around** a unit cell.

Заключать в себе I
The organic contents of these shales include conodonts and concretions which **enclose** phosphatic brachiopods, shark remains, and small cephalopods.

Заключать в себе II
The rapid motion observed in the superluminal sources may **hold** the key to the one-sided structure.
The amplitude and phase of the sine wave **embody** information on the structure of the celestial object.

Заключать в себе зародыш идеи
His illustration **carries the germ of the idea of ...**

Заключать в скобки
To put (*or* **enclose**) **in brackets** (*or* **in parentheses**) (*or* **To bracket**).

Заключать договор (*или* **соглашение**, *или* **контракт**)
To conclude an agreement.
The contract was awarded to another company.
They **had contracted for** 15 million barrels annually.
To make a contract for an installation with a construction firm.
To strike a contract (*or* **bargain**).

Заключаться в [*см. тж.* **В этом заключается, Состоять в**]
The essential difference between an incompressible and a compressible fluid **is in** the speed of sound.
The key to the structure **lay with** the arrangement of the heterocyclic amines.
This operation **consists in** heating the material to 50°C above ...
The chief advantage of the new device **lies in** its versatility.
The answer **resides in** the fact that ...
The greatest value of the periodic table **resides in** its ...
Another series of tests **involved** drawing of hard steel wire.

Заключаться в том, что
The uncertainty principle **implies that** even if ...
The importance of such structures **lies in the fact that ...**

Заключение [*см.* **Вывод, Выводить заключение, Приходить к выводу**].

Заключён в
The gas **is confined in** a container.
The compound **is embedded in** glass.
The capillary tube **is encased** (*or* **enclosed**) **in** an outer protecting tube.
The operating mechanism **is** totally **enclosed in** a case.
The apparatus **is housed in** a steel case.
The pipe **is housed** in a cylindrical cast-iron container.

Заключён в кожух
This section of the machine **is jacketed** for water cooling.

Заключён в оболочку
All members **are enclosed in a** lipoprotein **envelope** (*biol.*).

Заключённый в металлическую оболочку
Metal-encased capacitors ...

Заключённый в оболочку
The central organelle is a **membrane-enclosed** nucleus where genetic material is organized into chromosomes.

Заключённый в стеклянный колпак
The **glass-enclosed** switch is very compact.

Заключённый между [*см. тж.* **Ограниченный**]
These bearings are characterized by balls or cylinders **confined between** outer **and** inner rings.
The area **enclosed by** the curve **and** two straight lines ...
The angle **included between** the radius through the given point **and ...**

Закон [*см.* **Выводить закон, По закону, Подчиняться закону, Твёрдое правило**].

Закон о том, что
Archimedes' **law that** an immersed body ... is the principal law of aeronautics.

Закон регулирует
Ultimately what we can do here on the Earth will be limited by **the** same **laws that govern** the economy of astronomical energy sources.

Законно усомниться в том, что
One can **legitimately doubt that** this circulation is a primary process.

Закономерно повторяться
There is **a regular repetition of** the different layers.

Закономерный
The satellites exhibit some **regular** trends, such as increasing size with distance from Jupiter.

Закончен [*см. тж.* **Окончен**]
The aqueous phase can be left in the funnel until the procedure **is complete(d).**

Закончен на ... процентов
The plant **is 95% complete(d)** (*or* **finished**).

Законченная теория
The discovery finally led to **a full-blown theory of** plate tectonics.

Законченный [*см.* **Незаконченный**].

Закончить главу
Before **closing** this **chapter** we shall attempt ...

Закончиться [*см.* **Кончаться**].

Закорачивать
This capacitor **is shorted out** by a relay.
This action closes contacts which **short out** the amplifier input stages.
Such batteries can **be short circuited** without injury.

Закорачивать на корпус [*см.* **Заземлённый на корпус**].

Закрепление деталей
The universal fixture may be employed for **holding** (*or* **fastening,** *or* **clamping**) **workpieces.**

Закрепление на
This device is used for **securing** gears, pulleys and other components **to** shafts.

Закреплён [*см. тж.* **Жёстко закреплён, Прочно закреплён**]
The board should **be fixed** (*or* **fastened,** *or* **attached,** *or* **secured**) **with** screws.

Закреплён на
The propeller **is fitted to** the shaft.

Закреплён неподвижно
A horizontal boring machine **holds** the workpiece **stationary on** a movable table.
The hydrogens in cyclopropane **are fixed in position** and are not free to move.

Закреплённый на шпонке
A **keyed** shaft section ...

Закреплять I
Cylinder diameter at any point may be determined by **locking** the instrument at that point.
Tapes, rubber bands, etc., have been used **to secure** the mechanism in transit.
The insulation **is secured to** the deck.
All bolts must **be** properly **secured with** approved nuts.
The pipe should **be secured in** the jaws of the bending table.
The workpiece **is clamped on** the table.
The drill **is clamped in** a drill holder.

Закреплять II
Quenching **fixes** the structural changes which occurred under heating.

Закреплять в нужном положении
The screw **locks** the blade **in position.**

Закреплять в патроне
The drill **is held in a chuck.**

Закреплять на [*см.* **Прикреплять к**].

Закреплять на месте
The dummy is removed, the mould **is locked in place** and the melted bronze is poured in.

Закреплять на шпонках
The disks **are keyed to** the spindle.

Закреплять резец
The tool is held during grinding **in** a universal vice.

Закрепляться
A component **is** loaded and **secured by** a toggle clamp.

Закрепляться на тягах
Tall steel chimneys of small diameter cannot economically be made self-supporting and must **be guyed.**

Закрепляющий
It is recommended that, periodically, the nuts or screws **securing** the clamping plate should be checked.

Закруглённый
Grinding of **radiused** (*or* **rounded**) and flat portions on the work ...

Закруглять
Corners and edges **were rounded with** a file.
Round off rough edges.

Закручен
The beam **is curled into** a ring by the magnetic field.

Закручен вокруг
The two polynucleotide chains **were wound around** a common axis.

Закручивать
The magnetic field **curves** the particles **into** circular orbits.

Закручиваться
Positive and negative particles **curve** in opposite directions.

Закрывать глаза на
Just because a phenomenon cannot be reconciled with what we know, we need not **shut our eyes to** it.

Закрывать пробкой [*см. тж.* **Затыкать пробкой**]
Plug the exit **with a** plastic **stopper.**
The opening of the jug **is plugged by a** rubber **stopper.**

Закрыт с трёх сторон
The container **is closed on three sides.**

Закрыт со всех сторон
This chamber **is** completely **enclosed on all sides,** top and bottom **by** a circulating water jacket.

Закрытая кабина (*напр.* **экскаватора**)
An enclosed cab.

Закрытое помещение [*см. тж.* **В закрытом помещении**]
Gaseous agents are indispensable for disinfecting rooms or other large **enclosed spaces.**
The vehicle may have a body (**an enclosed compartment** for people or commodities).
Architectural acoustics is the science of planning and building **an enclosure** (*дальше приравнивается к room*) to ensure the most advantageous flow of properly diffused sound to all listeners.

Закрытый
Enclosed mercury switches control the heaters.
The panel-type compass consists of a **closed** glass cylinder filled with a liquid and ...

Закрытый кузов
Sedan is **a closed body** with two or four doors.

Закрытый сосуд
A closed (*or* **sealed**) **vessel.**

Закрытый стеклянной пробкой
The liquid chemicals are in **glass-stoppered** bottles.

Закупоривать

Organic slimes tend **to plug** (*or* **clog**) the filters.

Залегать
Anthracite **occurred** along the axes of deeply eroded synclines.
Coal **occurs** in layers.

Залегать на большой глубине
Beds of halite **are buried at great depth.**

Залегающий слоями
Anthraxylon consists of coal **occurring in layers** (*or* **bands**).

Залежи [*см.* **Соляные залежи**].

Залежи промышленного значения
The large masses of hydrocarbons found in the **commercial deposits ...**

Заливать
The clip screws must not be disturbed; for this reason they **are sealed with** shellac varnish.

Заливать в формы
The liquid **is poured into** sand **moulds.**

Заложен
An entire complex of biological servomechanisms **is built into** the body of every mammal.

Заложенный в [*см. тж.* **Вмонтированный, Встроенный**]
Steel bars **embedded in** the bottom lining conduct the current into a layer of molten aluminium.

Заложенный в нём
Every biological system has **built-in** controls to initiate or accelerate a process under some conditions and ...

Заложить [*см.* **Закладывать в**].

Заложить основу для [*см. тж.* **Закладывать основу**]
Let us describe these mechanisms in order **to lay a foundation for** our discussion of high-temperature deformation.
The objective of this chapter is **to lay the foundations of** an approximate method which ...
The paper **laid the groundwork for** the modern science of biology.

Замедленный [*см.* **В замедленном темпе**].

Замедленный рост
In plants high dosages of radiation result in **stunted growth.**

Замедлять [*см. тж.* **Задерживать**]
Lowering of temperature tends **to slow down** the reaction.
The positive-ion space charge **slows down** the incoming ions.
Gas backpressure in the mould **moderates** flow of the metal.

Замедлять ход
The machine **will slow down** or stop.

Замедляться
When the speed **falls** below this level, ...
The shock waves **slow down** (*or* **are retarded**) appreciably as they progress along the tube.

Замена [*см. тж.* **Для замены в случае необходимости**]
Aluminium alloys have been used as **alternatives to** copper for overhead lines.
Changing the plasticizer from nitroglycerine **to** diethylene glycol dinitrate produces better physical properties.
Machines with provision for very rapid **change-over** (*or* **changing**) **from** one component **to** another ...
Replacement of the OH group in acetic acid ...
Replacing the vacuum tubes **with** (*or* **by**) transistors offered the benefit of greater reliability.
Direct **substitution of** titanium fasteners **for** all the steel fasteners (*замена титановыми крепёжными деталями всех стальных деталей*) used in a heavy bomber results in an airframe weight reduction exceeding 1500 pounds.

Заменён
That system **has been abandoned in favour of** (*or* **replaced by**) the more familiar one in current usage.

Заменив
The next generation is certain to discard this model **in favour of** (*or* **replacing it by**) a better one.

Заменимый [*см.* **Взаимозаменяемые**].

Заменитель
This alloy is used as **a substitute for** silver.
Anhydrous sodium tetraborate prepared by high-temperature dehydration of borax is used as **a replacement for** the parent material.

Заменить его другим
Those who prefer to abandon the term "geosyncline" may **substitute another term,** such as "sediment trough".

Заменять [*см. тж.* **Вытеснять, Может служить заменой, Помещать вместо него**]
If the lamp can **be changed for** another source, ...
Better agreement is obtained if the constant of Eq. (22) **is changed from** 3/7 **to** 0.425.
Worn parts should **be renewed.**
The sleeve bearings **were replaced by** (*or* **with**) ball bearings.
An atom which **substitutes for** a regular atom of the material ...
When small-diameter cylinders have to be welded, an alternative round type arm can **be substituted for** the normal pattern.
Power's method **substitutes** ^{24}Na **for** the dye.
The worm drive **has** almost completely **superseded** other forms of gearing.
During the past thirty-five years positive-displacement rotary pumps **have** to some extent **supplanted** reciprocating pumps for pumping viscous liquids.
This unit **takes the place of** bulky tuning elements.
When automatics **take over from** manual machines ...

Заменять друг друга
Ions of similar size and the same charge commonly **substitute for one another** in crystals.

Заменять его
Table salt is the most common source, but other compounds may **serve instead** (*or* **replace it**).

Замерзать
When the lake **freezes over** in the winter ...
Gravity tanks may be liable **to freeze up** in cold climates.

Заметен
No evolutionary trends **are in evidence** here.

Заметно
Concentrated sulphuric acid does not react **appreciably** with alkanes at ordinary temperature.
The presence of the shaper did not **materially** (*or* **substantially**) affect the velocity of this portion of the wave.
The plate is thick enough to withstand atmospheric pressure without flexing **perceptibly** (*or* **markedly,** *or* **noticeably**).
This has contributed **measurably** to their position of leadership in the industry.
Saturn is **distinctly** smaller than Jupiter.
This salt has a **distinctly** higher solubility than ...

Заметно влиять на
The chemical reactions of dienes **are markedly** (*or* **distinctly**) **affected by** the isolation of ...
The solvation energy **materially affects** ΔG.

Заметно отличаться от
The new algorithm **differs noticeably from** the simple method.

Заметное влияние на
Trace contaminants on the base metals may **have a pronounced** (*or* **marked,** *or* **tangible**) **effect on** results.

Заметное действие [*см.* **Оказывать заметное действие на**].

Заметное количество
Continuous bubbling failed to produce any **detectable** aspartic acid.

Заметный [*см. тж.* **Значительный, Чётко выраженный**]
The hydrogen molecules here cannot emit **detectable** amounts of radiation.
The corrosion of an ancient metal object may continue at an **appreciable** rate in ordinary air.
The greater this velocity, the more **conspicuous** the Doppler shift.
A **distinct** drop was found at 86°F.
All these alloys possess **marked** ferromagnetic properties.
Acridine shows **marked** fluorescence.
If no **perceptible** (*or* **sensible**) change takes place in ..., the solution is saturated.

The influence of temperature is much more **prominent** than that of the reactor throughout.
The wood has been subjected to **pronounced** humidity changes.
Only one reaction occurs at a **detectable** rate without a catalyst.
The hydrogen contains **noticeable** amounts of ammonia and ... as impurities.
The tilt became more **pronounced** with time.
Many of these compounds are not formed in any **detectable** amount.
These changes **are** most **evident** in gases.
Such additional variables have no **noticeable** effect on ...

Заметный для невооружённого глаза [*см.* **Видимый невооружённым глазом**].

Заметьте
Notice (*or* **Note**) that no time element is involved.

Замечание
One additional **comment** (*or* **remark**) is necessary.
Two more **points** need to be made.

Замечателен
This plant **is notable** (*or* **remarkable**) **for** many reasons, including its unique control system.

Замечать [*см. тж.* **Обнаруживать, Следует отметить, что; Фиксировать**]
Excessive vibration **was noted** in the suction line to the machine.
A red scale **was noticed** to be attached to the surface.
At this stage the first significant changes in elongation at fracture **were observed** (*or* **detected**).

Замечен
If the snowflake is turned by 60 degrees, no change **will be perceived.**

Замещать
Nonmetals may **replace** (*or* **substitute for**) the hydrogen in ammonia.

Замкнутое пространство
The volume of **the closed space** in which the power is burned, is ...

Замкнутый выключатель
When **the switch is closed, ...**

Замкнуться на себя
It is even possible that space may **close on itself.**

Замкнутая орбита
The fluid circulates in **a closed orbit.**

Замкнутый на себя
The disk is provided with a coil **closed upon itself.**

Замкнутый объём
When a candle burns in **an enclosed volume** of air, ...

Замкнутый сосуд
The gas is confined in **a closed vessel** (*or* **container**).

Замораживание ядерных арсеналов
Nuclear freeze.

Замыкание выключателя
Closure of the switch will cause chart-drive motor to operate.

Замыкание на
A connector fastened to the coil is protected from **shorting against** the upper grip by ...

Замыкать выключатель
To close the switch, the spring is charged by means of ...

Замыкать контур
The switch **closes the** triggering **circuit** of the flash lamp.

Замыкать накоротко
The switch **shorts out** the first section of resistance.

Замыкать цикл
The Carnot cycle is closed by the hot body evaporating the liquid to ...

Замыкаться
The magnetic lines of force **close** along the axis of the torus.

Замыкаться через
The primary circuit of the transformer **is completed** through a trip switch.

Занесён
The material deposited may **be brought in** from remote sources.

Занижение
This can lead to **underestimating** (*or* **understating,** *or* **underrating**) the error.

Заниженного диаметра
Normal size taps will usually cut **undersize** threads.

Заниженный
The calculation will yield a **conservative** result.

Занимательная математика
Recreational mathematics (*or* **Mathematics for fun**).

Занимать I
The machine **will take** some seven years **to** complete ...

Занимать II
A one-mole sample of any gas **occupies** the same volume as ...

Занимать большое место в
The bicycle **figured prominently in** the early development of the automobile.

Занимать важное место в
Today, farm animals **fill** (*or* **occupy**) **a highly important place in** the life of man.
It seems clear that this engine **will loom large in** the future of the engine industry.
Stackers **have a significant place in** the development of this equipment.

Занимать ведущее положение
By 1920, electron tubes and their circuits **came to the forefront** and replaced other means of generating radio waves.

Занимать видное место в
Prominent among the heavy machinery **in** the plant **will be** two rail-feeding type plano-milling machines.
Modern forging **occupies a prominent place in** primary metalworking.

Занимать видное место в планах
The issue **is high on the agenda of** the industrial concerns.

Занимать *чьё-л.* **внимание**
Semiconductors **will occupy our attention in** the bulk of this work.

Занимать второе место за
As a conductor of both heat and electricity, copper **ranks next to** silver.

Занимать ... место
Astaine **fills** (*or* **occupies**) **the place immediately below** iodine **in** group VII.
Mercury **ranks 16th from** the bottom of the list of elements **in** abundance in the earth.

Занимать много времени
The procedure **takes a good deal** (*or* **plenty**) **of** (*or* **much**) **time.**

Занимать много места
To take (*or* **take up,** *or* **occupy**) **a great deal of** (*or* **considerable**) **room** (*or* **space**).

Занимать непропорционально большую часть пространства
In a small car the drive train **takes up a disproportionate share of the room.**

Занимать несколько строк
This number **takes up a few lines.**

Занимать одно из первых мест среди
Hydrogen **is high on the list of** candidates for ...

Занимать орбиту
Such an electron **takes up** (*or* **occupies**) **a** large orbit.

Занимать первое место
Coal **heads the list** [*or* **rates** (*or* **ranks**) **first,** *or* **comes first,** *or* **is first,** *or* **occupies the first place**] as fuel **in** this industry.
Of the new processes which have appeared, the basic oxygen process seems **to hold the lead.**

Занимать первое место в мире
We **have a world lead in** the development of ...

Занимать площадь
The machine **occupies a floor space of** 55 by 80 in.

Занимать положение I
Hydrogen **holds a** most unique **position among** the elements.

Занимать положение II
The atom can **take up** (*or* **occupy**) only certain distinct **positions** in relation to an external field.

Занимать промежуточное положение между

Alexandrite **is intermediate in** spectral composition **between** ruby **and** emerald.

Занимать промежуточную позицию
We attempted **to steer a middle course between** these views.

Занимать прочное место
Morphine continues **to hold a firm place in** relief of severe pain.

Занимать умы
The classification of Riemann surfaces **has occupied** mathematicians for more than a century.

Занимать центральное место в
These compounds **hold a central position in** organic chemistry.

Заниматься I [*см. тж.* **Активно заниматься, Изучать**]
Large numbers of students **are involved in** the interpretation of analytical data.
We **are concerned with** computer design problems.
The group **is engaged in** research on ...
He **was engaged on** scientific research in many European centres.
Today much of the chemical industry **is involved in** the production of synthetic compounds.
Although Callisto is more distant from Jupiter, I shall **take it up** first because it is easier to understand.
In this chapter we **are concerned** (*or* **concern ourselves**) **with** carbonium ion.
To correct this situation we **shall engage in** a bit of mathematical gerrymandering.
The problem **was** first **taken up** seriously **by ...**

Заниматься II [*см. тж.* **Рассматривать**]
Before we **turn to** these processes, we will review ...

Заниматься изучением
We **have inquired into** the embryonic origins of ...

Заниматься изучением вопроса
He **addressed himself to the question** whether ...

Заниматься этим вопросом
How much do you know about the water you drink? You might be surprised and even concerned, if you l**ooked into the situation.**

Занимающийся
Of great interest to those **concerned with** reactor design is ...

Занимающийся вопросами
Metallurgists, mechanical engineers, chemists, physicists, production engineers and others **involved with** metalworking lubrication technology will find this book a valuable reference.

Заново рассмотреть вопрос о
We decided **to take a fresh look at** symptom formation.

Заносить
Data **are entered in** the proper sequence.

Занятое состояние (*физ.*)
All **states** below **are occupied.**

Заняться [*см.* **Рассмотрим**].

Заодно с [*см.* **Вместе с, Выполнен заодно с**].

Заодно с корпусом
An important feature of the process is that it enables **integral** flanges to be provided, and the need for welding operations is thus eliminated.

Западный конец стрелки компаса [*см.* **Северный конец стрелки компаса**].

Запаздывать
That time the eclipse **fell** (*or* **was**) **behind schedule.**

Запас [*см. тж.* **Истощать запас, Мировые запасы, Разведанные запасы**]
Reserves of coal ...
A stock of 100 tons could be maintained in the bunker.

Запас ... истощается
Plants **run out of** phosphate.

Запас истощился
The shops **have run out of** (*or* **are out of**) paper.
The supplies of machine parts **are exhausted.**

Запас на коррозию
This provides a 3/16 in. **corrosion allowance.**

Запас прочности
Margin of safety (*or* **Safety factor,** *or* **Assurance factor,** *or* **Safety coefficient,** *or* **Safety margin**).

Запас энергии
A fluid flowing under pressure in a closed channel possesses **a store of energy** in three different forms.

Запасать энергию
The energy in a mechanical press **is stored in** a flywheel.

Запасённая энергия
The potential **energy stored (up) in** a pair of attracting bodies is ...

Запасной
The **standby** (*or* **emergency**) transmitter is brought into use should a failure occur in the unit.

Запасные части [*см.* **Набор запасных частей и принадлежностей**].

Запах [*см. тж.* **Не иметь запаха**]
This gas **has** neither colour nor **odour.**

Запиливать на радиус
File the corner of the blocks **to the desired radius.**

Запись [*см.* **Магнитная запись на плёнке**].

Записывается как
This **is written** 20 ft per second or 20 ft/sec.

Записывать в виде
The error voltage may **be written (as)** $\upsilon_e = \upsilon_2 - \upsilon_3(Q/Q_F)$.

Записывать на
The current **is recorded on** a strip chart recorder.

Запитка мотора
Powering a motor.

Запланирован как
The system **was** originally **envisioned** (*or* **conceived**) **as** a drafting tool.

Запланирован на [*см.* **Должен быть**].

Запланированный [*см.* **Планировать**].

Заплата [*см.* **Накладывать заплату, Ставить заплаты на**].

Заподлицо
The **flush-mounted** case takes up a minimum of panel space.

Заподлицо с поверхностью
Headless bushings can be installed **flush with the** jig plate **surface.**

Заполнен [*см. тж.* **Наполненный воздухом**]
The internal mechanisms of these jacks **are packed in** grease.
A column **is packed** (*or* **filled**) to a depth of 5 ft **with** ceramic spheres 5 mm in diameter.

Заполнен на 3/4
The levelling bottle should **be three-quarters full of** water before beginning to ...

Заполнен наполовину
The sublevel **is half full.**

Заполнение колонки [*см.* **Высота заполнения колонки**].

Заполнение пробела между
This is done by **bridging** (*or* **closing**) **the gap between** these two dates.

Заполненный жидкостью *и т.п.*
Hydrogen must diffuse into **the liquid-filled** pores.

Заполненный электронный уровень
A completed (*or* **filled**) **electron level.**

Заполнять анкету
The patient was asked **to fill out the questionnaire.**

Заполнять пробел в
This increasing amount of information **closes** (*or* **bridges**) **the gaps in** the geologic record.
Polymerase was needed **to fill gaps in** newly synthesized molecules.
To fill in the blanks in the catalogue of new particles, ...

Заполнять разрыв между
Quantum theorists began **to close the gap between** basic principles and practical applications.

Заполняющий
The material is used in the form of granules **packed in** a column.

Запоминать
You will have **to commit to memory** (*or* **to memorize,** *or* **to remember**) the names of ...

Запоминаться
Measuring results obtained from a number of production parts **are stored** and subjected to computer analysis to reveal cycle errors.

Запоминаться на
The pulse **is stored into** the permanent magnet memory matrix.

Запоминаться на магнитной ленте
The data **are stored on a magnetic tape.**

Заправка топливом
Before **refuelling** became necessary, ...

Запрессован
Parts with interference can **be pressed-in** at much lower cost than final machining to exact dimensions.
These bearings **are pressed into** bearing housing blocks.

Запрещать
There is nothing in the laws of energy conservation that **would forbid** a proton **from** decaying into ...

Запрещено использовать в качестве
Polychlorinated biphenyls **are banned as** plasticizers because they are known to be environmental hazards.

Запрещено пользоваться
Tools contaminated with short-lived products must **be barred from use.**

Запрос [*см.* **По заявке**].

Запросы удовлетворяются оперативно
Enquiries **are dealt with expeditiously** (*or* **promptly**).

Запуск
The start-up of an electric motor ...

Запуск и остановка
A special valve in the exhaust cuts off the swish of noise during **startup and slowdown.**

Запуск спутника
The first **launch(ing) of** such **a satellite** is projected for next year with a possibility of an experimental **shot** at an earlier date.

Запускать [*см. тж.* **Включать**]
The computer **triggers** the N_2 laser.
The relay serves **to actuate** (*or* **energize**) the dial mechanism of the clock.
The incoming start pulse **fires** the start blocking oscillator.
The compressor **was started.**
A controlled system that contains only inertia, or an analogous quantity,will keep moving forever once it **has been set in motion.**
The laser plasma is only the catalyst that serves **to turn on** (*or* **trigger**) the steady-state fusion process.
Chemical reactions can **be initiated** in less than a nanosecond by means of high-power pulsed laser.

Запускать аэростат
This **balloon** is to **be flown** next year.

Запускать в космическое пространство
Different types of instruments **have been launched into space.**

Запускать в массовое производство
It has been estimated that if and when these engines **are put into mass production,** they should cost about half as much per horsepower as a conventional engine.

Запускать или останавливать
The dispatcher may **start up or shut down** a generating unit.

Запускать машину
When **the machine is started up ...**

Запускать на орбиту
To put (*or* **send,** *or* **inject**) **into orbit** (*or* **To place in orbit**).

Запускать ракету
The rocket was fired (*or* **launched**) in September.
For a flight to Saturn **the vehicle was shot** in the direction that ...

Запутанный [*см.* **Громоздкий**].

Запущен
The two space instruments **were borne aloft** in 1989.

Запущенный в производство
This rectifier **is** not yet **in production.**

Запущенный на ракете
A **rocket-launched** spectrometer ...

Запчасти [*см.* **Набор запчастей и принадлежностей, Ящик для запчастей и принадлежностей**].

Заражать
These fungi can **attack** plants.

Заражаться
The mite **acquires** (*or* **contracts**) **the infection** (*or* **becomes infected**) when ingesting leucocytes.
Clovers may **be attacked by** bacteria, fungi, and viruses.

Заражён *чем-л.*
The chicks **were infected with ...**

Заражённый вирусом
Viral-infected animal cells ...

Заразителен для
These fungi **are infectious to** man.

Заранее
The identities of the compounds are not known **in advance.**
The properties of these materials can be specified **beforehand.**

Заранее не знать ничего о
The members of the team **have no prior knowledge of** the product.

Заранее устанавливать
The upper limit may **be preset** (*or* **specified,** *or* **prearranged,** *or* **predetermined,** *or* **preassigned**) according to the requirements.

Заранее установленный
A relief valve set at a **predetermined** (*or* **prearranged,** *or* **preassigned,** *or* **preset,** *or* **specified**) working pressure spills the excess back to the reservoir.

Зарегистрирован
Altogether, 22 polarity reversals **are documented.**
There are few **documented** examples (*Зарегистрировано мало примеров*) of this mechanism.
Earthquakes **have been recorded** from depths of 700 kilometres.

Зарегистрированный
This was the highest temperature **recorded** (*or* **on record**).

Зарегистрированы случаи
Cases are on record of death in animals exposed to microwave radiation.
There are cases on record of the failure of a complex, expensive system because of the failure of an inexpensive component.

Зародилась мысль
In the early 1870s W. Thomson **conceived the** basic **idea of** interconnecting ...

Зародыш идеи [*см.* **Заключать в себе зародыш идеи**].

Зарождаться
A new generation of particle accelerators **is** now **in prospect**.

Зарождающийся
He suggested that N_2 was the stable form of nitrogen in the **incipient** solar system.
To hold **incipient** cracks open, ...

Заряд [*см. тж.* **Поддерживать заряд**]
A conductor is said to have a capacity of one farad if **a charge of** one coulomb raises its potential by one volt.
The excess **charge on** the oxygen atoms ...

Заряжать до
The capacitor **is charged to** +6 volts.

Заряжаться положительно (отрицательно)
Some particles **go positive (negative).**

Заряжённый положительно [*см.* **Положительно заряжённый**].

Заселён (*физ.*)
Those states **are** fully **occupied with** known particles.
A variety of vibrational levels of the initial excited electronic state can **be populated.**

Заселённость
A pair of electrons represents a maximum orbital **occupancy.**

Заскакивать в
Move the valve positioning arm until it **snaps into** the notch.

Заслонять
The gases **obscure** (*or* **screen**) the object **from view.**

An absorbing screen of dust may **block our view of** the more distant quasars.
The question of ultimate sensitivity should not **obscure** the important aspect of ...

Заслонять звезду
The dust permeates the dark clouds and **shrouds the** newborn **stars.**
The stars were masked (*or* **hidden**) **by** the clouds.

Заслуга [*см.* **Большая заслуга принадлежит**].

Заслуга принадлежит
The credit (*or* **Credit**) **for** the discovery of oxygen **is given** (*or* **is due,** *or* **goes**) **to ...**
The credit for the discovery of this element **is shared by** two men.

Заслуживать
This report **warrants** (*or* **deserves,** *or* **merits**) careful study.
One of these alloys **appears worthy of** investigation.

Заслуживать внимания
Several points in this curve **are worthy of notice** [*or* **deserve** (*or* **merit**) **attention**].
Fruits and seeds also occur in coalfield fossils and **deserve** (*or* **are deserving of**) more **attention** (*or* **consideration**) than has been accorded them in the past.
The new device **merits notice.**

Заслуживать дальнейшего исследования
The problem **is a valid one for further investigation** (*or* **deserves further investigation**).

Заслуживать дополнительного изучения
These materials **are (well) worth another look.**

Заслуживать подробного рассмотрения
The classical features of Parkinsonism are too well known **to merit detailed consideration here.**

Заслуживать рассмотрения
This fact **merits** (*or* **deserves,** *or* **is worthy of**) **consideration.**

Засорённый частицами
A **particle-laden** gas stream ...

Засорять
To clog air passages ...
This material **clogs** (*or* **plugs**) the pores.
Long chips **clog** the wheel surface.

Засоряться [*см.* **Забиваться**].

Заставить задуматься
Craters on Mars **set one thinking.**

Заставлять [*см. тж.* **Что заставит нас искать**]
Wind and temperature gradients **cause** sound ray paths **to** curve.
Trochotrons can **be made to** count at very high speeds.
It is possible **to have** the velocity decrease with pressure ...
A solid ferromagnet can **be induced to** move.

Заставлять вращаться
This set of nozzles **imparts spin to** the missile.

Заставлять колебаться
To set a molecule **into vibration, ...**

Заставлять разлететься
Electrostatic repulsions should **send** these protons **flying apart.**

Застревать в
For superfinishes, lapping compounds may be used. But these may **become embedded in** the fluorocarbon and may be difficult to remove.

Застроенный район
In **builtup** and industrialized **areas ...**

Застывание
The gases released during **the consolidation of** the surrounding rock ...
The metal can flow freely and evenly into a mould before **freezing** (*or* **solidification**) prevents further flow.

Застывать
When the lava **congeals** to solid rock, ...

Затвердевать [*см.* **Застывать**].

Затем [*см. тж.* **Впоследствии**]
We **next** describe the waterfront shapes.
The steel is heated to a suitable temperature and **subsequently** (*or* **then**) quenched.
They first do ... **Thereupon** they take tools and dig ...
The measurement was repeated after five minutes and **thereafter** at intervals until ...

Затем идёт
Next is a modified printed circuit.

Затем переходим к
We start with the step profile and **progress to** graded profiles.

Затемнённый
The **shaded** cross section ...
A **solid** circle (triangle, bar) ...

Заткнут пробкой
The opening of the jug **is plugged by a** rubber **stopper** [*or* **closed** (*or* **stopped up**) **with a plug**].

Затрагивать
Many details of the global system of plates **will be touched on** (*or* **upon**) in later chapters.

Затрагивать вопрос [*см.* **Касаться вопроса о том**].

Затратить ... лет на
The several years that **went into** (*or* **were spent on**) the project ...

Затраты [*см.* **Не останавливаться перед расходами, Расходы**].

Затраты энергии
This can be achieved with a minimum **expenditure** (*or* **consumption**, *or* **input**) **of energy.**

Затраченный
The power **expended** (*or* **consumed**) is ...

Затрачивать энергию
To measure the amount of **power** that **would be expended** (*or* **spent**) **for** cooling the strands ...

Затрачиваться
This is possible only when work **is expended.**

Затрачиваться на [*см. тж.* **Идти на**]
The instrument measures power **consumed by** its own current.
A major portion of the energy **is expended in** heating the contacts.
Most of the energy **goes into** moving the two-particle system.

Затруднение [*см.* **Без затруднений, Вызывать затруднения, Выходить из затруднения, Испытывать затруднения** (*или* **трудности**), **Не представлять особых затруднений, Представлять затруднения, Создавать большие затруднения, Трудность**].

Затруднение устраняется при (*физ.*)
The problem disappears with a multilevel system.

Затруднение устраняется путём
The problem is eliminated by employing ...

Затруднять [*см. тж.* **Усложнять**]
Internal conversion **hampers** (*or* **hinders**) the use of IR emitting dyes as laser materials.
One difficulty that **plagues** the investigation of cosmic jets is that it is not known how much ...
This **makes** further substitution **difficult** (*or* **hard**).

Затрудняться
The careful investigation of these factors **is made difficult by** the fact that ...
Earlier investigations **have been hampered by** the fact that ...

Затуплять
The abrasives in the materials rapidly **dull** the sharp cutting edges of the reamer.

Затуплять острые кромки
Break all sharp corners.

Затупляться
Make arrangements to have 3 or 4 cutting tools on hand as they **are** quickly **dulled.**

Затухание волн
Attenuation (*or* **Damping out**) **of** earthquake **waves ...**

Затухание сигнала
To prevent **deterioration** (*or* **attenuation**, *or* **decay**, *or* **damping**) **of the signal** before measurement, ...

Затухать
There will be time for the transient oscillations **to die out** before the control system reaches the steady state.
Any random motions of the fluid **are damped out.**

Затухать и усиливаться

The fluctuation **is** alternately **damped out and amplified.**

Затыкать пробкой [*см. тж.* **Закрывать пробкой, Плотно затыкать пробкой**]
The ends of the tube **are closed** (*or* **plugged) by** rubber **stoppers** [*or* **stopped up** (*or* **closed) with plugs].**

Затягивать [*см.* **Туго затягивать гайку**].

Заусенец [*см.* **Снимать заусенцы**].

Захватывать
The F-centre **has captured** an extra electron.

Захватываться
These neutrons **are captured by** the concrete shield.
A large excess of vacancies can **be trapped** in the lattice.

Заходить за
The electron cannot **go beyond** the turning point.

Заходить за рамки
Detailed treatment of distillation **is beyond the scope of** the present text.

Заходить на одну ступеньку дальше, чем
Such a limit is known as the post-Newtonian limit of the theory because it **goes one step beyond** the original approximate Newtonian limit.

Заходить слишком далеко
If the electrolysis **is** not **carried too far,** the middle compartment will experience no change.

Захоронение отходов в землю
The burial (*or* **underground disposal) of wastes.**

Зацепление [*см. тж.* **Находиться в зацеплении**]
When gears (inter)mesh, one pair of teeth must remain **in engagement** until the following pair are in a position to carry the load.
The meshing of a pair of huge cogwheels ...
The engagement of the sprocket **and** chain must be smooth.

Зацеплять
Internal gear teeth in the spindle nose **engage** the teeth on the shank of the tool.

Зацепляться с
The trigger **engages with** the collar.
The horns **fall** by gravity **into engagement with** the chain links.

Зачастую
Overlap between the two categories can be noted **on frequent occasions.**

Зачаточное состояние [*см.* **В зачаточном состоянии**].

Зачаточный [*см.* **В зачаточном состоянии**].

Зачинатель
He is one of **the pioneers** (*or* **initiators,** *or* **trailblazers**) in the development of traffic flow theory.

Зашлифовываться
Defects of cracks **are** chipped out and **ground** before being welded.

Зашпонивать на
The wormwheel **is keyed to** the vertical shaft.

Заштрихованный
Positive rates of change are indicated by the **crosshatched** regions.
The **shaded** region is forbidden.
Regions of ... **shown by hatching ...**

Защита [*см.* **В защиту, Коррозионная защита, Обеспечивать защиту**].

Защита от
Defense against attacking aircraft ...
Protection against accidental break in the supply lines ...
Protection of niobium **from** oxidation ...

Защита от излучения
Radiation shielding.

Защита от коррозии
Protection against (*or* **from) corrosion** (*or* **Corrosion protection**).

Защита от опасности
Safeguarding of persons **from hazards** that may arise from the use of electricity ...

Защита от перегрузки
Overload protection of instruments ...

Защитник (*теории и т.п.*) [*см.* **Противник**].

Защищать от [*см. тж.* **Предохранять от**]
In this way, the steel **is protected against** corrosion.
These pipes **are protected from** extreme heat and damage.
Oil seals **safeguard** the bearings **against** dust and grit.
Interferon **protects** cells **against** virus infection.
The dust **shields** the incipient stars **from** ultraviolet radiation.

Защищать от излучения
To protect against radiation.

Защищать от контакта с
To protect the solution **from any contact with** air ...

Защищать от коррозии
Nickel coating **protects** plug valves **against** (*or* **from**) **corrosion.**

Защищать от окисления
Protect base metal **against** (*or* **from**) **oxidation.**

Защищать от перегрузки
This power supply system **is protected against** (**excessive**) **overloading.**

Защищать от проникновения влаги
Teflon seals **keep out moisture.**

Защищать от пыли
Oil seals **safeguard** (*or* **protect**) the bearings **against dust** and grit.

Защищать теорию
He **championed** (*or* **advocated**) **the** glacial **theory.**

Защищён от
The precision ball screws **are** fully **guarded against** dirt and chips.
The desert basins **are shielded from** fresh maritime air by high mountains.

Заэкранирован
The conductors **are shielded with** a copper braid.

Заявка на ... за неделю до
The wood supplier requires **a week's notice for** delivery.

Заявка на патент подана
Patent applied for.
Patent pending.

Заявлять [*см.* **Утверждать, что**].

Звезда [*см.* **Взрыв звезды, Изображение звезды, Положение звезды**].

Звено [*см.* **Связующее звено**].

Звёздная величина
Star magnitude.
+12 **stellar magnitude.**
Third magnitude stars are readily visible to the unaided eye.

Звёздочка [*см.* **Помеченный звёздочкой**].

Звёзды, видимые невооружённым глазом
Unaided (*or* **Naked**)**-eye stars.**

Звук [*см.* **Издавать звук**].

Звучать неубедительно
This argument **has little force** now that we know ...

Здесь
At this point (*or* **time**) (*or* **Here**), it is worth noting that ...

Здесь и далее [*см.* **В дальнейшем**].

Здесь означает
Stability **is herein taken to mean that** a small output disturbance will cause ...

Здесь показан
Presented (*or* **Shown**) **here are** the principal units of the teletype line.

Здесь также [*см.* **И здесь**].

Здесь уместно напомнить о том, что
It is appropriate at this point to recall that...

Здесь уместно сделать экскурс в историю
A note of historical interest is appropriate here.

Здоровая основа
This flexibility provides a **sound basis for** development.

Здоровье [*см.* **Вредный для здоровья**].

Здравый смысл подсказывает нам, что

Common sense guides us to suppose that gradient is an important factor.
Common sense seems to tell us that there is not enough rain to supply the continuous flow of a river.

Зеленеть
The solution **turns green.**

Зелёная улица
The manager was given **the green light.**

Землетрясение [*см.* **Подверженный землетрясениям**].

Землетрясение в 8 баллов
An earthquake of magnitude (*or* **with a magnitude of**) **8** or more might well result in ...
The earthquake measured 8 on the Richter scale.

Земля сплюснута у полюсов и выпукла у экватора
The Earth is flattened at the poles and bulges at the Equator.

Земная кора [*см. тж.* **Верхние слои земной коры**]
Common **crustal** materials ...

Земной день
The spacecraft was to operate 243 **Earth days.**

Земной и морской
The skeletal structures of **terrestrial and marine** vertebrates are remarkably similar.

Зенковать
Internal threads should **be countersunk** on one side only.

Зеркально отражаться
The energy **is reflected specularly.**

Зеркальное изображение
Molecules that **are mirror images of** each other are known as enantiomers.

Зеркальное отражение
The reflection is specular.

Зерно [*см.* **На границах зёрен**].

Зигзагообразно
The chains of atoms are arranged **in zigzag fashion.**

Зимняя спячка [*см.* **Впадать в зимнюю спячку**].

Злоупотребление [*см.* **Чрезмерное употребление**].

Знак [*см.* **До ... десятичного знака, Из ... знаков, Иметь обратный знак, Противоположный знак, Равны по величине и противоположны по знаку**].

Знак минус (плюс)
The minus (plus) sign.

Знаком с [*см.* **Близко знаком с, Хорошо знаком с**].

Знакомить с
The students **are introduced to** crushing, grinding and gravity concentration methods.

Знакомиться с
In this chapter **we shall become acquainted** (*or* **familiar**) (*or* **shall familiarize ourselves**) **with** the tools the chemists employ for ...

Знакомство
Organic syntheses require **(a) familiarity with** known organic reactions.

Знакомство с литературой
Faraday was impressed by the young man's **conversance with** the literature.

Знакомый [*см. тж.* **Быть знакомым с, Известный**]
The most **familiar** symmetries are spacial ones.
Engineers **familiar** (*or* **acquainted**) **with** the operation of such machines ...

Знание [*см. тж.* **Глубокое знание**]
A knowledge of reaction mechanisms is of more than theoretical interest.
The study of chemistry provides **a knowledge of** natural processes in ...

Знать [*см. тж.* **Быть знакомым с**]
The chemist must always **be aware of** isomeric differences.

Знать по опыту, что
We know from experience that ...

Знать совершенно точно, что
We now know beyond doubt that ...

Знать, что
Chemists **were aware that** some type of bonding must be present between ...

Значащая цифра [*см. тж.* **До ... значащей цифры**]
Calculate the formula weight of sodium chromate **to four significant figures.**
Express numerical answers with an accuracy of **three significant figures** (*or* **digits**).

Значение I [*см. тж.* **Иметь много значений, Присваивать значение**]
Some **values of** ... are listed in Table 3.
Values for relative electronegativities of different elements have been estimated.

Значение II [*см. тж.* **Всемирного значения, Второй по значению, Иметь значение для, Иметь первостепенное значение, Иметь практическое значение, Иметь принципиальное значение, Иметь решающее значение, Иметь физическое значение, Не иметь значения, Не придавать значения, Первостепенное значение, Придавать большое значение, Приобретать большое значение, Решающее значение**]
However great may be **the importance of** wireless telegraphy to shipping ...
The torsion resistance of porcelain enamels **is important for** such products as refrigerators.
The implications of the word component will be explored in the next section.

Значение III
What is **the meaning** (*or* **significance**) **of** this term?

Значение для
The discovery of the corona of our galaxy has important **implications for** a long-standing problem.

Значительная доля
Soda-glass membranes contain **a high proportion** (*or* **percentage**) **of** sodium ions.

Значительная роль [*см.* **Играть значительную роль в**].

Значительная степень [*см.* **В значительной степени**].

Значительная часть [*см. тж.* **В течение значительной части года**]
The soil is dry **during much of** the year.
For much of that time the number of spots on the Sun has been increasing.
A major portion (*or* **part**) **of** the earlier work was concerned with ...
Compression is responsible for the inversion in the Los Angeles basin **during a good fraction** (*or* **part**) **of** the year.
In much of this region yields of rice have doubled.

Значительно [*см. тж.* **Намного, Существенно**]
Rays belonging to modes **well** above cut-off ...
Saturn's atmosphere is **markedly** thicker than Jupiter's.
Pressures within Uranus and Neptune are **significantly** (*or* **much**) lower than within Jupiter and Saturn.
In the parallel-slot type the core is **materially** greater than in the radial.
Compounds of potassium are **decidedly** (*or* **far,** *or* **much,** *or* **considerably**) less common than those of sodium.
This factor can contribute **materially** (*or* **substantially,** *or* **appreciably,** *or* **markedly**).
33,000 ft lb/min is **rather** more than the average horse is capable of, but it has been adopted by engineers and is known as a horse-power.
The treatment effects are **significantly** (*or* **vastly,** *or* **greatly**) different from zero.
The Curie point of barium titanite is **substantially** (*or* **much**) higher.
The local temperature may be **vastly** greater than (*or* may **greatly** exceed) the macroscopic cathode temperature.
In every case the percent of absolute line pressure pulsation was **way** below [*or* **much** lower (*or* lower **by far**) than] the allowable 3% level.
The poles are cut down **materially.**

Значительно более
The events leading to the assembly of a biological membrane are **far** (*or* **vastly,** *or* **considerably**) **more** complex.
A sphere of fifty miles radius has a volume of **well over** half a million cubic miles.

Значительно больше
Astronautical engineers must be **vastly** (*or* **considerably,** *or* **much,** *or* **far**) **more** weight conscious than ...
Well in excess of 80% ...
Well over 250 nuts were rejected.

Значительно больше всех других
This pipeline is **by far the largest** in Indonesia.

Значительно выше, чем
The inductance is measured at a frequency **well** (*or* **much,** *or* **considerably,** *or* **far**) **above** (*or* **beyond**) the self-resonant frequency of the capacitor.

Значительно дальше
In this layout the vertical runners have been carried down **well past** the lower cavities ...

Значительно зависеть от
The comparisons **depend heavily on** the value of *k*.

Значительно замедлять
This process **constitutes a significant hindrance to** crystal growth [*or* **considerably retards** (*or* **inhibits**) crystal growth].

Значительно легче
This makes them **far** (*or* **much,** *or* **considerably**) **easier to** move.

Значительно лучше, чем
The reflecting telescope **was a great improvement over** the refracting telescope.

Значительно менее
Chemiluminescence is usually slow oxidation, **not nearly so rapid as** in a flame.

Значительно меньше
Even this figure **falls far short of** the modulus of the new fibers used for reinforcing composites.

Значительно ниже
These signals are **well** (*or* **substantially,** *or* **much,** *or* **vastly**, *or* **significantly**) **below** the amplifier-saturation amplitude.

Значительно опережать своё время
Steno **was far ahead of his time.**

Значительно ослаблять сигнал
The signals were heavily (*or* **greatly**) **attenuated.**

Значительно отклоняться от [*см. тж.* **Далеко отклоняться от**]
These relations **deviate widely** (*or* **considerably**) **from** the ideal laws.

Значительно отличаться *чем-л.*
Lathes rebuilt by the company **vary widely in** size and design.

Значительно отличаться от [*см. тж.* **Резко отличаться от**]
The metallic glasses **differ in significant ways** (*or* **significantly,** *or* **greatly**) **from** crystalline metals.
The configuration of the atom in the solid **is much different from** that in the liquid.
These loading conditions **differ markedly** (*or* **appreciably,** *or* **substantially,** *or* **considerably,** *or* **greatly**) **from** the test conditions.
The process **is significantly different from...**

Значительно отличающийся от
Large hills have **a significantly different** microclimate on their south slopes **from** that on their north slopes.
The product consisted of amino acids in proportions **widely disparate from** the original.

Значительно отставать от
The velocity of the charge on the spinning disk **would fall far short of** the velocity at which a current travels in a wire.

Значительно перевешивать
This advantage in overall speed **far outweighs** the few extra iterations necessary to ...

Значительно перекрываться
X-rays and gamma rays **overlap generously.**

Значительно переоценивать (*антон.* **недооценивать**)
We **have grossly overestimated** (*anton.* **underestimated**) the available reserves of ...

Значительно превосходить
These dynamic effects may **far exceed** the hydrostatic forces.
This production **is far in excess of** the output of ...
Titanium fasteners **are** often **vastly** (*or* **considerably,** *or* **greatly,** *or* **much,** *or* **far**) **superior to** identical steel fasteners.

Значительно превосходящий
This will lead to developments **far beyond** those which seem likely at the present time.

Значительно превышать
The compound's specific strength and specific modulus **far exceed** those attainable in monolithic structural materials.

Значительно превышающий
Values of α **significantly** (*or* **considerably,** *or* **much,** *or* **far**) **greater than** $b + 1$ are required.

Значительно продвигаться
Meanwhile the work on the new synthetic **was well on its way.**

Значительно различаться
The values **differed widely** (*or* **were widely different**).
These parameters may **vary (very) widely.**

Значительно различаться по
Aquifers **differ widely** (*or* **considerably,** *or* **greatly**) **in** shape, areal extent, and thickness.

Значительно раньше, чем
In that case, the photon must have been converted into a hadron **well before** reaching the nuclear surface.

Значительно содействовать
Piston ring expanders **are a great aid in** slipping rings onto the pistons.

Значительно способствовать [*см. тж.* **Играть значительную роль в**]
Such combinations **have gone a long way toward** improving the results.
The demonstration of reversals in nature **has done much to support** this explanation.
A knowledge of the internal structure of carbonate banks **is a great help in** finding and developing oil reservoirs.
This **makes a major contribution to** ageing.
An analysis of ... **has added extensively to** an understanding of chain elongation.
The new enterprise can **aid materially** (*or* **substantially,** *or* **considerably,** *or* **greatly**) **in** meeting the country's requirements for ...
These features **contribute largely** (*or* **greatly,** *or* **vastly**) **to** the first-rate performance of this electrode.
Certain practices can **do much toward** assuring trouble-free operation.
Improvements in design **have gone far to** overcome this effect.
The development of microbiological assay methods for vitamin B_{12} **was of great aid in** permitting ...
The new system **goes a long way to** relieve monotony.
The development of the detector **has benefited greatly from** the interaction of ...

Значительно увеличивать
Nuclear propulsion **has vastly multiplied** (*or* **improved,** *or* **enhanced,** *or* **increased**) the capabilities of the submarine.
Service life of the tubes **has been drastically** (*or* **greatly,** *or* **considerably,** *or* **substantially**) **extended.**
Useful life **is increased considerably.**
The ease with which the nuclear force field deflects particles of lower energy **adds greatly to** the difficulty of working backward from the experimental data to the probabilities of alpha scattering.

Значительно улучшать (*или* **повышать**)
This **yields a large dividend in** accuracy.

Значительно уменьшаться
Circulation losses may **be substantially** (*or* **greatly,** *or* **vastly,** *or* **considerably,** *or* **appreciably,** *or* **drastically,** *or* **seriously**) **reduced.**

Значительно упрощённый
In Fig. 1 is seen a **much-simplified** block plan of the factory.

Значительно усиленный
A **heavily** (*or* **greatly,** *or* **considerably**) **reinforced** rectangular cross section is used in the column design.

Значительное изменение
The wood has been subjected to **pronounced** (*or* **drastic,** *or* **considerable,** *or* **substantial**) humidity **changes.**
Wide temperature **changes** (*or* **variations**).

Значительное количество
The original electron may lose **a great deal of** (*col.*) its own energy.

Значительное количество работ
A considerable body of work existed in the technical literature on the vacuum evaporation of the semiconductor indium antimonide.

Значительное количество сведений о
The experiments have provided **a considerable body** (*or* **amount**) **of information** (*or* **data**) **on** heat transfer to spheres.

Значительное преимущество
This would provide **a** further **significant** (*or* **important,** *or* **considerable,** *or* **great**) **advantage.**

Значительное расстояние [*см.* **На значительном расстоянии от**].

Значительное увеличение
At lower currents there is **a marked** (*or* **pronounced,** *or* **drastic,** *or* **appreciable**) **increase in** (*or* **of**) absorption.
The gain is appreciable (*or* **considerable,** *or* **substantial**).

Значительные успехи
A notable (*or* **considerable,** *or* **substantial,** *or* **significant**) **advance** has been made **in** the studying of this phenomenon.

Значительный [*см. тж.* **Большой, В значительной степени, Заметный**]
In the gas phase negligible attraction exists between molecules, while in a liquid attractive forces become **important.**
A **sizable** proportion of the particles can attain...
It is most improbable that any **sizable** population of identical molecules could result from random chance processes.
Nonsilicate minerals seldom make up a **major** part of an igneous rock.
Costs of steam and power generation are an **important** (*or* **appreciable,** *or* **considerable,** *or* **substantial**) part of overall plant costs.
In spite of this **impressive** progress, solid fuel motors have certain disadvantages.
Such boundaries present **major** (*or* **considerable,** *or* **great**) obstacles to slip propagation.
No **marked** change has occurred in the properties of the metal.
This can have a **material** effect on our decision.
Notable improvements have been made in reducing the size and weight of ...
Dependence of ultraviolet radiation on solar and geometric altitude is **pronounced.**
Illuminating the entire retina with diffuse light does not have any **dramatic** effect on the pulse rate.
Mass transfer during the period of drop formation can be quite **significant.**

Значительный по величине
The relativistic effects begin to be **important** at the accelerating voltages that are used.

Значительный процент
This belting contains **a substantial proportion** (*or* **percentage**) **of** nylon.

Значительных размеров
The Moon is the only other **sizable** object in the solar system for which ...

... значный
The length of the wire to be employed is indicated on a 3-**digit** display of the control unit.

Зная
Given mechanical properties of the material, a limiting stress is decided upon.
Knowing two angles and the included side for a given triangle, calculate its remaining sides with trigonometry.
With a knowledge of the earthquake-wave velocities, it is possible to ...

Зона видимости [*см.* **В зоне видимости**].

Зона отдыха
A recreational area.

Зрение [*см.* **Попадать в поле зрения**].

Зрительное восприятие
Visual perception can play quite a few tricks.

Зубчатая передача [*см.* **Соединён зубчатой передачей, Сцепление**].

И

И [*см.* **А также**].

И более [*см. тж.* **И выше**]
Ultrasonic waves with frequencies of a billion hertz **and up** (*or* **over,** *or* **more**) are capable of travelling several centimetres through a solid medium.

И в то же время
Electronic equipment in space satellites must be expected to withstand considerable acceleration **while** functioning properly.
Analytical chemistry is a subject which is broad in scope **whilst** requiring a specialist approach.
This notation gives a simple **yet** precise name to particular enantiomers.
Special cooling stages are necessary to employ a superfluid film **and still** maintain the low temperature of the cell.

И в том, и в другом направлении
In either direction, positioning movements are made at a speed of 200 in. per min.

И в том, и в другом случае [*см. тж.* **В любом случае из двух**]
In either case the strength of the absorption band was related to ...

И в этом случае
Here (*or* **In this case**), **too,** ellipticity is apparent.

И впредь будет
Nickel alloys **will continue to** dominate applications in the 1000 to 2000°F range.

И всё же [*см.* **И в то же время**].

И выше [*см. тж.* **И более**]
These alloys are suitable for use at temperatures of 1000°F **and above** (*or* **up**, *or* **over**).
Glass-bonded mica is suited to applications at 400°C **(and) up(wards).**
There are 329 motors of 1 hp **or over.**

И далее [*см. тж.* **Начиная с ... и далее, И позже**]
These aspects are discussed on p. 96 **et seq.** (*or* **and further**).

И далее к
Radiation passes successively through a slit **and then on to** the detector.

И если да, то
We need to determine whether there were any daughter products present, **and if so,** how much.

И за его пределами
In the infrared region **and beyond ...**

И здесь
Here too (*or* **again**) the answer is yes.

И ..., и [*см.* **Как ..., так и**].

И менее
Larger sizes will crush 36-in. boulders to a product of 6 in. **and under.**

И многие другие
Modern studies have shown that sage, cloves, rosemary, and thyme, **to name but a few,** prevent peroxide development.

И наоборот
If the load is increased, the life of the bearing will be decreased, **and conversely** (*or* **vice versa**) if the load is decreased, the life of the bearing will be increased.
Conversely, (*or* **And vice versa**) it is possible to use measurements.
To put it in reverse, any algebraic number is a possible solution for some polynomial equation.

И обратно [*см.* **В ... и из него**].

И позже
From 1620 **onward ...**

И последующий
The usual production procedure consists in salt creaming **followed by** (*or* **and subsequent**) acid coagulation.

И поэтому
The fragments of Saturn's ring are much more sparsely distributed than those of the bright rings, **which is why** the crape ring seems so dim.

И, следовательно
A slight increase in the coil current **and hence** in its flux renders ...
Consequently, ...
Therefore, ...
A measurement of ... can yield a value of the rotational constant **and thus** a value for the moment of inertia.

И сотрудники
Ivanov **and his associates** (*or* **co-workers,** *or* **collaborators**) ...
Ivanov **and others** (*or* **et al.,** *or* **a. o.**) ...

И так далее

Out of the remaining n - 1 objects a second object may be chosen in n - 1 ways, **and so on** (**, and so forth**).
A particle whose spin half-integer values such as 1/2, 3/2, and 5/2, **and so forth,** is called a fermion.

И так далее, до бесконечности
The level of the activating substance must in turn be under the control of a second activator, and that one under the influence of a third, **and so on indefinitely.**

И, тем самым
The transformation (F.4) satisfies condition (F.3) **and so** (*or* **thereby**) defines a contact transformation.

И то, и другое [*см.* **Или и то, и другое**].

И тогда
Glass is an excellent electrical insulator — unless heat causes the glass to melt, **in which case** it becomes an effective ionic conductor.

И только
There is one **and only** one *A* for every *B*.

И тому подобное
The computer receives and stores data on inventory balances, manufacturing schedules, work authorization, **and the like.**

И тот, и другой
Overburden is removed by draglines or scrapers, **or (a combination of) both.**

И это действительно так
The flatness of the disk suggests that it rotates at a fairly rapid rate, **and that is the case.**

Ибо [*см.* **В том смысле, что**].

Игнорировать [*см. тж.* **Не принимать во внимание, Не учитывать, Пренебрегать**]
The transmittance term may **be disregarded.**
The homogeneous conversion in liquid hydrogen is slow and can **be neglected** (*or* **ignored**).

Играть большую роль в
Life-style differences **play a large role** (*or* **part**) **in** the causation of these cancers.

Играть важную роль [*см. тж.* **Занимать большое место в, Иметь важное значение**]
Iron **enters, in an important manner, into** the activities of living organisms.
Use of this technique could **have a profound impact** [*or* **could play a great role** (*or* **part**)] **in** colorimetric analysis.
Sensitivity **is of paramount importance** here.
This value **plays an important part** (*or* **role**) **in** calculation of ...
These propellants do not now **play a large** (*or* **significant,** *or* **major,** *or* **vital**) **part in** rocket propulsion.
Insulin **plays a leading role in** the body's use of sugar.
Sound waves **have been vital to** the transfer of information from one organism to another.

Играть важную роль в экономике страны
Polyethylene **is** a plastic **of economic importance.**

Играть весьма важную роль
The distribution of different sediment types **is of great concern** (*or* **importance**) **in** oil exploration.

Играть весьма незначительную роль
Chemical energy, which plays a major role in present-day human activities, **counts very little in** the universe as a whole.

Играть всё возрастающую роль
Electronic devices have continued **to play an increasingly important part in** the development of transmission plant.

Играть главную роль
It is the ultimate temperature that **is of first importance.**

Играть значительную роль в
This quantity **is of considerable importance in** the understanding of ...
The gravitational field **does much to** shape the outer edge of the satellite's ring.

Играть исключительно важную роль в
Permeability **is of primary importance in** determining the rate of ground water movement.
Turbulent flow in fluids **is of vital importance in** the geological activity of streams.

Играть незначительную роль
He believed that volcanic eruptions **were of minor** (*or* **little**) **importance.**

Играть некоторую роль в [*см. тж.* **Играть определённую роль в**]
The enzyme **has** (*or* **plays**) **a role** (*or* **a part**) **in** the breakdown of trinucleotides.

Играть определённую роль в
Each of these factors **plays a part in** determining the breakdown potential.

Играть основную роль в
Amplitude-modulated radio **has a dominant role** (*or* **plays a leading part**) **in** guidance and position location.

Играть решающую роль в
Hormones of the adrenal cortex **play a crucial** (*or* **decisive**) **role in** the sensory functions in man.
The reassociation of atomic hydrogen into molecular hydrogen **is** not **of crucial importance in** cooling the arc.
Such couplings **are crucial in** organogenesis.
The ability to distinguish between benign and malignant tumours **is crucial in** determining the appropriate treatment of the patient.

Играть роль [*см. тж.* **Иметь значение**]
This constituent **fulfils** (*or* **plays**) **the role of** an internal standard.
The pickup **acts as** a miniature generator.
The transport velocity **plays a** similar **part** (*or* **role**) **in** the theory of ...

Играть свою роль в
Symmetries in the laws of nature **have played a part in** the construction of ...

Идеал
Such gases will deviate from **ideality** to some extent.

Идеально подходить для
Centrifugal pumps of the horizontal volute type **are ideally suited for** removing condensate.

Идеальной чистоты
Rainwater, once considered **the ultimate in purity** for storage in cisterns, may now contain airborne pollutants.

Идеальный
This law is true only for an **ideal** gas.
The **ideal** contact screen will be one that automatically compensates for ...

Идеальный кристалл
A perfect crystal.

Идеальный с точки зрения
This car **is the ultimate in** performance, comfort and safety.

Идентично равен нулю
d_x **is identically (equal to) zero.**

Идентичный
The first term **is identical to** the excluded-volume term of Eq. (5).
Multilayer adsorption is assumed **to be identical with** (*or* **to**) vapour-liquid condensation.

Идея [*см.* **Зародилась мысль**].

Идёт [*см.* **За ним следует**].

Идёт речь о [*см.* **Если идёт речь о, О котором говорилось в**].

Идти [*см. тж.* **Затем идёт, Проходить**]
The reaction can **proceed** in either direction.

Идти в направлении [*см.* **Идти по направлению**].

Идти в ногу с [*см. тж.* **Не отставать от**]
Improvement of these components **will keep pace** (*or* **keep up**) **with** the improvement of the measuring elements.

Идти в ногу со временем
The publication **is kept up to date.**

Идти в производство
Before the product **goes into production ...**

Идти дальше
Before **proceeding further** some definitions are needed.

Идти до конца
The reaction **goes** (*or* **proceeds**) **to completion.**

Идти на
Fifteen percent of the energy **goes into** the vibrational excitation.

Идти на образование
The material that **went to form** the planets ...

Идти на производство
Two thirds of the Arline production **goes for** rubber chemicals.
A minor amount of ... **goes into** (*or* **is used in**) the manufacture of abrasives and refractories.

Идти на расходы по
It is time **to go to the expense of** changing the equipment.

Идти обычным путём
The addition of ... **follows the normal path** postulated by ...

Идти по направлению
Future developments in this field **will** probably **follow** two main **directions.**

Идти под названием
These alloys **go under** (*or* **bear**) **the name of** electron compounds.

Идти под наклоном к
The magnetic meridian **is inclined to** the true meridian.

Идти под общим названием
All the bodies in both positions **are lumped together as** the "Trojan asteroids".
All three relationships **go under the general name of** unconformity (*geol.*).

Идти рука об руку
These two aspects of scientific study **go hand in hand to** lead to a more profound interpretation of our physical world.

Идти своим ходом
The ships **proceed under their own power.**

Идти точно (*о часах*)
The clock **keeps perfect time.**

Идут споры о том
There is some controversy as to whether the use of ... will diminish.

Из [*см. тж.* **В ... и из него, Выходить из, Исключение из правила, Исходя из, Состоять из, Среди**]
Out of n numbered objects a_1, a_2, ... a_n, one object may be chosen in n ways.
Two **out of** every three molecules become negatively charged.
Of all the possible conformations, we can distinguish two general types.
One **in** ten growth layers has actual diagnostic value.
Among the 40 tubes, only a few are high-vacuum rectifiers.
The vessel is fabricated **from** steel.
It is evident **from** the curve that ...
The core is fabricated **of** aluminium-nickel alloy.
Of these three elements, Cd is the most effective.

Из ... видно, что
From these curves **it will be obvious** (*or* **noted,** *or* **noticed**) **that ...**
It has been apparent in recent reports **that ...**
It is evident (*or* **obvious,** *or* **clear**) **from** the curve **that ...**
One can see from the equation **that ...**
It is (*or* **can be**) **seen from** Fig. 2 **that ...**
Referring to Fig.5 **it will be observed that ...**
Reference to Eq. (18-35) **shows that...**
With reference to Fig. 16-5, **it can be seen that ...**

Из внимательного рассмотрения ... видно, что
Close inspection of these data **shows that ...**

Из всех
Of (*or* **Among**) **all the** igneous rock-forming minerals quartz survives the longest in the weathering zone.

Из ... выкачан
The tube **is evacuated of** gas.

Из ... вытекает [*см.* **Из ... следует, что**].

Из ... вытекает вывод
A consequence of the above discussion **is the fact that** such a system cannot be optically inverted.

Из вышесказанного (*или* **вышеприведённого) следует, что**
From the above (*or* **From the aforesaid,** *or* **From what has been said**), **it might be assumed that ...**
From the above discussion it appears (*or* **follows**) **that ...**

Из глубины земли
Convection currents carry hot mantle material **from deep within the earth.**

Из года в год
The use of plastic is growing **every year** (*or* **year after year**).
The distribution patterns of temperature and salinity change little **from year to year** (*or* **from one year to the next**).
For glaciers to form, the quantity of incoming snowfall — **year in and year out** — must exceed ...

Из ... знаков [*см. тж.* **... значный**] ·
Each dye is given a 5-**digit** number.

Из известных
This is the cheapest protein feedstuff **on record.**

Из какого бы ни
The plane angle of a dihedral angle has the same magnitude **from whatever** point in the edge the perpendiculars are drawn.

Из которого состоит
The practical steps **involved in** an analysis ...
The water particles **that make up** (*or* **comprise**) the wave ...
The materials **constituting** the fibre ...

Из которого удалён
Natural cotton **with** the fatty and waxy matter **removed** in order to increase its absorbing qualities ...

Из которых
Canonical transformations have a number of important applications, **of which** the more important (*or* the more important **of which**) are described in ...
This depends on a number of factors two **of which** we will consider here.

Из ... может получиться
Gaseous atomic systems **may make** excellent lasers.

Из ... можно видеть, что [*см.* **Из ... видно, что**].

Из ... можно извлечь некоторые сведения о том как
This observation **may tell something about** the way galaxies are formed.

Из него [*см.* **Оттуда**].

Из поколения в поколение
The variations — the longer neck, the stronger hoof — were preserved **across the generations** (*or* **from generation to generation,** *or* **from one generation to another**).

Из ... получают
Beryl **produces** the gemstones emerald and aquamarine.

Из предыдущего текста видно, что
From the preceding (*or* **foregoing**) **(text) it is seen that ...**

Из раствора
The sodium bromate may then be crystallized **from solution.**

Из ... следует
From Eq. (5) **follows** (*or* **it follows that**) $n = ...$

Из ... следует, что
It follows from these results **that** $x = ...$
From the laws of transformation **it follows that ...**

Из соображений
From operational **considerations ...**

Из соображений экономии
Nickel was chosen **for (reasons of) economy.**

Из стороны в сторону
The pendulum swings **from side to side.**

Из уважения к
To distinguish disubstituted benzenes, letters rather than numbers are usually employed **in deference to** tradition.

Из числа
Of 55 faint blue objects investigated, 32 turned out to have ...
To select a physically relevant solution **from among(st)** the admissible ones, ...
Of a list of 122 global hot spots identified in 1975, 53 are on oceanic crust and 69 on continental crust (*geol.*).

Из этого вытекает (*или* **следует**), **что**
From these facts it transpires that binary stars can be visually detected only ...
This suggests (*or* **From this it follows,** *or* **From this it is inferred**) **that** friction can considerably alter the flow forces.
It is therefore **concluded that ...**
It follows that the two defects disappear pairwise in this range.

From this results (*or* **follows**) **the conclusion that ...**

Из этого количества
Of this (amount), about 108,000 cu km falls as rain or snow upon the land surfaces.

Из ... явствует, что [*см. тж.* **Из ... видно, что**]
From this analysis **it is apparent that ...**
It is evident (*or* **clear,** *or* **obvious**) **from** these numbers **that** ultraviolet radiation has the energy per mole necessary to break bonds.

Избавлять... от расходов, связанных с
These salts **save** the dyer **the expense of** the vatting operation.

Избавлять от трудностей *и т.п.*
To spare future investigators **the** same **difficulties, ...**

Избавляться
These lines cannot **be got rid of** (*or* **eliminated,** *or* **removed**) **by** any form of heat treatment.
The large ports permit us **to do away with** the reducers sometimes used previously.

Избегать
Interference can **be obviated** (*or* **prevented,** *or* **precluded**) **by** a prior separation.
If a pathway can be made **to circumvent** direct formation of ...

Избегать затруднений (*или* **трудностей**)
We can **circumvent** these **difficulties by** using the approximate invariant.

Избегать ошибок при помощи
The use of such techniques **will avoid these errors.**

Избирательно поглощать
The pigment **selectively absorbs** light from ...

Избыток [*см. тж.* **В большом избытке, В избытке**]
Grignard reagents react with **excess** oxygen to form ...
The electrode with **an excess of** electrons is called the cathode.
All the combustible material is burned with the minimum amount **of excess** air.
Excessive froth passes under the splash baffle.
Surplus earth ...

Избыточное давление
Seventy pounds per square inch **(gauge) ...**
The mash was sterilized by autoclaving at 15 pounds per square inch **gauge** steam **pressure.**

Избыточный
Excess electrons move into the *p*-region.

Известен *чем-л.* [*см. тж.* **Быть известным** ***чем-л.***]
These lizards **are famed for** their ability to change colour.
This author **is famed** (*or* **famous,** *or* **renowned**) **for** his science fiction writing.
Jurassic rocks **are noted for** their wealth of well-preserved fossils.

Известен во всём мире
The Sierra Nevada **is renowned throughout the world for** its relatively young granite.

Известен как
These atoms **are known as** isotopes of the element.

Известен под названием [*см. тж.* **Быть известным под названием**]
These microorganisms **are** also **known** (*or* **referred to**) **as** *Acrasiae.*
The invention **is designated** Mark 3.

Известен под разными названиями
These devices **are variously known as** *filter photometers, absorptiometers* or *colorimeters.*

Известен своими вредными (*канцерогенными и т.п.*) **свойствами**
BaP **is a notorious carcinogen.**

Известен тем, что
These nuts **are reputed to** increase greatly the product's endurance.

Известно [*см.* **Давно известно, что; Насколько известно**].

Известно, что
It is common knowledge that light carries energy.
It has been known that ...
It is a matter of general (*or* **familiar**) **experience that ...**
It is well known that ...

Известны под общим названием
These microorganisms **are collectively known as** *saprophytes*.

Известный I [*см. тж.* **Из известных, Общеизвестный**]
Although the nuclear model of the atom **is familiar to** all of us today, ...
Write the **known** weight of the chemical.
Elementary reaction processes, similar to those **recognized for** gas-phase reactions, ...
The stimulant action of the plant's constituents **has been appreciated for** many centuries.
The most **familiar** characteristic of the sunspots is ...
Everybody **is familiar with** these simple units.
A **well-known** feature is ...
The best laser efficiency **reported** thus far is ...

Известный II [*см. тж.* **Всемирно известный**]
Most mining concerns **of eminence** have their own scientific departments.

Известный *чем-л.* [*см.* **Отличаться**].

Известный под названием [*см. тж.* **Быть известным под названием**]
Attachments **known as** "load multipliers" have been designed.

Известный широкой публике
No booster of higher thrust has yet become **public knowledge.**

Извлекаемая польза
The benefits that will accrue to the mine ...

Извлекать I
The interior of the solar nebula did not **derive** any significant quantity of energy from ...
The detector is a device employed **to recover** the desired signal **from** the modulated wave.

Извлекать II
A small amount of the liquid **is withdrawn** and replaced by ...
Wells are drilled **to tap** the hot water.
To extract cobalt **from** its ore, ...

Извлекать выгоду (*или* **пользу**) **из**
To gain the most **benefit from** the favourable effects, ...

Извлекать из [*см. тж.* **Получать энергию от**]
The computer **retrieves** data and instructions **from** the memory unit within a single cycle of the processor.
The necessary energy can **be drawn from** the thermal energy of the metal atoms.
Bromine **is** mainly **extracted from** sea water.
Specialized magnets are provided for **extracting** the particles **from** the ring.
To determine the amount of water that can **be withdrawn from** wells, ...
Parts must **be removed** (*or* **withdrawn**) **from** (*or* **taken out of**) the bath at frequent intervals.
When an atom **is plucked out of** a normal site and taken away from the crystal, ...
The energy the carrier **derives from** the electric field goes into vibrating the crystal lattice.
Fresh water **is recovered from** sea water.
Chemical energy **is derived from** fossil fuels, nuclear energy **is derived from** fission or fusion reactions, and solar energy **is derived** directly **from** the Sun.
Information about part machining **is drawn from** the computer memory.

Извлекать информацию из
Much of our **information comes from** diffraction experiments.
We have been able **to extract** (*or* **obtain**) a substantial amount of **information from ...**

Извлекать корень из двух
To extract (*or* **take**) **a root of two ...**

Извлекать максимальную пользу из
The country is determined **to make the most of** its resources.

Извлекать непосредственную пользу из
Other researchers could **benefit directly from** this experiment.

Извлекать пользу из
We **have profited from** comments by Dr. T.
Personnel in the Arctic or Antarctic especially **have benefited from** amateur radio service.
Advantages can **be gained from** such effects.

The chemical activities of yeast **have been put to good use.**

Извлекать сигнал из
The decoder **extracts the signal from** the modulated carrier energy.

Извлекать электроны из
To pull (*or* **extract**) **electrons out of** the metal, ...

Извлекать энергию
Nearly all **the** optical **energy** in the oscillator can **be extracted** as a single transform-limited pulse.

Извлечение [*см. тж.* **Получение**]
The material must be refractory enough to permit easy **extraction** (*or* **removal,** *or* **withdrawal**) **of** the casting **from** the mould.
Glycogen phosphorylase is the enzyme used when the need arises for **the retrieval of** glucose **from** storage.

Извлечение ... из
An electron beam is produced by **drawing** electrons **out of** a cathode plate and directing them to an anode.

Извлечение информации
The storage and **retrieval of information ...**

Извлечение корня
This can be achieved **by extracting** (*or* **the extraction of**) **roots.**

Извлечённый из
Hearts **isolated from** animals ...

Извне
External supply of food ...
Initial pressure can be applied **externally** (*or* **from the outside,** *or* **from without**).

Изгибаться
This portion of the sheet **curves** (*or* **bends**) so that it can enter the clamping jaws.

Изгибаться на ... градусов
A metal specimen **is bent through 90 deg.**
The ridge **makes** (*or* **takes**) **a 60° bend.**

Изгибаться по направлению к
The isotherm **curves towards** the concentration axis.

Изготавливать [*см. тж.* **Выполнять, Производить, Строить**]
These alloys can **be fabricated** at temperatures below 1000°C.
The frame **is fabricated from** (*or* **of**) steel.
These tools **are made from** (*or* **of**) stainless steel.
The ram **is manufactured from** (*or* **of**) solid bar steel.
Metal hose **is produced from** titanium strip.
A large portion of the shop work will be in connection with **turning out** replacement parts for machining on various machine tools.
Cast iron **is** often **made into** blocks of rough shape and called pig iron.
Open caissons **are** usually **constructed of** reinforced concrete.
Models can **be machined from** solid copper stock.

Изготавливать с нормальными допусками
The valve body **is produced to normal tolerances.**

Изготавливать сплавы [*см.* **Получать сплавы**].

Изготовитель
We applied **to the makers of** air compressors.

Изготовлен
The vessels **were made** (*or* **produced,** *or* **fabricated,** *or* **manufactured**) **from** aluminium through special techniques.
Electrodes responding to other halides **have been prepared.**

Изготовление ... подходит к концу
The machine **is nearing completion.**

Изготовленная деталь
A finished part.

Изготовленный [*см.* **Выполненный**].

Изготовленный им самим
Electromagnets **of his own making ...**

Изготовленный по индивидуальному заказу
Customized (*or* **Custom-made**) instruments.

Изготовленный специально для
The furnaces are usually **tailor-made** for the job.

Издавать
The Committee **issued** (*or* **published**) a decree ...

Издавать звук
A sound is emitted from ...
Strings of certain different lengths **give forth** (*or* **produce**) **sounds** that unite in pleasing harmony.

Издавна [*см. тж.* **Давно**]
In conventional aluminium oxide wheels **there has long been** a trend toward ...

Издание [*см.* **Выпуск в свет**].

Изделие [*см. тж.* **Готовое изделие**]
Pots and similar fire-hardened **artifacts ...**
Some of the **products** (*or* **articles,** *or* **items**) on which low-temperature enamels can be used include small appliances, ...

Из-за [*см. тж.* **Благодаря, В результате, Ввиду, Вследствие**]
These jigs have been selected **for** (*or* **because of,** *or* **owing to,** *or* **in view of**) their compactness.
All the energy dissipates **through** (*or* **owing to,** *or* **on account of**) inefficiencies in the turbine ...

Излагать [*см. тж.* **Формулировать**]
When Dirac first **propounded** the theory of negative energy states ...
The theory **expounded** (*or* **presented**) **in** this paper ...
A more detailed discussion **is presented in** Sec. 6.
He **put forth** his observations and interpretations in a book entitled ...
I will **set forth** some ideas on how ...

Излагать вывод
The main **conclusion** can **be stated** in a simple form.

Излагать задачу
It is best **to set out the problem** in such a way that ...

Излагать теорию
To outline a theory ...

Излагаться
The paper **presents** (*or* **describes**) the results of ...
Techniques of sample preparation **are set forth** clearly.

Излишек
With **excess** iron sulphide, the copper sulphide forms a molten solution called copper matte.
Surplus equipment ...

Излишек *чего-л.* **над** *чем-л.*
The excess of evaporation **over** precipitation has to be made up by underground drainage from the less arid areas that supply the water.

Излишне говорить, что
Needless to say (*or* **It is needless to say that**) detrital remnant magnetism is of great value in ...

Излишний I
The **excess** heat is absorbed by the water.
Excess alkali atoms enter the crystal as normal lattice ions.

Излишний II
The last two precautions were found **to be unnecessary.**

Излишняя смазка [*см.* **Чрезмерная смазка**].

Изложен
These principles **are set out** (*or* **outlined,** *or* **presented**) **in** Chapter 7.

Изложение
The presentation of this law in books ...
The presentation is designed to aid rapid assimilation.
This material can be used in **presenting** a course in ...

Изложенная теория
The outlined theory ...

Изложенный
The theory **given** (*or* **set forth**) **in** this paper ...

Излучать [*см.* **Испускать**].

Излучение [*см.* **Защита от излучения, Испускание света, Падающее излучение**].

Излучение звёзд
Stellar radiation.

Излучение Солнца
Solar radiation.

Измельчать [*см. тж.* **Размельчать в порошок, Тонкоизмельчённый**]
The balls **crush** the coal to reduce it to small size.

Измельчать в песок
Even the hardest rocks can **be reduced to a sand** by continued action of the process of crystal growth.

Измельчённый в порошок
The **powdered** ore is agitated with water in which ...

Изменение [*см. тж.* **Без изменения, Большие изменения, Вносить изменение, Вызывать изменение, Не вызывать изменений, Оставаться постоянным при изменении**]
By **varying** the operating frequency of the transmitter ...
The system requires minimum **modification to** existing aircraft.
The change in this parameter ...
Such **changes of** atmosphere may occur in ...
Variations in temperature.

Изменение в
The necessary **modifications to** the theory of dissociations ...

Изменение знака
The change of sign in the curve ...

Изменение климата
Climatic changes resulting from fluctuations in the oceanic circulation ...

Изменение на
A capacity **change** of 10 picofarads will ...

Изменение орбиты
The orbital changes resulting from collisions ...

Изменение по глубине
Depth-variation of temperature ...

Изменение по толщине
The variation of the mole fraction **across** the slab must be found next.

Изменение с ... на ...
This difficulty can be overcome by **changing** the variable of integration **from** S to Ψ.

Изменение с температурой (давлением)
The variation of the volume **with the temperature (the pressure) ...**

Изменение цвета
The change in colour of a piece of litmus paper ...

Изменять [*см. тж.* **Варьировать, Менять**]
When the angle **is varied from** 0° **to** 180°...
Oxygen can **modify** the path of carbon within the chloroplast.
The solution pH **has been adjusted** to convert the organic compounds into more soluble ionic forms.
Variations in r **will affect** the rotational term.
In quantum mechanics Planck's equation $E = h\nu$ **transformed** our view of the subatomic universe.
The shape of the flame may **be modified by means of** a sleeve fitted over the burner tube.

Изменять в корне
Space charges, in the form of ions and other charged particles, can **radically alter** the electric field.

Изменять направление движения на обратное
If all velocities **reversed direction, ...**
When reaching the free surface, the bubbles **reversed their direction (of motion)** (*or* **reversed the direction of their motion**).

Изменять направление реакции на обратное
The reaction can be reversed by heating.

Изменять наше понимание
The discovery thoroughly **revised our understanding of** stars.

Изменять от ... до ...
Discharge height can **be varied between** 1140 **and** 1950 mm.

Изменять по сравнению
We must **modify** the reaction conditions **from** those usually employed.

Изменять расположение
Should requirements demand, all the machines could **be resited** and incorporated in other groups.

Изменяться [*см. тж.* **Колебаться от ... до..., Мало изменяться, Меняться**]
Under these conditions, the braking distance could **be** considerably **affected.**
Nickel **changes** its magnetic permeability as a stress is applied.
As distillation continues, the distillate will continuously **change in** composition.
When the intermolecular distance **is changed** (*or* **altered**), ...
The observer's notions as to ... **have undergone a change.**

Изменяться в диапазоне
The magnetic field **is varied through a** small **range.**

Изменяться в зависимости от
The crystals **vary in** colour from yellow to red **according to** the amount of iron present.
Repair costs **vary with** the type of machine-tool.

Изменяться в несколько раз
The tracer diffusion coefficient may **vary several-fold.**

Изменяться в соответствии с кривой
The distribution **follows the curve of** Fig. 7.

Изменяться в соответствии с программой
The furnace temperature must **follow a program of** variation with time.

Изменяться в широких пределах
The length of the cylinder may **vary within** (*or* **over**) **wide limits** [*or* **over a wide** (*or* **broad**) **range**].

Изменяться во времени
These values **are time variant** (*or* **vary with time**).

Изменяться до неузнаваемости
A substantial degree of distortion can occur before the pattern **becomes unrecognizable** (*or* **until the pattern changes beyond recognition**).

Изменяться линейно с
The volume **varies linearly with** the temperature.

Изменяться монотонно [*см.* **Монотонно возрастать** (*антон.* **убывать**)].

Изменяться на I
The constant k_L **varies over** 14 orders of magnitude.

Изменяться на II
The orange colour of the solution **is changed** (*or* **changes**) **to** green.

Изменяться на ... градусов
The *r-f* polarity **changes** 180 **degrees.**

Изменяться обратно пропорционально
Times required for a specific penetration **vary inversely as** (*or* **with**) (*or* **are inversely proportional to**) D_{AB}.

Изменяться от ... до
The capacitance **ranges from** 300 **to** 500 mmf.
The chart speed **is variable from** 6 **to** 960 inches per hour.
The safety factor **varies between** 1.3 **and** 2.
The short-circuit current gain may **vary (anywhere) from** 30 **to** 200.

Изменяться от одного ... к другому
The mass being decelerated **varies from** operation **to** operation.
The distribution of molecules **varies from one** sample **to the next** (*or* **to another**).
The time **will vary with different** samples.

Изменяться по величине
These forces **vary in magnitude.**

Изменяться по форме
In beetles, the coxae **vary** considerably **in shape.**

Изменяться пропорционально
Thrust and engine weight **vary as** (*or* **with**) the square and cube, respectively, of engine diameter.

Изменяться прямо пропорционально
The volume of ... **varies directly as** (*or* **in direct proportion with**) the temperature of ...

Изменяться со временем (с температурой)
The current **varies with time (temperature).**

Изменяющийся
The material is received at a **varying** rate.

Изменяющийся во времени
Time-varying (*or* **variant**) magnetic fields induced inside the Moon could substantially perturb the flow of the solar wind.

Измерение [*см.* **Выполнять измерения, Делать измерения, Единица измерения, Проводить измерение**].

Измерение по точкам
The point-by-point measurements were slow and tedious.

Измерения с ракет
Rocket measurements put the height of the layer of continuous emission at about 90 kilometers.

Измеренный
A fuel injector feeds **a metered** (*or* **measured**) amount of fuel into the cylinders.

Измеряемый [*см. тж.* **Подлежащий измерению**]
The **metered** current ...
The fluid **under measurement** (*or* **being measured**) ...
If the capacity **to be measured** is connected across ...
To evaluate gamma doses **measured with** film dosimeters ...

Измерять I [*см. тж.* **Выполнять измерения, Делать измерения, Проводить измерение**]
The isotopic ratio of the lead **is measured with** (*or* **by**) a photoelectric cell.
There is no way of **gauging** the external gravitational field.

Измерять в гранах
Pearls **are weighed in grains.**

Измерять микроамперами
The d-c leakage current through the capacitor is quite small; **it is** usually **measured in microamperes.**

Измерять температуру
The flue temperature must **be taken** (*or* **measured**).

Измеряться
This does not mean that the duration of the failure should **be measured in** months.
The amount of each component part **is** separately **measured by** a photometer.
The storage of mechanical energy **is measured by** the height to which a given mass is raised.
Rate of fuel flow must **be metered.**
The driving force of a reaction **is measured by** the total free energy of ... minus the total ...

Измеряться в единицах [*см.* **Размерность**].

Измеряться в процентах
Porosity **is measured in percentage** — the ratio of open void space to the total volume of the rock mass.

Измеряться по
The energy **is measured by** the ionization potential.

Изнашивать
Moving work **will wear down** the measuring surfaces of the micrometer.
These conditions **wear out** an engine.

Изнашиваться
The plunger **wears (out)** rapidly.
The clutch lining can **be worn down** to almost paper.

Изнашивающийся
The compressor has few **wearing** parts.

Износ [*см. тж.* **Вызывать износ**]
The rate of **wear of** iron from the piston ring in mg/hr ...
There is no quality fall off in the product owing to **wear on** the bars.

Изношенный за пределами допустимых размеров
Parts that **are worn out of tolerance** can be restored to original size by ...

Изнутри [*см. тж.* **С внутренней стороны**]
Heat flows out **from the interior of** the solid.
To pass **from the inside** to the outside **of** the pipe, ...
Normal flow pressure **from within** the tank ...
The tubes will be insulated **on the inside.**

Изо дня в день
The same situation continued **day in and day out.**
Day-to-day changes ...
The production increased **from day to day.**

Изобилие [*см.* **В изобилии**].

Изобиловать [*см. тж.* **Встречаться в большом количестве**]
The materials left by the glacial ice **are well endowed with** alumino-silicate minerals.
The continental margins **abound in** thick geoclines.
The scientific literature **abounds with** suggestions as to how the positrons are made.

Изобилующий кратерами
The surface of Mercury consists of **heavily cratered** terrains and less cratered plains.

Изобилующий трещинами
The **heavily cracked** areas of the metal surface ...

Изображать графически в виде
Such equilibria may **be displayed graphically as** phase diagrams.

Изображать схематически [*см. тж.* **Схематически изображён**]
The arrangement of a typical bearing **is shown diagrammatically** (*or* **schematically**) (*or* **is sketched**).

Изображаться
This **is depicted** (*or* **portrayed,** *or* **pictured,** *or* **sketched,** *or* **shown,** *or* **exhibited,** *or* **displayed,** *or* **illustrated**) **in** Fig. 3.
Figure **7 depicts ...**
The electrical inpulse from the cell **is displayed on** an oscilloscope.
The separation scheme **is outlined** as follows: ...

Изображение [*см. тж.* **Зеркальное изображение, Отбрасывать изображение на**]
A display of the system at 18°C is given in Fig. 10-19.
See **the representation of** the engine on p. 5.

Изображение звезды
The measurement of **a stellar image ...**

Изображение, полученное со спутника
To extract more information from **satellite images of** the earth, ...

Изображение, полученное с более близкого расстояния
The closer views of Saturn showed ...

Изображение, полученное с большого расстояния
The distant views of the planet transmitted to the earth ...

Изображённый
Typical headers **are pictured** (*or* **portrayed,** *or* **depicted,** *or* **shown,** *or* **sketched,** *or* **exhibited,** *or* **displayed,** *or* **illustrated**) **in** Fig. 47.

Изобретательность [*см.* **При достаточной изобретательности**].

Изобретать [*см.* **Разрабатывать**].

Изогнут по кривой
The element **is flexed to a** predetermined **curve** by adjusting screws.

Изолированный
Rubber-**insulated** wire ...

Изолированный лентой
The joint should **be** soldered and well **taped.**

Изолированный от [*см. тж.* **Не соприкасающийся**]
These coils **are insulated against** ambient heat.
Cold junctions **are insulated from** the aluminium with mica plates.

Изолировать
Boyle added a little mercury through the open end of the tube **to seal off** a quantity of air in the closed end.

Изолировать от I
A thin film is formed on the surface of the water and **seals** it **off from** the air.
The dense vapours **exclude** air **from** the combustion area.

Изолировать от II
The rubber **insulates** the wire **from** the metal.

Изолятор от
They act as **insulators against** magnetic fields.

Изощрён в области архитектуры
Those ancients **were architecturally sophisticated.**

Из-под

Cuttings are removed **from under** the bit by water circulation.

Израсходовать
The trailers **run out of** fuel en route.

Изрезан трещинами [*см.* **Испещрён трещинами**].

Изрезанный [*см.* **Берег, изрезанный фьордами**].

Изучаемая проблема
The detector is best suited to **the problem in hand** (*or* **under study,** *or* **under investigation,** *or* **under discussion,** *or* **being discussed**).
The problem has been addressed (*or* **studied,** *or* **investigated,** *or* **explored**) **by ...**

Изучаемый [*см. тж.* **Интересующий нас, Исследуемый, Рассматриваемый**]
When a system **of interest** works, ...
The substance **to be studied ...**
In the range **covered** (*or* **under study,** *or* **under investigation,** *or* **under discussion,** *or* **being discussed**) the curves are in good agreement with experiment.
This quantity can be obtained from the phase diagram of the system **involved.**
The **test** substance.

Изучаемый предмет
Divisions of **subject matter** in all disciplines are arbitrary.

Изучать [*см. тж.* **Заниматься изучением, Исследовать, Рассматривать**]
I presume you **have taken** (*or* **studied**) plane geometry.
Laser saturation broadening in flames **has been treated** both theoretically and experimentally.
I never **took** any **courses in** astronomy.
One should **inquire into** the reasons for ...
Besides, chemistry **is concerned with** (*or* **addresses itself to**) individual enzymatic reactions that are involved in ...
Thermodynamics **deals with** the conditions under which transformation of heat energy into other forms of energy takes place.
They **explored** (*or* **studied,** *or* **investigated,** *or* **looked into,** *or* **examined**) the possibility of X-ray fluorescence.
Mechanics **treats of** the action of forces and their effects.
The subject of electrostatics **concerns itself with** properties of charges at rest.
The leading investigator of the biochemical aspects of starvation **has looked into** the changes in metabolism of obese people during fasting.
The problem can **be attacked** experimentally by three devices: ...
The subjects of geology and mineralogy **are covered in** this section.
This problem **was addressed by** Weyl in 1929.

Изучать более тщательно (*или* **подробно**)
Now we **investigate** pulse spreading **more closely** (*or* **thoroughly**).
We decided **to take a further look at** the properties of "anomalous" water.

Изучать возможность
About 18 years ago a number of workers began **looking into** the possibility of using electrons to ...

Изучаться [*см. тж.* **Интенсивно изучаться**]
The use of such materials **is under investigation** (*or* **under study,** *or* **under discussion,** *or* **being discussed**).

Изучаться химией твёрдого тела
Large numbers of the compounds involving such condensed polyhedrons **fall into the subject of solid-state chemistry.**

Изучающий
Astrobiology is the branch of biology **concerned** (*or* **dealing**) **with** [*or* **treating on** (*or* **of**)] plant and animal life on other planets.
As some **students of** vegetation believe, ...

Изучен [*см.* **Лучше изучен, Недостаточно исследован**].

Изучен лишь частично [*см.* **Частично изучен**].

Изучение [*см. тж.* **Более подробное изучение** (*или* **рассмотрение**), **Исследование, Ознакомляться с, При изучении, Становиться предметом изучения**]
An investigation of (*or* **into**) the effects of pressure ...
We are carrying on **research on** this subject.

A subminiature microphone for **the study of** intracardiac heart sounds ...
An examination of the use of ... will illustrate some of these problems.

Изучение под микроскопом
Examining in (*or* **under**) **the microscope** the chromosomes of ...

Изученный [*см.* **Полностью не изучен**].

Изученный лучше всего
The substitutional alloys **have received the most study.**

Изъян [*см.* **Без дефектов**].

Изымать [*см.* **Исключать из рассмотрения**].

Изыскивать пути
Operators started **searching** (*or* **looking**) **for** ways of cutting costs.

Изящный метод
For this purpose **an elegant method** has been devised.

Или [*см.* **Либо ...,**].

Или, вернее
This problem could have been treated as the transient response to an initial condition **or, more properly,** an initial value that is the result of ...

Или вообще не [*см.* **Или совсем не**].

Или другой
In considering changes, chemical **or otherwise, ...**

Или же [*см. тж.* **В качестве варианта**]
A machine can be supplied for welding either circumferential joints only, **or, alternatively,** a universal machine can be supplied.
In performing this function ceramic castings can permit the use of less expensive metals, **or else** raise the temperature limit of ...
Or, again, if through the H projection a plane is passed which ...

Или и то, и другое
A few of the clay minerals are tubular or elongate, **or both.**

Или и тот, и другой [*см. тж.* **И тот, и другой**]
By lowering the carbon content or the silicon content, **or both ...**

Или их сочетание
Glass and asbestos **or combinations thereof** have been used.

Или, наоборот
The dynamo is an electric machine for the conversion of electrical into mechanical energy **or, conversely** (*or* **vice versa**), mechanical into electrical energy.

Или не
This depends upon the presence of other elements, added intentionally **or otherwise.**

Или никогда не [*см.* **Редко, если вообще когда-л.**].

Или около того [*см.* **Приблизительно**].

Или почти
The strong interactions of matter remain invariant (**or nearly so**) when the identities of protons and neutrons are interchanged.

Или почти нерастворим
If the metallic salt formed **is insoluble in** water, **or nearly so, ...**

Или совсем не
Such circuits will perform their expected functions for only a short time **or not at all.**
The tip of the crystal whisker grows rapidly, while the sides grow very slowly, **if at all.**
These healing agents probably play only a secondary part, **if any.**

Или точнее
Copper is nonmagnetic; **or, more precisely,** it is slightly paramagnetic.

Или, что ещё лучше
Materials might be found that become superconductive at the higher temperatures of liquid hydrogen **or, better still,** of liquid nitrogen.
This may be called the Moon's solar day **or, better still,** the solar month.

Иллюстрация [*см.* **В качестве иллюстрации, В качестве примера, Для иллюстрации**].

Иллюстрирован
The publication **is illustrated with** explanatory drawings.

Иллюстрировать
This **is depicted** (*or* **shown,** *or* **portrayed,** *or* **exhibited,** *or* **displayed,** *or* **pictured,** *or* **illustrated**) **in** Fig. 3.
The following hypothetical mechanism **serves to illustrate ...**
This condition **is exemplified** most clearly **by ...**
The relations between ... can **be illustrated with** (*or* **by**) one of the cooling curves.
The determination of iron **is illustrative of** some practical problems which are encountered in ...

Иллюстрировать на примере глицина *и т.п.*
Let us use glycine to illustrate the type of evidence supporting this conclusion.

Имеем [*см.* **Если дан**].

Имеет место обратное положение
The opposite situation occurs with more favourable heating mediums.
Generally speaking, corrosion is slower in coarse-grained material than in fine-grained material, but **the reverse is** sometimes **true.**

Имеет смысл [*см. тж.* **Целесообразно**]
It is not unreasonable (*or* **It makes sense**) **to** repeat the test after a few days.

Имеется [*см. тж.* **Существует**]
A complete review **is available in** another paper.

Имеется большое число
Stars **are plentiful in** the galactic centre.

Имеется большой спрос [*см.* **В большом спросе**].

Имеется в продаже
A compact air filter **comes in** 1/4 and 3/8 **in.** pipe sizes.
A number of commercial models designed specially for shock tube work **are** now **(commercially) available** (*or* **are on sale**).
The book **is in print** (*anton.* **out of print**).

Имеется возможность
Since some materials are not damaged as easily as others, **the possibility exists of** developing radiation-resistant parts.

Имеется всё больше указаний на то, что
There is increasing evidence that the new material can withstand severe weather conditions.

Имеется мало данных
Initially, when **data were few (and far between), ...**

Имеется мало указаний на то, что
There is little evidence that this takes place.

Имеется масса примеров этого
Examples of this abound.

Имеется много типов
Sedimentary rocks **come in many varieties** [*or* **There are** (*or* **There exist**) **many varieties of** sedimentary rocks].

Имеется много данных в пользу
A strong case can be made for the hypothesis that ...

Имеется несколько типов
Cathodes **are of** (*or* **come in**) **several types.**

Именно [*см. тж.* **А именно**]
It has been (just) this research **which** has led to ...
It is in this range of concentration **that** the anomalous wave reaches its limiting height.
It is precisely these varied relaxation phenomena **that** are of prime chemical and physical interest.
It is because of their high threshold current density **that** such lasers are always run under pulsed conditions at room temperature.

Именно поэтому [*см.* **Вот почему**].

Именно так и обстоит дело
Such is indeed the case.

Именно тогда
It was then that the fraction 355/113 was first used as an approximation of π.

Именно тот, который
These **are precisely** the species **which** require ...

Именовать [*см.* **Называть**].

Именоваться
These capacitors **are referred to** (*or* **known**) **as** [*or* **are termed** (*or* **called**)] "memory" capacitors.

Именуемый [*см. тж.* **Называемый**]
Another type of steel **known** (*or* **referred to**) **as** (*or* **termed,** *or* **called**) titanium enamelling steel is also available.

Именуемый в дальнейшем
The Director of the Office (**hereinafter** in this section **referred to as** "Director") shall ...
This part, **subsequently referred to** in this article **as** Section 1, serves to ...

Иметь I [*см. тж.* **Не иметь, Обладать**]
This object **possesses** (*or* **has**) a symmetry axis.
Comets frequently **show** (*or* **have**) a tail.
Sulphur can **accommodate** more than eight electrons in its outer quantum shell.
This material **is of** high heat resistance.
The capacitor **features** (*or* **exhibits,** *or* **shows,** *or* **possesses,** *or* **displays,** *or* **has**) extraordinary stability.
Calcite may **exhibit** a wide variety of forms.
The instrument **features** eight data channels.
The cycloidal curve **exhibits** a higher pressure angle.
Many grains **show** slightly abraded edges.
The forklift truck **is** today **sporting** (*sl.*) such accessories as barrel handling devices, belt conveyors, ...

Иметь II
The reamer **is provided with** helical flutes.

Иметь III
If you **are given** a line of a fixed length, ...

Иметь более близкое отношение к
Eddy current measurement of conductivity **correlates more closely with** tensile strength than does hardness.

Иметь более продолжительный срок службы, чем
This machine **will outlast** any other similar machine.
The planer **is longer lasting than ...**

Иметь бóльшие возможности
The fragments that are produced **have considerable opportunity** to react with each other.

Иметь большое значение [*см.* **Важный**].

Иметь большое значение для сельского хозяйства, *и т.п.*
This technique **is of great agricultural importance.**

Иметь в виду [*см. тж.* **Важно иметь в виду, что; Следует иметь в виду**]
The student **must be** constantly **aware of** the possible errors that could be introduced by ...

Иметь в виду, что
We must constantly **bear** (*or* **keep**) **in mind that** all models are only representations of reality.

Иметь в запасе
We **stock** many vaneaxial blowers.

Иметь в наличии [*см.* **Иметь в распоряжении**].

Иметь в общем ту же форму, что и
This equation **has the same general form as** equation (10.2).

Иметь в распоряжении (*или* **в наличии**)
The astronomers do the best they can with the tools they **have at hand** (*or* **at their disposal**).

Иметь важное значение [*см. тж.* **Играть важную роль**]
The fact that heat is evolved when ... **is of great practical consequence** (*or* **importance**).
These results **hold much** biological **significance.**
The design of the casting **is of major importance.**
Of importance in the study of ... **is** the triple vector product.
The convergent-divergent nozzle **is critical to** the optimum performance of ...
Nitrogen purity **is of prime** (*or* **paramount,** *or* **great**) **importance.**

Иметь вид [*см. тж.* **Проявляться в виде**]
The region **has the aspect of** an undulating plane.

The exact notation **will look like: ...**
The reagents **are in the form of** solids, liquids, or gases.
The ammonium chloride formed **appears as** smoke or as a white deposit.
The total voltage applied to the plate **has the appearance** (*or* **shape**) shown in Fig. 2.
The resultant *rf* carrier **appears as** in Fig. 3.
The distribution of lattice modes **is of the form** *C*(*v*)*dv*.
The closure usually **takes** (*or* **has**) **the form** of a cap or plug.
In this case the equation **takes the form: ...**
The expression for the axial convective transport **is of the form of** Fik's law.

Иметь возможность
Then you **will have a (good) chance of** observing these particles.

Иметь все основания
We **have every reason to** believe that ...
The designer **is justified in** resorting to very thick slot insulation.

Иметь второстепенное значение
This induced magnetic effect **is of secondary importance.**

Иметь вырез
The insert tool holder **is dovetailed on** one side so that it can be used with quick change tool posts.

Иметь гладкую поверхность
An ice sheet **is** usually **smooth surfaced.**

Иметь ... делений
The scale beam **is graduated with** (*or* **has**) 100 **divisions** each side of the zero centre.

Иметь дело с
In absorption, where **we are concerned** [*or* **where we have to deal** (*or* **to do**)] only **with** the atoms in the ground state, ...
It is safe **to handle** an acetone-air mixture containing 6.0 mole percent acetone.
We **are dealing** here **with** both emission and absorption lines.
Often we **deal with** the volume of a gas sample at two different temperatures.

Иметь доступ к
The design engineer must **have access to** empirical design and cost data.
The mobile phase **has access** only **to** the outer layer of ...

Иметь другое название
In this industry the propeller **goes by another name.**

Иметь жёсткий допуск
These parts must **be held to close tolerances.**

Иметь значение [*см. тж.* **Важен для, Не иметь значения**]
In this case only the ratio **matters** (*or* **is of importance**).

Иметь значение для
The properties of coke that **are of concern in** metallurgical operations are its chemical composition ...
The torsion resistance of porcelain enamels **is important for** (*or* **is of importance in**) such products as refrigerators.

Иметь исключительно важное значение
The effects of pollution on the ocean systems **are of the utmost significance** (*or* **importance**).

Иметь канавку
The rims may **be grooved** to increase the surface.

Иметь конфигурацию
The device **is configured** as shown in Fig. 5.

Иметь короткий срок службы
The engine **is short lived.**
A **short-lived** engine ...

Иметь любую величину от ... до
The variable times *t* **may be anything from** zero **to** infinity.

Иметь максимум (*или* **пик**)
The curve **peaks** [*or* **has a peak** (*or* **a maximum**)] **at** temperatures greater than ...

Иметь мало [*см.* **Беден**].

Иметь мало общего с
The so-called chromosome of bacteria **has little in common with** its eukaryotic counterpart.

Иметь массу в ... раз больше, чем
The Earth **is 8 times more massive than** the Moon.

Иметь меньший диаметр, чем
Axial compressors **are smaller in diameter than** centrifugal ones.

Иметь место [*см. тж.* **Бывает, Если это так, Наблюдаться, Происходить, Существовать**]
The minimum value of t_d **occurs** when Eqs. (3-7*b*) and (3-7*c*) are equal.
A similar situation **exists** (*or* **prevails,** *or* **obtains,** *or* **takes place**) with regard to the total content of ...
Under certain conditions this actually **is the case.**
This **is** not always **the case.**
These ultraviolet effects **occur** at about 0.3μ.
The year 1959 **saw** a marked improvement in the world freight position.
The last quarter of the year **showed** a sharp increase in ...
A similar relation **holds for** the frequency of the heart beat.
The following relationships **are true** (*or* **hold true,** *or* **hold good,** *or* **hold,** *or* **are valid**).
Mass transfer **is involved** whenever a chemical reaction takes place.
The last few years **have seen** the first steps into the new territory of ...
At low pressures, second-order kinetics **obtain.**
Equation (8.1) **holds** throughout the flow.
Such a reaction **occurs** not only **with** aldose but also with ketose sugars.

Иметь много [*см.* **Богат**].

Иметь много значений
The energy $E(k)$ **will be multivalued** if ...

Иметь много общего с
Mass-transfer equipment employed in solvent extraction **has much in common with** that used for gas absorption and distillation.

Иметь много применений
The method **is rich in applications** (*or* **has many applications**).

Иметь много сторонников [*см.* **Быть весьма популярным**].

Иметь на складе [*см.* **Иметь в запасе**].

Иметь наклон
Piping **should** always **slope** [*or* **have a slant** (*or* **be inclined**)] **toward** the primary device to facilitate the draining of any condensate.

Иметь наклон ... градусов
On the dome flanks, the strata **dip** (*or* **are inclined**) **at angles from** 30° **to** 60°.

Иметь наконечник
Each tool **is tipped with** carbide (*or* **is** carbide **tipped**).

Иметь наружный диаметр
The gasification vessels are 13 ft **in outside diameter** (*or* **have an outside diameter of** 13 ft).

Иметь непосредственное отношение к [*см. тж.* **Иметь прямое отношение к**]
Such calculations **have a direct bearing on** our ability to produce a rational and enduring basis for life.
The cyclic code still **bears a direct relation to** the binary.
The reason **is directly relevant** (*or* **related**) **to ...**
I **was directly concerned with** this experiment.

Иметь низкую плотность
This oil **is of low density** (*or* **has a low density**).

Иметь номер
The points **are numbered** (*or* **have numbers**) 1, 2, 3, ...

Иметь обратный знак
The free end of the dipole **is** now **of opposite sign.**
The bending strains of the upper surface **are opposite in sign to** those of the lower surface.

Иметь общее поле с
These electrons **share the** positive **fields** of two or more nuclei.

Иметь общее представление о
Then you **will have a general idea** (*or* **grasp**) **of** the variety of reactions.

Иметь общие черты с
Eukaryotic tRNAs **share** a number **of traits with** prokaryotic species (*biol.*).

Иметь общий

Different cations **share** polyhedron elements **(with each other).**

Иметь общий ... с
Every form of life on Earth **shares a common** ancestry **with** every other form.
Each hydrogen atom **shares** its valence electron **with** the other hydrogen atom.

Иметь общую границу с
Plate *C* **shares a** plate **boundary with** Plate *B*.

Иметь общую особенность
The amino acids of proteins **share a common trait,** that of having a molecular structure of levorotary configuration.

Иметь ограниченное применение
Many of these units **are of limited application.**

Иметь ограниченную скорость *и т.п.*
Systems using paper tape **are limited in speed.**

Иметь один смысл [*см.* **Однозначный**].

Иметь одно значение [*см.* **Однозначный**].

Иметь одну общую черту
These systems **have one point** (*or* **feature**) **in common.**

Иметь острый максимум
The muscle tremor's spectrum **peaks sharply** in the range between 8 and 12 cycles.

Иметь отношение к [*см. тж.* **Относиться к**]
The best example of a simple molecule for which magnetic data **bear on** the electronic structure is provided by oxygen.
These logical deductions **bear on** almost every aspect of chemistry.
The secretion of posterior pituitary hormones may **have a bearing on** longevity.
This discovery **is pertinent to** our discussion.
The elements in the earth that **are relevant to** our story ...
It is necessary to identify the site of the lesion because of **the relevance of** this **to** the prognosis.
Analyses of coins, which in ancient civilization **bore a** more direct **relationship to** economic conditions than ...
This phenomenon **is related to** (*or* **has to do with**) valve stability.

Иметь первостепенное значение
When high thermal conductivity **is a prime consideration, ...**

Иметь под рукой
When you chip steel, **keep** a piece of the waste **handy** and rub the point of the chisel on it frequently.

Иметь под собой некоторую почву
Immunological studies have suggested that the foregoing proposal might **hold some validity.**

Иметь постоянное значение
If *u* **is constant (in value)**, ...

Иметь право
We thus **are entitled** (*or* **have the right**) **to** interpret ... according to ...

Иметь практическое значение
The emf produced in gravity cells is too small **to be of practical use.**
The information gained about this mechanism **is of practical significance** (*or* **importance**).

Иметь представление о
Anyone who wishes to fly an ultralight airplane should **have a grasp** (*or* **an idea**) **of** basic aerodynamics.

Иметь преимущество над
This design **offers** few **advantages over** the conventional engine.

Иметь применение
Sodium carbonate **enjoys** (*or* **has**) many commercial **uses** (*or* **applications**).

Иметь принципиально важное значение
This relationship **is of fundamental** (*or* **basic**) **importance.**

Иметь принципиальное значение
Since we are interested in the changes in the number of equivalents, and not concentration, the volume of the compartments **is** not **critical.**
This property **is of fundamental importance** in all such fields.

Иметь продолжительный срок службы
The final product **gives extended service.**
This hydraulic cylinder **lasts long.**
The engine **is long lived.**

Иметь промышленное значение
These carbohydrates **are** of great **industrial** (*or* **commercial) importance.**

Иметь простую структуру
The nuclei **are simple in structure.**

Иметь прямое отношение к
Injection of fuel at the bottom of the furnace **has a direct relationship to** (*or* **a direct bearing on**) reduced coke rates.

Иметь различные оттенки от ... до
Hematite **is** reddish brown **to** black.

Иметь различный состав
The precipitate **is variable in composition** (*or* **is of variable composition,** *or* **varies in composition**).

Иметь различный состав от ... до
These rocks **range** (*or* **vary**) **in composition from** gabbro **to** granite.

Иметь размерность [*см.* **Размерность**].

Иметь размеры
The mahogany case **measures** 16 × 9 × 18 inches.

Иметь решающее значение
The choice of absorbent, solvent, or adsorbent **is of critical** (*or* **decisive**) **importance.**

Иметь решение
The equations **possess a solution.**

Иметь ручное управление [*см.* **С ручным управлением**].

Иметь свойство [*см.* **Обладать свойствами**].

Иметь сезонный характер
In semidesert regions runoff **is seasonal** - copious in winter months, but absent in the dry summer.

Иметь силу
When the ideal-gas laws **hold,** we express ...

Иметь склонность к [*см.* **Иметь тенденцию к, Склонен к**].

Иметь сладкий запах [*см.* **Обладать сладким запахом**].

Иметь смысл
This concept **has a** quantum mechanical **meaning** (*or* **significance**).
The rate constant **is meaningful** (*or* **has meaning**) only when such variables are fixed.
This sentence, at last, **makes (some) sense.**
There is no point to (*or* **sense in**) pursuing this subject.
Replacement of m by μ **is worthwhile.**
Large capital investments into this enterprise **would be worthwhile.**
It would pay to put in air filters.

Иметь сомнительную ценность для
These sites **are of doubtful value in** providing a code for recognition (*biol.*).

Иметь состав
The lava **is** commonly **of** acidic **composition** (*or* **is** commonly acidic **in composition**).

Иметь существенное значение для
The new approach **is essential to** the development of ...

Иметь сходство с [*см.* **Обладать сходством с**].

Иметь тенденцию к [*см. тж.* **Проявлять тенденцию к, Склонен к**]
Such fuels **are likely to** knock.
Low-carbon steels **have a** greater **tendency to** sag.
These steels **are prone to** hydrogen embrittlement.
Chemical activity **tends to** increase.
The system **is apt to** go unstable upon switching back from manual to automatic operation.

Иметь техническую ориентацию
The society **is technically oriented.**

Иметь толщину до
The layer may **attain a thickness of** 500 m (*or* may **be as thick as** 500 m).

Иметь точные размеры
Such systems must **be dimensionally accurate.**

Иметь фаску
The ends of the inserts should **be chamfered** (*or* **bevelled**).

Иметь физическое значение
Only the real or the imaginary part of any

complex-valued function **is physically meaningful** [*or* **has a physical meaning** (*or* **significance**)].

Иметь форму
The coil **is** rectangular **in shape** (*or* **in form**).
The top rim of the trough **is formed into** a flange.
The conduit **is shaped like** (*or* **has the shape of**) a star in cross section.
The electro-pneumatic sewage unit **takes the form of** small receivers.
The variation may **take the form of** amplitude modulation.
Empirical correlations of heat-transfer data **are** frequently **of the form** (*or* frequently **have the form**) $Nu = f(R, Pr)$.
The ionized streams **take on a** treelike **form.**

Иметь форму палочки
These bacteria **are rod shaped** [*or* **rod-like** (**in shape**)].

Иметь целью [*см. тж.* **Направлен на**]
The program **is aimed** (*or* **directed**) **at** increasing the worldwide consumption of ...
The book **is designed to** aid all levels of management.
The method of characteristics **seeks to** replace the original system.
Several of these methods **are intended to** replace hydrogen with some less expensive substance.

Иметь что-либо общее с
Does plate tectonics **have anything to do with** (*or* **have any bearing on**) these problems?

Иметь широкое распространение
This species **has a wide distribution** [*or* **is widely distributed** (*or* **widespread**)] (*or* **occurs widely**).

Иметь штат
Leading manufacturers **maintain** (*or* **have,** *or* **keep**) their own **staffs** of expert designers.

Иметь ясное представление о том
The early geologists did not **have a clear notion** (*or* **idea**) **of** how crustal rock could be deformed during an orogeny.

Иметься [*см. тж.* **Есть признаки того, что; Наблюдаться, Не иметься, Существовать**]
A complete review **is available in** another paper.
The fans **are available in** five sizes.
The mountings listed above **are found on** both Scotch and water-tube boilers.
Such a fan **is** usually **to be found in** each room.
Enough theoretical knowledge **is at** (*or* **in**) **hand** for the design of ...

Иметься в изобилии
Basaltic volcanic rocks **are abundant in** this region.
Copper **is in abundant supply.**
Polyphosphate linkages and other bonds **abound** (*or* **are in abundance**) **in** such preparations.

Иметься в наличии
Such fixtures **are in stock** at present.
Motors **are available** in two forms, namely with fixed housing and ...
The technology **is at hand** for solving such problems.

Иметься в ограниченном количестве
These particles **are limited in number.**

Иметься в продаже [*см. тж.* **Продаваться**]
Such machines **are commercially available.**
The book **is in print** (*anton.* **out of print**).
The conveyor **is** now **being marketed** (*or* **sold**) with a 40 ft boom and 18 in. belt.
Special units making use of infrared heating **are** now **on the market** (*or* **on sale**).
These elements **are offered in** a range of sizes.

Иметься "на вооружении" (*жарг.*)
Two methods **are available.**

Имеются возможности для усовершенствования
There is still **room for development** (*or* **improvement**) in work handling systems between the machining systems.

Имеются все основания полагать, что [*см. тж.* **Есть все основания полагать, что**]
We have every reason to believe that this will lead to ...
We can safely assume that a glaciation is associated with ...

Имеются все признаки того, что
There is ample evidence that coordination does occur.

Имеются многочисленные указания на то, что
There is abundant evidence that sugars actually exist as cyclic compounds.

Имеются основания ожидать
It is reasonable to expect semicontinuity in problems of ...

Имеются основания полагать, что
There is reason to believe that this problem will not be difficult to control.
There are reasons (*or* **grounds**) **to assume that ...**

Имеются указания на то, что
There is evidence (*or* **Indications are,** *or* **There are indications**) **that** vitamin C may play an important role in ...

Имеются экспериментальные данные о том, что
There is experimental evidence that the shape of a molecule ...

Имеются явные доказательства того, что
The chloroplast genes of this organism **show clear evidence of** being transmitted to ...

Имеющий какое-либо значение
The only external force **of any consequence** (*or* **importance**) acts in the high-pressure chamber.

Имеющий непосредственное отношение к
Those **directly concerned with** machine shop practice are realizing that ...

Имеющий отношение к [*см. тж.* **Относящийся к**]
We will mention two lines of evidence **bearing on** this.
Most of the literature **having to do with** (*or* **relating to,** *or* **associated with**) diffusion employs this law.

Имеющий промышленное значение
This is a **commercially useful** reaction.

Имеющийся [*см. тж.* **Существующий**]
The holders were mounted in annular grooves **provided in** the bearing shields.
The distance bar guard for use on mechanical press brakes is lighter and more rigid that **existing** mechanical guards.

Имеющийся в наличии
The **available** material ...
The hammers **on hand** (*or* **at our disposal,** *or* **in our possession**) are too large.

Имеющийся в настоящее время
The evidence **to date,** (*or* **The currently available** evidence) suggests that ...

Имеющийся в продаже
Commercially available tools...
This separation plant has the most productive pool area of any separator **on the market.**

Имеющийся в распоряжении [*см. тж.* **Имеющийся в наличии**]
The data **available to** (*or* **at the disposal of**) our group ...
We hope that the experimental techniques already **in hand** (*or* **at our disposal**) will enable us to ...

Имеющийся у [*см.* **Имеющийся в распоряжении**].

Имея [*см. тж.* **Зная**]
With (*or* **Given**) these data, we can calculate ...
Given a circle, construct a square of the same area.

Имея в виду
We have been looking at other machining operations **with an eye to** replacing equipment with ...
With (*or* **Bearing**) these requirements **in mind** one can look at ...

Имея в виду возможность использования при
Various alloys used for furnace components must be chosen **with an eye to** elevated temperature operation.

Имея в виду это обстоятельство
With this in mind an attempt will be made to state ...

Имея в распоряжении
With this evidence **in hand** (*or* **at our disposal**) it becomes possible to ...

Имея "на вооружении" (*жарг.*)
Armed with these estimates, the experimenter now has a fresh field to explore.

Имитация
The simulation of gravity ...

Имитировать
To simulate normal conditions encountered in the cementing of oil wells, ...

Иммунитет к
Antibodies, which provide **immunity against** infection, are proteins.

Импульс и энергия сохраняются
Momentum and energy are conserved for the initial and final particles that endure long enough to be detected.

Импульсный режим
These lasers operate in **the pulsed mode.**

Имя [*см.* **Называть именем, Называть общим именем, Носить имя**].

Иначе I
Alternatively, this can be written as ...

Иначе II [*см. тж.* **В ином случае**]
This explains certain properties that would **otherwise** remain inexplicable.

Иначе III [*см.* **Дело обстоит иначе, Иначе обстоит дело с**].

Иначе IV [*см.* **Если не указано иначе**].

Иначе говоря [*см. тж.* **Другими словами, Иными словами**]
(To) put (it) otherwise [*or* **differently,** *or* **(in) another way**], ...

Иначе обстоит дело с [*см. тж.* **Совершенно иначе обстоит дело с**]
A different situation arises (*or* **obtains**) **with** solutions that show ...
When we deal with steel ...; **not so** (*or* **it is different**) **with** tin.
Metal removal from the components' exterior presented no problems. But the interior water passageways **were something else.**

Иначе, чем
We form these cutters **differently than** anyone else.

Ингредиент [*см.* **Компонент**].

Индивидуально изготовленная деталь
The cost of **a one-of-a-kind** (*or* **one-off**) **workpiece** may be very great.

Индивидуальное производство деталей
The machine is suitable for **one-off production.**
For **one-off jobs,** the sand is self-curing; for higher production it may be ...

Индивидуальные потребности [*см.* **В соответствии с индивидуальными потребностями**].

Индивидуальный [*см.* **На индивидуальной основе**].

Индивидуальный заказ [*см.* **Изготовленный по индивидуальному заказу**].

Индуцированный лазером *и т.п.*
Laser-produced (*or* **-induced**) ionization ...

Индуцировать ток
The resulting ionization **will trigger** (*or* **start,** *or* **induce**) **a current (flow)** from cathode to anode.

Инертный по отношению к
This lubricant **is inert to** most chemicals.

Инициатор
The use of load-bearing adhesives **was pioneered** (*or* **initiated**) **by** the aircraft industry.

Иногда [*см. тж.* **Время от времени**]
On occasion the explosive eruption of a volcano blows out an enormous mass of ...
Antibacterial treatment may **at times** (*or* **sometimes,** *or* **occasionally**) also be required.
Mercury bichloride has been used **on occasion** for suicide and homicide.

Иногда ..., а иногда
Multiple bonding may **at times** be present and **at other times** absent from compounds involving the same coordination number.

Иногда утверждают, что
It has been argued on occasion that the term "glass" should be reserved for materials ...

Иной [*см.* **Другой, Чем в ином случае**].

Иной формы
A somewhat **different-looking** (*or* **differently shaped**) cosmic jet (*or* A cosmic jet **of a different shape**) ...

Инструкция [*см. тж.* **Согласно инструкции**]
Complete **instructions for** the removal of the unit are given in Sect. 2.

Инструкция по установке
Installation directions.

Инструментальная погрешность
Instrument(al) error.

Интеграл [*см.* **Брать интеграл**].

Интеграл по
Line **integrals over** *C* ...
The integral of the current **over** the duration of electrolysis ...

Интегрирование [*см. тж.* **Проводить интегрирование**]
Upon **integrating** (43) **with respect to** the time (*or* **over** the area) we obtain ...

Интегрирование по частям
Integration by parts.

Интегрировать по
It remains that **to integrate** *A* **with respect to** *x* between the limits $x = a$ and $x = b$.
When **integrated over** φ **from** 0 **to** 2, ...
The expression **is integrated over** all possible values of ...

Интенсивно
Research in the utilization of ... is carried out very **actively** (*or* **intensively**).

Интенсивно изучаться
Considerable study is being given to propellers for ... (*or* Propellers for ... **are being studied intensively**).
The study of ... is proceeding vigorously.

Интенсивность реакции
The vigour (*or* **intensity**) **of the reaction** is governed by the proportion of chromic acid.

Интенсивный [*см. тж.* **Более интенсивный, чем**]
An **intense** red spectral line ...
Intensive studies are under way.

Интенсивный источник
An intense source of energetic neutrons ...

Интенсивный цвет
An intense colour.

Интервал [*см.* **В диапазоне, В интервале, Выдерживать интервал, Диапазон, Лежать в диапазоне, На интервале**].

Интервал между
The time separation (*or* **The interval**) **between** the two bursts is determined by many factors.

Интервал между импульсами
The code **pulse positions are spaced** 2.9 μs.

Интерес [*см. тж.* **Вновь пробуждать интерес к, Возбуждать интерес, Возрождать интерес к, Вызывать интерес, Живой интерес к, Не представлять интереса, Ослабление интереса к, Потерять интерес к, Представлять интерес, Пробуждать интерес к, Проявлять интерес к, Разжигать интерес к**]
Interest was created (*or* **aroused**) **in** derivates of salicylic acid.
Great **interest has been expressed by** American mining engineers **in** the British hydraulic roof-supports.
These tests **are of** particular **interest to** railroad engineers.
Less **interest is being shown in** these steels than in ...

Интерес возобновился
After a long hiatus **interest in** collective events **was rekindled.**

Интерес обострился
Interest in this source of energy **has quickened** in the past few years.

Интересен
The prospect of obtaining such spectra **is** exceptionally **intriguing** (*or* **interesting**).
The type of modification **is also of interest.**

Интересно
It is of interest to estimate the possible importance of these effects.
We **have been interested to** find that a number of ...

Интересно выяснить
It is instructive (*or* **of interest**) **to** consider what happens when ...

Интересно отметить, что
Interestingly (enough) (*or* **It is interesting to note that**) there is no problem in observing ...
It is notable that in this case classical mechanics and quantum mechanics would be in agreement.

Интересно, что
It is of interest (*or* **It is interesting**) that antioxidants for foods were known long before ...
Interestingly, similar leaflets exist in rods and cones of the eye.
It is intriguing that the paper immediately following this one described the first operation of ...

Интересный
A **fascinating** (*or* **interesting**) problem ...
We have been able to investigate a number of **intriguing** questions.
Some of the most **intriguing** recent suggestions have been for the utilization of ...

Интересовать [*см. тж.* **Нас в основном интересует, Нас интересует только**]
Such properties **will** not **concern** us in our study of ...
Of concern to us **is** the question: Which nuclei are stable and which radioactive?

Интересовать главным образом
Our **prime interest is in** the conversion of the electromagnetic energy of ...

Интересоваться [*см. тж.* **Заинтересоваться, Живо интересоваться**]
He **took an interest in** astronomy.
Chemists who **are interested in** the conversion of heat into work ...

Интересующий нас [*см. тж.* **Рассматриваемый**]
The diffusion coefficient may vary substantially over the concentration ranges **of interest (to us)** [*or* over the concentration range **concerned** (*or* **in question**)].
The problems we **are interested in** are ...

Интуиция подсказывает, что
Intuition suggests that ...

Информация о [*см. тж.* **Большое количество данных, Данные, Значительное количество сведений о, Из ... можно извлечь некоторые сведения о том, как; Извлекать информацию из, Сведения, Сообщать сведения**]
From **a knowledge of** the energy and power in each mode, we can deduce ...
There is little **information on** creep strength.

Информация о структуре *и т.п.*
The most useful source of **structural information** is ...

Информировать [*см.* **Разъяснять**].

Инъекция [*см.* **Вводить**].

Иными словами [*см. тж.* **Другими словами, Иначе говоря**]
To put it differently (*or* **another way**) (*or* **In other words**), ...

Ионно или молекулярно диспергированное состояние
For their separation, substances must be in **an ionically or molecularly dispersed state.**

Искажение [*см.* **Без искажения**].

Искать
We should **look for** evidence of such action in ...
We do not **pursue** other solutions here.
We **seek** an analytic solution in the form of a power series.
We **will seek for** clues that allow us to understand the landscape.
The obvious program is **to search for** global symmetries.

Искать в
The proof of this hypothesis was **to be looked for** in seismic activity.

Искать пути
Operators started **searching** (*or* **looking,** *or* **seeking**) **for** (*or* started **investigating**) ways of cutting costs.

Искать решения задачи
To seek the solution of the problem.

Исключать [*см. тж.* **Не включать, Не следует исключать, Опускать II, Предотвращать, Устранять**]
This **eliminates** a number of constants.
This term can **be eliminated from** the set of equations.
This **obviates** the necessity for stopping the test.

It would be possible **to omit** the transistor amplifier in this case.
The price of these torches **rules out** (*or* **excludes**) their application by smaller shops.
The general types of assembly methods do not **rule out** combinations of different types in producing the same product.
This does not **preclude** the use of a particular method.

Исключать возможность
This does not **preclude** (*or* **rule out**) the presence of ...

Исключать возможность создания
The need for individual feedback on each element **eliminates the possibility of** large parallel bistable arrays.

Исключать возможность того, что
We cannot **rule out** (*or* **exclude**) **the possibility that ...**

Исключать друг друга [*см.* **Взаимно исключать друг друга**].

Исключать из рассмотрения
We **exclude** (*or* **eliminate**) this phenomenon **from consideration.**
As for Jupiter and Saturn, we can **leave them out of** (*or* **omit them from**) **consideration.**
Its absence of chemical activity **bars** DNA **from** further consideration in the search for ... (*biol.*).

Исключать из уравнения
To obtain the shape of the trajectory, **eliminate** (*or* **drop**) t.

Исключать из числа
This **eliminates** argon **as** a candidate for this kind of laser.

Исключаться [*см. тж.* **Не исключаться**]
In the case of a single electron the change $L = 0$ **is ruled out** (*or* **excluded**).

Исключая [*см. тж.* **За исключением**]
The total cost of the part, **exclusive of** (*or* **less**) material costs, would be ...

Исключение [*см. тж.* **Без исключения, За исключением, За одним исключением, За редкими исключениями**]
The one **exception to** many of these drawbacks is represented by the semiconductor diode laser.

Исключение из правила [*см. тж.* **Являться исключением из правила**]
There are **exceptions to this rule.**

Исключением является
The (sole) exception is (provided by) the action of ...

Исключительная важность [*см.* **Представлять исключительную важность для**].

Исключительно I [*см. тж.* **Относиться исключительно к**]
The establishment was set up **solely** (*or* **exclusively**) for the development of engines.
They assert that the genetic code has a biological basis for its structural organization, **and no other.**
If the mantle were made of **nothing but** gem-quality crystals, ...
This choice is made **purely** on the basis of convenience.
This rule applies **strictly** to a harmonic oscillator.
These proteins occur **uniquely** in tissues in which gene transcription is severely repressed.

Исключительно II
This task can become **enormously** (*or* **exceedingly,** *or* **extremely**) complex.
Such monopoles would **be extraordinarily** (*or* **exceedingly,** *or* **exceptionally**) massive.
The sediments contain **remarkably** (*or* **extremely**) high concentrations of sulphide minerals.
The instrument is **exquisitely** sensitive.
Manganin is **eminently** suitable for standard resistors.

Исключительно важен
This component **is of crucial** (*or* **paramount**) **importance in** the interplay between ...
The shapes of molecules **are of the utmost importance** (*or* **are critically important**) **in** many biochemical events.

Исключительно важен для
The physical properties of a material **are crucial** (*or* **extremely important**) **to** a civil engineer.

Исключительно важная роль [*см.* **Играть исключительно важную роль в**].

Исключительно важное значение [*см. тж.* **Иметь исключительно важное значение, Решающее значение**]
The accuracy of measurement **is of fundamental importance to ...**
This provides data which **are of paramount** (*or* **prime,** *or* **great,** *or* **exceptional**) **importance in** studies of ...

Исключительно важный
Cleanliness **is all-important in** mould steels.
Complete dependence **is critical** (*or* **of critical importance,** *or* **of crucial importance**) **in** control components.
This is a method **of outstanding** (*or* **exceptional,** *or* **unique**) **importance.**

Исключительно наглядно
Geological processes are **dramatically** recorded in the appearance of Jupiter's satellites.
This fact is **strikingly** illustrated by a rock exposure ...

Исключительно разнообразны
The form and motions of the comet tails **are extremely varied.**

Исключительно сильный
Although material dispersion by itself is small, it can have a **dramatic** effect on pulse spreading when combined with ray dispersion.

Исключительно стойкий к
These colours **are outstanding in their fastness to** water.

Исключительный
The **exceptional** (*or* **remarkable**) accuracy of the feeder ...
The **outstanding** fatigue resistance of adhesives ...
Most copper alloys have **superior** casting qualities.

Искомый
We now have the **desired** result.
We can then calculate the **required** partial derivatives directly.
The solution **sought** is given by ...
This is the final form of the **sought-for** equation.

Искра [*см.* **Давать искру**].

Искусственное дождевание
Rain-making experiments ...

Искусственный
Whether natural or **man-made** (*or* **artificial**), some of these trace substances occur as gases, others as aerosols.
A **man-made** explosion ...

Искусственным способом
The cloves are picked by hand and dried in the sun or **by artificial means.**

Испарение [*см.* **Потерянный на испарение**].

Испещрён кратерами
The surface of Mercury **is (heavily) cratered** (*or* **strewn with craters,** *or* **crater-strewn,** *or* **pock-marked with craters** — *col.*).
The Moon surface **is studded with craters.**

Испещрён трещинами
Here the glacier ice **is scarred by crevasses.**

Исполняться [*см.* **Оправдываться I**].

Использован
This knowledge **was drawn on** to make good use of the new machines.

Использование [*см. тж.* **Для использования, Мирное использование атомной энергии, Область использования, По мере использования, Повторное использование, При использовании, Пригодный для использования, Применение, С использованием**]
Harnessing fission processes for production of electric energy ...
The harnessing of the steam engine in British mines and mills ...
The time required for half of the reactant to **be used up** is independent of ...
The tapping of solar energy ...
Alleviation of ... may be achieved by **adoption of** laminar-flow airfoil of small thickness.
The analysis is dependent **on the employment of** a satisfactory mixture law.
Another **use of** beryllium oxide is **as** a slurry for ...

One of **the uses of** these plastics is **in** instrument lenses.
Bombers may be of different types, depending on **the use to which they are put.**
Agriculturists showed a keen interest in **harnessing** isotopes and radiation **for** improving the production and protection of food.
The tapping of the world's oil resources.

Использование ... ограничивается
Packed beds **are limited in use to** collecting particles present in ...

Использование отходов
The recovery (*or* **utilization**) **of waste products ...**

Использовать I [*см. тж.* **Воспользоваться, Максимально использовать, Можно использовать, Наиболее эффективно использовать, Пользоваться, Применять, Широко использовать**]
We will show how these numbers can **be put to use.**
Advantage is taken of this fact **in** some turbojet engines.
Unique processes and equipment **have been** successfully **applied in** the mining and refining of potash salts.
The great majority of amplifiers are electronic and **depend** (*or* **rely**) **upon** transistors and chips for their operation.
These projects can **draw on** the data from five tests.
The new relay **employs** three sets of contacts.
We shall **follow** this method.
To harness atomic energy **for** peaceful uses, ...
This reaction may **be harnessed** to perform work.
The power unit **makes use of** a standard electric starter.
These vehicles **rely on** ambient air **as** a source of oxygen.
This nonreciprocity **has** as yet not **been turned to useful account in** antennas.
At present, these laboratories **are being utilized to** test timbers.
Such high precision makes it possible **to employ** (*or* **use,** *or* **utilize**) laser radiation **as** a primary standard of length and time.
With electricity farmers could **run** useful devices of all kinds.
This offers the possibility of **putting** hydrides **to work in** heat pumps.
These techniques **take advantage of** the laser's high spectral intensity.
Lasers **are exploited to** heat plasmas with short pulses of light.
Double-break or multibreak devices can **exploit** this effect even at higher voltages.
We **make use of** the generalized invariants.
The author's suggestions **were picked up by** the Japanese who ran some preliminary tests on eleven pure elements.
The steam from a dry field can **be put to use(s)** other than power production.
We can **draw on** the equation of general relativity **to** calculate ...
The newest accelerators **exploit** the same fundamental principles as the first ones.
Simplifying assumptions **have been invoked to** separate the two processes for individual study.
If this natural gas can **be tapped,** there would be a tremendous source of fuel.
This prevents defective parts from **being put into service.**

Использовать II
When all the even (or odd) integers **are used up,** there will still be half the series ...

Использовать в качестве
A charge-coupled delay line can **be made to serve the function of** a digital shift register.

Использовать в качестве основы для
Now this acid **is used as the basis for** a vast number of syntheses.

Использовать в качестве отправного пункта
We **have taken** this **as a starting point for** our investigation.

Использовать в медицине
This chloride **is used medicinally** (*or* **in medicine**) **to** neutralize ...

Использовать возможности
It becomes increasingly important to ensure that **the potentialities of** the very expensive equipment **are exploited** to the fullest practicable extent.

Использовать для
Aluminium enamels **are** primarily **used in** architectural applications (*or* **in** the manufacture of ...)
The material **is used in** (*or* **for**) the manufacture of ...

Использовать для многих целей
There are many uses to which this light **can be put.**

Использовать для разных целей
This machine is **to be put to a number of uses.**

Использовать для экспериментальных целей
This gas **will be put to (some) experimental use.**

Использовать должным образом
The floor space should **be turned to proper use** (*or* **used properly**).

Использовать компьютер в процессе
To computerize the process, ...

Использовать либо ..., либо ... по желанию
A flow splitter on the output **would allow the option of using either ... or ...**

Использовать методику
This **procedure will be followed** (*or* **used,** *or* **employed**) **in** subsequent chapters.

Использовать обстановку
To exploit (*or* **take advantage of,** *or* **make use of**) **the situation, ...**

Использовать опыт
Drawing on his operating **experience,** the operator may decide that the load will probably drop, etc.

Использовать повторно
The bags **are re-usable** (*могут быть использованы повторно*).

Использовать подход
For some diatomic molecules we **take** quite **a** different **approach from that** used in the preceding sections.
Following this **line of attack, ...**

Использовать принцип
By **applying the principle of** the flux trap, magnetic energy may be stored indefinitely in the magnetic coils.

Использовать термин в значении
Throughout this chapter, we **will use the term** *shoreline* **to mean** the shifting line of contact between water and land.

Использовать топливо
This machine **can run** (*or* **operate**) **on** (*or* **can use**) solar, nuclear or chemical **fuel.**

Использоваться [*см. тж.* **В котором используется**]
Advantage was taken of the new material.
This information **will be put to** (*or* **into**) **use in** the next chapter.
This basic action **is** still **of service in** several systems.
Use has been made of this invention **in ...**
Hydrogen can **serve in** a variety of energy converters.
This property **has been exploited** (*or* **utilized,** *or* **taken advantage of**) **in** numerous technical applications.
A few other antiknock additives **have seen some use** (*or* **have found applications,** *or* **have been applied**).
Solar cells **are harnessed to** drive cars.
The basins **have been in service** for eight years.
Such tubes **will continue in use.**
Devices of this kind **are** already **in service in** radar technology.
This chapter describes how these mechanisms **are made use of** (*or* **used,** *or* **utilized**) **in** the field-effect transistor.
Electromechanical devices can **be relied on in** a great variety of control applications.
Natural underground reservoirs of hot steam and hot water **are** now **being tapped** on a significant scale.

Использоваться в качестве
Erbium could also **be of use as** absorber.
The polyethylene sheets **served as** an insulation.
Here, the vibrational temperature T_{vib} **is employed** (*or* **used,** *or* **utilized**) **as** a measure of the vibrational energy.

Использоваться в качестве пищи
Abalones **are** often **used for food.**

Использоваться в основном для
The major use for cocoa butter **is in** the manufacture of ...

Использоваться в основном при
The principal use of ultraviolet spectroscopy **is in** quantitative studies.

Использоваться в промышленности
Adiabatic expansions **are used industrially.**

Использоваться вместо него [*см.* **Заменять его**].

Использоваться главным образом в качестве
The chief use of this chemical **is as** a fertilizer.

Использоваться главным образом для
Activated carbon **finds its major use** (*or* **is mainly used**) **in** solvent recovery ...

Использоваться для
Furfural **is used in** (*or* **for**) the production of synthetic rubber.
The series winding **offers a means of** compensating for voltage drop.

Использоваться для качественного анализа
The solution **is used as a qualitative test for** the sulphate ion SO_4^{2-} in solution.

Использоваться для многих целей
Low molecular weight glycols **have many uses.**

Использоваться для получения
Low clover species **is used for** hay.

Использоваться для практических целей
This is how advanced technology **is being turned to practical use.**

Использоваться полностью
This frequency band **is fully utilized.**

Использоваться человеком
This form of geothermal energy can **be put to human use.**

Используемый [*см. тж.* **Мало использоваться, Наиболее широко используемый**]
Another type of indicator **in use** (*or* **used**) **is** the diffusion type.
A single laser beam has many thousands of times the signal-carrying capacity of any other transmission medium **in service.**
The major design method **employed** is based on this principle.

Используемый в настоящее время
This unit takes the place of the bulky tuning elements **now in use** (*or* **in current use,** *or* **used at present**).

Использующие общий
Two or more communication channels **sharing** a **common** propagation path ...

Использующий компьютер
A **computer-aided** spectrometer ...

Используя
With this result we can obtain the effusion equation.

Исправить дело можно путём
If assembly techniques are not good, **the remedy is** better training for fitters.

Исправленный на активность
The **activity-corrected** D_{AB} (*or* **The** D_{AB} **corrected for activity**) varies widely with concentration.

Исправлять на
It is possible **to correct (the equation) for** the effects of ...
Current readings must **be corrected for** volume changes.

Исправлять недостаток
To correct this **condition** [*or* **To eliminate** (*or* **remedy**) this **defect**], proceed as follows: ...

Исправлять ошибки
Errors and misjudgements **can be** instantly **rectified.**

Исправлять погрешности
The control system automatically **compensates for** any mechanical **errors** in machine slide or table movement through servo feedback.

Исправлять положение
To remedy the condition (*or* **situation**), changes were recommended.
Matters can be straightened out (*or* **improved**) **by** the use of a laser having ...

Исправно работать
The instrument **is functioning properly.**

Исправный
An **operable** camera must be available.

Испускаемый газ

Surface defects are produced by gases **given off** (*or* **evolved,** *or* **liberated,** *or* **released**) **by** the reaction of ...

Испускаемый поток частиц
In these theories **a stream of** charged **particles emitted** (*or* **ejected**) **by** the star is assumed to be accelerated by the ambient fields.

Испускаемый свет
The light emitted (*or* **radiated,** *or* **given off**) **by** the sample is scattered in all directions.

Испускание света
The emission of light.

Испускать волну
Each television channel **emits a wave** which ...

Испускать дым
The bombardier beetle **emits** a cloud of acrid **smoke.**

Испускать излучение
The CO_2 laser **produces** intense monochromatic **radiation** at a set of infrared wavelengths.
The transmitter **sends out** (*or* **gives off**) electromagnetic **radiation.**

Испускать нейтрон
The unstable nucleus **ejects** (*or* **emits**) one of the surplus **neutrons.**

Испускать свет
In all likelihood superheavy magnetic monopoles would **radiate** (*or* **emit,** *or* **give off**) **light.**

Испускать частицы
Uranium **radiates** (*or* **emits**) **particles** which are helium nuclei.

Испускаться
Several neutrons **are given off** (*or* **emitted**) in fission.
Electromagnetic radiation **is sent out** (*or* **given off**) in discrete little bundles called "quanta".

Испускаться и распадаться
As for radioactivity, radon and thoron gases **emanate** (*or* **are emanated**) **from** the soil **and decay in** the atmosphere.

Испытание [*см.* **Во время испытаний, Выдерживать испытание, Жёсткое испытание, Лабораторное испытание, На испытаниях, Подвергаться испытанию, Приёмочное испытание, Проводить испытание, Проходить испытания**].

Испытание на долговечность
Endurance test.

Испытание на течь (*или* **утечку**)
Leak testing.
Testing of the piping **for leaks.**

Испытанная конструкция
A proven design.

Испытанный в полевых условиях
The components **are field proved** (*or* **field tested**).

Испытанный метод (*или* **способ**)
Proven ways (*or* **methods,** *or* **techniques**) **to** reduce wear ...

Испытательная установка
A test (*or* **trial**) **installation.**

Испытательный период
The trial period is over.

Испытываемый I
The gear **under test** (*or* **to be tested,** *or* **being tested**) is mounted coaxially with ...

Испытываемый II
The stress **experienced by** the rod ...
The force **exerted on** the structure ...

Испытываемый материал
The test material.

Испытываемый образец
The test specimen.

Испытывается нехватка
Low-sulphur oil **is in short** (*or* **critical**) **supply.**

Испытывать I [*см. тж.* **Подвергаться, Претерпевать**]
Magnetic fluids **exhibit** (*or* **undergo**) new instabilities ...
The Earth **must have endured** (*or* **experienced**) many more collisions than ...
Suppose a hadron **is subjected to** a gauge transformation.

Испытывать II [*см. тж.* **Проверять**]
To put these theories **to a test, ...**

Испытывать воздействие
The hydrogen atoms of the methyl group **experience** a magnetic field that depends on ...

Испытывать давлением
The sphere **will be pressure tested.**

Испытывать до разрушения
We **tested** these models **to failure.**

Испытывать затруднения (*или* **трудности**)
Considerable **difficulty has been experienced** (*or* **met with,** *or* **encountered**) in maintaining the arc at constant amplitude.
We **are faced with difficulties.**
We **have run into difficulties with** corrosion.
Problems were experienced in connection with the alignment of components ...
If you **have trouble** solving the problems, consult your instructor.

Испытывать на
Testing of the piping **for** leaks ...

Испытывать на дорогах
This rubber **is being road tested** in tyres.

Испытывать недостаток
The smokeless coals are **in short** (*or* **critical**) **supply.**
They **are short of** semifinished products.

Испытывать столкновение
The volume in which the *A* molecule can **suffer** (*or* **experience,** *or* **undergo**) **collisions with** *B* molecules in 1 second is ...

Испытывать ударами молотка
To hammer test.

Исследование [*см. тж.* **Ведутся исследования с целью, Вести исследования, Для научных исследований в области монокристаллов, Изучение, Область исследований, Обширные исследования, Проводить исследования, Широкие исследования**]
Every research group involved in **elucidation of** molecular structure must ...
Some of **the** earlier **inquiries into** this topic demonstrated that ...
Recent **work** indicates that some clay materials contain ...
In this **treatment** we consider *n* (*r*) in energy space.
Explorations into the replication of ...
We undertook **an** extensive **investigation into** videohead operation.
An investigation of the effects of pressure ...
A fundamental **investigation on** irreversible hydrogen embrittlement has been undertaken.
Research in building materials ...
Research into wood pulp production ...
The pressure of war stimulated **research on** agents suitable for the control of infectious diseases.
Several **studies on** the infrared dichroism of oriented cellulose have been made.

Исследование Земли из космоса
Remote sensing.

Исследование планет
Recent **planetary explorations** have uncovered ...

Исследования с целью
Investigations to find (*or* **with the aim of finding,** *or* **aimed at finding**) a more advanced technique reveal that ...

Исследователь
The discrepancies between the results of various **workers** (*or* **investigators,** *or* **researchers,** *or* **scientists**) ...

Исследовать [*см. тж.* **Вести исследования, Изучать, Осматривать, Рассматривать**]
Now let us use the methods of quantum mechanics **to attack** the hydrogen-atom problem.
The physicist can **probe** an atomic nucleus whenever laboratory apparatus is available.
This enabled the scientists **to probe** the floor of every ocean except the Arctic.
Four-component hydrocarbon mixtures **have been examined** (*or* **investigated,** *or* **studied**).
They **explored** the possibility of X-ray fluorescence.

Исследовать на
Samples **are tested for** the presence of bacteria.

Исследоваться
The use of such materials **is under investigation** (*or* **study**) [*or* **is being investigated** (*or* **studied,** *or* **examined**)].

The surface of Venus **has been probed by** radar signals.

Исследуемая проблема
This detector is best suited to **the problem in** (*or* **at**) **hand** (*or* **under study,** *or* **being studied**).

Исследуемый [*см. тж.* **Изучаемый, Рассматриваемый**]
This quantity can be obtained from the phase diagram of the system **involved** (*or* **in hand**, *or* **at hand,** *or* **under study,** *or* **under review,** *or* **under discussion,** *or* **being studied**).
The object **to be investigated** (*or* **being investigated,** *or* **under investigation**) ...

Исследуемый диапазон
In **the range covered** (*or* **under study,** *or* **in question,** *or* **being studied**) the curves are in good agreement with experiment.

Иссякать [*см. тж.* **Когда-то должен прийти конец**]
As the fossil fuels **run out,** they will become more expensive.
Following epinephrine treatment, the liver **is** not **depleted of** its glycogen stores.

Истекать [*см.* **Время истекло, Срок вышел**].

Истекать в камеру
The fluid **exhausts** (*or* **issues**) **into a chamber.**

Истекшее время
t is **the time elapsed after** introducing the test gas.

Истекший год [*см.* **В истекшем году**].

Истинный
Temperature changes were measured within 0.01°C of their **true** value.
The characteristic equation gives **genuine** eigenvalues.
Such systems are **true** dipoles.

Истолковывать
The opinions presented in this paper are the personal views of the author and should not **be construed to** represent the official policies of the government.

Истолковывать в том смысле, что
This work **has been interpreted as** demonstrating that ...
We **interpreted** this experiment **to mean** (*or* **as meaning**) **that** the enzyme that synthesizes DNA from the viral RNA template is already in existence before the infection.

Истолковывать как
The apparent different behaviour revealed in ... **was interpreted** merely **as** a difference in degree of dissociation.

Исторический [*см.* **В историческом плане**].

Исторический интерес [*см.* **Представлять исторический интерес**].

История изобилует примерами
The history of technology **provides many examples of** (*or* **abounds in**) (**cases where**) ...

Источник
The combustion of coal is thought to be **the** major **contributor of** sulphuric acid.

Источник неполадок [*см.* **Главный источник неполадок**].

Истощать
We cannot continue **to deplete** (*or* **exhaust**) our natural resources at the rate we have done without suffering ...

Истощать запас
Each species would multiply until it **outran** its food **supply.**
These stars **have exhausted** (*or* **drained**) their **supply of** ...

Истощаться
The supply of coal in the bin **is getting low** (*or* **dwindling,** *or* **running short,** *or* **nearly exhausted,** *or* **coming to an end**).
When an oil field **runs dry, ...**
The star may explode when most of the helium in the core **is used up.**

Истощающийся
The **dwindling** (*or* **depleting**) oil reserves ...

Истощение
Depletion of hemoglobin at the blood cell walls ...
This type of blood loss anemia will cause **depletion** (*or* **exhaustion**) **of** iron reserves of the blood necessary for hemoglobin synthesis.

Истощение природных ресурсов
The depletion (*or* **exhaustion,** *or* **dwindling**) **of** natural resources ...

Истощён
The oil field **is** badly **depleted.**

Исходить из I [*см. тж.* **Если исходить из предположения о**]
A paraboloid's light rays **originate at** the focus.
The light **originates** (*or* **emanates**) **from** a tungsten lamp.
The commands **emanate from** the locust's central flight motor.
This noise **emanates** (*or* **radiates,** *or* **issues**) **from** many sources.
All vectors **emanate from** a single point.
The lines **emerge** (*or* **issue**) **from** a point.

Исходить из II
We usually **proceed** (*or* **start**) **from** simple functions associated with ...

Исходить из предположения
We **assume** a diffuse source of illumination.
We **operate on the premise** (*or* **assumption**) **that ...**
We **proceed from the assumption that ...**
All previous analyses **started from** (*or* **were based on**) **assumptions of** fixed reactor temperature.

Исходное положение [*см. тж.* **Возвращаться в первоначальное положение**]
The starting position.

Исходный материал [*см. тж.* **Сырьё**]
Titanium is **an** ideal **source** (*or* **initial,** *or* **starting**) **material for** many processes.

Исходя из [*см. тж.* **Если исходить из, На основании**]
From theoretical principles they showed that ...
Based on this linear speed, the speed ratio of two pulleys is ...
Based upon an examination of the chart, it is believed that ...
On the basis that the radio signals ... he has calculated the distance ...
Reasoning from this knowledge of ... Mendeleyev stated ...
Using (*or* **Starting from**) the calculated data as the base, ...
On the basis of indirect evidence, ...

Исходя из вышеприведённых соображений
From the above (line of) reasoning it is clear that ...

Исходя из имеющихся данных
On the basis of present knowledge, the correlation given above appears valid.

Исходя из ..., он высказал предположение, что
Comparison of ... **led him to propose that** continental drift had taken place.

Исходя из ошибочного предположения, что
This value is much used **on the mistaken assumption that ...**

Исходя из предположения, что [*см. тж.* **В предположении, что; При предположении**]
We simplify this notation to ... **with the understanding that** the hydrogens are bound to ...
We start with isolated atoms **in the belief that** the electron wave ...
Forced circulation evaporators were studied, **based on the belief that** such evaporation would result in ...
The emitted resistance can be calculated **on the assumption** (*or* **assuming**) $N_e = N_l$.
On this assumption most experiments were made with specimens of window glass.
With this assumption we use the transformation of ...

Исходя из теоретических соображений
The strength of the magnetic field inside a star cannot be measured directly, but **on theoretical grounds** one would expect ...

Исходя из того, что
The order of magnitude of molecular dipole moments can be deduced **by recognizing that** these moments result from charges like that of an electron.

Исходя из этого
On this basis the tissue can be expected to manifest ...

Исходя из этого принципа
With these general **principles in mind,** we can turn to a classification of geosynclines.

Исходящий [*см.* **Вытекающий из, Выходящий**].

Исцеляющее действие
A curative (*or* **healing**) **effect.**

Исчезать
Turbulence **dies out** (*or* **disappears**) gradually as the surface is approached.
The disturbance created by the diaphragm **dies away.**
Civilizations based on irrigation **faded away** because of salination.
The first mineral resource to be totally mined out **became extinct** in 1969.
Such radioactive species as iodine 129 and plutonium 244 **are** now **extinct.**

Исчезающе мал
The apparent motion of the stars, with respect to one another as viewed from the Earth, **is vanishingly small.**

Исчезнувший
This means that there may be 10^3 to 10^4 as many **defunct** pulsars as live ones.

Исчерпывать возможности
The potentialities of this method **have been exhausted.**

Исчерпывающий
It is not possible here to give an **exhaustive** account of this reaction.

Исчисляться сотнями
Such observations may **number in the hundreds** (*or* **run into the hundreds**).

Итог [*см.* **В конечном счёте, Подводить итоги**].

Их
Certain missile nose cones or portions **thereof** are coated with ablative material.

К

К [*см. тж.* **Ближайший к, Обращённый к, Относиться к, Прижиматься к, Сродство к**]
Towards the end of the 19th century ...

К востоку от [*см.* **К западу от**].

К всеобщему удивлению
To everyone's surprise, the measurements showed that ...

К ... добавляется
This primary cause of pollution **is augmented by** the pollution that is produced by ...
To the test material in aqueous solution **is added** a solution of ... (*or* A solution of .. **is added to** ...).

К западу от
The mine is located **to the west of** the mountain range.
The Caledonian Geosyncline is terminated just **west of** Ireland.

К концу
This topography existed **at the close** (*or* **towards the end**) **of** the Precambrian time.

К концу 19-го века
Towards the end of the 19th century the use of ... was generally accepted as ...
By the turn of the 19th century ...

К концу (19)80-х годов
By the late (19)80s ...

К которому мы приступаем
The study of ..., **which we now undertake** (*or* **to which we now proceed**), is in keeping with ...

К которому приближается
The limit **approached by** the expression ...

К минимуму [*см.* **Сводить к минимуму**].

К .... можно добавить
To these measures **may be added** the construction of many small dams.

К моменту
By the time of body closure the embryonic neurons must ...

К настоящему времени [*см. тж.* **В настоящее время**]
By now the general pattern should be clear.
To review analytical methods and results **to date, ...**
On the basis of discoveries made **to date** it seems that ...
The experience **thus far** gained furnishes us with approximate cost figures for ...

К началу (20-го) века
By the early (20th) century ...

К началу (19)80-х годов
By the early (19)80s ...

К нашему удивлению
Surprisingly, we find that pulse spreading is significantly affected by material dispersion.

К ним относится
Among these are the accumulation and an increase in ...

К ... прилагается
The calculator **comes with** a handbook containing ...

К своему великому удивлению
Much to their surprise they discovered that ...

К северу от [*см.* **К западу от**].

К ... следует добавить
To the above drag **must be added** the sustenation drag.

К счастью
Luckily (*or* **Fortunately**), other chemical imprints can help to ...

К тому времени
By then ...

К тому времени когда
By the time the negative aperture is closed, the modulator shutters are usually in printing position.

К тому же [*см. тж.* **Кроме того**]
What is more [*or* **Moreover,** *or* **In addition (to that),** *or* **Besides**], short circuiting is eliminated.

К удивлению (учёных) оказалось, что
Surprisingly, it was found that ...

К числу ... относятся
Among the many organic acids **are** acetic and oxalic acids and phenol.

К этому времени
Segmentation is complete on the formation of ..., **by which time** the germinal plate covers ...

К этому можно добавить
To this we can add the large quantities of ...

К этому следует добавить
To this must be added the amount of head necessary to ...

К югу от [*см.* **К западу от**].

Кабель с металлическим экраном
Metal-sheathed cable.

Кабина для работы в любую погоду (*на строительном кране*)
An all-weather cab.

Каждодневный [*см. тж.* **В каждодневной практике**]
The **day-to-day** operation of the observatory ...

Каждому .... соответствует
For every contraction mapping ... this equation **has** a unique solution.
For every kind of particle **there is** an antiparticle.

Каждый [*см. тж.* **На каждый, Через каждые ... градусов**]
Three amino acids are encoded by six codons **apiece** (*or* **each**).
How many samples of 25.0 mg **each** could be prepared from ...?

Каждый в отдельности
Each of the loops is sufficient **by itself** to deliver 100 percent of the required cooling.
Although such resonant forces are **individually** small, ...
The corrections introduced will be treated one at a time.

Каждый день [*см.* **Ежедневно**].

Каждый должен сам найти ответ на этот вопрос
Each of us must determine the answer for himself after examining the potential value of the computer.

Каждый из
These atoms **each** have six valence electrons (*or* have six ... **each**).

Каждый из двух [*см. тж.* **Любой из двух**]
Either (of the two) process(es) could initiate a chain reaction.

Каждый из которых определяется
There will be n different simple wave solutions, **each (being) determined by** one of the n roots of Eq. (2.14).

Каждый конкретный
The expansion shall be allowed for in the die design for **each specific** (*or* **individual**) application.

Каждый ... отдельно взятый [*см.* **Каждый в отдельности**].

Кажущийся [*см. тж.* **Казалось бы**]
The duality of origin may be perceived to be more **apparent** than real.
The **apparent** position of a star ...
If the two diagonal pairs of lights are flashed alternately, it will appear to an observer as if the lights are moving. The **apparent** motion can take either of two forms: ...

Казалось бы
These fields are always present, even in **seemingly** perfect crystals.
This **seemingly** difficult task turns out to be relatively simple.

Как [*см.* **Каким образом**].

Как будто бы
This species will be treated **as though** it were a well-defined molecule.
The laser beam spot size increased **as if** a diverging lens **had been** placed in the resonator.
The effect is a horizontal shift in portions of the reproduced picture **as though** (*or* **as if**) **there were** a loss in horizontal synchronization.

Как будто бы он был
Where steeply dipping, layered rocks underlie a hillside, the upper edges of the layers are commonly turned downhill **as if** bent.
We subtract the two reactions **as though** (*or* **as if**) **they were** algebraic equations.
The liquid phase behaves **as if it were** a stationary medium.

Как бы велик ни был
The group velocity is less than the speed of light, **however** (*or* **no matter how**) **great** the phase velocity (**may be**).

Как бы ни был
Useful **as** these measures **may be,** we are faced with ...

Как бы то ни было
Be it as it may, we certainly know enough to sketch the broad outline of ...

Как в отдельности, так и вместе
Future progress with both processes — **individually and in combination** — will be followed with interest.

Как в случае
If, **as with** magnesium, alternating current is used, ...

Как вам известно
As you are well aware, ...

Как видно
The enthalpy of the reaction **is** (*or* **can be**) **seen to be** equal to ...

Как видно из [*см. тж.* **Как показано на рисунке, Как явствует из**]
There is but little difference, **as indicated by** (*or* **in**) Fig. 11.
As the statement **indicates ...**
As may (*or* **can**) **be seen** [*or* **As is seen** (*or* **obvious**), *or* **As will be seen**] **from** the diagram, ...
The calculator looks like a card index **as will be apparent from** the photograph.
The fixture moves in an anti-clockwise direction **as viewed** (*or* **seen,** *or* **observed**) **in** Fig. 3.
As evident (*or* **seen**) **from** the sketch, type 2 adaptors are intended for taper-shank tools.
As the following example **illustrates** (*or* **shows**), ...
As Fig. 14-5 **suggests, ...**
Half-life times vary greatly, **as exemplified by** the successive decay scheme for uranium-238 (Fig. 35-2).

Как видно из вышеизложенного
As is evident (*or* **obvious**) **from** (*or* **As evidenced by**) **the foregoing (account),** the answers to these questions are ...

Как видно из иллюстрации [*см.* **Как показано на рисунке**].

Как видно из названия
As its name implies (*or* **indicates,** *or* **shows**) (*or* **As the name suggests**) a pressure gauge is ....

Как видно из рисунка [*см.* **Как показано на рисунке**].

Как всегда
The variable arm IV, short **as it usually is,** has experienced some modifications.

Как его стали называть
The mineral sequences, or *Barrovian zones*, **as they have come to be called,** have been recognized in many metamorphic terrains.

Как и [*см. тж.* **Подобно тому, как**]
Here, **as in** the wet equatorial areas, the rainfall mechanisms are ...
The boiling point of a pure liquid, **like** the melting point of a pure crystal, represents a fairly sudden transition.
Like Boyle's law, this relation is followed by many gases.
These calculations, **along with** (*or* **as well as**) our findings, show that ...
The trains of meteors move with time **as do** noctilucent clouds.
The diameter required in order to fulfil this condition depends upon the reaction-zone length **as does** the critical diameter.
Presumably, **as for** the static case, the movement of the vibrating surface will be opposed in the manner of a spring.
The power unit is in a separate case **as is** the calibrated display unit.
Superconductors are **as** sensitive to changes in magnetic-field strength **as they are to** changes of temperature.
As with any chemical process, analysis is extremely important for process control.
Carbon dioxide **shares with** water vapour the property of absorbing infrared radiation.
In common with the other natural sciences chemistry is fundamentally concerned with ...

Как и было предсказано
We found that ICl is more soluble is chloroform, **as predicted.**

Как и в
Again, **as in** step 1, the temperature is constant.
As in wing theory, these components require an increase in blade angle.
As with all other kinds of theories, the foremost criterion here is ...

Как и в случае
As for a function of a real variable, the inverse of differentiation of a function of a complex variable is integration.
As in the case of silver and gold, platinum metals collect in ...
As with complete failure to deliver water, check first the whole pipe arrangement.
As is the case with methane, these three hydrogens are indistinguishable.
As with size and brightness, the form and motions of the comet tails are extremely varied.

Как и для [*см.* **Как и в случае**].

Как и должно быть
This term implies a dimensionless quantity **as it must** if its logarithm is to be taken.

Как и ожидалось
As (would be) expected, the response is a straight line with a slope.

Как и прежде [*см.* **Как и раньше**].

Как и при
As with (*or* As **in the case of**) normal reflection, the fluid is constrained.
As is the case with myxoedema, ...

Как и раньше
Cytidine is found rarely **as before** (*or* **previously**).

Как и следовало ожидать
As one would expect, Eq. 11 shows that ...
As would (*or* **could,** *or* **might**) **be expected** under these conditions, such engines received primary emphasis.
As (was to be) expected, the solid line fitted the circle well.
As we might expect, this difference is relatively large.

Как и у
As with (*or* **As in the case of**) tallium, the room temperature ductility of niobium is relatively high.
As is true of all proteins, **so with** hemoglobin the charge on the hemoglobin molecule depends on the hydrogen-like concentration.

Как легко заметить
As will readily be observed (*or* **As is easy to see**), there is no sharp line of demarcation between ...

Как может показаться с первого взгляда

These holes serve to support cylindrical guides for the top platen, and not for the rods, **as might appear at first sight.**

Как можно ближе
One set of gauges was placed **as close to the** junction as possible.

Как можно было ожидать
As one might expect, there is a strong general correlation between the two measures.
The evidence is not as strong **as might be hoped for,** but it is suggestive.
As might be expected from their nonpolar character, both of these forms are soluble in benzene.

Как можно быстрее
It is desirable to burn the mixture **as quickly as possible.**

Как можно дальше друг от друга
The *v*-values for the two glasses should lie **as far apart as possible.**

Как можно меньше
To have **as few** photon-electron conversions **as possible, ...**

Как мы увидим дальше
As we shall see subsequently (*or* **later**), ...

Как например
Incomplete combustion, **as in** the internal combustion engine, forms smokes.
Such reactions usually occur in polar solvents, **such as** water, methanol, or acetone.
Equipment designed to promote mass transfer between two liquids (**,as, for instance,) in** extraction processes, can be made quite compact.

Как насчёт [*см.* **А как насчёт**].

Как нетрудно понять
As can be readily appreciated, such contrast information is essential for ...

Как ни странно
Strangely enough (*or* **Strange though it may seem**), the first experiments employed a shock temperature rise of only 50 °C.

Как ни удивительно
Surprisingly, only one unidentified peak with substantial intensity is observed.

Как общее правило
As a general rule, the gold content ranges from 85 to 95%.

Как обычно [*см.* **Как всегда, Обычным путём**].

Как одно целое
The earth's crust and a significant portion of the upper mantle move together **as a unit.**

Как описано [*см.* **Как указано**].

Как отмечено выше [*см. тж.* **Как указано**]
As noted (*or* **indicated,** *or* **mentioned**) **above,** the lower value is ...

Как побочный результат
A theory of cell respiration has been developed **as a by-product of** the above-mentioned studies.

Как показано в
For two-dimensional flow, the hyperbolic condition may be obtained graphically, **as illustrated** (*or* **shown**) in Chapter 4.
As is shown in Sec. 14-3, ...

Как показано выше
As indicated (*or* **discussed**) **earlier** (*or* **above**), ...

Как показано на рисунке [*см. тж.* **Как видно из**]
The volume varies linearly with the temperature **in the manner indicated** (*or* **shown**) **in Fig. 5.**
As illustrated (**in Fig. 4**), these bearings are carried in ...
End flanges may be braced with a strap **as in Fig 2.**
As indicated in the picture, ...
The circuits were coupled together **as shown in** (*or* **by Fig. 3**).
Referring to Fig. 1, the thrust is equal to the mass of ...

Как показывает название [*см. тж.* **Как видно из названия**]
This publication, **as the title implies,** is primarily concerned with ...

Как правило
Hydrometallurgical processes, **as a rule,** are applied to ...
A field lens is **generally** placed behind the reticle.

Как предполагалось
When these molecules behave **as expected, ...**

Как принято
This reaction is written, **as is the convention,** as a reduction reaction.
As is customary, let ξ represent the degree of ...

Как раз такой, какой
These properties **are just the ones** predicted by ...

Как раз столько, сколько требуется для
For the Crab pulsar the energetic electrons produced in this way have energies of 10^4 electron volts, **just right to** produce the observed X-radiation from the nebula.

Как самоцель
Reaction mechanisms are not treated here **as an end in themselves.**

Как скоро выяснится
However, **as will soon become evident** (*or* **apparent,** *or* **obvious,** *or* **clear**), the logic was faulty.

Как сообщают
This machine **reportedly** operates [*or* **is reported** (*or* **said,** *or* **claimed**) to operate] at a speed of 20,000 cycles per minute.

Как средство против
This agent is effective **against** certain types of cancer.

Как стало ясно после
As was apparent after the acceptance of the quantum-wave relation, ...

Как ..., так и [*см. тж.* **Одинаково необходим для**]
Scientists **and** engineers **alike** (*or* Scientists **as well as** engineers, *or* **Both** scientists **and** engineers) **were** intrigued by ...
Just as the development of the electron microscope required the evolution of special sample techniques, **so** the flying spot scanner will stimulate a search for ...
Just as a shallow pot of water placed on a stove will boil faster than a deep pot of water, **so also will** a water tube boiler raise steam faster than a Scotch boiler.
The result applies **both to** molecules moving in random directions **and to** the directionally selected molecules.
Just as the Moon produces tides on the Earth, **so** the Earth produces tides on the Moon.

Как таковой [*см. тж.* **Сам по себе**]
This movement, **as such,** is not important to the navigator.

Как только
As soon as the crust becomes continuous, ...
Embryonic development begins **as soon as** the eggs are laid.

Как указано [*см. тж.* **Как отмечено выше**]
As already noted, ...
Adjust the proportional band **as in** par A.1 above.
The system should be filled with the fluid **as directed** (*or* **indicated,** *or* **stated**) above.
As discussed (*or* **stated,** *or* **pointed out,** *or* **outlined**) above, the amount of residual CO_2 in the lean amine can ...
As (previously) discussed (*or* **noted,** *or* **mentioned**), the threshold condition must be satisfied.
As stated above, ...

Как указано (показано) в
The width of the *F*-band changes with temperature **in the manner shown in** Fig. 4.
As suggested in Fig. 15-2, ...
These compounds may be grouped **as in** Table 3.

Как указано выше
As pointed out (*or* **indicated,** *or* **shown,** *or* **stated,** *or* **mentioned**) **above, ...**
Sodium hydrogen-carbonate precipitates and is treated **as noted** (*or* **indicated**) **above.**
As discussed (*or* **cited,** *or* **remarked**) **above, ...**

Как указано ниже
However, **as noted** (*or* **indicated,** *or* **remarked,** *or* **stated,** *or* **shown,** *or* **pointed out**) **later** (*or* **below**), special low-temperature enamels are fired at 1280 to 1350°F.

Как упомянуто в
As we have mentioned in Chapter 3, ...

Как упомянуто выше [*см.* **Как отмечено выше, Как указано**].

Как утверждают
The arch support **is claimed to** be less costly.

Как функция
H is plotted **against** (*or* **versus,** *or* **vs.,** *or* **as a function of**) *U*.

Как часто случается (*или* **бывает**)
If, **as is often the case** (*or* **as often happens**), a complexing agent is a weak acid, ...

Как чисто (*на чертежах*)
Mill or grind **to clean up** (*or* **until the surface "cleans"**).

Как это бывает
As is sometimes the case, ...

Как это делает
Synthetic chelates which absorb and desorb oxygen reversibly, **as does** hemoglobin, have been prepared in the laboratory.

Как это делается
This loss can be eliminated **as is done** at our plant.

Как это делается в случае отсутствия
The modulator shutters are not permitted to open as wide **as would be the case if** the undercorrection path **were nonexistent.**

Как это имеет место в
When the bonding atoms are rigidly positioned around the metal by the organic framework, **as (is the case) in** the porphins, the resulting increase in stability is unusual.
The electrons are hence not free to diffuse into a larger volume, **as happens with** homostructure lasers.

Как это имеет место при
Vapour-phase dehydrogenation of isoalcohols **as in** the preparation of acetone from ...
If the vertical velocity component is small, **as it is in** the large-scale motion of the atmosphere, ...

Как это ни странно
Strange as it may seem, ...

Как это обычно делается
As is customary when a new phenomenon is discovered, he tried to reproduce ...

Как это сделал
Consider now, **as was done by** Debye in 1912, the contribution to ...

Как это увязать с
How does all of this fit into the general scheme of things?

Как это часто бывает
Galvanic corrosion results from ..., **as is often the case,** for example, in hull piping systems.

Как явствует из [*см. тж.* **Как видно из**]
As may be inferred [*or* **As is clear** (*or* **evident,** *or* **obvious**)] **from** the graph ...
As the data of Table 5-5 **suggest, ...**

Какая-то доля
The refracting ray loses **a fraction of** its power at each reflection.

Какие происходят
The instrument cannot be used for sharp density changes **such as occur at** the shock front itself.

Каким бы ни казался
Bright **as** the future of composites **seem to be,** there is still a great deal of work to be done.
Significant **as** such a factor **might seem,** it is not as important as ...

Каким-либо другим путём
This device converts electric energy into light, heat, or mechanical energy, or **otherwise** consumes electric energy as in ...

Каким образом
This indicates **the manner in which** D_E varies with flow rate.
It is necessary to consider more closely **the way** the two types of microscope produce their images.

Каков бы ни был
Whatever (*or* **No matter what**) the initial direction of the particles **(may be),** they will soon be moving perpendicularly to the wave front.

Какова бы ни была причина этого [*см.* **Чем бы это ни было вызвано**].

Каково строение ... ?
How are such molecules **constructed?**

Каковы преимущества или недостатки ... по сравнению с ... ?
How does the new instrument **compare with** the other light detector?

Какое место он занимает в ... ?
What are fibre bundles and **how do they enter into** physics?

Какое расстояние покрывает ... ?
How far does a molecule **travel** between collisions?

Какой бы метод ни применялся
Whatever the method, ...

Какой бы ни
Whatever order you use, you will find ...

Какой бы он ни был
Floods can be catastrophic; disastrous **as they may be,** we must consider them as the expression of natural stream behaviour.

Какой-либо [*см. тж.* **В каком-либо направлении**]
When **any(one)** cock is opened, ...
The maximum rate of change of **a particular** (*or* **a certain**) characteristic of the orbit ...

Какой-нибудь [*см.* **Всего лишь, Какой-либо**].

Какой-нибудь один
The hydroxyl proton does not belong to **any one** molecule but to many molecules.

Какой-то [*см. тж.* **В какой-то точке, За какие-то секунды**]
At **some** point on the earth's surface ...

Какой-то момент [*см.* **В какой-то момент**].

Какой только можно себе представить
Any **conceivable** number can be represented by ...

Какую роль он играет в [*см.* **Какое место он занимает в**].

Калиброванный в единицах расстояния
Some FM radars use electronic frequency meters **calibrated in range** as indicators.

Калибровать по
The screens **are calibrated against** standard filters.
The analytical cells **were calibrated with** known mixtures of ortho- and parahydrogen.
The changes in temperature can **be calibrated from** the changes in resistance.

Калибровка по
Calibration against a black body radiator ...
Calibration with a standard solution of ...

Камень преткновения
The misapplication of pushbutton and selector switches has been **a stumbling block for** many control systems.

Канавка [*см. тж.* **Иметь канавку, С канавкой, С прямыми канавками**]
A tap having three **flutes** is recommended.

Капитальный ремонт
Major repairs (*or* **Overhaul**).

Капля [*см.* **Добавлять каплями, По капле**].

Карго
The first **shipload of** Russian coking coal reached Japan in ...

Кардинальный вопрос
The questions at issue for any food additive are whether or not it is necessary and, if so, whether or not it is safe.

Карманный
A **pocket(-sized)** test set.

Картина [*см.* **Набросать общую картину**].

Картина абсорбции *и т.п.*
Molecules with permanent dipoles often show complex **patterns of absorption.**

Картина вырисовывается [*см.* **Начинает вырисовываться картина**].

Картина потока
The surface drag changes **the flow pattern.**

Карьерный способ (*горн.*) [*см.* **Добывать карьерным способом**].

Касание [*см.* **Точка касания**].

Касательная к
The tangent to the curve ...

Касательный к
These trajectories are semi-ellipses **tangent to** the orbit of the Earth.

Касаться I
We will not **go into** (*or* **dwell on**) problems which ...
We have already **touched on** vapour pressure correlation forms.

Касаться II [*см. тж.* **Все, кого это касается; Относиться к,Поскольку это касается, Распространяться на, Справедливо , Это также относится к**]
Most of these design considerations also **apply** (*or* **refer**) **to** aluminium.
This paper **concerns** (*or* **is concerned with**) experimental control systems.
The article **deals with** (*or* **discusses**) the modifications at the power stations.
The same **holds true for** (*or* **of**) any sensitive device which ...
The investigation **concerned** the effect of shock waves propagating into air.
One project **is concerned with** the possibility of producing electricity in low-temperature geothermal fields.

Касаться III [*см. тж.* **Соприкасаться**]
The magnetic head **is in contact with** the surface of ...
The operating and equilibrium lines nearly **touch** (*or* **are** nearly **tangent to**) one another.

Касаться вопроса о том
We **have** not yet **touched on** how the cosmic jets are fuelled.

Касающийся
Further interesting information **relative to** (*or* **regarding,** *or* **relating to,** *or* **referring to,** *or* **concerning,** *or* **in relation to,** *or* **in respect to**) the equation of state may be found in Ref. 24.

Катализатор [*см.* **Над катализатором**].

Категорически отвергать
Why did they **reject** his hypothesis so **vigorously** (or **out of hand**)?

Категория [*см.* **В эту рубрику входят, Делить на категории, Относиться к категории**].

Катод [*см.* **На катоде**].

Качание маятника [*см.* **Колебание маятника**].

Качественные показатели
The qualitative characteristics of ...

Качественный [*см. тж.* **В количественном (качественном) отношении, Высококачественный, Доброкачественный**]
We can make some **qualitative** conclusions concerning ...

Качественный анализ
Qualitative analysis.

Качество [*см.* **В качестве, Высшего качества, Использоваться в качестве, Критерий качества, Служить в качестве**].

Качество снижается
The grade of ore used for copper production **has been going downward** (*or* **deteriorating**).

Качество ... снижено настолько, что
The quality is degraded to the point (*or* **extent**) **that** it is not useful for its intended purpose.

Квадрат [*см.* **Возводить в квадрат**].

Квадрат площадью 6 кв. дюймов
A square of 6 sq in.

Квадрат, построенный на
Therefore **the square on** *FB* = the squares on *FH, HB*.

Квадрат расстояния
The distance x **squared ...**

Квадрат со стороной в 6 дюймов
Imagine **a square six inches on a side.**
The test fixture consisted of a slab of plate glass **six inches square.**

Квадратичный по
H **is quadratic in** p_0.

Квадратного сечения
A **square** duct with water in turbulent flow was simulated.
A two-inch **square** bar (*со стороной в 2 дюйма*).
Positive clutches may consist of two or more jaws **of square section.**

Квадратный корень [*см.* **Корень квадратный из 2**].

Квадратура круга
The ancient Greeks formulated the famous problem of **"squaring the circle".**

Квантовать по
The angular momentum **is quantized in** magnitude and direction.

Кеплеровский
This is a true **Keplerian** orbit.

Кипение [*см.* **Доводить до кипения**].

Кислород воздуха
Atmospheric oxygen (*or* **Oxygen of the air**).

Кислотный, основной
Alcohols are less **acidic** than water; aromatic amines are less **basic** than aliphatic amines.

Кишеть
Paleozoic seas **were swarming with** highly differentiated aquatic plants.

Класс [*см.* **Делиться на категории**].

Класс отделки [*см.* **Высокий класс отделки поверхности**].

Классификация
Modern methods of malignancy **grading** take into consideration mitotic activity, ...

Классификация в соответствии с тем, является ли
The classification of tunneling rays **according to whether** the attenuation is effectively infinite **or** zero ...

Классификация по
The classification of human tumours **by** tissue type is given in ...

Классифицировать [*см. тж.* **Делить на, Относить к**]
Organic compounds may **be categorized according to** certain arrangements of atoms.
Chloramphenicol **is classed as** an antibiotic.
Acedobacter suboxydans **is classified among** the vinegar bacteria.
This error may **be classified as** a deformation error.
Fluid flow may **be classified under** two types, laminar and turbulent.
It is impossible **to categorize** *E. histolytica* **as** either a parasitic or as a commensal organism since it may be either.

Классифицировать в соответствии с его назначением
Dams may **be classified by** their purpose.

Классифицировать по размерам
Then the flows **are ranked according to magnitude.**

Классифицироваться по
The polar fluids **are rated in order of** their available power, toxicity, resistivity, ...

Класть [*см.* **Положить**].

Класть в основу [*см.* **Использовать в качестве основы для**].

Клеймо
High-temperature nuts **have** either an "H" or "A" **stamped on** the crown for identification.

Клепать [*см.* **Приклёпывать к, Склёпывать**].

Климат [*см.* **Изменение климата**].

Ключ к [*см. тж.* **Давать ключ к**]
A knowledge of these features **is the key to** planning a liquid-liquid extraction.
The clues (*or* **keys**) **to** this relationship lie in ...

Ключ к пониманию
The key to understanding how sediments are sorted ...

Ключём к ... является
The key to these questions **lies with** nucleic acids.

Книзу
The tube is tapered **from top to bottom.**

Кнопка [*см.* **Нажим кнопки**].

Кнопочное управление [*см.* **С кнопочным управлением**].

Ко времени писания этой книги (*или* **статьи**)
At this writing no one has proved the theorem.

Ковалентно связанный
Covalently bonded atoms ...

Ковать в горячем состоянии
The weld metal may **be hot forged** without difficulty.

Когда [*см. тж.* **В случае, когда**]
The fuel material is cooled **as** (*or* **while,** *or* **when**) it passes down through the steam generator.
Once these operating requirements have been established, the engineer should consult a porcelain enameller.
Where really large moulds are to be produced, a vertical band saw can be used advantageously.

Когда возможно [*см.* **Во всех случаях, когда это возможно**].

Когда, и только когда [*см.* **Если, и только если**].

Когда идёт речь о [*см.* **Когда речь идёт о**].

Когда он находится
Aquatic beetles have several accessory structures to aid their respiration **while** underwater.

Когда он не используется
The beetle's wings are carefully folded **when not in use.**

Когда речь идёт о
When it comes to moving a piston-engine airplane through the air, there is no alternative to the propeller.

Когда это не угрожает безопасности населения
The consequences can be extremely costly even **when public safety is not at issue.**

Когда это необходимо
Cold water circulates, **when required** (*or* **necessary**) in the outer jacket carrying away the excess heat.

Когда это целесообразно
Use the unity method **where appropriate.**

Когда-нибудь [*см. тж.* **В будущем, В какой-то момент**]
These are the first hot-headed beryllium fasteners **ever** produced.

Когда-то [*см.* **Одно время**].

Когда-то должен прийти конец
There is a limit to the amount of these resources.

Кодировать в виде
The scattering angle **is coded into** a ten-digit binary number.

Колебание I [*см. тж.* **Без колебания, Большие изменения**]
Fluctuations in climate are considerable in this area.
The costs remain practically unchanged with wide **variation in** production rate.

Колебание II
The vibration of the conveyor.
The oscillation of the atoms within the molecule with respect to one another ...

Колебание маятника
Oscillation (*or* **Swing**) **of a pendulum.**

Колебание напряжения в сети
Line voltage fluctuation.

Колебания относительно
Temperature **fluctuations about** the freezing point.

Колебания температуры
Fluctuations in (*or* **of**) **temperature.**
Variations in temperature.

Колебание функций (*матем.*)
Oscillation of functions.

Колебательное движение (*маятника и т.п.*)
Oscillatory motion.
Vibratory motion.

Колебаться
Populations **fluctuate in** size.
The temperature **fluctuates.**
The pointer **oscillates with respect to** the centre of the scale.
The atoms **oscillate** (*or* **vibrate**).
The prices **vary** (*or* **fluctuate**).
The conveyor **vibrates.**
In the steady state, *c* **oscillates** (*or* **fluctuates,** *or* **varies**) **between** upper **and** lower limiting values.
The controlled variable **will oscillate** forever **about** the desired steady-state value.

Колебаться от ... до ...
The amplitude of the radial velocity changes of stellar couples may **range from** a few kilometres per second **to** many hundred kilometres per second.
The output level **is variable from** 0.5 V **to ...**
The safety factor **varies between** 1.3 **and** 2.

Колебаться относительно
The object **oscillates about** the true Lagrangian point.

Колесо [*см.* **Установленный на колёсах**].

Количественно
The reluctance force can be expressed **quantitatively** in terms of ...

Количественные показатели
The quantitative characteristics of ...

Количественный
The **quantitative** results are obvious.

Количественный анализ
Quantitative analysis.

Количество [*см. тж.* **В количестве, В незначительном количестве, В огромных количествах, Граммовые количества, Значительное количество**]
A considerable **body of** data suggests that ...
The gaseous products contain large **proportions** (*or* **amounts,** *or* **quantities**) **of** propylene, butylene and butadiene.
These countries produce large **tonnages of** bentonite.

Количество уменьшается
As quartz **decreases in abundance,** dacite passes into andesite.

Колоссальный
The number of narcotics on the market is **legion**.
The stars emit radiation at a **prodigious** rate.

Комбинация [*см. тж.* **Сочетание**]
To obtain an adequate **compromise** (*or* **combination**) **of** oxidation resistance, refractory properties and resistance to impact, ...

Комбинированный
A **combined** magnetic spectrograph and spectrometer.

Комета [*см.* **Связанный с кометами**].

Комнатная температура [*см.* **При комнатной температуре**].

Компактный
A **compact** form.
This is a valuable machine **of small bulk** and low cost.
We use **space-saving** printed wiring.

Компенсация
Methods of **compensating for** changes in temperature ...

Компенсировать [*см. тж.* **Оправдывать расходы**]
The extra positive and negative charges could **compensate** each other.
The two trays are independently mounted and the movement of each is opposed to the other **to cancel out** the forces set up by each tray.
To compensate for the loss of steam, ...
This pump immediately adjusts its stroke **to compensate for** any variation in line pressure.
Voltage drop **is compensated by** a resistor.
This effect could **be counterbalanced by** using more material.
The valve supplies fluid **to make up for** external losses.
Blending sand had to be added **to make up for** a deficiency in fines.
The saving of steel might **offset** the high fabrication costs.
The moisture brought in with the air would **be offset by** the reduction in moisture diffusion.

Компенсировать недостаток
The impurity will attempt **to make up the deficiency** by taking an electron from a native atom near to it.

Компенсировать потери
The factor R denotes the ratio of energy output needed **to compensate for** (*or* **offset**) all possible plasma **losses**.

Компенсироваться
Usually the pressure force **is balanced out by** an opposing force.
Any increase in ... **would be** exactly **cancelled by** an equal decrease in ...

Any transmission loss must **be compensated for** by a linear aperture increase.
Reduced gain **is made up by** one amplifier stage.
The greater power cost may **be offset** (*or* **compensated for**) **by** the reduced investment.

Комплекс [*см. тж.* **Образовывать комплекс с**]
The climate of an area is **the totality of** atmospheric conditions of that area during ...
Automation and **the complex of** technological changes which are usually included in that concept ...
Bacterial metabolism is **the sum total of** the chemical changes carried out by living bacteria.

Комплексный
A **combined** program of therapy ...
Complete (*or* **All-round**) automation ...
Comprehensive instrumentation ...
The U-712-A is an **integral** drilling unit which includes a hoisting drum, a transmission, a rotary drive and an auxiliary brake.
An **integrated** and highly mechanized production line ...
How does the locust coordinate the movements of eight different body parts into a single **integrated** response?
A **diversified** high-energy physics laboratory ...

Комплект [*см. тж.* **В комплекте с, Серия**]
The satellite will carry microchannel plates as part of its **complement** of X-ray detectors.

Комплект данных
A set of data.

Комплектно
These boilers are to be supplied **complete** (*or* **as complete units**) **with** burner and controls.

Компонент
Sand is an important **constituent** (*or* **component,** *or* **component part,** *or* **ingredient**) **of** any block mix.
Gamma globulins are normal **constituents of** the circulating blood proteins.

Компонента, направленная под углом
Brewster-**angled components** will force oscillation into one direction of polarization.

Компьютер [*см.* **Закладывать в компьютер, Управляемый компьютером**].

Конвейер [*см.* **По конвейеру**].

Конвейерная сборка
Conveyorized assembly.

Конденсироваться в
Hydrocarbons from the cracking of ... may **condense to** aromatics.
The steam **condenses to** water.

Кондиционирование воздуха
The plant facilities are **air conditioned.**

Конец [*см.* **На противоположных концах, Положить конец, С коническим концом**].

Конец века [*см.* **В конце века**].

Конечная группа
An additional phosphate group is attached to **the terminal** phosphate **group.**

Конечная скорость
When the raindrops attained their **terminal velocity ...**

Конечная точка
The terminal point of the operating line ...

Конечная цель
This phase has as its **ultimate** (*or* **final**) **goal** (*or* **objective,** *or* **aim**) full-sized plants which ....

Конечно
These branches of science were, **to be sure** (*or* **of course**) clear precursors of plate tectonics.

Конечный [*см. тж.* **В конечном счёте** (*или* **итоге**), **Начальный и конечный, Окончательный**]
Valves, switches, relays, and so on have **finite** lives, i.e. are good for a limited number of operations.

Конечный продукт
The resulting (*or* **terminal**) **product** contained 99.6% $SrCO_3$.
The ultimate (*or* **end**) **products of** this reaction are water and carbon dioxide.

Конечный результат [*см. тж.* **Окончательный результат**]
The **end effect** would be that the top layer would contain ...
The end (*or* **final,** *or* **ultimate**) **result** will be to speed up practical applications.

Конкретнее
This invention relates to a broad class of novel organometallic compounds; **more particularly** (*or* **specifically**), the present invention relates to novel and useful metallic cyclomatic compounds.

Конкретно [*см.* **Подробно**].

Конкретность [*см.* **Для конкретности**].

Конкретный
Let us take the **specific** case of the Earth and the Moon.
With the **particular** (*or* **specific**) construction shown in Fig. 16, air filters are always supplied.
The **specific** properties of any particular ionic compound depend on the individual component ions.
The maximum rate of change of a **particular** characteristic of the orbit ...
The expansion should be allowed for in the die design for each **specific** (*or* **concrete**) application.

Конкретный пример
This is best illustrated by **a specific** (*or* **concrete**) **example.**

Конкурировать с [*см. тж.* **Вполне может конкурировать с**]
Hydrogen addition reactions **are in competition** (*or* **compete**) **with** elimination of carbon dioxide.
The tube **is competitive in** size **with** the transistor.

Конструирование
This seal has proved useful in **the design of** loudspeakers.

Конструирование с помощью компьютера
A system for **computer-aided design ...**

Конструировать [*см. тж.* **Проектировать, Сконструированный**]
The air hoists **are designed** (*or* **constructed**) to be easily moved and installed by one man.
Two new pumping systems **have been devised.**
This electrical equipment **is engineered for** a particular job.

Конструировать из
The machine **is built** (*or* **made**) **of** standard components.
The connectors **are constructed of** Neoprene.

Конструировать с запасом
Failures because of applied loads are relatively rare since most structures **are overdesigned.**

Конструктивные особенности
Test various **constructional features.**
It is possible to test out the **design features of** a future plant.

Конструкция [*см. тж.* **По своей конструкции, Проект, Прочная конструкция**]
The machine **is of** simple **design** (*or* **construction**).

Консультироваться у специалиста
A change of material is then necessary, and **specialist advice should be sought** (*or* **obtained**) (*or* **a specialist should be consulted**).

Контакт [*см. тж.* **Вступать в контакт, Находиться в контакте с**]
Good **exposure of** water surfaces **to** the passing air is achieved.

Контроль [*см. тж.* **Тщательный контроль**]
The restrictors can be adjusted to give precise **control over** the movements of the ball.

Контрольные цифры
Planned (*or* **Scheduled,** *or* **Target**) **figures.**
The target (*or* **goal**) **for** 1985 ...

Контрольный образец
The mice, both irradiated and **controls ...**

Контрольный препарат
The results are compared to those obtained using a **standard** (*or* **reference**) **preparation ...**

Контур (*эл.*) [*см.* **Цепь замыкается**].

Контуры ... совпадают
The outlines of these two continents **match** almost exactly.

Конус [*см.* **Сводить на конус, Сходить на конус**].

Конусность [*см.* **Овальность и конусность**].

Конфигурация [*см. тж.* **Иметь конфигурацию, Неправильная форма, Со сложной конфигурацией**]
In some meteorites the chondrules have very sharp **outlines.**
Specially **configurated** helicopters ...

Концентрировать внимание на [*см. тж.* **Внимание концентрируется на**]
Most investigations **have centred on** a single type.

Концентрировать до
Hematite **is concentrated to** 66% iron.

Концентрироваться [*см. тж.* **Группироваться**]
These investigations **focus on ...**

Концентричный с
The ring is kept in a position **concentric with** the shaft.

Кончать [*см.* **Заканчивать**].

Кончаться I [*см. тж.* **Заканчиваться**]
These two series begin with thorium and protactinium, respectively, and **end with** lead.
Some cracks **terminate** in another region.
After the acute phase **is over** and the patient has begun to return to normal life ...
The problem began with ploughing and **ended with** reaping.

Кончаться II
The fire will sustain itself until the fuel **runs out.**

Кончая [*см.* **Начиная ... и кончая**].

Координаты [*см.* **Привязывать к координатам, Проходить через начало координат**].

Копировать
The operator lets the tracer follow the template or master and the cutter **will duplicate** the pattern in the mould.

Коренное изменение в [*см. тж.* **Необходимо внести коренные изменения в**]
The effect would be **radical alterations in** the distribution of species throughout the world.

Коренным образом [*см. тж.* **В корне**]
The carbon dioxide problem is **fundamentally** related to the future consumption of coal.

Корень [*см.* **Извлечение корня**].

Корень квадратный из 2
The square root of 2.

Корень ... степени из
The axial concentration in the plume is inversely proportional to **the fifth root of** the time of sampling.

Корень уравнения
The root of an equation.

Кормо́й вперёд
The ship was towed **stern first.**

Корни уходят в древность
This concept **has roots stretching back into antiquity.**

Короткий
The life span of the Cambridge machine was **brief** (*or* **short**).

Короткий срок службы [*см.* **Иметь короткий срок службы**].

Ко́ротко останавливаться на
We **shall take a quick look at** these theories.
We **shall touch** (*or* **dwell**) briefly **on** the potential hazards to health from the devices.

Короткое замыкание [*см.* **Замыкание на, При коротком замыкании**].

Короткое расстояние [*см.* **На коротком расстоянии**].

Короткоживущий [*см.* **Долгоживущий** (*антон.*)].

Короче говоря
In brief we conclude that ...
In short (*or* **To make a long story short**) the results indicated that ...
In a word, gels are jellylike.

Корпус [*см. тж.* **Заземлённый на корпус**]
The heater is coiled around **the body of** the tube.

Корректировать [*см. тж.* **Вносить поправку на, Изменять**]
After a brief period of coasting the rocket **refines** (*or* **adjusts**) its trajectory.
The magnetic fields must **be adjusted** continuously as energy of the particles increases.

Корректировать на
A bond length calculated from covalent radii must **be adjusted for** the difference in electronegativity of ...

Корректировочные меры (действия)
Corrective action on the part of the pilot ...

Корректирующая команда
Corrective command.

Корректирующий сигнал
To transmit **corrective signals** into the control system ...

Корродировать
Chromium metal **attacks** (*or* **corrodes**) porcelain at 1600°C.
Wet bromine **is corrosive to** most metals.

Корродирующий
A **corrosive** (*or* **corroding**) acid.

Коррозионная защита
Corrosion protection.

Коррозионное воздействие
Corrosive attack.

Коррозионно-устойчивый
Corrosion-resistant (*or* **resisting**) steel ...

Коррозия [*см.* **Защита от коррозии**].

Коррозия под действием воздуха и воды
Corrosion by the atmosphere and by water ...

Косвенное доказательство того, что
This was **circumstantial evidence that** the gas and dust mark areas where new stars are forming.

Косвенное указание на то, что
There is good **indirect evidence that** the earth was molten.

Косвенные данные
The circumstantial evidence is interesting, but proof is difficult.

Косвенным путём
The process can be performed **by the indirect route.**

Космическая скорость [*см.* **Первая космическая скорость**].

Космическая техника
Space technology.

Космические масштабы [*см.* **В космических масштабах**].

Космические полёты (*или* **путешествия**)
Space travels (*or* **flights**).

Космический аппарат многократного использования
A space shuttle.

Космический полёт
Space flight.
Space(craft) mission.

Космический полёт с целью фотографирования
A photographic mission in space.

Космическое пространство
(Outer) space.

Космонавт в скафандре
A space-suited cosmo (*or* **astro**)**naut.**

Космос [*см.. тж.* **Космическое пространство, Полёт в космос**]
The "falling stone" was a guest from **(outer) space.**

Косое отверстие
A skewed hole.

Которому ввели
Test animals **injected with** bee venom can withstand ...

Которому всего лишь
Rocks **as young as** 40,000 years may also be dated by this method.

Которому подвергается
The repulsive force **experienced by** the particles ...

Которому подчиняется [*см.* **Правило, касающееся**].

Которому предстоит стать
All the residues were added to sectors **destined to become** mature rRNAs (*biol.*).

Которому способствует
A process **assisted by** the development of the Hudson ...

Который [*см.* **В котором, По которому**].

Который будет развит *и т.п.*
The theory of ... **to be developed** in the next chapter will show...

Который будет рассматриваться
The examples **to be considered** in the first half of the book ...

Который ещё предстоит изучить
To predict phenomena **yet to be studied ...**

Который иначе оставался бы неиспользованным
Auxiliary conductors occupy **otherwise wasted** spaces.

Который использовался
By virtue of the same reasoning **as was used for** the type 1 shock, ...

Который можно себе представить
The fastest **conceivable** velocity is equal to about Mach 930,000.

Который ... пришлось встретить (читать, видеть *и т.п.*)
This is the best article on the subject **that has come to my attention.**

Который сам [*см.* **Сам**].

Который характерен только для
The strong interactions, **which are unique to** hadrons, ...

Которым [*см.* **При помощи которого**].

Коэффициент полезного действия ... не превышает
Laboratory devices **do not surpass 8% efficiency.**

Краеугольный камень
Correct sampling is **the cornerstone of** reliable chemical analysis.

Край [*см.* **До краёв**].

Крайнее значение
The pressure may reach **a limiting** (*or* **extreme) value.**

Крайнее положение
The extremes (*or* **extreme positions**) **of** the pointer's swings ...

Крайний левый (правый)
If you turn the hexagon so that the 1 angle is **at the extreme left**, then the 4 will be **at the extreme right.**
The peak **farthest to the left (right) ...**
The laser wavelength is indicated by the line **on the far left (right) of** the figure.
The **left-most** (*or* **extreme left**) two columns show ...

Красиво отделывать хромом
The sockets **are handsomely finished in chrome plate.**

Красивое внешнее оформление
Using stone provides **an attractive appearance.**
The advantages of concrete are durability and the case with which **a pleasing appearance** can be obtained.

Красить [*см.* **Выкрашенный в ... цвет**].

Краска [*см.* **Наносить краску**].

Краснеть
The solution **turns red.**

Красное каление [*см.* **Нагревать до красного каления**].

Кратер [*см.* **Густо покрыт кратерами, Изобилующий кратерами, Испещрён кратерами**].

Краткая форма [*см.* **В краткой форме**].

Краткий [*см. тж.* **Сокращённый**]
The solution can be obtained in a **concise** geometric form.
The laws of thermodynamics are expressed in three **concise** statements.

Краткий обзор [*см.* **Делать краткий обзор**].

Кратко [*см. тж.* **Вкратце рассматривать, Коротко останавливаться на**]
This may be written **concisely** (*or* **briefly**) as ...

Кратко обобщим:
To summarize briefly, each model consists of functions ...

Кратко описан
The most important features **are (briefly) outlined** (*or* **described**) in the following paragraphs.

Кратко описывать
We **outline** the method for ...

Кратко останавливаться на [*см. тж.* **Коротко останавливаться на, Необходимо кратко остановиться на**]
It would be of interest **to mention briefly** some of the steps ...

Кратко рассмотреть
Let us **briefly run through** (*or* **consider**) (*or* **Let us take a brief look at**) some of the relay types available.

Кратковременного действия
It is best to use one of the **shorter-acting** drugs.

Кратковременный
Momentary breaks in transmission ...
A system is excited by an external pulse **of short duration.**
Organic laminates for continuous service at 200°C and **short-term** service at 250°C are found in ...
We are developing several laser systems for **short-run** fusion experiments.
A **short-lived** event ...

Краткое обозначение
A shorthand notation for the appearance of this spectrum is 'AX'.

Краткость [*см.* **Для краткости**].

Кратное
Multiples to the designed frequencies ...
R(t) contains some **multiple of** $\nabla \cdot S$.
The ion charge must be **a multiple of** the unit charge.

Кратный [*см. тж.* **В ... -кратном размере**]
The dilution may be one-**fold,** two-**fold ...**
The reactant is present in ten-**fold** excess.

Кратчайший [*см.* **В кратчайшее время**].

Крепко [*см.* **Прочно**].

Крепко связанный [*см.* **Прочно связан с**].

Крепление
The fine thread series is widely used in **fastenings,** such as bolts, nuts and screws.

Крепость
The strength of the ethyl alcohol is expressed by the term "proof".

Крепящий [*см. тж.* **Закрепляющий**]
The tool holders are provided with suitable mountings or **clamping** devices.

Кривая [*см. тж.* **Восходящая кривая, Крутая кривая, На кривой, Нисходящая ветвь, Пологая кривая, Семейство кривых**]
The curves for the saturated solution compositions ...

Кривая с двумя максимумами
A double-peaked curve.

Кристалл [*см.* **Внешний вид кристалла**].

Кристаллизоваться в
Magnoferrite **crystallizes in** black octahedra.
Diamond **crystallizes as** octahedra, dodecahedra, and cubes.

Кристаллизоваться в .... сингонии
Analcime **crystallizes in the** isomeric **system** (*or* **syngony**).

Критерий
The following strengths and weaknesses of relays can be used as **a** basic **guideline in** deciding which type of relay to employ.
These hydrides meet two **criteria for** strong inter-molecular attractions.

Критерий качества
Figure of merit.
Performance criterion.

Критика
Criticism has been levelled (*or* **voiced, or expressed) that** such curricula do not have ...

Критический пересмотр
The results were so unexpected that they demanded **a critical review of** the theory.

Кроме [*см. тж.* **Все, за исключением нескольких; Все, кроме одного; Если не считать, За исключением, Не включая, Помимо**]
This treatment is satisfactory at all **but** very high pressures.
Processes in which the system might do work **over and above** that of expansion ...

These meteorites have an appreciable amount of carbonaceous material **other than** free carbon.
Aside from (*or* **Besides**) 0.4-0.6% soda, calcine alumina contains ...
These miniatures compare in every way **except** size with the large connectors.
Except for (*or* **Apart from**) bubble caps, the plant was constructed entirely from carbon steel.
The resonator has the trivial resonance $F_1 = 0$ **in addition to** the usual free-free resonances.
This magnetic amplifier has no moving parts **other than** relays.
No special attention is required **other than** careful and frequent inspection.
There was little doubt about the good process performance of all the functional elements **with the exception of** the fluidized bed itself.

Кроме как (*разг.*)
Except at high temperatures the atoms have too little thermal energy to rupture the bond.

Кроме как в (*разг.*)
Covalent bonding, **except in** rare gases is most simply explained as ...

Кроме как для (*разг.*)
Chemical shift data are, **except to** the experienced operator, the least useful feature of the nmr spectrum.

Кроме того [*см. тж.* **Более того, Дополнительный, К тому же**]
Tile is classified as load-bearing or non-load-bearing; tile with a specially finished surface is face tile. **Again,** tile may be glazed or unglazed.
In addition (*or* **Furthermore,** *or* **Besides,** *or* **What is more,** *or* **Moreover**), the control of acidity is important in process streams.
There is **in addition** a friction drag.
The inadequacy of the Lewis structure is **further** indicated by the fact that ...
Furthermore, on addition of more water the concervate passes again into the sol state.

Кроме того, следует подчеркнуть, что
An additional point to emphasize is that one cannot predict ...

Кроме того, употребляется для
The salicylates relieve minor aches and pains and **have the added feature of** reducing elevated temperatures.

Круглого сечения
The use of an electrode **of circular section** enables it to be rapidly replaced.

Круглость
The operator is applying a gauge to check **the circularity of** a bore.

Круглосуточная работа
The apparatus includes powder storage capacity sufficient for **round-the-clock operation.**

Круглосуточно
The battery operates the charger **on a 24-hour basis.**
The plant operates **24 hours a day** [*or* **(a)round the clock**].

Круглый [*см.* **Отклоняться от круглой формы**].

Круглый год
This area is frozen **the year round.**

Круговое движение
Sanding should be done **with a** free **circular motion.**

Кругосветный рейс
The Beagle's **world-encircling** (*or* **round-the-world**) **voyage ...**

Кружиться вокруг
As the electron **whirls around** the proton, ...

Кружок
Cut two **disks** from a sheet of blotting paper.

Крупнозернистый
Coarse-grained rocks ...

Крупный [*см.* **Большой, Значительный**].

Крупный и средний уголь
For **large- and medium-sized coal ...**

Крупным планом
We have seen **close up** the crater-strewn surface of the Moon.
A close-up view of the machine ...

Крутая кривая
A steep(ly sloping) curve.

Круто
The potential-energy curve rises very **steeply.**

Круто падать
The observation curves **fall off steeply.**
The curve **slopes** (*or* **falls**) **steeply down.**
The curve **shows a steep decline.**

Круто подниматься
The free-energy surface **slopes** (*or* **rises**) **steeply up.**

Крутой [*см.* **Становиться круче**].

Крыть [*см.* **Покрывать**].

Куб [*см.* **В кубе**].

Кубический корень из
The cube root of 27.

Куда угодно
During machining coolant and chips can fall **where they will** without affecting accurate operation of the machine.

Кулоновские силы
These **forces** are **Coulombic.**

Л

Лабораторная посуда
Laboratory glassware.

Лабораторное испытание
Corrosion **bench test** shows that ...
The units are cable connected for **bench testing.**

Лабораторные масштабы [*см.* **В лабораторных масштабах**].

Лазер [*см.* **Работать в лазерном режиме, Усиленный лазером**].

Лакмус [*см.* **Реакция на лакмус**].

Лампочка [*см.* **Пережог лампочки**].

Левая часть уравнения
The left(-hand) side (*or* **The left member**) **of Eq.** 5 ...

Левый [*см.* **Правый верхний**].

Легко [*см.* *тж.* **Без затруднений, Нетрудно**]
The stylus head **is easy to** replace.
Some hydrocarbons **are readily** absorbed.
Aluminium foil can be welded **readily** to wire.
Solution particles pass through **with ease.**
It is a straightforward (*or* **simple,** *or* **easy**) **matter to** establish this.
This number can be written out **with ease.**
It is a straightforward matter to measure the capacitance of a condenser.
The equilibrium **is readily** established.

Легко видеть, что
It is easily (*or* **readily**) **seen** (*or* **It is easy to see,** *or* **It is clear**) **that ...**
It will readily be seen that ...
One can readily see that ...

Легко вступать в соединение с ... с образованием
Chromium **readily combines with** carbon **to form** chromium carbide.

Легко вычисляется по
The corresponding coefficient **is readily calculated from** the function ...

Легко доказать при помощи
D'Alembert's theorem **is easily proved from** Cauchy's integral formula.

Легко доступен
The visible wavelengths required **are immediately** (*or* **readily,** *or* **easily**) **available.**
All tooling areas **are readily** (*or* **easily**) **accessible.**

Легко доступный
Using **readily available** laser photons ...

Легко доступный для
The amino acids **readily available for** viral use ...

Легко обрабатываемый
Models are usually cut in an **easy-to-machine** (*or* **freely-machined**) material such as wood or high-density polyethylene foam.

Легко образовываться
This acid **forms readily** in rainwater.

Легко отличать от
Dolomite rock **is** not **easily distinguished from limestone.**

Легко поддаваться
The machine **readily lends itself** (*or* **is readily amenable**) **to** variations.

Легко поддаваться пайке
Cadmium **solders easily.**

Легко поддающийся обработке
Alloy 3003 is a moderately strong, **very** (*or* **readily,** *or* **easily,** *or* **highly**) **workable** alloy.
Parts can be manufactured of an inexpensive, **easy-to-machine** (*or* **free-machining**) base material.

Легко показать, что
It is easily (*or* **readily**) **shown** [*or* **easy** (*or* **straightforward**) **to show**] (*or* **It can easily be shown**) **that ...**

Легко получать
Greater signal levels **are easily** (*or* **readily**) **obtainable.**
Liquid nitrogen **can readily be obtained** commercially.

Легко получать из
Grignard reagents **are readily available from** halides and magnesium metal.

Легко понять [*см. тж.* **Как нетрудно понять**]
The occurrence of such obviously covalent compounds as PF_5SF_6 and many others **is easily understood** (*or* **is easy to understand**).

Легко понять, что
It is easily comprehended (*or* **understood**) (*or* **It is easy to understand**) **that** the lower the temperature of the furnace, the higher is ...

Легко проверить, что
It is easy to verify (*or* **check**) **that ...**
We may **readily check that ...**

Легко программируемый
Two **easily-programmable** industrial robots ...

Легко проницаемый
The capillary wall **is freely permeable.**

Легко работать с
This equipment **is simple** (*or* **easy**) **to operate** (*or* **handle**).

Легко реагировать с
Calcite **reacts readily** (*or* **avidly,** *or* **easily**) **with** sulphuric acid.

Легко себе представить
In such a system a local coordinate transformation **can readily be imagined** (*or* **visualized**).

Легко создать
The means for ... **are easily devised.**

Легко, трудно
The instruments **are easy to** make, but **difficult to** calibrate.

Легко убедиться (в том), что
It is easy to verify (*or* **check**) **that** a reflection of ... reverses the sign of ...

Легко устанавливаемый
The **simple-to-install** components illustrated on these pages ...

Легко установить
Radiometric ages of rocks became **readily available.**

Легко читается
The book **is written in an easy-to-read style** (*or* **reads fluently**).

Легковесный
Lightweight processors for airborne applications ...

Легкоплавкий
A **low-melting (point)** alloy.

Легкоразрешимый [*см.* **Более легкоразрешимый**].

Легкорастворимый [*см.* **Хорошо растворяться в**].

Легче воздуха
A **lighter-than-air** craft ...

Легче всего
The rotational motion of linear molecules **is easiest to** treat.
Such metals **are the most readily** extracted.
Such electrodes **are the easiest to** prepare.

Легче всего получать
The easiest geometric isomers **to prepare are** those of platinum (II).

Легче всего понять
The effect **is best understood** in terms of loops.
This **is most easily understood** if ...

Легче всего себе представить
This action **is most readily visualized** with the aid of ...

Легче понять
These problems **will be appreciated** (*or* **understood**) **more readily** after discussion of scale factors.

Ледникового происхождения
These pebbles **are of glacial origin.**

Ледниковый рельеф
Glacial topography.

Лежать в диапазоне
These signals **fall in** (*or* **within**) **the** broad **range** between 10^{-15} and 10^{-10} coulombs per pulse.
The charge collection time **lies in the range** of a few milliseconds.
The diffusion coefficient for binary liquid systems usually **falls** (*or* **lies**) **in the range** 5 to 2×10^{-5} cm^2/s in nonviscous liquids at 25°C.

Лежать в основе
The basis for the antibacterial effects of dyes **is** their ability to ...
Behind the Mullard invention **is** the notion that ...
Central to the theory **is ...**
Movement of charged particles in a magnetic field also **forms** (*or* **constitutes**) **the basis for** mass spectrometry.
These equations **form the basis** (*or* **foundation**) **of** the theory of ...
These theories **form** (*or* **provide**) **the foundation for** (*or* **are at the basis of**) colour television.
It is this form that **provides the basis** (*or* **is fundamental**) **for** a wide variety of TV antennas.
Let us consider the physical conditions that **underlie** the Sun's magnetism.
Boolean algebra **underlies** the theory of relations.
Microcomputers **are at the heart of** "transaction" telephones for checking customers' credit.
The general rule that the forces between two particles result from an exchange of other particles **is basic to** much of our present understanding of elementary-particle interactions.
This distinction between electricity and magnetism **is at the heart** (*or* **root**) **of** the theory of ...
The Periodic Table **provides the framework for** the whole study of inorganic chemistry.
Thermochemistry **is basic to** the study of chemical bonding.
An understanding of dye laser operation **is a building block for** understanding the principles of other tunable laser systems.
These interrelations **are the heart of** hydrodynamics.
The chapter describes the fundamental physics that **gives rise to** the behaviour of the single junction and the transistor as circuit elements.
The nature of energy **lies at the heart of** the mystery of our existence.
This reaction **is the basis for** the cyanamide process for ...

Лежать на (*антон.* **под**)
Younger layers **overlie** (*anton.* **underlie**) older ones.
Older layers **are overlain** (*anton.* **underlain**) **by** younger ones.
The perpendicular **will contain** the point *A* (*Точка A лежит на перпендикуляре*).

Лежать на одной прямой с
The two poles **are aligned with** the axis of rotation.

Лежать на ответственности
This phase **was the responsibility of** the engineering group.

Лежать на плоскости
Lines **lying in the** same **plane ...**

Лежать на прямой (линии)
All of the atoms of acetylene **lie along a straight line.**

Лежащие между
Electrons with energies **lying in the range from** 0.7 **to** 1.4 MeV ...

Лежащий в основе

The phenomena **underlying** the behaviour of materials ...
We faced the problem of finding the correct physical principle **to account for** all our observations.
The practical work is supplemented with a lecture course on the **underlying** theoretical principles.
This was a major factor **behind** the interest in developing digital optical computing techniques.

Лежащий на
A circle **resting on** a straight line ...

Лента [*см.* **Изолированный лентой**].

... лет тому назад
The first attempts to replace ... can be traced **back** 40 **years.**

Летать в воздухе
Aircraft **move through** free **air.**

Летающий по орбите
Distress signals are received by an **orbiting** satellite.
It is the largest telescope ever **orbited.**

Летучие вещества
Further heating reduces **the volatile matter** to about 1%.

Лечение в домашних условиях
Domiciliary care can be resorted to shortly after the stroke.

Лечение .... даёт хорошие результаты
Treatment is rewarding for such non-malignant conditions.

Лечение диетой
Dietary treatment.

Лечь [*см.* **Лежать, Ложиться**].

Лёгкая нагрузка
Space drills are suitable only for very **light-duty applications.**

Лёгкие работы
Light jobs.

Лёгкий I [*см. тж.* **Для лёгких грузов**]
The instrument **is light in weight.**
The new material **is lightweight** and flexible.

Лёгкий II
Keratin production provides a relatively **facile** (*or* **easy**) way to determine the degree of differentiation.

Лёгкий в обращении
This is a highly effective, practical and **easy-to-use** (*or* **handle**) instrument.

Лёгкое постукивание
The link length can be varied by **lightly tapping** the input lever arm of the control unit **with** a screwdriver.

Лёгкость [*см. тж.* **С одинаковой лёгкостью**]
Ease of adjustment to existing conditions ...

Лёгкость изготовления и установки
Ease in fabrication and erection.

Лёгкость обращения с
The flexibility of the laser beam and **the ease of handling** it ...

Ли
Whether or not a linear system is stable is determined completely by the roots of the characteristic equation.
These analyses will show **whether (or not)** the solution is being adequately stripped.
This depends on **whether (or not)** frequency doubling the laser output is important for the application.

Либо [*см.* **Или**].

Либо ..., либо ..., либо и тот и другой
If **either or both** acid **and** base **are** weak, ...

Ликвидировать недостаток
Now this **drawback has been** completely **overcome** (*or* **eliminated**).

Ликвидировать неисправность [*см. тж.* **Устранять неисправность**]
See to it that all **troubles should be** (*or* **are) eliminated** (*or* **remedied**).

Лимитирующий фактор
The atomic oxygen concentration was **the rate-determining factor.**

Линейно независимый
The corresponding n eigenvectors **are linearly independent.**

Линейно пропорциональный
These values **are linear with** the square of wavelength.
Output **is linearly proportional to** the bus current.

Линейный по
Here, the potential **is linear in** (*or* **with respect to**) the variable defining the amount transferred: (Y — Y*) **linear in** Y; Δt **linear in** t, etc.

Линия [*см.* **На линии, На одной линии с**].

Линия пересечения
The line of intersection of the two planes ...

Линия проходит
Lines of force **run** (*or* **pass**) **from** magnetic pole **to** magnetic pole.

Линия, проходящая через
The line passing (*or* **running**) **through** P is parallel to the axis of ...

Линия раздела
There is no sharp **line of demarcation** (*or* **demarcation line**) **between** the atmosphere **and** space.
The two parts are separated by **a dividing line.**

Линия раздела между
Stack gases leaving the chimney show sharp **lines of demarcation between** the opaque plume **and** the transparent air.

Литература [*см. тж.* **В литературе**]
Pertinent suggestions are made **in the literature ...**

Лить на
Condensation may be accelerated by **pouring** cold water **over** the cooling chambers and piping.

Литьё под вакуумом [*см.* **Отлитый под вакуумом**].

Лицензия [*см.* **По лицензии**].

Лишать *чего-л.*
The diffusive flow **will denude** the n-type side of the junction **of** the electrons making it positively charged.
This **denudes** the soil **of** nitrogen.

Лишаться
These sites **become depleted of** nearly all water in the layer above ...

Лишён
The sediments **are** almost **barren** (*or* **devoid**) **of** organic content.
In semiconductors at sufficiently low temperatures, the conduction band **is empty** (*or* **devoid**) **of** electrons.
What was left after combustion **was** completely **lacking in** oxygen and could burn no more.
The rock and iron which forms the main body of the Earth **was** once **stripped** (*or* **deprived,** *or* **depleted**) **of** volatiles.
The carbon atom **has been stripped of** three electrons.

Лишён возможности
Sodium chloride **is prevented from** diffusing through the membrane.

Лишённый [*см. тж.* **Будучи**]
"Amorphous" means **devoid of** crystalline structure.
When white light passes through a ruby it emerges **depleted of** its violet and yellow-green components.

Лишний
Excess (*or* **Surplus,** *or* **Superfluous**) ink should be wiped from the printing points.
This method can introduce **redundant** eigenvalues, which must be disregarded.

Лишь [*см. тж.* **Всего лишь, Исключительно, Не более чем, Один только, Только**]
The hydrogenation and hydroboration of alkynes are **but** two of many useful stereoselective reactions.
The cells employed as hosts by modern viruses are **mere** substitutes for ...
The crust of the continents is **merely** the uppermost layer of the continental lithosphere.
Many ions are required in **only** small amounts.
But (*or* **Only**) nineteen other units employ some transistors.
It is desired here **merely** to point out that ...
Maximum viscosity **was not** reached **until** September 1.
Here I can **do no more than** describe

briefly one example of these recent advances.
A good approximation of all the forces acting ... can be deduced from the force between **just** two stationary molecules.

Лишь в незначительной степени
This virus has been investigated **to only a small extent.**

Лишь вопрос времени
It seems **only a matter of time before** we have full-colour reproduction of high quality.

Лишь догадка
This can **only** be pure **conjecture** from the evidence shown.

Лишь незадолго до этого
As he had envisioned **only a short time previously, ...**

Лишь незначительно
Resistant rock has changed **but little** during 50–60 centuries of exposure to wave attack.
Bowing can affect the nuclear characteristics **only slightly.**

Лишь незначительное действие
The liquid rate has **but a minor effect on** $K_G a$.

Лишь незначительный
This heating has **only a slight** (*or* **an insignificant,** *or* **a negligible**) effect on luminescence.

Лишь немногие из
Solution foaming, loss in ability to accept the acrid gases, and excessive equipment corrosion **are only a few of** the problems encountered.

Лишь немногими примерами являются
We have to satisfy numerous small-lot requirements — production of special tools, dies, and replacement parts, **to name just a few.**

Лишь немного больше, чем
The driving heads cost **but little more** for a long rotor **than** for a short one.
The reaction factors will be **only moderately** (*or* **slightly**) **greater than** unity.

Ловить [*см.* **Поймать сигнал**].

Логарифм числа по основанию
Logarithms to the base *l* may be computed from a table of base 10.
The base *e* **logarithm of** *x* is called the natural logarithm of *x*.

Логарифмическая зависимость
Logarithmic relationship.

Логическая схема
The same **logic pattern** is followed for pressure decrease.

Логический вывод [*см.* **Делать логический вывод**].

Логичная мысль
Physically **the idea made sense** because the haemoglobin molecules are packed very tightly in the red cell.

Ложиться бременем на
The high cost **will** not **be burdensome** (*or* **a burden**) **on** the world economy if ...

Ложиться в основу
This noise can **form the basis of** (*or* **serve as a basis for**) a detection system.
Restrictions on angular momentum **provided the basis for** Bohr's quantum model of the hydrogen atom.

Ложиться выше, чем
The mass-transfer data for gases **fall** considerably **above** the heat-transfer data.

Ложиться на
The anthracene data **fall on** a straight line.
A straight line **fits** the seven dots rather well.

Ложиться на плечи
The task of establishing the phenomenon of plate subduction **fell to** the seismologists.

Ложный
His claim to this "discovery" proved **false.**

Локализовать пожар
The fire was brought under control in two minutes and was completely extinguished in a further couple of minutes.

Лом [*см.* **Сдавать в скрап**].

Ломаная траектория (*или* **линия**)
The polygonal path (*or* **line**) becomes a smooth curve.

Ломаться [*см. тж.* **Выходить из строя**]
When steel springs **fail,** they shrapnelize, placing personnel in danger.

Луна [*см.* **Ближняя сторона луны, На поверхности луны, Обратная сторона луны**].

Луч падает на
When **a beam is incident on** a medium, ...

Лучше I [*см. тж.* **Вдвое лучше, Ещё лучше, Или, что ещё лучше**]
Titanium fasteners **are superior to** (*or* **better than**) identical steel fasteners.

Лучше воспроизводиться
The resulting spectra **are more reproducible.**

Лучше всего
The microscope is **best** mounted on a low table so that the stage is on a level with the table top.
Lappa clover grows **best** in heavy dark marl soils.
It is best to redefine the amplification processes in terms of ...

Лучше всего было бы
The best plan to be followed is to make a motor with ...

Лучше всего подходить для
These clovers **are best suited for** grazing.
Axial-flow pumps of vertical design **are best suited to** large surface condensers.

Лучше всего согласовываться с
Model II **gave the best fit to** the data (*or* **fitted** the data **best of all**).

Лучше выдерживать
The ear **is more tolerant of** phase distortion **than** frequency distortion.

Лучше изучен
The origin of these rocks **is** now **better understood.**

Лучше использовать
The device should be **put to better use** [*or* **used more rationally** (*or* **efficiently**)].
They can now **take better advantage of** their resources.

Лучше отложить до тех пор, пока
The units and values of this quantity **are best left until** its determination from measurable quantities is considered.

Лучше отражать [*см. тж.* **Точнее отражать**]
These representations **more adequately depict** the actual molecular structure.

Лучше поддаваться
Plants **are more amenable to** study — they do not move, and so are easier to observe.

Лучше, чем [*см. тж.* **Превосходить**]
Dry drilling **is superior to** wet drilling.

Лучшее на что можно надеяться
The best that one can hope for is that the progress of the dementia will be retarded (*med.*).

Лучшее понимание [*см. тж.* **Для лучшего понимания**]
A concept, **giving a better insight into** the mechanism of ...
A better understanding has been gained of the way in which static electricity is generated.
The analytical results may **give a clearer insight into** the nature of the solution.

Лучшие показатели [*см.* **Давать лучшие показатели** (*или* **результаты**), **чем**].

Лучший [*см.* **В лучшем случае**].

Любая величина [*см.* **Иметь любую величину от ... до**].

Любой [*см. тж.* **В любой момент, В любом отношении, При любой нагрузке**]
The excitation purity of **any one** point on the diagram is given by ...
This ensures ease of welding under **all** (*or* **any**) service conditions.

Любой из
Any one of these machines may ...
To convert an ordinary number into **any one of** these other systems, ...

Любой из двух
Either of the two scalars records the output.

Любой из двух или оба вместе
It is easy to deal with **either or both** the quantities ΔE and ΔH.

Любой из нескольких
A given part can be made in **any one of several** different ways.

Любой из них (*двух*)
Synthesis of field and laboratory research has led to more understanding than **either** would have produced alone.

Любой из ряда
In an isolated atom each electron may have **any one of a number of** distinct energies.

Любой силы
Such an atom remains stable even in an **arbitrarily strong** field.

Любопытно отметить, что
Curiously, it was found that corticosterone and dexamethasone promoted extinction of ...

Любопытный
What is most **intriguing** is that the particles are not scattered randomly in all directions.

Люфт [*см. тж.* **Боковой люфт**]
The hinge should turn smoothly with no **free play.**
Grinding wheels should fit freely on their spindles but without unnecessary **play.**

М

Магнитная запись на плёнке
Tape recording.

Магнитная лента [*см.* **Запоминаться на магнитной ленте**].

Магнитное поле [*см.* **Направление магнитного поля**].

Макрокристаллический [*см.* **С макрокристаллической структурой**].

Максимальная польза [*см.* **Извлекать максимальную пользу из**].

Максимально
A molecule of methanol may form **a maximum of** three hydrogen bonds (*or* three hydrogen bonds **at the most**).

Максимально возможная точность
When **the ultimate in accuracy** [*or* **the maximum** (*or* **the greatest possible**) **accuracy**] is required, ...

Максимально возможный [*см.* **Находиться на большом расстоянии друг от друга**].

Максимально допустимый
The maximum allowable (*or* **permissible**) flank wear on the TiC-coated inserts was 0.032 in.

Максимально использовать
To make the most (*or* **the most use,** *or* **the best use**) **of** the cranes, tracks were laid along the whole length of the site.

Максимально повысить
To maximize the metal removal rates, use sharp wheels and the highest possible workspeeds.

Максимальный [*см. тж.* **Выдавать максимальную продукцию**]
The light intensity **was a maximum** in the centre of the laser beam.
Dip **is at its maximum** over the magnetic poles.
The peak blade speed ...
The production of this compound is attended with **the maximum** heat evolution.
In order to get **the most** heat economy, ...
Table 10 gives **the top** Curie temperature of various material systems.

Максимум [*см.* **В максимуме, Достигать максимума, Иметь максимум** (*или* **пик**), **От минимума до максимума, Самое большее**]
These molecular orbitals are restricted to **a maximum of** two electrons each.
The oxidation of one mole of glucose yields **a maximum of** 690,000 calories.
The head is limited between 30 and 40 ft **as a maximum.**
Such an electromagnet can reach 60,000 gauss **at most.**

Максимум до
Closed containers may be pressurized **to a maximum of** 900 psi.

Максимум и минимум
The cross sections build up a complex landscape of **peaks and valleys.**

Малая величина [*см.* **Бесконечно малая величина, Пренебрежимо малая величина**].

Малая глубина [*см.* **На небольшой глубине**].

Малая нагрузка [*см.* **Для малой нагрузки, При малой нагрузке**].

Малая серия
For prototypes or **short runs,** carbon steel tools are adequate.
A small lot (*or* **batch**).

Малейший
Even **miniscule** (*or* **infinitesimal**) perturbations in the osmotic pressure can lead to large amplitude fluctuations in polymer density.

Мало
The dominant tree species **are few** (**in number,** *or* **few and far between**).

Мало влиять на [*см.тж.* **Очень слабо влиять на**]
This galvanometer **is little** (*or* **only slightly**) **affected by** stray magnetic fields.

Мало вносить в
Other contributing structures also exist but they **add little to** the current theory.

Мало ..., если вообще имеет их
These fishes **have few if any** blue-sensitive cells.

Мало известно о
Not much (*or* **Little**) **is known about** the outline of this continent.

Мало изменяться
The hysteresis loop of Deltamax changes gradually but the squareness ratio **is little affected.**
The refractive index **varies only** (*or* **but**) **slightly.**

Мало изучен [*см. тж.* **Плохо изучен**]
These processes **are scantily** (*or* **poorly**) **known.**

Мало ... или вообще никакого
Stress concentration in the vicinity of a bolt **had little if any** (*or* **hardly any**) effect on the bending strength.
Few, if any relationships can be detected here.
No or little (*or* **Little or no**) hydrogen bonding has occurred.

Мало или совсем не
The quasars have a density distribution that **is only slightly or not at all** dependent on their radio properties.
Little or no absorption is observed for ...

Мало или совсем нет
There is little or no lava between the dikes.

Мало использоваться
The inverses of the secant and cosecant functions **are little used.**
Molecular fluorimetry **has received little use** as a qualitative procedure.

Мало напоминать
At first the concept of charge density in an atom seems **to bear little resemblance to** Bohr's picture of ...

Мало общего с [*см.* **Иметь мало общего с**].

Мало отличаться от
This definition **is little different** (*or* **differs little**) **from** our ordinary use of the word.
Such a wave **is little more than** an oscillating electric field.

Мало отличаться по
These solids **differ little in** density.

Мало подходить в качестве
Coal **had little to offer as** an illuminant.

Мало похож на
These models **bear little resemblance to** the planetary model.

Мало смысла
There is little point (*or* **sense**) **in** taking derivatives in the feedback loop in order to ...

Маловажный
The amorphous components **are of little importance.**

Маловероятен [*см. тж.* **Едва ли вероятен**]
Surface reaction-controlled dissolution **is unlikely.**
There is little likelihood of error.

Маловероятно, что
There is little likelihood that single crystals of gem quality will be developed.
It is unlikely [*or* **(highly) improbable**] **that** any further accident will result in ...

Малогабаритный [*см.* **Небольших размеров**].

Малого размера
Colloids are so **small in size** that ...

Малого сечения
Radial saws for cutting **light-gauge** structural steel ...
Pistons, connecting rods, and other **slender** elements ...

Малодоступный [*см.* **Труднодоступный**].

Малое [*см.* **В малом**].

Малозаселённый уровень (*физ.*)
A sparcely occupied level.

Малоизвестный
A **little-known** aspect of this mechanism ...

Малоизученный
This **poorly explored** (*or* **known,** or **understood,** *or* **studied,** *or* **investigated**) type of particle ...

Малоиспользуемый
Little used techniques have received minimal coverage.

Малоисследован
The planet remains **little** (*or* **scantily**) **explored** (*or* **investigated**).

Маломощный I
A **low-power** laser ...

Маломощный II
A **thin** deposit ...

Малонаселённый район
A sparcely populated (*or* **inhabited**) **area.**

Малоперспективный
The administration of exogenously produced interferon **has shown (very) little promise** up to the present.

Малопригоден в качестве
Such spectra **are of limited utility** (*or* **of little use**) **as** fingerprints for individual molecules.

Малораспространён
There must have been a time of the earth when all the volatiles **were in low abundance.**
Tropical trees **are of limited occurrence ...**

Малораспространённый
Tropical trees **of limited occurrence ...**

Малый [*см.* **Бесконечно малый, Небольшой, Пренебрежимо малая величина, Содержаться в недостаточном количестве**].

Малых размеров
Small-sized engines ...

Марка
These jibs can be fitted to coal cutters of any **make.**
Type 316 stainless steel.

Масса I [*см. тж.* **Имеется масса примеров этого, Много, Основная масса**]
Before the above means may be devised, **a host of** (*or* **a great many**) operational decisions must be made.
An electron beam can promote **a host of** chemical reactions.
A wealth of technological means is at hand; economic factors will determine the speed of progress.
Hot water has **a multitude of** potential uses.
The heat of many geothermal reservoirs comes from **a large body of** molted rock.

Масса II [*см. тж.* **Иметь массу в ... раз больше, чем; Обладать бóльшей массой**]
A molecule **of mass** *m* ...

Масса данных
There is now **a wealth of evidence** supporting that view.

Масса солнца
A million **solar masses ...**

Массовое производство
This switch is the only one of its type **mass-produced** (*or* **in mass production,** *or* **produced on a mass scale,** *or* **in quantity production**) in this country.
Large-scale production.

Мастерство
Facility will come with practice.

Масштаб [*см.* **В больших масштабах, В значительных масштабах, В космических масштабах, В лабораторных масштабах, В мировом масштабе, В ограниченных масштабах, В полузаводском масштабе, В промышленных масштабах, В увеличенном масштабе, В уменьшенном масштабе**].

Масштаб ... на километр
Scale 1/2 in. to the kilometre.

Масштабная модель
This **model is scaled** to represent the bond lengths and bond angles in that molecule.
A scaled model ...

Масштабный чертёж
A scale drawing.

Масштабы реакции
The extent of the reaction is limited by chemical equilibrium.

Математические выкладки
These cases are simpler to understand, though **the mathematics** (*or* **the mathematical treatment**) may become complicated.

Материал [*см. тж.* **Исходный материал**]
We obtained pure nickel from **stock** (*or* **material**) contaminated with cobalt.

Материал, разрушающийся при заданной силе удара или давлении
A controlled-break material.

Материя
Then these particles would be recognized as examples of a new form of **matter.**

Мах (число Маха)
The velocity is larger than **Mach 1.**

Маховик [*см.* **На маховике**].

Машина [*см.* **На машине**].

Машинное решение
An exact **solution by computer** [*or* **machine** (*or* **computer**) **solution**] gave the following results: ...

Маятник [*см.* **Колебание маятника**].

Медицина [*см* . **Использовать в медицине**].

Медицинский [*см.* **В медицинских целях**].

Медленно
The internal type of disturbance **is** usually **slow in** affecting the chemical process outputs.

Медленно растворяться
Alunite **is slowly soluble** (*or* **dissolves slowly**).

Медленно реагировать с
Benzene **is slow to react with** hydrogen.

Между [*см.* **Вкраплён между, Зазор между, Находящийся между ... и, Проведение реакции между, Разница между, Распределять между, Расхождение между**].

Между ... и ... есть много общего
There is much in common between the techniques used in quantitative **and** qualitative analysis.

Между ними
If the eye perceives colour by comparing longer and shorter wavelengths it must establish a balance point somewhere **in between** (*or* **between them**).
There are two periods of high water each day and two periods of low water **in between.**

Между прочим [*см. тж.* **Помимо всего прочего, Попутно отметим, что**]
This device, **incidentally,** is universally used by students.
We might observe **in passing** that the sequence under discussion occurred in a single good English sentence.

Между прочим следует упомянуть, что
In passing (*or* **Incidentally**) **it should be mentioned that ...**

Между центрами
The studs are placed about 12 inches **centre to centre.**
The distance of a planet from the Sun is measured **centre to centre.**

Межзвёздное пространство
Interstellar space.

Межпланетные сообщения
Interplanetary navigation (*or* **travel,** *or* **flight**).

Мелкая деталь
To record **fine details** in astronomical objects ...

Мелкая пыль
Fine dust.

Мелкая серия [*см.* **Малая серия**].

Мелкий [*см.* **Небольших размеров**].

Мелкий уголь
Small-sized coal ...

Мелкое деление [*см.* **С мелкими делениями**].

Мелкозернистый [*см. тж.* **Более мелкозернистый, чем**]
The mineral is **fine grained.**

Мелкоизмельчённый
Finely divided (*or* **ground**) metal particles increase oil oxidation.

Мелкосерийное производство
The company's activities include high-volume production as well as **small-batch** (*or* **-lot**) **production.**

Мелкосерийный
These clamps are best employed for some **short-run** production jobs.

Менее [*см. тж.* **(Всё) менее и менее, Значительно менее, Меньше, Не менее**]
Automatic welding time is **under** (*or* **less than**) 30 minutes.
Tractors **under** (*or* **below**) 10 hp ...

Менее важен, чем
Visible and uv spectrometry **are of secondary importance to** other spectral methods for ...

Менее важный
Reactions **of lesser importance ...**

Менее важный из двух
The enol-form **is the less important of the two.**

Менее густорасположенные, чем на
The craters here **are sparser than** the ones on the Moon.

Менее изучен
The formation of the earth **is less well understood.**

Менее мощный
Thinner salt deposits ...

Менее продолжительный
Precipitation from shower clouds **is of shorter duration than** that from layer clouds.

Менее распространённый
The sound velocities of some **less common** gases are listed below.

Менее точно
Structurally the coal bed (also called seam and, **less appropriately,** vein) is ...

Менее, чем
The device enables a template to be ready for use in **under** (*or* **less than**) an hour.

Менее чувствительный *и т.п.*
Iron-titanium is quite sensitive, while lanthanum-pentanickel **is** considerably **less so.**

Менее яркий, чем
Most of the time Mars is considerably **dimmer than** Jupiter is.

Меньше [*см. тж.* **В миллион раз, Значительно меньше, Менее, На ... меньше, Намного меньше**]
The life expectancy in this case is **under** (*or* **less than**) a year.
This coefficient is some 40% **below** unity.
They have energies **under** (*or* **less than,** *or* **below**) 1,000,000 eV.
The actual diameter of the shanks of commercial reamers may be from 0.002 to 0.005 in. **under** the reamer size.

Меньше атома
Electrons are **subatomic (in size).**

Меньше (*ант.* **Больше**) **в ... раз, чем**
The empirical values **are less** (*anton.* **more**) **than** expected **by a factor of** 10.

Меньше вполовину
Less by half.

Меньше всего
Sand is **least** impeded by particle size resistance.
That part of the shaft twists **the least.**

Меньше затруднений [*см.* **Вызывать меньше затруднений, чем**].

Меньше или равен
For waves in general the group velocity can **be less than or equal to** the phase velocity.

Меньше интересует
The simple ratio **is** usually **of less concern to** the circuit designer than is the slope of the *V*/*J* curve.

Меньше на бесконечно малую величину, чем
The external pressure **is infinitesimally less than** the internal pressure.

Меньше номинального размера
It will be necessary to recondition the crankshaft by grinding the journals to an **undersize** diameter.

Меньший [*см. тж.* **В меньшей степени**]
Metal chelates have a **more limited** (*or* **lesser**) solubility.
For **lesser** values of the coefficient of friction the angles lie between these extremes.

Меньший ...,чем [*см.* **Иметь меньший диаметр, чем**].

Менять I [*см. тж.* **Варьировать, Видоизменять, Изменять, Не вызывать изменений**]
Large departures from sphericity **will** not **affect** (*or* **alter,** *or* **change**) the result.

Менять II
Discharge height can **be varied between** 1140 **and** 1950 mm.

Менять знак
In the hyperbolic case the Jacobian may **change** (*or* **reverse**) **sign.**

Менять местами [*см. тж.* **Поменять местами**]
If we **interchange** the hydroxy group **and** the hydrogen on one carbon atom only, we obtain another pair of enantiomers.

Менять направление на обратное
The hydrogen flow **is reversed.**
The transverse magnetic field does not **reverse its direction** for magneto-acoustic shocks.

Менять порядок на обратный
We **reverse** the order of the integrals.

Менять русло реки
They **diverted** (*or* **re-routed**) **rivers** and irrigated arid lands to grow crops.

Менять цвет
The indicator **changes colour** when a slight excess of one reactant is added.

Меняться [*см.* **Изменяться**].

Меняться местами
Parts of chromosomes may **change** (*or* **switch**) **places** — the phenomenon termed translocation.
This atom does not **exchange places with** another atom.

Меняться на обратный
Sodium ion is present in much higher concentration than potassium ion, whereas their concentration ratio **is reversed** (i.e. $K^+ > Na^+$) in the fluid of muscle cells.
The direction along the x-axis **is reversed.**

Меняться ролями
When **the roles of** equivalent particles **are interchanged, ...**

Меняющийся
The material is fed at **a varying** (*or* **changing**) rate.

Мера I [*см.* **В значительной степени, В полной мере, Ни в коей мере не, По мере того, как**].

Мера II [*см.* **Принимать меры**].

Мери́ло
Intake manifold pressure is **a measure of** airflow to the engine.

Мерить [*см.* **Измерять**].

Мерка [*см.* **Мери́ло**].

Мероприятие
The term agricultural drainage refers specifically to **measures** intended to ...
The common goal of all these **undertakings** is to see ...
Expressing ... in terms of linear programming is not a trivial **enterprise.**

Меры по охране окружающей среды
To evaluate potential ways of **salvaging** our **environment, ...**

Меры предосторожности [*см.* **Принимать меры предосторожности**].

Меры сыпучих тел
Dry measures.

Места́ми
As a result, the Cambrian layers **in places** rest directly upon the Vishnu schists.

Местность
The composition of sediment in a given **area ...**

Местный источник
We found **a locally available supply of** aggregate.
The only **indigenous** (*or* **local**) **supply of** water ...

Местный перегрев
The fins ensure complete dispersal of heat and total absence of **hot spots.**
Heat should be applied slowly to avoid **localized overheating.**

Место [*см. тж.* **В другом месте, В месте, В некоторых местах, Занимать ... место, Иметь место, Меняться местами, На месте, Проверка на месте, Становиться на место, Удерживать на месте, Установленный на месте, Уступать место**]
Samples are collected at several different **localities** (*or* **locations**).
In each octave **there is room for** seven different notes.
The troposphere is **the seat** (*or* **scene**) **of** all important weather processes.
The spinal cord was viewed as **the seat of** many of these interactions.

Место взрыва
This device measures the radiation at various distances from **the blast site.**

Место входа в
The brine leaving at **the point of entry to** (*or* **into**) the evaporator ...

Место, где происходит
The principal **seat of** digestion is the crop.

Место, занимаемое ими в окружающей среде
Organisms may be classified according to **the ecological niche which they occupy.**

Место назначения
The place of destination of the ore ...

Место обитания
The available evidence suggests that this valley was **the habitat of** some of the earth's earliest living things.

Место происхождения
Electromagnetic waves radiate outward from **the point of origin.**
The place of origin of the ore ...

Место реакции
The concentration of the compounds at **the reaction site** may be influenced by some of these factors.

Место соединения
At **the junction of** the coating **and** the metal ...

Место соприкосновения
At **points of contact between** the liquid **and** irregular solids ...

Месторождение
Coal, petroleum and natural gas **deposits ...**
Coal **fields,** oil **fields ...**
The oldest important **occurrences of** coal (*or* coal **deposits**) are in ...

Металл основы
An example occurs in electroplating where trace contaminants on **the base metals** may have a pronounced effect on results.
The deposited metal is of approximately the same composition as **the parent metal.**

Металлический алюминий
Aluminium metal (*or* **Metallic aluminium**).

Металлический блеск
Chalcocite has **a metallic lustre.**

Метить
To label a chemical compound **with** a radioactive isotope, ...

Метка
A rope with **markers** at every foot ...

Метод [*см. тж.* **Изящный метод, Испытанный метод** (*или* **способ**), **Методом, Осуществляться по методу, По методу, Подход, Придерживаться метода, Скоростной метод, Способ, Средство для, Таким путём**]
The combustion **approach** gives good results.
Two **avenues** are available, (1) tilting propellers, (2) fixed propellers.
The normal **method of** (*or* **for**) producing an aerosol is by condensing a vapour.
Many improvements in bronze casting **practices** were reported.
Determine temperature effects by **the procedure** described in Paragraph (b).
This manufacturing **technique** is used in ...
Certain **strategies** can be adopted to reduce this loss.

Carbon-14 dating is **a** highly important **tool for** the geologist.
What we need is **a way to** keep track of such ores.
The determination of the latitude is possible by astronomic **means.**

Метод вычисления
Several **calculational** (*or* **computational**) **techniques** have been developed.

Метод исследования
The investigative (*or* **investigation**) **techniques** used showed that ...

Метод подбора
The interfacial concentrations are determined by **the trial-and-error method.**

Метод подгонки [*см. тж.* **Метод подбора**]
You can try to fit the powers of 2 into an ordinary number **by hit and miss.**

Метод попыток и ошибок [*см.* **Метод подбора**].

Метод устранения неполадки
The best **remedy for the trouble is** the use of mica insulation.

Методика [*см. тж.* **Использовать методику, По методике, Подход**]
In our experiment we use **a** different **strategy** (*or* **procedure**).

Методика эксперимента
Experimental procedure.

Методом
The rate of conversion was determined **by the** static **method.**
The wheel is impregnated **by an** undisclosed **process.**
Cobalt is purified **in the manner** described for arsenic ores.

Методом погружения
This treatment produces a fine microcrystalline coating **via immersion technique** [*or* **by the immersion procedure** (*or* **method**)].

Методом подбора [*см.* **Путём подбора**].

Метр (*линейка*)
A metre-stick.

Метраж
The capacity of the finished products warehouse has been doubled without the need for increasing **the floor area** (*or* **space**).

Метчи́к для грубой и чистовой нарезки
Formerly both **roughing and finishing taps** were required for the job.

Механизм [*см. тж.* **По механизму**]
The mechanism of (*or* **for**) the reaction is unknown.

Механика
Quantum **mechanics is** related to ...

Механическая обработка
Machining.
In this case the alloy becomes brittle and unsuitable for **mechanical working** (*or* **for machining**).

Механически прочный
This material is **mechanically strong.**

Меченный
Choline **labelled with** tritium (*or* Tritium-**labelled** choline) ...

Меченный радиоактивным изотопом
Metabolism studies with **radioactively labelled** substrate analogues ...

Мечтать [*см.* **О котором нельзя и мечтать**].

Мешать [*см. тж.* **Затруднять, Предотвращать, Препятствовать**]
The size of the ship **is** no **barrier** (*or* **hindrance,** *or* **impediment**) **to** the application of the principle.
This is **a** serious **handicap to** such a study.
This **hindered** (*or* **interfered with**) lathe operation.
The motor is placed so as not **to impede** the operator.

Микроколичество [*см. тж.* **Ничтожное количество**]
Mercury is found in **trace amounts** (*or* **quantities**) throughout the lithosphere.

Микроскоп [*см.* **Виден в микроскоп, Если рассматривать ... в микроскоп, Под микроскопом, Рассматривать в микроскоп**].

Микроскоп с увеличением в ... раз
A 45-**power microscope** objective lens was inserted in the beam of the one-milliwatt helium-neon laser.

Мимо
The movement of the magnetized elements of the tape **past** the read-out heads is sufficient to induce ...

Минимальное количество
Control gear components with **as few** moving parts **as possible** (*or* **with a minimum of** moving parts) can be seen on the stand.

Минимальный [*см. тж.* **При минимальном уходе**]
Humans require **a minimum** regular intake of Na^+.
The energy is **minimum** (*or* **minimal**) when ...
Holes for bolts should have a **minimum** diameter of 1/2 in.
These steels can be hardened with **a minimum of** scaling.
The power is **a minimum** when no water is being delivered.
The element is mounted on the wing where extraneous magnetic effects **are at a minimum.**
The job is done **in a minimum of** time.

Минимум [*см. тж.* **Минимальный, От минимума до максимума, Проходить через максимум (минимум), Сводить к минимуму**]
These openings may be holes of **a minimum 3/8 inch diameter.**

Миновать
The coal can **bypass** the crushers and screen and go directly to the belt conveyor to open storage.

Минус [*см. тж.* **Без**]
The total cost of the part **exclusive of** (*or* **less,** *or* **minus**) materials costs, would be ...
Upon reaching point *D* the full battery voltage **less** some small transistor drop is applied to winding 3.

Мир [*см.* **В мире, Во всём мире**].

Мир растений и животных [*см.* **Растительный и животный мир**].

Мирное использование атомной энергии
Peaceful uses of atomic energy.

Мировая слава [*см.* **Завоёвывать мировую славу**].

Мировой масштаб [*см.* **В глобальном масштабе**].

Мировые запасы
The world's supply (*or* **reserves,** *or* **resources**) **of** berkelium ...

Мнение [*см.* **Высказывать мнение о том, что; Не согласный с этим мнением, Широкораспространённое мнение**].

Мнения относительно ... расходятся
Opinions differ as to the quantities of mineral resources as yet undiscovered.

Мнения по вопросу о ... резко расходятся
Opinions differ widely on how the convection behaves.

Мнения расходятся
Opinions vary and the evidence is not clear.

Мнения учёных сходятся к тому, что
The concensus (presently) is (*or* **There is general agreement**) **that** the native nucleic acids are in the form of ...

Мнимый [*см.* **Действительный и мнимый**].

Многие из
Many of the clay minerals have been synthesized in the laboratory.

Многие не знают, что
It is not widely appreciated (*or* **known**) **that** red cell glycolysis may lower the sugar level by as much as a half if ...

Многие считают, что
There is much speculation that the particle does have a small mass.

Много [*см. тж.* **Большое количество, Намного**]
There is **a great deal of** (*or* **much**) evidence that ...

Много больше [*см.* **Значительно больше**].

Много внимания [*см.* **Большое внимание уделено**].

Много десятков километров
Drift will carry sediment for **many tens of kilometres.**

Много лет [*см.* **В течение многих лет, Ещё в течение многих лет, Издавна**].

Много ниже
These flow rates **are well below** those corresponding to flooding.

Много путешествовать
He **travelled widely** (*or* **much,** *or* **a great deal**).

Многовековой
A **centuries-old** tradition in science tells us always to test the simplest hypothesis first.

Многого можно достигнуть
Much can be gained by this approach.

Многое
We know **a great deal** (*or* **much**) about the physiological properties of ...

Многое в
Much of the behaviour of molecules is understandable.

Многое давать [*см.* **Давать многое**].

Многое можно сделать [*см.* **Ещё многое можно сделать в области**].

Многое нужно сделать [*см.* **Ещё многое нужно сделать, чтобы**].

Многое нужно узнать [*см.* **Ещё многое нужно узнать о**].

Многое узнать [*см.* **Хотя и удалось многое узнать**].

Многозначный
F is a **many-valued** function of *x*.

Многократно [*см. тж.* **Неоднократно**]
The **many times** repeated coal-forming conditions ...
When the wavelength is to be measured **repeatedly, ...**
By scanning the spectrum rapidly and **repetitively ...**
If you **repeatedly** divide this number by 2, ...

Многократного использования
The process uses a **nonconsumable** tungsten electrode.

Многократный
Repeated treatment with fresh batches of reagents will produce ...

Многолетней давности
Signs of chronic liver disease indicate **long-standing** hepatic damage.

Многолетний
A **long-standing** ambition of physicists is to construct ...

Многообещающий [*см.* **Быть перспективным, Весьма перспективный, Перспективный**].

Многосторонний
In exploiting the **manifold** capabilities of the computer the power industry has been understandably cautious.

Многоступенчатое преобразование (*мат.*)
Multistep conversion.

Многоцелевой [*см.* **Универсальный**].

Многочастичный
A **many-particle** system ...

Многочисленны
The problems that arise in all steel-making processes **are many** (*or* **numerous,** *or* **large in number**) and varied.
It was noticed that objects with excess ultraviolet emission **were** much more **plentiful** than known radio sources in typical star fields.
The causes of a low albumin **are legion.**
The **multitudinous** strands that comprise the chromosomes ...

Многочисленны и разнообразны
Industrial uses of closed-circuit television **are many and varied.**

Многочисленные данные [*см. тж.* **Большое количество данных**]
Much evidence points to this conclusion.
Abundant evidence (*or* **A large body of data**) shows that ...
There is now **ample evidence on** how the rate of cratering differed from one part of the solar system to another.

Многочисленные исследования
This has become the topic of **a large body of research.**

Многочисленные преимущества
The advantages of these batteries **are manifold** (*or* **numerous,** *or* **many**).

Многочисленные применения

This brass is machined into parts for **a multiplicity of uses.**

Многочлен [*см.* **Полином**].

Множество [*см. тж.* **Бесчисленное множество, Масса**]
This has been **a plethora of** conferences and symposiums.
Atoms "stick together" to form **the multitude of** substances found in the natural world.
This wall profile would break the normal shock wave into **a host of** oblique shock waves.

Множитель [*см.* **Разлагать на множители**].

Множить на
Multiply the annual change **by** (*or* **times**) the number of years.

Могут быть разделены
The components of colloidal dispersions **are separable by** the indicated procedures.

Могут свободно передвигаться
The charge carriers **are free to move through** the material.

Моделирование при помощи компьютера
The simulation of the fluids **with a computer** (*or* **The computer simulation of** the fluid).

Моделировать на компьютере
This motion **is computer simulated.**
It was decided **to simulate** (*or* **model**) the plant **on the** analogue **computer.**

Модель [*см. тж.* **Масштабная модель**]
The key to **the** modern **model for** (*or* **of**) electrons in atoms ...

Модификация [*см. тж.* **Видоизменён**]
The new hard anodizing process **is an adaptation** (*or* **a modification**) **of** the Hardas process.

Модулированный по амплитуде
Amplitude-modulated frequencies.

Модулированный по фазе
The transmitters **are phase modulated.**

Модулировать по амплитуде
The vector **is modulated in amplitude** (*or* **amplitude modulated**).

Можем [*см. тж.* **Иметь право**]
We are entitled to interpret this phenomenon is terms of ...
We are now **in a position to** state the problem.

Может [*см. тж.* **Способен**]
Steel tools **are** frequently **liable** (*or* **apt**) **to** give off sparks in certain conditions.
Steam should not be allowed to enter the recorder, as it **is liable to** damage the working parts.

Может быть I [*см. тж.* **А может быть и, Возможно**]
It may be that this structure serves as an orienting skeleton for ...

Может быть II [*см.* **Можно**].

Может быть выведен [*см.* **Можно вывести**].

Может быть использован для проверки
These results **provide a useful check on** numerical solutions.

Может быть получен в результате
Either the same olefin or a rearranged olefin **can result from** such a proton elimination.

Может быть приспособлен к
The compressor **is adaptable to** any power source.

Можеть быть это и так
Maybe so (*or* **It may be so**), but this argument has no meaning, since ...

Может дать богатую информацию относительно
This site **has much potential for yielding information about** human activities in the distant past.

Может дифференцироваться
H **is** obviously **differentiable** if *g* and *z* have ...

Может заменять [*см. тж.* **Может служить заменой**]
The use of Cerenkov light to detect proton decays **offers an alternative to** the direct observation of ...

Может и не быть [*см.* **Не обязательно должен быть**].

Может изменяться [*см. тж.* **Может меняться**]
The composition **is variable.**

Может изменяться в широких пределах
The speed of flow of ground water **is subject to wide variations.**

Может использоваться
The instrument **is usable** (*or* **operable**).

Может использоваться вместо [*см.* **Может служить заменой**].

Может конкурировать с
These superconducting motors **are competitive with** conventional units.

Может конкурировать с ... в отношении
This reactor **is competitive in** capital costs **with** many other designs.

Может меняться [*см. тж.* **Может изменяться**]
The ratio **is subject to variation.**

Может наблюдаться обратное явление
If, however, r(β) is a decreasing function, **the opposite situation may occur.**

Может передвигаться
The column **has movement towards and away from** the workpiece.

Может показаться, что
It may appear that this statement conflicts with the statement made above.

Может работать [*см.* **Может использоваться**].

Может свободно передвигаться
Although chloride **is free to move,** it can do so only in exchange for another anion.

Может служить заменой
The nitrile synthesis **offers an alternative to** the Grignard synthesis.

Может сравниться с
Few microcomputer software packages **compare favourably with** those available for larger and more expensive machines.

Может сравниться с ... по
Only comets **equal** Nereid in eccentricity.

Можно [*см.* **Имеются основания, Как можно ближе, Пригодный для**].

Можно быть уверенным, что
If we make up such a list, **we can be assured that** any particular fraction will be included.

Можно видеть на графике
This **can be seen graphically** in Fig. 6.

Можно видеть, что
One can see (*or* **recognize**) **that** the later steps in the mechanism are of no consequence.
It can be seen (*or* **It is seen**) **that** the rotational energy can be expressed as ...

Можно возразить, что
It may be argued that in some cases the forces result from ...

Можно вставлять
The fixture **accommodates** a wide variety of aluminium plates.

Можно вставлять вручную
The terminals **are hand insertable.**

Можно встретить
Such a fan is usually **to be found** in each room at the point where ...

Можно вывести
These equations **are derivable from** Hamilton's principle.

Можно выразить в виде
If so, π then **would be expressible as** a fraction.

Можно выразить путём
Many motion problems **are expressible by** posing an equation ...

Можно выразить через
The double integral **is expressible in terms of** two successive definite integrals.

Можно доказать непосредственной проверкой, что
It is a matter of direct verification to prove that ...

Можно допустить
Partial failures **can be tolerated** on 1 occasion in 50.

Можно допустить, что

Conceivably some linings will be effective for as long as 50 years, but ultimately one must expect them to fail.
If the earth consisted of a perfectly spherical lithosphere, **it is conceivable that** the entire lithosphere could move as a whole with respect to the rest of the earth.
Perhaps **one can concede that** a single molecule might be formed in the postulated manner, but it is most improbable that ...

Можно думать, что
Because of this great density **one is inclined to think** [*or* **it is believed** (*or* **thought**)] **that** there cannot be much of a remaining connection between ...

Можно использовать [*см. тж.* **Подходить**]
This result **is useful** (*or* **can be used**) **in** making gas-volume calculations.
Use could be made of the cells of ...
The method **will** also **be available for** screening new drugs for possible chromosomal effects.

Можно использовать для многих целей
Equation (12) **is useful in many applications.**

Можно использовать повторно
The rocket **is re-usable.**

Можно лишь высказывать предположения
The source of the dust **is open to speculation;** we cannot say whether it represents ...

Можно лишь упомянуть
We can do no more than mention a few of the theory's recent achievements.

Можно лучше уяснить из рисунка
The sequence of the events **is made clearer by Fig. 8.**

Можно надеяться, что
It is hoped that silicon carbide and boron phosphide may provide devices useful to 1000°C.

Можно надеяться, что при помощи ... удастся
A technique of carbon dating using a cyclotron **shows promise of** extending the time range of ^{14}C dating.

Можно найти в [*см. тж.* **Смотри**]
Data on titanium trichlorides **are available** (*or* **can be found**) **in** Bulletin TT2-S6.
A detailed discussion of ... **is found in** Chapter 5.

Можно написать целую книгу о [*см.* **О ... можно написать целую книгу**].

Можно объяснить *чем-л.*
The large fluctuations **are attributable to** scattered flight.

Можно ожидать
This effect **is likely** if the ligands are highly conjugated.
The two elements **would** thus **be expected to** form an ionic compound.
One would (*or* **might**) **expect** a linear term **from** internal sources if E_f / E_m is near unity or greater.

Можно определить так, как нам самим захочется
A formalist is likely to say that the real-number line **is whatever we define it to be.**

Можно оспаривать
This method **is open to argument.**

Можно осуществить путём
Such a process **is rendered possible by** the addition of ...

Можно отнести за счёт того, что
This success **is attributable to the fact that ...**

Можно отнести к
Among the plants the fungi **fit into** this group.

Можно перевести на
Every boiler **is convertible to** solid fuel firing.

Можно подвергнуть сомнению [*см.* **Вселять сомнение**].

Можно поделить на
Most of the chemical reactions of ammonia **may be classified under** three chief groups.

Можно подойти к ... с точки зрения ...
One way of looking at the formation of a covalent bond **is in terms of** the behaviour of ...

Можно показать, что
The matrices of Table 12-4 **can be shown to** represent the operations of the C_3 point group.
It can be shown that any given real numbers can be made to correspond to ...
The centre of mass of the system **can be shown to be** unaccelerated at all times (*or* **It can be shown that ... is** unaccelerated ...).

Можно полагать, что
It is felt (*or* **believed**) **that** the resulting values are reasonable.

Можно получить
These published works **are available from** the Institute.
The frequency of the radiation **is obtainable** (*or* **can be obtained**) **from** the following relationship.
Sensitivities between 400 and 7000 amp/lumen **are obtained by** this method.

Можно получить общее представление
A general idea can be had of the vehicle's utility and ...

Можно понять из
The junction reaction **is understood by reference to** Fig. 18-7.

Можно построить
A consistent non-Euclidean geometry **is constructible.**

Можно почти не сомневаться в том, что
There can be little doubt that a higher degree of complexity exists.

Можно приобрести в
This device **is available (commercially) from** a number of sources.

Можно продемонстрировать, что
It is demonstratable that ...

Можно продолжать без конца
This **may be continued endlessly.**

Можно разделить на
The pegmatites **are divisible into** two groups.
Biotic provinces **are divisible into** biotic districts.

Можно регулировать высоту
The burner **is adjustable for height.**

Можно с полным правом сказать, что
Thus in R^S **it is valid to say that** g is greater than n for all n.

Можно с уверенностью предположить, что
It is safe to assume that beetles hear sonic vibrations.
It may be safely suggested that covalent, ionic, and metallic bonds are stronger than ...

Можно с уверенностью сказать, что
It is safe to say [*or* **It can be said with confidence** (*or* **assurance**)] **that** diesel oil is preponderantly used.
We can state with assurance that ...

Можно свести к
This mathematical language **can be boiled down to the statement that ...**

Можно сделать вывод, что
From the result obtained **it may be deduced** (*or* **inferred**, *or* **concluded**) **that ...**

Можно себе представить [*см. тж.* **Который можно себе представить**]
A world populated solely by bacteria and blue-green algae **is conceivable.**
One can envision an interactive home terminal consisting of ...

Можно себе представить в виде
The potential surface **can be conceived of as** an undulating landscape.

Можно сказать и обратное
The reverse statement can also be made.

Можно сказать многое в пользу
Such devices **have much in their favour.**

Можно сказать с достаточной уверенностью, что
It is reasonably safe to suggest that molecular substances are usually lower melting than the typical ionic compounds.
We can say with reasonable confidence that the Moon's composition is different from the Earth's.

Можно сравнить с [*см. тж.* **Выдерживать сравнение с**]
The performance of furnaces in cold-metal shops ... **compares favourably with ...**

The carbohydrates as a group **are comparable with** the proteins and fats.
This speed **compares with** that of a rocket.

Можно судить о ... по ...
The presence of a black hole in space **could be inferred** only **by** the existence of ...

Можно считать, что
The evolution of integrated **circuits may be thought of** (*or* **considered**) **as** occurring in two phases.

Можно считать, что он
The β particle **may be thought of as** originating from the conversion of a neutron to a proton.

Можно также рассматривать *и т.п.*
Another way of considering the functioning of an accelerator **is** by analogy with a microscope.

Можно удовлетвориться
One can be content with this result.
It is satisfactory here **to** use an empirical expression to represent ...

Можно указать на
Cane or beet sugar, starch, ... **may be cited as** typical representatives of this group.

Можно упомянуть
Finally, **mention may be made of** four plastic injection moulding machines.

Можно усомниться в том, что
One is entitled to doubt whether any man will ever lay eyes on such planets.

Можно успешно использовать в качестве
Bubble columns **are attractive for** use as chemical reactors.

Можно часто видеть
The fireflies **are much in evidence** on warm summer nights.

Момент [*см. тж.* **В каждый момент времени, В любой момент, В момент вылета из, В момент написания этой книги, В тот момент когда, В этот момент, Начиная с этого момента**]
These forces act only **at the instant of** collision.
It was possible to predict **the** exact **moments at which ...**

Момент времени
The switch opens and closes electrical contacts **at** present **instants of time.**
The circuit identifies **the point in time at which** two input levels reach the same amplitude.
Staging defines the extent of tumour growth and progression **at** one **point in time.**

Момент относительно
If **the moments** of inertia **about** two of the principal axes are equal, ...

Моментально
Then all remaining resistance disappears **abruptly.**
This transition frees an electron, which **promptly** leaves the nucleus.
The atmosphere **instantaneously** adjusts itself to ...
These wheel-mounted machines can be placed anywhere in the factory **at a moment's notice.**
A high-speed photographic recording system gives **instantly** developed pictures for analysis of high-speed motion.

Монополия
The aeronautical engineer now works in fields which **were** once **the exclusive domain** of the physicist.

Монотонно возрастать (*антон.* **убывать**)
The pressure **increases** (*anton.***decreases**) **monotonically.**

Монотонно возрастающий
The temperature **is a monotonically** (*or* **monotone**) **increasing** function of the velocity.

Монотонный
f and g are **monotonic** (*or* **monotone**) functions.

Монтировать [*см. тж.* **Смонтирован**]
The bypass capacitors **are mounted** in the same unit.

Море наступает и отступает
The sea **advances and retreats.**

Морское судно
A sea-going vessel.

Морского происхождения
Most asphalts **are of marine origin.**

Морской
The coelenterata are mainly **marine** organisms.

Морской и земной
The zoosphere of the earth has been divided into **marine and terrestrial** faunal regions.

Мощное средство
The Mössbauer effect is **a powerful tool** (*or* **instrument**) in the hands of the physical chemist.

Мощное средство для
Thus esr spectroscopy provides **a powerful tool for** the study of chemical species with unpaired electrons.

Мощность [*см. тж.* **На половинной мощности, Работать на полную мощность, Средней мощности**]
This chain is recommended for machines of greater **horsepower.**

Мощность ... измеряется в л.с.
Motors **are rated in horsepower.**

Мощность меньше 1 л.с. [*см.* **Двигатель мощностью меньше 1 л.с.**].

Мощность на выходе
The transmitter **delivers 15 watts** (*or* **has an output of 15 watts**).

Мощный I [*см. тж.* **Достаточно мощный**]
Sodium is a **vigorous** reducing agent.
A **high-powered** laser system ...
Quasars are the most **energetic** objects known in the universe.
The most **energetic** (*or* **powerful**) propellants give values of about 13,000 fps.
This is a **potent** fissile material.
When **intense** gamma-ray sources became available, ...

Мощный II
A **thick** layer of coal ...

Мы ещё далеки от
We are a long way still from deciphering the chemical language of bullheads.

Мы знаем по опыту, что
We know from experience that there will be friction in the bearings.

Мы интересуемся [*см.* **Нас в основном интересует, Нас интересует только**].

Мы надеемся, что
Though intended primarily for the student, the book **will hopefully be found** interesting and useful by the practical engineer.

Мы не собираемся
It is not proposed (*or* **It is not our intention**) **to** deal at length with ...

Мы не хотим этим сказать, что
That is not to say (that) the erupting material resembles ...

Мысль [*см.* **Зародилась мысль**].

Н

На [*см. тж.* **Висеть на ... с, Вносить поправку на, Делить на, Закончен на ... процентов, Замыкание на, Затрачиваться на, Изменение на, Испытание на, Лить на, Масштаб ... на километр, Наложен на, Нанесение на, Нанесённый на график, Наносить на, Направлен на, Напряжение на, Насаживать на, Настраивать на, Обобщение на, Одевать на, Опорожнён на 2/3, Основываться на предположении о, Отражаться на, Падать на, Падение напряжения на, Повышать температуру на, Подвешивать на, Потерянный на, Продвигаться на, Произведение на, Работать на, Разлагать на, Разрезать на, Разряжаться на, Распространяться на, Рассчитанный на, Стандарт на, Сфокусирован(ный) на, Терять на, Увеличивать на, Умножать на, Умноженный на**]
The amplifier-supply current develops a voltage **across** the resistor.
The paper discusses the status of mechanical properties of tungsten-base alloys **as of** April 1982.
As of June 23, all recovery facilities were returned to normal operations.
Cylinders three inches in diameter **by** three inches long ...
Work is the product of force **by** distance.
The engineer increased the coercive force of the magnet **by** 7%.
A specification **for** (*or* **on,** *or* **covering**) nickel-chromium alloys ...
The engine delivers one power stroke **for** each full rotation of the shaft.

For every 1000 ft increase in altitude, there is a corresponding decrease in pressure of ...
A change **of** a few degrees may mean that icing conditions are imminent.
Five minutes were required to lift the 50-lb weight **by** (*or* **through**) 16 ft.
The control valve should be at least **one size** (*на один размер*) smaller than the control-agent pipe.
In this case the proper allowance **for** shrinkage is 3/16 inch **to** the foot.
If a 10-lb block is lifted (**на**) 3 ft.
Loops of nucleic acids may be lengthened or diminished (**на**) one nucleoside at a time.
There are four covalent bonds **to** each carbon.

На аноде [*см.* **На катоде**].

На базе которого
This has been the basic unit of equipment **around which** automated equipment has been built.

На базе теории [*см.* **Основываясь на теоретических данных**].

На безопасном расстоянии от
All personnel should **keep clear of** (*or* **at a safe distance from**) high-voltage equipment.

На берегу
Radio direction finder equipment may be installed either **on shore** or on board an aircraft.

На бесконечности
$\alpha + \beta + \gamma = 0$ is the line **at infinity.**

На ближайшем расстоянии от Земли
Venus **at its closest** is 42 gigametres away.

На ближайшие годы
A list of recommendations **for the years immediately ahead** has been published.

На близком расстоянии
The **short-range** repulsion between ions ...
The satellite was explored **at close range.**

На близком расстоянии от
Unlike the airplane, the magnetoplane can be flown **in close proximity to** a guideway.

На более поздней стадии
Stable precipitates are formed **in** (*or* **at**) **the later stages of** ageing.

На более поздней стадии процесса
Later in the process, some evidence has suggested that ...

На ... больше
This element has **one more** proton.

На ... больше кратеров, чем на
The Moon highlands **are more cratered than** the maria.

На ... больше, чем
The biological half-life of the new compound was 44% **higher than that of** tetracycline.
Nitrogen has **one** electron **more than** carbon.
The observed amplitudes **are greater by** 16.5% **than** those which ... (*or* **are** 16.5% **greater than ...**).

На большие расстояния
Then it is possible to understand how fine powder can move **(by) large distances** over the near side of the Moon.
Aggregates for concrete must be transported **(for) long distances.**

На больших глубинах
At great depths.

На больших расстояниях [*см. тж.* **Связь на больших расстояниях**]
When power and telephone lines are parallel **for long distances, ...**

На большой высоте
The balloon was flown **at high altitude.**

На большом расстоянии друг от друга
The storage facilities **are widely spaced** (*or* **separated).**
The particles must be kept **well** (*or* **far**) **apart.**

На большом расстоянии от [*см.* **Вдали от**]

На большом расстоянии от берега
Almost all of the earthquakes in this **area are well offshore.**

На борту космического корабля
Such systems are used **aboard spacecraft** (*or* **are space-borne**).

На борту ракеты
Direct measurements made with **rocket-borne** photometers are much more reliable.

На борту самолёта (вертолёта *и т.п.*) [*см. тж.* **Бортовой**]
Aboard the aircraft (helicopter, rocket, spacecraft).

На борту самолёта или судна
When radio direction finder equipment **is aloft or afloat, ...**

На борту судна
When radar **aboard a ship** (*or* **shipboard radar**) finds an oncoming target, ...

На весь срок службы
The major structural components will be designed **for the life of** the aircraft.

На ... виден
Liquid diffraction patterns **show** diffraction rings corresponding to ...

На ... влияет
The energies of chemical systems **are** mostly **influenced by** chemical reactions and ...
Photometric measurements **are susceptible to** interferences from numerous sources.

На внутренней стороне
The coating **on the inside of** the bulb ...

На волне
The iodine laser operates **at** (*or* **on**) **a wavelength of** 1.34 micrometres.

"На вооружении" (*жарг.*) [*см.* **Иметься "на вооружении"**].

На востоке, западе
The land surface extending from the Hudson Valley **on the east** to Erie **on the west ...**

На время [*см.* **На некоторое время**].

На всасе (насоса)
One side of the pump is connected **at its suction end** to the water tank.

На всех волнах
These infrared radiation detectors should absorb uniformly **at** (*or* **on**) **all wavelengths.**

На всё время
These bearings can be pregreased **for life.**

На всём протяжении от ... до
This gives the equipment more freedom of movement, **all the way from** the coal face **to** the outside.
Copper piping **all the way from** the orifice **to** the recorder is equally suitable.

На всю длину
A card advanced **its whole length** during one revolution of the shaft.

На всякий случай
To be on the safe side, we shall use a factor of 10 to 1 in the preliminary design.

На втором месте [*см.* **Вторым по значению после ... является**].

На втором месте по распространённости
Medullary carcinomas **are the second most frequent type.**

На входе [*см. тж.* **Давление на входе (выходе)**]
The dimensions of the strip **at entry ...**
At the point of entry into the tower ...
At the compressor **inlet ...**
At the amplifier **input ...**

На высоте
At a height of 5 km ...
The wire was suspended **at an elevation of** 6 metres.

На высоту
The total head includes **the height through which** the liquid is raised ...

На выходе [*см. тж.* **Мощность на выходе**]
This radiation produces no signal **at the output of** the amplifier.
The flue gas **exit** temperature is 248°F.
This depends on whether the flow is subsonic or supersonic **as it leaves** the throat.

На глаз
The dashed lines denote directions judged **by eye.**

На глазах [*см.* **У нас на глазах**].

На глубине
The sand formation lies 1200 m **beneath the surface** (*or* **at a depth of** 1200 m).
Solid igneous rock of a batholith is still hot **in a depth range of** 2 to 5 km.

На глубине 800 метров
At a depth of 800 m ...

На ... горизонте
These ores are mined **at** different **levels.**
An appreciable amount of development was conducted **on the** Nchanga **horizon.**
Electric locomotive haulage will be used **on the** main **levels.**

На ... градусов [*см.* **Изгибаться на ... градусов, Изменяться на ... градусов**].

На ... градусов не в фазе с
At 16.5 Hz, the engine **is** about 180° **out of phase with** the frame.

На ... градусов ниже, чем
Such substances have a melting point about 100 **degrees** Celsius **below that of** pure water ice.

На грани
The valve **was on the verge of** instability.

На границах зёрен
Failure does not begin **at grain boundaries.**
The specimens had a layer of second phase **on the grain boundaries.**

На границе фаз
For calculating the electromotive force **at the phase boundary** (*or* **interface**) ...

На график [*см.* **Наносить на график**].

На гусеничном ходу
A **caterpillar-mounted** chassis ...
Caterpillar-tracked drilling rigs ...
This loader is a **crawler-mounted** machine.
The machine **is mounted on caterpillar tracks.**

На данном этапе [*см. тж.* **На этой стадии**]
It is more pertinent **at this juncture** (*or* **point**) to see if ...
As things now stand, the two kinds of transistor complement one another.
As for now, a satisfactory explanation is as elusive as before.

На две половинки [*см. тж.* **Пополам**]
The cell **divides into** approximately equal **halves.**

На ... действует
A comet tail **is acted upon by** a repulsive force.
The glucose-1-phosphate **is acted on by** the phosphorylase present in the droplets.

На ... действует сила
The particle **experiences a force** acting in the z direction.

На ... длиннее, чем
This bond **is** 1.8 **times as long as** the intramolecular O—H covalent bond.

На длину [*см. тж.* **На расстояние**]
The valve should be filed, but only **for the length of** the valve travel.
The bolts are threaded **for a length of** 150 mm.

На дне [*см.* **Осаждаться на дне**].

На дно
Some of the ore spills **to the bottom of** the shaft.
We place a liquid *A* **at the bottom of** a tube containing a gas *B*.

На ... долготе [*см.* **На широте**].

На дому [*см.* **Лечение в домашних условиях**].

На достаточном расстоянии друг от друга
The two images will have **to be far enough apart** so that ...

На его место
The hot body is removed from the cylinder head, and an insulating cover is put **in its place.**

На единицу
e is the internal energy **per unit** mass.
... **per unit of** enclosed area ...

На единицу времени
The number of deaths **per unit time ...**

На единицу длины
Per unit length.

На единицу объёма
This provides a large contact area **per unit volume.**

На единицу продукта (реакции)
A lower cost **per unit (quantity of) product formed.**

На единицу смещения
The force constant is equal to the restoring force operating **for a unit displacement from** the equilibrium position.

На завершающем этапе
In the closing stages of World War II ...

На заднем плане
The feed conveyor belt **is in the background.**

На заказ [*см.* **По заказу**].

На западе [*см.* **На востоке, западе**].

На заре
Even **at the dawn of** the age of electricity power engineers saw ...

На земле
Almost all **terrestrial** hydrogen occurs in combination.

На значительном расстоянии от
Studies of the stock **at a distance well removed** (*or* **away**) **from** (*or* **at a considerable distance from**) the diaphragm have been conducted.

На ... или около него
On or near the surface ...

На ... имеется (*или* **находится,** *или* **смонтирован,** *или* **установлен** *и т.п.*)
The vertical shaft **carries** a number of small bar magnets.
A valve **is fitted to** the canister.

На индивидуальной основе
Because customers may request thousands of modifications to basic valves, the modifications are made **on a custom basis** according to the particular specifications desired.

На интервале (*мат.*)
On the initial **interval ...**

На испытаниях
On trials the tug achieved a speed of 12 knots.

На каждом из нас лежит доля ответственности за
All of us share in the responsibility for these choices.

На каждый
There are three hydrogens **for every** carbon in the sample.
For every *F*'-centre created, two *F*-centres are destroyed.

На каждый ... приходится
For each silicon **there are** three oxygens.

На катоде
The hydrogen is produced **at the cathode.**

На конус [*см.* **Сводить на конус, Сходить на конус**].

На концах обмотки
The voltage developed **across the winding** is approximately in phase with the mains.

На конце
A bolt is a rod with a head **at** one **end** and a screw thread **on the other.**

На корабле [*см.* **На борту судна**].

На коротком расстоянии
At short range, over distances of a few atomic spacings, ...

На корпус [*см.* **Заземлённый на корпус**].

На котором нож оставляет царапину
Calcite is a soft mineral **scratched with the point of a knife.**

На котором устанавливается
A device has a turret **that mounts** six pins.

На который
The time **for which** the electrons remain free ...

На который нави́т
An induction coil may simply consist of an iron bar **wrapped with** two insulated windings.

На который приходится (*или* **падает**)
The chief clove-producing countries are Zanzibar **with** 90 percent of the total output, Indonesia, ...

На который способен только [*см.* **Который характерен только для**].

На кривой
There is one peak **in the** frequency **curve.**

На лакмус [*см.* **Реакция на лакмус**].

На линии

In this case the centre of buoyancy and the centre of gravity are **in the** same vertical **line.**

На маховике
The traxcavator delivers 100 hp **at the flywheel.**

На машине
Only one spindle at a time is operated **on** this **machine**.

На ... меньше
The average power of the N_2-laser-pumped dye laser is ≈ **10^2 less.**
This element has **one less** neutron.

На ... меньше, чем
Carbon has **one** electron **less than** nitrogen.

На месте [*см. тж.* **Проверка на месте, Удерживать на месте**]
The principal dimensions of the arch may be dictated by the conditions **at the site.**
These units will be assembled **at site.**
The magnetic field was scanned with plugs **in position.**
This is a method for **in situ** insulation.
The units may be fitted to an existing valve **in situ.**
We found a **locally available** supply of aggregate.
On-the-site casting of concrete.
An **on-the-spot** investigation was conducted.
Towers are assembled **on the spot** by the erecting crew.
An extensive theoretical analysis was followed by a detailed **on-site** measurement programme.

На место
The sample is ready for lowering **into place.**
The device moves the sample **into position.**
The units will go on stream when they are delivered **to location.**
The caisson was floated **to the site.**

На минуту
I would like, **for the moment,** to leave out of consideration the 32nd satellite, which ...

На минуту предположим, что
Assume for the moment that ...

На молекулярном уровне
True solids are not fluid **at the molecular level.**

На начальной стадии (*или* **ступени**)
Early in (*or* **In the initial stage of**) the test no such data were available.
In (*or* **At**) **the early stages of** ageing, nitrogen atoms diffuse to ...
In the opening stage of the search, the resource is found in ever-increasing amounts.

На начальной стадии развития
This method **is** still **in a primitive state of development.**

На начальном этапе развития [*см.* **На начальной стадии развития, На раннем этапе развития**].

На ... не влияет [*см. тж.* **Не влиять на, Оставаться неизменным при**]
The optogalvanic effect **enjoys immunity from** scattered laser light.
The space telescope **is immune to** (*or* **is unaffected by**) the blurring effects of atmospheric turbulence.

На небольшой глубине
A chain of magma chambers is present **at shallow depth** (*geol.*).

На него
Estimate the required depth of packing and the effect of counterdiffusion **thereupon.**

На некоторое время
We will delay the detailed consideration of acid-base theory **for the present.**
Let us concentrate **for a while** on two of these terms.
If, **for the time being,** we ignore reality, ...

На некоторое время предположим, что
Assume a nonrotating Earth **for the time being.**

На некоторое расстояние
The stone will rise **part way** up the mound and then ...

На некотором расстоянии
X-radiation can produce a darkening of a photographic plate **some distance away.**

На некотором расстоянии друг от друга
The antennas are placed (*or* spaced) **some distance apart.**
Numerous gauging (*измерительные*) stations are located **at intervals** on rivers.

На некотором расстоянии от
The capsule is mounted **some distance from** the actual pressure pickup.
Points **somewhat removed from** the wing ...
The point **is some distance away from** the optical axis of the lens system.

На неопределённое время
The wastes would remain there **for indefinite periods.**

На неопределённое расстояние
The ray path extends **indefinitely** beyond r_{rad}.
The waveguide extends **indefinitely** in all directions.

На неопределённую глубину
The sand extends **downward indefinitely.**

На несколько порядков (величины) выше (больше), чем
Its viscosity **is several orders (of magnitude) greater than ...**

На нет [*см.* **Сводить к нулю**].

На нём
The revolving superstructure consists of the rotating frame and the operating machinery **thereon.**

На никелевой основе
Nickel-base alloys of chromium are of particular importance.

На ничтожную величину
The temperature of the cold body is **only infinitesimally** lower than ...

На нужное расстояние
To pull the cutter into the work **the required distance, ...**

На нуль [*см.* **Устанавливать на нуль**].

На ... оборот [*см.* **Повернуть на один полный оборот**].

На обороте
As shown in Fig. 130 **overleaf, ...**

На обратном пути
This picture of the Moon was taken **on the homeward** (*or* **return**) **journey.**
To clean the belt **on its return trip, ...**

На один [*см. тж.* **На каждый**]
The vibrational energy **per** degree of freedom ...
Machining three parts at a time required only 3.02 hr, as compared to 8.02 hr **apiece** conventionally.

На один меньше
There will be **one fewer** intensive variable for that phase.
Decarboxylation of acids to form hydrocarbons containing **one less** carbon ...

На одной линии с
Off-loading cannot proceed unless the rails on the elevator platform **are in line with** the rails on the reciprocating track.

На одной оси с
Mount the laser generator and the see-through detector **in line with** the laser beam.
Steam cylinders **are in line** (*or* **coaxial**) **with** air cylinders.

На одном уровне с [*см.* **Находиться на одном уровне с**].

На одну часть
This method produces two parts of butyl alcohol **to each** (*or* **per**) **part of** acetone.

На орбите
A star **in orbit** is continuously accelerated about its companion.

На опыте
These arguments are tested **by experiment.**

На орбиту [*см.* **Выводить на орбиту, Выходить на орбиту**].

На основании [*см. тж.* **Исходя из**]
Instead of the pair of peaks that we might expect **based on** the chemical shift difference between..., we observe ...
Relying on such experiments, he concluded that ...
Based on a study of the molecular configuration of the compounds, G. Bertrand formulated a rule ...
These equations were derived by Baker

based on (*or* on the basis of) work by Ridenberg.
Product yields can be predicted **from** feedstock properties.
On the strength of these data some scientists suggested that.
This relation was developed **from** experimental observations.

На основании ряда .... соображений
They concluded, **on several** geochemical **grounds,** that ...

На основе I [*см. тж.* **Сплав на основе кадмия**]
Compositions **based on** ammonium nitrate are used for gas generators.

На основе II [*см. тж.* **Возникать на основе, Исходя из**]
These methods have been developed **around** conventional incoherent sources.
This machine has been developed **from** the famous gathering-arm Joy loader.
Enzymes may be classified **on a basis of** the types of substrates.
This permits transfer of power between two separate power systems **on a** variable-ratio **basis.**
The reaction was performed by ... **starting from** methyl-cyclohexane and utilizing ... as catalysts.
Using the calculated data **as the base ...**
A relatively simple system is built **around** a single microprocessor.
These pocket calculators were designed **around** metaloxide-semiconductor circuits.
A similar classification **on the basis of** ... is done in terms of ...

На основе гипотезы
Many of the properties of binary alloys ... can be explained **on the hypothesis that ...**

На основе которого [*см.* **На базе которого**].

На основе которого можно строить
The triple point is a convenient condition **on which to base** a temperature scale.

На основе ... соображений
The range of values of β_i for ... can be derived **on** physical **grounds.**

На открытом воздухе
This equipment is suitable for installation **out of doors.**
The new pallet is suitable **for** indoor and **outdoor use.**
The burner is designed **for outdoor service.**
View cameras are used in studios or **outdoors.**

На ощупь [*см. тж.* **Жирный на ощупь**]
The amount of heat contained per pound of fluid that can be detected **by feel** or by a thermometer is known as sensible heat.
These lines can often be recognized **by touch** as steps on the smooth polished surface.
Graphite **has a greasy feel** (*жирный на ощупь*), marks paper and acts as a lubricant.

На ... падает
Packaging **accounts for** a disproportionate amount of the total manufacturing cost.

На парашюте
The telescope is cut free from the balloon and returned **by parachute.**

На первой стадии
Early in [*or* **In the first** (*or* **initial**) **stage of,** *or* **In an early stage of**] the test no such data were available.

На первый взгляд
Certain structures that might appear **at first glance** (*or* **sight**) to be simply different confirmations actually represent two different chemical compounds.
At first glance it would seem that there is little correlation.
On the face of it, measuring the vibrations of a body seems a simple matter.

На первый план [*см.* **Выдвигать на первый план**].

На передней панели
One of three modes can be selected by means of push buttons **at the front of** the unit.

На переднем плане
The two ball mills **are in the foreground.**

На пересечении
The equivalence points are located **at the intersection of** lines of ...

На периферии
Centrifugal force is greatest **at the periphery.**

На петлях
A **hinged** door.

На плоскости
The coordinates of a point **in** (*or* **on**) **the plane ...**
Integrals are used to compute areas bounded by curves **in a plane.**

На площади
Apply the solution **over** a small **area.**
The impact force is distributed **over** a large **area.**

На поверхности I
Interactions between water molecules and ions **at the** crystal **surfaces ...**
The first product of combustion **at the surface of** coke is carbon monoxide.
Amorphous silicon oxidizes only **superficially.**

На поверхности II
Twenty five percent of the practical work is carried out underground while the **surface** and office work is carried out at ... (*min.*).

На поверхности Луны
The automatic chemical analyses were conducted directly **on the lunar surface.**

На поверхности раздела
Y_i is the mole fraction **at the interface.**

На ... поддерживается постоянная температура
The inner surface of the tube **is maintained** (*or* **kept**) **at a constant temperature.**

На подъёме
Oxygen steelmaking **is on the rise.**

На поздней стадии болезни
Bronchial adenocarcinomas often do not produce signs of pulmonary involvement until **late in the disease.**

На поздней стадии беременности
The manufacture of alpha-lactal-bumin is initiated **late in pregnancy.**

На полной скорости
The machine is running **at full speed.**

На полном ходу
When **in full operation,** the factory is intended to have an annual output of ...

На полную мощность [*см.* **Работать на полную мощность**].

На половине расстояния между ... и [*см.* **На полпути между ... и**].

На половинной мощности
Operations were conducted at half **capacity.**
The amplifiers operate **at half power.**

На полпути к
The temperature of the Moon is only about 1000°C at a depth **halfway to the centre.**

На полпути между ... и
This temperature fell **midway between** Venus **and** the Earth.
Free radicals lie **midway** (*or* **halfway**) **between** carbonium ions **and** carbanions.

На пользу человечеству
This energy can be used **for man's benefit.**
They used this knowledge **for the benefit of mankind.**

На полюсе
The south magnetic pole is not located **at the** true south **pole.**

"На попа" (*жарг.*) [*см.* **Поставленный "на попа"**].

На пороге
The phenomenon of superconductivity **is on the threshold** of large-scale technological application.
Today this technique **is on the threshold of** becoming a tool of fundamental importance in ...

На ... порядков длиннее, чем
The recognition time of the nucleotides by the polymerase **is** two **orders of magnitude longer than** in RNA synthesis (*biol.*).

На последнем курсе
The student **in his final year** considers ...

На постоянном уровне [*см.* **Поддерживать на постоянном уровне**].

На правильном пути [*см.* **Быть на правильном пути**].

На практике
This system is proving **in action** the benefits of applying modern technology to ...

In (actual) practice, ionic activities are often determined by ...

На ... предъявляется большой спрос [*см.* **В большом спросе**].

На прилагаемом рисунке
The type 30 unit is shown **in the accompanying figure.**

На примере [*см. тж.* **Иллюстрировать на примере глицина, Показано на примере**]
This type is illustrated by **the example of** diamond.
Using rhodamine 6G **as an example,** it can be shown that ...

На ... приходится
It is found that most of the mass **is accounted for by** particles whose radius is between 0.1 micron and 10 microns.
The more developed countries **account for** most of the world's environmental pollution.
The four types of hydrogenation **account for** the production of billions of pounds of ...
The cobra **is responsible for** the majority of the 25,000 deaths occurring each year from snake bite in India.
For every 100 grams of molecular hydrogen **there is** a gram of dust.

На продвинутой стадии [*см.* **Находиться на продвинутой стадии**].

На промежутке
If f is a function defined **on the** finite **interval from** x_1 **to** x_2, ...
If q_s varies **over the distance** s, ...

На противоположных концах
These groups **are at the opposite ends of** the benzene ring (*chem.*).

На протяжении
The magnetic field was uniform **over a length of** 12.5 cm.
Over the course of half an hour there were seven reductions in ...
The earthquake affected the level of the land **over a** 900-km **stretch of** shoreline.

На протяжении ... лет
Benign tumours often grow slowly **over** several years.

На ... процентов [*см. тж.* **Насыщенный на ... процентов**]
This reduces the labour for cleaning approximately **80 percent.**
To increase ... **by 5 percent**, ...
The contraction **of 2 percent of** the balloon volume ...
This bond is **50 percent** ionic.

На ... процентов меньше
The chemical bonds **are less** ionic **by a few percent** (*or* **a few percent less** ionic).

На пути [*см. тж.* **Помещать на пути**]
The number of molecules **in the path of** the light ...

На пути к [*см. тж.* **Находиться на пути к**]
The interstellar material through which the light passes **on its way to** the Earth ...
The light must pass through the solution **on the way to** the eye of the operator.

На равном расстоянии друг от друга
The holes **are evenly spaced** (*or* **equidistant**).
The posts **are located at regular intervals.**

На равных основаниях (*или* **правах**)
Shaft horsepower is a term which can be used almost **interchangeably** with brake horsepower, the difference being ...
Competing **on equal terms,** SO_3 and P_4O_{10} are stronger acidic compounds than silica.

На радиус [*см.* **Запиливать на радиус**].

На различные периоды времени
We immerse the part **for varying lengths of time** in a vat of blue dye.

На ракете [*см.* **Установленный на ракете**].

На раннем этапе развития
Early in the development of the egg, two protective envelopes are formed.

На ... раньше
Then the pulsar should arrive at periastron 0.04 second **early.**

На расстояние [*см. тж.* **Действовать на расстоянии**]
The atoms move back and forth **over a distance** that is ...

The stud should be screwed into the plate **a distance** equal to ...
When the rolls were separated **by this distance ...**
A pilot tunnel was driven ahead of the main tunnel **for a distance of** 9 ft.
Streams of incandescent hydrogen are shot out from the Sun's surface **for distances of** thousands of miles.
The mercury falls **(for) a short distance** within the tube.
The grinding heads can be moved transversely **through a distance of** 6 ft.

На расстоянии [*см. тж.* **Находиться на расстоянии**]
An image of Saturn made **at a range of** 162,000 kilometres shows ...
The distance through which the force acts ...
This explains how particles can act on one another **at a distance.**
The picture was made **from a range** (*or* **distance**) **of** 700.000 kilometres.
The nonuniformity must vary slowly **over distances of** the order of ...
The marker is readily visible **at 100** ft.
We shall be able to detect tornadoes **at a distance** by means of radar.
The dial is boldly marked and can be read **from a distance.**
The telemotor provides a means of moving the control valves **from a distance.**
Within a few feet of the obstacle ...

На расстоянии вытянутой руки
Hold the instrument **at arm's length.**

На расстоянии до ... километров от
The spacecraft passed **within** 700 **km of** Venus' surface.

На расстоянии ... друг от друга [*см. тж.* **Расположенные на расстоянии ... друг от друга**]
The grooves **are** *d* **apart.**
The two detectors **are placed** (*or* **spaced**) 100 ft **apart.**
The holes are spaced **at** 10 ft **intervals.**

На расстоянии от
The retarder **is** installed (**at**) 100 m **from** the surface.
The resistance measuring bulb can be located **at** any **distance** up to 3000 ft **away from** the instrument.
The switch is closed except when a descending cage is **within** a fixed **distance of** the shaft bottom.
The pitot-static tube is located **a** considerable **distance from** the airspeed indicator.
The transmitters were positioned **at** various **distances from** the ground track of the satellite.
The flame, seen **at a distance of** a few kilometres, may ...
A diffuse source of radius r_d is situated **distance** f **from** a fibre.

На расстоянии ... от Земли
The two galaxies appear **to be** about three million light years **away.**

На рисунке не показан [*см.* **Не показан**].

На рисунке показан (*или* **приведён**)
Figure 1 gives radiation lengths as a function of atomic number.
Figure 2 illustrates (*or* **demonstrates,** *or* **shows,** *or* **depicts,** *or* **exhibits,** *or* **displays,** *or* **presents**) a system that ...
A simple design **is illustrated** (*or* **shown,** *or* **presented,** *or* **displayed,** *or* **depicted**) **in** (*or* **on**) **Fig. 3.**
In Fig. 10 is shown (*or* **Shown in Fig. 10 is**) the circuit of ...
Referring to Fig. 17, we have the following pattern: ...

На самолётах (вертолётах *и т.п.*)
Air conditioning equipment for ground and **airborne** use ...

На самом близком расстоянии от Земли
Mars when **it is at its closest,** is briefly brighter than Jupiter.

На самом верху
At the extreme top ...

На самом деле [*см. тж.* **А на самом деле это не так, И это действительно так, Фактически**]
Now it is time to admit that the spacing between ... is not **in fact** constant ...

На самом же деле
What actually happens is that the accelerated proton keeps moving and ...

На север (запад, юг, восток) [*см.* **Направляться на север** *и т.п.*].

На севере [*см.* **На востоке, западе**].

На сжатом воздухе
The press can be operated **on air** alone for low-energy forming work.

На складе [*см.* **Иметь в запасе, Иметься в наличии, Храниться**].

На случай
The large quantity of water contained in an economizer provides reserve space **in the event** (*or* **in case**) **of a** sudden boiler overload.

На случай аварии
A 150 kW Diesel alternator is provided **for emergency use.**

На современной ступени развития
It is not possible, **in the present state of the art,** for a single-stage rocket to reach the speeds required.

На солнечной энергии
A **solar powered** water pump ...

На солнце
Unshielded thermometers **in sunlight** may indicate temperatures far above that of the air.

На ... сравнительно мало влияет
The threshold and saturation voltage levels **are relatively unaffected by** temperature variations.

На среде
The organisms are easily grown in the laboratory **(up)on** simple **media.**

На стадии (*или* **ступени**)
At this stage, there is very little increase in the resistance.
The process is still **in the** experimental **stage.**

На стадии проектирования
At the design stage.

На станке
The valve seat must be machined **in** (*or* **on**) **a lathe.**
Only one spindle at a time will be operated **on** this **machine** (*or* **machine-tool**).

На станке можно установить
The machine can take (*or* **accommodate**) a workpiece up to 4 ft long and ...

На стене [*см.* **Настенный**].

На стойке [*см.* **Смонтированный на стойке**].

На столе [*см.* **Настольный**].

На стыке между
Modulator-demodulators are needed **at the interfaces between** the communication network **and** the terminals and the data-centre equipment.

На судне [*см.* **На борту судна**].

На суше
On land, geothermal gradients have been measured in deep mines and boreholes.

На схеме показан (приведён)
The diagram (re)presents the three-component system.

На счётчике
This monitor provides a continuous indication of level **on a meter.**

На теоретической основе [*см.* **Ставить на теоретическую основу**].

На территории университета
On the campus of Columbia University ....

На топливе [*см.* **Работать на топливе**].

На трение [*см.* **Потери на трение**].

На углах
The centres of the atoms are supposed to lie **at the corners of** a cube.

На угол [*см. тж.* **Повернуть на угол**]
The coil was capable of rotating **through 180°** about an axis.

На ... указывает [*см.* **Указывать на**].

На уровне
The cold water cistern is fixed **at a** high **level.**
Raise the gauge to a height at which the sharp edge of the notch **is** exactly **level with** the top of the valve connection.
The surface of the liquid **is flush with** the floor of the tunnel.
Oxygen could have been maintained **at a level of** about 0.02% of the total composition of the atmosphere.
For electrons **in the** same principal **level ...**
On the molecular **level,** diffusion is the result of ...

На уровне глаз
The vacuum gauges are mounted **at** operator **eye level.**

На уровне земли
The airflow measured **at ground level** is due to ...
There is a chain-operated conveyor **at ground level.**

На уровне моря
At sea level.

На уровне полёта
At flight level.

На фоне [*см. тж.* **Вырисовываться на фоне**]
The telescope photographs the flashing light **against** (*or* **on**) **the background of** the stars.
We shall discuss these findings **against the backgrounds of** the trends shown in the preceding decades.
Any measurement must be made **against a background of** this noise.

На фото
The board shown **in the photo ...**
Shown in the photograph is ...

На ходу́
The adjustments can be made **while (the machine is) running.**

На холоде
Potassium reacts violently with water **in the cold.**

На холостом ходу́ [*см.* **Работать вхолостую**].

На целых 10 процентов
Small quantities of tin increase the ultimate strength of the cast iron **by as much as 10%.**

На ... частей
A solution of one part cleaner **to** three **parts** water ...

На частоте
A charged particle can oscillate **at** any **frequency.**
Stations transmitting **at** different **frequencies ...**
The signal was received **on a frequency of** 20.005 Mc.
Amplitude modulation is used **on frequencies** below 30 Mc.

На ... число
As of March 1, 56 plants were under construction.

На что указывает
The ammonia hydrate is a weak electrolyte in aqueous solution **as indicated by** an ionization constant of 1.65×10^{-5} at 25°C.

На шарнирах
A **hinged** bracket.

На широких просторах
In the vast expanses of the Pacific Ocean ...

На широте
These deposits are located **in the** middle **latitudes.**

На шкале
The pressure is read directly **on the** meter's **dial.**
The critical angle is read off **on the scales.**

На электроде
Chlorine is formed **at the** positive **electrode** and sodium hydroxide at the negative.

На этой стадии
At this point, a comet comes under the influence of Jupiter.
At this point (*or* **stage,** *or* **juncture**) we needed a new procedure.

На этом фоне
Against this background ...

На этом этапе
At this point (*or* **stage,** *or* **juncture**) in our research we began efforts to verify the existence of ...

На этот вопрос нельзя дать определённого ответа
The answer to this question is not known with certainty.

На 20% эффективнее, чем
1 g of manganese in the form of ... **is 20 percent as effective as** (*or* **20 percent more effective than**) the same weight of iron in the form of ...

На юге [*см.* **На востоке, западе**].

На 2/3 длины заклёпки
Drill a hole about **two thirds of the way through the rivet shank.**

На 1 октября 1982 г.
Data **are as of October 1, 1982.**

Набирать высоту (*авиа.*)
To gain height (*or* **altitude**).
As the airplane **climbs, ...**
The pilot attempted **to gain altitude** during takeoff.

Набирать скорость
To gather (*or* **pick up**) **speed.**

Набирать энергию
Here the electron has more time **to gain energy.**

Наблюдаемый
Benzedrine produces effects similar to those **seen** (*or* **observed**) when the sympathetic nervous system is activated.
The term amoeboid movement refers to the type of movement **seen in** animals.

Наблюдаемый объект
The object under observation.

Наблюдается тенденция к
The trend has been toward bigger and more sophisticated airplanes.

Наблюдатель видит
The equivalent image **appears to the viewer** two or more times during a rotation of 360°.

Наблюдать
No appreciable change in the rate of work hardening **was detected** (*or* **observed**).
Excessive vibration **was noted** in the suction line.

Наблюдать за [*см. тж.* **Следить за**]
During rocket firing the test stands can **be viewed** through a periscope.
The mine fans can **be watched** (*or* **observed**) from the central power station.

Наблюдать за ходом реакции
To follow the course of the reaction, ...

Наблюдаться [*см. тж.* **Иметь место, Происходить**]
Another major effect of topography **is seen** (*or* **observed**) in lowland sites.
Naturally occurring infections caused by ... **have been seen** in cattle, rodents, ...
Very little wear **is evident** (*or* **observed**).
The above effects **were noted** after irradiation of about 10^7 *r*.
These absorption bands do not **occur** in the vapour phase.
Frog skin **exhibits** (*or* **shows**) a potential difference of 20-90 mV with the inside positive.
An interesting situation **obtains** in connection with an externally heated cathode.
These sources **are** not **found** in rich clusters of galaxies.
High-output cardiac failure can occur, but **is** only **seen** infrequently (*med.*).
More than simple bonding between amino acids **was evidenced** in these reactions.
Also **present** in the spectrum were lines not familiar to me.

Наблюдаться в
Complex conservation **is exhibited** also by the same system.

Наблюдаются признаки
All coast lines **show evidence of** repeated rise and fall of the land relative to the sea.

Наблюдающийся
Graphite softening is a corrosion effect often **noted** (*or* **observed**) on cast iron pipes.

Наблюдение [*см.* **Беспрепятственное наблюдение над, Данные наблюдений, Находиться под наблюдением, Тщательное наблюдение**].

Наблюдение без приборов
Non-instrument observation.

Наблюдение за солнцем и звёздами
Solar and stellar observations.

Наблюдение с земли
The two stars are quite hot, as judged both from the rocket spectra and from **ground-** (*or* **earth-**)**based observations.**

Наблюдён
Most asteroids with a diameter greater than 50 kilometres **have** now **been surveyed.**

Набор [*см. тж.* **Ассортимент, Ряд, Серия**]
The laps are available individually or in six different **sets of** various sizes.
The plate holds **an assortment of** filters.

Набор данных
A set of data.

Набор запчастей и принадлежностей
A spares and accessories kit.

Набор термопар
A set of thermocouples.

Набросать общую картину
We **have sketched the broad outlines of** plate tectonics.

Наверно
It is likely that this range extends considerably.

Наверняка
The next generation **is certain** (*or* **sure**) **to** discard this model.
Such a deposit **is certain to be of** glacial origin.

Наверху [*см. тж.* **Внизу и наверху**]
The most oxidized carbon **is at the top.**
Control gear is housed in a compartment **on top of** the machine.
The operator sits **atop** the welder.

Наверху, внизу
The heat source **is at the top of** the system rather than **at the bottom.**

Наверху таблицы
The electrodes **at the top of the table** have a tendency to ...

Навеска
A charge (*or* **batch**) **of** 5.5 g **of** ... was placed in a glass tube.
A weighted sample (*or* **specimen**).

Навести [*см.* **Наводить**].

Навивать [*см.* **На который навит**].

Навигационные средства
Navigation aids.

Навинчивать на
Screw the complete assembly **onto** the threaded clock spindle.
Screw the union nuts **on to** the valve bodies.

Навит [*см.* **Намотан на**].

Навитый на
A heating coil **wrapped around** the column established a stable gradient of temperature.

Наводить на мысль
This suggests that ...

Наводить на правильный след
The event that happened **to put us on the right track** was the finding of ...

Наводить на фокус
The radiation **is brought to a focus** on the front face of the plate.

Наводить напряжение
The changing flux will **induce an** alternating **voltage** in ...

Наводить порядок в [*см.* **Приводить в порядок**].

Наводить телескоп на звезду
We pointed the telescope at (*or* **toward**) **the star.**

Наглухо скреплять
These two surfaces **are held securely together by** the clamps.

Наглядно [*см. тж.* **Исключительно наглядно**]
The difference is **conveniently** illustrated by expressing ...
In describing the state of positronium and quarkonium **it is** more **illuminating to** specify the orbital angular momentum, ...
The figure illustrates this difference **dramatically** by comparing the butene isomers.
This latter type is illustrated more **emphatically** by the example of diamond.
It is more **informative** to use a three-dimensional plot.
These considerations are summarized **pictorially** in Fig. 5.14.

Наглядно демонстрировать
This **has been clearly demonstrated** for methionyl-accepting types.

Наглядно иллюстрироваться
This statement **is readily illustrated by** the operation of a refrigerator.

Наглядно указывать на
The peak intensities **are descriptive of** the relative amounts of each amino acid ...

Наглядное изображение
Figure 5 is **a pictorial rendition of** the

proportions of crystals and liquid as a function of temperature.

Наглядный [*см. тж.* **Яркий**]
The term ... **is** more **descriptive** (*or* **illustrative**).
A **dramatic** proof of this is provided by ...
A **pictorial** model ...
A **lively** (*or* **vivid**) presentation of these ideas ...

Наглядный пример
A graphic (*or* **vivid,** *or* **striking**) **example of** what can be achieved with the plastic repair process ...
An illustrative example is furnished by Table 6.
As **a pictorial** (*or* **graphic**) example we consider flow around a convex wall.
The green paramecium provides **an apt illustration.**
There are two **clear examples of** tissue-specific alterations in ...

Нагнетать
Each pump is capable of **delivering** (*or* **supplying**) 510 tons of water per hour.
The air **was provided by** a blower.
The grout **is forced** (*or* **pumped**) **into** the voids in the foundation rock through holes drilled into the rock.

Наготове [*см.* **Быть наготове**].

Награждать
The Academy **bestowed** the prize **on** the discovery of ...

Нагревание [*см.* **При нагревании**].

Нагревание до ... градусов
Alkali halide crystals may be additively coloured by **heating to** several hundred **degrees** Centigrade.

Нагревание с помощью лазера
The feasibility of **laser-heating** a small dense plasma to thermonuclear conditions is discussed.

Нагревать до красного каления
To heat to redness.

Нагревать на [*см.* **Повышать температуру на**].

Нагреваться
The acid **heats up** considerably.

Нагреваться до белого каления
The fuel cups **attain white-hot incandescence.**

Нагретый до красного каления [*см.* **Накалённый докрасна**].

Нагружать предварительно [*см.* **Предварительно нагружён**].

Нагрузка [*см.* **Выдерживать нагрузку, Для большой нагрузки, Для малой нагрузки, Нести нагрузку, Под нагрузкой, Полезная нагрузка, При расчётной нагрузке**].

Нагрузка на
Loads on the transformer secondaries ...

Нагрузка при разрушении
Load at collapse.

Нагружённый
Bearings are used at all **load-carrying** points.

Над [*см.* **Алгебраическое действие над, Непосредственно над**].

Над водой
An **overwater** flight.

Над головой
The star **was** directly **overhead.**

Над катализатором
Dehydrogenation of a reduced azulene **over a** platinum **catalyst ...**

Над ... расположен
These strata **are overlain by** a sandstone layer.
In the Los Angeles area cool air **is overlain by** warmer air.

Над уровнем земли
At a specified altitude **above the ground ...**

Над уровнем моря
The volcano rises to an elevation over 4000 m **above sea level.**

Надводное судно
Ocean liners and other large **surface ships ...**

Надвое [*см.* **Пополам**].

Надевать на [*см.* **Одевать на**].

Надежда [*см. тж.* **В надежде на то, что; Возлагать надежды на, Оправдывать ожидания**]
There is no **hope for** advances in this field.

Наделять свойством
Dirac's quantization condition **endows** the magnetic monopole **with** certain **properties.**

Надеясь
In the hope of answering these questions, we embarked on a study of ...

Надеяться [*см. тж.* **Есть основания надеяться на то, что; Можно надеяться, что; Мы надеемся, что**]
One can **look forward to** a successful solution of ...
We **were hopeful of** finding (*or* We **hoped to** find) something of interest.

Надеяться на то, что [*см.* **Следует надеяться, что**].

Надёжные данные
Solid (*or* **Firm**) **data** are available only from the earth and other planets.

Надёжный
In order that Eq. (2) shall give a **good** value of *C* for an actual capacitor, ...
These burners are **dependable** (*or* **reliable**) and efficient in operation.
A **foolproof** method was needed for focusing the telescope.
We supply **high-reliability** capacitors.
This assumption is supported by **solid** evidence from actual processes in bacteria.
Trustworthy values must be calculated.

Надёжный в пределах
These values must be considered **reliable to** 0.05°A.

Надёжный в эксплуатации
The machine has proved completely **reliable in service** (*or* **operation**).

Надлежащий [*см. тж.* **Заданный, Соответствующий, Указанный**]
Appropriate amounts of solution were added to ...
Selection **of the proper** metal thickness is extremely important.

Надлежащим образом [*см.* **Должным образом**].

Надо [*см.* **Следует**].

Надобность [*см.* **По мере необходимости, При необходимости**].

Надрез [*см.* **С надрезом, Без надреза**].

Нажат
When the button **is (de)pressed, ...**
If the levers **are depressed** further, ...

Нажим кнопки
Depression of a push button initiates the welding cycle.

Нажим на
The flow is started by a few **squeezes on** the rubber bulb.

Нажимать кнопку
The operator **pushes** (*or* **depresses,** *or* **punches**) **a button** on the console.
Press the push button to initiate gas and water flow.
The scientists on Earth will **push the controls.**

Нажимать на
Bear down on the pneumatic hammer only sufficiently to hold the chisel against the work.
Do not **bear** heavily **on** the handle of the lapping tool.

Нажимать на рычаг
(De)press the lever.

Нажимом кнопки [*см. тж.* **Одним нажимом кнопки**]
The table is braked to rest **upon depression of the** stop **button.**

Назад [*см. тж.* **Вперёд**]
Tilt the shell **rearward** to pour off slag.

Назван в честь
The montmorillonite group **gets** (*or* **derives**) **its name from** Montmorillon, a town in France.
The name "illite" **honours** the state of Illinois.

Назван именем
The Shpolsky effect **is named for** its discoverer.

Назван по
The centrifugal casting process **is named from** the manner in which the metal is distributed in the mould.

Назван по имени
The Jurassic system **is named for** the Jura Mountains.

Название [*см.* **Быть известным под названием, Идти под названием, Идти под общим названием, Известный под названием, Как видно из названия, Носить название (*или* имя), Получать название, Это название объясняется тем, что**].

Название которого не указано
They used an **unspecified** (*or* **unnamed**) polymer at 100°C.

Название объясняется
The name "lithographic limestone" **is derived from** the use of the rock for lithography.
Historically, **the name** "aromatic" **arose from the fact that ...**
Aliphatic compounds **owe their name to** their original derivation from ...

Наземный
The new system is incorporated in two models, one airborne, the other a **ground-** (*or* **land-**)**based** unit.

Назначение [*см. тж.* **Двойная цель, Общего назначения**]
The function (*or* **purpose**) **of** the foaming agent is to cover the surface of the solution with ...

Называемый [*см. тж.* **Известный под названием**]
These are two Bessel functions of the third kind **designated** (*or* **referred to**) **as** (*or* **termed,** *or* **named,** *or* **called**) first and second Hankel functions.

Называется более точно [*см.* **Более точно называется**].

Называть [*см. тж.* **Получать название, Так назван потому, что**]
By a long slug **is meant** one which is long enough to be the subject of a steady-state extrusion.
Wiener **credited** the vacuum tube **as being** the major instrument of ...
This portion of the wave **will be denoted** (*or* **named,** *or* **designated,** *or* **called**) the stable section.
When the ratio is unity, the propeller **is described as** a square propeller.
This system **is designated as** Model M-50.
Such a plot **is** generally **identified as** a "Stress-Number of Cycles Curve".
This phenomenon **is known** as piping.
Such absorption **is termed** chemical.
This type of magnetism **is given the name** temporary magnetism.
Actinomycetales **are** often **spoken of as** "higher", "filamentous", or "mouldlike" bacteria.
This relationship **has been labelled as** Stefan's law.
When there are more than two alleles of a given gene, they **are said to be** multiple alleles.
The minimum current density needed to start lasing action in a diode **is termed** (*or* **referred to as**) the threshold current density.

Называть именем
The comet **was named for** (*or* **after**) the discoverer.

Называть общим именем
Other intermolecular forces **are** often **lumped together as** van der Waals forces.

Называться [*см. тж.* **Известен под названием, Носить имя**]
Terrestrial photogrammetry **denotes** that branch wherein photographs are taken from ...
This component **is designated** the solvent.
Such processes **are said to be** isothermal.
Such a case **is referred to as** coordinate covalent bonding.
Together, the rational numbers and irrational numbers **are spoken of as** (*or* **are said to be**) real numbers.

Называться именем
This function was developed by P. Langevin and **is** often **referred to by his name**.

Наиболее вероятно
The cracking **is most likely to** occur where the metal is weakest.

Наиболее вероятный [*см. тж.* **Вероятнее всего, Наиболее правдоподобный**]
The **most likely** (*or* **probable**) fuel for a fusion-power energy source is deuterium.

Наиболее густонаселённый
The most populous countries ...

Наиболее заметен [*см.* **Ощущаться больше всего**].

Наиболее известен как
This quantity **is most familiar as** the proportionality constant.

Наиболее известный
The best known example for this type of excitation is the helium-neon laser.

Наиболее известный в области
Most prominent in the investigation of neutron bombardment of uranium was Enrico Fermi's group in Italy.

Наиболее изученный [*см. тж.* **Изученный лучше всего**]
The Canadian shield is one of **the most extensively studied** areas of ...
The ammonia synthesis reaction is one of **the best-understood** (*or* **studied,** *or* **investigated**) cases.

Наиболее наглядно показан
The economy of the method **is best shown** (*or* **demonstrated**) **by** the following example.
The limitations of these arrangements **can best be appreciated from** the patterns in Fig. 15-4.

Наиболее напоминать
This machine **most closely resembles** the unit described in ...

Наиболее перспективный в отношении
The compounds **exhibiting the most promise for** storing energy are listed below.

Наиболее подходить для
This product **is best suited to** our operation.

Наиболее полезный в практической работе
The coefficient **of greatest practical utility** is the mutual-diffusion coefficient.

Наиболее правдоподобный
The most plausible (*or* **credible**) hypothesis is that ...

Наиболее пригодный для
Hyperbolic cooling towers **are best suited to** regions with high humidity.

Наиболее распространён
This disease **has a peak incidence** after the age of 55 to 60.

Наиболее распространённый [*см. тж.* **Наиболее широко используемый**]
Three of **the most commonly encountered** shapes are shown in Fig. 13.
The isotope **of greatest abundance** is ...
The two **most abundant** (*or* **widespread**) elements in the universe are hydrogen and helium.
Tables 1 and 2 list **the** ten **most plentiful** elements in the Earth's crust and in the human body.
We have starters in all **popular** sizes.

Наиболее редко
Colon cancer occurs **least often** in the descending colon.

Наиболее соотвествовать
This approach **is best matched to** the problem at hand.

Наиболее точно соответствовать
Find the number **to** which the mantissa **most closely corresponds.**

Наиболее удалённый
Aphelion is the point in a planet's orbit around the Sun where **it is farthest** (*or* **most distant**) **from** the Sun.
The farthest removed layer ...
These include **the** seven **outermost** satellites of Jupiter.

Наиболее удобный для
The quantity **best suited to** express the energy at which ...

Наиболее целесообразно [*см.* **Лучше всего**].

Наиболее часто [*см.* **Чаще всего**].

Наиболее часто встречаться [*см.* **Наиболее распространён**].

Наиболее широко использоваться
Optical view finders **are in most common use.**

Наиболее широко используемый
This is **the most-used** single-lens reflex camera.
Where mechanical or magnetic separation is not used, the process **most generally** (*or*

universally, *or* **extensively) employed** is that known as wet gravity concentration.
The reaction **that has enjoyed the widest application** is ...

Наиболее эффективно [*см. тж.* **Рекомендуется**]
This **can best be done** in a rotating turbine.

Наиболее эффективно использовать
In order **to make the best (use) of** the equipment ...
We can use this versatile machine **to best advantage** (*or* **most efficiently**).

Наиболее эффективно работать
The instruments **performed at their best.**

Наибольшая важность [*см.* **Представлять наибольшую важность для**].

Наибольшее количество
The two uses which have consumed **the most** [*or* **the greatest amount** (*or* **quantities**) **of**] argon are ...

Наибольшее приближение к
At its **nearest approach to** Neptune, Nereid comes to within 800,000 miles of the planet.

Наибольшее промышленное значение
The minerals of **chief commercial importance are** borax and kernite.

Наибольший [*см. тж.* **В максимуме**]
These parts show **the most** (*or* **the greatest,** *or* **the worst**) wear.

Наивысший расцвет [*см.* **Достигать наивысшего расцвета**].

Наилучшее приближение
The resulting substance may represent **the closest (possible) approach to** the ideal quantum gas.

Наилучший ... достигается путём
The mixing of fluids in pipe flow **is best accomplished** (*or* **achieved**) **by** employing high velocities.

Наилучший из них
Prior to 1920, reliance was placed mainly on mercury and other expansion thermometers. The Beckman thermometer represents **the acme among these.**

Наилучший метод
It may seem that the brewer's **best plan is to** devote all his resources to the production of beer.

Наилучшим образом [*см.* **Лучше всего, Наиболее эффективно**].

Наилучшим образом подходить для
This product **is best suited to** our operation.

Наилучшим образом соответствовать
"Simple" liquids **show the best correlation with** the linear plot.

Наименее известный
Of the three methods this one **is the least known.**

Наименее изученный
Pluto **is the least known** member of the solar system.
This subject **is the least understood** aspect of sedimentary rocks.

Наименее устойчивый к
Berseen **is the least tolerant of** the clovers **to** winter freezing.

Наименее часто [*см.* **Наиболее редко**].

Найден [*см.* **Находить, Обнаружен**].

Найдено, что
The average value **was found to be** 16 ± 3.
Similar hairpin loops **have been deduced to** exist in ... (*biol.*).
A crystal of potassium chlorate **was found neither to** float nor sink in a solution of bromoform at 25°C.

Найти [*см.* **Находить**].

Найти применение
Then mika wrapper type of insulation **was** again **taken up.**

Найти своё отражение в
All of this **was reflected in** a remarkable expansion of the computer industry.

Накалённый докрасна
The free halogen gas is passed over a mixture of the oxide with carbon or some carbonaceous material **at red heat.**
Red hot platinum ...

Накапливать [*см. тж.* **Собирать**]
We use a condenser **to build up** sufficient charge from the strobe's batteries.

Накапливать данные для
They **amassed the data for** a map of ...

Накапливать информацию
We **are compiling** (*or* **accumulating**) **information on ...**
The greatest amount of **information on** (*or* **about**) **... has been gathered** (*or* **amassed,** *or* **accumulated**) in temperate forests.

Накапливать опыт
As construction companies **gained** (*or* **accumulated**) **experience ...**

Накапливать энергию
The device **stores** mechanical **energy.**

Накапливаться [*см. тж.* **Скапливаться**]
Moisture **builds up** until the thawed soil is saturated.
Large amounts of tritium **are stockpiled** for nuclear weapons and for research in fusion power.
Moisture, oil and dirt **collect** (*or* **gather,** *or* **accumulate**) in the bottom of the air-filter sump.

Накачивать
The pump **delivers** (*or* **supplies,** *or* **feeds**) this water at a rate of 400 gal/hr.

Накладывать друг на друга
Three curves **are superimposed** for comparison.

Накладывать заплату
To apply patches to the tank wall, ...

Накладывать на предметное стекло микроскопа
The tissue **is mounted on a microscopic slide.**

Накладывать ограничение
When no quantum **restrictions apply, ...**

Накладывать ограничение на
There is no **restriction on** the way in which particles can be distributed over the individual energy levels.
Transfer inefficiency **imposes** (*or* **places**) **a limit(ation) on** the speed and number of transfers for a practical charge-coupled device.

Накладывать сетку на
A net was applied over the whole surface of the rock.

Накладывать слой на
Layers can **be put down on** a substrate quickly.

Накладывать условие [*см.* **Налагать условие, Ставить условие**].

Накладываться [*см. тж.* **Налагаться**]
Transverse waves **are superimposed on** the motion of the gas behind the shock.

Накладываться друг на друга
These two patterns **super(im)pose on one another** on the screen.

Наклон [*см. тж.* **Величина наклона, Иметь наклон, Пологий наклон, С наклоном**]
The slope of the line ...
The tilt of the vapour surface ...

Наклон к
The inclination of line *AB* **to** the horizontal also is indicated.

Наклон касательной к кривой
We shall henceforth speak of **"the slope of the curve"** as implying **"the slope of the tangent to the curve".**

Наклон кривой
This value can be obtained from **the slope of the curve.**

Наклон орбиты
The tilt (*or* **inclination**) **of the orbit with respect to** the orbital plane of the Earth ...

Наклон оси
The axial tilt (*or* **The tilt of the axis**) **of** Mercury ...

Наклон относительно оси
Changes of speed cause **a tilting of** the compass card **about** the north-south axis.

Наклонён на ... градусов по отношению к
The spin axis of comet Enoke **was tilted five degrees with respect to** the plane of ...

Наклонён относительно оси
When the compass card system **is tilted about** the north-south **axis, ...**

Наклонён по отношению к
The neodymium-glass disks **are tilted** (*or* **inclined**) **(with respect) to** the incoming laser beam.
The Earth's axis **is tipped to** the plane of its orbit.

Наклонён под углом
The plane of the Earth's Equator **is inclined to** the Sun's apparent orbit **by 235°.**
The plates a**re inclined at a** small **angle to** one another.
The pump operates best when **tilted at an angle of 10 or 15°.**
The orbit **is inclined 14 degrees (with respect) to** the equatorial plane.
The disk **is tilted at an angle of 15 degrees to** the plane of the galaxy.

Наклонный [*см. тж.* **В вертикальном или наклонном положении**]
The derrick has a **slanted** boom.
The feeder discharges the rock on an **inclined** belt.

Наклонять
Figure 18 shows how the electrode holders can **be inclined to** facilitate entry to curves, flanges, etc.
The furnaces can **be tilted** to facilitate pouring.
Bulldozer blades can **be tipped** forward or backward.

Наклоняться на ... градусов
The swivel type of milling head is normally arranged **to tilt 45 degrees** each side of the centre line.

Наконец
Finance, transportation, and **lastly** (*or* **finally**) communications are comprehensively discussed.

Наконечник [*см.* **Иметь наконечник, С наконечником**].

Накопить ряд убедительных доказательств того, что
Many investigators **have amassed a convincing body of evidence that** such interactions in the primitive atmosphere of the Earth are capable of producing ...

Накопление
Accretion (*or* **Accumulation**) **of** knowledge ...
The swift **accrual of** word power (*learning new words*) ...
A build up of mineral deposits resulting from the water evaporating on the hot piping ...
A piling up of deleterious mutations ...
This prevents **build up of** static electricity on one part of the structure, which can ...

Накопленный опыт [*см. тж.* **Весь накопленный опыт**]
There was little **backlog of** (*or* **accumulated**) **experience** on which to base new theories.
Experience (which has been) gained (*or* **accumulated,** *or* **gathered**) over a number of years ...

Налагаемый
The symmetry of the **imposed** field ...

Налагать друг на друга
We **superimpose** the two beams by the use of ...

Налагать на
If that diagonal **is laid down on** the line, ...
If a protractor **is laid over** a geometric angle ...
The frequency of the pitch **is superimposed on** the 5 megacycle impulse, ...

Налагать ограничение
The boundary conditions **impose** (*or* **place**) **the restriction** that ...
Similar **limits are** also **imposed** (*or* **placed**) **by** the detector.
The competing processes **set limits on** the injector signal.

Налагать отпечаток на
Magnetic reversals of the earth's field **leave their imprint on** rocks.

Налагать требование (*или* **условие**) **на**
This **places a constraint on** the design of a power supply for the computer: it must be capable of ...

Налагать условие [*см. тж.* **Ставить условие**]
We **impose the** following initial **condition: ...**

Налагаться (друг на друга)
The two probability distributions **superpose** (*or* **are superimposed**) at large *n*.

Налагаться на
A convective flux **is super(im)posed on** that due to diffusion.

Налево [*см.* **Направо**].

Налетать на [*см. тж.* **Падать на**]
Deuterons **strike** (*or* **impinge on**) stationary tritons.

Налетающий
The **impacting** meteorite left a deep crater.

Наличие [*см. тж.* **Имеющийся в наличии, Обеспечение**]
The availability of proper materials ...
The availability of powerful pulsed tunable dye laser has made it possible to ...

Наличный
The energy resources **(now) at hand** are sufficient to sustain ...

Наличный ассортимент состоит из
There are thirty models **to choose from.**

Наложен на
The radiofrequency interference **is superimposed on** the signal.
Superimposed on the outer shells **are** layers defined according to the physical state of the rock.

Наложение ... на
Superposition of Figs. 16 **and** (*or* **on**) 17 reveals good agreement of the results.

Наложение поля на
Consider the effect of **the imposition of a field of** O_h symmetry **on** the orbitals of an atom.

Наложение слоя
We found that we could protect the indium antimonide by **laying down a** third **layer of** silicon monoxide.

Наложенный на [*см.тж.* **Накладывать, Налагать**]
Heyn's printing method uses sheet silk **laid over** the specimen.

Наложить [*см.* **Накладывать, Налагать**].

Нам встречался
We have come across equipment where we found it very difficult to assemble the seals without damaging them.

Нам повезло
We were fortunate (enough) to discover the first source of X-rays ...

Нам удобно
We can conveniently discuss such reactions in terms of ...

Нам хотелось бы
We would like to see engineering included within the framework of ...

Наматывать на
The cables **are coiled around** the pipes.
The coil **is wound on** a metal form.

Наматывать плёнку
To wind a film.

Намечать на
The launching **has been set** (*or* **planned**) **for** October.

Намечать отверстие
It is good practice first **to locate the hole** with a drill of smaller diameter.
The location for each **hole** should **be spotted on** the pipe **with** a centre punch.

Намечать пути к
The study **directed the way to** improvements in the technique.

Намечаться
No similar trend **is evident** among the moons of Saturn.
The theory will take years to develop, though its elements **have surfaced** already for the glow discharge and the flame.

Намеченный [*см. тж.* **Предполагаемый**]
The improvements **intended** (*or* **contemplated,** *or* **planned,** *or* **envisaged**) must be weighed against the savings that they may provide.
The operation **to be performed.**

Намеченный к
Such units **are contemplated** (*or* **scheduled,** *or* **planned,** *or* **slated**) **for** installation in the near future.

Намеченный срок
The target date for completion is January.

Намного [*см. тж.* **Значительно**]
This makes the machines **far** (*or* **much,** *or* **considerably**) easier to move.

The inductance is measured at a frequency **well** above the self-resonant frequency of the capacitor.

Намного более [*см.* **Значительно более**].

Намного более продолжительный, чем другие
Precambrian was the first and **by far the largest** interval in geological history.

Намного больше [*см. тж.* **Значительно превосходящий**]
Matter would then be capable of attaining a velocity **far beyond that of** light.

Намного больше всех других
The pipeline **is by far the largest** in Indonesia.

Намного больше, чем
A diver can do useful work down to 5000 ft — **far in excess of** (*or* **vastly larger than**) all previously predicted limits.

Намного больший
And this is in spite of the **vastly greater** mass of the Sun.

Намного выше
A laser operating **far above** the threshold ...
Some of the new superconductors will be superconducting **well above** the present region.

Намного меньше
Usually **many fewer** microgametes are produced than macrogametes.

Намного меньше, чем
This density is **far** (*or* **much**) **less than** is obtainable by ...

Намного превосходить
Titanium fasteners **are** often **vastly** (*or* **much**) **superior to** identical steel fasteners.

Намного раньше, чем
The spark-plug electrodes ignite the mixture **far in advance of** the normal ignition spark.

Намотан на
The electric heating cables **are coiled round** the pipes.
The conductor **is wound on** (*or* **around**) an iron cylinder.

Намотанный на [*см.* **Туго намотанный на каркас**].

Нанесение на
The process of **applying** a coating of zinc **to** the surface of steel ...
The application of a fused vitreous coating **to** metal surfaces ...
By **spreading** a monomolecular layer of oleic acid **upon** an aqueous solution of egg albumin ...
Capillary columns may be prepared by **coating** the stationary phase **on to** the walls of the tube.
The application of a drop of hydrochloric acid **to** the mineral surface ...

Нанесение слоя ... между
By **coating** gelatin **layers between** the emulsion layers ...

Нанесён
A scale (*шкала*) ranging from 0 to 3/32 **is marked off on** each of the faces.

Нанесён на
The stationary phase **is coated on to** a solid support.
A thin film of the liquid **is supported on** a filter disc.

Нанесённое повреждение
Damage wrought (*or* **inflicted**) **by** explosions ...

Нанесённый ветром [*см. тж.* **Отложения, нанесённые ветром**]
The sea floor is often dominantly **wind-blown** dust.
A **wind-built** dune ...

Нанесённый на
A liquid **coated on(to)** a solid support ...

Нанесённый на график
Experimental points **entered** (*or* **plotted**) **on** the graph are ...

Нанести последний удар по
Faucault's experiment was widely interpreted as **having placed the final nail in the coffin** of the particle theory of light.

Нанизанный на
A digital computing device usually consists of counters **strung on wires.**

Наносить [*см.* **Покрывать**].

Наносить деления с интервалами в ... минут
The rotary dial **is calibrated in 3-minute increments ...**

Наносить информацию на ленту
The information **is entered on** standard tape.

Наносить краску
Printing presses are not able to **apply** layers of **ink** of different strength.

Наносить на
Apply the solution **over** a small area.
Gold dissolved in mercury **is applied to** the article to be coated.
The gaseous mixture **is deposited on** a surface.
The liquid stationary phase **is coated on to** an inert solid support.

Наносить на график
A plot is sketched for the plate darkening as a function of ...
In a rubidium-strontium diagram, the ratio of strontium 87 to strontium 86 **is plotted against** (*or* **versus,** *or* **vs**) the ratio of rubidium 87 to strontium 86.
Using the above data, we **plot** sensitivity curves.
Crystal frequencies **are plotted against** (*or* **versus,** *or* **vs**) channel frequencies.
The energy of a group **is graphed** as a function of the electric field.

Наносить на карту
These stars **have been mapped** (*or* **plotted on a map**).

Наносить наибольшие потери
These species **are the costliest of** insect pests.

Наносить огромные потери
Volcanic eruptions and earthquakes **have taken enormous tolls in** lives and property throughout the ages.

Наносить повреждение
To inflict damage on the machine ...

Наносить разбрызгиванием
The paper **is sprayed with** colouring reagents.

Наносить серьёзный вред
This pollutant may **have a severe impact on** the population.

Наносить сетку
If a square **grid is marked on** the face of a slug which is then extruded, the grid will be deformed.

Наносить слой на [*см. тж.* **Покрывать слоем**]
A thin **layer** (*or* **film**) **of** semiconductor **was applied on** the surface of ...
Books **are** then **given a coat of** glue along the sewed back edge.
Another **coat of glue is applied over** the back of the book.

Наносить ущерб
The potential productive capacity of the mine **will** not **be impaired** [*or* **(adversely) affected**] **by** the experiment.

Наносить черту
The barrel on which the knob turns **is inscribed with** horizontal **lines.**

Наносить шкалу
The gauges **are calibrated with** both pressure and corresponding temperature **scales.**
The glass tube is mounted on a piece of wood which **has a scale marked on it.**
The circumference of the protractor **is graduated with a scale** marked in degrees.
The ruler **is graduated to an** inch **scale.**
The straightedge portion of the plotter **is engraved with** a number of **scales.**

Наносить эмульсию на
To apply emulsion to a specimen ...

Наноситься на
Corrosion-resistant pure aluminium **is clad to** a strong duralumin base.
The coating **is installed to** the inside walls of laminated resin tubing.

Наоборот I [*см. тж.* **А не наоборот, В противоположность этому**]
The propulsion engines for aeroplanes must operate continuously during the flight. **In contrast** (*or* **By contrast**), space vehicles coast freely during practically all of their useful lives.
Such methods are difficult as well as tedious and require large amounts of starting material. Chromatography, **on the other hand,** is simple, rapid, and ...
Quite the reverse.

Наоборот II [*см. тж.* **Бывает и наоборот, В противоположность этому, И наоборот**]
For many professionals, it was love of high country which attracted them to geology, rather than **the other way (a)round** (*or* **about**).
Conversely, efficiency increases as the cut-off ratio decreases.
To the contrary, both polynucleotides reacted more strongly with ...
The abdominal ganglia, **on the contrary,** vary greatly.

Написание формулы в виде
The arrangement of the formula in this form is in accord with ...

Наполнен [*см. тж.* **Заполнен**]
Such columns **are packed with** a solid stationary phase.

Наполненный [*см. тж.* **Заполненный**]
Turbidity currents are dense masses of water **charged** (*or* **filled**) **with** sediment.

Наполненный воздухом
Air-filled parts of an aerostat ...

Наполненный на 3/4 [*см.* **Заполнен на 3/4**].

Наполнять и опорожнять
A single pump serves **to fill and empty** the vessel.

Наполнять сжатым воздухом
A rubber bag **is inflated by** compressed air.

Наполняться
The depression **fills with** water to form a lake.

Наполовину выполнен
The work **is half done.**

Наполовину дешевле
This machine **is half as expensive** (*or* **twice as cheap**), although capable of the same duty.

Наполовину заполненный
The glass **was half-filled with** water.

Наполовину меньше [*см.* **В два раза меньше, чем; Меньше вполовину**].

Наполовину уменьшать
Redesigning cuts the number of operations **in half.**
This **reduces** residence time **by (one) half.**

Напоминать [*см. тж.* **Близко напоминать, Больше напоминать, В общем напоминать, Несколько напоминать**]
This behaviour **is reminiscent** (*or* **reminds one**) **of** that of graphite.
This relationship **bears a resemblance to** (*or* **resembles**) Beer's law for light absorption.
This is called a delta system, because its configuration **is suggestive of** (*or* **like**) the Greek letter Δ.

Напоминать в отношении [*см.* **В отношении**].

Напоминать во всех подробностях (деталях)
The second experiment **resembles** the first **in every detail.**

Напоминать друг друга [*см.* **Внешне напоминать друг друга**].

Напоминать по своему принципу действия
The unit **resembles** the Ludlow machine **in its principle of operation.**

Напоминающий
These inclusions give agate an appearance **reminiscent of** familiar natural scenes.

Напомним, что
Recall (*or* **It will be recalled,** *or* **You will recall**) **that** this control system is unstable.
The spin-down ladder, **it will be remembered** (*or* **recalled**), extends one rung lower than ...
We are reminded that the fields in this expression are those of the absorbing waveguide.

Направлен в сторону
The arrow **points toward** the more electronegative element.
The two vectors **point in** opposite **directions.**

Направлен в сторону, противоположную Солнцу
Comet tails **point away from the Sun.**

Направлен вверх
The arrow **is pointing up(wards).**

Направлен вдоль или против
Its magnetic field **is aligned with** the external field **or is opposed to it.**

Направлен вниз
The arrow **is pointing down(wards).**

Направлен к
The force of gravity **is directed toward** the centre of the Earth.

Направлен на
The report **is aimed at** promoting a better understanding of ...
Primary X-rays **are directed on to** a secondary target.
A beam **is directed at** a target.
The telescopes **were trained on** quasars.

Направлен на цель
When the beam **is on the target ...**
All this **is directed to** increasing production.
Considerable research **is** currently **directed towards** the operation of ...
When the telescope **is directed towards** a radiant surface, ...
The antenna **will be pointed towards** the Earth when the satellite is too low.

Направлен наружу
The radiation from the solar nebula **is directed outward.**

Направлен одной стороной к
The Moon **keeps the same side toward** (*or* **presents one side to**) the Earth.

Направлен от нас
The stream **is aimed away from us.**

Направлен под углом
If polar bonds **are directed at** such angles, ...

Направлен противоположно
The bar magnet **is in opposition to** an applied magnetic field.

Направление [*см. тж.* **В западном направлении, В направлении, В обратном направлении, В одном направлении, В продольном направлении, В противоположном направлении, В различных направлениях, Вдоль направления, Идти по направлению, Менять направление на обратное**]
An aerodynamic moment of the opposite **sense to ...**
The sense of the lines **is** clockwise.

Направление вращения
The pulleys have **the** same **sense of rotation.**

Направление исследований
This **line** (*or* **avenue**) **of inquiry** (*or* **investigation**) was very fruitful.

Направление магнитного поля
The sense of the magnetic field.

Направление полёта
The course of the flight (*or* **The flight direction**).

Направленная сила
A directional force.

Направленность
One of the detector's drawbacks was the lack of **directionality.**

Направленный
In the presence of a **directional** field ...

Направленный в сторону, противоположную
The side of the Moon **facing away from** the Earth ...
The register portion of the mandrel is **facing away from** the machine.

Направленный вверх (вниз)
Upward- (Downward)-directed jets ...

Направленный вдоль оси
Enough **axially directed** light goes back into ...

Направленный влево (вправо, вверх, вниз)
The **leftward (rightward, upward, downward)** line ...

Направленный внутрь (наружу)
Macromolecules are positioned here with an **inwardly directed** negative and **outwardly directed** positive end.
An **inward- (outward)-directed** pressure ...

Направленный к северу *и т.п.*
The **northward-directed** polar axis ...

Направленный к центру

This **centrally directed** acceleration is necessary to ...

Направленный луч
This neutron star emits **a directional** radio **beam.**

Направленный на [*см. тж.* **Предназначен для**]
Increasing attention must **be directed to** the elimination of such defects.
A parabolic mirror **aimed at** the transmitter ...

Направленный на север *и т.п.*
The **north-seeking** end of the needle ...

Направленный наружу
An **outward-directed** force ...

Направленный под углом [*см.* **Компонента, направленная под углом**].

Направленный противоположно
Electrons induce a magnetic field **in opposition to** the applied field.

Направлены в противоположные стороны
The particles must **be oppositely directed** after collision.

Направлять [*см. тж.* **Повёрнут в направлении**]
It is usually found more efficient **to lead** (*or* **direct**) the vapour **to** the low-pressure casing.
The light **is led** (*or* **guided**) **to** the slit.
Many patients **are referred to** a geriatric clinic with the diagnosis of ...
In this way the energy, spread over a wide range of frequencies, **has been channelled** (*or* **directed**) **into** a narrow band.
The liquid **is directed to** the proper tanks.
The carbon dioxide **is** then **sent to** the ammonia synthesis reactor.

Направлять в больницу на
Where there is doubt, **hospital referral for** bone biopsy is necessary.

Направлять в отвал [*см.* **Отправлять в отвал**].

Направлять излучение на
A pattern is impressed on the photoresist by **shining** ultraviolet **radiation on** it through a mask.

Направлять к
These ions can **be directed toward** a detector.

Направлять на
If a high-power laser beam **is applied to** a particle, ...
Further research should **be directed to** optical focusing systems.
The efforts **are directed toward** finding the optimum solution.
A laser beam **was directed at** (*or* **to(ward)**) a particle a few microns across.
The device **directs** a 150 psi stream of high-velocity coolant **at** the wheel to remove chips.
The beam of electrons **is directed onto** the surface of the crystal.
The jet of hot air can **be focused on** individual components.
To play a jet of water **over** (*or* **on to**) the surface of ...
The arc **is played against** the work.
Metal spraying is a process in which a very fine spray of molten metal **is projected on to** the material to be galvanized.
With the television cameras **trained on** him ...

Направлять на правильный путь
It was Hooke's method that **set** Newton **on the right track.**

Направлять свет на
This backward motion can be readily seen if one **shines** laser **light on** smoke particles floating in the air.

Направлять телескоп на
We **aimed** (*or* **pointed**) **the telescope at** (*or* **directed the telescope toward**) the star.

Направляться
If the ship **is headed** downstream, ...
When an electric field is applied, the ions **set off to** the oppositely charged electrode.

Направляться на север *и т.п.*
The group of geologists **headed North,** etc.

Направляющийся на север *и т.п.*
Imagine a plane **heading due north.**

Направо
The entire plate moves **toward the right** (*or* **rightwards**).

Напрашиваться
In simple cases only one logical bonding arrangement **suggests itself.**

Напрессовывать на
The shaft sleeve **is pressed onto** the shaft by means of a hydraulic press.

Например [*см. тж.* **В качестве примера, Для примера, Как например, Скажем**]
Among other things, the paper stated that ...
The direction of a light ray can be changed by passing it from one medium to another, **as** from air to water.
For iron, **as an example,** the density would be equal to ...
Michelangelo, **for one,** protested against ...
This Group was previously known as the Inert Gases or Rare Gases. As will be seen, argon **for one** is certainly not rare, and xenon and krypton are not inert.
Once the ordered arrangements have been disrupted, **such as** by melting (or dissolving) the compound ions can move more freely.
Thus for a rectangular or square aperture the wavefront may be subdivided into ...
For one example (*or* **thing**), they were able to synthesize a number of amino acids from ...
By way of example (*or* **By way of illustration,** *or* **To cite an example,** *or* **For example,** *or* **For instance**), ...
To illustrate, ...
To take an illustration, ...
To take one (*or* **an**) **example, ...**
After capturing one type of carrier, **say,** an electron, the centre would become negatively charged.
These materials include some of the rare earth elements, **such as** caesium.

Напруживать кольцо
The ring is then ready for **springing over** the bucket **into** its groove.

Напрягать предварительно [*см.* **Предварительно напрягать**].

Напряжение [*см.* **Выдерживать напряжение, Давать напряжение, Наводить напряжение, Повышать напряжение, Подвергать напряжению, Снимать напряжение**].

Напряжение на клеммах
The voltage across the terminals.

Напряжение на конденсаторе
The voltage across the capacitor.

Напряжение, приложенное к
Voltage impressed (*or* **imposed**) **across** the capacitor must be limited.

Напылять
A thin layer of metal **is evaporated onto** the sample.
This product can **be sprayed** (*or* **sputtered**) **on.**

Наравне с
The term "neoplasm", meaning "new growth" is often used **interchangeably with** the term "tumour" to signify a cancerous growth.

Нарастание давления
The build-up (*or* **increase**) **of pressure.**

Нарастание тока
The build-up of current.

Нарастать
As pressure **is built up,** the blank is bulged to fill the die cavity.

Наращивать
In this way layers of semiconductor can **be built up.**

Нарезанный под болт
The device has a tapped plunger **to accept a** standard **bolt.**

Нарезать под
The burner bodies **are** drilled and **tapped for** a 1/2 in. standard pipe oil line.
These valves consist of a casting **threaded** at each end **for** standard pipe.
The plate should **be threaded to receive** the bolt.

Наружная поверхность
The exterior of the tube is spray coated.
The outside of the airship envelope is coated with aluminium paint.
The inner and **outer surfaces of** the membrane ...

Наружная часть
Both **the** interior and **exterior** are coated with enamel.
The outer part of the Solar System ...

Наружное освещение
Outdoor lighting.

Наружный
All **exterior** parts are finished in polished nickel.
Combination tools are arranged for cutting an **external** thread and tapping a hole at the same time.
The capillary tube is encased in an **outer** protecting tube.
The **outer** circumference of a gear wheel ...
The pressure at the bottom of the storage tank is always greater than that of the **outside** air.

Наружный диаметр
The outside (*or* **outer**) **diameter.**

Наружный слой [*см.* **Внутренние и наружные слои**].

Наружу [*см. тж.* **Направлен(ный) наружу**]
To pass from the inside to **the outside of** the fuel tube, ...
The liquid entering ... is thrown **outward** by centrifugal force.

Нарушать I
This approach **violates** the basic principle for optimum performance.

Нарушать II
Substrate analogues can **disrupt** normal cell metabolism.

Нарушать атомную решётку
The high-energy particles will **disrupt** (*or* **break down**) **the lattice of atoms** (*or* **the atomic lattice**).

Нарушать параллелизм
Heavy pressure **will force** the two scales **out of parallel.**

Нарушать правило
Only for molecules exposed to strong magnetic fields **is** this selection **rule** easily **violated** (*or* **broken**).

Нарушать принцип
It is possible that a rarefaction shock **would** not **violate the** entropy **principle.**

Нарушать работу
This **will** not **disturb** (*or* **upset,** *or* **disrupt**) **the** normal **operation of** the system.

Нарушать равновесие
The impeller has become partially clogged so that **the balance is disturbed.**
Any movement of the hand-wheel displaces the slider, and thus **upsets the** electric **balance.**

Нарушать связи [*см. тж.* **Разрывать связи**]
To break bonds in complex protein, ...

Нарушать симметрию
The anisotropy **breaks the symmetry of** the fibre.

Нарушать структуру
This **disrupts the** electronic **structure of** the molecules.

Нарушаться
The law **breaks down** at high voltages.
Parameter quantization can be done in such a way that stability **is** not **impaired** (*or* **affected**).

Нарушен
Once the ordered arrangements of the solid state **have been disrupted, ...**

Нарушение вакуума
Deterioration in vacuum.

Нарушение плёнки
When **the film is ruptured, ...**

Нарушение правила
We cannot write similar structure for ... without **violating the** octet **rule.**

Нарушение решётки (*физ.*)
The disruption of a lattice.

Нарушение связей [*см.* **Разрыв связей**].

Наряду с [*см. тж.* **А также**]
The reaction produces, **among** other products, copper nitrate, ...
This gas contains the hydrogen and nitrogen components **along with** gaseous impurities.
Figure 1 shows a neutron-gamma log **alongside** the corresponding natural-gamma-ray log.
In parallel with the increase in carbon-dioxide in the atmosphere there also has been a rise in suspended particulate contamination.

Наряду с ... он обладает
The strength of copper **is accompanied by** high ductility.

Наряду с ... происходит
Hand in hand with an increase in E_g with increasing x **is** a decrease in the refractive index.

Нас в основном интересует
Our prime (*or* **main**) **interest here is with** the practical aspect of the results.

Нас интересует только
Our concern (*or* **interest**) **is only with** the scalar quantity U.

Нас ожидают сюрпризы в области
Some surprises are in store in hot and cold forging of metals.

Насаженный на ось
The compass in its simplest form consists of a small bar magnet, **pivoted** in the centre, and mounted on bearings.

Насаживать на I
These tyres **are clamped on to** special wheels.

Насаживать на II
A burner tube **is extended by** a silica tube (*На трубку ... насажена*).

Населённый [*см.* **Густонаселённый район**].

Населять
Many of these fishes **inhabit** warm or cold fresh waters.

Населять одну и ту же среду
Even animals that **shared the same environment** were not identically affected.

Насквозь
To obtain good heating efficiency, this ratio is usually 3:1 when the work is to be heated **all the way through** and 10:1 when it is to be surface hardened.

Насколько видит глаз
The new seismic scar runs **as far as we** (*or* **one**) **can see.**

Насколько возможно [*см. тж.* **По мере возможности**]
Extend the line **as far** across the board **as possible.**
All these instruments should **so** (*or* **as**) **far as possible** be grouped together.

Насколько известно
Eastern Quebec and, **so** (*or* **as**) **far as is known,** the Asbest region in the Urals produce chrysolite.

Насколько можно установить
As far as could be determined, the action of this protein was specific for ...

Насколько нам известно
To our knowledge (*or* **To the best of our knowledge,** *or* **As far as we know,** *or* **So far as we know**) such methods have never been employed.

Насколько ошибочный
How much would the calculated packed height **be in error** if axial dispersion were ignored?

Наследственные черты [*см.* **Передача наследственных черт**].

Настаивать на
There is considerable pressure from environmental groups **to** reduce pollution of the river.

Настало время [*см. тж.* **Пора**]
The time is right (*or* **ripe**) **to** try ...

Настенный
The section is served by **wall-mounted** cranes.

Настолько
The Sun **is so much** bigger than any other body in the vicinity that ...

Настолько выше, что
This ratio **is so much larger that** the core volume is considerably greater for the same magnetic densities.

Настолько глубоко войти в нашу жизнь, что
Synthetic polymers **are so much a part of our everyday lives that** we would have to make some drastic changes to get by without them.

Настолько горяч, что до него нельзя дотронуться
Rock in the walls of deep mines **is too hot to touch.**

Настолько же [*см.* **Ничуть не менее**].

Настолько, что
Provision is made for indicating the point at which the honing stones have become worn **to an extent that** they need to be replaced.

Настольная ЭВМ
Another typical microcomputer application **is the desk-top** (*or* **-type**) **computer.**

Настольный
We are already witnessing the advance of the **desk-top** microcomputer to capture the middle ground of calculation work.
A **tabletop** version of the Van de Graaff generator is widely seen in classroom demonstrations.

Настоятельно рекомендовать
They **strongly recommended** three-phase motors.

Настоятельно рекомендуется
It is strongly recommended that the air supply to the controller be clean, dry and oil free.

Настоящее время [*см.* **В настоящее время, До настоящего времени, Используемый в настоящее время, К настоящему времени**].

Настоящий
The model demonstrates a number of features that are characteristic of **full-scale** tornadoes.

Настраивать на
The battery-supply bridge **is set to** the most sensitive range.
The circuits should **be tuned to** 3.58 Mc.
The instrument **is set at** the chosen wavelength.
When the laser radiation **is tuned to** specific frequencies ...

Настраивать на волну
Then the laser **is tuned to** this **wavelength.**

Настраиваться
The amplifier **is tunable over** the entire 6-gc satellite communication band.

Настроен в пользу [*см.* **Высказываться в пользу**].

Настроен на
If the applied laser radiation **is tuned to** the centre of the Doppler profile ...

Настроенный на
Consider a laser beam **tuned to** resonance for an atom at rest.

Настроить на частоту
Another possibility would be a tunable laser that could **be placed on the** precise **frequency** desired.

Наступает время
There comes a time when the cluster traverses the galactic disk.

Наступает момент
As the flight speed increases, **there comes a point** (*or* **a time**) **where** the flow reaches the local speed of sound.

Наступать
A change **comes** when you raise this number to a ... power.
The repulsion between molecules **sets in** at small intermolecular distances.
Convection **sets in** (*or* **begins**) **when ...**

Наступать на
The sea **encroaches upon** the continent.

Наступать после
In the elderly this malaise commonly **follows** thyroid ablation.

Наступление [*см. тж.* **С наступлением**]
Onset of the infection is preceded by trauma of the area.
The upward migration of methane may contribute to **the triggering** (*or* **onset**) **of** earthquakes.

Наступление болезни
Onset of the disease is usually rapid.

Наступление эры
The superiority of Democritus' model was not recognized until **the dawning of the age of** science.

Насухо протирать [*см.* **Протирать насухо**].

Насчёт [*см.* **А как насчёт**].

Насчитываться
No less than 60 offsets **can be counted** on the eastern boundary of the Pacific plate (*geol.*).

Насчитываются миллионы
Other galaxies **number in the millions.**

Насыпа́ть
Pour in the requisite amount of catalyst.

Насыщенный бромом
Bromine-laden air ...

Насыщенный на ... процентов
Dry air would become **90 percent saturated with** water.

Наталкивать на
I **was led to** investigate such devices by three considerations (*На изучение этих устройств меня натолкнули...*).

Наталкиваться на [*см.* **Ударяться о**].

Наталкиваться на барьер
The electrons **are confronted by** a potential-energy **barrier.**

Натуральная величина [*см.* **В натуральную величину**].

Натуральных размеров
A **full-size** propeller.
A **full-sized** dummy or structural model.

Натыкаться на
We **have** accidentally **stumbled** [*or* **hit** (*sl.*)] **on** the form of graphite with the best properties for our purpose.

Натыкаться на препятствие
This is what happens when water waves **run into** (*or* **meet with**) **an obstacle.**

Натягивать
Pull the thread **taut with** the pencil and draw ...

Натягивать на [*см. тж.* **Одевать на**]
When the belt **is stretched over** the pulley ...

Натяжение [*см.* **Подвергаться натяжению или сжатию**].

Натяжение пружины
The reduced pressure acts on the valve and will rise until it is just balanced by **the pull of the springs.**

Натянутая пружина
The pull of **a stretched spring.**

Натянутый [*см. тж.* **В натянутом состоянии**]
The coil is supported by a fine wire **in tension.**
The wires stretched along the street **are** as **taut** as harp strings.

Наука о
Aerostatics is **the science concerned** (*or* **dealing**) **with** (*or* **the science that treats of**) the equilibrium of ...
Acoustics can be defined as **the science of** sound.

Наука о планетах
Planetary science.

Наука физика
The science of physics.

Научный сотрудник [*см.* **Исследователь**].

Находить I [*см. тж.* **Вычислять, Искать, Можно найти в, Найдено, что; Обнаруживать, Определять, Прийти к**]
Once the function **has been arrived at** (*or* **found**), ...
The general shape of the ray paths **can be deduced from ...**
It would be important **to identify** the pathways by which ...
To help you **locate** specific terms in the text, ...
These two unknowns cannot **be evaluated** (*or* **found**) **from** the single equation.
The mass of the Earth **was worked out** (*col.*) by another method.
The designers's goal is **to arrive at** a proper economic balance of investment and operating costs.
The instrument quickly **locates** (*or* **localizes,** *or* **detects,** *or* **spots**) lost circulation zones.
The torpedo **locates** its target by acoustic means.
The rocket **seeks** its target by acoustical homing.

Находить II [*см. тж.* **Дано ... , Найти**]
Given: The engine consumes 27.5 gallons per hour ...
Required: Amount of gasoline consumed.

Находить III
Look up the logarithm of the number preceding the power of 10.
We **deduce** (*or* **find**) **from** Eq. (11-47) that these parameters are related to ...

Находить всё более широкое применение
These steels **are finding ever-widening application in** metallurgy.
New fibres **find expanding applications in** engineering and industry.
Carbides **are finding increasing use** (*or* **application**).
For acetylation, ketene **is finding ever increasing favour.**
Today **a growing number of uses are being found for** these units.
Aluminium **is being used more and more.**
Zinc **will find increased usage on** these cars.

Находить дефект в
When **trouble is traced to** such a unit, the entire unit is removed.

Находить много применений
Such tubes **find many applications.**
The machines described **have many uses in** the production of ...

Находить нефть (*или* **жилу**)
To strike oil (*or* **a vein**).

Находить объяснение
Therefore **some** other **explanation must be invoked to account for** additional absorption.

Находить оптимальное сочетание между
To strike a compromise between column efficiency **and** speed of separation ...

Находить ответ на вопрос [*см. тж.* **Решать вопрос**]
This provides the means for **tackling** one of the fundamental **questions of** chemistry.

Находить отражение в
The conservation principles **are embodied in** sets of differential equations.

Находить положение [*см.* **Определять положение**].

Находить практическое применение
Both the Seebeck and the Peltier effects **have found practical use.**

Находить применение [*см. тж.* **Применяться**]
Such measurements **find use** (*or* **application**) **in** molecular-mass determinations.

Находить применение в качестве
Inorganic and organic tin compounds **find use** (*or* **application**) **as** catalysts in many industrial processes.

Находить применение в промышленности
These bromides **have found industrial use.**
Coatings of this alloy could **find commercial application** this year.

Находить решение
He **hit on** (*col.*) (*or* **discovered,** *or* **found**) **a solution** by pure accident.

Находить широкое применение
Gravimetric methods **have found a wide utility in** chemical analysis.
Such devices **may be used extensively in** computers.
This machine **has a wide application** (*or* **is widely used**) **in** workshops.
Vermiculite **has widespread application as** lightweight concrete and plaster aggregate.
Transformer coupling **finds wide** (*or* **extensive**) **application** (*or* **use**) **in** tuned amplifiers.
Such devices **may have extensive** (*or* **frequent**) **applications in** computers.

Находиться [*см. тж.* **Лежать, Расположен**]
The camera **can be contained in** an artificial satellite or **positioned on** the moon or a planet.
Such a fan **is to be found** in each room **at** the point where ...
The screw **is situated** (*or* **located**) at the rear of the clamp.
The lactose carrier **resides in** the membrane.
The transform fault **occurs** between the ends of the boundary.
This point **lies in** a two-phase region of the phase diagram.
This electron pair **is localized within** the central internuclear region.
These points **occur in** the cubic element.
The amount of water **present as** vapour in the atmosphere is ...
The negative electrons should **spend** more **time** between the nuclei than in other regions.

If the observer **is stationed** above the equator, ...
The space in which the electron **finds itself** at the moment ...

Находиться близко друг к другу [*см.* **Расположены близко друг к другу**].

Находиться в [*см. тж.* **Помещаться**]
Some control mechanism must **reside in** the RNA molecule (*biol.*).
The proportion of time the solute **spends in** the mobile phase ...
These elements now **reside in** the continental crust.

Находиться в ... виде
Most of the carbon dioxide in the oceans **is in the form of** carbonate.

Находиться в воздухе
The aircraft **was airborne** for eight hours.
Balloons **stay aloft** for long periods of time.

Находиться в движении
The free electrons in a bar of metal **are in** incessant random **motion** at high thermal velocities.
All segments of the alimentary tract **show** peristaltic **movements.**

Находиться в довольно хорошем согласии с
These results **are in reasonably good agreement with** the experimentally deduced energies.

Находиться в зацеплении
The rack **engages** a pinion.
The wheels **are geared to** the counter.
A considerable number of teeth **are in** constant **engagement.**
This quadrant **meshes with** a spur gear.

Находиться в квадратичной зависимости от
The vibrational contribution to ... **depends quadratically on** the sample concentration.

Находиться в контакте
The two surfaces **contact** (*or* **are in contact**).

Находиться в массовом производстве
The switch is the only one of the type **mass-produced** in that country.

Находиться в начальном периоде развития
This theory **is (still) in its infancy.**

Находиться в непосредственной связи с
Specific gravity of a liquid **may be related directly to** [*or* **associated** (*or* **connected**) **directly with**] its significant properties.

Находиться в обратной зависимости от
The mobility **depends inversely on** mass.

Находиться в обратной пропорции [*см.* **Обратно пропорционален**].

Находиться в однозначном соответствии
The transformations from the Cartesian coordinate system to the curvilinear coordinate system **are in one-to-one correspondence.**

Находиться в продаже
Such glass bulbs **are on the market.**

Находиться в противоречии с [*см. тж.* **Противоречить**]
This **is in contrast with** earlier work on anthracene.
Here, stability of the product and the "basicity" of the reactant **are in conflict.**
These findings **are in conflict** (*or* **contradiction**) **with** the "steady-state" hypothesis.

Находиться в процессе зарождения
It is clear that these methods **are** only **in their infancy.**

Находиться в равновесии с
The liquid **is in equilibrium with** a residue ...

Находиться в резком противоречии с
But this possibility **is sharply contradicted by** evidence.
The new view **is in sharp** (*or* **marked**) **contrast to** the one that had prevailed earlier.

Находиться в резонансе с
These molecules **are resonant with** the laser.

Находиться в сложной зависимости от
The appearance of these spectra **depends in a complex manner on ...**

Находиться в смеси с

Cobalt **is mixed with** nickel in many of the minerals found in Canada.

Находиться в соответствии с [*см. тж.* **Согласовываться с, Соответствовать**]
The planet's image **conforms to** this prediction.
These rules **are consistent with** our understanding of ...
This finding **is consistent with** the theoretical model.
It has been proved that the capacity, efficiency and strength of the boiler **are as guaranteed by** the manufacturer.
The discovery was shown **to be in accord** (*or* **agreement**) **with** the general principles of ...
The dimensions adopted **are in accordance** (*or* **compliance,** *or* **conformity**) **with** the latest recommendations of the IEC.
This finding **is in line** (*or* **in keeping**) **with** that of other investigators.
These facts **are in line with** the decrease in the heat of formation of ...
The earth terminals were designed **to be compatible with** the satellite's characteristics.
The observed radial temperature dispersion **was found to fit** (*or* **to correspond to**) Eq. (4.35).
The procedure **was in keeping with** Kepler's hunch about the role of the Sun.

Находиться в соотношении
The respective reverberation times for axial, tangential and oblique waves **are in the ratio 6:5:4** (*or* **in the 6:5:4 ratio**).

Находиться в стадии разработки
Extra low-temperature enamels **are under development** (*or* **are being developed**).
The processes **are** still **under development.**

Находиться в стадии строительства [*см. тж.* **Строиться**]
The machine **is under construction.**

Находиться в тесной связи с
The secretory cells **are in close association** (*or* **are intimately connected**) **with** blood vessels.
Each of these components **bears an intimate relation to** (*or* **is intimately related to**) every other.

Находиться в тесном контакте с
The pipe surface **should be properly contacted by** the brine to be cooled.
When heat flows from one material to another **with which it is intimately in contact ...**

Находиться в удовлетворительном согласии с
The predictions of the theory **are in gratifying agreement with** the experimental results.
The curve **is in fair** (*or* **reasonable,** *or* **good**) **agreement with** the mass-transfer data.

Находиться в химическом соединении с
Oxygen and hydrogen **are combined chemically with** carbon on the surface of the particle.

Находиться в хорошем согласии (друг с другом)
The results **agree closely with each other** [*or* **are in close** (*or* **good**) **agreement**].

Находиться в хорошем соответствии с
The decreasing bond strengths in the lithium halides **correlate well with** the decreasing charge densities of the halide ions.

Находиться в центре внимания
Leeches **were a major focus of interest for** the 19th-century pioneers of modern experimental embryology.
The problem of life's beginnings **has been the focus of attention** for at least several millennia.
Such interactions **have been a central preoccupation of** physicists in the 20th century.

Находиться в эксплуатации
The plant **has been in operation** for seven years.
These valves **are** still **in service.**
By the 1820s much more efficient hydraulic motors **were** already **at work.**

Находиться в эмбриональном состоянии
This science **is** still **in its infancy.**

Находиться далеко друг от друга
The particles **are far apart** [*or* **widely spaced** (*or* **separated**)].

Находиться за пределами
Any number which **lies outside** the dynamic range ...

Находиться между
When the fluid **is sandwiched between** two glass plates, ...

Находиться на [*см. тж.* **На ... имеется** (*или* **находится,** *или* **установлен** *и т.п.*)]
The south magnetic pole **falls on** the Antarctic Continent well south of Australia.

Находиться на безопасном расстоянии от
All persons **should keep clear of** (*or* **keep at a safe distance from**) high-voltage equipment.

Находиться на большом расстоянии друг от друга
The storage facilities **are widely spaced** (*or* **are wide apart**).

Находиться на одном уровне с
When the liquid-air interface **is level** (*or* **even**) **with** the calibration mark on the container, ...

Находиться на продвинутой стадии разработки
Laser systems designed to monitor air pollution **are well along in development.**

Находиться на продвинутой стадии строительства
The construction of the station **is well under way.**

Находиться на пути к
The probe **is on its way to** the planet.

Находиться на равном расстоянии друг от друга
The teeth **are equally** (*or* **uniformly**) **spaced.**

Находиться на равном расстоянии от
Every point on the circle **is equally distant** (*or* **equidistant**) **from** the centre.

Находиться на ранней стадии развития [*см.* **Находиться в процессе зарождения**].

Находиться на расстоянии
This star **is 11 parsecs distant** (*or* **is at a distance of ... from the Earth,** *or* **is separated from us by a distance of ...**).

Находиться на расстоянии ... друг от друга
The layers **are 5 cm apart.**
Two elements of fluid **are separated by a distance** Δ_y (*or* **are** Δ_y **distant from each other**).

Находиться на расстоянии ... друг от друга по вертикали
The trays **are spaced 18 in. vertically.**

Находиться на расстоянии ... километров
The block's western end **is thirty kilometres away.**

Находиться на ... расстоянии от Земли
Venus **is 42 gigametres away** (*or* **distant**).

Находиться на уровне
The level of globin production **stood at 20%.**

Находиться под атмосферным давлением
The top of the column **is at atmospheric pressure.**

Находиться под давлением
The metering system **is kept under pressure.**

Находиться под действием [*см. тж.* **Испытывать воздействие**]
If the metal **is exposed to** a magnetic field, ...
When such a structure **is subjected to** an external force, ...

Находиться под действием атмосферных условий
Old glass tends to be weaker than new material, particularly if it **has been exposed to weather.**

Находиться под наблюдением
The animals **were under observation** for two weeks.

Находиться под сомнением
The position of the station is known and that of the aircraft **is in doubt.**

Находиться при ... температуре
The part **is kept at a** constant **temperature.**

Находка для
The ion source **is a boon to** experimenters.

Находясь в полёте
While in free flight, the projectile is charged electrically.

Находящиеся в равновесии (друг с другом)
Concentrations of two phases **in equilibrium (with each other)** are usually quite different.

Находящиеся на максимально возможном расстоянии друг от друга
For groups **at maximum possible separation, ...**

Находящиеся на равных расстояниях от
If the point of control and the point of measurement **are equidistant from** the axis of table rotation, ...

Находящиеся на расстоянии ... друг от друга
An electron passes between two electrodes **5×10^{-3} cm apart.**
The force of attraction between two parallel wires **1 metre apart** (*or* **spaced at 1 metre,** *or* **separated by 1 metre**) is ...

Находящийся [*см. тж.* **Расположенный**]
Among the metal elements in animals are potassium and magnesium, **found** chiefly in cells.
Placed, situated.

Находящийся в нашем распоряжении
This body could not be observed by any technique now **at our disposal.**

Находящийся в помещении
The occupants of the room (*or* **building,** *or* **office,** etc.).

Находящийся в равновесии
The two systems **in equilibrium ...**
Diffusion does not occur in a system **at equilibrium.**

Находящийся в равновесии с
The first substance **in equilibrium with** the second ...

Находящийся в распоряжении
The best system now **available to** (*or* **at the disposal of**) experimenters is ...

Находящийся в скрытом состоянии
The solar energy **latent** in carbohydrates and other organic matter can be employed.

Находящийся вне
Usually these devices are elaborate installations **external to** the engine.

Находящийся между ... и
The clutch, **interposed between** engine **and** transmission, has ...
The plate **sandwiched between** the jaws was released.

Находящийся под влиянием диффузии
A **diffusion-affected** reaction.

Находящийся под действием разрывного усилия
Subatomic particles can initiate cavitation in liquid **under tensile stress.**

Нахождение I [*см.* **Время пребывания**].

Нахождение II [*см. тж.* **Обнаружение**]
Much research has been directed to **pinpointing** the carcinogenic factors associated with ...
This method of testing has proven most satisfactory in **locating** (*or* **detecting**) cracks at the root of the gear teeth.

Нахождение дефектов (*или* **неполадок**)
Trouble shooting.

Нахождение формулы ... связано с трудностями
The formula of this compound **poses many problems.**

Нацеливать на
The jet of hot air can **be focussed on** individual components.

Начал изучаться
The less striking varieties of abnormal behaviour **have come under the scrutiny of science** only in recent years.

Начало [*см. тж.* **Брать начало в, В самом начале, Вести своё начало от, Для начала**]
Fracture and **the onset of** twinning (*двойникование кристаллов*) appeared to be coincident.
The onset (*or* **commencement**) of emission coincides with the passage of the shock front.

Начало было положено в
Practical applications of the method **originated in** automotive die foundries.

Начало координат [*см.* **В начале координат, Проходить через начало координат**].

Началось с древних времен
The investigation of clay materials **goes back into antiquity.**

Начальная стадия [*см.* **На начальной стадии** (*или* **ступени**)].

Начальная точка
The initial point of a ballistic path ...

Начальное положение [*см.* **Возвращаться в первоначальное положение**].

Начальный и конечный
Energy differences between **initial** (*or* **original**) **and final** stages of a process ...

Начальный период развития [*см.* **Находиться в начальном периоде развития, Находиться в эмбриональном состоянии**].

Начальный период существования
The early life of the planet ...

Начат
A start has been made on the exploration of ...

Начинает вырисовываться картина
A fuller picture of ... is beginning to emerge.

Начинать [*см.* **Положить начало**].

Начинать действовать I
As starvation is prolonged, other sources of energy for the brain **come into play.**

Начинать действовать II
There is often a delay before a density-dependent mechanism **takes effect.**

Начинать действовать через ... часов
Thyroxine takes three to four hours **to begin to work** (*or* **to take effect**).

Начинать колебаться
If the sample gas has enough gain at a certain frequency, it should **break into oscillation** at that frequency.

Начинать критиковать
The internal-combustion engine **is coming under criticism** because of its substantial contribution to air pollution.

Начинать применяться
Solid fuel motors **are coming into use.**

Начинать с
We **begin** (*or* **start**) **with** van der Waals' equation for 1 mol of gas.

Начинать сначала
To explain that, I will have **to begin at the beginning.**

Начинаться
Before transcription of the genes can **commence** (*or* **begin,** *or* **start**), ...
Before the development of the North Sea oil fields **got under way, ...**
If a high reverse voltage is applied to a *p-n* junction very rapidly, avalanche multiplication may **set in.**

Начинаться ... и кончаться
A sequence of demonstrations that **begins with** the law of areas **and ends with** the proof that ...

Начинаться с
The chemical sequences of metabolism **begin with** digestive processes.
The word *ether* has had a long history, **dating back to** the time of Aristotle.

Начиная ... и кончая I
The entire combined mill department, **from** the raw mill feed **to** the slurry blending, is operated from a central control room.
Products ranging **from** toothpaste **to** missile nose cones ...
You can use these machines to grind everything **from** small parts **to** heavy pieces.
Adults of various species show great diversity in size **ranging** from 1 mm in some species found in fish **to** over 400 mm in length found in some mammalian species.

Начиная ... и кончая II
A fluvial denudation takes place, **beginning with** a rapid tectonic uplift **and ending with** the development of a peneplain.

Начиная ... и кончая III
With the metals still in contact there can be a potential difference between them of

anywhere from a tiny fraction of a volt **to** several volts.

Начиная от
Beginning at the centre of the board, mark each 60-minute interval on ...

Начиная отсюда
From this point on(ward), relief declines and slopes become more gentle.

Начиная с
Label your parallels **starting with** 30°N at the mid-latitude.
This section will include, **as from** the January 1983 issue, ...
Beginning in 1825, several integrating devices were developed.
Beginning on October 25, the plant will operate on a two-shift basis.
Beginning with this batch, the rotors will be manufactured by the new method.
A course of lectures on ... **commencing** September 6, ...
Starting in 1984, ...
Each symbol is given a subscript, **beginning with** zero.

Начиная с ... и далее
From 5/10000 **(and) on,** we have a decreasing geometric progression.

Начиная с этого момента
From this time on, the current will be limited by ...

Начнём с того, что
What are the available energy options for the future? **To begin with** there are the known finite and irreplaceable energy sources: the fossil fuels and ...

Нашедший свое отражение в
The assumptions about fluid motion **embodied in** the theories may not be precisely correct.

Наши дни [*см.* **В наши дни**].

Нащупывать
A radar illumination beam **seeks out** the attacking plane.

Не [*см. тж.* **А не, А не на, А также не, Далекó не, Или совсем не**]
The model **fails to** (*or* **does not**) explain many observations of this phenomenon.
This optical processor **fails to** use all the parallelism which optics has to offer.
No detailed study has been made of methods by which ...
Many shapes **other than** round are formed by extrusion through dies of suitable contour.
The particle managed to travel through the box **without** hitting another particle.
The article **neglects to** consider some additional factors.

Не ..., а ...
A liquid corresponds **not** to a single crystal phase **but** to a continuous series of such phases (*or* A liquid corresponds **to** a continuous series of such phases **(and) not** (*or* **rather than**) to a single crystal phase).

Не без недостатков
This method **is not without disadvantages** (*or* **is not infallible**).

Не без основания
We view this plant with pride and **for good reason!**
The parallel efforts of these two laboratories will undoubtedly be seen as another race, and **with some justice.**

Не без преимуществ
The method **is not without merit.**

Не безграничен [*см.* **Возможности не безграничны**].

Не более I [*см. тж.* **Максимально**]
Oxygen normally forms **no more than** two covalent bonds.

Не более II [*см. тж.* **Всего лишь**]
Zooplankton **are no more than** four centimetres long.

Не более и не менее, чем
The strong force **is nothing more than** the system of interactions needed to ...

Не более чем [*см. тж.* **Всего лишь**]
The conventional numerical control **is nothing more than** a special-purpose data processing system.
The calculated absorption rate **is no better than** a good estimate.
The effect of individual tectonic events is, **at most,** regional (*geol.*).

Не больше [*см.* **Но не больше, Самое бóльшее**].

Не больше, чем [*см. тж.* **Самое бóльшее**]
The total harmonic distortion **shall be no more than** 3%.
A rugged tool with a rate of wear **no greater than** that of conventional tools ...
Sampling, of course, is important, but **no more so than** in the other methods described.
The boilers must be filled with water at a temperature **of no more than** 100°F.

Не бояться перегрузки и короткого замыкания
The instrument **is overload- and short-circuit proof.**

Не бояться проколов
These tyres **are puncture proof.**

Не бояться ударов
The device **is not susceptible to shock** (*or* **is shock proof**).

Не был обнаружен
The electron could be readily observed, but the neutrino, having no mass and being electrically neutral, **escaped detection.**

Не было
Unfortunately, tunable continuous-wave lasers **were not available** (*or* **were unavailable**) at that time.

Не быть опознанным [*см.* **Оставаться неопознанным**].

Не в
If a line intersects the cone's axis at a point **distinct from** the apex, ...
The pointer **is off** its equilibrium point.

Не в масштабе
In this arrangement of the process **(not to scale)** the colour outline shows ...

Не в порядке
There **may be** something **out of order with** the steam valve.

Не в равновесии с
The charge carriers **are out of equilibrium with** the lattice.

Не в фазе
This depends on whether the arriving radio waves **are** in phase or **out of phase ...**

Не в фазе с [*см. тж.* **На ... градусов не в фазе с**]
If the path of one beam is made slightly longer or shorter than that of the other, the light waves in one beam **will be out of phase with** the waves in the other.

Не в фокусе
The teloblast lies deep and **is out of focus.**
An **out-of-focus** photograph ...

Не вдаваясь в подробности [*см. тж.* **Не входя в подробности**]
The effect of the dielectric can be understood, **without going into** the molecular behaviour, by supposing that ...
Without going into details I can give you the results.

Не вечен [*см.* **Когда-то должен прийти конец**].

Не видеть возможности
I **see no way of** predicting a major catastrophe.

Не видно
When a star is forming, **it is hidden from** view; it is surrounded by the opaque cloud of dust and gas.

Не включать [*см. тж.* **Исключать, Опускать II**]
For air *S* is unity and **may be omitted** (*or* **excluded,** *or* **dropped**) **from** the formula.

Не включая [*см. тж.* **За исключением, Исключая, Минус, Не считая**]
The entire unit weighs 8.5 lb, **not including** the hydraulic actuators.
The time required for the complete cycle, **exclusive of** curing, is from 10 to 15 sec.
The cost of storage tanks, **less** (*or* **minus**) foundations, is shown in Fig. 7.

Не влиять на [*см. тж.* **Не оказывать влияния на**]
The gas-jet laser cutter **has little or no effect on** areas adjacent to the cut.
The transducer material **is unaffected** (*or* **not affected**) **by** temperature.

Не внушать доверия
The assumption that Y* is zero under dynamic absorption conditions **is suspect.**

Не водорастворимый [*см.* **Не растворимый в воде**].

Не воздействовать на
Chloric (I) acid **has no action upon** carbon particles.
Nitric acid **is** almost **without action on** aluminium.

Не все
Particles in liquids **do not all** have the same kinetic energy.

Не всегда
It does not always happen that a quantity of sea water is evaporated away completely.
The amount of cytosine incorporated **was not consistently** equal to the total guanine.
Such attempts **are not necessarily** successful.

Не всегда справедлив
This statement **is** sound but **not universally true.**

Не всегда так
Such **is not necessarily the case for** active second-order systems.

Не встречать препятствий
The layer is so thick that **no barrier is encountered by** diffusing molecules.

Не встречая сопротивления [*см.* **Абсолютно не встречая сопротивления**].

Не входить в
Both the light-year and the parsec **are outside** the metric system.

Не входя в подробности
Without going into detail we shall simply note that ...

Не входящий в систему СИ
They have added special units **outside the SI system** (*or* **nonsystematic units**).

Не выводя из
The seals can be replaced **without taking** the valve **out of** the system.

Не выдерживать испытания
The component part specification allows a certain number of units **to fail the tests.**

Не выдерживать критики
None of these objections **stand up.**
This chain of reasoning **does not stand up (under scrutiny).**

Не вызывать больших затруднений
Mechanical transfer of the cut-off forgings to a subsequent grinding machine **should present few problems** (*or* **difficulties**).

Не вызывать затруднений
Overdriving a system with proportional control of the basic first-order system **creates no problems** (*or* **difficulties**) at all.
Starting and stopping **would** usually **not be a matter of concern.**

Не вызывать изменений
A change in concentration of the aqueous solution **leaves** the concentration of the ion in the nonaqueous solution **unaltered** (*or* **unchanged,** *or* **invariant**).

Не вызывать особых затруднений [*см.* **Не представлять особых затруднений**].

Не вызывать сомнения
This fact is beyond question.

Не выносить критики
He **tolerated no criticism.**

Не выполняться
In this type of model, Cantor's hypothesis **fails** (*or* **does not hold**).

Не выполняться для
Close correlation **breaks down for** a number of examples.

Не выходить за пределы [*см.* **Ограничиваться**].

Не выходить из строя
This material **remains serviceable from** –85 to 500°F.

Не говоря уже о
Thousands of types of wheels are made with different combinations of the above characteristics, **not to mention** (*or* **to say nothing of,** *or* **let alone**) the multitude of sizes and shapes available.

Не говоря уже о многих других [*см.* **И многие другие**].

Не годиться [*см.* **Не подходить, Не пригоден**].

Не гореть
This compound **will not burn.**

Не давать [*см.* **Препятствовать**].

Не давать больших результатов
So far this research **has met with only limited success.**

Не давать возможности [*см. тж.* **Не позволять**]
This law **gives no way of** deducing the contribution of ...

Не давать желаемого эффекта [*см.* **Неэффективен**].

Не давать никакого эффекта [*см.* **Не приводить ни к чему**].

Не давать распадаться
The mass of these quarks is comparable to the binding energy that **holds** the quarks **together in** the hadron.

Не двигаться [*см.* **Неподвижный**].

Не действителен [*см.* **Не выполняться, Оказываться несостоятельным**].

Не действовать
The tide gauge **was inoperative** during two storms.

Не действовать на [*см.* **Не влиять на**].

Не делать *чего-л.* [*см. тж.* **Если это не будет сделано**]
Addison's disease results from **a failure of** the cortex **to** produce its steroid hormones.

Не должен
The total load **may not** exceed 80 percent of the branch circuit capacity.

Не должен нагреваться
There must be no heating of the unburned gases.

Не допускается [*см.* **Недопустим**].

Не допускать
This temperature **allows no** overload.

Не допускать в [*см. тж.* **Препятствовать**]
The suction is designed to assist in air **exclusion from** (*or* **keeping** air **out of**) the impeller inlet.

Не допускать загрязнения
The ball bearings **should be kept free from dirt.**

Не допускать попадания [*см.* **Изолировать, Препятствовать попаданию**].

Не допускать проникновения
Cofferdams are made sufficiently high **to exclude** the flood waters.

Не достигать [*см. тж.* **Далеко не достигать**]
The moon's shadow **fell short of** the earth.
The transfer of iridium to the earth by such a mechanism **would fall short of** the required amount.

Не достигнув
The composition will move along the line **and stop short of (reaching)** the equilibrium line.

Не единственный, кто
We **were not alone in** suggesting that ...

Не за горами
Now the solution to this problem **is (close) at hand.**
Beam welding **was** also **within sight** [*or* **was around the corner** (*col.*)].

Не зависеть от
The constant of proportionality **is unaffected by** the geometry of the sample.
The system **is independent of** (*or* **does not depend on**) power line variations.
The rate **was** essentially **temperature independent.**
These properties **are invariant with** (*or* **independent of**) the direction.

Не зависящий от времени *и т.п.*
The **time-independent** equation ...

Не загрязнять окружающую среду
This fuel cell **is** virtually **pollution free** (*or* **nonpolluting**).

Не загрязняющий окружающую среду
Control of toxic fumes, the closed system of solution circulation and the air filtration system, all contribute to the formation of an **ecologically clean** (*or* **nonpolluting**) process.

Не замечать

The base pairing has become so reduced that the researchers **overlooked** it (*biol.*).

Не знать заранее [*см.* **Заранее не знать ничего о**].

Не знать, что
Many engineers **are unaware (of the fact) that** there is a lower limit for ...

Не зная
The characteristic may be determined immediately **without knowledge of** the solution.

Не идти в сравнение с
The early metal-vapour lasers **did not compare with** other types of laser for experimental and commercial applications.

Не идти дальше
The approach **did not advance beyond** the traditional doctor-patient relationship.

Не играть роли [*см. тж.* **Безразлично, Не иметь значения**]
In some instances a series of operations on a workpiece must be undertaken in a predetermined order, and in others the order **is immaterial.**
The latter fact **plays no part in ...**

Не известен
The origin of the linear magnetic anomalies in the ocean **remained a mystery** for several years.
The function of these poly(A)-rich regions still **remains an open question** (*biol.*).
The source of such motions **is a puzzle.**
The biochemical role of ascorbic acid **is obscure** (*or* **unknown**).

Не известно [*см. тж.* **О котором не было известно, Остаётся тайной**]
How this occurs **is** still **a question.**

Не известны случаи
No case of destruction of one of these windings through heating **has come to our notice.**

Не изменять [*см.* **Не вызывать изменений**].

Не изменяться [*см. тж.* **Оставаться неизменным**]
Only the equilibrium bond lengths **are unaffected.**

Не изменяться при [*см. тж.* **Не вызывать изменений**]
The snowflake **is invariant (with respect) to** 60-degree rotations.

Не изменяться с
This exponent **does not vary with** solar distance.

Не изучен
The relation of the adrenal steroids to normal sex functions **is not understood.**

Не изученный [*см.* **Полностью не изучен**].

Не иметь [*см. тж.* **Без, Не обладать, Отсутствовать**]
Venus **lacks** known satellites.
Caecilians **lack** limbs entirely.
The welds **were free from** defects.
The new bottles **are free of** (*or* **from**) cracks.

Не иметь абсолютно ничего общего с
This **has nothing (whatever) to do with** the loss of energy.

Не иметь большого значения [*см. тж.* **Маловажный**]
The positions of hydrogen atoms **are of little consequence** (*or* **importance,** *or* **significance**).

Не иметь возможности
We **have no way of** proving that some cosmic event might not have altered this process.

Не иметь запаха
The new coolant **is odour free** (*or* **odourless**).

Не иметь значения [*см. тж.* **Безразлично**]
The source of the anomaly **is of no concern:** it could be a concentration of mass in the earth or a distant object in space.
It makes no difference whether type 400 **or** 399 is employed.
The direction of motion **is immaterial** [*or* **is of no importance** (*or* **significance,** *or* **consequence**)].

Не иметь ни малейшего понятия
They **have not the foggiest** (*or* **slightest**) **notion** (*or* **idea**) what this drug may have in it.

Не иметь ни того, ни другого
The neutron has a mass and a magnetic moment, whereas the photon **has neither.**

Не иметь ничего общего с
The measured rise of the photon-proton cross section **has nothing to do with** such a saturation.

Не иметь отношения к [*см. тж.* **Не относящийся к**]
This role has been shown **to be unrelated to** translational properties (*biol.*).
Fixed nitrogen might even be a by-product of a process whose primary function **is unrelated to** nitrogen metabolism.
In that case the resulting micrograph may **bear no relation to** topography.

Не иметь под собой почвы [*см.* **Не выдерживать критики**].

Не иметь поля
Here, the image space **is field free.**

Не иметь понятия о [*см.* **Понятия не иметь о**].

Не иметь последствий [*см.* **Оставаться без последствий**].

Не иметь практического значения
Such activity **is of no practical importance.**

Не иметь прецедента
The quantum assumption **had no parallel** (*or* **precedent**) in familiar systems.

Не иметь себе равного
The fishes **are unrivalled among** the vertebrates in the ability to adapt to unpromising living conditions.
On all these scores the device **has no equal.**
This mould-making process **is unparalleled.**

Не иметь смысла
This argument **is meaningless** (*or* **makes no sense**) since this series will never be used up.
It would serve no purpose (*or* **make no sense**) **to** present here large amounts of data on ...

Не иметь смысла поскольку это касается
This expression **is meaningless for** comets.

Не иметь успеха [*см.* **Не увенчаться успехом**].

Не иметься [*см. тж.* **Отсутствовать**]
If these values **are not available** (*or* **are unavailable**), they may be estimated by the following rules.
Chemical and physical methods for biotin analyses **are not available.**

Не имеющий ... вообще
A particle **with no spin at all ...**

Не имеющий себе равных в отношении
This results in a compact boiler **unrivalled for** economy and reliability.

Не исключаться
The development of a temporary CO_2 cap **was not ruled out.**

Не исключено, что
It is not inconceivable (*or* **improbable**) **that ...**

Не использован
Many of the potentialities of the shock tube as an experimental tool **are** still **untapped** (*or* **unused**).

Не использоваться
Always keep straight edges in their box when they **are not in use.**

Не испытывать
The valves **are free from** excessive vibration.

Не испытывать боли
There are no complications and the patient **is pain free.**

Не исчерпывать
This list **does not exhaust** the possibilities.

Не касаться
Computer techniques **will be omitted** in the present discussion.

Не касаться благодаря
The magnetic head **is kept from touching** the medium **by** the air-bearing effect.

Не лучше, чем
Static molecular models represent molecules **no better than** a modernistic statue represents a real, live, moving person.

Не менее
A shield of **no less than** 2 in. ...
They synthesized **no fewer than** ten amino acids.
If the reasons for the development of this art are remarkable, the reasons for its precipitous decline **are no less so.**

Не менее, чем
By the end of the century the number of people aged 85 and over will increase by **no less than** one half.

Не менее, чем в ... раз превышать
These reserves **are fully ten times larger than** the proven U.S. crude oil reserves.

Не меньше [*см.* **Но не больше** (*антон.* **Но не меньше**)].

Не меньше, чем [*см.* **Самое бóльшее**].

Не менять [*см. тж.* **Не вызывать изменений**]
The transformation **leaves** this value **unchanged** (*or* **unaltered**).

Не менять свойства
The material **retains its properties** over a wide temperature range.

Не меняться [*см.* **На ... не влияет, Оставаться неизменным**].

Не меняться по длине
The stem of arm *V* appears to **be invariable in** length.

Не меняя
The parametrization would again give this result, **leaving** the characteristic equations **unchanged** (*or* **unaltered**).

Не мешая
Removal of scrap **without getting in the way of** the die-setter ...

Не можем не
We **cannot but** express (*or* **cannot help** expressing) our delight at this achievement.

Не может [*см.* **Ни один ... не способен**].

Не может быть достигнут [*см.* **Вне пределов досягаемости**].

Не может быть и речи о
The distillation of the enormous quantities involved **is out of the question.**

Не может быть использован
The system **is** neutrally stable and, therefore, **unusable as** a control system.
For this purpose time averages of the wind and the humidity **will not do.**

Не может быть обнаружен
The underlying mass has such a low luminosity that **it escapes** (*or* **eludes**) **detection.**

Не может занимать ... состояние (*физ.*)
If one fermion occupies a certain state, all other identical fermions **are excluded from** that **state.**

Не может позволить себе
Society **can ill afford** unreliable communication networks.

Не может сравниться с
Although the performance of this recorder **does not equal that of** most commercial instruments, it is adequate for experiments of many kinds.

Не можете не
You **will not fail to** note the syllable *benz* in this compound.

Не найден
Complete proof **is not yet at hand.**

Не намного больше, чем [*см.* **Лишь немного больше, чем**].

Не намного превышать
This amount **is little more than** the biological minimum.

Не нанося ущерба
Without detracting (**in any way**) **from** the resolution of the microscope the collecting and sorting procedure can significantly increase ...

Не наоборот [*см.* **А не наоборот**].

Не нарушая установки
The applications include checking workpieces on a machine **without disturbing the set-up.**

Не нуждаться в
The solid stationary phases **have no need of** a support if ...
This device **dispenses with the need for** a metal cladding.

Не обладать
Elliptical galaxies **are** generally **devoid of** structural features.
This property **is not shared by** particles with a finite mass.

Не обладать достаточными знаниями
We **lack sufficient knowledge to** discriminate between ...

Не обладающий
The mesentron is the only portion of the alimentary tract **lacking** a cuticle.

Не обнаружен
Such quasars **escaped detection** by radio telescopes.

Не обнаруживать
Hypoparathyroidism **is** often **missed** since the scar is almost invisible.

Не обработанный после литья [*см.* **Не подвергнутый обработке после литья**].

Не обращать внимания
This report **has escaped the attention of** the researchers.

Не обременять [*см.* **Не утруждать**].

Не обслуживаться
Many substations **are unattended** and use automatic or remote control.

Не обсуждаться [*см.* **Не касаться**].

Не объяснять
This hypothesis **leaves unexplained** (*or* **fails to explain**) the mechanism of ...

Не обязательно
The computer **need not be** located next to the machine.
The corresponding pulse **need not be** transmitted by the radar.
Lasers **do not necessarily** offer any advantage in ...
Artesian water **is not of necessity** deep.

Не обязательно должен быть
The laser **does not need to be** very powerful.
The coacervating agent **need not be** a micromolecular substance that can form hydrogen bonds.
The reactant **does not have to be** a stereoisomer.
It is not necessary that the X_k **be** independent.
It is not necessary for these liquids **to be** totally immiscible.

Не ограничен
The function is **unbounded on** the interval $0 < x < 1$.

Не ограничиваться [*см. тж.* **Этим не исчерпывается**]
The differences between microcomputer software and minicomputer software **go beyond** the support level.

Не один
Most biologically important compounds contain **more than one** functional group.
There is **more than** one reason for this.

Не один раз [*см.* **Несколько раз**].

Не один человек
More than one person has suggested that ...

Не оказывать влияния на
Chemical reactions involving such solutions often **leave** some of the ionic species **unaffected**.
The measurements **were unaffected by** (*На измерения не оказывали влияния*) changes in ...

Не оправдываться [*см.* **Не подтверждаться**].

Не оставаться незамеченным
The virtues of metal hydrides in this respect **have not gone unnoticed.**

Не остаётся
We can no longer make sets when we **run out of** components.

Не останавливаться перед расходами (*или* **затратами**)
Titanium is used in supersonic aircraft and in various military applications where **expense is no object** (*or* **where no expense is spared**).

Не останавливая
All structural members can be inspected visually **while** the reactor **is operating.**

Не осуществляться [*см.* **Не выполняться**].

Не отличаться от
In this sense, an aircraft **is no different from** any other machinery.

Не отличаться по внешнему виду от
These breccias **are not dissimilar in aspect to** sedimentary breccias.

Не относиться к
Most of the details of the story **are irrelevant to** communication.
The question **is not pertinent to** this discussion.
This reasoning **does not hold for** tunneling rays.

Не относящийся к
The unit was discharged by an effect **unrelated to** that under consideration.

Не отставать от
The rate of sediment deposition **kept pace with** the rate of crustal subsidence.
A skilled abacus operator can easily **keep pace with** a desk calculator operator.
The reaction rate must be sufficient **to keep up with** the rate of absorption.
Just **to keep up with** the increase in world population the water demand will increase by about 100 billion cubic metres per year.

Не охвачен
A number of important features of NMR spectroscopy **have not been dealt with** in this brief introduction.

Не очень высок
The stress levels **are moderately high.**

Не очень далёк от действительности
Since we have a good knowledge of stream flow, the estimate of maximum capacity **is** probably **not much in error.**

Не очень отличаться друг от друга
These values **are not much different from each other.**

Не очень хорошо растворяться в
ICl **is not very** (*or* **appreciably**) **soluble in** water.

Не параллельны друг другу
The two vectors **are nonparallel.**

Не поверить в
The discovery **was met with disbelief.**

Не подающий радиосигналов
A **radio-silent** pulsar companion ...

Не подвергать действию
Keep the Vynolite board **out of** the direct rays of the Sun.

Не подвергаться
Cyclohexane in this conformation **is free of** torsional strain.

Не подвергаться влиянию
The line intensity **is unaffected** (*or* **not affected**) **by** the gas.

Не подвергаться выветриванию
The resin **is** completely **unaffected by (outdoor) weathering.**

Не подвергаться напряжению
The middle plane of the bar **is free of stress.**

Не подвергнутый обработке после литья
The **as-cast** surfaces of the magnet ...

Не подвержен
This grade of steel **is not prone** (*or* **subject,** *or* **susceptible**) **to** intergranular corrosion.
Liquids that sustain laser action **are not vulnerable to** permanent structural damage.

Не подвластен
The flux of particles is diffuse and **is beyond the control of** the experimenter.

Не поддаваться
Venus **had** long **resisted** telescopic investigations.
This law **defies (all attempts of)** mathematical formulation.

Не поддаваться анализу
To assess some aspects of chemical reactions that hitherto **eluded analyzing, ...**

Не поддаваться (воз)действию
The metal **is unaffected by** the extreme flame heat.
The balance is of all-metal construction and **is immune from the effects of** weather vibration.
All these alloys **are resistant to** corrosion by sea water.

Не поддаваться объяснению
This feature **has defied explanation.**

Не поддаваться решению
This problem **has** long **defied** (*or* **resisted**) **solution** by ordinary means.

Не подкрепляться
Such proposals **are not supported** (*or* **are unsupportable**) **by** factual evidence.

Не подлежит сомнению, что
It is beyond question that this depends on ...
There is no question that this project made the higher energy economically feasible.

Не подтверждаться
This hypothesis **lacks support from** any known factual evidence.

Не подходить
For horizontal and rising holes this system **would not do.**

Не подчиняться управлению
There is a break in the block diagram, and the system **is out of control.**

Не позволять [*см. тж.* **Не давать возможности, Не давать распадаться**]
To keep water circulation **from** washing the core, ...
An interlocking mechanism **prevents** the discharge door **from** being opened [*or* **prevents** (*or* **precludes**) the opening of ...].
Diamonds with imperfections that **prohibit** their use as gems ...

Не показан
Amortisseur starting windings of the rotor **(not shown)** combine with ...
For simplicity the reflecting curtain **is omitted.**

Не покидая
The welder can adjust the value of the welding current **without leaving** the place where he is working.

Не полностью изучен
Many aspects of ionic behaviour in biochemical systems **are** still **not fully** (*or* **completely**) **understood.**

Не пользоваться популярностью
This insulating material **has been in disrepute** (*or* **in disfavour**) for the last few years.

Не помогать
An oral cholecystogram **is unhelpful** if the patient is clinically jaundiced.

Не понятно [*см.* **Не совсем ясно**].

Не похож на
The values obtained **bear no resemblance to** each other.

Не правило, а исключение
Degeneracies **are not the rule** in quantum mechanics **but the exception.**

Не представлять затруднений
Maintenance of the computer **should present no problems.**

Не представлять интереса
The negligible concentration of the one species **is of no interest.**

Не представлять опасности для жизни
These trace amounts **pose no hazard to life** (*or* **are not lethal**).

Не представлять особого интереса
The remaining earthquakes **are of little interest.**

Не представлять особой угрозы для здоровья и безопасности населения
Such reactors **offer no significant threat to the health and safety of the general public.**

Не представлять особой ценности
These minerals **are of no particular** economic **value.**

Не представлять особых затруднений
The supply of potential **presents no special problems.**
This **is not a particular problem.**

Не представлять собой
The bonding in 1.3-butadiene appears **to be something other than** two isolated carbon-carbon double bonds separated by a single bond.

Не представлять ценности для
Then separation techniques **would be of no value to** the analytical chemist.

Не представлять ценности для биологии *и т.п.*
These studies **hold no biological** (etc.) **value.**

Не препятствовать
Abnormalities in the nucleus **are no bar to** (*or* **do not preclude**) cell division.

Не прибегая к
It is useful to have a method of evaluating this integral **without resort(ing)** (*or* **recourse**) **to** graphical integration.

Не приближать к
Keep the Vynolite board **away from** hot surfaces.

Не приближаться к
All personnel **should keep clear of** high-voltage equipment.

Не приводить ни к чему
All of this **was to no avail.**

Не пригоден [*см. тж.* **Оказываться несостоятельным**]
These sulphides **are unsuitable for** treatment by the ordinary "hypo" process.
Pots **were totally unsuited for** machine manufacture of glass containers.
Such steels **are completely unsuitable** in many cases.
This technique **will not work for** the Earth.
This method **would never do for** moving vehicles.
A dish-shaped reflector **is ruled out** for X-rays.

Не пригоден в качестве [*см.* **Нельзя использовать в качестве**].

Не пригоден для изучения
This method **is unsound** (*or* **unsuitable,** *or* **not valid**) **for** strong shock waves.

Не придавать значения
No significance should be attached to the positioning of ...

Не признаваться
The possibilities of superconductivity **went unrecognized** for a surprisingly long time.

Не прикасаться [*см.* **Не приближаться к**].

Не принимать во внимание [*см. тж.* **Не учитывать, Пренебрегать**]
The transmittance term **may be disregarded.**
Various physical factors **are neglected** (*or* **ignored**) in the simplified model.

Не принимать всерьёз
This suggestion **was not taken seriously** by astronomers.

Не принимать пищи
Some obese individuals **have gone without food** for as long as eight months.

Не принимать сигнал
Black and white TV receivers **are blind to the** chrominance sideband **signals.**

Не приходится удивляться тому, что [*см.* **Не удивительно, что**].

Не производиться
This amplifier **is** practically **extinct (now).**

Не пропускать [*см.* **Непроницаемый для**].

Не проходить незамеченным
This change **has not gone unnoticed.**

Не прошло много времени с тех пор как
No great length of time has yet elapsed since the solar nebula condensed from the cloud.

Не проявляя признаков
All the newborn infants touched and grasped real objects **without any sign of** being disturbed.

Не работать
That mine was a cassiterite producer but **is (now) inactive.**
The tide gauge **was inoperative** during two storms.

Не равны по величине
The time intervals between polarity reversals **are irregular in length.**

Не равный единице
In solutions with densities **other than unity ...**

Не равный нулю [*см. тж.* **Ненулевой**]
This image has a **nonzero** diameter.

Не раз [*см.* **Неоднократно**].

Не развит в достаточной степени чтобы
The theory **is not far enough advanced to offer ...**

Не разлагаясь
This compound boils **undecomposed** (*or* **without decomposing**) at 270°C.

Не разрешаться [*см.* **Недопустим**].

Не распадаясь
This is faster than a neutron star could rotate **without breaking apart.**

Не распространяться за пределы
The rise in temperature **is confined to** this region.

Не рассматриваться
Thus far, **no consideration has been given to** the role of ...

Не растворимый в воде
Carbasole (III) is a **water-insoluble** solid.

Не реагировать на
Calcium carbonate **is** almost completely **unreactive to** hydrogen sulphide.
The material **is unresponsive to** a magnetic field.

Не реагировать на сигнал [*см.* **Не принимать сигнал**].

Не реагировать с
Most of the non-metals **show no reaction** (*or* **do not react**) **with** water.
Calcium **has no reaction with** alkalis.

Не рекомендуется
The patients suffered from diseases of the alimentary tract where oral feeding **is ill advised** (*or* **is discouraged**).

Не родственные
"Chameleon" is a common name applied to two **unrelated** groups of lizards.

Не родственный ему
Electrical measurements play a major role even in such **unrelated** fields as medicine.

Не самый маловажный из
Not least among these questions is the nature of the earth immediately after its formation.

Не связаны между собой
In the lower classes of vertebrates, cortical and medullary adrenals **are divorced from each other.**

Не скоро [*см.* **Ещё не скоро**].

Не следует допускать
The temperature **should not be allowed to** go above 290°F.

Не следует забывать, что [*см. тж.* **Следует иметь в виду**]
It should be remembered that ...

Не следует исключать
This possibility **must not be ruled out.**

Не следует путать с
An EMF-generating selenium cell (**not to be confused with** a device that changes resistance in response to light) has ...
"Fine" silver **should not be confused with** London "standard" silver, which is 92.5% pure.

Не следует считать, что
It is not to be supposed that all integrals of analytic functions are zero.

Не слишком высокий
At **not-too-high** temperatures ...

Не слишком отличаться от
Our simple "working" models **are not too far removed** (*or* **too different**) **from** those of our colleagues of the past.

Не слишком трудно
It **was not unduly difficult.**

Не смешивающийся с водой
A **water-immiscible** fluid.

Не снижая [*см.* **Без ущерба для**].

Не совпадать с [*см.* **Не согласовываться с, Отличаться от, Расходиться с**].

Не совсем
These devices are **not entirely** (*or* **not quite**) adequate for ...

Не совсем правильный
This result **is not exactly** (*or* **quite**) **correct.**

Не совсем точно называют
The response to seasonal changes in the length of the day **is** sometimes **loosely called** photoperiodism.

Не совсем хорошо известен
The mechanisms of antibody formation and activity **are not (yet) entirely known.**

Не совсем ясно
Why such a plume is initiated in any particular area **has been something of a mystery** (**is unknown,** *or* **is not known**).

Не согласный с этим мнением
There were a few **dissenters from this view.**

Не согласовываться с
These conclusions **are at variance** (*or* **do not agree**) **with** those of previous workers.
This **is inconsistent with** the data of Run No. 9.
This concept **is not reconcilable** (*or* **cannot be reconciled**) **with** the morphological features of ...

Не содержать
The lunar rocks **are** waterless, hydrogen-poor and **free of** (*or* **from**) organic matter.
One fraction **lacked** two polypeptides of molecular weight 48,000 and 37,000.

Не содержащий
Cells **deprived of** amino acids ...
Producing sulphur dioxide **free from** (*or* **containing no**) impurities ...
A copper-**free** (*or* copper**less**) aluminium alloy ...

Не соответствовать [*см. тж.* **Абсолютно не соответствовать, Совершенно не соответствовать**]
The experimental evidence **is inconsistent with** the "expected" formula.

Не соответствовать действительности
This statement **is contrary to fact.**

Не соприкасаться [*см.* **Без соприкосновения с воздухом**].

Не соприкасающийся
A potential difference will appear between the ends **not in contact.**
Antimatter **out of contact with** ordinary matter would be stable.

Не сработать
If the emergency cooling systems should **fail to function, ...**

Не сразу стало очевидным
The applicability of the observation to living systems **was not apparent immediately.**

Не сталкиваясь с
These particles can travel far enough **without colliding with** other particles.

Не столь идеальный
Most procedures **fall short of this ideal.**

Не сулить
These factors **do not offer opportunities** for improvement of ...

Не существенно [*см.* **Не иметь значения**].

Не существовать [*см. тж.* **Отсутствовать**]
These tree species **are not found** elsewhere in the region.
All of these elements **are** either very rare or **nonexistent** in nature.
The particle **is** simply **not there.**
The World Health Organization certified that Somalia **was free of** smallpox.

Не существует чёткого различия
No clear-cut distinction exists.

Не считать необходимым
Newton **saw no need to** acknowledge Hooke's statement of ...

Не считая [*см. тж.* **Если не считать, За исключением, Кроме, Минус**]
But for a few substances, the state of the art has not advanced sufficiently.
Except for (*or* **With the exception of**) the bubble caps the plant was constructed entirely of carbon steel.
The delivered cost of a 20,000 lb/hr steam unit is about 120,000 dollars **excluding** buildings, water treating facilities, stacks, and outside piping.
The total cost of the part, **exclusive of** (*or* **less,** *or* **minus**) material costs, would be ...
Not counting optical isomers, there are two butanes with ...

Не так [*см.* **А на самом деле это не так, Если это не так**].

Не так уж
Fortunately, the rocks **are not** all **that** complex.

Не так уж долго осталось ждать того времени, когда
It should not be long before important letters are sent as electrical messages having the appearance of an ordinary typed letter.

Не так уж удивительно, что
It is no great surprise that sand-sized sediments are predominantly quartz.

Не такой, какого можно было бы ожидать
The behaviour of ... **is not that which is normally expected.**

Не такой сильный
Chlorite **is not as strong** an oxidizing agent **as** sodium hypochlorite.

Не терять эффективности
The compound solutions **do not become inoperative by** saturation.

Не только [*см. тж.* **А не только**]
It is not the mere attainment of low temperatures **that** stimulates attempts to achieve them.
The new cooling systems **do more than** speed the heat treating operation.
Not only is background interference being reduced by choice of wavelength, but ...

Не только ..., но и
Thus the histories may be compared **not only** between regions on a given continent, **but** between continents **as well.**
Not only do these histone modifications occur at specific sites in the molecules, **but** they **also** occur at specific times during the cell cycle.

Не требовать высокой квалификации
Lathe operation is fast, automatic and **requires little (operator) skill.**

Не требовать ухода
The relays **offer freedom of maintenance.**

Не требуется
A high degree of precision **is not warranted** (*or* **needed,** *or* **necessary**) here ...

Не требующий обслуживания
A **maintenance-free** triple filtration system ...

Не увенчаться успехом
Such attempts **have not met with success** (*or* **have not been successful,** *or* **have been unsuccessful,** *or* **have failed**).

Не удаваться
Early attempts to understand the properties of matter by solving the wave equation **fared poorly** (*or* **have not met with success**).
With a laser, this approach **fails.**
They **failed to** establish an immediate connection.

Не удивительно что
It comes as no surprise (*or* **It is not surprising) that ...**
Small (*or* **No**) **wonder that** we have witnessed an enormous increase in scientific knowledge of ...
After such a success **it is little wonder that** plans were drawn up for ...

Не указывать названия [*см.* **Название которого не указано**].

Не указывая [*см.* **Без указания**].

Не упоминаться
No mention has been made of the fact that ...

Не успевать
The explosive force moves so fast that air **has no time to** leave the die.
Sorbite is a form of pearlite in which the iron carbide **has not had time** (*or* **has not managed**) **to** segregate.

Не успевать следить за
These motions **are too fast for the eye to follow.**

Не установлен [*см.* **Неясен**].

Не уступать
The output of the machine **is highly competitive with** that of a motorized scraper.
Copper **is as good as** mercury **for** the reduction of sorbic acid.
The capacitance uniformity of our diode **compares well with** CaAs epitaxial diodes.

Не утруждать
I **will spare** you the actual calculations.

Не учитывать I [*см. тж.* **Без учёта, Игнорировать, Не принимать во внимание, Пренебрегать**]
No account has been taken in this calculation **of** heat production from Th, U.
These calculations **ignored** the vast quantities of salt which are present in sedimentary sequences.

All these theories **fail to account for** the actual behaviour of the muscle tremor.
The homogeneous conversion in liquid hydrogen is slow and **can be neglected** (*or* **disregarded,** *or* **ignored**).
The theoretically predicted pressure **takes no account of** [*or* **does not take into account** (*or* **consideration**)] the roughness of the punch.

Не учитывать II [*см. тж.* **Упускать из виду**]
The amateur tends **to overlook** the importance of the thermometer.

Не учитываться
The higher harmonics **are disregarded** [*or* **are not taken into consideration** (*or* **account**)] here.
Amplitude variations **are ignored by** such systems.
Periodic fluctuations in gauge **have been neglected.**

Не ущемляя интересов
The salt imported with irrigation waters should be exported **without harming the interests of** water users downstream.

Не хватает для обеспечения
This amount **falls short of** the basic requirements of the body.

Не хватать
Vegetable proteins **are deficient** in amino acid lysine.
The smokeless coals **are in short supply.**
It wanted but a few days before he should ...
A number of details **are** still **lacking.**

Не центруется с
If the milling spindle **is off-centre relative to** the workpiece, ...

Не часто [*см.* **Редко**].

Не что иное как
These furnaces **are nothing more nor less than** (*or* **nothing but,** *or* **simply**) ovens lined with ...

Не чувствовать боли [*см.* **Не испытывать боли**].

Не являться исключением
Geology **is no exception.**

Не являться неожиданностью для
This kind of reaction **comes as no surprise to** a physicist.

Не являться чем-то новым для
Cosmic jets **are not new to** astronomers.

Не ясно
However, how the stimulus produces the generator potential **is not understood.**
What function this element played **was not evident** (*or* **clear**).

Неабсорбированный
The **nonabsorbed** beam of X-rays ...

Небесное тело
The Moon is the only **heavenly** (*or* **celestial**) **body** that is not self-luminous.

Неблагоприятно влиять на [*см. тж.* **Отрицательно влиять на**]
Such generators **are adversely affected by** wide temperature changes.
For applications where large clamps **would be detrimental to** (*or* **would impair**) general appearance ...

Неблагоприятное влияние [*см.* **Вредное влияние, Оказывать неблагоприятное влияние на**].

Неблагоприятные последствия
Beetles can withstand wide ranges of temperature without **ill effects.**

Неблагоприятные условия
This provides reliable electrical power **under adverse** (*or* **unfavourable**) flight **conditions.**

Неблагоприятный
If the temperature falls below 1300 K, two **adverse** factors develop: ...

Неблагоприятный для существования живых существ
On Mars, the surface temperature **is unfavourable for life.**

Небольшая глубина [*см. тж.* **На небольшой глубине**]
At shallow depths ...
The common cockle is found **at moderate depths.**

Небольшая жертва, принесённая ради
It would be **a small price to pay for** solving the radioactive ash disposal problem.

Небольшая нагрузка
If the motor starts to run away **under light load, ...**

Небольшими партиями
The turret is ideal for large work **in small lots.**

Небольшими порциями
Carefully add concentrated nitric acid, **a little at a time.**

Небольших размеров
These fishes **are of small size** (*or* **are small in size**).
The sun is a **modest-sized** member of a family of some 100 billion stars which make up our galaxy.

Небольшого объёма
Small-volume samples ...

Небольшое количество
The igneous rocks and metamorphic rocks, which constitute 95 percent of the volume of the earth's crust, are made up of **a bare handful of** silicate minerals.

Небольшой [*см. тж.* **Малых размеров, Невысокий, Незначительный, Ограниченное количество**]
Although the time-resolution is **modest,** this laser is a popular excitation source for ...
To produce a **small-scale** turbulence, ...
Casting alloys also usually contain **minor** (*or* **small**) amounts of a variety of metals.
To increase the die life at a **reasonable** cost, ...

Неважно [*см.* **Не иметь значения**].

Невелик [*см.* **Недолго существовать**].

Невероятный
Here is dependability and versatility that **is** almost **beyond belief** (*or* **unbelievable,** *or* **incredible**).

Невидимый для глаза
Ultraviolet rays **are invisible to the eye.**

Невозможен
These calculations would be **impracticable** (*or* **impossible,** *or* **impractical,** *or* **unfeasible**) without optical computing.

Невозможно [*см. тж.* **Если это невозможно, Нельзя, Почти невозможно, Практически невозможно, Трудно или даже невозможно**]
There is no way to check this out empirically.
The viscous damping **is** almost **impossible to** achieve.
Blind rivets **do not lend themselves to** automatic feeding and insertion, and therefore cost more to install.
The organism **defies** identification or assignment to any known taxonomic category.

Невозможно использовать [*см.* **Непригоден**].

Невозможно наблюдать
When the comet **is no longer observable** (*or* **can no longer be observed**), ...

Невозможно обнаружить
These defects **are not detectable** (*or* **cannot be detected**) by zero-setting checks.

Невозможно определить
There is no way of telling the width of such an ocean.

Невозможно ответить на этот вопрос
This question is unanswerable.

Невозможно переоценить важность [*см. тж.* **Нельзя переоценить**]
It is impossible to overestimate (*or* **overstate**) **the importance of** analysis.

Невозможно сказать
There's no way of telling when the next disaster will come.

Невозможный [*см. тж.* **Исключаться, Практически невозможный**]
The switch makes possible heretofore **impracticable** (*or* **unfeasible,** *or* **impossible**) applications of ...

Невооружённый глаз [*см. тж.* **Видимый невооружённым глазом, Звёзды, видимые невооружённым глазом**]
The observations were made by **the unaided** (*or* **naked**) **eye.**

Невоспламеняемый (*антон.* **Воспламеняемый**)
The cutting fluid is **nonflammable** (*anton.* **flammable**).

Невыполнение

This may be attributed to **a failure of** the above assumption.

Невыполненные заказы
The outstanding (*or* **The backlog of**) **orders.**

Невысокий
Carbon dioxide is an inert gas at **moderate** temperatures.

Невыясненный вопрос
Still **unanswered** (*or* **unclarified**) are many **questions** of importance.

Неглубокий поток
Drainage canals usually have **a shallow flow of** water.

Негорючий
The **nonflammable** (*or* **noncombustible**) gas was introduced as an arc-extinguishing medium.

Недавнего происхождения
Few of the visible craters in the planet's images are **recent.**

Недавно образовался
Some craters **are** comparatively **recent (in age).**

Недавно опубликованный
Two **recent papers** support this view.

Недалеко от
Mount Pelee lies **a short distance from** the city of St. Pierre.

Недалеко от побережья
It is a small island **off the coast of** Iceland.

Недействительный [*см.* **Оказаться несправедливым**].

Недолго служить [*см.* **Иметь короткий срок службы**].

Недолго существовать [*см. тж.* **Существовать недолго**]
The life span of the Cambridge machine **was brief.**

Недолговечный [*см.* **Иметь короткий срок службы, Существовать недолго**].

Недопустим
In high-performance systems, $c_0/r_0 = 0.98$ **may** well **be intolerable.**
If the hole will be exposed, the chipped edge **cannot be tolerated** (*or* **is impermissible**).
No leaks **can be tolerated** in the lines between...

Недорогой
The instrument is **moderately** (*or* **reasonably**) **priced** (*or* **inexpensive,** *or* **not expensive**).
The machine **is of moderate cost.**

Недосмотр
Because of **an oversight in** construction, the shells were ...

Недоставать [*см. тж.* **Обладать недостатком**]
What **was lacking** (*or* **missing**) **in** the mutants was a protein that has...

Недостает
The accounts of these observers **fall** somewhat **short of** objectivity.

Недостаток I [*см. тж.* **Дефект, Достоинства и недостатки, Серьёзный недостаток, Страдать недостатком, Устранять дефект**]
The trouble with this hypothesis is that the clouds would have collapsed completely ...
Unfortunately, there was one **flaw** in this theory.
The drawback to this process is that ...
There are obvious **pitfalls** in this method.
The chief **drawback** (*or* **disadvantage,** *or* **shortcoming**) **of** hydrogen is the hazard of fire if ...
A limitation (*or* **failing,** *or* **weakness,** *or* **flaw**) **of** this method is that a breakdown at any station stops the entire line.

Недостаток II [*см. тж.* **Восполнять недостаток, Испытывать недостаток, Ликвидировать недостаток, Нехватка**]
A deficiency of this vitamin in the diet leads to scurvy.
The electrode having **a deficit of** electrons is called the anode.
Drilling was discontinued because of **lack** (*or* **shortage,** *or* **scarcity**) **of** adequate equipment.

Недостаток кислорода в атмосфере
Oxygen-deficient atmospheres can lead to suffocation.

Недостаток места [*см.* **Ввиду нехватки места**].

Недостаток рабочей силы
Shortage of hands (*or* **labour**).

Недостаточно [*см. тж.* **Мало, Не хватать**]
The nearby islands **are inadequate to** give the harbour full protection from the seas.
Vegetable proteins **are deficient in** amino acid lysine.
Where fuel **is lacking ...**
We **are short of** high-speed drills.

Недостаточно вентилируемый [*см.* **Плохо вентилируемый**].

Недостаточно изучен [*см.* **Недостаточно исследован**].

Недостаточно исследован
The region very near the wall **has not been adequately explored** (*or* **investigated,** *or* **studied**).
The mechanism of the process **is** as yet **imperfectly** (*or* **little**) **understood.**
The factors influencing gas release **are** still **not clearly understood.**

Недостаточно разработан
This theory **is not sufficiently advanced** to permit ...

Недостаточное понимание
Our **lack of understanding of ...** prevents us from obtaining ...

Недостаточный [*см. тж.* **Обладать недостатком**]
Deficient air supply is indicated by ...
The rate of response of the conventional synchronizing system **is** quite often **inadequate to** synchronize the motor.
Uranium resources appeared **scarce** in relation to the projected needs.
The most critical deterrent of the use of martensitic steels is their **inadequate** corrosion resistance.
Deficient (*or* **Poor**) nutrition associated with fire diseases.
No qualitative interferences owing to **a lack of** solvent purity have been observed.

Недостижим
Absolute zero **is** thus **unattainable.**

Недостижимость
The unattainability of absolute zero ...

Недоступен для наблюдения [*см.* **Невозможно наблюдать**].

Недоступный
The cost of placing transmission systems underground **is prohibitive.**

Недоступный для
Such toughness levels previously **were beyond the reach of** iron foundry products.

Недра земли [*см. тж.* **В недрах земли**]
The interior of the Earth (*or* **The Earth's interior**) contains an appreciable amount of ...

Нежелательная примесь
The compound is free from **troublesome** (*or* **unwanted,** *or* **undesirable**) **impurities.**

Нежелательно
This **is undesirable** from the corrosion standpoint.

Нежелательный
To reduce **unwanted** (*or* **undesirable**) side effects, ...
The two sidebands, one wanted and the other **unwanted,** can be separated.
Delays of this order **would be objectionable.**

Независимо друг от друга
The jaws are operated **independently of one another.**

Независимо от
Navigation equipment operates totally **independent of** terrestrial navigation aids.
The thickness of the coils was recorded **independently of** the gaugemeter from a contact micrometer.
For maintaining the same direction of flow **irrespective** (*or* **regardless**) **of** the direction of the pump rotation, ...
Under these conditions one of the three filters is never required, **no matter what** the colour of the negative.
The fatigue limit is the highest stress which, **regardless of** the number of times it is repeated, will not cause fracture.
Whatever the material (is), the walls of the vessel must ...

The change from one method of steering to the other can be made **without regard to** the relative positions of ...

Независимо от его напряжения
The spin state of an electron cannot be changed by a uniform magnetic field **no matter how strong (it is).**

Независимо от того [*см. тж.* **Будь он ... или нет, Будь то**]
However old the earth **might be,** many events had to be included in its history.
Combustion is the burning of any substance, **whether it be** gaseous, liquid, **or** solid.
A particular wavelength has a particular energy and a particular set of properties **regardless of** what you call it.
An attractive aspect of this class of machine, **be it** (*or* **no matter whether it is**) 100 tons or 1000 tons, is its long life.
The plate will have approximately the same percentage of printing area on each tone, **irrespective of whether** it is made of zinc **or** magnesium.
You can rely on this gauge **no matter how** severe the conditions of service.
Whether dispersing agents **are** used **or not,** the quality of ... depends upon ...
The results are valid **whether or** not the fields **are** aligned.

Независимо от того, в каком порядке они следуют друг за другом
The final result will be the algebraic sum of all the shifts **no matter what their sequence.**

Независимо от того, из какого
"Single-ion" properties are often of importance **without regard to** the particular compound **from which** the ions were obtained.

Независимо от того как [*см.* **Как бы ни был**].

Независимо от того, является ли он ... или
The foods that we eat, **whether** natural **or** artificial, are compounds of carbon.

Независимость в отношении нефтеснабжения *и т.п.*
Self-sufficiency in oil will help to eliminate that deficit.

Независимость от
Although mathematics is sometimes called a science, it is usually distinguished from science by its relative **independence from** empirical considerations.

Независимый от
The system **is independent of** power line variations.
Length-**independent** losses ...
Time-**independent ...**

Незагрязнённый
Initial tests showed that the hydraulic fluid systems remained **contamination free** (*or* **uncontaminated**).

Незадолго до этого [*см.* **Лишь незадолго до этого**].

Незаконченный
The fourth stand remains **incomplete** (*or* **unfinished**).

Незамеченный [*см.* **Оставаться незамеченным**].

Незамкнутая цепь
An **open-chain** compound.

Незанятое состояние (*физ.*)
All **states** above this level **are empty** (*or* **unoccupied**).

Незачем [*см.* **Нет необходимости**].

Незначительная роль [*см.* **Играть весьма незначительную роль**].

Незначительно [*см. тж.* **Лишь незначительно**]
The surface temperature of the nebula would have increased **moderately** from 3,500 K to 4,000 K.

Незначительный [*см. тж.* **Лишь незначительный, Небольшой**]
The structural differences are of a **minor** nature.
This component is present in **minor** (*or* **insignificant**) amounts.
The solubility of sodium chloride in ethanol is **slight.**
Only a fair (*or* **moderate**) current value is passed through ...
A great many modifications can be introduced with **little** or no additional labour cost.

Except for **minor** difficulties the work proceeds smoothly.
With **modest** increases in exhaust velocity ...
This is a beryl mine, but it has also produced **minor** amounts of spodumene.
When **only moderate** accuracy is required, ...
Such a catalyst would have only a **marginal** effect on the cost of ammonia.
Of the three gradients, the pressure gradient is found to have **only a slight** (*or* **an insignificant**) effect.

Неизбежно [*см. тж.* **В силу необходимости, Обязательно**]
The steam cycle is **necessarily** less efficient than is theoretically possible.
Such changes **inevitably** (*or* **are bound to**) occur at the plate-making stage.
The volume of the open-hearth furnace is insufficient to contain all the charge in the form of cold metals and the charge of scrap must **of necessity** be spread over a period of time.
Physical and nervous disorders which almost **unfailingly** accompany infectious diseases ...
Their distinctive features **cannot help but** contribute greatly to the overall picture.

Неизбежно напрашивается вывод о том, что
There seemed no escaping the conclusion that there was also a transverse force drawing particles into the centre of the laser beam.

Неизвестен [*см.* **Оставаться неизвестным**].

Неизвестное [*см.* **Уравнение с одним неизвестным**].

Неизвестный
Solve the equation for **the unknown** terms.

Неизменно [*см. тж.* **Всегда, Постоянно**]
Excessive crankshaft speed **invariably** reduces engine life.
Homonuclear diatomic molecules like H_2, N_2, and O_2, **necessarily** have a zero dipole moment for any bond length.

Неизменный [*см. тж.* **Оставаться неизменным, Постоянный**]
If the Hamiltonian **is invariant** under the transformation, ...

Неиспользованный [*см. тж.* **Оставаться неиспользованным**]
In this way the country will be able to exploit **untapped** (*or* **unutilized**) coal deposits.
The continental margins should be investigated as storehouses of **untapped** information relating to ...

Неисправно работать
The instrument may **malfunction.**

Неисправность [*см. тж.* **Выявление неисправностей** (*или* **неполадок**), **Ненормальность в работе, Устранять дефект**]
A malfunction in the lines of hydraulic control ...
This prevents valve **troubles.**

Неисправный
This allows quick replacement of a **faulty** (*or* **defective,** *or* **an inoperative**) system by standardized standby thermometers.

Неисследованный [*см. тж.* **Нетронутый**]
Mapping in previously **unexplored** parts of the country ...

Неистощимый
An **unexhaustible** supply of solar energy ...

Неисчезающий
Provided that the Jacobian is **non-vanishing,** the equation may be solved to obtain ...

Неквалифицированный
Inexpert work can cause irreparable harm.

Некоторая свобода
The tether system allows **a degree of** lateral motion.

Некоторая часть
At least **a portion of** these molecules are located in ...

Некоторое время [*см.* **В течение некоторого времени**].

Некоторое время тому назад [*см.* **Одно время**].

Некоторое количество
A quantity of sodium hydroxide solution is divided into two equal parts.

Некоторое применение
Titanium finds **a limited** (*or* **some**) **use** in spite of its high cost.

Некоторое сходство между
There is **a vague similarity between** this technique and ...

Некоторое число
X is **some number** between *x* and *a*.

Некоторые
A selection of practical applications is given in Table 5.

Некоторые из
Certain of the reactions discussed are specific to only one functional group.
Certain of the amino acids may undergo structural changes ...

Некоторые сведения о
Something of the nature and importance of these molecular properties will be mentioned afterwards.

Некоторый [*см.* *тж.* **В некотором смысле**]
Radar can provide **a degree of** information about the size of raindrops and hailstones.
The size of the hole has always been **something of** a handicap.
The potential energy will be **some function of** this one dimension.
For each crystal plane there will be **some one** angle at which the Bragg law will be satisfied.
The presence of polar hydroxyl groups results in **a measure of** adsorption.
Two aspects need **slight** amplification.

Некоторым образом
The tides, **in a way,** affect time.

Некруглость
Deviations from circularity were found.

Некруглый
Cylinder liners which are **out-of-round** can be remachined.

Нелегированный
For **unalloyed** iron the greater grain growth seems to occur above ...

Нелегко
It is not (an) easy (matter) to reconstruct ...

Нелегко объяснить
These factors **are not easily explained** (*or* **accounted for**).

Нелегко себе представить
Although the engine is simple its basic geometry **is not easy to visualize.**

Нелинейный по
This equation **is nonlinear in** u_0, u_1, u_2.

Нельзя [*см.* **Невозможно, Этого нельзя сказать о**].

Нельзя допускать
If the hole is to be exposed, the chipped edge **cannot be tolerated** (*or* **is impermissible**).

Нельзя и мечтать [*см.* **О котором нельзя и мечтать**].

Нельзя исключать [*см.* **Не следует исключать**].

Нельзя использовать в качестве
The column **is** then **inoperable** (*or* **unusable**) **as** an absorber.

Нельзя наблюдать [*см.* **Невозможно наблюдать**].

Нельзя не прийти к выводу о том, что
There is no escape from the conclusion (*or* **One cannot but infer**) **that** reef growth kept pace with ...

Нельзя отличить от [*см.* *тж.* **Никак нельзя отличить от**]
The eggs of most species **are indistinguishable from** those of other insects.
The effects of gravity on masses and electromagnetic radiation **are indistinguishable** (*or* **cannot be distinguished**) **from** the effects of uniform acceleration.

Нельзя отрицать привлекательности
The idea **is not without (strong) appeal.**

Нельзя переоценить
The importance of this **cannot be overemphasized** (*or* **overestimated,** *or* **overrated,** *or* **overstated**) (*or* **cannot be too strongly emphasized**).

Нельзя применить [*см.* **Неприменим**].

Немедленно обращаться за помощью
Such patients **should seek help promptly** (*or* **immediately**).

Немедленно отразиться на
The availability of continuously tunable lasers **has had an immediate impact on** chemical implications.

Немногие [*см.* **Лишь немногие из**].

Немного I [*см.* **Мало**].

Немного II [*см. тж.* **Несколько**]
The water level is **slightly** (*or* **somewhat**) below the level of the spray jet.

Немного больше
The capacity was only **a trifle** (*col.*) **over** half of ...

Немного ниже [*см.* **Несколько ниже**].

Немногочисленны
Such assemblies **are few in number** (*or* **few and far between**).

Немыслимый с экономической точки зрения
A fixed stator winding along the track **is economically unthinkable.**

Ненормальность в работе
Air leaking into the pump from any source is likely to cause **erratic running** (*or* **faulty performance**).

Ненужный
To remove the **unneeded** core, ...

Ненулевой
Molecules of **nonvanishing** (*or* **nonzero**) size ...
In that case $J(e)$ for any e **not zero** is ...
Distinct from zero (*or* **nontrivial,** *or* **nonzero**).

Необнаружение
The failure to detect the signal ...

Необоснованный
An **unjustified** assumption ...

Необработанные данные
Useful results may be developed from **raw** (*or* **untreated,** *or* **unprocessed**) experimental **data.**

Необратимая реакция
An irreversible reaction.

Необратимо превращаться в
Diphenylamine **is irreversibly converted to** diphenylbenzidine.

Необратимый во времени
The class of such weak solutions **is irreversible in time.**

Необходим [*см. тж.* **Совершенно необходим, Требоваться**]
Cobalt **is required** in small amounts **by** plants and animals.
In science, as opposed to pure philosophy, observable facts **are requisite.**
To attain the high performance, powerful turbojets, rockets, or ramjets **became a necessity.**
It takes at least a minute **for** the chamber **to** come to equilibrium.
New approaches **are called for.**

Необходим для
Consideration of the ordered array of atoms or ions **is basic to** an understanding of the results.
Complex numbers **are necessary to** the mathematical treatment.
Artificial ventilation **is required to** maintain a normal atmosphere.
The presence of an inert strand **is requisite for** these processes.
Considerations of phase equilibria **are essential to** (*or* **necessary for**) an understanding of any mass-transfer process.
Calcium **is** also **essential in** many biological functions of the vertebrates.
Carbon dioxide **is essential to** synthesis.
Minute in amount but **indispensable for** life **are** the hormones and vitamins.

Необходим для понимания
Some knowledge of ... **is necessary to an understanding of** the formation of ...

Необходим опыт
It takes experience to build a crane like this.

Необходимо [*см. тж.* **Для этого необходим, Когда это необходимо, Нужно, Следует**]
There is a need to examine the significance of ...

If steroids are used **it is essential to** reduce the dose as soon as possible to 7.5 mg of ...
The bed **needs** (*or* **has**) **to be** regenerated before it can be used for another 10-min adsorption cycle.
A very powerful magnetic field **is required to ...**
It is essential that the insulation **should be** well packed.
Much **needs to be** done to satisfy these requirements.
Much **remains to be** done in this area.
It takes a very powerful magnetic field **to** control the path of a particle.

Необходимо более внимательно изучать данные
A closer look at the data is called for.

Необходимо внести коренные изменения в
There has to be a radical change in the construction of the cars.

Необходимо выяснить
It needs to be ascertained if these acids are actually requisite for protein synthesis.

Необходимо кратко остановиться на
Brief mention should be made of the glass electrode.

Необходимо особенно подчеркнуть, что
It cannot be too highly stressed (*or* **It should be particularly emphasized**) **that** the rate at which metal can be removed is largely dependent on ...

Необходимо особенно тщательно следить за тем, чтобы
Special care must be used to eliminate ...

Необходимо подчеркнуть, что
It is necessary to stress (*or* **It should be stressed**) **that** we are dealing with ...
It must be emphasized (*or* **underscored**) that no other sequence of events ...

Необходимо понимать, что
It should be realized that the properties of some elements ...

Необходимо провести
A new survey **is in order.**

Необходимо проявлять большую осторожность
Great care must be exercised in selecting ...

Необходимо сделать несколько замечаний
There are a number of points to be made.

Необходимо сделать следующее [*см. тж.* **Для этого необходимо сделать следующее**]
To renew the ink pads **the following procedure should be adopted.**
To remove the circuit-supply unit **proceed as follows.**

Необходимо сделать следующее замечание
A remark is in order [*or* **It should be noted** (*or* **remarked,** *or* **pointed out**) **that ...**].

Необходимо следить за тем, чтобы не
(Care should be taken to) see that [*or* **Take care** (*or* **Make sure**) **that**] oxidation of the amine **does not** occur in storage.
Care must be exercised (*or* **taken**) **to** avoid overheating the work.

Необходимо учесть
Proper allowance must be made for (*or* **Account must be taken of**) the processing tolerances.
In the comparison of these results, **consideration must be given to** the temperature differences (*or* **the temperature differences must be taken into account**).

Необходимо, чтобы
It is essential (*or* **necessary**) **that** the body of the machine **is** [*or* **(should) be**] effectively earthed.
It is requisite that the α-helix of the molecules **become** completely straightened.

Необходимое условие
Then **a necessary condition for** f to attain a minimum is ...

Необходимость [*см. тж.* **Без необходимости, В силу необходимости, В случае необходимости, Вызывать необходимость, Нет необходимости, По мере необходимости, По необходимости, При необходимости, Устранять необходимость в**]
Because of **the need for** great strength and rigidity ...

Необходимость ... вызвана тем, что
The **necessity of** considering this effect **stems from the fact that ...**

Необходимый [*см. тж.* **Требуемый**]
In order to carry out **the needed** (*or* **required,** *or* **necessary**) numerical estimates ...
Appropriate amounts of malt sprouts were added to ...
In this case high tensile strength and corrosion resistance **are (critical) requirements.**
Some revisions seem **imperative.**
Having set **the requisite** number of bolts in ...
The potentiometer offers **the wanted** performance characteristics.

Необходимый для того, чтобы
He has measured the time **it takes** a compression wave **to** travel from ... to ...

Необходимый и достаточный
This indicates sets of properties that **are necessary and sufficient for** para-unitariness.

Неограниченно
When a variable increases **beyond all bounds,** it is said ...
As *m* increases **indefinitely, ...**
As *n* is increased **without bound, ...**
The gas would expand **without limit.**

Неограниченное количество [*см.* **Вмещать неограниченное количество**].

Неограниченный
These machines have been designed to permit almost **limitless** possibilities in the field of ...
The wave propagates in an **unbounded** medium.

Неограниченный по протяжённости
The cladding **is unbounded in extent.**

Неодинаково [*см.* **По разному**].

Неодинаковые [*см. тж.* **Разные**]
Two **dissimilar** (*or* **distinct,** *or* **different**) conducting materials are joined in a continuous loop.

Неоднозначность
The non-uniqueness (*or* **ambiguity**) **of** this reduction may be seen by considering ...

Неоднозначный
As a result of ... the coil may exhibit several resonance modes, and a self-resonance determination **is then ambiguous.**

Неоднократно [*см. тж.* **Многократно**]
We have spoken **repeatedly** of ...
This belting has proved **time and again** (*or* has **repeatedly** proved) its complete reliability.

Неоднократно повторяться
This process **was repeated over and over again.**

Неоднородной толщины
These fibres **were irregular in thickness.**

Неоднородный [*см.* **Неодинаковые**].

Неопределённая глубина [*см.* **На неопределённую глубину**].

Неопределённое время [*см.* **В течение неопределённого времени**].

Неопределённое расстояние [*см.* **На неопределённое расстояние**].

Неопределённость
By averaging many exposures **the uncertainty** may be reduced to ...

Неопределённый
Let φ be the manifold across which the normal derivative of *U* **is indeterminate.**
The position of the electron within the wave train **is uncertain.**
The prospects for ... seem **dim** at the moment.

Неопровержим
The principal conclusion that amino acids and the genetic code coevolved seems **irrefutable.**

Неопровержимое доказательство того, что [*см.* **Неоспоримое доказательство того, что**].

Неоспоримое доказательство того, что
This **is decisive evidence that** the surface

layers of the Moon are quite different from the surface layers of the Earth.
Such a spectrum **can furnish unambiguous** (*or* **unassailable**) **proof of** the compound's identity.

Неотличим от [*см. тж.* **Нельзя отличить от**]
Many living species **are** almost **indistinguishable** in structure **from** species that flourished a billion or more years ago.

Неотъемлемая часть [*см. тж.* **Составлять неотъемлемую часть**]
A calibrating device and a recorder **are integral parts of** the unit.
Today, synthetic polymers **are an integral part of** our lives.

Неотъемлемая часть нашей жизни [*см.* **Настолько глубоко войти в нашу жизнь, что**].

Неоценимое преимущество
An inestimable advantage.

Неочищенный газ
Sulphur contained in **crude** coke-oven **gas ...**

Непараллельный
The reflector **is** sufficiently **off parallel with** the other reflector.
The measuring surfaces of the micrometer may thus be forced **out of line** (*or* become **nonparallel**).

Неперетачиваемая пластинка (*в резце*)
The new cutter with **throwaway inserts** is set up quickly on a simple and easy-to-use fixture.

Неплотно закупоренный
The glass tube **is loosely plugged with** cotton.

Неплотно прилегающие друг к другу
Adhesives of heavy-body consistency can be used in the joining of **loosely mating** structure parts.

Неплотный
The gas had escaped through a **leaky** valve.

Неповреждённые детали
In this way you can produce **damage-free workpieces.**

Неповреждённый [*см.* **Оставаться нетронутым**].

Неподвижен [*см.* **Быть неподвижным по отношению к**].

Неподвижная точка
Let *0* be **a fixed point.**

Неподвижно закреплённый [*см.* **Закреплён неподвижно, Прочно закреплён**].

Неподвижное состояние [*см.* **В состоянии покоя**].

Неподвижный [*см. тж.* **Оставаться неподвижным**]
The Earth's magnetic poles **are** not **fixed,** but tend to move at a known rate.
The model pertains to transport between an **immobile** surface and a turbulent stream of fluid.
We studied mass transfer inside a completely **stagnant** drop.
The rim of the brake rotates with the shaft; the remaining parts of the assembly **are static.**
Planed work, bolted to the machine table, reciprocates, while the tool remains **fixed.**
A **"motionless"** satellite.
The drill is moved from one hole to another in a piece of work, while the work remains **stationary.**
If at the points *A* and *B* there are two **stationary** clocks, ...
Stagnant air ...
The magma source in the mantle remains **fixed (in position),** while the lithospheric plate above it moves steadily over the source (*geol.*).
The **stationary** coordinate system is referred to as the laboratory system.

Неподвижный вал
Three of the pulleys are on **fixed shafts.**

Неподвижный слой
A gas flowing in a tube forms **a stationary layer** in contact with the walls.

Неполадка [*см. тж.* **В случае неполадки, Выявление неисправностей, Главный источник неполадок, Метод устранения неполадки, Устранять недостатки**]
When **a fault** arises, ...

Owing to technical **hitches ...**
Maladjustment ...
Malfunction in the lines of hydraulic control ...
This prevents valve **troubles** (*or* **mishaps,** *or* **upsets**).

Неполадки в работе
These characteristics must be taken into account if **faulty operation** is to be avoided.

Неполностью
An **imperfectly** evacuated space ...

Неполностью изучен
This phenomenon **is** still **understood incompletely.**

Неполностью симметричный
Nontotally symmetric.

Непонятен
Our most advanced theoretical models **are incomprehensible to** the layman.

Непоправимо повреждён
This "protective O_3 shell" **could be permanently** (*or* **irreparably**) **damaged.**
If a blade **becomes damaged beyond repair, ...**

Непоправимый вред
Inexpert work can cause **irreparable harm.**

Непоследовательный
The use of an **inconsistent** terminology ...

Непосредственная близость [*см.* **В непосредственной близости от**].

Непосредственная причина
Immediate causes of rockslides are not often evident.

Непосредственно I
The derivatives could be obtained **at once** by differentiation.
These expressions can be found easily from Eqs. (2.3) and (2.4) **by inspection.**

Непосредственно II
It is the usual practice not to record the deviation **as such,** but to indicate ...

Непосредственно в области
Conditions **in the immediate region of** an interface are difficult to observe.

Непосредственно впереди [*см.* **Непосредственно перед**].

Непосредственно за
A sample cell **(placed) just** (*or* **immediately**) **beyond** the focus of a convex lens produced a strong thermal lens.
The atom temperature **immediately behind** the shock wave was measured.

Непосредственно над
The top fuller is placed **directly** (*or* **immediately**) **above** the bottom fuller.

Непосредственно отвечать за
This operation **is the direct responsibility of** the refrigerating engineer.

Непосредственно перед I
The box is located **immediately ahead of** the drive head.
A separator is installed **just ahead of** the main turbine shop.
The work material is passed through an induction heating coil **immediately in advance of** the forging rolls.

Непосредственно перед II
The minerals are added to the basic solution **just before** infusion.
The reaction mixture was prepared **immediately** (*or* **just**) **prior to** (*or* **before**) use.

Непосредственно перед тем как
Just before the valve started to oscillate, the number of bubbles increased.

Непосредственно под [*см. тж.* **Чуть ниже**]
The filter unit is mounted **immediately** (*or* **just**) **below** the input-resistor unit.
The wave can travel **immediately under** the ground surface.

Непосредственно позади
The detector cannot be placed **directly behind** the filter.
There is a switch **immediately behind** each stop.

Непосредственно получать
Thus we **obtain** (*or* **have**) **immediately** (*or* **at once**): $A + b^2 + ...$

Непосредственно после

The precursor RNA molecule received proteins **immediately following** (*or* **after**) transcription (*biol.*).
These isotopes emit gamma rays **immediately on** decay.

Непосредственно после литья [*см.* **Не подвергнутый обработке после литья**].

Непосредственно после того как
Screening begins **the moment** (*or* **as soon as**) the material is placed at the feed end.

Непосредственно предшествующий
The period **immediately preceding** the launching of the missile ...

Непосредственно прилегающий к
The pollutant was found in the soil **immediately adjacent to** the factory.

Непосредственно примыкающие друг к другу
The sites **immediately adjacent to one another ...**

Непосредственно связан с [*см.* **Тесно связан с**].

Непосредственно сзади
The detector cannot be placed **directly behind** the filter.
There is a switch **immediately behind** each stop.

Непосредственно следовать из
From this **it readily** (*or* **immediately**) **follows** (*or* **it follows at once**) that ...

Непосредственно соприкасаться с
Each ganglion **lies in direct contact with ...**

Непосредственно соприкасающийся с
The fluid **in immediate contact with** the fixed surface can properly be said to be stagnant.

Непосредственно спереди (*антон.* **сзади**)
The two adrenals of mammals **lie immediately anterior** (*anton.* **posterior**) **to** the kidneys.

Непосредственно явствовать из [*см.* **Явствовать непосредственно из**].

Непосредственный I [*см. тж.* **В непосредственной близости от**]
ATP serves as **the immediate** source of energy for the mechanical work performed by muscle.

Непосредственный II
The student should be provided with **first-hand** experience of the types of software and computer systems that he may meet in industry.

Непосредственный III [*см.* **Иметь непосредственное отношение к**].

Непосредственный интерес [*см.* **Представлять непосредственный интерес для**].

Непостоянный
The tests gave **variable** results.

Непохожий на
Asymmetry makes the image extremely **dissimilar to** the object.

Неправильная установка
Malalignment (*or* **Maladjustment,** *or* **Misalignment**).

Неправильная форма
Irregular shape.

Неправильно оценивать
Bell **had misjudged** the electrical properties of mercury.

Неправильно сконструированный
Improperly designed.

Неправильно употребляемый термин
The term “soft packing” **is** really **a misnomer,** as the packing is only soft in the uncompressed state.

Неправильное использование (*или* **применение,** *или* **употребление**)
Misuse of fasteners ...

Неправильной формы
Where a very hard rock is subjected to severe stresses, it may rupture into **(highly) irregular** angular blocks.
Crystals of highest purity are often **irregularly shaped** (*or* **irregular in shape**).

Неправильность
The irregularity of the liquid structure ...

Неправильный [*см. тж.* **Ошибочный**]
Any drastic changes are indicative of **improper** operation.
This conclusion **is in error.**

Неправильный термин
The terms "die cushion" and "press cushion" **are misnomers.**

Неправильных размеров [*см.* **Нестандартных размеров**].

Непревзойдённый
This machinery offers **unmatched** durability.
Stainless steel has **unsurpassed** corrosion resistance.
The selection can provide **unexcelled** solutions to such problems.
The *g* factor can now be measured with **unexcelled** accuracy.

Непредвиденное обстоятельство
Allowance must be made for various **contingencies** that may jeopardize the lifting operation.

Непременно [*см.* **Обязательно**].

Непреодолимое препятствие [*см. тж.* **Представлять непреодолимое препятствие для**]
The supporters of this model will face **insurmountable** (*or* **insuperable**) **obstacles** in producing an explanation.

Непрерывно [*см. тж.* **Постоянно**]
If adequate ventilation is provided **at all times, ...**
The old rubber types improve **steadily.**
The process of growth can continue **uninterruptedly.**

Непрерывно меняющийся
What lies behind the Sun's **ever changing** visible features?

Непрерывно растущий
To provide for **progressively increasing** output, the capacity of the finished products warehouse has been doubled.
The **ever-growing** refractory materials industry ...
The world's **ever-expanding** population ...

Непрерывно уменьшаясь
The tension applied to the wire is varied during the winding, **being reduced progressively** as successive layers are applied.

Непрерывный
Electrons are in **ceaseless** (*or* **continuous**) motion by virtue of their heat energy.
The concept of **continual** (*or* **continuous,** *or* **permanent**) creation of stars in the Universe ...
Uninterrupted (*or* **Continuous**) movement of coal from the face to the loading point ...

Непрерывный в
A function f is called **continuous at** x_0 if ...

Непрерывный по Липшицу
U remains **Lipshitz continuous.**

Непрерывный поток
A mechanical feeder ensures **a steady flow of** material.

Непрерывный рост
The unabated growth of the plastics industry ...

Непригоден [*см. тж.* **Не подходить, Неприменим**]
This procedure **fails** only if ...
These cleaners should be used when all other methods **fail.**
Porous metal bearings are frequently used when plain metal bearings **are impractical.**
The device **is unsuitable** (*or* **unfit,** *or* **not fit**) **(for use)** in its present form.
Many physicians prescribe simple analgesics, although they are considered **inappropriate** by some rheumatologists.

Непригоден для
Much of the water in natural sources **is unsuitable for** humans to drink.

Непригоден для заселения
Such regions **are unsuited to human settlement.**

Непригоден для использования человеком
Such streams and lakes **are unfit for human use.**

Непригоден для употребления
This water **is unfit for use.**

Непригодность
This indicates **a** basic **inadequacy** (*or* **unsuitability**) **of** the procedure employed.

Неприемлем с точки зрения охраны окружающей среды
Generating power on board the vehicle **is ecologically unacceptable.**

Неприемлемый [*см.* **Делать непригодным для**].

Неприкрытый [*см.* **Оставлять неприкрытым**].

Неприменим [*см. тж.* **Непригоден**]
Henry's law **does not apply** (*or* **is inapplicable**) in this case.
Such steels **are** completely **unusable** in many cases.

Неприятный вкус
This is done to remove **the objectionable tastes.**

Неприятный запах
Carbon dioxide is a gas with **an obnoxious** (*or* **objectionable**) **odour** and ...

Непродолжительный [*см.* **Кратковременный**].

Непрозрачный для
The plasma **should be opaque to** the incident radiation.

Непроизводительно затраченный на
Allowing 50% extra for work **wasted in** friction, James Watt arrived at ...

Непроницаемость для
Impermeability to minority carriers ...

Непроницаемый для
All push buttons **are dust and oil tight.**
This surface **is impervious to** dirt and moisture.
The pipe **is opaque to** radiation.
Water tight, Air tight, Gas tight, Liquid tight.
Although the membrane of the red cell lets water pass freely, it **is impermeable or impenetrable to** large molecules such as hemoglobin.

Непроницаемый для звука
Sound proof.

Непропорционально большой [*см.* **Занимать непропорционально большую часть пространства**].

Непропорциональный
The effect **is out of proportion to** the quantity of ...

Непрореагировавший
Some dimethylacetylene remains **unreacted.**
The **unreacted** gases are recycled.

Непрямой
Out-of-straight bars.

Неработоспособный
Friction may make the device completely **inoperative.**

Нерабочее состояние [*см.* **Приводить в нерабочее состояние, Приходить в нерабочее состояние**].

Неравномерно
World coal reserves are most **unevenly** (*or* **nonuniformly**) distributed among the continents.
The pressure **is nonuniformly** distributed.

Неравномерный
Attempts to heat the rivet too quickly will give **uneven** (*or* **nonuniform**) heating.

Неразгаданный [*см.* **Неразрешённая загадка**].

Неразрешённая загадка
It would be gratifying to feel that **the backlog of** cosmic **puzzles** is not accumulating at a hopelessly rapid rate.

Неразрешённая проблема
An outstanding (*or* **unsolved,** *or* **unresolved**) **problem.**

Неразрешённый [*см.* **Оставаться неразрешённым**].

Неразрешим
This is useful in problems which **would** otherwise **be intractable.**

Неразрешимая задача
The determination of the optimal profile **is an intractable problem.**

Неразрывно связан с

Some of the most fundamental activities of life **are inextricably entwined** [*or* **intimately associated** (*or* **connected,** *or* **linked**)] **with** the properties of the lipids.

Inexorably associated with, Indissolubly related to ...

Deep scarring of the land **goes hand in hand with** open-pit mining of ores.

Неразумен

This choice **is not well advised** (*or* **is ill advised,** *or* **is unreasonable**).

Нераспространение (ядерного оружия)

Non-proliferation (of nuclear weapons).

Нерастворимый в воде

If the amine **is water insoluble** (*or* **insoluble in water**), ...

Нереальный

Such a jet of particles with a total momentum of 6 GeV will be recorded only in the **unlikely** circumstance that all the momentum has been invested in a single particle.

Нередкий

Exceptions to Veer's law **are not uncommon** (*or* **not infrequent,** *or* **not rare**).

Gout and pseudogout are **not infrequently** encountered in the elderly.

It is not unusual to find 2 or 3 tanks for each product.

Нередко встречаться

This expression **is not uncommon** (*or* **rather common**) **in** the literature of chemical engineering.

Нерешённая проблема

An unsettled (*or* **unresolved**) **problem.**

Нерешённый вопрос

There are many other **outstanding questions** that remain to be answered.

Неровная поверхность

When travelling over **uneven surfaces ...**

Неровности поверхности

Surface imperfections (*or* **irregularities**).

Неровность

The drawing shows how the glue fills microscopic **irregularities** between seemingly smooth surfaces.

Несколькими путями

The alkali bromides can be manufactured **by several processes.**

Несколько I [*см. тж.* **В некоторой степени, Немного, Слегка**]

The corresponding pressure ratio is **somewhat** (*or* **slightly**) higher for real gases.

The temperature changes **somewhat** when ...

The air pressure must **slightly** exceed the hydrostatic head.

Несколько II [*см. тж.* **Один или несколько**]

Many clay minerals are composed of **more that one** (*or* **of several**) clay minerals.

The ability of ... to punch **multiple** holes in one stroke ...

Несколько десятков

Several tens of kilometres ...

Несколько иной

A **somewhat different** restriction is necessary.

Несколько напоминать

Milled cereals **bear some resemblance to** the beetles' normal environment.

Stress corrosion **is somewhat similar to** pitting.

Fired enamels **somewhat resemble** [*or* **resemble to some extent** (*or* **to a degree**)] organic coatings.

Несколько ниже [*см. тж.* **Чуть ниже**]

The metal is heated to a temperature **just below** the critical range.

The water level **is slightly** (*or* **somewhat**) **below** the level of the spray jet.

Несколько процентов

In lavas containing **several percent of** water ...

Несколько раз

A single analyte atom may be ionized **more than once** during the laser pulse.

Несколько сбивает с толку

These examples **are somewhat misleading.**

Несколько севернее

Just north of the equator ...

Несколько секунд [*см.* **За несколько секунд**].

Несколько снижать
If manufacturing costs **can be lowered somewhat, ...**

Несколько сомневаться в
The existence of *f* synapses **was (still) in some doubt** at the time.

Несколько сот(ен)
For some dielectrics *k* ranges from one to **several hundred.**
A temperature of **several hundred** degrees Celsius ...
Several hundreds of metres ...

Несколько тысяч
Platforms contain **several thousands of** feet of such deposits.

Несложный [*см.* **Простой**].

Несмотря на [*см. тж.* **Даже при**]
In spite of (*or* **Despite**) repeated attempts, no instance has ever been observed to violate ...

Несмотря на всё
Life may succeed **against all the odds** in moulding the universe to its own purposes.

Несмотря на то, что
These colours are also being used **despite** (*or* **in spite of**) **the fact that** relatively expensive raw materials are sometimes required.
The radiant power differs in wavelength, **even though** the monochromator is set to the same nominal wavelength.
The subesophageal and thoracic ganglia, **even though** near one another, usually remain distinct.
Although most common minerals are relatively inactive, ...
Notwithstanding the fact that ...

Несовместим с
The temperature and pressure in the thermionic diode cell **were incompatible with** a purely thermal collisional energy augmentation process.
The results of some of the experiments **are not compatible** (*or* **are incompatible**) **with** the filter theory.
The phenomenon **was (totally) irreconcilable with** the most elementary physical laws.

Несовпадение [*см.* **Расхождение между**].

Несомненно [*см. тж.* **Бесспорно самый лучший**]
These impressions in the lunar surface **are indubitably** craters.
There is no question (that) the devices could be made much smaller.
Without question (*or* **Unquestionably,** *or* **Doubtless(ly),** *or* **Undoubtedly,** *or* **Undeniably**) the major source of man's intake of mercury is his food.
This is **far and away** your best buy.
To be sure (*col.*), the ratio of ... is 100 times greater in the sun than ...

Несоответствие [*см. тж.* **Расхождение между**]
Failure to meet the specifications ...
A gap (*or* **discrepancy**) **between** estimated **and** observed ultraviolet radiation ...
There is still **an unbalance between** the development of these two branches of industry.
To avoid **an inconsistency between** quantum mechanics **and ...**

Несостоятельный [*см.* **Оказаться несостоятельным**].

Неспособен
Carbon **is incapable of** possessing more than an octet of ...

Неспособность
The failure of such methods **to** resolve energy differences ...
The inability of the molecules **to** acquire ...

Несправедливый [*см.* **Оказаться несправедливым**].

Несравненно больше, чем
The gravitational influence of Neptune on Triton **is overwhelmingly** (*or* **incomparably**) **greater than ...**

Несравненно меньше
Early blimps **were only a fraction of the size of** the rigid airships of that period.

Нестандартное содержание
Then the analyzer signals that **the** molybdenum **content is out of range for** this type of steel.

Нестандартной формы
This facilitates the accurate machining of **odd-shaped** surfaces.

Нестандартный
Sometimes the new part demands a gauge or jig that **must be custom built.**

Нестандартных размеров
When an **off-dimension** part has been produced, ...

Нестационарное состояние
The **unsteady-state** diffusion equation.

Нестационарный
Non-steady-state conduction ...

Нести в себе информацию
This message **carries** more **information** than ...

Нести заряд
The fragment B^- **bears** (*or* **carries**) **a** negative **charge.**

Нести нагрузку
Both worms **bear** equal **loads.**

Нести потери
Certain losses in efficiency **may have to be borne** (*or* **incurred,** *or* **sustained,** *or* **suffered**).
The resonator **will suffer some loss.**

Нести расходы
One must **incur** considerable **expense** in gathering the data to be used in the model.
The development **costs have been borne** primarily **by** the government.

Несущая поверхность
The carrying surface of the belt.

Несчастный случай со смертельным исходом
A fatal accident.

Нет [*см. тж.* **Не существовать**]
For such gases an equation of state **is not available** (*or* **is unavailable**).

Нет большого выбора
We **have little choice.**

Нет в продаже [*см.* **Имеется в продаже, Распродан**].

Нет готовых рецептов [*см.* **Для ... нет готовых рецептов**].

Нет данных о том, что
The electron **gives no evidence** yet **of** having an internal structure (*Пока нет данных о том, что электрон обладает внутренней структурой*).

Нет двух одинаковых
No two of the four groups attached to the central carbon **are the same.**

Нет единого мнения относительно [*см.* **Нет согласия между ... относительно**].

Нет единого мнения среди ... относительно
There is no agreement (*or* **consensus of opinion**) **among** mineralogists regarding the origin of ...

Нет конца
There is no end (in sight) to the continuing evolution of ...

Нет недостатка в
Fortunately, **there is no lack of** examples of geosynclines being formed at the present time.
There is no shortage of questions to be answered.

Нет необходимости
The chamber **need not** be removed.
We **need not** go into the details here.
There is no need for a stiff pendulum rod.
There is no need to mount the pendulum.

Нет необходимости останавливаться на
I **need not dwell on** the elaborateness of the network.

Нет ни малейшего сомнения в том, что
It cannot be doubted that this process contributed to ...

Нет ни малейшего указания (*или* **признака**)
There is not a grain of evidence to suggest the Triassic appearance of western Utah.

Нет никакого сомнения в том, что
There is no question (*or* **doubt**) **that** nuclear power is a saving technical development.
There can be no doubt that ...

Нет ничего похожего на
There is nothing like tunneling in classical mechanics.

Нет оснований
It is beyond reason to hope for extraction of ferrous metals in significant quantities to provide substitutes for ore deposits of the continents.

Нет пределов
With more powerful radar systems **there is** almost **no limit to** the resolution that can be obtained.

Нет причин
It is unjustified to link these differences to chemical pollutants.

Нет смысла [*см. тж.* **Едва ли целесообразно**]
There is no point in going through all the details of ...

Нет согласия между ... относительно
There is no agreement among clay mineralogists **regarding** proper nomenclature for the halloysite minerals.
There is no general agreement (*or* **consensus of opinion**) **among** authors **as to** the details of this classification.

Неточная градуировка
Errors due to **imperfect** (*or* **inaccurate,** *or* **faulty**) **calibration of** the instrument ...

Неточно применять слово
The word back-mixing **is used (somewhat) loosely** in the literature.

Неточный
This assumption **is inexact.**

Нетронутый [*см. тж.* **Оставаться нетронутым**]
In this way the country will be able to exploit **untapped** (*or* **unutilized**) coal deposits.
A wide and **virgin** field is here open and ...

Нетрудно
It is an easy matter to enumerate all six possibilities.

Нетрудно понять
There is no difficulty in understanding (*or* **It is not difficult to understand**) how these elements happened to be at the surface.

Нетрудно убедиться [*см.* **Легко убедиться (в том), что**].

Неубедительно звучать [*см.* **Звучать неубедительно**].

Неудача [*см.* **Обречён на неудачу**].

Неудачный [*см.* **Не увенчаться успехом**].

Неудачный вариант
Sodium cyanide **would be a poor choice.**

Неудобно пользоваться
This instrument **is inconvenient to use.**

Неудовлетворительный
A year ago it was decided that the training methods **were inadequate.**
Improper measuring technique is a common cause of erroneous conclusions about accuracy.

Неуклонно развиваться
Research in this field **is making steady headway** (*or* **is advancing steadily**).

Неуклонно расти
The need for this product **will grow steadily.**

Неуклонно растущий
Ever greater (*or* **Ever-increasing**) quantities of electric energy must be provided.
The **ever-growing** application of air-borne electronics ...

Неупорядоченно [*см.* **Беспорядочно расположены**].

Неурожай
Such **a crop failure** can lead to famine.

Неучёт
Failure to take account of (*or* **to take into account**) this variation in the osmotic coefficient would cause false conclusions.
Neglect of this factor was responsible for the failure of early estimates.

Неуязвимый
The radar designers try their best to make their sets **immune to** enemy countermeasures.

Нефтедобывающий
Every **petroleum producing** area in the world ...

Нефть [*см.* **Давать нефть, Добыча, С нефтяным отоплением**].

Нехватка [*см. тж.* **Испытывается нехватка, Недостаток**]
At very low temperatures no electrons will be excited from the valence to the conduction band because of **the lack of** thermal energy.
The dearth of the technological personnel ...
A deficit of electrons ...
Drilling was discontinued because of **lack** (*or* **shortage,** *or* **scarcity**) **of** adequate equipment.
For lack of new equipment we have to use old machines.

Нецелесообразно [*см.* **Мало смысла, Нет смысла**].

Нечто большее, чем простая случайность
This **is something more than a mere incident.**

Нечто вроде
Many so-called colour-blind individuals have trichromatic vision **of a sort.**
In this respect the planet offers **what amounts to** an immense natural laboratory.

Нечто среднее между
Transfer moulding **is a cross between** compression moulding **and** injection moulding.

Нечувствительный к
Such amplifiers **should be insensitive to** system disturbances.

Неэкономно использоваться [*см.* **Пространство используется неэкономно**].

Неэффективен
In such applications digital electronic hardware **is inadequate** (*or* **ineffective,** *or* **inefficient**).

Неявно
The emf of the cell is **implicitly** included in ... terms.

Неясен
The reason for the small size of the molecule **is** still **elusive** (*or* **unclear,** *or* **vague,** *or* **obscure**).

Неясный [*см.* **Неопределённый**].

Ни [*см.* **Как бы велик ни был**].

Ни в коей мере не
This **is in no way** (*or* **by no means**) detrimental to the elements.

Ни в коей мере не связан с
These factors **are in no way related to** natural causes.

Ни в коем случае не
On no account must steam be allowed to enter the recorder.
Guniting **is not, under any circumstances,** to be regarded as ...
Under no circumstances should error-rate compensation be used.

Ни в одном из
In none of the cases for which these calculations were done does instability occur.

Ни в одном случае [*см.* **Ни разу**].

Ни малейшего сомнения [*см.* **Нет ни малейшего сомнения в том, что**].

Ни малейшего указания [*см.* **Нет ни малейшего указания**].

Ни ..., ни ...
Energy can be **neither** created **nor** destroyed.

Ни один из
None of the materials under study is more than a few millimetres from a metal surface.
One form of tin shows **none of the** typical metallic characteristics.

Ни один из двух
Neither of the two proteins demonstrated any exonuclease activity.
Neither reactant **is** a charged species.

Ни один ... не способен
Creating such heavy particles **is beyond the capabilities of** any existing accelerator.

Ни одного из
The fresh solvent contains **none of** these compounds.

Ни разу
When these prominent neurons were stimulated, **in no case was** there an obvious motor response.

Ни то, ни другое [*см.* **Не иметь ни того, ни другого**].

Ни тот, ни другой [*см.* **Ни один из двух**].

Ниже I [*см. тж.* **Значительно ниже, Падать ниже, Приводиться ниже**]
Below this level there can be another domain.
Deactivation can drop the energy **past the point of** intersection of ...
The pressure drops **below** 3 mm.
If the skip is accidentally lowered **beyond** the lowest point of the chute's travel, ...

Ниже II
Such a coordinate system is assumed **below** (*or* **in what follows,** *or* **in the following**).
The theory of cohesion in solids is discussed **later** (*or* **below**).

Ниже III [*см.* **Вниз и вверх по течению от**].

Ниже нуля
Below zero.
An icy **minus**-60 degrees ...
Sub-zero temperatures.

Ниже перечислены [*см. тж.* **Перечислены ниже**]
The liquid propellant chemical fuels **are listed below.**

Ниже по течению
Figure 4 is a photograph of the eddying wake **downstream of** (*or* **from**) a shock-induced separation of ...

Ниже приводится
Below is a summary of ...
Below is shown (*or* **given**) the relationship between ...
Seen (*or* **Illustrated**) **below is** a complete pilot plant for ...
Following are brief discussions of ...

Ниже среднего
In an area with a negative magnetic anomaly, the earth's magnetic field intensity **is below average** (*or* **lower than average**).

Ниже стандарта
They claim that the quality of the product carburized at over 1750°F **is substandard.**

Ниже точки замерзания
The average temperature here **is below freezing.**

Ниже уровня земли
Fume extraction channels have been provided **below ground level.**

Ниже уровня моря
Below sea level.

Ниже, чем [*см.* **На ... градусов ниже, чем**].

Нижеприведённый [*см. тж.* **В последующих главах, Дальнейший**]
The discussions **which follow** point out the meaning of ...
The following study will be limited to a sharp-edge valve.
In the analysis of the data **that follow** (*or* **given below**) the logarithmic form is used.

Нижнее положение [*см.* **В нижнем положении**].

Нижние слои земной коры
The lower crust is denser than the upper crust.

Нижний
See **bottom** photo ...
The lower row of the matrix ...
The lowermost layer of the soil ...

Нижняя поверхность
The insecticides are sprayed on plants in such a way that **the undersides of** the leaves are also coated.
The undersurface of the crust ...

Нижняя сторона
The test piece has a notch **on the underside.**

Нижние слои атмосферы
These bands are absorbed by the O_2 **in the lower atmosphere.**

Низ [*см.* **Книзу, Снизу**].

Низкая концентрация
When spherical particles are **sparsely distributed** in vacuum ...

Низкая точность
These methods have **poor** (*or* **low**) precision.

Низкие значения вплоть до
Values as low as (*or* **Low values down to**) 10^{-9} have been reported for solids.

Низкое содержание [*см. тж.* **Беден, С низким содержанием**]
These ores **are low in** metallic **content** (*or* **have a low** metallic **content**).
These bauxites **are poor in** aluminium.

Низкокипящий (*антон.* **Высококипящий**)
A **low-boiling** (*anton.* **high-boiling**) compound.

Низколежащий (*антон.* **Высоколежащий**)
These quenchers have **low-lying** (*anton.* **high-lying**) triplet states ...

Низкопористый (*антон.* **Высокопористый**)
Roofing tile **is of low porosity** (*anton.* **of high porosity**).

Низкосортный (*антон.* **Высокосортный**)
Low-grade (*anton.* **High-grade**) materials must be ...

Никак нельзя отличить от
These molecules **can in no way be distinguished from** each other.

Никакой
No pure substance has permeability approaching this.

Никакой другой
Every even integer is assigned one particular number and **no other.**

Никакой другой, кроме
No body other than the Sun and the Moon can have any significant tidal effect on the Earth.

Никогда
At no time (*or* **Never**) should thermoplastics and thermosets be stored in the same room.

Никоим образом не
This pressure **was by no means** the limit of what could be achieved.
Not all chelates are volatile **by any means.**
This **in no way** affects the operation of the machine.

Никто не сомневается в
The importance of quantitative measurement **has never been doubted.**

Нисходящая (*антон.* **Восходящая**) **ветвь** [*см. тж.* **Спадающая кривая**]
We studied **the falling** (*or* **descending,** *or* **down-tending**) [*anton.* **the rising** (*or* **ascending,** *or* **up-tending**)] branch of the curve.

Ничего не говорит о том, что
The fact that a particular isotope is "unstable" **says nothing about** how quickly it will disintegrate.

Ничего не даёт
This analysis **accomplishes nothing.**

Ничего не знать о
We are still **in the dark about** the location of ...

Ничего не упомянуто о том, что
No mention has been made of (*or* **Nothing has been said as to**) what happens to the shock waves when they reach the walls.

Ничего подобного не произошло с
Nothing of the kind (*or* **of this sort**) **has happened to** the first observer.

Ничем не оправдываться
The postulate **had no justification** except "to make the theory fit the data".

Ничем не отличаться от [*см. тж.* **Совершенно не отличаться от**]
Calcium carbonate in shells is a true mineral and **is no different from** calcite formed by ...

Ничем не отличаться от нового
The repaired tool **is as good as new.**

Ничто не может препятствовать
There is nothing to prevent the electron **from** drifting parallel to ...

Ничтожная величина [*см.* **На ничтожную величину, Пренебрежимо малая величина**].

Ничтожно
The pressure of the gas **is (only) infinitesimally** different from that of the piston.

Ничтожное количество
The process can be applied to **minute amounts** as well as to relatively large quantities.
For **micro amounts** (*or* **quantities**) chromatography on filter paper is used.

Ничуть не менее
This precision **is every bit as** important **as** the extension in energy.

Ничуть не отличаться от [*см.* **Совершенно не отличаться от**].

Но [*см.* **Однако**].

Но не
A buoy is an anchored moored floating object, **other than** a lightship, intended as an aid to navigation.

Но не больше (*антон.* **Но не меньше**)
These equations have four solutions **but no more** (*anton.* **but no less**).

Новатор
He was **a pioneer** (*or* **a trail-blazer,** *or* **an innovator**) in this field.

Новаторские исследования
In this field, invaluable **pioneer research** was carried out.

Новаторский
Telecommunication technology can play an important role in the development of **innovative** systems for delivering medical care.
An **innovative** (*or* A **novel**) method of filling the storage ring ...
A **novel** attempt at the description of such systems ...
A **pioneering** experiment has recently been carried out by ...

Новейшей конструкции
All the fishing gear **is of the latest design.**

Новейший [*см. тж.* **Самый современный**]
Recent research has shown that ...

Новичок в области
As **a newcomer to** the science of geology, he was ...

Нововведение
This is the most recent **innovation.**
These techniques are **newcomers to** the field of nondestructive testing.

Новшество [*см.* **Нововведение**].

Новый [*см. тж.* **Совершенно новый**]
A **fresh** portion of the solution is introduced into the first unit.
This technology **is young.**
This is **a fresh** approach to gear shaving.
Martensitic stainless steels are relatively **new to** the aircraft industry.
The present invention relates to **novel** and useful metallic cyclomatic compounds.

Новый клиент
The low cost surprises our **first-time customers.**

Ножницы
A 12-gauge **shear.**

Ножной
The welder is motor driven through a **foot-operated** clutch.
A **foot-operated** switch is provided for reversing the motor.

Номер [*см.* **Иметь номер, С чётным номером**].

Номинальная мощность
Generators with **power ratings** from 150 to 1200 watts ...

Номинальное напряжение
Voltage ratings (*or* **Rated voltages**) **are** 500 V at sea level.

Номинальный размер [*см.* **Меньше номинального размера**].

Норма [*см.* **Отвечать стандартам**].

Нормально
When the amplifier operates **properly, ...**

Нормально к [*см.* **Перпендикулярно к**].

Нормально работать [*см.* **Исправно работать**].

Нормального размера
Normal sized or slightly enlarged kidneys must be...

Нормальный к [*см.* **Перпендикулярный к**].

Нормированный к
The plot **is normalized to** the intensity of bare uranium.

Нормировать к
This spectrum **was normalized to** laser power fluctuations.

Носить в себе
Man can **harbour** at least six species of amoebae.

Носить имя
The depression **bears the name** Meteor Crater.

Носить на себе следы
The oldest sedimentary rocks exposed on land **bear evidence of** deposition in water.

Носить название (*или* **имя**)
Each mineral variety **bears a name.**
Such a plot **is** generally **identified** (*or* **classified**) **as** (*or* **termed,** *or* **referred to as,** *or* **called**) a "Stress-Number of Cycles Curve".

Носить общее название
Electrons, muons and neutrinos **are collectively called** leptons.
Epinephrine and norepinephrine **are referred to collectively as** catecholamines.

Носить различные названия
This form of petroleum **goes under various names.**

Нужда [*см.* **Необходимость, Потребность в, Удовлетворять потребности, Устранять необходимость в**].

Нуждаться в
A one-megahertz, one-megabit charge-coupled memory device **would require** a power of somewhat between a milliwatt and a watt to sustain it.
Mariners, aviators, ... **have need for** a compass.

Нуждаться в дальнейшем рассмотрении
These observations **need further consideration.**

Нуждаться в дополнительных комментариях
Several features **deserve further comment.**

Нуждаться в объяснении
It was this multiplicity of hadrons that **stood in need of explanation.**
This relationship **needs clarification.**

Нужды городского хозяйства
This water supplies **urban needs.**

Нужен для [*см.* **Необходим для**].

Нужно [*см. тж.* **Необходимо, Следует**]
When the density of the gas **is to be** measured, ...
To determine ... we **need** only perform the division of ...
If purchased power **is to be** used, then only the transformers, substations and distribution facilities **need be** provided.
Much **needs** (*or* **remains**) **to be** done to satisfy these requirements.
We provide such units exactly where **they are wanted.**

Нужно лишь
All one need to do is to apply the above rule.

Нужно найти
What **is wanted is** the density of points within ...

Нужно признать, что
It must be admitted that such calculations cannot be carried out with similar success for ...

Нужный [*см. тж.* **Время, необходимое для; Требуемый**]
To maintain **the requisite** (*or* **the required**) temperature, ...
This potentiometer offers **the wanted** performance characteristics.

Нулевого порядка
A **zeroth-order** differential equation.

Нулевой
In terms of "**zeroth** ionization potential", ...

Нуль [*см.* **Везде равен нулю, Выше нуля, Не равный нулю, Ниже нуля, Падать до нуля, Сводиться к нулю, Устанавливать на нуль**].

Нумерация
A new method of **numbering** sites is employed.

Нумеровать
Label the meridians, starting with 70°W on the right.

Нумероваться по порядку
Sometimes the σ_g orbitals **are numbered sequentially,** the first being $1\sigma_g$.

Ньютоновский
Newtonian mechanics.
The **Newtonian** formulation.

Ныне исчезнувший
The lakes bordered on **now-vanished** glaciers.

О

О [*см. тж.* **Информация о, Наука о, Относительно III, Трение стали о сталь**]
Of such machines it can be said that ...

О котором говорилось в
This results from cathode sheathing **as discussed in** the preceding section.

О котором идёт речь [*см. тж.* **Рассматриваемый**]
The symmetry **at issue** (*or* **involved**) **is** isotopic-spin symmetry.
The term "foliated" is used to indicate that the material **referred to** (*or* **dealt with,** *or* **in question,** *or* **in hand,** *or* **at hand**) consists of thin, separable lamellae or leaves.

О котором можно только догадываться
The two processes interact in ways **that can only be guessed at.**

О котором не было известно
The primary system of the reactor now had a leak **unknown to** the operator.

О котором нельзя и мечтать [*см. тж.* **Достигнуть совершенно неожиданного успеха**]
These instruments extend the chemist's studies to a scope **undreamed of** a few years ago.

О которых никогда раньше и не мечтали
Trouble-free performance **never before thought possible** was achieved.

О ... можно написать целую книгу
The story of the growth of the synthetic chemical industries **would make a book by itself.**

О ... не может быть и речи
Studies of superconductors placed under very high pressures at ultralow temperatures **were out of the question.**

О том, что
The reader will encounter statements **to the effect that** introducing error-rate control makes the system respond faster.
There are theories **to the effect that** the Moon was once much closer to the Earth.

О чём свидетельствует
These earthquakes originate in the cold interior of the subducting plate **as demonstrated** (*or* **evidenced,** *or* **witnessed**) **by** seismic wave velocities within the slab (*geol.*).

Оба
Both of these forms are soluble in benzene.
This enzyme can attack **either** terminus of single-stranded DNA (*biol.*).

Обведённый кружком
Special taps are to be marked with the letter *S* **enclosed in a circle** (*or* **with a circled** letter *S*).
Letters **within circles ...**

Обводить
The paper mask is laid on the metal sheet and **traced,** after which the metal is cut.

Обволакивать
Colloidal smokes and smogs **blanket** urban and industrial areas.
The star **is shrouded by** a cloud of gas.

Обгонять
The uplift of the continents **has** always **kept ahead of** erosion.

Обдумывать
He **pondered** the problem during 30 years.

Обеднение
Depletion of the Moon **in** gold ...

Обеднён
The albic horizon **has been depleted of** clay minerals, iron oxide, ...
The meteorites' parent body **is depleted in** alkalis.
The mantle **has been impoverished in** radioactive elements during ...

Обеднять
The fractionation process **depleted** the lunar core **of** radioactive elements.

Обедняться
The soils of cultivated lands **have been depleted of** their natural phosphate.
When the water vapour in the atmosphere **is depleted** to the point at which ...
The environment under the deposit **becomes exhausted of** oxygen.

Обедняться вследствие
The cometary shell **is being depleted by** these stellar perturbations.

Обезврежен
These compounds **may be rendered harmless by** treating with ...

Обеспечен I
The cells **are fitted** (*or* **provided,** *or* **equipped,** *or* **supplied**) **with** interlock systems.

Обеспечен II
The supply of phosphate **is assured** (*or* **provided for**).

Обеспече́ние [*см. тж.* **Для обеспече́ния**]
The provision of adequate plant facilities for ...

Обеспече́ние совместимости ... с
This problem is to be considered when **interfacing** the electromechanical limit switch **to** solid-state circuitry.

Обеспе́чивать [*см. тж.* **Давать**]
The combination of so many properties is difficult **to achieve.**
A coating of zinc is deposited on the wire **to afford** protection against corrosion.
The unit **assures** electrical system reliability.
Reliability is a difficult thing **to build into** equipment.
It may become necessary to reduce the amine concentrations **to effect** easier stripping of the amine solution.
The system is used **to ensure** a constant rate of flow.
The cylinder **furnishes** radiation shielding.
To **gain** the flexibility needed for ...
Four-wheel steering **gives** exceptional manoeuvrability.
The hard metal and ceramic structures adopted **make for** mechanical ruggedness.
To obtain correct filter operation, ...
These gases **offer** better performance than nitrogen.
The machines have been designed **to permit of** almost limitless possibilities in the field of ...
The diffuser **provides** a uniform illumination of the negative.
The use of very large antennas **will secure** high efficiency in the radiation of ...
The above engineering features **have given** these boring mills a leading position throughout the country.
To maintain high accuracy in milling operations, ...
The machine **provides for** copying intricate masters.
Tunable dye lasers **afford** (*or* **ensure**) temporal resolution.
The engine **delivers** (*or* **gives**) enough power.
The overall goal is **to realize** the following characteristics: ...
In most finishing operations it is only necessary **to impart** a smooth finish **to** the wheel.
The electronegativity difference between carbon and hydrogen is insufficient **to produce** a bond polarity high enough for effective hydrogen bonding.

Обеспечивать безопасность
The concrete reactor vessel **affords** (*or* **provides**) **a high degree of safety.**

Обеспечивать более глубокое понимание
This **will give new insight into** the phenomenon.

Обеспечивать бо́льшие возможности для
The species are interchangeable, thereby **providing great scope for** experimentation.

Обеспечивать возможность [*см. тж.* **Давать возможность, Позволять**]
Thermocouples made of semiconductors **offer the prospect of** operation at high temperatures.
It is not unusual to find two or three tanks for each product **to allow for** receiving in one while pumping from or settling in another.
The testing machine **makes possible** testing of (*or* **makes it possible** to test) large components.
This **provides a means for** the removal of corrosive compounds.

Обеспечивать высокую разрешающую способность
The method **yields a high resolution.**

Обеспечивать доступ к
Access to the under-chassis components **is gained by** removal of the base plate.
A turnout from the machine hall pilot tunnel **provides access to** the transformer hall.

Обеспечивать защиту
The optimum **protection would be afforded** (*or* **provided,** *or* **given**) **by** the addition of ...

Обеспечивать значительное повышение
This precision **can pay a big bonus in** production speed and quality.

Обеспечивать лёгкий доступ к
This **allows** the dye-setter **easy access to** his group of machines.

Обеспечивать наиболее эффективное использование
Reflectors are especially designed **to give the** most **effective use of** the light.

Обеспечивать напряжение
The sections can be connected in series **to furnish** (*or* **provide,** *or* **supply**) 240,000 **volts.**

Обеспечивать необходимый эффект
Short-duration irradiation **will do the job.**

Обеспечивать оптимальное сочетание
A compromise had to be reached between the sensitivity, precision **and ...**

Обеспечивать понимание
This description **gives** physical **insight into** the difference between ...

Обеспечивать превышение предложения над спросом
The previous techniques that geologists developed **to keep supply ahead of demand ...**

Обеспечивать преимущества
Britain's impressive resources **could give it an edge in** the economic competition with ...

Обеспечивать путём
A considerable OH^- concentration **is available by** hydrolysis of ...

Обеспечивать работу двигателя
To keep the engine running, ...

Обеспечивать стимул
Incentives should be offered to speed development ...

Обеспечивать широкие возможности для
The use of empirically determined parameters **allowed much room for** manipulation of the models.

Обеспечивать экономию
These factors **effect a saving in** operating costs.
This **provides a saving in** power consumption.
A saving in timber **can be obtained.**

Обеспечивающий экономию
Enamels permit the use of thinner gauge metals **with resulting** [*or* **which provide** (*or* **yield**)] cost and weight **saving.**

Обесточивание [*см.* **В случае обесточивания**].

Обесточиваться
The contacts may remain closed when one coil **is de-energized.**

Обёртывать
Wrap the sandpaper **around** a wooden block.

Обзор
We give **a** brief **overview** (*or* **survey,** *or* **review**) **of** the fundamental properties of ...

Обзор по вопросу о
We have presented **an overview of** electron and hole motion.

Обзор ... приводится в
The extensive **literature on** this shift **is reviewed in** Rev. [5].

Обильно
Another substance that is **copiously** (*or* **lavishly,** *or* **abundantly**) produced by combustion is carbon monoxide.

Обильно выделяться
Carbon monoxide and carbon dioxide **are** both **given off copiously** when lunar fines are intensely heated.

Обильно снабжён
The medulla **is richly supplied with** nerves.

Обильно снабжён рёбрами
The cross-stay **is liberally ribbed.**

Обильные осадки
Ample (*or* **Abundant**) **precipitation.**

Обильный
Sulphur is an **abundant** constituent of ocean water.
There is **a wealth of** [*or* **a great deal of** (*or* **abundant**)] information about ...
An **ample** (*or* **copious**) supply of air is provided.
Copious brown fumes appear.
These available raw materials **are** cheap and **plentiful.**
The bursts release **prodigious** amounts of energy.

Обитать в
All six species of amoebae **inhibit** the gastrointestinal tract.

Обитающий на дне
Bottom-dwelling organisms ...

Обладать [*см. тж.* **Иметь**]
These types of lavae **are of** high viscosity.
The observer **is equipped** (*or* **provided**) **with** a device that makes it possible to ...
This material **is** abrasion **resistant** (*обладает высоким сопротивлением истиранию*).
The steel **displays** embrittlement at elevated temperatures.
These refractories do not **exhibit** acidic or basic properties.
The automatic press **embodies** (*or* **has,** *or* **includes,** *or* **incorporates**) all the regular features of the semi-automatic press.
The capacitor **features** extraordinary stability.
The corrugation **offers** an enlarged area and so increases total heat transfer from ...
These alloys **possess** good tensile strength.
Carbon-fibre materials **offer** nearly all the attractive features of glass-fibre materials.
The adrenals **show** remarkable similarity of structure.
This type of capacitor **affords** greater capacity for a given volume.

Обладать бóльшей массой
Deuterium is chemically similar to hydrogen except that it **is more massive.**

Обладать большой энергией
Such pions **are particularly energetic.**

Обладать глубокими познаниями в области [*см. тж.* **Изощрён в области архитектуры**]
He **had an intimate knowledge of** the physiology of human speech.

Обладать горьким вкусом
This compound **tastes sour.**

Обладать значительным преимуществом
Such processes **possess considerable merit.**

Обладать исключительной стойкостью к [*см.* **Исключительно стойкий к**].

Обладать меньшей энергией, чем (*физ.*)
Two-thirds of the octaves **are less energetic than** light.

Обладать недостатком (*физ.*)
Wilson cloud chambers **have the disadvantage** (*or* **shortcoming**) **of** a long dead time.

Обладать недостаточной гибкостью
Such instruments **lack flexibility.**

Обладать общим свойством
All earthquake waves **share the common property that ...**

Обладать ограниченной растворимостью
Water **is of limited solubility** in ethers.

Обладать ограниченной чувствительностью
The experiments **were limited in sensitivity.**

Обладать ограниченными ресурсами
They **are limited in resources.**

Обладать одинаковой энергией
The two structures **are of equal energy.**

Обладать отличными рабочими характеристиками
The "sonic press" **should be an outstanding performer in** the fabrication of ...

Обладать преимуществами по сравнению с

These multilevel residue systems **offer several advantages over** analogue systems.

Обладать преимуществом
A charge-coupled delay line **offers** (*or* **has**) **major advantages over** the more conventional glass delay line.
The fractional weight carrier **incorporates all the advantages of** the Keyboard type.
Each type **offers** (*or* **displays,** *or* **holds**) certain **advantages over** other methods.
For atomic samples, lasers **are a great advantage** because of ...

Обладать преимуществом по сравнению с
A tunable laser **has an advantage over** a conventional source because ...

Обладать свойствами
Over 200 alloys **offer** (*or* **possess**) mechanical and physical **properties** in just the right combination.
Organic glasses **possess** many **properties** (*or* **qualities**) **of** an ideal medium for ...
The mineral **shows** (*or* **exhibits**) expanding structural **characteristics.**

Обладать сладким запахом
This compound **smells sweet.**

Обладать способностью I
Montmorillonite **has the property of** absorbing various amounts of water between individual unit layers.

Обладать способностью II
He **has a knack** (*col.*) **for** getting to the root of a problem.

Обладать стойкостью к
This grade of steel **offers (high) resistance to** oxidation.

Обладать структурой
Leaves of trees **are structured so that** if we fold a leaf along its stem the two sides appear identically matched.

Обладать сходством с
These models **bear similarities to** living things.

Обладать также
This property **is shared by** the other particles.

Обладать тем преимуществом, что
An interpreter **has the advantage that** the result of each operation can be seen individually (*comput.*).

Обладать точностью до
The computer **will be accurate to within** 0.1 percent.

Обладающий наибольшей массой
Jupiter **is the most massive** planet.

Обладающий опытом в области
Operators **experienced in** preparing tapes for ... are wanted.

Обладающий самыми элементарными навыками
This can be done by a mechanic **with only rudimentary training.**

Обладающий свойствами
In order to produce coke **having** (*or* **possessing**) **desired properties, ...**

Область I [*см. тж.* **В данной области, В области, Во всей области, Относиться к области, Сфера**]
This is **an area of** spectroscopy in which ...
Developmental work is being carried out in two new **areas** (*or* **fields,** *or* **spheres**).
This skill is necessary to every **department** of life.
To extend this linear concept into **the domain of** nonlinear systems, ...
In several **domains of** science ...
Thus we enter into **the territory of** metaphysics.
New aspects of multiple coloumb excitation are among **the realms** that can be advantageously explored.

Область II [*см. тж.* **В диапазоне, В интервале**]
The flux is uniform **over the** whole **area.**
To supply power in remote **locations** (*or* **regions,** *or* **areas**), such as the Arctic, ...

Область знаний
We cannot deprive the student of **an** important **area of knowledge.**

Область использования
This opens up **a** wide **field of uses** (*or* **application**) for such machines.

Область исследований
An expanding **area of** scientific **exploration ...**
In several **areas of** nuclear **study ...**

Another **line of investigation** has now been opened.
This **realm** (*or* **field**) **of research** is flourishing.

Область, лишённая электронов
The charge density in **the electron-denuded region** will be $+qN_D$.

Область применения
The process has three major **areas of application.**
The fields of application of thyristors and relays and contactors overlap to some extent.

Область спектра
The blue and red **regions of the** visible **spectrum ...**

Область стыковки
An extraordinary new **meeting ground of** astrophysics, general relativity and elementary-particle physics has been found.

Область физики
The study of collisions of ... is **an** important **field of physics.**

Область энергий
An energy region.

Облегать
The cable **follows** the rock face more **smoothly** and is easier to fasten.

Облегчать I
This **made** the erection of the steel lining much **easier.**
The lower part is milled **to assist** (*or* **aid,** *or* **promote**) the inflow of air.
The weight of the torch has been reduced **to facilitate** the work of the welder.

Облегчать II
To lighten the construction of the aircraft, one has to ...

Облегчать положение
Prescribing this medicine **improves matters.**

Облегчать работу
The instruments **reduce the work load on** laboratory technicians.
A simpler form of loading equipment is used, **to lighten the work of** the operator.

Облегчать решение задачи
Lowering the basic repetition frequency **alleviates the problem.**

Облегчать труд рабочего
There is the substitution of mechanical power for manual effort, which **takes some burden from the worker.**

Облегчение [*см.* **Для облегчения**].

Облегчение боли [*см.* **Ослабление боли**].

Обледенение
The possible **build-up of ice on** (*or* **frosting of**) the coil ...

Облетать ... за ... дней
The satellite **circles** (*or* **orbits**) the planet **every** 1.77 days.

Облетающий землю
With the development of rocket technology it became possible to place magnetometers on **Earth-orbiting** spacecraft.

Облицованный
Bearing surfaces on the reciprocating head are Teflon **lined.**
The strip is low-carbon steel **faced** (*or* **lined**) on both sides with nickel claddings.
A lead-**lined** steel cylinder ...

Облучать
Several grams of plutonium-239 **have been irradiated with** neutrons.

Облучаться
The nuclear emulsion **was exposed to** monoenergetic neutrons.

Облучение [*см. тж.* **Вызванный облучением, Под облучением, При облучении**]
The air molecules were stripped of some of their electrons by **exposure to** X-rays.

Облучение светом (*лучами, частицами*)
F-centres may be produced in uncoloured crystals by **irradiation with** ultraviolet light, X-rays, γ-rays and high-speed particles.

Обматывать
Cool off the casing by **wrapping** cold wet rags **around** it (*or* by **wrapping** it **with** ...).

Обмениваться
The individual atoms can **trade** (*or* **exchange**) electrical charges.

Обме́р [*см.* **Выполнять измерения, Делать измерения, Проводить измерение**].

Обмерять [*см.* **Измерять**].

Обнадёживающий
Preliminary experimental results are extremely **encouraging.**

Обнажённый
The **exposed** rocks ...

Обнаружен [*см. тж.* **Наблюдаться**]
Some interesting data **have come to light** in the examination of ...
Coal **is** also **found** in Jurassic strata.
Several hundred polypeptides **have been seen** on such gels after electrophoresis of ...
No rock **has turned up** with an age of crystallization from its magma younger than 3 billion years.
Carbon monoxide **was** first **identified** (*or* **detected**) in interstellar space by ...

Обнаружение
The detection of tumours ...

Обнаружение дефектов
Trouble shooting.

Обнаруженный
Another characteristic of the proteins **revealed by** *in vitro* studies was an ability to ...

Обнаружено, что [*см. тж.* **Установлено, что**]
It **has been found** experimentally **that ...**

Обнаружено, что ... происходит
F-centre luminescence with high efficiency **has been found to occur in** KCl and KBr at low temperatures.

Обнаруживаемый
The booster pilot valve translates pressure changes **sensed** (*or* **detected**) **by** the balancing unit into output pressure changes.
The change in temperature **detectable by** this instrument may be less than 0.0001°C.

Обнаруживается [*см.* **Сразу обнаруживается**].

Обнаруживать I [*см. тж.* **Выявлять, Замечать, Находить, Что обнаружено**]
Nozzles are checked **to detect** any defects.
This deflection **is detected by** a mechanical relay.
Further investigation **disclosed** (*or* **revealed**) that ...
Copper **was** first **discovered** at ...
X-ray film for **pinpointing** the smallest manufacturing defects ...
They **revealed** the presence of 20 similar stars.
Huygens **made out** (*col.*) the fact that Saturn was surrounded by ...
At the time he **hit upon** (*col.*) a new method for grinding lenses.
On Christmas night 1758 a comet **was sighted.**
Recent planetary explorations **have uncovered** significant differences in ...
He reported **spotting** two luminous patches in the night sky.
A recent study **has uncovered** an account of an annular eclipse.

Обнаруживать II
The recombination reactions **display** (*or* **exhibit,** *or* **show**) a zero or negative temperature dependence.
The length of the uniform flow region **revealed** several interesting characteristics.

Обнаруживать III
The colour and texture of distinctive soils may serve **to locate** an underlying rock unit.

Обнаруживать дефекты
The tester **detects** internal **flaws.**

Обнаруживать неисправность
When **a fault is detected,** the carriage is stopped immediately.

Обнаруживать, что
Thus we **have discovered that** the molecular orbitals must be of the symmetry types A_1 and B_1.

Обнаруживаться
The ablastic activity **is found in** the globulin portion of the serum.
Two interesting aspects of the dissociation process **have come to light** (*or* **have revealed themselves**).
The two types of chromatin **are made evident by** a large number of staining techniques.

Обнаруживаться в форме (*мед.*)
Thyrotoxicosis does not always **present in** the elderly with classical symptoms and signs.

Обнаруживаться у
Osteoporosis should be suspected when the typical symptoms **present in** any patient with a predisposing medical history.

Обновлять
For this edition the original figures **have been brought up to date** (*or* **updated**) and some new material added.
The minicomputer **updates** machine instructions.

Обобщать [*см.* **Кратко обобщим**].

Обобщать на
This rule **can be extended** (*or* **generalized**) **to** curved spaces of any number dimensions.
This permits **the extension** (*or* **generalization**) **of** the resulting equations **to** systems involving mixtures.

Обобщение на
The extension of the principle of evolution **to** the fundamental molecules of life ...
A useful **generalization for** (*or* **to**) the simpler elements is ...

Обобщённый на
One should use the following scheme **generalized to** other cases: ...

Обогащать
Hematite **is concentrated to** 66% iron.
These crystals settle, thereby **enriching** the residual melt **in** silica, alumina, and alkalis.
The concentrator **will treat** 60,000 tons of ore per day.

Обогащён
The UO_2 **is enriched to** 98% **in** ^{235}U.
As the solidification proceeds, the liquid composition **becomes enriched with** metal *B*.

Обозначать [*см. тж.* **Означать**]
Entropy **is symbolized by** (*or* **as**) *S*.
Standard electrode potentials **are indicated by** the symbol $V°$.
This term **implies** a dimensionless quantity.
Molality **is represented by** *m*.
Calling its mass *m* and its velocity *v*, the angular momentum is *mvr*.
(Let us) denote the energies **by** 1, 2, ..., *n*.
m **denotes** (*or* **designates**) mobility.
The area of the triangle **is denoted by** *A*.
The device **is designated** *AN*/*SPS*-35.
This volume **is designated as** *S*.
U.S. Air Force aircraft **are designated by** both numbers and letters.
The subscript *K* **identifies** the force contributed by ...
The long and short records **are labelled** *l* and *s*, respectively.
Ln **signifies** the natural logarithm.
In this formula *X* **stands for** fluorine, chlorine, bromine or iodine.

Обозначать буквами
The fixture plate *B* **is lettered** to correspond with Fig. 3.

Обозначаться
Quantities of the sides $x > 0$ and $x < 0$ **are specified** (*or* **denoted,** *or* **designated**) **by** the subscripts 0 and 1, respectively.
The frequency **is** usually **symbolized by** the Greek letter ν.

Обозначен [*см. тж.* **Выражен через, Хорошо обозначенный**]
The three positions in which the plug can be placed **are labelled** (*or* **marked**) *'DSD, ND, USD'*.
This *emf* **is labelled** (*or* **denoted**) *C* in Fig. 23.
The instrument should read the temperature **marked** on the test-coil.

Обозначение [*см. тж.* **Для обозначения**]
The following **designations** are used: $\alpha = l/a$, $\gamma = a/t$ and $\beta = c/a$.
Adjacent lines of the six-phase system may be determined by **the** Roman-numeral **labelling** of the vector diagram.
Notation (*or* **Nomenclature**): *C* = specific heat capacity, *G* = rate of heat generation per unit volume, ...
The notation $P(x, y)$ denotes a point *P* with coordinates (x, y).
Symbols: θ = temperature, θ_0 = undisturbed ground temperature.
The excitation of a three-axis magnetic dipole source is most conveniently described **in** vector **notation.**

Обойтись [*см.* **Обходиться**].

Оболочка
The earth is surrounded by **an envelope of** gas, the atmosphere.

Обоняние [*см.* **Острое обоняние**].

Оборот [*см.* **Повернуть на один полный оборот, Полоборота, С малым числом оборотов**].

Оборотов в минуту
The engine develops 340 hp at 1900 **rpm (revolutions per minute).**

Оборудован [*см. тж.* **Приспособлен(ный) для, Снабжён**]
The unit **is equipped** (*or* **supplied,** *or* **provided**) **with** a turbocharger.
The vehicle **was fitted out with** a pressurized cabin.
The wheels **are fitted with** roller bearings.
The aeroplane **is instrumented with** thousands of strain gauges.
The power unit **incorporates** standard electric starting equipment.

Оборудован для
The satellite **was fitted out for** X-ray observations.

Оборудование [*см. тж.* **Аппаратура, Бортовое оборудование, Противопожарное оборудование, Технологическое оборудование**]
This technique is not used as widely as UV due to the high cost of **instrumentation.**

Оборудование, снабжённое ЭВМ
The system makes it easy for even an inexperienced employee to operate **computerized equipment.**

Оборудованный
The firm has developed a special transducer **featuring** a plug-in terminal for lead wires.
Inexpensive lasers, **aided by** light-deflectors, will be key elements in scanning and printing terminals.
A glider **thus fitted out** was launched.

Оборудованный приборами
An **instrumented** enclosure ...

Оборудованный транзисторами [*см. тж.* **Полностью оборудованный транзисторами**]
A **transistorized** amplifier ...

Обоснован
The view that ... **is justified.**
If this explanation **is valid,** there should be two other ridges ...
This conclusion **is warranted.**
Thus the earlier assumption **is substantiated.**

Обоснование
The whys and wherefores (*col.*) **of** the design of cascade control systems can best be presented in terms of actual problems.

Обоснованность [*см.* **Правильность**].

Обоснованный
A **justified** assumption ...

Обосноваться на
At the same time more semiconductor manufacturers sought **to establish a foothold in** the rapidly expanding microprocessor market.

Обосновывающий
Some data **substantiating** the proposed sequence of events can be offered.

Обострять [*см. тж.* **Усугублять сложность**]
These factors may **aggravate** the hyperglycaemic tendency (*med.*).

Обостряться
Interest in the origin of life on earth **gained momentum** in the first half of the twentieth century.

Обрабатываемая деталь
The piece [*or* **work(piece)**] is made the positive terminal and the electrode negative.

Обрабатываемость [*см.* **Способность поддаваться обработке**].

Обрабатываемый материал
Speeds of working vary according to **the material being worked** (*or* **machined**).

Обрабатываемый обычным способом
These plastics possess physical properties unlike those of any other **commonly machined** material.

Обрабатываемый с помощью перфоленты
Fixtures made for one **tape-run part ...**

Обрабатывать [*см.. тж.* **Действовать, Легко поддающийся обработке**]
They can **farm** any piece of unclaimed soil here.

The pickle plant **handles** (*or* **processes**) 100 tons of pickles a season.
The rods **are machined** on a turning lathe.
Processes which **work** the metal by means of rolls ...
The life of timber depends upon the way in which it **is** felled, seasoned and **worked.**
Cylindrical rolls are used for **working** flat stock.
More than 15,000 tons of sea water **must be processed** (*or* **treated**) to obtain one ton of bromine.
The machine **will accept** workpieces up to a maximum of 7 ft wide by 7 ft high.
The electrolyte **is** next **treated with** zinc dust.

Обрабатывать всухую
Do not **machine dry** except for very light finishing cuts.

Обрабатывать данные
The computer **processes** (*or* **handles**) **data** simultaneously from eight gas chromatographs.

Обрабатывать землю
To work (*or* **farm**) **land.**

Обрабатывать на станке
In this department the parts **are machined.**

Обрабатываться
Two components **are completed** at each cycle.

Обрабатываться в холодном (*антон.* **горячем**) **состоянии**
The material **is cold** (*anton.* **hot**) **worked.**

Обрабатываться на станках
Polyimides **machine** very well if proper precautions are taken.

Обрабатываться паром
Bones **are steamed** (*or* **treated with steam**) to remove gelatine.

Обрабатываться под выступы
The additional top plates **are machined to accept** (*or* **accommodate**) **part projections.**

Обработанная информация
Printers display **processed information** for the human user.

Обработанный на бесцентровом шлифовальном станке
Centreless-ground rods ...

Обработка [*см. тж.* **Без обработки, Грубая и чистовая обработка, Легко поддающийся обработке, Механическая обработка, Не подвергнутый обработке после литья, Поверхностная обработка, Способность поддаваться обработке**]
Machines are available for **handling** strip materials up to 3 in. wide.
Alumina is extracted from bauxite by **digesting** (*or* **treating**) it at elevated temperature and pressure **with** a strong solution of caustic soda.
The handling of goods at the railway junction ...
Surface **treatment of** the bearings ...
The processing of the part from blank to finished shell ...
Equipment used in **processing of** milk ...
Cobalt is precipitated as the hydroxide by **treatment with** sodium hypochlorite.
The extraction and **working of** metals ...

Обработка воды
Water treatment (*or* **processing**).

Обработка данных
Data handling (*or* **treatment,** *or* **processing**).

Обработка ... деталей одновременно
Four-at-a-time machining.

Обработка отходов
The chromic acid **wastes are handled** (*or* **treated**) in a different manner.

Обработка тяжёлых деталей
Such tools are used in **heavy machining.**

Обработка шлифованием
Abrasive machining.

Образ жизни
The way of living (*or* **of life**) **of** these organisms is totally unexplored.

Образец [*см.* **Брать образцы, Испытываемый образец, Контрольный образец, Отбирать образцы, Проверка по контрольному образцу**].

Образец для испытания на растяжение
A tension test specimen.

-обра́зный
Tubing with a D-**shaped** cross section ...

Образование [*см. тж.* **Приводить к образованию, Распадаться с образованием, С образованием, Создание**]
The displacement process leads to **the production of** interstitial atoms and vacancies.
This prevents **the occurrence** (*or* **formation**) **of** continuous oxide films.
These examples of shock wave **production** illustrate two methods which can be used for **the generation** (*or* **formation**) **of** shock waves.

Образование и нарушение хим. связи
Bond making and breaking ...

Образование ... из
The formation of a compound **from** its elements ...

Образование поперечных связей (*хим.*)
Cross linking.

Образованный
The surface **generated by** the rays ...

Образовывать [*см. тж.* **Давать**]
Hydrogen chloride **forms** ions in aqueous solution.
The roof collapsed **giving rise to** a crater (*geol.*).
As the seawater evaporates, the remaining salt and water **make up** a brine that is denser than seawater.
Aldehyde sugars **give rise to** (*or* **produce**) sugar acids.
The red and green images **combine into** a black image.
The three instruments **form** (*or* **comprise,** *or* **make up**) a signal generator assembly.
As $\Delta_0 \upsilon_z$ changes, the circles **generate** a surface, which ...

Образовывать волну
Thus, no severe blast **wave would be generated.**

Образовывать комплекс с
The salt **will complex** (*or* **will form a complex**) **with** double bonds.

Образовывать сплавы с
Chromium is known **to alloy with** many metals.

Образовывать угол с
The angles which the ray **forms** (*or* **makes**) **with** the axis ...

Образовываться [*см. тж.* **В ... образуется, Возникать**]
Neutrons **are generated by** the reaction between ...
A potential difference **is set up** at the membrane.
No lather **can occur** until this precipitation has been completed.
A film **forms** on the surface of the commutator.
When hydrogen sulphate is passed into cold concentrated nitric acid, considerable heat **is developed.**
A laminar layer **builds up** (*or* **is built up,** *or* **forms**) near the leading edge.
Aspartate **arises** (*or* **is formed**) principally **by** transamination of oxaloacetate.
If a defect **should develop** in the cladding, ...
The pipe **developed** a leak.
Too hard a wheel **develops** a smooth, glazed surface that will not cut.
Steam **forms** continuously.
The West Antarctica ice mass **originated** as two separate icecaps.
As a result, a black precipitate of silver nitride **is produced.**
A fog **may appear** in the gas if condensation nuclei are present.

Образовываться в результате
The amine **arises** (*or* **is formed**) **by** hydrolysis of ...
The quartz pebbles **were derived from** long continued erosion of ...
Part of the earth's atmosphere **was derived from** volcanic activity.

Образовываться из
The amphibians **evolved from** fishes and gave rise to reptiles (*or* the reptiles **evolved from** amphibians).
This expression **comes from** Eq. (6) by setting $H' = 0$.
ATP **is generated** (*or* **produced,** *or* **obtained**) **from** adenosinediphosphate and organic phosphate.
These conglomerates **are derived from** weathered limestone.
Manganese nodules **are formed from** manganese and iron derived from ...

Образующие его
All **its constituent** molecules are stacked in ...

Образующийся
The resulting (*or* **resultant**) paste is passed over roll refiners.

Образуя [*см. тж.* **Давая**]
These compounds react with water **to give** (*or* **giving**) simple hydrocarbons.
A number of elements combine with uranium **to form** (*or* **forming**) intermediate phases.

Обратимая (*антон.* **Необратимая**) **реакция**
A reversible (*anton.* **irreversible**) **reaction.**

Обратить *чьё-л.* **внимание на**
The astronomer Daniel Kirkwood **called attention to** these gaps.

Обратная величина [*см. тж.* **Величина, обратная**]
Provided A_0 is non-singular, **its inverse** A_0^{-1} exists.
The reciprocal of the volume ($1/v$) **is ...**
The reciprocal of electrical conductivity **is** resistivity.
The converse of streaming potential ...

Обратная зависимость [*см.* **Находиться в обратной зависимости от**].

Обратная пропорция
An inverse proportion.

Обратная реакция [*см. тж.* **Прямые и обратные реакции**].
A reverse reaction.

Обратная реакция по отношению к
The step $CH_4(g) \rightarrow C(s) + 2H_2(g)$ **is the reverse of** the formation of methane from its elements.

Обратная сторона Луны
The far (*or* **back,** *or* **dark,** *or* **invisible,** *or* **other**) **side of the Moon.**

Обратно квадрату
This pull varies **inversely with the square of** the distance to ...

Обратно пропорционален
The grain size of a casting **is inversely related to** cooling rate.
The amplitudes of the radial velocity curves of both components **are in inverse proportions to** their mass ratios.
The heights of the columns **are inversely proportional to** the two densities.

Обратно пропорционально [*см. тж.* **Изменяться обратно пропорционально**]
The gravitational force varies **in inverse proportion to** the square of the distance.
The intensity varies **as the reciprocal of** the diameter.
At constant temperature, the volume of gas varies **inversely as** (*or* **with**) the pressure.

Обратное можно сказать о
The reverse (*or* **opposite**) **is true for** (*or* **of**) left circularly polarized light.

Обратное отношение
An inverse ratio.

Обратное положение [*см. тж.* **Имеет место обратное положение**]
The reverse situation is observed only when ...
The reverse (*or* **converse**) **is true in** catalytic alkylation.

Обратное положение имеет место в отношении
The reverse holds good for the *L*-series.
The opposite situation occurs over the middle and low latitudes.

Обратный [*см. тж.* **В порядке, обратном; Величина, обратная; Имеет место обратное положение, Противоположный, Реакция; обратная**]
In the southern hemisphere the effect **is reversed.**
The series of reactions, which takes place in microorganisms, **is the reverse of** that used for cysteine formation in animals.
Stripping **is the reverse** of absorption.
The inverse power dependence r^{-n} ...

Обратный ему
This theorem, together with **its converse,** proves that ...

Обратный поток
There will be **a counterflow of** electrons.

Обратный процесс [*см. тж.* **Процесс, обратный**]
Subtraction and division are defined as **the**

inverse processes of addition and multiplication.
This is called evaporation, **the reverse process** being condensation.

Обратный путь [*см.* **На обратном пути**].

Обратный ход
Reverse motion.

Обращать внимание на I [*см. тж.* **Следует обратить внимание на, Уделять внимание**]
We **call (your) attention to** the extensive Supplement.
Attention is drawn to the fact that the new material does not ignite.

Обращать внимание на II
Special **attention** (*or* **consideration**) **must be given to** waves with a zero phase velocity.

Обращать внимание читателя на
The author **calls** (*or* **draws,** *or* **directs**) **the reader's attention to** the recent emphasis in the literature on ...
We **have already called attention to** the fracture zones that cut across ...

Обращать мало внимания на
Little attention is given to the reactive character of ...

Обращать на себя внимание
The properties of water in biological systems **have engaged our attention** primarily because of our interest in cell membranes.

Обращать особое внимание на [*см. тж.* **Уделять главное внимание**]
Our principal concern will be with the areas of molecular spectroscopy that stem from ...
We should focus (*or* **concentrate**) **our attention on** plastics.
(Particular) emphasis is placed upon accuracy.

Обращаться за помощью [*см.* **Немедленно обращаться за помощью**].

Обращаться исключительно осторожно
You must **handle** these compounds **with extreme care.**

Обращаться к [*см. тж.* **Заглядывать в, Переходить к, Пользоваться**]
In the 1840s European engineers **addressed themselves to** the concept of axial flow.
To solve this problem **we** now **turn to** the finite-difference method.
We now **direct** (*or* **turn**) **our attention to** the above-mentioned systems.
The reader may wish **to refer to** published papers in which ...
The interested student **should consult** some of these articles.

Обращаться к ... в поисках
Under these circumstances **we should look at** the electron theory **for** clues.

Обращение с [*см. тж.* **Безопасное обращение с, Лёгкость обращения с**]
Bromine **handling** and storage ...

Обращён ... к
The reproducing stylus **presents** a spherical surface **to** the groove.

Обращённый к
The area of an asteroid **presented to** (*or* **facing**) the Sun ...

Обращённый к Земле [*см.* **Ближняя сторона Луны**].

Обреза́ть
The wires **are cropped by** knives.

Обрести
On further processing the mixtures **assumed** the full characteristics of ...

Обречён на неудачу
All our attempts **were doomed to failure.**

Обрушение почвы
A caisson foundation protects the workers against water pressure and **collapse of soil.**

Обрываться
The equilibrium line **terminates at** *C*.
The rate at which chains **are terminated** ... (*chem.*).

Обслуживание [*см. тж.* **Оперативное обслуживание, Техническое обслуживание**]
The machine requires practically no **maintenance** apart from electrode dressing.
Factory work consists largely of **tending** machines.

Обслуживание в порядке живой очереди
Orders will be accepted **on a first-come, first-served basis.**

Обслуживать
Two of these shovels are used in the shaft, one **delegated** to each shift.
The chip wringer can **service** a number of machine tools.
One operator **attends** several presses.
Such systems should be able **to cater for** (*or* **to**) thousands of channels.
The oscillator **covers** the range 1 kc/s-10 Mc/s.
The operator **can handle** up to six machines.
A 30-ton derrick **serves** No. 2 hatch.
The meter **can be serviced** without shutting down the pipeline.
The laboratory **will service** the pigment department.
The accumulators **take care of** several presses.
The second operator **is tending** the open dies — applying lubricant where necessary, for example.

Обслуживать станок
Each apprentice **looks after** three **automatics.**
The lathe is manned (*or* **operated**) **by** a skilled turner.

Обслуживаться
All the machines in a group **are served by** a work transportation system.
The telephone service **is manned** around the clock **by** trained operators.
Control boards for the two kilns **are attended by** one operator.
The power house **is serviced by** a 20-ton crane.

Обслуживающий персонал [*см. тж.* **Без обслуживающего персонала**]
Operating and **maintenance personnel** received exposures to radiation.

Обстановка [*см.* **Использовать обстановку**].

Обстоятельно
The observed behaviour is very **neatly** explained by this mechanism.
These factors will be more **appropriately** summarized in a later section.

Обстоятельство [*см.* **В зависимости от обстоятельств, Если учесть все обстоятельства, Непредвиденное обстоятельство, При некоторых обстоятельствах**].

Обсу́дим
Let us take up first the case of an active orogenic belt along a continental margin.

Обсуждаемый вопрос
The subject under discussion (*or* **being discussed,** *or* **under consideration**).

Обсуждать [*см. тж.* **Рассматривать**]
We **have not yet addressed** the specific question of where and how magmas are generated.
This process is rather a technical one, and **will not be taken up** (*or* **discussed,** *or* **considered**) here.

Обсуждаться
This paper **deals** (*or* **is concerned**) **with** the development of ...
Another chapter **covers** (*or* **discusses**) the problems of ...
Abrasive wear **was treated** (*or* **discussed**) in two papers.
This mechanism **is dealt with** (*or* **discussed,** *or* **treated**) in Chapter 7.

Обсуждение
Speculation (*or* **Discussion**) continues concerning the nuclear properties of ...

Обтекание
Below we give the diffusion equation for Stokes **flow past** [*or* **(a)round,** *or* **over**] a sphere.

Обтекать
The ball is a loose fit in the body, so that air can **flow (a)round** (*or* **past,** *or* **over**) it.
The cooling water passes through tubes **around** which the exhaust steam **flows.**
The liberated air **flows** (*or* **passes**) **around the outside of** the tubes.

Обтекающий
The flow about (*or* **past,** *or* **around,** *or* **over**) the wings ...
The fluid **streaming past** it ...

Обтирать
The specimen **is swabbed** (*or* **wiped**) **with** cotton wool.

Обуздывать
Before man began **harnessing** the rivers ...

Обусловленный
The fluctuations **are due to** (*or* **are caused by,** *or* **result from**) roll eccentricity.
Improved coal quality **stemming from** better washing techniques ...

Обусловливать [*см. тж.* **Определять**]
Heat **causes** (*or* **is responsible for**) the continuous evaporation of the solid.
These elements **define** (*or* **determine**) the geometry of the orbit.
Two criteria **should determine** the choice of the solid.
The rate at which the furnace can melt scrap **governs** the rate at which ...
Recent interest in the development of such insulating structures **has motivated** extension of the study of ...

Обусловливаться [*см. тж.* **Определяться**]
The behaviour of the dashpot **is conditioned by** the viscosity of the oil used.
The usefulness of this gypsum **depends upon** the fact that it hardens slowly.
The interplanetary navigator's most difficult problems all **derive from** the following fact: ...
The plasma volume **is determined by** this equilibrium.
The design of the anvils **is dictated by** the specific requirements that ...
The choice of the lathe **is governed by** the type and size of work to be performed.
The increased pressure drop **results from** hole friction.
These problems **spring** (*or* **arise,** *or* **stem**) **from** a number of different demands.

Обучение
Only limited **training of** the operator is needed.
Training in the analytical methods ...

Обучение с помощью ЭВМ
Computer-assisted instruction.

Обходить
The mains supply is connected direct to the instrument circuit, **bypassing** the fuses and switch.
Depending on the complexity of the part, it may have to be directed to only two or three of the six machines, **bypassing** the others.

Обходить препятствия
The gauge jaws **get around** (*or* **about**) **obstructions** (*or* **obstacles**).

Обходиться
We can **get by with** two simple rules: ...
It is then possible **to make do** (*col.*) **with** one ring.

Обходиться без
It is possible **to dispense with** (*or* **do without,** *or* **omit**) a separate getter.
The body cannot **do without** glucose.
By using ..., you can **do away with** trial runs on the machine-tool.
It is frequently possible to use a simple mean driving force or potential and thereby **obviate the need for** the integration.

Обширная литература [*см. тж.* **Появилась обширная литература**]
The literature on the subject **is quite voluminous** (*or* **extensive**).

Обширное пространство [*см.* **Огромное пространство**].

Обширные исследования
We have conducted **extensive studies of** fluid mechanisms.

Обшит
The air receiving box **is lined with** sound-absorbing material.

Общая длина
The overall (*or* **total**) **length of** the plug is 2 inches.

Общая картина (*биол.*)
The overall picture of biosynthesis of tRNAs strongly resembles that of ...

Общая площадь
The combined (*or* **total**) **area of** the openings must be at least ...

Общая реакция
The general (*or* **overall**) **reaction is** $acid_1 + base_2 = base_1 + acid_2$.

Общая сторона
The triangles *KAH*, *KGH* are equal because $AH = HG$, *HK* **is common** and the angles at *H* are right.

Общая формула
Carbon forms compounds with the halogens which have **the general formula** CX_4.

Общего назначения
This oscilloscope is a **general-purpose** instrument.

Общее имя [*см.* **Называть общим именем**].

Общее мнение
At present, **the consensus** regarding polymerase activities appears to be as follows: ...

Общее название [*см.* **Носить общее название**].

Общее представление [*см.* **Иметь общее представление о**].

Общее представление можно получить [*см.* **Можно получить общее представление**].

Общее признание [*см.* **По общему признанию**].

Общее свойство [*см.* **Обладать общим свойством**].

Общее устройство
Figure 1 shows **the general arrangement of** the ammeter mechanism.

Общеизвестный
The dependence of ... **is a matter of common knowledge.**
Adenosine triphosphate **is** now **universally known as** ATP.

Общей формы
Generally shaped curves (*or* molecules, etc.) (*or* Curves **of the general shape**) ...

Общей чертой ... является то, что
What all the nodules **have in common is that** they tend to collapse.

Общепризнанный
This **is the (generally) recognized** way of eliminating the effect.
His interpretation of the earth was taught as **received fact.**

Общепринятое обозначение
We shall use **the convention of** capital T to represent temperature on the Kelvin scale.

Общепринятое представление [*см.* **В противоположность общепринятому представлению**].

Общепринятый [*см. тж.* **Обычный, Традиционный**]
These definitions **have been universally accepted.**
Universally adopted standard conditions require that ...
The accepted industry standard is a cushion capacity of ...
So far we have described only **conventional** heat-transfer methods for generating electricity in a laser-power plant.
The commonly (*or* **universally**) **accepted** model of the F-centre is an electron trapped at a negative-ion vacancy.

Общеупотребительный [*см.* **Входить в употребление**].

Общие замечания
General observations concerning heat effects ...

Общие черты [*см. тж.* **Иметь общие черты с**]
These phenomena have certain **features in common with** convection.

Общий I [*см.* **В более общих выражениях, В общей сложности, В общем случае, Иметь мало общего с, Иметь много общего с, Иметь что-либо общее с, Суммарный**].

Общий II
The aggregate mass of very small asteroids is only a minor fraction of the total.
The combined effect of creep and slippage is ...
Several tanks with **a combined** capacity of 10,000 gallons ...
This factor has been included in **the overall** computation program.
The equation merely represents **the overall** transformation by which all bacteria secure energy.
The overall voltage gain was 5000.
Seven new centres were opened, making **the total** number 83.
This would have less **all-round** flexibility.

Общий III [*см. тж.* **Иметь общий ... с**]
Ionizing solvents **have** one property **in common,** self-ionization.

The two curves **have** a point **in common** (*or* **a common** point).
Several species may have **a common** ancestry.
The components of the analyzer are assembled in two basic units, an optical unit and an electronic unit, in **a common** housing.
The engine, the transmission and the differential could use one oil reservoir **in common.**

Общий вес
The overall weight of ...

Общий вид
The general view of the enlarger ...

Общий для
The time attenuating factor **is common to** (*or* **the same for**) both wavefronts.
Common to both systems **are** the problems of corrosion and scale deposition.
The amplifier **is common to** all the eight converters.
The edge **shared by** two faces ...

Общий для всех
Automotive vehicles **have** five functional components **in common.**

Общий ... с [*см.* **Иметь общее поле с**].

Общий случай [*см.* **В общем случае**].

Общий термин
Rock deformation is **a blanket** (*or* **broad**) **term** referring to any ...

Общность [*см. тж.* **Без потери общности, Для общности**]
This **commonness of** morphology was found in ...

Общность утеряна
Since **generality is lost for** nonlinear systems, ...

Объединение
The integration of the six major areas of manufacturing technology ...

Объединены в
The pitot and static tubes **are combined in** the pitot-static tube.
The motor and generator **are combined into** a single machine.

Объединён с
The reduction gear may be either mounted separately or **made integral with** the motor.

Объединённый
The **pooled** resources of many nations ...

Объединять
Several small classes **may be pooled to form** one large class.
It is often necessary for several departments **to pool resource**s on a computer system which is compatible to all their needs.
The Graphical Numerical Control **combines** many commands **into** often-used sub-program groups of macros.
Oil tanks **are combined within** a single shell.

Объединять в
The unit **integrates** data from several sources **into** a single tape.
The various units described **are now being combined into** an operating circuit.
Furnaces **will be integrated into** production lines.

Объединять в себе
The new engine **combines** low fuel consumption **with** simplicity.
The new automatic optical micrometer **has combined** the speed of video processing technology **with** the data processing and ...
Solid-state detectors **combine** the functions of monochromator **and** detector.
The synchronously pumped mode-locked cavity-dumped *CW* dye laser **combines** the desirable characteristics of both of the above lasers.

Объединять в схему
They tried **piecing** these models together **in a pattern** consistent with the data contributed by others.

Объединять с
This rule **may be combined with** the chain rule.
The analytical procedure **must be coupled with** some form of ...
The reactor **could be coupled to** a conventional steam system.
Assaying **is integrated with** ore testing.

Объединять свои усилия
The two scientists **joined forces** in order to try again.

Объединять уравнения
A new tensor can be introduced **by combining Eqs.** (22) **and** (23).

Объединяться в [*см. тж.* **Сливаться с**]
Eight ganglia is the maximum number; they **may unite into** one or more ganglia.

Объединяться с
The production of sulphur dioxide from anhydrite **is combined with** the manufacture of cement.

Объект I [*см. тж.* **Являться объектом исследования**]
This sequence **has been the subject** (*or* **object**) **of** much experimentation.

Объект II
On **projects** using large amounts of concrete, such as dams, ...

Объект III
The ring-shaped **features** observed on Venus ...

Объект научного исследования
Only such phenomena are rightly **a matter for scientific enquiry.**

Объектом исследования является
The investigation is concerned with precision grinding techniques.

Объём
After evaporation to small **bulk** and cooling, the solution will deposit crystals.
The passage of the electric current through **the body of** the solution ...

Объём воды (*или* **жидкости**)
The exchange of heat between **parcels of water** (*or* **liquid**) ...

Объём воздуха
The ratio of the amount of water **a body of air** holds to the amount it can hold ...
The warm ascending **parcel of air** rises into an environment where the pressure is lower.

Объёмный
Three-dimensional magnetic fields.

Объёмный процент
Air contains 78 **volume percent** nitrogen (*or* 78% nitrogen **by volume**).

Объёмом
A container **of volume** *V* ...
A crystal **with a volume of** 130 cubic centimetres ...

Объявить запрещённой зоной
The regions containing collected radioactive wastes **should be marked off-limits.**

Объяснение [*см. тж.* **Давать объяснение, Для объяснения**]
This is **a** plausible **explanation for** the heat of formation of ...

Объясним
This lack of kinship between ... **appears explicable only on the basis of** separate origins.

Объяснять [*см. тж.* **Можно объяснить** *чем-л.*, **Приписывать**]
The actual sequence of events **is clarified** later.
The theory **gave an insight into** why ...
A look at ... further **illuminates** the causes of these shifts.
This seems difficult **to justify on the basis of** simple electrostatic forces.
The hypothesis **provides an explanation for** the magnetic symmetry that appears ...
This action **accounts for** (*or* **explains**) the name of the instrument — “contrabarometer”.
This discrepancy **is accounted for by** the difference in ...
The difference **may be ascribed** (*or* **attributed**) **to** recombination in ...
We **attribute** this phenomenon **to** the formation of ozone.
The reduction in failures **can be credited to ...**
The poor quality of the mirrors **is explained by** (*or* **is due to**) two causes.
The reduction in mortality **can be put down to** better living conditions.
Microcrack formation **may be responsible for** the lower density of cold-worked metals.

Объяснять иначе, чем
The cross section through the Atlantic sediments is very difficult **to interpret in any other way except by** constant creation of new oceanic crust at the crest of the ridge.

Объяснять на примере
The second factor limiting the occurrence of electrovalent salts **is** best **explained in terms of an example.**

Объяснять то одним, то другим

The Balmer lines of hydrogen **are variously attributed to** excitation at the contact surface **and to** a residual impurity in the argon.

Объясняться [*см. тж.* **Вызван, Вытекать, Связан с**]

The higher density of Jupiter **is due to** its larger mass.
This fact **owes to** the ≈ 100 ns effective time constant for ...
The usefulness of this gypsum **depends upon the fact that** it hardens slowly.
Use of the ballistic range for aerodynamic investigations **derives from the fact that ...**
The wheel wear **was due to** attrition of the grits.
The value of asbestos **ensues from** (*or* **arises out of**) the incombustible nature of the products fabricated from ...
This **is explicable on the basis of** imperfect chemical separation.
This increase **results from** (*or* **is caused by,** *or* **stems from,** *or* **is due to,** *or* **arises from,** *or* **is brought about by,** *or* **is explained by,** *or* **is associated with**) the rise of prices.
These metals **owe** their electrical conductivity **to the fact that ...**
The superior high-temperature performance of the cast alloys **is attributable to** the high carbon content and ...
This capability **flows from** the use of parallel computation.

Обычай [*см.* **Входить в обычай**].

Обычно I [*см. тж.* **В каждодневной практике, Принято, Типичный**]

Such a stringent standard **is** now **routinely** met.
Liquid diffraction patterns **characteristically** show one or two maxima that correspond to ...
The great majority of **routinely** detected events can be classified as earthquakes.
The receptacle **is conventionally** 2-wire, 120-volt, 15-ampere.
That is how the logarithms **are conventionally** tabulated.
This inert phase **is normally** a gel structure.
Engineering **practice is** to express quantities in lb/h.
Group I members **tend to** have relatively few nucleosides of this sort.
Such lasers **typically** generate pulses of 5–10 ns duration.
Traditionally, the residual bottoms have been blended with lighter stocks.
It is usual to check the ... level whenever there is any doubt.
In this application **it is common** (*or* **usual**) **to** employ ...
It is common for metabolic pathways **to** exhibit some form of cyclic pattern.
The atomic weight **is commonly** called the mass number.
The **commonly** used gases are seldom pure enough for use with these sensitive detectors.
The head gain **is customarily** measured in inches of water.
It is customary to install a pump having two or three stages.
The factor k **is generally** taken to be equal to unity.
A field lens **is generally** placed behind the reticle.
Floating roof tanks **are normally** employed for prevention of loss through evaporation.
The temperature at this point **is ordinarily** the same as that of the forward cylinder section.
Where it is suspected that ... **it is the practice** (*or* **custom**) **to** steam out the coils.
In large marine installations **it is standard** (*or* **usual**) **practice to** use ...
The sensitivity for detection **is typically** (*or* **usually,** *or* **generally,** *or* **commonly,** *or* **as a rule**) five times as great as ...
In designing such packed columns, **it is common** (*or* **general**) **practice to** assume “piston”, or “plug” flow.
The regions of strongest divergence **tend to be** found over the subtropical regions.
Many plant breeders **make a practice of** having different batches of seed treated with gamma rays, neutrons and one chemical mutagen.
For a long time questions related to insulation **were apt to be** ignored.
The usual way to stop the intrusion **has been to** drill ... (*geol.*).

Обычно II

In this way dye molecules can enter more freely **otherwise** inaccessible dye-sites.

Обычно бывает
Axial compressors **tend** (*or* **are apt**) **to be** longer than centrifugal ones.

Обычно встречаться на
Tidal pools **are common to** rocky coasts.

Обычно встречающийся
In **commonly encountered** electromagnetic brakes ...

Обычно известный как
Dripstone and flowstone accumulate as elaborate encrustations, **known popularly as** "formations".

Обычно использоваться
The procedure **is in routine** (*or* **common**) **use by** several networks.
For an oven, a temperature differential of several degrees **is common.**

Обычно используемый
Many airfoil profiles **in common use** (*or* **commonly used**) are comparatively thin.

Обычно используется для
The method **is common for** controlling ...

Обычно используют [*см.* **В основном принято использовать**].

Обычно практиковаться
Use of small loops ... **is a standard practice** in areas where ...

Обычно применяемый
Commonly employed materials include arsenic, silicon and ...

Обычно применяться
This term **is** still **in common usage.**

Обычно считают, что
It is generally believed that ...

Обычного размера
Ordinary-sized systems ...

Обычного типа
These installations **are of the conventional** (*or* **usual,** *or* **standard,** *or* **normal,** *or* **regular**) **type.**

Обычное дело
By the early thirties, communications between points on opposite sides of the globe had become **commonplace** on wavelengths of 80 through 20 m.
Automatic ganging will become more and more **common.**

Обычное явление
Floods **are common** but always limited in extent.

Обычной формы
Diamond wheels **made in conventional shapes** (*or* **of ordinary shapes**) will ...

Обычные ошибки
This information will help you to avoid **common mistakes.**

Обычный [*см. тж.***Довольно обычный, При обычной температуре, С обычными покрышками**]
The standard enthalpies of some **common** compounds ...
Using either **conventional** or laser excitation sources ...
With the advent of new engineering techniques, X-ray diffraction has become a **commonplace** tool for studies of ...
This phenomenon **is** rather **common** in plants.
Customary (*or* **Conventional**) techniques can be...
We used **familiar** methods.
Ordinary paint is of little value in ...
The new product outperforms **regular** lubricants.
The automatic press embodies all the **regular** features of the semi-automatic press plus ...
Another **standard** technique is vacuum fusion.
The **usual** practice is ...
If an electric field is applied to an **ordinary** atom, ...

Обычный для
Electron capture **is** more **common with** heavy isotopes.

Обычный приём
This form of exaggeration **is standard practice** to focus attention on the details which ...

Обычным путём
The rectifiers give full wave rectification **in the normal fashion** (*or* **in the regular way,** *or* **in the ordinary way,** *or* **in the usual fashion**).

These loads can be weighed **routinely** with a reasonable accuracy.

Обязан [*см. тж.* **Вытекать из**]
I am greatly indebted to Dr ..., **for** fruitful discussion of the paper.
Amethyst **derives** its colour **from** a hole colour centre.
Insulators **owe** their high resistivity **to** the small carrier population they have.
The process of photosynthesis **is responsible for** the existence of plants.

Обязан своим происхождением [*см. тж.* **Быть обязанным своим происхождением**]
The term phosphor **owes its origin to** the chemiluminescence of phosphorus.

Обязан своим существованием тому, что
Supercooled water **owes its existence to the fact that ...**

Обязанность [*см.* **Ответственность лежит на**].

Обязательная принадлежность
The power hacksaw is practically **a "must"** (*or* **indispensable**) **in** the stock-preparing section of ...

Обязательно [*см. тж.* **Не обязательно**]
The equipment used with these systems must **necessarily** be small.
Were the DNA molecule to participate actively in metabolism, it would **of necessity** undergo ... (*biol.*).
Future experimental programs **are certain to** include such searches.
It is imperative that the plating operation **be** closely controlled.
Be sure to adhere to the steps specified in the instructions.

Обязательный
There is no proof that cholesterol **is** an **obligatory** (*or* **mandatory**) intermediate in the synthesis of ...
Vacuum treatment is not **essential for** treating ...
Increased axle loadings are now allowed, but stronger axles **are imperative.**
A thorough understanding **is** not **mandatory** at this stage of presentation.

Овальное отверстие
Remove the drill bushing and you are guaranteed to get **an out-of-round** slightly mislocated or oversize **hole.**

Овальность и конусность
The machine checks **out-of-roundness** at the top and bottom of each bore and **taper** from top to bottom.

Овладевать
A tool engineer can **master** the programming technique in a few hours.
It is not necessary **to master** all the theory.

Овладевать умами
The erroneous theory **had a** strong **hold on the minds of** chemists.

Овладевший
Persons **trained in** transmission line theory find it useful to apply it to ...

Оглядываясь назад
In retrospect it is surprising that the above principle was not extended earlier in this fashion.

Оговаривать [*см.* **Если не указано иначе**].

Огонь [*см.* **Локализовать пожар**].

Ограждаться
The live terminals **are shrouded** (*or* **protected**) **by** a barrier to prevent accidental handling.

Ограничен
The Sinai Peninsula **is bounded** (*or* **bordered**) **by** two fault trenches.
The coordinates of the molecules' position **are bounded by** the finite size of the container.
The disturbance **is confined to** a closed surface.

Ограничение [*см. тж.* **Налагать ограничение**]
The rate of growth of the population is high when there are no environmental **constraints** such as shortage of food or space.
There is **a limitation** (*or* **restriction**) **on** the size of particles which may constitute an aerosol.

Ограниченная область пространства
Let R be **a bounded region of a space** of m variables.

Ограниченное количество [*см. тж.* **В ограниченном количестве, Иметься в ограниченном количестве**]
Some scientists suggested that clays are composed of extremely small particles **of a limited number of** crystalline minerals.

Ограниченное применение
This method **is of limited usefulness** (*or* **utility**).

Ограниченный I
In its own **circumscribed** domain ...
In the **confined** space of ...
These units have **a restricted** (*or* **limited**) speed of response.
The need to obtain increased output from a **restricted** labour force ...
Such converters have **limited** applications.

Ограниченный II
The area **enclosed by** the curve line and the straight line ...
We assume a region *R* **bounded by** the axis $t = 0$, the line $t = t_0$, and a characteristic issuing out of the origin.
A crystal is an organized solid **bounded by** crystal faces.
These rocks are characterized by successive layers or beds of material **limited** above and below **by** planes called bedding planes.

Ограничивать I
Insulators are used **to confine** the passage of electricity **to** the desired paths in any circuit.
The transformer **limits** (*or* **restricts,** *or* **confines**) the bandpass **to** 2 Mc.
The sample size has **to be restricted to** prevent overloading the column.
Considerations of symmetry **constrain** the choice of terms.
In a room-temperature computer the signal transmission properties of metallic conductors can severely **constrain** the maximum operating speed.
Our orbital model of the atom **restricts** the centralized nuclear region **to** a single electron pair.

Ограничивать II
The duration of usable laser energy for heating dense, freely expanding, small plasmas **is bounded by** two characteristic times.
Any line segment that partially **bounds** a plane geometric figure ...

Ограничивать внимание
We **restrict our attention to** this nucleus.

Ограничиваться [*см. тж.* **Сводиться к**]
The use of these manipulators **is** not **confined to** welding.
Accuracy **is limited** only **by** that of the original data.
The duties of the operator **are limited to** feeding the work into the machine.
Practical use of porcelain enamels **is limited to** metals with ...
The use of these detectors **is restricted to** applications where ...
We **have restricted ourselves to** the simplest case of spherical molecules.
The disturbance **is confined to** a surface enclosing the origin.
This technique **is limited by** the large amounts of vapour that must be pumped off.
We **restrict** the discussion **to** the case of ...

Ограничиваться рассмотрением
We **shall restrict our consideration to** the specific type of ...

Ограничивающий
The surface **bounding** the occupied volume of ...
The subduction zones **bounding** the Pacific plate form a “ring of fire”.

Огромное большинство [*см.* **Подавляющее большинство**].

Огромное значение [*см. тж.* **Первостепенное значение**]
This provides data which **are of paramount** (*or* **prime,** *or* **cardinal,** *or* **great,** *or* **tremendous**) **importance in** studies of magnetism.

Огромное количество [*см.* **Масса**].

Огромное пространство
Vast expanses of the continents ...

Огромное число
Examination under a light microscope revealed **an abundance of** microscopic particles.

Огрубляющий пищу продукт
Agar is used as **food roughage.**

Одевать на
A rubber hose **is fitted** (*or* **slipped**) **over** the end of the sampling tube.
A bearing **can be mounted on** a shaft by means of ...

Одеваться на
The sockets easily **slip over** nuts.

Один [*см. тж.* **В одном лишь**]
Cyclic hydrocarbons with more than thirty members in **a single** ring of carbon atoms have been prepared.

Один-единственный
The system consists of **a single** arrangement.
The amino acid arm almost always consists of seven pairs of nucleosides, plus **a solitary one** before the -*CCA* terminus (*biol.*).

Один в другом
The telescoping rolls are concentrically mounted **one inside the other.**

Один за другим [*см. тж.* **В приведённом порядке, По одному, По очереди, Последовательно**]
By the early 20th century experimental and theoretical developments were appearing **at a rapid pace** (*or* **one after another**).
Fragment ions of different masses are "focussed" through the exit slit **in turn.**
Telegraph cables on the flat sea floor were broken **one by one.**
Numerous other solid-state laser materials were discovered **in rapid succession.**
The use of each system will be discussed **in turn** (*or* **by turns**).
Large quarry and tunnel blasts require that the charges be detonated **in sequence** (*or* **sequentially**).
The welding passes are made **one after the other.**
These missiles can be fired **repetitively** almost as fast as a bolt-operated rifle.
The sets of coils may be subjected simultaneously or **successively** to the inducing action of the field magnets.

Один, и только один
There are controlled systems to which energy must be supplied in **one** direction, **and one** direction **only** (*or* in **one, and only one,** direction).

Один и тот же [*см. тж.* **Общий для**]
When power and telephone circuits are carried on **common** poles, ...

Один из
This screen is acknowledged **to be among** (*or* **one of) the** most efficient devices available.
One such group is the hydroxyl.

Один из возможных вариантов состоит в том, что
One possibility is that cosmic jets are made by a nozzle.

Один из главных
Silica is **a major** (*or* **an important**) component of glass.

Один из двух
Galvanic action is combatted by **either** (*or* **one**) **of two** ways: ...

Один из десяти
One in (*or* **out of**) **every ten** hospital beds is filled by a patient with a mental disorder.

Один из лучших
He was **a top-level** mathematician.

Один из основных
Loss of mobility is **a central** problem in old age.
The flat faces on crystals, inclined in various ways to each other, are **a principal** feature of real or idealized crystals.

Один из первых
He **was among the first to** suggest ...

Один из первых конструкторов
He **was among the first to design** interdigital transducers.

Один из решающих факторов
The location of the bridge **is a controlling consideration.**

Один из ряда
This boron-silicon similarity **is one of a number** (*or* **a series**) **of** diagonal relations in the Periodic Table.

Один из следующих
These effects will be studied in **a later** chapter.

Один из способов
One way to decrease (*or* **of** decreasing) the damage **is to** remove ...

Один из способов выйти из положения состоит в том, чтобы
One way out is to concentrate our wastes into a small portion of space.

Один из способов осуществления этого
One way of doing this is to send up a rocket with ...

Один или несколько
A hardener is an alloy containing a high percentage of **one or more** alloying elements which ...
Small caissons are used **singly or in groups** to carry such loads as ...

Один лишь [*см. тж.* **Один только**]
The mere presence of this histone is not sufficient to explain ...
This mechanism **alone** is not a sufficient explanation.
The van der Waals force **is solely** responsible for holding uncharged molecules together.
Here, the current is determined **solely** (*одним лишь*) by the rate of high diffusion of ...

Один на другой
The successive bundles are placed **one on top of the other.**

Один на другом
For a series of beams lying **one upon the other ...**

Один над другим
The layers are arranged **one above the other.**

Один только I
Density measurements **alone** do not reveal the actual conditions in a crystalline lattice.

Один только II
More 3-methyl-1-butene is formed than we might expect **merely** from (*на основании одних лишь*) statistical considerations.

Один ... уже
This peculiarity **alone** makes our galaxy remarkable.
This observation **is by itself** sufficient for the statement that ...

Один шанс из
One chance in a billion ...

Одинаково легко [*см.* **С одинаковой лёгкостью**].

Одинаково необходим для
Proteins **are essential to** the replicatory process of DNAs and RNAs **alike** (*biol.*).

Одинаково относиться к [*см.* **В равной мере относиться к**].

Одинакового размера
Blast furnace coke **should be uniform in size.**

Одинакового состава
All rocks **of like composition** develop the same minerals in the same range.

Одинаковые размеры
The reflecting bases of the mirror and the prism **are (of) the same size.**

Одинаковый [*см. тж.* **Обладать одинаковой энергией, Общий для**]
No two electrons may have all their quantum numbers **alike.**
End flanges should be **equal in** width.
The distance between adjacent holes **should be the same.**
The crystals were **of uniform** thickness.
Equal volumes of gases and vapours under the same conditions of ... contain identical numbers of molecules.
Electrons **are identical in** charge.

Одиночная частица
A unit particle.

Одиночный [*см.* **Индивидуальное производство деталей**].

Одна из основных проблем
A primary consideration is high spectral irradiance in the analyte volume.

Одна часть на тысячу
Linearity errors **are** approximately **one part in a thousand.**

Одна часть ... на ... частей
One part (of) molybdenum **for** (*or* **per**) **two parts (of)** tungsten ...

Однако [*см. тж.* **В то же время, Но**]
The resulting forces are repulsive, **except that** at a nuclear separation of about four angstrom units there is a small attractive force.
The isothermal calorimeter is simple, **and yet** it can yield excellent data (*or* **however** it can ...).

Одним из которых является [*см.* **В частности**].

Одним из примеров которых является
Some polysaccharides, **of which** cellulose **is an example,** are completely insoluble in water.

Одним из примеров является [*см. тж.* **Примером является**]
Fresh water **is an example.**
This fire-extinguisher **is one example,** now being produced under contract.
An example exists in machining stainless steel bars for valve parts.

Одним из таких примеров является
One such example is the application of plate tectonics to ...

Одним нажимом кнопки
At the touch of a button he can select ...

Одним словом [*см.* **Короче говоря**].

Одним ударом
Newton solved three problems **in one stroke.**
A mechanical press usually achieves a forging **with one stroke.**

Одно время
At one time it was even suspected that ...
Transformer coupling was **at one time** used in audio amplifiers.

Одно дело ... Другое дело
It is one thing to predict too little osmotically effective water in the cell; that can be explained by a number of hypotheses.
It is quite another matter to predict too much water because there is no explanation.

Одно и то же
Some scientists believe that energy and matter **are one and the same** (*or* **the same thing**).

Одно целое с
The cams are ground **as an integral part of** the shaft.
Priming is effected by a small mechanical pump arranged **integral with** the pumping equipment.
These gears **are integral with** their shafts.

Одновременно [*см. тж.* **В то же время**]
This led to the decision to interconnect large numbers of processors which can work **concurrently.**
It is necessary to use two or three filters **at a time.**
Beads of 1/2 in. diameter are formed ten **at a time.**
This setup can produce three different parts **at once.**
The machine processes two units **simultaneously.**
An atomic gas laser about 0.15 m in length can only have a single mode oscillating **at one time.**
$F(x)$ and $G(x)$ are never **both** zero **together.**

Одновременно ... и
This was at once a statement of a metaphysical view of the world **and** a demonstration of ...

Одновременно обеспечивать
A maser amplifier **combines** very high gain **with** extremely low noise.

Одновременно с
Coincidentally with the arrival of a digital data pulse, an operating pulse is supplied to the stepping motor.
Concurrent with the increased use of detergents, many new formulations have been developed.
Double and multiple stars must have originated **concurrently with** single stars.
Again with Breit and **contemporaneously with** Bohr (1936) he invented ...
Synchronous with the arrival of the cosmic-ray flux, there occurred ...
Coincident with the development of the hydrogen bomb, the search for a more controlled means of releasing fusion energy was begun.
Laplace proposed that the planets and satellites were formed **contemporaneously** (*or* **simultaneously**) **with** the Sun.

At the same time as, Simultaneously with ...

Одновременный
The use of these detectors would be quite limited if it were not for **concurrent** advances in computer technology.

Одного возраста
The two rocks **were of an age** (*or* **of the same age**).

Одного знака
For both waves, X and X^1, **are of the same sign.**
Dislocations **of like sign ...**

Однозарядный
A singly (*or* **single**) **charged** cation ...

Однозначная функция
A single-valued (*or* **one-valued**) **function.**

Однозначно
The magnitude of steady-state values **is** always **uniquely** (*or* **unambiguously**) determined by the damping ratio.

Однозначно определённый
The disturbance **is uniquely determined.**

Однозначно определять
The chromaticity **is uniquely** (*or* **unequivocally**) **determined by** x and y.

Однозначно отображаться на
A sufficiently small cube in ε-space **is mapped one-to-one** (*or* **in a one-to-one way**) **onto** a neighbourhood of U_0.

Однозначное соответствие [*см. тж.* **В однозначном соответствии с, Приводить к однозначному соответствию с**]
This is called **placing** two series **into "one-to-one correspondence".**

Однозначное соответствие между
There is a **one-to-one correspondence between** the terms in the characteristic equation and ...

Однозначность
The uniqueness of the solution of certain problems ...

Однозначный
This equation **is single** (*or* **one**) **valued.**
Thus we obtain an **unambiguous** solution.
This variation in angle may be related to the modulating wave in any predetermined **unique** manner.
E is a **single-valued** function of F.

Одноимённый
Like magnetic poles repel and unlike magnetic poles attract.

Одной из разновидностей является
Streams following major faults **are one variety.**

Однокомпонентный
A **single-component** gas ...

Одномерный
We have solved the **one-dimensional** problem.

Однонаправленный [*см.* **В одном направлении**].

Однородного состава
The vapour **is uniform in composition.**

Однородность
The homogeneity of the field ...
The uniformity of the surface finish ...

Однородный
A **homogeneous** structure (*or* mixture, etc.) ...
The extra low-temperature enamels have a **uniform** finish.
A **uniform** (*or* **homogeneous**) magnetic field ...

Одностадийный процесс
A one-step process.

Одноступенчатый
A **single-stage** rocket ...

Одноцелевой
A **single-purpose** lubricant ...

Одобрять
We **favour** the idea of giving ...

Ожесточённо дискутировать
The relative importance of partial melting as opposed to metasomatism **has** long **been furiously** (*or* **heatedly**) **debated.**

Ожесточённые споры [*см. тж.* **Вызывать ожесточённые споры**]
Heated debates (*or* **arguments**).

Ожидаемое время жизни [*см. тж.* **Время жизни**]
Life expectancy (*or* **expectation**).

Ожидание [*см.* **Вопреки ожиданиям, Оправдывать ожидания**].

Ожидать [*см. тж.* **Как и следовало ожидать, Нас ожидают сюрпризы в области**]
The chemical resistance **to be expected from** the bond ...
These diodes achieve the long life we **expect of** transistor circuits.
The patient can **look forward to** a normal life-span after a successful operation.

Ожидать своего решения
The problem **remains to be solved.**

Ожидаться
It is anticipated (*or* **expected**) **that** the thermal efficiency of the units will be 40 percent.

Озабоченность [*см.* **Вызывать озабоченность населения**].

Озаглавлен
The second column of the first table **is headed** *g*.
The book **is (en)titled** "Introduction to ..."

Озадачивать
This dilemma **has plagued** various philosophers throughout history.

Ознакомившись с
With a knowledge of (*or* **Having familiarized ourselves with**) both igneous and sedimentary rocks we are ready to ...

Ознакомление [*см. тж.* **Беглое ознакомление, Рассмотрение**]
Inspection of the Periodic Table reveals that ...
Exposing readers **to** new ideas can heighten their appreciation of the subject matter.

Ознакомлять с
An introduction to simple units of measurement and simple concepts of heat will be necessary.

Ознакомляться с [*см. тж.* **Ближе (п)ознакомиться с, Более подробно ознакомиться с, Знакомиться с**]
As we learn more about the subject of chemistry, we **will** gradually **acquire a familiarity with** many structural features.
Students **become acquainted** (*or* **familiar**) **with** the rarer minerals.
The navigator **should familiarize himself with** these publications.

Ознаменовать
The paper **marked** the discovery of the atomic nucleus.

Означать I [*см. тж.* **Здесь означает, Под этим подразумевается, что; Указывать**]
The term thermodynamics **implies** a study of the flow of heat.
This sharp enhancement **signalled** the existence of a new kind of quark.
Such a low level does not necessarily **mean** (*or* **signify**) that ...
These bands **signify** the presence of a vinyl group.
Equation (8.2) **implies that ...**
For ligands of rather similar type an increase in ligand basic strength **implies** an increase in its metal-chelating ability.
Bonding also **refers to** the fastening together of two prices by means of adhesives.

Означать II [*см. тж.* **Обозначать**]
m **denotes** mobility.
y(t) **stands for** the input.
In this paper "mining" **will be taken to mean** "coal mining".
B **signifies** the concentration of ...
Here, *u* **represents** the radiant energy density.

Означающий
Cohesion is often used incorrectly as a term **to denote** strength of materials.

Оказаться за пределами
If the ratio **falls outside of** these values, ...

Оказаться несостоятельным
Aristotle's model **collapsed** when tested by experiment.

Оказаться несправедливым
This calculation is liable **to break down** at the very lowest pressures.

Оказаться неэффективным
The success of mutation breeding where all other methods **had failed ...**

Оказаться пригодным для
The idea **may** even **work for** a single-axis control system.

Оказаться справедливым [*см.* **Оправдываться I**].

Оказываемое давление
Further movement of the pedal will increase **the pressure brought to bear upon** the work.
Pressure exerted on the frame is controlled by turning the knob.

Оказываемое сопротивление
Resistance offered by the diode ...

Оказывается, что
It turns out that alanine given by injection can increase the production of glucose.

Оказывать бесценную помощь при
Aryl hydrazines **were of inestimable value in** structure determination in sugar chemistry.

Оказывать благоприятное влияние на
The lower oxidation **had a beneficial** (*or* **favourable**) **effect on** die life.

Оказывать важную услугу
In these processes, DNA **renders vital service** (*biol.*).

Оказывать влияние на [*см. тж.* **Влиять на**]
Parallel advances in the development of computer graphics **will have** (*or* **make**) **an** even greater **impact on** the work of the designer.
Aldosterone **exerts some action** (*or* **effect,** *or* **influence**) **on** the metabolism of carbohydrate.

Оказывать вредное влияние
These impurities **may prove deleterious.**

Оказывать вредное влияние на
The green tarnish which sometimes forms on the surface **has** no **detrimental** (*or* **deleterious,** *or* **harmful,** *or* **unfavourable,** *or* **adverse,** *or* **untoward,** *or* **ill**) **effect upon** the method.

Оказывать главное влияние на
These factors **exert primary control over** a biotic community.

Оказывать давление на
Since the laser **exerts** no **pressure on** the work, it can be turned sharply in any direction.
The die cushion **delivers** uniform **pressure to** the blank during drawing.

Оказывать действие на [*см. тж.* **Влиять на**]
The compounds that **exhibit** this **effect ...**
Theoretically, one charged object **exerts a force on** all other charged objects in the universe.
Camphor **has a** local **action on** the gastrointestinal tract.
The magnetic oscillations in the waves **act on** charged particles causing them to vibrate.
To exert (*or* **have**) **influence (up)on ...**
To have (*or* **produce**) **an effect (up)on ...**

Оказывать заметное действие на
Trace contaminants on the base metals **may have a pronounced** (*or* **marked,** *or* **appreciable,** *or* **perceptible**) **effect on** results.

Оказывать неблагоприятное влияние на
To affect adversely (*or* **exert an adverse effect on**) ...
The sealed tube stage **was very detrimental to ...**

Оказывать обратное действие
Placing the cells in a concentrated salt solution **has the opposite effect.**

Оказывать обратное действие на
The electric and magnetic fields generated by the beam **can act back on** the beam in a variety of ways.

Оказывать отрицательное действие (*или* **влияние**) **на**
Entrainment of liquid from one tray to the next tray above **has an adverse effect on** the composition change across the tray.

Оказывать плохую услугу
This kind of publicity **does** science **a disservice.**

Оказывать помощь при
The Periodic Table **provides a useful guide to** estimating the relative electronegativity of common elements.

Оказывать решающее действие на
The interaction of these electric charges **can have a determining effect on** the physical properties of the gel.

Оказывать сильное влияние на
Climate **has a great deal to do with** the way fluvial processes act.
Absorption processes **have an important bearing on** the interpretation of primary emission.
The achievement of a practical fusion-power reactor **would have a profound impact on** almost every aspect of human society.
The temperature at which cells live and grow **can have a pronounced effect on** the amount of unsaturated fatty acid in their membranes.

Оказывать сопротивление
Rough channels **set up** (*or* **exhibit,** *or* **offer**) more **resistance to** flow.

Оказывать такое же действие
Many other impurities **act the same way.**

Оказываться I
About 30 percent of the 3000 nuclear tracks measured **fell** within the cone of tritons.

Оказываться II
More than half of the objects identified on the basis of their radio position usually **turn out** (*or* **prove**) **to be** quasars.
The approach to equilibrium of any degree of freedom **is found** (*or* **proves,** *or* **appears**) **to be** approximately exponential.
Laser radiation **was found (to be)** capable of exciting ...

Оказываться в [*см. тж.* **Попадать в**]
The fifth carbon atom must be rotated so that the oxygen atom in the OH group on this carbon atom **is brought into** the plane of the first five carbon atoms.

Оказываться в поле зрения [*см.* **Попадать в поле зрения**].

Оказываться недействительным
The correlation **breaks down for** hailstones with a small radius of growth.

Оказываться несостоятельным
Neutrinos are now seen as an ideal probe for examining the weak interaction at high energies, where present theories **break down** (*or* **fail**).

Окаймлён
The edges of the polygons **are fringed with** tiny droplets.

Окаймлён с севера
The plateau **is fringed on the north by** high mountain chains.

Окаймлять
The system of beaches which **fringe** large portions of eastern United States ...

Окалина после ковки
Forging scale.

Окаменевший
Fossilized (*or* **Petrified**) tree trunks ...

Оканчиваться
Some foam stabilizers have long hydrocarbon chains which **terminate** (*or* **end**) **in** a polar group.

Окисляющее действие
The oxidative action of chlorine ...

Около [*см. тж.* **Порядка, Приблизительно**]
The total value of the shipment will come **close to** $178 billion.
For this kind of telephony, frequency differences **approaching** (*or* **approximately,** *or* **about,** *or* **around**) 10 cps are permissible.
In the neighbourhood of 100 in. ...
Missions such as journeys to the planets may take **in the order of** a year to accomplish.
Silicones retain **some** 80% of their original properties at 315°C.

Оконтуривать
Prospecting by drilling is continuing **to outline** the areas to be opened in the future.

Окончание [*см. тж.* **По окончании**]
After **the completion of** hydrogen burning ...

Окончательная обработка
Before being passed to the assembly area for **finish machining** and incorporation into units, ...
This facilitates **the finishing of** parts that must be held to close tolerances.

Окончательная отделка поверхности
External surfaces are finished on plunge grinding machines.

Окончательно не доказан
The existence of ... must be taken as probable, but **not certainly** (*or* **conclusively**) **proved.**

Окончательно установлен
The existence of maximum flux in the vicinity of 0.15 MeV **is** not **conclusively established by** the spectrometer data.

Окончательный [*см. тж.* **Конечный**]
The eventual (*or* **ultimate,** *or* **final**) appearance of the comet's tail will depend on ...
The net result is that the titanium carbide tool has significantly better life when machining grey cast iron.

Окончательный ответ
Nuclear power plants were once hoped to be **the ultimate answer to** man's needs for electric energy.

Окончательный размер
The die sections are machined very close to **finished dimensions.**

Окончательный результат
The net result is an increase in the translational temperature of the system.
The net result is that a photon at ω_L is annihilated while a photon at ω_S is created.

Окончен
Then the star's life **is over** (*or* **finished**).

Окрашен
The cell **was stained with** peroxidase.

Окрашен в ... цвет
The bench **is painted grey.**
The rock fragments **may be coloured brown to black,** etc.

Окрашивание
A staining technique makes the chromosomes fluorescent.

Окрашивание лакмусовой бумажки в ... цвет
The turning of litmus paper blue, etc.

Окрашивать
The dials **are painted with** a substance containing a trace of a radium salt.

Окрашивать в ... цвет
The indicator **will turn** the water **to a yellow,** etc. **colour.**
Hypochlorites **yellow** and damage wool.
By igniting the product in a burner flame to which the calcium **imparts** a brilliant **crimson colour** one achieves ...

Окрашивать в самые различные цвета
When pure, calcite is either colourless or white but impurities **can introduce a wide variety of colours.**

Окрашивать лакмусовую бумажку в синий цвет
The litmus paper turns blue.

Окрашиваться
Phosphide **colours** more slowly than cementite.
The solution **changes to a red colour.**
If the water is alkaline, it **will turn red.**

Окрашиваться в ... цвет
Starch **produces a blue colour** when treated with ...
Glycogen **gives a reddish-brown colour** with this reagent.
A violet-red colour develops when these sugars are treated with ...

Окрестность [*см.* **В окрестности**].

Округление
Errors entering into each numerical operation as a result of **rounding off ...**

Округлённый до ... знаков
We will use atomic weights **rounded (off) to** five, etc., **figures** (*or* **digits**).

Округлённый до секунды
1 rad = 57°17'45'' **to the nearest second.**

Округлять до
We then **round (off)** the answer **to** the desired four figures.

Округлять до ближайшего
The tabulated values **are rounded off to the nearest** 10°C.

Округлять до ближайшего целого (числа)
Round (off) all numerical quantities **to the nearest whole number** (*or* **integer**).
The result **is rounded off to an integer.**

Округляться
The sum **is** then **rounded off.**

Окружающая среда [*см. тж.* **При температуре окружающей среды, Температура окружающей среды, Условия окружающей среды**]
The character of the clay minerals changes in passing from one **environment** to another.
The bath was insulated from **the surroundings.**
To understand how these molecules interact with **the (surrounding) medium** (*or* **environment**), ...
The rate of heat flow is proportional to the temperature difference between an object and **its environment.**
The activity of the solute **in the (ambient) medium** is high.

Окружающие условия
This difference arises from **environmental** (*or* **ambient**) **conditions.**

Окружающий I
We studied mass transfer between a sphere and **an ambient** (*or* **a surrounding**) liquid.

Окружающий II
The properties of the electron together with its **enveloping** cloud of virtual particles ...
Such synclines form continuous belts **circling** the continents.
In the countries **ringing** the Baltic Sea ...

Окружающий воздух
The temperature of **the outer air** through which the aircraft is moving ...

Окружающий его
Bitumen remains immobile in **the enclosing** (*or* **surrounding**) sand.

Окружение [*см. тж.* **Окружающая среда**]
Chemical reaction between a metal and its **surroundings ...**
This value depends on **the** chemical **environment of** the carbon atoms.
To see the simplest elements in **their** simplest natural **setting, ...**

Окружён
The molybdenum tube **is surrounded by** concrete tubes of the same metal.
An incipient star **is embedded in** a shell of gas.

Окупать расходы на
These chucks help **to pay off** machines faster.

Окупаться [*см. тж.* **Оправдывать себя**]
The welding gun **has already paid for itself.**
The system **pays out** quickly because of its high productivity.

Окутан облаком
Venus **is shrouded in a blanket of** carbon dioxide.

Омывать
The concentration of potassium ions in human cells is more than 100 times greater than it is in the blood **that bathes** them.
The eastern boundary current **sweeps** the west coast of North America.

Омываться
The grooves **are washed by** line fluid.

Опасение [*см.* **Вызывать озабоченность населения, Вызывать опасения, Высказывать опасения**].

Опасное напряжение
Such **stresses** are not **critical** in heavy sections.

Опасности, грозящие рабочим
To lessen **the exposure of workmen to hazards, ...**

Опасность [*см.* **Подвергать большой опасности, Подвергаться опасности, Представлять опасность для, Существует опасность**].

Опасность для здоровья
The presence of radioactive contamination **is a (potential) health hazard.**

Опасность для окружающей среды [*см.* **Представлять опасность для окружающей среды**].

Опасность для здоровья людей
The release of carbon monoxide constitutes a serious **hazard to human health.**

Опасность для человека [*см. тж.* **Представлять опасность для жизни человека**]
Personal hazards in the handling of sodium peroxide ...

Опасность пожара
In order to reduce **the fire hazard** (*or* **danger**), ...

Опасные последствия [*см.* **Вызывать опасные последствия**].

Опасный [*см. тж.* **Быть опасным**]
This substance **is dangerous to** health.
Dry active substances **are** the most **hazardous** (*or* **dangerous**).

Оперативное обслуживание
Prompt service.

Оперативный
Means for providing for the safe and **expeditious** movement of aircraft ...

Операция [*см. тж.* **Выполнять операцию, За одну операцию**]
One additional **manipulation** converts Eq. (6-49) into ...
The square root can be constructed by straightedge and compass in a finite number of **manipulations.**
With one drilling machine you can perform hundreds of drilling **assignments** in up to 2 in. steel.

Операция с
The rules for **dealing with** sums, products, and quotients ...
A mathematical **operation** performed on a function ...

Опережать
The phase of one pendulum **is** 180° **ahead of** the other.

Оперирование
The instrument is intended for **operating on** rabbits, rats, etc.

Оперировать
Such derivatives **can be manipulated** like fractions.

Опираться на
The cover has a flat surface which **bears up against** the inside of the inward projecting lips of the drumhead.
The metal frame **rests on** the bottom plate.
The technique of differentiation **leans upon** facts about inverse functions.

Описан
These fermentations **may be depicted by** the following equations: ...
Three useful methods **are outlined** below.

Описание
The Bohr **description** for the energy of ...
This brief **sketch** should be sufficient to assess the public reaction to the accident.
An **account of** typical cells is given on p. 56.

Описанный [*см. тж.* **Кратко описан**]
The reactions **outlined** above ...
Even though the procedure **discussed** (*or* **described**) for the taking of a flue-gas analysis may seem complicated, ...

Описываемый
In the region **covered by** these characteristics ...
The angular velocity is the number of radians **swept through** per second.

Описывать I [*см. тж.* **Освещать, Приближённо описывать**]
We **have covered** this event in Chap. 12.
The purpose of this chapter **is to give an account of** the movement of energy in the astronomical world.

Описывать II
This equation **governs** the flow under such conditions.
This enabled the Newtonian mechanics **to represent** (*or* **describe**) planetary motions to a high degree of approximation.

Описывать III
This paper **is concerned with** experimental control systems.
The book **covers** (*or* **describes**) the principles of soldering.
The article **deals with** (*or* **outlines**) the modifications at the power station.
The article **presents** (*or* **describes**) a method ...
The point on the flywheel **traces** (*or* **describes**) a circle with a circumference 2π.

Описывать в общих чертах
We certainly know enough **to sketch the broad outline of ...**

Описывать вокруг
We can **circumscribe** a regular polygon **about** a circle.

Описывать дугу
On the beach face the sand particles carried by an uprush **describe an arc** in the direction of ...

Описывать окружность вокруг треугольника
To circumscribe a circle about a triangle, ...

Описывать траекторию
The spot of light **describes** a circular **path** when the lens assembly is rotated.
The point **will trace out a trajectory** in this space.

Описываться уравнением
The surface generated by ... **has** [*or* **is given** (*or* **described**) **by**] **the equation** x^2+ ...

Описывающий
Then the appropriate equations **descriptive of** the process can be written.

Оповещать о
Alarm systems are used **to signal** the presence of danger.

Опознавать
To enable identification of a substance of analytical interest, ...

Опознавать по расцветке
The giant cells **are identifiable by colour.**

Опорная точка I
The string hangs freely from two **points of support.**

Опорная точка II
There are no **points of reference** (*or* **reference points**) against which the changes in elevation could be measured.

Опорожнён на 2/3
When the float **is** about **two-thirds empty, ...**

Опорожнять [*см. тж.* **Спускать воду**]
The lock chamber **is** filled and **emptied** by means of ...

Оппозиция [*см.* **Вызывать оппозицию**].

Оправдавший себя на практике
Well-proved designs ...

Оправдан
We are undecided whether the expense of a second launching **is warranted.**
These assumptions **are justified.**

Оправдывать себя за ... лет
Although the machine cost about 1 million dollars, it is expected that **the write-off period will be** less than four **years**.

Оправдывать
The difference is not large enough **to warrant** changing the reaction conditions.
These parts are expensive enough **to warrant** extra machining costs.
The volume of work does not **warrant** (*or* **justify**) having an operator at each station.

Оправдывать ожидания
If these wells **live up to expectations,** they will open up new areas for drilling.
Their **expectations were realized.**

Оправдывать расходы
The cost of the plant is so great that most railroads are unable **to justify the expenditure.**
The recovery of some valuable material from the process was necessary in order **to offset the cost of** operation.

Оправдывать свою репутацию
The Italian pasta does not **live up to its reputation** unless one uses special kinds of durum wheat.

Оправдывать себя I
It will pay to inspect the tube bundles.
The installation actually **paid for itself.**
Tests indicate that the valve **can pay out** in 7 to 8 months.
Recovery equipment costs less than 40,000 dollars with **a payout of** less than five months.
Waste recovery **pays off.**
The investment **will** amply **repay itself** in efficient service and utter reliability.

Оправдывать себя II
If this block **proves out,** it will undoubtedly lead to adoption of such blocks for other cars.
Total intravenous feeding **has proved itself** in the treatment of 1300 adults and more than 100 infants.
Dye lasers still **have to prove themselves** in this area.
The preceding generations of accelerators **have proved their worth.**

This machinery **has been proven** throughout the world.

Оправдывать себя III
Such efforts **are** always **rewarding.**

Оправдывать себя на практике
The kinetic-rate expression **works very well** despite its questionable form.

Оправдывать усилия
A designer **may be justified in going to great** (*or* **fantastic**) **lengths to** convert a pound of dead weight into a pound of payload.
The results **justified our efforts.**

Оправдывать эту потерю (*или* **жертву**)
The scanning rate is lower, but the improvement in focusing **is worth the sacrifice.**

Оправдываться I
That prediction **was borne out** (*or* **justified**).

Оправдываться II [*см.* **Ничем не оправдываться**].

Определение [*см. тж.* **По определению**]
To assess the carcinogenic risk associated with this contamination, ...
Impingement tests are often used **to assess** (*or* **determine,** *or* **estimate,** *or* **evaluate**) the resistance of condenser tube material to sea water.
When **deciding** the correct path of the propeller ...
This provides a basis for **rating** the effectiveness of lubricants.

Определение возраста пород
This method of **dating** (*or* **age determination of**) **rocks** is widely used.

Определение возраста с помощью углерода ^{14}C
The ^{14}C dating of fossil animals ...

Определение структуры
Accurate **structural determinations** are limited to substances that form crystalline compounds.

Определённо указывать на [*см.* **Указывать со всей определённостью на то, что**].

Определённое количество
Since only **so much** metal can be formed in one blow, ...
Any given vessel of air can only hold **so much** water and no more.

Определённость [*см.* **Для определённости**].

Определённый I [*см. тж.* **В определённых пределах, Тот или иной**]
These particles can have only **certain** energies.
Any particular layer always contains **distinctive** fossils.
Each absorption band is associated with a **distinct** (*or* **definite**) type of electrical oscillator.
Each of the materials comprising the Earth's surface has **distinct** elastic properties.

Определённый II [*см. тж.* **Заранее установленный**]
A counter may be located at a **fixed** (*or* **set**) distance from the source.

Определённый III [*см. тж.* **Тот или иной**]
The maximum rate of change of a **particular** characteristic of the orbit ...
Apparatus suitable for **specific** test methods ...
The conveyor feeds a **specified** amount of coal into ...

Определённый таким образом
The quantity u, **thus defined**, may depend on ...

Определять I [*см. тж.* **Вычислять, Невозможно определить, Обусловливать**]
Magnitude of the principal stresses **controls** (*or* **governs**) the degree of birefringence.
Covalent bonds **are responsible for** atomic combinations in many elements.
θ is the angle **defining** the position of the rotor with respect to the stator.
These elements **define** the geometry of the orbit.
The take-off condition **dictates** (*or* **determines,** *or* **defines**) the amount of wing area required for an airplane.
The armature of the rudder motor **dictates** the direction in which the rudder motor rotates.
The rate at which a furnace can melt scrap **governs** the rate at which it can accommodate successive portions of the charge.

These equations **govern** simple waves.
It is the naval architect who **settles** (*or* **decides on**) the form of the vessel.
Three points **determine** a circle.
The geometry of the small ring compounds **fixes** their configuration.
The equation **specifies** the topography of the potential surface.

Определять II [*см. тж.* **Оценивать**]
These variables are difficult to **appraise** accurately.
The cost of steam generation required by the power plant **can be arrived at** (*or* **defined**) **from** Fig. 2.
A number of coils were rolled **to assess** the performance of the controller.
The pressure **was determined** (*or* **deduced**) **from** the weight of steam and ...
Reserves **are estimated** (*or* **evaluated**) **at** 100,000,000 bbl.
To assess the distribution and level of the pollutant ...
This knowledge enables the analyst **to gauge** the meaning and reliability of the results obtained.
Information about temperatures below the surface **can be inferred from** the magnetic properties of rocks.
The adequacy of the global supply **can be gauged through** a simple analysis of the per capita need for water.

Определять III [*см.* **Классифицировать**].

Определять IV
If the wavelength composition of the light is known, its colour **can be specified** (*or* **determined,** *or* **identified**).
Identify the two chemicals in the equation for which ...
The closer you want **to pinpoint** the exact orbit, the more corrections you must make.

Определять возраст [*см.* **Возраст ... определяется**].

Определять как
It is convenient **to define** the relief angle **in terms of** the angle between the flank and a plane perpendicular to the drill axis.
The mobility μ **is defined as** the average drift velocity when E1 = 1.

Определять на глаз
Estimate by eye the ratio between ...

Определять по
The Rydberg constant **is determined** (*or* **inferred**) **from** the spectrum of hydrogen.
The quantity of liquid delivered **is determined from** the change in weight.
The dimensions of clay particles **are determined by** the rate at which they settle in a still column of water.

Определять по дальномеру
The distance **is judged by a range-finder.**

Определять положение
Three coordinates are needed **to locate** each atom.
The coordinates *X, Y, Z* **locate** the centre of gravity of the molecule.
Two measurements **fix** the position of a plane with respect to the earth.

Определять предел
The effects of collimator thickness **place** (*or* **impose,** *or* **set**) **a** lower **limit on** the sensitive energy range.

Определять расположение
Neutron diffraction can be used **to locate** light atoms.

Определять сорт
Originally, cast iron **was graded by** examination of fracture characteristics.

Определяться [*см. тж.* **Обусловливаться, Подчиняться**]
The experimental methods of measuring dielectric constants **depend on** the frequency range under investigation.
The divergence of *v* **is defined** (*or* **determined,** *or* **described**) **by** the following expression: ...
The plasma volume **is determined by** this equilibrium.
The number of oxygen atoms coordinating with a modifying cation **is dictated by** the size of that cation.
The choice of the lathe **is governed** (*or* **controlled**) **by** the type and size of work to be performed.
In the special theory of relativity an event **is specified by** the three space coordinates and the time.
The initial state ahead of the piston **is specified by** *H*.

Определяться в процентах
The conductivity of commercial copper **is rated on a percentage basis.**

Определяться как
Burning velocity **is defined as** the normal velocity of ...
The angular momentum **is defined as** Iμ.
In statistical mechanics entropy **is interpreted as** a measure of ...

Определяющий фактор [*см. тж.* **Решающий фактор**]
In high-speed machines, the internal forces may be **the controlling** (*or* **deciding,** *or* **decisive,** *or* **determining**) **factor** in design of members.
Noise in the measuring circuit **is the governing** (*or* **crucial**) **factor.**

Опреснение морской воды
This energy could be used for **desalting** (*or* **desalination of**) **seawater.**

Опрессовывать
To pressurize (*or* **pressure test**).

Опробовать
These areas **have been sampled by** drilling.

Опровергать
The experiment seemed **to** effectively **rule out** the alternative hypothesis.
Experimental results **argued against** (*or* **were at variance with**) this conclusion.
This finding **demolished** (*or* **toppled**) the boundwater hypothesis in its original form.
This **invalidates** the assumption of constant fluid density.
The discovery of radioactivity in 1896 **dispelled** the belief that all atoms are permanent and immutable.
This **refutes** the assumption that rivers flowing through the more arid regions carry the most salt.

Опровергать существование
Another experiment that may measure or **rule out** a host of gravitational effects ...

Опровергающий [*см.* **Подтверждающий и опровергающий**].

Опровергнут
Classical prediction of ... **is (completely) disproved.**

Оптимальное сочетание [*см.* **Находить оптимальное сочетание между, Обеспечивать оптимальное сочетание**].

Оптимальный вариант [*см.* **Лучше всего было бы**].

Опубликованный
No such data can be found in **the available** (*or* **published**) literature.
No quantitative data of this kind **have** previously **been reported.**
Books **in print ...**

Опускать I [*см.* **Погружать в**].

Опускать II [*см. тж.* **Отбрасывать**]
We **drop** all subscripts.
For richer concentrates, roasting **is omitted** at many plants.
Let us now **pass over** the distribution of molecular speeds in two dimensions and proceed directly to ...
Terms like this **can be thrown** (*or* **dropped**) **out.**
It is conventional **to leave out** all the high powers of 2.
Chemists have the tendency to shorten long names by **leaving out** syllables.
For air *S* is unity and **may be omitted from** the formula.
The second term in Eq. (10.35) **can be dropped** (*or* **discarded**).

Опускать в воду *и т.п.*
The assembly **is lowered** (*or* **immersed**) **into the water.**

Опускать в скважину
The spectrometer **was lowered down a borehole.**

Опускать перпендикуляр
From *C* **drop a perpendicular to** *AB*.

Опускать перпендикуляр с линии ... в точке
Drop a perpendicular from line *AB* **at point** *C*.

Опускаться
When the Sun **has dropped** (*or* **sunk**) well below the horizon, ...

Опускаться в
The *–e* ending **is dropped from** the name of the parent hydrocarbon chain.

Опускаться на
An amphibian plane arises from and **alights on** either water or land.
The space vehicle **descended to** the lunar surface.

Опускаться на дно
The impurity coagulates and **sinks to the bottom.**

Опускаться ниже
As air temperatures **go below** –35°C, ...

Опущен I
The instrument **is immersed in** the water.
The cask **is lowered into** the transfer basin.

Опущен II
In the following discussion of Kepler's theory the problem of latitudes **will be left out** (*or* **omitted**).

Опущен в
Some minor types of stable vegetation **are omitted from** this general classification.

Опыт I [*см. тж.* **Богатый опыт, Весь накопленный опыт, Использовать опыт, Накапливать опыт, При наличии некоторого опыта, При опыте, Ставить опыт**]
In another **run** (*or* **experiment**) the procedure of Example I was repeated.
This formula is in good agreement with **experiment.**

Опыт II
A new engineer has no **experience of** ships (*or* **in** designing ships).
Experience on automatic equipment makes it easier to ...

Опыт говорит, что
The author's **experience suggests that ...**

Опыт на (*или* **с**)
The experiments were performed **on** animals.

Опыт по
In his **experiments on** liquid diffusion Graham showed that ...

Опыт подсказывает, что
Experience leads us to conclude that there is no zeroth-order term.
Our **experience tells us** (*or* **suggests**) **that** only a few of ... can be arbitrarily fixed.

Опыт показывает, что
Experiment shows that a mass of hydrogen peroxide proportional to 34 decomposes into ...

Опыт работы с
This computer requires no **computer expertise.**

Опыт эксплуатации
Operating experience.

Опытно-конструкторские работы
Development work.

Опытное исследование
This little township has been selected for **a pilot study.**

Опытные данные
Experimental findings (*or* **data,** *or* **results**).

Опытный участок
The firm drilled one well in **the pilot area.**

Опытным путём
The best size of the bead can be determined only **by experiment** (*or* **experimentally**).

Орбита [*см.* **Вращаться вокруг солнца по эллиптической орбите, Выводить на орбиту, Выходить на орбиту, Двигаться по орбите, Изменение орбиты, На орбите, Наклон орбиты, По орбите, Полёт по орбите**].

Орбита вокруг Земли
An Earth-circling orbit [*or* **An orbit (a)round** (*or* **about**) **the Earth**].
A circumtellurian (*or* **circumterrestrial**) **orbit.**
Putting the spacecraft into **an Earth orbit** requires that ...

Орбита вокруг Солнца
In **the orbit of** a planet or comet **about** [*or* **(a)round**] **the Sun ...**
A solar (*or* **circumsolar**) **orbit.**

Орбита кометы
A cometary orbit.

Орбитальная плоскость
The orbital plane of the Earth ...

Организация по борьбе с загрязнением среды
An environmental (*or* **anti-pollution**) **group.**

Организм
The red blood cells of **the human body ...**

Организовывать I
In the 1930s he **established** (*or* **set up**) a research institute.
He **put together** (*or* **set up**) a team to make an analysis of ...
Many states **have instituted** studies of ...

Органического происхождения
Organically derived deposits ...

Оригинальный
The process has some **unconventional** aspects.
All this is provided by the **unique** thread design.
He used an **ingenious** method not requiring a probe to measure the surface temperature.

Ориентация в пространстве
The orientation of a molecule **in space ...**

Ориентирован в том же или в противоположном направлении
The nuclear magnetic fields **are aligned either with** the external field **or opposing** the magnetic field.

Ориентировать на север или юг
The centre line of the plotter **may be oriented either north or south.**

Ориентировать прибор на карте (по параллели)
The instrument **should be oriented to the chart (to a parallel).**

Ориентироваться
These controls enable a locust **to orient itself** in flight.

Ориентироваться на
Producers **are oriented to** rimmed, capped and killed steels.

Ориентировочно
These compounds may be **broadly** subdivided into two classes.
Tentatively, we conclude that the planet has evolved much as the earth has.
We prefer to think **provisionally** that ...

Ориентировочно определять
In this article we **will infer** the chemical composition of ... on the basis of the seismic data.

Ориентировочный
The **estimated** extent of the canyon ...
These figures **are speculative** (*or* **tentative**), but they give some idea of ...

Ориентируясь по
Project the point up, **using** the nearest vertical grid **as a guide.**

Орошаться дождём
This land is watered exclusively **by rainfall.**
These crops **are rain fed.**

Орто- по отношению к (*хим.*)
Here, the hydroxyl groups **are ortho to** each other.

Осадок [*см.* **Давать осадок**].

Осаждаться
Cadmium **is precipitated from** the electrolyte of ...

Осаждаться на
The vapour **deposits on** the face of the sand mould.
The pure metal **deposits at** the cathode.

Осаждаться на дно
The compound tends **to settle to the bottom of** the pot as solid crystals.

Осаждаться слоями
The sample **is deposited in layers.**

Осаждение накипи
The deposition of scale on boiler tube surfaces ...

Осваивать
This subject **can be mastered** in a few months.

Освежать
For this edition the original figures **have been brought up to date** (*or* **updated**) and some new material is added.

Освежаться
The computerized information **is updated** annually.

Освещать I
The discovery **illuminated** (*or* **elucidated**) the cause of some diseases.
This is a complicated procedure and **cannot be covered** in detail here.
The book **covers** all fields of petroleum technology.

One great literary masterpiece often **illumines** a civilization.
This mechanism **has not been** fully **elucidated.**

Освещать II
Shine a light on a cockroach and it will scurry away.
In this microscope a beam of electrons **illuminates** the specimen to be studied.
When white **light is shone on to** many complexes, ...

Освещаться I
The literature on studies of continuous-flow resistance **is covered** (*or* **surveyed**) in the excellent review by ...

Освещаться II
The plate **is exposed to light.**

Освещение [*см.* **Внутреннее и наружное освещение, Естественное освещение, Наружное освещение, Яркость освещения**].

Освещение образца
Sample illumination.

Освещение шахты
Mine lighting is done from lx a 110-V a-c circuit.

Освещён
This problem **has not been** adequately **addressed** (*or* **elucidated**) in the literature.

Освобождать [*см. тж.* **Высвобождать**]
The column which supports the spindle head withdraws **to clear** the working area.

Освобождать винт
Loosen, without removal, **the** two **screws** at the right-hand end.
Slacken (do not remove) **the screws** securing the chassis to the case.

Освобождать гайку [*см.* **Отпускать гайку**].

Освобождать место для
If the new molecules are not strongly bound to the surface, **they can** leave it and **make room for** more reactants.

Освобождать от
The enriched bismuth dross **is freed of** (*or* **from**) calcium, magnesium, and lead by chlorination.
In purging mathematical philosophy **of** metaphysics ...
Open the drain cock **to rid** (*or* **drain,** *or* **empty**) the steam cylinder **of** water of condensation.

Освобождать ... от забот и расходов, связанных с
The stabilizer salts **save** the dyer **the trouble and expense of** this operation.

Освобождать от необходимости
A high-level language **relieves** the programmer **of having to** adapt a procedure ...

Освобождать энергию
As **the energy is liberated** (*or* **released**) in the oxidation reaction, ...

Освобождаться от I
With the help of Eq. (16-17), one **eliminates** σ and obtains ...

Освобождаться от II
The asthenosphere is not fluid because it manages **to rid itself of** the radioactive heat.

Освобождаться от III
To break free of the gravitational attraction by the planet, ...

Освобождённая энергия
Energy liberated (*or* **released**) **by** the explosive ...

Оседание пыли
Dust settlement.

Оседать [*см.* **Давать осесть**].

Оседать на дне [*см.* **Осаждаться на дно**].

Осколки
After each face blast, a traxcavator is used to load **the broken ground** into ...

Ослабление [*см.* **Уменьшение**].

Ослабление боли
Analgesics are used primarily for **the relief of pain.**

Ослабление звука
The rate of growth and **decay of sound** in a room ...

Ослабление интереса к
With **the erosion** (*or* **loss**) **of interest in** this enterprise ...

Ослабление сигнала
To prevent **deterioration** (*or* **decay,** *or* **attenuation) of the signal** before measurement, ...

Ослабление тока
The current continues to flow without **decay** (*or* **deterioration**).
This causes **a** sharp **fall in the** transistor **current.**

Ослаблять
Slacken the unions between the pressure pipes and the upstream and downstream valves.
The drain plug only requires **slackening,** not completely removing.
These effects may **depress** (*or* **attenuate**) line intensities.

Ослаблять боль
This medicine **allays pain.**
It **eases the aches** (*or* **relieves the pains**) **of** rheumatism.

Ослаблять винт
Loosen by 1/2 turn **the** two **screws of** the adjustable link.
Release (*or* **Slacken,** *or* **Back up**) **the screw.**

Ослаблять гайку
Slacken (*or* **Loosen,** *or* **Release,** *or* **Back up**) **the nut.**

Ослаблять сигнал
Ferrite magnetic fields **may attenuate** (*or* **weaken**) **the signal.**

Ослабляться
The repulsive force **falls off** with distance.
The polarization **decays** when ...

Ослабнуть I
The resistance of the rock may change, causing the anchoring **to give way.**

Ослабнуть II
Interest in optical logic elements **waned** in the late 1960s.

Осложнение [*см.* **Вызывать осложнения**].

Осложнять положение
Hydrogen is high on the list of candidates, but the problem of storing it safely and compactly **stands in the way.**

Осложняться тем, что
The constancy of supply **is complicated by the fact that** electric energy cannot be stored economically on a large scale.

Осматривать
The samples recovered from the wells **were inspected by** the geologist in the field.

Осмотр [*см. тж.* **Визуальный осмотр**]
The machine can be rapidly opened up for rotor **inspection** (*or* **examination**).

Оснащать [*см.* **Обеспечивать, Оборудован**].

Оснащён [*см. тж.* **Снабжён**]
The tool **is fitted with** ball racings and needle bearings.

Оснащённый приборами [*см.* **Хорошо оснащённый приборами**].

Основа I [*см. тж.* **В качестве основы для, В основе ... лежит, Здоровая основа, Металл основы, На базе которого, На никелевой основе, На основе, Положен в основу, Служить основой для, Составлять основу для, Сплав на основе кадмия**]
The methods presented form **a groundwork** (*or* **basis,** *or* **foundation**) **for** analysis of polyphase circuits.
The heart of the theory is ...

Основа II
Refractory metals can be sputtered on glass or ceramic **substrates.**

Основа для
We use this result as **a building block to** study the effect of ...

Основа для ... заложена в
The stage for the events preliminary to life's origin **was set on** a sterile earth devoid of large continents.

Основан
In the present form, the plant **had its origin** (*or* **was founded**) in 1975.

Основан на [*см. тж.* **Быть основанным на, В основе ... лежит**]
Our work **was founded on** experiments with ...
This system of nomenclature **is founded on** the names of ...

The general technique of differentiation **is built upon** the rules for differentiating combinations of ...
Policy objectives **rest on** widely differing assumptions.
This technique **depends** (*or* **is based**) **on** the above principle.
The process **depends on** the flow of electricity between the wheel and the workpiece.
The measurement of the rate of a chemical reaction by interferometry **relies on** following the change in total density as the reaction proceeds.
The choice of lasers for ... **is based on** three considerations: ...
The earlier method **has its origins in** the valence-bond approach.

Основан на данных по
The two theories **had their bases in** quantitative analytical **evidence.**

Основан на общих принципах
All antennas **share basic principles.**

Основан на предположении о том, что
The test **rests on the assumption that ...**

Основан на том, что
Another consideration favouring crossflow towers **stems from the fact that ...**

Основание [*см.* **Давать достаточные основания для, Есть все основания полагать, что; Иметь все основания, Исходя из, На основании, На равных основаниях** (*или* **правах**)].

Основание для
The electromotive series cannot serve **as a guide for** predicting corrosion behaviour of metals.

Основание института
The establishment (*or* **founding**) **of the Institute.**

Основание перпендикуляра
The foot of the perpendicular.

Основание степени
The base number.

Основание треугольника
The base of the triangle.

Основанный на
The optogalvanic effect is compared to two other **laser-based** selective ionization methods in Fig. 2.
We use a method **derived from** the balanced chemical equation.
Electric power is supplied by an integrated system of generation, transmission and distribution **built around** carefully designed components.

Основаны на аналогичном принципе
The charge-coupled device **shares much the same** technological **base with** the transistor.

Основная единица
The fundamental unit of mass in the metric system is the gramme.

Основная забота [*см.* **Уделять главное внимание**].

Основная и производная единицы
The basic and derived SI **units ...**

Основная масса I
The effect was related to the difference in surface tension between **the bulk** and the surface of the liquid.

Основная масса II
The overwhelming bulk of the phenols, cresols, and xylenols is obtained from coal tar.
The main body of ground water lies at deeper levels.
The bulk of the heavy nuclei are formed by the fusion of ...

Основная мысль
The central (*or* **basic**) **idea is** that the device ...

Основная особенность
The key feature.

Основная реакция
The fundamental reaction is the oxidation of luciferin.

Основная роль [*см.* **Играть основную роль в**].

Основная трудность заключается в
The central problem with my instrument **was** finding a readily available sphere.

Основная цель
The prime object (*or* **objective**) **of** most industrial concerns **is ...**

Основная часть [*см. тж.* **Бóльшая часть**]
The Sun emits **the bulk** (*or* **most**) **of** its energy output at optical wavelengths.
When a new design is required **the bulk of** the equipment can be used again.
The basic part of this laser apparatus **is** a quartz tube.
Water constitutes **the greater part of** most organisms.
The greater part of our work **was** carried out indoors.
These components are adding **the major portion of** the corrosion products to the system.

Основное внимание [*см.* **Привлекать к себе главное внимание, Уделять главное внимание**].

Основное внимание уделяется
The emphasis is on the detection of the maximum number of elements.

Основное оборудование
It is anticipated that **major** (*or* **the basic**) **equipment will be** delivered in the spring.

Основное положение
It is **a fundamental** (*or* **central**) **tenet of** chemical kinetics **that ...**

Основное правило
The fundamental (*or* **basic**) **rule.**
A set of **ground rules for** switching over to ...

Основное преимущество [*см.* **Преимущество**].

Основное содержание
This constitutes **the dominant bulk of the subject matter of ...**

Основное соображение
The major consideration in determining the condition for forging is ...

Основное требование, предъявляемое к ... состоит в том, чтобы
The essential feature required of any aromatic compound **is that** there be extensive delocalization of ...

Основное уравнение
The basic (*or* **general,** *or* **fundamental**) **equation** of the heat balance ...

Основной I [*см. тж.* **В основном, Главный, Определяющий фактор**]
Refrigeration and heating require **the major** portion of the energy.
It is the look into the molecular world that is our **principal** interest.
We wish to point out a few **salient** features of this theory.
General descriptions of **the basic** (*or* **main,** *or* **principal**) types of cooling towers have been published.
Liquid wastes can be divided into two **broad** classes, sewage and industrial liquid wastes.
That country is **the dominant** (*or* **predominant,** *or* **chief,** *or* **principal,** *or* **leading**) producer and consumer of this metal.
The foremost consideration in the design of the furnace **is** ...
The key step in the production of antibiotics **is** fermentation.
Major uses of alum **are** as astringents, styptics and emetics.
Major parts **are** the crankcase, crankshaft, pistons, ...
The primary purpose **is to** determine the hardening characteristics.
Two **salient** differences **are to be** noted.
The time constant is not **a fundamental** parameter in the system.
Some of **the essential** features of the apparatus are illustrated in Fig. 3.

Основной II [*см.* **Кислотный, основной**].

Основной для (*или* **при**)
The concept of coordination **is basic to** the formulation of the structure of polyatomic molecules and ions.

Основной металл
Cladding can be added to both sides of a sheet or strip of **base metal.**
The base (*or* **basic**) **metal of** an alloy ...
Fusion of **the parent metal** and the addition of metal to the joint ...

Основной металл и покрытие
Parts can be designed with **a base metal of** the required structural properties, allowing **the overlay** to meet wear and corrosion needs.

Основной текст
This will not be considered further in **the main body of the text.**

Основной упор [*см.* **Делать основной упор на**].

Основной элемент
The column is **the heart of** the gas chromatograph.

Основные детали
Key (*or* **Principal,** *or* **Chief,** *or* **Main**) **components.**

Основные принципы
The basic principles of ...

Основные размеры
The essential (*or* **principal,** *or* **basic**) **dimensions.**

Основные сведения
We shall give you **basic facts about** bushings.
The essentials of the system's operation in response to stress are as follows: ...
It is planned to give **a groundwork of** the physical, structural and economic properties of the better known minerals.

Основные факты
Fundamental (*or* **Basic**) **facts.**

Основные черты
Let us begin by considering some of **the salient** (*or* **prominent,** *or* **main**) **features of** particle accelerators.
The fundamentals of the basic oxygen steelmaking process **are** as follows.

Основные элементы
The essentials of an electrolytic cell **are** shown in Fig. 10.1.

Основу ... составляет
At the heart of the simulator **are** 23 minicomputers.

Основы
This chapter discusses **the basics** (*or* **elements,** *or* **rudiments**) **of** machine control.
The essentials of these radio systems **are** discussed in this article.
The foundations of mathematics ...
In earlier papers the author has explained **the fundamentals of** such a method.

Основываться на предположении о
All previous analyses **started from** (*or* **were based on**) assumptions of fixed reactor temperature, throughput and conversion.

Основываясь на теоретических данных
He has estimated, **on theoretical grounds,** that the shrinkage lies between ...

Особенно [*см. тж.* **В особенности**]
The smooth surface of the conveyor makes it **particularly** suitable for ...
In many cases, **especially** (*or* **particularly**) with reactions of organic compounds, ...
The components of Jupiter's atmosphere, **notably** the ammonia and methane, are opaque to infrared.
These drugs should **specifically** be avoided.

Особенно бросаться в глаза
Particularly striking is the presence of innumerable vertical basalt dikes.

Особенно важен
Of prime importance is the growing role of the chemical engineer.
This **is of particular valu**e (*or* **importance**) (*or* **particularly important**) **for** plastics.

Особенно высокий *и т.п.*
Three classes of carbonium ions owe their **pronounced** stability to ...

Особенно интересен
Of particular (*or* **special**) **interest is** the theory that ...

Особенно интересовать
It is the factors determining the rate of interphase transfer that **have been the particular concern of** (*or* **have attracted the particular attention of**) many chemical engineers.

Особенно перспективный
This method appears to be **particularly promising.**

Особенно подходить для
This device **is particularly appealing** (*or* **attractive**) **for** use as artificial muscle.

Особенно подчёркивать [*см.* **Необходимо особенно подчеркнуть, что**].

Особенно полезный
The system **should be of particular assistance in** the preparation of drawings.

Особенно следует отметить
Of special note is the very large value for the proton.

Особенно тщательно сконструирован
Particular care has been taken in cross-slide **design.**

Особенно ярко проявляться
This effect **is most pronounced at** the edges of the air ducts.

Особенность [*см. тж.* **Конструктивные особенности, Отличительная черта, Характерная особенность**]
The peculiarities of tRNAs ...
This **trait is** also true for benzene.
A **peculiarity** (*or* **special feature**) **of** this type of wave is that ...
To study geological **features** in nearby mines, ...

Особое внимание уделено [*см. тж.* **Упор делается на**]
Particular emphasis has been placed on (*or* **Particular attention has been given to**) the use of shock tubes.
Part II provides the electromagnetic theory approach, **with emphasis on** waveguides that propagate ...

Особую ценность представляет
Of particular value is the clear determination of ...

Особый
There are some dozens of lipids, each with its **distinctive** (*or* **peculiar,** *or* **own**) chemical pattern.
Most of the amino acids contain an asymmetric carbon in a **particular** configuration called "*L*".
The sand-sized grains may bear **distinctive** surface markings such as microstriations, ...
In the **special** case where the exchanged quantum is massless the range is infinite.
The generation of hydroelectric power is a **distinctive** industrial use of water in that it is entirely unconsumptive.

Особый интерес [*см.* **Представлять особый интерес**].

Особый интерес представляет
Of special interest is the availability of an on-line tape punch arrangement.

Особый случай
These particles **are a special case** because they are massless and move with the speed of light.

Осознать [*см. тж.* **Понять**]
Aristotle **perceived** the importance of water in shaping the land.
We (have come to) realize that geology is a dynamic science.
As time passed, aircraft builders **became cognizant** (*or* **aware**) **of** the importance of aircraft fastener fatigue testing.

Оспаривать [*см. тж.* **Можно оспаривать**]
This role **was** much **disputed** until ...

Оспаривать целесообразность
Few doctors **would dispute the value of** attempting to treat this disease when it is first discovered.

Осреднять [*см.* **Усреднять**].

Оставаться [*см. тж.* **В результате ... остаётся мало, После ... остаётся, Сохраняться**]
Chemicals which **are left** (*or* **remain**) too long in contact with ...
Much **remains to be** done in this area.
This steel will never have to be painted and it **will stay** bright and clean.
When these numbers are used up, half of the series **will (still) be left over** (*or* **there will (still) be** half of the series **left over**).
In the interior of the dielectric material between the condenser plates such charges cancel out, and **one is left with** only the charges on the surface of ...
One difficulty **persists.**

Оставаться без изменений [*см.* **Оставаться неизменным**]
Air and water rates **are** (*or* **remain**) **unchanged** (*or* **unaltered,** *or* **constant**) on crossing ...

Оставаться без последствий
In some states of the positronium such an exchange **is of no consequence;** in other states, however, it changes the sign of the wave function.

Оставаться безрезультатным
Our research efforts often **go unrewarded.**

Оставаться в растворе
Borax and other salts **remain in solution.**

Оставаться в силе
The previous equations **(still) stand** [*or* **remain valid** (*or* **in force**)].

If the filters were not matched, the same result **would hold (good).**
This approximation **holds** (*or* **is valid**) within the indicated limits.

Оставаться в состоянии покоя
No particle as light as the electron **can hold still** for very long.

Оставаться в тени
This side of the telescope **is kept away from the sun** (*or* **is kept in the shade**).

Оставаться загадкой
The origin of the Gulf Coastal Plain **remains (something of) an enigma.**

Оставаться на месте
The vapours escaped, whereas the solids **remained on the spot.**
Seawater could be evaporated locally, and the chemical compounds **would** then **be left behind.**
The remaining rods **were left in place.**
The asteroid always moves in and out of the zone; it never **stays put.**
The inclination of a slope on which boulders **would stay put** is the angle of repose.

Оставаться недоказанным
This statement **stands** (*or* **remains**) **unproved.**

Оставаться незамеченным [*см. тж.* **Не оставаться незамеченным**]
The neuropathy of diabetes often **seems to escape notice.**
The rapid fall of the water table **goes (largely) unheeded** because people cannot see the water table.
Another capability of polymerase 1 **went unnoticed** for nearly a decade.

Оставаться неизвестным
The origin of these clusters **remains a mystery** (*or* **unknown**).

Оставаться неизменным [*см. тж.* **Без изменения, Оставаться без изменений**]
This benzene ring **has remained intact.**
In this way the positioning of the optics **can be left untouched** (*or* **intact**).
The total number of atoms **is** (*or* **remains**) **fixed** (*or* **unchanged,** *or* **the same**).
The analogue-to-digital interface **must remain invariant** (*or* **unaltered,** *or* **constant,** *or* **unchanged**) despite modifications or changes in the computer.
The velocity of the centre of mass **does not change** during collision.
Today a number of details in the original paper have been revised, but the basic mechanism of ... **remains intact.**

Оставаться неизменным при
The positional isomerism **is unchanged on** oxidation.
The angles **are unchanged** by rotation.
Rotation of the plane **leaves** all angles **unchanged.**
The correlation **is invariant to** distortion.

Оставаться неиспользованным
Additional petroleum accumulations **remain untapped.**

Оставаться неопознанным
This was argon, but it **went unrecognized.**

Оставаться неподвижным
We only deal with the displacement vectors on the atoms that **stay put.**
All the other molecules **remain stationary** (*or* **immobile**).

Оставаться неразрешённым
A number of problems **(still) remain to be solved** (*or* **remain unsolved**).

Оставаться нетронутым
When the base is dissolved in acid the gold shell **is left** (*or* **remains,** *or* **is preserved**) **intact.**

Оставаться постоянным [*см. тж.* **Оставаться неизменным**]
The slit width of the instrument **is kept** (*or* **held,** *or* **remains**) **constant** for a series of measurements.
These laws deal with a condition in which some quantity **is held** (*or* **kept**) **constant.**

Оставаться постоянным при изменении
The transmission loss **is** not **constant with frequency.**

Оставаться постоянным при преобразовании
The characteristic manifolds of a system **are invariant under the transformation of ...**

Оставаться преданным
They **remained devotees of** (*or* **devoted to**) the phlogiston theory.

Оставаться прежним
All observable properties of the hadron **would remain as before.**

Оставаться справедливым
The previous expressions **still stand.**
The law of conservation of mass always **holds.**

Оставаться таким
The sub-boundary corrosion susceptibility is low and has been observed **to remain so** after ageing four years at room temperature.

Оставить стоять
Set the solution **aside** (*or* **Allow** the solution **to stand**) for a week.
When fresh milk **is allowed** (*or* **left**) **to stand** several hours, ...

Оставляет желать лучшего
The internal consistency of the method **leaves something to be desired.**

Оставляет желать много лучшего
Both theories **leave much** (*or* **a lot**) **to be desired** (*or* **are far from perfect**) in their correlation with experimental data.

Оставлять в стороне
Leaving aside the special case of superconductors, we shall try to describe the electronic ground state of the crystal.

Оставлять за собой
The high-field region in its passage across the diode **leaves behind it** a dense "plasma" of electrons and holes.

Оставлять на усмотрение
The finish **can be left to discretion of** the manufacturer.

Оставлять неприкрытым
The sample **was left exposed to the air.**

Оставлять след
Lead **makes a mark on** paper.

Оставшийся неизменным
Each **intact** benzene ring ...

Остаётся
It remains (*or* **It only remains for us**) **to** compute N_T according to Eq. (9.10).

Остаётся выяснить
It remains to be seen whether similar reactions operate in other cells.
Whether this will be an economical method **remains to be seen.**
It remains (now) to see how the values of such ... change.

Остаётся исследовать
One related possibility **remains to be investigated.**

Остаётся ответить на вопросы
Many other **questions remain to be answered.**

Остаётся тайной
How these genes are controlled **remains a mystery.**

Остальная часть [*см. тж.* **Остальные элементы**]
The symbols used in **the remainder** (*or* **the rest**) **of** this discussion are shown in the table.
Of the newly transcribed mRNA, about 80% was found associated with ribosomes, while **the remainder** apparently **was** not associated with... (*biol.*).
The rest of the day **is** spent in polishing the parts.
The remainder of the plant **is** arranged on a unit basis.

Остальное I
Filler metals for brazing aluminium and aluminium alloys usually contain 4–13% silicon, with copper 0.3–4%, **(and the) balance aluminium.**
Monel, an alloy of approximately 67% nickel, **the balance** (*or* **rest,** *or* **remainder**) **being** copper, is a well-known corrosion-resistant alloy.
Seventy percent of the upper baffle was laid down by the pump method, **and the balance** (*or* **the rest**) was completed by hand.

Остальное II (*не оговоренное на чертеже*)
... **unless (otherwise) specified** (*or* **stated**).

Остальной
The remainder of the energy stored in the bond is covalent in character.
The rest of the time is represented by diastems.

Остальные
We thus have four characteristics, two associated with the fast wave front and **the**

remaining (*or* **the other**) two with the slow wave front.
These are metals; **the remaining** (*or* **the other**) elements **are** metalloids.
Most of the elements are solids at room temperature, two of them are liquids **and the rest are** gases.

Остальные элементы (*структуры и т.п.*)
The wavenumbers are independent of **the rest of the structure.**

Останавливать [*см. тж.* **Выводить из эксплуатации, Прекращать**]
The table is fed to the right and up to a dead stop, which **arrests** its movement.
Movement of the indexing cam **can be arrested by** a preset stop.
Brakes **bring** the vehicle **to a stop** (*or* **to rest**).
A signal is automatically transmitted **to bring** the elevator **to a halt.**
Pressure **keeps** the pump **inoperative** when coolant reservoirs are full.

Останавливать поступление [*см.* **Отрезать поступление**].

Останавливаться [*см. тж.* **Прекращаться**]
The planet **would come to a halt** (*or* **to a stop**), and then start falling toward the Sun.
The gas is accelerated through a nozzle and **is** there **brought to a standstill** at the head of a pitot tube.
The process will eventually **come to a halt.**
This valve absolutely shuts off steam every time the engine **comes to rest.**
The motor **will be shut down** (*or* **will stop**) automatically.
The depth at which projectile ions **come** (*or* **are brought**) **to rest** within the solid target can be predicted only within ...

Останавливаться на [*см. тж.* **Сосредоточиваться на**]
We **dwell on** this equation because it is quite successful.
I **will enlarge on** the subject of ventilation.

Остановившийся
Electrical energy is needed to restart **the dead** engine.

Остановка [*см.* **Аварийная остановка, Запуск и остановка**].

Остановлен
The machine **was shut down** for the holiday.

Остатки [*см. тж.* **Остальной**]
Fusain consists essentially of **the remains of** decomposed plants.

Остаток ряда (*матем.*)
Remainder of an infinite **series** after the n-th term ...

Остающаяся часть
Geothermal energy will probably not become a major source of energy during **the remainder of** this century.

Остерегаться
The operator **should guard against** accidental contact of ...
Tube failure and leakage, and dirty tubes are the main things which **must be guarded against.**

Осторожная оценка
A conservative estimate.

Осторожно
The zero-setting system should be used **with care** (*or* **with caution**) and only for flights of short duration.
Dioxin **should** always **be** prescribed **with caution.**

Осторожно обращаться с [*см.* **Обращаться исключительно осторожно**].

Осторожность [*см.* **Проявлять исключительную осторожность**].

Острая нехватка
The shortage of the substances for research **is acute.**

Острая проблема
The transportation **problem** did not become **pressing** until large oil reservoirs were discovered in the North Sea.

Острая проблема, стоящая перед
The detection of trace components has always been **a challenge to** the analytical chemist.

Остро заточен
Tools **should be kept very sharp**, and frequent hand stoning is recommended.

Остро необходимый
The measurements will provide **much-needed** clues to the evolution of the system.

Остро реагировать на
The calcium carbonate crystallites in this solid **are extraordinarily reactive to** hydrogen sulphide.

Остро сознавать
One **must be keenly** (*or* **acutely**) **aware of** environmental hazards.
Britain **has a keen awareness of** the importance of technology in fostering economic development.

Остро сознавать опасности загрязнения
We are (only too) painfully aware of the threats of air and water **pollution**.

Острое обоняние
Many animals **have an acute sense of smell.**

Острое отравление
The effect **of acute** lead **poisoning of** the kidneys can be serious.

Остроумное решение вопроса
He found **an ingenious solution to that problem.**

Остроумный метод
An ingenious method for ...

Острый
The problem of contaminants in the gas is **acute.**
The treatment of a **severe** anaemia ...

Острый максимум [*см.* **Иметь острый максимум**].

Остывать
The volcanic rocks that form on the surface can **cool (down)** very quickly.

Осуществим в промышленных условиях при помощи
The process has been made **industrially possible by** the laser.

Осуществимость
To predict **the** technical **feasibility of** larger projects, ...

Осуществимый [*см. тж.* **Возможный, Практически возможный, Экономически осуществимый**]
Every physically **realizable** (*or* **feasible**) capacitor has ...

Осуществление [*см. тж.* **Выполнение, Проведение**]
The execution (*or* **implementing**) **of** a program ...
It is well to have an electric hoist for **handling** (*or* **performing,** *or* **carrying out**) this operation.
Some of the overall potential must be used in **accomplishing** (*or* **effecting**) the phase change.
In the early 1960s packaging technology did not allow **the realization of** practical devices with ...

Осуществление плана
The execution of a plan.

Осуществлён
This saving already **has been effected** in most of the urban sections.

Осуществлённый
The assemblies **completed** in this manner must ...

Осуществлять [*см. тж.* **Вести записи** (*или* **регистрацию**), **Выполнять, Проводить, Производить**]
The combination of so many properties is difficult **to achieve** (*or* **attain,** *or* **realize**).
Consolidation of powder **is** most commonly **brought about by** hot pressing.
These operations **were** often **carried on** simultaneously.
This survey **is being conducted by ...**
All operations **will be performed** (*or* **completed**) on time.
The new plan **was put into effect.**
Similar experiments **will be run** (*or* **carried out,** *or* **performed**) in our laboratory.
Machining **is completed** in one chucking (*за одну установку в патроне*).
Such communication links **should be** easily **realized.**
Preparation of 2,3-butanediol **has been by** fermentation.
Activity or concentration gradient is employed **to effect** (*or* **accomplish**) mass transfer between two phases.
One method of **arranging** head-on collisions is to build two storage rings that ...
These reactants **effect** oxidation.

Specific halogenation **can be made to occur** in sunlight ...
Quantitative analysis **is practised by** every analytical laboratory.
Such measures **were** ultimately **effectuated.**

Осуществлять вращение
The CH_3 group **executes a rotation** relative to ...

Осуществлять движение
The molecules **engage in** Brownian **motion.**
The point **executes** (*or* **carries out**) harmonic **motions.**

Осуществлять контроль
Strict **controls must be exerted** in hypochlorite bleaching to avoid oxidation of the cotton.
To exercise control over workshop operations, ...

Осуществлять операцию
These operations can be done (*or* **performed,** *or* **carried out,** *or* **accomplished**) under pressure.

Осуществлять план
To carry out (*or* **execute**) **a plan.**

Осуществлять программу
The program is being carried out.

Осуществлять реакцию [*см. тж.* **Проводить реакцию**]
The reaction is hard **to achieve** (*or* **accomplish**) under laboratory conditions.
The reaction might be performed in the cell.
We prefer **to conduct** (*or* **run**) **this reaction** at a higher temperature.

Осуществлять регуляцию (*биол.*)
The manner in which hormones **exert control** is easily explained by ...

Осуществлять управление
Management of such airports **rests in** [*or* **is the function** (*or* **responsibility**) **of**] a city department.
The cell cytoplasm **exerts control over** the timing of synthesis.

Осуществлять функцию
The activated kinase **performs the** same **function** for a related enzyme, phosphorylase kinase.

Осуществляться [*см. тж.* **Вестись, Достигаться, Производиться**]
Loading **is** direct **into** railroad cars.
Control of the welding current **is by** a trip-switch.
Transmission of power from the engine to the wheels **is accomplished by** the clutch.
Traction **is effected by** the winding action of the cables.
Routine maintenance **is handled** in the same way.
Conditions under which the test **is run** should be improved.
A program of component tests **is underway.**
Our internal communications **are handled by** a network with nervous and metabolic subsystems.
Fine control of carrier-gas pressure **is achieved by** ...
The determination of position by dead reckoning **is** commonly **performed by** plotting on ...
This reduction **is** most conveniently **performed** at the cathode.
Cross pollination of flowers **is effected** principally **by** bees.
The reaction **is carried out** (*or* **conducted,** *or* **run**) **by** the above-described mechanism.
Controls **are exercised by** the cell.
This substitution **is realized** under acidic conditions.
Conduction usually **occurs** through a metallic wall.
The manufacture of dyes **proceeds from** simple raw materials.

Осуществляться по методу
The calculation **follows the method** given by ...

Осуществляться посредством
Regulation of enzyme synthesis **is (effected) by way of** post–transcriptional events.

Осуществляться путём
The transport through the film **is** solely **by** molecular diffusion.

Ось [*см. тж.* **Вращаться вокруг оси, Насаженный на ось, Откладывать на** (*или* **по**) **оси**]
The centreline of the workpiece ...

Ось вращения
The rotational axis (*or* **The axis of rotation**) **of** Venus ...

От [*см.* **В отличие от, Гарантирован от, Зависеть от, Защита от, Изолировать от, Независимо от, Отклонять от, Отличать от, Предохранять от, Работать от**].

От времени до времени [*см. тж.* **Время от времени**]
From time to time optical astronomers would succeed in identifying ...
Provision must be made for defrosting the pipes **at intervals** (*or* **from time to time**).

От ... до [*см. тж.* **Изменяться от ... до, Иметь различный состав от ... до**]
Between 25 and 30 rivets can be fixed per minute.
The plant was required to operate at loads **between 10 and 100%** (*or* **from 10 to 100%**).
The width of the land of the cutting edge should be about one-fifth the distance **from tooth to tooth.**
The tubes have an outside diameter **of (from) 10 to 25 cm.**
The wavelengths range **between a few millimetres and 15 metres.**
A group of devices used for detecting infrared radiation requires energy gaps **from 0.5 down to 0.1 eV** or even less.
The automatic and semiautomatic drills are good for a variety of materials **ranging from** soft wood and synthetic products **to** mild steel and cast iron.
The estimates range anywhere **from $50,000 to $500,000.**
Dense shale and limestone have porosities **in the range from 1% to 10%.**
The tube is anything **from a few metres to several hundred metres** long.
The aggregate has a **gray-to-black** colour.

От ... до ..., включительно
On the finite interval **from** x_1 **to** x_2, **inclusive, ...**
As shown in Secs. 5 **through** 7, ...

От ... ещё далеко до
The description of the monomer units **was a long way from** the determination of ...

От ... к [*см. тж.* **Изменяться от одного ... к другому**]
Pressures **vary with each** station.
The magnitude of this change will **vary from** mill **to** mill.
The catalyst volume **varied** somewhat **from** sample **to** sample.

От которого зависит
The features **governing** this stereoscopicity indicate that ...

От ... мало пользы
Direct conductance measurements **are of little use** unless ...

От минимума до максимума
Ripple voltage **is** less than 20 mV **peak to peak.**

От начала до конца
The concentration of a highly reactive intermediate has been followed **from start to finish.**

От обратного [*см.* **Доказательство от обратного**].

От одного ... к другому
The concentration of water vapour varies widely **from cylinder to cylinder** (*or* **from one cylinder to another**).

От одного конца до другого
The hardness gradient is uniform **from end to end of** the shell.
The fibril may traverse the chromosome 200 or more times **from one end to the other.**

От одного места к другому
The permanent fields measured by the Apollo instruments vary **from place to place.**

От одной партии деталей к другой
The treated product will not vary **from one lot to the next.**

От руки
Portions of the tape can be deleted or replaced with **manually** entered data.

От себя
Always use the plotting board with North **away from you.**

От сети [*см.* **Работающий от сети**].

От случая к случаю
The appropriate functions are different **from case to case** (*or* **from one case to another**).

От средних до крупных размеров
Particles **of medium to coarse size ...**

От удара
The diaphragm breaks **on impact.**

От электропривода [*см.* **Работать от электропривода**].

Отапливаемый газом
Gas-fired furnaces ...

Отапливаемый углём
A **coal-fired** boiler ...

Отбивать молотком
The lead bottom **is hammered free from** the slag.

Отбивать образец (породы) молотком
The geologist **sampled** the slate **with his hammer**.

Отбирать образцы [*см. тж.* **Брать образцы**]
The gas **was sampled** periodically.
Samples of metal **were drawn** (*or* **taken**) at 10 min intervals.
To take samples.
Samples were withdrawn from the fermentor.

Отбирать пробы [*см.* **Брать образцы**].

Отбор образцов
The sampling of such gases is just beginning.

Отбраковка
Streaks and other flaws causing **rejection of** moulded items often result from improper storage.

Отбраковывать дефектные детали
The tester automatically **rejects the flawed parts.**

Отбрасывать [*см. тж.* **Отказываться от**]
We **drop** (*or* **discard**) the infinitesimal term (*math.*).

Отбрасывать изображение на
The lens **throws the image of** a lamp filament **on to** the drawing.

Отбрасывать резкую тень
Light travels in straight lines and **casts sharp shadows.**

Отбрасывать тень
The luminous part of the flame **casts a shadow** if placed between ...

Отбрасываться
Questionable data **should be rejected.**

Отбрасываться к
Because of the change of direction, the particles **are flung to** the outer wall.

Отбуксировать
The caisson **was** built on shore and **floated to** the site.

Отвал [*см.* **Отправлять в отвал**].

Отведённый [*см. тж.* **Время, отведённое на**]
The bands of frequencies **assigned** (*or* **allocated**) **to** the amateur service ...

Отвергнут
The theory **fell into disrepute.**
In the case of the Sea of Japan, the entrapment hypothesis **has been rejected** (*or* **discarded,** *or* **denounced,** *or* **overthrown,** *or* **ruled out**).
That possibility **was** quickly **denied.**

Отвернуть до конца
When the regulator **is screwed full out, ...**

Отверстие
Wire screen **openings.**

Отверстие для болта
There is **a hole** in the bearing cap **to receive the bolt.**

Отверстие под
Holes to receive these pins are drilled by means of ...

Отверстие сита
A 7/8 in. **screen** (*or* **sieve**) **opening ...**

Ответ [*см.* **В ответ на, Давать ответ на**].

Ответ на вопрос [*см.* **Находить ответ на вопрос**].

Ответственная деталь
A critical part.
Clutch plates, bearings and other **vital** (*or* **essential,** *or* **important**) **parts ...**

Ответственная операция
For **exacting services,** the compressor may be sealed with chilled water to prevent condensation in lines.

Ответственность лежит на

The responsibility for what may happen afterwards **will be on** you.
The responsibility of maintaining the boiler in first-class condition **rests with** the operating engineer.

Ответственный

Oscilloscopes of better than ±2% system accuracy for the most **demanding** applications ...

Отвечать критерию

The species reported **fitted** (*or* **met**) all **the criteria.**

Отвечать нормам [*см.* **Отвечать стандартам, Полностью отвечать нормам**].

Отвечать описанию

If the lead (*свинец*) from an object of unknown age **fits the description of** a meteoritic lead ...

Отвечать потребностям

Answering this need was the water-tube boiler.
This approach **is** quite **adequate for our needs** (*or* **meets our needs**).

Отвечать стандартам

The dimensions **should be in conformity** (*or* **compliance**) **with the** relevant **standards.**
These capacities **meet** (*or* **conform to,** *or* **comply with**) government **standards.**

Отвечать техническим требованиям

The tube **meets** (*or* **conforms to,** *or* **complies with,** *or* **corresponds to**) **specifications.**
The equipment **lives up to its specifications.**

Отвечать требованиям [*см. тж.* **Удовлетворять требованиям**]

The design **was adequate.**
The connectors **(fully) conform to** (*or* **comply with,** *or* **meet,** *or* **correspond to**) **the requirements of ...**
Only in the past ten years **have** instruments and techniques **become equal to the job.**
The pickup **fills the requirements of** operational use.
Samples will be supplied **to fit** (*or* **suit**) **your requirements.**
These parts **fulfil requirements of** our specifications.
Control materials **must be capable of meeting** (*or* **satisfying,** *or* **fulfilling**) several **requirements.**
The relays **are compatible with** environmental **requirements of** both military and industrial applications.
The machines **suit** customers' **requirements.**

Отвечать требованиям конструкции

The methods of calculating the height or packed volume, required **to meet design criteria, ...**

Отвинчивать

To unscrew the cutter **from** the bar, ...
The base of the trap **can be screwed off** by hand.
Unscrew the plastic cap.

Отвинчивать винт

Remove the right-hand amplifier mounting bracket **by extracting the** two **screws** in the side of the instrument case.
Remove (*or* **Take out**) **the screws** at the left-hand end.
Undo the four **screws** at the four corners of the plate.
Unscrew (*or* **Withdraw**) **the screws** securing the clock base to the plate.

Отвинчивать гайку

Remove the washer **by** first **taking off the nut.**
If **the** two **nuts are** completely **undone ...**
Unscrew (*or* **Remove**) **the nuts** securing the tube to the chamber.

Отвлечься [*см.* **Если отвлечься от технической стороны вопроса**].

Отвод тепла

The heat-rejection (*or* **-removal**) unit maintains the water temperature at the level required for the process.

Отводить I

These pipes **divert** the brine **from** any one circuit **into ...**
Swing the pen arm **to** the left, and fit the chart over the chart post.

Отводить II

A different frequency band **is allocated** (*or* **assigned**) **to** each channel.

Отводить III [*см. тж.* **Подводить и отводить**]
A spring in the tool then automatically **withdraws** the roller head **to** the starting position.

Отводить в сторону
A drawbridge can be raised, lowered, or **drawn aside** to provide a clear passage.

Отводить от
The spindle assembly is arranged in such a manner that **it is moved clear of** the workpiece in the event of failure of the power supply.
Before the micrometer is returned to stowage, **back** the spindle **away from** the anvil and ...
The worktable moves to the left, this **bringing** the tool **clear of** the workpiece.

Отводить тепло
At currents of about 1000 to 3000 amperes per square centimetre much **heat** still **must be removed** (*or* **carried away**) **from** the laser during operation.
The latent **heat** necessary for evaporation **is extracted from** the space to be cooled, and then **rejected to** sea water on condensation.
To withdraw heat from a hot body, ...

Отводиться
The oil provides for lubrication of the bearings and **escapes** by way of a passage in the shaft.
When the tool has been transferred to the spindle, the arm **retracts** and the tool carrier remains vacant.

Отворачивать [*см.* **Отвернуть до конца**].

Отгоняться
The carbon disulphide **is distilled away.**
If these materials are heated strongly with hydrogen chloride, $GeCl_4$ **distils** (*or* **is distilled**) **off.**

Отградуированный в делениях величиной
Micro-dials **are graduated in** 0.001 in.

Отградуированный в единицах расстояния
The scale **is marked in distances.**

Отградуированный в километрах
The dial of the airspeed indicator **is calibrated in kilometres.**

Отгружать
Very radioactive samples **are shipped** (*or* **transported**) in lead containers.

Отгрузочный вес
Shipping weight.

Отдавать
The water condensed from the steam after it **has given up** its energy can provide a supply of fresh water.
Acids **give up** cations.
As the nucleus **loses** (*or* **gives up**) kinetic energy **to** the electron, ...

Отдавать должное за
We **must give** him **credit for** a rather simple model of ...

Отдавать и присоединять
The substance which **donates** (*or* **gives up**) hydrogen or electrons is said to be oxidized and the one which **accepts** (*or* **adds**) the hydrogen is said to be reduced.

Отдавать или присоединять
The molecule **can either lose** (*or* **give away**) *or* **gain** (*or* **take up**) protons.

Отдавать предпочтение [*см. тж.* **Предпочитать**]
Preference is given to the largest group.
The proximate analysis **is preferred.**
In this age of computers **the attraction is toward** a two-based system.
Mechanical seals **are** increasingly **favoured by** industry.
The approach **favoured by** our group is a much more empirical one.
To decide between two theories, ...
The spark **was preferred to** the arc.
Polarization helps us to understand why some molecules **are favoured over** their ionic counterparts.

Отдавать тепло
The molten metal **is losing heat to** the cavity surface throughout the filling period.
Steam flows around the outside of the tubes, **giving up its** latent **heat.**

Отдавать электроны
A base is an ion or a molecule that **can donate** a pair of **electrons.**
The iron **loses electrons to** tin.

Отдавать энергию

The accelerated ions **give up energy to** the molecules of ...

The atom **gives up** (*or* **releases,** *or* **liberates**) **its energy as** radiated light.

Microwaves in a wave guide **lose energy to** the walls of the guide.

Отдалённо напоминать

Many malignant neoplasms **only vaguely resemble** their normal counterpart tissue.

Отдалённое будущее [*см.* **В весьма отдалённом будущем, В далёком будущем**].

Отдалённый

The force is transmitted to **distant** points on the plate.

To analyse the interstellar gas in **remote** parts of our galaxy, ...

Отданный

The energy **lost to** the gas may be sufficient to bring the particle to rest.

Отдача [*см. тж.* **Давать наибольший эффект**]

Lasers are difficult to keep operating with good **performance.**

Отдача тепла

Rejection (*or* **Loss**) **of heat to** a cold body occurs ...

Отдача тепла путём проводимости

Loss of heat to the walls **by conduction** was observed.

Отдача электрона

The loss of an electron.

Отделение ... от

Both processes require physical **separation of** the liquid phase **from** the solid phase.

Отделённый от

At each end of the shell is fitted a cast-iron endpiece **divided** (*or* **separated**) **from** the shell by a brass tube plate.

Отделены друг от друга

The conductors **are separated by** thin mica sheets.

Отделка [*см.* **Высокий класс отделки**].

Отделка поверхности

The castings have uniform **surface finish.**

Отдельно [*см. тж.* **В отдельности**]

Despite this, proteinurea should be considered further **in its own right.**

Отдельно и вместе [*см.* **Как в отдельности, так и вместе**].

Отдельно или вместе

We are interested in a response where *r* and *l* act **singly or together.**

The three basic techniques may be used **singly or in combination.**

Отдельные

Longitudinal and transverse cracks break the rock into **discrete** (*or* **separate**) blocks.

Отдельные лица

Research is no longer carried out by **isolated individuals.**

Отдельный [*см. тж.* **В отдельных случаях, Каждый в отдельности**]

The components of the sample separate into **individual** spots or bands.

We tabulated these values for **individual** ions.

Diorite occurs as **isolated** small bodies (*geol.*).

This will lessen the need for memorizing many **isolated** details of factual information.

Отделывать [*см. тж.* **Красиво отделывать хромом**]

The unit **is handsomely finished in** walnut or mahogany.

Electrocoating approach can be used **to give** a surface **a velvet finish.**

Отделять от

This transition is extremely difficult **to resolve from** the laser-excited molecular fluorescence.

The demodulator **separates** the audio-frequency signal **from ...**

Отделяться

As the sperm mature, they **break away** and often circulate in the tail cavity.

Отделяться от I

A yeast cell develops a protuberance which gradually enlarges and then **breaks away** (*or* **separates**) **from** the mother cell.

Отделяться от II

The cross bunker **is segregated** (*or* **sepa-**

rated) **from** the after end of No. 2 **by** a cofferdam.

Отдых [*см.* **Зона отдыха**].

Отечественный
Domestic oil production ...

Отказ [*см.* **Выход из строя**].

Отказ от [*см. тж.* **Упразднение**]
This paper led to **the** eventual **abandonment of** the old theory.
The steam engine epitomized Britain's **break with** the traditional European "wood and water" technology.
The competing antenna development and construction began, resulting finally in **shelving** (*or* **abandoning**) the former system.

Отказываться от [*см. тж.* **Отменять, Прекращать**]
We must **do away with** the present system.
The ruby laser **must be ruled out** for fusion purposes.
Here, the engineer **should discard** (*or* **rid himself of,** *or* **abandon,** *or* **give up,** *or* **dismiss**) many old concepts.
This practice **has** long **been discontinued.**
The process **was dropped** as uneconomic.
This design **was rejected** (*or* **ruled out**).

Отказываться от ... в пользу
The "interlock" model **was** soon **abandoned in favour of** "attractive force" descriptions.

Откачанный
The tube contains a cathode and an anode in an **evacuated** envelope.

Откачивать
An air pump **draws away** the condensate.
The instrument **is evacuated** (*or* **purged**) with a dry gas.
The water **was pumped out.**

Откидное дно
A **drop-bottom** bucket ...

Откладывать [*см.* **Отложить до**].

Откладывать на (*или* **по**) **оси**
On the abscissa the equivalent local length of each objective **is plotted.**
The abscissa is the temperature of the source.
Operating frequencies **are laid off** (*or* **plotted**) **on** (*or* **along**) **the** vertical **axis.**
They **are plotted as ordinates and ..., as abscissas.**

Откладывать обсуждение [*см.* **Переносить обсуждение**].

Откладывать обсуждение на некоторое время
We **shall set these problems aside for the time being.**

Откладываться на графике [*см.* **Отражаться на графике в виде**].

Отклонение [*см. тж.* **Расхождение с**]
The magnetic field produces **a** strong **deflection** in the carrier's trajectory.

Отклонение (стрелки) на полную шкалу
Full-scale deflection.

Отклонение наружу
The shock waves are associated with **outward diversions of** the airflow.

Отклонение от
The countertorque increases in proportion to **the excursion of** the coil **from** its zero position.
Large **departures of** the equipotential surface **from** sphericity will not affect the result.
When there is **a departure of** the controlled pressure **from** the set value, the out-of-balance force moves a multiplying valve.
The constant reported in this work **may have a deviation of** 1.1% **from** the absolute valve.
These errors account for **the deviation of** the measurements **from** theory.
Variations from this composition are found in commercial steels.
h **is the variation of** the strip thickness **from** the required value.
It appears that building such a large device is feasible and would require no major **departures from** present practice.

Отклонение от круглой формы
The cylinder gauge can be used for determining **out-of-roundness.**

Отклонение от нормального режима [*см.* **Ненормальность в работе**].

Отклонение стрелки прибора
The deflection of the needle (*or* The throw of the point).

Отклонять
The mirror **deflected** the laser beam.

Отклонять от
A malfunction in the lines of the hydraulic control of the rocket could **send it off** its programmed trajectory.
The resulting force **deflects** the pendulum **from** the vertical.

Отклоняться [*см. тж.* **Форма капли отклоняется от сферической**]
The particle's path **is deflected by** the gravitational field of Jupiter.
The arc **is deflected** downwards magnetically.
Special taps **varying** (*or* **deviating**) only slightly **from** standard dimensions are to be marked with the letter *S*.
The behaviour of shock waves **diverges from** that predicted by ideal theory.
The field lines **deviate from** a simple dipole configuration.
The behaviour definitely **departs from** what is observed at lower energies.
In order to show how this can be carried out, I must **digress** for a while to discuss some definitions.

Отклоняться на
The angular positions of the new distances were not quite right, but they **were** never **off by** more than eight minutes.

Отклоняться на большой угол
Some of the particles **were deflected through wide angles.**

Отклоняться от [*см. тж.* **Далекó отклоняться от, Значительно отклоняться от**]
These coefficients **depart (very appreciably) from unity.**
When the polarization begins **to depart from** linearity, ...
Group I **has diverged** only slightly **from** the original arrangement (*biol.*).
The composition of the crystal **deviates from** stoichiometric proportions.

Отклоняться от вертикали
If the stick **tips (too far) out of vertical,** it will fall.

Отклоняться от инструкций
The special properties of these alloys will not permit **bending the rules** as much as with ordinary machining.

Отклоняться от истины на
The lag introduced in such a case can produce altitude readings which **are** more than 20,000 ft **in error.**
With this method of calculation you **would be off by** 3,000 miles.

Отклоняться от круглой формы
If the furnace **is out of round, ...**

Отклоняться от курса
The rocket **went off course.**

Отклоняться от своего пути
A shock wave **is deflected from its line of travel** as it emerges from a material of certain density into ...

Отключать
The transformer **was taken out of service.**
The automatic feed **can be disengaged for** manual **operation.**
Disconnect the amplifier-output plug.
Unplug the connecting cable.

Отключаться от
The rheostat **is cut out of the circuit** as the motor approaches full speed.
The transformer **is** automatically **disconnected from the supply** during the idling periods.

Отколовшийся от
It is assumed that eucrites are fragments **spalled from** smaller bodies in the asteroid belt.

Открывать
Boiler pressure **pushes** the valve **open.**

Открывать возможности
This **offers (considerable) scope for** further improvements.
The addition of silver **offers (strong) possibilities of** providing alloys with ...
These transistors **open up possibilities for** new circuits.
These tyres **open up (new) possibilities to** vehicle designers.
Lasers **offer (outstanding) possibilities in** this field.
The increase in rotor current **opens the way to** a reduction of the stator current.

The ready availability of this synthetic product **opens the door to** large-scale exploratory investigations.

Открывать новую область
The laser has **opened up new fields of** optical research.

Открывать новую область экспериментальных исследований
This concept **opens up a new area to the experimenter.**

Открывать новую эру
That **was an opening shot in a new chapter of** space exploration.
The construction of an atomic clock **opened (up) a new era** (*or* **chapter**) **in** the study of ...

Открывать новые возможности для
The application of the shock tube techniques to the investigation of this reaction **has opened up fresh opportunities** (*or* **new avenues**) **for** detailed study.
The sealant **opens up new fields of use in** high-pressure sealing.

Открывать новые пути
The search for new silicon controlled rectifiers **has opened up brand new vistas for** the entire industry.
The unprecedented heating capability of high-power pulsed lasers **opens a new avenue of attack on** this problem.

Открывать путь к
Synthetic chemistry **will open (up) the way to** (*or* **for**) the development of ...

Открыт с одного конца
The tube **is open at one end.**

Открытая поверхность
The arrangement of the metal atoms on **an exposed surface ...**

Открытие
In recent years neurophysiologists have made some important experimental **findings** (*or* **discoveries**).

Открытое пламя
When preparing zinc electrolytes, smoking and carrying **naked flames** is forbidden.

Открытый [*см. тж.* **Без герметической оболочки**]
The quasars **uncovered** (*or* **discovered**) in the survey **are ...**

Откуда
They could not tell **from whence** their dangers came.
From where can such an immense amount of gas come?
How do we know all this?
Whence came life on the surface of the Earth?

Откуда следует, что
The effect exerted upon ... will be proportional to ...; **whence it follows that ...**

Отливать
In this workshop molten metals **are cast into** the required shapes.

Отливать в виде
The cadmium metal **is cast into** bars.

Отливка из
This is a patented method of producing high-quality **castings in** bronze, gun metal, etc.

Отлитый заодно с
A slab **cast integrally with** a concrete beam is assumed to assist the beam in carrying loads.

Отлитый из
We had a model of the water passage-way **cast in plaster.**

Отлитый под вакуумом
Vacuum-cast beryllium ingots ...

Отличать
We must be able **to distinguish between** elastically and inelastically scattered electrons.
Bromine **can be distinguished by** the following facts: ...

Отличать друг от друга
One can easily **tell** the cars **apart.**
The proton and the neutron **can be distinguished by** their differing electric charges.

Отличать от [*см. тж.* **Нельзя отличить от, Следует отличать от**]
What **differentiates** animals **from** plants?
The measuring instrument cannot **differentiate** (*or* **distinguish**) **between** reflected **and** emitted energy.

Lactose **may be differentiated from** many sugars **by the fact that** it is not fermented by ordinary yeast.
The engineer **should be able to discriminate between** satisfactory **and** unsatisfactory products.
This property **distinguishes** the precipitate **from** the yellow sulphides of ...
The terrigenous muds are silty, and their silt and lack of complete oxidation **set them apart from** brown clay.
One of the problems that plagued early chemists **was how to tell** an element **from** a compound.
It is difficult **to tell the difference between ... and ...**
To **separate** earthquakes **from** explosions, it is necessary to ...

Отличать по
These materials **can be distinguished by** their crystal form.

Отличаться I
Titanium **is noted for** its light weight, corrosion resistance, and many other desirable properties.
The surfaces **are characterized by** their smooth appearance.
Engineers are engaged in the design of superconductive bearings **distinguished by** the absence of friction.
Aluminium **is distinguished for** its light weight.
This bearing **excels in** low friction and reliability.
The capacitor **features** extraordinary stability.
The gearboxes **are noteworthy for** small size and ease in mounting.
Fraunhofer diffraction **is distinguished by** the simplicity of the mathematical treatment required.

Отличаться II
These isomeric structures **differ in** the position of the methyl group attached to the five-carbon chain.
Sand storms **differ by** the large mass, **and by** the stronger transporting winds required.

Отличаться высокой чистотой
Calcite **is** commonly **of high purity.**

Отличаться друг от друга
The two figures **diverged** considerably.
These products **vary in** size and value.
Two signals applied to the phase detector **will differ (from one another) by** this phase delay of one symbol.
The orbits **are distinguished** geometrically **by** their eccentricities.
The effects of the errors on the results **will differ.**
Scalar quantities **differ** only **in** magnitude.
Individual plants and animals **are,** usually, physically **distinct (from each other).**

Отличаться друг от друга в том смысле, что
The forces between ions and those between molecules **differ in that** ions carry full charges ...

Отличаться на
Compass headings **differ from** true headings **by** compass error.

Отличаться на величину
The two heat capacities **differ by the value of** R:
$C_p - C_v = R.$

Отличаться на ... от
The largest coded number **varies** (*or* **differs**) **by** only one bit **from** the smallest.

Отличаться от [*см. тж.* **Значительно отличаться от, Не слишком отличаться от, Расходиться с**]
The internal angular momentum **is distinct from** the external one.
Their properties **are unlike** those of any other materials.
The attitude of the American worker toward machines **has been different from** that of the European worker.
The nomenclature adopted for research and development purposes **must necessarily depart from** that in current use in industry.
The high melting point and greater strength of brazing filler metals **differentiate** brazing **from** soldering.
Chalcopyrite **is distinguished from** pyrite **by** its lesser hardness.
The composition of the Moon **is distinct from** that of the Earth.
Vycron **differs from** other polyester fibres **in** chemical constitution.
The lifetime appropriate to large values of $(N - N_l)$ **may be different from** τ_{01}.

A shock only **differs by** a third-order term **from** the adiabatic transition.
This **contrasts with** the enthalpy properties.
Coastal outlines of deltas **are** often **other than** the traditional triangle, depending upon ...
Structural isomers are compounds that **differ from** each other **by** the positioning of atoms or ...

Отличаться от ... в том смысле, что
Vermiculites **differ from** montmorillonite **in that** only a limited degree of expansion can take place.

Отличаться от других
The drive mechanisms of these conveyors **are distinctive,** especially their large pulleys.

Отличаться от ... на
Compass heading **differs from** true heading **by** compass error.

Отличаться от него
In spite of the eucrites' resemblance to terrestrial basalts they **are distinctive in** several respects.

Отличаться по [*см. тж.* **Мало отличаться по**]
The input signal and the feedback **differ in** (*or* **as to**) phase.
These circuits **differ according to** their purpose and function.
The two strands of the DNA **are** markedly **distinct in** weight.
The elements *A* and *B* **diverge in** relative positive or negative characters.

Отличаться по внешнему виду от
The absorption bands in Titan's infrared spectrum **have an appearance different** (*or* **differ in appearance**) **from** that of ...

Отличаться по конструкции *и т.п.*
The two synchrotrons **differed in design.**

Отличаться по своей природе от
All these spores **are distinct** (*or* **differ**) **in nature from** the bacterial endospores.

Отличаться тем, что
This method **differs from** the above **in that** it commences with the shock Mach number.
This solution **differs in (the fact) that** only certain amounts of vibrational energy are allowed.
Constant-pressure processes **are different in that** the volume of the system changes.
Some minerals **are distinctive in that** they are common in metamorphic rocks and rarely found in igneous rocks.

Отличающиеся друг от друга [*см.* **Неодинаковые, Разные**].

Отличающийся от [*см.* **Значительно отличающийся от, Отличный от**].

Отличие [*см.* **В отличие от, В противоположность, Расхождение с**].

Отличие от
The early atmosphere's complete **dissimilarity from** that of today ...
By its **variation from** unity the activity coefficient shows the nonideality of the solution.
Perhaps **the** most outstanding **distinction** has been found during the infective processes.

Отличительная особенность [*см.* **Особенность, Отличительная черта**].

Отличительная черта
The distinctive property (*or* **feature**) **of** calculators is that ...
This semi-permeability is **the characteristic property of ...**
A distinguishing feature of this animal is its small size.
These behavioural relationships **are distinctive of** animal communities and are not found in plant communities.
The cytoplasm often loses its **distinguishing characteristics,** for example, the cross striations in muscle.
A feature of this machine is the automatic centring device.

Отличная работа
The machines offer the customers **top performance.**

Отлично [*см. тж.* **Прекрасно согласовываться с**]
Fine pole chucks **excel at** holding this part.

Отлично полироваться
Marble **may be given a high polish.**

Отлично пройти лабораторные испытания
The new alloy **has passed its lab tests with flying colours.**

Отлично согласовываться с
Both models **give excellent agreement with** experimental results.

Отличный [*см. тж.* **В отличном состоянии**]
The modern mechanical feed unit provides **the ultimate in** smooth, uniform feed action.
Top performance ...
The first-rate (*or* **first-class,** *or* **high-class,** *or* **superior**) performance of the electrode ...
This results in **excellent** (*or* **superb,** *or* **remarkable,** *or* **exceptional**) tube performance.

Отличный от
The products of the reaction may have a **different** distribution **than** the original substances.
The numerical value **will be something other than** 1.0.
The chemical characteristics of the original substances **are different from** those of the new substances formed.
Some of the flakes are composed of structural units **different** (*or* **differing**) **from** those listed above.
At temperatures and pressures **other than** those existing under ...

Отличный от других
There are some dozens of lipids, each with its **distinctive** (*or* **unique,** *or* **peculiar**) chemical pattern.

Отличный от нуля
Different (*or* **Distinct**) **from zero** (*or* **Nonzero**).
The first term **not being zero, ...**
Nonvanishing.

Отложен на графике в зависимости от
The surface finish **is plotted versus** (*or* **vs,** *or* **as a function of,** *or* **against**) the stock removal rate.

Отложения, нанесённые ветром
Wind-laid deposits.

Отложить до
As this topic will be reviewed again in Sec. 5, we **shall defer** (*or* **postpone,** *or* **put off**) our discussion until then.

Отложить до тех пор, пока [*см.* **Лучше отложить до тех пор, пока**].

Отменять
This system of measurement **has been abandoned.**
Orders for 55 nuclear plants **have been cancelled.**

Отмерять
A specified amount of water **is measured out** in the measuring cylinder.

Отметка I
A rope with **markers** at every foot ...

Отметка II [*см. тж.* **На высоте**]
A meter is the distance between two **scribe marks** on a platinum bar which ...
The crane was placed **at** zero **elevation.**

Отмечать I [*см. тж.* **Важно отметить, что; Интересно отметить, что; Как отмечено выше, Как указано, Необходимо подчеркнуть, что; Следует отметить, что; Указывать**]
As **has** already **been intimated,** most of the basic molecules of ...

Отмечать II [*см. тж.* **Фиксировать**]
When the temperature conditions are steady, **note** the thermometer reading.
The time required for a film to form on the surface **is noted.**

Отмечать III
Among these antibodies **may be listed** (*or* **quoted**) synnematin, *XG*, streptothricin, etc.

Отмечать IV
We **shall** now **highlight** the design features of the relay types available.
We **will point out** some features of ...

Отмечать V
The compass serves **to mark off** equal segments of lines.
The left limit **is marked off by** the dotted line.
Lengths of $\lambda/4$ and $\lambda/2$ **are marked off** on the axis for comparison.
The diagonal line **marks** the equilibrium boundary between the two forms.

Отмечать на карте
The former ice limits **can be mapped** in great detail.

Отмечать, что
The author **pointed out that** a wave of zero velocity must be regarded as ingoing.

Отмечено
As **discussed** (*or* **noted,** *or* **mentioned**) below, ...
Excessive vibration **was noted** (*or* **noticed**) in the suction line.
At this stage the first significant changes in elongation at fracture **were observed** (*or* **recorded**).

Отнесение к
This facilitates **the assignment of** loci **to** particular chromosomes.
Referring plate motions **to** the volcanic hot spots makes sense only if ...

Отнесён к I [*см. тж.* **Относить к**]
Many molecules **can be related by** chemical and physical investigations **to** substances whose structures have already been determined.

Отнесён к II
Basin and Range faulting **can be dated to** the late Miocene.

Отнесён к координатам [*см.* **Привязывать к координатам**].

Отнимать много времени
This analysis **is (very) time consuming.**

Отнимать от
Drag opposes the motion of the body and **robs it of** (*or* **takes away**) some of its energy.

Относимый к
The spectral lines **attributed to** the high velocities of ... are being measured.

Относительно I [*см. тж.* **Довольно, Сравнительно**]
Relatively high values of N are attained.

Относительно II [*см. тж.* **В отношении, Колебаться относительно, Мнения относительно ... расходятся, О, По отношению к, Симметричный относительно**]
A driving force that is symmetrical **about** the centre of the swing ...
The side groups are arranged in various directions **about** the polymer axis.
If the last line is not resolved **from** its close neighbours, use ...
This spectrum is displaced **from** the origin by ...
$4xy^2$ is of degree 1 **in** x, degree 2 **in** y ...
This result allowed determination of the apparent velocity of any small section of the wave **in reference to** (*or* **as related to**, *or* **relative to**, *or* **in relation to,** *or* **with respect to**) the velocity of the stable section.
Further interesting information **relative to** (*or* **regarding,** *or* **relating to**) the equation of state may be found in Ref. 24.
The voltages are **with reference to** the chassis.
The pointer oscillates **with respect** (*or* **reference**) **to** the centre point of the scale.
The moment of the force **about** point *0* ...
There is no agreement among ... **regarding** proper nomenclature for ...
To push the fluid **relative to** the stationary layer, ...
No information is available **as to** the mechanism involved in ...
It is necessary to make a few remarks **with reference to** ...

Относительно III [*см. тж.* **По вопросу о**]
Nothing definite is known **regarding** (*or* **about**) these enzymes.
Little has been said **as to** the speeds obtained in...

Относительно высокая точность
The diamagnetic susceptibility may be computed with **reasonable** accuracy from ...

Относительно друг друга
The movements of the component atoms **relative to each other ...**

Относительное положение
The relative positions (*or* **mutual arrangement**) **of** the particles ...

Относительное положение атомов
The determination of **relative atomic locations** (*or* **relative positions of the atoms**) within molecules ...

Относить за счёт [*см. тж.* **Объяснять, Приписывать**]
Many bands **can be assigned to** the vibration of particular chemical groups.

The observed HCl absorption **can be assigned to** the vibrational transition from $v = 0$ to $v = 1$.
The positive time lags **may be attributed to** (*or* **explained by**) errors introduced by ...
The electronic absorptions of organic compounds **can** often **be identified with** a group within the molecule.
The Moon's influence on the tides **was put down to** astrological superstition by the astronomers of early modern times.

Относить к I [*см. тж.* **Классифицировать**]
It is possible **to assign** each electron **to** a particular group according to the kind of interaction it has experienced.
This plant **has been assigned to** the genus Kakabekia.
Rocks of lower metamorphic grade **were assigned to** the Archeozoic era.
Magnesium **is** sometimes **classed with** the alkaline earths.
Apophyllite closely resembles the zeolites, **with which it is** sometimes **classified.**
Calcarenites **are grouped with** the limestones.
Most lipids **may be placed into** one of two categories.
These bacteria **were** once **placed in** the genus Aerobacter.
Charophyta **are** generally **classified with** the green algae.
Such expressions **can be carried over to** any rotating system.

Относить к II
Those readers interested in ... **are referred to** Chapter 6.

Относиться в равной мере к [*см.* **В равной мере относиться к**].

Относиться враждебно к
His idea **got a hostile reception from** the geologists.

Относиться друг к другу как
Any two volumes **are related as** $n_a/n_b = V_a / V_b$.

Относиться исключительно к
Certain types of fossils **are restricted to** certain layers of rock.

Относиться к I [*см. тж.* **Все, кого это касается; К ним относится, Касаться, Не относящийся к, Охватывать, Падать на, Равным образом, Распространяться на, Справедлив для, Это особенно относится к случаям, когда**]
Evidently Einstein's restriction **should not apply to** this wave.
The laboratory rules **are concerned with** noncritical operations.
The following rules of centrifugal machines **hold true for** all centrifugal pumps.
Henry's Law **refers** only **to** the effect of pressure.
Faraday's laws **relate to** the electrolysis of solutions and fused salts.
The term "computer-aided engineering" **refers to** a "total" system concept, in which ...
The result **is** only **appropriate for** a finite time interval which is undetermined as yet.
The same situation **pertains to** H^2.
The above example **pertains to** the diffusion of liquids.
The result **applies** (*or* **refers,** *or* **relates**) **to** mass transfer from plate to fluid, or fluid to plate.
The book **deals with** (*or* **treats on**) distillation.
Another question **has to do with** diseases arising from dietary deficiencies.
This **will be true for** (*or* **of**) very high electric fields.
Lines 1a and 2a **apply to** a 47-microfarad, 35-volt polar capacitor.
The term caisson **covers** a wide range of foundation structures.
Similar considerations **hold for** emitting molecules.
This **is** particularly **true** in humid regions.
These properties **are** not **pertinent to** the problem at hand.
This is especially **the case with** wide armature cores.
The differences **are a matter of** degree rather than of type.
These terms **are related to** certain atomic groupings.
The discoveries **concern** the properties of electric charges.
This discussion **has** so far **concerned itself with** the experimental results obtained.
The common names *isobutane* and *isopentane* **apply to** those isomers having ...
The third factor **concerns** the bulky nature of ...

The most significant developments of that period **centred around** the field of communications.

Относиться к II

The basic principle of the device **dates from** (*or* **back to**) the 15th century.
The first trials **go back to** 1912.
These mummies **are dated to** 2800 B.C.

Относиться к III [*см. тж.* **Принадлежать к**]

Most abrasive materials **fall in** the region at the top of the scale.
All the above forces **fall in(to)** this category.
All forms of anemia **fall into** two main types.
The discussion of pseudovectors **belongs to** the domain of the tensor calculus.

Относиться к IV

Mathematical biophysics **stands in the same relation to** experimental biology **as** mathematical physics **to** experimental physics.

Относиться к ... как ... к

The length of the plank **is** (*or* **relates**) **to** the length of a standard yardstick **as** 21 **to** 8.

Относиться к категории

All of these devices **come under the heading of** digital computers.
Many practical problems **fall in this category.**
Many different mineral and organic substances **qualify as** sediment.

Относиться к классу

The powerplant **is rated in the** 50,000-lb-thrust **class.**

Относиться к области

All these questions **fall within the realms** (*or* **domains**) **of** analytical chemistry.

Относиться конкретно к

The discussion **is specific to** packed gas-liquid contacting devices.

Относиться с должным вниманием к

I hope this suggestion **will receive the attention it deserves.**

Относиться с интересом к

The transportation community **viewed** the proposal **with interest.**

Относящиеся друг к другу как [*см.* **В отношении 3:2**].

Относящийся к [*см. тж.* **Связанный с**]

The determinant Δ **associated with** the matrix should be zero.
Standards **pertaining** (*or* **relevant**) **to** radio frequencies ...
Aeronautics is the art and science **relating to** the flight of aircraft.
D_1^0 and D_2^0 are the diffusion coefficients **relating to** standard state conditions.
Further interesting information **relative to** (*or* **concerning,** *or* **regarding,** *or* **as to,** *or* **as regards**) the equation of state may be found in Ref. 24.
This article considers resting potentials, action potentials, and other phenomena **concerned with** bioelectricity.
Several thousand papers have been published on topics **related to** offshore oil platforms.
Relationships **involving** (*or* **dealing with**) gas volumes are discussed in ...
The laws **dealing with** reflection of light from ...
This provides data **relevant to** the distribution of ...

Относящийся к изучению *и т.п.*

Some basic ideas **that enter into the treatment of** charged particles in a vacuum must be reviewed.

Относящийся к информации *и т.п.*

Information-related activities ...

Относящийся к нему (ним)

The landing gear and all **the related** instruments ...
The chambers and **the associated** amplifiers ...
Television transmitters and **their associated** transmission lines ...

Относящийся к этому

In order to evaluate these theories let us look at some **relevant** data.

Отношение [*см.* **В других отношениях, В количественном (качественном) отношении, В некоторых отношениях, В одном и в другом отношении, В различных отношениях, В химическом** *и т.п.* **отношении, В этом отношении, Взаимосвязь, Во всех отношениях, Зависеть от ... в отношении,**

Иметь отношение к, Инертный по отношению к, Обратное отношение, Соотношение].

Отношение ... к
Ratio between room-temperature **and** 500° resistivities is 2.52 for silver, 2.71 for gold and 2.9 for copper.
The ratio of height **to** diameter is extremely low.
The measurement of **ethane to ethylene ratio** was required.
Gas-oil ratio of 550:1 ...
Steam-hydrocarbon feed weight ratio ...
The plate thickness to hole diameter ratio ...
They found **the temperature-pressure relation(ship).**
Relation(ship) between counting efficiency **and** average energy ...
Normally the densities of fresh water and salt water **are in the ratio of** 40:41.

Отнюдь не [*см.* **Далекó не, Никоим образом не**].

Отнюдь нет
But it is not only alcohol; **far from it.**

Отображать на (*матем.*)
This operation **maps** C **onto** a curve Γ.
The region **can be mapped onto** a disk.
This constitutes **a mapping of** the space **upon** (*or* **into**) itself which **maps** a figure **into** (*or* **upon**) some other figure.

Отображать однозначно на
A cube **is mapped (in a) one-to-one (way) on ...**

Отображаться на [*см.* **Однозначно отображаться на**].

Отображение на себя
The mapping of φ **into itself** is called a contraction if ...

Отодвигать на задний план
After the war the acetone-ethanol fermentation **was relegated to the background.**
The high power-handling ability of these devices **overshadows** their frequency limitations.

Отождествлять с
The coordinate x° **will be identified with** the time t.
We solve the problem **by identifying** the time origin **with** the moment of collision.

Отопление [*см.* **С нефтяным отоплением**].

Отопление домов
Anthracite is used mainly for **domestic heating** (*or* **house-heating**).

Отопление помещений
The reactor and the steam generator will provide 7 million Btu per hour for **space heating.**

Оторван от I
Under such conditions the scientist **will be divorced from** the practical problems.
The outermost electron is no longer merely excited but **is torn loose from** the atom entirely.

Отпадать (*мат.*) [*см.* **Выпадать**].

Отполированный [*см.* **Хорошо отполированный**].

Отполированный до яркого блеска
The nonhardenable grades of ferrite **can be buffed to a high lustre.**

Отправлять в отвал
The top 12 ft of the overburden **is** first removed and **wasted.**

Отправная точка
In nonstandard analysis one takes as **the starting point** the finite real numbers.
The starting point for the development of this relationship is ...

Отправной пункт [*см.* **В качестве отправного пункта**].

Отпускать винт [*см.* **Освобождать винт**].

Отпускать винт на ... оборота
To remove the tool block manually it is necessary **to back off the** clamp **screw one-third turn.**

Отпускать гайку
A special spanner is provided **to allow the nut to be loosened** without removing the nozzle.
Slack off the locknut.

Отпускать на пол-оборота
The absorption chamber has a screw plug

which, when **backed off a half turn,** serves as a vent.

Отработанный газ
The objective is to replace **spent gases** with fresh air.

Отравление металлом
Metal poisoning from mercury, etc. ...

Отражать
The coefficient *k* **accounts for** the heat conducting ability of a substance.
These formulas do not **take account of** (*or* do not **take into account,** *or* do not **make allowance for**) the higher local rigidity.
These questions **reflect** (*or* **are representative of**) the major problems.

Отражать действительность [*см. тж.* **Хорошо отражать действительность**]
One could clearly see that **the model was valid.**

Отражаться
The real process **is well represented by** this equation.

Отражаться в
The relative strength of ionic and covalent bonds **(is) reflected in** a number of properties.

Отражаться на I [*см. тж.* **Влиять на, Не влиять на, Немедленно отразиться на, Отрицательно влиять на**]
The results **may reflect on** the validity of the theory.

Отражаться на II
The light **is reflected** from the galvanometer mirror **on to** a graduated scale.
The point scanned by a mirror **is reflected to** an infrared detector.

Отражаться на внешнем виде
The silicon content **is reflected in the way the rock appears to the eye** (*or* **in the external appearance of the rock**).

Отражаться на графике в виде
Such a pair of images **will plot as** a straight line.

Отражаться на себя
The laser field **was reflected back on itself** by means of a mirror.

Отражаться от
The core path **reflects** (*or* **is reflected**) **from** the interface.
The shock wave **reflects at** the end-wall.
The laser beam **bounces from** the cone **to ...**

Отражение
The NMR spectrum **is a portrayal** (*or* **reflection**) **of ...**

Отрасль [*см. тж.* **Область**]
They work in different **segments** (*or* **branches**) **of** the aviation industry.
This procedure is essential to every **area** (*or* **branch,** *or* **domain**) **of** chemistry and chemical engineering.
The study of carbon compounds **is one of the oldest fields of** chemistry.

Отрасль знаний
From all **divisions** (*or* **fields**) **of knowledge ...**

Отрасль промышленности
All phases (*or* **branches**) **of the** plastic **industry ...**

Отрегулировать [*см. тж.* **Регулировать**]
During the assembly the end-plates **must be adjusted so that ...**

Отрегулировать в соответствии с
The photographer **can adjust** the light of the flash unit **to suit** the aperture.

Отрезать поступление
The effect of ... **would be to cut off the supply of** carbonaceous material for ...

Отрезок
Cap the opening with **a** short **length of** rubber tubing.

Отрицательно влиять на [*см. тж.* **Неблагоприятно влиять на**]
Such generators **are adversely affected by** wide temperature changes.
This permits an unusual amount of contaminant to be pumped without seriously **affecting** performance.
Application of melamine resins **adversely affects** sunlight resistance.

Отрицательно заряжённый
Negatively charged aerosols ...

Отрицательное влияние (*или* **действие**) **на**
Increasing boiling point elevation **has** (*or*

exerts) a detrimental (*or* **adverse) effect on** the product rate [*or* (**adversely**) **affects,** *or* **impairs** the product rate].

Отрицать всё это
Kepler believed in ... and Galileo **would have none of that.**

Отрыв [*см. тж.* **Отделение ... от**]
Hydrogen **abstraction** (*or* **Abstraction of** hydrogen) **from** propane ...
After formation and **release,** single drops soon reach their terminal velocity.

Отрыв электрона
The detachment (*or* **abstraction,** *or* **removal) of the (outermost) electron ...**

Отрывать
The capillary is tapped (*постукивать*) every seven seconds **to detach** the drop.
The energy required **to remove** (*or* **detach,** *or* **abstract**) an electron **from** an atom (*or* **to tear** an electron **away from** an atom) ...

Отрывать атом от
Free radicals **break the atoms loose** (*or* **tear the atoms away,** *or* **abstract the atoms**) **from** their covalent bonds, ...

Отрывать друг от друга
Rydberg atoms **can be pulled apart by** a relatively weak electric field.

Отрывать электроны от
When X rays pass through tissue, they ionize atoms in it by **removing electrons from** them.
The radiation **strips electrons off** the nuclei of atoms.

Отрываться
The bubble **is released** (*or* **detached**) when the buoyant force just overcomes the surface tension.
The vibrational energy of the atoms is so great that they begin **to break away.**
The main flow **breaks away** (*or* **separates**) **from** the surface.
This coating does not **break away from** machine surfaces.
The Moon **must have broken free of** Mercury's gravitational field.

Отрывочные данные
This kind of information must often be estimated from **fragmentary data.**

Отрывочные сведения о
Prior to 1915 most so-called chemical engineering curricula combined purely descriptive courses in industrial chemistry with **smatterings of** mechanical, electrical, and civil engineering.

Отсасывание пыли
The difference between blowing the dust around and **vacuuming it off ...**

Отсасываться
The dust **is sucked** (*or* **drawn**) **off** and discharged.

Отсеивание
Examination of fluorescence emission only within a narrow time window involves **throwing away** most of the spectroscopic information generated by ...

Отсекаемый
The length of the normal **cut off by** the x-axis ...
The portion AB **intercepted on** the x-axis **by** the two characteristics ...
The part of the line **intercepted by** the half-circle ...

Отсекать
If you **lop off** the first 3 integers, the series still remains endless.
The supply regulators **chip** the peaks **off** the sinusoidal waveform, giving each half cycle a trapezoidal form.

Отскакивать друг от друга
The electrons and the positrons **bounce off each other.**

Отскакивать от
The electrons repeatedly **bounce off** moving magnetic clouds that act as magnetic mirrors.
Some of the particles **bounced back from** the foil.

Отслаивание
Exfoliation is **the flaking off of** the outer layer of a specimen. It is also referred to as **peeling** or **spalling.**

Отставание во времени
This device has a preset **time delay** (*or* **time lag**).

Отставать
The country **has been falling behind in** research since the 1930s.

Отставать на
The steady-state response **lags behind** the zero-inertia response **by** the following value: ...

Отставать от I [*см. тж.* **Не отставать от**]
This coating **breaks away from** machine surfaces.

Отставать от II
Techniques for determining costs **have not kept pace with** changes in manufacturing.
The output voltage **lags (behind)** the input voltage in time.
It frequently happens that catalogues **are outstripped by** the developments.

Отстоять [*см.* **Далеко отстоять друг от друга**].

Отстоять друг от друга на расстоянии
The holes **are (spaced) 15 ft apart** (*or* **spaced at 15 ft**).

Отстоять на ... сантиметров от
The pivot point **should be offset by six centimetres from** the centre of the grating.

Отступать [*см.* **Море наступает и отступает**].

Отступать к
The ice margins **receded toward** the central highland areas.

Отступать от
Then the seas **would recede from** the continents.

Отсутствие [*см. тж.* **В присутствии и в отсутствие, Ввиду отсутствия, За отсутствием, При отсутствии**]
Coherent scattering implies **no** exchange of energy between the beam and the scattering centres.
The lack of any crystal growth makes the glass highly reproducible.
The lack of information about the exact position of the particle ...
The advantages of the new system lie in **the freedom from** (*or* **absence of**) human errors.
Drilling was discontinued **because of lack of** (*or* **for the lack of**) adequate equipment.
We assume **no** instrument error.

Отсутствие в
The absence of adenosine **from** site 1 ...

Отсутствие массы у
The **masslessness of** the photon ...

Отсутствие утечки [*см.* **Плотный**].

Отсутствие учёта [*см.* **Неучёт**].

Отсутствовать [*см. тж.* **Не иметь, Не обладать, Нет, Опущен в**]
These dispersions **were free from** coarse aggregates.
The new bottles **are free of** cracks.
Information on these conditions **is lacking.**
In places plant growth **may be lacking** completely.
Antennules **are lacking in** the adult, and cement glands are much reduced.
In many areas the means for crossing rivers **are** either **nonexistent** or only of a primitive nature.
In the 1958 TV receiver, transistors **are** almost **nowhere to be seen.**
There is freedom from porosity on vital machined surfaces.
When a box **is not provided,** rests should be so placed as to ...
Data **are not in hand** (*or* **are not available,** *or* **are unavailable**) to estimate the extent of this effect.
The needed data and correlations **are** often **missing.**
These fossil plants **lack** growth rings (*у ... отсутствуют ...*).
The current in coil *C* **is nil.**
Fortunately, astronomers are not halted in a practical sense; theory **may be lacking,** but they can get along.
No experimental values **are available.**
The heat is stored to permit continuous operation when sunlight **is unavailable.**
There are bands within the zone that **are** virtually **empty of** matter.
The probability of tunnelling through the barrier **is nil.**

Отсутствовать в
Tree and shrub strata **are absent from** some communities, for instance, the grassland.
Infinities **were absent in** Feynman diagrams.
The parent peak **is** often **missing from** the spectrum.
This crustal layer **is missing from** oceanic lithosphere.

Отсутствует единое мнение относительно [*см.* **Нет согласия между ... относительно**].

Отсутствует подтверждение
Adequate empirical **support for** the theory **is lacking.**

Отсутствующий у
These metals offer advantages **not found in** single metals.

Отсчёт [*см.* **С прямым отсчётом**].

Отсчитываемый
One can use the entire 360 degrees of the compass, **counted** clockwise.

Отсчитывать
These angles **are measured** (*or* **reckoned**) **from** *v*.

Отсылать читателя к [*см.* **Смотри**].

Отсыхать
Yellow patches appear on the leaves, and mottled areas turn brown and **dry out.**

Отсюда [*см. тж.* **Начиная отсюда**]
Power canals are placed on minimum grade to conserve head, **hence** (*or* **thus,** *or* **therefore**) velocities are usually lower.

Отсюда видно, что
The states formed from the t_{2g}^2 configuration **are thus seen to be** A_{1g}, E_g, T_{1g}, and T_{2g}.

Отсюда непосредственно следует, что
It immediately follows that matrix multipliers of v_x are symmetric.

Отсюда следует, что [*см. тж.* **Из этого вытекает** (*или* **следует**), **что**]
It follows (herefrom) (*or* **Hence it follows**) **that** the molecule must have six degrees of freedom.

Отталкивание электронов (*взаимное*)
Interelectron repulsion.

Отталкиваться от
These paint particles **are repelled from** the other atomizing head.

Оттенок [*см.* **Иметь различные оттенки от ... до**].

Оттеснять
The advancing cosmic jet must **push** the matter **out of the way.**

Оттуда
Output from the detector is fed into a cathode follower and **thence** through a clipping network.

Отфильтровывать
The flow **is filtered for** graphite dust and iron oxide.
Such stray signals **cannot be filtered off** (*or* **out**).
He **filtered off** the sediment.

Отфильтровывать частоты
Acoustic filters **filter out** certain **frequencies.**

Отходить назад
Immediately after completing the reading the micrometer screw **backs off** automatically to clear the workpiece.
Owing to compression of the oil in the chamber during the feeding stroke, the piston **backs off** very slightly.

Отходы городского хозяйства
The urban wastes are collected as sewage.

Отходящий от
In many cases branch pipes **off** the main stream pipe are required to carry a reduced pressure.

Отчасти
The final thickness of the extruded product depends **in part** (*or* **partly,** *or* **to some extent,** *or* **to a degree**) upon the speed of the conveyor.

Отчётливо заметный [*см.* **Ярко выражен**].

Отщепление
This reaction may be visualized as **the splitting out of** H_2O.

Отщепляться
A molecule of water **is split out** when a peptide bond is formed.

Отъединять подачу
A depth gauge with an adjustable stop automatically **disengages the power feed** when preset drilling depth has been reached.

Оформление [*см.* **Красивое внешнее оформление**].

Охарактеризовывать вкратце
The effect **can be summarized** (*or* **briefly outlined**) **as follows: ...**

Охарактеризовывать как
The cohesive energy in solids **may be defined as** the difference between ...
The third era of electrical engineering **can be classified as** the era of engineering research.

Охватывать I [*см. тж.* **Относиться к**]
We have assumed that covalent bonds **encompass** only two atoms.
Floods never **engulf** an entire continent.
This curve **encloses** the same area as ...
Each colour is considered as **stretching over** a certain range of frequency.
The term marine life **embraces** the plants and animals that drift in the open sea.
A very broad band of wavelengths **brackets** most of the terrestrial infrared radiation ...
The oscillator **covers** (*or* **embraces**) the range 1 kc/s–10 Mc/s.
Investigation **will cover** the fields of nuclear structure, reactor design and material damage.
The mean lives ... **encompass** a tremendous range.
To span the same energy range a proton synchrotron would need to accelerate protons from ... to ...
Oceanography **encompasses** the study of all aspects of the oceans.

Охватывать II
The chain **is wrapped on** the sprocket.
An outer part, the cortex, **envelops** (*or* **encloses**) an inner, the medulla.

Охватывать область от ... до
The emission spectrum roughly defines the tunability range, which **spans** approximately 570–650 nm for rhodamine 6*G*.

Охваченный патентом [*см.* **Охраняться патентом**].

Охлаждать
Allow the part **to cool** (*or* **Cool** the part).
The material is heated and then **allowed to cool** in still air at room temperature.
Liquid nitrogen **chills** bearing components to minus 300°F for shrink-fit assembly.

Охлаждать на воздухе
Then the part **is allowed to air cool to** room temperature.

Охлаждать ниже
Liquid water **can be cooled below** its freezing point.
It is most practical **to chill** the gas **below** 60°F.

Охлаждаться [*см. тж.* **Остывать**]
As the vapour **is chilled** it again condenses onto the surface.
This allows the welding set **to cool down** rapidly.

Охлаждаться маслом
The pistons **are oil cooled.**

Охлаждение [*см.* **С ... охлаждением**].

Охлаждение до комнатной температуры
Cooling to room temperature.

Охлаждён
The palladium **was allowed to cool** in the gas.

Охлаждён до
The bar **is cooled to** room temperature.

Охлаждённый с печью
Furnace cooled.

Охотно [*см.* **Легко**].

Охотно реагировать с
Formaldehyde molecules **react readily** (*or* **avidly,** *or* **briskly**) **with** each other.
These bonds **are susceptible to reaction with** electron-deficient reagents.

Охрана окружающей среды [*см. тж.* **Меры по охране окружающей среды**]
Environmental protection.

Охраняться патентом
These designs **are covered by patents** in all major countries.

Охрупчиваться
Conventional caulking materials **embrittle** and lose bond in ...

Оценивать [*см. тж.* **Определять**]
It is necessary carefully **to assess** those factors which ...
To make an estimate of the maximum conversion of ...

In order **to evaluate** these theories ...
The losses of gas **can be assessed** (*or* **set**) **at** about 2.7 kg.
Reserves **are estimated** (*or* **evaluated**) **at** 10,000,000 bbl.
The lower limit **is estimated at** 0.002 mg.
It is not possible with this information alone **to judge** the effectiveness of an existing system.

Оценка [*см. тж.* **Определение,. Осторожная оценка, Приближённая оценка**]
An initial **appraisal** (*or* **assessment**) **of** the magnitude of this contamination ...
Impingement tests are often used **to assess** the resistance of ...
Audiometry is **the** quantitative **assessment** (*or* **evaluation**) **of** individual hearing.
The existing **estimates of** future capacity ...
The estimation of the natural stock ...

Оценка эффективности
Performance evaluation of a satellite-linked experimental network ...

Очевидно, что
Clearly (*or* **Obviously**) saturation will occur only for ...
It is apparent (*or* **obvious**) **that** such stress can have major consequences.
Evidently (*or* **It is evident that ...**).

Очевидный
The advantages of lasers **are (so) apparent** (*or* **evident,** *or* **compelling**) **that** they have almost completely replaced ...

Очень [*см.* **Весьма**].

Очень близкий к [*см. тж.* **Весьма аналогичный**]
The community includes the five species at depths **much like** those they occupy in ...
The gas-pressure curve **would be very nearly** (*or* **very much like**) an adiabatic curve.

Очень близко к
The disk **is in close proximity to** the poles.

Очень близок к
The molar percent of the purine adenine **is closely matched by** that of the pyrimidine thymine.

Очень важно
It is of first importance that the alignment of piston, rod and compressor is absolutely true.
Of prime (*or* **singular,** *or* **paramount,** *or* **critical,** *or* **fundamental,** *or* **vital**) **importance ...**

Очень важно для
This **is crucial** (*or* **quite important**) **for** the purposes of the present article.

Очень важный [*см. тж.* **Исключительно важный, Решающее значение**]
Porosity **is** a property **of great importance** (*or* **significance**) **in** petroleum geology.

Очень легко
It is a very simple matter (*or* **It is very easy**) **to** construct this curve.

Очень медленно
The wires will sag **ever so** (*or* **very**) **slowly.**

Очень опытный
An operator **with (very) wide experience** and skill ...

Очень помогать
This passage **gives us a strong clue to** (*or* **is very helpful in**) understanding where the meaning of language really resides.

Очень похожий на [*см.* **Весьма аналогичный**].

Очень слабо влиять на
Ordinary atoms **are scarcely affected by** an applied electric field.

Очень трудный
Machining large complex parts like ship screws **is a** slow, **arduous** task for any machine shop.

Очень широко использоваться
This bond **is in very regular use** (*or* **is used very widely**).

Очень яркий
Such stars **would be highly luminous** (*or* **very bright**).

Очень ярко выражен
The nucleus of our galaxy **stands out conspicuously** at wavelengths of 20 and 100 microns.

Очередь [*см.* **В первую очередь**].

Очерченный [*см* **Резко обозначенный, Чётко обозначенный**].

Очистка от
The cleaning (*or* **removal**) **of** oxide scale **from** the surfaces of metals ...
Sweeping the apparatus **free of** hydrogen for weighing ...

Очищать от [*см. тж.* **Освобождать от, Удалять**]
To clean the rust **from** the surface (*or* **To clean** the surface **of** the rust), ...
Cleanse it **of** bacteria and humidify.
The screen **can be cleared of** stone after the belt is stopped.
The carbon is saved and the countryside **is freed of** soot.
The difficulty of **freeing** the enzyme **from** impurities ...
To remove the impurities **from** the solution, ...
This **rids** oil **of** corrosive gases.
The gas begins to flow before the arc is started **to purge** the joint **of** atmospheric contaminations.

Очищать пескоструйным аппаратом
The bell **is sandblasted** and polished.

Очищать с помощью ультразвука
Scaled parts **are ultrasonically cleaned.**

Очищать сточные воды
To treat sewage.

Очищенный
A **cleansed** stream ...

Ошибка [*см. тж.* **В пределах ошибки эксперимента, Вносить ошибку в, Инструментальная погрешность, Отклоняться от истины на**]
You have **a fallacy** (*or* **an error,** *or* **a mistake**) in your proof somewhere.

Ошибочно
Galileo **mistakenly** (*or* **erroneously**) thought that ...

Ошибочно принимать за
These seismic waves **could be (mis)taken for** those of an earthquake.

Ошибочное предположение [*см.* **Исходя из ошибочного предположения, что**].

Ошибочное толкование
This can lead to **misinterpretation of** experimental data.

Ошибочность ... состоит в том, что
The fallacy in these calculations is that Kelvin also assumed that ...

Ошибочный [*см. тж.* **Неправильный**]
The calculation **was in error.**
He showed this assumption **to be untrue.**
Hall's observation **was** just as **erroneous** (*or* **wrong,** *or* **faulty**) as Newton's.
These data **may be in error** (*or* **invalid**) because of the variation of Reynolds number with size.

Ошибочный термин
The so-called graphitization of cast iron **is a misnomer;** actually, the removal or corrosion of iron occurs, leaving the graphite network.

Ощутимо
The presence of the shaper did not **materially** (*or* **tangibly,** *or* **perceptibly**) affect the velocity of this portion of the wave.

Ощущается нехватка
Axles **are in short supply.**

Ощущать
These forces **cannot be perceived** directly.

Ощущать недостаток [*см.* **Испытывать недостаток**].

Ощущать необходимость в
We **feel the need for** a source of advice.

Ощущаться больше всего
It is here that the benefits of data-processing technology **are most pronounced.**

Ощущение глубины
The distinguishing feature of binoculars **is the depth perception** obtainable.

П

Падать [*см. тж.* **Сокращаться, Уменьшаться**]
The albumin **sinks to** a lower level.
If the suction pressure **declines** (*or* **decreases,** *or* **drops,** *or* **diminishes**) **to** 0.4 in. of water, ...
At greater heights atmospheric pressure progressively **falls off.**

If the temperature **sinks** below the critical point, ...

Падать до нуля
The flux **goes** (*or* **reduces**) **to zero** as the concentrations equalize.
The velocity **decays to zero.**

Падать на I [*см. тж.* **Луч падает на, Попадать на**]
When a ray **hits** one of the scatterers ...
The Moon **has been impacted by** meteorites for an extended period of time.
An intense laser beam **is incident (up)on** a gas-filled sample cell.
When the bubbles **are hit with** a laser beam, ...
A stack of five "thick" platelets reflects only 20% of the light that **strikes** it.
The laser beam **impinges on** a stainless steel cone.
Radiant energy **strikes** the emitting surface.
These two beams **strike** (*or* **fall on**) the screen.

Падать на II [*см. тж.* **На который приходится, На ... падает, На ... приходится**]
Engine parts **accounted for** (*or* **constituted,** *or* **comprised,** *or* **made up**) 11.3% of the deliveries.
Ninety percent of the storage cost **is due to** tanks.

Падать на дно
The entrapped soil particles are released and **drop** (*or* **fall**) **to the bottom of** the bath.

Падать на землю
The raindrops **fall to earth.**

Падать на прямую линию
All the points **would fall on a straight line.**

Падать ниже [*см. тж.* **Опускаться ниже**]
When the signal-to-noise ratio **drops below** a point that can be tolerated, ...

Падающее излучение
Incident radiation.
The radiation incident (*or* **falling,** *or* **impinging**) **(up)on** the surface ...

Падающий на
The photon flux **impinging on** the sample yields a value of ...
The total flux **incident (up)on** the vessel ...
The extent to which a sound wave **incident on** a plane interface is refracted is determined by ...

Падающий свет
Light impinging on the retina.
This model enables us to estimate how thick a dense plasma must be to absorb all **the incident** laser **light.**

Падение давления на [*см. тж.* **Перепад давления на**]
Pressure drop across the valve ...

Падение напряжения на
The voltage drop (*or* **The drop in voltage**) **across** the resistor is 0.1 volt.

Падение напряжения на переходе (*полупров.*)
The potential drop (*or* **The potential difference**) **across the junction.**

Падение уровня жидкости
The drop in the liquid level is measured.

Память [*см.* **Запоминаться**].

Панель [*см.* **На передней панели**].

Пар [*см.* **Генерировать пар, Упругость паров**].

Паразитировать на
Several groups of beetles **are parasitic on** other insects or animals.

Параллельно I [*см. тж.* **Наряду с, Проходить параллельно**]
Molecular and eddy diffusion take place **in parallel.**
Two valves are connected **in parallel.**
A thermistor can be placed **in parallel with** a load.
The target consisted of a grid work of wires mounted **parallel** on a block of wood.
This line is drawn **parallel to** the x-axis.
The third element is aligned **parallel to** the magnetic field.
When a point moves **parallel to** the axis, ...
The force acts **parallel with** the line joining ...
Surface diffusion occurs **in parallel with** diffusion in the gas.

Параллельно II
The machine carries out many similar operations **in parallel** (*or* **concurrently**).

Параллельно включать [*см.* **Включать параллельно**].

Параллельно с [*см.* **Одновременно с**].

Параллельно соединённый [*см.* **Соединён(ный) параллельно**].

Параллельное сопротивление
A capacitor with **a** high **resistance in parallel ...**

Параллельность
Maintain **a** strict **parallelism.**

Параллельный
Motion **parallel to** the magnetic field ...
In some species the proboscis **is parallel with** the main axis of the body.

Параметры пара
The preset top **steam conditions** are 2400 lb per sq in. and 1050°F.

Пáрами [*см. тж.* **Попáрно**]
Sunspots usually appear **in pairs** or groups.

Паровой привод [*см.* **С паровым приводом**].

Парообразное состояние
The vapour state.

Партия
We examine every **lot** (*or* **batch**) **of** material by spectrographic techniques.
The first **shipload of** Russian coking coal reached Japan in ...
Production of the first **batch of** 30 aircraft is continuing.

Партия деталей
The production **of parts in** small **batches ...**

Пассивен по отношению к
If the gases **are indifferent to** each other, ...
Iron **is passive to** concentrated nitric acid.

Патент [*см.* **Заявка на патент подана, Охраняться патентом**].

Патент на
The first **patent on** the electrical telegraph ...

Патрон для деталей диаметром до полудюйма
A 1/2-in. capacity chuck.

Первая космическая скорость
The orbital (*or* **circular**) **velocity.**

Первая стадия [*см.* **На первой стадии**].

Первое место [*см.* **Занимать первое место**].

Первое приближение [*см. тж.* **В первом приближении**]
A first approximation still yields a value of ...

Первоначально [*см. тж.* **Вначале, Сначала**]
Consider the case where the system is **initially** (*or* **originally**) at rest.
The vapour occupies the space **originally** (*or* **initially**) filled with liquid.
Originally the idea arose through investigation of ...

Первоначальное значение
When the temperature returns to its **initial value, ...**

Первоначальное положение [*см.* **Возвращаться в первоначальное положение**].

Первоначальный
Count the number of digits between **the original** (*or* **initial**) and new decimal point positions.
When a malignant tissue no longer resembles the tissue **of origin ...**

Первоначальный вид [*см.* **Восстанавливать до первоначального вида**].

Первооткрыватель
Newton was **a pioneer** (*or* **ground breaker,** *or* **trail blazer**) **in** mathematics.

Первостепенное значение [*см. тж.* **Иметь первостепенное значение, Огромное значение**]
This provides data which **are of paramount** (*or* **critical,** *or* **vital,** *or* **cardinal,** *or* **fundamental,** *or* **prime,** *or* **first**) **importance in** studies of ...

Первые исследования
Since these **pioneering** (*or* **early**) **studies** there have been several attempts to find the solution to the problem.

Первые исследователи
Early investigators believed anauxite to be an interlayer mixture of ...

Первый [*см. тж.* **Впервые**]
Early investigators believed anauxite to be ...
A succession of **pioneering** storage-ring projects was built at Novosibirsk.
The data came from **the pioneering** work of *A*.
Early airships were moved around on the ground by crews of many men.
Race and ball surfaces of the bearings are **the first to** show attrition.
Military aircraft **pioneered** flying in bad weather.

Первый в истории
The first-ever International Conference on ...

Первый в мире
The unit is **the world's first** shape-cutting machine (*or* **the first** shape-cutting machine **in the world**) that can ...

Первый в своём роде
This dye penetrant is **the first of its kind** ever developed.

Первый исследователь
One of **the pioneer investigators of** this problem was K.

Первым был исследован
The first to be investigated was an adiabatic explosion.

Первым долгом [*см. тж.* **В основном, В первую очередь, Во-первых, Прежде всего**]
First and foremost, Britain has vast energy reserves.
What they did **first of all** (*or* **first off**) was to call the local geologist.
The final acceptance of this interpretation will depend **in the first instance** (*or* **place**) on confirmation of their results.

Переведён из ... состояния в
Within that part of the zone uranium **is changed from** the hexavalent **state to** the quadrivalent one (*chem.*).

Перевод ... в [*см.* **Превращение ... в**].

Переводить в
The concentrate is roasted **to transform** cobalt sulphide **to** cobalt sulphate.

Переводить в ... состояние
The energy required **to take** (*or* **transfer,** *or* **carry**) the reactants **to the desired state,** ... (*chem.*).

Переводить на [*см.* **Можно перевести на**].

Перевозить [*см.* **Отгружать**].

Перевозка [*см.* **Во время перевозки**].

Перевоплощать в
The chemical engineer is often called upon **to translate** the results of laboratory research **into** large-scale manufacturing operations.

Перегибаться по прямой
Sheet metal **bends along a straight line.**

Перегрев [*см.* **Местный перегрев**].

Перед I [*см. тж.* **До, Непосредственно перед**]
A mirror is mounted **in front of** the lamp.
The box is located **ahead of** the drive head.
The three evaporators are located **forward of** the engine room.
A trap was placed **upstream of** (*or* **from**) the absorber.

Перед II
Following a deglaciation, but **preceding** the next glaciation, is a period of time in which ...
The electrophile is produced in the reaction solution **prior to** its attack on ...
Preliminary to annihilation the positron-negation pairs form bound systems called positronium atoms.
Prior to (*or* **Before**) testing, all specimens were dried.
Preparatory to die casting a heated core is loaded vertically to ...

Перед нами встал вопрос
We were confronted with a question: ...

Перед ... ставится
The number of each of these element notations **is prefixed with** the letter *n*.

Перед ... стоит проблема
One unsolved **problem** remains **to face** (*or* **confront**) the trajectory designer.
The industry **is** now **being confronted** (*or* **faced**) **with an** acute ventilation **problem** (*or* The industry **is facing** an acute ...).

Передаваемый
The maximum energy **imparted to** the lever by the wheel ...
Explosive energy **transferred to** the rock ...
The **transmitted** signal ...

Передавать
The piston **conveyed** the pressure **to** the sample in a smaller chamber.
Animals **transmit** their useful characteristics **to** their offspring.

Передавать движение
Motion is applied to the lower track by means of two pneumatic cylinders.
Movement of the hand steering wheels **is transmitted through** the worm.

Передавать знания
To impart knowledge to students, ...

Передавать изображение
Photographs (*or* **Images**) **were transmitted** (*or* **relayed**) **from** the spacecraft **to** ground-based stations.

Передавать импульсы
Nerve **impulses are transmitted from** one cell **to** another.

Передавать информацию
The amount of **information transmitted** (*or* **conveyed,** *or* **relayed**) ...

Передавать мощность
Power from the transmission **is carried** (*or* **conveyed**) **to** the axle **by** a chain or propeller shaft.
According to the movement of the wheel on the bridge **power is communicated to** the worm-wheel, which in turn **transmits power to** the main pinion.

Передавать по трубам
Hydrogen **can be pipelined** (*or* **piped**) **over** any distance required.

Передавать сигнал
The nerve fiber **conveys** (*or* **transmits**) the signal **to** the spinal cord.

Передавать тепло
The hot combustion gases **transfer heat to** the environment.
The heat is transmitted through the walls.

Передавать усилие
The large wheel, by a rack and pinion system, **transmits** this manual **effort to** an injection piston.

Передаваться
Linear motion **is imparted to ...**
The signal from the clipper **is passed to** a cathode follower output stage.
Determine the amount of energy **transferred to** the electron.
The heat **is** rapidly **transmitted** (*or* **transferred**) **to ...**
This plant disease **is transmitted by** two species of aphids.
Minimum of vibration **is transmitted to** supporting structures.
The development role of the teloplasm **is passed on to** cell *D*.
Any disturbance of the electron-pair waves at one junction **is** immediately **communicated to** the other junction.

Передаваться из поколения в поколение
How could these variations be passed on **from generation to generation** (*or* **from one generation to another**)?

Передача
The passing of individual characteristics **from** parent cells **to** their progeny ... (*biol.*).

Передача информации
This allows **communication of** phase **information from** one phase **to** the next.
The transmission (*or* **conveying**) **of information** along optical fibres ...

Передача мощности
A belt drive is a means for **the transmission** (*or* **transfer**) **of power between** shafts.

Передача наследственных черт
The transmittance of hereditary traits.

Передача работает плавно
The drive runs smoothly.

Передача сигнала
These characteristics are optimum for **the conveyance** (*or* **transmission**) **of a** rapidly changing **signal.**

Передвигать на расстояние
The force of gravity **moves** the grains **a** very slight **distance** down the slope.

Передвигаться [*см.* **Двигаться**].

Передвигаться на далёкие расстояния
The electrons **can move over long distances.**

Передвигаться на расстояние
The particle **travels a distance** v each second.

Передвигаться по компасу
To navigate by compass.

Передвигаться продольно
The optical setting head spans the bar and **can be moved lengthwise** along the latter.

Передний конец
The crank shaper has a reciprocating ram, with a head or tool holder **at its forward end.**

Передний и задний ход
Forward and reverse motion of the spindle are selected automatically.

Передний план [*см.* **На переднем плане**].

Передовой [*см.* **Новаторский**].

Передовые методы
Advanced (*or* **Progressive**) **methods of** assembly are described.

Пережить
In the 1960s the geological sciences **experienced** a revolution comparable to ...

Пережог лампочки
A bulb burnout.

Перейти рубеж
It is not clear how the neutron-capture chain **could** ever **get past** this **point.**

Перекантовывать на 180°
Before being loaded on the spindle, the work piece **is turned end-for-end,** so that the boss portion is outwards.

Перекачивать в
The necessity **to pump over** half of the system **into** E_2 ...

Переключать
It will be necessary **to reverse** the connections **to** the potentiometer.
The unit **is switched to** (*or* **for**) normal operation.
This controller **can be switched from** direct **to** reverse-action control.
Flip (*or* **Set,** *or* **Throw,** *or* **Turn**) switch **to** ... (*in instructions*).

Переключать внимание на
He **redirected** (*or* **switched**) **his attention to** animal behaviour.

Переключать на
The device **can be reset to** the zero-resistance state by ...

Переключать с ... на
These devices **can be switched** quickly **from** one state **to** another.

Переключаться на I
A major part of the production of the earliest nitrogen fixation plants **was diverted to** the manufacture of munitions.
We are unable **to switch** rapidly **to** nuclear sources.

Переключаться на II
We **turn our attention to** the two enormous ice masses ...

Переключаться с ... на
These versatile machines **are** easily **changed over from** one process **to** another.
The integrator **is switched from** the initial-condition mode **to** the compute mode.

Переключение [*см. тж.* **Переход**]
The signals effect **change-over from** coarse **to** fine rate.
Change-over from one range **to** the other is effected manually.

Переключение с ручного на автоматическое управление
There are switches for **manual/automatic change-over.**

Перекрывать I
It is assumed that the eigenvectors of A **span** the n-dimensional space.
The two parallel lines on the lapped area **straddle** the hair line on the graticule.

Перекрывать II
The air supply **is cut** (*or* **shut**) **off** immediately.
The air blows to atmosphere until **it is shut down.**

Перекрывать III
In order **to override** the natural and man-made noise the pulse had to be very intense.

Перекрывать плотиной
The Zambezi river **has been dammed** to create a large reservoir.

Перекрываться I
The emission spectra **overlap.**

Перекрываться II
Such waves could not be detected because they **were obscured by** the background earth noise.

Перекрываться с
The *p*-orbital on the benzylic carbon **can overlap with** the *p*-orbitals of the benzene ring.

Перекрыть промежуток
A plasma arc momentarily **bridges the gap** when a pair of contacts is opened.

Перемежаться с [*см. тж.* **Слои ... перемежаются со слоями**]
Layers of minerals having a granular structure **alternate with** thinner layers of fibrous minerals.
The iron plates **are interleaved with** scintillation counters.

Перемежающиеся I [*см. тж.* **Чередующиеся**]
Metals that have been subjected to continuous **alternating** heating **and** cooling ...

Перемежающиеся II
Pearlite consists of **interstratified** (*or* **alternating**) layers of ferrite and cementite ...

Перемена полярности
Polarity reversal (*or* **Reversal of polarity**).

Переменный [*см. тж.* **С переменной скоростью**]
If this **variabl**e distance is *r*, ...

Перемешивание
Stirring is continued during the course of reaction.

Перемешивать [*см.* **Тщательно перемешаны**].

Перемешивать мешалкой
The solution **is agitated by a stirrer.**

Перемешиваться
The solution **is** mechanically **stirred** (*or* **agitated**).

Перемешивая
Add calcium carbonate to dilute hydrochloric acid, **with stirring.**
With stirring, add dilute sulphuric till ...

Перемещаться
The electron can now **transfer to** the point *C'* without any change in energy.

Перемещаться в наклонное положение
The plane **moves into an inclined position.**

Перемножать друг на друга
How many 2's **should be multiplied together** to obtain ...

Перенесение на [*см.* **Обобщение на**].

Перенесёмся назад к
Now **let us move back in time to** the ancient Egyptians.

Перенести [*см. тж.* **Отложить до**]
The lasing material **can survive** (*or* **withstand**) the increases in energy without damage.

Переносимый насекомыми
This is **an insect-transmitted** disease.

Переносить [*см.* **Выдерживать**].

Переносить болезни
Mites **transmit** innumerable **diseases.**

Переносить в ... часть уравнения
The directly measurable quantities **are rearranged to the left side of the equation.**

Переносить на I [*см. тж.* **Распространять на**]
The analogy between positronium and quarkonium **can be extended to** one additional phenomenon.

Переносить на II
Transfer two drops of solution **to** each disk.

Переносить обсуждение
We **reserve** the more complex molecules **for** later sections.

Переносить тепло
A considerable amount of **heat must be transferred** (*or* **transported**).

Переносить энергию
The energy that **can be transferred** (*or* **transported**) **to** the mechanical reservoir ...

Переноситься
For this reason discussion of ... **is deferred for** a later section.

Переноситься в другой мир
We can use these pictures **to transport ourselves into new worlds.**

Переносчик болезней
Ticks are the most important **vectors of disease to** domestic animals.

Переоборудовать
The machine **is** now **being engineered to accommodate** 50-ton heats.
The plant **has been (completely) retooled** (*or* **re-equipped**) **with** new furnaces.

Переосмысливаться [*см.* **Термин переосмыслился**].

Переоценивать [*см.* **Нельзя переоценить**].

Перепад давления на
To minimize the magnitude of **the differential in pressure** (*or* **pressure drop,** *or* **pressure differential,** *or* **pressure difference**) **across** the valve, ...

Перепад напряжения [*см.* **Разность потенциалов**].

Перепад температуры [*см.* **Разность температур**].

Перепад температуры на граничном слое
The temperature difference across the boundary layer.

Переплетающиеся
The DNA molecule consists of two **intertwined** helical chains of many nucleotides (*biol.*).

Переполнен [*см.* **Битком набит**].

Перепроверять
To ensure against error, there is a TV camera at each truck loading point, so that the clerk **can double check.**

Перерабатываться
The shale **may be** mined and **processed** in surface plants.

Переработка
The processing of food, chemicals, plastics and petroleum ...

Пересекать
The time required for the flame front **to cross** the combustion space ...
This tangent **cuts** (*or* **intersects**) the axis at the point Q.
The current in the rotor of an induction motor is induced as the rotor conductors **cut** lines of magnetic flux created by the stator.
If the bisector does not **meet** DE, they are parallel.
A laser beam **intersects** a beam of sodium atoms from ...

Пересекать на продолжении
EF and HK are not parallel, therefore they **will meet if produced.**

Пересекать по линии
The surface **intersects** adjacent surfaces **in** straight **lines.**

Пересекаться
When power and telephone circuits **cross each other, ...**
The lines **meet** (*or* **intersect,** *or* **cross**).

Пересекаться в точке
The two lines **meet** (*or* **intersect**) **at point** B.

Пересекаться под углом
The Ox''-axis and the fluid velocity q **intersect at the** Mach **angle** a.

Пересечение [*см.* **До пересечения с, Линия пересечения, На пересечении**].

Перескакивать с орбиты на орбиту
The electron can gain or lose energy only by **jumping from one** allowed **orbit to another.**

Перескочить через запрещённую зону
The manner in which increasing temperature causes more electrons **to leap up the energy gap** between bands can be understood by considering ...

Пересматривать свои взгляды
In that case astrophysicists **will have to rethink matters** [*or* **revise** (*or* **reconsider**) **their views**].

Пересматриваться
The sea has long been taken to be a stagnant pool, but today this view **is giving way.**
These concepts **are** currently **undergoing revision** (*or* **are being revised**).

Переставать
Beyond a certain point elastic deformation **ceases to** obey (*or* **no longer** obeys) Hooke's law.
The particles **cease to move.**

Переставать быть справедливым
Under these conditions the law **ceases to be true.**

Переставлять
Reset the decimal point so that there is a single digit to its left (*e.g.* 00004.4).

Переставлять местами
The transpose *A'* of the matrix *A* is obtained **by interchanging** rows and columns.

Перестановка
Surfaces up to 14 ft high can be milled without **repositioning** the part.

Перестановка резца между операциями
The turret can be used for permanent mounting to reduce **tool setup from job to job.**

Перестать пользоваться популярностью
The theory soon **fell from favour** (*or* **fell into disfavour**).

Перестать поступать
The clamps are operated by hydraulic arrangements, and they are not released if air **fails** while machining is in progress.

Перестать существовать
An adult knows that the object is still there, that it **has** not **ceased to exist.**

Перестраиваться
The atoms **rearrange themselves** at the Curie temperature.

Перестройка
The changes within the hemoglobin subunit cause **a realignment of** the subunits **with respect to one another.**

Пересчёт с ... на
A list of **conversions from** English **to** metric units ...

Пересчитывать с ... на
If you wish **to convert from** metric **to** English units, ...

Перефразировать
The argument **can be restated in a different way.**

Переход I [*см. тж.* **При переходе к бóльшим и бóльшим значениям**]
The transfer of an electron **from** the lowest level **to** the next level ...
The transition of an electron **from** one orbit **to** another ...

Переход II [*см. тж.* **Переключение**]
A change to processes that are easier to mechanize ...
The change-over from one fuel **to** the other ...
A change-over to circumferential welding merely necessitates the loosening of ...
Conversion to investment casting permitted strict tolerances to be held.
The retooling **to convert to** die casting ...
The major **swing to** turbojet aircraft occurred in late 1958.
The difficulty was corrected **by changing** (*or* **switching**) **to** another suitable oil which did not foam.
The shortage of skilled labour is forcing **the switch to** automated systems.
By going to much finer and more closely-sized powder particles, the porosity was greatly reduced.

Переход на
This problem can be circumvented **by going** (*or* **changing**) **to** a digital system.

Переход от ... к ...
A method has been obtained for **going from** a crystal structure **to** a calculated X-ray pattern.

Переходить I
These materials **transfer to** the fibre **from** a water suspension.
This electron may be caused **to pass into** a larger orbit.
The interstitial atoms **leave** their positions **for** the regular ones.

Переходить II
To change from one fuel **to** the other, it is only necessary to manipulate the fuel control valve.
To convert to die-casting, we had to reequip the plant.

Переходить в I [*см. тж.* **Постепенно переходить в**]
When heating is continued beyond 1403°C the gamma iron **changes** (*or* **converts,** *or* **transforms**) **to** delta iron.

As abundance of phenocrystals increases, the rocks **pass into** andesite porphyry.
Here, red light **grades into** infrared radiation.
Under a linear transformation the points z_1, z_2, z_3 **go over into** distinct points w_1, w_2, w_3, and z **goes into** w.

Переходить в II [*см. тж.* **Сливаться с**]
The mountainous terrain **gives way to** a lowland area.
The lateral bending movements **give way to** a more complicated cycle of motions (*biol.*).

Переходить в III
The hot material **switches to** a less dense form.

Переходить в избыток
When potassium cyanide **passes into excess, ...**

Переходить в раствор
Iron **goes** (*or* **passes**) **into solution as** ferrous sulphate.

Переходить в ... состояние
The layer of soft clay **turned** (*or* **transformed**) **into a** near-liquid **state.**

Переходить к [*см. тж.* **Затем переходим к, Приступать к**]
We **are coming (now) to** the question of heating.
As one **goes to** higher and higher bases, numbers become shorter and shorter.
If we **pass on to** equations of the second degree, ...
We **(now) turn (our attention) to (the discussion of)** the element hydrogen.

Переходить к ... и обратно
Anyone who knows fourth-grade arithmetic **can switch back and forth between** ordinary numbers **and** two-based numbers.

Переходить на
At this speed it is advantageous **to shift to** the lighter-weight turboprops.

Переходить на метрическую систему
Most British scientists **have turned to the metric system (of measurement)** (*or* **have gone metric**).

Переходить от ... к
Let us (now) turn from the PVT behaviour of gases **to** two properties of a different type.
Now we must see how we can **go from** measurable properties of the solution **to** quantities attributable to the components.

Переходить с ... на
If we **switched from** a ten-based system **to** an eight-base system, ...
To change over the present telephone system **to** the new switching system, ...

Переходная область
In **the transition region,** a nearly circular fibre starts to ...

Переходная стадия между
Heavier welding is in **the transition stage between** development **and** application.

Переходя к
Going to the next number, we can say that ...

Перечисленные
The three kinds of geosynclines **listed** here are associated with ...

Перечисленные выше [*см.* **Вышеперечисленные**].

Перечислены
The uses of coal tar **are outlined** in Table 2.
The biological properties of this enzyme **are listed** (*or* **set out,** *or* **enumerated**) below.

Перечислены ниже
The methods that are most often used for preparing amines **follow: ...**

Перечислять
We need not **list** all the disciplines.

Период [*см. тж.* **В период, В рассматриваемый период, В течение длительного времени, Время, За период, Продолжительное время**]
The neutrons are delayed **for intervals** ranging from a fraction of a second to more than a minute.

Период вращения Земли
The terrestrial rotation period (*or* **The Earth's rotation period**).

Период времени [*см. тж.* **На различные периоды времени**]
In such **a span** (*or* **length**) **of time** many transformations could have taken place.
The period of time over (*or* **during**) **which** energy can be accumulated as ... is limited.

These rocks were deposited **during the** same **period** (*or* **time interval**).

Период хранения
Miniature mercury cells with **a** long **shelf life** can be used to advantage.

Периодически [*см. тж.* **От времени до времени**]
Vehicles should be cleaned **at regular intervals.**

Перпендикулярно к
The set of electrodes is located **at right angles to** the magnetic field.
The load carried by the beams acts **transversely to** the principal axis of the beams.
Position the autocollimator **square** [*or* **perpendicular(ly)**, *or* **normally**] **to** the reflecting surface.
The jets **are directed across** the line of sight.

Перпендикулярный к
The lines of force **are normal** (*or* **perpendicular**) **to** the surface of the rotor.
The flange **must be** properly lined up and **square with** the pipe axis.

Персонал [*см.* **Без обслуживающего персонала**].

Перспектива [*см. тж.* **В перспективе имеется**]
The prospects for (*or* **of**) building such a device depend on ...
The outlook for the world's fuel supplies is rather gloomy.

Перспективные потребности в
To explore their **potential needs for** satellite communications, ...

Перспективный [*см. тж.* **Быть весьма перспективным, Быть перспективным, Весьма перспективный**]
Lasers are a **promising** source **for** fluorescence excitation.
This process appears **to have considerable promise.**
For these areas titanium **holds much promise.**
Such processes **hold the greatest promise for** increased acetylene yields.
Radiation energy **offers promise as** a processing tool.
These steels **show promise for** aircraft.

Перспективный для применения в области
These materials **are candidates for** computer technology.

Перфорировать
These data **are punched into** computer input cards.

Пескоструйная обработка [*см.* **Подвергать пескоструйной обработке**].

Пескоструйный аппарат [*см.* **Очищать пескоструйным аппаратом**].

Петля [*см.* **На петлях**].

Печать [*см.* **В печати**].

Пешеходы и транспорт [*см.* **Движение транспорта и пешеходов**].

Писать прописными (заглавными) буквами
The terms Q and W **are written with uppercase letters.**

Писать строчными (маленькими) буквами
The terms q and w **are written with lowercase letters.**

Питательное вещество
The circulatory system carries **nutritive materials** to the organs and tissues of the body.

Питательный для
Most clovers **are nutritious to** livestock.

Питать
Such cables **could feed power to** transformers.

Питаться
Abalones **feed on** algae (*or* **use** algae **for food**).
These insects **are nurtured** upon plant **foods.**
The field of the generator **is fed from** the exciter.
The supply of nutrients **on** which plants **feed ...**
The larvae **live on** phytoplankton.

Питаться от
The field winding of the motor **is energized from** a source ...

The solar cells **draw current from** the battery.
The indicator **is operated from** a dry battery.
This radio equipment **is powered by** batteries.
The driving motor **takes its current from** the ship's main supply.

Питаться путём
Most plants **nourish themselves by** photosynthesis.

Питаться растениями
The majority of beetles **are plant feeders.**

Питающий
The **feed** gas stream flowed at the rate of 1.85 cm^3.

Питающийся от
An a-c **line-operated** unit ...
A **battery-operated** radio set ...

Питающийся растениями
Plant-feeding (*or* **-eating**) mites (*or* Mites **feeding on plants**) destroy billions of dollars worth of ...

Питтинг
A **pitted** surface ...

Пища [*см.* **Употреблять в пищу**].

Пища для размышлений
We have presented some new ideas as **"food for thought" on** such topics as ...

Плавать
Vessels **plying** (*or* **sailing**) between this country and East ...

Плавиться под вакуумом
These ball bearings **are vacuum melted.**

Плавная работа
These roller bearings give **smooth running.**

Плавно [*см.* **Постепенно**].

Плавно соединяться
The straight line and the curve join **smoothly.**

Плавное снижение
The smooth fall of intensity ...

Плазма, генерируемая лазером
To obtain **laser-generated plasmas** for thermonuclear research, ...

Пламенем
Hydrogen burns **with a** very hot **flame.**

Пламенная резка
The plate **is flame cut** to the required shape.

План [*см.* **В историческом плане, В плане, Выдвигать на первый план, Выдвигать план, Выполнять план, Досрочно выполнять план, Крупным планом, На заднем плане, На переднем плане**].

Планета [*см.* **Исследование планет, Наука о планетах**].

Планирование [*см. тж.* **При планировании опыта**]
This method of **scheduling** (*or* **planning**) is called ...

Планировать [*см. тж.* **Запланирован как**]
A 30% increase **was projected for** 1987.
Installation of the equipment **was scheduled for** June.
The unit **is scheduled for** operation in March.
Tests **are scheduled to** start next year.
Delivery of the equipment **is slated to** begin in September.

Планируемый [*см. тж.* **Намеченный**]
During the period of **projected** use ...
Many institutes would participate in the design and development of the **proposed** observatory.

Плоскость [*см.* **На плоскости**].

Плотина [*см.* **Перекрывать плотиной**].

Плотно затыкать пробкой
The end of the tube **is tightly stoppered.**

Плотно упакованы
In condensed phases metallic atoms **are packed closely together** (*or* **closely packed**).

Плотное прилегание
Fixtures for forming adhesive joints must be designed to ensure **intimate mating of** the bonding surfaces.

Плотный
An **air-tight** joint.
Valves should **be** kept **leak free.**

Плохо вентилируемый
Ill-ventilated [*or* **Poorly** (*or* **Inadequately**) **ventilated**] rooms ...

Плохо изучен [*см. тж.* **Мало изучен**]
The effects of microwave radiation on biological systems **are poorly understood.**

Плохо подогнан
The patient's dentures **were ill fitting** and caused him pain.

Плохо проводить (ток)
Some ionic solids **show weak conductivity** when ...

Плохо растворяющийся
A **sparingly** (*or* **poorly**) **soluble** compound.

Плохо сконструированный [*см.* **Неправильно сконструированный**].

Плохо согласовываться с [*см.* **Довольно плохо согласуется с**].

Плохо сохраняться
Hydrogen peroxide solution **keeps badly** in a glass bottle with a rough inner surface.

Плохое влияние (*или* **действие**) **на**
Increasing boiling point elevation **has a detrimental** (*or* **adverse,** *or* **ill,** *or* **untoward**) **effect on** the product rate.

Плохое качество
The inferior (*or* **poor**) **quality of** these mirrors ...

Плохой вариант [*см.* **Неудачный вариант**].

Плохой урожай [*см.* **Неурожай**].

Площадь [*см. тж.* **Занимать площадь, На площади, Производственная площадь**]
The flux density at any point in a magnetic field is the flux passing through **an area of** one square centimetre.

Площадь цеха
The furnaces occupy only 5.5 × 100 feet of **floor space.**

Плюс-минус
This value may be well in error by about 30 degrees **either way.**
Accuracies better than **plus or minus** 50 ft ...
The value found was 299,895 **plus or minus** 30.

Пневматический
Stepping motion is applied to the conveyor by means of an **air-operated** (*or* **pneumatic**) mechanism.

По [*см. тж.* **Аналогичен по, В соответствии с, Вычислять по, Дифференцировать по, Задача по акустике, Инструкция по установке, Интеграл по, Исследование, Калибровать по, Линейный по, Определять по, Опыт по, Отличаться по, Подсчитывать по, Предсказывать, Проверять по, Производная по, Распределение по, Скользить по, Степенной ряд по, Усреднять по, Циркулировать по**]
The molecular cloud is known only **by** its designation in the catalogue.
The fluxes were calculated **from** the known thermal flux.
The pressure was determined **from** (*or* **by**) the weight of steam and ...
The thickness of the layer was measured **from** the photograph.
This effect might have been predicted **from** the change in the viscosity of ...
The input and feed-back signals must be equal **in** magnitude and in phase.
Crystallized alumina is excelled **in** hardness only by diamond and carborundum.
The weights differ only **in** sign.
The slider moves **over** a series of contacts.
The measured voltage is fed to the amplifier **via** a coaxial cable and a pair of twisted leads.
The file has today been completely standardized **as to** shape, grade of teeth and weight.
Adhesives are also classified **by** physical form.
The refractive index is measured **by** deflection of the light source.
Visual binary stars can be recognized **by** their orbital motion.
Identification **by** colour is not always reliable.

По (*фрезе и т.п. – на чертеже*)
Radius **to suit** cutter.

По амплитуде [*см.* **Модулированный по амплитуде**].

По аналогии
By analogy, we may assume that ...

По аналогии с
By analogy with Eq. (1-5) we can write, ...

По ... в каждом ряду
Commercial cement is stored in eight storage silos arranged **in two rows of four each.**

По величине [*см. тж.* **Изменяться по величине**]
In dc circuits the voltages and currents are constant **in magnitude.**

По весу [*см. тж.* **Весовой процент**]
Silicon makes up about 1/4 of the rock **by weight.**

По ветру
A balloon may float freely in the air **with the wind.**

По внешнему виду [*см. тж.* **Не отличаться по внешнему виду от**]
Ilmenite resembles magnetite **in (outward) appearance.**

По возможности
The required compression symmetry is achieved by irradiating the pellet **as** uniformly **as possible** (*or* **practical**) with multiple laser beams.
It is good practice to use **the** shortest **possible** connecting tubing.
It is desirable, **where possible,** to avoid the use of such oils.
In general fabricating practice, the use of large lathes is avoided, **wherever possible.**

По возрасту
In age, the blue stone approaches 500 million years.

По вопросу о [*см. тж.* **Относительно, По поводу**]
Several studies **on** the infrared dichroism of oriented cellulose have been made.

По вполне понятной причине [*см.* **По понятной причине**].

По всей вероятности [*см. тж.* **Вероятнее всего**]
In all likelihood (*or* **probability**), this is not so, particularly near a tube wall.
Most likely the truth lies between the two opinions.

По всей длине
The roof sprays consist of three rows of 14 nozzles disposed **along the (whole) length of** the building.
To stiffen the floor, steel angles are welded **along its full length.**
The strips run **the entire length of** the frame.
Electrons can travel **the full length of** the tube.
A canal 200 ft long runs **(all along) the length of** the building.
The flange should be brushed **over its entire length.**
Protection must be provided **through the whole length of** the pipe.
The heating current must be chosen to give correct heat distribution **throughout the length of** the rivet in a reasonable time.

По всей толще
To ensure even pressure **across the whole width of ...**

По всей шкале
The present instrument is linear in response with respect to load to within 2.5%, **over the whole scale.**

По всему [*см. тж.* **Во всём**]
The emission is uniform **throughout** the layer.
Mechanical ventilation is installed **throughout** the accommodation.
The conduction electrons are spread **over** the metal.
The pressure is maintained equally **all along** the line.

По всему диаметру колонки
The pressure is uniform **across the diameter** (*or* **section**) **of the column** (*or* **across the column**).

По всему контуру (*эл.*)
Over the entire circuit (*or* **Throughout the circuit**).

По всему организму
Haemoglobin has the function of distributing oxygen **round the human body.**

По высоте [*см. тж.* **Распределение по высоте**]
The liquid maintains a nearly uniform concentration **from top to bottom** [*or* **throughout (the height of)** the column].

To provide uniform application of the coating materials **along the full vertical extent of** the object, ...

По высоте (длине *и т.п.*)
The mass velocities vary considerably **through** the tower.

По вышеуказанным причинам
The first elements of each group cannot, **for the reasons given above,** attain these oxidation numbers.

По глубине
These zones range **in depth** from 10,700 to 10,800 ft.
The distribution of the alloying elements **in depth** can be adjusted by ...

По границам зёрен
The formation of a second phase **along the grain boundaries ...**
Accumulation of hydrogen **at grain boundaries ...**
The specimen had a layer of a second phase **on the grain boundaries.**

По графику
The integration is performed **from a plot of** C_p versus *ln I.*

По данным [*см. тж.* **Воспроизводить по данным**]
The existence of modification systems has been suggested **on evidence** derived from ...

По два *и т.п.* [*см.* **Взятые по два**].

По диаметру
The rings are made **to the** new **diameter.**

По длине I [*см. тж.* **По высоте**]
Each plate is bent **lengthwise.**
The web may be perforated **lengthwise,** similar to postage stamps.
There are 19 supports **along (the length of)** the upper panel jig.

По длине *и т.п.* **II**
The Rio Grande **is the third longest** river in the U.S.

По догадке
The ancient scientists did not know much about body systems, except **through conjecture.**

По дуге
The lever can be moved **in an arc,** and the boring tool consequently moves **through an arc,** but through one half of the distance.

По его словам
He visited the laboratory, where **as he put it** the necessary conditions appeared to exist.

По его собственному признанию
Charles Darwin **by his own admission** liked to think of himself as a geologist.

По желанию
Additional machines may require additional memory capacity in the computer system, which can be added **as an option.**
The height of the working position can be varied **to suit** the operator.
The basic pattern of fracture can be produced **at will** by establishing appropriate experimental conditions.

По желанию заказчика
With this unit, there is a basic form and **optional** variations can be made.

По заказу [*см. тж.* **Выполнять на заказ**]
Parts which are not available from stock can be produced **to order.**

По закону
From Kirchhoff's **law** we have the formula: ...

По замыслу [*см.* **По идее**].

По запаху
We may detect some gaseous molecules **by odour.**

По заявке
Prices can be supplied **on application.**
Other head styles can be furnished **on request.**

По идее I
The simplest **in principle,** and the first to be applied to meteorites, is the uranium-helium method.

По идее II
Conceptually, the method is the modal analogue of the ray analysis for ...

По имени [*см.* **Называть именем**].

По индивидуальному заказу
Assembly of **custom-built** apparatus is usually by hand.

По инициативе [*см.* **Предприниматься по инициативе**].

По истечении некоторого времени
After a lapse of time the relative abundance of lead^{206} will be greater than ...
As time passes the pressure and volume ratios are unchanged, but radioactivity is detected in both the liquid and vapour phases.

По какой-либо (*или* **той или иной**) **причине**
If **for some reason** (*or* **other**) (*or* **for whatever reason**) a non-spherical detonation front is formed, ...

По капле
Water is added **drop by drop** (*or* **dropwise**) to the solution.

По касательной к
A sluice supplied large quantities of water **at a tangent to** the wheel.

По команде
The thrust cannot be altered **on command** during flight.

По компасу [*см.* **Передвигаться по компасу**].

По конвейеру
Fresh cucumber pickle slices go **by conveyor** to the hand-pack filler.

По конструкции
The machine is simple **in construction** (*or* **design**).

По которому
The mechanism **whereby** (*or* **by which**) the pallets are accelerated is not yet completely understood.

По крайней мере
Recombination is reduced by **at least** three orders of magnitude.

По кругу (эллипсу) [*см. тж.* **Двигаться по кругу**]
The thrust bearing is made up of many tilting pads located **in a circular position** (*or* **in a circle**) (*or* **circularly positioned** tilting pads).
The point travels **around a circle.**
The assembly turns **in a circle.**

По лицензии
They make use of the machines **under licenses** from the manufacturers.

По массе
Sea water contains about 0.13 percent of magnesium **by mass.**

По меньшей мере I [*см. тж.* **Не менее, По крайней мере**]
At least some asteroids were heated up to a temperature of ...

По меньшей мере II
The notion of a triangle with an infinitely small base is elusive, **to say the least.**

По мере
The pressure is seen to rise **as** hydrogen dissolves.

По мере возможности [*см. тж.* **Насколько возможно**]
Each commodity has its own specific storage condition which, **so far as is practicable** (*or* **as far as possible**), should be strictly adhered to.
The absorption should be reduced **as much as possible.**

По мере износа
Bushing materials tend to lose accuracy further **as they wear.**

По мере использования
The scrubbing medium becomes diluted and less effective **with use.**

По мере необходимости
Adjust the blade up or down, **as (may be) necessary.**
These amalgams are prepared by the dentist **as needed.**
These are tanks into which oil is transferred **as needed** from the main storage tanks.
The pump raises and lowers its speed of operation **as required.**

По мере поступления информации
As new information becomes available the magnitude of geothermal energy resources is beginning to be appreciated.

По мере приближения к
As the surface **is approached,** the field lines depart from a simple dipole configuration.

По мере создания
As more powerful lasers **are developed** the detection limits should be improved even further.

По мере того как
As the steam pressure **increases** (*or* **is increased**), the reflector height decreases.

По мере того, как глубже изучается
As one-dimensional systems **come to be better understood, ...**

По мере увеличения [*см.* **По мере того как**].

По мере удаления от
As the material **moves (farther and farther) away from** (*or* **As ... recedes from**) the centre of ...

По мере ускорения или замедления
The strip thickness varies **as** the mill **is accelerated or decelerated**.

По методике
The relative amounts of the two phases can be calculated **by the** following **procedure.**

По методу [*см. тж.* **Методом, Осуществляться по методу**]
In (*or* **With**) another **method,** antimony (III) sulphide is first roasted in air.

По механизму
Addition of HBr to alkenes may proceed **by a** free-radical **mechanism.**
Ammonia molecules add to other molecules or ions **through the mechanism of** covalent-bond formation.

По мнению [*см. тж.* **С точки зрения**]
The very low concentrations on the Earth represent **in my view** (*or* **opinion**) the maximum retention of volatiles by the terrestrial rocks.

По мнению автора
It is the author's opinion that ...

По названию
This is called the Mediterranean forest **after** the area where it was first studied.

По направлению [*см.* **Идти по направлению**].

По направлению к полюсу (экватору)
Warm water moves **poleward,** and cool water moves **equatorward.**

По нашему мнению
It is our opinion that (*or* **In our opinion**) they should ...

По неизвестным нам причинам
For reasons unknown (to us) ...

По не совсем понятным причинам
For reasons not well understood, unusually large quantities of iron oxides were brought to the seafloor.

По некоторым причинам
For some reason there are more available states corresponding to B.

По необходимости [*см. тж.* **В силу необходимости**]
Since we are a cold-metal shop, we **of necessity** use a large amount of cast iron.

По нескольку капель
Add silver nitrate, **a few drops at a time.**

По ... нормам
The ancient methods of handling fractions were not very efficient **by** our **standards.**

По обе стороны [*см. тж.* **Расположенные по обе стороны**]
With the straightedge placed along this line, make pencil marks at 60 and 120 units **each way from** the centre.
The cells lie **on each side of** the midline.
The potential energy rises parabolically **on either side of** the equilibrium position.

По общему мнению
It is generally agreed that the colours seen on the surface of the satellite are consistent with ...

По общему признанию
The screen **is acknowledged to** be among (*or* **is recognized to** be one of) the most efficient devices available.

По общему согласию
5,570 years is the "accepted value" **by common agreement.**

По объёму
By volume, these layers make up 3 percent of the continental crust.

По обычаю [*см. тж.* **По традиции**]
The solvent term is **by convention** omitted.

По одному [*см. тж.* **Один за другим**]
Virtual gluons can be emitted **singly.**
The investigator can go on to test various cell components **one at a time** (*or* **one by one**) to determine just which are affected by the hormone.

По одному или партиями
Workpieces can be suspended from hooks or loaded into fixtures **singly or in multiples.**

По окончании
With these machining operations **completed,** the transfer arm was traversed away from the secondary turret.
After completing the check, connect the test coil and ...
On completion of the injection sequence, the guard is opened and the dies are separated.
After completion of the working stroke ...
By the time the end of the wave is formed **at the completion of** the oscillation, ...
At the close (*or* **conclusion**) **of** synthesis, long continuous DNA molecules are the end product.

По определению
The speed ratio of a belt drive is, **by definition,** the ratio of the angular speed of ...
p-Aminophenol reacts with both acids and bases, and is therefore amphoteric **by definition.**

По опыту
We know **from experience** that ...

По орбите [*см. тж.* **Двигаться по орбите, Полёт по орбите**]
The space station continually travels **in an orbit** about the Earth.
The vehicle was travelling **on** the Earth's **orbit.**

По оси [*см. тж.* **Откладывать на** (*или* **по**) **оси**]
This causes measurable expansion **along the** *c* **axis.**

По основанию [*см.* **Логарифм числа по основанию**].

По отношению к [*см. тж.* **Вогнутый по отношению к, Инертный по отношению к, Относительно, Реактивный по отношению к**]
Substituents **para to** the displaced group provide ...
This result allowed determination of the apparent velocity of any small section of the wave **in reference to** the velocity of the stable section.
The skip is positioned at the correct loading point **in relation to** the chute.
The placement of the transducer **relative to** the site to be irradiated ...
Specific gravity **relative to** air ...
The fluid is at rest **relative to** a contact discontinuity.
The voltages are **with reference to** the chassis.
The instrument indicates the tilt of the aircraft **with reference to** the horizon.
The position of the film curve **with relation to** the curves for component parts may be explained by the fact that ...
Care should be taken to set the throttle valve in the correct position **with** (*or* **in**) **respect to** the pressure governor spindle.
If the solution is now made 0.2 *M* **with respect to** sodium chloride, ...
The metal is positively charged **with respect to** the solution.

По оценкам [*см.* **По приближённым оценкам**].

По очереди [*см. тж.* **Один за другим, Поочерёдно**]
There are 130 lines which must make use of this network **in turn.**

По памяти
Answer **from memory.**

По периметру
Four recording heads are mounted **around the periphery** (*or* **circumference**) of a drum.
Wall panels have been installed **along the perimeter of** each floor.

По поверхности [*см. тж.* **Двигаться по поверхности**]
Mass transfer **over the** entire plate **surface** is observed.

По поводу [*см. тж.* **В отношении, Относительно**]
There was much speculation **as to** the origin of ...

По поводу того
Before a conclusion can be reached **on whether or not** this province has always been a part of ...

По понятной причине
Those deposits have not been explored, and **for good reason.**

По порядку
If you number the carbon atoms of the hexagon **in order,** then ...

По порядку важности это:
At present the water existing on the Earth is distributed in three separate reservoirs; **in order of importance they are** the oceans, the continents and the atmosphere.

По последним измерениям
The equatorial diameter of Neptune is about 28,000 miles **at latest measurement.**

По последним подсчётам
A considerable number of gene loci (79 **at the last count**) have now been definitely assigned to the X chromosome.

По построению
By the construction of ψ, any element is ...

По праву [*см.* **Завоёвывать принадлежащее ему по праву место**].

По приближённым оценкам
Most large reservoirs behind big dams have an **estimated** useful life of a century or two.

По приблизительным подсчётам
An **estimated** 455,000 cu km of water evaporates annually from the ocean surface.

По прибытии на
On arrival at the roasting plant, coffee beans are blended to achieve ...

По привычке
Many of the trivial terms are still used **through habit.**

По принципу
These fields are constructed **on the model of** electromagnetism.
The device operates **on the** same **principle** as the electron-positron rings.
By the same **token,** for any operation that can be applied to a pair of operands there is a corresponding ...

По причине [*см. тж.* **Благодаря, В результате, Ввиду, Вследствие, Из-за**]
This assumption can be dismissed **on** two **counts.**
For this **reason** a rapid-scan spectrometer is essential.
The destruction of the insulation **by reason of** static discharges ...

По причине, не зависящей от
In some cases random error occurs **for reasons beyond the control of** the experimenter.

По программе [*см.* **Действовать в соответствии с программой, Изменяться в соответствии с программой**].

По проектам
We build such machines **to** our **designs.**

По протяжённости
A plane wave is infinite **in extent.**

По прошествии ... лет
When ten **years have elapsed** (*or* **After a lapse of** ten **years**) the fuel cost will ...

По прошествии некоторого времени [*см.* **По истечении некоторого времени**].

По прямой [*см. тж.* **Двигаться по прямой, Перегибаться по прямой**]
The particle moves **as a crow flies** (*col.*).
The chain pitch is measured **on a straight line** between the centres of adjacent pins.
The satellite model was moving **in a straight line** over a stationary Earth.
The particle moves **in** (*or* **along**) **a straight line.**

По радиусу [*см. тж.* **Загибать по радиусу, Расстояние по радиусу**]
Each set is made up of six valves **arranged on a radius** round the centre.

По различным причинам [*см.* **По разным причинам**].

По размерам I
Air classifiers are used to separate particles **by size.**
The particles differ **in size.**
The particles are sorted out **by sizes.**

По размерам II
The grooves are machined **to the dimensions** given in Fig. 3.

По размеру
The tubes are cut **to length.**
The ram is accurately machined and ground **to size.**
The material is drilled and punched **to suit the size of** the rivet.

По разному
The coat is constructed of identical molecules, **variously** called subunits or capsomers.

По разным причинам
For a variety of reasons (*or* **For various reasons**), this involved a number of invalid assumptions.

По распространённости
Barium is eighteenth **in abundance** in the Earth's crust.
The ninth **most abundant** element is titanium.

По реакции [*см. тж.* **Путём реакции**]
The free arsenic sublimes **according to** (*or* **in accordance with**) **the reaction** 4FeAsS + ...
This compound was obtained **by the** Grignard **reaction.**

По ряду причин
This terminology can be confusing **for a number** (*or* **a variety,** *or* **several,** *or* **a diversity**) **of reasons.**

По ряду пунктов
Although the fission hypothesis seems satisfactory **on a number of counts,** there are strong objections.

По самым скромным подсчётам
By the most conservative estimate, continental crust has existed for ...

По своей конструкции
The connectors are coaxial **in construction** (*or* **design**).

По своей массе
Jupiter is far larger **in mass** than the Moon is.

По своей природе [*см. тж.* **По своему характеру**]
This situation is strongly contrasted with that in nuclear fission, which **by its (very) nature** must produce ...
The charge-coupled device is basically analogous **in nature.**
The generation of turbulence is random **in nature** (*or* **in character**).
In that case you might better consider some of the newer controllers, which **inherently** possess a high degree of flexibility.
Row *B* **by its nature** cannot distort ...
Optical processors are **inherently** two-dimensional and parallel.

По своей структуре
Both belts are homogeneous **in structure** (*or* **structurally**).

По своей функции
This form of mRNA is not really messenger **in function** but may play some other role in the cell (*biol.*).

По своему желанию
They applied patterns of light to the silicon film and changed its conductivity **at will.**

По своему составу
These rocks are **compositionally** equivalent to the familiar rock types.

По своему характеру [*см. тж.* **По своей природе**]
Field effect transistors are more similar **in concept(ion)** to the thermionic valve than bipolar transistors.
The proximate analysis is empirical **in character.**
The most direct and **conceptually** simple way to describe ...

По своим масштабам
The device is similar to the ISR in conception but much larger **in scale.**

По свойствам и составу
In properties and composition the *A-31* system is quite similar to ...

По сезонам [*см.* **Распределение по сезонам**].

По системе
For small units without a circulatory lubricating system, the oil is often treated **on the** batch **system.**

По склону [*см.* **Вниз по склону, Стекать по склону**].

По скорости [*см.* **Взвешенный по скорости**].

По скромной оценке
According to a conservative estimate, ...

По совпадению
The Sun has an overall dipole field of about one gauss; **by coincidence** this is about the same as the Earth's field.

По современным нормам (*или* **понятиям**) [*см. тж.* **Согласно современным взглядам**]
The first computers were crude and very expensive **by today's** (*or* **present**) **standards.**

По соображениям
Gamma sources will be preferred **for** technical **reasons.**
For given conditions three-bladed propellers are better **from considerations of** efficiency than four-bladed ones.
From technical **considerations ...**

По соображениям безопасности
For safety reasons (*or* **For reasons of safety**), ...

По составу
The vapour is uniform **in composition.**
The standards are similar **in composition.**

По состоянию на
Data are **as of** October 1, 1983.

По спектру
The photomultiplier moves **across the spectrum.**

По сравнению с [*см. тж.* **Преимущество по сравнению с ...**]
The asteroid would then have a period of revolution of about six years **as compared with** (*or* **to**) Jupiter's period of twelve years.
The hopper machine gives a substantial increase in loading rate **as against** the standard loader.
These fuels are scarce **(as) compared to** (*or* **with**) coal.
The first part outlines the distinctive characteristics of nuclear **as opposed to** conventional fuel.
Compared to conventional enamels, low-temperature enamels have proper resistance to ...
A reduction in width of the heads **from** standard can produce an increase in noise level.
The variations are even smaller **in** (*or* **by**) **comparison with** (*or* **to**) **...**
Improvements **on** the original torches concern new types of heat elements.
Roof bolts have several advantages **over** other methods of roof support.
This is a very elaborate receiver greatly improved **over ...**
Relative to chemical methods of analysis, chromatographic methods have many unique features.
Even **by comparison with** a white dwarf a neutron star is tiny.
The heat loss through the wall of the oven will be small **in relation to** the energy-delivery capability of the final control elements.
When compared to the copper wire in a cable, the cellular core is a poor conductor.
This volume is small **when compared to** the volume in cans.

По сравнению с ... выглядит миниатюрно
The hypothetical shell of planetoids **dwarfs** the known Solar System (*известная Солнечная система выглядит миниатюрно ...*).

По сравнению с ним
The four inner planets differ greatly from the four outer planets, which are giants **by** (*or* **in**) **comparison.**

По сути дела [*см. тж.* **В принципе, По существу, Фактически**]
Inorganic chemistry is **properly** a study of ...

По существу [*см. тж.* **В основном, В принципе, Фактически**]
This method is **conceptually** identical with the one described in ...

At that time **essentially** nothing was known about ...
The physics of Rydberg atoms is **essentially** the physics of hydrogen.
Composite propellants are **essentially** mixtures of an inorganic oxidizer and a fuel.
In essence (*or* **In substance**), bacterial metabolism is a model from which the results are likely to be applicable to plants and animals.
The adaptive principle consists **in essence** of three things: ...
A demonstration of an optical bottle in air would **in essence** be a demonstration of optical levitation.
The radiation from the explosion zone is **substantially** black body radiation.

По существу представляет собой
This equipment **amounts to** a closed-circuit feedback system.

По существующей шкале
The accepted atomic weight of oxygen **on the present scale** is 159994±0.0001.

По тем же причинам
For similar reasons we do not discuss ...

По тем же соображениям
By the same reasoning Uranus would be dimmer than Saturn.
By a similar argument, the number of odd integers is equal to the number of all integers.

По тем же соображениям, что и в отношении
By the same reasoning (*or* **token**) **as for** the pure gas limit the flow is a backward-facing rarefaction wave.

По течению [*см.* **Вверх по течению, Вниз и вверх по течению от**].

По типу [*см.* **Построен по типу, Происходить по типу, Разработан по типу**].

По той же причине [*см. тж.* **По тем же соображениям**]
The laser beam has no mass and can be easily moved and controlled; **by the same token** (*or* **for the same reason**) it does not generate mechanical responses.

По той или иной причине
Such schemes will fail **for any of several reasons** (*or* **for one reason or other**).

По той причине, что
Mixtures of paint are known as subtractive mixtures **for the reason that** each paint absorbs ...
This version has been discarded **on the grounds that** it requires ...

По тому же принципу
The design of ... **follows the same pattern.**

По тому же принципу, что и при
The gas can be purified **on the same lines as** in the earlier preparation.

По точкам [*см. тж.* **Измерение по точкам**]
Recording the intensity of light **point by point** across the spectrum ...

По традиции [*см. тж.* **По обычаю**]
By convention, all thermodynamic state functions are represented by capital letters.
As a matter of convention, G is used to designate a transfer function in the forward loop.

По траектории
The missile is guided through space **along its trajectory.**
The particle is moving **in a** circular **path.**

По требованию
This provides a means for calling upon the memory of a flip-flop **on demand.**

По трубе
The flow **through a pipe ...**
Liquid flowing **in a pipeline ...**

По уравнению [*см. тж.* **По формуле**]
The Na_2CO_3 decomposes into CO_2 and sodium hydroxide **according to the (following) equation: ...**
The lattice spacing is determined **by** (*or* **using**) Bragg's **relation.**
The surface concentration of paramagnetic oxide calculated **by equation** 7 is too large.

По фазе [*см. тж.* **Модулированный по фазе, Сдвинут по фазе, Смещён по фазе**]

The wave motion is different **in phase** from that of the primary waves incident on the medium.

По Фаренгейту
At 68 **degrees Fahrenheit ...**

По форме [*см. тж.* **Изменяться по форме**]
The punches are machined **to the shape of** the door panel.
Equation (9.107) is identical **in form** to Eq. (9.106).

По форме и размеру
The aggregate produced should be cubical **in shape** (*or* **form**) and uniform **in size.**
They are **of the** same **size and conformation.**

По формуле [*см. тж.* **По уравнению**]
It can be computed **from the formula: ...**
The thermal efficiency of the boiler is calculated **with** (*or* **by**) **the (following) formula: ...**

По химическому составу [*см.* **Аналогичный по химическому составу**].

По центру
Holes are drilled **through the centres.**
The discharge tube was placed **through the centre of** the slot.

По циклу
Turboprop engines work **on the** Brayton **cycle.**

По часовой стрелке, против часовой стрелки
Clockwise rotation of the shaft will move the paper in an **anticlockwise** (*or* **counterclockwise**) direction.
The cylinder rotates **clockwise, anti**(*or* **counter**)**clockwise.**

По частям [*см.* **Интегрирование по частям**].

По шаблону [*см.* **Резать по шаблону**].

По ширине
The flow is not uniform **across the width.**
The value of λ changes **across the width of** the band ...

По ширине и долготе
The location of an earthquake **in latitude and longitude ...**

По шкале I
The angle through which the cell has turned is observed **by the scales** *A* and *B*.
The critical angle is read off **on the scales.**

По шкале II
The hardness of amber is 2–2.5 **on** Mohs' **scale.**

По шкале времени
On the time scale of atomic phenomena ...

По эллипсу
The interplanetary vehicle will proceed **along an ellipse.**
The apparent positions of stars move **in** small **ellipses.**

По этим данным
On this evidence, a complete cycle might require 2000 to 4000 years.

По этой причине [*см. тж.* **Вследствие этого, Поэтому**]
Because of this [*or* **For this reason,** *or* **That** (*or* **This**) **is why,** *or* **Therefore**] the refraction method is known as "The First Arrival Method".

По этому вопросу
Information **on this point** will be very important.
There is little information **on this subject** [*or* **matter,** *or* **problem,** *or* **score** (*Amer.*)].

По этому принципу
Only a small percentage of all known metals have been investigated **along these lines.**
The unit is designed **on this principle.**

Побережье [*см.* **Недалеко от побережья**].

Поблизости [*см.* **Близлежащий**].

Побочное явление [*см.. тж.* **Давать побочные явления**]
The extraction of petroleum may seem to have little impact on the land surface, but there are important undesirable **side effects** in some instances.

Побочный продукт
As an important **by-product** of the Bohr model ...

Побочный эффект (*или* **Побочное действие**)
There were other **side actions** (*or* **effects**) as well.

Поведение [*см.* **Вести себя нормально**].

Поведение ионов
Many aspects of **ionic behaviour** in biochemical systems are still not fully understood.

Повернуть на один полный оборот
The motor **turns** all print wheels **by one complete revolution.**

Повернуть на угол
The analyzer **must be rotated** to the right **111°** for a solution of glucose.
The rollers **swing** the cases **through 90 deg.**
The conveyor **may be swung 45°** to either side of centre.

Повернуть на четверть оборота
Rotate the disk **a quarter turn.**

Поверхностная обработка
The surface finish of the TV cabinet was superb.
Surface treatment of the bearing ...

Поверхностное ознакомление [*см.* **Беглое ознакомление**].

Поверхностный осмотр [*см.* **При поверхностном осмотре**].

Поверхностный слой
A superficial oxide **layer ...**

Поверхность [*см.* **Внешняя поверхность, Внутренняя поверхность, Двигаться по поверхности, На поверхности, Несущая поверхность, По поверхности**].

Поверхность вращения
A surface of revolution.

Поверхность земли
About 70 per cent of **the Earth's surface** is covered by ...

Поверхность раздела [*см. тж.* **На поверхности раздела**]
An oil-metal interface ...

Поверхность склеивания
A bond area.

Поверхность соприкосновения
A contact surface.

Поверхность твердого тела
If a particle comes in contact with **a solid surface, ...**

Повёрнут в направлении
The steering gear controls **the direction toward which** the front wheels **are pointed.**

Повёрнут одной стороной к
The Moon always **presents one face to** the Earth.
Both Mercury and Venus **turn** (*or* **keep**) **one face** eternally **to** the Sun and have no solar day.

Повёрнутый к
The Jupiter-**facing** hemisphere of Callisto seems to be ...

По-видимому [*см. тж.* **Вероятно, По всей вероятности**]
There appears to be little difference in the oxidation properties of ... and ...
The segment **supposedly** carried two genes.
The oxidation **is likely to be**: R—S—H ...
The gases **appear to be** [*or* **are apparently** (*or* **evidently**)] insoluble in the polymer crystallites.
It seems likely that a substantial correction for transpiration may be required.
These vessels **presumably** carry the secretory products of the cortical cells.

По-видимому есть основания утверждать, что
It seems reasonable to say that the problem has been resolved.

Повинен в
The flame atomization source **is to be blamed for** a high incidence of large, unvapourized particles in the analyte region.

Повлечь за собой [*см.* **Влечь за собой**].

Поворачивать [*см.* **Вращать ..., Повернуть, Резко поворачивать**].

Поворачивать за угол
This permits one wheel of the car to rotate

faster than the other when **turning a corner.**

Поворачивать на ... градусов
The fixture **is turned** (*or* **rotated**) **through** 90 **degrees by** a swivelling unit.

Поворачивать на один полный оборот
The disks **are turned through one complete revolution** for each operation.

Поворачиваться
The cutter **is indexed** (*or* **turned**) **in** steps of 90°.

Поворачиваться вверх.
The curve **turns up** in the vicinity of the loading point.

Поворачиваться на ... градусов
When a compass point **is rotated through 180°, ...**

Поворачиваться на угол
When the magnetic induction B is applied, the direction of current flow **swings** (*or* **turns**) **through** some **angle** due to the Lorentz force.

Поворачиваться под различными углами к
The workpiece **can be presented to** the machine **at various angles.**

Поворот [*см.* **Большое достижение, В области ... произошёл поворот**].

Поворотный пункт
Darwin's Origin of Species is **a turning point in** our understanding of the development of life.

Повреждать [*см. тж.* **Выводить из строя**]
The laser does not **damage** parts.

Повреждаться [*см.* **Выходить из строя**].

Повреждение [*см. тж.* **Выходить из строя, Не в порядке, Устранять дефект**]
The obelisk had endured thirty centuries without visible **deterioration.**
This will cause serious **damage to** the cylinders.
These storms frequently cause tide gauge **failure.**
Such steels can be hardened without **injuring** (*or* **affecting**) the finished surfaces.
There is no evidence of **injury to** the cells.

Повреждение в результате
Damage to the hoist **from** overrun of the chain ...

Повреждение при перевозке
The risk of **damage in transit** is thus reduced.

Повреждён [*см. тж.* **Выходить из строя**]
The thread **was mutilated** (*or* **damaged**).

Повреждённый
Abrasive grit blasting removes the **impaired** surface.
This enzyme system repairs the **affected** strand.

Повседневный контроль
The tester is designed for **routine inspection.**

Повсеместно использоваться [*см. тж.* **Широко использоваться**]
The indicator **is in general** (*or* **common,** *or* **universal**) **use.**
Ammeters of this type **are used universally.**

Повсеместно принят
During the 1800s the concept of atoms and molecules **became generally** (*or* **universally**) **accepted.**

Повсеместно присутствовать среди
Two minor proteins, L and NS, **are universal among ...**

Повсеместно распространяться
This idea **gained universal currency.**

Повсюду [*см. тж.* **Везде, Встречаться повсеместно, Повсеместно, Широко использоваться**]
We employ heavy-duty bearings **throughout.**

Повторение
If the output signal from an amplifier is not **an** exact **replica of** the input signal, distortion has occurred.

Повторно использовать [*см.* **Использовать повторно, Можно использовать повторно**].

Повторно использоваться
The coolant is collected by a large trough, and after being filtered, it **is recirculated.**

Повторное использование
The truck enables empty bogeys to be returned from the unloading end for **reuse.**
Recycling of appropriate plastics must be encouraged.

Повторный
The problem of producing **repeat** batches of components in fairly small quantities ...
These corrections could be made by a **second** experiment.

Повторный заказ
Repeat orders can be quickly handled.

Повторный эксперимент
Replicates of the experiment showed immediately that ...

Повторять [*см.* **Точно повторять**].

Повторять опыт
A recent **replica of this experiment was made.**

Повторять путь
Under these circumstances the proton **retraces the** same **path** in the opposite direction.

Повторять снова и снова
By **proceeding to do this over and over again** a regular polygon with 12, 24, 48, ... sides can be inscribed.

Повторяться
Floods **recur,** and the recurrence interval is predictable.
Sedimentary rock associations are of several kinds and **may occur over and over.**
If such zones **are repeated, ...**

Повторяющаяся последовательность
Polymers are enormous molecules made by connecting small molecules in **repetitive sequences.**

Повторяющееся действие
The recurring action of a mechanical clock ...

Повторяющийся
The individual atoms are bound to each other in a **repetitive** three-dimensional array.
A set of **replicate** results is a representative sample.

Повышать [*см. тж.* **Увеличивать**]
The synchrotron **boosts** the energy of the protons for injection into a larger synchrotron.
To raise (*or* **elevate**) the boiling point, ...
The kaolin **adds** strength, abrasion resistance, and rigidity.
Molybdenum **enhances** the resistance of stainless steels to pitting corrosion.
Niobium **improves** the heat resistance of ...
The addition of the new unit **will raise** (*or* **increase**) the capacity from 80 to 135 mln lb/yr.
Production **could be stepped up** quickly.
He **upped** the payload to ...

Повышать до
This program **brought** the rate of copper output **to** a level commensurate with ...
The concentration **was brought up** (*or* **raised,** *or* **elevated**) **to** the desired level.

Повышать напряжение
A transformer is used **to step up** (*or* **raise,** *or* **increase,** *or* **build up**) **the voltage.**

Повышать температуру на
The amount of heat required **to raise** 1 lb of the material **1°F** is ...

Повышаться [*см.* **Нарастать, Подниматься, Увеличиваться**].

Повышение [*см. тж.* **Выигрыш, С повышением, Увеличение**]
The upper section is cooled for **better** (*or* **increased**) absorption efficiency.
With further **gain** (*or* **increase,** *or* **rise**) **in** vehicle speed ...
Five percent **gain in** productivity ...
Upgrading of fastener quality and reliability ...
To prevent **the building up** (*or* **buildup**) **of** pressure in the cell, ...

Повышение в два раза
A doubling of the concentration would cause ...

Повышение на

With **a rise of** several degrees C ...

Повышение точки кипения

Adsorption on activated carbon improves with **increasing boiling point.**

A rise in (*or* **An elevation of**) **the boiling point ...**

Повышенная температура [*см. тж.* **При повышенной температуре**]

The salicylates relieve minor pains and reduce **elevated temperatures.**

This reaction will proceed only at **elevated temperatures.**

Повышенное давление

An elevated (*or* **heightened**) blood **pressure.**

Повышенный

Steels containing up to 1% chromium give **enhanced** (*or* **increased,** *or* **improved,** *or* **better**) resistance to atmospheric corrosion.

Higher than usual, Rather high.

Погибать

The plant **dies** when the seeds mature.

Погибнуть в результате

When a teloblast **dies of** malfunctions, ... (*biol.*).

Поглотитель энергии

The controlled system is **the sink for the energy** (*or* **the energy sink**).

Поглощать

^{211}At **is** readily **taken up** (*or* **absorbed**) **by** the thyroid gland.

The nutrients **are taken up by** the plants.

When the amount of air passed over a surface is sufficient **to take up** the heat dissipated from, ...

Поглощаться атмосферой

The convected heat **is lost to the atmosphere.**

Поглощаться и высвобождаться

Carbon dioxide **is taken up by** plants during their growth cycle **and released by** the decay of plant material.

Поглощающий инфракрасные лучи

Infrared-absorbing gases ...

Поглощение

The take-up (*or* **absorption**) **of** oxygen **by** the plants ...

There should be air-conditioned cooling so that there will be a minimum of moisture **pick-up by** the material.

Поглощение в инфракрасной области

Infrared absorption.

Поглощенный

Only a small fraction of the water **taken up by** the roots serves as a reactant in photosynthesis.

Погодоустойчивый

The equipment **is weather-proof** (*or* **weather resistant**).

Погрешность [*см.* **В пределах ошибки эксперимента, Вносить ошибку, Инструментальная погрешность, Отклоняться от истины на**].

Погружаемый аппарат

Manned and unmanned **submersibles ...**

Погружаемый в

The geothermal gradient is measured by a probe **dropped into** the soft sediment.

Погружать в

The components **are dipped in** (*or* **into**) molten metal and ...

The container **may be immersed in** cold water.

The test specimens **were submerged in** the solution.

The interacting mass **was plunged into** the water.

Погружаться на дно

Then the sphere **sinks to the bottom.**

Погружение

Neither on this **dive,** nor on others ... (*of frogmen*).

They regretted the brevity of their **plunge** (*in a bathyscaphe*).

The record **submersion** (*or* **submergence**) (*of a submarine*) ...

The process of **downsinking of** the plate beneath the edge of another is called subduction.

Погружение в

This is accomplished by **dipping** the part **in** a two-layer liquid.

The coatings are obtained by **immersing** the part to be coated **in ...**
The lowest temperature was obtained by **immersion of** the specimen **in** liquid hydrogen.

Погружён в
The pump mechanism **is** entirely **immersed** (*or* **submerged**) **in** oil.
The metal electrode **dips** (*or* **is dipped**) **into** a solution containing ions of the metal.

Погружённый наполовину
A ball floats on the surface exactly **half submerged.**

Под I
The steel cylinder lies **beneath** an electrostatic field.
A tray is fitted **underneath** (*or* **below,** *or* **under**) the electrodes for storage of unheated rivets.
The region **beneath** the dotted curve represents ...

Под II [*см.* **Нарезать под, Отверстие под, Сверлить под**].

Под III [*см.* **Отделывать**].

Под IV [*см.* **Подразумеваться под**].

Под V
The storage ring was later moved to the Orsay Laboratory **outside** Paris.

Под атмосферным давлением [*см.* **Находиться под атмосферным давлением**].

Под болт [*см.* **Нарезанный под болт**].

Под вакуумом [*см. тж.* **Плавиться под вакуумом**]
The melting was carried out **under vacuum.**
The stripper operates **under a** slight **vacuum.**

Под влиянием [*см. тж.* **Под действием**]
The device changes resistance **in response to** (*or* **under the effect of**) light.
Electric charges move **in response to** electric fields.

Под водой
The rocket is launched **underwater.**

Под вопросом
The degree of further development **is open to question** because of increasing technological difficulties.

Под вороток
The tap shank has a square end **to accommodate** (*or* **receive,** *or* **fit**) **a tap wrench.**

Под давлением [*см. тж.* **Находиться под давлением**]
The calorimeter is filled with oxygen **under a pressure of ...**
The molten metal is injected into moulds **under pressure.**

Под давлением ниже атмосферного
Potable water can be produced **by subatmospheric** boiling.

Под действием [*см. тж.* **Находиться под действием, Находящийся под действием, Под влиянием**]
Lead (II) nitrate is often used to make nitrogen dioxide **by the action** of heat (*or* **under the action of** heating).
The enzyme accepts histidine **when acted upon by** (*or* **under the action of**) an appropriate ligase.
Corrosion **by** acids ...
Chrysotile is subject to progressive embrittlement **on exposure** to temperatures above 400°C.
The motions of objects **under the influence** (*or* **effect**) **of** gravity ...
Then the electron starts falling back toward the proton **under the attraction of** the Coulomb force.

Под действием вибрации
Electrical characteristics **under** strong **vibration ...**

Под действием излучения [*см.* **Под облучением**].

Под действием света
Only **under exposure to light** will the material permit electron flow.

Под действием силы тяжести [*см. тж.* **Под действием собственного веса, Самотёком**]
The incline is insufficient to cause the bogey to run away **under gravity.**

Flow occurs from a higher to a lower elevation **by action of gravity.**

Под действием собственного веса
The material flows **by gravity.**
The concrete is forced down the vertical pipe **by gravity.**
Fresh water **is gravity fed** to the whirlpool casing.
This permits **gravity feed to** trucks.
The feeders employ **the natural fall of** material through the date.
The platform is tilted and the car runs into the cage **under gravity.**

Под действием ультрафиолетового излучения
Under UV (*or* **ultraviolet) light.**

Под заклёпку
The material is drilled and punched **to receive** (*or* **fit,** *or* **accommodate,** *or* **suit the size of) the rivet.**

Под землёй
The miners spend their working days **belowground.**
A few locomotives were used **underground.**

Под ключ I
The screw cap is milled to an octagon at the top **to receive a** box **wrench.**

Под ключ II [*см.* **Для сдачи "под ключ"**].

Под континентами
The composition of the crust **beneath** (*or* **under) the continents ...**

Под микроскопом [*см. тж.* **В микроскоп, Изучение под микроскопом**]
Examining samples of his own white blood cells **under the microscope,** he noticed that ...
Colloidal particles cannot be seen even **with an** optical **microscope.**

Под наблюдением [*см.* **Находиться под наблюдением**].

Под нагрузкой
When the engine operates **under load, ...**
Under a load of 100 g applied for 5 seconds ...

Под названием [*см. тж.* **Быть известным под названием, Известный под названием**]
This mineral is also known **by** (*or* **under**) **the name** orthite.

Под наклоном [*см.* **Идти под наклоном к**].

Под напряжением
The heads are charged **at** 140 kV.

Под облучением
Most plastics tend to lose tensile strength **under irradiation.**
Under radiation, most metals become harder and stronger.

Под общим названием [*см.* **Идти под общим названием**].

Под острым (*антон.* **тупым**) **углом**
Nonuniform bending can be induced by placing the strips **at an acute** (*anton.* **obtuse**) **angle.**

Под открытым небом [*см.* **На открытом воздухе**].

Под поверхностью
Magma cools **beneath the surface.**

Под ... подразумевается [*см. тж.* **Означать**]
By a region or domain **is meant** an open connected point set *E*.
This **is considered to mean** distortion produced by ...
The term landslide **is** often **used in reference to** any form of rapid mass wasting.
Linearity **is taken to mean that** the process can be described by means of linear differential equations.

Под председательством
We attended a symposium **chaired** (*or* **presided over**) **by** Dr. P.

Под прямым углом
This permits transmission of power from the shaft to the axle **at a right angle.**
The set of electrodes is located **at right angles to** the field.

Под прямым углом друг к другу
These polarization directions **are at right angles.**

Под прямым углом к
The waveguide extends **orthogonal to** the *x*-axis.

Под руками [*см.* **Иметь под рукой**].

Под руководством
The discussion is being organized by our Institution **under the aegis of** the Ministry.
Geiger worked **under the direction** (*or* **supervision**) **of** Lord Rutherford.

Под руководством специалиста
Each student obtains **supervised** practice on surveying equipment.

Под собственной тяжестью
The plate sinks **of its own weight** (*or* **by gravity**).

Под сомнением [*см.* **Находиться под сомнением**].

Под током
When the coil **is energized, ...**

Под углом [*см. тж.* **Видеть ... под углом, Направлен под углом**]
The screws are inserted **at an angle.**
The film normal is tilted **at an angle to** the X-ray beam.
This is accomplished by positioning each filter **at a** different **angle to** the beam.
The boundaries of the shaft pillar descend **at 70°** (*or* **at an angle of 70°**, *or* **at a 70° angle**) **to** (*or* **with**) the horizontal.
This requires each eye to view the object **from** different **angles.**
A swash plate is a disk mounted **at a slant** on a revolving shaft.

Под углом зрения [*см. тж.* **В свете, С точки зрения**]
Observations are made **at** viewing **angles of** 10 degrees.

Под угрозу [*см.* **Ставить под угрозу**].

Под управлением
The trains are started, operated, and stopped **under the control of** a computer.

Под эгидой
The International Committee for Future Accelerators operates **under the aegis of** UPAP.

Под этим подразумевается, что
By this is meant that the composition of each phase is ...

Подавать [*см. тж.* **В ... подаётся**]
The drum from which wire **is fed** during winding ...
The air **is conducted to** the tool through a hose.
Conveyors have been erected **to convey** coal **to** the appropriate site.
Each pump is capable of **delivering** 510 tons of water per hour.
The ripping head **discharges** coal **onto** an intermediate conveyor.
The coal **is fed to** the bunker.
Vibration pickups **feed** their voltage **into** amplifiers.
A distribution valve **feeds** compressed air **into** the bottles.
The ore **is released** through a chute **into** the skip.

Подавать давление
The pressure is delivered by a centrifugal compressor.

Подавать по трубам
The steam **can be piped from** the field right **to** the turbine.

Подавать самотёком [*см. тж.* **Под действием собственного веса**]
The catalyst **is fed by gravity into** a regeneration vessel.

Подаваться [*см. тж.* **Поступать**]
Power from the four generators **is delivered to** the main bus.
The filter cleans the fuel before it **enters** the engines.
The output from the photocell **is fed into** the galvanometer.
The signal **is fed to** the second transmitter.
The signal from the clipper **is passed to** a cathode follower output stage.
The air **was provided by** a blower.
The hydrogen **is supplied to** the flame through a small orifice.
An operating pulse **is supplied to** the stepping motor.
A liquid **is delivered at** the top of a vertical tube.
Materials **feed onto** belt conveyors from hoppers.

Подаваться на
The steam **flows to** the turbines.

Подаваться под давлением
The nutrient solution **is forced through** the glass filter **into** the growth tube.

Подаваться под действием собственного веса [*см.* **Под действием собственного веса**].

Подавлять
The resistance of the material quickly **suppresses** the eddy currents.

Подавлять вибрацию
With its massive frame, the machine **dampens vibration** and runs smoothly.
The mechanical hysteresis damping **holds the vibrations in check.**

Подавляющее большинство [*см. тж.* **В основном**]
The great **bulk of** these deposits consists of the sulphate of calcium.
(By far) the majority [*or* **The vast** (*or* **great,** *or* **overwhelming**) **majority**] **of** technical investigations using the shock tube have employed a technique of this type.

Подавляющее большинство данных
The preponderance of the evidence (*or* **data**) indicates that the complexes are quite young by galactic standards.

Подать мысль о том, что
This finding **suggested that** small particles are suspended in ...

Подача [*см.* **Прекращать подачу**].

Подача плёнки (*фото*)
The **film advance** mechanism ...

Подача самотёком [*см.* **Под действием собственного веса**].

Подача тепла
Heat supplied or removed largely depends upon ...

Подача энергии
The rate of **energy delivery** (*or* **supply**) to do useful work ...

Подбор [*см.* **Метод подбора**].

Подбор крови по типам
This makes **blood matching** (*or* **typing**) a difficult procedure.

Подбрасывать [*см.* **Бросать монетку**].

Подведём итоги
In sum(mary) (*or* **To sum up,** *or* **To summarize**) groups I and IV members are well known, those of group III are reasonably well determined, but ...
To summarize: The combustion experiments are all exothermic and ...

Подвергаемый термообработке
Heat-treatable steels ...

Подвергать
Off-axis loads **subject** a column to combined bending.

Подвергать большой опасности
Geologic processes **impose severe hazards upon** people and their structures.

Подвергать действию света
The cells **were exposed to light.**
The number of free electrons in a semiconductor can be greatly increased by heating or **shining light upon** it.

Подвергать действию силы
If the spinning rotor **is subjected to a force** perpendicular to ...

Подвергать напряжению
Temperature changes **place** (*or* **impose**) a terrific **strain on** all conduit runs.

Подвергать обработке ... методом
The components **were put through** a special thermomechanical **process.**

Подвергать пескоструйной обработке
The riveted areas **were sandblasted** to provide a clean surface.

Подвергать преобразованию Фурье *и т.п.*
This product **can be Fourier transformed.**

Подвергать проверке
As these methods **are put to the test, ...**
It is desirable to undertake explorations **to test** this theory.
To check (*or* **verify**) the results, ...

Подвергать сомнению [*см. тж.* **Сомнительный**]
The validity of the maxima **is questioned by** some authors.
Some investigators **have cast doubt on** (*or* **questioned**) this finding.

Подвергать удару
If a piece of steel **is subjected to pounding** (*or* **a blow,** *or* **an impact**) ...

Подвергаться [*см. тж.* **Испытывать, Претерпевать**]
The star **may go through** a series of contractions.
Platform strata deposited in earlier periods **were subject(ed)** to erosion by running water.
The sealant **is subject** to abrasion and tearing.
This body **experiences** (*or* **undergoes**) acceleration.
The material **suffers** temper embrittlement.
Certain nuclei **may undergo** amitotic division (*biol.*).
This transition **has been the subject of** intensive investigations.

Подвергаться воздействию [*см. тж.* **Испытывать воздействие**]
The sample **is exposed to** a laser pulse.
A unit positive charge **experiences** a force equal to ...
While the needle **is subjected** to the electric field, ...
The enamels do not fade **when exposed to** salt spray.
The fans **are exposed to** high temperatures.
These bearings **are subjected to** axial forces.

Подвергаться воздействию света
Many chemical substances change drastically **when exposed to light.**

Подвергаться воздействию силы
The particle **experiences a** restoring **force** pulling or pushing it back to its equilibrium position.

Подвергаться воздушному охлаждению
After tempering, the plates **are allowed to air cool.**

Подвергаться грубой расточке
One cylinder **is rough bored** in the castings.

Подвергаться действию [*см. тж.* **Подвергаться воздействию**]
When the molecules **are subjected to** a magnetic field...
The entire earth **is subject to** the force of gravity.
Electrons drifting from the negative electrode will enter the notch where they **experience** the higher field and become heavy.

Подвергаться действию атмосферных условий [*см.* **Находиться под действием атмосферных условий**].

Подвергаться действию *чего-л.* **в течение короткого времени**
Liquid flowing over a single packing element **is exposed briefly to** the gas.

Подвергаться дефектоскопии
The part **is examined for flaws** by an X-ray technician.

Подвергаться естественному старению
The assemblies **must be aged naturally** after forming.

Подвергаться жёстким испытаниям
The trestles **were put through** (*or* **subjected to**) **arduous** (*or* **severe,** *or* **rigorous**) **tests.**

Подвергаться жёсткой (*или* **суровой**) **критике**
The Commission report **came under a storm of criticism.**

Подвергаться износу
The two kinds of polymer differed markedly in the amount of **wear they sustained.**

Подвергаться испытанию
The gaskets **were subjected to this test.**
The unit **is under test** (*or* **is being tested**).

Подвергаться исследованию
This is now **the subject of** extensive **research.**

Подвергаться критике
The proposal **came under criticism.**

Подвергаться механическому разрушению

The winding **could** thus **be mechanically ruined.**

Подвергаться наибольшему износу
Chuck keys **receive the greatest amount of wear.**

Подвергаться наклёпу
If the tube **is work hardened** (*or* **cold worked,** *or* **strain hardened**), anneal it first.

Подвергаться напряжению
The concrete at the base of the dam **will undergo** (*or* **will be subjected to**) minor temperature **strains.**

Подвергаться натяжению или сжатию
There is a point where the belt **is in tension or compression.**

Подвергаться обдирке
On this machine, various diameters **are rough ground.**

Подвергаться облучению
The nuclear emulsion **was exposed to** (*or* **irradiated by**) monoenergetic neutrons.

Подвергаться обработке [*см.* **Не подвергнутый обработке после литья**].

Подвергаться опасности
To obtain the best lift/drag ratio without **running into the danger of** flow breakdowns, ...

Подвергаться пересмотру [*см.* **Пересматриваться**].

Подвергаться преобразованию
Sugar **goes through** (*or* **undergoes,** *or* **is subjected to**) **a series of transformations.**

Подвергаться разложению
Cocain cannot be sterilized without **undergoing** some **decomposition.**

Подвергаться распаду
Ribosomes **undergo a breakdown** after a period of service.

Подвергаться сомнению
The authenticity of these data **is open** (*or* **subjected**) **to question** (*or* **is in doubt**).

Подвергаться термообработке
The belts **are heat treated.**

Подвергаться тщательному изучению
The matter **was** not **brought under close study** until this century.
The spiral arms **have been subjected to intense scrutiny.**

Подвергаться фракционной перегонке
If liquefied air **is fractionally distilled, ...**

Подвергаться холодной обработке [*см.* **Обрабатываться в холодном** (*антон.* **горячем**) **состоянии**].

Подвергаться электролизу
When a fused chloride **is being electrolysed** (*or* **is subjected to electrolysis**), ...

Подвергающийся
The behaviour of columns **under** inelastic stress depends on ...

Подвергающийся большому напряжению
This material is not used in structures **where considerable stresses occur.**

Подвергающийся действию
The area **exposed to** heat ...

Подвергнут
This gel **has been exposed to** hydrolysis.

Подвержен [*см. тж.* **Весьма подвержен**]
The soft-metal threads **are prone to** stripping.
Hard faces **are prone to** thermal shock if they...
The product **is liable to** distort or warp when ...
The adrenals **are susceptible to** certain infections.
The external-combustion engine **is** not **susceptible to** contamination or damage from dust or salt in the environment.
Even the hydrogen nucleus **would be subject to** decay.

Подвержен вибрации
Self-tapping screws **are not vibration proof.**

Подвержен действию
Air **is acted upon by** gravity, like all matter.
Many patients **are** not **exposed to** these side-effects.

Подвержен коррозии
The pins, being unstressed, **are** less **prone** (*or* **subject,** *or* **liable**) **to corrosion.**

Подвержен ошибкам
Our compasses today **are subject to** the same inherent **errors** as ...

Подвержен поражениям
The alkyl mercurials attack the brain cells which **are** particularly **susceptible to injury by** this form of mercury.

Подвержен разрушениям
At elongation approaching this limit rubber **is** extremely **prone to damage.**

Подверженность
Susceptibility to progressive failure is called fatigue.

Подверженный землетрясениям
An earthquake-prone region.

Подверженный износу
The areas **subjected to wear** are flame hardened.

Подвешен I
Two metal spheres **are suspended from** threads.
The float **is suspended (up)on** a flexible pendant from a valve and rod.
The platform **is suspended from** the ceiling by steel wires.

Подвешен II
The particles **are suspended in** the fluid.

Подвешен над
The reactor **is suspended over** the cooling pond.

Подвешенный в воздухе
Air-borne colloidal particles ...

Подвешивать на
Aerials **are** usually **suspended on** buildings, towers, or poles.
In drilling oil wells a cutting tool **is suspended on** a wire line.
The chip **was suspended** by wires.

Подвижное равновесие
Flowing equilibrium.

Подвод тепла [*см. тж.* **Подача тепла**]
The heat input must all appear as ...

Подводить
The required input and output connections of the logic element **were brought out to** the terminals of the integrated-circuit package.
The contact point of the dial gauge **is brought to** the centre-line of the drill.
Bring the micrometer spindle **into contact with** the anvil.

Подводить базу под теорию
This section **provides the** necessary **background to** the **theory of ...**

Подводить и отводить
When energy **must be supplied** (*or* **delivered**) **to and removed** (*or* **withdrawn**) **from** the control system, ...

Подводить итоги
The second law **sums up** our experiences with equilibria.
Section II **reviews** previous work on optical computing.

Подводить к существу дела
That at last **brings** me **to the point.**

Подводить энергию к
Power from the four generators **is delivered to** the main bus.

Подводиться к
The inner end of the first workpiece **is presented to** the stationary tools on the headstock.
A precision orifice **is brought close to** the surface to be measured.

Подводная конструкция
Sodium nitrate inhibits corrosion of **underwater structures.**

Подводный хребет
A submarine ridge.

Подводя итоги, можно сказать
In summary [*or* **To summarize** (*or* **sum up**)] the efficiency of the cutoff operation has been greatly increased.

Подгонка данных к *чему-л.*
Forcing the data to fit the diffusion model is somewhat of an empirical approach.

Подгонять друг к другу
The sections of the blanket **are fitted together.**

Подгонять к

The experimental data **are fitted to** the calculated values.

Kepler first proceeded to try **to fit** a theory of Ptolemaic type **to** the data.

To fit a straight line **to** a series of points ...

We choose different values of *a* and *b* **to give a good fit to** observed data.

Neither candidate **could be fitted into** the χ meson model.

If a part **is to be mated with** other parts during assembly, ...

Подгонять теорию к данным

To make the theory fit the data, ...

Подготавливать почву для

The development of the steam engine **set the stage for** the true mechanization of mining.

To set the stage for a discussion of ... let me briefly review ...

Подготовительная стадия

An essential **preliminary to** all these experiments in turning, etc., was accurate control of tool shapes.

Подготовка [*см. тж.* **В порядке подготовки к, Для подготовки к, Обучение**]

The material covered in this textbook has been designed **to give you an adequate background** for further study.

Подготовка в области

These sections contain supplemental information for those who do not have **a background in** biology.

The programmer does not require special **training in** computer techniques.

Подготовка почвы для

Inversions form the essential ingredient in **setting the stage for** air pollution.

Подготовлена почва для

As atmospheric oxygen continued to accumulate, **the stage was set for** the initial appearance of eukaryotic cells.

Поддаваться I [*см. тж.* **Лучше поддаваться, Не поддаваться**]

The cell **is susceptible to** thermodynamic treatment.

Such polymers **are amenable to** heat setting treatments.

These problems **are** not **amenable to** theoretical treatment because of their complexity.

Viral vaccines do not **lend themselves to** filter sterilization.

Heating by warmed air **lends itself to** automatic control.

Поддаваться II

The denatured material **is** much more **susceptible** (*or* **prone,** *or* **liable**) **to** degradation than ...

Often the tool in such an operation is a costly diamond grinding wheel, since nothing else **will attack** the hard material (*твёрдый материал не поддаётся ничему другому*).

Поддаваться лечению

Continental blood vessel defects that **are curable by surgery ...**

These diseases **are treatable** through this approach.

This disease **responds** rapidly **to treatment.**

Поддающийся вычислению

A **computable** capacitance standard, ...

Поддающийся изгибу

Bendable cast iron ...

Поддающийся механической обработке

Machinable materials ...

Поддающийся наблюдению

Most of the **observable** characteristics ...

Поддающийся программированию

A robot is a **programmable** machine capable of ...

Поддержание

The insulin makes possible **the maintenance of** a relatively constant blood-sugar concentration.

Поддержание жизни

The process of photosynthesis is also responsible for **the maintenance of** animal **life.**

Поддержание существования

Water is important to the creation and **sustenance of** every living thing.

Поддерживать [*см. тж.* **В котором поддерживается температура, На ... поддерживается постоянная температура**]
Hold the drill **up** by hand to prevent its dropping onto the work.
The weight of a dirigible **is sustained** (*or* **supported**) **by** buoyant forces which sustain a ship in water.

Поддерживать в рабочем состоянии
This staff can **keep** the assembly **operating** (*or* **working,** *or* **going**).

Поддерживать во влажном состоянии путём смачивания водой
The upper surface of the plate **is kept wet with water.**

Поддерживать горение
To sustain combustion.

Поддерживать дугу
A single-phase a-c **arc is maintained** between the tips of two adjustable electrodes.

Поддерживать жизнь
The ability of carbohydrates **to sustain** (*or* **support**) **life ...**

Поддерживать заряд
This energy **maintains the charge of** a storage battery.

Поддерживать здоровье
Veterinary medicines **maintain the health of** livestock.

Поддерживать колебания
A slight impulse is needed **to maintain oscillation** for another 30 sec.

Поддерживать на высоком уровне
This becomes important when power **must be kept high** (*or* **at a high level**).

Поддерживать на максимально высоком уровне
The output working velocity of the tool **must be kept as high as possible** (*or* **at the highest possible level**).

Поддерживать на постоянном уровне
The temperature **is held** (*or* **maintained,** *or* **kept**) **constant.**

Поддерживать на уровне
The water temperature **was maintained** (*or* **held,** *or* **kept**) **at** 600°F.

Поддерживать постоянное напряжение
The anode **is maintained** (*or* **held,** *or* **kept**) **at a constant potential.**

Поддерживать постоянную температуру
The temperature is held (*or* **kept,** *or* **maintained**) **constant.**
The tube **is held at a constant temperature.**

Поддерживать постоянным
The local gradient of the partial pressure **is held** (*or* **kept,** *or* **maintained**) **constant.**

Поддерживать работу
In many cases the voltage required **to keep** the motor **running** is significantly lower than that required to start the motor.
The power necessary **to maintain** a charge-coupled memory device ...

Поддерживать равновесие
The temperature change required **to maintain equilibrium ...**

Поддерживать репутацию
High-pressure moving-part logic systems **have upheld the reputation of** pneumatics.

Поддерживать самолёт в воздухе
The thrust from the power plant necessary **to** propel or **sustain an aircraft ...**

Поддерживать скорость
This speed can be indefinitely **sustained** (*or* **maintained**).

Поддерживать существование [*см. тж.* **Поддерживать жизнь**]
Each irrigated region **supported** over a million people.

Поддерживать температуру
If one junction **is maintained at a** known **temperature ...**
Cooling water inside the tubes **maintains the** solution (**temperature**) **at** 30°C.
A high **temperature is maintained.**

Поддерживаться I
Electrical neutrality **is maintained by** the hydrogen ions.

Growing clouds **are sustained by** upward air currents.

Поддерживаться II
At present the salinity of the oceans **is sustained at** a fairly constant value.

Поддерживаться III
This supposition **received support among** researchers.

Поддержка [*см.* **В защиту**].

Поделён на [*см. тж.* **Делить на**]
The analogue operation region **is divided (up) into** *N* distinguishable levels.

Поджимать винт [*см. тж.* **Туго поджимать винт**]
To tighten a screw, ...

Подземная часть строительного объекта
The subsurface portion of a construction project.

Подкисленный
In these cases, water **acidified with** nitric acid should be used as solvent.

Подкислять
The solution **is** then **acidified by** dilute sulphuric acid.

Подкреплять [*см.* **Подтверждать**].

Подкрепляться
This conclusion **is strengthened by** the evidence ...

Подлежащий анализу
The mixture **to be analyzed ...**

Подлежащий измерению
The interval **to be measured ...**

Подлинно
Truly (*or* **Genuinely**) homogeneous rock masses are a rarity in nature.

Поднимать
An industrial robot is designed **to pick up** (*or* **lift,** *or* **raise**) heavy sheets of metal from a conveyor.

Поднимать вопрос [*см. тж.* **Выдвигать вопрос**]
Cable television **has raised** a number of **issues** that remain to be finally resolved.

Поднимать давление
Various pumps are operated **to build up the pressure** in the cylinder.

Поднимать до уровня
The programme **brought** the rate of copper output **to a level** commensurate with ...

Поднимать на высоту
If the bigger stone **is raised through a height** *h*, ...

Подниматься
When the glucocorticoid level in the circulating blood **is elevated,** the central nervous system shuts off ...
This electron cannot escape unless its energy **is boosted** higher than the top of the barrier.

Подниматься на I
The airplane **climbed to** 60 thousand feet.
An air-cushion vehicle **rises a few feet** above the surface.

Подниматься на II
Since that time the Great Basin **has been elevated** about 1.5 kilometres.

Подниматься на поверхность
Deeper magma **rises to the surface** and erupts.

Подносить к
When a uranium compound **is brought near** the knob of the electroscope ...

Подносить пламя к
If **a flame is applied to** a mixture of ...

Поднятие
These clouds are produced by **the ascent** (*or* **lifting**) **of** damp air over large mountain barriers.
Uplift of land occurs rapidly along many coasts.

Подобно [*см. тж.* **Как и**]
Similar to the histones, specific phosphorylation enzymes regulate ...
The generator potential, **much like** the graded local response, is produced at ...

Подобно тому, как [*см. тж.* **Аналогично тому, как**]
Just as poisonous compounds, if handled improperly, can cause accidents, **so** can radioactive isotopes.

The computer system can lead the questions to the necessary data **much as** a librarian helps a student.

Подобный [*см.* **Аналогичный**].

Подогнаны друг к другу [*см.* **Быть хорошо подогнанными (друг к другу)**].

Подогнать к [*см.* **Подгонять к**].

Подогревать паром
The anhydrite is placed in water which **is steam heated** and forms a suspension.

Подопытное животное
Test animals have survived very deep dives.

Подпадать под категорию
Our investigation does not **fall in(to) this category.**

Подпадать под рубрику [*см.* **Относиться к области**].

Подпираться пружиной
The located pin **is backed by a spring.**

Подразделять на [*см. тж.* **Делить на**]
Energy **can be classified as** potential or kinetic energy, and **can be broken down** (*or* **subdivided**) further **into** such forms of energy as mechanical, electrical, radiant, and chemical.
The table **categorizes** plastics **into** 29 families.
These compound sugars **are subclassified into ...**
Broaching machines **are classed as** either horizontals or verticals.

Подразумевать под [*см. тж.* **Под этим подразумевается, что**]
This term does not **imply** actual contact.
We take the word rays **to mean** ray tubes whenever discussing power.

Подразумевать, что
We should write not ψ^2 but $\psi^*\psi$ **implying that** the probability function is obtained by ...
By the statement that a matrix is positive definite we **mean that ...**

Подразумеваться под [*см. тж.* **Под ... подразумевается**]
By a long slug **is meant** (*or* **implied**) one which is long enough to be the subject of a steady-state extrusion.
This consideration **is implicit** (*or* **implied**) **in** what has already been said.

Подробнее [*см. тж.* **Ближе (п)ознакомиться с**]
This type of hydrolysis will be discussed **at greater length** (*or* **in greater detail**) in Chapter 17.
This is described **more fully** in the Appendix.

Подробнее смотри в
For more details, see the Appendix.

Подробно [*см. тж.* **Более детально, Весьма подробно, Детально**]
We now investigate this question **more closely.**
Examining this sequence **more fully** (*or* **carefully,** *or* **thoroughly**) it is naturally found that ...
Senile dementia is considered **at length** elsewhere.
Fusion power has been discussed **at length** (*or* **in detail**) in several articles.
The maintenance of electrical equipment is covered **in great** (*or* **considerable**) **detail** (*or* is covered **comprehensively**) in a later section.
Such reactions have been studied **in some detail.**
The size distribution of ice crystals has been studied less **extensively** (*or* **comprehensively**).
The paper will describe **more specifically** the research efforts ...

Подробно излагать
This aspect of millimetre wave research **will be detailed in** a special article.

Подробно изучать
We decided **to look into** the problem **in detail.**

Подробно изучен
These reactions **have been studied extensively** (*or* **thoroughly,** *or* **comprehensively**).

Подробно ознакомиться с
In this section we **shall take a close look at** the nonlinearities commonly found in controlled systems.

Подробно описан
The model **has been detailed in** a recent publication.

Подробно рассматриваться
These preparations **are fully considered in** Chap. 5.

Подробности [*см.* **Не входя в подробности**].

Подробные данные
The industrial history file comprises **in-depth** (*or* **detailed**) **data on** every industrial firm in the state.

Подробные сведения о
That rocket has provided the first **comprehensive** (*or* **detailed**) **data** (*or* **information**) **on ...**

Подробный [*см. тж.* **Более подробный, Детальный**]
The author gives **a comprehensive** (*or* **detailed,** *or* **thorough,** *or* **in-depth**) analysis of transport to and from spheres.

Подрывать основы
The experimental proof of this violation **will shake the foundations of** our description of such interactions.

Подряд (*нареч.*)
Direct current was kept constant often for two weeks **at a time** (*or* **running,** *or* **on end,** *or* **in succession**).
Soil moisture is frozen for several **consecutive** winter months.

Подсказывать [*см.* **Интуиция подсказывает, что**].

Подскакивать
The cost of importing oil **has escalated to** ... dollars a barrel.

Подсоединять вольтметр к клеммам
The voltage of this cell can be measured **by placing a voltmeter across the terminals.**

Подсоединять к
The coil **is connected to** a suitable circuit.
Filters **can be switched** (*or* **connected**) **into** the circuit.

Подсоединять к сети
The armature of the instrument **is connected across the** supply **mains.**

Подставлять в
Substitute (*or* **Insert**) this value **in(to)** Eq. (8).
Substituting $v = 0$ **in** Eq. (13.1) shows that ...

Подстановка
Insertion of 80°C **for** the freezing point of naphthalene **in(to)** Eq.(10–22) gives: ...
Substitution of (*or* **Substituting**) these data **in(to)** Eq. (1–9) gives: ...

Подстановка N **вместо** M
The substitution of N **for** M.

Подсчёт [*см.* **Согласно подсчётам**].

Подсчитывать
We can **tally up** the electrical charge on the silicate frame: two oxygens at –2 and one silicon at +4 give a net charge of zero.

Подсчитывать по
The reaction rate **was estimated** (*or* **calculated**) **from** the concentration.

Подтверждать [*см. тж.* **В значительной мере подтверждать**]
These observations **reinforce** the statement that ...
This fact **substantiates** our conclusion.
These findings **are evidence in favour of** an assumption that ...
Our experience **has verified** several important advantages of the new processor.
This result **lends credence** (*or* **support**) **to** the view that the alga-like organisms probably were photosynthetic.
Switches housed in aluminium continued to operate freely, thus **attesting to** aluminium's superior corrosion resistance.
The tabulated values **bear out** (*or* **confirm,** *or* **corroborate**) this relationship.
The two investigations **provide support for** this view.
The continuous nature of the frequency shifts **supports** the conclusion that ...

Подтверждать или опровергать
Much more research must be done **to** either **validate or disprove** the hypothesis.

Подтверждать мнение о том, что
The bulk of evidence **favours the view that** each fibre is a single component containing ...

Подтверждать правильность метода
The result **lends support to the validity of the** aerological **method** used.

Подтверждать теорию
This **has strengthened the case for** seafloor spreading.
These findings **strengthen** (*or* **support,** *or* **confirm**) our **theory.**

Подтверждаться [*см. тж.* **В пользу ... говорит, Явствовать из**]
The possibility that either effect can dominate **is borne out** (*or* **corroborated,** *or* **confirmed,** *or* **attested to**) **by** the results achieved.
This hypothetical scheme **is supported** (*or* **backed**) **by** experimental results.
This is **supported** (*or* **sustained**) **by** the fact that, ...
The Earth's wrinkled surface suggests that the solid rock bends and breaks; this impression **gains substance from** earthquakes.
We felt confident that the basic findings **would stand.**

Подтверждающие данные
Some of **the supporting** (*or* **confirmatory,** *or* **corroborative**) **evidence for** asymmetry comes from viruses.

Подтверждающий
Fossils provide basic evidence **in support of** the concept of evolution.

Подтверждающий и опровергающий
Much evidence exists both **in support of and against** a concept that ...

Подтверждение [*см. тж.* **В подтверждение**]
Experimental **verification** (*or* **corroboration**) **of** this suggestion followed just a year later.

Подтверждён
The hypothesis **was borne out** (*or* **confirmed,** *or* **corroborated**) **by** our experiments.
This observation **has been substantiated by** the discovery of ...
The prediction **was borne out by** experiment.

Подтверждённый документами
The statements are **documented** facts at three major plants.

Подтягивать гайку (винт) [*см. тж.* **Туго подтягивать гайку**]
Tighten the nut (screw).

Подушка [*см. тж.* **Воздушная подушка**]
Some types of varnish must be cooked **under a blanket of** an inert gas.
A vehicle **on an air cushion ...**
The engine mechanism is mounted **on** rubber **cushions.**

Подхвачен I
From here coal **is picked up by** the rear conveyor.

Подхвачен II
Darwin's theory **was** again **taken up** and strongly supported by Davis in the 1920s.

Подход [*см. тж.* **Другой подход**]
In experimental studies of shock wave attenuation, three different **lines of attack** (*or* **approaches**) can be distinguished.

Подход к решению проблемы
The method of attack.

Подходить [*см. тж.* **Пригоден**]
The source of the chloride ion is seldom important; any soluble chloride **will do.**
This description is quite generalized and does not necessarily **fit well** in all cases.

Подходить для [*см. тж.* **Больше всего подходить для, Особенно подходить для, Пригоден для**]
This method **is appropriate** (*or* **suitable**) **for** describing the propagation of shock waves in solids.
For quantitative calculations of the energies the Bohr model **is** not **adequate.**
Porcelain enamels **are** ideally **suited for** this purpose.
Both methods **are suited to** new mills.
Ionization methods **are** rarely **suited to** the static measurement of gas concentration.

Подходить к I
We **come now to** the problem of assigning loci to their particular autosomes.
The problem **is** best **approached by** a consideration of dispersion curves.

Подходить к II
The hybrid orbitals were constructed **to fit** the geometry of particular molecules.

Подходить к концу [*см. тж.* **Изготовление ... подходит к концу**]
As the 19th century **came** (*or* **drew**) **to a close** electrical ignition was added to internal-combustion engines.
The railway **is nearing completion.**
To come (*or* **draw**) **to an end.**

Подходить к проблеме с двух сторон
He **attacked the problem in two ways.**

Подходить к решению проблемы
They **addressed (themselves to) the problem by** comparing the frequencies of ...

Подходить лучше всего [*см. тж.* **Лучше всего подходить для**]
These values of *a* and *b* **give the best fit.**

Подходить под углом зрения
For some diatomic molecules we **take** quite **a** different **approach** from that used in the preceding sections.

Подходить скептически к
The theory **was received with skepticism.**

Подходящий
A device with the **apt** name "Digs" was designed for use with coal mining equipment.
The following classification has proved to be **a workable one.**
A more **appropriate** (*or* **suitable,** *or* **proper,** *or* **fitting**) term is the separation energy.
The speed selected **is** that best **suited to** the prime mover.
The alkanes require reaction conditions **suitable to** the substitution of a hydrogen by ...

Подчёркивать [*см.* **Необходимо особенно подчеркнуть, что; Следует отметить, что**].

Подчёркивать необходимость
This **underlines the need for** careful matching of ...

Подчинение закону
The obedience of a gas **to** Gay-Lussac's **law** constitutes another feature of ...

Подчинять себе
This might be the best way **to tame** a plasma arc in a circuit breaker.

Подчиняться
Momentum transport **is governed by** different equations.
These values are not independent, but **are subject to** the algebraic relation: ...

Подчиняться граничным условиям
These functions **are subject to boundary conditions.**

Подчиняться закону
Comets seemed **to be amenable to** no **law.**
The distribution of errors **adheres to the law of** probability.
The current **follows the** ideal rectifier **law.**
Flow phenomena **are governed by** special **laws.**
The particle **obeys** Hooke's **law.**

Подчиняться правилу
This structure **fulfils** (*or* **follows**) **the** octet **rule.**
Boron does not **conform to the** usual **rules of** valence in forming these compounds.

Подчиняться требованию
Now let us see how magnetic-bubble devices **lend themselves to the requirements of** memory systems.

Подчиняться уравнению
Throughout these regions the dispersion is normal and **adheres to** Cauchy's **equation.**
The hole current in the 1-region **obeys** (*or* **is governed by**) the equation: ...

Подчиняться условию
The jumps of density and pressure **are subject to the condition: ...**

Подчиняющийся
A wave **subject to** some initial conditions is called hyperbolic.

Подъём и спад
In the 20th century we have seen a series of **ups and downs in** the population growth.

Подъёмная скорость
Serving the sub-assembly area there is a gantry crane with **a** maximum **hoisting speed of** 70 ft per min.

Подытоживать [*см. тж.* **Можно сказать с достаточной уверенностью, что; Резюмируя**]
The three laws of thermodynamics **sum up** our experiences with energy and natural processes.

Пожинать плоды
We have only begun **to reap the harvest of** our previous investigations.

Позаботиться о том, чтобы
Care should be exercised to see that there **is** no ingress of dust.
Make sure (*or* **See to it**) **that** there **is** no collection of moisture.
We **must take care to** exclude water in the reaction (*or* **must take care that** water **be** excluded in the reaction).

Позади [*см. тж.* **Сзади**]
Another lens is employed **back of** the point of greatest intensity.

Позволять [*см. тж.* **Давать возможность, Допускать, Не позволять, Обеспечивать возможность**]
The motor mercury interruptor **admits** control of the rate of make and break.
For a given gross weight a reduction in engine specific weight **allows** a corresponding increase in payload.
This **allows** (*or* **permits**) zero-setting the meter.
The bottom plunger moulding press **allows for** loading when the mould is in the open position.
This **enables** (*or* **permits,** *or* **allows**) the temperature **to be** found at any point.
This **enables** an easy replacement of the drum section.
The alloying elements **make it possible** to co-deposit substantial quantities of tungsten.
A central focusing screw **makes possible** the focusing of both barrels simultaneously.
Electric-motor drives **permit** efficient power generation ...
The right-angle milling attachment **permits (of)** milling in the horizontal plane.
Aircraft model testing **provides** (*or* **furnishes**) a means for rapidly evaluating ...
A laser-anemometer **enables one to** make two-dimensional velocity-component measurements optically.
This arrangement **has enabled** tooling costs **to be** reduced.
A multi-bender arrangement **permits** making a sequence of different-angle bends.
A modification of the square-jaw clutch **permits** more convenient engagement.
The first step **lets us** describe the dependence of ...
These curves **allow one** (*or* **us,** etc.) to write ...

Позволять более чётко понять
Recent advances in geochemistry **offer a clearer view of** how the continents have arisen.

Позволять ввести
The development of such instruments **made feasible** a new method for ...

Позволять делать вывод
The results are not yet sufficient **to allow** definite **conclusions.**

Позволять использовать
Charge-coupling **makes possible** comparably sized memory components.
The system **permits** (*or* **allows**) **the use of** one or more cutters for any width of cut.
The smaller fraction of Na **will allow (for)** (*or* **permit**) a hydraulic scheme.

Позволять осуществлять [*см. тж.* **Обеспечивать возможность**]
The tenfold improvement of resolution **makes possible** more detailed observations of ...
This **permits** (*or* **allows**) two checks within the five-minute period, one at the beginning and one at the end.
Free oscillations **have made** a direct determination of density **possible.**

Позволять понять
This **will allow an understanding of** the role of ...
This analysis **gives an insight into** what happens if ...

Позволять предположить
The bonding predicted **suggests** a coplanar geometry that includes ...

Позволять проводить исследования
The existence of thermometers **allowed investigations to be made of** the variation ...

Позволять создавать
This **makes possible** all the devices of solid-state electronics.

Поздний [*см.* **Более поздний**].

Поздняя стадия [*см.* **На поздней стадии**].

Позже I [*см.* **Как мы увидим дальше**].

Позже II
More recently (*or* **In more recent times**), another type of DNA polymerase was found in ...
Subsequently, it was reported that ...
More recently, detailed interferrometric studies were made.
The samples were placed in glass storage bulbs and analyzed **at a later time** (*or* **date**) [*or* **later (on)**].

Поиски [*см. тж.* **При поисках**]
To continue **the quest of** the ancestral molecule, ...
They continued **an** active **search** (*or* continued **searching,** *or* **looking**) **for** oil and gas.
The scanner will stimulate **a search for** other methods.

Поиски неполадок
Trouble shooting.

Поймать сигнал
To pick up a signal.

Пока I [*см. тж.* **А пока, До настоящего времени, До сих пор, На некоторое время**]
Disregarding the horizontal movements..., consider **for the moment** only the lifting of ...
For the time being (*or* **For the present**) we are interested primarily in ideas and not particularly in details.
This ratio has **thus far** been determined only in the case of ...
The physiologic importance of glucose will be discussed under biologic chemistry. **For now,** let us say that glucose is used in ...
Up to now (*or* **Until now,** *or* **So far,** *or* **Up to the present,** *or* **As yet**), there has been no detailed work done to find ...

Пока II [*см. тж.* **До тех пор пока**]
This is not found to be true experimentally **as long as** the similar atoms are otherwise equivalent.
As long as the energy is high enough, its particular value is irrelevant in determining ...

Пока III
It is desirable to burn the mixture **while** the piston is near top centre position.

Пока ещё I
Whilst (*or* **While**) **still** warm the work is painted with the primer.

Пока ещё II
The conditions for the formation of this centre are **as yet** unknown.

Пока не [*см.* **До тех пор пока не**].

Пока не высохнет
The books are kept in press **until dry.**

Пока не выяснено
Whether or not this type of approximation remains valid for ... **remains to be seen.**

Пока не доказано обратное
Initially these diseases should be considered to be drug induced **until proved otherwise.**

Пока не изучен
Most of the substance's actions in animal cells **remain to be explored.**

Пока не ясно
What triggered the eruption **is yet to be explained.**

Пока он находится в расплавленном состоянии
The copper is protected from air **while molten.**

Показ
The detected output is suitable for **presentation** on the screen.

Показан I
Some of the elements of such a system **appear** in Fig. 17.
The indispensability of acetylcholine esterase for nerve function **has been demonstrated by** Dr. N.
The proposed design **is depicted in** the accompanying drawing.
The current **is** amplified and **displayed** (*or* **shown**) **on** the meter.
The loader **was displayed at** the recent mining machinery exhibition.
In Fig. 5 **are shown** four views of ...
The instrumentation used in the experiment **is diagrammed** (*or* **sketched**) **in** Fig. 4.

Показан II
Digoxin is rarely **indicated** in elderly patients in sinus rhythm (*med.*).

Показан на графике
This relationship **is plotted in Fig**. 5.2.

Показан на иллюстрации
One of these crushers **is illustrated** above.

Показание [*см.* **Давать показания, Снимать показания**].

Показание шкалы
The reading of the scale.

Показанный [*см. тж.* **Здесь показан, Как показано на рисунке**]
The apparatus **depicted** (*or* **shown,** *or* **presented**, *or* **exhibited,** *or* **pictured,** *or* **displayed,** *or* **illustrated**) **on** the preceding page ..
The NH_3 molecule has a pyramidal structure of the type **illustrated in** the diagram.

Показанный на рисунке
The apparatus **of Fig.** 8.4 (*or* **presented,** *or* **shown in Fig.** 8.4) is suitable.
The device **in Fig.** 14 functions as ...

Показанный пунктиром
By following paths like those **shown dashed** (*or* **as a dashed line**) ...

Показано [*см. тж.* **Как показано на рисунке**]
As illustrated (*or* **displayed,** *or* **depicted,** *or* **shown**) **in** Fig. 1, ...
In the figure **it is intimated** why the number of sites had to begin at ...
As **will be discussed** (*or* **described**) somewhat later, ...

Показано на примере
This **has** now **been demonstrated with** alanine.

Показано, что
The isotope **was demonstrated to have** properties like those of ...

Показатель [*см. тж.* **Давать лучшие показатели, чем**]
Fossil content **may be an** additional **guide to** water clarity.
The Mach number **is an index of** compressibility.
Because coral reefs form only in very shallow water, they **are** important **indicators of** changes in sea level.

Показаться (в поле зрения)
Finally, the tunnel **appeared in view.**

Показывать I [*см. тж.* **Демонстрироваться на экране, Доказывать, Здесь показан, Как показано на рисунке, На схеме показан, Указывать**]
These machines **will be on view at** the Exposition.
Figure 7 **depicts** the particle size distribution.
Further inspection of Fig. 1 **discloses that** there are two points of inflection on the curve.
The spectrograms **evidence** only a trace of ammonia vapour.
The successive frames **portray** the motions of ...
The instrument **should read** the temperature marked on the test coil.
Adjust the valve until the supply air gauge **reads** 20 psi.
Density measurements alone do not **reveal** the actual conditions in a crystalline lattice.
The thermometer **shows** (*or* **reads**) 25° below zero.
The instrument **will indicate** the altitude of not less than ...

Показывать II
Examples **will bring out** the significance of this definition.

Показывать графически
Show by graphical display the extent to which these data conform to Raoult's law.

Показывать на примере
We **can demonstrate** this **with a** simple **example.**

Показывать точное время [*см.* **Идти точно**].

Показывать, что [*см. тж.* **Из ... видно, что**]
Further investigations **disclosed** (*or* **showed,** *or* **demonstrated**, *or* **revealed**) **that ...**
Figure 4 **indicates that** the yield of lactic acid decreases with ...
The experimental evidence **points to the fact that ...**
Our study **revealed that** the phosphate was incorporated in ...
The preliminary results **suggest that ...**
The study **made it apparent that** the frequency of occurrence ...
More precise measurements **intimate that** this is not probable.
The nature of the experiments conducted on various colloidal droplets **intimates that** they are models of how living things came into being.

Покидать [*см. тж.* **Выходить из**]
To escape the gravitational field of the Earth, ...
Thus the atoms **escape from** the cell.

Покоиться на
The metal frame **rests on** the bottom plate.

Покой [*см.* **В состоянии покоя**].

Поколение [*см.* **Из поколения в поколение**].

Поколение за поколением
Through its stability the DNA molecule is capable of providing the same information to **generation after generation of** cells (*biol.*).

Покрывать
Coat (*or* **Cover**) the object **with** a protective layer of wax.
The seats of these valves **are surfaced with** a new alloy.
The unit **is given a coat of** priming paint.
The coarser fragments sink fairly rapidly and **blanket** the lake floor **with** a thin layer of silt and sand.

Покрывать коркой
The effective removal of the foreign matter that **encrusts** these buried objects ...

Покрывать огромные пространства
Today systems of messages that can be recorded and widely transported enable man **to bridge vast reaches of space.**

Покрывать расстояние
Within this time light **goes** (*or* **covers,** *or* **travels**) **a distance of** 193,000 miles.

Покрывать расходы на
Improved performance and safe conditions for the workforce **will** quickly **recoup the cost of** specialist advice.
The recovery of some valuable material from the process was necessary in order **to offset** (*or* **recover**) **the cost of** operation.

Покрывать слоем смазки [*см. тж.* **Наносить слой на**]
The part **should be given a (lubricating) coat of** watchmaker's **oil.**

Покрывать тонким слоем
After using a centre, **give it a light coat of** lubricant and put it in a box for storage.

Покрывать флюсом
The metal is cleaned by pickling in an acid bath, washed, **fluxed** and dipped into molten zinc.

Покрываться
The alloy **becomes coated with** a protective layer of ...
A perfectly clean surface of aluminium is very active chemically and **covers itself** in the air in a few seconds **with** a very thin protective coating of oxide.

Покрываться накипью
The boil tube **has become coated with scale.**

Покрыт
The copper surface **is coated** (*or* **covered**) **with** a layer of silver.
The tank **is coated with** an enamel paint.
The junction **is plated with** platinum.
All surfaces **are silver plated.**

Покрыт накипью
Because some tubes **are scaled up,** the rate of flow might be reduced.

Покрыт растительностью
All the earth's surface **is occupied by vegetation.**

Покрытие
Cladding aluminium **with** copper ...

Покрытие дороги бетоном
Surfacing roads with concrete.

Покрыть тонким слоем
Give the workpiece **a light coat of** lubricant.

Покрытый
Cadmium-**coated** (*or* **plated**) articles.
Ferrolum is a lead-**clad** steel (*or* a steel **clad with** lead).
The calomel electrode consists of Hg **covered with** a layer of ...

Покрытый кратерами [*см.* **Густо покрыт кратерами**].

Полагать, что [*см. тж.* **Есть все основания полагать, что; Имеются основания полагать, что; Можно полагать, что; Предполагать, Считать**]
Herodotus **reasoned that** the Nile River Delta must be thousands of years old.

Поле [*см.* **Внешнее поле, Направление магнитного поля**].

Поле зрения [*см. тж.* **Держать в поле зрения, Попадать в поле зрения**]
To provide **a** wide **field of vision** to the front and rear, ...

Поле притяжения Земли
The Earth's gravitational field.

Полевые условия [*см.* **В полевых условиях, Испытанный в полевых условиях**].

Полезен [*см. тж.* **Быть полезным, Весьма полезен**]
This knowledge **is useful to** the biologist.

Полезная нагрузка
The spacecraft has **an** instrument **payload of** 152 pounds.

Полезно I[*см. тж.* **Целесообразно**]
Before beginning this task **it would be well** (*or* **we would do well**) **to** consider ...
It turns out **to be profitable to** deal with ...
It is worthwhile to be able to predict whether or not ...
It is helpful (*or* **advisable,** *or* **useful**) first **to** consider a simpler system.
It is good (*or* **sound**) **practice** [*or* **It is wise** (*or* **well**)] **to** rinse off the solution.
It may be beneficial (*or* **useful,** *or* **expedient,** *or* **advantageous**) **to** reduce the mass velocity.

Полезно II
To see the relative role of ..., **it is instructive to** compute these parameters for a 1 metre cuvette.

Полезно было бы
It might be well to examine ...

Полезный
The ladybird beetles are among the most **beneficial** of all animals because ...
The **usable** length of the thread ...
This feature of the centrifugal pump **may be of advantage** (*or* **of use,** *or* **useful,** *or* **helpful,** *or* **beneficial,** *or* **advantageous**) where the quality delivered must be ...
These effects **may be of utility** (*or* **of service**) **to** the organism in times of violent effort and emotion.

Полезный для
The crossflow tower **benefits** particularly **from** increased height.
The Reynolds number is a flow parameter **useful in** determining the extent of laminar boundary layer flow over a surface.

Полезный для химиков
The second law can be expressed in a **chemically useful** form.

Полёт без экипажа
An unmanned flight.

Полёт в воздухе
Technology of **flight through the air ...**

Полёт в космос
Flight into (outer) space [*or* **Space flight** (*or* **mission**)].

Полёт на Сатурн
A Saturn flight (*or* **mission**).

Полёт по орбите
An orbital flight.

Полёт по приборам
An instrument flight.

Полёт по прямой
A straight-line flight.

Полёт с экипажем
A manned flight.

Поливать струёй воды
To play a jet of water over (*or* **on to**) the surface of ...

Полимеризоваться в
Furfuryl alcohol **polymerizes into** a solid resin.

Полином от n неизвестных (переменных)
A polynomial (*or* **multinomial**) **in n variables.**

Полином степени n по производным
A polynomial of degree n in the derivatives p_i.

Полная амплитуда
The peak-to-valley (*or* **peak-to-trough**) **amplitude.**

Полная мощность [*см.* **Работать на полную мощность**].

Полное отражение
Regardless of whether partial or **total reflection** occurs, ...

Полное отсутствие
A total (*or* **An utter**) **absence of** segmental neurons ...

Полное представление о
The paper gives the reader **a comprehensive idea of** all the work which ...

Полное сгорание
Where **combustion is complete ...**

Полномасштабный
This system could be enlarged to **a full-size** power plant.
Full-scale tests were made.

Полностью [*см. тж.* **Весь, Выписывать полностью, Выполненный целиком из алюминия, Целиком**]
We ignore polarization effects **altogether.**
Copper loss is converted **entirely** into heat.
The system is **totally** dependent on a coding device.
This investment will **amply** (*or* **fully,** *or* **completely**) repay itself.
It was necessary to replace **the entire** bottom of the tank (*or* **completely** replace the bottom ...).
These parts are made of uniform material **throughout.**
A **fully** parallel computing system ...
The background may obscure some lines **altogether.**

Полностью автоматизированный
In present-day machines arithmetical operations **are completely** (*or* **fully**) **automatic.**
The **all-automatic** magnetic tape recording systems are ...
These machines can be semi-automatic or **completely** (*or* **fully**) **automated.**

Полностью автоматически
The rollings are obtained **fully automatically.**

Полностью аналогичен
The process **is identical with** the decay of positronium.

Полностью закрытый
Drive is transmitted by **a totally-** (*or* **completely-**) **enclosed** gearbox.

Полностью или частично
In some lower animals, magnesium replaces **either totally or partially** the skeletal calcium.
To pay for the equipment **in full or in part, ...**
The assembly operation may be transferred to a machine **in whole or in part** (*or* **wholly or in part**).

Полностью использовать
This arrangement **takes full advantage of** solar energy.

The work of expansion **uses up** the thermal energy of the gas.
Full advantage can be taken of modern methods of mechanization.
The authors **made full use of** this theory.
A full benefit is taken of this feature by the department.

Полностью не изучен
The factors influencing gas release **are** (still) **not clearly** (*or* **completely**) **understood.**

Полностью не объяснён
This phenomenon **is not (yet) properly explained.**

Полностью оборудованный
A **wholly** (*or* **fully**, *or* **completely**) **refrigerated** liner ...

Полностью оборудованный транзисторами
An all-transistor radio set.
This equipment **is completely** (*or* **fully**) **transistorized.**

Полностью оборудованный ЭВМ
We have completed testing a **fully** (*or* **completely**) **computerized** engine control system for ...

Полностью оборудованный электронными устройствами
All-electronic equipment ...

Полностью оправдывать
A quantitative analysis **fully justifies** this omission.

Полностью определять
This equation **completely determines** (*or* **defines**) the variation of ...

Полностью освещён
Few other features of these processes **have come into full light** as yet.

Полностью отвечать нормам
The polarity dots **are in full accord with accepted standards.**

Полностью отличаться от [*см.* **Абсолютно отличаться от**].

Полностью отражаться
The incident wave **is totally reflected.**

Полностью отсутствовать
Some half ganglia **are entirely absent in** these specimens.

Полностью охарактеризовывать
It would be impossible **to do the subject justice** in a few paragraphs.

Полностью перейти на
After that steam power **took over completely** (*После этого человечество полностью перешло на паровую энергию*).

Полностью подготовлен к
We **are all set for** new experiments.

Полностью понять
It is essential that we **fully grasp** (*or* **comprehend**, *or* **understand**, *or* **realize**) the meaning of this definition.
To fully appreciate the significance of these data ...

Полностью прореагировать
To react completely with the metal, ...

Полностью развитый
The **fully developed** shock front deviates from linearity.

Полностью разделять
We **fully share** the outrage that many people feel about the pollution of the environment.

Полностью симметричный
Totally symmetric (*TS*).

Полностью согласовываться относительно
Not all reports **are in complete agreement as to** the details of the process.

Полностью согласовываться с
The results **are in complete agreement with** experiments.

Полностью транзисторный [*см.* **Полностью оборудованный транзисторами**].

Полностью удовлетворять каждодневным потребностям
The communications **are completely adequate for the day-to-day needs of** the city.

Полностью устранён
These limitations **can** never **be fully eliminated.**

Полностью учитывать
This **takes into complete account** the effect of the charge, mass, magnetic moment, and ...

Полностью электронный [*см.* **Полностью оборудованный электронными устройствами**].

Полнота [*см.* **Для полноты**].

Полнота смешивания
The process is controlled by **the intimacy of mixing.**

Полный
The net work done by the working substance is equal to the **net** heat absorbed.
The **total** number of degrees of freedom is not less than 6.
The **total** electric charge of the particles ...

Полный комплект
A full range of attachments has been provided for these machines.

Полный оборот [*см. тж.* **Повернуть на один полный оборот**]
A radar signal makes **a round trip** between the Earth and a planet or a spacecraft.

Полный цикл
A complete cycle is accomplished within an hour.

Пол-оборота
When the clutch was rotated **one-half revolution, ...**

Половина
All plastic materials were obtained in sheet form of thickness **one-half** inch.
The distance between any two adjacent rivets is equal to **one-half** (*or* to **half**) the pitch.
This reduces the volume of the gas sample to **half** its original value.
A neutral hydrogen atom loses **half as much** energy per centimetre **as** the proton in passing through ...

Половинная мощность [*см.* **На половинной мощности**].

Половинная степень [*см.* **В половинной степени**].

Пологая кривая
The potential-energy **curve is** comparatively **flat,** that is it has a low rate of change.
A flattened (*or* **gently sloping**) **curve.**

Пологая поверхность
A gently inclined (*or* **sloping**) **surface.**

Пологий наклон
Sedimentary layering may have **a gentle** initial **dip.**

Пологий склон
This kind of deposit forms on **the gentle slope of** the continental rise.
Continental shelves with **gently sloping** floors ...

Полого (*антон.* **Круто**) **наклонённый**
A **gently** (*anton.* **steeply**) **inclined** side of a hill ...
A **gently descending** slope ...

Положен в основу
These equations **form the basis** of the theory of ...

Положение I [*см.* **В нижнем положении, Ведущее положение, Возвращать в первоначальное положение, Занимать положение, Исправлять положение, Исходное положение, Определять положение, Основное положение, Принимать положение, Рабочее положение, Среднее положение**].

Положение II [*см.* **Принцип**].

Положение в пространстве
The position of a molecule **in space ...**

Положение звезды
The determination of **the stellar position** depends on ...

Положение меняется
At a concentration close to 1.5, **the situation reverse**s and the crystal becomes more stable.
If, on the other hand, the electron is moving more slowly than the wave, **the reverse is true.**

Положение о том, что
The foundation of Maxwell's theory is **the proposition that** an electric charge is surrounded by ...

Положение "пара" (*хим.*) [*см.* **В положении "пара"**].

Положение с добычей урана удовлетворительное
We **do well on uranium,** mining substantially more than we need at the moment.

Положение ухудшится
In terms of the availability of resources and energy, **things will get worse,** not better.

Положив
Putting (*or* **Setting**) $\partial\Omega/\partial t = 0$, we obtain ...
On putting a certain term equal to zero ...
Setting $n = 2$, we arrive at ...

Положим [*см. тж.* **Предположим**]
Let (us assume that) $Z_x - Z_y - 1 = ...$

Положительно (*антон.* **Отрицательно**) **заряжённый**
Positively (*anton.* **Negatively**) **charged** particles ...

Положительно определённый
A is a **positive definite** $n \times n$ matrix.

Положительное свойство
Leeches have their **good points:** they inject anticoagulant substances into one's bloodstream.

Положить
Then **place** (*or* **set,** *or* **put**) $p = 0$.

Положить в основу [*см* **Использовать в качестве основы для**].

Положить конец
These failures **might have brought** (*or* **put**) **an end to** mutation breeding had it not been for a few investigators who ...
Man's earliest mastery of metallurgy **marked the end of** one great cycle of prehistory.

Положить начало [*см. тж.* **Начало было положено в**]
To initiate (*or* **trigger**) the halogenation reaction, ...
It was believed that science, having "split the atom", **had ushered in** a new era of abundant, inexpensive energy.
This achievement **marked the beginning of** active research on ...
The first theoretical investigation of optical fibres **dates back to** Hondros and Debye in 1910.
A beginning has now **been made** in providing an explanation for the relation between reality and the mind.
The new approach to enzyme technology **has initiated** a remarkable volume of work.
They **pioneered** investigations into ...

Поломка
Breakdowns of pumps have caused delays in production.
These storms frequently cause tide gauge **failure.**

Полоскать
All the glassware **was** thoroughly washed and then **rinsed with** distilled water.

Полтора [*см.* **В полтора раза больше**].

Полузаводское испытание
In order to obtain needed design data, **pilot tests have been carried out in** a small scrubber.

Полузаводской [*см.* **В полузаводском масштабе**].

Полуцелый
The magnitude of the spin can assume only integer or **half-integer** values.

Получаем (что)
For a pure gas rarefaction wave **we have** (*or* **obtain**) ...

Получаемый
The **resulting** metal is called alloy steel.
In 1954 the percentage of total benzene **derived** (*or* **obtained**) **from** petroleum was 36%.
Lysine is formed from α-ketoglutaric acid plus a C_2 fragment **derivable from** acetate.
The capacitive current **drawn by** the capacitance must ...

Получаемый в результате

The amount of OH^- **generated** (*or* **produced**) in the hydrolysis ...
The evaluation of coal for particular uses is based upon the information **provided by** the ultimate and proximate analyses.
The heat **available from** this reaction ...

Получается впечатление, что
It is as if one signal were acting as a reference code for the other.

Получается, что
From such calculations **it turns out that** the luminosity of the primordial Sun rose from ...

Получать I [*см. тж.* **В результате чего получаем, Извлекать, Можно получить, Обеспечивать путём, Приобретать**]
Several methods were used **to arrive at** an estimate of earth age.
Van der Waals' equation **is arrived at** (*or* **deduced,** *or* **derived**) **by** assuming that ...
Additional resolution **can be gained by** using ...
You can substitute ... and **come up with** a true equality.
This value **is found** (*or* **obtained**) **from** the eigenvalue equation.
To secure information on ...
Related equations **can be worked out** in the same way.
From (A3) we **have** (*or* **get,** *or* **obtain**): ...

Получать II
The natural dyestuffs **are derived from** plants or animals.
By drilling hundreds of holes they **recovered** 50,000 core samples.
They **were able to secure** about a 20% yield of ...
Bromate **may be formed from** bromide electrolytically.
The operating pulses **could be derived** (*or* **obtained**) **from** a contact breaker.
A more uniform production of acetylene gas that **can be had from** the untreated calcium carbide ...
In that period, many antibiotics **were isolated** in pure form.
Ammonium chloride **is made** (*or* **prepared**, *or* **produced**, *or* **obtained**) **by** absorbing ammonia in hydrochloric acid.
The weight of ... **is derived from** the ratio of ...

Получать впечатление
The impression gained from a study of ...

Получать всеобщее признание
It was not until the nineteenth century that his principles **received** (*or* **gained**) **general acceptance.**

Получать доступ к
Following this adsorption the phage **gains access to** the cell.

Получать доходы
The airlines **derive** (*or* **obtain,** *or* **get**) 85% **of their revenues from** that source.

Получать значение
We **arrived at** (*or* **obtained**) three different **values.**

Получать из
The force to drive such generators **derives from** the flow of water.
Certain metals **are extracted from** low-grade ores.
The number of nuclei per square centimetre **is found** (*or* **derived**) **from** Avogadro's number and the mass of the sample.

Получать информацию
Valuable **information can be gleaned** (*or* **derived,** *or* **obtained**, *or* **extracted,** *or* **gained**) **from** a measurement of the shock velocity.

Получать название
Hence, *axb* is not a true vector and therefore **is given the title** pseudovector.
Alberite **derives** (*or* **takes,** *or* **gets**) **its name from the** Albert Mines.
Alkaloids **draw their name from** a variety of sources.
A cyanoethyl group on *Y* **gave** the process **the name** cyanoethylation.
Apophyllite exfoliates when heated, is losing water, and **is named from** this characteristic.
Borite thus **received the name** Bologna stone.
The experimental tests of baryon-number conservation **have come to be known as** proton-decay experiments.

Получать наибольшую отдачу от
In order **to get the most out of** the abrasive wheel, ...

Получать обратно
The base seeks **to regain** the lost proton.

Получать ответ
In order **to arrive at** a useful **answer, ...**

Получать представление о
A simple way **to visualize** the use of such a spirit level is shown in Fig. 104.

Получать представление о том, как
To gain an impression of how the quasars are distributed let us look at ...

Получать путём
Phosphorus trichloride oxide **is manufactured by** heating ...

Получать распространение
Another type of fill that **is gaining acceptance** for smaller cooling towers is called film fill.

Получать результат
Although quite different **results from** the dimerization of isobutylene **are realized** (*or* **obtained**), ...

Получать сведения о
To gain insight into the origin of the genetic code, ...

Получать сплавы
These alloys can be fabricated (*or* **produced,** *or* **obtained**) at temperatures below 1000°F.

Получать у [*см.* **Приобретать у**].

Получать финансовую поддержку
The inventor **secured the financial backing of** the government.

Получать функцию
We **derive** two new **functions by** performing the following integrations: ...

Получать широкое признание
The process **has gained** (*or* **received**) **wide acceptance** (*or* **recognition**).

Получать энергию от
The energy is derived (*or* **comes**) **from** sunlight.
An atomic bomb **derives its energy from** nuclear reactions.
The chargers **are powered by** dry batteries.

Получаться I [*см. тж.* **Из ... может получиться**]
What **works** (*or* **succeeds**) in one mine may not be successful in another.

Получаться II
The by-products **result** in several ways.

Получаться в результате
A similar product **results from** the purification of ...
Blue and green colours **result from** the presence of ferrous iron oxide.

Получающийся
Equation (6) gives the Klein-Nishina global cross section σ, **resulting** when σ_ψ is integrated over all directions.

Получен
This result **has been arrived at** (*or* **obtained**) in a number of papers.
Confirmation of the symmetrical magnetic stripes **was gained** in the course of oceanographic surveys.
The laser dyes **were obtained from** a different firm.
The values and curves presented here **are due to** Landau.

Получен в результате [*см.* **Может быть получен в результате**].

Получен из
The value of *s* **has been derived** (*or* **obtained**) **from** Eq. (5.9).

Получение [*см. тж.* **Выделение**]
The recovery of cadmium in zinc-smelting operations ...
To obtain the new product much reequipment had to be done.
For X-ray **production** (*or* **generation**) the source is a simple filament.
Preparation of vinyl halides from alkynes ...
The production of ionic compounds ...
Some of the more common ways of **securing** pure chemical compounds from natural sources are: ...

The **production** (*or* **creation**) of neutrinos requires that ...

Получение данных
A more recent development in **data securing** (*or* **acquisition,** *or* **retrieval**) ...

Получение дуги
Arc production.

Получение металлов
Refining processes applied in **winning** non-ferrous **metals ...**

Получение спектра
The production (*or* **acquisition**) **of a spectrum.**

Получение формулы I
Formulating the structures of these species ...

Получение формулы II
Derivation of an equation.

Получение энергии
This was never considered seriously as a practical method of **power generation** (*or* **production**).

Полученный
Nevertheless, **what data have come to hand are** highly instructive.
Molecular orbitals like those **deduced for** benzene can be used as ...
The size and shape of a casting have considerable influence on the cooling rate and **resulting** microstructure.
The previously **derived** (*or* **obtained**) solutions for the potential remain ...
The information **gained** (*or* **obtained**) about this mechanism is of practical significance.
The **resultant** rotation has twice the original value.
The definition **arrived at** must ...
The greatest pressure **realized in** such experiments ...

Полученный в результате
Figure 2 presents a plot of comparative *S-N* curves **resulting from** these tests.

Полученный в результате этого
The resulting solution was satisfactory.

Полученный из
The values of *H.P.* **derived** (*or* **obtained**) **from** the above formulae are only approximate.

Полученный пиролизом
"Bitumen" is a term used to designate naturally occurring or **pyrolytically obtained** substances ...

Полученный при помощи
Knowledge of the size, etc. of molecules **deduced from** experimental methods ...

Полученный с помощью лазера
Laser-produced plasma can serve as ...

Получивший широкое признание
Molecular fluorescence spectrometry is a **well-established** method.

Получить дальнейшее подтверждение благодаря
This assumption **has received further support through** the discovery of ...

Получить дальнейшее подтверждение в виде
This point of view **has received further support through** certain results ...

Получить некоторое представление о
In order **to gain some insight into** (*or* **get some idea of**) the effect of ...
Some idea (*or* **notion**) **of** ... **can be gained from** the weight of ...

Получить ожог
Some patients **suffered burns** over half of the body's surface.

Получить ответ
In order **to secure** (*or* **obtain**) **answers** with a given level of precision ...

Получить полное признание
The evolutionary component **must receive ample recognition.**

Получить приблизительное представление о
The functions enable us **to gain** (*or* **get**) **a rough idea** (*or* **notion**) **of** these magnitudes.

Получить признание
This design **has gained recognition** (*or* **acceptance**).

Support reaction does not seem **to have received** much **recognition** in the past.

Получить своё название благодаря
The polydyne method **derives** (*or* **takes**) **its name from** employment of a polynomial displacement curve that ...

Получить стимул для развития
Real **impetus was given to** fluidics in 1959 with the publication of ...

Получить хороший отзыв
His paper **was favourably reviewed.**

Получить широкое распространение в
The use of jigs and fixtures fabricated from plastic materials **has received wide acceptance** (*or* **recognition**) from industries engaged in ...

Польза [*см. тж.* **В пользу ... говорит, Высказываться в пользу, Извлекать пользу из, На пользу человечеству, Приносить пользу**]
The utility of the theory has yet to be demonstrated.
The benefits (*or* **advantages**) **of** tin addition to cast iron ...

Пользоваться [*см. тж.* **Использовать**]
More precise tables **must be consulted for** accurate data.
For now, we **may rely on** a set of tabulated equations given in Appendix *D*.
It is not always possible **to refer to** (*or* **use**) stars for orientation.

Пользоваться большим уважением
He **was held in high esteem** in the geological profession.

Пользоваться вниманием [*см.* **Относиться с должным вниманием к**].

Пользоваться меньшей популярностью
This alternative **has declined in popularity.**

Пользоваться осторожно
This concept **must be used with care.**

Пользоваться поддержкой
The theory **received support from** a group of astronomers.

Пользоваться популярностью
One of the reasons why tools did not **find favour** was a "failure to recognize the role of phase composition".
For years this hypothesis **was favoured** (*or* **enjoyed popularity**).

Пользоваться растущей популярностью
The digital computer **has found increasing favour in** real-time applications.
Another type of relay which **is growing in popularity** is the dry reed relay.

Пользоваться спросом
These sizes **are in demand.**

Пользоваться широкой популярностью
His principles **were widely accepted** (*or* **favoured**) **in** Europe and North America.

Пользуясь
The lines of the spectra are identified **by reference to** frequency correlation tables.

Полюс [*см.* **На полюсе**].

Поменять местами
The machine can be operated above synchronism **by interchanging the position of** the brushes.
The motor can be reversed **by reversing** two of the leads supplying the primary.

Поместить ... между
We **interposed** (*or* **placed**) a nonmagnetic bar **between** the piston and the sample.

Поместить на пути луча
The object was **placed** (*or* **interposed**) **in the path of a** parallel **beam** of light.

Помеха
The size of the ship **is** no **barrier to** the application of this principle.
This is **a** serious **handicap** (*or* **hindrance**) **to** such a study.
Radio reception was poor on account of static **interference.**
Interference with the operation of the pump owing to the proximity of ... was eliminated.

Помечать [*см. тж.* **Указывать**]
The outer scale **is labelled** (*or* **marked**) "miles".

Помеченный [*см. тж.* **Обозначен**]
Five terminals on the terminal plate **are marked** (*or* **labelled**) *L, N, E, N, L* (*L* = line, *N* = natural, *E* = earth).

Помеченный звёздочкой
The **starred** (*or* **asterisked**) quantities ...

Помещать [*см. тж.* **В котором размещён, Вставлять**]
A resistance is **inserted between** cathode **and** earth.
The cabinet **may be located** (*or* **placed,** *or* **positioned,** *or* **situated,** *or* **sited**) near the mill.
The sample **is mounted** (*or* **placed**) **in** a holder.

Помещать вместо него [*см. тж.* **Заменив**]
One can eliminate the laser **by substituting** a small white lamp at the point where the mercury bead is normally placed.

Помещать между
A sheet **is interposed** (*or* **placed,** *or* **sandwiched**) between the input and output series elements.
A thin layer of the fluid **is confined** (*or* **inserted,** *or* **sandwiched**) **between** two plates.

Помещать на пути
The filters **are interposed** (*or* **put,** *or* **placed**) **in** the beam.
Various thicknesses of some material **are placed across** a beam of beta rays.

Помещать перед
In front of a telescope **are placed** two fixed mirrors shown in Fig. 10.

Помещаться
The new plant **will accommodate** engineering and processing facilities.
The amplifier **is contained in** an aluminium case.
The welding transformer **is enclosed in** a cast iron box.
The instrument **is housed in** a case.
Insulation **is placed** (*or* **sandwiched**) **between** the commutator bars.
The entire computer **will have to fit in** a box.

Помещаться на ладони
The instrument **fits into the palm of** your hand.

Помещение [*см. тж.* **В закрытом помещении, Внутри и вне помещения**]
Excellent laboratory **facilities** are provided and a variety of equipment is available.

Помещён
A filter **is interposed** (*or* **placed,** *or* **inserted**) **between** the lamp and the lens.
The column **is enclosed in** an oven.
When a hydrogen atom **is put** (*or* **placed**) **in** an electric field ...

Помещён вплотную к
The source **abuts** (*or* **is placed directly against**) the endface of the fibre.

Помещён на
The base **on which** the apparatus **rests ...**

Помещённый в центре
Gases pass from the combustion chamber into a **centrally located** (*or* **positioned,** *or* **disposed**) flue.

Помещённый на пути луча
Consider a crystal **mounted in (the path of)** an X-ray beam.

Помимо I [*см. тж.* **Кроме, Сверх**]
There are a number of sizeable satellites **apart from** the Moon that are large enough to ...
One of the disadvantages in the use of this oxidizer, **apart from** its hydroscopic nature, is the crystal phase change which occurs at 32°C.
This indicator offers many outstanding features **aside** (*or* **apart**) **from** (*or* **besides**) the great sensitivity.
The resonator has the trivial resonance $F=0$ **in addition to** the usual free-free resonances.
Impact resistance is dependent on a number of factors **other than** enamel formulation.

Помимо II [*см. тж.* **За исключением, Не включая**]
Except for (*or* **Aside from,** *or* **With the exception of**) the bubbling caps, the plant was constructed entirely of carbon steel.
The total cost of the construction, **exclusive of** material costs, would be ...

The capital cost of the conversion, **over and above** the cost of the control equipment, may be considerable.
This magnetic amplifier has no moving parts **other than** relays.

Помимо всего прочего
These properties make it possible, **among other things,** to focus a laser beam to a spot with ...
The new evidence revealed, **among other things,** four large volcanic mountains on the Martian surface.

Помимо тех, которые
Amino acids **other than those that** make up proteins are also present in ...

Помимо того [*см.* **Кроме того**].

Помимо того, что
Apart from the fact that chopped carbon fibers provide a stronger filler than most alternatives, the wear characteristics of the component are improved ...

Помимо того, что ... является ..., он ещё и представляет собой
As well as being the solution of an eigenvalue equation, the propagation constant **is also** an explicit function of the model fields.

Помимо этого
There are several instances of a fairly well-developed family life, but **other than these,** little can be found to illustrate any development of societies among the beetles.
Beyond that point no basic differences from the other proposals can be noted.

Помножить на [*см. тж.* **Умножать на**]
The value of the cross section **should be multiplied by** the fraction of ...

Помогать [*см. тж.* **В помощь, Облегчать положение, При помощи, С помощью**]
Each piece of information **aids** (*or* **helps**) **in** the determination of total molecular geometry.
This **can be a help in** deciding ...
The method **assisted** the operation **in** speeding up the process.

Помогать понять
These developments **furnish insights into** the nature of ...

Помогать при
This information **aids** (*or* **helps**) **in** the reconstruction of ancient plants.
This result **is helpful in** the deduction of ...

Помогать уточнить
The distribution of salinity in the sea **gives a (further) elucidating glimpse into** the structure of eddies.

Помощь [*см.* **Оказывать помощь при**].

Понадобится много времени для того, чтобы
One will have to go a long way to find the unmetamorphosed equivalent.

Понадобится некоторое время для того, чтобы
It will take some time before we overcome this problem.

Понижать [*см. тж.* **Снижать**]
To bring the pressure **down to** this value, one must ...
This will heat the thermistor enough **to lower** (*or* **decrease,** *or* **reduce,** *or* **diminish,** *or* **cut**) the resistance **to** 200 ohms.
The transformer is suitable for **stepping down** (*or* **reducing,** *or* **decreasing**) the supply voltage **to** 85 volts on open circuit.

Понижение точки кипения
Boiling point depression (*or* **lowering**).

Понижение (*антон.* **Повышение**) (*содержания ... в организме*)
A significant potassium **lowering** (*anton.* **elevation**) ...

Понижение уровня моря
Depression (*or* **Lowering**) **of sea level.**

Пониженный
The products have **reduced** (*or* **lessened**) combustibility.

Понимание [*см. тж.* **Глубокое понимание, Для лучшего понимания**]
For reading with **comprehension ...**
If we wish **to gain a (more penetrating) insight into** our physical environment, ...
The realization of these difficulties did not stop them from further research.

An understanding of the chemical problem of bioluminescence involves isolating ...
Awareness, Grasp ...
Experimental work **has given us (great) insight into** the mechanism of ...

Понимать [*см. тж.* **Осознать**]
In order **to (better) appreciate** the physical mechanism for ...
It is easy **to perceive** (*or* **see,** *or* **realize**) why the cost is enormous.
It is important **to realize** (*or* **recognize,** *or* **understand,** *or* **be aware of the fact that**) real processes impose problems in addition to ...
Newton **perceived** (*or* **came to perceive**) **that** the planets ...
It is important **to grasp that** the nature of seeds depends on ...
In order **to gain (some) insight into** (*or* **an understanding of**) the effect of the number of plates on evaporation performance ...

Понимать буквально
These simplified "visualizations" should not **be taken (too) literally.**

Понятие [*см. тж.* **Не иметь ни малейшего понятия**]
In such cases it is convenient to introduce **the concept of** a train tensor.
The notion of the atomicity of electric charge was then developed.
The complete change in **the ideas on** the origins of ...

Понятия не иметь о [*см. тж.* **Не иметь ни малейшего понятия, Ничего не знать о**]
We **have no idea of** the answer to these questions.

Понять
One **can** now **appreciate that** the planets of the inner solar system occupy only...
In order **to appreciate** the meaning of ...

Поочерёдно [*см. тж.* **Один за другим, По очереди**]
The gas should be passed **in turn** through (1) alkali solution, (2) sulphuric acid, **and** (3) ...
The steel is subject to **alternat**e contact with oxygen **and** water.
By **alternately** starting **and** stopping the machine ...
In such processes the iron oxide is **alternately** subject to absorption **and** regeneration.

Поочерёдный
Alternate freezing **and** thawing ...

Попавший в
Objects **caught in** (*or* **captured by**) a force field ...

Попадание [*см. тж.* **Препятствовать попаданию, Проникновение в**]
To prevent water **entering** is one of the aims of mine drainage.
Adhesives seal against **entrapment of** moisture between surfaces ...
The counter-gravity flow of the inhaled air reduces **the entry of** heavier dust particles into the filtering medium.
Motors on the milling heads are totally enclosed to exclude **ingress** (*or* **penetration**) **of** metallic dust generated by the cutters.

Попадать в I [*см. тж.* **Относиться к III, Проникать в**]
Does your product **fall into** this category?

Попадать в II [*см. тж.* **Оказываться в**]
Suppose that N points **are thrown into** the μ space; what is the probability that just n_1 points **will end up** (*or* **find themselves**) **in** cell 1, n_2 in cell 2, and so on?
The points **fall on** a straight line.
These harmonics **may fall within** the pass band of the receiver.
The particles **arrive at** the screen on a line which ...
Then uranium **finds its way into** sedimentary rocks.
This will enable dirt **to work into** the threads of the micrometer.
There is no risk of dirt **becoming trapped between** the surfaces.
In case contamination **enters** the nitrogen stream, ...
These electrons do not necessarily **land in** the corresponding region of the anode.

Попадать в поле зрения
Each operator controls the cars until they **come into the view of** the other operator.
When two objects **fall within** an observer's **view, ...**

Попадать в фокус
The image **comes to a focus** several feet behind the primary mirror.

Попадать на
When the particle **strikes** the photographic plate, ...
The number of molecules that **hit** a section of the wall per second ...
If allowed **to fall on** a red-hot, inert surface, the distillate decomposes.
When one of the scattered atoms **lands in** an empty site, ...

Попадать на орбиту
Some of these comets **will be thrown into** hyperbolic **orbits** and be lost from the solar system.

Попадать под влияние
At this point, a comet **comes under the influence of** Jupiter.

Попадающий к
Only a minor fraction of petroleum products **reaching** the consumer has not been chemically changed from its original state.

Попа́рно
An operator feeds the rods **in pairs** onto the charging conveyor.
The rods **are arranged in pairs.**
The stars in a cluster tend **to unite by pairs** into binary systems.

Поперечное движение
Automatic positioning of worktable **cross** (*or* **transverse**) **movement ...**

Поперечное сечение рассеяния *и т.п.*
The electron's **cross section for scattering** (*or* **scattering cross section**) **is** given by ...

Поперечные связи [*см.* **Образование поперечных связей**].

Поперечный
The truss is capable of resisting **transverse** shear.
A **transverse** magnetic field.

Поперёк
The engine is mounted **crosswise** (*or* **transversely**) on the frame.

Пополам
The pipes are cut **in two.**
The cell breaks **in two.**
The fruit is cut **in half** (*or* **into halves**).

Пополнять
We **augment** (*or* **supplement**) these equations **by the addition of ...**

Пополняться
The solution **undergoes replenishment** (*or* **is replenished**) twice.

Поправка к
A correction to enthalpies ...

Поправка на [*см. тж.* **Вводить поправку на, Внесение поправки, Вносить поправку на, Исправленный на активность**]
The correction for scattering in the lower atmosphere is difficult to make accurately.

Поправочный коэффициент
A correction factor.

По-прежнему
Such tubes **will continue in use** (*or* **will be used as before**).

Попросту говоря
Put very simply, the three-level system has the potential of ...

Популярность растёт
Pneumatic gauging continues **to grow in popularity.**

Популярный [*см. тж.* **Быть весьма популярным**]
A **well-accepted** hypothesis maintains that ...

Попутно
Let me note **in passing** that the lighter components do give rise to etchable tracks.
Retinopathy is often discovered as an **incidental** finding when examining the fundus (*med.*).
A great deal of carbon dioxide is made **incidentally** during the heating of limestone to produce lime.

Попутно отметим, что
We mention in passing that the radioactive thorium-lead decay series is an important heat-producing system.

Попутно упоминаться
The soluble system **has** already **received passing mention** in connection with ...

Попытаться
An effort must be made to reduce the scatter noise.

Попытка [*см. тж.* **В попытке**]
This has led to **attempts at** dividing the tube into segments.
Many **attempts to** mechanize the welding procedure led to ...

Попытка не удалась
Attempts at air sterilization **have not been successful in** preventing colds.

Попытки
A century-long **effort to** understand the structure of ...

Попытки раскрыть тайну происхождения
The search for "how" and "when" of the origin of our universe intrigues us all.

Порá
The time is ripe (*or* **It is high time,** *or* **It is an appropriate time**) **to** accept this principle.

Поражать I
One **is struck by** the similarities between the speculations of 50 years ago and the better-understood concepts of today.

Поражать II
Several diseases **attack** the coconut plant.
If the tumour **invades** surrounding tissues, the latter ...

Поражать в первую очередь
This disease **primarily strikes** children.

Поражён раком
This tissue is suspected **to harbour cancer.**

Поразительно
The genetic code system is **breathtakingly** simple.
It is a striking fact that the system's activity can be evoked by all kinds of stresses.
The development of missiles and aircraft has been **astoundingly** (*or* **amazingly,** *or* **remarkably**) rapid during the past thirty-five years.

Поразительно похож на
The van't Hoff equation **bears a striking resemblance to** an equation used to represent ...

Поразительный I [*см. тж.* **Блестящий II**]
The cell wall of a collenchyma cell is its most **striking** feature.
This will not impair the **dramatic** (*or* **amazing**) reliability advantages of the miniature radar unit.
The use of such drugs has increased over the past three decades, with **dramatic** (*or* **striking**) success in some cases.

По-разному
Haliotus fulgens are **variously** called blue abalone, green abalone or the splendid ear shell.

Поровну делиться [*см.* **Делиться поровну между**].

Порог [*см.* **На пороге**].

Порода, залегающая горизонтальными слоями
Horizontally layered rocks.

Порождать [*см. тж.* **Вызывать**]
This coupling **gives rise to** the multiplicity of lines in the naphthalene spectrum.

Порождать проблему
Radioactive materials **pose** a unique **problem:** they must be stored in such a way that ...

Порочный
The phlogiston theory **was fallacious.**

Порошкообразный [*см. тж.* **В порошкообразной форме**]
The **powdered** catalyst is removed by filtration.

Порошок [*см. тж.* **Превращать в порошок, Размельчать в порошок**]
Powdered aluminium (*or* Aluminium **powder**) ...

Поручать работу
The work was entrusted to our company.

Поручен
Our company **was charged with** the construction of the telescope.

Поручено
The Committee **is charged with** coordinating the plans of ...

Порча

The deterioration of buried objects is largely the result of chemical change.
These storms frequently cause tide gauge **failure.**

Поршень [*см.* **Ход вниз**].

Порядка [*см. тж.* **Около, Приблизительно**]

If *A* and *B* are square matrices **of order** *n* (*or* **of the** *n***th order**), then the product *AB* is ...
The decay is **first-order** (*or* **of the first order**).
Calculations indicate that laser energies **of** (*or* **on,** *or* **in**) **the order of** 5,000 joules will be needed.
These steels have yield strengths **in the** 200,000 psi **area.**
At temperatures **in the neighbourhood of** 1000°C ...
Usual burning times **are of (the) order (of)** 150 sec.
The thermal efficiency of these units **will be in the region of** 40%.

Порядок [*см. тж.* **В порядке увеличения, В следующем порядке, В стройном порядке, В указанном порядке, Приводить в порядок**]

The order in which derivatives are taken indicates that ...
In accordance with **the** established **procedure ...**

Порядок величины

These two **values are of** (*or* **on,** *or* **in**) **the** same **order** (*or* **magnitude**).

Посадка с зазором в

For brazing steel with copper **a press fit to** 0.002 in. **clearance** may be used.

Посвятить усилия *чему-л.*

We have devoted our efforts to measurements of ...

Посвящать всё свое время изучению вопроса

He decided **to pursue the matter on a full-time basis.**

Посвящён

Much research **is devoted** (*or* **dedicated**) **to** variations of reaction conditions.
The direct utilization of coal as a source of such... **has been the objective of** much research.
This section of the book **is concerned** (*or* **deals**) **with** [*or* **is dedicated** (*or* **devoted**) **to**] conveyor belting.
As bacteriophage T7 has been more thoroughly studied than T3, much of the discussion **centres on** that form (*biol.*).

Посвящённый

Haemolysis is discussed further in the section **on** [*or* **devoted** (*or* **dedicated**) **to**] jaundice.

Посещение объекта

An on-site visit.

Поскольку [*см. тж.* **Ввиду того, что; Так как**]

Inasmuch as (*or* **Because,** *or* **Since**) laser light is highly monochromatic, it is evident that ...
Having no electrons, the proton is the smallest possible ion.
By virtue of the fact that ... the wave possesses a different form upon exit from the shaper than it had at entry.
Considering that d = ..., expression 2 may be written in the form ...
Equation (1) is a particularly convenient choice **as** (*or* **in so far as**) it expresses this value in terms of ...

Поскольку это касается

The installations of these shafts are completely automatic **as to** loading and dumping.
Each machine is designed for a particular service, especially **as to** (*or* **as regards**) the kinds of materials for which it is best suited.
The two types are equivalent **insofar** (*or* **so far,** *or* **as far**) **as** discrimination among various gases is concerned.
So far as the wave front velocity **is concerned,** linear and semi-linear equations are the same.

Поскольку это так

This being the case, the predictions of any metric theory for the solar system can be analyzed using ...

После [*см. тж.* **Вслед за**]

Following these two methods, four chemical analysis methods have been tried.

To overcome the pressure expected **following** (*or* **after**) an accident ...
On evacuating, gas must flow out through 5-mm. holes.
Once installed, this heater operates automatically.
Subsequent to exposure at the desired temperatures the specimens were baked at 400°F.
Upon leaving the tank, the flow divides into four streams.
This, **when** integrated (*or* **upon** integration), yields: ...
On substitution of the expression for β from Sec. 17-15, we obtain ...

После вычета
This gives, **on subtraction,** the desired enthalpy value.

После завершения строительства
The lock (*шлюз*) will have a vertical lift of 103 ft **upon completion of** the dam.

После обработки [*см.* **До и после обработки**].

После ... остаётся
Evaporation of the lake water **leaves behind** dissolved salts.

После преобразования
On rearrangement, this result can be written as ...

После рождения [*см.* **До и после рождения**].

После того, как
Once a given compound **has been** identified, the analysis is repeated.
Nowhere in the junction may carrier densities increase or decrease **once** the dynamic equilibrium **is** established.

После чего
There is a specific displacement of electrons with a resultant rearrangement of bonds **following** (*or* **after**) **which** the coenzyme and products dissociate.
These products are allowed to remain long enough to obtain assays, **whereupon** (*or* **then**) they are sent to the proper pile.

После этого
Production declined rapidly **thereafter.**
Thereafter the magnet currents will be held fixed.

Последнее время [*см.* **В последнее время, До последнего времени**].

Последнее нововведение
This **is the most recent** (*or* **the latest**) **innovation.**

Последние достижения
Recent (*or* **The latest**) **advances in** optical bistability ...

Последний [*см. тж.* **За последние годы**]
Those portions of the casting that **are last to** solidify ...
In **the last-mentioned** group these are found in ...
The two diesel engines **last mentioned** (*or* **named**) have also seen service elsewhere.
This isotope is called deuterium and its ions are called deuterons; **these latter,** when moving with high energy, ...
According to **recent** (*or* **the latest**) experiments ...

Последний из двух
These coefficients can be found either as ... or as ...; **the latter** approach is adopted in Section 35-14.

Последний из нескольких
In the last-named disease there is paroxysmal labirinthine ...

Последний по порядку, но не по значению
Last but not least, man's internal electrostatic processes rival in ingenuity any that man has been able to devise.

Последний удар по
That was **the last** (*or* **final**) **blow to** the phlogiston theory.

Последовательно I [*см. тж.* **Нумероваться по порядку**]
The glassware was then rinsed **successively** (*or* **sequentially**) with distilled, deionized water.
The carbon atoms of the basic chain are numbered **sequentially.**
Firing **sequentially,** this laser arrangement could achieve unparalleled repetition rates.
The system requires the red, blue and green components to be printed **in succession.**
Operations are performed on two components **in tandem.**

The machine performs all operations on the stationary workpiece simultaneously rather than **consecutively.**

Последовательно II
For large objects several spray guns can be used **in tandem.**
Used **in tandem with** a sock-type filter, the charcoal performs two functions.

Последовательно включённый [*см.* **Включённый последовательно**].

Последовательно соединённый [*см.* **Соединён(ный) последовательно**].

Последовательно установленный [*см.* **Установленный последовательно**].

Последовательное сопротивление
A capacitor with **a** low **resistance in series ...**

Последовательность [*см. тж.* **В следующем порядке**]
The sequence of processes is intake, compression, addition of heat, expansion, and exhaust.
The numerals indicate **the consecutive** order in which the lines are drawn.
The order of the principal steps in the treatment of ...

Последовательность операций
The operating sequence (*or* **The sequence of operations**).

Последовательные и параллельные реакции
Consecutive and parallel reactions.

Последовательные приближения
The successive approximations used in interpreting X-ray data ...

Последовательный I [*см. тж.* **В последовательном порядке, Ряд реакций**]
Three **consecutive** five-hour runs ...
A number of **successive** measurements are usually sufficient.
The solution is made acid with **successive** additions of HCl.
Automatic functions include **sequential** or simultaneous positioning of ...

Последовательный II
The **series** resistance in the winding ...

Последовать за этим
A furious controversy **ensued.**

Последствия [*см. тж.* **В результате, Вызывать опасные последствия, Далеко идущие последствия**]
The ecological **impact** (*or* **consequences**) **of** pollutants ...
Such a rise of sea water **could have** serious **repercussions for** coastal areas.

Последствия, отрицательно влияющие на окружающую среду
Extraction of mineral resources from the earth **has** many **serious environmental impacts:** deep scarring of the land, ...

Последующий [*см. тж.* **В последующие годы, В последующих главах, И последующий, С последующим**]
These problems are discussed in **later** sections.
Subsidence of the basin continued **through** the **ensuing** Devonian, Mississippian, and Pennsylvanian periods (*geol.*).
In **succeeding** years several other designs appeared.
The **ensuing** (*or* **subsequent,** *or* **succeeding,** *or* **following**) chapters discuss ...
Some of these rules will be used in the discussion **that follows.**
This will be investigated in the **following** sections.
In **subsequent** experiments ...
All the **ensuing** development ...
Such films must be removed by **subsequent** cleaning operations.
Forecasts normally cover a period of 24 to 30 hours with an outlook for the **succeeding** 24 hours.

Послойный
Layer-by-layer adsorption ...

Посмотреть на [*см.* **Заглядывать в**].

Посмотрите внимательно на
Take a good (*or* **detailed**) **look at** the parts shown here.

Посредине [*см.* **В центре, Внизу посредине**].

Посредине между
The point **halfway between** the ambilicus **and** the anterior prominence of the right hip bone ...

The line drawn **midway between** the upper **and** lower surfaces ...

Посредством
This includes the formation of estrogen **through** a series of oxidation and reduction reactions.
Neutralization of the acid **through** the addition of (*or* **by** adding) ...
These data can be obtained **through** long-term observation.
The spring acts on the valve spindle **via** (*or* **through the medium of**) the yoke.
The relay controls large values of current and power **through the utilization of** a special cold cathode tube.

Поставить перед собой задачу
He **set himself the task of** proving the possibility of self-duplicating automata.

Поставить под сомнение
Some recent studies **have thrown** (*or* **cast**) **doubt on** the ideal treatment of reflection at a plane wall.

Поставленная цель
The computer should be given a specific statement of **the goal to be sought.**
This method is well suited for **the purpose in hand.**

Поставленный "на попа" (*жарг.*)
The machine looks something like an engine lathe **turned up on end,** with the faceplate at the bottom and with the work mounted vertically.

Поставлять
The wire **was supplied in** rolls.

Поставлять в собранном виде
The panel **is supplied assembled.**

Поставлять по заказу
Larger sizes **are available on special order.**
Ranges beyond these **are furnished** (*or* **supplied**) **on order.**

Поставляться
Such accelerators **are** now **available from** a number of commercial firms.
Normally, stove bottles **come with** square nuts.
The pump **comes in** single, duplex or triplex configurations.

Lead **is obtainable in** sheets and pigs.

Постадийно
The combustion of solids such as coal and wood occurs **in stages** (*or* **steps**).

Постановка вопроса (проблемы)
In **the definition of problems ...**
Formulation (*or* **Statement**) **of the problem.**

Постановка задачи
The method for **setting up a problem** is as follows: ...

Постепенно
The difference in temperature levels will be **progressively** (*or* **gradually**) reduced along the length of the unit.
These values increase **in a gradual manner** (*or* **gradually**).
The voltage may be **smoothly** varied from ... to ...
A **smoothly** (*or* **gradually**) ascending trajectory ...
Rotating hydraulic motors were improved **by degrees,** over the years.

Постепенно переходить в
Coastal marshes lie within the tidal zone and **grade into** fresh-water marshes above sea level.

Постепенно уменьшать дозу
Cimetidine is very effective, but it is best **to tail it off** when the course has finished rather than to abruptly stop the patient taking it (*med.*).

Постепенный
The **progressive** removal of a species from solution by precipitation ...

Постороннее вещество
Intake screens protect the oil pump from **foreign material** (*or* **substance**).
This design reduces the risk of **foreign matter** entering the manometer.

Постороннее включение
The successive growth stages of dolomite have different amounts of **included foreign matter** (*or* **foreign inclusions**).

Посторонние лица
Enclosures are used to prevent **unauthorized persons** from entering ...

Посторонний
The input signal should be free of **extraneous** high-frequency components.
Extraneous noise sources interfered with antenna evaluation.

Постоянная (величина)
"S" is (**a**) **constant** here.

Постоянно [*см. тж.* **Всё время, Всегда, Ежедневно, Неизменно, Непрерывно, Неуклонно**]
The surface of Venus is **perpetually** (*or* **constantly**) hidden by clouds.
Such devices will be **routinely** available.
One problem arose **repeatedly** in any attempt to calculate ...
Erosion, transportation and deposition **persistently** carry mineral matter from higher places on the continents to ...
The forces are changing **constantly.**
Later researchers have **consistently** reported that no such change could be detected.
Special storage places should be provided in which the temperature can be held below 60°F **at all times.**
The entire sensitive portion of the bulb must be immersed **at all times** in the medium being measured.
What lies behind the Sun's **ever** changing visible features?
The need for this product will grow **steadily.**

Постоянно ведётся регистрация
At the gauging stations, **continuous records are kept of ...**

Постоянно находиться в движении под действием
In a fluidized bed, solid particles **are kept in constant motion by** a blast or air or gas.

Постоянно проверяться
The harmlessness of the food colourings to the human system **is under constant check by** a federal agency.

Постоянно следить за
The orbits of these objects **may be kept under steady watch.**

Постоянно соприкасаться с
This surface **is in continuous** (*or* **constant**) **contact with ...**

Постоянно существовать
In a swamp or bog environment, where water saturation **persists, ...**

Постоянный I
A structural member of **uniform** cross-section ...

Постоянный II [*см. тж.* **Неизменный, Оставаться неизменным, Поддерживать постоянное напряжение**]
The pressure and temperature have been presumed **to be fixed.**
The composition **is fixed** and the two variables are temperature and pressure.
A **steady** difference of potential exists across ...

Постоянный III
This assures complete control of rods and caps **at all times.**
In areas of **sustained** shortage of water ...

Постоянный во времени
The number of particles in any given element **is constant in** (*or* **with**) **time** (*or* **temporally constant**).

Постоянный и переменный
We assume that the pressure and temperature **are fixed** (*or* **constant**) and that only the amounts of the components **are variable.**

Постоянный спутник Земли
A permanent Earth satellite.

Построен по типу
This theory **is modelled on** quantum electrodynamics.

Построение кривых
Next comes **the construction of curves.**

Построение теории
These assumptions provide the basis for **the derivation** (*or* **development,** *or* **construction**) **of an** interesting **theory.**

Построенный [*см.* **Строить**].

Построенный по типу
Parallel to this psychological theory, and **patterned after it,** is the anatomical scheme of primary receptive centres.

Постукивание [*см.* **Лёгкое постукивание, Слегка постукивать**].

Постулировать

Graham's Law of Diffusion **postulates** (*or* **states) that** the velocity of diffusion is inversely proportional to ...

Поступать [*см. тж.* **В ... поступает, Подаваться**]
The gas **arrives at** the station.
The ions **arrive at** the detector.
Input signals **come from** a digital typewriter.
The sweep signal **is derived from** two oscillators.
The fuel **is drawn from** the main tank.
The centrifuge cleans the fuel before it **enters** the engines.
When the water **enters** the canal, ...
The information **originates from** radar instrumentation.
After hoisting, the ore **is admitted to** a dressing plant.
Where the expected response to therapy **is** not **forthcoming, ...**
The depression **receives** (*во впадину поступают*) sediments **from** adjacent mountain slopes.

Поступать в продажу [*см. тж.* **Иметься в продаже**]
The new device **was offered for sale** in March.
The automatic brake **will be on the market** by spring.
Some new types of packages **have come on the market** in recent years.

Поступать в продажу в виде
The alloy **comes in** bar, wire and forging billets.
The steel **is available in** rolled strip form.

Поступать из
Air supply **is taken from** shop air lines.
These fossils **come from** widely separated parts of the world.
The oxides of sulphur **come** mainly **from** electric power plants.

Поступать на
The first waves **to arrive at** a seismometer are compressional waves.

Поступать на Землю
The solar energy that **falls upon** (*or* **arrives at**) **the Earth ...**

Поступать на рынок [*см. тж.* **Поступать в продажу**]
Supplies from outside the U.S. **could come** (*or* **go**) **on the market** at a much lower cost than ...

Поступать от
Orders for book manufacturing **emanate** (*or* **come**) **from** book publishers.
The input to the processor **is derived from** a time varying electrical signal.

Поступать с
Virtually all our energy supply **is derived from** the Sun.

Поступать самотёком [*см. тж.* **Под действием собственного веса**]
The rods **gravitate (down) to** an indexing workset.
A drainage bucket from which the sink products **gravitate into** a discharge chute ...

Поступать следующим образом
To prove this statement, we **proceed as follows: ...**

Поступающий
One can thus reconstruct the method the brain uses to analyze **incoming** information about ...
The output **available from** the flip-flops ...
The current **drawn from** the power supply ...
The **incoming** (*or* **arriving**) fuels will be handled in ...
On the basis of 1 lb mole/h of air in the **feed** gas we calculate ...
The enthalpy of the **entering** (*or* **arriving**) air is 34.09 Btu/lb.

Поступающий в
This cuts off current **to** the cell.

Поступающий сигнал
An incoming signal.

Поступление [*см. тж.* **Отрезать поступление, При поступлении**]
The device cuts off **supplies of** coal.
The arrival of the ore **at** the plant ...
The delivery of the tracer **to** an organ ...
The energy **receipts from** the Sun ...

Поступление питательных веществ в
This insures **an** adequate **nutrient supply for** the central region of the nervous system.

Посылаемый на Землю
Data **brought back** by artificial satellites indicate that ...

Посылать на Землю
The photographs **sent back by** Mariner probes showed that ...

Посыпать
If iron filings **are sprinkled on** a piece of paper held over a bar magnet ...

Посыпать порошком
The liquid **has been sprinkled with a** fine **powder.**

Потенциальные возможности в области
It was not until the late 1950s that organic chemists really began to appreciate **the potential of** this device **for** structural studies.

Потери на испарение
Losses through (*or* **due to,** *or* **by**) **evaporation** are regarded as trifling.

Потери на отражение
Losses by reflection.

Потери на трение
The friction(al) losses in the drive mechanism ...

Потери плазмы, вызванные неустойчивостью
Instability-initiated plasma losses.

Потеря [*см. тж.* **Восполнять потерю, Нести потери**]
If the fabric is thoroughly rinsed after washing no **loss in** tensile strength need be expected.
Loss in equilibrium water capacity ...
Higher angular resolutions could be achieved but only at the cost of a severe **sacrifice in** sensitivity.
The sacrifice of one power stroke out of every two is a frequent deterrent to the selection of ...

Потеря в весе
A weight loss of 6% ...

Потеря воды образцом
There **is a loss of water from the sample.**

Потеря общности [*см.* **Без потери общности**].

Потеря управления
Serious problems, such as **a** complete **loss of control, ...**

Потерянный на испарение
Water **lost** (*or* **losses**) **by** evaporation ...

Потерянный на трение
The energy **lost to** (*or* **in**) **friction ...**

Потерять интерес к
These innovations **disengaged** any further British **interest in** hydraulic-motor theory (*Ввиду этих нововведений Великобритания потеряла интерес к теории гидравлических двигателей).*

Потерять смысл
The whole analysis **loses its meaning.**

Поток [*см. тж.* **Воздушный поток, Возникновение потока, Выходящий поток, Испускаемый поток частиц**]
A mechanical feeder ensures **a** steady **flow of** material.
The sulphur is burned off the iron ore by **a stream of** fluidizing air.
The coal-proportioning system blends individual **streams of** coal **from** the two mines into uniform feed for ...
A flux of heat ...

Поток внутрь
The inward flux of heat was determined.

Поток наружу
The outward flow of the gas ...

Поток частиц
This wave could be associated with **a stream of particles** moving with velocity.

Поток электронов
Current, in the form of **an electron stream,** is drawn from the cathode to the anode.

Потомство
The function of the organism and its **offspring ...**

Потому что [*см. тж.* **Ввиду того, что; Поскольку, Так как**]
The stem of arm *V* appears to be invariable in length **for** (*or* **since,** *or* **because,** *or* **as**) all known sequences contain five pairs.

Потребление

For a man weighing 175 lb **the** critical total **uptake of** CO will occur in 1.4 h total exposure.
The human **consumption of** ascorbic acid depends on ...

Потребление в домашнем хозяйстве
Water **for domestic consumption ...**

Потребление для бытовых нужд [*см.* **Потребление в домашнем хозяйстве**].

Потребление и расход
There is no way of achieving a permanent weight reduction without reducing **the intake of** calories to less than **the outgo.**

Потребляемая мощность
Power requirements (*or* **demand**) **of** the furnace **are** (**is**) 230 volts/60 cycle/3 phase/70 kilowatts.

Потребляемая энергия
The energy consumed in magnetizing and demagnetizing magnetic material ...

Потреблять большое количество
A modern industrial society **is a heavy user of** energy.
The power station **handles** (*or* **consumes**) **great quantities of** fuel.

Потребляться
A chemical equation may simply indicate what substances **are consumed** and what new substances are produced.

Потребности высоки [*см.* **В большом спросе**].

Потребности промышленности
Industrial demand (*or* **needs**) ...

Потребности сельского хозяйства
Much of the **agricultural demand** is supplied directly by rainfall.

Потребность в [*см. тж.* **Возникла потребность, Необходимость, Отвечать потребностям**]
The demands for electric energy will increase ...
A continuing **demand for** increased flight speed ...
To establish **the** human **requirements for** vitamin *C*, ...

Потребность в кислороде
These beetles have **a** low **oxygen demand.**

Потребоваться
It has taken the high photon flux of tunable lasers **to** overcome ...

Потребуются годы для
This theory will **take years to** develop.

Потухнуть
When the air was released, the candle **went out.**

Потухший вулкан
It was demonstrated that the crater was not **an extinct volcano.**

Похож на [*см. тж.* **Аналогичен, Весьма напоминать ... по, Мало похож на**]
The punkish flower head **looks like** (*or* **resembles**) a strawberry.

Похожи друг на друга
The two comets **are similar in appearance.**

Похожий на [*см. тж.* **Аналогичный, Весьма сходный с, Не похож на**]
This process **is akin to** choosing from a menu.

Почва [*см.* **Благодатная почва для, Готовить почву для, Иметь под собой некоторую почву, Подготавливать почву для**].

Почивать на лаврах
Herschel did not **rest on his laurels.**

Почленно
This expression may be integrated or differentiated **term by term.**

Почленный
A **term-by-term** summation ...

Почти [*см. тж.* **Близкий к, Практически, Приблизительно**]
If the reaction system is one of constant or **near-constant** (*or* **nearly constant**) volume, then ...
The two new galaxies **are all but** (*or* **almost**) hidden by dense clouds of dust.

Почти безразлично
They found that **it made little difference whether** the 1000-m **or** 2000-m depth contour was used.

Почти вертикальный
A canal may have vertical or **near-vertical** sides.

Почти всегда [*см. тж.* **Бóльшую часть времени**]
Almost without exception ...

Почти идеальный
A **near(ly) ideal** system ...

Почти или совсем не
This device is highly reliable and requires **little or no** maintenance.

Почти как [*см. тж.* **Аналогично**]
The process is carried out **in much the same way as** (*or* **very similarly to**) silver plating.

Почти круговая, почти полярная орбита
A near-circular near-polar orbit.

Почти не [*см. тж.* **Едва**]
B. subtilis yields **scarcely any** glycerol.
Calcium carbonate is **hardly** affected by heat at ...

Почти не влиять на [*см.* **Очень слабо влиять на**].

Почти не зависеть от
The initial bubble size **depends almost not at all on** the original size.

Почти не требовать
The pumps **require little or no** attention.

Почти невозможно
In the nonhardenable 400 series grades, **little can be done to** dissolve carbides.
Often **it is next to** (*or* **almost**) **impossible to** guarantee ...

Почти неразличим [*см.* **Едва различим**].

Почти нет
There is scarcely any air to disperse pollutants.

Почти никогда
Rarely, if ever, is a large body of data collected and suddenly explained at a stroke by an inspired theory.

Почти ничего больше не сообщалось
Little else has been reported regarding these viruses.

Почти нормальный
When the pituitary was excised, the animal returned to **near-normal** behaviour.

Почти пропорционален
The attraction of bodies to the Earth **is closely proportional to** the mass of the body.

Почти равен
Its activity **will be very nearly equal to** its pressure.

Почти столько
The strength of the wave field in the nebula would be approximately 10^{-4} gauss, **just about** the value required earlier to explain ...

Почти так же, как
It seemed reasonable to suppose that life could have originated on Mars **much as it had** on the Earth.
In elastic scattering the target particle recoils **much as if it were** a billiard ball.
Objects seen in the scanning electron microscope at a magnification of 15 diameters look **much as they do** when they are viewed with a strong magnifying glass.

Почти таким же образом
Tryptophan decomposes **in much the same manner.**

Почти такой же
Relative acid strength **is very nearly** (*or* **almost**) **the same** in these solvents **as** it is in water.
Backlash can occur in any part of the system, with **much the same** effect.
Some realistic estimates led to **(very) nearly the same** values **as** did the laminar theory.

Почти точно совпадать с [*см.* **Очень близкий к**].

Почти целиком
Coal microscopy technique depends **almost entirely** on the use of thin sections of coal.

Поэтапно [*см.* **Этапами**].

Поэтому [*см. тж.* **Вследствие этого, Следовательно**]
It is not surprising, **then,** that ...
Much of the light is directed upward and **so** is lost.

Thus we can write: ...
The cross-bedding is usually concave upward; **this being so,** one can tell ...
The reactions are usually rapid and **in consequence** (*or* **as a consequence**) have wide application in diagnosis.
Because of this, the refraction method is known as ...
Heavy water is the oxide of the hydrogen isotope deuterium and **hence** (*or* **therefore,** *or* **consequently**) is called deuterium oxide.

Поэтому считают, что
This has led many people to believe that the environmental agents responsible for cancer are chemicals that we inhale or ingest.

Появилась мысль [*см.* **Прийти в голову**].

Появилась обширная литература
Today, **an extensive** (*or* **a substantial body of**) **literature has evolved** which traces the role of ...

Появился ... лет тому назад
Magnetic theory **dates back about 70 years.**

Появился спрос на
When the high-speed, large-capacity units **came into demand, ...**

Появление [*см. тж.* **Возникновение, Образование, Приводить к появлению, С момента его появления, С появлением**]
This transfer leads to **the production of** a chloride ion.
Before **the emergence of** quantum mechanics ...
Until **the advent of** complex metal-oxide semiconductor circuits most desk computers were assembled from ...

Появляться I [*см. тж.* **В ближайшем будущем появится, Возникать, Образовываться**]
A thriving cottage industry supplying computer programs **has evolved.**
This effect **arises** because the materials have a refractive index which varies with ...
Where do these comets **come from?**
This theory **made its appearance** in the late 1960s.
If some of the neurological complications **ensue, ...**
If relevant symptoms **emerge** at a later date, ...
Soon high-power pulsed lasers began **to emerge** as a working system.
If a defect **should develop** (*or* **appear**) in the cladding, ...
New types of chips **are** now **making their appearance** in commercial equipment.

Появляться II
Finally the north pole of the satellite **came (in)to view.**

Появляться на свет [*см. тж.* **Рождаться**]
In 1903 the Owen machine **came into being** (*or* **existence**).

Права гражданства [*см.* **Завоёвывать права гражданства**].

Правая верхняя часть [*см.* **В правой верхней части**].

Правая часть уравнения
The terms **on** (*or* **in**) **the right(-hand) side** (*or* **member**) **of** Eq. (2) were obtained.

Правда
True (enough), these enzymes are themselves made by way of ...

Правдоподобен
If this model **is realistic** (*or* **true,** *or* **approaches reality**), it explains how ...

Правдоподобно
It is more realistic to suppose that ...

Правдоподобное предположение
The most **credible speculation is that** the gamma bursts are caused by ...

Правдоподобный [*см. тж.* **Наиболее вероятный**]
A **reasonable** (*or* **likely,** *or* **plausible**) explanation is that all of the four processes melted the earth.
The theory offers a **valid** explanation for ...
Some **credible** (*or* **realistic**) models have been proposed.
This is a **likely** (*or* **plausible**) explanation.

Правила
Present **practice** does not (*or* **Present rules,** *or* **regulations** do not) permit more than 1700 grams of uranium in ...

Careful observation of **the do's and dont's** (*sl.*) listed below will enable you to take proper care of the micrometer.
Rules for writing "net" equations ...

Правило [*см.* **Выводить правило, Как общее правило, Как правило, Нарушать правило, Соблюдение правил, Твёрдое правило**].

Правило, касающееся
This expression is to be expanded by **the rules governing** determinants.

Правильнее
These items **would be more properly** (*or* **correctly**) classified as ...

Правильно
See that the "earth" is **properly** (*or* **correctly**) connected.
This phenomenon could be **realistically** explained only on the basis of ...
If the modes are selected **adequately, ...**

Правильно ли предположить, что
Are we correct in assuming that ...

Правильно называть
Light-green stones **are properly termed** green beryl.

Правильно поставленная задача
A properly (*or* **correctly**) **posed problem** needs to be ...

Правильной формы
The dimensions of a **regularly shaped** room (*or* of a room **of regular shape**) ...

Правильность
The validity (*or* **correctness**) **of** this substitution is obvious.
The excellent agreement between experiment and theory supported **the validity of** the model.

Правильность теории [*см.* **Проверять правильность теории**].

Правильный I [*см. тж.* **Справедлив, Точный**]
This nomenclature is the only **proper** nomenclature for these compounds.
In this method, the **proper** (*or* **correct**) choice of solvents is important.

Правильный II
Those ions form a **regular** crystalline lattice.
A **regular** tetrahedron ...
The earth is not a **true** sphere.

Править
The wheels **are** automatically **trued with** a rotary diamond wheel dresser.

Право [*см.* **Иметь право**].

Право принадлежит
Final **authority for** issuance of standards **should reside with** departments that will use ...

Правый верхний
The **upper right(-hand)** corner ...

Практика [*см.* **В современной практике, Входить в обычай, На практике**].

Практиковаться [*см.* **Обычно практиковаться, Применяться, Широко практиковаться**].

Практическая возможность
This demonstrates **the feasibility of** protein-directed synthesis of ...

Практическая применимость
Consideration is given to **the (present) practicality** (*or* **feasibility**) **of** laser ionization mass spectrometry.

Практически [*см. тж.* **По существу, Почти**]
Essentially all types of plant fossil are encountered here.
Solution time is **essentially** independent of the problem being solved.
This limits the reaction, **for all practical purposes,** to simple alcohols.
The repaired tool is, **for all practical purposes,** as good as new.
The angle is so small that, **for practical purposes,** sensitivity of the scale can be defined as the number of ...
These parts are free of stress **for all intents and purposes.**
The dielectric constants of these materials remained **practically** (*or* **virtually**) constant.
Some of the detection methods employed with gas chromatography are applicable to **virtually** all kinds of gases and vapours.

Практически возможно
It is rarely **feasible** (*or* **practicable**) **to** determine ...

Практически возможный (*или* **осуществимый**)
Measuring such displacements to within five percent demands a good metrology laboratory, but **is hardly practicable for** most shops.
The closeness of the curves to one another indicated that fatigue test standardization **was feasible** (*or* **practicable**).
Lasers make it **practical to** machine small holes in ...

Практически всё, что угодно
We make systems that will monitor and control **(just) about anything.**

Практически вытеснивший
All American steam ocean-going vessels use the water-tube boiler **to the practical exclusion of** fire-tube boilers.

Практически невозможно
It is not practical (*or* **feasible**) **to** draw a precise line of distinction.

Практически невозможный [*см. тж.* **Почти невозможно**]
Geographical and other conditions make the building of such structures financially or physically **impracticable** (*or* **unfeasible**).

Практически осуществимый
Such calculations are too difficult to be **practical.**

Практически применимый
No **usable** formula for the cooling effect of open air on average individuals can be derived because ...

Практическое значение [*см.* **Иметь практическое значение**].

Практическое применение
A practical implementation of the method ...

Практичный [*см. тж.* **Целесообразный**]
Caissons are used where they provide **the** most **feasible** method of passing obstructions.

Практичный подход к
A pragmatic approach to mathematical operations ...

Пребывание [*см.* **Время пребывания**].

Пребывание в состоянии покоя
Being at rest in a gravitational field **is** equivalent to ...

Превосходить I [*см. тж.* **Значительно превосходить, Не намного превышать**]
The features move at a speed that **is in excess of** the speed of light.
The total horse power **is in excess of** (*or* **exceeds,** *or* **is over,** *or* **is more than**) 5000.
The repulsive forces always **exceed** the attractive ones.
Shipments are expected **to top** $2 billion.

Превосходить II
Crystallized alumina **is excelled** (*or* **surpassed**) **in** hardness only **by** diamond and carborundum.
Such magnets **can outperform** wirewound fields **for** accuracy.
This product **has outstripped** the standards of the industry.
The timer greatly **surpasses** pneumatic timers **in** reliability.
In this one respect, the system with bang-bang control **is superior to** the system with on-off control.
Electric locomotives **can outperform** (*or* **are superior to**) their diesel counterparts **in** almost every respect.

Превосходить во много раз [*см.* **Во много раз больше**].

Превосходить по производительности и рабочим характеристикам
These tools **out-produce and outperform** any comparable machine.

Превосходить по эффективности
The composite materials **will outperform** the traditional monolithic materials.

Превосходный
This results in **superior** (*or* **excellent**) tube performance.

Превосходство над
The superiority of C-135 fasteners **over** (*or* **to**) those made from other materials surprised even the most optimistic.

Превосходящий [*см.* **Свыше**].

Превратиться в конечном счёте в
As a result of denudation the continent **would end up as** a shallow submarine platform.

Превращать в [*см. тж.* **Преобразовывать**]
The explosion tends **to make** heavier nuclei **out of** lighter ones.
Further weathering **may turn** goethite **to** hematite.
The paste **is formed into** a thin film **by** compressing it between ...
This DNA polymerase **converts** the single-stranded DNA **into** a duplex molecule.
Collapse of a mass of sediment **causes** it **to become** a turbid liquid.
We **render** this equation exact **by** multiplication by $w(x, y) = xy$.
Alchemists believed that lead **could be turned to** gold.
One pound of water requires about 970 Btu **to change** (*or* **convert**) it **to** steam.
The propeller accelerates the air passing through it, thereby **changing** (*or* **transforming**) engine power **into** useful thrust.
To convert heat **to** (*or* **into**) electricity, ...
The amplifier **converts** direct current **to** alternating current.
The machine **can be converted into** a projection welder.
A microprocessor **can be made into** a general-purpose microcomputer.

Превращать в порошок
Tin **can be powdered** at about 470 K.

Превращаться в [*см. тж.* **Преобразовываться в**]
The anhydrous solid **turns (in)to** a pool of solution.
All eigenfunctions for ... **transform** according to ...
As quarts decreases in abundance, dacite **passes into** andesite.
Already existing minerals **may be altered to** new ones.
Mass spectrometers quickly **evolved (in)to** systems specifically designed for the analytical laboratory.
The larvae **metamorphose into** pupae near the surface.
Hydrogen **is turned to** helium.

Превращаться в конечном счёте в
Uranium-235 and uranium-238 decay successively into other radioactive elements until they **finally end up as** nonradioactive isotopes of lead.

Превращаться друг в друга [*см.* **Взаимно превращаться друг в друга**].

Превращение [*см. тж.* **Преобразование**]
We can write a qualitative equation to represent **a** chemical **change** involved.
The conversion of nonaromatic **to** (*or* **into**) aromatic hydrocarbons ...
Complete **transformation of** steel **from** austenite **to** (*or* **into**) martensite ...
Change, Transmutation ...

Превращение тепловой энергии в механическую
Heat-to-work conversion (*or* **conversion of heat to mechanical energy**).

Превращён в
Many sorbents **may be made into** a slurry with the solvent and poured into the tube.

Превышать [*см. тж.* **Больше, Значительно превышать, Не намного превышать, Превосходить**]
The signal **stands out above** the background "noise".
This limit **should not be exceeded.**
The value of the ore **is** considerably **in excess of** the average grade.
The break strain of the strap **exceeds** [*or* **is over** (*or* **more than**)] half a ton.
One operator with a new centreless grinding system **can top** the output of 13 operators with old grinders.

Превышать в два раза [*см.* **В два раза больше, чем**].

Превышать допуск [*см.* **Если допуск в ... превышен**].

Превышать ... на слишком большую величину
The Raleigh number **exceeds** the critical value **by too large a margin.**

Превышающий [*см. тж.* **Свыше**]
The elements operate at speeds **in excess of** 1 kc per sec.
Yield strengths **in excess of** the specified value were obtained.

Предварительно I [*см. тж.* **Заранее**]
To distinguish between ..., **first** add calcium chloride solution in excess to precipitate normal carbonate.
Remove the washer **by first** taking off the nut.
A hermetic seal is obtained by rolling together the lid flange, **previously** coated with a sealing compound, and the flanged open end of the case to form a tight double seam.

Предварительно II
If this proposal is **tentatively** accepted as valid, ...

Предварительно нагружён
The bolt **is pre-loaded** during insertion.

Предварительно нагружённый
Pre-loaded ball-bearings ...

Предварительно напрягать
In order **to pre-stress** the bolts, ...

Предварительно напряжённые железобетонные конструкции
Developments in building construction with **pre-stressed concrete components ...**

Предварительно очищенный
Prepurified.

Предварительно удалив
A cobalt concentrate is obtained by ore flotation **after prior removal of** most of the copper mineral.

Предварительный I
Some high-temperature reactions require **the prior** dissociation of a molecule to produce ...
By this method functions can be obtained immediately, without **first** (*or* **previously**) solving the differential equations.
Previous cleaning of the metal is required.

Предварительный II
Some **tentative** (*or* **preliminary**, *or* **provisional**) general conclusions from experimental observations can be made.

Предвестник
The splitting of the comet was apparently **a forerunner of** complete disintegration.

Предвидимое будущее [*см.* **В предвидимом будущем**].

Предвосхищать
We **are looking forward to** the launching of the probe.
Carnot's ideas on air as a working substance **foreshadowed** the development of the internal combustion engine.
We **anticipated** the pleasure of seeing the new model.

Предел [*см. тж.* **В более узких пределах, В определённых пределах, В пределах, В узких пределах, В указанных пределах, В широких пределах, Вне пределов, Выходить за пределы, Далеко за пределами, До предела, За пределами, Изменяться в широких пределах, Не распространяться за пределы, Нет пределов, Определять предел, Устанавливать предел**]
This represents **an** upper **limit to** the size of the orbit.

Предел видимости [*см.* **В пределах видимости**].

Предел допуска
The limits of tolerance may be indicated on a dial.

Предельная величина
The pressure may reach **a limiting value.**

Предельная величина, которую может выдержать человек
This corresponds to a pressure of 3 1/2 atmospheres, which **is** about **the limit of human endurance.**

Предельный случай
Two **limiting cases** have been considered.
The physically relevant solution may be obtained as **a limiting case of** Eq. (3.2.14).

Пределы досягаемости [*см.* **В пределах досягаемости**].

Предлагаем самостоятельно вывести
The exact relationship **is left for the student to work out** (*or* **derive**, *or* **develop**).

Предлагать
He **proposed that** reconstructions of the continents **should be** made using submarine contours.
Several schemes **have been proposed** (*or* **suggested**, *or* **advanced**).

Niels Bohr **put forward** his model of the atom.
The chemists **have come up with** new compounds.

Предлагать вниманию
I have the pleasure of **bringing to** your **notice** a novel system of ...

Предлагать гипотезу [*см.* **Выдвигать гипотезу, Высказывать гипотезу о том, что**].

Предлагать объяснение
We shall summarize **the explanations** that **have been put forward for** the results obtained.

Предложен
The following definition **is due to** [*or* **was proposed** (*or* **put forward,** *or* **advanced,** *or* **suggested**) **by**] Saint Venant: ...

Предложение [*см.* **Вносить предложение**].

Предложенный
A Type II superconductor is depicted here according to a model **put forward by** *C*.

Предложено
It has been suggested that the term allophane **be** used for all such materials.

Предмет [*см. тж.* **Изучаемый предмет, Являться предметом**]
This constitutes **the subject matter of** electrophysiology.

Предмет изобретения (*в патенте*)
What we (*or* **I**) **claim is:** ...
We (*or* **I**) **claim as our** (*or* **my**) recent **invention: ...**

Предмет исследования
The electronic structure of the nitrogen molecule **has been the subject** (*or* **theme**) **of** much **investigation.**
The shapes of such curves **have** long **been subjects for study.**

Предмет науки
The subject matter of astronautics **is** flight in regions where ...

Предмет разногласия
The allocation of the water of the Rio Grande **has** long **been a matter of contention between** the U.S. and Mexico.

Предназначаться для
These explosives **are designed for** coal blasting.
The instrument **is designed to** operate with a minimum input.
Such units **are (intended) for use on** grounded circuits.
These methods **are intended** (*or* **meant**) **for** performance evaluation of spectrometers.
Motor over-current protection **is intended to** protect motor windings and branch conductors from overheating.
The centre aisle **is reserved for** the movement of personnel only.
The tray **is destined for** the far end of the first operation line.

Предназначен для
Each cell **is dedicated to** the production of ...
This water **is destined** (*or* **meant**) **for** irrigation.

Предназначен для одного
Instrumentation **is** often **peculiar to one** particular technique.

Предок
Those four-hoofed creatures **were ancestral to** (*or* **ancesters of**) the modern horse.

Предоставилась возможность
In 1979 palaeontologists interested in the problem of reptilian extinction **were presented with a** new **possibility.**

Предоставить его самому себе
As a stream erodes downward, it would, **if left to its own devices,** fashion a vertically walled canyon.

Предоставлять [*см. тж.* **Распределять**]
These diagnoses **are** best **left to** the urologist.

Предоставлять в распоряжение
We **place** (*or* **put**) **at** your **disposal** a collection of interchangeable components.

Предоставлять разрешение
Permit has been granted.

Предотвращать [*см. тж.* **Избегать, Мешать, Не давать распадаться, Препятствовать, Удерживать от распада**]
Extensive baffling is used **to prevent** laser scatter **from** reaching the photomultipliers.

In a fast crosswind the wing cannot be raised quickly enough **to forestall** a skid.
Motors on the milling heads are totally enclosed **to exclude** (*or* **prevent,** *or* **guard against**) ingress of metallic dust.
A duplicate radar system is the obvious way **to guard against** the possibility of grounding due to equipment failure.
The installation **insures against** dehydration of the gypsum.
The resulting gyroscopic stabilization **keeps** the projectile **from** tumbling.
The filter **keeps** stray radio-frequency signals **from** entering the amplifier.
The closed vacuum system **precludes** oxidation.
The presence of titanium **prevents** the formation of martensite.
The non-return valve **prevents** air **being** drawn back into the main-pump suction.
This requires shutdown of the reactor **to safeguard** it **against** the release of contaminants.
The rams are situated on the outside of the main chassis members **to ensure that no** twisting arises at ...
Properly executed roof bolting **will inhibit** loosening.

Предотвращать возможность [*см. тж.* **Исключать, Устранять**]
Care should be taken **to guard against** (*or* **prevent**) water hammer in steam piping.
To guard against any possibility of introducing pathogenic organisms from the Moon, the lunar samples were placed in quarantine for seven weeks.
The factor of 1/2 **prevents** each ion-ion interaction **from** being counted twice.

Предотвращать доступ
A long tube suffices **to exclude** air.

Предотвращать изгиб
The stringers of an open-floor railroad bridge should be braced **to relieve** them **of bending** due to lateral forces from the train.
The floor beams should be provided with bracing **to relieve the bending** due to tractional forces.

Предотвращать ошибку
This **error is overcome by** making the altimeter case airtight.

Предотвращать попадание [*см. тж.* **Изолировать от**]
Change the toweling in the filters **to keep** them **clear of** foreign matter.

Предотвращать трудность
The problem can be forestalled by using a direct-current link to tie.

Предотвращение [*см. тж.* **Для предотвращения**]
Keeping the gas **from** leaking posed a production problem.
To maintain the high water velocity desirable for **suppression** (*or* **prevention**) **of** fouling, ...

Предохранять от [*см. тж.* **Защищать от, Предотвращать**]
Keeping dust **away from** delicate components ...
This **kept** the solution **from** coming in contact with air.
Teflon seals **keep out** moisture.
This resistance **protects** the contacts **against** accidental overload.
Nickel coating **protects** plug valves **against** (*or* **from**) corrosion.
Oil seals **safeguard** the bearings **against** dust and grit.

Предохранять от загрязнения
These materials **must be kept free from contamination.**

Предохранять от ударов
The vehicle **must be cushioned against shocks** for the comfort of passengers.

Предохранять от яркого света
Such cells **should be kept from bright light.**

Предполагаемое время жизни [*см.* **Время жизни**].

Предполагаемый [*см. тж.* **Намеченный**]
The definition is based on **the assumed** (*or* **inferred,** *or* **presumed**) properties of the real numbers.
This **conjectured** (*or* **assumed,** *or* **proposed,** *or* **inferred**) interaction, if it proves actually to occur, must be considered ...
The design of the keyboard depends on its **intended** use.

The proposed impact probably took place between 2.7 and 2.0 billion years ago.
These forms **can be surmised to be** activated states.

Предполагается
Each ion **is taken to be** spherical.
The molecule in bacteria **is perceived to be** circular.

Предполагается выпустить в продажу
These materials **are targeted for the market** early next year.

Предполагается, что
The bacteria **have supposedly** (*or* **presumably**) distinctive physiological abilities.
It is suggested that the boron **is** located in the cavities of the metal lattice.
It is anticipated (*or* **expected**) **that** the thermal efficiency of the units **will be** 40%.
Such boilers **are assumed** (*or* **presumed**) **to** generate saturated steam at the same pressure.

Предполагать [*см. тж.* **Высказывать предположение о том, что; Полагать, что; Считать**]
This mechanism **is presumed to be** adequately represented by ...
You **may anticipate that** the stream discharge **will** increase with increasing basin area.
It **was** originally **conceived** (*or* **conjectured**) **that** the hydrogen bonds **were** responsible for ...
These forms **can be surmised.**
He **speculated that** the lower mantle **was** inhomogeneous.
The concept of a delocalized π bond **suggests** orbital occupancy by more than two electrons.
The existence of superclusters **has** long **been conjectured** (*astron.*).
The design procedure **assumes** uniform pressure.
It can be inferred (*or* **assumed**) **that** the absorption **will be** different as well.
One **can infer that** craters have been erased.
The theory **proposes that there are** three or more types of ...
One **may speculate that** these two satellites **are** richer in water than ...
The liquid temperature **will be assumed (as)** constant at 122°F.
In such cases covalent bonding **may be inferred.**
If "1" **be taken as** 10 cm, ...
If a homogeneous medium **is thought of as** being constituted of ...
Conventional definitions of environmental extremes **presuppose** protection of electronic gear by cooling and heating.
He **surmised that** the amount of methane on Titan **must be** far greater than ...
For weakly guiding fibres, we **anticipate that** ε **will be** small...
The heat death of the universe that **was contemplated by** physicists in the 19th century ...

Предположение [*см. тж.* **В предположении, что; Высказывать предположение о том, что; Если исходить из предположения о, Исходить из предположения, Можно лишь высказывать предположения, Основываться на предположении о, При предположении**]
This theory includes **the premise that** a strong lithosphere rests upon ...
Reasonable **guesses** (*or* **conjectures,** *or* **inferences,** *or* **suppositions,** *or* **assumptions,** *or* **presumptions**) **as to** the shapes of molecules can be made.
A large number of geologists were skeptical about **the proposal that** the crust of the ocean floor **is** spreading apart ...
The most likely **conjecture** (*or* **speculation**) **is that** the very centre of the Milky Way harbours a black hole.

Предположение о том, что
The assumption that only a molecule *A* moves implies ...

Предположение относительно
Assumptions of force constants for bond stretching can lead to ...

Предположив, что
(By) assuming that $E_s = 0$, one obtains the local field $E_l = E_r$.

Предположим [*см. тж.* **Пусть**]
(Let us) suppose (for argument's sake) that all these students had their picture taken for the yearbook, where ...
Say an optical reader is mounted on the spindle.
Let (us assume that) $Z_i - Z_l = ...$

Put $P_1P/P_2P = r$.
(Now) suppose the initial design calls for ...
T **is taken to be** 2 hr.

Предпоследний
The next to last (*or* **The last but one**) carbon atom ...

Предпоследний по величине
The second-smallest protein ...

Предпосылка для
A prerequisite for a precise titration is the reproducible identification of ...

Предпосылка к
This is **an** essential **prerequisite to** the comprehension of ...

Предпочитать [*см. тж.* **Отдавать предпочтение**]
In radiant tube service cast tubes **are favoured over** wrought.
The shells structure **is favoured** today.
Small units **were preferable** (*or* **preferred**) **to** large ones.
Analytical methods **are preferred over** the more complicated assays.

Предпочитать использовать ... для
For these reasons iron-titanium hydride **has been the material of choice for** most energy storage applications.

Предпочтение [*см.* **Отдавать предпочтение, Предпочитать**].

Предпочтительно пользоваться для лечения
The drug of choice for treatment of chronic myelocytic leukaemia **is** bisulfan.

Предпочтительный
Nonionic complexes have been resolved by **preferential** adsorption on quartz or sugars.

Предпочтительный метод лечения
The treatment of choice for this tumour is surgery.

Предпринимать
We **embarked on** (*or* **launched**) a series of control experiments.
They **undertook** (*or* **initiated**) the present investigation in order to ...
No similar census **has been attempted** south of the stream.
The first step **was taken in** 1989.

Предпринимать исследование
Some social scientists **undertook** a number of **studies of** hospital units practising milieu therapy.

Предпринимать усилия в области
Eighteen years ago **a** serious **effort was mounted** (*or* **made**) to calculate the probability of a major reactor accident.

Предприниматься по инициативе
The new programme **was pioneered by** this laboratory.

Предсказание
The prediction that the proton will decay into other particles ...

Предсказывать
Product yields **can be predicted** (*or* **forecast**) **from** feed-stock properties.
The positron was discovered four years after Dirac **foretold** its existence.
Dirac's theory **made** no **prediction about** the mass or size of the magnetic monopoles.

Представитель
Acid halide is **one of** a large group of organic substances possessing ...

Представить вопрос на референдум
The issue **should be submitted to a referendum.**

Представить себе [*см. тж.* **Можно себе представить**]
A bistable device **can be envisioned** (*or* **thought of**) **as** an optical nonlinearity combined with feedback.
If an accelerator **is conceived** (*or* **visualized**) **as** a large microscope, ...
Picture a listener 30 kilometres from the transmitter.
We **can conjure up** (*or* **imagine**) a whole series of numbers which ...
To appreciate the extent of the information available from binary stars, consider ...
It is difficult **to conceive of** (*or* **imagine**) an enamelled product that will not be subject to ...
We **picture** the ionization of ... **as** involving reaction with ...
Curves **may be thought of as** intersections of two surfaces.
Above 120°C the barium titanate crystal

may be visualized as a cube with a barium ion at each corner, ...
When we think of a spectrum, we usually **visualize** bands of colours.
Imagine a laser beam striking a plastic sphere.
The simple wave **may be visualized** if the initial functions are given.
One **can** readily **visualize** the following broad uses of the computer in the control of power systems: ...
One **may envision** applications of the multicoloured helium-selenium laser to devices designed for ...

Представить себе ... как
Any mechanical system **may be conceived** (*or* **imagined**) **as** a set of N particles in space subject to a certain number K of constraints.
Think of a molecule **as** a collection of atoms held firmly in ...

Представлен [*см. тж.* **Показан**]
The proposed design **is presented** (*or* **exhibited,** *or* **shown,** *or* **displayed,** *or* **depicted**) in the accompanying drawing.
The potential-energy term **can be represented by** $U(r)$.

Представлен в таблице
The results of exposing silicon, germanium ... rectifiers to radiation hazards **are tabulated in** Table V.

Представлен схематически [*см.* **Схематически изображён**].

Представление [*см. тж.* **Давать лишь приблизительное представление о, Давать точную картину, Иметь представление о**]
Our present **view** (*or* **notion**) **of** electronic structure **is** far from complete.
The definition of a shock employed here is not based on **the** usual physical **notion** (*or* **concept**).

Представление о ... можно получить по
Erosion of the countryside **can be inferred from** the sediment carried by this stream.

Представленный [*см. тж.* **Показанный**]
The papers **submitted to** the Conference ...
Examination of the reactions **outlined in** Table 29.1 reveals a number of potentially useful processes.

Представляет для нас наибольший интерес
The special case when these equations are homogeneous **has been of our main interest** here.

Представлять [*см. тж.* **Изображать, Передавать**]
To depict the structure of ethane, ...

Представлять благодатную почву для
Artificial transmutations **offer a fertile field for** research.

Представлять более непосредственный интерес для
The formulation for first-order quasilinear systems **is of more direct interest to** us.

Представлять в виде
Such ions **are represented as** spheres.
The description of *PVT* behaviour **is** usually **reported in terms of** the thermal expansivity.

Представлять данные о том, что
Some scientists **have presented evidence that ...**

Представлять затруднение для
Complex compounds **present a** real **challenge to** the synthetic chemist.

Представлять затруднения
This calculation **presents** (*or* **involves**) no **difficulties** (*or* **problem**).
Measuring distances in astronomy **has** always **been a problem.**

Представлять интерес
Diffusion in polymers **is of interest to** chemical engineers.
This trend **may be of interest in** future technical experiments.
Of (some) interest is the following phenomenon: ...
Our **interest is in** describing the by-products of ...

Представлять интерес для химиков
The study of ... **is of** obvious **chemical interest.**

Представлять интерес для промышленности
The process **is of** considerable **industrial interest.**

Представлять интерес с точки зрения математики
These problems **are of mathematical interest.**

Представлять исключительную важность для
The ecology of the oceans **is of profound** (*or* **great**) **importance for** all life on earth.

Представлять исторический интерес
This statement **is** mainly **of historical interest.**

Представлять мало интереса [*см.* **Не представлять особого интереса**].

Представлять наибольший интерес
It is the theories with local symmetry that **hold the greatest interest** today.
Radiocarbon dating **is of chief interest.**
Colour centres **are of most interest in** alkali halide crystals.

Представлять наибольший интерес для
The method **is of prime interest for** fusion power applications.

Представлять наибольшую важность для
It is the transitional wave that **is of primary concern to** designers of protective structures.

Представлять непосредственный интерес для
The results **are of immediate interest to** the experimentalist.

Представлять непреодолимое препятствие для
These conditions **presented an impenetrable barrier to** astronomers.

Представлять опасность для [*см. тж.* **Опасность для здоровья**]
Meteoric particles do not appear **to be a serious hazard to** space craft.
Cosmic rays **may constitute a threat to** space travel.

Представлять опасность для жизни человека
Earthflows **are** rarely **a threat to human life.**

Представлять опасность для окружающей среды
Radioisotopes with very long half-lives **are** not **environmental hazards.**
Alluvial rivers **have long posed an environmental problem** because of the overbank flooding.

Представлять особый интерес
Of particular (*or* **special**) **interest is** the tape which ...

Представлять себе [*см.* **Представить себе**].

Представлять серьёзную опасность для
Dust storms **present a severe hazard to** transportation.

Представлять собой [*см. тж.* **Являться**]
The ratio $k/wc = \alpha$ **is defined as** the thermal diffusivity.
Sand and sandstone formations **make** excellent reservoirs.
Electrometallurgy **refers to** recovery of a metal which is first obtained by ...
Table 3 **presents** a list of ...
The two following statements **constitute** the second law: ...
Communication equipment **comprises** (*or* **is,** *or* **represents**) an essential item of nearly all space vehicles.
An electric current **consists in** the flow of free electrons through ...
Heating up to about 600°C **constitutes** a secondary hardening.
Such atoms **would constitute** antimatter.
Exact analysis of the situation described **presents** a difficult mathematical problem.
The outer rim **makes up** one pole and the inner area is the opposite pole.

Представлять собой опасность для окружающей среды
These volcanoes **are an** extreme **environmental hazard.**

Представлять собой угрозу для
A volcano in eruption **brings the threat to** life and property.

Представлять сомнительную ценность
The data **are of questionable** (*or* **dubious**) **value for** use in the design of large equipment.

Представлять ценность [*см.* **Не представлять ценности для**].

Представляться в виде
Pluto is so small that it **shows up as** merely a dot of light (*astr.*).

Представляющий важность для промышленности
The atmosphere **provides the industrially vital** gas oxygen.

Представляющий для нас интерес
For the semiconductor **of interest (here),** the predominant process is electron injection.
In all cases **of present interest** this factor can be neglected.

Представляющий значительный интерес в настоящее время
This is a subject **of much current interest.**

Представляющий интерес [*см. тж.* **Интересующий нас**]
Only the metal **of interest is** deposited.
For such absorption spectra, the only part of the selection rule **that is of interest** is $\Delta J = +1$.

Представляющий наибольший интерес
The amines **of principal** (*or* **particular,** *or* **primary**) **interest** are those of the transition metals.

Представляющий особый интерес
The products **of specific interest ...**

Представьте себе
Picture (*or* **Imagine**) a large continent.

Предстоит [*см. тж.* **Который ещё предстоит изучить**]
As yet, none of the phenomena suggests that a large eruption of the volcano **is pending.**
Laser **is (destined) to** play an increasingly important part in facilitating ...
A real revolution in this field **lies ahead.**

Предупреждать [*см.* **Предотвращать**].

Предусматривается в случае необходимости
Micrometer adjustments **can be built in, as necessary.**

Предусматривать [*см. тж.* **Обеспечивать, Следует предусмотреть, Устанавливать**]
An exceptional degree of accuracy **has been designed** (*or* **built**) **into** this machine.
Future plans **call** (*or* **provide**) **for** an additional filter.
The new system **contemplates** (*or* **envisages**) mining primary ore.
Equation 8 **incorporates** (*or* **includes**) the normal losses.
Usually air spaces **were allowed** between adjacent coils.
This method **involves** increasing the pressure of the superheated steam.
It is necessary **to provide** a concrete lining.
Another scheme **called for** injecting thin trails of smoke into the airstream of a wind tunnel.
These superb valves **were designed into** the engine by our engineers.
The treaty **provides that** the U.S. shall deliver to Mexico ...

Предусматривать возможность [*см. тж.* **Принимать меры**]
The constructional arrangement **allows for** the adjustment of ...
By elongating the stud holes, **allowance is** usually **made for** some adjustment to the pitch of the blades.
Provision is made for the ventilation of the storage space.
Provision is made within the circuitry **to** limit the transistor voltage.
This consists of a piston in a closed cylinder **with provision for** fluid to pass through a small opening ...

Предусматривать при проектировании
These stresses **must be considered in the design.**

Предусматривать устройство для
Provision is made for removing the dust.

Предусматриваться
A three-year period **was allowed for** attainment of thermal stability.

Предусмотрен
Two pumps **are provided,** one of which supplies pressure fluid for operating the machine, and the other for operating auxiliary equipment.
The Tornado aircraft has a high internal fuel capacity, both self-sealing bags and integral tanks **being incorporated in the design.**
Provision is made for transverse movement of the lower die assembly.
These factors of safety **are built** (*or* **designed**) **into** the set-up.

The mill **has provision for** installation of a fifth stand.

Предусмотренный

A lubricating unit with **built-in** safety features ...
Various safety devices **incorporated in** the design ...
The holders were mounted in annular grooves **provided in** the bearing shields.

Предусмотрено устройство, благодаря которому

Provision is made for the condensate to spread out in thin films.

Предшественник

Precursors to life on earth ...
The Mark I, **predecessor of** the Mark II detector ...
Lime muds **are precursors** (*or* **forerunners,** *or* **predecessors**) of limestone.
The Atomic Energy Commission **was the predecessor of** the Department of Energy.

Предшественник землетрясения

A search for **predecessor events to earthquakes ...**

Предшествовать I

Use of animals for bioassay **antedated** (*or* **preceded,** *or* **predated**) use of microorganisms.
The first appearance of living organisms **was preceded by** the gradual development of a complex chemical environment.
The dust and gas that **came before** the protostars ...
The study of diffraction by crystals **will be preceded by** treatments of the classification of crystals.

Предшествовать II

For singlet states a superscript 1 **is prefixed to** the letter designation of the state.

Предшествующий [*см. тж.* **Предыдущий**]

The four zeros **preceding** the 2 (0.0002) are not measured quantities, but ...

Предъявлять высокие требования к

Mechanized mining **places** (*or* **imposes**) **heavy demands on** underground illumination.
This **placed** more **stringent requirements upon** the protecting devices.

Предъявлять требования к

The most general **requirements that can be placed** (*or* **imposed**) **upon** the control are ...
The following demands are made on a suitable shock detector: ...

Предыдущий [*см. тж.* **Предшествующий**]

The results described in **earlier** sections appear to support our conclusion.
In **the above** examples the orbit is circular.
It is evident from **the foregoing** equations that ...
Section 7 contains a number of applications of the theory given in **the preceding** (*or* **previous**) section.
Pre-existing (*or* **Previous**) abnormalities may lead to serious consequences.

Преемник

A direct **descendant of** the classical finite state machine is a parallel pipelined processor.

Прежде [*см. тж.* **В прошлом, Как и раньше**]

This relationship has been discussed **previously** (*or* **before**).

Прежде всего [*см. тж.* **В основном, В первую очередь, Главным образом**]

It was the beginning of a journey that **above all (else)** was physiographic.
First and foremost ...

Прежде чем [*см.* **Перед**].

Прежде чем идти дальше

Before we proceed (*or* **Before proceeding**) **(any) further,** we consider a synthesis example.

Прежде чем приступить к

Preparatory to solving Eq. (1.3.4), we will first discuss ...

Прежде чем приступить к рассмотрению

Before proceeding to an important application of ...

Преждевременный

The danger of **premature** shots is reduced, because the cord cannot be set off by sparks or stray currents.

Прежний [*см. тж.* **Возвращать в перво-начальное положение**]
Thus **the earlier** (*or* **previous**) assumption is substantiated.

Преимущества и недостатки [*см. тж.* **Достоинства и недостатки**]
For different applications, lasers have characteristic **advantages and disadvantages** (*or* **shortcomings**) (*or* **merits and demerits**).

Преимущественно [*см.* **В основном**].

Преимущество [*см. тж.* **Двойное преимущество, Извлекать пользу из, Обладать тем преимуществом, что**]
The special **convenience of** γ is that it shows explicitly the importance of nonideality.
This concept has **the advantage of** lighter weight.
The advantages of composite over double-base propellants are lower cost and easier manufacture.
The system is proving in action **the benefits of** applying modern technology to ...
The merits of plastic propellants are their chemical stability and good storage properties.
The metric system **has** many **points** in its favour.
The virtues of ammonium nitrate are its cheapness and ...

Преимущество для
There are important **benefits to** the user of the pump.

Преимущество над [*см.* **Иметь преимущество над, Обладать преимуществом**].

Преимущество по сравнению с ... в отношении
Chlorite **has** some **advantages over** hypochlorites **for** bleaching.

Прекрасно согласовываться с
This assumption **is in excellent agreement** with historically dated events.

Прекрасно справляться с задачей
The great optical telescopes **do** this **brilliantly.**

Прекратить деятельность
Cutting the loop on the efferent side **would abolish all activity of** the muscle.

Прекращать [*см. тж.* **Останавливать, Отказываться от**]
About five percent of the ions would fuse before plasma expansion **terminated** (*or* **stopped**) the reaction.
If nothing is done **to arrest** (*or* **stop**) the deposition of silt, ...

Прекращать подачу
The device **cuts off supplies of** coal.
Shut off the hydrogen.
Turn off the nitrogen flow.

Прекращать поступление [*см.* **Отрезать поступление**].

Прекращать работу
The spaceborne laboratory **will cease to operate** in 1994.

Прекращаться [*см. тж.* **Останавливаться**]
Drilling **was discontinued** (*or* **stopped**) because of lack of adequate equipment.
The etching **was terminated** to avoid excessive impingement of ...
The hub still rotates until power **is shut off ...**
The air supply **is cut off.**
If the residue is cooled, combustion **ceases.**
Since hand milking **has come to an end, ...**
The reaction **arrested itself** (*or* **ceased,** *or* **was terminated**) in the usual fashion.
If the arc is not struck within the present time delay limit, then the gas and water flow **will cease** (*or* **stop,** *or* **discontinue**).
Without multiplication of the parasites, the infection **must** ultimately **terminate.**

Прекращение
As the well cools after **cessation** (*or* **termination**) **of** drilling, ...
A discontinuance of tests by both sides ...
The suspension of traffic during prolonged frosts ...

Преломляться
A large fraction of a ray's power is lost each time it **refracts** (*or* **is refracted**).

Премия в области ... присуждена
The prize for chemistry **has been awarded to** M.

Пренебрегать [*см. тж.* **Не принимать во внимание, Не учитывать**]
Even if ultraviolet light **is discounted** as an energy source, two other sources remain.
The higher harmonics **are disregarded** here.
Amplitude variations **are ignored** (*or* **neglected**) **by** such systems.
The homogeneous conversion in liquid hydrogen is slow and **can be neglected.**
This factor is unimportant for ... and **is** often **overlooked.**
The wires have been put up **with no regard for** public safety.

Пренебрежение
Neglect of (*or* **Ignoring**) this factor may introduce large errors.

Пренебрежимо мал
This quantity **is negligible** (*or* **negligibly small**).

Пренебрежимо малая величина
A negligible (*or* **A negligibly small**) **quantity.**

Преобладание
Dullness (*тусклый оттенок*) may result from **a predominance of** mineral matter.

Преобладать
The forest **is dominated by** oaks and hickories.
Where this form of contamination **is paramount,** rapid filtration is essential.
If the latter view **prevails, ...**
Above that zone hydrogen and helium **prevail.**
As the temperature rises, lattice collisions **become dominant** and the mobility will begin to fall.
Where oolites **are dominant,** the rock is called an oolite limestone.

Преобладать в
The complex molecules **dominated** the mixture.

Преобладать над
One process **dominates** the other depending on local circumstances.
Here, erosion **dominates over** deposition.
At higher densities adverse factors **override** these beneficial effects.

Преобладать у
The cold antibody variety **is prevalent in** the elderly (*med.*).

Преобладающее большинство
The overwhelming majority of studies of neurotic symptoms ...

Преобладающее представление о том, что
The following discussion is based on **the prevailing concept that** the chromosome consists of ...

Преобладающий
Open-hearth steelmaking was the **(pre)dominant** method.
The **prevailing** hypothesis is that the primordial atmospheres ...
The **prevailing** winds blow from the west in the middle latitudes and ...
The **dominant** component of the rock.

Преобразован в
The vertical water wheel **had evolved into** three basic types: ...

Преобразование [*см. тж.* **Превращение**]
Substituting from Eq. (2.3) into Eq. (2.29) and **rearranging** gives ...
These same relations, one for **changing** a γ **to** a Δ and the other for **changing** a Δ **to** a γ, ...
Conversion to corresponding pulse heights ...
The transformation (*or* **change**) of elements **into** one another ...
Rearrangement of Eq. (16-7) gives a relation that ...
With a little **manipulation** this formula can be shown to depend on ...
Conversion from the amino **to** an acedamido group ...

Преобразователь
Digital-**to**-analogue **converter.**
Heat-**to**-electricity **converter.**

Преобразовывать [*см. тж.* **Превращать в**]
The converter **changes** the liquid **to** gas.
The amplifier **converts** direct current **to** alternating current.
To convert heat **to** (*or* **into**) electricity, ...
All fractional equations **can be transformed** (*or* **recast**) **to** (*or* **into**) rational integral equations.
These devices **translate** digital data **into** analogue voltages.

The booster pilot valve **translates** pressure changes sensed by the balancing unit **into** output pressure changes.
This form of equation (1.6.10) is not the most convenient one, and we now **recast** it for the benefit of later work.
Equation (9.16) **may be rearranged to give ...**
The surface finish equation **can be reworked as follows: ...**
Equation (9.16) **may be rearranged to give ...**
The surface finish equation **can be reworked** (*or* **developed,** *or* **converted,** *or* **rearranged,** *or* **modified**) **as follows: ...**

Преобразовываться в [*см. тж.* **Переходить, Превращаться в**]
At a temperature where the liquid **is** rapidly **changing to** gas ....
This result **rearranges to** the derivative forms of ...
Less stable carbonium ions **rearrange to (form)** more stable carbonium ions.

Преодолевать
A rocket moving 7 miles per second **will defeat** (*or* **overcome**) the Earth's gravity and never return.
The arrangement allows cars **to negotiate** acute curves.

Преодолевать барьер
The energy needed **to overcome** (*or* **clear,** *or* **surmount,** *or* **climb over,** *or* **penetrate**) **the barrier ...**

Преодолевать силу
To overcome the attractive **forces, ...**

Преодолевать сопротивление
When the forces **overcome the resistance of ...**

Преодолевать трудности [*см. тж.* **Устранять затруднение**]
The difficulties to be surmounted are great.
To overcome this **impediment, ...**
This **difficulty may be obviated** (*or* **resolved**) **by** connecting ...
One might try **to get over** (*or* **minimize**) **the difficulty** without departing from classical mechanics.
How do they **master these difficulties?**
They **met the difficulty by** placing ...
It was to overcome these difficulties that the sequence circuit was evolved.
The new technique **gets around the problem by** limiting the penetration of the alloy.
Steps **to counter** (*or* **overcome**) **this problem** were taken.
Two means of **tackling** (*or* **coping with**) **the difficulty** are: ...
We **have this problem licked** (*sl.*).

Преодоление трудности
One way around this problem is to ...

Преподнесение [*см.* **Изложение**].

Преподносить
We **present** the subject as we understand it.

Препятствие [*см. тж.* **Наталкиваться на барьер, Помеха**]
The size of the ship **is** no **barrier** (*or* **obstacle**) **to** the application of this principle.
The most critical **deterrent to** the use of martensitic steels is ...
This is **a** serious **handicap to** such a study.
Such boundaries **presented obstacles to** slip propagation.
The main **impediment to** the development of such a theory was ...

Препятствия, стоя́щие на пути
Obstacles placed (*or* **interposed**) **in** steady flows ...

Препятствовать [*см. тж.* **Задерживать, Затруднять, Значительно замедлять, Мешать, Не препятствовать, Ничто не может препятствовать, Предотвращать**]
An excess of alkali in the solution **will retard** the formation of HOCl.
This **hindered** (*or* **interfered with**) lathe operation.
The oil pockets **impede** (*or* **retard**) the flow of air.
Sodium nitrate **inhibits** corrosion of underwater structures.
This concentration of sugar is sufficient **to inhibit** the growth of most microorganisms.
An interlocking mechanism **prevents** (*or* **keeps**) the discharge door **from** being opened (*or* **prevents** the opening of the discharge door).

There are no **obstacles to** obstruct movement.
The use of optics in a computer **was hindered by** the lack of a suitable optical memory.
The ions **are inhibited from** moving towards the photocathode **by** collisions with the walls.

Препятствовать попаданию [*см. тж.* **Изолировать от**]
The baffle **keeps** stray light **from** entering the photomultiplier.
The box **keeps out** room light.
The canal intake is designed **to keep out** silt.

Препятствовать протеканию процесса
Large bulky groups **interfere with this process.**

Препятствовать прохождению
The disk **blocks** part of the light falling on the slit.

Прерываться
Drilling **was discontinued** (*or* **suspended**) because of lack of adequate equipment.
The chain **is interrupted.**
The particles **are interrupted in** their journey (*движение частиц прерывается*).

Преследовать цель
The objectives to be pursued by extensive research ...
We **pursue** well-defined **goals.**

Претворять в жизнь [*см. тж.* **Проводить в жизнь**]
The new plan **was put into effect** (*or* **operation**).
Measures were taken **to implement** this method.
In this way we **will make** our theory **work.**

Претерпевать [*см. тж.* **Испытывать, Подвергаться**]
The gas **experiences** a temperature rise.
Under such conditions the material **is subject to** great strains.
During cooling, some metals and alloys **undergo** transformations in the solid state.

Претерпевать искажение
The original shape of the waveform **suffers distortion** (*or* **is distorted**).

Претерпевший изменения под влиянием канцерогена
A **carcinogen-altered** cell ...

Преувеличивать
These expressions **overestimate** (*or* **overstate**) the losses.

Преуменьшать
These expressions **underestimate** (*or* **understate**) the losses.

Прецедент [*см.* **Не иметь прецедента**].

При [*см. тж.* **Во время, Встречающийся при, По мере, После**]
$I(\alpha, \varphi)_{200}$ is the intensity of the 200 reflection **at** a given α and φ.
The engine develops 340 hp **at** 1900 rpm.
For a given centre distance, the length of a crossed belt will be a constant.
In starting up, the starter should be set at ...
Certain precautions must be taken to obtain satisfactory results **in** using this equipment.
On ignition the ingredients must vaporize.
On interruption of the electric current the valve closes instantly.
The temperature is read **(up)on** entering and leaving the water jacket.
Bentonite shrinks **upon** drying.
When added to aluminium, germanium produces a better hardening effect than silicon.
When employing these compounds as fuel additives, we ...
When tuning a system for optimum performance one must ...
With an overall length of 18 ft the machine weighs 15 tons.
The compressor operates **with** one suction valve open.
Both shot core drilling and rotary drilling methods are used **in** shaft drilling.
Given comparable costs for raw materials, the manufacturing cost is determined largely by the weight of the component.
The breakdown of bias voltage decreases by a few tenths of a millivolt **for** every °C increase in temperature.
With the proper combination of resistors and capacitors, the voltage will be ...
With (*or* **In**) this method, the amount of material to be removed can be closely controlled.
Given the extraordinary resolution of the Space Telescope, it is possible to detect ...

The conductance increases linearly **with** the addition of H^+.
The lower inertia of the cone clutch elements permits rapid reversal **with** low energy loss.
In moving through the tube the atoms collide with ...
The potential energy is taken as zero **for** (*or* **as,** *or* **with,** *or* **when**) a $\to \infty$, ...
The equation is useful **in** comparing diffusion currents from electrodes with different capillary characteristics.
Neutron stars are apparently born **in the** explosions of supernovas.
Such a function is real **for** real z.

При атмосферном давлении
Distillation **at atmospheric pressure** can yield ...

При благоприятных условиях
Given a suitable opportunity, the free edge of a plate may plunge into the asthenosphere (*geol.*).
Under favourable conditions calcite is precipitated as a mineral deposit.

При более тщательном рассмотрении выясняется, что
On closer inspection (*or* **examination**) those achievements **are noted to be** concentrated exclusively within ...
A closer look at the data **shows that ...**

При большом увеличении
At high magnification, tiny points of light are observed ...

При введении через рот
Amphotericin B is essentially non-toxic **by oral administration.**

При включённом свете
With the room **light on ...**

При внимательном рассмотрении
Under close examination the plates exhibited a shiny film of ...
(When) viewed closely, such a mixture readily reveals ...

При возвращении [*см.* **На обратном пути**].

При воздействии [*см. тж.* **Под действием**]
On exposure to flowing heat, the outer surface absorbs much of the heat.

При вращении
As (*or* **When**) the disk **rotates** its blades block.

При входе в
The monopole would slow down much sooner **on entering** a substance than ...

При входе и выходе
The refrigerant evaporating temperature **at entry and exit** (*or* **at inlet and outlet**) ...

При выборе
In deciding on a particular vehicle fuel, it is necessary to consider ...

При выдерживании
The supersaturated solid solution breaks down **on standing** [*or* **on being kept** (*or* **held**)] at room temperature.

При выключенном свете
With the room light off ...

При горении
The heat liberated **in combustion ...**

При давлении
The mean free paths of gases **at 1 atm (pressure)** (*or* **at a pressure of 1 atm**) ...

При давлении и температуре
Hydrogen flows through the line **at 100 psia and 15°C** for several days.

При дальнейшей обработке
On further processing the mixtures assumed the full characteristics of ...

При дальнейшем нагревании
On further heating, $CuSO_4$ is produced.

При данном [*см.* **При заданном**].

При движении
The region in which each particle can move **in** its vibrational **motion** is restricted.
φ increases **when moving** in the direction from upstream toward P.

При деформации
To predict the behaviour of various metals **under deformation, ...**

При длительном выдерживании
On long standing in aqueous solution, a small amount of basic copper sulphate is formed.

При длительном хранении
The powder decomposes at 350°C and at room temperature **on long standing** (*or* **storage**).

При дневном свете
Communication by this infrared link will be possible **in (bright) daylight.**

При добавлении ... к
On addition of purified *IF*-3 **to** isolated 30 *S* ribosomal subunits (*biol.*) ...

При достаточной изобретательности
Given enough ingenuity, the construction could be worked out.

При других условиях [*см.* **В других условиях**].

При заданном [*см. тж.* **Зная, Имея**]
At given conditions of temperature and pressure ...
Given *S* and *m* as defined above, R^S/m contains both infinitesimals and infinite elements.
A convenient way to calculate the temperature distribution in a fuel element, **given** the heat flux and mass flow rate, is ...

При замене
With μ **in place of** *m*, the Schrödinger equation is: ...

При изменении [*см. тж.* **Оставаться постоянным при изменении**]
As the laser wavelength **changes,** the conformations excited also change.
Correction of the metering function **under changes of** altitude and temperature ...

При изучении
This information is of interest **in studies of ...**

При использовании
With a laser, this approach fails.
In use (*or* **When in use**), a rotating shaft is inserted in ...
Used (*or* **When used**) in tandem with a sock-type filter, the charcoal performs two functions.
Experiments were conducted **using** (*or* **with the use of**) the optimum quantities of ...
All the stripping is done with the scraper fleet, **utilizing** a D8 tractor with ...
When employing these compounds as fuel additives, ...

With (*or* **In**) most methods, the precise regulation of carrier gas flow is rarely necessary.

При испытаниях
On trials the tug achieved a speed of 12 knots.

При какой-то определённой температуре *и т.п.*
We want to record the way the atoms in a rock would arrange themselves **at any particular temperature,** etc.

При калибровке
When calibrating spectrophotometers, the same instrumental setting should be used as ...

При комнатной температуре
The specimens were prestrained **at room temperature.**

При концентрации
At a high **concentration of** water ...

При коротком замыкании
The voltage induced in the coil **while short-circuited** should be negligible.

При котором
We may choose a coordinate system **such that** the *x*-axis **is** oriented along $H_{t,o}$.
Conditions can be attained **wherein** the diffusion current is dependent on ...
Conditions may be chosen **whereby** no current flows through a cell.

При котором ... является
The momentum vector can assume only those orientations in space **which result in** its component in the direction of the field **being** an integral number of ...

При любой нагрузке
The motor maintains the same speed **at all loads** (*or* **at any load**).

При любых условиях
The martensitic stainless steels are magnetic **in** (*or* **under**) **all conditions.**

При малой нагрузке
A diesel engine is most efficient **at light loads.**

При методе [*см. тж.* **По методу**]
With (*or* **In**) **this approach** the sample is irradiated with ...

При минимальном уходе
The equipment is capable of several hundred hours operation **with the minimum of maintenance.**

При мощности
The fluorescence excitation profile was obtained **at a low** laser **power.**

При нагревании
Mercuric oxide, **on being heated** [*or* **when** (*or* **if**) **heated,** *or* **on heating**], yields mercury and oxygen.

При нагревании до красного каления
Tungsten steel **in a red-hot condition** (*or* **at red heat**) can be used to cut other metals.

При наличии
This will inevitably take place **given** sufficient time.
With the availability of higher-power lasers it will be possible to ...
With a computer, this is an easy task.
Given (*or* **With**) that specific information, we would do a pretty good job.
With this information **at hand** the design of a desired apparatus needs only a bit of arithmetic.

При наличии возможности
It is desirable, **where** (*or* **whenever,** *or* **if**) **possible,** to avoid the use of such oils.

При наличии времени и желания
All those quasars can be studied telescopically **given the time and the inclination.**

При наличии некоторого опыта
With some experience, a pilot may interpret the radar indicator to obtain ...

При наличии опыта
With practice (*or* **experience**), it is usually possible to allocate like individuals of plant or animal to individual species.

При наличии соответствующих возможностей
Given the opportunity, the present building can be expanded.

При наступлении
Estrogen is released by secretory cells in the ovary of the female animal, particularly **at the onset of** puberty.

При не слишком низких температурах
At not-too-low temperatures ...

При некоторых обстоятельствах
Some waves can **under certain circumstances** (*or* **conditions**) have phase velocities greater than ...

При необходимости [*см. тж.* **Если потребуется, По мере необходимости**]
The plant permits inclusion of other elements for crushing, grinding, screening and concentration **as may be required.**
This equipment could be moved elsewhere **as the need arose.**
The bobbins may be put in parallel, **if need be** (*or* **should the need arise**), to increase the field strength.
The table shaft is hollow so that **if required** (*or* **necessary**), hydraulic lines can be ...
The device converts moderate pole spacing to fine pole spacing **when needed.**

При нормальной работе
In (*or* **Under**) **normal operation,** the arc voltage is approximately 25 volts.

При нормальных условиях
The instrument will indicate the altitude of the aircraft above sea level **if standard** (*or* **normal**) **conditions prevail.**
The properties of the mantle **at standard conditions ...**

При облучении [*см. тж.* **Под облучением**]
During neutron **exposure ...**
The disappearance of vinyl unsaturation **on irradiation ...**

При обработке
If treated with certain electrophilic reagents benzene undergoes substitution.
The DNA-bound ribosomes were released from the cellular membrane fraction **on treatment with** deoxyribonuclease (*biol.*).

При образовании [*см.* **Во время его образования**].

При обычной температуре
At ordinary temperatures ...

При обычных условиях
Bromine exists **under ordinary** (*or* **normal**) **conditions** as a dark red liquid.

При одинаковых размерах *и т.п.*
Size for size, the *K-Prene* springs are more expensive than the steel springs, but **pressure for pressure** they cost the same.

При одной установке
It is sometimes most convenient to undertake as many machining operations as possible **at one set-up.**

При одной установке в патроне
Jobs which require two chuckings are now completed **in one chucking.**

При одном прикосновении
The rollers spin **at a touch.**

При определённых обстоятельствах
Time resolution will, **in certain** (*or* **specific**) **situations,** serve as a useful ...

При опускании
A pump and valve arrangement raises the D_2O column **as** the Hg **is lowered.**

При опыте
They supply energy to operate a charger **in experiments.**

При открытом
It is preferable to start the pump **with** the discharge valve **open.**

При отсутствии
This would be true **in the absence of** a spacially distributed background.
In the absence of the atmosphere ...
Estimate the vaporization rate **with no** air leakage.
This new orbit would be permanent, **barring** additional stellar perturbation.

При охлаждении
The *C—H* absorption might be expected to decrease **on cooling.**

При оценке
In (*or* **When**) **evaluating** voltage losses ...

При первой попытке
They experimented with the system and achieved excellent results **on their** (*or* **at the**) **first try** (*or* **attempt**).

При первом появлении
Scientific terms are defined **as they first appear.**

При первоначальных исследованиях
During the early work with clay minerals the name allophane came to be associated with ...

При первых признаках
The rove beetles appear in large numbers **at the first signs of** putrefaction of animal flesh.

При перевозке [*см. тж.* **Во время перевозки**]
Formaldehyde in water solutions should be kept warm **in** (*or* **during**) **transit** (*or* **transportation**).

При перегрузке
The iron vanes tend to saturate magnetically **on overload** and thereby act as further overload protection.

При пересечении
These functions become discontinuous **at** such **intersections.**

При переходе
Tunable dye lasers provide high spectral irradiance at atomic **transitions.**
In these **transitions** the radiation is ...

При переходе из ... в
In going from state *a* **to** state *b*, ...

При переходе к бóльшим и бóльшим значениям
As one goes higher and higher in the scale of numbers ...

При переходе от ... к ...
The physical properties of the free elements show a regular gradation from nonmetallic to metallic as one **passes** (*or* **goes**) **from** nitrogen **to** bismuth.
When passing from forced circulation **to** natural convection ...
The differential change in the individual components of v **in moving** (*or* **going**) **from** $P(x, y, z)$ **to** $0(x + dx + du, z + dz)$ is given by ...
The character of the clay minerals changes **in passing from** one environment **to** another.

При планировании опыта
In the design of a spectroscopic **experiment,** it is important to consider ...

При поверхностном осмотре
Iodine crystals appear blue-black **on cursory examination.**

При повышении [*см. тж.* **По мере того, как**]
The sweep component beats with the second, third and fourth harmonics of the crystal oscillator **as** the sweep frequency **increases.**

При повышенной температуре
This material showed thermoplastic properties **at elevated temperatures.**

При подготовке к
In preparation for the second step, ...

При поисках
In the search for such a property it turns out to be profitable to ...

При полёте
In flight over the ocean the pressure reference setting is 29.92 in. of mercury.

При полёте по приборам
When flying under instrument conditions ...

При полной нагрузке
Efficiency is better than 96% **at full load.**
Output of the machine **on full production** is 120 racks per hour.

При полном отсутствии
It is rare for one reaction to occur **to the total exclusion of the others.**

При помощи [*см. тж.* **Посредством, Путём, С помощью**]
With this microscope the particles can be magnified up to 15,000 times.
The age of very ancient rocks may be measured **using** the potassium-argon method.
By (*or* **With**) such a method ...
The dry box is evacuated **by** a vacuum pump.
The bearings are mounted on the shaft **by the use of** a hydraulic system.
Refuelling is accomplished **with [the aid** (*or* **help**) **of]** (*or* **by means of**) a simple machine.
Solid state bonds can be achieved **with (the use of)** ultrasonic welding.
The surface of normal velocity may often be constructed **by means of** the reciprocal surface.
Circular polarization is obtained **through the use** of the slots ...
Irregular surfaces can be treated **by use of** the servo control system.
We can introduce the curves **through** Eq. (1.14).
The stereochemical relationships between ... can be determined **by reference to** the Fischer projection of ...
The gas laws can be understood **through** a model.

При помощи которого
This is a technique **whereby** a clearance is measured.

При помощи ... метода
With (*or* **In**) **this method,** it is possible to make ...

При помощи ультразвука
Ultrasonically assisted wire drawing ...

При помощи уравнения
With (the aid of) the Bernoulli **equation** one can ...

При попытке
On attempted isolation (*or* **In attempting to** isolate) ...

При постоянной температуре
These data have been obtained **at constant temperature.**

При постоянном
Differentiation must be performed **holding** φ **= constant** [*or* **with** φ **(held) constant**].

При постоянном давлении
If the pressure is kept constant (*or* **At a constant pressure**) the volume varies linearly with ...

При построении
In the construction of (*or* **When constructing**) Fig. 2, ...

При поступлении
Beta detectors may give a signal **at the advent of** each individual particle.
Dissolved oxygen in the feed water can be scavenged **as it enters** the drum.

При правильном использовании
Computers are valuable pieces of machinery that, **when properly used,** may do much to upgrade the quality of modern life.

При предельной растворимости
At the limit of solubility ...

При предположении [*см. тж.* **В предположении, что; Исходя из предположения, что**]
If the assumption is made that ...
These equations can be combined into a single equation **under** three different **assumptions ...**
Even **with the** most optimistic **assumptions ...**

При предположении о
The only potential-energy contribution, **assuming** a ball-and-spring type of model for the molecule, arises from ...
With the supposition of frictionless pulleys, no energy is transferred to ...

При преобразовании
The manifolds are invariant **under transformations of** the variables.

При приближении к [*см. тж.* **По мере приближения к**]
This becomes more difficult **as** the centre of the point **is approached.**
The angle tends to be very large **as** the divergence speed **is approached.**

При приливе, отливе
This area is completely covered **at high tide,** but exposed **at low tide.**

При приложении усилия
Nickel changes its magnetic permeability **as a stress is applied** (*or* **on application of a stress**).

При применении к
The reduction becomes particularly simple **when applied to** systems involving ...

При проектировании
These stresses must be considered **in the design.**

При производстве
The salt is used **in the manufacture of** explosives.

При пропускании через
Acetylene, **when passed through** a hot tube, yields benzene.

При прохождении через
These radiations from the nucleus, **in their passage through** the atom, excite ...
Oil is picked up by steam **in its passage through** the engine.
Sunlight is refracted and dispersed **in passing through** the raindrops.
The heat that was picked up by the steam **in transit through** the superheater ...
In the transmission electron microscope the electron beam is modified in various ways **as it passes through** thicker and thinner sections of the specimen.

При прочих равных условиях [*см.* **При равных прочих условиях**].

При работающем двигателе
The adjustment can be made **while the motor is running.**
With the chart-drive **motor running,** the chart-speed selection knob can be set to the desired position.

При работе
In the case of pumps **on** salvage **duty ...**
If (*or* **When**) **operating at** the maximum absorption ...
When operated at 20 Hz ...

При работе без нагрузки
Terminal voltage **for no load** is 2 VN.

При равновесии
The figure shows the potential distribution **at equilibrium.**

При равных прочих условиях
Harder workpieces will produce better finishes, **all (other) things** (*or* **factors**) **being equal** (*or* **the same**).

При разнообразных условиях
The experiments were run **under a variety of conditions** (*or* **under various conditions**).

При разомкнутом
With the relay switch contacts **open,** a potential appears across the load.

При разряжённом конденсаторе
With the capacitor discharged the switch is closed.

При разложении
Two additional molecules of *ATP* are formed **in the breakdown of** glucose **to** pyruvic acid.

При распространении по
This equation determines the variation of the discontinuity strength in the Alfven mode **as it propagates** (*or* **travels**) (*or* **during its propagation**) **along** a tube.

При рассмотрении в микроскоп
An aqueous solution of copper (II) chloride appears homogeneous **on examination under a microscope** (*or* **when observed with a microscope**).

При растворении
Each mole, **on solution** (*or* **on dissolving**), yields one mole each of silver ion and chloride ion.

При расходе
At a flowrate of 16 gpm/ft^2 ...

При расчётной нагрузке
The output voltage may be varied from 0 to 5,000 V **at rated load.**

При реакции с
These compounds yield predominantly acetylene **on reaction with** H_2O.

При ... рекомендуется
The upper gastro-intestinal tract ulceration **is a good reason for** avoiding tablets and prescribing a liquid preparation.

При решении уравнений
Addition is often used **in the solution of** (*or* **in solving,** *or* **when solving**) ordinary differential **equations.**

При самой большой длине
The Galaxy as a whole has a diameter which is, **at its longest,** 30,000 parsecs.

При сборке
In the assembly of (*or* **When assembling**) the engine after overhaul, care must be taken to ...

При свете
Alkanes react with halogens **in the (presence of) light.**

При сильном нагреве
Under intense heat, quicklime becomes incandescent.

При совпадении
With the 0 of the vernier **and the 0 of** the graduated column **coincident** (*or* **When... coincide**), the vernier hook can be made to ...

При согласии
Barium studies can be organized **if** the patient **is cooperative** (*med.*).

При созревании
The eggs in the ovaries increase in size **at maturity.**

При солнечном свете
In (the presence of) sunlight, methane reacts with ...

При соответствующих условиях
Given proper conditions, we should be able to ...
Under appropriate (*or* **proper**) **circumstances** (*or* **conditions**) ...
The impurity content should be constant **under suitable conditions.**

При соприкосновении
On coming in contact with the respective electrode, the colloidal substance loses its charge.
The freshly cut surface darkens **on exposure to** air.
These alloys obtain an oxide layer immediately **(up)on contact with** air.
The dissolved gas reacts instantly with OH^- **on contact.**
The process by which ethylene oxide and water react **in contact with** (*or* **when contacting**) an ion-exchange resin is discussed in the following section.
Meshing does not result **on contact,** unless the jaws are aligned.

При сохранении
On retention of only the first-order terms one would obtain ...

При срабатывании
On operation of the extra-low-water-level switch the control unit will shut down the automatic firing equipment.

При сравнимых условиях
Steam is far less "ideal" than helium **under comparable conditions.**

При столкновении (*яд. физ.*)
A number of different processes may happen **at collision.**

При ... стремящемся к

As (*or* **For,** *or* **With,** *or* **When**) $\alpha \rightarrow 1$, β is given by the following expression: ...

При строительстве здания следует учитывать
Considerations of health and safety **must** also **be embodied in a building.**

При существующем
At least three comets have orbits with eccentricities so close to unity that, observational errors **being what they are,** the orbits might be hyperbolic.

При существующем положении [*см.* **В данной ситуации**].

При существующих условиях
Under prevailing conditions of recovery technology ...

При таком предположении
On (*or* **Under**) **this assumption,** i_{pc} is equal to ...

При температуре [*см. тж.* **В котором поддерживается температура**]
The air circulates through the coil **at (a temperature of)** 17°C.

При температуре, близкой к комнатной
Water is vaporized into air **at near-room temperature.**

При температуре окружающей среды
These alloys can be more easily worked **at ambient temperatures.**

При температуре опыта
The tube is filled with a liquid **at the test temperature.**

При транспортировке [*см.* **Во время перевозки**].

При тщательном изучении
On close examination of these tissues it was found that ...

При увеличении I
The pressure will fall to the equilibrium value **as** the density **increases** (*or* **with increasing** density).

При увеличении II
The etched groove is not visible **at this magnification.**

При удалении от [*см.* **С увеличением расстояния от, С удалением от**].

При указанных условиях
To obtain the collision properties **at the specified** (*or* **indicated**) **conditions, ...**

При условии
With the constraint $X_3 = z^{-1}Y_3$ it can be shown that ...

При условии соблюдения
We consider Eq. (3.3) **subject to** the boundary conditions.

При условии, что [*см. тж.* **Если**]
With the proviso that $V >> 1$, it is possible to ...
The equation admits a solution of constant state **subject to the condition** (*or* **requirement**) **that ...**
Such a plant in a remote location can justify its cost **provided (that)** it is kept in service for a long enough time.
Tin-base solders are acceptable for radiation environments **providing** (*or* **on condition that**) the temperature is low.
The beam proved very suitable for alignment tests, **provided (that)** certain difficulties could be overcome.
Mining companies make the data available to the Government **with the understanding that** data would be released without identifying individual companies.

При условиях [*см. тж.* **В условиях**]
An absorption coefficient is defined as the amount of gas dissolved **at** standard **conditions** by 1 cm^3 of the solvent.
Some water can **under** (*or* **in**) certain **circumstances** (*or* **conditions**) have phase velocities greater than ...

При условиях эксперимента
Determine the value of D_{AB} for helium in nitrogen **under the test conditions.**

При учёте
These data show a linear relationship **if** the residual current **is accounted for** (*or* **taken into account,** *or* **allowed for**).

При хорошей видимости
The resolving power of large optical telescopes **under good seeing** (*or* **visibility**) **conditions** is about one arc-second.

При хранении
Aviation gasoline must be stable **in storage.**
On keeping, cyanic acid soon polymerizes to cyanuric acid.

При частоте
At a given collision **frequency** all protons will absorb ...

При этих условиях
Under (*or* **In**) **these conditions ...**

При этом [*см. тж.* **Причём**]
Suppose a red quark changes its colour and in **the process** emits ...
It changes into a proton **emitting** an electron as it does so.
As this takes place, a certain amount of liquid enters the chamber.
This effect could be counterbalanced by using more material; **in so doing** (*or* **in doing so,** *or* **in this case**) the result would be a sacrifice of speed.
The gamma quantum itself disappears **in the process.**
The dissipation of energy **therewith** slows down.
The compass will point to the magnetic pole, but **in so doing** will point well to the west of the north.
Let us examine the solution adjacent to a constant state and **in doing so** (*or* **this**) follow the proof given above.

Прибавлять и вычитать
The quantity RT/P **can be added to and subtracted from** the integrand to give ...

Прибегать к [*см. тж.* **Не прибегая к**]
To appreciate these special cases one **must resort to** quantum theory.
Recourse was made (*or* **We resorted,** *or* **We made recourse**) **to** a propulsion unit incorporating ...
The 19th century industrialists **resorted to** a two-step combustion process in order to ensure that...
Again gas chromatography and mass spectrometry **were called on,** and they revealed that ...
Because of this, **recourse to** much simpler models **is** often **necessary** [*or* **it is** often **necessary to take** (*or* **have**) **recourse to** much simpler models].
The thermal reservoir **will be called upon** to supply this heat.
We **resorted to** the trial-and-error procedure.

Приближать к
This **brings** the phase **closer to** chemical equilibrium.
As the cell **is moved closer to** the lens focus, ...
To bring some internal residues **into proximity with** the growing end of the chain, ...

Приближаться
As the end of the Mesozoic **drew near** (*or* **close**), ...

Приближаться к I [*см. тж.* **Близкий к, Не приближаться к**]
The liquid **may come close to** equilibrium.
By inadvertently **approaching** a radiobeacon station...
The comet **nears** the Sun.
When the pulp **nears** (*or* **approaches**) the bottom of the standpipe ...
This force becomes greater **as** the particle **nears** the core.

Приближаться к II
These density conditions **approximate** average conditions existing at ...
The operator rotates the antenna until the modulation of the trace appears **to approximate** (*or* **approach**) zero.
Both coefficients **approach** the values appropriate to molecular diffusion.
The distribution **approximates to** the normal Gaussian curve.

Приближаться к завершению
The railway **is nearing completion.**
As the reaction **nears completion,** the second term becomes small.

Приближаться к ... по точности
The machine **approaches** jig-borer **accuracy.**

Приближаться к ... снизу (сверху, справа, слева)
A series of numbers that **approached** π **from below (from above, from the right, from the left) ...**

Приближаться по размеру к
These asteroids **were similar in size to** those in ...

Приближающийся к [*см.* **Близкий к, Близко приближающийся к**].

Приближение [*см. тж.* **Более точное приближение, В весьма хорошем приближении, В грубом приближении, В качестве приближения, В первом приближении, В хорошем приближении, Грубое приближение, С хорошим приближением**]
The fine image of an optical system **is an approximation of** a two-dimensional Dirac delta function.
The computed stresses at the centre of the load should be considered as **a** reasonable **approximation to** the stresses at the edge of the attachment.
Their weighted mean closely **approximates** the true daily mean.
The true daily mean **is** closely **approximated by** the mean of 24 hourly readings.
φ **is the** first **approximation to** the solution of the ... equation.

Приближение к [*см.* **По мере приближения к, При приближении к**].

Приближённая оценка
From these correlations it is possible to make **rough** (*or* **approximate,** *or* **tentative**) **estimates of** gaseous product compositions.

Приближённо выражать
The curve thus obtained **can be approximated by** this equation.

Приближённо вычислять
It has been possible **to calculate in a crude way** (*or* **crudely,** *or* **approximately**) the maximum difference in ...

Приближённо описывать
The flow **may be approximated by** nonisentropic flow.
The first expression **may be approximated by ...**

Приближённо равный
The spaces *A* and *B* are filled with water at a pressure **approximating** (*or* **approximately equal to**) the discharge pressure of the pump.

Приближённый метод
A crude (*or* **An approximate**) **method.**

Приблизительно [*см. тж.* **Около, По приближённым оценкам, Порядка, Приближённо, Примерно, Согласно подсчётам**]
The distribution of craters agrees **broadly** with estimates of ...
The world's chemical industry then marketed **an estimated** 1000 new synthetic chemicals each year.
The conglomerate was tilted to **something like** 45 degrees.
In a million years **or so** even the most rapidly spinning neutron star slows down.
This concept appeared **near** the middle of the 19th century.
Theoretically iron crystals should resist deformation at stresses **approaching** [*or* **of about** (*or* **around**), *or* **in the neighbourhood of**] several million psi.
The machine age in the glass container industry started **around** 1890.
These steels have yield strengths **in** the 2,000,000 psi **area** (*or* **in the area of** 2,000,000 psi).
The maximum strain was **in the neighbourhood** (*or* **vicinity**) **of** 2%.
The thermal efficiency of these units will be **in the region of** (*or* **approximately**) 40%.
These disturbances are propagated **at roughly** the speed of sound.
The "dilute form" in percent of total concentration was calculated **roughly.**
Some 250 Mcf of nitrogen was pumped into the line.
An expression for the sound speed in a gas may be obtained very **crudely** as follows.
The terminal velocity is **roughly** constant.
The focal length is 50 mm **or thereabouts.**
The laser output pulses have **an estimated** power of over 1 MW.
The strip should be heated **at around** 1200°F.

Приблизительно в ... направлении
The cosmic jet points **in the approximate direction of** one of the source's radio lobes.

Приблизительно равен
The size of the synthesized RNA usually **approximates** that of the parental molecule (*biol.*).
The frequency of such a vibration **will be something like** the rate with which the complex breaks up.

Приблизительно совпадать с ... по составу
Low-density rock **of the approximate composition of** granite ...

Приблизительно согласовываться с
These diameters **are in rough agreement** (*or* **roughly agree**) **with** those obtained from ...

Приблизительно таким же путём, как и
This compound decomposes **in much the same manner** (*or* **fashion,** *or* **way**) (*or* **in about the same manner,** etc.) **as ...**

Приблизительно такой же
It was considered to be an amorphous substance with **about the same** chemical composition as the mineral kaolinite.

Приблизительно то же самое можно сказать о
Much of the same is true of deep-water molluscs.

Приблизительно установлен
The actual age of the rock **may be approximated by** measuring ...

Приблизительное представление [*см.* **Давать лишь приблизительное представление о**].

Приблизительное представление о ... даёт
A rough measure (*or* **idea**) **of** the resistance of a glass to crystallization **is given by** the displacement of ...

Приблизительный [*см. тж.* **По приблизительным подсчётам**]
If a monopole is detected, **rough** information on its direction can be recorded.

Приболчивать [*см. тж.* **Прикреплять болтами**]
The baseplates **are bolted onto** the machine saddle.

Прибор [*см. тж.* **Оборудованный приборами, Точный прибор, Хорошо оснащённый приборами**]
A device (*or* **An instrument,** *or* **A unit**) that measures ...

Прибыльный
This company should be **a profit-maker.**

Приведение к виду
The highest derivative is separated **by putting** (*or* **recasting**) the equation **in the form ...**

Приведём один пример
To cite (*or* **To take**) **one example,** two photons with opposite charges might ...
To cite one example of how this view has changed, ...

Приведён [*см. тж.* **Показан, Представлен**]
The proposed design **is depicted** (*or* **exhibited**, *or* **displayed,** *or* **illustrated,** *or* **pictured**) **in** the accompanying drawing.
Ag-base alloys **are listed** (*or* **given**) **in** Table 3.
Details **are presented** elsewhere.
Additional discussions of thermodynamics **will be found in** subsequent sections.

Приведён в движение
Once the fluid **is set in motion, ...**

Приведён в таблице
These data **are listed** (*or* **shown,** *or* **given**) **in Table** III.

Приведённый [*см. тж.* **Показывать, Указанный**]
Data **presented in** the literature vary widely.
The constants **reported in** this work ...
Many reactions, such as the one **cited** above, occur ...
The reference **cited in** this article ...

Приведённый в колебательное движение
A particle **set in oscillation** would continue in this motion indefinitely.

Приведённый выше
In the list of fractions **above** (*or* In **the above** list of fractions), you will see that ...

Приведённый пример
In the example cited (above) ...

Приветствовать новшества
Even engineers and businessmen who **are** particularly **open to innovation** approach major expenditures in a conservative mood.

Привёрнутый [*см.* **Привинчивать**].

Прививать к
Strains of bacteria of... **are inoculated into** a nutrient medium.

Привинчивать
The machine **should be** placed in a convenient working position on the bench and **screwed down.**
In some instruments, the chart post **may be screwed to** the floor.

Привиться
The name **caught on in** Germany.

Привлекательность [*см.* **Нельзя отрицать привлекательности**].

Привлекательный
The potential uses of such a fusion-torch capability **are intriguing;** for one thing, it could be used to ...
Investment casting **is** particularly **inviting** (*or* **attractive,** *or* **appealing**) when intricate shapes, with close tolerances, have to be produced.

Привлекать
To understand the surface paradox, observed with strongly interacting photons, we **must** once again **invoke** the uncertainty principle.

Привлекать внимание
Such streaks of light are bound **to fix** (*or* **attract**) **the attention of** the astronomer.
The scene **arrested our attention.**
Recent efforts to ... **have drawn attention to** the absence of ...
The scientist **has called attention to** a curious oversight on Dr. M's part.
An outstanding phenomenon **came to the attention of** physicists.

Привлекать к себе значительное внимание
The subject **has attracted considerable interest** (*or* **attention**).

Привлекать к себе главное внимание
Protective coating research **is commanding the major attention in** this area.
Among liquid lasers the dye laser **has attracted the most notice.**
The high-energy processes and objects that **command the attention of** modern astronomers, such as supernovas, neutron stars and ...

Привлекать особое внимание [*см.* **Особенно интересовать**].

Привлекать с эстетической точки зрения
Cantilevers are used in many special cases when they **appeal aesthetically to** the designer.

Привлекать талант
Good technologies for providing clean power gas will be developed only if a great deal more **talent is recruited for** the work.

Привлекать широкое внимание
The first antibiotic **to receive** (*or* **attract**) **widespread attention** was penicillin.

Привлечение
It can be shown, without **invoking** the parallel postulate, that only one such perpendicular can be drawn.

Привлечь внимание ... к
This chapter is designed **to bring to the attention of** the reader the problems which are likely to...

При́вод [*см.* **С гидравлическим приводом, С дизельным приводом, С ножным приводом** (*или* **управлением**)**, С паровым приводом, С ручным управлением, С турбоприводом, С цепным приводом, С электрическим приводом**].

Приводимый в движение
A space vehicle **powered by** a rocket ...
Tractors **powered with** an internal combustion engine ...

Приводимый в движение соленоидом
A final electrical output signal serves to operate a **solenoid-actuated** hydraulic spool valve.

Приводимый в действие
A drill **operated by** compressed air ...
Combines **powered by** gasoline engines were then introduced.

Приводимый в книге
All of the profiles **appearing** (*or* **presented,** *or* **given**) **in this book** fall into two classes.

Приводимый здесь
The properties of a number of these materials are summarized in the **accompanying** table.

Приводимый от двигателя
A tachometer **driven off the motor ...**
Various types of **engine-driven** arc-welding generator sets ...

Приводить [*см.* **На схеме показан, Указывать**].

Приводить аргумент (*или* **довод**) [*см. тж.* **Выдвигать аргумент**]
To adduce (*or* **To bring forward,** *or* **To advance**) **an argument, ...**

Приводить без вывода и доказательства
This rule **is presented without derivation or proof.**

Приводить в движение
Vacuum tubes which **activate** the mechanisms ...
To actuate, *or* **to cause to move,** *or* **to bring into action,** *or* **to set in motion ...**
The relay serves **to actuate** the dial mechanism of the clock.
The machines in these plants **are** largely **driven by** a-c motors.
This **initiates the operation of** the governor mechanism.
The motors **operate** the caterpillar tracks.
A separate motor **powers** the hydraulic pumps.
All American passenger cars **are powered with** (*or* **propelled by**) 6- or 8-cylinder engines.
When the machine member **is set** (*or* **put**) **in motion, ...**
The rocket **is propelled** in the same way.

Приводить в действие [*см. тж.* **Задействовать, Приводить в движение**]
The equipment **is powered** (*or* **driven**) **by** electric motors.
The transducer **actuates** the relay to disengage the motor drive at the preset size.
The hammer head **is activated by means of** compressed air.
The switch **brings into operation** the printing mechanism.
The instructions will enable the user to install, **set to work** and maintain the recorder in first-class working order.
The clutch **is operated by ...**
The oscillograph **can be triggered by ...**

Приводить в качестве доказательства того, что
This event **was cited as evidence that** the nebula must be within our galaxy.

Приводить в качестве примера
The protoplasmic membrane of the biological cell **has been cited as an example of** coacervation phenomena.
We **shall exemplify** one of these methods.

Приводить в колебательное движение
A tuning fork **is set in(to) vibration by** sound waves.

Приводить в негодное состояние
Oil or moisture in the tubing **will make** the abrasive **unusable.**

Приводить в нерабочее состояние
The filling fluid will leak out **making** (*or* **rendering**) the system **inoperative.**

Приводить в однозначное соответствие с
The *n* elements of any finite set obviously **cannot be put** (*or* **set**) **into one-to-one correspondence** (*or* **matched one to one**) **with** its subsets because ...

Приводить в порядок
To straighten out the existing system of ...

Приводить в правильное положение
"To align" means **to bring parts into proper position.**

Приводить в рабочее состояние
Damaged drills **may** easily and rapidly **be made serviceable** again by using this method.

Приводить в равновесие
The bed **has been brought to equilibrium with** the feed gas.
A crank **brings** the balance **to** perfect **equilibrium** easily and quickly.

Приводить в соприкосновение
The gas and the liquid **are brought together** (*or* **in contact**) in a suitable contacting apparatus.
When two metals **are placed** (*or* **brought**) **in(to) contact,** electrons pass from one to the other.

Приводить в соприкосновение с
A small fluid element **is brought into contact with** a phase boundary.
When a very dilute gas **is contacted with** a large quantity of solvent, ...

Приводить доводы в пользу *чего-л.*
Arguments in favour of this treatment **were advanced** (*or* **adduced**).

Приводить доказательство того, что
One **can cite evidence that** the gas plays a part in ...

Приводить к I [*см. тж.* **Влечь за собой**]
This method **offers** savings in production time.
Removal of the denaturing conditions **brings about** the formation of ...
This **causes** the input voltage **to** rise and fall.
This research **has culminated in** the discovery of ...
The use of a driving belt **could give rise to** vibrations.
This **involves** an increase in ...
This **leads to** new concepts.
If solute concentration varies over many atomic distances, a variation in lattice parameter **will result.**
Flapping of the belt **could result in** poor finish.
The current in the motor increases, and **the result is** overheating.
Uneven removal of excess metal **tends to** redistribute stresses.
In areas where present climates **are** not **conducive to** the deposition of ...

Приводить к II
The mixture **is adjusted to** pH 6.8.

Приводить к III [*см. тж.* **Благодаря которому происходит**]
Biotin deficiency in animals **is associated with** dermatitis, loss of hair, ...
Thermal stresses sometimes **produce** surface cracking.
A small error in ψ **will** eventually **produce** a significant error in the fields.
The change in contact resistance **effects** the desired current change.
These collisions **can involve** either a gain or loss in mechanical energy.
Continued condensation **causes** the period of rotation to shorten.

Приводить к виду
We use ... **to bring** these equations **(in)to the form: ...**
This expression **can be put** (*or* **recast**) **in a** more convenient **form.**

Приводить к возникновению
The observation of ... **gave birth** (*or* **rise**) **to** the new science of radioastronomy.

Приводить к выводу [*см. тж.* **Аналогичные рассуждения приводят к выводу о том, что**]
Application of this principle **suggests** (*or* **leads to the conclusion**) **that ...**
This improvement through utilizing dye lasers **suggests** the possibility of extending ...
This **leads us** (*or* **One is led**) **to the conclusion that ...**
This difference **suggests** [*or* **leads us to conclude** (*or* **to recognize**)] **that** the heat of solution ...

Приводить к желаемому результату
The proof of this statement **furnishes the desired result.**

Приводить к непроизводительной затрате энергии
This technique **is wasteful of energy.**

Приводить к образованию
The combination of ... **gave rise** to the mass 243 isotope of berkelium.
The second cleavage **gives rise** to four cells.
It is this motion that **is responsible for** the volcanoes of the Cascades.
This distortion **may result in** a molecule of HCl.

Приводить к однозначному соответствию с
The counting numbers **can be matched one to one with** a subset of integral fractions.
To bring these two values **into "one-to-one correspondence", ...**

Приводить к лучшему соответствию
This **brings** theory **and** experiment **into better agreement.**

Приводить к появлению
Transcription of the DNA molecule **brings into existence** the several types of RNAs (*biol.*).
The decay of such nuclei **gives rise** to gamma rays.

Приводить к предположению
This fact **suggested** (*or* **led to the suggestion**) **that ...**

Приводить к путанице [*см. тж.* **Вызывать путаницу**]
Using *db* in relation to control systems only **confuses the issue.**
Too many lines **tend to be confusing.**

Приводить к разрушению
Further increases in blank diameter **terminate** (*or* **end**) **in failure.**

Приводить к совпадению
The segments of the two curves **were brought into coincidence.**
To **fit** the experimental data **into** a quantitative theory, ...
Incorporation of $(\sigma_w/\sigma)^3$ in the abscissa of the usual correlation **brings** the data on liquids of low surface tension **in(to) line with** the data on water.

Приводить к созданию
This **brought** the ultralight airplane **into being.**
Our research **has** already **come up with** plating solutions that permit faster deposition rates.

Приводить к увеличению
The addition of further enthalpy terms **will cause** the value of β **to increase.**
High flow rates **tend to increase** K.

Приводить к форме
This equation **can be brought (in)to** conservation **form.**
We **can put** the Langmuir formula **in the** same **form** as the formula for ...

Приводить обзор [*см.* **В ... приводится обзор**].

Приводить пример
One additional **example can be given** (*or* **adduced,** *or* **cited,** *or* **offered**).

Приводить ссылки
We **cite** those **references** which ...

Приводиться [*см. тж.* **Показан, Приводить**]
Table 12 **sets out** the data on which these conclusions are based.
An energy level diagram for dye laser operation **is illustrated** (*or* **given,** *or* **exhibited**) **in** Fig. 5.
The partition function **will be cited** without derivation.
Typical ranges for stretching bond absorptions **appear** below.
Table I **lists** the density of polyethylenes.
The physical properties of calcium metal **are given** in Table 2.
The tables **cover** the characteristics of the materials.
The specification **is set out** herewith: ...

Приводиться в движение
Motion is imparted by means of a double-acting hydraulic ram.
Spindle **drive is taken from** a 3-hp motor.
The converter **is actuated by** electrohydraulic means.
The machine **is driven by** a diesel engine.
The aircraft **is powered by** two engines.
The worktable **is set in motion** and the roughing cut taken.
The discriminators **are operated from** a regulated power supply.

Приводиться в таблице
Included (*or* **Given**) **in Table** I **is** the calculated product of ...
In Table I **are listed** the major calcium minerals and their formulas.
Some of the important properties of beryllium **are tabulated** (*or* **given,** *or* **displayed**) **in Table** I.

Приводиться ниже
The details **are as follows** (*or* **are given below,** *or* **follow**).
Examples of the simplest cycloalkanes **follow** (*or* **are given below**).

Приводиться от [*см. тж.* **Приводиться в движение**]
A central roll **is power driven from** an electric motor through a transmission unit.
The alternator **is driven off** the main shaft.
These machines **may be powered from** portable units.
The press has a capacity of 1000 tons and **drive is taken from** a 125-hp motor.

Приводнение (*космич. аппарата*)
After **the splash-down** the capsule was delivered to ...

Приводняться
The spacecraft **is due to splash down** in the ocean in two hours.

Привыкать

The organism **is said to be habituated to** the stimulus.

Привязывать к координатам
Here, diffusion and flow **are to be related to** cartesian coordinates.

Пригоден [*см. тж.* **Весьма пригодный для, Вполне пригоден для, Не пригоден, Подходить для, Применим**]
The tool rest **is adequate for** small jobs.
The method **is appropriate in the case of** strain-ageing.
Rockets are particularly **attractive for** aircraft launching.
This method **is capable of** analyzing most hydrocarbon samples.
The analyzer **is suitable for** a 625-line system.
Because of its greater stiffness the fixed arch **is** better **suited for** long spans than hinged arches.
Ceramic, glass-ceramic and glass-bonded micas **are suited to** applications at 400°C and up.
The gasket **was** not **suited to** 575°F temperature.

Пригоден для производства
Coir **is suitable for** sailcloth.

Пригоден только для
The data plotted in Fig. 12.4 **are adequate only for** rough approximations.

Пригодность
Many astronomers question **the validity of** this model.
The suitability of coal **for** gas-making ...

Пригодный для [*см. тж.* **Можно успешно использовать в качестве**]
This makes metal hydrides **feasible for** the storage of energy.
In view of the inconsistancies in ..., this alternative **can** scarcely **be** considered **tenable.**
These raw materials **are satisfactory for** the manufacture of ...
A computer-aided draughting system assists in converting sketches or concepts into working drawings **suitable for** use in manufacture.
The alloy **is good for** bearings and ...
The result **is appropriate for** a finite time interval.

Пригодный для использования
Semi-metallic powders **are applicable to** flame spraying and other coating processes.
These filters **are feasible for** large-scale industrial applications.
Glass-ceramics **are serviceable at** high temperatures.

Пригодный для повторного использования
With **re-usable** mandrels a new coating is applied for the next part.

Приготавливать
Triple superphosphate of lime **is prepared by** the action of phosphoric acid on crushed phosphate rock.
Make up (*or* **Prepare**) a solution of ...

Приготовление
This is **the** usual laboratory **preparation of** the gas, **by** apparatus shown in Fig. 25.

Придавать [*см.тж.* **Сообщать**]
The units **endow** the structure **with** a hydrophilic nature.
These landforms **lend** variety and beauty **to** the scenery of the continents.
The properties **imparted by** the bentonites **to** the drilling fluid are very important to ...

Придавать более привлекательный вид
The appearance of many foods **is enhanced by** artificial colouring.

Придавать большое значение
We **attach much importance to** (*or* **place strong emphasis on**) this matter.
Aeronautical engineers **have** always **been weight conscious.**
A premium is placed upon careful calibration of ...

Придавать вид
This abrasive **imparts** better **finishes** in grinding very hard materials.

Придавать заданную форму
Cast iron **is** usually **made into specified shapes.**

Придавать значение [*см.* **Не придавать значения**].

Придавать наклон [*см. тж.* **Наклонять**]
If **a tilt is given to** the film, ...

Придавать направление
If **a direction is imposed on** the rotating system, ...

Придавать особое значение
You **should attach particular** (*or* **special**) **significance to** the letter sequence.

Придавать прочность
These metals **impart strength to** steel.

Придавать свойства [*см. тж.* **Наделять свойством**]
Carboxyl groups **confer** ion-exchanging **properties on** the paper.
This attribute **imparts** (*or* **gives**) some unique physical **properties to** the clay materials composed of these minerals.

Придавать смысл
Each word we use **has been assigned a (specific) meaning.**

Придавать форму [*см. тж.* **Приводить к форме, Формировать**]
This **gives a** ridgelike **form to** the healed fault (*geol.*).
The work of wind in **shaping** the shorelines ...
The thermoplastic **is** heated and then **shaped to** the contours of a mould.
The top rim of the trough **is formed into** a flange.
The first instrument **should be shaped so that ...**
Solid-rib arches **can be shaped to** almost any required **form.**

Придавать цвет
To impart a blue **colour to** these products, one has to ...

Придерживать
The airship net **is held down by** sand bags.

Придерживаться [*см. тж.* **Использовать методику**]
In our discussion we **have adhered to** classical mechanics.
Let us **entertain** the hypothesis **that ...**

Придерживаться диеты
Such patients have difficulty in **sticking to** (*or* **observing**) **their diet.**

Придерживаться метода
We **shall follow this method.**

Придерживаться мнения (*или* **точки зрения**)
They **hold to the idea that ...**
We do not **hold this viewpoint.**
A group of authors that **follow this point of view ...**

Приемлемый [*см. тж.* **Подходящий, Пригодный для**]
A **workable** (*or* An **acceptable**) theory must recognize ...
A more **plausible** configuration would be realized by twisting the torus.
The total radiation of a black body at the temperature chosen can be determined with **reasonable** (*or* **tolerable**) accuracy.
The result is appreciable capacitance in a **reasonable** volume.

Приём [*см. тж.* **В ... приёмов, Метод, Обычный приём**]
By **the** simple **expedient of** changing from cathode rods to plates, the tolerance of ...was increased.

Приёмочное испытание
The system was installed nine days after **acceptance test** (*or* **checkout**) at the factory.

Прижимать к
Apply the grinding wheel **to** the work **with** gentle pressure.
The water pressure behind the rings **keeps** them **close against** the pump barrel walls.
Press a sheet of emulsion **against** the plate.
Loosen the link which **retains** the terminal plate **against** the door.
The air cushion is capable of exerting forces up to 160 tons for **holding down** the strip during piercing the blanking.

Прижиматься к
The ball **is held (up) against** the seat **by** the pressure acting on ...
The straightedge **should rest against** the pencil.
The rolls **are forced against** the strip **by** the screws.

Признавать
Today most geologists **accept** continental drift.

Признак [*см. тж.* **Есть указания на то, что; Имеются все признаки того, что; Указание**]
A high level of aspertase transaminase **is** usually **a marker of** hepatocellular pathology.

This **is** a good **indicator** (*or* **indication**) **of** the growing use of ...

Признаки
They observed no **evidence of** an interfacial barrier.

Признание [*см.* **Завоёвывать всеобщее признание, По общему признанию, Получить признание**].

Прийти в голову
It occurred to us that infusing the solution directly into a large vein would allow the use of ...

Прийти к
We **have arrived at** a satisfactory method for compensation.
The quantum restriction **can** also **be arrived at by** considering the wave nature of ...

Прийти к выводу о том, что
It was concluded that H_2S had an inhibiting effect on the synthesis of hydrocarbons.

Прикасаться [*см.* **Касаться**].

Прикинуть значение
In order to obtain the equilibrium alcohol concentration in a liquid, **a guess of** $A_{A.2}$ is needed.

Прикладывать [*см.* **Прилагать**].

Прикладывать давление к
The pressure which was **impressed on** (*or* **applied to**) the diaphragm capsule **by** rotating the knob ...

Прикладывать к
Rake and relief angles are measured by **bringing** small contact points of the protractor **against** the tool face and flank, respectively.

Прикладывать напряжение к переходу (*полупров.*)
If **an** external **voltage is applied across the junction, ...**

Прикладывать усилие к
An external magnetic field **exerts a** twisting **force on** the electron.

Прикладывать электрическое поле
These electrical charges are free to move when **an electric field is applied.**

Приклеенный к
Safety glass consists of a layer of glass **cemented to** each side of ...

Приклёпывать к
The ring **is riveted to** the rim of the boiler.

Прикреплён к
The electrodes **are clamped to ...**

Прикреплён снаружи
Temperature sensors **are attached** (*or* **clamped**) **to the outside of** the pipe.

Прикреплённый на шарнирах
An aileron **hinged to** the trailing edge of a wing ...

Прикреплять к
A hot-wire anemometer **was fitted to** the boom of ...
A diagram of the internal connections **is affixed to** the panel.
The base plate **is attached to** the chassis.
The filtering funnel **was fastened to** a suction flask.
The brackets **are fixed to** the rear case.
The board **should be fixed with** screws.
The insulation **is secured to** the deck.

Прикреплять болтами [*см. тж.* **Приболчивать, Скреплять болтами**]
Fenders **are bolted to** the car body.

Прилагаемая нагрузка
The loads imposed (*or* **applied**) **to** the airship in flight ...

Прилагаемая сила
The imposed (*or* **applied**) **force.**

Прилагаемое напряжение
The forcing function is analogous to **the impressed** (*or* **applied**) **voltage.**

Прилагаемое поле
The applied magnetic **field ...**

Прилагаемые пункты патентной формулы
The appended claims ...

Прилагаемые чертежи
The accompanying (*or* **attached**) **drawings ...**

Прилагаемый [*см.* **На прилагаемом рисунке**].

Прилагать
We **have appended** an atlas of graphs **to** our report.

Прилагать большие усилия к
A great deal of effort is going into the investigation of the detailed nature of these events.
The company **is making a major effort to** capture the market.

Прилагать большие усилия к тому, чтобы
Blondlot **went to great lengths** to respond to Wood's criticism of his experimental procedures.
Great pains were taken to detect the exact day on which successive new Moons appeared.

Прилагать большие усилия с целью
Much effort has been directed toward producing better amplifiers.

Прилагать все усилия к тому, чтобы
He **was bending his every effort to** discovering this piece of information.

Прилагать давление к
To apply (*or* **impose**) **pressure to** the cylinder walls, ...

Прилагать заряд
These factors determine **the charge which can be put on** the plates.

Прилагать максимальные усилия к тому, чтобы
Unless **great care is taken to** eliminate all sources of impurities, it is very unlikely that ...
Maximum effort has been expended to produce ...

Прилагать напряжение к
If a direct **voltage** (*or* **potential difference**) **is applied to** the combination of a resistor and ...

Прилагать поле к
When **a** crystal **field is applied to** a free ion (*or* **across** the gel) ...

Прилагать свои способности
Electrical engineers **apply their abilities in** other fields.

Прилагать сигнал
The input **signal is applied between** the common terminal **and** the grid.

Прилагать силу к
The laser beam **exerts a** vertical **force** of several *g* **on** the particle.

Прилагать усилие
If **a force is applied** to create an asymmetry between the split beams, ...

Прилагать усилия
Battery manufacturers **are** already **hard at work to** produce batteries that need not be recharged.
Considerable **effort has been devoted to** the collection of data on ...
An effort should be made to obtain such data.
Most of the mining companies **have put** more **effort into** remote ore-sensing than ...

Прилагать энергию
The binding energy is **the energy** that **must be supplied** (*or* **applied**) to ...

Прилагаться [*см. тж.* **К ... прилагается**]
The magnetic field **is applied** externally.
The transverse impulse **is impressed on** (*or* **applied to**) the electron passing between ...

Прилегать вплотную к
Steel rods are screwed in until the rod head **is tight against** the surface.

Прилегать к
The plateau **is flanked on** the north, east and south **by** mountains that rise to 4,000 meters.

Прилегающий к [*см. тж.* **Непосредственно прилегающий к, Примыкающий**]
We single out the thin fluid layer **adjacent** (*or* **next**) **to** the wall.

Прилив и отлив
During **the rise and fall of tide** (*or* **During tide and ebb,** *or* **During high and low tide**) ...

Прилипание
To prevent **seizure of** the liquid metal **against** the mould walls, ...

Прилипать к
The molecule **adheres to** the surface ...
The ions **cling to** the colloidal particles.

Приложенное напряжение
A potential difference V **applied across** its length ...

For **a** fixed **impressed** (*or* **applied**) **voltage ...**
A steady **potential difference impressed across** the terminals ...

Приложенный
Under a load of 100 g **applied for** *5* seconds ...
The **applied** field increases.

Применение [*см. тж.* **Иметь применение, Использование, Находить применение, Область использования**]
The analysis is dependent on **the employment** (*or* **application**) **of** a satisfactory mixture law.
The tester is designed for laboratory **use.**
The alloy has a large number of **uses** (*or* **applications**) as a substitute for silver.
Computer-aided design refers to any **application of** a computer **to** the solution of design problems.
The application of this tool **to** metal-working jobs ...
The implementation of this technique ...

Применим
This statistical description **applies** when the system has ...
The phase rule **applies to** all systems.
The same principle **is adaptable to** other work that involves ...
These constants would **be applicable for** testing other tubes.
The equation **is applicable to** the new system.
This method **is appropriate in the case of** strain-ageing.
The author proposes an improved correlation **to cover** different gases and liquids.
The analyzer **is suitable for** a 625-line system.

Применимость [*см.* **Практическая применимость**].

Применительно к [*см. тж.* **В применении к**]
This safety regulation, **as applied to** steel plants, states that ...
The process has been developed **to fit** the type of material available.

Применяемый [*см. тж.* **Используемый**]
Aerostat is a term **applied to** any "lighter-than-air" aircraft.
The design principles **employed** (*or* **used,** *or* **applied**) are similar to those already proved in ...

Применяемый в настоящее время
In general, the microwave sources **now in service** (*or* **now in use,** *or* **being used**) are expensive.

Применять [*см. тж.* **Использовать, Неприменим**]
A basic principle that **needs to be invoked** here is ...
Both these methods **are implemented.**
In such cases this lemma **may be applied.**
The same procedure **is followed** in the case of ...

Применять впервые [*см.* **Впервые применить**].

Применять для практических целей
Although the basic phenomena were understood, a considerable time elapsed before they **could be put to practical use.**

Применять метод
Both **approaches have been taken** (*or* **applied**).
A similar **procedure may be followed** to show that ...

Применяться [*см. тж.* **Использовать, Начинать применяться, Широко использоваться**]
This process **is employed** (*or* **used**) **by** our firm.
Unique processes and equipment **have been** successfully **applied in** the mining of ...
The spectrometer **can be applied to** the measurement of ...
This term also **applies to** reactions involving ...
A system such as this **is** already **in operation at** repair shops.
This method **is in use** [*or* **is being used** (*or* **applied**)] **at ...**
The chief **use of** calcium **is in** the production of ...
The term "binding energy" **is** sometimes **used** (*or* **applied**) to describe the energy which ...
The charge-coupling principle **can be applied to** fulfil a number of information-processing requirements.

Experimental procedures in heterogeneous catalysis **involve** specialized techniques.
Various types of antennas **find use** (*or* **application**) **in** Doppler radar.

Применяться в ограниченных масштабах
The algorithm **finds limited use** with second-order controlled systems.

Применяться в основном (*или* **главным образом**) **в**
Leading uses of copper compounds **are in** agriculture, ...
The principal use of cadmium **is in** the plating of ...

Применяться в промышленных масштабах
The preparation of ... **has been used commercially.**
The process **is commercially available.**

Применяться во многих случаях, когда
Calcium hydroxide **is used in many applications where** hydroxide ion is needed.

Применяться главным образом в качестве
The major uses of butanols **are as** chemical intermediates in ...

Применяться ежедневно
Such techniques **are (now) in daily use.**

Применяться к
The technique for solving a first-order equation **is** readily **extended for** the solution of ...
Freeze-drying **has been extended to** a great variety of foodstuffs.

Применяться наиболее широко [*см.* **Наиболее широко использоваться**].

Применяя
By applying (*or* **using**) the principle of the flux trap, magnetic energy may be stored indefinitely.

Пример [*см. тж.* **Брать пример из, В качестве примера, Для примера, Конкретный пример, Наглядный пример, Например, Одним из примеров является, Приводить в качестве примера**]
There are no **instances of** old sediments having been recovered.
The crystal **furnishes** (*or* **provides**) **an** excellent **example of ...**

Пример которого приведён на рис.
One obtains a two-dimensional vibronic/mass spectrum, **as exemplified in Fig.** 5.

Пример сказанного
The blue-white Type *0* and Type *B* giant stars **are a** good **case in point.**

Пример того, как
This **is an example of how** we are making our contribution to ...

Примерами которых являются
There may be many social groups of animals in a single community, **exemplified by** ant colonies, flocks of birds, and herds of elk.

Примерами этого являются
The relay, the toggle switch, the transistor flip-flop, and the ferrite core **are examples.**

Примерно [*см. тж.* **Около, Ориентировочно, Порядка, Практически, Приблизительно**]
The sphere will dissolve completely in **roughly** 10^7 s.
Evaporation was cut **an estimated** (*or* **by approximately**) 80%.
The cost of such a unit would be **in the vicinity** (*or* **neighbourhood,** *or* **region**) of 15% ...
Some (*or* **About,** *or* **Around**) 250 Mcf of nitrogen was pumped into the line.
The omega-meson breaks down **in something like** 0.0001 attosecond.
A Bragg angle of, **say,** between 20 and 30 degrees ...

Примерно в то время, когда
About the time the detailed location phase for this project **was** started, a new application of seismic surveying was investigated.

Примерно в то же время
At about the same time the group reported finding ...

Примерно одинаково
They look **much the same.**

Примерно с ... года
Since about 1950, continuous casting of many alloys has increased.

Примерно таким же образом
Each of the atoms will act as a radiation-

scattering centre **much as** each of the slits acts as a centre of radiation.
The hot well is used **in much the same manner** (*or* **fashion,** *or* **way**) (*or* **in a very similar manner,** etc.).

Примерно такой же
In this case, the procedure **will be about** (*or* **much**) **the same.**
With plastic plates, **much the same** procedure **is** followed.

Примерно такой же, как и
Jupiter and Saturn are the only planets that possess hydrogen and helium **in much the same** concentrations **that** the Sun does.

Примерный
A **sample** voltage-current characteristic for this circuit ...

Примером которого является
There is a class of molecules (**typified by** the noble gases) that is attracted to most other substances more strongly than ...

Примером этого является [*см. тж.* **В качестве примера можно указать на**]
Thus an inundation can ensue. **A case in point is** the valley of the Rio Grande.
Examples are provided by gas mixtures in which ...
Another **example is seen in** the nickel ores of ...
An example of such a structure **is found in** the myelin sheath of nerve.
Oxidation-reduction reactions of ammonia of the second type **are exemplified** (*or* **typified**) **by** reactions of ...
An example (*or* **An instance**) **of** this type of process **is ...**
The Bunsen ice calomiter **is a** good **example.**
The lac transcription process **provides** (*or* **is**) **an example.**
The case to be considered **is typified by** gas absorption in carbon.

Примесь [*см. тж.* **Беспримесный, Добавлять примесные элементы, С примесью**]
Tellurium atoms were introduced as **a dopant.**
Emery is a greyish black variety of corundum containing much **admixed** magnetite or hematite.
Many **impurities** in the aggregate **are** lighter than the good stone or sand.

Примесь типа *n*
The *n*-**dopant.**

Примечательно, что
It is particularly **remarkable that** the melting point of ice VII ... **is** over 100°C.

Примешивать
Stir in the ammonium sulphate till it is dissolved.
Hydrated barium peroxide **may be stirred** slowly **into** ice-cooled water ...

Примиряться с
We **must put up with** those thermal drops in the insulation; there is no way to avoid them.

Примитивный
The early **crude** instrument of our ancestors ...

Примыкать к
The antenna site **is adjacent to** the main plant.

Примыкающий [*см. тж.* **Ближайший к, Прилегающий к**]
Transferring heat from the flame to the **adjacent** layers of unburned mixture ...
The region **adjacent to** a constant state ...

Принадлежать [*см. тж.* **Большая заслуга принадлежит**]
This statement **is due to** Lord Kelvin.

Принадлежать двум или более
These electrons **are shared by two or more** atoms.

Принадлежать к [*см. тж.* **Не входить в**]
Amphibians **are among** the so-called cold-blooded animals.

Принадлежать к категории [*см. тж.* **Относиться к**]
Telegraph and data messages **are** commonly **in this category.**
These substances **were found to belong in the** carbohydrate **class.**
Any analogue computer employing ... **falls in(to)** (*or* **belongs to**) **the category of ...**

Принадлежать к типу
In the first **type are** branched-chain acids which ...

Принадлежать к числу
Acids and bases **are among** the most important chemicals of commerce.
Clostridium kluyverii **belongs among** the anaerobic organisms.
These microscopic organisms **rank among** the most fruitful of the domesticated plants.

Принадлежать по праву [*см.* **Завоёвывать принадлежащее ему по праву место**].

Принадлежащий
The lone pair of electrons **possessed by** the oxygen atom ...

Принадлежит заслуга
He **deserves the credit for** the design of ...

Принадлежит значительная часть работ по
This author **is responsible for much of the work on** dispersion.

Принадлежность [*см.* **Обязательная принадлежность**].

Принесённый ветром
These basins receive **wind-blown** dust.

Принести мало успеха
Subsequent attempts to solve this problem **met with little success.**

Принимается за
The mass of the unknown **is taken as** (*or* **is assumed to be**) M_1M_2.
The size of the indentation **is taken as** a measure of the material's hardness.

Принимается равным
Standard pressure **is taken** (*or* **assumed**) **to be** 760 mm.
The factor k **is** generally **taken to be equal to** unity.

Принимается, что
This field **is assumed (to be)** fixed in space.
"l" **is taken as** 10 cm.
Potential energy **is taken as** zero.
J **is taken to be** negative.
It **is assumed that** Eqs. (1) and (2) **are** single valued.

Принимать I [*см. тж.* **За ... принимается**]
We **set** (*or* **put**) $dv = z_{x,j}dx_j$.
We **adopted** this **as** a standard procedure.

Принимать II [*см.* **Если принять, Считать**].

Принимать III
This smooth and adherent oxide directly **accepts** a one-coat porcelain enamel.
It is essential that aluminium surfaces be cleaned and **made receptive to** the enamel.

Принимать в расчёт [*см.* **Принимать во внимание**].

Принимать вид
The embryonic cells **take on the appearance of** the normal fibroblast cells.
With these substitutions Eq. (5) **becomes** [*or* **takes** (*or* **assumes**) **the form**]: ...

Принимать во внимание [*см. тж.* **Если принять во внимание, что; Если учесть, что; Не принимать во внимание, Не учитывать, Учитывать**]
These factors **should be taken into account** (*or* **consideration**).

Принимать все возможные меры к тому, чтобы
Take as great care as possible to avoid ...
Extensive care must be taken to reduce radiofrequency interference.
Every effort should be taken (*or* **made**) **to** minimize side-effects.

Принимать за I [*см. тж.* **Считать**]
The difference between the compass reading and the magnetic direction **is taken as** the deviation for each heading.

Принимать за II
These organisms **can be (mis)taken for** (*or* **confused with**) pathogenic bacteria.

Принимать за III [*см. тж.* **Если принять за**]
The potential energy **is taken as** zero.

Принимать за единицу
$\partial \ln a_A / \partial \ln X_A$ **can be taken to be unity.**

Принимать за стандартное состояние
Taking pure water **as the standard state, ...**

Принимать значение
This function **takes the value** *0* at all points on ...
The parameters a, b, and c are adjustable,

taking on (*or* assuming) different **values** for each depth.

Принимать как должное
The inhabitants are used to the tides and **take them for granted.**

Принимать меры
Provision has been made for supplying more highly developed systems.
Care was taken to maintain a low concentration of ...
Make sure (*or* **See to it that**) all screws **are** tightened up.
Precautions have been taken to reduce effects of vibrations in the analyzer.
Steps should be taken to ensure proper filtration.
The airship net which is held down by sand bags is permitted to rise slowly, **care being taken that** the envelope **does not** slip out from under the net.

Принимать меры к тому, чтобы [*см. тж.* **Следить за тем, чтобы**]
Precautions must be taken to insure that stimulated emission **does not** dominate the decay.
Efforts are being made (*or* **taken**) **to** modify the manufacturing process.

Принимать меры предосторожности
(Some) precautions against the explosion hazard **must be taken.**
Caution should be exercised in handling carbon monoxide.

Принимать на веру
Unless one can confidently diagnose a neurological abnormality, any patient **should be given the benefit of the doubt.**
Since the numbers are so strange there is no reason **to take for granted** the theory that predicts them.

Принимать (на вооружение) (*разг.*)
This method **was adopted** after the discovery of ...

Принимать на себя
When a teloblast dies, its developmental role **is taken over by** another cell (*biol.*).

Принимать направление
The axis of rotation **may assume** any **direction** in space.

Принимать окончательную форму
After the clouds **take shape ...**

Принимать положение
The cooling system must be capable of operation in **any position** an aircraft **may assume** (*or* **take**).

Принимать равным [*см.* **Приравнивать к**].

Принимать сигнал
These devices **accept** (*or* **receive,** *or* **pick up**) **a** low-energy **signal** and modify it.

Принимать тщательные меры к тому, чтобы
Much care has been taken to avoid contamination of the liquid sample with suspended solid impurities.

Принимать участие в [*см.. тж.* **Участвовать в**]
GTP **has** not **been** directly **implicated in** chain termination (*biol.*).
When gases **take part** (*or* **participate,** *or* **are involved in**) chemical reactions ...
This procedure **involves** (*в этой процедуре принимает участие*) an olefin as the starting agent.

Принимать форму
Such glaciers **are shaped into** long, narrow ice streams.
The image **can take** several **forms.**
In a certain range of Reynolds numbers, the wake **arranges itself into** a double row of vortices.
The trajectory **will assume the form of ...**
The variation may take **the form** (*or* **shape**) **of** amplitude modulation.
The airship tail surfaces **have taken on** three typical **configurations** (*or* **forms**).

Принимать через рот
Mercury bichloride may result in death from kidney failure when it **is taken by mouth** (*or* **per os** — *Lat.*) in a substantial dose.

Принимать чрезвычайные меры
We shall have **to institute emergency measures.**

Приниматься [*см.* **Считаться**].

Приниматься за
The corresponding load **is taken as** a minimum value of the collapse load.

Принимающий
All patients **on** vitamin *D* should have their calcium levels monitored regularly.

Принимая во внимание, что
Considering (*or* **In view of the fact**) [*or* **Taking into account** (*or* **consideration**)] **that** d = ..., expression (2) may be written in the form ...

Принимая, что [*см. тж.* **Исходя из предположения, что**]
Taking z_0 **to be** the position where ..., we will show that ...

Приносить больше вреда, чем пользы
Topical antibiotics **may do more harm than good.**

Приносить неоценимую пользу
This theory **was of immeasurable service** in the earlier days of ...

Приносить пользу
These water resources **are of (great) benefit to** man.

Принудительная смазка [*см.* **С принудительной смазкой**].

Принцип [*см. тж.* **В принципе, Использовать принцип, По принципу, По своему характеру**]
The theoretical **concepts** embodied in Burdin's approach to turbine design ...
Another engineer applied these **precepts** to the vertical water wheel.
The general **principle** (**of operation**) **of** pumps is . ..
Computers based on this **concept** (*or* **principle**) are called data-driven processors.

Принцип работы прибора [*см.* **Работа прибора**].

Принципиальная конструкция
Various modifications of **the basic design of** a burette have been introduced.

Принципиальная разница между
The fundamental difference between absorption **and** emission processes ...

Принципиальная схема
Figure 1 is **a basic** (*or* **key,** *or* **theoretical,** *or* **schematic**, *or* **skeleton,** *or* **circuit**) **diagram** showing the principle of ...
A conceptual sketch of an optical processor ...

Принципиально [*см. тж.* **В принципе**]
The photons described by these fields differ **in a crucial respect** (*or* **radically,** *or* **fundamentally**) from the known properties of the photon.

Принципиально важный [*см.* **Иметь принципиально важное значение**].

Принципиально новый
A **crucially** (*or* **radically,** *or* **fundamentally**) **new** physical situation then arose in the deep interior of the primordial Sun.
We must create **radically** (*or* **fundamentally**) **new** technology.

Принципиально новый метод
This system is **a radical departure from conventional practice.**

Принципиально отличаться от
This spectrometer is **of a radically** (*or* **fundamentally**) **different kind from** those prism instruments which are used for ...
Optical computing systems **differ fundamentally from** electronic systems.

Принципиально разные
There are two **fundamentally** (*or* **radically**) **different** kinds of acarines.
It is impossible to have more **essentially different** game-situations than there are orders-of-cards.

Принципиальное значение [*см.* **Иметь принципиальное значение**].

Принципиальное различие между
It soon became apparent there were **fundamental differences between** the two areas.

Принципиального характера
One modification **of a fundamental nature** was needed.

Принципиальный [*см. тж.* **С принципиальной точки зрения**]
The difference **is crucial**: molecular clouds are typically much colder and denser than atomic clouds.

Принято [*см тж.* **В основном принято использовать, В современном языке принято называть ископаемым**]
The trend in the masonry block industry **is to** use high-pressure steam autoclaves.

It is common practice to clamp the box standard to the worktable of the measuring machine.
It is conventional to display this information in the form of plots of the source-to-drain current.

Принято выражать ... в
It is the practice to express sound intensity **in** decibels.

Принято пользоваться
A convention uses the unit torr **as** the equivalent of 1 mm of mercury.

Принято считать, что [*см. тж.* **Обычно считают, что; Считается, что**]
It is (generally) agreed (*or* **taken**) that the relativistic particles are ejected from ...
It is customary to assume that the energies are isotropic.
It is commonly supposed that Euclid wrote only one book.

Принять за [*см.* **Ошибочно принимать за**].

Принять (на вооружение) (*разг.*)
The technology of the system **has been adopted by** many manufacturers.

Принят(ый) в качестве
Agreement should be obtained with the method **accepted as** standard for the particular substance.
This standard **has been adopted as** a commercial standard.
The ampere **is (now) taken as** the fundamental unit.

Принятый в настоящее время
This **is the presently accepted** value.
Pressure sore **is the current name** for bed sores (*med.*).

Принятый во внимаине
The volume of the preheat zone **was** not **considered** [*or* **taken into account** (*or* **consideration**), *or* **taken account of**] **in** the computation of reaction time.

Приобретается с опытом
The knack of reading maximum and minimum indications of the oscillating pendulum **comes with practice.**

Приобретать [*см. тж.* **Присоединять**]
Atmospheric gases **have assumed** (*or* **acquired**) their present concentration as a result of ...
One electron volt is the energy that a particle carrying the charge of one electron **receives** (*or* **gains**) when ...
Molecules **can gain** excess energy ...
Positive particles **gain** electrons.

Приобретать большое значение
When the company's daily production of 200,000 units is considered, this die performance **takes on great significance.**
Carbon monoxide **has assumed great importance in the field of ...**
The binary system **has come into** (*or* **has acquired**) **importance** because of its value in computer applications.
The new method **is gaining in importance.**

Приобретать вид
Then the interface **develops a** comblike **appearance.**
This relationship **takes** (*or* **acquires,** *or* **assumes**) **the form** shown in Fig. 2.

Приобретать вновь [*см. тж.* **Вновь приобретать**]
The crystal **regains** (*or* **resumes**) its original dimensions.

Приобретать жёсткость
Members are designed on the principle of a bridge truss **to gain stiffness.**

Приобретать заряд
The fragment thus **acquires a** positive **charge.**

Приобретать знания
To gain such **knowledge, ...**

Приобретать значение
This **has assumed a (new) significance** (*or* **importance**).
Automation began **to take on** (*or* **acquire**) **a new meaning** with publication of ...

Приобретать конфигурацию
Each hydrogen atom **attains the** stable helium **configuration.**

Приобретать красный цвет
The solution **turns red.**

Приобретать новые черты
Abrasive cleaning **is taking (some) new twists** (*or* **features**).

Приобретать опыт [*см.* **Накапливать опыт**].

Приобретать права гражданства (*разг.*)
Polymer chemistry did not **come into its own** until World War II.

Приобретать свойство
A moving magnetic monopole **would begin to take on the properties of** an electric charge at a speed approaching the speed of light.

Приобретать способность
The neurons then **gain the capacity to** synthesize acetylcholine.

Приобретать у
Strong organic acids **are** not **available from** commercial suppliers.

Приобретать цвет
Although large-gap semiconductors are colourless when they are pure, they **can take on colour** when they are "doped" with traces of an impurity.

Приобретать энергию
A magnetic monopole **would acquire** more **energy** than ...

Приобретение
The gain of energy ...

Приостанавливать [*см. тж.* **Останавливать**]
Drilling **was discontinued** (*or* **suspended**) **for** three months.

Приостановить развитие (болезни)
Treatment with beta-blockers can be discontinued when the thyrotoxicosis **has been brought under control.**

Приписываемый
If the bosons have the properties **ascribed** (*or* **attributed**) **to** them, ...

Приписывать [*см. тж.* **Объяснять, Относить за счёт**]
Historians **trace** both ideas **to** ancient Greeks.
Perhaps the ancients knew more about astronomy than we **give them credit for.**
He was the first to study the gas systematically and so he **gets credit for** its discovery.
We **ascribe to** $r(\beta)$ **and** $s(\alpha)$ the values determined at points A and B, respectively.
The boundary values **are assigned to** the term uv.
The amber **was assigned** a negative charge.
Not long ago these diseases **were accredited to** our dizzy pace of living.
Anderson **ascribes** this disagreement **to** the oversimplified model.
The increased boron content **may be attributed** (*or* **ascribed**) **to** the dissolution of the samples.
A large number of early investigators **are credited with** the invention of the mercury thermometer.
If we **put it down to** chance (*случайности*), ...
The same type of structure **can be assigned to** many other molecules with unsaturated six-member rings.
The elementary particles can be classified **by assigning** quantum numbers **to** each of them.

Приповерхностный
With time, the **near-surface** rocks are eroded.

Припуск на
Enamel thickness **must be allowed for** in the design of a product.
Corrosion **allowance.**

Приравнивание
100% modulation can be obtained **by making** the modulation voltage **equal to** the plate supply voltage.

Приравнивать друг к другу
We **equate** the two expressions.

Приравнивать к
We **set** the coefficient **equal to** B_V.
The time derivative **is set** (*or* **taken**) **equal to** zero.
We **equate** the solid input **and** output for the element.
The process permits **equating** their ratio **to** (*or* **with**) that of their values at column outlet pressure.

Природа [*см. тж.* **Встречаться в природе, Встречающийся в природе, По своей природе**]
Most of the organic substances within plant and animal tissues **are of a** colloidal **character** (*or* **nature**).

Природный [*см. тж.* **Встречающийся в природе**]
Native gold occurs as nuggets or as grains in alluvial sand.
Some **naturally occurring** clays will absorb ions from aqueous solutions.

Присваивать
We **assign to** (*or* **give**) each tooth one and only one number.

Присваивать буквенное обозначение
It is possible **to assign** the coefficients **letter names** with unspecified values.

Присваивать значение
The factor k **is assigned a value of** 10^{-7} weber/amp.m.
An arbitrary **value is assigned to** m.

Присваивать название
The scientists **have given** the cycle **the name** galactic fountain.
Communities **are** usually **named after** two or three predominant species or the type of vegetation or habitat.
A permanent **name is assigned** (*or* **supplied**) after the comet has passed perihelium.
These compounds **take** (*этим соединениям присваивают*) special **names.**

Присваивать номер
The two sites for each pair of nucleosides **are assigned** (*or* **allocated**) **the** same **number** (*biol.*).

Присваивать общее название [*см.* **Идти под общим названием**].

Присоединением
This sol can be coacervated **by the addition of** alcohol.
The different atoms tend to react with each other **by gaining** (*or* **adding**) or losing electrons or sharing pairs of electrons.

Присоединён к
When a benzene ring **is attached to** some other structure, ...

Присоединять [*см. тж.* **Включать**]
When ferrous iron **takes on** oxygen, it turns a ferric red.
Ammonium chloride **can add (on)** 3 to 6 molecules of ammonia to form complex salts.
These materials have no tendency **to gain** protons.
Thin conductors **can be joined to** members of similar thickness ...
The isoalloxazine ring of *FAD* **picks up** a hydrogen ion from the solvent.
An impurity atom which **can accept** (*or* **take up**) one or more electrons ...
The sulphur hexafluoride molecule readily **acquires** (*or* **adds on**) free electrons, forming a heavy negative ion.

Присоединять и отдавать [*см.* **Отдавать и присоединять**].

Присоединять к
We **connect** each of the two parts of the system **to** separate heat reservoirs.

Присоединяться
Hydrogen iodide always **adds** in the normal manner.
Acetylene **adds to** alcohols to give vinyl ethers.
Acids **add themselves to** anions **and to** free electrons.
One of the water molecules is broken off and **adheres to** the other water molecule.

Присоединяться к мнению
Giordano Bruno **espoused the** Copernican **view that** Earth revolved around the Sun.

Приспосабливать [*см. тж.* **Может быть приспособлен к**]
The characteristics of lasers **can be matched with** the needs of atomic fluorescence spectrometry.
Our ovens **may be arranged for** electric or gas heating.
The machine **can be adapted for use as** a spot welder.
The machine **can be** easily **converted for** spot welding.
This coupling **can be fitted to** any make of tractor.
Equipment **must be tailored to** a specified problem.
Magnetic materials **are tailored to meet** special requirements.
The proper distribution of the suction allows a designer **to tailor** the development of the boundary layer **to** his particular demands.

Приспосабливать к требованиям заказчика
You **can customize** your system with these standard units.

Приспосабливаться к
Animals **adapt to** new environments.
How does the body **accommodate** (*or* **adapt**) **itself to** prolonged starvation?

Приспособлен(ный) для
The process **is** particularly **adapted to** welding heavy work.
The unit **is equipped for** push-button or manual starting.
These dosimeters **are (well) suited to** (*or* **for**) such measurements.
MF broadcasting requires arrays **tailored for** special local conditions.
Our instruments **can be customized for** your exact needs.
This formulation **is** most **suitable for** numerical simulation.
The photomultiplier tube **can be conditioned to** operate at higher voltages.
Indirect dryers **are** especially **suited to** drying under reduced pressure.
Persian clover **is** particularly **adapted to** wet, heavy soils.
The metric system **is geared to** human needs.

Приспособление [*см.* **Зажимное приспособление, Устройство**].

Приспособление для
The microscope has **a provision for** still photography.

Приспособленный специально для
In a system of scanning **adapted to** count random size particles ...
The proportion of equipment **tailored to suit** (*or* **adapted specially for**) each installation is comparatively small.

Приступать к [*см. тж.* **Обращаться к, Прежде чем приступить к рассмотрению**]
We now **turn to** a close examination of ...
The thermodynamic treatments that we now **take up** are concerned with ...
In many cases treatment of this disease **can be instituted** without further investigation.
Eventually, astronomers **got around to** making such maps.
We now **proceed to** a study of hyperbolic systems.
We **have embarked on** an extensive research project.
Trial under anticipated operating conditions is advisable before **embarking upon** extensive use.
After cleaning it is necessary to remove loose paint before **proceeding to** the next operation.
The approval of the Inspector must be secured before **proceeding with** drilling and repairs.
In **initiating** infrared observations one of our earliest hopes was to discover ...
The company **entered the field of** die casting in 1982.
Chemists **set out to** prepare new aromatic systems other than ...
Before **going into** a detailed description of the system ...

Приступать к выполнению (*или* **проведению**)
To initiate (*or* **launch,** *or* **embark on**) **a program for ...**

Приступать к измерению
We next **undertook to measure** both components in a variety of samples.

Приступать к изучению
We **embarked on a study of ...**

Приступать к обсуждению
Before **entering into a discussion** of irradiation effects in metals...
Before **proceeding to** the next subject let us determine ...

Приступать к производству или продаже
Long before the company **went into** computers ...

Присутствие [*см.* **В присутствии**].

Присутствовать в большом количестве в
Glucose **is abundant in** liver and muscle tissue.

Присутствовать в виде
In aqueous solution the Ti^{3+} ion **is present as** the octahedral $Ti(H_2O)_6{}^{3+}$ ion.

Присутствовать в изобилии
Organic molecules **exist copiously in** the interstellar clouds.

Присутствовать везде
Air and water **are omnipresent.**

Присущий [*см. тж.* **Свойственный, Характерный для**]
The **inherent** rigidity of nonfluid colloids is the principal factor determining their stability.
The capacitor **features** extraordinary stability.
Such restrictions **are inherent in** [*or* **typical** (*or* **characteristic**) **of**] earlier machine-tools.
The delay **inherent in** the production of a single side band ...
The second kind of asymmetry **is intrinsic in** the design of the system.
This valve eliminates the constant leakage **peculiar to** all steam steering engines.

Присущий ему одному
The rate of decay is **an inherent characteristic of each unique** isotope.

Присущий только
Several features **unique to** LEI deserve further comment.

Притупление
Patients with Cushing's syndrome suffer **a** considerable **dulling of** the senses.

Притягивать
The Sun **pulls on** (*or* **attracts**) the Earth.

Притягиваться
The charged particles of the smoke **are drawn** (*or* **attracted,** *or* **pulled**) **to** the plate of opposite charge.

Притягиваться друг к другу
The ends assume opposite polarities so that they **are attracted together** (*or* **to one another**).

Притяжение [*см.* **Поле притяжения Земли**].

Притяжение Земли Солнцем
The Sun's (gravitational) pull on the Earth ...

Притяжение к магниту
The attraction of liquid oxygen **for a magnet ...**

Приходится
We are thus **led to** modify the picture that emerged from lower-energy experiments.

Приходится лишь сожалеть, что
It is a cause for regret that Ptolemy gives only brief extracts from ...

Приходится признать, что
One is forced to accept the fact that little is presently understood about ...

Приходится считаться с
When the internal-combustion turbine becomes a force **to be reckoned with** in the marine-engineering world, ...

Приходить в голову
This is the first possibility that **comes to mind.**
It was then that they **conceived the idea of** forming ...
This idea occurred to several investigators.

Приходить в действие
It is during this portion of the cycle that the spring washers **come into operation.**
In this case a slipping device **comes into action.**
The intermolecular forces which **come into play** in crystals of ...

Приходить в нерабочее состояние
Under such temperature conditions electronics and other equipment **would become inoperative.**

Приходить в равновесие
Phases in contact **tend to equilibrate** by mass transfer from one to the other.
It takes at least a minute for the chamber **to come to equilibrium.**
The plant communities that **come into equilibrium with** the high moisture conditions are very stable (*botan.*).

Приходить в соприкосновение с [*см. тж.* **Вступать в соприкосновение с**]
Clay is carried to the sea, where it **contacts** salt water.
If a particle **comes in contact with** a solid surface, ...
The condensate seal prevents steam from **coming in(to)** direct **contact with** the Bourdon tube.
It normally does not **make contact with ...**

Приходить в состояние покоя
At this time the system **comes to rest.**

Приходить во взвешенное состояние
Particles of a given size **are lifted into suspension.**

Приходить к
A new discovery **is** often **arrived at** simultaneously **by** two or more workers.
Thus we finally **arrive at** the result $F \equiv 0$, which was to be shown.
Thus we **are led to** the following definition.

Приходить к выводу [*см. тж.* **Выводить заключение, Делать вывод**]
We **have drawn** (*or* **reached,** *or* **arrived at,** *or* **come to) the** same **conclusion.**
One can **come to recognize that** these quantities do play an important role in ...

Приходить к выводу о том
Ultimately, the geologists **will infer** why, how, and when certain strata were folded.
We **deduce from** Eq. (2.52) **that** there are no paths in the cladding if ...
As the reaction was sensitive to RNase, **it was deduced to be** dependent on tRNA.
Thus, we **get the conclusion that** most of these materials ...
He **was led to conclude that** for a given geologic period ...
It was concluded that ...
He **arrived at the conclusion that ...**
They **concluded that ...**

Приходить к противоположному выводу
The Canadian scientist **reached the opposite conclusion.**

Приходить к согласию относительно
The two observers **agree as to** when the event took place.
The chemists and engineers **cannot agree** completely **on** the types and causes of ... problems.

Приходить на помощь
As starvation continues, a number of general factors **come to the aid of** the organism.
The company **has come to the rescue of** photographers with a new strobe flash unit.

Приходиться на I [*см. тж.* **На каждый ... приходится, На который приходится** (*или* **падает), На ... приходится, Падать на**]
Engine and machine parts **accounted for** 11.3% of the deliveries.
A large fraction of the mass of the asteroidal belt **is accounted for by** the few large asteroids.
Ninety percent of the storage cost **is due to** tanks.

Приходиться на II
About 30% of the 3000 nuclear tracks measured **fell within** the cone of tritons.
The 120 mark in the straightedge **falls on** the central parallel.

Приходящий и уходящий
The **ingoing** (*or* **incoming**) **and outgoing** waves are defined in terms of ...

Причём [*см. тж.* **При этом**]
Biotite is readily transformed to chlorite, **during which** change by-product magnetite and sphene may also be produced.
Slip the instrument into the cylinder, **with** the dial at right angles to the cylinder wall.
Frog skin exhibits a potential difference of 20–90 mV **with** the inside positive.
Each detector cell is made in two sections which are bolted together **with** a gasket (placed) between them.
The tubing is laid in slots on the moving table **with** the sheet held in position by clamps.
The pipeline runs from North to South, two side lines branch**ing** off at right angles to it.

Причина [*см. тж.* **Быть причиной, Вызывать, Есть основания полагать, что; По причине, По той или иной причине, По той причине, что; Являться причиной**]
There are no pathological **reasons for** the lower level of albumin.
Carbon dioxide **is the** chief **cause of** (*or* **for**) corrosion in ...
Microcrack formation **may be responsible for** the lower density of cold-worked metals.

Причина и следствие
Cause and effect.

Причина состоит в [*см.* **Объясняться**].

Причина состоит в том, что
This is because (*or* **The reason is that**)

the two compounds have the same crystal structure.

Причина того, что
This structure **is the reason why** cyclohexane has no strain energy.

Причиной оказался
The blackout **was traced to** the tripping of a circuit breaker.

Причиной этого является [*см.* **Вызван**].

Причиной является
The reason has to do with (*or* **is**) the agility of the metallic electron.

Пришла пора
After seven years **it is timely to** examine the mining activities of the corporation.

Приятно отметить, что
It is encouraging (*or* **pleasant**) **to note that** another means for ... is now emerging.

Проба [*см.* **Брать образцы**].

Пробегать
The electron beam **sweeps from** the top of the picture tube **to** the bottom twice in a thirtieth of a second.

Пробел
Bodé pointed out the presence of **a gap in** the law ...

Пробивать [*см.* **Перфорировать**].

Пробивать себе путь в
The induction coil **was finding its way into** engineering.

Пробиваться через
A core of mobile rock **has broken through** the overlying strata.
Oil under pressure **may force its way through** faults in weak rock.
If a pulse of high positive voltage is applied to the gate, electrons **tunnel through** the oxide layer.

Пробит молнией
The insulating jacket **was punctured by lightning.**

Пробка [*см.* **Закрывать пробкой, Затыкать пробкой**].

Проблема [*см. тж.* **Вопрос, Задача**]
The issue (*or* **The problem**) **is** unresolved.
For an investigator of meteorites **the** basic **challenge is** deducing the history of the meteorites from ...

Проблема заключается только в
The problem is only one of data acquisition.

Проблема, связанная с заражением окружающей среды
In recent years, much attention has been devoted to **environmental problems** resulting from gasoline additives.

Проблематичный
The origin of continental crust **is** highly **conjectural.**

Пробуждать интерес к [*см. тж.* **Вновь пробуждать интерес к**]
This **awakened** (*or* **aroused**) **interest in** celestial mechanics.

Пробурить скважину
Over the last 30 years, drillers **have put down** 40 **holes into ...**

Проваливаться I [*см.* **Не увенчаться успехом**].

Проваливаться II
The roof **gave away** (*or* **collapsed**).

Провар
Thus, uniform **melt-through** (*or* **penetration**) **is** obtained.

Проведение исследований
Pursuance of research.

Проведение программы [*см.* **В порядке проведения программы**].

Проведение реакции между
The manufacture of this plastic consists essentially of **reacting** phosgene **with** diethylene glycol.

Проведение эксперимента [*см. тж.* **Методика эксперимента**]
A more precise confirmation would require **the performance of the experimen**t with man-made mesons.

Проверить факт присутствия
We must use other methods **to verify the presence of** a carbonium ion in these processes.

Проверка [*см. тж.* **Для проверки, Можно доказать непосредственной провер–кой, что; Повседневный контроль, Подвергать проверке, Производить проверку на**]
The engineers have completed **a check of** all patches on the tank.
A routine **check on** air contamination **was** carried out.
These tests were instituted as **a check upon** the accuracy of ...
Checking for contamination yielded no results.
Checking of transistors **for** instability is mandatory.
Weekly **check-ups ...**
To test this hypothesis, field observations were made.

Проверка на месте
On-the-spot (*or* **On-site**) **inspection.**

Проверка по контрольному образцу
Checking against a master standard.

Проверка установки на нуль
To check for zero setting, place ...

Проверять [*см. тж.* **Испытывать, Пере–проверять**]
It can be easily **verified that** Eq. (15-29) reduces to Eq. (15-28) when ...
The level of radioactivity **is** carefully **monitored.**
Check the micrometer **for** zero setting.
In this way, **a check on** the accuracy of the gauge-glass reading **is made.**
The magnetic field **was checked against** that of a permanent magnet.
The pressure recorded **was checked** periodically **against** a water manometer.
All bearings **should be checked for** wear.
Examine the edges of the measuring faces **for** burrs.
To keep check on the angle of bend, ...
The interior of the boiler **should be examined for** tools that might have been left inside.
Steam lines **should be examined** frequently **for** corrosion.
The crankcase **should be inspected for** excessive gases.
To test these conclusions, we carried out several experiments.
The above theory **was tested by** results of three experiments.
This formula permits **verification of** the value of *K*.

Проверять на
The experimental data **can be tested for** conformity to ...

Проверять на заражение
The entire area around the chamber **is monitored** continuously **for** alpha particle **contamination.**

Проверять на лакмус
Use the test by blue **litmus paper.**

Проверять на трещиноватость
Rotors **are** then **inspected for cracks.**

Проверять по
Check the calibration **against** a standard potentiometer.
The indicators **should be checked against** actual chemical analysis.

Проверять правильность теории
To test the validity of the theory, ...

Проверять путём
That the function satisfies the Schrödinger equation **can be tested by** substitution in Eq. (5).

Провероять точность расчётов
Check the calculations for accuracy.

Провисание [*см.* **Забирать слабину**].

Проводимый
The studies **done** at our Laboratory ...
It is expected that in the near future developments now **under way** will yield better techniques.

Проводится работа по
Work is underway to determine ...

Проводить I [*см. тж.* **Выполнять, Осу–ществлять**]
The absorption of HCl **is** often **conducted** (*or* **carried out**) without cooling.
Much research work **has been accomplished.**

Проводить II
A piece of iron or steel can be magnetized by **stroking it** in one direction **with** a magnet.

Проводить абсорбцию

It might be preferable **to run** (*or* **conduct,** *or* **carry out**) **the absorption** at a higher temperature.

Проводить анализ
Satisfactory **analysis can be performed** (*or* **carried out,** *or* **made**) on samples having ...

Проводить аналогию с
He **drew the analogy to** convention in the atmosphere.

Проводить в жизнь
The new plan **was implemented** [*or* **put into effect** (*or* **operation**)].
If such developments **can be brought to fruition,** there should be great potentialities for ...

Проводить вычисление [*см.* **Выполнять вычисления**].

Проводить дифференцирование по
The differentiation is performed with respect to this variable.

Проводить дорожные испытания [*см.* **Испытывать на дорогах**].

Проводить измерение
We used laser-excited fluorescence **to perform the measurement.**
Always stop the work before **taking a measurement.**
Measurements were taken (*or* **made,** *or* **conducted,** *or* **carried out**).

Проводить изучение
The studies were conducted (*or* **done,** *or* **carried out**) by means of ...
We **have made studies into ...**

Проводить интегрирование
Now **perform the integration** with $n = 1, 2, 3, ...$
Integrate over the volume of ...
In the latter case **integration is to be taken** (*or* **carried out,** *or* **performed**) **along** an arbitrary curve in the z plane.

Проводить испытание [*см. тж.* **Испытывать**]
Thousands of fatigue **tests were conducted** (*or* **carried out,** *or* **performed,** *or* **run**).

Проводить исследования [*см. тж.* **Вести исследования, Исследовать**]
As actual **investigations are pursued, ...**
The studies were conducted with the actual support structure.
We **are engaged in research on** (*or* **into**) ...
The laboratory **instituted a** thorough **investigation** to find out ...
One can use computers for **making** such **investigations.**
We **have made studies into** computer uses for oil.
The Institute is equipped **to perform** (*or* **to do**) **research on** foamed plastics.

Проводить кабель
The cables for each circuit **are led** (*or* **layed,** *or* **run**) by independent routes.

Проводить линию
Draw (*or* **Pass**) **a line** connecting the two pairs of points.

Проводить операцию
These **operations were** often **conducted** (*or* **performed,** *or* **carried out**) simultaneously.

Проводить опыт
It is necessary **to conduct** (*or* **do,** *or* **carry out,** *or* **make**) **the experiment** under conditions such that ...

Проводить преобразование
The same **transformation is applied to** the same hadron.

Проводить различие между [*см. тж.* **Следует проводить различие между**]
One **must discriminate between** these **and** other theories.
Distinction is drawn between the permeability **and** the mean coefficient of diffusion in the polymer matrix.
A distinction is made between a "Fourier Describing Function" **and** a "Hamilton Describing Function".
It is necessary **to distinguish between** electronic **and** atomic polarizabilities.

Проводить реакцию
We prefer **to conduct** (*or* **carry out,** *or* **run,** *or* **perform**) this **reaction** at 150°F.

Проводить резкое различие между
The dividing line between what is called emerald **and** green beryl **is sharp.**

Проводить рукой вдоль
Draw your **hand along** the tube as it revolves.

Проводить черту между
In order **to draw a line between** marketed grades of copper **and** copper alloys, the ASTM has adopted specifications in which ...

Проводить эксперимент
Experiments have been pursued (*or* **performed,** *or* **conducted,** *or* **carried out**) to determine ...

Проводиться
The measurements **are in progress** [*or* **are being conducted** (*or* **carried out**)].
Work **is proceeding on** the development of a new system.
A series of experiments **has been under way** (*or* **run,** *or* **conducted,** *or* **performed,** *or* **carried out**) for some years.

Проводиться в обычном порядке
A conventional procedure is followed for planning ...

Проводиться весьма интенсивно
The study of such forces **is currently an active area of** investigation.

Проводиться по методу
The calculation **follows the method** given by ...

Проводка к двигателю
If the direction of rotation is incorrect, **the wiring to the motor** must be altered.

Прогибать заготовку
A tool that is not sharp **may tend to pull the stock out of line** during machining.

Прогноз климата
Climatic prediction.

Прогонять I
After leaving the assembly line the complete chassis **are given a running-in trial.**

Прогонять II
Helium **is forced** (*or* **circulated**) **through** each coolant loop.

Прогрев
After switching on, allow five minutes for the instrument **to warm up.**
After **an** initial **warming-up period** the instrument shows no drift for six hours.

Продавать
Suppose a manufacturing concern wishes **to market** (*or* **sell**) bolt sets ...

Продавать в розницу (*антон.* **оптом**)
Hydrogen peroxide **is sold retail** (*anton.* **wholesale**) in‘20 volume’ and ‘10 volume’ solutions.

Продаваться [*см. тж.* **Иметься в продаже**]
This product **finds a market as** an oxidizing agent for ...
Bromine **is available in** 6.5-lb bottles.
Bacitracin **is** normally **marketed** (*or* **sold**) **as** a mixture of ...
This model **sells for** 89 cents each.

Продавливать через
The liquid **is forced through** a capillary tube.

Продажа [*см. тж.* **Иметься в продаже, Поступать в продажу, Торговля**]
Finished steel is steel that is ready for **marketing** (*or* **sale**) without further work or treatment.

Продвигаться
Construction at Fermilab **proceeded** faster than at CERN.
The cascade of secondary electrons grows exponentially as it **progresses along** the inside of the tube.
The art of manufacturing **has progressed** (*or* **advanced**) greatly within the last few years.
The flame front **travels** (*or* **propagates**) too slowly.

Продвигаться на
The rotary switch **advances** one contact for each impulse it receives.
The leavers permit the scrape wheel **to advance** one tooth.

Продвижение
The rate of **advance of** the drilling bit ...
The progress is of order of 1000 linear feet per week.

Продвижение по
The fast progress of a part **through** the factory ...

Продвинутая стадия [*см. тж.* **Находиться на продвинутой стадии разработки**]
A still grander device **is in an advanced stage of** development.

Продевать через
We **thread** one end of the wire **through** the tube.

Проделана большая исследовательская работа
A considerable volume of research has been carried out.

Проделанная работа
If *y* **is work done** (*or* **performed**) **by** a force ...

Проделанный в
Rollers become wedged between the sleeve and recessed pockets **machined in** the hub.

Проделать анализ
We **have done** (*or* **performed,** *or* **carried out**) **an analysis of ...**

Проделать вычисления
In applying this notion Kepler **went through** (*or* **carried out**) tedious **calculations.**

Проделывать работу
No **work of** expansion **is performed** (*or* **carried out,** *or* **done**).

Проделывать работу над
For a reversible expansion, **work** *w* **done** (*or* **performed,** *or* **carried out**) **on** the gas **is** ...
Work must be done on the molecular pair to drive them together.

Продемонстрировано [*см.* **Показано**].

Продет сквозь отверстия
Platinum wire electrodes **were laced through the holes** in the paper.

Продиктован
His analysis **was inspired by** experimental observations made by ...

Продифференцировав
(Up)on differentiating (*or* **differentiation**) we obtain ...

Продлевать
The space mission **was lengthened** (*or* **prolonged**) **for** another eight months.

Продлевать срок службы
The copper in the bond **adds** considerably **to** grinding wheel **life.**
The coating considerably **extends** (*or* **prolongs**) **the life of** these alloys.
The programme was designed **to improve** tool **life.**
The users **can** thus **stretch service life for** parts subjected to wear.

Продолжать I
We now **pursue** our discussion in more detail.

Продолжать II
We **extend** the line **by** the distance *fg*.
The straight line **must be produced into** the opposite quadrant.

Продолжать верить в то, что
They **persisted in the belief that ...**

Продолжать двигаться
Such particles **will continue in motion** (*or* **moving,** *or* **to move**).

Продолжать исследование
Let us **explore** this equation **further** so that we can apply it to ...

Продолжать обсуждение
In Chapter 12, we **shall have more to say** (*or* **shall continue discussion**) about hot spots on the continental lithosphere.

Продолжать свой путь
The stone **will** surmount the obstacle and **continue on its way.**
The neutrinos pass through the object and **continue on their way to** vast distances.

Продолжать существовать
This fish was especially well developed in the middle Mesosoic and **persists to the present.**
These terms **persist today.**

Продолжать увеличиваться
As the number of variables **increases further** (*or* **continues to increase**) ...

Продолжаться I [*см. тж.* **Длиться**].
The course **covers** three years.
The laboratory course **extends over** the first two years.
Each pulse **lasts for** 5×10^{-9} second.

Продолжаться II
These investigations **are being continued.**
Although this study **is (still) in progress,** the experimental results appear to be sufficiently significant to ...

After use, the gas flow **persists** long enough to allow ...
The volcanic activity here began in the Eocene and **(still) persists today.**
Production of sediment and sedimentary rock **has gone on throughout** the past years.

Продолжение
The upper curve **is an extension of** the lower curve to negative values of the abscissa.

Продолжительное время [*см. тж.* **В течение продолжительного времени** (*или* **периода**)]
Ageing **for a more or less extended time ...**
Prolonged intervals.

Продолжительное выдерживание
Long standing in an excess of alcohol converts the hemiacetal into a complete acetal.

Продолжительность
The duration of the laser pulse is determined by ...
The length of the induction period ...

Продолжительность жизни
Plants that first colonize bare ground will have short **life spans** (*or* **expectation of life,** *or* **life expectancy**) (*botan.*).

Продолжительность существования [*см. тж.* **Время жизни**]
Estimates of **the life (expectancy) of** these energy sources vary.

Продолжительный [*см. тж.* **Иметь продолжительный срок службы**]
The microscope makes possible **lengthy** (*or* **prolonged,** *or* **protracted**) investigations with small objects.
The unit will function **for extended** (*or* **prolonged**) periods.
Over the **extended** trial period the enlarger has exhibited ...
Long-term storage ...
Prolonged heating at such a temperature favours further grain growth.
Prolonged service testing has proved that ...
Long-term measurements ...
The Plummer-Vinson syndrome is usually found in women after **long-standing** iron deficiency.

Продолжительный период [*см. тж.* **В течение продолжительного времени**]
A circuit may have different characteristics after **an extended** (*or* **prolonged**) **period of** use.

Продолжить, включив
The current-voltage curve **can** now **be extended to include** this region.

Продолжить линию до
Extend (*or* **Produce**) **the line to** values $K < 1$.

Продольная и поперечная подача
The worktable is 42 × 10 in. with **a** 22-in. **longitudinal traverse and a** 10-in. **cross traverse.**

Продольное направление [*см.* **В продольном направлении**].

Продувание воздухом
After **being blown with air** the copper is subjected to poling.

Продувать
The pipes should be flushed out with water instead of **blown out with** steam.
The pipes **must be blown through** in order to clean out ...

Продувать воздухом
Air is blown through the molten metal.

Продукт соединения
These compounds **are addition products of** ammonia **and** the acid.

Продуктивен [*см. тж.* **Полезен**]
It was indicated that extensive investigations into ... **would be** highly **profitable.**

Продукты распада от испытания оружия
Radioactive substances introduced by man's activity include **fission products from weapons tests.**

Продумывать
One **must think out** each step of the method.

Проект
The study of several advanced reactor **concepts ...**

Проектирование с помощью ЭВМ
Computerized design.

Проектировать [*см. тж.* **Конструировать, При проектировании, Создавать**]

Such installations **are** invariably **engineered** (*or* **designed**) **to** specific requirements.

Проектировать на плоскость
To project an image of ... **onto the plane of ...**
Projected area is that area bounded by the outline of the blades **when projected into an** athwartship **plane.**

Проектировать с таким расчётом, чтобы
It was decided **to design** the column **to be packed with** 2-in. Raschig rings for ...

Проектный срок службы
The communication satellite has exceeded its **design life** and is still operating.

Проекция на
Projection of the model image **onto** the film ...
The projection of this distance **on** a plane normal to the stream direction ...

Прозрачность для
Because of its **transparency to** ultraviolet and infrared radiation phosphorescent fluoride has important applications in spectroscopy.

Прозрачный для [*см. тж.* **Непрозрачный для**]
No medium **is transparent to** the whole electromagnetic spectrum.
There is a time by which the plasma has expanded to a point when it becomes **transparent to** (*or* **for**) the incident laser light.

Произведение на
Work is **the product** of force **by** distance.
Momentum is defined as **the product of** the mass **into** the velocity.
This force is proportional to **the product of** the mass **times** the radius.
The **product** of the velocity **and (of)** cos β ...

Производимый в промышленных масштабах
The **commercially produced** metal reacts with many ...

Производительность в 12 раз выше
At this speed 12 workpieces could be machined using a coated insert, so for this application coated inserts **outproduced** uncoated inserts **12 to one.**

Производительность станка
The capacity of a machine-tool.
Machine-tool productivity.

Производить I [*см. тж.* **Выполнять, Делать, Осуществлять**]
These operations **were** often **carried on** (*or* **out**) simultaneously.
Drilling **is done** from barges.
The machine **performs** computations for navigation.
To perform division.

Производить II [*см. тж.* **Выпускать, Изготавливать**]
Each week the plant **turns** (*or* **puts**) **out** (*or* **produces**) thousands of such units.

Производить арифметическое действие
Even though ∞ is not a number, we **can put it through (certain) arithmetic operations** (*or* **paces**).
The computer **can perform** (*or* **carry out**) thousands or millions **of arithmetic operations** per second.

Производить в массовых количествах
Some die details **can be mass produced.**

Производить вычисления
Here we **shall** not **carry out** (*or* **perform,** *or* **make,** *or* **do**) any calculations.

Производить измерение
Always stop the work before **taking a measurement.**

Производить интегрирование
Now **perform the integrations** with $n = 1, 2, 3, ...$
Integrate over the volume of ...

Производить проверку на
Check for valve blow or any unusual noises.

Производить работу для
The work done in overcoming (*or* **to** overcome) the attraction ...

Производить работу по
The total **work done in** moving ...

Производить разложение
We **take the** Fourier **transform of ...**

Производиться
Loading and unloading **is performed by** one operator.

This type of chain **has been in production** for some time.
Delivery of the material from the mill **is by** rail.
Diamond drilling **is proceeding** with the object of ...
Calcium oxide **is made by** the thermal decomposition of ...
Calcium sulphide **is formed** industrially **by** the reduction of ...

Производиться в промышленных масштабах
The acid **is manufactured** (*or* **obtained,** *or* **produced**) commercially.
Such castings **are in commercial production.**
Sodium hydroxide **is made commercially by** the electrolysis of ...
Aldehyde **is produced** (*or* **prepared**) **industrially** at the rate of ... per year.

Производиться путём
Addition of two complex numbers **is effected by ...**

Производная по [*см. тж.* **Брать производную по**]
The current gain is the **derivative of** the total current **with respect to** the minority carrier current.

Производная по времени
Time derivative.

Производственная площадь
An enlargement of **floor area** (*or* **space**) was recommended.

Производственные возможности
The production potentialities of the plant are enormous.

Производство [*см. тж.* **Идти в производство, Идти на производство**]
Building (*or* **Construction,** *or* **Production**) **of** machinery ...
Derrochrome is used in **the making of** chrome steel.
The manufacture of many steels ...
The preparation of such metals as chromium, uranium, ...
BaO_2 is a starting material for **the preparation of** hydrogen peroxide.

Производство обгоняет потребление
Production is outrunning (*or* **outstripping**) **consumption.**

Производство ... связано с затруднениями
These steels **cause** many **problems during production.**

Производство электроэнергии
To sharply increase **the output of electric energy, ...**

Произвольно [*см. тж.* **Задан произвольно**]
The nonuniformity may be **arbitrarily** large.
When the isotopic-spin arrow is rotated **in an arbitrary way ...**

Произвольный
John Dalton's suggestion of assigning an **arbitrary** value of 1 for the lightest element, hydrogen ...

Проинтегрировав
(Up)on integrating we obtain ...

Проистекать из [*см. тж.* **Вытекать из**]
The error **results** (*or* **arises,** *or* **stems**) **from** neglecting ...

Проистекать из того, что
The interplanetary navigator's most difficult problems **derive** (*or* **stem,** *or* **arise,** *or* **result**) **from the fact that ...**

Происходивший ... лет назад [*см тж.* **Относящийся к**]
Sediment cores reveal older epochs of polarity reversals **dating back** tens of millions of **years.**

Происходит взрыв
If a spark has enough energy, **an explosion is set off** (*or* **occurs**).

Происходит образование
Meanwhile **the formation** of the embryonic gut **is under way** (*or* **is taking place**).

Происходить I [*см. тж.* **Наблюдаться**]
Anaplastic cells **are derived from** adult, differentiated cells.
This change **comes about by virtue of** the force acting on ...
Such explosions **come (about)** (*or* **occur**) each 100 years.

Происходить II [*см. тж.* **Иметь место, Наблюдаться**]
No major breakthrough **has come about** (*col.*).

Most of the world's volcanic activity **is found** near the boundaries of ...
We know from experience that this does not **happen.**
This process **has been going on for** 3 billion years.
The change from melt to crystalline rock **happens** (*or* **occurs**) rapidly.
Here, fluvial denudation **has been in progress for** long periods of time.
Expansion of the clay mass **results** when more water penetrates ...
The Mediterranean Sea **was the site of** extensive evaporite depositions (*В Средиземном море происходили* ...).
Processes of fluvial denudation **are at work** from the very beginning.
Such an event **will never come to pass.**
Two processes **operate** simultaneously.
Every living cell **is a seat of** numerous metabolic reactions.
Combustion **will occur** (*or* **proceed**) at any pressure if a suitable catalyst is added.
If a leak **occurs** urgent measures should be taken.
Under these conditions the transformation of heat energy into other forms of energy **takes place.**
The 1930s **saw** a marked spurt in the technological applications of catalysts.
The past 20 years **have witnessed** an amazing increase in the number of molecules detected.

Происходить в
The clavicle **is a** frequent **site of** fracture.
This **is the case in** the region marked as *A*.

Происходить в ограниченном масштабе
Although some differentiation **occurs** in eggs of ..., **it is of limited extent.**

Происходить в результате
Generally such failures **stem** (*or* **arise,** *or* **result**) **from** [*or* **are caused** (or **brought about**) **by,** *or* **are due to**] improper circuitry.

Происходить в следующем порядке
The chemical shift of ...**follows the order:** Cl > Br > I.

Происходить в течение короткого времени
The collision process **takes place in a short time interval.**

Происходить гораздо реже, чем
The disasters **are far outnumbered by** the nuisance effects.

Происходить за счёт
As starvation continues, a progressively greater proportion of the weight loss **is accounted for by** the consumption of body fat.

Происходить из [*см. тж.* **Образовываться из**]
The designation *F-centre* **comes** (*or* **derives,** *or* **is derived**) from the German word *Farbe.*
Coal **may originate from** isolated fragments of vegetation.

Происходить непрерывно
The basic turnover of proteins in the body **goes on at all times.**

Происходить одновременно
The two processes **go on** (*or* **proceed**) **concurrently** (*or* **simultaneously**).

Происходить одновременно с
Consumption of sea floor **keeps pace with** production of new sea floor.

Происходить от
The word *infinity* **comes** (*or* **derives**) **from** a Latin word meaning *"endless"*.

Происходить по причине
Failures in rubber seals **can be traced to** two main causes: ...

Происходить по типу
The known catabolic transformations of corticosterone **follow the pattern seen in** the catabolism of ...

Происходить с
Figure 4 shows what **happens to** the signal.

Происходящие время от времени
If it were not for the tides, and **an occasional** hurricane, ...

Происходящий
The geologic processes **at work** (*or* **operating**) today can be best understood by ...
This is not the only process **going on in** the collision.
Proton transfer should be analyzed in terms of the specific change **involved.**

We can observe vertical motion **happening** today.
The developments **(now) in progress** (*or* **under way,** *or* **taking place**) indicate that ...
This electrical activity is produced by the many electrified storms continuously **in progress** over the Earth.

Происходящий из
Well-known species include the domestic pigeon **descended from** the rock dove.

Происходящий под действием
Water is brought to high elevations on land by atmospheric processes **which are powered by** solar energy.

Происхождение [*см. тж.* **Быть обязанным своим происхождением, В месте происхождения, Вести своё происхождение от, Внеземного происхождения, Ледникового происхождения**]
The genesis (*or* **origin**) of some lunar craters may be clarified by radar images.

Происхождение жизни
They propose that the nucleic acids arose first before **life had its origins.**

Происхождение которых относится к
Among the cotylosaurs are found the most primitive known reptiles **which date from** the Late Carboniferous.

Происхождения
Ordinary coal is **of** organic **origin.**

Пройден I
The severest part of the railway grade **was negotiated** with ease.

Пройден II
Two repair shafts **were sunk.**

Пройденная траектория
The path traversed (*or* **covered**) **by** the particle ...

Пройденное расстояние
This can be determined by plotting **the distance travelled** (*or* **covered**) against time.

Пройдёт еще много времени прежде, чем
We **have a long way to go before** we reach our goal.

Пройдёт некоторое время прежде, чем
It will be some time [*or* **Some time will pass** (*or* **elapse**)] **before** direct investigations will be really feasible.

Пройдя часть пути
Part way down the cylinder, the piston stopped.

Пройти I [*см. тж.* **Время истекло, Проходить**]
Several hours **must elapse** (*or* **pass**) **before** the circuit is completed.

Пройти II
The British pneumatic control industry is less than 40 years old, and yet it **has gone through** a number of phases during its development.

Пройти незамеченным
Failure at two interfaces is obvious, but a single weakness **can pass undetected** (*or* **unnoticed**).

Пройти расстояние в
It would take an ion about 30 min **to travel 1 m** in the direction of the applied voltage.

Пройти через
After the neutrons **have made the trip** (*or* **have passed**) **through** the collimator ...

Прокаливать до
The oxalate **is** then **ignited to** the oxide.

Прокатывать в холодном состоянии
The equipment **will cold-roll** mild steel.

Прокатываться в фольгу
Lead easily **forms foil** (*or* **is** easily **rolled into foil**).

Прокладывать [*см. тж.* **Проложен между**]
The frame grid tubes **forged** (*or* **paved**) the way for high-performance, low-cost black-and-white TV.

Прокладывать курс
We know how **to lay off a course** or measure one which is on the chart.
The drafting machine aids the navigator **in plotting courses.**

Прокладывать между
Alternate plates of metal **are stacked with** the dielectric.
A disk of heavy carbon paper **is sand-**

wiched between the pointed end of the stylus and the paper tape.

Прокладывать трубопровод
We have finished **laying** 87 miles **of the pipeline.**

Прокол [*см.* **Не бояться проколов**].

Пролетать мимо
The Pioneer mission **flew by** (*or* **past**) Jupiter.

Проливать новый свет на
This work **has provided fresh insight into ...**
Laser **sheds new light (up)on** molecular structure.

Проливать свет на
The Mössbauer effect **can shed light (up)on** this problem.
Data from satellites **have clarified the** origin of the radiation belts.
These studies **have helped to elucidate** the structure of the flame.
Further investigation of budding in yeast promises **to throw light on** the universal process of cell division.
Such a catalyst **might help to illuminate** the nature and mechanism of the enzymes.

Проложен между
A core layer is **sandwiched between** two layers which form the cladding.
Sheets of metal foil **are clamped between** the mica sheets.

Проложенный
The electrodes are sheets of metal foil **stacked** alternately **with** the mica sheets.
This cartridge is formed by a pile of circular disks **interleaved by** thin washers.
Dufelt incorporates layers of Hycar, **sandwiched with** standard felts.

Проложенный в земле
Cables **buried in the ground** may be more subject to ...

Промежуток [*см. тж.* **В интервале, На промежутке, С равными промежутками, Через некоторые промежутки времени, Через равные промежутки времени**]
An air **gap of** 1 centimetre can withstand about 3000 volts.

Промежуток времени [*см. тж.* **Интервал между**]
The time lapse between first-filled **and** last-filled castings **is** a few milliseconds.

Промежуток между импульсами
The amplitude of the pulses from the objects was uneven, but **the interpulse spacing** (*or* **the spacing between pulses**) was quite regular.

Промежуточная дисциплина
A border(line) (*or* **An interdisciplinary**) **science.**

Промежуточное звено для стыковки
An interface between numerical control **and** machine-tool relay panels.

Промежуточное положение [*см.* **Занимать промежуточное положение между**].

Промежуточное пространство
Thermal conduction may bring energy directly from the coronal regions of the Sun to Earth's atmosphere, if coronal gases fill **the intervening space.**

Промежуточный [*см. тж.* **В промежуточный период, Граничный**]
HF is a **borderline** case ...
Information is passed to the minicomputer via **an interface** device.
During the **intervening** stages the core supports the outer cylinder.

Промежуточный между
The pulses move at a velocity **intermediate between** the sound speeds of the hot and the cold gas.
The properties of metalloids are **intermediate between** those of metals and nonmetals.

Промежуточный по массе *и т.п.* **между**
A particle **intermediate in mass between** the electron and the proton ...

Промежуточный продукт
Sodium chlorate is used as **an intermediate (product)** in perchlorate production.

Промежуточный цвет
Red, green, and blue lights can be chosen to produce any of the various **intermediate** colours.

Промер
The "quick setup aids" eliminate trial cuts and repeated **gauging** during setup.

Промерять [*см.* **Измерять**].

Промывать
The pipes **should be flushed out with** water instead of being blown out with steam.
If the cells **are** not properly **rinsed,** a film may be formed.
The solid residue **was washed with** ether.

Промывка
Always disassemble the unit first for proper cleaning and **rinsing.**
Carbon dioxide is removed from gas mixtures by **washing with** alkaline solutions.

Промышленная операция
In most **commercial** nickel electroforming **operations ...**

Промышленная скважина
Exploratory and **producing wells ...**

Промышленная эксплуатация [*см.* **Вводить в промышленную эксплуатацию**].

Промышленного значения
The **industrially** (*or* **commercially**) **important** process of formation of ...

Промышленного производства
Industrially prepared acetyl chlorides are much used.

Промышленное значение [*см. тж.* **Иметь промышленное значение, Наибольшее промышленное значение**]
Naturally occurring mullite has no **commercial significance** (*or* **importance**).

Промышленное производство [*см.* **Производиться в промышленных масштабах**].

Промышленность [*см.* **В промышленности**].

Промышленные залежи [*см. тж.* **Залежи промышленного значения**]
There are **minable** cinnabar **deposits** in many regions around the world.

Промышленные масштабы [*см.* **В промышленных масштабах**].

Промышленный [*см. тж.* **Имеющий промышленное значение**]
This can be achieved by the use of **commercial** dye lasers equipped with ...
A **commercial** process for beryllium production ...

Пронизан
The resulting wafers **are penetrated by** thousands of channels.

Пронизывающий
When the explosives are detonated, the tube collapses and the field lines **threading** the tube are squeezed together.

Проникать в [*см. тж.* **Понимание**]
These caves collapse before we **can gain access to** them from the surface.
The light **penetrates into** the cladding from the core.
The large chromate ions **would** not **penetrate** the smaller pores.
Usually long extended tooling **reaches into** otherwise completely inaccessible areas.
The air **finds its way into** the pump suction.
Should air **gain access to** the suction, ...

Проникать в ... на небольшое расстояние
The beam of electrons **penetrates** the crystal **a short distance.**

Проникать в существо проблемы
He always **gets to the root of a problem.**

Проникать в тайны
We were equipped with appropriate instruments for **probing the mysteries of** superconductivity.

Проникать вглубь
When the heat front **penetrates to the** comet's **interior, ...**
Cold ocean water **penetrates deep into** the crustal rock.

Проникать глубже в
Investigators **probed deeper into** the nature of electricity.

Проникать глубоко в
Alpha particles do not **penetrate deeply into** living tissue.

Проникать на поверхность земли
These rays **penetrate to the surface of the earth.**

Проникать через

The virus **enters via** the upper respiratory tracts.

Проникновение в [*см. тж.* **Не допускать проникновения, Попадание, Препятствовать попаданию**]
The non-return valve prevents **ingress of** air **to** (*or* **into**) the main pump from the air-pump.
The penetration of a totally reflected light wave **into** a medium ...
The penetration of the outer orbital electron **within** the closed shells of other electrons ...

Проницаемость для
The successive layers differ in their **permeability to** solutions.

Проницаемый для [*см. тж.* **Легко проницаемый**]
Hot palladium **is permeable to** hydrogen.
The membrane **is** about a million times more **permeable to** the chloride anion than to ...
Paper capacitors **are pervious to** moisture.

Проницаемый для газов
The wrappings **are gas permeable.**

Пронумерованы [*см.* **Иметь номер**].

Пропитан(ный)
Keep a piece of waste **saturated with** oil handy.
The fabric **is impregnated with** rubber.

Пропитанный водонепроницаемым составом
When **waterproofed by** tarring, canvas can be made into ...

Пропитывать
The emulsion must be completely removed from the fabric so that it **can be** uniformly **penetrated** (*or* **impregnated**) **by** solutions.
Alumina spheres **were soaked with** nitrobenzene.

Пропитываться водой
When a mass of the dry clay **becomes soaked with water** it undergoes a large volume expansion.

Пропорционален
The liquid velocity near the wall **is proportional to** the distance from the wall surface.

Пропорционально [*см. тж.* **Изменяться пропорционально, Обратно пропорционально, Прямо пропорционально**]
This increases the rate of hydrolysis **in proportion to** the concentration of ...
The density decreases **as** $(\rho)^{-1/2}$.
The force of ... varies **directly with** the first power of distance.
For oils of greater viscosity at atmospheric temperatures, the distances should be reduced **in proportion.**
The voltage will vary **proportionally** (*or* **in proportion**) **to ...**
If dy/dx varies **proportionally** with y, ...
The duties vary **proportionately with** the speed of the main engine.

Пропорционально квадрату
The impact pressure, caused by ... varies **with the square of** the velocity.
The cost of area meters tends to increase **as the square of** the pipe size.

Пропорционально ... степени
It **is proportional to the** fourth **power of** the wavelength of the radiation.
The power loss increases **as the** third or fourth **power of ...**
In quadruped animals the width of the body should vary **as the** 3/2 **power of** its length.

Пропорционально степени 4/3
The penetration increased **with the four-thirds power of** the velocity.

Пропорциональность [*см.* **Прямо пропорционально**].

Пропорциональны друг другу
Intensity and concentration **are proportional (to each other).**

Пропорциональный [*см.* **Линейно пропорциональный, Прямо пропорционален**].

Пропорция [*см.* **В пропорции, Соотношение**].

Пропускаемый свет
Transmitted light.

Пропускание
The resulting water is acidic and must be neutralized **by passage through** an anion-exchange resin containing OH^-.

A dew point of less than –70°C was obtained **by passing** tank argon **through** a tower containing ...

Пропускание тока
Current measurement is achieved **by passing the current through** an accurate resistor and ...

Пропускать [*см. тж.* **Прозрачный для**]
The filter **passes** the probe beam.
Air **is passed through** a flow counter.
The input signal **is passed through** a conventional rectifier.
This filter **transmits** green light.
The slotted disk serves **to permit the passage of** compressed air between ...
Some of the positive ions **were allowed to pass through** the cathode canal.

Пропускать или отбраковывать
The monitoring system is adjusted **to pass or reject** tubes according to molybdenum content.

Пропускать над
Gas *B* **is passed over** the top end of the tube.

Пропускать свет
No **light is transmitted** (*or* **passed**) **by** the crossed polarizers.

Пропускать свет через
Light is allowed to pass through a solution of ...

Пропускать ток по цепи
Refrigeration can be effected if **a current is passed** (*or* **sent**) **round the circuit.**

Пропускать ток через
When the coil **is energized, ...**
He **ran a current through** the mercury.
A constant **current is passed through** the specimen.

Пропускать через
Microwaves **can be passed** with very little loss **along** metal tubes.
Water **is passed through** a bed of particles.
A sterilizing solution **may be run through** the machine just before milking.
When light from a point source **is sent through** the negative, ...
The mixture **is made to flow through** a tube.

Пропускать через насос
The mixture **was put through a pump.**

Пропускаться через
When a gas **is allowed to pass through** a small hole, ...

Пропускающий [*см.* **С утечкой**].

Пропущенный контролем
The component **has been** tested and **o.k.'d** (*sl.*) (*or* **approved**).

Прореагировать [*см.* **Полностью прореагировать**].

Прорываться через
The steam **must force its way** up **through** this layer.

Просачиваться в
Air **may leak in at** the apparatus.
The part to be tested is first immersed in a special penetrant which **seeps into** the finest cracks.

Просачиваться в почву
As rain falls on a slope, it will begin **to seep into the soil.**

Просачиваться из
The first possibility was that some solute **might** unexpectedly **leak out of** the cell when it shrank.

Просачиваться через
Ammonium nitrate **washes** rapidly **through** soil and causes pollution of waterways.
The water **seeps** (*or* **percolates**) **through** the ground.

Просверлить [*см.* **Высверливать**].

Просверлить глухое отверстие в стенке
To drill a hole part way through the wall (*or* **To drill a blind hole in the wall**).

Просветы в облаках
Breaks in clouds.

Просвечивать рентгеновскими лучами
The nozzles **are X-rayed** to check ...

Проскакивание
To prevent the drillpoint from **breaking through, ...**

Проскакивать и задерживаться

Pellets smaller than the gap **will fall through it and** those with diameters that are larger than the gap **will be held back.**

Проскальзывание
Slippage in such a clutch produces heat.

Проскальзывать
Should the tap meet an obstruction, the clutch **slips**, eliminating tap breakage.

Прослеживать
To follow (*or* **trace**) the fate of the labelled elements, ...
We have attempted **to trace** the history of continental movements.

Прослеживать от ... до
The isotherm **can be followed from** the low-pressure side **to ...**

Прослеживать ход болезни
It is possible **to follow** (*or* **trace**) **the course of the disease.**

Прослойка [*см.* **С прослойкой**].

Просматривание
Viewing and recording the image ...

Просматривание с воздуха
The reconnaissance includes **airborne** infrared **scanning** over a large area.

Просматривать
The new telescope **could sample** (*or* **scan**) 12 times more sky.

Прост в обращении
Pulsed dye lasers **are straightforward to use.**

Прост в эксплуатации и обслуживании
The air conditioners **are easy to operate** (*or* **handle**) **and maintain.**

Простаивать
On the average, cutting tools **are idle** about 70% of the time.
It is necessary to know which machines are running and which **are down** and why.
If a machine **is** temporarily **out of action** for tool changing or because of a breakdown, ...

Простаивать из-за неполадок
Stand-by pumps and by-pass systems ensure that machines **will** not **be idled by a malfunction.**

Простая случайность
It does not seem **to be mere random chance** (*or* **accidental**) **that ...**

Простейшей конструкции
The compass **in its simplest form** consists of ...

Простираться
The ligament sacks are hollow tubes which **extend** most of the length of the cavity of the trunk.
The ventilation shaft **extends to** 200 ft below sea level.
The resulting fluorescence spectra **extend over** an appreciable wavelength range.
The isotherms **extend into** the region where condensation occurs.

Простираться в направлении
The mountain range **runs in a direction** just west of ...

Простираться до
The San Andreas Fault **extends** (*or* **goes out**) **to** sea 150 km north of San Francisco.
This sea **reached** eastward **to** Manitoba, ...

Простираться до бесконечности
The medium through which the wave propagates **extends to infinity.**
The line **stretches to infinity** in both directions.

Простираться от ... до
The range of absorption maxima **extends from** 620 nm **to** 490 nm.

Просто [*см. тж.* **Легко, Лишь**]
The Vapour-Pressure Thermometer is **merely** a bulb connected to ...
In this multiplier vacuum tubes are used **merely** (*or* **simply**) as switches.

Просто путём
The two allotropes are directly convertible into each other **by mere** temperature change.

Просто устанавливать
The pumps **are simple to install.**

Простой I [*см. тж.* **Иметь простую структуру**]
We obtain the desired expression by **straightforward** integration.
The adaptation of roof bolting to ripping faces has not been so **straightforward** (*or* **simple**) as it might at first sight appear.

Простой II [*см. тж.* **Аварийная остановка**]
Dead time is the time a worker loses from lack of materials or equipment breakdown.
After long periods of **idleness** (*of a motor, etc.*) ...
The transformer is automatically disconnected from the supply during **the idling periods.**
To oil the working surfaces and thereby minimize corrosion when **standing, ...**
Breakdown time, Standing time ...
This ensures that the loading shovel has **the** minimum **waiting time** between empty cars arriving at the bottom.
In this way you eliminate **downtime** that would be needed to change inserts.
This permits different parts to be set up while others are being machined, to reduce **the idle time.**

Простой машины
Dies can be changed in as little as 5 min, and **machine downtime is** thus kept to a minimum.

Простота [*см. тж.* **Для простоты**]
The ease of fabrication ...

Пространственное распределение
Spatial distribution.

Пространственное расположение
The spatial arrangement of atoms ...

Пространство [*см. тж.* **Водное пространство**]
During periods of low water, the flood plains were unvegetated **expanses of** gravel, sand, silt, and clay.

Пространство используется неэкономно
This assembly **is wasteful of space** (*в этой сборке пространство ...*).

Просуществовать
Nematodes **have survived** 48 hours in a vacuum.

Просыпаться
Some of the ore **spills to** the bottom of the shaft.

Протекать I [*см.* **В ... протекает ток**].

Протекать II [*см. тж.* **Течь**]
This valve is known **to be leaky.**

Протекающий клапан
A leaky valve.

Протест [*см.* **Вызывать бурный протест**].

Против [*см. тж.* **На одной линии с, Направлен вдоль или против**]
This hole **is opposite** another hole in the lifting plate.
The brackets are welded **opposite to** the external frames.

Против ветра
In using the instrument one stands with the right shoulder **facing into the wind.**

Против часовой стрелки
In an anti- (*or* **counter-)clockwise direction.**
Anti- (*or* **counter-)clockwise.**

Против этого говорит то, что
Against this practice is the fact that the working pressure ...

Противник (*теории и т.п.*) (*антон.* **Защитник**)
The opponents (*anton.* **Proponents**) (**of this theory**) insisted that ...

Противодействовать [*см. тж.* **Препятствовать**]
There are always two opposing tendencies or actions which **counteract each other.**
Plate current variations cause the cathode potential to vary in such a way as **to oppose** the effect produced by ...
The calcium ion is able **to counter(act)** the toxic effects of ...

Противопожарное оборудование
Fire-fighting equipment.

Противоположен
Motion on the transform fault **is the opposite of that** in the simple transcurrent fault (*geol.*).
The substitution in this reaction **is the opposite of** (*or* **is opposite to**) **that** realized under acidic conditions.

Противоположен по знаку
Twice the kinetic energy **is** equal but **of opposite** (*or* **but opposite in**) **sign to** the potential energy.

Противоположная сторона Луны
The back (*or* **other,** *or* **far,** *or* **opposite**) **side of the Moon.**

Противоположно [*см.* **Направлен противоположно**].

Противоположно заряжённый
The charged particles are drawn to the plate **of opposite charge.**
The charged ions migrate from the sample solution to **the oppositely charged** electrodes.

Противоположно направленные
The two **opposing** (*or* **oppositely directed**) beams pass through each other.
One pair of forces will excite the radial mode and the **oppositely sensed** pair will act in the thickness direction.

Противоположного заряда [*см.* **Противоположно заряжённый**].

Противоположного знака [*см.* **Противоположно заряжённый**].

Противоположность [*см. тж.* **В противоположность, Прямая противоположность**]
In this case fluorescence **is the converse of** absorption.
This thesis **is (quite) the opposite from** (*or* **to**) the concept widely held in the past.
Adiabatic **is the reverse of** diabatic.

Противоположны по знаку
The fluxes N_A and N_B are frequently **of opposite sign** (*or* **opposite in sign**).

Противоположны(е) друг другу
Two almost **antithetical** views ...
These two processes are **the reverse of each other.**

Противоположные заряды притягиваются
Unlike charges attract (each other).

Противоположные процессы
Two **contrary processes ...**
Radiation and reception of radio waves **are inverse** (*or* **reverse,** *or* **opposite**) **processes.**

Противоположный [*см. тж.* **В противоположном направлении, Действовать в противоположные стороны, Диаметрально противоположный, Направленный в сторону, противоположную; Обратный, Прямо противоположный, Равный и противоположный, С противоположных сторон**]
The configuration of the product **can be opposite to** (*or* **from**) **that of** the starting material.
The ions with charges **opposite that** of the central ion ...
The **opposing** strands differ in width.
There are always two **opposing** tendencies which counteract each other.
The force **opposite to** the direction of motion ...

Противоположный заряд
Unlike (*or* **Opposite**) **charges** attract each other.

Противоположный знак
If we mix two colloids **of opposite sign,** the particles of one will attract the particles of the other.
An error voltage **of the opposite sign** is derived.

Противоположный по знаку
A constant voltage drop across the barrier which is equal in magnitude but **opposite in sign to** the height of the $p = n$ barrier ...

Противоположный по направлению
Opposite in direction to ...

Противоречивый
Reversibility data in one system may lead to **conflicting** (*or* **erratic**) conclusions.
Various and **discrepant** (*or* **contradictory**) accounts have been preserved.

Противоречие [*см.* **Вступать в противоречие с, Находиться в противоречии с**].

Противоречить
This seems **contrary to** (*or* **to contravene,** *or* **to contradict,** *or* **to run counter to**) the basic principles of chemistry.
All other feasible mechanisms **are in conflict with** the experimental evidence.
These rules **are at variance** (*or* **in contradiction**) **with** those which stemmed from ...
This **is inconsistent with** the data of Run No. 9.
The observed results **are contradictory to** the genetic theory.

Противоречить здравому смыслу
It **defies common sense to** argue that a lava flow would produce ...

Противоречить самому себе
It has been claimed that the theory of relativity **is self-contradictory.**

Противопоставлять
This is **to be contrasted with** the nonselective fragmentation of ...

Противостоять I
The force of the constrained cylinder **is opposed by** the springs.

Противостоять II
Monel **withstands** (*or* **resists**) corrosion by ...

Противотоком
The gas and liquid are passed **countercurrent (to one another).**

Противоточная система
A countercurrent system.

Протирать
If your balance sticks, **wipe off** all places where moving parts touch.

Протирать насухо
The surface **must be wiped dry.**

Протирать начисто
The cells **should be wiped clean.**

Прототип
This will be **the progenitor of** a whole family of supersonic transport engines.

Протравливать [*см.* **Травить**].

Протягивать бумажную ленту
The transport mechanism **advances the paper chart** under the pen.

Протягивать через
To pull the cable **through** this conduit, ...

Протянут через
Parallel wires **extend through** a cylindrical volume.

Профилактика
The plan had been to replace the valve at **the** next routine **maintenance of** the equipment.

Проход [*см. тж.* **За один проход**]
The container has an opening for **the passage of** the ore.

Проходимое расстояние
The distance *d* **travelled** (*or* **traversed**) **by** a given species ...

Проходить I [*см. тж.* **Пройденная траектория**]
The platinum contact **extends into** the mercury reservoir **through** a glass seal.
The cable **runs from** the transformers **into** each room.
The red line **runs across** the chart.

Проходить II
The trucks easily **cover** two miles in 25 minutes.
The wide range of horizontal and vertical angling allows cars **to negotiate** acute curves.
The current **passes through** the bias resistor.
The light **passes through** the water.
The shock wave **travels through** the ground.
The light **traverses** a stack of three filters.
This tyre is capable of **traversing** terrain hitherto uncrossed by vehicles.
As the molecule **traverses** this length, ...

Проходить III [*см. тж.* **Проникать в, Пропускать**]
The shock wave **travels into** the low-pressure chamber.

Проходить IV
The wire **runs from** north **to** south of the compass scale.

Проходить V
Reactions **occurring** in aqueous solutions ....
The process **will progress** (*or* **proceed,** *or* **take place**) **in** the tube.

Проходить VI
After a pre-set period **is elapsed,** air is applied to ...

Проходить вдоль всего
A canal **runs the (entire) length of** the building.

Проходить весь путь
In a counterflow tower the air **travels all the way from** the bottom **to** the top.

Проходить дорожные испытания
This rubber **is being road tested** in tyres.

Проходить жёсткие испытания

The trestles **were put through arduous** (*or* **severe**) **tests.**

Проходить испытания
The trestles **were put through tests.**
The rig **has undergone** (*or* **has been subjected to**) standard **tests.**
The theory **has been put to** many experimental **tests.**

Проходить к ... через
From the magma chambers the molten rock **finds its way to** the surface **through** fractures.

Проходить контроль
The parts **have passed inspection.**

Проходить мимо
General relativity predicts that a light ray will be bent as it **passes by** a massive object.

Проходить насквозь I
Certain proteins penetrate the lipid layer and others **extend all the way through it.**
The bolt holes **extend** (*or* **go all the way**) **through** the plating of the boiler.

Проходить насквозь II
See to it that the bit does not drill into the table when it **breaks through** the work.

Проходить незамеченным
His finding **went unnoticed.**

Проходить параллельно
The bar **runs parallel to ...**

Проходить путь
The magnetic line **traverses a** long **path** around the torus.

Проходить расстояние [*см. тж.* **Покрывать расстояние**]
The molecule **travels** (*or* **traverses**) **a distance** u_x.
The light **travels a distance** $2L$.
The distance traversed (*or* **travelled**) **by** the shock wave was estimated.

Проходить туннель
There were two **tunnels to be driven.**

Проходить через I
Let the plane λ **go through** $P_0(x_0, y_0, z_0)$.

Проходить через II
The Earth's atmosphere **has gone through** three main stages.

Проходить через III
When a charged particle **travels through** a transparent medium ...

Проходить через блоки
The belt **passes over** two or more **pulleys.**

Проходить через максимум (*антон.* **минимум**)
HTU_{OG} increases with gas-flow rate, but **passes** (*or* **goes**) **(through) a maximum** (*oppos.* **minimum**) in the vicinity of the loading point.

Проходить через начало координат
This line **passes through the origin** (**of the coordinates**).

Проходить через цикл
Each of the three spaces **experiences** two operating **cycles** per revolution.

Проходка
The average daily **advance was** 32 ft.
A new tunnel **drivage** record ...
In driving headings (*штреков*) on both levels an effort is made to ...
This increases **drilling footage** per man-shift.

Проходка шахтного ствола
Shaft sinking.

Проходящий длительный курс лечения
Patients **on long-term** diuretic **therapy ...**

Проходящий испытание
The chassis **under test** are placed in groups of six.

Проходящий свет
Transmitted light.

Проходящий через [*см. тж.* **Линия, проходящая через**]
The equilibrium curve is a straight line **(passing) through** the origin.
A generator (*образующая*) **through** point P of a generalized cone ...

Прохождение [*см. тж.* **Беспрепятственное прохождение, При прохождении через**]
The temperature of the fluid is increased **by the passage of** the shock waves.
After **traversing** glass plate G, the two waves **pass through** a compensator.

Прохождение на близком расстоянии от
The comet exhibited a large decrease in period after **a close** Jupiter **encounter.**

Прохождение спутника
The transmitter frequency must be sufficiently stable over the duration of **the satellite pass.**

Прохождение через[*см.* **При прохождении через**].

Процент [*см. тж.* **В процентах, Выражать в процентах, Доля в, Значительный процент, На 20% эффективнее, чем; Насыщенный на ... процентов, Несколько процентов, Определяться в процентах**]
Adenocarcinomas account for **a** larger **proportion** of cases in women than in men.
The two particles differ in mass by **a tenth of a** (*or* **one**) **percent.**
The high **incidence of** death from heart disease ...
This alloy contains 62 **percent (of)** tin and ...
The belting contains **a** substantial **proportion** (*or* **percentage**) **of** nylon.
The gaseous products contain large **proportions of** propylene, butylene and butadiene.

Процент брака
The reject rate of the coil forms was high.

Процент выживания
In the case of hypothermia **the survival rate is** low.

Процент заболевания
White Americans have **a** higher **incidence rate of** female breast cancer.

-процентный
This indicates seasonal precipitation increases **of** 20 **percent.**

Процентный состав
The percent(age) composition of alloys and rocks may be derived from such observations.

Процесс [*см. тж.* **В процессе, Вести процесс, Головной процесс, Обратный процесс**]
Processes for conversion of liquid fossil fuels to utility fuel gases ...

Процесс, обратный
The reversal of vaporization **is** condensation.
We can think of bond formation as **the reverse of** cleavage.

Процесс производства [*см.* **В процессе производства**].

Процесс размножения
Sporogony **is an** important **multiplicative process.**

Процессы, происходящие в организме
We need energy in the form of molecules of adenosine triphosphate for all our **bodily processes.**

Прочее [*см.* **Помимо всего прочего**].

Прочёсывать (*жарг.*) [*см. тж.* **Просматривать**]
In 1781 Herschel was engaged in **sweeping of** the skies **with** a telescope.

Прочная конструкция
The unit is **of robust** (*or* **rugged**) **construction** (*or* **design**).

Прочная основа
This system provides **a firm basis for** initiating discussion.

Прочно
The core support is mounted **firmly** on the tank floor.
The controller is **robustly** (*or* **ruggedly**) constructed.
The races are held **securely** in place.
The centrepieces **securely** hold the top and bottom jaw sections.
Strongly constructed buildings ...
A hobbing press is more **sturdily** built than ordinary presses.

Прочно закреплён
The instrument **is firmly secured.**
A pointer **is rigidly attached to** the centre of the scale beam.
The engine **is securely** (*or* **firmly**) **fastened to** the hull.

Прочно закрепляться
The coupling **is clamped solidly.**

Прочно прикреплять к
The cord **must be firmly attached** (*or* **fixed**) **to** the ball.

Прочно связан с
The mercury **is firmly bonded to** (*or* **bound with**) a carbon atom.
The valence electrons **are tightly bound to** the nuclei.

Прочно удерживать
Such a solid surface **holds** each adsorbed molecule as **tightly** as all the others.

Прочное положение [*см.* **Завоёвывать прочное положение**].

Прочностные свойства
Strength properties.

Прочность [*см. тж.* **Запас прочности**]
The durability (*or* **strength**) **of** the hardened cement **is** excellent.
The integrity of solder joints subjected to vibration and shock **is** best preserved by ...
Mechanical **robustness** (*or* **rigidity**) test ...
The sphere will be pressure tested to prove its **soundness.**
Lucalox has been found to retain its **strength** at high temperatures.
In this problem **toughness** and reliability are closely related.
The ruggedness of freight elevators ...

Прочный [*см. тж.* **Высокопрочный**]
The supporting structure must have a **secure** foundation.
The concrete structure must be built on **sound** rock.
A **rigidly built** saw-frame ...
The housing is covered with vulcanized rubber, leather-like in appearance, but much more **durable.**
High-strength steels.
The transmitter is a **robust** (*or* **rugged**) unit.
The weld must be **sound** and free from cracks.
At speeds and altitudes where only **the staunchest** materials will serve ...
This material **is** mechanically **strong.**
The relays **are ruggedly built.**
Such systems **must be rugged** enough to withstand shocks.
Sturdy latches, substantial handles ...
A **stiff** construction can be obtained by ...

Прошедший [*см. тж.* **Время, истекшее с**]
t is the time **elapsed after** introducing ...

Прошло время [*см.* **Не прошло много времени с тех пор, как**].

Прошло много времени
A considerable amount of time has elapsed (*or* **passed**) between ...

Прошлое [*см.* **В прошлом**].

Прошлые века
To reconstruct the geology of **past ages, ...**

Проще говоря
A planetary satellite, or **more simply,** a moon, is a solid object orbiting a planet.
Simply stated, a rock is younger than the youngest rock which it cuts or within which it is intruded.

Прощупывать
During the ground runs the pilot **feels out** the aircraft to evaluate its adequacy.

Проявление [*см. тж.* **Внешнее проявление**]
This phenomenon is **a manifestation of** the a-c effect.

Проявлять [*см.* **Иметь**].

Проявлять активность
Peptides **may exhibit** (*or* **show,** *or* **display**) **activity** which is greater than ...

Проявлять большой интерес к
The UN **is taking an active interest in** geothermal energy.

Проявлять интерес к
Great **interest has been expressed** (*or* **demonstrated,** *or* **displayed**) **by** mineral engineers **in** this roof-support system.
Some **interest is being shown in** these steels.

Проявлять исключительную осторожность
Use extreme care (*or* **caution**) **in** handling the foil so as not to bend it.

Проявлять осторожность
Personnel **should exercise caution when** measuring parts machined from fluorocarbon resins.
Care (*or* **Caution**) **must be exercised** (*or* **is required**) **in** the interpretation of shock tube measurements made at low pressures.

Проявлять признаки
Malignant tumours generally **show evidence of** significant growth.

Проявлять свойство
The nonreducing sugars do not **exhibit** (*or* **manifest,** *or* **show**) **this property.**

Проявлять склонность к [*см.* **Склонен к**].

Проявлять способность к
As a rule, microspheres do not **show a capacity for** concentrating materials (*or* do not **possess the ability to** concentrate materials).

Проявлять тенденцию к [*см. тж.* **Склонен к**]
If the sands are siliceous, the soils **tend to have** a reduced nutrient content.

Проявляться
Most of the oxygen, nitrogen and sulphur in the coal **appear as** water, ammonia, and hydrogen sulphide in the gaseous products.
When atomic energy is released quickly in a bomb, **it manifests itself as** heat, shock wave, ...
Radiation damage of the nitrilites **would be reflected by** changes in the rate of fermentation.
The mass effect **shows itself as** a slight difference of the terms of ...
This reduced adhesion **shows up** most vividly when ...
External corrosion **shows (up) as** rusty or pitted spots on the metal.
These antibodies are too weak **to reveal themselves in** test tube reaction.
The relative scarcity of volatile elements in eucretes (*a type of meteorites*) **shows up in** the composition of ...
Acoustic neuroma **can present in this way** (*med.*).
This form of the disease **can be manifested by** a wide range of signs and symptoms.
This uncertainty **makes itself evident in** the range of values found for ...
All these characteristics **are exhibited by** arsenic.
A number of interesting properties **emerge in** the vicinity of the critical point.

Проявляться в виде
Weathering **manifests itself as** a reduction of the material to ...
This form of narrow saturation resonance **manifests itself in** the output signal of a gas laser.
Temporal arthritis occasionally **presents with** localizing neurological signs (*med.*).
This neoplasm **may present as** weight loss.
This activity **is** often **manifested in** the production of cosmic jets.
Such deviations **show as** a curvature of the calibration graph.
Autonomic neuropathy **is** most usually **evident as** postural hypotension and ...

Проявляться в том, что
The diffusion law **makes itself evident** (*or* **manifests itself**) **in the fact that** the system may fail to hold gases.

Проявляться в других формах
Osteoarthrosis **may** also **present in other ways,** for instance, as the rupture of a Baker's cyst.

Проявляться наиболее ярко
Edema and other symptoms of acute protein deficiency **were most conspicuous in** the children.

Проявляться путём
In the spatial transient, the power in the tunneling rays **manifests itself by** adding a tail to the pulse.

Пружинный
A **spring-driven** clock ...
A **spring-loaded** valve ...

Прямая (линия) [*см.* **Двигаться по прямой, По прямой**].

Прямая противоположность
The effect of monsoon control **is the exact antithesis** (*or* **reverse**) **of** the Mediterranean regime of rainfall...
The maximum eccentricity program **is the exact** (*or* **diametrical**) **opposite of** the circularizing thrust program.

Прямая реакция
A forward reaction.

Прямо пропорционален
The energy content of one quantum of a particular radiation **is in direct proportion** (*or* **directly proportional**) **to** its frequency.
The frequency of mutations induced by X-rays **is** almost **directly proportional to** the dosage of radiation.

Прямо пропорционально [*см. тж.* **Изменяться прямо пропорционально**]
The volume of a gas **varies directly as** the absolute temperature.
Echo intensity **varies directly as the square of** the target diameter and inversely as the fourth power of the distance.
The rate of conversion **increases directly with** the surface concentration.
The amplitude **varies in direct proportion to ...**

Прямо противоположен
The direction of magnetization of some rocks **is exactly the opposite of that** in adjacent strata.
The electron-releasing resonance effect **is in direct opposition to** the electron-withdrawing inductive effect.
This observation **is in direct opposition to** the statement that ...
This situation **is in complete contrast to** what would be expected if ...
This process **is just the reverse of** that already described.

Прямо противоположный [*см. тж.* **Диаметрально противоположный**]
Some rocks possessed a polarization **quite the reverse** (*or* **the exact reverse**) **of that** of today.
Two **diametrically** (*or* **directly**) **opposed** (*or* **opposite**) theories ...

Прямой отсчёт [*см.* **С прямым отсчётом**].

Прямой угол [*см.* **Под прямым углом**].

Прямолинейность
The curves approach **straightness** (*or* **linearity**) at the top.

Прямолинейный
The **straight line** (*or* **rectilinear**) portion of the curve ...

Прямоугольный
Sharp, round, and **right-angled** blades can be fitted.

Прямые и обратные реакции
Forward and reverse reactions.

Пуск
The relay serves **to actuate** (*or* **start**) the dial mechanism.

Пускать [*см.* **Запускать**].

Пускать в ход [*см. тж.* **Запускать машину**]
Set the clock **going** (*or* **Start** the clock) **by** swinging the pendulum.
When the lathe **is set in motion, ...**
The compressor **was started (up).**

Пускать в эксплуатацию [*см. тж.* **Вводить в эксплуатацию, Пуск**]
The instrument **can** now **be put into commission.**
The station **will be commissioned** in 1992.
These instructions **will** enable the user to install, **set to work,** and maintain the recorder in first-class working order.
A new haulage system **will** soon **go into operation.**
The third unit **goes on line** in December.
These units **will go on stream** when they are delivered to location.
This permits the diffusion pump **to be placed in operation.**
Two tractors **were put into operation.**
The ship **was put into service** in April 1982.
To put the boiler **into service, ...**

Пускать станок
Then we **start (up) the lathe.**

Пускаться в рассуждения о
I **will** not **launch into a discussion of ...**

Пусть [*см. тж.* **Предположим, Скажем**]
Let U_0 **be** (*or* **Let us assume that** U_0 **is,** *or* **Assume that** U_0 **is**) the initial velocity.
Let $A = A(\rho/\rho_1)$.
To each pair (x_1, x_2) in ... **let there** correspond a certain definite number y.

Пусть будет
Let there be N molecules per unit volume.

Пусть это будет
When an industrial effluent has to be discharged to any water course, **be it** [*or* **whether** (*or* **no matter whether**) **it is**] a stream or a river, some form of treatment is essential.

Путаница [*см.* **Во избежание путаницы, Вызывать путаницу**].

Путать [*см.* **Не следует путать с**].

Путём [*см. тж.* **Обычным путём, Посредством, При помощи, Различными путями, Таким образом, Химическим путём**]

To project the image of the slit of the lamp housing onto the slit of the multiplier **by way of** reflection from the grating, ...

The moving air acquires water from the land **through** evaporation and transpiration.

This is accomplished **by** increasing the preload.

In fungi, lysine is formed **by a** different **route.**

Harris process is a process for softening lead **by** the use of salts of sodium.

The relay controls large values of current and power **through** the use (*or* **utilization**) **of** a special cathode tube.

The wave will reach the detector **by way of** the more direct route.

These data can be obtained **through** long-term observation.

The most important commercial synthesis of anthranilic acid is **via** the Hoffmann degradation of ...

Solid state bonds can be achieved reliably **with** ultrasonic welding.

When androgens are produced by this **pathway** in the adrenal, one additional reaction occurs.

The most efficient way to replenish soil nitrogen is **through the application of ...**

It is possible to compute definite integrals by an easier **procedure.**

Moisture transport occurs **by** water vapour diffusion.

Friction power can only be reduced **at the expense of** increasing the pumping power.

Путём введения (*или* **внесения**)

The improvement of soil **through incorporation of** organic matter ...

Путём воздействия ... на [*см. тж.* **Воздействие**]

Triple superphosphate of lime is prepared **by the action of** phosphoric acid **on** crushed phosphate rock.

Путём добавления [*см. тж.* **Добавлением**]

Cadmium is precipitated from the electrolyte of ... **by the addition of** zinc dust.

Путём использования

Measurements **are made by reference to** a calibration curve.

This determination **can be made through the use of** the chart.

Путём конвекции

The water circulates **by convection.**

Путём ... можно получить

Addition of a commercial brightener **gives** sound, mirror-like deposits.

Путём перехода

The electrons can increase their energies **by going** (*or* **transferring**) **to** higher energy levels.

Путём подбора

The best electrode pressure to use with any particular size of rivet can be found only **by trial and error.**

Путём присоединения ... к

A white precipitate is obtained **by adding** (*or* **by addition of**) disodium hydrogen phosphate **to** calcium chloride solution.

Путём проводимости [*см. тж.* **Отдача тепла путём проводимости**]

Heat flows out of the earth **by conduction.**

Путём рассмотрения

The regions were defined **through consideration of** the rainfall probabilities.

Путём реакции

This compound is obtained **by the reaction of** acetic acid and bases.

The best method for the preparation of chlorine monoxide **is by the reaction of** chlorine **with** mercuric oxide.

Boron trifluoride is most readily obtained **from the reaction of** boric acid, hydrogen fluoride, **and** sulphuric acid.

Путём совместного использования

It is **through the interplay of** observation, prediction **and** comparison that the laws of nature are slowly clarified.

Путём экстраполяции от

Predict the properties of astatine **by extrapolation from** the known properties of the common halogens.

Путь [*см. тж.* **Быть на правильном пути,**

Идти обычным путём, Изыскивать пути, Искать пути, Метод, На обратном пути, На полпути между ... и, На пути к, Отклоняться от своего пути, Помещать на пути, Пройденное расстояние]
Fuel cycles that release most of their energy in the form of charged particles offer still other **avenues for** the recovery of fusion energy.
The actual metabolic **pathways by** which amino acids are synthesized are presented in ...
Operators started searching for **ways** (*or* **means**) **of** cutting costs.

Путь к ... свободен
The way is cleared toward resolving this problem.

Путь луча
The path (of travel) of the ray ...

Путь, проходимый газом
The pathway traversed (*or* **taken**) **by the gas ...**

Путь распространения волны
The wave propagation path ...

Путь реакции
The rate of the reaction via **the** third **reaction (path)-(way)** can be expressed by the term ...
Thermodynamics cannot predict what **path the reaction will take** if it does proceed.

Путь решения проблемы
A different **line of attack on the problem of** control of the atmospheric branch of the water cycle has been advanced.

Пучок лучей
To convert **a** diverging **bundle** (*or* **beam**) **of rays** to parallelism, ...

Пыленепроницаемый
All push-buttons **are dust tight** (*or* **dust proof**).

Пыльный
The **dust-laden** air enters ...

Пытаться
We **seek** (*or* **strive**, *or* **endeavour**, *or* **attempt**, *or* **try**) to identify ...
They **attempted** the production of elements beyond uranium.

Пытаться получить
We **shall attempt** a graphical solution first.

Р

Работа I [*см. тж.* **В процессе работы, Ведётся большая работа по, Выполнять работу, Действие, Круглосуточная работа, Нарушать работу, Опытно-конструкторские работы, При нормальной работе, Режим, Эксплуатация**]
The normal **operation** (*or* **performance**) of the system ...
To ensure steady **running** (*or* **work**) **of** the crusher, ...
Work at (*or* **on**) the project ...
Some **work has** already **been done on** this problem.

Работа II [*см. тж.* **Исследование**]
In this **paper** (*or* **work**, *or* **investigation**, *or* **study**) the rotary dispersion of ... is reported.

Работа без смазки
Dry operation.

Работа для одного человека
A one-man job.

Работа, затраченная на преодоление силы трения
The work done against friction ...

Работа ... основана на
The bolometer **depends for its operation on** the change in resistance of ...

Работа по
Work has begun on the bonding of the dispersion-hardened tin to ...

Работа по созданию
This was a milestone in **the quest for** an organic super-conductor.

Работа по чертежам
Working from drawings.

Работа прибора
The figure shows **the operation of the instrument.**

Работа продвинулась настолько, что сейчас
Work has progressed to the point where two companies now plan ...

Работа, произведённая над
The work done on the gas is ...

Работа с большой нагрузкой
Heavy-duty service (*or* **operation**).

Работа со смазкой
Wet operation.

Работать [*см. тж.* **Может использоваться, Не работать, Успешно работать**]
More than a million combines **were** then **at work** on American farms.
We **are active in** the design and application of ...
The machine **has been functioning** (*or* **operating,** *or* **working,** *or* **running**) properly.
When the pump **is in service ...**
The tubes **operate at** 350°C.
The plant **is operated** 24 hours a day.
The transformer **performs** well.
The air grinder **performs** at 1/4 hp, 17,500 rmp, 100 psi.
The belt **can be run at** speeds up to ...
The adjustment can be made while the machine **is running.**
Machines with this equipment **are** already **in operation.**

Работать безаварийно
The conveyor system **is trouble free.**

Работать безукоризненно
The valves **function flawlessly.**

Работать в диапазоне
These components **can operate over frequency ranges** far broader than ...
Several communication satellite systems **are to operate at** *K*-band.

Работать в лазерном режиме
Sodium fluorescein **will** not **lase** without a triplet quencher present.

Работать вхолостую
A governor makes it possible to operate grinding wheels at their most efficient speed and prevents overspeeding when **running idle.**

Работать на нас
Many accidents of physics and astronomy **have worked** together **to our benefit.**

Работать на переменном токе
The logic array of the computer **can be powered by alternating current.**

Работать на полную мощность
When **in full production** (*or* **at full load,** *or* **at full blast** — *sl.*) the station will provide ...
The machines are **in full operation.**
The plant **was operated at full power.**
The mill is expected **to be running at (full) capacity** by 1992.

Работать на сжатом воздухе
The system **is operated by compressed air.**

Работать на срез *и т.п..*
The bolt **is in shear .**
The rib **is subject to compression.**
Concrete **is** relatively **weak in tension.**

Работать на станке
To run (*or* **work,** *or* **operate**) **a lathe.**

Работать на топливе
The converter **operates on** diesel **fuel.**
This machine **can run on** solar, nuclear or chemical **fuel.**
The plant **is fired with** fossil **fuel.**

Работать на трение
The clutch **operates by friction.**

Работать на холостом ходу
When the engine **is idling, ...**

Работать наиболее эффективно [*см.* **Наиболее эффективно работать**].

Работать одной рукой
The solder is automatically fed which permits rapid, **one-handed operation.**

Работать от
The tachometer **is driven off** (*or* **by**) a motor.
The demodulator **operates** directly **from** the supply.
This machine **operates** from the compressed air main.
The discriminators **are operated from** a regulated power supply.
The motor **operates on** ordinary alternating current.

Работать от электропривода
These moving components **are electrically powered.**

The bins are equipped with feeders **operated electrically.**

Работать по чертежу
To work from a blueprint (*or* **drawing**).

Работать под нагрузкой
When **operated under load ...**

Работать против себя
If the air velocities are carried too high the method **defeats its own object.**

Работать с полной нагрузкой
The machines **are used to capacity.**

Работающий
We have a few reactors of this type **in operation.**

Работающий двигатель [*см.* **При работающем двигателе**].

Работающий от
A **battery-operated** radio set.
The **a-c line-operated** unit employs ...

Работающий от сети
This is a **mains-operated** unit.

Работающий по этому принципу
A pilot plant **embodying this concept** was operated by ...

Рабочая позиция
The tool holder has eight **positions** (*or* **stations**).

Рабочая температура
Operating temperature.

Рабочее давление
Operating (*or* **Working**) **pressure.**

Рабочее испытание
The fully assembled chassis is subjected to **a test run.**

Рабочее место
Telescopic sights permit the operators to read all positions of the columns from their **work stations.**

Рабочее положение
The mechanism can be set so that the pen remains **in the operative** (*or* **working**) **position** when the door is opened.
The rotary tool holder has eight **positions** (*or* **stations**).

Рабочее состояние [*см. тж.* **Поддерживать в рабочем состоянии, Приводить в рабочее состояние**]
Brackets must be oiled and always kept in good **operating** (*or* **working**) **condition.**

Рабочее тело
After liberation, the high-temperature internal kinetic energy must be transferred as heat to **a** suitable **working substance** (*or* **working material,** *or* **working medium,** *or* **working fluid**) such as air, water, or steam.

Рабочие условия [*см.* **В рабочих условиях**].

Рабочий диапазон
"Mylar" has an effective **operating range of** from –80° **to** 300°F.

Рабочий режим [*см.* **Режим**].

Рабочий ход
The working stroke of the spindle can be varied steplessly.

Равен [*см. тж.* **На равных основаниях** (*или* **правах**), **Не иметь себе равного, Одинаковый, При равных прочих условиях**]
The power level **equals** (*or* **is equal to**) the heat loss.
The power in the radiation field **is** the difference between ...
The electronegativity difference between chlorine and hydrogen **is as great as** that between nitrogen and hydrogen.

Равен или больше
If the electron energy **is equal to or greater than** an electronic transition of the atom, ...

Равен нулю
On an asteroid, gravity **is** virtually **nil** (*or* **zero**).

Равен по величине
The maximum error **must equal** the step **in magnitude** (*or* **must be equal to** the step **in magnitude**).

Равен по величине и противоположен по знаку
The heat effect **is equal in magnitude but opposite in sign to** that of ...
The flux linkage induces a voltage pulse **that is equal but opposite to** the one induced during the approach.

Равен по мощности
Ten solar energy plants **match the power output of** a large hydroelectric installation.

Равно как и [*см. тж.* **А также**]
This calculation, **along with** our findings, shows that ...
Generally, cutting tools for shapers, planers and lathes are similar, **as are** the mounting mediums.
The diameter required in order to fulfil this condition depends upon the reaction-zone length **as does** the critical diameter.

Равновесие [*см.* **В состоянии равновесия, Выводить из равновесия, Достигать равновесия, Находящиеся в равновесии, Не в равновесии с, Подвижное равновесие, При равновесии, Приводить в равновесие, Приходить в равновесие**].

Равновесие нарушено
This delicate **balance is disrupted** in cancer tissue.

Равновесие устанавливается
An equilibrium is established according to the reaction of Eq. (17-77).

Равновесие фаз
Equilibrium between two **phases ...**

Равновесное положение
The particle is restored to its **equilibrium position.**

Равное расстояние [*см.* **На равном расстоянии друг от друга**].

Равномерно
The adsorbed chromia is **evenly** distributed over the surface.
A **uniformly** impregnated substance was obtained.
The hot metal fills the mould cavity gradually and **uniformly.**

Равномерное распределение
This ensures **even** (*or* **uniform**) **distribution of** materials.

Равномерный
To ensure **even** (*or* **uniform**) pressure across the width of ...
To ensure **steady** running of the crusher under fluctuating feed conditions, ...

Равномерный по толщине
The plate **is uniform across the width** (*or* **in thickness**).

Равноотстоять от
All five carbons in the ring **are equidistant from** the manganese.

Равноотстоящий
Equally spaced (*or* **Equidistant**) notches indicate...

Равноотстоящий от
All points on the plane **should be equidistant** (*or* **equally spaced,** *or* **at an equal distance**) **from** a remote point at the right.
A point **equidistant from** two given intersecting lines ...

Равноправный [*см.* **На равных основаниях** (*или* **правах**)].

Равносильно заявлению о том, что
This **is tantamount to stating that** the enzyme binds only single-stranded DNA.

Равноудалённый
The rotational spectra consist of **equally spaced** absorption lines.
All points on a profile **are equidistant from** a common centre.

Равноценен [*см. тж.* **На равных основаниях** (*или* **правах**)]
Magnesium perchlorate **is the equal of** (*or* **is equal to**) any desiccant from the standpoint of drying efficiency.

Равны
The two series **are equal.**

Равны по величине
The controlling air impulses **are equal in magnitude** (*or* **size**).
These fractions **are equal in value** (*or* **have the same value**).

Равны по величине и противоположны по знаку
N_A and N_B **are equal** (**in value**) **but opposite in sign.**

Равны по высоте
The resulting chromatographic peaks **were equal in height.**

Равный [*см.* **Приравнивать к**].

Равный и противоположный

There is an **equal and opposite** charge on the other plate.
In a circular orbit the gravitational force **is equal and opposite to** the centrifugal force.

Равный или меньший
This diameter **must be equal to, or smaller than,** the distance between ...

Равный нулю
It **is equal to** (*or* **equals**) **zero.**

Равный по величине и противоположный по направлению [*см. тж.* **Равны по величине и ...**]
This force **is equal in magnitude and opposite in direction to** the Coriolis acceleration (*or* **and opposed to it in direction**).

Равным образом
It has been shown already how electromagnetic radiation can interact with the ground state to produce an excited state. **In an equivalent manner** a photon can interact with an excited state to produce a ground state.

Равняться
Substituting..., we find that the period of revolution **comes out** (*or* **is equal**) **to** 27.3 days.

Радар, предотвращающий столкновения
A collision-avoidance radar.

Ради [*см.* **Для**].

Радиация [*см.* **Защита от излучения, Падающее излучение, Под облучением**].

Радиус [*см.* **Загибать по радиусу, Запиливать на радиус, По радиусу, Расстояние по радиусу**].

Радиус действия
R **is the radius of action of** the active conductors.
The range of the nuclear force.

Радиус кривизны
The grating has **a radius of curvature of** 50 centimetres.

Радиус поворота
The turning radius is reduced when using leaning front wheels.

Радиусом
The inner core of the earth, 3475 km **in radius,** consists of ...
An orbit **of radius** *r*.
A shaft pillar **of** 50 m **radius.**

Раз [*см. тж.* **В два раза больше, чем; В два раза выше, чем; В два раза меньше, чем; В миллион раз, В ... раз, Во много десятков раз меньше, Во много раз больше, Ещё раз, Уменьшать вдвое**]
The specific goal for chemicals is a 17-**times** (*or* a 17-**fold**) increase.
Doubling the load will reduce the life of the bearing **by a factor of** eight.
For the amplitude to decrease **by the factor** 1/e (*в* 1/*e раз*) ...

Раз в восемь лет
(Once in) every (*or* **Once every**) **eight years** all valves must be removed from ...

Раз в два года
Biennially (*or* **Every two years**).

Раз в полгода
Ships are repaired **semiannually** (*or* **each half year**).

Раз в смену
Flue gases must be analyzed at least **once a watch** (*or* **a shift**).

Раз в шесть месяцев
The governor should be tested at least **every six months.**
Under normal operating conditions, the instrument should be lubricated **at six-monthly intervals.**

Раз и навсегда
They decided to resolve the problem **once and for all.**

Разбавление [*см.* **Большое разбавление**].

Разбавленный [*см. тж.* **Бесконечно разбавленный раствор**]
A dilute acid ...

Разбавленный водой
Diluted with water (*or* **Water diluted**).
Water-thinned latex paint (*or* Latex paint **thinned with water**).

Разбавленный раствор
A dilute solution.

Разбавлять до безопасной концентрации
Such gases **can be diluted past harm** by using ...

Разбивать на [*см. тж.* **Делить на**]
The enthalpy function **can be broken up into** a temperature-independent term and a temperature-dependent term.
It is necessary **to break** the image **up into** dots.
The procedure **can be broken down** (*or* **divided,** *or* **subdivided**) **into** the following steps: ...
The gross weight of an airplane **can be broken into** component weights.
These methods **can be grouped as follows** (*разбить на следующие группы*): ...
The outer loop **breaks** the integration range **down into** a number of integrals.

Разбивать на части
The integral **can be split** (*or* **divided**) **into** two **parts.**

Разбирать
These ferries **can be broken down** into units which can easily and swiftly be transported from point to point.
Always **disassemble** the unit (*or* **take** the unit **apart**) first for proper cleaning and rinsing.
Blowers **should be** removed, **dismantled** (*or* **taken apart**) and inspected for wear.

Разбираться в
The trace is so complicated that the observer may not be able **to make sense** (*or* **to make head or tail** — *col.*) **of** it.
This situation may be difficult **to unravel.**

Разбит на
In Fig. 2 the system **is broken down into** its elements.

Разбить на два раздела
The scientific work **can be classified under two heads** — that concerned with control and that entailing research.

Разброс [*см. тж.* **Большой разброс**]
The dispersion of the experimental points is about the average.
The scatter in the data is most evident in Run No. 7.
The scatter of points may be due to variation of ...
There is always **a spread of** energies **about** a mean value.

Разброс по частоте
The beam has **a spread in frequency about ...**

Разброс траекторий (*снаряда*)
Dispersion of trajectories.

Разбросаны I
The data for heating times **are scattered.**

Разбросаны II
Rock fragments **are strewn over** the entire Martian surface.

Разбрызгивать на
$CaCl_2$ is often **sprinkled on** icy roads to help melt the ice.

Разведанные запасы
The proved (*or* **proven,** *or* **known,** *or* **explored,** *or* **prospected**) **reserves.**

Развёрнутое уравнение
An expanded equation.

Развиваемая сила
The force exerted (*or* **developed**) **by** air in motion ...

Развивать силу
The air cylinder is capable of **exerting** (*or* **developing**) **a** maximum **force of** 600 lb.
The model was rotated in a centrifuge **to induce** centrifugal **forces.**

Развивать тему
This is **a subject** we **will elaborate upon** (*or* **develop**) later in the chapter.

Развиваться
The concept of chemical substances as being composed of particles **evolved** gradually ...
This type of brazing **is progressing** rapidly.
Electroplating **is heading** in several new directions.

Развиваться в двух направлениях
Platform technology then **took two paths.**

Развиваться естественным путём
This disease ought to be treated rather than be allowed **to run its natural course.**

Развиваться с нарастающей силой

A technological revolution **is gathering force** (*or* **momentum**) in our industry.

Развивающийся
The exciting and still **evolving** (*or* **developing**) technology appears to be the logical solution.

Развитие I [*см. тж.* **В процессе развития**]
Life of the geologic past shows **an** orderly **progression of** forms from primitive to advanced types.
The advancement of science ...
There has been **a** tremendous **growth in** atomic physics.
The control of frictional heat has been one stumbling block in **the progress** (*or* **development**) **of** this method.
In keeping with **the** expected **progression of** manned space flight from single to multimanned vehicles ...
The continuous **evolution of** reactor technology ....

Развитие II
The VSERP theory **is an outgrowth of** the Pauli exclusion principle.

Разгадать
We will try **to puzzle out** the origin of the orebody.

Разгадать загадку
To unravel the puzzles of planet origin, ...

Разгонять до
The protons **are raised** (*or* **accelerated**) **to** high energies.

Разграничение
There is **a** sharp **distinction between** measuring and gauging.
There **is** now no **distinct line between** brass and bronze.

Разграничивать
We **should establish a (strict) line of demarcation between** mechanics' work and the work of mechanics' helpers.

Разгромлен окончательно
The ether concept **was shattered past retrieval.**

Разгрузочная сторона
The view shows **the discharge end of** the press.

Раздаваться
The inner face of the bearing is adjusted axially along the spindle, and as it moves along the taper it **expands.**

Раздваиваться
The ray **bifurcates,** part of it being reflected at angle O_z and part of it being transmitted into ...

Раздвигать
Braking pressure **forces** the plates **apart.**

Раздвигать на ... расстояние
When the rolls **were separated by** this **distance, ...**

Раздвигаться
The two metal strips **are pushed apart by** the cam.

Раздел [*см.* **В разделе о, Граница раздела между, Линия раздела, На поверхности раздела, Область, Поверхность раздела**].

Раздел науки
The principal **divisions of** botanical **science are** as follows: ...

Разделение [*см. тж.* **Деление**]
Choosing *k* objects out of *n* is equivalent to **partitioning** the *n* objects **into** two groups of sizes *k* and *n-k.*
A rifting apart (*or* **separation**) **of** the continents (*or* **A** continental **rifting**) ...
The separation of an aqueous solution of ... **into** two liquid phases ...

Разделение на
The problem of interpreting the universe is considerably simplified by **breaking** it **down to** smaller problems.

Разделены во времени
To distinguish events that **are separated in time by** only 10 microseconds ...

Разделён на
A processor **is partitioned into** modules.

Разделённые
The region consists of two continental rock sequences **separated by** a marine sequence.

Разделённый на [*см.* **Делить на**].

Разделённый на сантиметры
It is a ruler **with centimetres marked off (on it).**

Разделённый на сектора
A rotating **sectored** disk ...

Разделка кромки
Vertical seams are welded in one pass without need for elaborate **edge preparation.**
Preparing (*or* **trimming**) **the edges of** the workpiece for welding ...

Разделять I [*см. тж.* **Делить на**]
It remains to see how the values of Table 6-9 **can be divided up** so that contributions from the separate ions can be obtained.
In a colour camera an optical system **separates** the red, green and blue image components of a picture.

Разделять II
As two charges **are pulled apart, ...**

Разделять взгляды
Their **views are reciprocated by** enlightened mining men.

Разделять мнение
Not all workers **share** this **judgment** (*or* **opinion**).

Разделять на
The machines to be served **should be broken down** (*or* **divided,** *or* **subdivided,** *or* **classified**) **into** three groups.
These crystals **can be classed into** three sections.
Melting furnaces **can be separated into** two main groups.

Разделять на категории
It is generally convenient **to separate** charge-coupled sensors **into** two **categories:** linear sensors and area sensors.

Разделяться I
The rock tends **to split or part along** these planes of weakness.
Where plates **pull apart** and new oceanic crust is formed ...
Evidently, North America and Gondwanaland were together 1.15 billion years ago, but **split** (*or* **rifted**) **apart** (*or* **separated**) shortly thereafter.
Constituents having different densities **separate** under the influence of gravity.

Разделяться II
The container is within the jacket, the two **being separated by** a 1-cm air space.
The stream **is split at** *B*.

Разделяться на
When a liquid system **breaks down into** two phases ...

Разделяться на части
A single large continent (*Pangaea*) formed during the Proterozoic and remained as a single unit until it **broke apart** during ...

Разжигать интерес к
These vivid descriptions **sparked** (*or* **stimulated**) his **interest in** science.

Раззенковывать [*см.* **Зенковать**].

Разлагать
This enzyme **breaks down** starch.
In scanning, the picture **must be broken down into** lines of successive elements.
A pure substance that **can be broken down into** two or more ...
The picture **is broken into** the sequence of elemental parts by the process of scanning.
Hydrogen, oxygen, ... **cannot be resolved into** simpler substances.
Forces acting on an aerodynamic surface **can be resolved into** a lift **and** a drag, **and** a pitching moment.
Thus the white sunlight **is spread out** (*or* **dispersed**) **into** a spectrum.

Разлагать в ряд
A continuous function ... **can be expanded in(to) the** Fourier-Bessel **series.**
Expand this function **in** a Taylor **series.**

Разлагать в степенной ряд по
To expand F **as a power series in** r/ρ ...

Разлагать до
The starches and cellulose **may be broken down** (*or* **degraded**) **to** *D*-glucose.

Разлагать на [*см. тж.* **Разбивать на**]
Bacterial activity **breaks down** the carbohydrate molecules **into** carbon dioxide **and** water.
This catalyst is used **to dissociate a** halogen molecule **into** a halide ion **and** a positive halogen ion.
An element is a substance **which cannot be broken down to** simpler substances **by** chemical reactions.
To decompose water **into** oxygen and hydrogen, ...

We **decompose** (*or* **resolve**) the electric field **into** plane-wave components.
The distortion term **is broken down into** its components.
This motion can be analyzed **by resolving** it **into** components.
The action of the prism in **resolving** white light **into** its constituent colours is called colour dispersion.

Разлагать на множители
To expand the number **into** factors ...

Разлагать по степеням
The exact Hamilton-Jacobi equation **may be expanded in powers of** φ_1.

Разлагать свет
White light is composed of various colours that **can be spread out** (*or* **decomposed**) **into** a rainbow by a prism.

Разлагаться [*см. тж.* **Не разлагаясь, Распадаться**]
Freons **are decomposed by** ultraviolet light.
The rise in amino acids is an indication that proteins in the skeletal muscles **are being broken down** to provide material for the production of glucose for the liver.

Разлагаться на
In the reverse reaction, water **breaks down (in)to** hydrogen **and** oxygen.
If heated, nitrogen dioxide **dissociates into** nitrogen oxide **and** oxygen.

Разлагаться на компоненты
A beam of white light on passing through a prism **is separated into its component colours.**

Разлагаться на элементы
B_2H_6 **can be** completely **decomposed to its elements** at 500–600°C.

Разлетаться
These nuclei contain so much positive charge and so much electrostatic energy that they are ready **to fly apart** at the slightest provocation.
The particles **bounce apart.**

Разливать в формы
The burden **is poured out** for distribution **into moulds.**

Различается несколько семейств (*биол.*)
Several families are differentiated (*or* **distinguished**), mainly **by** the method of attachment and ...

Различать I [*см. тж.* **Отличать от**]
A distinction is made between the boiling point and the condensation point.
Colour vision is the ability **to discriminate** (*or* **distinguish**) lights on the basis of their wavelength composition.
To discriminate between a fluorescence signal **and** a background interference, ...
The eye **can distinguish among** (*or* **identify**) a great number of shades.
The light microscope **cannot distinguish** objects smaller than about 10^{-5} centimetre.
Geologists **recognize** (*or* **differentiate**) three major classes of rocks.

Различать II
The normal eye readily **distinguishes** the figure.
To perceive the subtle differences between them, ...

Различать III
We **recognize** four major classes of geosynclines.

Различать по
The passenger cars **are distinguished** by the horsepower of the engine, the number of cylinders, ...

Различаться
Four functional groups of adrenocortical steroids **are recognized** (*or* **distinguished**).

Различаться по
These chambers **vary in** size.

Различаться по своей структуре *и т.п.*
These isomers **differ structurally** (*or* **in structure**).

Различаться по составу
The extractable species **vary in composition.**

Различают
Three general types of comet tails **are recognized** (*or* **distinguished**).

Различие [*см. тж.* **Проводить различие между, Разница между, Резкое различие между**]
Although these viruses show many similarities, they also exhibit a number of **distinctions.**

Различие во взглядах [*см.* **Нет согласия между ... относительно**].

Различие между [*см. тж.* **Проводить различие между**]
In chromosomes, **distinctions between** chromatin and heterochromatin acquire significance.
Measured neutron cross sections show considerable **variation from** one nucleid **to** another.

Различимый
Iron wire burns in oxygen with no **discernible** flame.
The Mississippi river has formed five clearly **discernible** delta complexes.
Distinguishable features, such as jets, are seldom observed.

Различно [*см.* **По разному**].

Различного цвета
Variously coloured pieces of wood ...

Различной длины
Sequences from a single source **were heterogeneous in length** (*or* **of different length**) (*biol.*).

Различной формы
Variously shaped orbits ...

Различные I [*см. тж.* **Выполнять самые разнообразные функции**]
Varied responses are obtained.

Различные II [*см. тж.* **Отличаться друг от друга**]
Each processing element has more than 100,000 **distinct** electronic components.
Examples are found in such **diverse** cells as the algae *Valonia Halicystis* and *Nitella.*
Galvanic corrosion occurs when two **dissimilar** metals in contact are exposed to ...
This mathematical language seems to apply to all critical phenomena, even in the most **disparate** physical systems.

Различный [*см. тж.* **Иметь различный состав, Разнообразные**]
The beetles are adaptable to **a variety of** media.
Even these few **disparate** and undeveloped examples ...
This term describes substances that **are** chemically **distinct** (*or* **dissimilar,** *or* **different**), but exhibit similarity of crystalline form.
Beds of bentonite show a **variable** (*or* **varied**) thickness.
Tryptophan and **variable** (*or* **different**) amounts of tyrosine are destroyed by acid hydrolysis.
A variety of techniques are used.
Automatic gain control makes it possible to receive incoming signals of **varying** (*or* **differing**) strength at nearly the same volume.
A range of five standard milling heads of **varying** power is available.

Различными путями I
This back pressure may be applied **in a variety of** (*or* **in various,** *or* **in different**) **ways.**
Amplitude modulation can be produced **in a number of (different) ways.**
This can occur by **a variety of processes.**
Water moves from the world ocean to the lands and back, **following various paths.**

Различными путями II
This is achieved **by various means** (*or* **in various ways**).

Различных размеров и форм
The bellows can be made **in various sizes and shapes.**

Разложение [*см. тж.* **Биологическое разложение отходов**]
Carbon dioxide is also prepared by **the decomposition of** a metal carbonate with an acid or by heat.
Breakdown of complex substances **to** simpler substances by living cells ...
Yeasts obtain energy **by breaking down** sugars **into** simpler compounds.
Complete **breakup of** the molecule ...
To prevent peroxide **decomposition** in the vessel during processing ...
The resolution of the original light **into** its component frequencies ...

Разложение по (*матем.*)

The expansion of the elastic energy density **in terms of** the strain invariants ...

Разложение соединения
The method involves **degrading the compound into** smaller compounds, breaking them down further, ...

Размазанный
The energy levels of the impurity atoms represent the discrete levels of single atoms or molecules as opposed to the **smeared-out** energy levels of a liquid or a solid.

Размельчать [*см. тж.* **Измельчённый в порошок**]
The grinding teeth serve **to break** the food **into finer particles.**

Размельчать в порошок
The gold-bearing quartz **is crushed to powder.**
Crude barite **is ground** (*or* **reduced**) (**to fine powder**).

Размельчать до
The ore **is crushed to** 6 in.

Размер [*см. тж.* **Аналогичного размера, Бесконечных размеров, Бывают разных размеров, Габариты увеличиваются, Доводить до заданного размера, Иметь размеры, Малых размеров, Меньше номинального размера, Нестандартных размеров, По размерам, Рассчитывать размеры, Точность размеров**]
Supertankers range **in size** from 350 M to 400 M bbl and more.
The device is small **in size.**
The new product is offered **in four sizes.**
The balloon basket is 3.5 ft **high by** 3 ft **wide by** 3.5 ft **long.**

Размер ... растёт
The continent **was growing in size.**

Размерность
K has **dimensions** of energy per Kelvin per mole.
P has **dimensionality** (mass) × $(\text{length})^{-1}$ $\times(\text{time})^{-2}$.

Размерный допуск
Dimensional tolerance.

Размером
Then the set *P* is a subset of R^S **of size** *c*.
These cameras are made **in sizes** down to 35 min.
Micron- and submicron-**sized** particles ...
For particles **of size** 1 micrometre the resulting speed would be ...

Размером с [*см. тж.* **Величиной с**]
Fragments **the size of** pebbles and cobbles litter the surface of ...
Boulders **as big as** a house ...
Sand-**sized** mineral grains ...

Размером с Луну
There are six other satellites in the solar system that **are Moon-sized** or a little larger.

Размеры
Most alluvial rivers have a yearly flood **of such proportions that** the water cannot any longer be contained within the channel.

Размеры атома
What we know about **atomic sizes** (*or* **dimensions**), ...

Размеры молекулы
The molecular dimensions (*or* **sizes**) **of** the organic solvent ...

Размеры ... составляют
The worktable **measures** 15 **by** 20 in.

Размеры уменьшаются
Today's warehouses **are shrinking in size.**

Разметочная синька
Apply a coat of **layout blue** to the work.

Разметочный стол
A marking-off (*or* **laying-out**) **table.**

Размечать
Locate and drill holes in the reinforcement plate.
The plate **is marked out** and cut to the required shape.

Размечать для сборки
All pieces **are match-marked for assembly** at their destination.

Размешивать
A paddle arrangement **stirs** the cement slurry.

Размещать I [*см. тж.* **В котором размещён**]
Only a limited number of detectors **can be accommodated in** an instrument.
The usual method is **to enclose** all circuits **in** a metal cabinet.
To accommodate all *N* electrons in the lowest available states, ...

Размещать II
The canal intake **must be located at** a point where ...

Размещаться [*см. тж.* **Помещаться**]
The engine controls **are housed in** a separate capsule.
The avionics-and-control van **houses** all communications and control equipment.
The installation **is sited** next to a railway line.

Размещение [*см. тж.* **Для размещения**]
To plan **the location of** factories, ...
Placement of loudspeakers ...
The siting of a power station ...
Positioning of the coil centre ...

Размещение объекта
This should reduce costs and greatly ease **siting** problems.

Размещён
The transmitters **were positioned at** various distances from ...
Electrical controls **are arranged on** a panel.

Размещённые заказы
There was a significant increase in **orders placed by** utility companies for new power reactors.

Размывать изображение
These electrons come to a focus at a slightly different point and **blur the image.**

Размыкать
A limit switch is fitted **to break** the primary circuit at ...
The switch **opens** the contactor.

Размыкаться
As the contacts begin **to move apart** (*or* **open**) the surface area that remains in contact begins to decrease.

Разница [*см.* **Различие, Расхождение между, С той только разницей, что**].

Разница должна быть устранена
Any **variation in** the width between different ring grooves **should be corrected.**

Разница между
The difference in tension between the tight and loose sides of a flat belt equals ...
The difference in the magnitude of the five coefficients ...
There is **a** significant **disparity** (*or* **difference,** *or* **divergence,** *or* **discrepancy**) **between** the grades of ...
Wide **variations in** life **between** circuits that have different functions ...
The distinction between heterogeneous and homogeneous mixtures is an arbitrary one.
As yet nobody has been able to produce direct evidence of any structural **difference among** cones.

Разновидность [*см. тж.* **Вариант**]
Emery is **a** greyish black **variety of** corundum containing ...
A new **version** (*or* **modification**) **of** a phosphate coating chemical ...
A variation of this method **is** to heat ...

Разногласие по поводу
There is some **disagreement on** the nature of the flow.

Разного цвета [*см.* **Бывает разного цвета от ... до**].

Разноимённые
Like magnetic poles repel and **unlike** magnetic poles attract.

Разнообразие [*см. тж.* **Большое разнообразие**]
Examples of **the** great **diversity of** available switching plans are shown in Fig. 1.
The enormous **variability in** vapour and particle content of the air ...
The variety of bands results from the variety of different electronic states that can be ...

Разнообразны [*см.* **Весьма разнообразны, Исключительно разнообразны**].

Разнообразные [*см. тж.* **Весьма разнообразные формы, Выполнять самые разнообразные функции, Самые разнообразные**]
Three general classes of stainless steel have been developed to provide such **varied** properties.

The many and **varied** observations of ...
This equation has many applications **in a variety of** fields.
The tool is capable of meeting **a variety of** requirements.
The use of boron has been patented for such **diversified** (*or* **diverse**) applications as in motor-starting devices, phonograph needles, ...
The development of a more **diversified** guidance system ...
The **diversified** organisms which roam the land ...
The DNA of viruses occurs in **a diversity of** molecular states.

Разнообразными способами
Molecules are emitted from the comet's nucleus **in a variety of fashions.**

Разнообразных размеров
Globules **of assorted sizes** are characteristic inclusions.

Разнородный
This thermoelectric engine is based on the temperature differential between **dissimilar** metal plates.

Разность между
The angular dispersion of a prism in the ratio of **the difference in** angular deviation of two rays ...
The difference of two terms ...

Разность потенциалов [*см. тж.* **Падение напряжения на, Создавать разность потенциалов**]
V_d is **the** total **voltage difference across** the junction.
The voltage drop across the capacitor ...

Разность температур
The temperature difference (*or* **drop,** *or* **differential,** *or* **gradient**) **across** the element ...

Разные [*см. тж.* **Неодинаковые**]
When two **dissimilar** solids are in contact, they...
Three **distinct** mineral species are represented by this group.

Разные знаки [*см.* **Противоположные по знаку**].

Разные пути
The same result may be obtained by **alternative** (*or* **different**) **pathways.**

Разный
Items of **dissimilar** material are stored in separate bins.

Разными способами
Boron nitride may be prepared **in a number** (*or* **variety**) **of ways.**

Разных размеров [*см.* **Бывают разных размеров**].

Разобранный [*см.* **В разобранном виде, Разбирать**].

Разового использования
Metal inert gas welding uses **consumable** electrodes.

Разогрев [*см.* **Прогрев**].

Разойтись [*см.* **Расходиться**].

Разомкнутая цепь [*см.* **Незамкнутая цепь**].

Разрабатываемый
Aircraft **under development** (*or* **being developed**) ...

Разрабатывать [*см. тж.* **Выводить закон, Конструировать, Проектировать, Создавать**]
Newton **elaborated** (*or* **worked out**) his own theory of gravitation.
In the second phase Kepler **set up** a theory for the longitudes of Mars.
When steel-making techniques **were discovered ...**
Several hardness scales **have been developed.**
This technique **was developed** (*or* **devised,** *or* **worked out,** *or* **evolved**) originally for metallurgy.
A tentative hypothesis **was devised.**
To draw up (*or* **elaborate,** *or* **develop,** *or* **work out,** *or* **map**) a plan (*or* a programme), ...
We **formulate** special compositions for ceramic bodies.
We **are working up** techniques for warm forging.

Разрабатывать в соответствии с индивидуальными потребностями
The firm **has custom engineered** a new processing system.

Разрабатывать метод
To devise a technique for measuring ...
New methods of energy conversion **are being devised.**
A method is currently being sought to induce vortex breakdown behind wide-bodied transport jets.

Разрабатывать методику
The general **procedure for** constructing the modes of ... **was laid down** in Section 13-5.

Разрабатывать на основе
A workshop instrument **has been developed from** the original design.

Разрабатывать проблему
He **is working on the use of** the system as an aid in ...

Разрабатывать теорию
To evolve (*or* **develop,** *or* **work out,** *or* **elaborate,** *or* **devise**) **a theory.**

Разрабатывать эксперимент
Experiments must be devised (*or* **worked out**) **to** test this suggestion.

Разрабатывать шахту
To work a mine.

Разрабатываться I
Doppler radar, laser anemometers, and acoustic detectors **have been developed for** measuring both the strength and the location of vortices.
Extra low-temperature enamels **are under development** (*or* **are being developed**).

Разрабатываться II
These petroleum resources **are** already **under development.**

Разработан [*см. тж.* **Недостаточно разработан**]
A variety of new experimental tests of gravitation theories **has been devised.**
This method **is due to** Landau.
The procedure **was worked up by** our firm.

Разработан в ... году
This classification **dates from** 1894.

Разработан по типу
The theory **is patterned after** QED.

Разработанный
No other system so far **devised** (*or* **developed,** *or* **elaborated**) can give such an effect.
The process **evolved by** them ...
An alternative method, **due to** Pauling, makes use of ...

Разработанный на основе
The machines **developed from** a smaller twin-wheel tool grinder ...
The instrument, **which stems from** the one designed for ...

Разработка [*см.* **Находиться в стадии разработки**]
The elaboration of a successful theory ...

Разрастаться в
Rapidly, this information **snowballed into** an enormous accumulation of details.
As a result the polyacrylamide **grows into** a complex web of interconnected loops and branches.

Разрез [*см. тж.* **В разрезе**]
A sectional view of a phonograph cutter is shown in Fig. 15.
Figure 3 **is a section through** the converter.

Разрезать на
The foil **was cut into** squares.

Разрешается
It is permissible to run mains and alarm leads in a single conduit.

Разрешать
The local legislature **authorized** the construction of the canal.

Разрешать вопрос (*задачу, проблему*) [*см. тж.* **Решать проблему**]
To resolve (*or* **solve**) **a problem.**
This **would settle** some vital **issues.**

Разрешать противоречие
The presence of deep-earth gas **could resolve this contradiction.**

Разрешать сомнение
Computer studies **may settle this doubt.**

Разрешать спор
Published experimental work **has resolved this controversy.**

Разрешение (*проблемы и т.п.*)

Blind nuts provide **a** simple **solution to** replacement of ...

Разрешённый [*см.* **Допустимый**].

Разрешимая проблема
A tractable problem.

Разрешить вопрос
Our laboratory may be capable of **laying this question to rest** (*or* **solving this question**).

Разрушать [*см. тж.* **Нарушать**]
Moderate earthquake motions **can collapse** (*or* **destroy**) walls and ...
Such tumours **are destructive to** adjacent tissues.
Only molten alkali metals and gaseous fluorine at high temperatures and pressures **attack** TFE resin.
The maximum stress applied **to rupture** the material is called ultimate stress.
Such forces of expansion **can break down** the strongest material.

Разрушать окружающую среду
To destroy the environment.

Разрушать связь (*хим.*)
This process **breaks** (*or* **ruptures**) one of the two carbon-carbon **bonds.**

Разрушаться
The atom **would collapse** on collision with the sphere.
Sudden forcing may cause the grinding wheel **to disintegrate.**
The material **will fail** if the load is applied and removed many times.
It was believed that titanium strip **would rupture in** drawing.

Разрушаться вследствие
A short compression member **may fail by** twisting of the section.
Rock **is broken up by** chemical action.

Разрушен
As the comet approached the earth **it was disrupted by** gravitational forces.

Разрушение [*см. тж.* **Испытывать до разрушения, Подвергаться механическому разрушению**]
Collapse of a crystal ...
The chemical weathering of these minerals involves **the disruption of** their structures.
High temperatures cause **disintegration of** the electrode material.
Breakage of rock **by** explosives.
The breakdown of the coating ...
Severe **damage to** homes was announced.
This would lead to **a** complete **shattering of** the oxygen atom.
Break-up, Degradation ...
Failure of walls or other effects of blast ...
Some **fracture of** the rock will occur.

Разрушение вследствие
Failure by local buckling or by twisting ...

Разрушившийся
The pieces of the **failed** part ...
Mechanically **degraded** rocks ...

Разрыв во времени между
There is no **time lag between** pressure and density changes.
The lapse of 30 **years between** invention and production of ...

Разрыв связей
The breaking (*or* **rupture,** *or* **disruption,** *or* **dissociation**) **of** hydrogen **bonds ...**

Разрывать на части
Reactions in which molecules **are torn** (*or* **pulled**) **apart** and new ones are assembled ...

Разрывать связи
To break (*or* **rupture,** *or* **disrupt**) **bonds in** complex proteins ...

Разрываться
The bond **may** finally **disrupt** (*or* **be disrupted**).

Разрывное усилие [*см.* **Находящийся под действием разрывного усилия**].

Разряжаться на
The capacitor **discharges into** the primary circuit.

Разумеется [*см.* **Излишне говорить, что; Само сабой разумеется, что**].

Разумно
This problem must be dealt with **intelligently.**
It **would be prudent** (*or* **reasonable,** *or* **proper**) **to** begin thinking now about ...

Разумно выбранный
A **judiciously chosen** spectral band ...

Разумно задать вопрос
A rational question at this point **is**: If so much is known about earthquakes, why cannot they be prevented?

Разумно предположить, что
The basalt is rich in calcium, and seawater contains less calcium, so that **it is reasonable** (*or* **it stands to reason**) **that** the seawater **would** take calcium out of the rock.
It is reasonable (*or* **appropriate**) **to suggest** (*or* **assume**) **that** this sequence may reflect ...

Разумное использование
Supplement evaporation **by judicious** (*or* **rational**) **use of** chemicals ...

Разумное существо
If there were any **sentient beings** on that planet, ...

Разумный
If **intelligent** feed-water treatment is exercised, ...
The **judicious** use of antidepressants is recommended.
This is an absurd idea for a particle but completely **rational for** trains of waves.
Such calculations provide **reasonable** explanations for the observed formation of ...
This is a **sound** statement.

Разупорядоченный (*антон.* **Упорядоченный**)
The lattice structure of glass **is** highly **disordered** (*anton.* **ordered**).

Разъедать [*см. тж.* **Корродировать**]
The aqueous solution of HF rapidly **attacks** glass and most metals.
A nail **will be eaten up** if dropped into an acid.

Разъединять
The quarks are bound so tightly that they **cannot be pried apart.**
To separate the molecules completely ...

Разъяснение [*см.* **Нуждаться в объяснении**].

Разъяснять
In that paper he **clarified** his ideas.
As **was made clear** (*or* **explained**) in the previous chapter, ...
I **will enlighten you upon** many features of ...

Ракета [*см.* **Установленный на ракете**].

Ракета для исследования Луны (Марса)
A lunar (Martian) probe.

Ракета на лазерной энергии
The system is **a laser-powered** spherical **rocket** whose payload is ...

Рамки [*см.* **В рамках, Выходить за рамки**].

Ранее
To study one-photon forbidden transitions to **hitherto** (*or* **previously**) inaccessible electronically excited molecular states, ...
The sources discussed **previously** (*or* **before**) ...

Ранний период [*см.* **В начале развития**].

Ранний этап [*см.* **На раннем этапе развития**].

Раньше [*см. тж.* **В прошлом, До, Значительно раньше, чем; Одно время**]
Previously (*or* **Formerly**) we said that ...

Раскалывать
Water freezing in a crack in the rock **will tend to split** the rock **apart.**

Раскалываться
Great stresses cause hard rock **to break apart.**

Раскладывать
The airship envelope **is spread out on** the floor of the hangar.

Раскручивание
This substance is known to serve in **unwinding** superhelical molecules.

Раскрывать
These sea shells **cannot be pried loose** when given warning.

Раскрывать возможности
This feature of laser-excited atomic fluorescence spectrometry **unveils its potential** as a trace element analytical technique.

Раскрывать природу молекулы
The results of these measurements **are a guide to the nature of** (*or* **reveal the nature of**) **the molecule.**

Раскрывать тайны материи
Our efforts **to unravel the secrets of matter ...**

Раскрытие
This phenomenon can be understood only by **untangling** the intricate relations among temperature, viscosity, and ...

Распад [*см. тж.* **При разложении**]
The tyrosine formed undergoes further **degradation** (*or* **breakdown,** *or* **disintegration**).

Распад кометы
Disruption (*or* **Break-up**) **of a comet.**

Распад на элементы
Bi_2S_3 is not very stable, and **decomposition to the elements** takes place slightly above 100°C.

Распадаться I [*см. тж.* **Разлагаться**]
The five *d* orbitals **break up into** two sets.
The gas has **to dissociate into** single atoms.
A χ-meson **decays** (*or* **breaks down**) **into** several charged particles.
These silicone fluids do not **decompose into** gums or tars.
Glucose **is broken down into** carbon dioxide and water with the release of energy.
The glucose-phosphate compound **breaks down** to pyruvic and acetic acids.
The crystal **broke into** three pieces.
The hydrogen molecules **are dissociated** (*or* **degraded**) **to** hydrogen atoms in the arc.
The substance of that star **disintegrated** and spread out into space.

Распадаться II
These graphs **fall into** two groups.

Распадаться с образованием
Samarium 147 **decays to yield** neodymium 143.

Расплываться
When a drop strikes a surface, it **spreads out.**

Расплывчатый
The term chromatin **is broad and indefinite.**

Располагать [*см. тж.* **Размещать**]
Mendeleev **arranged** the 63 known elements **in** eight groups.
Suppose a number of electrically charged particles **have been set out in** some definite configuration.
It remains only **to locate** pairs of Geiger counters.
It is desirable **to position** (*or* **locate,** *or* **accommodate,** *or* **place**) the atomizers so that ...
The order in which **we have listed** the sections in the table ...

Располагать в порядке трудности
The problems in the text **are graded in difficulty.**

Располагать в форме кольца *и т.п.*
We **arrange** many magnets **in a ring.**

Располагать далеко друг от друга
The two parts of the loop **are** as **widely separated** as possible.

Располагать информацией
If **information on ... is available, ...**

Располагать основными сведениями о
You **must know the basics of** flight before you venture aloft alone.

Располагать под небольшим углом к
The rolls **are slightly skewed with respect to** the longitudinal axis of the work.

Располагать последовательно
Several accelerators **are lined up** (*or* **arranged**) **in series.**

Располагаться [*см. тж.* **Находиться**]
The figure shows how these detergents **line up in** water.
How **are** subatomic particles **arranged within** the atom?
The waves **align themselves on** a straight line.
The molecules **are aligned so that** charged plates attract oppositely charged ends of the dipole.
Atomic *p* orbitals that **lie along** the molecular axis ...
The tanks **are arranged** (*or* **positioned,** *or* **located,** *or* **placed**) horizontally.
The anthracene data **fall on** a straight line.

Располагаться в виде
The regions of star formation **are arranged in** a spiral galaxy.

Располагаться в определённом порядке
The beads **fall into a certain order.**

Располагаться в том же порядке, что и
The transition lines **are ordered like** the expected components of a rotation-vibration band.

Располагаться в форме шестиугольника
The six carbon atoms **are arranged in a hexagon.**

Располагаться вокруг
Groups of atoms **are arranged about** the central carbon atom.

Располагаться группами
The species included in the tables **are arranged by groups.**

Располагаться на
Some of these bodies **took up** orbits around Saturn.

Располагаться над [*см.* **Над ... расположен**].

Расположен [*см. тж.* **В ... расположен, Находиться, Установлен**]
When installing the thermometer, the tip **should be arranged** (*or* **placed,** *or* **sited**) as near as possible to ...
Loudspeakers **are so disposed as to** give a three-dimensional effect.
Pollution sources **should** not **be located in** valleys.
The luminous reaction zone **occurs** very close to the solid surface.
The cabins **may be placed** (*or* **located,** *or* **sited**) near the mill.
The thermocouple **is positioned in** the outflow pipe.
The atomizers **are positioned to** apply a multi-colour finish.
The blade **is set at** right angles to the handle.
The screw **is situated at** the rear of the clamp.
The turns **are spaced** 1/8 in. **apart** (*or* **at** 1/8 in. **intervals**).
Four sets of burners **are patterned around** the inner periphery of each furnace section.
When atoms **are arranged in** a solid ...
Volcanic islands often **occur in** long, straight chains.
The boxes **are aligned** (*or* **arranged**) parallel to the optic axis of the telescope.

Расположен бесконечно далеко от
The apex of the cone **is infinitely distant from** the base.

Расположен в виде геометрической фигуры
The bonds **are arranged in a** symmetrical **geometric pattern.**

Расположен далеко от
This taxonomic group **is far removed from** the taxon to which the genus Escherichia belongs.

Расположен между
Intervening between the black bands **are** layers of bright or dull coal.

Расположен на
The fluidized bed **rests on** a travelling grate.

Расположен над [*см.* **Над ... расположен**].

Расположен под углом к
"Angular" means that the strata of one rock group **are set at an angle to** the strata of the other group.

Расположен таким образом, что
The liquid crystal molecules **are aligned with** their long axes parallel **to** the electrode surface.

Расположение [*см. тж.* **Важно только знать расположение, Взаимное расположение, Положение, Пространственное расположение**]
Diamagnetic anisotropy is dependent on **the alignment of** the molecule **in** the magnetic field.
When melting occurs **the** regular **arrangement in** the crystalline lattice becomes **the** random **array of** particles of the liquid.
The disposition of the dikes **in** the rock ...
The layout of material **in** the book ...
Engines differ **in the positioning** (*or* **arrangement**) **of** their cylinders.
The layout of the section is shown in Fig. 4.

Расположение ... вдоль и против направления
Lining up the nuclear moments **with and against** the magnetic field ...

Расположенные близко друг к другу
Electronic interactions may occur among **closely spaced** groups (*or* groups **located in close proximity**).

Расположенные в соответствующем порядке
The illusion of motion can be created by sequentially illuminating stationary objects of similar shape **arranged in an appropriate pattern.**

Расположенные далеко друг от друга
Specially designed equipment has been set up in two **widely separated** (*or* **spaced**) locations.

Расположенные друг на друге
There are actually three spectra **on top of one another.**

Расположенные на равном расстоянии (друг от друга)
A series of **regularly** (*or* **equally,** *or* **evenly**) **spaced** lines ...

Расположенные на расстоянии ... друг от друга [*см. тж.* **На расстоянии ... друг от друга**].
The computers actuate transformers and solid-state switches **positioned at** one-mile **intervals** along the guideway.
Conducting brushes **are spaced at intervals of** ... cm.

Расположенные по обе стороны
The cromaffin masses **disposed bilaterally along** the dorsal aorta ... (*biol.*).

Расположенные последовательно
An assembly of two cushions **in tandem** is designated *"CC"*.
The cooler consisted of two shell-and-tube units **in series.**

Расположенный [*см. тж.* **Атомы, расположенные в узлах; Беспорядочно расположенные, Находящийся**]
The furnace consists of several hearths **arrange**d (*or* **positioned,** *or* **situated,** *or* **located,** *or* **placed**) one above the other.
The roof sprays consist of three rows of 14 nozzles **disposed** along the length of the building.
Ultrasonic energy is obtained from a generator **housed in** the base.

Расположенный в центре
Each flagellum consists of a circle of paired microtubules surrounding one **centrally located** pair.

Расположенный вблизи [*см.* **Близко расположенный, Близлежащий**].

Расположенный далеко [*см.* **Далеко расположенный**].

Расположенный дальше от
The choice is more limited for dyes **farther away from** the centre of the visible region.

Расположенный на далёком расстоянии
A **remotely located** command station ...

Расположенный поблизости [*см. тж.* **Близко расположенный, Близлежащий**]
Reflections occur from lenses, **nearby** instruments, and so on.

Расположенный рядом с
The hydrogen atom **adjacent to** the carbonyl group ...

Расположены близко друг к другу
The housing for the photomultiplier and the lamp **should be close together** (*or* **to each other**) (*or* **closely spaced**).

Расположены близко или далеко друг от друга
The boards **are spaced closely and widely.**
The anodes and cathodes **could be close together or far apart.**

Расположены в виде
The hydroxyl ions **are arranged to form** (*or* **in the form of**) a tetrahedron.

Расположены в виде кольца
A compound in which six carbons **are arranged in a ring ...**

Расположены далеко друг от друга
The atoms **are far apart (from each other).**

Расположены на ... расстоянии друг от друга
Identically oriented antennas **are separated** (*or* **spaced at**) 500 ft (*or* **are** 500 ft **apart**).

Расположены параллельно (друг другу)
The optic axes of the binocular halves **must be (aligned) parallel (to each other).**

Расположены по обе стороны
The chromaffin masses **are disposed bilaterally along** the dorsal aorta and ...

Расположены через промежутки в [*см. тж.* **На расстоянии, Расположены на расстоянии ... друг от друга**]
The repeater stations **are located at intervals of** 165 miles.

Распределение по I
The distribution of the molecules **throughout** the available energy levels ...
The radial **distribution of** bound-ray power **over** the core cross section .:.

Распределение по II
The distribution of coal **by** rank, geologic age, and district ...

Распределение по высоте
The distribution of electrons **with height** can thus be measured.

Распределение по размерам
The size distribution of the oil fields ...

Распределение по сезонам
The distribution of water **from season to season ...**

Распределение по уровням
The distribution of gas molecules **over** (*or* **throughout) the** energy **levels ...**

Распределение пор по размерам
Pore-size distribution.

Распределение ресурсов
The allocation of resources.

Распределённый среди
The positive ions uniformly **distributed among** the negative ones ...

Распределять
Special equipment **to spread** the load **among** the three phases of a power line ...
To distribute the load uniformly **over** the entire area of ...

Распределять между
The available water **is allocated to** those who need it most.

Распределяться между
Light power **is distributed among(st)** all bound **and** leaky rays.

Распродан [*см. тж.* **Имеется** (*антон.* **Нет**) **в продаже**]
The edition soon **went out of print.**
The book **is out of print.**

Распространение
Resistance to crack **propagation ...**
The propagation of radio waves.
To prevent **the transmission of** vibration, ...

Распространение информации
Our aims are collection and **dissemination of information on ...**

Распространение на [*см.* **Обобщение на**].

Распространение света
The propagation of light.

Распространены по всему миру
These environments **are distributed throughout the world.**
These mollusks **are world-wide in their distribution** (*or* **are distributed worldwide,** *or* **throughout the world**).

Распространён [*см.* **Наиболее распространён**].

Распространён среди
This disease **is common in** elderly women.

Распространённость
The incidence of mental disorders in the U.S.A. is hard to assess.

Распространённость в земной коре
Both metals have roughly the same **crustal abundance.**
The abundance (*or* **The occurrence**) **of** this element **in the Earth's crust ...**

Распространённость в природе
The natural occurrence of boron ...

Распространённость во всём мире
The global abundance of uranium ...

Распространённость на земле
The terrestrial (natural) abundance of deuterium **is** 1 part in 6700 parts of ordinary hydrogen.

Распространённый [*см. тж.* **Наиболее распространённый, Широкораспространённый среди**]
Naturally occurring carbonates **are the most abundant of** the calcium minerals.
One **popular** error is to regard the absolute zero as ...

Распространённый во всём мире
This is an extinct group of Cambrian organisms **with world-wide distribution.**

Распространять
The Office **will distribute** a list of authors among ...

Распространять на
The qualitative conclusions regarding ... **can be carried over** (*or* **extended**) **to** liquids and solids.
All attempts **to extend** the approach **to** atoms with more than one electron were unsuccessful.
We **can extend** this model **to** a broad spectrum of covalent species.
The summation **should be extended over** the possible combinations of arguments.
This enables the results **to be extended to cover** (*or* **include**) the finite currents.
Within the past ten years the use of seismic survey methods **has been extended into** the field of ...

Распространяться [*см. тж.* **Проходить через, Свет распространяется со скоростью**]
The waves **would propagate** (*or* **progress**) downward.
Strain energy **is propagated through** the rocks.
The crack **propagated** at a high rate.
Each end of the crack is drilled so that the crack **will** not **spread.**
The flame **travels** forward.
The two rays of light **travel** at different velocities.
The shock wave **travels** (*or* **is propagated**) **through** the ground.
Solar radiation **streams out** in all directions from the Sun.

Распространяться волнообразно
Light **travels in waves.**

Распространяться на I
The rate at which the flame **advances into** the combustible mixture ...
Practical applications of the method **are expanding to** other casting fields.
The atmosphere **extends for** about 200 miles above the surface of the Earth.

Распространяться на II
The term "chilled iron" **spreads to** the part-white, part-grey types of cast iron.
This requirement does not **cover** (*or* **extend to**) bacterial spores.
The guarantee **cannot be extended to** cases of mechanical damage.

Распространяться на большие расстояния
The wave **runs to great distances.**

Распространяться на ... километров
These disturbances **may extend for** many **kilometres from** the airplane.

Распространяться по всему
The disturbance **extends over the whole** space.
Devonian reefs **ranged across** central Europe and ...

Распространяться по поверхности воды
Ripples caused by a stone dropped into water **travel out** in all directions **over the surface of the water.**

Распространяться через
As the optical signal **traverses** the sample, ...

Распространяющийся в воздухе
Air-borne sound ...

Рассеивать ... в форме тепла
The eddies **dissipate** their mechanical energy **as heat.**

Рассеивать страх
Even the economic revival did not **dispel this fear.**

Рассеивать тепло
Fluorocarbon resins do not rapidly absorb and **dissipate heat** generated in cutting.

Рассеиваться
Because the heat **cannot be dissipated to** the surroundings, ...
An X-ray beam **is scattered by** (*or* **from**) **the sample.**

Рассеиваться на ... угол
The electrons **may be scattered through** large **angles.**

Рассечён
If a right circular cone **is sliced by** a plane parallel to its base, ...

Рассеяние вперёд
Forward scattering of particles ...

Рассеяние на
X-ray **scattering by** (*or* **from**) electrons ...

Рассеяние частицами (*или* **на частицах)**
The **scattering of** light **by** (*or* **from**) **the particles ...**

Рассеяние энергии на трение *и т.п.*
It is impossible to eliminate completely all **energy dissipation through friction.**

Рассеянный на
Secondary electrons **scattered from** (*or* **by**) the quartz are collected at ...

Рассматриваемый [*см. тж.* **В рассматриваемом случае, В рассматриваемый период, Изучаемый, Интересующий нас, Исследуемый**]
In the range **covered** the curves are in good agreement with experiment.
The device is best suited to the problem **in** (*or* **at**) **hand** [*or* **(being) considered** (*or* **studied,** *or* **investigated**)].
This quantity can be obtained from the phase diagram of the system **involved** (*or* **of interest**).
The range **under consideration** (*or* **in question,** *or* **under review,** *or* **under examination,** *or* **under investigation,** *or* **under study,** or **under discussion**) ...

Рассматриваемый ниже
These processes employ one or more of the steps **discussed below.**

Рассматривать I [*см. тж.* **Изучать, Исследовать, Обсуждать**]
We **shall cover** these compounds in the next chapter.
Here we **examine** the combined effect of ...
We **shall deal with** this subject in the next chapter.
To fully appreciate the significance of these data, each aspect of the genetical processes **must** first **be scrutinized.**
The question **could be approached from** two angles.
In this paper **we will** not **concern ourselves with** those problems.
We **have considered** this problem carefully.
Mechanics **treats of** the action of forces and their effect.
Since subtraction is the same process as addition, subtraction **is** not **treated** separately here.
We **will** now **look at** the basic principles used in fluid logic.
Let us **take a look at** the individual components of ...
The formation and properties of shock waves **will be discussed in** the following chapter.
The effect of these differences on ... **will be covered** later.
At the moment enzyme catalysis forms a separate subject; we **shall** not **take it up** here.
The next section **takes care of** Case 1.
The durability of the material **must be viewed** from two standpoints — the mechanical and the electrical.

Рассматривать II
When an object **is viewed with** both eyes, it looks like ...

Рассматривать III
This series **can be considered** a result of the substitution of ...
Then luminiferous ether **could be viewed as** an exceedingly subtle gas.

Рассматривать более внимательно
We **will** first **look more closely at** the mechanical weathering processes.

Рассматривать в микроскоп
If a colloidal dispersion **is viewed through a microscope, ...**

Рассматривать довольно подробно
In the preceding chapters we **considered at some length** (*or* **in some detail**) the materials of ...

Рассматривать как
A ton **can be considered as** a unit of volume.
Some scientists **look (up)on** matter **as being** concentrated energy.
The photons **can be thought of as** a wave with ...
The shock front constitutes a sufficiently sharp transition **to be regarded** (*or* **viewed**) **as** a mathematical discontinuity.
We **take it as** convincing evidence that single heavy atoms are ...
The ions in certain salts **may** not **be treated as** hard spheres.
These trajectories **are seen as** the shortest paths that ...
The theory **treats** these forces **as** different manifestations of ...

Рассматривать как будто бы он
The small increases in pressure **can be treated as if** they obeyed the acoustic approximation.
The motion of the piston **may be thought of as** divided into a number of moments.

Рассматривать по-новому
Since the confirmation of Einstein's General Theory of Relativity, physicists **have taken a new view of** gravitation.

Рассматривать с точки зрения
A crystal **can be inspected for** elements of symmetry.

Рассматриваться I [*см. тж.* **Рассматривать, Считаться**]
An isolated hydrogen atom **can be treated as** a composite boson.
This force **can be considered as** a spring force.
The problem of the nature of the real-number line **is viewed** quite differently by adherents to ...

Рассматриваться II [*см. тж.* **Обсуждаться**]
The previous chapter **discussed** (*or* **was concerned with**) perturbations due to ...
These questions **are the concern of** the present chapter.
This subject **will be dealt with** (*or* **taken up**) **in** the next chapter.
Consideration is being given to the use of shapes other than ...
Abrasive wear **was treated** (*or* **considered,** *or* **discussed**) **in** two papers.
This branch of science **treats of** the motion of air.
Simultaneous diffusion and chemical reaction **is the subject of** Chapter 8.

Рассматриваться как
This **is considered** a convenient range.
Infrared radiation **is** commonly **thought of** (*or* **regarded,** *or* **considered**) as "heat".
Pollutants **are seen as** one small part of the total.
Water vapour **can be treated as** an ideal gas.
The laser **can be viewed as** a problem-solving tool for atomic fluorescence spectrometry.
Electrons **are** often **visualized as** small loops.

Рассматриваться подробнее
This subject **is pursued further** in Chapter 17.

Рассмотрен
Optical methods **will be dealt with** first.

Рассмотрен достаточно подробно
This matter **has been given adequate consideration.**

Рассмотрение [*см. тж.* **Внимательное рассмотрение, Из внимательного рассмотрения ... видно, что; Ознакомление, При внимательном рассмотрении**]
For **a consideration of** the nature of plastic sulphur, see p. 316.
Further **inspection** (*or* **examination**) **of** Fig. 1 discloses that ...
We must now subject the concept of equivalent weight to **a** somewhat closer **scrutiny.**
Any theoretical **treatment** (*or* **consideration**) **of** the problem is complicated.

Рассмотренный выше
The apparatus **discussed above** has formed the basis of ...

Рассмотреть более тщательно
In such cases it would be a good idea **to take a second look at** the whole corrosion problem.

Рассмотреть возможность использования
It is often advisable **to consider** an abrasion-resisting steel.

Рассмотрим [*см. тж.* **Обсу́дим**]
(We) consider (*or* **Let us consider**) such loops where ...

Расстояние [*см. тж.* **Выдерживать интервал, На близком расстоянии от, На значительном расстоянии от, На некоторое расстояние, На расстоянии, Находиться на расстоянии, Покрывать расстояние, Связь на больших расстояниях**]
m is the mass of the particle and *r* is **its distance from** the axis of rotation.
The mean **distance of** the planet **to** the Sun ...
The distance of the image plane **from** the exit pupil ...

The mean **separation** (*or* **spacing**) **between** atoms increases beyond the static equilibrium distance.
To measure **the separation of** one star **from** another, ...

Расстояние до
The photographer must estimate **the distance to** his object.
Distant galaxies appear to be receding from us at a rate proportional to **their distance.**

Расстояние между
The spacing of (*or* **between**) various electronic levels ...
The separation between neighbouring atomic structural units ...

Расстояние между атомами
The interatomic distance.

Расстояние между выступами и впадинами на поверхности
The peak-to-valley distance of the finished workpiece ...

Расстояние между Землёй и кометой
The Earth-comet distance (*or* **The distance between the Earth and the comet**).

Расстояние между зубьями
Variations in **tooth spacing ...**

Расстояние между ионами (атомами, ядрами, молекулами)
The interionic (-atomic, -nuclear, -molecular) spacing.

Расстояние между молекулами
The molecular separation (*or* **The intermolecular distance**).

Расстояние между обкладками конденсатора
The voltage breakdown value for **a** given **plate spacing ...**

Расстояние между осями
The interaxial distance.

Расстояние между центрами
Flat belts may be used to transmit power between pulleys whose **centre distance is** as much as 30 ft.
With diameters D_1 and D_2 of the pulleys and their **centre distances** known the length of the belts can be calculated.
The centre-to-centre distance of the lathe must be ...

Расстояние между электродами
The electrode separation (*or* **The interelectrode distance**).

Расстояние между ядрами
Internuclear separation (*or* **spacing,** *or* **distance**).

Расстояние, на которое перемещается
The work involved is the force times **the distance that** the charge **is moved.**

Расстояние, на которое поворачивается вал
The distance the engine shaft turns ...

Расстояние от выступа до впадины
Peak-to-valley measurements are obtained by fitting a double prism objective lens to the microscope.

Расстояние от Солнца
This exponent does not vary with **solar distance.**

Расстояние по воздуху между ... и
The air distance between Boston **and** San Francisco is 4.33 megameters.

Расстояние по радиусу
Let r be **the radial distance from** the centre of the sphere.

Рассуждать
His reasoning is as follows (*он рассуждает следующим образом*).

Рассуждая таким образом, пришли к выводу о том, что
Using this line of reasoning, the age of the Earth was placed at 100 million years.

Рассуждение [*см. тж.* **Аналогичные рассуждения приводят к выводу о том, что**]
Simple physical **reasoning** provides the necessary insight.
By a more complicated **argument** we may show that ...

Рассуждения, лежащие в основе
The reasoning behind his proposal is as follows: ...

Рассчитан на

The first superconductivity systems **will be tailored for** metropolitan areas where ...
This power supply system **is designed for** steady loads.
The instrument **is designed to** operate with a minimum input.
These methods **are intended** (*or* **meant**) **for** performance evaluation of spectrometers.
The compressor **is rated at** 26 tons refrigeration.
The reducer **is rated at** 154 hp and 75 rpm.
The riveter **accepts** rivets up to 3/32-in. diameter, 5/16 maximum length.
Very little strength **can be built into** spade drills.
The cabin **is configured for** four seats.
The lamp **is rated for operation at** 12 volts.

Рассчитан на обработку
The machine **is built to accommodate** huge workpieces.

Рассчитан на работу под давлением
The absorber **is designed to be operated at** 470 psig.

Рассчитанный на
The installation consists of 40 capacitors **rated at** 20,000 volts.

Рассчитанный с помощью ЭВМ
A **computer-calculated** cycle time ...

Рассчитывать
Work out (*or* **Calculate**) the amount of angular momentum which the solar nebula must have had.

Рассчитывать на
Writing this book proved a tougher task than I **had bargained for** (*or* **expected,** *or* **anticipated**).
Alkaloids are complex organic amines, so the chemist **can count** (*or* **rely**) **on** their ability to form salts with acids ...

Рассчитывать размеры
The foam segments **are sized** (*or* **dimensioned**) **to** pass through an 18-in. diameter manhole.

Рассчитывать с запасом
The gauges **are conservatively rated.**

Рассчитывать таким образом, чтобы
The design **must be such as to** permit the casting to be ejected from the mould cavity.
The trajectory **was devised (so as) to** bring the spacecraft closer to ...

Рассыпаться в порошок
In extreme cases, the glass **may collapse into powder.**

Растачивать под
The housing **is bored to receive** a thrust bearing.

Раствор [*см.* **В растворе, Переходить в раствор**].

Растворение [*см.* **При растворении**].

Растворимость в воде
Water solubility.

Растворимый в
Such cadmium **is soluble in** sulphuric acid.

Растворимый в воде
One end of the molecule **is hydrophilic** (*or* **water soluble,** *or* **soluble in water**).

Растворимый в жирах
Fat soluble.

Растворитель
Acetone is used as **a solvent for** cellulose ether.

Растворяться [*см. тж.* **Плохо растворяющийся**]
Gold and silver **dissolve in** this solution.
Acids that **are dissolved in** water are represented as ...

Растворяться с образованием
Carbon dioxide gas **dissolves in** water **to form** a weak acid.

Растёт беспокойство относительно
Within recent years **concerns have been growing with respect to** the quality of the water we drink.

Растёт убеждение в том, что
The belief is growing that recently formed stars ...

Расти [*см. тж.* **Нарастать, Увеличиваться**]
The energy in the laser cavity **is** first **built up** and then decays.
The light wave **grows in** amplitude (*амплитуда световой волны растёт*).

Растительное вещество
Fossilized tree trunks and other **vegetal** matter ...

Растительный
In early societies, covalent compounds for medicines, etc., were usually obtained from **plant** (*or* **vegetative**) or animal sources.

Растительный и животный мир
All **plant and animal life is** composed of complex organic compounds.

Растительный покров
Soil condition depends on **vegetative cover** and ...

Расточка резцом
On large holes **single-point boring** gives the best accuracy.

Растущий [*см.* **Всё больше (и больше)**].

Растягивать
The increasing load **stretches** the wire rope **by** several feet.

Растяжение и сжатие пружины
On **stretching** (*or* **extending**) **and compressing the spring ...**

Растянутая шкала
The **stretched-out** (*or* **extended**) time **scale.**

Расход устанавливается на таком уровне, при котором
The flow of gas *A* **is set at a rate which** does not disturb the velocity profile of the flowing gas *B*.

Расход энергии [*см. тж.* **С большой затратой энергии**]
This device will provide more gain at higher frequencies with less **power supply drain.**
Expenditure (*or* **Consumption**) **of energy.**

Расходиться [*см. тж.* **Отличаться, Разделяться**]
When stresses are exerted upon jointed rock, the rock **comes apart** rather readily along these planes.
When the rolls **were separated by** this distance ...
If new oceanic lithosphere is being formed and the plates **are moving apart, ...**

Расходиться во мнениях о том
The geologists **disagree on** (*or* **about**) how these movements have taken place.
There is (some) disagreement [*or* **no consensus (of opinion)**] **among** geologists **on the question of** why ...

Расходиться на большое расстояние
Here the curve portions **become widely separated.**

Расходиться от
Other cracks **radiate outward from** the centre.

Расходиться с [*см. тж.* **Отличаться**]
The densities **disagreed with** those obtained from the shock velocity.
This **is at variance with** current experience.
This is inconsistent with the data of Run No. 9.
Theoretical predictions **have failed to agree with** experiment.

Расходовать [*см. тж.* **Затрачивать энергию**]
In the future, more companies **will lay out** money for automation.

Расходоваться [*см.* **Использоваться**].

Расходуемый
Routine maintenance is mainly limited to the replacement of **expendable** items, for example, the chart and recorder ink.

Расходы [*см.* **Идти на расходы по, Не останавливаться перед затратами, Оправдывать расходы, Покрывать расходы на**].

Расхождение во мнениях относительно
The present **diversity of opinion regarding ...**

Расхождение между [*см. тж.* **Разница между**]
The main **discrepancy between** the predicted and experimental value is due to friction in the fluid.
There is **a** significant **disparity** (*or* **difference**) **between** the grade of the ore being currently mined **and** the grade of the total ore reserves.
A gap between estimated **and** observed ultraviolet radiation ...

Discordance between the observed **and** computed positions of the Moon ...

Расхождение с

Such apparent **disagreement with** the theory does not mean that ...

Расцвечен

The three input leads **are colour-coded** green, grey and black.
Busbars **are marked** — red, white, blue and black.

Расчёт [*см. тж.* **Алгебраические выкладки, Математические выкладки, С таким расчётом, чтобы**]

Calculation of a boiler.
Chemical reactor **design.**
The reckoning of future positions of the vessel by means of this speed ...

Расчёт размеров

Dimensioning (*or* **Sizing**) **of** electronic component parts.

Расчётный

The **design** (*or* **rated**) temperature **for** the heating system is 65°F.
The voltage **rating is** 600 V.

Расчёты

The machine performs **computations** (*or* **calculations**) **for** navigation.

Расширение и сжатие газов

The expansion and compression of gases.

Расширение производственной площади

An enlargement of floor area.

Расширение технологических возможностей станка

Widening the scope of working of the machine.

Расширенный

A bell is closed at one end and **flared** at the other.

Расширенный (*антон.* **Суженный**) **участок трубы**

An expanded (*anton.* **A contracted**) **section of a tube.**

Расширенный вариант

An extended version, often called Cauchy's formula, **is ...**

Расширилось применение

The use of engineering plastics **has expanded** rapidly over the last 15 years.

Расширять

When Maxwell's equations of electromagnetism **are augmented to include** magnetic charges and magnetic currents, ...
The tape processing systems **may be augmented by** the use of disk storage devices.
To expand the nuclear industry, ...
This **extends** the useful working range of ...
The plant **was being enlarged** (*or* **expanded**) **to include** full gasoline-plant facilities.
The investigations **will be** considerably **extended.**
The slot **was widened by** filing.
The caisson bottom **may be belled up to** 30 ft in diameter.

Расширять возможности

When the development of improved materials **extends** (*or* **enhances**) the capabilities of titanium carbide tools, ...

Расширять диапазон

To extend the range of the instruments ...

Расширять шкалу прибора

To increase the precision of absorption measurements **by expanding the scale of the instrument, ...**

Расширяться

A salinometer **bulges out to** a fairly large diameter.
The combustion products **expand to** produce power.
The gas **is expanded** isothermally.

Расширяться и сжиматься

The metal **expanded and contracted with** temperature changes.
If the gas **expands, ..., and** if it **is compressed, ...**

Расщепление подуровней

Further **splitting of sublevels** will be discussed later.

Расщепление связей (*хим.*)

Cleavage of the silicon-carbon **bonds ...**

Расщепление спектральных линий

Splitting of spectral lines.

Расщеплять на

The enzyme **splits** the glucose molecule **into** two molecules of pyruvic acid.

Расщеплять связь (*хим.*)
To cleave a bond.

Расщепляться на
The original lines of the spectra **were split into** two or more lines.

Рациональное зерно [*см.* **В этом что-то есть**].

Рациональный [*см. тж.* **Разумный**]
A **sound** (*or* **rational**) theory was formulated.

Рваное отверстие
Punching causes **ragged holes.**

Реагировать I [*см. тж.* **Охотно реагировать с, Полностью прореагировать**]
Hydrazine does not **react** (*or* **interact**) **with** oxygen under such conditions.

Реагировать II
The servo system **responds to** the difference between ...
This emulsion **responds** (*or* **is responsive**) chiefly **to** green light.
The other interlock **responds to** the slightest horizontal movement of the beam.
Specialized taste receptors **are responsive to** water-soluble chemicals.

Реагировать с образованием
Hydrogen from the solar wind and carbon from the solar wind **can react to form** (*or* **produce**) methane.

Реагирующее вещество
The initial **reactants** (*or* **reacting substances,** *or* **reagents**) **are** hydrogen and light nuclei.

Реагирующий на
The hadrons are the only particles **responsive** (*or* **reacting**) **to** the strong force.

Реактивный по отношению к
White phosphorus **is** so **reactive toward** air that it should be stored under water.

Реакция I [*см. тж.* **Бурная реакция, Бурно реагировать с, Быстрая реакция, Интенсивность реакции, Основная реакция, Осуществлять реакцию, По реакции, Проведение реакции между, Проводить реакцию, Путём реакции, Скорость реакции**]
A large portion of **the reaction proceeds** (*or* **takes place,** *or* **occurs**) **in** the bulk phase.
The reaction proceeds vigorously.

Реакция II [*см. тж.* **В качестве реакции на**]
The response of the reactor **to** an increase in reactivity ...
Chemoreception is **the response of** most organisms **to** a change in their chemical environment.

Реакция даёт [*см. тж.* **В результате реакции образуется**]
In this **reaction** only one organic product **results.**

Реакция идёт
The reaction proceeds (*or* **occurs,** *or* **takes place**) until ...

Реакция идёт до конца
The reaction goes (*or* **proceeds**) **to completion.**

Реакция идёт направо
The reaction goes towards the right.

Реакция между
The reaction of hydrogen **and** (*or* **with**) bromine ...
A product of **a reaction between** ammonia **and** various acids ...

Реакция на
The response of living organisms **to** physical forces ...
Structural damage may result from **a** structure's **response to** the vibration.

Реакция на лакмус
The solution shows **a** neutral **reaction toward litmus.**

Реакция, обратная
The reverse of the addition **is an** elimination **reaction.**

Реакция, представляющая интерес для химиков
A reaction of chemical interest.

Реакция продвигается настолько, что
Let us assume that **the reaction proceeds by an amount that** produces a great change in ...

Реакция с
The reaction of potassium amalgam **with** (*or* **and**) anhydrous $AlCl_3$.

Реализоваться
Stage efficiencies close to unity **can be realized** (*or* **achieved**).
If such conditions **are realized, ...**

Реалистичный [*см.* **Отражать действительность, Правдоподобный**].

Реальное ощущение полёта
The space-shuttle simulator creates **a true sensation of flight.**

Реальные условия [*см.* **В реальных условиях**].

Реальный
Let us see how this is related to **actual** experimental conditions.
A discussion of major forms of **actual** electrical communication systems ...

Ребристая конструкция
The finned design of the water tubes ...

Ребро [*см.* **Снабжён рёбрами**].

Регистрация [*см.* **Вести записи**].

Регистрировать [*см. тж.* **Вести записи**]
Keep a record of the variation of the room temperature.
It is planned **to register** (*or* **record**) the results on sensitive instruments.
The solution level **was followed by** instruments.
The thickness of the coils **was recorded from** a contact micrometer.

Регулирование
Water is of critical importance in **controlling** body temperature.
Monitoring of the reaction so that the alkene alone can be isolated ...

Регулирование по высоте [*см. тж.* **Можно регулировать высоту**]
Height adjustment of the fixtures ...

Регулировать [*см. тж.* **Можно регулировать высоту, Осуществлять управление**]
Pressures **were adjusted to** obtain the same flow rate throughout.
The knob **controls** (*or* **governs**) the volume of combustion air.
The adjustable filters **control** the colour of the light.
The temperature **is** carefully **regulated**.

Регулироваться пирометром
All heaters **are pyrometer controlled.**

Регулируемый диффузией
The deposition of cadmium on the mercury surface **is diffusion controlled.**

Регулирующий
The laws **governing** the arrangement of atoms in molecules ...

Регулярно
Vehicles should be cleaned **at regular intervals.**

Редкий
Stable atomic hydrogen **is** by no means **scarce** in the universe as a whole.

Редко бывает, чтобы
It is rare for one reaction **to occur** (*or* **It is seldom that** one reaction **should occur**) to the total exclusion of the others.

Редко встречаться [*см. тж.* **Встречаться очень редко**]
Rings of seven or more members, though comparatively **uncommon,** are well established.
These minerals **are rare in occurrence.**
Natural streamcuts **are few and far between.**
Such rock masses **are a rarity in nature.**

Редко, если вообще когда-л.
Dolomite **is seldom if ever** precipitated directly from seawater.

Редко случаться
Fire **is of infrequent occurrence** (*or* **is rare,** *or* **rarely occurs**) on the major deserts.
This **is seldom the case.**

Реже всего [*см.* **Наиболее редко**].

Реже встречаться
Aragonite **is less common** (*or* **less abundant**) [*or* **occurs** (*or* **is encountered**) **more rarely**] **than** calcite.

Режим [*см. тж.* **В жёстких условиях, Вводить в режим**]
The oscillator **behaviour was** described by ...
The operating conditions of the boiler ...
Under d-c **operation** the grid is negative.

The flow is within **the** turbulent **regime.**
He is active in the field of lunar and interplanetary flight **regimes.**
An opportunity for studying grass and forest **regimes** alongside one another.
A high-protein, limited carbohydrate, and plenty of water **regimen** is prescribed.

Режим работы
The mode of operation [*or* **The operating condition** (*or* **mode**)] **of** each machine is identified for each element.

Режим смазки
Relubrication intervals.

Резание [*см.* **Глубина резания**].

Резать на [*см.* **Разрезать на**].

Резать по шаблону
Slabs **are cut to templates.**

Резать точно по заданной ширине
The material **can be cut to the exact required width.**

Резервный
The chemist now has an **alternate** means at his disposal for speeding up reactions.

Резкие колебания
The widest swings in annual precipitation from year to year occur in ...

Резкие колебания температуры
Adhesive joints in service may be subjected to a number of deteriorating influences such as weathering, **temperature extremes** (*or* **wide fluctuations in temperature**), or chemical fluids.

Резкие отличия
Nonetheless, **sharp distinctions** do exist.

Резкий
The wood has been subjected to **pronounced** (*or* **drastic,** *or* **dramatic,** *or* **abrupt,** *or* **sharp**) humidity changes.
The **steep** rise in the cost of coal ...
A conventional enamel can withstand a **sudden** temperature change without failure.

Резкий поворот
The discovery that interferon is induced by double-strand RNA provided **a (major) breakthrough in** the understanding of interferon induction by viruses.

Резкий скачок (*матем.*)
As x changes gradually, y must either change gradually, or not at all; **abrupt jumps** are forbidden.

Резко
Permeability fluctuates **drastically** (*or* **dramatically,** *or* **sharply**).
These loading conditions differ **markedly** (*or* **sharply,** *or* **widely**) from the test conditions.
The heat capacity changes **abruptly.**
Jupiter's great mass **dramatically** increases the velocity of incoming objects.

Резко возрастать
The potential energy **rises steeply** (*or* **sharply**).

Резко выделяющийся
These lines, especially a **prominent** yellow line, were found in the spectrum of ...

Резко выраженный
The **marked** dependence of the structure on ...
These copolymers have a less **pronounced** block structure.
In this area very slight changes of temperature cause **sharply defined** changes in the resistance of ...

Резко изменяться
The mass velocities **change drastically** through the column.
The treatment of mental illness in the U.S. **has changed profoundly in** the past 30 years.
The situation **changed abruptly** with the developments in nuclear physics and...
The extent of adherence **varies widely.**

Резко обозначенный [*см. тж.* **Чётко обозначенный**]
The smallest details of the ridges and valleys **are sharply outlined** (*or* **defined**).
The berm usually has **a well-defined** edge.

Резко обрываться
Several geosynclinal belts **end** (*or* **terminate**) **abruptly.**

Резко останавливаться
The eruption **came to an abrupt halt** (*or* **halted abruptly**).

Резко отличаться

These phenomena **differ markedly** (*or* **sharply,** *or* **greatly,** *or* **drastically**) **from** supersonic flow.
The two types of engines **differ widely in** their combustion requirements.
The properties of many carbohydrates **differ enormously** (*or* **vastly**) from one substance to another.

Резко отличаться друг от друга
The nonhistone proteins **showed marked distinctions** (*or* **differed widely**).

Резко отличаться от
These larvae **differ radically** (*or* **widely**) **in** appearance **from** their parents by having no wings.
This behaviour **contrasts with** (*or* **is distinctly different from**) that of carbon monoxide.
The Sun's chemical composition **is in marked contrast to** that of the innermost planets.

Резко поворачивать вниз
Here, the intestine **takes a sharp downward turn.**

Резко поворачивать налево (направо)
The band **makes a sharp left (right) turn.**

Резко прекращаться
At this point the surface laser action **abruptly ceases.**

Резко сокращать
The drug **drastically reduced** the digestive system's secretion of acid and pepsin.
Maintaining a large inventory **would cut deeply into** profit.

Резко сокращаться
The duration of the uniform flow **decreased drastically.**

Резко увеличиваться
The number of hadrons emitted **abruptly increased** a hundred-fold.
The pressure difference **increases steeply** (*or* **sharply,** *or* **dramatically**).

Резко улучшаться
Then the world food supply **could be drastically improved.**

Резкое изменение
Our atomic age has suggested some **drastic** (*or* **dramatic**) **changes in** fundamental thinking.

Резкое различие между
In relation to transport through polymers, **the distinction between** gases and liquids **is** by no means **sharp.**

Резкое увеличение
A drastic (*or* **sharp**) **increase in ...**

Резкое уменьшение
A severe (*or* **drastic,** *or* **sharp**) **decrease in** the silver content ...

Результат [*см. тж.* **В результате, Возникать в результате, Давать лучшие показатели, чем; Давать необходимый эффект, Давать результаты, Данные, Конечный результат, Повреждение в результате, Полученный в результате, Являться результатом** (*или* **следствием**)]
The most unexpected **outcome of** the above work was the discovery of ...
This method **is an outgrowth of** broad studies of ...
This book **is the result of** research in the field of ...
Much of the bad posture of adults **is the sequel of** rickets in childhood.
Electrical resistance **is a result of** the scattering of ...
This **is a** direct **consequence of ...**

Результаты исследования
The findings (*or* **results**) **of an investigation into ...**

Результаты экспериментов одних исследователей отличаются от результатов других
The results of the experiments vary from one investigator to another.

Резьба [*см.* **Срывать резьбу, Тонкая резьба**].

Резьба любого направления
The spindle is for cutting **threads of either hand.**

Резюмировать [*см. тж.* **Охарактеризовывать вкратце, Подводить итоги**]
The above results **may be summed up** as **follows: ...**
We **shall** now **summarize** some of the basic theorems.

Резюмируем:
In summary, 1° alcohols are oxidized to ...

Резюмируя, можно сказать, что
In summary (*or* **Summarizing,** *or* **Summing up,** *or* **To sum up,** *or* **To summarize**), **(we can say that)** the paleomagnetic data vindicate all the details of the drift hypothesis.

Рекомбинация [*см.* **В результате рекомбинации**].

Рекомендовать [*см. тж.* **Настоятельно рекомендовать**]
The serious student of the subject **is recommended** (*or* **advised**) **to** read ...

Рекомендуемая литература
We have included **suggested reading** at the end of each chapter.

Рекомендуемый
Suggested (*or* **Recommended,** *or* **Advisable**) starting concentration is 10 to 100 parts of ...

Рекомендуется [*см. тж.* **Настоятельно рекомендуется, Полезно, Целесообразно**]
It is therefore **best to** apply the Debye equation to ...
These antifoams **are best added** before foaming starts.
Such calculations **are best conducted by** digital computer.
It is advisable (*or* **advised,** *or* **wise**) **to** have as much slope in the piping as possible.
In some cases **it is good practice** first **to** locate the hole with a drill of smaller diameter.
It is well to have an electric hoist for handing this operation.
It is recommended that these values **be** measured at ...
It will be well for you to become thoroughly versed in tool handling.
Boroxines **have been proposed** as extinguishing agents.

Рекомендуется для использования в
Materials with high dielectric constants **are desirable for** capacitors.

Рекомендуется использовать
If the effect of high velocity is dominant, then titanium **is indicated.**

Рекомендуется использовать в качестве
Some of these compounds **have been suggested** (*or* **proposed**) **as** polymerization catalysts.

Реконструировать
It was decided **to redesign** (*or* **revise the design of**) the cooler fans.

Реконструкция
Only slight **revision** (*or* **re-designing**) **of** the system was needed.
Modernization, Reconstruction, Renovation ...

Ремонт [*см. тж.* **Аварийный ремонт, Капитальный ремонт**]
These parts need frequent **maintenance** due to corrosion.
Repairs to the leaking areas have been successful.

Ремонт "домашним способом"
Do-it-yourself repair can be disastrous.

Ремонтная бригада
In case of a fan failure **a maintenance crew** (*or* **gang**) can be despatched immediately.

Рентабельно [*см. тж.* **Добывать рентабельно**]
Only 1/10 of this amount can be mined **on an economically successful** (*or* **profitable**) **basis** (*or* **mined economically**).

Рентабельный
Development of this resource **is** not **economically feasible** at this time, but the ultimate potential is great.

Рентгеноскопия
$BaSO_4$ is used in **X-ray studies** (*or* **examination**) **of** the gastrointestinal tract.

Рессорный
Some English cars **are of a sprung type.**

Рессоры [*см. тж.* **Устанавливать рессоры**]
Independent **springing of** the front wheels to the frame ...

Рецепт [*см. тж.* **Для ... нет готовых рецептов**]
The standard **recipe for** renormalization would not solve the problem.

Речь идёт о [*см. тж.* **Если идёт речь о**]
The case in point (*or* **at hand,** *or* **in hand**) is the core plate.
When chemical reactions **are dealt with** the Δ notation means ...
Here, **we are dealing** (*or* **have to do**) **with** a dichroic material.

Решать вопрос
At first these were suspected to be ..., but later it was proposed that ...; **to settle the question,** a study was made.
We know enough **to tackle** (*or* **solve**) some relevant **questions.**

Решать задачу I
One should always draw such diagrams when **working (out) problems.**

Решать задачу II
A given **problem is attacked by solving** a differential equation ...

Решать задачу на
If the pilot **is working a problem in** fuel consumption, the figures will represent gallons of gasoline.
To solve (*or* **do**) **problems in** multiplication, division and proportion, ...

Решать на ЭВМ
The equation **can be solved with a computer.**

Решать пример
Let us **work through an example.**

Решать проблему [*см. тж.* **Разрешать вопрос (задачу, проблему)**]
If an initial effort does not **crack the problem** (*sl.*)...
We **tackled** (*or* **solved**) **the problem by** applying ...
The laboratory **has dealt with the problem by** sucking water out of ...
Thus the student will be better prepared **to handle** quantitative design **problems.**
Fastening **problems should be (re)solved** while they are in the design stage.

Решать проблему в несколько приёмов
One **has to approach the problem in stages.**

Решать уравнение относительно
The preceding equation **can be solved for** the unknown velocities v_2 and v_1.

Решающая роль [*см.* **Играть решающую роль в**].

Решающее значение [*см. тж.* **Играть решающую роль в, Иметь решающее значение, Исключительно важен**]
Reliability **is of crucial** (*or* **critical,** *or* **decisive**) **importance in ...**

Решающий
The **pivotal** (*or* **decisive**) role of the microprocessor in advanced system design today offers ...

Решающий фактор [*см. тж.* **Один из решающих факторов**]
Here, the laser pulse energy would be **the deciding** (*or* **governing**) **factor** instead of peak power.

Решение [*см. тж.* **Семейство решений, Строгое решение**]
It has not proved feasible to obtain **a solution of** this equation.
This grader is **the** economical **answer to** all haul-road maintenance problems.
To make use of this vaporization in **overcoming** the terminal problems of re-entry, one has to ...

Решение вопроса
The resolution of the issue will have to await further study of ...

Решение, выполненное на ЭВМ
The authors obtained **computer solutions.**

Решение задачи
The method for **handling** (*or* **tackling,** *or* **solving**) **a problem ...**
One **solution of** (*or* **to**) **the problem** was proposed by ...
One of the first modes of **attacking the problem** was that of removing the water by ...

Решение уравнения
Various **solutions to the** simple diffusion **equation** may be employed.

Риск [*см.* **Без риска**].

Рискованно
It is hazardous (*or* **risky**) **to** offer any sweeping generalization.

Рисковать
In these circumstances we **risk** (*or* **run the risk of**) losing ...

Рисунок [*см.* **Как показано на рисунке, На рисунке показан** (*или* **приведён**)].

Ровно столько ..., сколько нужно для
Only (*or* **Just**) **enough** heat must be added **to** maintain conditions of constant temperature.

Ровно столько ..., сколько он может
Then Jupiter could acquire **just as much** angular momentum **as it could** store.

Ровное покрытие
An even coating of slurry is deposited.

Родиной ... является
About 80 species of clover **are native to** the United States.
Collard **is of** Mediterranean **origin.**

Родственный
This group includes sugar, starches, and cellulose, along with many other **related** substances.
Hydraulic jumps **are akin to** shock waves.
This board is used in the building and **allied** (*or* **related**) industries.
Papers on mining practice and **kindred** subjects ...
Gamma rays are electromagnetic radiation **related to** light rays and X-rays, but ...
There is an **allied** problem.

Рождать
Since pions and kaons are unstable, some of them decay as they proceed down the tube, usually **giving rise to** a muon and a neutrino.

Рождать надежду
The discovery of superconductivity **gave birth to hopes that** this phenomenon might eventually be put to many practical uses.

Рождаться
Planets may **come into being** when small planetesimals fall together.
The electronic differential analyzer **had its genesis** during World War II.
This technology **is** just **emerging.**

Роковая ошибка
There was **a fatal flaw in** his calculations.

Роль [*см. тж.* **Важная роль, Играть роль**]
The function of the foaming agent is to cover the surface of ...
The part played **by** (*or* **The role of**) this factor in the development of ... **is** great.

Роль повысилась
The spring washers **have increased in importance** with the trend towards smaller, more compact machinery.

Рост [*см. тж.* **Задерживать рост**]
With (a) rise of (*or* **in**) temperature ...

Рубрика [*см.* **В эту рубрику входят**].

Рука об руку [*см.* **Идти рука об руку**].

Руководитель группы
The leader of the team for astrometry ...

Руководство [*см.* **Под руководством**].

Руководствоваться
The choice of carrier frequency **is governed by** the ionization time.
In doing this we **are guided by** efficiency considerations.

Руководствоваться знанием
Land managers **can be guided by a knowledge of** potential end points.

Руководящие работники
The shortage of electronics technicians is acknowledged by **key personnel** in manufacturing.

Руководящий персонал
These reports are read by **top executives.**

Рулон плёнки (*фото*)
35-mm **film in rolls** giving 20 to 36 exposures ...

Ручное управление [*см.* **С ручным управлением**].

Ручной [*см. тж.* **Вручную, С ручным управлением**]
A **hand-held** remote control.
A **hand** saw.
The brake is released by a **hand-operated** (*or* **manually operated**) lever.
This method saves **manual** (*or* **hand**) labour.

Ручной калькулятор
A hand-held calculator.

Рушиться под собственной тяжестью
Such a structure **would collapse** (*or* **topple**) **under its own weight.**

Рывками
When an air pump works **with a jerky motion** (*or* **runs in jerks**), ...

Рыхлый
The originally **loose** sediments were made solid subsequent to deposition.

Рычаг [*см.*. **Нажимать на рычаг**].

Ряд I [*см. тж.* **Один из ряда, По ... в каждом ряду, Серия, Степенной ряд по, Целый ряд**]
The accelerator has **an array of** rectifiers and condensers.
A number of new machines ...
A sequence (*or* **series,** *or* **succession**) **of** long and short alternating pulses ...
This research extended over **a series of** years.
A series of holes at the rear of the case provide for ...
Oxalic acid is present in the form of salts in **a variety of** plants.
A succession of extrusions of this type may lead to the development of extensive lava plains.
A set of functions ...
A series of runs (*or* experiments) ...

Ряд II
The figures are arranged **in** two **rows.**

Ряд лет
My own tests upon this point, covering **years of time, ...**

Ряд последовательных ступеней
The reaction proceeds by means of **a sequence of steps.**

Ряд реакций
In processes which involve **successive** (*or* **a succession of**) **reactions** the speed of the whole process is determined by ...

Ряд сочетаний
A wide **array of** (*or* **A number of,** *or* **A variety of**) possible **combinations ...**

Ряд убедительных доказательств того, что [*см. тж.* **Накопить ряд убедительных доказательств того, что**]
For many years there has been **a body of compelling** (*or* **convincing**) **evidence that** the water in human red blood cells has anomalous properties.

Рядами
The storage silos are arranged **in** two **rows.**

Рядом
The unit cells are placed **alongside each other.**
The plants growing **side by side** were suddenly separated by several metres.

Рядом с
Permanent shops will be located **adjacent to** No. 2 shaft.
One of these units was to be placed **alongside** the first station.

С

С аналогичной структурой
All these eukaryotes have **similarly structured** chromatin.

С большей и большей точностью
Machine tools will be built **to closer and closer limits of accuracy.**

С большей точностью, чем
Astronomers cannot compute ...**closer than** a tenth of a degree.
The *g* factor is now known **to greater accuracy than ...**

С большим выходом
To produce esters **in high yields, ...**

С большим трудом
As a result of waste disposal animals **are** sometimes **hard put to** find adequately oxygenated water.

С большим увеличением
Examination of fossil tools **at high magnification ...**

С большим усилением
A **high-gain** amplifier.

С большим успехом
Aluminium has been used **to great advantage** (*or* **very successfully,** *or* **with great success**) for sour crude oil storage tank roofs.

С большой затратой энергии
At a considerable cost (*or* **expenditure**) **of energy ...**

С большой лёгкостью
These molecular fragments react **with great ease.**

С большой массой
Massive stars (*or* Stars **with a large mass**)...

С большой осторожностью
Great care should be exercised in handling all blueprints.
These data must be used **with (a) great (deal of) caution.**

С большой скоростью
As the tool rotates **at high speed, ...**
The controller input is changing **at a high rate.**

С большой точностью
These standards must be calibrated **to a high accuracy.**
This instrument is designed to measure, **to a high (degree of) accuracy,** the parameters of ...

С введением
With the advent (*or* **introduction**) **of** high-frequency heating, new techniques were developed in the field of ...

С внешней стороны
The tubing is coated **on the outside** with pure block tin.

С внутренней стороны
The bolt head should be fitted **on the inside.**
Dissolved material is precipitated **on the inside of** the cavity.

С воздуха [*см.* **Вид с воздуха**].

С возникновением [*см.* **С созданием**].

С возрастающим [*см.* **С большей и большей точностью**].

С востока [*см.* **С запада**].

С входной (*антон.* **выходной**) **стороны**
On the upstream (*anton.* **downstream**) **side of** the final control elements ...

С выделением
The HOCl will decompose **with the release of** oxygen.
The HOCl will decompose **to liberate** (*or* **release**) [*or* **with the liberation** (*or* **release**) **of**] oxygen.
Sodamite reacts with cold water, **liberating** ammonia.

С выделением тепла
Thus the reactants are converted to LiF **with the evolution** (*or* **release,** *or* **liberation**) **of heat.**

С выдержкой
Several photographs should be taken **at** different **exposures.**

С вырезанным
An iron disk **having** a segment **cut away** on each side ...

С высоким содержанием
High-iron (*or* **Iron-rich**) bauxite ...
Glasses **high in** (*or* **with a high content of**) silicates ...
Alloys **rich in** nickel ...
Compounds **high in** bromine content are nonflammable.
Ductile iron is a product **of high** carbon and silicon **content.**

С высоким содержанием кислоты
Fish cannot live in waters **of high acidity.**

С высокими рабочими характеристиками
High-performance plastics are noted for their resistance to chemical attack.
High-performance lathes ...

С высокой разрешающей способностью
The planet was photographed **at high resolution.**

С высокой степенью точности
The centre frequency of the laser transition can be established **with a high degree of accuracy** (*or* **precision**).

С высотой
The atmosphere becomes increasingly ionized **with elevation** (*or* **altitude**).

С гидравлическим приводом
This machine **is hydraulically operated** (*or* **driven,** *or* **powered**).

С гладкой поверхностью
A **smooth-surfaced** ice sheet ...

С глубины
The wells produce oil **from a depth of** about 9000 ft.

С годами
As years went by, such deposits would thicken.

The percentage of photographic discoveries has steadily increased **over the years.**

С ... граничит
The uplifted mass **is bordered by** low areas.

С грубой поверхностью
We used **rough-surfaced** objects.

С грузом [*см.* **Вес с грузом**].

С давних пор
Corrosion caused by ... has been a **long-standing** problem.

С датчиком
The modular components include a **transducerized** diaphragm ...

С двойной (одинарной) связью
The **doubly bonded** oxygen should be closer to the central carbon atom than the **singly bonded** ones.

С двойными стенками
The nematocysts are **double-walled** capsules.

С двумя максимумами [*см.* **Кривая с двумя максимумами**].

С дизельным приводом
A **diesel-driven** (*or* **-powered**) generator must be ...

С добавкой
Neodymium-**doped** glass (*or* Glass **doped with** neodymium).

С должным учётом
It is convenient to grind ... **after due allowance has been made for** the working position of the tool.
The best SNRs are obtained by using beam-forming optics, **with proper consideration of** (*or* **with due regard for**) individual atomic saturation spectral irradiances.

С дополнительным
The manned orbiting laboratory was made up of a spacecraft **with** a cylindrical section **added for** instruments and crew space.

С допплеровским уширением
Interaction of laser light **with a Doppler-broadened** spectral line is depicted in Fig. 3.

С допуском
Normally, fluorocarbon resins are machined **to tolerances of** about ±0.005 in.
The glass cones were ground **to the** proper **tolerance** after cooling.

С допуском на
These components are machined **to tolerances of** 0.002 in. for size and concentricity.

С доставкой [*см.* **Стоимость с доставкой**].

С достаточной точностью
To sufficient accuracy the luminosity of the solar nebula was equal to ...

С достаточной уверенностью можно сказать, что
One can say with a fair degree of confidence (*or* **assurance**) **that ...**

С древних времён
Crude extracts of various alkaloid-bearing plants have been used **since antiquity.**

С другой стороны
Salt, **on the other hand,** presented a more complex problem.
Alternatively (*or* **On the other hand**), a more open structure can be produced in which ...

С дурным запахом [*см.* **Дурно пахнущий**].

С единичным усилением
An amplifier **with unity gain.**

С жёсткими допусками
This complex component must be produced **to close tolerances.**
To produce **close-tolerance** balls, ...

С запада *и т.п.*
These fragments of lithosphere are bounded by the Pacific mid-oceanic ridge **on the west.**

С запасом [*см. тж.* **Конструировать с запасом**]
The structure must be designed **with a safety margin of** ...

С заусенцами
Burred edges.

С Земли
Ground- (*or* **Land-**)**based** observations ...

С избытком
n-Propylbenzene gives benzoic acid **with an excess of** oxidizing agent.

С известной структурой
Crystals **of known structure ...**

С излишком [*см.* **Более чем**].

С изобретением [*см.* **С появлением**].

С интервалами
Samples of metal were drawn **at** 10-min **intervals.**
The turns are spaced 1/8 in. **apart** (*or* **at** 1/8 in. **intervals**).

С интервалом в ... дней
Successful reinductions of interferon were obtained when the poly I:C injections were given six or seven **days apart** in two subjects.

С интервалом в ... секунд
The particles come out in pulses only **a few seconds apart.**

С интервалом в ... часов
The two pictures of the satellite were made 11 hours **apart.**

С использованием
Experiments were conducted **using** [*or* **by** (*or* **with**) **the use of**] the optimum quantities of various dispersing agents.
These calculations can be carried out **with** (*or* **using**) the data accumulated in Table 6-5.

С использованием приборов
Instrumentally based methods ...

С использованием ЭВМ
The company has been operating **a computerized** production control system.

С каждой стороны
Semiradial compressors have horizontal double-acting cylinders **on each** (*or* **either**) **side.**
The scale beam is graduated with 100 divisions **(on) each side of** the zero centre.
The swivel type of milling head is normally arranged to tilt 45° **(on) each side of** the centre line.

С каждым годом [*см.* **Из года в год**].

С какой угодно скоростью
We can make the system respond **arbitrarily fast.**

С канавкой
The pulleys **are grooved** or flat wheels which ...
Three-**fluted** taps produce the best results.

С кнопочным управлением
A **push-button(-operated)** lock secures the spindle sleeve.

С коммерческой точки зрения
Commercially, coffee is the most important caffeine beverage plant in the world.

С коническим концом
The cutter is held by a **conical-ended** screw.

С которым мы имеем дело
This equation can be modified to apply to other phase equilibria besides **the one dealt with (here).**

С красным смещением
A single line could represent almost any emitting atom **red-shifted** by any arbitrary amount.

С кратерами
Mars has two hemispheres, a **cratered** and an uncratered one.

С круглой головкой
A **round-headed** screw.

С крутым наклоном
When bucket conveyors operate **at steep inclines, ...**

С крутыми склонами
Most of the world's great **steep-sided** (*or* **-sloped**) volcanic cones are composed of ...

С крутыми стенами
A **steep-walled** canyon ...

С крыльями
A **winged** vehicle.

С кулачковым приводом
A **cam-driven** carriage moves around the periphery and across the face of the work.

С ... легко обращаться
Thionyl chloride **is easy to handle.**

С любой степенью точности
In this way π could be determined **with any degree of exactness** (*or* **accuracy**).

С макрокристаллической структурой
Bismuth is a **coarsely crystalline** metal.

С максимальным эффектом [*см.* **Наиболее эффективно**].

С малым ... или совсем без
They may elute rapidly **with little or no** resolution.

С малым увеличением
Fast photography **at low magnification**.

С малым числом оборотов
A **slow-speed** electric motor.

С мелкими делениями
A **finely-graded** rheostat for fine variation ...

С меньшими затратами
By modifying specifications we can produce parts **at less cost.**

С металлическим экраном [*см.* **Кабель с металлическим экраном**].

С минимальными усилиями
The turbine components can be removed **with minimum effort.**

С минуты на минуту
An individual's blood composition will vary somewhat almost **from minute to minute.**

С момента
Since the invention of the wave digital filters ...

С момента его появления
The diesel is about to enter a period of development more significant than any other **since its inception** (*or* **advent**).

С надрезом, без надреза
The test bar **may be notched** or **unnotched.**

С наклоном
The tube is placed **at an inclination** (*or* **at a slant**).
The equator of Mars **is tipped** (*or* **inclined,** *or* **tilted**) ...
A straight line **with a slope** equal to ...

С наклоном в ... градусов
It was necessary to sink a shaft **inclined at** 17 deg.

С наклоном от
Install the supply-air lines **to slope away from** the controller so that condensed moisture cannot drain into the instrument.

С наконечником
Carbide-**tip(ped)** drills are often used.

С намоткой из
A rheostat **wound with** just one wire size requires...

С нарушением допусков [*см. тж.* **Деталь, изготовленная с нарушением допусков**]
Parts that have been machined **out of tolerance** can be built up to the required size and geometry.

С наступлением
With the advent of the space and atomic age.

С наступлением войны
With the advent of war, the demand for these products increased.

С начала своего существования
The firm has been interested in training **since its inception.**

С небольшим числом кратеров
One of Mars' hemispheres is heavily cratered, and the other **lightly cratered.**

С небольшими оговорками
The theory is **(with minor reservations)** reliable enough for accurate extrapolations to be made.

С незапамятных времён
Since gravitational radiation is not appreciably absorbed by matter, it should have been accumulating **since the beginning of time** (*or* **from time immemorial**).

С незначительным ... или совсем без него
The chambers distribute the water over ... **with little or no** cavitation.

С неизвестным (*матем.*)
The case of a single equation **in one unknown** is considered.
This is a complete system of five equations **in the unknowns** p, q, and ...
An equation **with two unknowns** (*or* **unknown quantities**) ...

С неослабной интенсивностью
The transient change in membrane potential is propagated **with undiminished intensity.**

С неполной нагрузкой
The machines were operating **below capacity.**

С нефтяным отоплением
An **oil-fired** (*or* **-fuelled**) boiler ...

С нечётным массовым числом
Odd-mass-numbered species ...

С нижней стороны
Water enters **on the underside of** the valve.

С низким содержанием
Low-iron bauxite.
Medium-carbon steel nuts **low** (*or* **poor,** *or* **deficient**) **in manganese** (*or* **with a low content of manganese**) are hard to tap.
The lunar rocks are waterless and **hydrogen poor** [*or* **poor** (*or* **low**) **in hydrogen**].
The silicothermic reaction is generally employed to produce ferrochromium **of low-carbon content** (*or* **low-carbon ferrochromium**).

С ножным приводом (*или* **управлением**) [*см. тж.* **Ножной**]
A **foot-operated** valve.

С нормальными допусками [*см.* **Изготавливать с нормальными допусками**].

С обеих сторон
The teeth have the same form **on both sides.**
The dialyzing chamber is placed between two electrodes, with pure water in compartments **on either side.**
The plates lie **on both sides of** the fault.

С обильным выделением тепла
Sodium hydroxide dissolves **with great evolution of heat.**

С обоих концов
An open caisson is a shaft open **at both ends.**

С образованием [*см. тж.* **Легко вступать в соединение с ... с образованием, Соединяться с образованием**]
Styrene is polymerized **to give** polystyrene.
The acetyl chloride reacts with the water **to form** (*or* **yielding,** *or* **giving,** *or* **with the formation of**) acetic acid.
The potassium chloride and the sulphate of potash magnesia will react **to yield** (*or* **produce**) potassium sulphate and magnesium chloride.
Electromagnetic radiation can interact with the ground state **to produce** an excited state.

С обратным знаком [*см.* **С противоположным знаком**].

С обслуживающим персоналом или без него
Substations **may be attended** (*or* **manned**) **or unattended** (*or* **unmanned**).

С обычными покрышками
A **conventional-tyred** truck.

С одинаковой лёгкостью
Macro- and trace amounts of sulphur are determined **with equal facility** (*or* **ease**).

С одинаковым зарядом
An **equally charged** proton ...

С одинаковым знаком [*см.* **Одного знака**].

С одинаковым успехом
Hence, this arm could **as appropriately** be named the “invariable” **as** the “dihydrouridine” arm (*biol.*).

С одного взгляда
These variables reveal **at a glance** whether the system is in a normal state.
The truth of this theorem can be seen **at a single glance.**

С одного конца [*см. тж.* **Открыт с одного конца**]
A cantilever is a beam or truss supported **at one end (only).**

С одной стороны
A single track is laid **to one side of** the shaft excavation.
All accessories are located **on one side of** the engine.

С одной стороны ..., с другой стороны
On the one hand, ... and **on the other (hand) ...**

С основанием длиной ***r***
We construct a triangle **having as base the length** *r* and the perpendicular of *pl* units.

С особым упором на
The purpose of this article is to examine ... **with particular reference to** (*or* **emphasis on**) mankind’s future energy needs.

С остановками
Automatic transmission is widely used on buses engaged in **stop-and-go** city travel.

С осторожностью [*см. тж.* **Осторожно**]
This method must be used **with caution** (*or* **care**).

С острой кромкой
A **sharp-edge** tool ...

С отводом от середины
The thermistor-potentiometer unit is supplied from a **centre-tapped** 10-0-10 V winding.

С отрицательным зарядом
A **negatively charged** particle ...

С оттенком
The colour is white, occasionally **tinged with** blue, yellow, or red.

С ... охлаждением
The pistons **are oil cooled.**
A **water-cooled** reactor ...

С паровым приводом
The deck machinery **will be steam driven.**

С первого взгляда
Such clusters are recognizable **at a glance.**
In a snowflake, the presence of a symmetrical pattern can be detected **at a glance.**

С первого раза
Dies can now be designed for **"first-shot"** (*sl.*) success, so avoiding expensive trial-and-error modifications.

С переменной скоростью
A **variable-speed** motor.

С перерывами
He worked **off and on** for five years.

С плохим запахом [*см.* **Дурно пахнущий**].

С пневматическими покрышками
Pneumatic-tyred wheels.

С ... по [*см.* **От ... до**].

С повышением [*см. тж.* **По мере того как, С увеличением**]
The amount of carbon formed tended to increase **with increase in** (*or* **with increasing**) reaction temperature.
Corrosion rate increases **with increased** temperature.
The equilibrium constant will fall **with a rise in** temperature.
The strength of the metal falls off quickly **as** temperatures **go higher** (*or* **rise**).

С подогревом
Dissolve the iron sulphate, **with heat,** in dilute sulphuric acid.

С позиций
A unified approach to the study of analytical chemistry **in the context** of present-day industrial practice ...

С полной определённостью
To demonstrate **unambiguously** that a chemical change has occurred, ...

С полной уверенностью
Such samples can be identified **with certainty.**
Machining of such castings is carried out **with full confidence** that there will be freedom from porosity on vital machine surfaces.

С полным основанием [*см. тж.* **Вполне**]
One might **realistically** expect to detect ...

С полным основанием можно сказать, что
It is fair to say that even aeronautical engineers have had difficulty in ...

С положительным знаком
A **positively charged** particle ...

С помощью [*см. тж.* **При помощи**]
These problems have been solved **using** (*or* **employing,** *or* **by application of**) the Schrödinger equation.
This is usually accomplished **via** internal conversion.
These compounds may be separated **by** fractional crystallization **or through the agency of** enzymes.
Samples are prepared **by** different methods.
The levers are operated **by (means of)** precision cams.
The low-frequency components are attenuated **by the use of** a coupling capacitor.
The temperature coefficients were determined **through the use of ...**
This is more easily achieved **with (the use of)** inorganic phosphors.
The readings are made **with the help** (*or* **aid**) **of** a microscope.

С помощью вычислительных устройств
Computerized design of structures ...
Computer-assisted instruction ...

С помощью которого [*см.* **При помощи которого**].

С помощью спутника
We determine the position of an emergency transmitter in a **satellite-aided** search and rescue system.

С помощью уравнения
The surface concentration of paramagnetic oxide calculated **by equation** 7 is too large.

С пониженным уровнем шумов
A new group of **noise-reduced** pneumatic hand tools has been designed.

С поправкой на [*см. тж.* **Исправленный на активность**]
This reading, **corrected for** instrument error, is the pressure altitude.

С последующим
Perchlorates may be produced by electrolysis of sodium chlorate **followed by** conversion to any desired salt.
The reactor would shut down, **accompanied** (*or* **attended**) **by** the release of fission products.

С постоянной скоростью
A liquid flows **at a steady** (*or* **constant**) **rate of** 3.14 cm^3/s.

С постоянной температурой
Gauge blocks are often kept in special, **constant-temperature** rooms.

С постоянным фокусом
A lens **of fixed focus ...**

С появлением
With the advent of high-power tunable lasers, multiphoton ionization spectroscopy was developed.
The percentage of discoveries has increased **as** more sensitive photographic emulsions **have become available.**

С практической точки зрения
As a practical matter [*or* **From the practical standpoint** (*or* **point of view**)], it is desirable to arrange an analogue computer for a solution time in the range of 30 s to 2 min.
In practical terms, a laser is an obvious requirement for site-selection spectroscopy.

С превышением допуска
Bores **that are out of tolerance** are ink marked.

С преобладанием
Attritus may contain ... **with** clay minerals usually **predominating** (*or* **predominant**).

С приближением к
The component gradually decreases **as we approach** the magnetic poles.
Going toward the equator, the prevalence of skin cancer increases in proportion to ...

С примесью
The addition of ... precipitates cobalt as the hydroxide, initially pure, and finally **admixed with** (*or* **with an admixture of**) nickel hydroxide.
The **boron-doped** diamond appears blue.

С примесью типа *n*
The *n*-**doped** material ...

С принудительной смазкой
All bearings are **force lubricated.**
Bearings are of the plain type **force lubricated** under a pressure of 20 lb/sq in.

С принципиальной точки зрения
This type of writing is preferred **from a conceptual point of view.**

С приходом весны
With the advent of spring, growth is rapid.

С приятным запахом
Carbon tetrachloride is a colourless, **pleasant-smelling** liquid.

С продвижением реакции
As the reaction advances, ξ increases to 1.

С промежутками в несколько лет
It is advisable to carry out such measurements **at intervals of several years.**

С прослойкой
The deposit consists of two beds of borate minerals **interspersed with** shale.
Most agate is composed of two or more tones of brownish red, often **interlayered with** white.

С простой структурой
Structurally simple compounds ...

С противоположным знаком
The collimation corrections will be nearly equal and **of opposite sign** for these two stars.

С противоположных сторон
Two repair shafts were sunk **on opposite sides of** the damaged shaft.

С прочными стенками
The calorimeter bomb is a **strong-walled** metal container.

С прямым отсчётом
A **direct-reading** millivoltmeter ...

С прямыми канавками
Counterbores for brass **are fluted straight.**

С рабочего снимается значительная часть ...
The operator is relieved of much responsibility for accuracy.

С равной лёгкостью
The machine can be applied **equally readily** for rotating-tool fixed workpiece **and** rotating workpiece fixed tool operations.

С равными промежутками
A series of **equally-spaced** energy bursts and ...
The surface of the crystal may have facets **spaced at regular** (*or* **equal**) **intervals.**

С радиусом [*см.* **Радиусом**].

С разветвлёнными цепями (*хим.*)
Branched-chain acids ...

С развитием
With advances in (*or* **With the advance of**) microelectronics the computer became much smaller and cheaper.

С разрушением образца
Destructive methods ...

С ракетным двигателем
Rocket-propelled vehicles ...

С расстоянием от [*см. тж.* **С увеличением расстояния от**]
When $n(x)$ decreases **away from** the waveguide axis ...

С ребром в 10 миллиметров
A cube 10 mm **on an edge ...**

С резиновыми покрышками
The complete machine is mounted on **rubber-tyred** wheels.

С ручным управлением
The compressors were equipped with **hand-operated** bypass.
The press **is manually controlled.**
The equipment **is manually operated.**

С самого начала
Although we separated these scales, it was clear **from the outset** that there might be a close relation between two or more of them.
The collision theory is **from the outset** tied to the kinetic-molecular theory.

С ... связан
The A_1 vibrations **have associated with them** an oscillating dipole that is directed along ...

С ... связями
Double-bonded or **triple-bonded** carbons ...

С севера [*см.* **С запада**].

С сечением
Caissons **of** rectangular **cross section ...**

С созданием [*см. тж.* **С появлением**]
With the advent of satellites these systems became of paramount importance.

С соответствующим ему
The system undergoes a further expansion **with its associated** pressure drop.

С сорванной резьбой
Thread-stripped nutplates ...

С таким же успехом
The same treatment may be applied (equally well) to most polyatomic aggregates containing ...
Equation (4.20) **can (just) as readily** (*or* **easily**) be deduced from physical considerations.
We could **equally well** say that ...

С таким расчётом, чтобы [*см. тж.* **Так, что(бы)**]
Design parameters have been scaled **so as to** be comparable.

The unit **is so** constructed **that it can be** moved from place to place.
Parts should always be designed **so that** minimum stress **is** imposed on the enamel.

С такой же лёгкостью
Soft iron is easily magnetized, and loses its magnetism **(just) as easily.**

С такой же скоростью, с какой
Radioactivity supplies heat **as fast as** it is lost by ...

С тем, чтобы [*см. тж.* **С таким расчётом, чтобы; С целью**]
The two phases should be adjusted **so as to** regain ...

С теоретической точки зрения
Theoretically, ...

С тех пор
It has **since** become clear that such outflows are common.
Since then (*or* **Since that time** [*or* **Ever since (then)**] ...
Over the years the industry has improved this process considerably.

С течением времени [*см. тж.* **Со временем**]
Such experiments will become more precise and more numerous **as time passes.**
Since all machines wear, their defects worsen **as time goes on** (*or* **by**).
Such optical binaries (stars) can be distinguished from real couples only **in the course of time.**
In (*or* **With**) **time** some of these bacteria developed metabolic pathways that led to ...
As time elapses, the concentration profiles take on a different shape.
Over the years the electronic micrometer instruments have become more and more automatic.
The magnetic poles of the Earth tend to move slowly **with the passage of time.**
These substances have accumulated **through time.**
The pole of relative rotation can change its position **through time.**
These properties vary **with time.**

С той лишь (*или* **только**) **разницей, что**
The treatment of dispersion according to quantum theory is essentially similar to that outlined, **with the** (**only**) **difference that** the natural frequencies are now identified with ...

С той точки зрения, что [*см.* **В том смысле, что**].

С торговой маркой
Nylon rod, **trademarked** *Monocast,* had just appeared on the market.

С точки зрения [*см. тж.* **В свете, В смысле, По, По мнению**]
The laser drilling process is expensive **in terms of** energy.
Communities may be classified **in respect to** their complexity and extent.
In energy **terms,** an air conditioning system is a series of independent energy processes ...
The characteristics of this laser are excellent **with respect** (*or* **with relation**) **to** time resolution.
First, the sequences of various regions are analyzed **as to** the evolution of the bases.
The South, **in the view of** President Roosevelt, was the nation's No. 1 economic problem.
These resins were the best **as regards** [*or* **from the point of view** (*or* **from the viewpoint**) **of**] adhesion strength and transparency.
The question could be approached **from** two **angles.**
This might be undesirable **from the standpoint of** leakage.
This is undesirable **from the corrosion standpoint** (*or* **corrosion-wise**).
Quantum theory explains the Zeeman effect **in terms of** the behaviour of atoms in magnetic fields.
As far as the strength of the structure **is concerned, ...**
From our **standpoint** (*or* **point of view,** *or* **viewpoint**) waves with zero velocity are ...
To choose the best bridge location **for** design and economy, ...

С точки зрения промышленного использования
The first two oxides are the more important **from an industrial standpoint.**

С точки зрения структуры [*см. тж.* **В структурном отношении**]
Structurally, the chlorites are regular interstratifications of ...

С точки зрения теории вероятности
Probabilistically, this represents ...

С точки зрения теории групп
From the group theoretical standpoint, this requires ...

С точки зрения эволюции
These results are analyzed **from an evolutionary standpoint.**

С точностью до [*см. тж.* **В пределах ошибки эксперимента**]
Linear coordinates of ... are measured **accurate to** 0.003 in.
This apparatus **is accurate within** microseconds.
Angle *"A"* **may be read to** 0.01.
In these methods weighings are made **to** ±0.0002 mg.
The time scale **can be read to** (*or* **with**) **an accuracy** (*or* **a precision**) **of** 10 milliseconds.
The length of the tube **is measured to better than** 0.0025 cm.
The cam cannot be installed **to** the required **precision.**
The balance is capable of weighing **to the nearest** 0.1 mg.
Vacuum-tube voltmeters were calibrated **to within** 1%.
These parameters are known **with an accuracy of** 5%.
With a precision of 1 part in 1,000,000,000 ...
For this angle the measurements agreed **within** 0.1.
The contemporary instruments can measure the angular position of stars **to a thousandth of a second of arc.**
Thus it should be possible to obtain a numerical answer **good to** ±25%.
Readings can be obtained **to an accuracy of** 1 micron.
One can predict **with an accuracy of** 90% **or better** whether the child will be afflicted with the disorder.
Angle settings **are accurate to five minutes of arc.**

С точностью до ... десятичных знаков
The data will be displayed **to the fifth decimal place.**
Calculate **to three-place accuracy.**

С точностью до одного градуса
Determine, **to the nearest degree,** the mid-latitude of ...

С точностью до ... значащих цифр
The calculation is done **with a precision of** 10 **significant figures.**

С точностью до пятого десятичного знака
The data will be displayed **to the fifth decimal place.**

С точностью до ... порядка
We expand Φ (ω) about ω_0 and, **correct to first order,** obtain ...

С точностью до ... раз
Within a factor of 3 or **4** all nuclei scatter neutrons to the same extent.

С точным допуском
When a forging is to be made **to close tolerances, ...**

С трансмиссионным приводом
A **transmission-driven** hydraulic system must be ...

С трёх сторон
The container is closed **on three sides.**

С ... трудно работать
Such lasers **are difficult to operate.**

С трудом поддаваться намагничиванию
Hard iron **is difficult to magnetize.**

С трудом поддаваться обработке
This part **is difficult to machine.**

С турбоприводом
A **turbine-driven** pump ...

С увеличением [*см. тж.* **По мере того как, С повышением**]
The potential energy outside the metal decreases **with distance from** the surface.
Drill speeds decrease **as** drill diameters **increase.**
The sweep component beats with the second, third, and fourth harmonic **as** the sweep frequency **increases.**
As the length of the chain between ... **increases,** so does the tendency of ...
The amount of carbon formed tended to increase **with increase in** reaction temperature.

Corrosion rate increases **with increasing** (*or* **increased**) temperature.
The live load decreases **with an increase in** the floor area.

С увеличением в ... раз
Facets on the minute single crystals are clearly visible when viewed through a microscope **of** at least 30 **power.**
A 17-**power** telescope ...

С увеличением расстояния от [*см. тж.* **С расстоянием от, С удалением от**]
The thickness of the loess deposits decreases **away from** the rivers (*or* **as the distance from** the rivers **increases**).
With distance from the centre the concentration decreased.

С уверенностью [*см. тж.* **Можно с уверенностью сказать, что**]
It can be predicted **with certainty** (*or* **confidence**) that ...
It is not yet possible to predict k_c **with any assurance.**
This **can confidently be** ascribed to ...

С удалением от [*см. тж.* **С увеличением расстояния от**]
The magnetic energy increases **with distance** (*or* **away**) **from** the centre.
As we **recede from** the magnetic poles ...

С удалением от центра
The shells decrease in density **outward from the centre.**

С уменьшением [*см. тж.* **В уменьшенном масштабе, По мере того как, С увеличением**]
The free period of the accelerometer decreases **as** the mass **is reduced** (*or* **with reduction in** the mass).
Note how rapidly the volume must increase **as** the pressure **is reduced** [*or* **with decreasing** (*or* **decreased**) pressure].

С упором на
The company plans an extensive test programme **with an emphasis on** cyclic endurance testing.
The course deals with the principles of geology **with (special) reference to** its application in mining.

С условием, что [*см.* **При условии, что**].

С успехом
Tracers are used **to advantage** (*or* **successfully**) in several ways.
An observing screen **is** often **advantageously** replaced by a magnifier.

С установкой [*см.* **Стоимость с установкой**].

С утечкой
A **leaky** condenser *(in boilers)* ...
A **leaky** valve ...

С участием
Consider a reaction **involving** (*or* **with the participation of**) four gases.

С учётом [*см. тж.* **Исправленный на активность, Учитывая**]
Rewriting Eqs. (1.6.1) **in terms of** the result (1.6.5) we obtain: ...
The indicators are calibrated to read true airspeed **subject to** instrument error.
Based on accumulated experience the method was used for ...
The material of the tank was specially selected **having regard to** the extremely low temperature of the cargo.
With allowance made for ...
Selection of materials **with consideration for** their heat-storage capacities ...
The system should be designed **with due regard for** safety.
Material of the stock screw is selected **with regard to** the chemical requirements of ...
This term can be written, **in view of** Eq. (5.10), as: ...

С учётом удобства для облуживающего персонала
The tool room is laid out **for convenience of personnel.**

С физической точки зрения
Physically (speaking), a wave of this kind corresponds to ...

С формулой
Acrolein is the simplest member of the class of unsaturated aldehydes, **formula,** CH_2=CHCHO.
Acetone is a chemical compound **of formula** CH_3COCH_3.
The most important group of alicyclic hydrocarbons are the terpenes **of the (general) formula** $C_{10}H_{16}$.
Amide (acid) is a derivative of carboxylic

acid **with** (*or* **of,** *or* **having**) **the (general) formula**

$$R{-}\overset{\overset{\large O}{\|}}{C}{-}NH_2.$$

С химическим составом
Brochantite is a mineral **with the chemical composition** $Cu_4(SO_4)(OH)_6$.

С химическим топливом
Chemically-fuelled generators ...

С химической точки зрения
Chemically (speaking), carotenes are carotenoid hydrocarbons.

С хорошей резкостью
When the spectrum falls on the slit **in good focus ...**

С хорошим приближением
The minority carrier current can be calculated **to a good approximation.**

С целью [*см. тж.* **Для, Исследование с целью**]
The mixture is cooled **to** bring about the crystallization of ...
This substance is added to foundry sand **for the purpose** (*or* **for purposes**) **of** retaining (*or* to retain) moisture.
The stages are cascaded **with the goal of** (*or* **with the aim of,** *or* **for the purpose of**) maximizing the power gain of each stage (*or* **with the aim to** maximize ...).
These units have been developed **with a view to** speeding repairs.
The heat treatment is carried out **with the object** (*or* **intent**) **of** producing ...
Numerous laboratory experiments have been conducted **in an effort to** substantiate what is...
Suppose one raises the temperature **in an attempt to** get ...

С целью максимального увеличения
Special drill rods were developed with a maximum possible inside diameter **so that** the inner tube and the core **could be kept as large as possible.**

С целью повышения
To improve gear tooth surfaces **for greater** wear resistance, ...

С ценой деления
The wheel has a dial **graduated** in 0.0001 in.
An **inch-graduated** depth gauge.

С центром в
A small sphere **centred at** the molecular site ...
Draw a circle **with its centre at** *A*.

С центром на
In an area **centred at** the North pole ...

С центром при
The resonance absorption **centred at** 3.95λ consists of two lines.

С цепным приводом
A **chain-driven** carriage ...

С частичной нагрузкой
The economy of operation **at partial load** is good.

С частотностью
Adenosine occurs in this group **with a frequency of** 66%.

С чётным массовым числом
Even-mass-numbered species ...

С чётным номером
In the **even-numbered** tubes ...

С шарнирами [*см.* **На шарнирах**].

С экипажем
Manned (*or* **Human-operated**) **flight** (*or* **vehicle**).

С экспериментальной точки зрения
Experimentally, more laser power does not necessarily mean greater SNR.

С электрическим приводом
An **electric(-motor)-driven** pump.
The machine operates from an **electrically driven** (*or* **operated**) compressor.
The moving components **are electrically powered.**

С электрической точки зрения
In electrical terms (*or* **Electrically**), the living cell is known to consist of a low-resistance interior, separated from ...

С электронным управлением
Some of these machines are **electronically operated** (*or* **controlled**).

С этого момента
From this point on(wards) the computer takes charge.

С этой точки зрения
From this standpoint (*or* **viewpoint,** *or* **point of view**) present-day viruses appear to possess ...

С этой целью [*см. тж.* **В этих целях, Для этого**]
It is desirable to alter the integrated transmitted energy control of one of the colour components; **to(wards) this end,** there are nine pneumatic switches on the encoder.
With this in mind (*or* **With this object in view,** *or* **For this purpose**) an attempt will be made to state ...

С юга [*см.* **С запада**].

С 1982 г. [*см.* **Начиная с**].

Садиться на седло (*о клапане*)
When pressure is reduced to that exerted by the spring, the valve disk **seats** again.

Салазки [*см.* **Смонтированный на салазках**].

Сам испытал
The students who have **experienced** earthquakes **first-hand ...**

Сам по себе [*см. тж.* **Как таковой**]
Let us imagine that each molecule of a magnetic substance is a tiny magnet **in itself.**
These two features **alone** do not provide an adequate description of ...
The average result has little value **by itself.**
Catalysis is so important that the chemist considers it a subject **by itself.**
The rays are not **in themselves** colour making.
Each of the density ranges is quite broad **in itself.**
Isotope sources are not competitors of machines **per se.**
The large clouds and large globules will probably collapse **on their own** under the force of their own gravitation.
Each processing element of the computer is a powerful computing unit **in its own right.**
Chronological age **on its own** is not a contra-indication to surgical intervention.
The silicate framework is electrically neutral and can exist **by itself.**
The molten material did not burst out **on** (*or* **of**) **its own accord.**
This explanation is correct **as far as it goes,** but it is hardly satisfying.
None of these phenomena would seem **by itself** to be a convincing cause of the reptilian extinctions.
Taken alone, this shift is insufficient for describing ...

Сам по себе тот факт, что
The mere fact that the pictures show no signs of life on Mars means nothing.

Самая большая трудность состоит в том, что
The crux of the difficulty is that the Fermi theory is not finite.

Само собой разумеется, что [*см. тж.* **Излишне говорить, что**]
It is axiomatic that natural selection cannot act on nonheritable features.
Needless to say (*or* **It is self-evident that,** *or* **It goes without saying that,** *or* **It stands to reason that**) the use of such pigments...

Самого низкого сорта
The coal with the least amount of carbon **is the lowest ranking.**

Самодельный
Ranging from **"make-it-yourself"** gadgets to expensive commercial devices ...

Самое бóльшее [*см. тж.* **Максимум**]
These systems will have only one, or **at most** a few turbines.
Such an electromagnet can reach 60,000 gauss **at most** (*or* **at best**).

Самое важное [*см.* **Главное**].

Самой высокой энергии
A few of **the most energetic** cosmic rays have energies more than a billion times greater than ...

Самой различной формы
The bourdon pressure element may be made **in any one of a number of shapes.**

Самолёт [*см.* **Доставлять на самолёте (вертолёте)**].

Самонаводиться на луч
Anti-radiation missiles **will home in on the** radar **beam.**

Самонаводиться по шуму
To home on the noise produced by ...

Самоподдерживающаяся реакция
A self-maintaining reaction.

Самопроизвольно возгораться
Sulphur **ignites spontaneously** in fluorine at room temperature.
Amorphous boron **is spontaneously flammable** (*or* **combustible**) at 800°C.

Самопроизвольное возгорание
Coal is subject to **spontaneous combustion.**

Самостоятельно
In order to investigate these figures **on your own ...**
He was urged to observe the experiments **for himself.**

Самостоятельный I
We must look upon the Moon, then, as neither a true satellite of the Earth nor a captured one, but as a planet **in its own right.**

Самостоятельный II
One must first take dual instruction before making a **solo** flight.

Самотёком [*см. тж.* **Двигаться самотёком, Под действием собственного веса, Поступать самотёком**]
The water supply enters the pump suction **by** (*or* **under,** *or* **by the force of**) **gravity.**
In order to introduce the material into units **by gravity flow, ...**
From the tank the oil **gravitates** to the bearings.

Самоходный
A **self-propelled** vehicle ...

Самоцель [*см.* **Как самоцель**].

Самые разнообразные [*см. тж.* **Выполнять самые разнообразные функции**]
A great variety of broken or worn tools can be restored by this process.
Reclaiming arid lands and controlling rivers requires **a great diversity of** structures such as dams, power plants, canals, ...
Stainless steels are used in **diversified** industries such as the dairy, chemical processing, food processing, ...
A wide diversity of mRNA species appear to be present simultaneously in cells (*biol.*).

Самый близкий к [*см.* **Ближе всего**].

Самый большой
By far the greatest number of atomic control systems in use today are those controlling temperature.

Самый большой из известных
They are **the largest known** structures in the universe.

Самый важный
Mitotic cell division was **the crucial** step towards further evolutionary advance.
The all-important factor in amphibian life is water.

Самый верхний
When the reaction is irreversible, **the uppermost** (*or* **the top-most**) curve applies.

Самый высокий [*см. тж.* **Максимальный**]
This was **the top** (*or* **the highest,** *or* **the maximum**) speed for an uncoated insert.

Самый высококачественный
Top-quality (*or* **First-grade**) products ...

Самый длинный *и т.п.*
Longest of all is the Peru-Chile Trench (*or* The Peru-Chile Trench **is longest of all**).

Самый лучший [*см. тж.* **Бесспорно самый лучший, Наилучший**]
This system **is (by far) the best** choice for what is ...

Самый лучший из существующих
This process **is the best available for** CO_2 removal.

Самый маленький
It would still have been **(far and away) the smallest** planet in the system.

Самый нижний
The lowermost layer ...

Самый низкосортный [*см.* **Самого низкого сорта**].

Самый первый
This kind of genetic apparatus probably existed in **the very first** forms of life.

Самый последний [*см.* **Последнее нововведение**].

Самый сильный
The most pronounced (*or* **The strongest**) effect occurs in aromatic compounds.

Самый современный
Advanced molecular orbital theory provides the best bonding description of O_2.
Most up-to-date techniques are used here.

Самый старый из известных
Since the time of **the oldest known** stromatolites ...

Самый удалённый [*см.* **Наиболее удалённый**].

Самый яркий
Comets are **at their brightest** when near the Sun's position in the sky.

Сбалансированы
When the attractive and the repulsive interactions **are in balance ...**

Сбалансировать
High-order asymmetry errors **must** frequently **be balanced out over** the whole field.

Сбивать
With a cold chisel, **knock off** the rivet head.

Сбивать с толку
The terminology applied to neoplasms **can be confusing.**
The rate law **can be misleading in** determining mechanisms.

Сбился с курса
The rocket **went off** course.

Сближать
To start the arc the carbons **are brought together** for a short time.
If two atoms **are brought close together,** they...
Work must be done on the molecular pair **to pull** (*or* **drive,** *or* **move,** *or* **force**) them **together.**
Gibbs' elegant results **bridge the gap between** two great world views: the mechanical and the thermodynamic.

Сближаться
The molecules **approach each other.**
As a result, these two elements **are brought into proximity.**
Before two HCl molecules **can approach closely** enough for interaction to be sufficiently strong, ...
The ends of a six-carbon chain **approach each other** (*or* **draw close together**).
The two points *F* and *F'* **come (close) together** as the solvent rate approaches its minimum value.
The atoms **are brought closer together.**
The peaks **come closer and closer together.**
The particles **draw** (*or* **move**) **closer together.**

Сближаться на короткое расстояние
As two molecules **come within short distances of each other ...**

Сблокирован с
The isolating switch **is interlocked with** the cubicle door handle.

Сбоку [*см. тж.* **Вид сбоку**]
The switch **is on the side of** the machine.

Сболчивать [*см.* **Скреплять болтами**].

Сборка [*см.* **При сборке**].

Сбрасывание ... в
The disposal of organic material **into** a stream ...

Сбрасывать
The ripping head **discharges** coal **into** an intermediate conveyor.
The ore **is released through** a chute **into** the skip.
A portion of the air **was vented to** atmosphere.
Waste rock **is discarded into** lorries.
4,000 liters of hydrochloric acid **was spilled into** the Ohio river and 1,500 liters of paper-mill waste **was dumped into** a Texas lake.

Сбрасывать в отвал
Before the treated concentrates **are** finally **discarded,** they may be ground in a ball mill.

Сбрасывать груз сбоку или с конца
Self-loading scrapers **are** either **side dumping or end dumping.**

Сбрасывать давление
When **the pressure is released** (*or* **relieved**), ...

Сбрасывать листья
Deciduous trees **shed their leaves** in winter.

Сбрасывать на
The coal **is dumped to** the surface.

Сбрасывать на нуль
This pulse **resets** the device **to zero.**
The logic device **must be reset (to zero)** at the end of each machine cycle.

Сбрасывать тепло [*см.* **Отводить тепло**].

Сбрасываться в [*см.* **Выпускаться**].

Сброс в
Reports were received of six different **spills of** oil **into** inland rivers and lakes.

Сбываться
The prediction **was borne out.**

Сваренный вручную
A **hand-welded** joint ...

Сваренный точечной сваркой
Two steel plates **were spot welded.**

Сваривать в дуге
To arc weld.

Сваривать точечной сваркой
The machine is used **to spot weld** the back of ...

Сваривать электродуговой сваркой
The bench **is arc welded.**

Свариваться
The components **are welded together.**

Свариваться в атмосфере инертного газа [*см.* **Сварка с газовой защитой**].

Сварка за один проход
To make a one-pass weld, ...

Сварка с газовой защитой
Gas-shielded welding.
Welding in an inert gas atmosphere.

Сварная конструкция
The vessel is supported by **a** large **weld-fabricated** (*or* **welded**) **structure.**

Сварное соединение
A welded joint (*or* **A weld**).

Сварной
A **weld-fabricated** (*or* **welded**) machine bed occupies a floor space of ...

Свéдения [*см. тж.* **Большое количество данных, Данные, Знание, Значительное количество сведений о, Из ... можно извлечь некоторые сведения о том, как; Информация о, Накапливать информацию, Сообщать свéдения**]
These **insights into** the strength of materials obtained from experiments show that ...

Сведения о происхождении
These **findings have provided new clues to the origin of ...**

Сведены в таблицу
A number of the more useful relations **have been summarized** (*or* **collected**) **in Table 4.**

Сведённый [*см.* **Сводить в таблицу**].

Свежеприготовленный
A **freshly prepared** solution ...

Сверлить [*см.* **Высверливать, Просверлить глухое отверстие в стенке**].

Сверлить до глубины
Holes **are drilled to a depth of** 1 in.

Сверлить до заданного размера
Using the new material, the holes **could be drilled to size** without reaming.

Сверлить под
The burner bodies **are drilled** and tapped **for** (*or* **to receive**) a 1/2 in. standard pipe oil line.

Сверлить предварительно и окончательно
A hole **is rough drilled** on the first machine **and finish drilled** on the second.

Сверлить спиральным сверлом
Five cross holes **are twist drilled** in two parts.

Сверх [*см. тж.* **Выше**]
Then x_0 increases **beyond** a critical value.
The excess of the transferred energy **over and above** what is required to detach the electron ...
The lens speed can be increased **in excess of** f 1.9.

Сверхвысокая прочность
Ultra-high strength.

Сверхгибкий
Super-flexible cable ...

Сверхминиатюрный
The transmitter is a **subminiature** (*or* **subminiaturized**) unit.

Сверхнадёжный
Safe operation is enhanced by **fail-safe** circuitry.

Сверхнизкий
Extra-low temperature enamels ... under development.

Сверхпрочный
Ultra-high-strength alloys ...
Ultrastrong steel ...

Сверхскоростной
Ultrafast tensile testing machines ...
Ultra-high-speed automatic machines ...

Сверхтвёрдый
Ultra- (*or* **extra-**)**hard** tools ...

Сверхточный
Super precision gears ...

Сверху I [*см. тж.* **Вид сверху, Выходящий снизу (сверху), Если смотреть сверху, Приближаться к ... снизу (сверху ...)**]
Materials feed onto the belt conveyors **from overhead.**
The material to be crushed is fed in **at the top.**
The liquid enters **from above.**

Сверху II
From aloft, the immensity of the atmospheric ocean makes ...

Сверху III
Atop (*or* **On top of**) the entire assembly **is** a third conductor.

Сверху вниз [*см. тж.* **В направлении вниз**]
The degree of interaction of different organisms in the community increases **from the top down.**
The three photographic layers contain, **from top to bottom,** yellow, magenta, and cyanazo dyes, respectively.

Сверхчистый
A gram of **ultrapure** natural bee venom ...

Сверхчувствительный
The device **is supersensitive to** temperature changes.
A reliable **ultrasensitive** counting system.

Сверять с
Kepler **checked** the theory **against** the observations and found the concordance very good.

Свет [*см.* **В свете, Испускать свет, При свете, Проливать свет на, Пропускать свет**].

Свет распространяется со скоростью
Light travels at a speed of 300,000 km/s.

Светить ярче
The Moon **outshines** Jupiter in the deep night.

Светиться
The coating on the end of the tube **will fluoresce** under the impact of the electrons ...
The neon signal light **glows** only when current is on.
Phosphorus has the unusual property of **glowing** in the dark.

Светлый
The oil **should be light coloured** for clear viewing of the work.

Светонепроницаемый
A camera is a **light-tight** enclosure containing ...

Светящееся пятно
The ions strike a fluorescent screen producing **a luminous spot.**

Святящийся
Some volcanoes produce **incandescent** ash flows.
The Orion Nebula is a huge cloud of **luminous** dust and gas.
The anode is made of a **fluorescent** material.

Свидетельство [*см.* **Есть указания на то, что**].

Свидетельствовать [*см. тж.* **О чём свидетельствует**]
Newton, whose continuing allegiance to corpuscularism **is** repeatedly **attested by** his letters, ...
A clustering around this limit of secondary components of ... **attests** (*or* **suggests**) **that** the tendency to expand ...
The physiographic differences between the

Earth and the Moon **bear witness to** (*or* **point to**) the geological significance of ...
The smooth-flowing text **betokens** an excellent job of translation.
The wide disagreement with the facts **is demonstration that** the simplified notion ...
This predominates, **as evidenced by** the progressive decrease ...
Figure 4 **indicates** (*or* **points to the fact**) **that** the yield of lactic acid decreases with the increase of ...
The number of papers concerned with perforated-plate performance **is indicative of** a lively interest in ...
This in itself **is testimony to** the size and intricacy of ...
Today a fossil record has been found **to bear witness to** three of the key events in the earliest stages of ...

Свидетельствовать о том, что
The occasional occurrence of mischarging **testifies that** the problem deserves attention.

Свинчивать гайку с
Remove (*or* **Unscrew**) **the nuts from** the bolts (*or* **Screw the nuts off** the bolts).

Свобода выбора
The designer has unlimited **freedom in choosing** an architecture to suit his needs.

Свободно [*см. тж.* **Беспрепятственно**]
The rams of the power-control receiver **freely** (*or* **are free to**) travel backwards and forwards.

Свободно входить в
The chisel has a shank which **fits loosely into** the ram of the pneumatic hammer.

Свободно двигаться
The molecules **are free to move in** this volume.
The prothorax **is** often **freely movable.**
The molecules **move freely about.**

Свободно колебаться
One end of the lever **is free to oscillate** (*or* **freely oscillates**) **in** a suitable pivot.

Свободно падающий предмет
A free-falling object.

Свободно сидеть
Grinding wheels **should fit freely on** their spindles.
The piston above the valve disk **fits loosely in** its cylinder.
The ring **should be a loose fit on** the pipe.

Свободный [*см.* **Беспрепятственное прохождение**].

Свободный от I
The furnace should be perfectly **clear of** foul gases.
This air **is dust free.**
The tests indicate that these parts **are free from** (*or* **of**) defects.
The dielectric oil must be kept **clean of** chips.
A bacteria-**free** solution ...

Свободный от II
Die cushions **are not subject to** the drawbacks of springs and rubber bumpers.

Свободный полёт
Whenever a space vehicle **is in free coast** (*or* **is coasting**) ...

Сводить в таблицу
The data **are accumulated in Table** 6-5 ...
The results **are summarized in the table.**
Properties of these alloys **are tabulated** below.

Сводить в точку
The rays of light **are brought to a point.**

Сводить к
The new process **holds** warpage **to** 0.032 in.
This principle **reduces** the problem of centroid location **to** that of two points.
This substitution **reduces** the integral **to** the form of Eq. (37-116).

Сводить к классам
In most point groups, symmetry operations **can be organized into classes.**

Сводить к минимуму
The silicone fluid's resistance to oxidation **keeps** maintenance **to a minimum.**
The oxide preparation was closely controlled **to minimize** the chlorides.
Setup times **are held to a minimum.**
The number of acting gates **is reduced to a minimum.**
The use of the new varnishes **reduces** maintenance cost **to a minimum.**
Steam requirements **are kept to a minimum** by means of ...

To keep the bending stresses **as small as possible, ...**
We design shock tube equipment in such a way as **to minimize** oblique interactions (*or* **to reduce** oblique interactions **to a minimum**).
We must **render** the noise sources **as small as possible.**
The silicone fluid's resistance to oxidation **keeps** (*or* **holds,** *or* **reduces**) maintenance **to a minimum.**
The oxide preparation was closely controlled **to minimize** the chlorides.

Сводить к нулю [*см. тж.* **Аннулировать**]
The extra machining and handling costs **would negate** (*or* **nulify**) the steel's advantages.
The resulting elliptical orbit **reduced** the symmetrical errors **to zero.**
The new Hamiltonian can be made **to vanish** (*or* **to be reduced to zero**).

Сводить на конус
Hand reamers **are tapered** slightly on the end to facilitate ...

Сводить на нет
The small advantages conferred by these methods **are** often **offset** (*or* **reduced to zero**) **by** increased contamination.
Liquid quenching of air-hardened steels is a serious mistake, because it **sacrifices** almost all the basic advantages of ...

Сводить погрешность к 1%
The errors in multipliers of this design **can be held** (*or* **kept**) **to 1%** or less.

Сводиться к [*см. тж.* **Ограничиваться**]
Under these conditions Eq. (6) **reduces to** $\alpha = (b + 1) + 4b\tau_l/\chi^2 e$.
The investigation **amounts** (*or* **boils down**) **to** finding out the causes of ...
The calculation **reduces to** the solution of the following equation: ...
It was not long ago that the subject of star formation **was limited to** theoretical speculation.

Сводиться к минимуму
Wear of the thread **is minimized** (*or* **is reduced to a minimum**) since the only load placed on ... is the constant weight of the spindle itself.

Сводиться к нулю
Cohesion is greatest in fine clays and **diminishes to nothing** (*or* **vanishes**) [*or* **reduces** (*or* **goes**) **to zero**] in sand.

Сводная таблица
A summary table.

Своевременно
It is timely (*or* **appropriate**) at this point to express ...

Своевременный
How **timely** this innovation **is**!

Своего времени
He was a leading palaeontologist **of his day.**

Своего рода
Venus has continents **of a sort.**
Protenoid microspheres have a surface membrane **of sorts.**

Своеобразный
The propeller **is a peculiar kind of** wing.

Своим ходом [*см.* **Идти своим ходом**].

Своими глазами
They decided to go to the glaciers and **see** the evidence **first-hand.**

Свой собственный [*см. тж.* **Особый, Собственный**]
Long before the rise of copper metallurgy prehistoric Europe had an advanced mining technology **all its own.**
Such particles have fields **of their own,** and the fields of many particles add up.
Antiparkinsonian therapy introduces additional side-effects **of its own.**

Свойственен только человеку
The ability to substantially alter the environment **is uniquely man's.**

Свойственный [*см. тж.* **Присущий**]
To avoid the interference **inherent in** (*or* **typical of,** *or* **characteristic of**) combustion methods, ...

Свойственный только
This reaction **is unique to** hydrogen bromide.

Свойство [*см. тж.* **Наделять свойством, Особенность, Отличительная черта, Придавать свойства, Улучшенные свойства, Характерная особенность**]

High-bromine compounds often impart self-extinguishing **characteristics** to other materials.
The mechanical **properties of** polymeric materials are very complex.
The features of the new material will be described below.

Свойство, проявляемое
Diamagnetism **is a property exhibited by** substances with a negative magnetic susceptibility.

Свыше [*см. тж.* **И более, Сверх**]
The sheet is not recommended for applications in which temperatures **in excess of** (*or* **above,** *or* **exceeding**) 50°C are required.
More than 300 tubes failed.
The break strain of the strap **is over** (*or* **exceeds**) half a ton.
A wind tunnel which produces airflows to Mach 20-**plus ...**
The construction of 90-**plus** such plants ...
Temperatures **upwards of** 50 million degrees are required.
Generators having outputs of **upwards of** 1500 kW per set ...
Small hollow fibers can provide **over** 10,000 ft^2 of membrane surface in a cubic foot of equipment volume.
Expenses **over and above** the capital outlays ...
A gram of this venom would cost **in excess of** $10,000.

Связан I [*см. тж.* **Быть связанным с**]
This subfraction **binds to** the tissue DNA (*biol.*).
These stars **are bound by** mutual attraction.
The two carbon atoms **are linked to** a third.
The piston of the power cylinder **is linked to** the damper.
The two plants **are connected by** a railway.
The bundle **was tied with** string.
The camera range finder **is coupled with** the focusing mechanism.
The enamel coating **is bonded to** metal **by** fusion.
The protons **are attached to** carbon.

Связан II [*см. тж.* **Находиться в непосредственной связи с, Неразрывно связан с**]
This phenomenon **is associated** (*or* **connected**) **with** (*or* **is due to**) magnetic storms.
Control **is** directly **related to** the steam generation rate through the temperature coefficient.
This is an intricate process which **entails** the consideration of approximating sums.
The acceptance or rejection of the food depends upon its taste, which **is** usually **related to** its nutritive or harmful qualities.
The rate of bleaching **must be connected** (*or* **correlated**) **with** the formation and decomposition of HOCl.
All these tests **involve** the breaking of a test piece.
A final limitation of chemical lasers **has to do with** the state of knowledge.
Doubtlessly this constancy **is correlated to** the active role played by ...
The momentum carried by a photon **is related to** the photon's energy by the equation ...
Cancer patterns in Europe do not **correlate with** industrialization.
The collision theory **is tied to** the kinetic-molecular theory.
These are the electrons that **are** most directly **involved in** the chemical characteristics of molecules (*с которыми непосредственно связаны ...*).
The production and use of ionic compounds **are** inevitably **linked to** (*or* **with**) the deterioration of the environment.
Another uncertainty **stems from** the difficulty of ...
One difficulty **concerns** the use of hydrogen cyanide as a condensing agent.

Связан III
The rope **is tied into** a knot.

Связан с
A number of difficult problems **centre around** these processes.

Связан с большими трудностями
The direct measurement of temperature behind the shock front still **presents** (*or* **involves**) **severe difficulties.**
The study of an organism that cannot be readily maintained in the laboratory **is fraught with great difficulties.**
Supplying power to a high-performance computer **can be a major challenge.**

Связан с затруднениями [*см.* **Нахождение формулы ... связано с трудностями**].

Связан с трудностями [*см. тж.* **Представлять затруднения**]
This process **involves** (*or* **presents**) **(some) difficulties** (*or* **problems**).
Each new problem **poses** its own unique **challenges.**
The location of new substations **has been a problem** because of space restrictions.

Связан со значительными трудностями
The analysis of naturally occurring solutions often **presents a considerable challenge** (*or* **problem,** *or* **difficulty**).

Связан со спутником
An important cause of outage **was satellite related.**

Связанный водородом
Surrounding water molecules form **hydrogen-bonded** clusters.

Связанный глиной
The corresponding **clay-bonded** material is known as quartzite.

Связанный двойной связью с
In these compounds a terminal oxygen atom **is doubly bonded to** a carbon atom.

Связанный с I [*см.* **Быть связанным с, Жестко связан, Занимающийся, Прочно связан с**]
To risk the possible frustrations **attendant upon** so formidable a problem, ...
Thus we avoid delays **incident to** procuring items of material or parts.
We are working on problems **involving** (*or* **associated with**) automation, electronics, etc.
It is convenient to replace k by a new factor μ_0 **related to** k **by** the equation $\mu = 4\pi k$.

Связанный с II [*см. тж.* **Имеющий отношение к, Находиться в непосредственной связи с, Относящийся к, Тесно связан с**]
Mills **associated with** coal-mines ...
Symptoms of **age-related** diseases ...
The first serious investigation **pertaining to** boron was carried out at ...

Связанный с кометами
Various **cometary** phenomena ...

Связанный с ним
Pumps and **allied** equipment ...
The board is used in the building and **allied** industries.
The welding heads **and (their) associated** transformers ...
The basic mining process with the **attendant** problems of roof support and ...
The book describes detonation processes and **related** phenomena.
One overhead crane serves all these mills **and their related** equipment.
The discharge pulses are applied when the over-voltage of polarization and **its attendant** increase in impedance reach a predetermined voltage level.

Связанный с этим
It is very difficult to remove radioactive material once it is fixed inside the body, and the **ensuing** hazard depends very little on ...

Связаны I
The chains **are bound together by** aluminium atoms.

Связаны II
All three angles **are related by** the following equation: ...

Связаны друг с другом
We need to know how these properties **are related to each other.**
The two conductivities **are related by** the law ...

Связаны обратной зависимостью
Energy and wavelength **are inversely related.**

Связующее звено
This bond serves as **a coupling agent** (*or* **a connecting link**) **between** different metabolic processes.

Связь I [*см.* **Двусторонняя связь**].

Связь II [*см.* **Нарушать связи, Образование поперечных связей, Разрыв связей, Расщепление связей, Соединение с тройными связями**].

Связь III [*см. тж.* **Взаимосвязь, Зависимость между, Тесная связь, Устанавливать взаимосвязь между**]
Ship-to-ship and ship-to-shore **communications ...**

In very diffuse gases **the relation between** temperature and ionization may be much weaker.
The linkage between mathematics **and** pictorial representation ...
The association of electricity **and** magnetism ...

Связь между клетками
The biochemical apparatus of the cell membrane is responsible for **cell-to-cell communication.**

Связь на больших расстояниях
Long-range communication(s).

Связь с
The association of specific ions **with** the several phases of the action potential has been demonstrated.
The association between skin cancer **and** exposure to sunlight was observed over 100 years ago.

Связывать I
Some of the spikes **have been associated with** disturbances on the Sun.
The theory of wings **relates** the drag **to** the aspect ratio.
This quantity **relates** the area of a peak on a chromatogram **to** the quantity of test substance eluted from the column.

Связывать II
Greensand should contain the minimum amount of clay that is sufficient **to bind** the particles **together.**
The bars **tie** the separate elements **together.**

Связывать III
This theorem **links** derivatives **and** integrals.

Связывать атомы в молекулы
What **binds atoms together into molecules?**

Связывать в
The solute particles **tie up** the solvent **in** solute-solvent clusters.

Связывать друг с другом
The six types of chemical bonds that **hold** atoms **to each other** are covalent, polar covalent, coordinate covalent and ... bonds.

Связывать с
Absolute dating has enabled geologists **to relate** the history of the earth **to** that of the other planets of the solar system.
The odor we **associate with** a substance is determined by ...
This phenomenon **may be linked to** certain mathematical properties of ...
The gravitational attraction that **binds** a planet **to** the Sun ...
The nuclear force **binds** neutrons **and** protons **together.**
These expressions **relate** the flow velocity **and** (*or* **to,** *or* **with**) the pressure.

Связываться [*см.* **Соединяться с**].

Связываться с
The phenomenon of oxidation **was closely associated with** oxygen in the early days of chemistry.
Colon cancer **has been linked by** some studies **to** dietary practices.
The scientists **contacted** (*or* **got in touch with**) the local geologist.
The 5.8 *S* rRNA of eukaryotes has been reported **to bind to** two prokaryotic proteins (*biol.*).
Hydrogen atoms **can bind** quite strongly **to** such a surface.

Связывающий ... с
So far the only evidence **linking** the optical object **with** the binary pulsar system is ...

Сглаженный
Smoothed-out beam profiles ...

Сглаживание
Smoothing off welds on the engine nose sections ...

Сглаживание волны
There will be **flattening of** the *T* **waves.**

Сглаживание пика (кривой)
Flattening of the peak.

Сглаживать
Edges of rivet holes **should be smoothed off** with a file.
A scored cylinder **may be smoothed up** by stoning.
To feather out small scratches a spot blast mode is employed.
In the shock front, the particles tend to diffuse forward **to smooth out** the concentration gradient.

Сгорание [*см.* **Полное сгорание**].

Сгорать
The length of the tungsten electrodes when new is 4 in., and they **can be burnt away** until a length of 1 in. remains.

Сгруппированы [*см. тж.* **Группироваться**]
In "functional layout", all machines **are grouped together into** sections.

Сгруппированы под названием
The remaining vertebrates **are grouped together as** the *Anamnia*.

Сгруппировывать
All controls **are** conveniently **grouped together on** this truck.
These molluscs **are** commonly **grouped together in** the family *Cardiidae*.

Сгруппировывать в серии
These lines **can be grouped in series.**

Сгруппировывать по типу
Building wires **are grouped by type in** several classifications.

Сгущаться в
The solution **thickens into** a gelled material.

Сдавать в скрап
The faulty cylinder **should be discarded** or sent back for replacement of the valve.
If the part cannot be repaired, it **should be scrapped.**

Сдавать в эксплуатацию
This will depend upon how rapidly aircraft **are introduced into service** (*or* **enter service**).
To get the aircraft **into** airline **service** in 1985, ...

Сдвиг [*см.* **Большой шаг на пути к**].

Сдвигаться по частоте
The lines of the atomic spectrum **are** then **shifted in frequency.**

Сдвигаться с места
Make sure that the micrometer anvil **was** not **moved out of position** while the set screw was being tightened.

Сдвинут в область резонанса в силу доплеровского смещения
If the laser frequency is higher than the centre frequency of the resonance, molecules ... **will be Dopplershifted into resonance.**

Сдвинут влево
Each base pair **is offset to the left by** 36°.

Сдвинут по фазе
The plot for star *A* **would be** mutually **displaced in phase by** half a period.
The current **is phase shifted.**

Сдвинуться по фазе
The radiation and oscillator **become** 180° **out of phase.**

Сделан кустарным способом
At the time, many instruments **were home-made.**

Сделанный [*см.* **Выполненный**].

Сделать всё возможное, чтобы
A good engineer **will do his utmost** (*or* **best) to** minimize friction.

Сделать выбор
The problem arises when you have **to decide** (*or* **choose**) **between** several machines all designed to do the same type of job.

Сделать вывод
It may be inferred that the standards were reproducible within ±0.15μm.
We **can conclude** (*or* **draw,** *or* **make a conclusion**) **that** the system is a very effective low-pass filter.

Сделать недействительным
The operating line may be distorted by local vaporization of the solvent sufficiently **to invalidate** the method.

Сделать полный оборот
Turn the circle until the point you have marked **makes a complete circuit.**

Сдерживать
The shearing forces **retard** the flow.

Северный конец стрелки компаса
The north-seeking end of the compass needle.

Седло [*см.* **Возвращаться в седло, Садиться на седло**].

Сейсмостойкая конструкция

An earthquake-proof (*or* **-resistant**) **structure.**

Сейчас преобладает мнение о том, что
The prevailing view today is that rubbing merely enhances the effect by bringing more tiny areas together.

Семейство кривых
A set (*or* **A family**) **of curves.**

Семейство решений (*матем.*)
A family of solutions.

Сенсационные последствия
The impact of the experiment **was dramatic:** DNA was suddenly in and protein was out.

Середина [*см.* **В середине 80-х годов, Помещённый в центре**].

Середина века [*см.* **В середине ... века**].

Середина июня *и т.п.* [*см.* **В середине июня** *и т.п.*].

Середина 50-х годов [*см.* **В середине 80-х годов**].

Серия [*см. тж.* **Ряд, Тип**]
The first in **a succession of** pioneering storage-ring projects at Novosibirsk was completed in 1965.
The error signal may be transmitted as **a sequence of** long and short alternating pulses.
A set of data.
The procedure differed only slightly for the two **sets of** experiments.

Серьёзная опасность для [*см.* **Представлять серьёзную опасность для**].

Серьёзная проблема
Buffeting flutter of a wing is **a problem of great concern** [*or* **a serious** (*or* **grave**) **problem**] in transonic flight.

Серьёзное влияние на
Interstitial displacements **may have profound** (*or* **serious**) **effects on** crystal properties.

Серьёзное возражение
A strong objection.

Серьёзные последствия
The slackening of the river flow **could have grave consequences.**

Серьёзные трудности [*см.* **Более серьёзные трудности, чем**].

Серьёзный недостаток
Such a structure **has the grave** (*or* **material**) practical **disadvantage** (*or* **drawback**) that ...

Сетка [*см.* **Наносить сетку**].

Сеть [*см.* **Работающий от сети**].

Сечение [*см. тж.* **В сечении *А-А*, Квадратного сечения, Круглого сечения**]
Section through liquid receiver (*in a drawing*).

Сжатие [*см. тж.* **Подвергаться натяжению или сжатию**]
The contraction of specimens when the vacancies are annealed ...

Сжатие и расширение газов (*или* **пружины**)
The compression and expansion of gases (*or* **of a spring**).

Сжатый воздух [*см.* **На сжатом воздухе**].

Сжигание
Carbon dioxide is manufactured by **(the) burning (of)** high-purity fuels.
Carbon dioxide is prepared by **the combustion of** carbon in air or ...
Charcoal is prepared by **the ignition of** wood, sugar, ...

Сжижаться
This lubricant does not **thin out** excessively up to 200°F.

Сжимать пружину (*или* **газ**)
To compress a spring (*or* **a gas**) ...

Сжиматься
Air **is compressed** until the piston reaches the top of the stroke.
The "island" domains suddenly **contract into** the small circles we call bubbles.
If stretched rubber is warmed, it tends **to contract.**
The spheres are either growing or **shrinking.**
This domain **shrinks to** an angular region.
The initial closed surface **shrinks to** the origin.

Сжиматься и расширяться
The metal **contracted and expanded with** temperature changes.
The Earth **may shrink or expand** as a whole.

Сзади [*см. тж.* **Позади**]
The engine of a large bus may be placed **in** (*or* **at**) **the rear.**
The connecting box is mounted **on the rear of** the main case.
The bellows **is back of** the shock absorber.
The luggage compartment **is (located) aft of** the helicopter's engine.

Сигнал [*см. тж.* **Затухание сигнала, Ослабление сигнала, Поймать сигнал, Принимать сигнал**]
Visual and audible **signals.**

Сигнал посылается с
A signal is sent out from the transmitting antenna.

Сидеть свободно [*см.* **Свободно сидеть**].

Сила [*см.* **В силу необходимости, Развивать силу, Сохранять силу**].

Сила взаимного отталкивания электронов
The electron-electron repulsive force.

Сила действует
A force is exerted on the carriers.

Сила, действующая вниз (вверх)
When **the downward force** exceeds **the upward force, ...**

Сила, действующая на
In analyzing **forces exerted** (*or* **acting**) **on** structures ...

Сила земного тяготения
The force of gravity (*or* **of the Earth**).
The (Earth's) gravitation force.
The pull of (the Earth's) gravity on a body ...

Сила притяжения Земли Луной и Солнцем
The tides are driven by **the gravitational pull of the Moon and Sun on the Earth.**

Сила тока
Most plating equipment cannot operate at **amperages** [*or* **current intensities** (*or* **strengths**)] needed to maintain ...

Сила удара увеличивается
The shock increases in strength.

Сильная боль
A severe pain.

Сильная вибрация
Severe vibration.

Сильная коррозия
Severe corrosion.

Сильная струя
A powerful jet of water ...
A high-pressure jet stream of oil coolant ensures ...

Сильная утечка [*см.* **Большая утечка**].

Сильно [*см. тж.* **В значительной степени, Резко**]
The tinning pots have become **badly** (*or* **severely**) contaminated with iron.
The signals were **heavily** attenuated.
The presence of the shaper did not **materially** affect ...
The average number of zero crossings **is strongly** (*or* **heavily,** *or* **highly**) dependent on ...

Сильно влиять
These treatments **markedly** (*or* **significantly,** *or* **drastically,** *or* **strongly,** *or* **heavily,** *or* **badly,** *or* **dramatically**) **affected** the animal's later behaviour.

Сильно действовать
When bromide **acts** too **vigorously on** a molecule, ...

Сильно зависеть от
The future of laser application **will depend critically** (*or* **crucially,** *or* **highly,** *or* **strongly,** *or* **heavily**) on the time required for ...

Сильно загрязнённый
Heavily (*or* **strongly,** *or* **severely**) **polluted** air ...

Сильно загрязнять
A large quantity of crude oil **severely polluted** the beaches.

Сильно заражённый
The leaves of **badly infected** plants ...

Сильно изменяться

The velocities of rotation of Venus and Mercury **have been grossly changed** (*or* **profoundly altered**) **by** the tidal friction of the Sun.

Сильно ионизирован
The solution **is highly ionized.**

Сильно корродированный
Severely corroded.

Сильно мешать
These studies **will be severely hampered by ...**
This characteristic **would interfere drastically with** free unwinding.

Сильно нагревать
When fats **are strongly heated, ...**

Сильно нагреваться
Cold ocean water **becomes highly heated.**

Сильно наклонённый
Phoebe has a **highly inclined** orbit.

Сильно ограничен
The selection of a lens **was severely limited.**

Сильно ограничивать
This can **severely restrict** (*or* **limit**) the effectiveness of ...

Сильно отклоняться от
Other liquid solutions **deviate widely** from ideal behaviour.

Сильно отличаться по [*см. тж.* **Резко отличаться**]
The eyes of these animals **differ dramatically** (*or* **greatly**) **in** size.
The molecules **differ widely in** molecular weight and ...

Сильно отражаться на
The increased band gap **has severe** (*or* **dramatic,** *or* **profound**) **effects on** the behaviour of ...

Сильно повреждён
The micrometer **was severely damaged.**

Сильно поглощать
The interstellar dust does not **heavily** (*or* **strongly**) **absorb ...**

Сильно подвержен
Such a surface **becomes highly susceptible** (*or* **subject**) **to** attack by fatigue or stress corrosion.

Сильно преувеличивать
At high density the approximation **grossly overestimates** the pressure.

Сильно притягивающий молекулы воды
That portion of a molecule **having a strong attraction for water molecules** is hydrophilic.

Сильно разбавленный *чем-л.*
Mixtures of hydrogen and oxygen **highly** (*or* **very,** *or* **quite**) **diluted with** argon ...

Сильно разбавленный раствор
A very dilute solution.

Сильно разветвлённый полимер
A highly branched polymer.

Сильно страдать от
The industry **was hard hit by** foreign competition.

Сильное влияние [*см. тж.* **Большое влияние**]
The electrode material **may have a profound** (*or* **dramatic**) **effect on** the arc characteristics.
Glucocorticoids **have potent** (*or* **strong**) **effects on** carbohydrate metabolism.

Сильное землетрясение
A violent earthquake.

Сильное искажение сигнала
A severe (*or* **bad**) **distortion of a signal.**

Сильное разбавление
The high dilution of ...

Сильное уменьшение [*см.* **Резкое уменьшение**].

Сильный [*см. тж.* **Исключительно сильный, Мощный I, Острый**]
A (very) potent insecticide ...

Сильный ветер
High winds are common here.

Сильный катализатор
The most **potent catalysts** are: ...

Сильный нагрев [*см.* **При сильном нагреве**].

Сильный ожог
Leuisite caused **severe** (*or* **bad**) **burns** on contact with the skin.

Сильный окислитель
Bi(V) **is a powerful oxidizing agent.**

Сильный растворитель
Molten cryolite **is a powerful solvent.**

Сильный реагент
A powerful reagent.

Сильный ток
A high (*or* **large,** *or* **strong,** *or* **heavy**) **current.**

Силы действуют
It is assumed that molecular **forces operate** (*or* **act**) only **through** fixed centres of molecules.

Силы, действующие между
The strength of adhesive **forces (operating) between** different materials ...

Силы, действующие между частицами
The types of **interparticle forces** (*or* **forces acting between particles**) ...

Силы притяжения молекул воды
The attractive forces among water molecules ...

Символ [*см.* **Выражать символом**].

Симметричный относительно
The hyperbola **is symmetric about** the *x*- and *y*-axes.

Симметрия [*см.* **Нарушать симметрию**].

Синоним
Automation is sometimes used as **a synonym for** any technological advance that can be seen in ...

Синонимичный
A term **synonymous with** meteorology ...

Синусоидально
The current at a given point in an a-c circuit varies **sinusoidally with** time.

Синусоидально изменяющийся
Sinusoidally varying alternating currents increase ...

Синхронно
Synchronous motors run at a fixed speed **in synchronism with** the frequency of the power supply.
This antenna is rotated **in synchronism with** the radar antenna.
The phage genome replicates **in synchrony** (*or* **synchronously**) **with** the host DNA (*biol.*).

Синхронный
The motion of the disc **is synchronous with** that of the armature.

Система координат
A frame of reference (*or* **A system of coordinates**).

Система поисков и спасательных операций с помощью спутников
A satellite-aided search and rescue system.

Система с ЭВМ
The computerized system is capable of diagnosing itself.

Система уравнений
A set (*or* **system**) **of equations.**

Систематически повторяться [*см.* **Закономерно повторяться**].

Ситуация [*см.* **В данной ситуации, Положение**].

Скажем [*см. тж.* **Например**]
The velocity near the axis was, **say** (*or* **perhaps,** *or* **approximately**), 1.2 times the average velocity.
If we use, **say**, a single-point tool, ...
Suppose that the conditions are changed, **as by** a sudden jump in temperature.

Сказанное выше [*см.* **Вышесказанное**].

Скапливаться [*см. тж.* **Накапливаться**]
Proper drainage should be provided wherever condensate **can collect** (*or* **gather**).

Скафандр [*см.* **Космонавт в скафандре**].

Сквозной болт
A through bolt.

Сквозные и глухие отверстия
Through and blind holes.

Скептически настроен в отношении
Some engineers **were skeptical of** this new technology.

Складывать [*см. тж.* **Сложить вместе**]
To add up the factors of particular integers, ...

Складывать вдвое
The plate **should be folded in two.**

Складывать или вычитать
Algebraic equations **may be added or subtracted.**

Складывать уравнения
We **combine these equations.**

Складываться
The waves **add up** (*or* **together**) **to give** a net resultant wave.
This velocity **is added** vectorially **to** the stream velocity.
The two resultants **are** then **combined** vectorially.

Склеивать
The pieces **are bonded** (*or* **glued**) **together to** build up the shape required.

Склёпывать
The machined faces **are riveted together.**

Склон [*см.* **Пологий склон**].

Склонен
We **are** often **apt to** overlook the difficulties that were encountered in ...

Склонен к
Those *d* orbitals not involved in hybridization **are favourably disposed towards** π-bond formation.
Austenitic steel **is** not **prone to** embrittlement.
The crystals **tend to** oxidize in a moist atmosphere.
These bonds are rich sources of electrons and, therefore, are **susceptible to** reaction with electron-deficient reagents.

Склонен считать, что
Most scientists **are inclined to believe that** such is the case.

Склонность
An abnormal **tendency to** thrombosis ...

Склонный к
The features of the beta-tungsten structure **that make it favourable to** superconductivity are subtle.
Steps which the **coronary-prone** (*люди, склонные к сердечно-сосудистым заболеваниям*) can take ...

Склонный к математике
A **mathematically inclined** person ...

Скобка [*см.* **Брать в скобки, В скобках, Заключать в скобки**].

Сколь угодно малый *и т.п.*
The range can be made **as small as is wished** (*or* **as one likes**).

Скольжение [*см.* **Без скольжения**].

Скользить один по другому
When two blocks of the earth's crust **slide past each other, ...**
Silicate sheets in talk **can slide over each other** fairly easily.

Скользить по
The vernier **slides over** the fixed scale.

Сколько-нибудь
There are no internal movements of rock inside the Moon that **are at all** comparable with ...
For water treatment **to be anywhere near** efficient, one should ...
Few generalizations **of any value** (*сколько-нибудь ценных*) are given here.

Сконструирован [*см. тж.* **Сконструировать**]
The parts **are designed for** long wear.
This requires apparatus **patterned after** that used in ...

Сконструированный
This is the heaviest platform yet **conceived.**

Сконструированный по специальному заказу
In many cases microcomputers have replaced systems based on **custom-designed** large-scale integrated circuits.

Сконструированный по типу
He worked with a nebular spectrograph **patterned after** the 150-ft instrument.

Сконструировать [*см. тж.* **Конструировать**]
A clamp exerting a controlled force **could be devised** (*or* **designed**).

Сконцентрировать [*см.* **Концентрировать внимание на**].

Сконцентрировать внимание на
We **concentrated (our attention) on** an attempt to find this pathogenic agent.

Скопление
Very short columns sometimes show **a buildup** (*or* **an accumulation**) **of** immobilized surfactant near ...

Скорее
More likely the bulk of the outflow consists of ...
What is most significant is not the philosophical appeal of ...; **rather** it is the growing conviction that ...

Скорее ..., а не
When a salt dissociates in solution, it is the ions **rather than** the molecules **which** (*or* **that**) diffuse.

Скорее всего [*см.* **Вероятнее всего, По всей вероятности**].

Скорее даже
At least three, **and more likely** four such bends have been observed.

Скорее похож на
A joint fracture **is more in the nature of** a tensional crack.

Скорее правило, чем исключение
This pattern **is the rule rather than the exception for** the mid-oceanic ridge system.

Скорее ..., чем
A process of this type **is more likely to be** spontaneous at a high temperature **than** at a low temperature.
The charge-coupling concept **is basically** of semiconductor electronics **rather than** one of electro-optics.
They concluded that thymidine diphosphate **was more likely than** the triphosphate **to be** the direct raw material for DNA.

Скоро [*см.* **В скором времени**].

Скоростной метод
A rapid (*or* **fast,** *or* **shortcut**) **method** (*or* **technique**).

Скорость [*см. тж.* **Взвешенный по скорости, Набирать скорость, С переменной скоростью, Со скоростью**]
Metal removal **rate** is directly proportional to **the** wheel **speed.**
The rate of evaporation.
The resistance varies with **the rate of** loading.
The reaction **rate.**
The speed (*or* **velocity**) **of** air flow.
The speed (*or* **velocity**) **of** light.
The velocity of propagation of the wave.

Скорость звука (света)
The speed (*or* **velocity**) **of sound (light).**

Скорость изменения
The rate of change of the momentum ...

Скорость образования
The rate of photon **production ...**
The rate of formation of acetylcholine ...

Скорость под водой
Submerged speed.

Скорость подъёма (*аэростата*)
Ascensional rate.
Rate of climb (*or* **ascent**).

Скорость проходки (*скважины*)
Rate of penetration.

Скорость реакции (*хим.*)
The rate (*or* **velocity,** *or* **speed**) **of a reaction.**

Скорость резания
At **cutting speeds** from 30 to 150 strokes per minute ...

Скорость резания, скорость подачи, глубина резания
Turning was carried out **at a speed of** 750 ft per min with **a feed of** 0.0053 in. per rev and **a** 0.05-in. **deep cut.**

Скорость роста
The growth rate of the mollusks ...

Скорость снятия стружки
The machine is capable **of metal** etc. **removal rates** in excess of ...

Скорректировать [*см.* **Корректировать**].

Скошенная кромка
A bevelled edge.

Скрап [*см.* **Сдавать в скрап**].

Скреплены
These structural materials **are held together by** fasteners.
The glass fibers **are held together with** a suitable binder.
The two halves of the clamp **are secured together by** studs.

Скреплять [*см. тж.* **Наглухо скреплять**]
A bolt is used **to fasten** objects **together.**
Twenty-seven of the plates **are** then **fastened** (*or* **clamped**) **together.**

Скреплять болтами
The plates **could be bolted together.**

Скромная оценка
This estimate is conservative.

Скромные подсчёты [*см.* **По самым скромным подсчётам**].

Скрывать от нашего взора
Clouds **conceal** most of Jupiter's surface.
The surface features of Venus **have been veiled from view by** a permanent cloak of clouds.

Скрытый
It is not yet possible to estimate how many other such fields may **lie hidden in** the Earth's crust.
Energy **latent in** the nucleus of an atom ...

Скудно покрытый
In environments **covered only scarcely by** brush ...

Скудный
Meagre experimental data suggest that ...
The paucity of data on comets ...
Scant(y) information ...

Слабая связь с
This nucleoside shows **only** rather **loose correlation to** groups.

Слабина́ [*см.* **Забирать слабину́**].

Слабо
The formaldehyde molecule **is only weakly** (*or* **slightly**) attracted to benzene molecules.

Слабо абсорбировать
If the waveguide **is only slightly absorbing, ...**
This ion shows **a weak absorption** in the visible region.

Слабо влиять на [*см.* **Очень слабо влиять на**].

Слабо гидрализован
Sodium trichloracetate **is only slightly hydrolyzed.**

Слабо зависеть от
The rates of such processes **depend only slightly** (*or* **weakly**) **on** the molecular diffusivity.
The composition of the melt **has only a weak dependence on** the composition of the mixture.

Слабо изученный [*см.* **Мало изучен**].

Слабо ионизированный
Simple organic acids **are only slightly** (*or* **weakly**) **ionized** in aqueous solution.

Слабо обогащённый
Slightly enriched uranium ...

Слабо представлен [*см.* **Мало**].

Слабо притягивающий молекулы воды
The portion of a molecule **having little attraction for water molecules** is hydrophobic.

Слабо проявляться
These tendencies **appear only slightly in** arsenic and more strongly in antimony.

Слабо растворим в
These compounds **are poorly** (*or* **sparingly,** *or* **only slightly**) **soluble in** water.

Слабо растворимый [*см.* **Слаборастворим**].

Слабо связанный
Metals are characterized by **loosely held** (*or* **bound**) valence electrons.

Слабое место
The weak point in this suggestion lay in the fact that ...

Слабокислый
Weakly acidic.

Слаборастворим
Hydrogen **is only slightly** (*or* **poorly,** *or* **sparingly**) **soluble.**
Helium **has only a slight solubility.**

Слабый
A **dilute** solution.
Nylon is resistant to some **mild** acids.
Ordinary turbulent eddies **are** too **feeble** to sustain large sand particles.
Dimerization **is only slight** (*or* **weak**) in oxygenated solvents.

Слабый астероид (*или* **звезда**)
A faint asteroid (*or* **star**).

Слабый ветер
A gentle (*or* **low**) **wind.**

Слабый запах *и т.п.*
Carbon dioxide is a colourless gas with **only a slight smell.**

Слабый наклон, крутой наклон
The wheelwear behaviour can be represented as two linear regions: a **shallow-slope** and a **steep-slope** region.

Слабый сигнал
This equipment receives **low-power** (*or* **weak,** *or* **feeble**) **signals** from the spacecraft.

Слабый синеватый оттенок
Cadmium is a silvery-white metal with **a faint bluish tinge.**

Слагаться из
The particles **that make up** (*из которых слагаются*) nuclei ...

Сладкий запах [*см.* **Обладать сладким запахом**].

Сладкий на вкус
The sugars are easily soluble, **sweet-tasting** and crystalline.

Слева [*см. тж.* **Приближаться к ... слева**]
The illustration **at the left ...**
The open ocean **is to the left.**
The ion source **is on the left,** and the collector is on the right.

Слева на рисунке
At the left of Fig. 5 ...

Слева направо
As we read **from left to right, ...**

Слева от
All elements **to the left of** the grouping B-Si-Ge-Sb-Po are classified as metals.

Слева спереди
The clutch plate is **in the left foreground of** the figure.

Слегка [*см. тж.* **Немного**]
When the suspension is heated **mildly** (*or* **gently,** *or* **slightly**), ...
Boiling occurs when the vapour pressure of the liquid **just** (*or* **slightly**) exceeds the external pressure.
The magnetic lines are **slightly** (*or* **gently**) curved.

Слегка ионизированный [*см.* **Слабо ионизированный**].

Слегка колебаться
The abundance of each species **fluctuates mildly** around some definite level.

Слегка нагревать
If the rock **is heated mildly** (*or* **gently,** *or* **slightly**), the magnesium carbonate decomposes.

Слегка нажимать на
Use only gentle pressure on the adjustment screw.

Слегка наклонён в сторону моря
These layers **dip gently seaward.**

Слегка наклоняться к востоку и западу от
The surface of the peninsula **slopes gently east and west from** a central divide.

Слегка обогащённый [*см.* **Слабо обогащённый**].

Слегка постукивать [*см. тж.* **Лёгкое постукивание**]
Gently tap the reaction tube.
If the clock fails to start, **tap** the chart plate **lightly with** the knuckles.

Слегка тереть
Rub the surface **gently with ...**

Слегка щелочной
Mildly alkaline.

Следить за [*см. тж.* **Наблюдать, Не успевать следить за, Необходимо следить за тем, чтобы не; Тщательно следить за**]
Hurricanes **are** carefully **tracked** and offshore crews are removed in time.
To track (*or* **keep watch on**) the spacecraft, ...

Следить за изменением
What we need is a way **to keep track of** the laser beam diameter and divergence.

Следить за тем, как
There is a method for **keeping track of how** a given state responds to charge conjugation.

Следить за тем, чтобы [*см. тж.* **Необходимо следить за тем, чтобы не**]
Be careful not to allow the air hose to become kinked.
Care must be taken to align the ends of the wires correctly.
Care should be exercised to see that there **is** no rundown ...
One must be careful that the added circuits **do** not produce leakage currents.
Ensure that good contact **is** maintained with the holders.
It should be seen that the tubes **are** completely dry.
Make (*or* **Be**) **sure there is** no collection of moisture.
When adding the mercury **see that** nothing interferes with the free movement of the pen.
Take care when the boss is welded on **that** the inside of the pipe **does not** become distorted by the heat.

Следить за ходом
To follow the course of the titration, ...
The only way **to keep track of** the process is with the aid of flow diagrams.

Следить за чистотой
Keep the welding dies **clean.**

Следить при помощи спутника
They **have tracked** the buoys **by satellite** for eight months.

Следовало бы
It would be well to put these theories to a test.

Следовало ожидать
This difference **was to be** (*or* **would be**) **expected.**

Следовательно [*см тж.* **А, следовательно, и; Вследствие этого; И, следовательно; Поэтому**]
Consequently, it is not necessary to read every chapter.
If a given line represents 1, **it follows that** a line representing any algebraic number ...
Changes would occur in the depositional environments and **thus** in the lithofacies.

Следовать [*см. тж.* **За которым последует, За ним следует, За ... последовал, За ... следует, За этим следует, Из ... следует, Из этого вытекает, что; Использовать методику, Последовать за этим**]
From the principle of superposition, **it is evident** (*or* **it follows**) **that** the Algonkian sedimentary strata are younger than ...

Следовать за ... в указанном порядке
Boron carbide, silicon carbide, tungsten carbide, and aluminium oxide **rank below** boron nitride in hardness, **in that order.**

Следовать закону [*см.* **Подчиняться закону**].

Следовать из [*см. тж.* **Явствовать из**]
This **is evident from** Eq. (2-5).

Следовать непосредственно из
These conclusions **follow immediately from ...**

Следовать одному и тому же принципу при решении *и т.п.*
The solutions of all analytical problems **follow the same basic pattern.**

Следовать примеру
Other industries **should follow** the airlines' **example.**

Следовать рекомендациям
Bromine can be handled safely, but **the recommendations of** the manufacturers **should be respected.**

Следствие [*см.* **Результат, Являться результатом**].

Следует [*см. тж.* **Необходимо, Нужно**]
One additional feature **needs to** (*or* **should**) **be** recognized.

Следует иметь в виду
It is well to bear in mind that the net radiative contribution of carbon dioxide is to cool the atmosphere.

It should be borne in mind (*or* It should be remembered) that this will result in higher temperatures.
The effect of firing temperatures **must** always **be kept in mind.**

Следует искать признаки
This disease **should** always **be searched for.**

Следует лечить эту болезнь обычными способами
(Appropriate) treatment of this disease is along the standard lines.

Следует надеяться, что
Hopefully, we can find other energy sources before the fossil fuels are gone.

Следует не забывать, что [*см.* **Следует помнить, что**].

Следует обратить внимание на
The selectivity afforded by this method **is noteworthy.**

Следует ожидать поступления
Much additional information **should be forthcoming.**

Следует отличать от
Bus-bars **are distinguished from** connection bars, which interconnect ...
Fine solder **should be distinguished from** soft solder in which equal parts of lead and tin are present.

Следует отметить, что
We emphasize that this is of special importance.
Notice that such products have just appeared on the market.
It might be well to point out [*or* **It should be pointed out** (*or* **remarked,** *or* **mentioned**)] **that ...**
It should be recorded (*or* **noted,** *or* **recognized**) **that** there are some inherent ...
It is worth noting (*or* **It is worthy of note**) **that** the scalar equation of this type is exceptional.
Noteworthy also **are** the very large values that ...
It is pertinent to note that the genetic mechanism always remains encapsulated.

Следует относить за счёт [*см.* **Вызван**].

Следует относиться к нему с осторожностью
Special terms are commonly used, although **a cautionary note is appropriate,** since many of the terms have a range of meanings.

Следует подчеркнуть [*см. тж.* **Следует отметить, что**]
It must (*or* **should**) **be emphasized that ...**

Следует помнить, что [*см. тж.* **Следует иметь в виду**]
It should be remembered (*or* **One important point to remember is**) **that** these deviations are constant.
Remember, this process is efficient because ...
It must be remembered that a mild elevation of blood pressure might be the result of ...

Следует понимать как
The subscript y **should be read as denoting** the tangential component.

Следует предпочитать
Metformin **should be used in preference to** *phenformin.*

Следует предусмотреть
In designing the cooling die, **provision should be made for** 40-50% increase in ...

Следует прибегнуть к ... для
When the known properties of S are expressed in terms of these coordinates **it is then the province of** differential geometry **to** investigate their consequences.

Следует признать, что
Admittedly, the probability of success under these circumstances had to be regarded as very small.

Следует проводить различие между
A distinction needs to be drawn between what are ...

Следует рассмотреть
This possibility **is worth consideration.**

Следует сделать ещё одно замечание
One further comment is in order (*or* **should be made**).

Следует считать доказанным
The existence of ... **must be taken as proved.**

Следует уделять должное внимание
Due attention should be given to the dimensions of ...

Следует указать [*см.* **Следует отметить, что**].

Следует упомянуть
A point that should be mentioned is (*or* **It should be mentioned**) **that** one can write ...
Worthy of mention are the supercooling and freezing of water.
Some of these features **bear mention (here).**
Mention should be made of another unique achievement.

Следует учитывать
When checking the calibration of the measuring instrument against a standard potentiometer, **account must be taken of** [*or* **one should take account of** (*or* **take into account**)] the effect of ...
As with all internal combustion engines, **allowance must be made for** the effects of (*or* the effect of **... should be allowed for**) every ...
In the comparison of these results, **consideration must be given to** the temperature difference.
Piezo-electric crystals tend to be very sensitive to temperature changes and this **must be allowed for** during calibration.
The period of time to which measurements relate **also deserves consideration.**
In adding ... **due regard must be had to** direction.

Следующего вида
A directional derivative in the direction of λ is an expansion **of the form: ...**

Следующее поколение
The coming generation of detectors ...

Следующий I
The precise formulation of the limit concept used here **is as follows** (*or* **the following**): ...
The following procedure is used: ...

Следующий II
Each **successive** electron is held by a larger positive field.

Следующий III [*см. тж.* **В одном из следующих разделов, В последующих главах, В следующем десятилетии, В следующем разделе, В течение следующих нескольких недель**]
The ensuing (*or* **next,** *or* **following**) chapter suggests that ...
The present status of ... is discussed in the two chapters **which** (*or* **that**) **follow.**

Следующий по важности
Second in importance is the matter of temperature.

Следующий по распространённости за
Next in abundance after oxygen **is** the chemical element silicon.
Carbon monoxide **is the next-commonest** molecule.

Следующий по сложности за
Next in order of complexity to structures involving simple monatomic ions **are ...**

Следующим образом
The switches feeding each department were connected **as follows** [*or* **in the following manner** (*or* **way**)]: ...
Remove the door **by proceeding as follows: ...**
The paramagnetic oxide concentration was determined **in the following manner** (*or* **way**): ...
The gravitational force differs with height **in this fashion: ...**
The regenerative feature may be explained **thus: ...**
The best way of purifying salt **is as follows** (*or* **the following**): ...
The above equation may be rewritten **thus: ...**
The compound needs purification **on** (*or* **along**) **the following lines: ...**

Следующим по частотности является
The next most frequent (*or* **in frequency**) **is** uridine.

Следы [*см.* **Носить на себе следы**].

Следы обработки
The use of a file would cause undesirable **marking(s)** on the surface of the work.

Сливаться I [*см. тж.* **Выпускаться**]
Sodium sulphate crystallizes out and the solution **is decanted away from** it.
The fluid **is discharged from** the plant inlet scrubber to ...

Сливаться II
The charge and recharge steps **are merged into** one longer charging operation.
Below 0.1A all curves **coalesce** (*or* **merge together**).
At very high rates of alternation the two colours **appear to be fused** because the eye cannot resolve them temporally.
On returning to their starting point the two rays **would merge into** one beam again.
Over the Cordilleran ranges, ice caps and alpine glaciers **coalesced into** a single ice body.
Certain chromosomes **can fuse into** a chain.
The foci of the ellipse **have merged to become** the centre of the circle.

Сливаться с
The intensity and composition of galactic cosmic rays in the region where the solar system **merges into** the interstellar space will be studied.
The Interior Plains **merge with** the Atlantic and Gulf Coastal Plain.

Сливаться с фоном
The most common form of protection among beetles is coloration that **blends into the background.**

Слипаться
In a perfectly inelastic collision the colliding bodies **stick together** after collision, as two colliding balls of putty would do.

Слишком [*см. тж.* **Не слишком трудно, Чрезмерно**]
Most chemical reactions of molecular species **are (far) too** slow **to** sustain a biochemical chain of events.
An inexpensive airplane that **is** not **unduly** difficult to fly ...

Слишком ... для того чтобы
These lines **are too** broad **to be** analytically useful.

Сложилось впечатление, что
They **were under the impression that** no such experiments had previously been carried out.

Сложить вместе
If the Moon, Triton, Pluto and Mercury **are all lumped together,** you would have a body which would be nearly twice as massive as Mars.

Сложная деталь
A complicated part.

Сложная операция (*по обработке металла и т.п.*)
For **tough** (*or* **complicated**) **jobs,** the latter lubricant works best.

Сложная проблема
Molecular spectral interferences are **a complicated** (*or* **intricate**) **problem** (*or* **a challenge**).

Сложная форма
Castings **of intricate** (*or* **complex**) **shapes** involve ...

Сложно
The change of period **is complicated to** calculate.

Сложно устроенный
The **complexly built** *Ciliophora* **...**

Сложной формы
The process is especially applicable in producing **intricately** (*or* **complex-**)**shaped** parts.

Сложность I
The complexity of the reaction ...
The severity of the problem is often influenced by psychological factors.

Сложность II
Telescopes of increasing **sophistication** (*or* **complexity,** *or* **intricacy**) ...

Сложность окружающих условий
As **the severity of the environment** increases the austenitic grades are generally superior.

Сложные отливки и поковки
Complex castings and forgings.

Сложные рассуждения
This requires more **sophisticated reasoning.**

Сложный I [*см. тж.* **Глубокий анализ, Громоздкий, Трудоёмкий**]
The calculations become more **intricate** (*or* **tedious,** *or* **involved,** *or* **cumbersome**).
This is a much more **elaborate** procedure than is necessary for the coal material itself.

One of today's most important and **challenging** problems is the development of ...
A combination magnetic/filter separator cuts down costs, but is an **elaborate** piece of equipment.
The surface wind system ... is much more **complicated** and **complex** than ...
Fairly **elaborate** computations are necessary.
Techniques which are common in the motion-picture business have been adopted for many of the more **involved** (*or* **intricate**) television productions.
Very **sophisticated** mathematical techniques ...
Sophisticated equipment ...

Сложный II
A **composite** two-fibre waveguide ...
The transition is a **compound** one (both the spin and the orbit must change).
A **composite** particle ...

Сложный вопрос
This is an **involved** (*or* **intricate,** *or* **complicated**) **question.**

Сложный предмет
The theory of magnetism is **a complex subject.**

Сложный процесс
This is a rather **intricate** (*or* **complicated**) **process.**

Сложный эксперимент
Sophisticated experiments have shown that ...

Слои ... перемежаются со слоями ...
In the crystal lattice of this mineral, ions of calcium **lie in alternate layers** (*or* **alternate**) **with** carbonate ions.

Слоистая структура
A layered structure.

Слой [*см. тж.* **Внешний слой, Наносить слой на, Осаждаться слоями**]
The thermocouples are placed in the catalyst **bed.**
The process of applying a **coating** of zinc to the surface of steel ...
The protective **film** of oil ...
The gypsum deposit is made up of thin **strata** (*or* **layers**).

Слой материала
The fabric of the main envelope or pressure hull of an airship is usually made up of two or three **plies of cloth.**

Сломаться [*см.* **Выходить из строя**].

Слоями
Beds of sedimentary rock are initially deposited **in** horizontal **layers.**

Служба [*см.* **Срок службы**].

Служить [*см.* **Использоваться**].

Служить в качестве
The polyethylene sheets **served as** an insulation.
A corona discharge creates numerous free radicals that **go to work** (*or* **serve**) **as** chemical catalysts.

Служить для
This **serves to** average the statistical fluctuations.

Служить для передачи *и т.п.*
This current can **serve as** the torque-**transmitting** means.

Служить дольше, чем
Although ceramic and carbide coatings are brittle, they may be durable enough to **outlast** the softer substrate ...

Служить заменой [*см.* **Может служить заменой**].

Служить мерой
This portion of the coating **is taken to be a measure of** the oxygen content.

Служить основой для
This method can **form the basis of** (*or* **serve as the** (*or* **a**) **basis for**) a separation process.
The first law of thermodynamics **provides the basis for** the calculation of the necessary enthalpy balances.
The resulting wave functions are accurate enough to **serve as a basis for** perturbation studies ...

Служить полезным целям
Such models **serve useful purposes.**

Служить примером [*см.* **Являться примером**].

Служить той же цели [*см.* **Заменять его**].

Служить цели
To what purpose can a computer of this large size **be applied?**
This cement **serves** a number of useful **purposes.**
The purpose that is served by this process is ...

Служить этой цели
Only protons and neutrons contained in nuclei **will serve the purpose.**

Случается [*см.* **Бывает и наоборот, Как часто случается**].

Случай [*см. тж.* **В большинстве случаев, В других случаях, В ином случае, В исключительных случаях, В крайнем случае, В лучшем случае, В любом случае, В обоих случаях, В общем случае, В первом случае из двух, В последнем случае, В рассматриваемом случае, В редких случаях, В случае, В таком случае, В том случае, если; В этом случае, Во всех случаях, Во многих случаях, И в этом случае, Как и в случае, На случай, Ни в коем случае не, Предельный случай, Частный случай, Чем в ином случае**]
Explanations are offered in a few **instances** (*or* **cases**) where ...
This is the first **occasion** where we have to contend with wave effect.

Случайно
This enables the pump to be started up without danger in the event of the discharge valve being **inadvertently** left closed.
Many discoveries are made **by accident** (*or* **accidentally**).
The tools must have been burnt **by accident.**
The pipe ruptured either **by chance** or as a result of another event.

Случайный
The resemblance is **coincidental** (*or* **accidental**).
To prevent **accidental** loosening of the fastening by vibration, ...
This led Oersted to the **accidental** discovery of ...
There will be many **chance** distortions in the pattern of the network.
Random errors result in ...

Случайный наблюдатель
Mass movement can be extremely slow and pass unnoticed to **the casual observer.**

Случаться [*см.* **Это происходит потому, что**].

Случилось так, что
As it happened (*or* **It happened that**) the problem was resolved in spite of ...

Смазка [*см. тж.* **Без смазки, Работа без смазки, Работа со смазкой, С принудительной смазкой, Со смазкой, Чрезмерная смазка**]
The initial **greasing** (*or* **lubrication**) **of** the shaft should be sufficient for at least one year.

Смазывать
Joint surfaces of all unions **should be smeared** (*or* **lubricated**) **with** graphite paste.

Смачивать
This equation applies when the liquid **wets** the orifice.
If the paper **is moistened with** ammonia, it is coloured blue-black.

Смачивать водой
This variety of opal is opaque but becomes transparent when **soaked in water.**

Смежные науки
Interdisciplinary sciences.

Смежный [*см. тж.* **Соседний**]
The distance between **adjacent** holes should be the same.

Смена резцов, скоростей и подачи [*см. тж.* **Быстрая смена резцов**]
Automatic **tool changing and speed and feed changing** are controlled from small programming panels.

Сменный
Renewable bushings are designed for ...
The burner is supplied with three **interchangeable** nozzles.

Сменяться
Then the cold climate **gave way to** moderate conditions.

Сменяющие друг друга
The seafloor was spreading during **alter-**

nating periods of normal and reversed polarity.

Смертельный случай
A number of **fatalities** (*or* **fatal cases**) at the plant were attributed to gas poisoning.

Смесь [*см. тж.* **В смеси с , Тесная смесь**]
Five **blends** (*or* **mixtures**) of toluene **and** (*or* **with**) methylcyclohexane were prepared.
This concrete **mix** was of a better quality.

Смесь газа с воздухом
A gas/air (*or* **gas-air**) **mixture.**

Смета [*см.* **Составление сметы на**].

Сметная стоимость
The estimated cost of the project is £5 thousand million.

Смешанный с
Expanded pearlites **blended** (*or* **mixed**) **with** cement are effective blocking agents.

Смешиваемость
The system shows complete liquid and solid **miscibility.**

Смешивать [*см.* **Перемешивать**].

Смешиваться с [*см. тж.* **Не смешивающийся с водой**]
Liquid hydrogen peroxide **mixes with** water in all proportions.
No. 2 feed gas **is blended** (*or* **mixed**) **with** the cracked, cool No. 1 gas.
In such heaters, steam and feed water **mix together.**

Смешиваться с водой
These disinfectants **are miscible with water** (*or* **water miscible**).

Смещаться
The zero **is shifted to** a higher position.
The equilibrium **must be displaced** in the direction of ...
The two ions **have become displaced from** their normal lattice position.
With rising temperatures the anomalous wave **shifts to** more negative potentials.

Смещение во времени
A corresponding **time displacement of** the pulse peak ...

Смещение равновесия
Displacement (*or* **Shift**) **of equilibrium.**

Смещён вперед, назад
The emitter **is forward biased,** while the collector **is reverse biased.**

Смещён на величину
The next plane **is displaced** an amount a/h along the *x*-axis.

Смещён на ... километров от
The centre of the Moon's mass **is offset by** about 2 **km from** the geometric centre of the Moon's outline.

Смещён относительно
This spectrum **is displaced from** the origin by ω_1.

Смещён по фазе
The two coils **are displaced in phase by** 90°.

Смещён по энергии
The fluorescence spectra **are shifted in energy.**

Смонтирован
The coil **is mounted in** a long silver tube (*or* **on** a support).

Смонтирован на панели
The recorder **is panel mounted.**

Смонтирован на передней панели
All controls and indicators **are front mounted.**

Смонтированный на гусеницах
A **crawler-** (*or* **track-**)**mounted** machine is used in ...

Смонтированный на салазках
A **skid-mounted** drill ...

Смонтированный на стойке
A **rack-mounted** model ...

Смотреть [*см.* **Если смотреть на**].

Смотреть на будущее через розовые очки
Remember we **are viewing the future through rose-coloured glasses.**

Смотреть сверху [*см.* **Если смотреть сверху**].

Смотри [*см. тж.* **Можно найти в**]
For a detailed discussion of this subject **see** Chapter VI.
See Section 3.9 **for** a more detailed discussion of ...
Refer to Fig. 728.
This increases with the concentration, **figure** 8.12.

Смотри в разделе
For a discussion of this **see under** Potassium Cyanides.

Смотри выше
See above.

Смоченный
Barium minerals **moistened with** hydrochloric acid give ...
Cotton wool **moistened with** strong ammonia may be used as a swab.
The specimen is swabbed with cotton wool **soaked in** the etchant.
The cloth **is wetted with** hot alkali.

Смутно представлять себе
The biological role of morphine in the body **is only hazily understood.**

Смывать
Oil is flooded on the honing area **to flush away** chips.
A cleaner component **is rinsed from** (*or* **washed off**) metal surfaces.
This product can be sprayed on and **rinsed with** warm water.
The apparatus **is washed free of** nitrate ion.

Смывать в
Rains **wash** large quantities of loose soil **down** mountain slopes **into** the adjacent canyons.

Смывать с
The lighter gangue material **is washed off** the table.

Смываться в море
Many salts which are washable in water **will be washed into the sea** over many years.

Смыкать контакты
A current produces a magnetic field to magnetize the reeds and **close the contacts.**

Смысл [*см. тж.* **В некотором смысле, В общем смысле, В полном смысле слова, В смысле, В том смысле, В химическом смысле слова, В этом отношении, Важен в том смысле, что; Иметь смысл, Не иметь смысла, С точки зрения**]
This concept has no quantum mechanical **meaning** (*or* **significance**).

Смягчать удар [*см.* **Предохранять от ударов**].

Снабжаться энергией [*см.* **Получать энергию от**].

Снабжён [*см. тж.* **Обладать, Оборудован**]
Insulated electric conductors **are provided with** a covering of flexible material.
Those three amino acids **are provisioned** (*or* **provided**) **with** six codons each.
The cell **is completed with** a reference electrode.
Such a sewage unit usually takes the form of small receivers **complete with** float gear.
The instrument **is complete with** a carrying case.
The unit **is equipped** (*or* **furnished,** *or* **provided**) **with** a turbocharger.
The space vehicle **is fitted out with** a pressurized cabin.
The cylinder **is fitted with** a detachable head.
The chamber **is fitted with** an opening.
The element **is furnished with** a knob.
The instrument **incorporates a** safety device.
The thermocouples **are supplied with** sheaths.
Spindle units **feature** angular contact bearings.

Снабжён наконечником из
Each tool is **tipped with** carbide (*or* **is** carbide **tipped**).

Снабжён приборами
Some closures **were instrumented.**

Снабжён противовесом
One of the ends of the lever **is counterweighted.**

Снабжён пружиной
The instrument anvil **is spring loaded** to simulate pressure.

Снабжён рёбрами
The outer surface of the drum **is finned.**

Снабжён цветной маркировкой
The wires **are colour coded.**

Снабжённый ЭВМ
An automatic **computerized** reader can check ... in 40 minutes.

Снаружи [*см. тж.* **Вне, С внешней стороны**]
A sample cell placed **outside** the laser cavity produced a strong thermal lens.
The pressure is applied **externally.**
There will be a flow of particles into the crater **from outside.**
A telescope will be attached **to the outside of** the laboratory.
The wire is fed from the handwheel mounted **externally.**
The outside of the boiler is sprayed with ...
The name of the contents is painted **on the outside.**
The scale might collect **on the outside of** the tubes.

Сначала [*см. тж.* **Вначале, Начинать сначала, Первоначально, Предварительно**]
With sea water, bromine must **first** be concentrated before the steaming-out process becomes economically practical.
The lateral stress decreases **initially** with time until ...
At first, these results should be surprising, but a closer look shows that ...
First we consider fundamental modes and then high-order modes.

Сначала займёмся
The simplest case of a diatomic molecule **will be our initial concern.**

Сначала появился
First came nylon strapping to replace steel in many applications.

Сначала применялся как
Laser-excited atomic fluorescence spectrometry **had its beginning as** an analytical method.

Снижать [*см. тж.* **Понижать, Уменьшать**]
The liquid film **impairs** the efficiency of the column.
The grade of rock must be kept high **to hold down** the shipping cost per unit of phosphate.
The internal voids **detract from** the engine's performance.
Efficiency **was depressed** (*or* **reduced**) **by** increases in liquid viscosity.
The presence of carbon **depresses** the melting point of iron.
The presence of nickel **lowers** the critical temperatures.
Air resistance **would whittle away** the speed of ...

Снижать до минимума
The use of the new varnishes **reduces** maintenance costs **to a minimum** (*or* **minimizes** the maintenance costs).

Снижать значительно ниже
This delocalization of charge **reduces** the charge density **significantly below** that of an "isolated" ion.

Снижать качество
Strong interactions significantly **degrade** the communications quality.

Снижать напряжение
The arm overcomes rotational drag, and **relieves tension** on the coil lead.
The primary voltages **are stepped down** through transformers.

Снижать прочность
Plastic flow **can be detrimental to** (*or* **can lower,** *or* **decrease,** *or* **impair**) **the strength of** a material.

Снижать скорость
This fouling **retards the speed of** the ship.

Снижаться [*см. тж.* **Падать, Сокращаться**]
The velocity **reduces** from F to G.
Cooling occurs when the pressure **is reduced.**
The mountains gradually **decrease in elevation.**
Productivity **tapered off** markedly towards the end.
Production has continued **to decline.**
The suction pressure **declined to** 0.4 in. of water.
The collector current **drops (off)** (*or* **falls (off),** *or* **decreases**).

The yield **falls to** 80% at 1000°.
The pressure on the cylinder **is relieved.**
The electron's energy **is** slightly **lowered.**

Снижаться до безопасного уровня
Then the radiation **would die down to undangerous levels.**

Снижение [*см. тж.* **Понижение**]
A **drop in** pH ...
The increase in sensitivity is not accompanied by **reduced** detection limits.
If helium atoms are slowed down by **lowering** the temperature, ...
The **fall** (*or* **decline,** *or* **reduction**) **in** (*or* **of**) resistivity ...
A **decline in** productivity ...
A **drop in** production ...

Снижение качества
This assures low-cost production with no **loss of quality.**
There is no **quality fall-off** (*or* **loss**) **in** the product due to wear.
Reduction in the quality of work in a machine tool is often observed.

Снижение номинальных параметров
Derating germanium transistor circuits should permit their operation at fluxes of ...

Снижение эффективности
Changes in strain that would indicate a **deterioration in performance ...**

Снизу [*см. тж.* **Вид снизу, Выходящий снизу, Приближаться к ... снизу**]
The rotor is shrouded **on the underside.**

Снизу (*антон.* **Сверху**) **колонки**
The gas is introduced **at the bottom** (*anton.* **top**) **of the column.**

Снизу вверх [*см. тж.* **В направлении вниз**]
The strata are arranged in order of decreasing age **from bottom to top.**
After casting, pressure is exerted **from the bottom upwards.**

Снимать [*см. тж.* **Считывать**]
The door **can be lifted off** the hinge pin.
The engine crankcase **is removed** and the crankcase inspected.

Снимать заусенцы
The parts **must be deburred** and polished.

Снимать измерения с
Voltage **measurements are taken from** a high-impedance source.

Снимать информацию с
The **information is retrieved from** the disk by a recording head.

Снимать напряжение
Annealing **relieves** internal **stresses.**
A short-time anneal did not **remove the residual stresses.**
It has been necessary **to stress-relieve** all chimneys in the absorbers.
After heat treatment, the plates **must be stress relieved.**

Снимать ограничение
These steps allow us **to lift** (*or* **remove**) **the restriction.**

Снимать окалину
We had **to descale** the steel by shot-blasting.

Снимать показания
To take a thermometer **reading,** open the door.
Readings can be taken without opening the meter case.

Снимать с поверхности
Impurities oxidize before the lead and **are skimmed from the surface.**

Снимать с эксплуатации
The shells **were removed from** (*or* **taken out of**) **service.**

Снимать спектр
Spectra were taken (*or* **obtained,** *or* **appropriated**) **from** two standards.

Снимать стружку
Large planers **remove a chip** 1/32 in. long and 3/4 in. deep.

Снимать толстую стружку
Take a deep cut — about 1/8 in. per pass.
Heavy cuts can be taken in one pass.

Снимать фаску
The nibbler **bevels edges** on large parts.

Снова [*см. тж.* **Заново рассмотреть вопрос о**]
Once again, we include the Earth for purposes of comparison.
Hence, the *in vivo* functions of all the poly-

merases need investigating **anew,** using natural complexes rather than purified enzymes.

Снова воспылать интересом к
My **interest in** the thermal lens **was rekindled** at the new laboratory.

Снова заполнять
The cell **is** then **refilled with** the same solution.

Снова и снова
Here's a unit that proves itself **time and again.**

Снова обрести своё прежнее значение
As petroleum becomes scarcer, this process **may regain its former importance.**

Снова охладиться до
After the apparatus **has cooled back to** room temperature ...

Снова превращаться в
On attempted isolation, hydrates lose water and **revert back to** the carbonyl compound.

Снова привести в рабочее состояние
The drill **can be restored to service** by the removal of ...

Снова приобретать
The crystal **regains** its original dimensions.

Снова проходить тот же путь [*см.* **Повторять путь**].

Снова пустить в эксплуатацию
Inject water into the boiler, and **restore** it **to operation.**

Снова работает нормально
The plant **is (now) back to normal (operation).**

Снова установить
Reset the instrument **for** zero reading.

Снова формулировать
We **re-state** the problem for an *m*th-order equation.

Снятие давления
Pressure release.

Снятие деталей со станка
The robots can be used for handling operations including the loading and **off-loading of machines.**

Снятие заусенцев
Here, the need for **deburring** is reduced.

Снятие материала
Reducing (*or* **Removal of**) **material** by grinding ...

Снятие металла
The **metal-removal** capacity of the planer has increased.
The cutter **is removing metal** the whole cutting time.
Slip the hub **off** the bearing sleeve.
Then the inner face expands and **can be slipped off** the journals.

Снятие напряжения
Stress relieving consists in flash tempering at ...

Снятие окалины
This is an electrolytic process for **descaling** and producing a bright silvery surface on iron and steel.

Снятие показаний прибора
The taking of readings.

Снятие стружки (*или* **материала**)
These studies determined the basic relationship between **stock** (*or* **chip**) **removal** (*or* **chip cutting**) rates and available horsepower.

Снятие толстой стружки
A grinder for **heavy stock removal.**

Снятие характеристики
It is preferable **to obtain the characteristics** by independent measurement.

Со взрывом [*см. тж.* **Воспламеняться со взрывом**]
Hydroxylamine decomposes **explosively** if heated.

Со временем
Some isotopes are unstable and **with time** will decay into ...
The direction of the magnetic field varies **with time.**
In due course, an ageing population decreases in size.
After-effects will appear **in the course of time.**

In time, the copper strip will be consumed.
The device will **in time** help to overcome these difficulties.
With the passage of time ...

Со времени [*см. тж.* **С момента**]
Since their discovery, viruses have been viewed in several ways.

Со всей Европы
Scientists came **from all over Europe.**

Со всей очевидностью [*см.* **Вытекать со всей очевидностью из**].

Со всей полнотой
The wide versatility of the shock tube **is amply** (*or* **fully**) demonstrated by different experimental techniques.

Со всех сторон
Inserts require sufficient surrounding wall thickness **on all sides** to prevent strains and breakage.
The chamber is completely enclosed **on all sides,** top and bottom by a circulating water jacket.

Со значком "прим"
The **primed** variables p' and q' ...

Со своей стороны
The planet, **for its part,** has never shown any effect due to the comet's gravitational attraction.

Со склада
These types of transistors are available **from stock.**

Со скоростью [*см. тж.* **Двигаться со скоростью**]
Mild steel rings could be ground **at** 350 pieces **per hour.**
The pump delivers this water **at the rate of** 500 Mcf daily.
The body is moving **with** (*or* **at**) a constant **speed** (*or* **velocity**).
If the molecules **are** all moving **with speed** u, ...
If a plane is moving **at** 800 km **an hour, ...**
The reaction rate is proportional to **the rate with which** these molecules are formed.

Со следами метеоритов
A **meteorite-scarred** surface ...

Со сложной конфигурацией
Complex-shaped parts ...

Со смазкой
The disk clutch may be operated dry or **wet.**

Со спиральными канавками
Spiral-fluted cutting tools ...

Со средним содержанием
Medium-carbon steels ...

Со стандартными покрышками [*см.* **С обычными покрышками**].

Со стороной
A cubic container **of side** l ...
It is possible to build a charge-coupled unit cell with dimensions of less than a millimetre **on a side.**
The first integrated circuits consisted of about a dozen components on a "chip" **measuring a** few millimetres **on a side.**
It is a cube, one meter **on a side.**
If you construct a square **with each side equal to** 3 cm, ...

Со стороны
The picture shows pin numbers **as viewed from** wiring connections.
Fuses **on the source side of** the protector are required.

Со шлицом для отвёртки
Screwdriver-slotted shafts ...

Со штрихом (*антон.* **Без штриха**)
The **primed** (SF', m') and **unprimed** (SF, m) symbols indicate ...

Собирать [*см.* **При сборке**].

Собирать в узел
When **assembled together as a unit,** the structure can be ...

Соблюдать [*см. тж.* **Точно соблюдать**]
It is necessary that we **abide by** the rules of logic.
The dimensional criteria shown in the table **are adhered to.**
To comply (*or* **conform**) **with ...**

Соблюдать жёсткие технические требования
Manufacturers are obliged **to meet rigid specifications.**

Соблюдать правила
Services are being inaugurated to help you

observe (*or* **comply with**) **the regulations** (*or* **rules**).

Соблюдать условие
The characteristics of *FM* tend to produce a more rapid deterioration in performance if this **condition is** not **met.**

Соблюдаться
If the conservations law for charge **is obeyed, ...**

Соблюдение правил
This can be avoided by **following** (*or* **fulfilling**) certain **rules.**
With **the observance of** (*or* **compliance with**) proper **rules ...**

Собранный [*см.* **Поставлять в собранном виде**].

Собранный на заводе
Factory-assembled rheostats ...

Собственный
Every fraction has **its own** number (*or* has **a** number **of its own**), ...
The firm reported results on cooling towers **of their own.**
The circuit reduces the **inherent** noise of transistors.
To obtain a measure of **intrinsic** activity of the catalyst, ...
The total volume available is much larger than the **proper** volume of the particles.

Событие ... вида (*физ.*)
The average time between **events of** either **sort** will be: ...

Совершать возвратно-поступательное движение
The workpiece **reciprocates,** while the tool remains fixed.

Совершать движение
Mechanical systems **execute a** periodic **motion.**

Совершать полный оборот
How many seconds does it take the planet **to make a complete turn** (*or* **circuit**) in its orbit?

Совершенно [*см. тж.* **Вообще**]
There is no moisture exchange **whatsoever** (*or* **at all**).

Совершенно аналогично
Such an atom would be formed **in perfect analogy to** the ordinary atom.

Совершенно другое дело
It is quite another matter (*or* **thing**) to predict too much water, because there is no explanation.

Совершенно другой
The organs change to fit the insect for a **much different** (*or* **quite** a **different**) mode of life.
This can cause some delay in setting up the instrument for a part with a **widely different** dimension.
A **distinctly different** process operates in the system which ...

Совершенно иначе обстоит дело с
A completely different type of situation occurs in such substances as silicon.

Совершенно иначе, чем
The diode laser produces light **in a manner quite different from** the way the incandescent lamp does.
A glacier flows **much differently than** water.

Совершенно не оправдываться
At 3.095 MeV the assumption that the quark and the antiquark act as free particles **fails badly.**

Совершенно не отличаться от
In this respect the phenomenon **differs not at all** (*or* **does not differ in the least**) **from** that of ternary systems.

Совершенно не соответствовать
The response of the press to the accident **was all out of proportion to** the actual damage.

Совершенно независимо от
These clouds have motions of their own, **quite apart from** the motion of ...

Совершенно необходим
Careful design to prevent the leakage of tritium fuels **is mandatory.**
Thin sections **are a prime necessity** in the study of ...
The equations of general relativity **are indispensable to** a detailed analysis of ...

Совершенно необходимо
In aerospace manufacturing **this is a necessity** (*or* **a must**).
Money for scientific research is a scarce resource and **it is imperative that it be** used as efficiently as possible.

Совершенно необходимо, чтобы
It is important that the components offer the ultimate in reliability.

Совершенно необходимый [*см. тж.* **Необходимый**]
This is "a must" instrument **for** such studies (*or* This instrument **is "a must" for** such studies).

Совершенно непригоден
Such steels **are completely unusable** in many cases.
Pots **were entirely unsuited for** machine manufacture of ...

Совершенно нерастворим
Calcium carbonate **is quite insoluble in** water.

Совершенно новый
These **all-new** (*or* **entirely new**) specifications ...
We must create **radically new** technology.
The models **are totally** (*or* **altogether**) new.

Совершенно обратное
All the evidence proved **just the reverse.**

Совершенно отличаться от [*см.* **Абсолютно отличаться от**].

Совершенно отсутствовать на
The images of the satellite **show no** craters **what(so)ever** (*на изображениях спутника ...*).

Совершенно очевиден
The tendency toward negative values **is quite marked** (*or* **obvious,** *or* **evident,** *or* **pronounced**).

Совершенно очевидно, что [*см. тж.* **Совершенно ясно, что**]
It is apparent (*or* **obvious,** *or* **clear,** *or* **evident**) **that** Fig. 9.33 is fully analogous to Fig. 9.23.
As can well be imagined, smooth progress during drilling operations depends largely on their efficiency.
It is amply evident that living things are chemical entities.
Quite apparently, the characteristics may be different.

Совершенно ясно, что [*см. тж.* **Совершенно очевидно, что**]
It is amply clear that there is no direct interaction between ...
Therefore, **it is evident that** the Earth's atmosphere was not solely derived from ...
It is now **well understood that** a careful treatment of this assumption is the key to ...
Clearly (*or* **Plainly**), r is negative for each point between ...
It should be readily (*or* **clearly**) **apparent that** this type of valve is not suitable on ocean-going vessels.

Совершенный [*см. тж.* **Усовершенствованный**]
More **elaborate** presentation of time-resolved spectral data can be prepared by computer.
As more **sophisticated** (*or* **perfect**) diagnostic techniques become available, ...

Совершенство
The level of this text does not require a high degree of mathematical **sophistication.**
The precision of measurements depends on the degree of **sophistication** of the equipment.

Совершенствовать [*см.* **Улучшать**].

Совместим с
The collector's shaker mechanism **is compatible with** existing units in operation.

Совместить с
The gravitational attractions of the Sun and the Moon produce a torque required **to bring** the equatorial plane **into coincidence with** the ecliptic plane.

Совместно [*см. тж.* **В сочетании с**]
For most efficient removal of air, these two methods are used **in combination.**
An additional resistor should be used **in conjunction with** a single capacitor.
Present trends are toward water-tube boilers used **in conjunction with** high-pressure steam turbines.
The governor functions **integrally with** the fuel control system.

A decision on the method of analysis should be taken by the client and the analyst **in consultation.**
The discovery was made **jointly** by two observers.
The two phenomena **combine to** create ...

Совместно выполняться
In microprocessing, a certain kind of task **can be shared by** several machines.

Совместно с [*см. тж.* **В сочетании с, Вместе с**]
Clovers may be grown **in combination with** grasses and other legumes.
Seafloor spreading may operate independently or **in association with** continental drift.
The analyst must decide **in conjunction with** his technological colleagues how ...
In collaboration (*or* **cooperation**) **with** Dr ... we synthesized ...

Совместное действие
The strain produced **by the joint action of** two or more stresses is the sum of ...

Совместное мероприятие
Many physicists think such **joint ventures** are already working well.

Совместное решение
Simultaneous solution of these equations must be ...

Совместные уравнения
By using this technique the infinite system can be reduced to a single pair of **simultaneous equations.**

Совместные усилия
The National Electric Code was the result of **united** (*or* **joint**) **efforts of** various organizations.

Совместный
Both axial and radial dispersion are due to the **combined** effects of molecular diffusion and mixing.
In this **collaborative** (*or* **joint**) experiment photons were directed against ...
The **joint** resistance of resistances in parallel is ...
The **joint** magnetizing effect of both sets of coils ...

Совмещать
Set air temperature on the scale *A* **opposite** pressure on the scale *B*.
The movement of the steering-motor armature **brings** the slider **into coincidence with** the new position of ...
The zero of the vernier is then **made coincident with** the zero of the dial.
The abrasive machinery **combines** turning and grinding **in** a single grinding operation.
This type of ventilation is **combined with** the new method.

Совмещать в себе
This method of high-speed metal deposition **combines** electroplating **and** honing.
The antennae **combine** several sense organs (*zool.*).

Совпадать [*см. тж.* **Близко совпадать, Контуры ... совпадают, На одной линии с, Находиться на одном уровне с, Согласовываться с**]
Rotate the inner disk until the figure 20 on the minutes scale **is opposite** the figure 40 on the miles scale.
The results **agree** (*or* **coincide,** *or* **accord**) very closely.
If the micrometer readings do not **agree with** the gauge dimensions, wear is indicated.
Turn the knob until the pointer **is coincident with** zero of the index.
Hold the bottle alongside the graduated scale until the two water levels **are in line.**
The level in the bottle **should be in line with** zero on the burette.
— These observations **fit** two quite diverse sets of facts.
The two invariants **agree** (*or* **coincide**) **with** those found previously.
The milling head is moved transversely until the spindle **is coincident with** the centre line of the workpiece.
The part is clamped onto the machine with its axes **aligned with** those of the machine.

Совпадать по фазе
The reference oscillator **must be in phase with** the desired signal.

Совпадение [*см. тж.* **До совпадения с, При совпадении**]
A qualitative **agreement between** theory **and** experiment ...
Good **agreement is** observed **with** values computed from ...

The figures show a good **fit** of the equation **to** the data.

Современная ступень развития [*см.* **На современной ступени развития**].

Современное состояние
We shall review the **current status of** research on the application of high-power lasers to the generation of fusion power.
It will be instructive to review **the (current) state of the art in** the development of high-power pulsed lasers.

Современной конструкции
Figure 37 shows a two-throw pump **of present-day** (*or* **up-to-date**) **design.**

Современные нормы [*см.* **По современным нормам**].

Современный [*см. тж.* **В современном виде**]
One **modern-day** solution to these problems involves ...
An **up-to-date** textbook ...
In **recent** devices the conflicting demands of speed and sensitivity are met by ...
Present-day processes of mineral accumulation are extremely slow.
Present views are outlined below.
Even the **current** models of the atom must be viewed as imperfect.
Contemporary crystal rectifiers resemble what is ...
In **modern** practice, the evaporators are usually worked by bled steam.
Those boilers resembled the water-tube boiler **of today.**
Cycle temperatures greater than 2300°R have not been found to be practical because of limitations **of the present** high-temperature materials and **present** turbine-blade cooling techniques.
Present-day merchant vessels ...
Present-day (*or* **Modern**) amphibians are highly specialized animals.
Current engines ...
Today's aircraft ...

Современный метод
This can be attained by **currently available methods.**

Современный уровень [*см.* **Доводить до современного уровня**].

Совсем [*см.* **Совершенно**].

Совсем другое дело
The strain caused by meteorite impact **is another thing altogether** (*or* **is something else again**).

Совсем или почти не [*см.* **Почти или совсем не**].

Совсем наоборот
Quite to the contrary, evidence has been presented that ...

Совсем не [*см. тж.* **Или совсем не**]
The type of cutting tool **is by no means** new.
Neopentane reacts very slowly or **not at all** with bromine.
At such times the currents were flowing weakly or **not at all.**

Совсем не ... или мало
Norepinephrine produces **little or no** change in cardiac output.

Совсем не отличаться от [*см.* **Совершенно не отличаться от**].

Совсем не похож на
This piece of equipment **looks nothing like** a hydraulic press.

Согласие [*см. тж.* **Единое мнение относительно того, Находиться в хорошем согласии с, Нет согласия между ..., Соответствие**]
This remarkable **accord between** theory **and** observation ...
The figures show **a good fit of** the equation **to** the data (*or* **good agreement between** the equation **and** the data).

Согласно [*см. тж.* **В соответствии с, По**]
Every minor formed from the first three rows is zero **by** property (ii).
These proteins appear, **from** X-ray diffraction patterns, to be "linear" molecules.
Navy aircraft designations **by** function are given in Table 2.
The buttons are produced **to** [*or* **in accordance** (*or* **compliance,** *or* **conformity**) **with**] the established requirements.
The degree of vacuum can be adjusted **to suit** individual requirements.

Согласно взглядам
In that **view** the universe was filled with ...

Согласно вычислениям ... составляет
The lattice energy of AgCl **is calculated to be** 211.0 kcal/mole.

Согласно вышеприведённому определению
The wave, **as defined above,** implies the existence of ...

Согласно гипотезе
This equation has, **by hypothesis,** *n* distinct roots.
On another **hypothesis** the difference results from ...
One hypothesis states (*or* **asserts**) **that** the basaltic magma undergoes ...
Under this hypothesis, seismic activity should be observed along ...

Согласно его заявлению [*см.* **По его словам**].

Согласно закону
By (*or* **According to**) Newton's second **law,** the force is proportional to ...
The orbital periods of stars of average masses are, **by virtue of** Kepler's third **law**, 10^6 to 10^7 years.
The total mass of the system is, **from** Kepler's third **law**, m_1 + ...

Согласно заявлениям (утверждениям)
It has been claimed that the theory of relativity is contradictory.

Согласно земным нормам
All the simple compounds would be present on Jupiter in unbelievable quantity **by earthly standards.**

Согласно инструкции
The plates were processed **as prescribed** (*or* **directed**) **by the makers** [*or* **as prescribed** (*or* **directed,** *or* **stipulated**) **by the instructions,** *or* **in accordance with** (*or* **according to,** *or* **in compliance with,** *or* **in conformity with**) **the instructions**].

Согласно интерпретации
On (*or* **According to**) **this interpretation** the extended radio sources are observed at large angles to the direction of their jets.

Согласно критерию
By (*or* **According to**) **these criteria,** the main mass of the lunar highlands is older than the mare (*seas*).

Согласно механизму [*см.* **По механизму**].

Согласно наблюдениям
As observed in a spectrograph of moderate dispersion, the width of the atomic emission lines is usually determined by ...
It has been observed that an increase in double bonding increases ...

Согласно нашим нормам
This speed is considered fast **by our standards.**

Согласно нашим подсчётам
Our estimate is that (*or* **According to our estimates**) geothermal energy will be ...

Согласно обычаям [*см.* **По традиции**].

Согласно одной точке зрения
One view holds that the granite was derived by reworking of a primitive granite segregation.

Согласно оценке [*см.* **По приближённым оценкам, Согласно подсчётам**].

Согласно оценке ... должен составлять
One recent **guess** (*or* **estimate**) **places** the output of these wells **at** a possible 130,000 megawatts by 1995.

Согласно оценке ... составляет
Assessment (*or* **Estimate**) **of** ... **comes to** only 1% of the energy potential available through hydropower development.

Согласно подсчётам
The average amount of boron in the Earth's crust **is estimated as** three parts per million.
The friction factor **was calculated to be** 0.00923 [*or* **According to the calculation** (*or* **estimates**) the friction factor is 0.00923].
Evaporation was cut **an estimated** 80%.

Согласно правилу
By convention (*or* **According to the rule**), cations are written before anions.

Согласно предположению
This equation has **by hypothesis** *n* distinct roots.
The activation energy associated with ... is about 0.12 eV **as suggested by** our scientists.

Согласно принципу
Under (*or* **According to**) this **principle,** rock of the cold slab must be denser than mantle rock of ...

Согласно современным взглядам
In the modern (*or* **present**) **view**, this theory is obsolete.
According to present views ...
According to current concepts, the sequence of amino acids ...
The current concept is that most of the dikes are injected along a narrow zone.

Согласно современным нормам
The forming of these metals was crude **by modern standards.**

Согласно сообщениям
According to the manufacturer, etc.
Titanium carbide cutting tools, **it is stated,** have been used "intermittently" for about 45 years.
These space charges **reportedly** (*or* **are said to**) have influenced results of physiological tests.
One species **is said** (*or* **reported**) **to** produce xerosin.
The system **is claimed to** be particularly suitable to ...

Согласно теории
This **theory holds that** the earth started hot, but has been losing heat ever since.
The wave **theory supposes that** this radiation consists of ...

Согласно терминологии
Chemical **terminology would have it that** (*or* **According to chemical terminology**) spontaneous processes are those in which every instance of ...

Согласно техническим условиям
Tools ground **to our specifications ...**
The test report is performed **in accordance** (*or* **compliance,** *or* **conformity**) **with the specifications.**
The equipment is designed and built **to the** most exact **specifications.**

Согласно указаниям [*см.* **Согласно инструкции**].

Согласно экспериментальным данным
Experimentally, formaldehyde boils at –21°C at 1.00 atm.

Согласован
The new unit of luminous intensity **was agreed upon** at the meeting.

Согласованный
The use of thermometers with **agreed (-upon)** scales ...

Согласовывать с
One of the solutions to providing special contacts is **to interface** the electronic gear **with** the environment at higher circuit voltages.
We attempted **to fit** equation 1 **to** our experimental data.
The above sequence of events is difficult **to reconcile with** data from other laboratories.

Согласовываться с [*см. тж.* **Близко совпадать, Довольно плохо согласуется с, Прекрасно согласовываться с**]
The general scheme of lithospheric motion **conforms with** modern plate tectonics (*geol.*).
The descriptions of the proteins **concur with** analyses of the RNAs.
This observation **correlates well with** the above suggestion.
This assumption **fitted well with** the generally accepted idea.
Any model **must be consistent with** experiment.
These factors **are** not easily **compatible with** the model.
Each method **is agreed upon by** oncologists.
Be sure that the circuit load **matches** the switch.
The results **check well** [*or* **agree,** *or* **are in (good) agreement**] **with** those obtained previously ...
The results **were** sufficiently **consistent to** permit us ...
This **is consistent with** the idea that stable precipitates are ...
All available data **correlate well.**
The data **fit** the present curves **(reasonably) well.**
This finding **is in line** (*or* **harmony**) **with** that of other investigators.

Согласующийся с
The theory gives results **in agreement with** (*or* **in conformity with,** *or* **conforming to**) experimental results.

Соглашаться с
They could not **go along** (*or* **agree**) **with** Newton when he said that ...

Содействовать [*см. тж.* **Значительно содействовать, Способствовать**]
Radiometric determinations **can be of assistance in** assigning dates to rocks.
All these factors **aid in** achieving a reduced lasing threshold in ...
The method **assisted** (*or* **aided,** *or* **helped**) the operator **in** speeding up ...

Содержание I [*см. тж.* **Низкое содержание, Основное содержание, С высоким содержанием, С низким содержанием, Со средним содержанием**]
Some carbon steels used in the manufacture of taps have **a** vanadium **content of** about 0.25%.
The rate of absorption is proportional to **the** total liquid **holdup in** the apparatus.
The salt **content of** the river is high.

Содержание II
The content of Hamilton's principle is not changed if ...

Содержание бактерий
The production of milk of **an** acceptably low **bacteria count ...**

Содержание ... в
The vapour **content of** the air ...

Содержание лактозы мало́
In the whale **the lactose in** milk **is low.**

Содержать I
The gases which **contain** such molecules ...
The van **contains** both heating and air conditioning equipment.
The zone **can hold** two electrons per atom.
The free 40 *S* particles **bear** (*or* **contain**) a protein absent from the 60 *S* units (*biol.*).
The cells that **hold** the pigment ...
Ice sheets and mountain glaciers **hold** 2% of the world's water.
The molecule **incorporates** four sulphur atoms.

Содержать II
The table **lists** some values of ...

Содержать большое количество
Histones of sperm **are abundantly supplied with** cysteine.
The planet's atmosphere **contains** H_2 **in abundance.**

Содержать большое количество примесей
This material **is very impure.**

Содержать в себе
The galactic centre **harbors** (*or* **contains**) a large number of pulsars.

Содержать в среднем
Ocean water **averages** about 3.5 percent of dissolved solids.

Содержать в хорошем состоянии
The pump buckets **should be maintained** (*or* **kept**) **in good condition.**

Содержать в чистоте
The electrodes **should be kept clean.**

Содержать информацию [*см.* **Нести в себе информацию**].

Содержать массу информации
The data of Table (12-1) **constitute** (*or* **contain**) **a wealth of information on ...**

Содержать небольшое количество примесей
If the calcium sulphide **is slightly impure,** its use ...

Содержаться в
About three-fourths of the energy supplied **resides in** the carbohydrate product.
Europium **is found** (*or* **occurs,** *or* **is contained,** *or* **is present**) **in** small quantities in monazite.
Most of the comet mass **is contained in** the solid nucleus.
Most of the world's water, 97%, **is held in** the oceans.
In this machine, all of the processing logic **is contained in** the central processing unit.

Содержаться в большом количестве
Carbon, nitrogen, oxygen, sulphur and hydrogen **are (all) abundant in** solar wind.
Above that zone hydrogen and helium prevailed, but methane, etc. also **abounded.**

Содержаться в недостаточном количестве
Sulphur **is deficient in** the Earth's crust.

Содержаться в чрезмерном количестве
If the foreign material in the coal **is excessive, ...**

Содержащий
Indium-**bearing** (*or* **containing**) metals ...
Large systems **involving** hundreds of equations have been successfully solved.
Ionic crystals **involving** (*or* **incorporating**) polyatomic ions ...
Natural suspensions **bearing** the necessary amino acids ...

Содержащий новейшую информацию
It is the world's **most up-to-the-minute** journal.

Содержащийся в
The free energy **inherent in** hydrogen gas is the driving force of this process.

Содержащийся в хорошем состоянии
Well-maintained roads ...

Содержится больше, чем
Aspartic acid **was more abundant in** the proteinoid **than** glutamic acid.

Соединение I [*см. тж.* **В месте соединения, Соединён(ный) параллельно (последовательно)**]
A fish plate is a simple bar used for **joining** rails in tracks.
A welded **joint ...**

Соединение II [*см. тж.* **Вступать в соединение**]
Linking together the monomer units ...
Oxidation is defined as **the combination** (*or* **union**) **of** oxygen **with** some other element.
A chemical **compound.**
The term "hydride" is used to describe **a compound of** an element **with** hydrogen.

Соединение с тройными связями
A triply bonded compound.

Соединены
When the two continents **were joined together, ...**
The electrodes **are connected to** the grid.
The ends of the tube **were connected to** (*or* **with**) steel castings by ball-and-socket joints.

Соединён
The transmitter **is coupled to** the shaft.
This conductor **can be joined to** members of similar thickness.

Соединён зубчатой передачей
The indicator pointer **is geared to** the hand-wheel.

Соединён кабелем
The meter **is cable connected to** the main assembly.

Соединён ординарной (*или* **простой**) **связью** (*хим.*)
Each carbon **is singly bonded with** both adjacent carbon atoms.

Соединён(ный) параллельно
Filter capacitors **are connected across** each resistor.
The two triodes **are connected** (*or* **placed**) **in parallel.**
Two **parallel-connected** valves ...

Соединён(ный) последовательно
The arrangement uses a thermostat **in series with** the solar cells.
A resistor **is (placed) in series with** the output lead.
The current passes through the bias resistor and the **series** control valve.

Соединён с
The spectroscope **is attached to** a telescope.
The ferrous ion **is linked to** a porphyrin molecule.

Соединён шестернёй с
The traction motor **is geared to** the driving axle.

Соединённые (друг с другом)
The clutches have hinged shoes **connected together by** a kinematic mechanism.
A set of balls **joined together by** springs ...

Соединённые болтами
The plates **bolted together ...**
The ducts **bolted to** the covering ...

Соединённые концами
A regular curve is the union of a finite number of regular arcs **placed end to end.**

Соединённые на резьбе
The valve is made of two portions **threadedly connected together.**

Соединённые рёбрами

The arrangement of atoms is similar to that of Al_2Cl_2, that is two **edge-shared** tetrahedra.

Соединённый водородными связями
A **hydrogen-bonded** water structure.

Соединённый с
An integrator pen **coupled to** a ball ...

Соединять [*см. тж.* **Подсоединять к**]
Connect points *A* and *C* **with** a straight line.
The first line **joins** points P_1 and P_2.
The line **joins** *dl* **to** *P*.
The machine **joins together** the edges of plastic flooring.
A cable **connects** the loop **to** the control unit.

Соединять болтами [*см.* **Скреплять болтами**].

Соединять в себе [*см. тж.* **Объединять**]
The parts **combine** impact strength **with** dielectric strength.

Соединять гранями
These are solid figures created by **joining** cubes **at their faces.**

Соединять при помощи связи
To unite two amino acids **by means of a** peptide **bond, ...**

Соединяться с I
The exhaust hood **connects** (*or* **is connected to**) the condenser.
The other end of the propeller shaft **connects with** another set of gears.
A rudder motor **is coupled to** the rudder through gearing.
The anchor base is located where the arm **meets** the shoulder.

Соединяться с II
A number of elements **combine with** uranium.

Соединяться концами
In a series circuit, all the components **are connected end to end.**

Соединяться прямой (линией)
Two adjacent points **may be connected by a** straight **line.**

Соединяться с
The iron oxide formed in the reactions **unites** (*or* **combines**) **with** silica in the ore to form a slag.

Соединяться с образованием
One volume of chlorine and one volume of hydrogen **combine to give** (*or* **to form,** *or* **with the formation of**) two volumes of hydrogen chloride.

Соединяться, образуя
Many metals **combine with** sulphur **to form** sulphides.
Rings of silica tetrahedra **are linked (together) to form** beryl.

Соединяться углами, гранями, рёбрами
In addition to the **sharing of corners,** coordination polyhedra may **unite by the sharing of faces or edges.**

Создаваемый [*см. тж.* **Вызван**]
The current **induced by** a magnetic field ...
The distortion **due to** the quadrature component is less than ...
The differential pressure **produced** at the measuring point ...
The lines of force **set up by** the stator coils are perpendicular to ...
Oscillations **set up in** an aircraft **by** a momentary disturbance ...

Создавать I [*см. тж.* **Вызывать, Образовывать, Организовывать, Проектировать, Разрабатывать**]
The compounds that nature can **produce ...**
The magnetic moment **produces** a diamagnetic effect.
It is this reaction which **builds up** the reservoir of activated molecules.
Displacing a particle in one direction **brings about** a force in the opposite direction.
Within a short time of this discovery a whole new field of research **had been launched.**
This vibrational resonance **can create** new photons.
Industrial and professional societies **have brought into being** (*or* **existence**) a wide variety of standards.
Where the valley is narrow the earthflow toe **forms** a dam, sometimes **creating** a lake.
To build up (*or* **produce**) sufficient pressure so as to ensure ...

These forces cannot **develop** torque.
If the rotor is given the shape of a polygon, the lines of force **exert** the desired torque.
In large crystals the dislocations interact **to generate** new ones.
The detonation wave upon impacting the wave shaper **generates** a shock wave.
The heat **generated by** magnetization ...
The feedback **generates** parasitic laser oscillations.
The resistance element **generates** precision voltages.
The use of a driving belt could **give rise to** vibration.
The model was rotated in a centrifuge **to induce** centrifugal forces.
The pump **produces** a vacuum of 0.1 mm.
When a current passes through a wire, it **sets up** a magnetic field around the wire.
The magnetic field **sets up** a magnetomotive force.
The flywheels **set up** in the spring-mounted screen a motion which ...
The heating of the coils **sets up** a ventilating draught.
The object of the experiment **is to build up** a high current of charged particles.
The gradient of viscous shear stresses **establishes** a steady-state concentration gradient.
These energy transitions **give rise to** pockets of photons.
This **brings with it** acute problems of electrical interference.
In the past 20 years the electronics industry **has generated** many completely new technological systems.
The media **bring into existence** and cultivate a new form of common consciousness.

Создавать II
Systems with odd numbers of channels **can** also **be devised.**
An instrument **has been created** (*or* **devised**) for ...
The research staffs **are evolving** workable designs.
The engineers **have come up with** an improved technique for ...
He **originated** the projection method.

Создавать большие затруднения
Aerodynamic heating **is** (*or* **presents**) **a severe problem** at high flight speeds.

Создавать большие трудности для
Various industrial wastes **pose major problems for** modern society.
This requirement **presented a considerable challenge to** the experimenters.

Создавать вакуум
This **gives rise to a vacuum.**

Создавать возможности [*см.* **Открывать возможности**].

Создавать волну
The combustion **wave was initiated** (*or* **set up**) **by** a spark.

Создавать впечатление, что
He tried **to give the impression that** the experiment was original with him.

Создавать давление
Then the pump fails **to build up** (*or* **produce**) adequate **pressure.**

Создавать затруднения
In steel grinding, the chemical reactivity of diamond **may be** (*or* **present**) **a problem.**
The possible role of phosphorus in prebiotic syntheses **poses (great) difficulties.**

Создавать избыток
The more rapid diffusion of ammonia **leaves** hydrogen chloride **in excess.**

Создавать крутящий момент
This attraction **produces a torque.**

Создавать магнитное поле
To produce (*or* **induce**, *or* **create**) **a magnetic field, ...**

Создавать напряжение [*см. тж.* **Наводить напряжение**]
Internal **stresses are set up** (*or* **induced**, *or* **produced**) **by** uneven contraction.

Создавать основу
This molecular concept of matter **provided the basis** on which the behaviour of gases could be studied.

Создавать поле
When a voltage is applied to this device, it **sets up** (*or* **creates,** *or* **induces**) **an** electric **field.**

Создавать полюса
The coil **establishes** (*or* **induces**) **poles** that generate currents in ...

Создавать потенциал
To generate a potential.

Создавать поток
In order **to initiate the flow** a second perturbation is required.

Создавать почву для
By the time the Sun had become a true star **the stage for** the formation of the planets **had already been set.**

Создавать разность потенциалов
Difference in temperature between ... **sets up a difference in** (electrical) **potential.**

Создавать свойство
A similar tempering cycle **develops the** desired physical **properties.**

Создавать теорию
One way **to establish** (*or* **develop,** *or* **elaborate**) **a theory** is to make predictions ...

Создавать термин
The lunar soil is **a term coined by** lunar geologists to avoid saying "power" or "dust".

Создавать токи
Eddy **currents are set up** inside the Moon.

Создавать трудности
Gravity would be so small as **to give rise to** technological difficulties (*or* **to present ...problems**).

Создавать усилие
These **forces may be established by** the compression of axial springs.

Создавать шумы
Sudden increases in the rate of pressure rise sometimes **produce noise**s which are confused with combustion knock.

Создаваться [*см. тж.* **Возникать**]
The internal circulation **is set up** (*or* **caused**) **by** the gas-liquid surface shear forces.
Surface defects **are produced by** gases.
The magnetic field **is set up** (*or* **induced,** *or* **produced**) **by** the current flowing through ...
The convective currents **are set up by** the temperature difference.
New cable systems **are** now **in the making.**
The pressure **is created by** detonation.
These forces **are exerted by** the stars.

Создаваться благодаря
Additional stability **is conferred by** delocalization of ...

Создалось впечатление
Many people **have formed an impression of** the Earth as a uniquely beautiful oasis in a harsh and hostile universe.

Создан
Some of our rock names **were coined by** miners in the Middle Ages.

Создание [*см. тж.* **Появление, С появлением, С созданием**]
They observed small numbers of ionization events before **the advent of** lasers.
Optical elements for **realizing** low-cost processors ...
The energy required for **creating** such a charge ...
The generation of such vortices ...
The preparation of new compounds ...
The evolution of the personal computer followed **the advent of** the microprocessor.

Создание и разрушение химических связей
Making and breaking of chemical bonds.

Созданный
The new beam **created at** ω_A can further combine with ω_L.

Создатель
Lord Kelvin, **the originator of** this temperature scale, ...

Создать новую область
The transistor **opened a new area of** solid-state electronic technology.

Создать себе репутацию в области
They **have built up a reputation for** the manufacture of heavy-duty gears.

Создать термин
The term *phi* phenomenon **was coined by** an experimental psychologist.

Создающий
The number of protons **responsible for** the signals ...

Сознавать [*см. тж.* **Остро сознавать, Понимать, Чётко представлять себе**]
We **are aware of** the need to protect the ecological balance.

Сознавать, что
You **are** probably **aware that** the time dimension is extremely important in geology.

Созревать
That technique **has (now) come of age.**
The conditions **are ripe for** the formation of ...

Сокращать I [*см. тж.* **Уменьшать**]
To keep the setup time **down, ...**
This **cut** (*or* **reduced,** *or* **decreased**) cleaning time over 50 percent from old methods.
The device **cuts down** engineering man hours.
To cut (*or* **trim,** *or* **reduce**) the cost of ...
Coalescence into the Gulf Stream often **cuts short** the life of an eddy.

Сокращать II (*матем.*)
Like factors **can be cancelled from** the numerator and denominator.
We **cancel** two out of that fraction.

Сокращать III
The electron volt **will** (now) **be abbreviated to** eV.

Сокращать вдвое [*см.* **Сокращать вполовину, Уменьшать вдвое**].

Сокращать вполовину (наполовину)
This method **can cut** metal wear **in** (*or* **by**) **half.**

Сокращать время обработки вполовину (наполовину)
We **have cut machining time in** (*or* **by**) **half.**

Сокращать по начальным буквам
We **abbreviate** these directions **by initial letters** *SE, NW,* etc.

Сокращаться I [*см. тж.* **Сжиматься, Снижаться, Уменьшаться**]
The range in water level between high and low tide **is cut down.**
The base flow declines slowly as the ground-water supply **dwindles** (*or* **goes down,** *or* **reduces**).
Production **will be down** (*or* **reduced**) in the aircraft industry.
Production has continued **to decline** (*or* **drop,** *or* **fall off**).
The yield **falls to** 80 percent at 1000°.
In this atmosphere oxygen **is reduced to** 100 ppm.
The life of the machine **is impaired by** excessive heating.

Сокращаться II (*матем.*)
The fraction 4/8 **can be cancelled by** 2.
The first terms **cancel out** only because the second terms do not **cancel.**
These terms appear both in the numerator and the denominator, so that they **cancel.**

Сокращаться III (*анат.*)
The muscles **contract** under the action of the acid.

Сокращение [*см. тж.* **Падение**]
The rhythmic **contractions** of the heart are controlled by (*anat.*)...

Сокращение дробей
Reduction of fractions.

Сокращение мышц
Then the medusa is ready to repeat **muscular** (*or* **muscle**) **contractions** (*or* **the contraction of muscles**) that lead to movement.

Сокращение объёма
A contraction of the volume of the balloon ...

Сокращение расходов на
To save on the wiring **cost, ...**

Сокращённо выражать в виде формулы
This compound **is abbreviated by** the chemists **with the formula** CO_2.

Сокращённое обозначение
"Bit" is **a contraction of** binary digit in the binary number system.

Сокращённый [*см. тж.* **В сокращённом виде**]
Here, $фД^2$ is a **shorthand** symbol for the last term in the equation.

Солнечная энергия [*см.* **На солнечной энергии**].

Солнечный свет падает на

That portion of the Moon's surface **was exposed to the sunlight.**

Соляные залежи
Salt from **salt beds** is obtained by mining.

Сомневаться [*см. тж.* **Едва ли можно сомневаться в, Никто не сомневается в**]
This kind of instruction is costly and some teachers **are doubtful of** its educational value.

Сомнение [*см.* **Вне всякого сомнения, Внушать сомнение относительно, Возникают сомнения относительно, Вселять сомнение, Вызывать сомнение относительно, Высказывать сомнение относительно, Находиться под сомнением, Не вызывать сомнения, Не подлежит сомнению, что; Нет ни малейшего сомнения в том, что; Ставить под сомнение**].

Сомнительная ценность [*см.* **Иметь сомнительную ценность для**].

Сомнительно
It is doubtful (*or* **questionable**) **if** (*or* **whether**) any detectable amount of this element occurs in nature.

Сомнительный
The authenticity of these data **is open to question** (*or* **is questionable**).

Сомнительный случай
In **questionable cases,** the tower height may be obtained by ...

Соображение [*см.* **В силу ... соображений, Высказывать соображения относительно, Из соображений, На основании ряда ... соображений**].

Соображения, лежащие в основе
To understand **the reasoning behind** this suggestion, ...

Соображения, связанные с загрязнением окружающей среды
Environmental considerations such as exposure to moisture, oils, or chemicals ...

Сообщать I [*см. тж.* **Придавать**]
The telemotor shaft **communicates** rotation **to** the power shaft.
The presence of hydrogen ions **endows** such compounds **with** acidic properties.
Very minute traces of metallic impurities in crystalline substances **endow** them **with** the power of emitting light ...
By **forcing** the partition **into** vibration ...
The main pinion **gives** the required speed **to** the rudder.
High-pressure oil **is given** a rapid whirling motion.
Energy **can be imparted to** the gas molecules in the form of ...
Some of these properties **can be imparted to** linear polyamides.
This set of nozzles **imparts** spin **to** the missile.
The high velocities which must **be imparted to** a missile ...
An aileron **impresses** a rolling motion **on** the airplane.
This energy **must be supplied to** a nucleus in order to ...

Сообщать II
In the next chapter we **fill in** many details about plate tectonics.
The astronomers **will communicate** (*or* **report**) their findings **to** other scientists.
We **presented** our results in a paper.

Сообщать высокую скорость
A particle **is brought to high speed.**

Сообщать движение
When **a** rotary **motion is imparted to** the fluid ...

Сообщать заряд
If we **impart** positive **charges to** both spheres, ...

Сообщать крутящий момент
An induction motor **supplies torque.**

Сообщать сведения
A great deal of **information** about an amplifier **is conveyed** (*or* **communicated**) **by** stating the coupling method used.

Сообщать свойство [*см.* **Придавать свойство**].

Сообщаться [*см.* **В ... сообщается о**].

Сообщаться с
The openings **are in communication** (*or* **communicate,** *or* **are connected**) **with** an annular passage.

Сообщают, что
It is stated that test running in this way corresponds to ...

Сообщающийся с атмосферой
The reaction is carried out in a container **open to the atmosphere.**

Сообщение [*см. тж.* **Согласно сообщениям**]
Photoacoustic spectroscopy is the subject of **a** separate **presentation** at this symposium.
According to one **account,** the aftershocks were a constant trembling.

Соосный
The outboard support bearing is honed to ensure that it **is** accurately **in line with** the bearing bores.

Соответственно I
Flares are about 20 times more frequent than sunspots, but their duration is **correspondingly** (*or* **accordingly**) much shorter.

Соответственно II
There are basically three types of extrusion known **respectively** as direct, inverse and impact.
m_1 and m_2 are the **respective** masses of the two bodies.

Соответственно III [*см.* **Должным образом**].

Соответствие [*см. тж.* **В однозначном соответствии с, В соответствии с, Находиться в соответствии с, Однозначное соответствие, Согласно**]
To maintain reasonable **consistency between** the nomenclatures for ...
A qualitative **agreement between** theory **and** experiment ...
The figures show **a** good **fit of** the equation **to** the data.
Compatibility between the packing **and** the sealed fluid is essential.
Agreement between the two estimates is excellent.
However, *A* is chosen for **consistency with** the weak-guidance results.
He found **an** excellent **correlation** (*or* **correspondence**) **between** the observed **and** computed magnetic profiles.
The correctness of ... is determined by **the match between** the calculated frequencies **and** the positions of ...
This **correspondence** (*or* **agreement**) **with** observation may give us some confidence.
The compliance of the instrument reading **with** the true value of ...

Соответствовать [*см. тж.* **Вписываться в, Находиться в соответствии с, Согласовываться с**]
The results **are consistent with** what is expected.
The results **check with** observations.
These trends in properties **correlate** (*or* **accord**) **with** our model of the atom.
When the energy difference between the two levels **is matched by** the energy of the photons (*когда энергия фотонов соответствует* ...).
The molecular dimensions of the organic solvent **match** those of the solute.
To every organism **(there) corresponds** an abstract topological space and ...
The core identification tapes **shall comply with** the requirements for insulating papers.
The instrument **conforms to** the specification.
The data **fit** the present curves reasonably well.
Equation (6.26) **fits** the data fairly well.
The numbers given to the contact blades **are in line with** the pin numbers on the octal base.
Their analyses **are in agreement** (*or* **in keeping**) **with** experimental observations.
The tooling **is peculiar to** the product being machined.
This feed rate **is appropriate to** the length to be delivered.
The position of the bulb **corresponds to** the true horizon.
This will make the controlled variable response **fall within** the specifications.
Because all chemical processes are reversible **there is for** every exoergic reaction a **corresponding** endoergic one.
For each signal **there is** only one response.

Соответствовать действительности
This assumption **will** approximately **represent the facts.**

Соответствовать наиболее точно [*см.* **Наиболее точно соответствовать**].

Соответствовать по своей структуре
Any three-dimensional array **must correspond in structure to** one of the 14 Bravais lattices.

Соответствовать требованиям
This combination **is** ideally **suited to the requirements of ...**

Соответствующий I [*см. тж.* **При соответствующих условиях**]
Examine the **corresponding** values of ...
These effects must be limited to a magnitude **compatible with** the desired accuracy.
The extinct bird had massive legs, **in keeping with** great body weight.
Test equipment **appropriate to** each test is installed.
To maintain the **requisite** temperature, ...
Steel **conforming to** (*or* **complying with**) the specifications ...

Соответствующий II
We supplied the hydraulic equipment and **associated** control systems.
Noise in electrical circuits arises because all the mechanisms **involved** are in dynamic and not absolute equilibrium.
Television transmitters and **their associated** transmission lines ...
The liver, spleen, kidneys ... with **(their) associated** nerves and blood vessels, are located in ...
Specialists trained in the **pertinent** (*or* **relevant**) branches of engineering ...
A cold storage plant is a large insulated building, with **its attendant** refrigeration equipment.

Соответствующий III
Selection of the **proper** aluminium alloy is extremely important.
Such results can be produced by exposure to hydrochloric acid of **appropriate** composition.
One end of the sling stay is held in a **suitable** bracket.
This variation can be measured by **suitable** photometers.
Appropriate substitutions should be made.
These numbers may be written with the **appropriate** algebraic signs.

Соответствующий IV
This will be discussed in the **relevant** (*or* **corresponding,** *or* **appropriate**) sections of the book.
Pertinent information is available in ...
The ions move to their **respective** electrodes under the influence of the applied voltage.
P_1 and P_2 are the periods of revolution of planet-1 and planet-2, D_1 and D_2 are their **respective** distances.

Соответствующий описанию
A rock mass **answering this description** is said to have homogeneous structure.

Соответствующим образом [*см. тж.* **Должным образом**]
Recognition of this symmetry **correspondingly** simplifies the study of ...
Cokes are produced from a wide variety of coals, and their properties vary **accordingly** (*or* **correspondingly**).
Start the main feed-water pump and adjust the feed-water check valve **as needed** (*or* **required**).
See that the "earth" is **properly** connected.
This effect is taken into account **suitably** changing the value of *m*.

Соотношение [*см. тж.* **Выводить уравнение, Находиться в соотношении, Отношение**]
For proper operation of the pump, **the relation(ship) between** speed **and** heat should be fully understood.
There is **a** definite mathematical **relationship among** the masses of all substances involved in chemical reactions.

Сопоставление
A **correlation** was made **between** impact strength **and** impurity content.
The relative basis must be determined by **correlation with** other types of tests.

Сопоставлять ... с
We **correlated** our measurements **with** the results of ...
The fluorescence intensity obtained from the solid **can be related to** the rare earth concentration in solution.

Соприкасаться [*см. тж.* **Касаться, Не соприкасающийся, Непосредственно соприкасающийся с**]
The metallic surfaces that **are in contact** during sliding friction ...

Every particle of oil **should come** directly **in** (*or* **into**) **contact with** a particle of air (for combustion).
The cold air **comes in contact with** hot brickwork.
When it is undesirable for the process fluid **to contact** the instrument, ...
When the work **contacts** (*or* **touches**) the grinding wheel, ...
It normally does **not make contact** with ...
The surface **is exposed to** a hot gas.

Соприкасающиеся вещества
The behaviour of different **substances in contact** (*or* **contacting substances**) is greatly affected by ...

Соприкасающиеся поверхности
The contact(ing) surfaces of the valve seat and disk ...

Соприкасающийся с
The activity of the phase **in contact with** the surface was low.

Соприкосновение [*см.* **Без соприкосновения с воздухом, Вступать в соприкосновение с, Контакт, Поверхность соприкосновения, При соприкосновении, Приводить в соприкосновение, Приходить в соприкосновение с**].

Сопровождать
The vibrational-energy changes **accompany** (*or* **attend**) the energy change due to ...

Сопровождаться
Such tests **must be accompanied by** other tests that are more ...
The production of this compound **is attended with** (*or* **by**) the maximum heat evolution.
The initial etch **is followed by** a second, or fine etch.
All natural processes **must occur with** an increase of entropy.

Сопровождающий
Melting **attendant on** (*or* **involved in**) the formation of igneous rocks ...

Сопротивление [*см. тж.* **Абсолютно не встречая сопротивления, Оказывать сопротивление**]
Abrasion (*or* Corrosion, etc.) **resistance ...**
A coil of wire **of 100 Ω resistance ...**
The metal **offers** a high **resistance.**

Сопротивляемость [*см.* **Стойкость к**].

Сопрягаться с
The upper (male) section **mates with** the lower (female) section.

Сопряжённые детали
Mating parts may need clearance if they are to be assembled freely.

Сопутствовать
Flame is not **a** necessary **accompaniment of** combustion.

Сопутствующий
All other **attendant** problems can be solved easily.

Сорт [*см.* **Высокосортный, Низкосортный**].

Сорт ... определяется по
Coals **are ranked according to** the percentage of carbon they contain.

Сортировать по размерам
The vibratory screen **sizes** the material **into** -3/8 in., -1/4 in., and dust.

Соседний
Interactions between **neighbouring** nuclei occur when ...
This construction lets you remove any major assembly without disturbing **adjacent** assemblies.
The distance between **adjacent** holes should be the same.
The fire affected some **neighbouring** installations.

Сосредоточен
Operating controls **are grouped on** a pendant unit.

Сосредоточивать внимание [*см. тж.* **Концентрировать внимание на**]
Attention must be centred on the removal of industrial wastes.
Up to this point **we have concentrated** (*or* **focussed our attention**) **on** single-particle properties of matter.
We now **need to focus** (*or* **centre**) **upon** the mechanisms of ...
It will be **to** such systems that we now **direct out attention.**

Сосредоточивать усилия на

The investigators **focussed their efforts on** the last century.

Сосредоточиваться на
Much of the current interest in the subject **is centred on** the details of ...

Состав [*см. тж.* **Входить в состав, Иметь состав, Фазовый состав**]
The constitution of various hydrocarbon groups ...
Depending on **the formulation** (*or* **composition**), the hardness of enamels ranges from ...
Synthetic resin glues **are of** many **formulations.**
The atomic **makeup** of the molecule ...

Состав атмосферы
The atmospheric composition.

Состава
Brucite is a mineral **of** (*or* **having**) **composition** $Mg(OH)_2$ and ...
The silica tetrahedral groups are arranged to form a tetrahedral network **with the** (*or* **of**) **composition** $Si_4O_6(OH)_4$.

Составлен из
This series of compounds **is formulated from** [*or* **composed** (*or* **made up**) **of**] several types of resins.
The solution **was made up from** liquid components.

Составление
The preparation of maps (solutions, tables, etc.).

Составление сметы на
The method of **costing** mechanization processes ...

Составлять I [*см. тж.* **Представлять собой**]
The three instruments **form** (*or* **comprise,** *or* **represent**) a signal generator assembly.
Fourteen die castings **make up** (*or* **constitute**) the principal components of ...
There are a number of plausible ways in which nucleons might be grouped **to make up** a nucleus.
These particles **compose** the hazes observed on Jupiter.
These three bonds **comprise** the triple bond.

Составлять II [*см. тж.* **Достигать**]
A mean sidereal day **comprises** 23 hr 56 min and 4 sec.
The apprentices' full term of training **covers** five years.
The canyon **forms** 5 percent of the satellite's surface.
The average planetoid diameter **would run** close **to** a mile.
Nitrogen, oxygen and argon together **account for** 99.97% of ...
The cost of cooling towers **may amount** to 50% of the total cost of ...
The value of this merchandise **comes to** only 10.4% of the total.
Argon **constitutes** (*or* **makes up**) almost 1% of the air.
The housing **measures** 12 in. in length.
The kinetic energies **range from** zero **(up) to** 3.5 MeV.
The build-up at edges **may run as high as** 0.05 in.
The investments **total** 10 mln dollars.
In man the adrenals **comprise** 0.0002% of the body weight.
In many such materials the clay-size grade and clay-mineral fractions **comprise** less than 50% of the total rock.
The figure **represents** about 27% of the gross national product.
The world's supply of californium **is in the range of** millionths of a gram.
Electrons **contribute** (*or* **constitute**) the bulk of ordinary matter.

Составлять III
The computer **generates** production reports.

Составлять IV
We **formulate** (*or* **make up**) special compositions for ceramic bodies.

Составлять V
These errors may be allowed for by **making up** a calibration card for the instrument.
When **drawing up** a drill nomenclature ...
A design diagram **may be prepared** by plotting ...
To compile a map, a dictionary, a report ...

Составлять более [*см.* **Превышать**].

Составлять в среднем
The size of the feed **averages between** 18 in. **and** 21 in. cube.

The honing time **averages** 1 minute.
Production of steam **amounted to an average of** 900,000 lb per hour (*or* **was** 900,000 lb per hour **on the average**).

Составлять в сумме
The semicircles grow smaller and more numerous, but they always **add (up) to** *pi*.
Global reserves of fresh water **add up to** 37 million cubic kilometres.

Составлять график
Plot the free energy of mixing of chloroform and ethanol at 45°C.
Make a graph showing the volume of ... versus ...

Составлять до
Production speeds of such machines **range up to** 600 parts per minute.

Составлять долю
The length of this region **is (only) a fraction of** a chemical bond length.

Составлять единое целое с
The cascade thrust reverser **is an integral part of** the exhaust nozzle.
The particle counter **is integral to** the console.

Составлять карту
Charts have been prepared (*or* **compiled**) which show ...

Составлять неотъемлемую часть
Each machine has a worktable, which **is** either **integral with** it, or is accurately located in relation to it.
This equipment **makes** (*or* **is**) **an integral part** of many advanced systems.

Составлять основную часть
Gypsum **constitutes the major portion of** portland cement.
The heavy parts that **make up the bulk of** the engine ...

Составлять основу для [*см. тж.* **Лежать в основе**]
The flow **forms the basis for** (*or* **lies at the basis of**) most calculations.

Составлять от ... до
The power output **may run** (*or* **range**) **between** 2 and 20 (*or* **range from** 2 **to** 20) watts.
The polymer concentration **varies** (**in the range**) **from** 30 **to** 175 g/l.
The amplifier bandwidth **extends from** 20 **to** 20,000 cps.
The dielectric constant of mica **is** (*or* **lies**) **in the range of** 6–8.
The cadmium content of these byproducts **runs** (*or* **ranges**) **from** 2–3 **to** 25%.
The results **fall between** L **and** μ_S.

Составлять планы
Plans for the new factory **have been drawn up.**

Составлять половину
This series **is (only) half as great as** the series of all integers.

Составлять приблизительно
The gene **approximated** 400 nucleotides in length (*biol.*).

Составлять ряд
We **set up a series.**

Составлять ... сантиметров в длину
This meteorite **measures** 12 **cm in length**.

Составлять спецификацию
The specification was drawn up.

Составлять список
Geochemical researchers are gradually **putting together** (*or* **compiling,** *or* **making up**) **a list of** ingredients that go into ...

Составлять суть
This mode of electron transfer **is the essence of** charge-coupling.

Составлять схему
A *YX* **diagram is set up** as shown in Fig. 9.9.

Составлять таблицу
The following **table is prepared** containing ...

Составлять тему главы
The results of these investigations **provide the subject matter for** the present **chapter.**

Составлять угол с [*см. тж.* **Образовывать угол с**]
The scattered beam **makes an angle** ψ **with** the original direction.

Составлять уравнение
It is now possible **to set up an equation.**

Составлять часть
The slidewire **forms** (*or* **is,** *or* **comprises**) **(a) part of** the potentiometer.

Составляющая [*см. тж.* **Компонента, направленная под углом**]
The axial flow **component** is directed towards ...
At least one ion **constituent ...**

Составляющие его [*см. тж.* **Образующие его**]
The mass of an atom is less than the sum of the masses of **its constituent** (*or* **component**) protons, neutrons and electrons.

Составляющий I
Make sure that all the **component** (*or* **constituent**) amino acids are identified.
The particles **comprising** (*or* **making up**) the aerosol may remain liquid.

Составляющий II
One of the detectors consists of a solid cylinder **measuring** three feet in diameter and five feet in length.

Составляющий III
The **component** peaks of a chromatogram must be ...

Составляющий его
The rocks could have been melted when **their constituent** material was first added to the Moon.

Составляющий одно целое с
The deck-girder bridge consists of a concrete slab **built integrally with** a large series of ...

Составная часть
Sand is **an** important **constituent** [*or* **component (part),** *or* **ingredient**] **of** any block mix.

Составной элемент
Chalcopyrite **is an** original **constituent of** igneous rocks.

Состояние I [*см.* **В ... состоянии**].

Состояние II [*см.* **В зачаточном состоянии, По состоянию на**].

Состояние III [*см. тж.* **В отличном состоянии, Приводить в нерабочее состояние, Приводить в рабочее состояние, Содержать в хорошем состоянии**]
The metamorphosed **condition of** the rocks indicated that ...

Состояние готовности [*см.* **В состоянии готовности к**].

Состояние исследований в области
The (present) state of the art of predicting volcanic eruptions ...

Состояние покоя [*см.* **В состоянии покоя**].

Состоятельность [*см.* **Правильность**].

Состоять в [*см. тж.* **Заключаться в**]
The advantage of the method **lies in** its simplicity.
Until 1965 all high-energy physics experiments **involved** the bombardment of a stationary target with ...
The operation **consists in** trimming the ends of the slab.
One kind of deformation **involves** only volume change.
The difference between ... and ... **is in** the need for ...
The method **calls for** the injection of ammonia into ...

Состоять в следующем
The operation of the instrument **is as follows: ...**

Состоять в том, что [*см. тж.* **Заключаться в**]
The problem **lies in the fact that** the northern set of stripes runs at right angles to ...
The chief merit of this treatment of conjugated systems **is that** it offers an easy approach to ...

Состоять из I [*см. тж.* **Из которого состоит, Представлять собой**]
In each year, **there are** about 31,557,000 seconds.
Pink ruby **is comprised of** Al_2O_3 doped with 0.005% Cr_2O_3.
The rest of the plant **involves** (*or* **consists of**) typical mass transfer equipment.
Production of aluminum metal **involves** two steps.
Carbohydrate analysis **involves** separation of the carbohydrate mixture, identification of the individual carbohydrates, and estimation of their quantities.

The measuring system **is built up from** a number of standard units.
The element **is composed** (*or* **is made up,** *or* **consists**) **of** equal numbers of protons and neutrons.
Most of the common gaseous elements **are constituted by** diatomic molecules.
The rock **is made up of** the calcite shells of microorganisms.
The machine **is made up of** two subassemblies — a drive unit and ...
This class **is made up** almost entirely **of** metals.
The machine **is comprised of** three automatic drill units, two lead-screw tapping units, and a rotary-indexing turntable.
The stress tensor **comprises** the mechanical part **and** the viscous part.
The attachment **incorporates** a microscope **and** a protractor.
The hologram **comprises** (*or* **consists of**) 16 subholograms.

Состоять из II
These graphs **fall into** two groups.
The satellite's atmosphere **is** 90 percent methane.

Состоять на ... процентов из
Salmine **consists of** arginine **to the extent of** 88%.

Состояться
The exhibition **will be held** (*or* **will take place**) in the Kelvin Hall.

Состоящий в (*или* **из**)
Processes **involving** only mechanical changes ...

Состоящий в том, что [*см. тж.* **Заключаться в том, что**]
The theory is based upon an observation **to the effect that** the uniformity of water depth in coral lagoons might be well explained by ...

Сосуществовать
The two opposite properties usually **go together** (*or* **coexist**).

Сотрудничество между
Research and development **interplay** (*or* **cooperation**) **between** electronics manufacturers **and** educational institutions ...

Сохранение
The rearrangement proceeds with **retention of** configuration.
The conservation of energy ...

Сохранять [*см. тж.* **Выдерживать интервал**]
In all modern furnaces a double bell and a hopper are used **to conserve** the large volume of gas which ...
The angular momentum of this star **would be conserved** until the final stages of collapse.
This material **maintains** low loss characteristics throughout the entire spectrum.
The liquid metal **retains** (*or* **preserves**) its silver colour.
The material **retains** its properties over a wide temperature range.

Сохранять желаемую форму
When released from its mould, the alloy **holds** (*or* **retains**) **the desired shape.**

Сохранять свою форму
The rock **will hold its shape** when resting on a flat surface.

Сохранять силу [*см. тж.* **Действителен для**]
The approximation **holds** (**good**) (*or* **is valid,** *or* **retains its validity**) within the limits.
This relationship **was preserved** after deformation.
This condition **is valid** (*or* **holds true**) **for** other materials.

Сохранять тепло
In order **to conserve heat, ...**

Сохранять энергию, момент
To conserve energy, impulse, ...

Сохраняться [*см. тж.* **Всё ещё существует, Импульс и энергия сохраняются, Плохо сохраняться**]
Water converts these salts back to graphite, in which some oxygen **is** still **retained.**
Remanent magnetism is the magnetism that **persists** when the magnetic field is absent.
This same relationship between major lake basins and rock type **holds** northwestward as we follow ...
Although roofs collapsed under the weight of the ash, walls and contents of the buildings **survived.**

Assume that angular momentum **is conserved** during collapse.
The basic design **has been retained** with no modifications.
With this method the chisel **will stand up** longer.

Сохраняться постоянным
The pressure **is kept** (*or* **held**) **constant.**

Сочетание [*см. тж.* **В соединении с, В сочетании с, Совместно с**]
These properties are best represented by **a combination of** all three structures.
The design values chosen for this counter represent **a compromise** (*оптимальное сочетание*) **between** high neutron sensitivity, uniform pulse size, low gamma sensitivity **and** conventional dimensions.
The condenser type offered **the** best **compromise on** sensitivity, stability and reproducibility.
The way system **is a cross between** conventional oilhydrostatic ways **and** pneumatic ways.

Сочетание условий
The set of conditions where the phases of the gel first separate **is** the critical point of the gel.

Сочетать [*см. тж.* **Объединять**]
The problem of **combining** a high degree of mechanization **with** reasonable versatility ...

Сочетать в себе [*см. тж.* **Объединять в себе**]
A micrometer screw system **combines** high sensitivity **and** long range.

Сочетаться [*см. тж.* **Хорошо сочетаться**]
The formalism **meshes (perfectly) with** de Broglie's work.

Сошлифовывать
When a drill has broken in the shank the broken ends **are ground away** (*or* **off**).

Сошлифовывать до толщины
Tungsten carbide electrodes **are ground to a thickness of** 0.020 in.

Спад
The fluorescence-**decay** curve ...

Спадать I
Then the pulse **decays (away).**
Later on, interest in theoretical ideas about the nature of matter **waned** (*or* **subsided**).
The curve **slopes down from** 0°C **toward** the eutectic point.
The charge and the voltage **decay** with the same time constant.
When the speed **falls** (*or* **drops**) below this level, ...
The observation curves **fall off** steeply.
The current grows to two maxima in opposite directions and **dies away to** two minima during each cycle.

Спадать II
Sand may be deposited as the wind **dies.**

Спадающая кривая
A descending (*or* **dropping**) **curve.**

Спарен с
An element **is paired with** a subset that includes that element.

Спаренные
The **twin**-lens reflex camera is essentially two similar cameras coupled together.

Спаренные электроны
These two **electrons** have their spins pointing in opposite directions; in other words, they **are paired.**

Спарены
The adrenal glands **are** always **paired.**

Спаривание
The pairing of electrons of opposite spins requires ...

Спаривать
Either worktable can be used separately while work is being set up on the other, or they **can be coupled together** to support one very large workpiece.

Спариваться с
Uridine frequently **pairs** (*or* **is paired**) **with** quanosine.

Спаяны
The diaphragms **are soldered together.**

Спектр
The infrared **spectrum of** a chemical substance may be related to ...
The complete absorption **spectrum for** a pure compound ...

Спереди [*см. тж.* **Впереди**]
Plugs and sockets are provided **at the front of** the machine.
The container has an opening **in the front.**
The beam is focussed by a lens **in front of** the sample.
The instrument **was ahead of** a line between ...

Специализированный
To facilitate this work, a variety of **special-purpose** units is provided.

Специализироваться в области
They **specialize in** the design of ...

Специалист
No individual can hope **to be expert in** all areas of chemistry.

Специалист в области науки о земле
An earth scientist.

Специально [*см. тж.* **Изготовленный специально для, Приспособленный специально для**]
The equipment is **expressly** designed for the metalworking industry.
The pumps are **purpose** designed for mine duties.
The gauge is **specially** (*or* **specifically**) designed to measure ...
The pump is designed **specifically** (*or* **explicitly**) **for** use with the Doxford engine.

Специально оборудованный
Mines are launched by **specially fitted** (*or* **equipped**) ships.

Специально приспособленный
These tools are **peculiarly** (*or* **specially**) **adapted to** the study of such problems.

Специального назначения
A **special-purpose** analogue computer (*or* machine) ...

Специального состава
A **specially formulated** cast nylon is used for ...

Специальной конструкции
Should this approach be unsatisfactory, a **tailormade** burner head may be tried.

Специальный
Lead, zinc, silver and other metals are often added for **special-purpose** bronze.
Other more **specialized** aspects of colloidal properties are discussed in ...

Специальный курс
A specialized course in ...

Спецификация на [*см. тж.* **Выполнять согласно техническим условиям, Согласно техническим условиям**]
Specifications for (*or* **on**) gears ...
The switches meet **specifications on** contact resistance.

Специфическая черта
Peculiar features of (*or* **Features peculiar to**) this type of laser are ...

Специфичность по отношению к
Specificity toward (*or* **for**) particular compounds ...

Специфичный для
Forms **specific** (*or* **peculiar**) **to** lysine ...

Спешить или отставать
The navigation timepieces are subject to **a** daily **gain or loss.**

Спиливать
File down the points of the teeth.

Спираль [*см.* **Двигаться по спирали**].

Сплав на основе кадмия
A cadmium (*or* **Cd**)**-base(d)** alloy.

Сплавление с
The alloying of copper **with** other metals requires ...

Сплавленный с
The generator uses silicon **alloyed with** cobalt.

Сплавлять с
Gold **is** usually **alloyed with** silver or copper.

Сплошная линия
A continuous (*or* **unbroken,** *or* **solid**) **line.**

Сплошной
The metal at the joints is **continuous** — no holes are required.
The flywheel is of **solid** disk type.
Then the barrier island would extend as a single **unbroken** island from ... to ...

Сплюснут у полюсов
The Earth **is flattened at the poles.**

Сплюснутость у полюсов
The polar flattening of our planet ...

Спокойное солнце [*см.* **Год спокойного солнца**].

Спокойный
Subsequently the lunar core cooled, and it **is** now **quiescent.**

Спор [*см. тж.* **Идут споры о том**]
Uncertainty about these values was at the centre of theoretical **controversies** (*or* **debates,** *or* **arguments**) in those days.

Спорный
The nature of quasars **is controversial.**

Спорный вопрос
The place, manner, and time sequence of adding these characteristic segments to the precursor **are** still **controversial subjects** (*biol.*).
It is a moot point (*or* **a point open to question**) how much competition actually occurs within populations.

Способ [*см. тж.* **Испытанный метод, Метод, Различными путями**]
The mode of preparation of the reagent ...
It was necessary to find **a means of** transmitting the colour signal components without ...
The stylus is heated and ...; this **expedient** results in ...
Techniques for predicting how a machine will behave ...
Other **means** (*or* **ways,** *or* **methods**) **of** (*or* **for**) improving ...
The procedures that yield denatured DNA **are: ...**

Способ выйти из положения [*см.* **Один из способов выйти из положения**].

Способ преодоления трудности
A cure for this difficulty is to obtain ...

Способ устранения
The defect cannot be easily **removed,** and the best cure is prevention.
The remedy for the harmful eddy currents involves ...

Способен
The press **is capable of** making only one piece at a time.
The infrared camera **is capable of** giving temperature indications.
The mercuric ion **has the (cap)ability** (*or* **is able**) **to** form ...
This element **has the (cap)ability of** producing very large, complex molecules.
A quark **is free to** change its colour.

Способен конкурировать с
Nuclear reactors **are competitive with** fossil fuels.

Способность [*см. тж.* **Обладать способностью**]
This **capacity for** interaction is largely overlooked.
The virions are alive as long as they retain **the capability for** duplicating their proteins (*biol.*).
A surface with **propensity to** capture hydrogen atoms is needed.
The capacity (*or* **ability**) **of** a medium to absorb radiation ...
The energy of a body is defined as its **capacity to** do work.

Способность подвергаться протяжке
Drawability of copper ...

Способность поддаваться обработке
The elements lead, sulphur and some others are commonly added to metals to improve their **machinability** (*or* **workability**).

Способность поддаваться пайке
Solderability.

Способный
Suppose we have a laser **capable of** producing a million joules of optical energy.

Способом
The curves should be plotted **in the manner** shown (above).
Phosphors are stimulated electrically or **by** some other **means.**

Способствовать [*см. тж.* **Значительно способствовать, Помогать, Содействовать**]
Intermolecular hydrogen bonding **is favoured by** a high solute concentration.
Emission **is aided by** placing a probe on the cathode.

Suppression of termination by this codon **was mediated by** a tRAN (*biol.*).
Cleavage **is** frequently **instrumental in** segregating ...
High pressure **is favourable to** the production of ammonia.
This feature **is an aid to** (*or* **is useful in**) interpretation of ...
Rubber gaskets and compounds **will aid** (*or* **assist**) **in** reducing vibration.
The lower part is milled **to assist** the inflow of air.
Slow feeds **are beneficial** (*or* **favourable**) **for** producing smooth finishes.
The belief may be encouraged, as it **conduces to** the welfare of ...
Windy nights **are** not **conducive to** surface-air cooling.
Nuclei ... are highly hygroscopic and **encourage** condensation.
This **will serve to** increase the hydraulic pressure.
Prolonged heating at such a temperature **favours** (*or* **benefits**) further grain growth.
By **fostering** development of fishing ...
The employment of independent pins **makes for** (*or* **contributes to**) resistance to corrosion.
This radiation **may promote** certain chemical reactions.
It is desirable **to promote** passage of all combustible particles through the flame.
Grooves in the stones **facilitate** motion of materials.
These researches **contributed to** the development of ...
A very slight amount of mixing **can** greatly **enhance** (*or* **improve**) the transport.

Способствовать одному ... за счёт другого
By varying reaction conditions and reactant ratios, chemists **can** often **favour one** mechanism **over another** and thus control a reaction.

Способствовать пониманию
This relation **gives** (*or* **offers**) **some insight into** the way the configuration of the magnets can be optimized.
The method **will provide (useful) insight into** the corresponding analysis of heat effects in packed towers.
These quantities **provide** additional **insights into** the properties of substances.
This **enhances** the understanding of ...
Dating by the ^{14}C method **has** greatly **advanced our understanding of** human prehistory.

Способствовать созданию
The incorporation of landing gear **made for a** complete ultralight airplane.

Способствовать этому
Abnormally cold weather in those years **may be a factor.**

Способствующий
This has been considered as **a contributory factor for** the ageing process.

Справа налево [*см.* **Слева направо**].

Справа от
The electron configurations **to the right of** Fig. 12-17 ...

Справа от него
The superconducting transition temperature of titanium is increased by combining it with transition-metal elements **to its right** in the Periodic Table.

Справедлив
If this hypothesis **is true, ...**
This approximation **holds (good)** within the limits.
This assumption **will** no longer **be valid** (*or* **legitimate**).

Справедлив для [*см. тж.* **Быть справедливым для**]
This explanation **holds (good) for** thionine and ...
This **is** also **true for** (*or* **of**) excessive leakage.

Справедлив с точностью до [*см.* **Выполняться с точностью до**].

Справедливо
The method can be **justly** (*or* **with good reason,** *or* **rightly**) criticized for ...

Справедливо предполагать
It was correctly reasoned (*or* **suggested,** *or* **supposed**) **that ...**

Справедливость [*см. тж.* **Правильность**]
The truth of the hypothesis ...
To demonstrate **the validity of** the laws of motion, ...
They proclaimed **the verity of** his theory.

Справляться
Rats subjected to shocks and other stresses in early life developed normally and **were able to cope (well) with** stresses later.
The amount of cooling surface must be adequate **to cope with** the maximum possible heat loading.

Справляться в
Tables of solubility data **should** always **be consulted** (*or* **referred to**) before unfamiliar solutions are prepared.

Справляться с задачей
Modern data processing techniques are powerful enough **to cope with the task** (*or* **to meet the challenge**).

Справляться с работой [*см.* **Выполнять работу**].

Справочник
This encyclopaedic work is **the** major **reference (book) for** the dye chemist.

Справочник по
A handbook of chemistry ...

Справочный материал
Table 11.7 is **a** good **reference source for** your study of organic reactions.

Спрессован из
The pellets **were pressed from** a mixture of powders.

Спрессовывать в
The powder **can be (com)pressed into** pellets.

Спроектированный [*см.* **Сконструированный**].

Спроектированный по специальному заказу
A **custom-designed** aircraft ...

Спрос [*см.* **В большом спросе, Появился спрос на**].

Спрос на
Demand for aircraft engines ...
If there is **a market for** these items, ...

Спускать I
Moisture, oil and dirt **should be drained out** (*or* **off**) daily.

Спускать II
A steel pipe **is lowered into** the hole.

Спускать воду [*см. тж.* **Опорожнять**]
After **the water has been emptied** (*or* **drained**) **from** the boiler ...

Спутник с телескопом на борту
A telescope-toting satellite.

Срабатывание
Radio altimeters are used in bombs, missiles and shells as proximity fuses to cause **functioning** (*or* **operation**) at predetermined altitudes.

Срабатывать
The circuit-breaker **comes into action** when the voltage falls below a predetermined value.
Current overload relays **operate at** about 125% motor current.
The relay **is tripped by** increasing current when a fault occurs.
The temperature switch **actuates** if the internal water temperature becomes excessive.

Сравнение [*см. тж.* **Выдерживать сравнение с, Для сравнения, По сравнению с, Успешно выдерживать сравнение с**]
This was verified **by reference to** (*or* **comparison with**) published spectra.
A frequent **checking against** a master standard ...
A comparison between (*or* **of**) core-measured porosities **and** log-derived porosities shows that ...
The relative basis must be determined by **correlation with** other types of tests.

Сравнение ... с ... показывает, что
When this result is compared with that of Eq. (2), it is apparent that ...

Сравнивать с [*см. тж.* **Можно сравнить с**]
Contrast this spectrum **with** those in Figs. 8 and 9.
We tried **to match** the laboratory absorption spectrum of these molecules **to** the observed astronomical sources.
This part of the rock **has been likened to** a pack of cards standing on edge.
This expression **should be confronted with** Eq. (12).
We **correlated** (*or* **compared**) our measurements **with** the result of ...

Сравни́м по
Sulphur trioxide **is comparable to** (*or* **compares with**) the proton **in** electrophilicity.

Сравни́м с [*см. тж.* **Вполне сравним с, Выдерживать сравнение с**]
The sensitivity of this telescope **matches** the sensitivity of ...
Stellite alloys have a modulus of elasticity **comparable to** steel.
This method **compares favourably with** the classical approach.

Сравнимый с ним
Cyclopropanes are less reactive than **comparable** olefins.

Сравнимый с ним по размерам
For a **comparable-sized** paper chromatogram ...

Сравнительно [*см. тж.* **Довольно, Относительно**]
A telescope of **moderately** long focal length ...
The strain increases **fairly** (*or* **rather,** *or* **comparatively**) rapidly.

Сравнительно легко
This material emits electrons **with relative ease.**

Сравнительно небольшой
These systems deliver 100 kW pulses at **moderate** repetition rates (~100 Hz).

Сравнительно точно аппроксимировать
Many of the properties of gases **can be closely approximated by** simple expressions.

Сравнительно хорошо отражать
This equation **follows** the behaviour of a gas **reasonably well.**

Сравнительно хорошо совпадать
The data of the two authors **are in fairly good agreement.**

Сравнительное изучение
Comparison studies of a large number of alloys ...

Сравнить с
The coating **can be likened to** a layer of snow covering ...

Сравниться с
It seems unlikely that solid compositions **will** ever **equal** liquid propellants in performance.
No other high-density polyethylene **can match** the stresscrack resistance of ...

Сразу [*см. тж.* **Одним ударом, С первого взгляда**]
Bismuthine decomposes **instantaneously** on heating.

Сразу видно, что
It is immediately obvious that the volume of the air decreases.

Сразу же [*см. тж.* **Моментально**]
We see **at once that ...**

Сразу обнаруживается
When the results are scanned, some correlation between the two parameters **is immediately apparent.**

Сразу после [*см.* **Непосредственно после**].

Сразу после напыления
The coating **is in the as-sprayed condition.**

Сразу после того как [*см. тж.* **Непосредственно после того как**]
Immediately the tool reaches the inner end of the boss on the workpiece, the rollers expand and release their grip.
Movements of the rock are stopped **immediately** they commence.
Screening begins **the moment** (*or* **as soon as**) the material **is** placed at the feed end.

Сразу после этого
Immediately afterwards ...

Среда [*см. тж.* **На среде, Окружающая среда, Температура окружающей среды, Условия окружающей среды**]
Such systems provide models of how enzymes behave in their natural **milieu** (*or* **medium,** *or* **environment**).

Среда обитания
When **the habitat of** these animals is invaded by bad air ...

Среди
Of [*or* **Among(st)**] the new processes which have appeared, the basic oxygen process seems to hold the lead.

Среди которых имеются
The shale contains abundant fossil organisms, **among which are** condonts, shagreen granules of sharks, ...

Среднего радиуса действия
Medium-range missiles ...

Среднего размера
Our sun is a typical **medium-size(d)** star.

Среднее
The encounter rate that we should expect can be written as **the mean** (*or* **average**) **of** these results.

Среднее положение [*см. тж.* **В среднем положении**]
Set the fine-grain control **to its mid-position.**

Средней мощности
A **medium-powered** tractor ...

Средний I [*см. тж.* **В среднем, Со средним содержанием, Составлять в среднем**]
In the U.S. the **average** (*or* **median**) age of the population declined between censuses.
The **average** gas-oil ratio is 1400 cu ft per barrel.
M is the **mean** molecular weight of the product gases.
A **median** lethal dose of radiation ...
At low Reynolds number the value of *C* is small, it increases toward unity at **medium** Reynolds number.
In the **medium** exposure ranges maximum development occurs.
Small and **medium-size(d)** castings.
The process has proved successful for the production of grains of **moderate** size but is not suitable for very large grains.

Средний II
Cadmium is the **middle** member of group IIb in the Periodic Table.

Средний III
At **intermediate** and slow rates of exchange ...

Средний квадратичный
A 0.01-g mass has at 300 K a **root-mean** square velocity of ...

Средний срок выживания
The median survival of untreated patients is about 2 months.

Средних размеров
Bubbles **of intermediate** (*or* **medium**) **size** [*or* **Medium-size(d)** bubbles] become distorted.

Средняя линия
The centre line of the plotter ...

Средняя продолжительность жизни
Average (*or* **Mean**) **length of life** (*or* **Mean life time**).
Expectation of life.
Life expectancy.

Средняя точка
The machine base and the vertical posts are joined together near **the midpoint of** the base.

Средняя широта (долгота)
The mid-latitude (longitude).

Средство для [*см. тж.* **Метод, Навигационные средства, Являться средством**]
A softening **agent ...**
This provides **a means for** the removal of corrosive compounds.
The use of transistors is evaluated as **a means of** alleviating this problem.
The twentieth century's potent technological **media of** mass communication ...
The representation of electrical quantities as ... is **a** useful **tool of** circuit analysis.
The reflected shock technique is **a** valuable **tool for** chemical kinetic studies.
Electron diffraction is also used as a research **tool in** studying ...

Средство связи
The telephone is **the** major **vehicle for** personal **communication.**

Срез
Thin **sections** were prepared for microscopic analysis.

Сродство к
The great **affinity of** this element **for** halogens ...
This compound has **an affinity for** free electrons.

Сродство к электронам
The electron affinity of fluorine ...

Срок [*см.* **В короткий срок, Время**].

Срок выходит
Time is running out.

Срок вышел
The time is up.

Срок службы [*см. тж.* **Время жизни, На весь срок службы**]
The battery has greater reliability and increased **expectation of life** (*or* **life expectancy**).
This tank bottom **is expected to last** indefinitely.
Highly abrasive flowing media can shorten bearing **life.**
The lower operating temperature makes the bath **long lived** (*oppos.* **short lived**).
The plastic bottom **should outlast** (*or* **outlive**) for many years the side walls of the tank.
Service (life) up to 20 years can be anticipated.
The useful life of automobile engines ...
It is difficult to predict the **life-in-service of** the components.

Срок существования
Other pollutants have **a** relatively short **life.**

Срок хранения
The shelf life is the length of time after manufacture that the product will remain in good usable condition.

Срок хранения скоропортящихся продуктов
To increase **the storage life of perishables, ...**

Срочная необходимость [*см. тж.* **В случае необходимости**]
There is **a** particularly **pressing** (*or* **urgent**) **need for** such a resource estimate.

Срочно
It is necessary to terminate the chain reaction **promptly** in order to prevent damage to the reactor.

Срывать провода
Telephone **wires were torn down by** windstorms.

Срывать резьбу
A coarse **thread** is recommended to reduce the possibility of **its being stripped.**

Ссылка
A discussion of ... may be found in **Brown**[1].

Ставится задача
It is proposed to recover acetone from an acetone-air stream by absorption in water, using ...

Ставить вопрос о том
This **raises** (*or* **poses**) **the question as to** whether there exists a smoother transition from ...

Ставить задачу [*см. тж.* **Излагать задачу**]
Then we **can pose the problem** in a more tractable way.

Ставить заплаты на
To apply patches to the tank wall, ...

Ставить на пути луча
The slide **is inserted** (*or* **interposed**) **in the beam.**

Ставить на теоретическую основу
To place the concept of intelligence **on a theoretical footing, ...**

Ставить опыт
Experiments were run (*or* **carried out,** *or* **performed,** *or* **made,** *or* **staged,** *or* **set up**) **to** determine the effect of ...

Ставить ... перед
We can sufficiently describe substitution by **prefixing** the amide name **with** *N*-(*e.g. N-bromoacetamide*).

Ставить под сомнение
This finding did not **cast** any **doubt on** our previous statement.
Recent experiments **have cast some suspicion** (*or* **doubt**) **on** the importance of hydrogen bond patterns in this role.
Quantum fluctuations of space-time **call into question** the very meaning of ...

Ставить под угрозу
Various contingencies **may jeopardize** the lifting operation.

Ставить проблему
Isomeric differences **pose** numerous **problems** in various aspects of the chemist's work.

Ставить условие

The condition laid down in Sec. 5 requires that ...

Ставить часы по
Set your **watch against** the accepted standard.

Стадии прохождения реакции
The description of **steps by which a reaction proceeds** is called the reaction mechanism.

Стадия [*см.* **Двустадийный, Достигать стадии, На более поздней стадии, На первой стадии, На этой стадии, Одностадийный**].

Стадия проектирования (*или* **конструирования**)
Starting with **the conceptual phase,** rigid controls on weight and size are needed.

Стал использоваться
Cinnabar **came into use** at first as a pigment.

Стал широко применяться
The cotton stripper **came into wide use** in 1926.

Стали называть [*см. тж.* **Как его стали называть**]
Any compound containing the aldehyde group **came to be called** an "aldehyde".

Стали рассматривать как
These minerals **came to be regarded as** metamorphic index minerals.

Сталкиваться (друг с другом)
Then the two continents **collided (with each other), ...**

Сталкиваться с I
I have often **come up against** the problem of trying to explain that ...
Here again one **is up against** the thermal problems of laser experiments.

Сталкиваться с II
When the atoms **encounter** the walls of the cell they exchange energy with the walls.
When this electron **strikes** (*or* **collides with,** *or* **impinges on**) an atom, ...

Сталкиваться с трудностями
Washer users often **run into** (*or* **face**) **problems** (*or* **obstacles**) when specifying a washer for a particular job.

Стало известно о
A new crystalline modification of boron **was reported.**

Стало ясно, что
Now **it has been made** (*or* **has become**) **clear that** synthesis of protein in prophase is essential also.
It has become evident (*or* **apparent,** *or* **clear**) during the past few years **that ...**
It is now appreciated that this is an oversimplification.

Стандарт(ный образец)
The reference (*or* **standard**) chosen is usually tetramethylsilane.

Стандарт на [*см. тж.* **Отвечать стандартам**]
Standards for (*or* **on**) reamers were established.

Стандартизировать по
The solution **has been standardized against** known concentration of ...

Стандартный I [*см. тж.* **Обычный, С обычными покрышками**]
The exciter is **of conventional** (*or* **standard**) design.
We used **regular** muriate of potash.
The machine is built **of standardized** components.

Стандартный II
It is convenient to have a set of **reference** conditions (**standard** temperature, **standard** pressure) for comparison of gas properties.
The difference in thermal conductivity between the **reference** and sample streams is small.

Стандартных размеров
Plain thrust-washers **in standard sizes** are available from stock.

Становится ясно, что
If the foregoing observations are reconsidered, **it becomes apparent** (*or* **evident**) **that ...**

Становиться [*см. тж.* **В результате чего ... становится**]
Liquid crystals **can turn** opaque under electrical stimulation.
Then the grid voltage **goes** (*or* **becomes**) positive ...

A considerable amount of sulphur dioxide emitted to the atmosphere **ends up as** sulphate ions or ...
Fine pole chucks lose effectiveness as a part **gets** thicker.
The cadmium **is** thus **rendered** soluble.

Становиться более разнообразным
As the applications **diversified ...**

Становиться возможным благодаря
The determination of the shape of ... **has been made possible by** the use of ...
New types of computing architectures that **were made possible with** optical processors ...

Становиться всё меньше и меньше
The gradient **diminishes** (*or* **reduces**) **progressively** downstream.

Становиться горизонтальным
The curve **flattens out** at high Mach numbers.

Становиться доступным в результате
New information **has become available from** a recent study by ...

Становиться жертвой
These vegetarian animals **fall prey to** carnivorous animals.

Становиться известным
A number of interesting facts **are coming to light.**

Становиться круче
The velocity profile on the wave front **steepens** (*or* **becomes steeper**).

Становиться на место
The coupling bolts **should go into place** (*or* **into position**) when tapped lightly with a hammer.
More pieces of the puzzle **fell into place.**

Становиться недействительным
When the angle α_1 is increased beyond a certain limit, this model of shock reflection **breaks down** (*or* **fails**).

Становиться особенно заметным
Centrioles **come into particular prominence** during mitosis (*biol.*).

Становиться предметом изучения
The less striking varieties of abnormal behaviour **have come under the scrutiny of science** (*or* **have become the subject of study**) in the last 25 years.

Становиться совершенно невидимым
So thin are the rings that they then **disappear completely from view** even in the best telescopes.

Становиться таковым
Some molecular compounds are partially ionized or **become so** when dissolved in solvents.

Станок [*см.* **На станке**].

Старший научный сотрудник
A senior research scientist (*or* **researcher**).

Стать [*см.* **Становиться**].

Стать возможным благодаря
This structure **was made possible by** our investment in ...

Стать настолько неотъемлемой частью нашей жизни [*см.* **Настолько глубоко войти в нашу жизнь, что**] .

Стать первой мишенью для
Airplanes and helicopters **become a prime target for** a lightning stroke.

Стационарное состояние [*см. тж.* **В стационарном состоянии**]
The temperature of the liquid in the beam achieves **a steady state** when ...
The ocean is **in a steady state,** in which inputs and outputs are balanced.

Стационарный [*см. тж.* **В стационарном случае**]
The **steady-state** population of the excited state ...
Steady-state conduction ...

Ствол [*см.* **Проходка шахтного ствола**].

Стекать в
Make sure that the mercury does not **drain down into** the pressure element.

Стекать по склону
The lava **flows downslope** (*or* **downhill**).

Стеклообразное состояние
Many alloys remain in **the glassy state** indefinitely at room temperature.

Стеклянная бумага [*см.* **Шлифовать стеклянной бумагой**].

Стеклянный блеск
Vitreous lustre.

Стенка [*см.* **С двойными стенками**].

Степени
The equation is homogeneous **of degree one** (*or* **of the first degree**).

Степени ... по
Equation (1.6.9) is homogeneous **of degree** n **in** λ^r.

Степенной ряд по
A power series in M-1.
The total aberration is expressed as **a power series in** the field variables.

Степень I [*см. тж.* **В значительной степени, В меньшей степени, В некоторой степени, В одинаковой степени, Высокая степень развития, До некоторой степени, С большой точностью**]
The extent (*or* **degree**) **to** which antibiotics may exert bacterial effects ...

Степень II [*см. тж.* **В степени, Возведение в степень, Возводить в степень, Корень ... степени из**]
The degree of the term **is** the sum of the exponents of the unknowns.
The acoustic power of the noise varies as the eighth **power of** exhaust velocity.
The penetration increased with **the four-thirds power of** the velocity.

Степень III
An equation **of the first degree** (*or* a **first-degree** equation) ...

Степень влияния ... зависит от
The extent to which charge **is affected by** the interaction **depends on** the nature of this interaction.

Степень завершённости (*или* **законченности**) **реакции**
The extent to which the reaction proceeds plays an important role in ...

Степень прохождения реакции
The degree of advancement of the reaction ...

Степень свободы
The industrial robot has five **degrees of freedom.**

Степень точности
Even the artificial satellites have not supplied us with measurements within that **range of accuracy.**

Стереть с лица земли
An avalanche can **wipe out** a whole town.

Стимул
Their confidence in our products is **a** constant **spur in** our efforts to ...
This investigation provided further **impetus** (*or* **incentive**) **to** technological progress.

Стимулировать
This finding **lent impetus to** a successful search for ...
Taxation and high fuel costs **have spurred** (*or* **fostered,** *or* **stimulated**) the development of ... (*or* **have given impetus to**) the development of ...
The nutrient **is stimulatory to** growth of the test organism.
The first photon **has stimulated** the system **into** emitting a second photon.

Стоимость рабочей силы
Only one man was needed for assembly, and **labour costs** were halved.

Стоимость с доставкой
Delivered cost.

Стоимость с установкой
Installed cost.
The data processing system **costs** $30,000 **installed.**

Стои́т задача [*см.* **Перед ... стои́т проблема**].

Стойка [*см.* **Смонтированный на стойке**].

Стойкий [*см. тж.* **Устойчивый**]
All connections in the relay **are resistant to** heat, shock and vibration.

Стойкость к
The stability of saturated fatty acids **toward** (*or* **to**) oxidation ...

Стойкость к резким температурным колебаниям
Resistance to extremes of heat and cold.

Сток
Mercury salts in **runoff from** agricultural lands threaten the fishing industry.

Столб воздуха
Column of air (*or* **Air column**).

Столбец [*см.* **В виде столбца**].

Столбцы и строки таблицы
Columns and rows of Table 6-3 ...

Столкновение между частицами
An interparticle collision (*or* **A collision between particles**).

Столкновение с
The impacts of the small planetesimals **on** the large ones ...

Столкновение со стенками
Collisions of molecules **against the walls of** the container ...

Столь же важен
Change of sea level **is equally important in** the explanation of existing reef features.

Столько же, сколько
If **as many** protons were emitted **as** electrons, the Crab nebula would now be ...
As many gas molecules will hit the back **as** the front of the mirror.
There are **as many** integers divisible by a trillion **as** there are integers altogether .

Столько ..., сколько
The mole is the amount that contains **as many** particles of a specified type **as** there are ^{12}C atoms in ...

Столько-то
The result of combining **so many** parts of colour *A* with **so many** of colour *B* ...

Сторона [*см.* **Аспект, В стороне от, Из стороны в сторону, С внешней стороны, Со всех сторон, Со стороны**].

Сторона уравнения
The left **member** (*or* **The** left-hand **side**) **of an equation.**

Сторонник
The proponents (*or* **adherents,** *or* **supporters,** *or* **advocates**) **of** nuclear power contend that these installations are accident proof.
Defenders of this theory insist that ...

Стороны равны
Hence the triangles *KDA, KCG* **have their sides equal.**

Стоять
When the lift **is at rest, ...**
At present one plant **is shut down** (*or* **is idle**).

Стоять в одном ряду с ... по важности
Entropy **stands with** internal energy **in importance.**

Стоять на правильном пути [*см.* **Быть на правильном пути**].

Стоять на следующем месте по
Guanosine **ranks next in** frequency.

Стоять перед [*см. тж.* **Перед ... стоит проблема**]
This can help to answer questions that **challenge** (*or* **face,** *or* **confront**) investigators today.

Стоять перед лицом
Britain **faces** intense competition from ...

Стоять перед необходимостью
Industrial nations **face the need to** curtail air pollution.

Стоящий в начале списка
A mineral **high on the list** could strongly react with ...

Стоящий перед [*см.* **Задача, стоящая перед**].

Страдать
Old people rarely **suffer with** hereditary spherocytosis.
People who **suffer from** chronic disease ...

Страдать недостатком
The grid detector **suffers from** (*or* **has**) many **disadvantages** (*or* **drawbacks,** *or* **shortcomings**).

Страдать некоторой неточностью
It is useful to group rock materials on the basis of their resistance to erosion. True enough, the arrangement **lacks precision** since different members of a single rock type will not always have the same resistance.

Страна происхождения

Fermentation of cocoa beans is carried out in **the country of origin.**

Страна-член
The member nations of this organization have stated that ...

Странно [*см.* **Как это ни странно**].

Стрелка [*см.* **По часовой стрелке, Против часовой стрелки**].

Стрелка, направленная от ... к
An arrow pointing from reactants **to** products ...

Стремиться I [*см. тж.* **При ... стремящемся к, Проявлять тенденцию к**]
Potassium ions **tend to** diffuse out.
This force **tends to** bend the drill.
Segments of the rigid lithosphere **seek** an equilibrium.

Стремиться II
This gain is worth **striving for.**
The investigators **seek** (*or* **endeavour**) **to** discover ...
Theoretical physicists **have** long **sought to** establish some relationship among ...
Geologists **are striving** (*or* **trying,** *or* **making efforts**) **to** develop skill in predicting ...

Стремиться к бесконечности
For (*or* **When,** *or* **With**) $m \to \infty$ ...
At high field strengths the current **tends to** (*or* **approaches**) **infinity.**

Стремиться к нулю
As adhesive layer thickness **approaches** (*or* **tends to**) **zero,** the stress also **approaches zero.**

Стремление [*см. тж.* **В стремлении**]
The quest for speed has led to the development of ...

Стремящийся к обеспечению
An engineer **in search of** maximum strength must ...

Строгая проверка
Example 9.10 below provides **a severe test of** the foregoing hypothesis.

Строгие правила
Stringent safety **regulations ...**

Строгие требования [*см. тж.* **Жёсткие требования**]
The instrument meets **the exacting** (*or* **rigid,** *or* **stern,** *or* **stringent,** *or* **severe**) **requirements of** the modern laboratory.

Строгий
The suggested initial conditions **are** too **severe.**

Строгий допуск
The airport pavement surface is finished **to exacting tolerance.**
Conversion to investment casting permitted **strict tolerances to be held.**

Строгий контроль
Very **close** furnace **control** is required.
Rigid (*or* **Exacting**) quality **control** assures a minimum of rejects.

Строгий критерий
A rigorous criterion.

Строго говоря [*см. тж.* **В строгом смысле слова**]
Strictly speaking (*or* **In the strict sense**), chemical reactions are always stoichiometric.

Строго научно
The system of complex numbers can be defined **rigorously.**
Neither set of equations can be solved **rigorously.**
These spectra are difficult to interpret **rigorously.**

Строго научный
A **rigorous** treatment of the interaction of light with such electron systems is beyond the scope of this text.

Строго определённый
Each peak belongs to a pair separated by a **well-defined** distance.
Each electron in an ion moves in **strictly specified** ways.

Строго последовательный
He developed the first **fully consistent** theory of evolution.

Строго придерживаться
To be consistent with the molecular interpretation of entropy, we take the entropy at absolute zero to be zero.

Строго следовать хронологии
If this book **were strictly faithful to the chronology of** events, ...

Строго соблюдая
Intra-articular inspections must be performed with **scrupulous attention to** sterility (*med.*).

Строгое наблюдение
The loading of foodstuffs **is rigidly supervised by** inspectors.

Строгое ограничение
Because of **the severe** (*or* **rigid,** *or* **stringent**) weight and space **restrictions** in aircraft ...

Строгое рассмотрение
Any more **rigorous treatment** requires the use of algebraic signs for the wave function describing ...

Строгое решение
A rigorous solution.

Строгое требование
A strong requirement.

Строение [*см.* **Иметь простую структуру**].

Строительный материал
Various metals are used for **structural materials.**

Строительство
In this way lime is produced for **the building trade.**
The construction of residential houses ...

Строить
We use these functions **to build up** functions appropriate to the whole molecule.
Construct (*or* **Build**) a rectangle.
Activation energy curves **were constructed** (*or* **plotted**).
This subject matter **is patterned** along similar lines.
To erect (*or* **build,** *or* **construct**) such a house, ...

Строить модель
Models of ... have been constructed.

Строить на основе
We **base** our presentation **on that** given by Stokes.

Строить перпендикуляр к
Construct perpendiculars to the parallels of latitude.

Строить теорию
In **constructing** (*or* **elaborating,** *or* **building,** *or* **developing**) **a theory of** the nucleus ...

Строить уравнение
To set (*or* **build**) **up an equation.**

Строиться
Some reactors of this type **are under construction.**

Строй [*см.* **Вступать в строй, Выводить из строя, Выход из строя**].

Стройный [*см.* **В стройном порядке**].

Строки и столбцы таблицы
Rows and columns of a table.

Структура [*см.* **В структурном отношении, Обладать структурой, Определение структуры, По своей структуре, С макрокристаллической структурой**].

Структурная единица
The building block of a metal-oxide semiconductor integrated circuit is the field-effect transistor.
These enzymes catalyze the synthesis of RNA from **its building blocks:** four different ribonucleoside triphosphates.

Струя [*см. тж.* **Сильная струя**]
A stream (*or* **blast,** *or* **jet**) **of** air ...
High-pressure **jets of** water can be used to mine coal.

Студени́стый
A **jelly-like** substance such as gelatine or silicic acid ...

Студент последнего курса [*см.* **На последнем курсе**].

Ступенчатая форма
The cylinder is given **a stepped configuration.**

Ступенчатое изменение
A step change in m from zero to m_0 ...

Ступенчатый
The two waves represent the **stepwise** reduction of oxyphenazine.

Ступенчатый метод
A step-by-step procedure.

Ступень [*см.* **Достигать ступени, на которой; На первой стадии, На стадии**].

Ступенями
Some tumours may progress **in a stepwise fashion.**
The stored energy is released **in a stepwise manner** (*or* **step by step**).
The concrete lining was poured **in lifts of** 5 ft.
The process is carried out **in stages** (*or* **in steps,** *or* **stepwise**).
Narrow down the proportional band **in** small **steps.**

Стык [*см.* **На стыке между**].

Стыкован I
Each gauging machine is equipped with a process controller that **is interfaced with** a general-purpose minicomputer.

Стыкован II
The units **may be butted end-to-end** (*or* **butt joined**) to form a continuous trough.

Стыковать I
The two pieces **can be butted together** and then joined.

Стыковать II
The environment and radar operation simulator **has** recently **been interfaced with** a more convenient pulsed radar.

Стыковаться I (*в космосе*)
The spaceship **docked** (*or* **linked up**) **with** the rocket.

Стыковаться II
This computer **can interface to** (*or* **with**) instruments.

Стыковка I
The docking of the spacecraft **in** the rocket ...
The link-up of the spacecraft **with** the rocket ...

Стыковка II
Interfacing the two instruments presents difficulties.

Судить о
To judge the conformity of ... to this expression, ...

Судить по
The degree of filling **can be judged from** (*or* **by**) the picture.

Судовое оборудование [*см.* **Бортовое оборудование**].

Судовой [*см.* **На борту судна**].

Судя по
Such metals can show both metallic and non-metallic properties **as judged from** the properties of their compounds.
Judging from (*or* **by**) the large number of different gene functions, ...
The nucleoside must serve a particularly vital function in protein synthesis, **to judge from** (*or* **by**) the extremely complex modifications that have evolved.

Су́женный
The **necked-down** section of the nozzle ...
Failure of these specimens occurred at a **necked** (*or* **narrowed**) section.

Суживать до
Tunable dye laser bandwidths **can be narrowed down to** 0.0001 mm.

Сумма [*см.* **В сумме, Комплекс**].

Сумма по
The sum of such fractional quantities **over** all the components of the mixture is unity.

Суммарная реакция
An overall reaction.

Суммарный [*см. тж.* **Общая площадь**]
The **combined** effect of all the magnetic fields causes the compass magnet to be displaced from magnetic north.
The **net** effect of the two captures will be the removal of ...
Then the X-ray emission from quasars alone could explain the **integrated** X-radiation from the entire sky.
The **total** strata thickness was 6 ft.
The **aggregate** service life of ...
The **combined** energy of the electrons ...
The **overall** rate of changes of the photon density can be written as ...
The **net** charge is the algebraic sum of all ionic charges shown.

Суммирование по
The summation is **over** all the nearest neighbour pairs.
The equation can be extended to a polyatomic molecule **by summing over** all pairs of atoms.

Суммировать [*см.* **Складывать**].

Суммировать по
Then we **sum over** all classes of symmetry operations.

Суточные и годовые колебания
Daily and yearly temperature **variations.**

Сушить на солнце
After fermentation, the beans **are sun dried.**

Сушиться
The crystals **are** washed with water and **allowed to dry** (*or* **dried**).

Существенно [*см. тж.* **Значительно, Намного**]
Nitrogen did not **significantly** (*or* **materially,** *or* **tangibly,** *or* **substantially**) affect the sulphide titre.

Существенно зависеть от
Equation (5.3) **essentially depends on** the density.

Существенно отличаться от
The diesel engine **differs essentially from** the mixture engine.

Существенный для
This assumption, **essential to** shallow water theory, is ...
A well-known fact **fundamental to** this science is ...
Factor *A* **is essential for** the binding of formylmethionyl-tRNA.

Существо [*см.* **Углубляться в существо вопроса**].

Существо ... состоит в следующем
The problem, in essence, is this: ... (*or* **Essentially, the problem is as follows: ...**).

Существовавший тогда
The migration of the **then existing** forms of animal life ...

Существовал ещё в ... году
Records of solar and lunar eclipses **go back as far as** 750 B.C.

Существование I [*см. тж.* **В течение всего существования, Время существования**]
It may be that a typical quasar is a strong radio emitter for only a small part of its **life-span.**

Существование II
The occurrence (*or* **existence**) **of** coloured compounds indicates absorption of ...

Существовать [*см. тж.* **В какой бы форме ... ни встречался, Встречаться, Если он существует, Иметь место, Иметься, Не существовать**]
Such stresses **obtain** when ...
Many such systems **are in existence** (*or* **are found,** *or* **exist,** *or* **are available**), (*or* **There are many such systems,** *or* **There exist many such systems**).
Electromechanical devices **are (still) with us (today),** and **will be around** for a long time to come.
The Solar System **has been in existence** for five billion years.
Olivine is unstable under the low temperatures and pressures that **prevail** at the surface.
Such eddies have been known **to persist** for two years.
Although corrosion by gases is similar to corrosion by liquids, two important differences **are found.**
Both polymeric and dimeric hydrogen bonding structures **can occur** in solution.
Cold climates **occurred** in regions that are hot at the present time.
Such factors **are** always **found** in pairs.

Существовать в ... состояниях
The weakon (*a particle*) **comes in** three charged **states,** designated W^+, W^-, and Z^0.

Существовать долго
Such stars **are long-lived.**

Существовать за счёт
During the famine in Biafra the population **was subsisting** almost solely **on** the roots of the cassava plant.
Truly ancestral metazoans presumably **subsisted on** smaller organisms or organic debris.

Существовать недолго
Such stars **are short-lived.**

Существовать пáрами
All the leptons **come in pairs.**

Существует [*см. тж.* **Имеется**]

The vibrations of the molecule **are** of three types.

Существует возможность
The possibility exists of using mineral deposits of ...

Существует опасность
In this case, **the risk of** committing an error **is run.**
This kind of dehumidifier is used for small areas where moisture damage **may be a problem.**

Существует разногласие [*см.* **Нет согласия между ... относительно**].

Существует тенденция
The tendency has been for each group **to** construct its own device.

Существует теория о том, что
It is theorized that heating converts the organic matter into petroleum.

Существуют различные типы
Such dryers **occur in a variety of types.**

Существующее положение
The situation as it stands (at present) (*or* **The existing situation**) ...

Существующий [*см. тж.* **В существующем виде**]
Since the time these satellites took their **current** form ...
By the end Herschel had the best telescopes **in existence.**
With **(currently) available** (*or* With **existing**) lasers, detection limits may be as low as ...

Существующими темпами
If the construction continues **at the present rate,** ...

Существующий в виде
Materials **occurring as** crystalline solids ...

Сущность
The principle (*or* **essence**) **of** the process is that ...

Сфера
The detailed laboratory investigation on meteorites is largely **a province** (*or* **field,** *or* **realm,** *or* **sphere,** *or* **domain,** *or* **an area**) **of** microanalytical chemistry.

Сфокусирован(ный) на [*см. тж.* **Фокусироваться на**]
The **focus(s)ed** solar rays heat the chamber to around 800°C.
The diameter of the target image **focus(s)ed on** the reticle is ...
The eyepiece is **focus(s)ed on to** the graticule.
Light from the lamp **is focus(s)ed by** a small lens **on** one of the knife-edges.

Схема I [*см. тж.* **Логическая схема, На схеме показан, Принципиальная схема**]
With this **hookup** there is always enough air passing through the machine.
The phototube circuit **schematic** (*or* **diagram**) is shown in Fig. 4.

Схема II
A hadron can be built out of quarks according to either of two **blueprints.**

Схематически изображён
Newton's experiment **is diagrammed** (*or* **represented schematically**) at bottom.
It **schematically** (*or* **diagrammatically**) **depicts ...**

Схематически иллюстрируется
This **is illustrated diagrammatically** (*or* **schematically**) **by** (*or* **in**) Fig. 118.

Схематически представлен
The responses from Eqs ... **are sketched** (*or* **schematized**) on p. 34.

Схематический
The illustration **is** purely **diagrammatic.**
A **schematic** representation of the apparatus ...

Схематическое изображение
A diagrammatic (*or* **schematic**) **sketch of...**

Схематическое описание
Only **sketchy descriptions of** the new mines are currently available.

Сходен [*см.* **Весьма аналогичен**].

Сходен по своему принципу с
This device **is similar in function to** a time-delay relay.

Сходен с [*см.* **Аналогичен по конструкции**].

Сходить на конус
The thread **tapers** upward until it reaches a dimension of ...

Сходить с рельсов
The car **left the track** (*or* **was derailed**).

Сходиться
The membrane is curved until the two free edges **meet.**

Сходиться в
The magnetic meridians **converge at** the magnetic poles.

Сходиться в точке
The rays of light **are brought to a point.**
The three beams **converge to a (common) point.**

Сходиться в фокусе
The rays **come together to a focus.**

Сходиться вместе
Where the states of Colorado, Utah, and Wyoming **come together,** a large lake existed in Eocene time.

Сходиться во мнении по этому вопросу
The astrophysicists **are agreed on this point.**

Сходиться во мнении, что [*см. тж.* **В общем сходятся во мнении, что**]
It is (now) agreed by geologists (*or* Geologists **are agreed (now)**) **that ...**
There is a consensus (of opinion) that ...

Сходиться к
The iterative scheme **converges to** a unique solution.
The lines of sight **converge at** the object.
The higher powers of V **will converge on** zero.

Схóдны по форме
The shorelines of South America and Africa **are similar in shape,** but they do not match exactly.

Сходный [*см.* **Аналогичный, Весьма сходный с**].

Сходство по составу с
The compositional resemblance of these acids **to** DNA ...

Сходство с [*см. тж.* **Обладать сходством с**]
The similarity of these rocks **to** one another ...
The resemblance of these particles **to** bacteria is striking ...

Сходство структур
This is possible because of **the structural similarity of** these minerals.

Сцепление I
A bronze worm is cast on the crank-shaft with machine-cut teeth **to engage with** the wormwheel.

Сцепление II
Adherence is the quality of clinging or sticking together of unlike particles.

Сцепление зубьев
The meshing of the teeth.

Сцеплённый [*см.* **Соединён зубчатой передачей**].

Сцепляться [*см. тж.* **Зацепляться с, Находиться в зацеплении**]
Three gears **will engage** with no backlash.
The pinion **engages with** segments of two bevel gears.
When gears **intermesh,** one pair of teeth must remain in engagement until ...
The gear **meshes with** the pinion.
The roller has parallel grooves which **mesh with** the spiral gear of the worm.
Peripheral teeth on this member **are engaged with** internal teeth on an outer member.
The multi-tooth ring **mates with** a similar ring provided on the underside of the fixture.
The caging knob **engages** the azimuth gear.

Счастливая случайность
Since Rutherford did not know that quantum mechanics governed his scattering experiment, **it is (only) a happy accident that** his formula correctly describes low-energy scattering.

Считается, что
It is agreed that this formulation is correct.
It is thought (*or* **deemed**) **that** the largest fraction of carbon dioxide is dissolved in the oceans.
It is believed (*or* **assumed**) **that** these organisms do not produce disease.

Two tensors **are said to be** of the same kind if ...
These two varieties **were visualized as** forming a continuous thread ...

Считать [*см. тж.* **Есть основания полагать, что; Утверждать, что**]
This point **may be considered** the point of zero purity of ...
These organic accumulations **are interpreted to be** ancient reefs.
We normally **think of** such phenomena **as** "physical changes".

Считать, что [*см. тж.* **В предположении, что; Не следует считать, что; Полагать, что**]
It is my belief (*or* **I believe**) **that** the schemes proposed are not convincing.
He **conceived of** molecular attraction **as** due to an instantaneous arrangement of ...
The amplitude factor f_j **can be taken as being** approximately proportional to ...
We **can consider** singlet methylene **as** being formed from ...
The surface of the earth **can be looked upon as** being divided into two predominant levels.
Almost all lunar geologists **are of the opinion that** molten rock emerged from ...
Until about 1750 everyone **held that** the Earth originated in one or more catastrophic events.
They **reasoned that** the development of the Earth's crust could be best understood by ...

Считаться I
Coacervation **is held to** have a widespread biological significance.
Certain structural changes **are recognized as** diagnostic in determining ...
The difference **might (well) be reckoned as** negligible.
This need **is perceived as** being so important that ...
This method **is thought to** give the most accurate results.
The average composition of continental crust **is judged** (*or* **speculated**) **to be** petrologically intermediate.
The difference in variance **is deemed** (*or* **considered,** *or* **believed to be**) statistically significant.
If there is one peak in the frequency curve, the distribution **is said to be** unimodal.
The radial eddy diffusion coefficient **was taken to be** equal to the eddy viscosity.
All fluxes **are taken** [*or* **assumed (to be)**] positive in the direction of increasing *y*.

Считаться II [*см.* **Приходится считаться с**].

Считаться III
The pure component **was taken as** the standard state.

Считаться доказательством того, что
The colour shifts of remote galaxies **are taken as evidence that** the universe is expanding.

Считаться правильным
These values **are (now) (generally) accepted as correct.**

Считывать
Read the number of minutes **from** the straightedge scale.
The values of the *x*'s **are read** directly **from** the potentiometers.
The number of millimetres of acid **is read off** the scale.
The density **is read on** the corresponding scale.
Readings can be taken without opening the meter case.

Считывать показания [*см.* **Снимать показания**].

Счищать [*см. тж.* **Очистка от**]
The accumulated zinc **is stripped from** the cathode sheet.

Съедобный
The ormer is important as **a food** (*or* **an edible**) animal.

Съёмный
The microscope incorporates a **demountable** (*or* **detachable,** *or* **removable**) secondary electron multiplier.
The saddle is fitted with **replaceable** ways.

Сыграть [*см.* **Играть**].

Сыграть свою роль
The protein skin **has (now) served its purpose** and can be removed from the cell surface.

Сыпучие тела [*см.* **Меры сыпучих тел**].

Сырьё [*см. тж.* **Исходный материал**]
Titanium is **an (ideal) source** (*or* **raw,** *or* **initial,** *or* **starting**) **material** for many processes.
This light gasoline **would be a (good) starting material for** ethylene or acetylene production.
We obtained pure nickel from **stock** contaminated with cobalt.
Gas oil is commonly used as catalytic-cracking feed **stock.**

Т

Таблетка
Pellets of sodium hydroxide are often used for removal of acids from the atmosphere.

Таблица [*см.* **В виде таблицы, В таблице перечислены, В форме таблицы, Представлен в таблице, Сводить в таблицу**].

Табличные данные
Tabulated data.

Таинственный
The long-standing problem about the light of the **enigmatic** quasars ...

Так [*см. тж.* **Таким образом**]
At gun pressures the rate of burning of cordite depends on the calorific value but at rocket motor pressures this **is** not always **the case** (*or* **so**).

Так быстро один за другим, что
The two deposits of ash erupted **so close in time that ...**

Так же
Although the system responds much better to high-temperature targets, it is almost **as** sensitive to the reflected energy of the Sun.

Так же давно, как и
Earthquakes at sea have been known **as long as** seismometers have existed to detect them.

Так же, как и [*см. тж.* **А также, Аналогично, Наряду с**]
Physogastry may occur in larvae **as well as** in adults.
This calculation, **along with** (*or* **as well as**) our finding, shows that ...
The retorts are made of fire-clay, **as also are** the condensers.
The theories of colour vision are clearly represented, **as are** explanations of ...
The diameter required in order to fulfil this condition depends upon the reaction zone length **as does** the critical diameter.
The catalyst was washed and dried **in the same manner** (*or* **way,** *or* **fashion**) **as** the chromium catalyst.

Так же легко, как и
The diffusion of ... can proceed **as easily as** it does on the smooth regions.

Так и есть (на самом деле) [*см. тж.* **Именно так и обстоит дело**]
Such, indeed, is the case.

Так или иначе [*см. тж.* **В любом случае**]
In any event (*or* **case**), the stress finally reached the point where ...
There are several other types of uranium deposit, but **in one way or another** they all owe their origin to ...
One way or the other, the answer should be known soon.

Так как [*см. тж.* **Ввиду того, что; Поскольку**]
The manufacturer builds for possible temperatures of 70 to 90 deg., **for** (*or* **because,** *or* **as,** *or* **since**) he expects to find fairly high temperatures in some cases.

Так назван потому, что
The binary system of numbers **takes its name from the fact that** it employs only two symbols: 0 and 1.

Так называемый
This population inversion, **as it is called,** has the unique property of ...
The spectral line is split into two parts, each exhibiting **what is known as** (*or* **so-called**) circular polarization.
The air-speed indicator presents **what is termed** (*or* **called**) indicated air speed.

Так называется
This amplifier **is so named** because ...

Так обстоит дело с
Such is the case for the "torsional" motion in ethane.
This is how matters stand in implementing the Clean Air Act.

Так что

The corresponding expression is z_0 = ..., **so that** the transient extends a factor of 2π further than ...

Так, чтобы

Heterojunctions tend to trap holes and electrons **in such a way as to** prevent recombination from occurring with the production of useful light.
The valves are adjusted **so that** both are slightly open.
The unit **is so** constructed **that** it can be moved from place to place.

Также [*см. тж.* **А также, Аналогичным образом, Кроме того**]

This technique can be applied to ... **as well** (*or* **can also be** applied to ...).
The structure **could equally be** written: ...
An analytic function *F* [*f(z)*] of an analytic function f(*z*) **is likewise** analytic.
Because the atoms are very tiny, their masses **likewise are** very small (*or* **are also** very small).

Также не

The outcome **also does not** single out one observer as being "better" than the other.

Также показан

Also shown are curves for conventional abrasive grinds.

Такие далёкие друг от друга как

Attempts to stimulate the coalescence process have been made in places **so far apart as** Australia, the Caribbean, East Africa, and Pakistan.

Таким же образом (*или* **путём**)

The lower part of the oval can be constructed **by the same procedure.**

Таким же образом, как и

The emission will be dependent upon the field **in the same fashion that** the emission from thermionic cathodes is dependent upon the temperature.
Thread cutting in lathes is accomplished **in (exactly) the same manner as for** brass or steel.

Таким образом

By this means network requirements are greatly simplified.
In such a manner the synchronous motor pulls into step and ...
The rate of change of the potential energy can be maximized **in this fashion.**
In this manner (*or* **way**) a maximum amount of sound steel is produced.
The liquid **so** produced is practically pure heavy water.
Hence the material is conductive.
To explain why populations change **(in) the way they do, ...**
The random motions of the air **thus** heated are recorded by ...
By this means certain regions of DNA can be amplified (*biol.*).

Таким образом, чтобы [*см. тж.* **С таким расчётом, чтобы; Так, что(бы)**]

The chamber is designed **so** (*or* **is so** designed) **that** part of the piston head comes close to ...
Arrange the system **in such a way** (*or* **so**) **that** electrons flow through a wire.

Таким путём [*см. тж.* **Таким образом**]

Tremendous current densities can be obtained **by this means** (*or* **strategy**).
It is along this pathway that the usual image is transformed into a visual percept.
By this expedient a catalyst can be used continuously.

Таково положение

That was how matters stood in the summer of 1989.
This is the situation in the analysis for toluene.

Такого рода

Experiments **of this sort** (*or* **type,** *or* **kind**) are quite common.

Такого типа

Experiments **along these lines** have revealed a strong protective effect of poly I:C in mice.
All reactions **of this sort** (*or* **type,** *or* **kind**) lead to ...

Такое большое количество

That much oxygen does not seem to be present.

Такой большой

There is no contradiction in supposing that the main refractory material could form particles **as large as this.**

Такой же
Gamma rays have effects almost **identical with** (*or* **to**) those of X-rays.
At the same time as the outer wheel on a turn overruns the differential case, the inner wheel lags by a **like** amount.

Такой же как и
Short reaction times and low partial pressure have **as** favourable an influence on limiting methane formation **as** they have on limiting carbon formation.

Такой же как при
By using a procedure **identical to that for** absorption ...

Такой как
When iodine is dissolved in a solvent **like** carbon tetrachloride, ...
The activation energy for some chemical reactions, **like** the thermal conversion of ..., is equal to ...
When lighter nuclei are assembled into elements **as** heavy **as** iron, ...

Такой, какой встречается в
Well-formed single crystals, **as occur in** natural minerals, ...

Такой, при котором
The preferred arrangement **is that which** maximizes the distance between the electron pairs.
x is a number in the domain of g **such that** $x \neq x_0$ and $[x - x_0] < \delta$.

Там, где
Where (*or* **Wherever**) really large moulds are to be produced, a vertical band saw can be used advantageously.
Where the curve shows a maximum or minimum, the equilibrium vapour has ...

Там, где требуется
Plastics and rubber are employed **where** flexibility **is desired.**

Там есть
We do not usually see water on slopes, but the water **is there.**

Твёрдо уверен
I firmly believe (*or* **I am strongly convinced,** *or* **I am firmly impressed with the belief**) **that ...**

Твёрдо установлен
Techniques for forming ...**are well established.**
This principle **has been securely** (*or* **firmly**) **established by** experiment.

Твёрдо установленный
There **are well-established** empirical rules saying that ...

Твёрдое правило
There are few **hard-and-fast rules** governing the machining of ...

Твёрдое тело
A solid (body).

Твёрдость по Моосу
The hardness of chabazite **is 4 to 5 on Mohs scale** (*or* **4 to 5 Mohs**).
The hardness is 6 (Mohs scale).

Твёрдые частицы
The atmosphere contains **solid matter** (*or* **particles**), liquid drops, etc.

Творческий
These opportunities could be provided through the **imaginative** application of telecommunication technology.

Тем более
Generation in this region is not possible by causing electrons to oscillate either in conductors or vacuum, **much less by** mechanical movement.
The more so (*or* **Especially**) **as ...**
This makes the quarkonium system **all the more** important for studies of ...

Тем временем
In the interim (*or* **In the meantime**) the primary system was heating up.

Тем или иным образом
A very large part of chemistry is concerned, **in one way or another,** with the state of equilibrium.

Тем или иным путём
In one way or another (*or* **In some way or other**) the protostar must get rid of some of the angular momentum.
A large number of experiments have employed thermality **(in) one way or another.**
By one means or another some fraction of the gravitational energy released by the collapse is transferred outward.

Тем не менее [*см. тж.* **Всё же**]
Nonetheless (*or* **Nevertheless,** *or* **Just the same**), this must be considered a real possibility.

Тем самым [*см. тж.* **Таким образом, Что приводит к**]
A sodium atom loses one electron and a chlorine atom gains one electron because, **by doing so,** a more stable electronic configuration is formed by both elements.
Magnetostatic fields always oppose the magnetization and **in doing so** (*or* **in so doing**) they reduce the overall magnetization of ...
No clamping device is needed and the reliability of the sets is **thereby** greatly increased.
The balance weight for the side head is completely enclosed in the column **thus** affording complete protection to operator and machine.

Тема
The subject matter of the book is outlined in Chap. 1.

Темнеть
When the tissue is exposed to hydrogen peroxide, the injected neuron **turns dark** (*or* **turns a dark colour**).

Темнота [*см.* **В полной темноте**].

Температура [*см. тж.* **Высокая температура, Измерять температуру, Колебания температуры, Повышенная температура, При давлении и температуре, При комнатной температуре, Разность температур**]
The inlet (*anton.* **outlet**) **temperature is** 68°F.

Температура окружающей среды
Select a location as dry as possible, where **the ambient temperature** does not exceed 50°C.
The surrounding [*or* **environment(al)**] **temperature** will reach 300°F.

Температура опыта [*см.* **При температуре опыта**].

Температура повышается
Inside stars plasmas of ordinary hydrogen and other light elements **are raised** (*or* **increased**) **to** ignition **temperatures.**
The solvent **undergoes a temperature rise** (*or* **rises in temperature**) as it passes through the tower.

Темпы
The pace of development continues to increase.

Тенденции ... противостоит
This **tendency is opposed by** the thermal motions of the molecules.

Тенденция [*см. тж.* **Иметь тенденцию к, Наблюдается тенденция к, Проявлять тенденцию к**]
The tendency for a decrease ...
The tendency to leak is a serious defect.
The tendency toward instability ...
Today **the trend is to** unitized construction.
The trend today is to differential counting.
Two major **patterns appear to be** followed.

Тенденция к сохранению
There is **a tendency for** the unsaturated ring structure **to be preserved.**

Теорема [*см.* **Доказывать теорему**].

Теоретик
Most **theorists** (*or* **theoreticians**) consider an aqueous environment to be most probable.

Теоретическая основа [*см.* **Давать теоретическую основу**].

Теоретически
In theory (*or* **Theoretically**) this type of deficiency is possible.

Теория завоёвывает признание
In the late 1960s, **the case for** plate tectonics **gained strength.**

Теперь, когда
Now that we have presented ..., we need to focus upon ...

Тепло [*см.* **Выделение тепла, Отводить тепло, Подача тепла**].

Тепло выделяется
Heat is given out (*or* **released,** *or* **liberated**) when all elements and compounds are formed from their atoms.

Теплоотвод
The laser was mounted on a diamond to allow very efficient **heat removal.**

Тереть
Amber acquires an electric charge when **rubbed with** fur.
If one substance **is rubbed with** (*or* **against**) another, ...

Тереться друг о друга
The journal and the bearing **will rub against each other.**

Термин переосмыслился
The term has changed its meaning.

Термин прочно вошёл в литературу
The term "aromaticity" **is deeply embedded in the** chemical **literature.**

Терминология ... несколько расходится
Different crystallographers **vary somewhat in the nomenclature of** crystal systems.

Термозащитное покрытие
Extra **heat-shielding for re-entry (into the atmosphere)** will be needed.

Термообработка [*см.* **Подвергаться термообработке**].

Термостатируемый
In such cases operation in a **temperature-controlled** (*or* **thermostated**) room may be necessary.

Терпеть [*см.* **Не выносить критики**].

Терпеть фиаско
Such schemes **will fail.**

Территория университета [*см.* **На территории университета**].

Терять [*см. тж.* **Потери**]
These rays **suffer** power **loss by** tunneling.

Терять зрение
If the patient **has failing eyesight, ...**

Терять на
The body **loses** heat **by** radiation.

Терять свой обычный смысл
The gas is so tenuous that the term temperature **ceases to have its conventional meaning.**

Терять силу
In most molecules, the electrons are not moving in a single field of force, and the Larmor theorem **breaks down** (*or* **fails,** *or* **does not hold**).

Терять смысл
These concepts **lose their meaning** (*or* **significance**) on a molecular scale.

Терять энергию на
A beta particle **loses its energy by** excitation and ionization of atoms.

Терять энергию при столкновениях
The electrons **have lost (much) energy by** (*or* **in**) **collisions.**

Теряться
This advantage **is** somewhat **offset by** increasing wear.
This enables the components to be separated, but some sensitivity **is sacrificed** (*or* **lost**).

Теряться в догадках [*см. тж.* **Учёные теряются в догадках**]
One is left wondering how the underlying mass can have such a low luminosity.

Теряться в результате
Some energy **is lost as** friction in the operation of the generator.

Теряться на радиацию
All the power of the ray **has been lost to** (*or* **by**) **radiation.**

Тесная связь
There is **an intimate connection** (*or* **relationship**) **between** dispersion **and** absorption.
The intimate linkage among (*or* **connection between**) mathematics, art theory **and** philosophy ...
Because of the **close association of** soil horizons **with** (*or* **and**) climate ...

Тесная смесь
A solution is a homogeneous mixture; in order to predict whether or not two substances can form such **an intimate mixture, ...**

Тесно переплетаться
The effects of mechanization on productivity and on working conditions **are deeply intertwined.**

Тесно связан с
Supernovas **may have much to do with** the triggering of star birth.

Closely allied (*or* **related,** *or* **connected**) **to** noise control **is** vibration control.
The problem **is closely allied to** [*or* **connected** (*or* **associated**) **with**] seepage control.
Flow rate and pressure **are closely (inter)linked** [*or* **(inter)related**].
The response to most compounds **is closely related to** the mass of ...
Other auxiliary systems **are intimately connected.**
Intimately related to the economics of the accelerators **are** the technological factors that ...
Hemophilia **is closely linked to** colour blindness in some families.
The electron **is tightly bound to** the atom.

Тесно связанные
Two **tightly coupled** ions ...

Тесно связанные между собой
Two **closely related** questions arise.

Тесно связаны друг с другом
The studies of electronic spectra and photochemistry **are intimately related.**

Тесно сотрудничать с
Geologists **work closely with** hydrologists in studying water on and beneath the lands.

Тесные взаимоотношения
A key constituent of the method **is a close relationship between** the staff **and** the patients.

Тесный контакт [*см.* **Находиться в тесном контакте с**].

Техническая ориентация [*см.* **Иметь техническую ориентацию**].

Технические требования [*см.* **В соответствии с техническими требованиями**].

Технические условия [*см.* **Спецификация на**].

Технический
Commercial(-grade) aluminium ...
Technical(-grade) toluene ...

Техническое обслуживание
Much of the repair and **maintenance work** required by the equipment underground is done in temporary shops.

Технологическая вода
Process water.

Технологическая информация
The lack of background **know-how** has caused some users to question the process effectiveness.

Технологические трубы
Process piping.

Технологическое оборудование
Pipelines, storage tanks, reaction vessels and other types of **process equipment ...**

Течение [*см.* **В нижнем** (*антон.* **верхнем**) **течении реки, Вверх по течению, Вниз и вверх по течению, С течением времени**].

Течение реакции [*см.* **Ход реакции**].

Течь I [*см.* **Давать течь, Испытание на течь** (*или* **утечку**), **Протекающий клапан**].

Течь II [*см. тж.* **В ... протекает ток**]
When a current **flows along** a rectangular conductor, ...
When the unit is switched off no current **flows in** the cell.
The current **flows through** a modulator coil.

Тип [*см. тж.* **Вид, Имеется много типов**]
The most common positive clutch is **the** spiral jaw **type.**
This is **an** open **type of** system.
There are two **types of** indicator electrode.
The simplest **type of** colour centre is one called an *F*-centre.
Butt Welding Machine-**Type** MS 301.
The V-12 **types** were developed on this basis.
The **Type** 3M Amplifier is identical to the Type 1M.
Other similar **type** valves (*or* valves of **a** similar **type**) have only an accuracy of ±20% of ...
We are fabricating **a** new **line** of cooling towers.
The horse was replaced with motors of various **descriptions.**

Типа
This is true for any equation **of this sort** (*or* **type,** *or* **kind**).

The experiment was performed in an apparatus **like that** depicted in Fig. 2-13.
The fourth bond must be **of the π type.**
The branched-chain **type of** explosion ...

Типа слюды *и т.п.*
This is a general term for the **mica-like** (*or* **mica-type**) clay minerals.

Типично [*см. тж.* **Для которого характерно**]
These are **characteristically** substitution reactions.

Типичный [*см. тж.* **Характерный для**]
Representative circuits of these detectors are shown in Fig. 1.
Representative steels of the various types now in use ...
These formations will contain known quantities of potassium in amounts **representative of** average sedimentary formations.
High-moisture smog seems **typical for** London.
This feature **is typical of** such assemblies.

Типичный для
These properties **are typical of** the nonmetals.

Типичный пример
Figure 2 shows some **representative** (*or* **typical,** *or* **characteristic**) examples.

Типичным представителем ... является
A group of amoebas that has a shell **is typified by** *Arcella.*

Типичными симптомами (заболевания) являются
Hemorrhages, perforations and related changes **are typical.**

То вперёд, то назад
The marine shoreline shifted **back and forth** many times.

То есть
Subsequent heating processes would be inherently more likely to melt the upper layer; **that is** (**to say**), the first few hundred kilometres below the surface would be susceptible to melting, whereas ...

То же (самое) относится к [*см. тж.* **Это также относится к**]
It is well known that the heart rate of an adult changes when he is surprised, **and the same is true of** (*or* **for**) infants.

То же (самое) произойдёт и с
The period of the satellite going around the Earth will lengthen; **so it will also be for** the disk moving around the solar nebula.

То же (самое) происходит
A similar situation holds when we observe an object move behind another object.
As the number of layers in a single platelet increases, **so does** the reflectivity of the platelet.

То одним, то другим [*см.* **Объяснять то одним, то другим**].

То ..., то [*см. тж.* **По–разному**]
The rate at which individual sunspots migrate is **alternately** faster and slower.

То туда, то сюда
These planktons exhibit no special pattern and are blown **hither and thither** by the wind.

То, что
That the extinction coefficient is increased by denaturation **is** well known.
The fact that surface diffusion may be important in such cases **is** suggested by ...

Тогда и только тогда, когда
This is true **if and only if** U is a function of x/t.

Тогда как
The outer shell of the wave front is not convex, **whereas** the inner one is.
Pig pancreas is rich in amylase, **whereas** cattle, sheep and dog pancreases have lower concentrations.

Того времени
These losses were not noticed by the aeronautical engineers **of the day.**

Того или иного типа
A tremendous number of counters **of one kind or another** was manufactured.

Тождественность
The study showed virtual **identity of** the cytoplasmic enzyme **with** that extracted from ...

Тоже [*см.* **Также**].

Ток [*см.* **В ... протекает ток, Включать ток, Давать ток, Под током, Пропускание тока**].

Ток течёт [*см.* **Течь**].

Толкать в
Any input of energy **propels** an electron **into** one of the empty states of higher energy.

Толстый слой
Air and steam were blown through **a deep bed of** coal to obtain a fuel gas.

Толчок [*см.* **Давать толчок**].

Толща [*см.* **В толще, По всей толще**].

Толщина ... составляет от ... до [*см.* **Ширина ... составляет от ... до**].

Толщиной
This includes various types of scrap 3/8 in. **thick** (*or* **in thickness**).
A 5 μm **thick** layer (*or* A layer 5 μm **thick**) was ...

Толщиной в один атом
A coating **one atom thick** ...

Только I [*см. тж.* **Всего лишь, И только, Исключительно, Никакой другой, кроме; Один лишь, Просто**]
The absorption of hydrogen atoms **alone** (*or* **of only** hydrogen atoms) is studied.
No band can be assigned **solely** to any particular group of atoms.
The electrode is sensitive to this ion **only.**
If a sample is irradiated with **just** one laser, ...
The electron's transitions are confined to **just** one of the ladders in the energy diagram.
But nineteen other units employ some transistors.
In plants absorbing carbon dioxide **only** the stripping problem is more acute.
The magnitude of the shifts depends **solely** upon some property of the solvent.
The ultimate resolution is determined **exclusively** by the objective lens.
Such filters **have not** been used **except in** experimental manner.

Только II
Maximum viscosity **was not** reached **until** September 1.
Cases are known in which beryliosis **did not** appear **until** 15 years following exposure.
Several of the items listed **cannot** be adjusted **except** during manufacture.
It **was not until** the early part of this century **that** the glass container became modernized.
Only then did we find out that ...
Only when these factors are eliminated **can** cohesion be considered as ...

Только в ... году
As late as 1633 (*or* **It was not until** 1633 **that**) Galileo found that the Earth rotated.

Только изредка упоминается
This phenomenon **has received only occasional attention** in the literature.

Только лишь
The heating and cooling parts of the cycle **do nothing but** cancel each other.

Только после того как
The effort to develop metal-vapour laser **never** gained momentum **until** the authors obtained a quasicontinuous output of laser light in a helium-cadmium a.c. discharge.

Только слегка касаться проблемы
This problem is only touched (up)on in the later chapters.

Только ... способен
The ability to make this distinction **is unique** to our new instrument.

Только через ... лет
It was not until 30 **years later that** the study of these viruses became popular.
It was another 17 **years before** the first engine was developed.

Только что упомянутый
In the reaction **mentioned immediately above** (*or* **just mentioned**) ...

Томсоновский
The scattering per electron **is** substantially **Thomsonian.**

Тонкая проволока
Fine wire.

Тонкая регулировка
Microbore cartridge tools are being employed to provide for **fine adjustment.**

Тонкая резьба
Fine threads lack strength and are difficult to tap.

Тонкий вал
The method is especially useful when turning **slender shafts.**

Тонкое различие между
There is **a subtle** (*or* **fine**) **difference between** a soft solid **and** a highly viscous liquid.

Тонкоизмельчённый
Finely divided (*or* **Pulverized**) material ...

Тонкостенный (*антон.* **Толстостенный**)
Turning **thin-walled** (*anton.* **thick-walled**) parts ...

Тонуть
The diamonds float, while the hydrophilic gangue minerals **sink.**

Топливо [*см.* **Заправка топливом, Работать на топливе**].

Торговля
Commerce (*or* **Trade**) in disinfectants is subject to regulation ...

Тормоз [*см.* **Включать тормоз**].

Тот
A commutator is **that** part of a d.c. motor which serves the dual function of providing ... and ...

Тот или иной
By the application of **one or other** type of grinding process, it should be possible to complete ...
Figure 3 shows the result of raising the temperature on a **given** column.
This excites **one or another of** the natural modes of vibration.
The maximum rate of change of **a particular** characteristic of the orbit ...
In order to remove **a specified** (*or* **specific**) particle to infinity, ...
Molten lava being erupted from **one** volcano **or another** solidifies into ...
In some situations **one or the other of** these agencies predominates, but more usually both operate together.

Тот, который
The stars lie half a parsec from **those** discovered earlier.

Точечная сварка [*см.* **Сваренный точечной сваркой**].

Точка [*см.* **Внутренняя точка, Отправная точка, Средняя точка**].

Точка, в которой
There is **a point** on the circle **such that** $|G(e^{i\omega_0})| = 1$.

Точка замерзания [*см.* **Ниже точки замерзания**].

Точка зрения [*см.* **Придерживаться мнения, С точки зрения**].

Точка касания
The point of tangency (*or* **of contact**) **of** the two circles ...

Точка на графике:
Светлая точка — open circle.
Темная точка — solid circle.

Точка перегиба
Inflection point.

Точка пересечения
Find **the point of intersection** (*or* **the intersection point**) **of** these two lines.

Точка равновесия
To determine the length of time a plasma must be confined at a given density and temperature to produce **a "break-even" point** in the power balance ...

Точка расхождения между
Here is one **point of departure between** information theory **and** problems of human communication.

Точная копия
Each molecule **is a precise replica of** the original.

Точная корректировка
Precision adjustment of space vehicle orbit characteristics ...

Точнее [*см. тж.* **Более точно называется; Или, точнее**]
Such orbitals are designated as σ molecular orbitals or **more specifically,** (*or* **more precisely**) as pσ orbitals.
There are approximations **that do better than** the Raleigh theory.

Точнее говоря

To be (more) specific, we will now examine a junction found between ...
More precisely (*or* **More exactly**) (*or* **To be more precise**) we shall substitute for the absolute notion of truth and more flexible concept of ...
In more exact terms ...

Точнее отражать
These representations **more adequately depict** (*or* **more nearly approximate**) the actual molecular structure.

Точно I
A **precision**-fitted seal prevents leakage.
The array **is precision** tuned.
The accuracy of a **properly** calibrated declinometer ...
Heavy ions follow the electric field lines more **closely** than do electrons.
Heavy atoms are easier to locate **with precision** than light atoms.

Точно II
It is **well** established that strain-ageing in low-carbon steel is due to ...
These variations can be predicted reasonably **well.**

Точно III
To solve the problem **exactly, ...**

Точно воспроизводить
The vibratory current **faithfully reproduced** the various frequencies of speech.

Точно выполненный
The colloid mill consists of two **accurately machined** disks rotating in ...

Точно вычислять
Ordinary geometry suffices **to calculate exactly** the perimeter of that triangle.

Точно как [*см.* **В точности как**].

Точно наводить на фокус
In the scanning electron microscope a beam of electrons **is brought to a fine focus** and is scanned across the specimen.

Точно не известен
The molecular formula of this material **is not known with certainty.**

Точно не предсказуем
The theory of probability deals with events whose occurrence **is not precisely predictable.**

Точно не установлен
The driving forces **have not (yet) been clearly identified.**

Точно определённый
These comets have **well-determined** orbits.

Точно определять (положение)
To pin-point (**the target,** etc.).

Точно повторять
The piston of the power cylinder **faithfully copies** the movement of the differential piston.

Точно подгонять к
Standards **should be matched to** the gross composition of the sample **as closely as possible.**

Точно предсказывать, что
One **can predict (rather) closely that ...**

Точно регулировать
The intensity of each light source **can be closely controlled.**

Точно решать
To solve the problem **exactly, ...**

Точно соблюдать
Follow carefully the instructions given below.

Точно так же [*см. тж.* **Аналогичным образом**]
Measurements of the conductive heat flow are complicated by the flow of water in the crust; **by the same token** the thermal energy transported by convective circulation in hot springs can disturb measurements of the conductive heat flow.
In (just) the same way polynomial equations of the fourth degree can be constructed.
Likewise, among deactivating groups certain substituents are much more deactivating than others.
In similar fashion (*or* **Similarly**), the sum of the four next-smallest semicircles is *pi*.

Точно так же, как (и)
Such microassociations occur in the various zones of lakes **just as they do** in other environmental subdivisions.
Just as water **is** the equilibrium form of hydrogen, carbon dioxide **is** the equilibrium form of ...

Точно такой же
In olivine an ion of either magnesium or iron always occupies **precisely the same** position in space with respect to ...

Точно указывать
Such perturbations make it difficult **to pinpoint** the time of a comet's return.

Точно указывать на [*см.* **Указывать со всей определённостью на то, что**].

Точно укладываться в
Each of the numbers 1, 2, 3, 4 and 6 **will go evenly into** 12.

Точно установлено, что
It is well established that among fishes, amphibians and reptiles the pineal organ is sensitive to light.

Точно учитывать
It is difficult **to keep close track of** plant resources.

Точно центроваться с
The milling head **is accurately in line with** the milling spindle.

Точное представление
We attempt to give the student **as authentic a view of** the subject **as possible.**

Точное решение
The exact solution of the problem ...

Точное уравнение (*или* **решение**)
An exact equation (*or* **solution**).

Точность [*см. тж.* **В пределах точности анализа, Выдерживаться с точностью до, Выполняться с точностью до, Высокая точность, Добиваться точности, С точностью до**]
This equation gives the motion of the Moon **with (reasonable) exactness.**
The validity of all such dates rests upon four factors.
The sensing device **must be accurate to** 1 part in 10,000.
Such systems **may be accurate to better than** 50 ft.
Mercury barometers **may be accurate to within** 0.0005 in.
The faithfulness (*or* **accuracy**) **of** such a reconstruction is proportional to the number of projections.

Точность до трёх десятичных знаков
A precision of three decimal places is typical for analogue computers.

Точность размеров
Dimensional accuracy.

Точность регулирования
The fineness of control.

Точные измерения
Precision (*or* **Precise,** *or* **Exact**) **measurements.**

Точные исследования
Most of **the precise work in** beta spectroscopy is done with double focusing spectrometers.

Точные размеры [*см.* **Иметь точные размеры**].

Точный [*см. тж.* **Близкий к действительности, Более точное приближение, Достаточно точная картина**]
The 4n + 2 rule **is precise.**
This was 0.1% above **the true** value.
This expression **is** thermodynamically **exact.**
A **faithful** (*or* **exact,** *or* **true**) copy of each message ...
These instruments **are precise.**
A **precision** method.
The defect can be corrected by lapping the measuring faces on a **true** flat surface.
Squaring fixtures are used on grinders to produce **true** square edges required on ...

Точный до
The measurement of a stellar image **will be accurate to within** 0.02 arc-second.

Точный допуск [*см.* **С точным допуском**].

Точный прибор
A precision instrument.
More **refined instruments** are available with maximum errors of 1%.

Травить
The metal to be coated **is pickled** (*or* **etched**) in dilute hydrochloric acid.

Традиционно
It is customary to express this great quantity in ...

Традиционный

A synthesis following **well-established** (*or* **traditional,** *or* **conventional**) routes would produce ...

Традиция [*см.* **В соответствии с традицией**].

Траектория частицы
The path of a particle is made well visible by ...

Трактовать [*см.* **Рассматривать**].

Транзистор [*см.* **Полностью оборудованный транзисторами**].

Транспорт и пешеходы [*см.* **Движение транспорта и пешеходов**].

Транспортировать [*см.* **Доставлять, Отгружать, Передавать по трубам**].

Транспортировка [*см.* **Во время перевозки, Повреждение при перевозке**].

Транспортируемый по трубопроводу
Coal gas **is** a convenient **piped** gaseous fuel.

Транспортное средство
The coal may now be loaded into **transportation facilities** for the market.

Тра́та [*см.* **Бесполезная тра́та**].

Требование [*см. тж.* **В соответствии с требованиями, Жёсткие требования, Отвечать требованиям, Предъявлять требования к, Строгие требования, Удовлетворять требованиям**]
The general **requirements for** an oven **are that it be** clean ...
The basic **requirement of** any frame **is that it be** strong enough.
Requirements on quality of parts **are** greater than ...
A final **constraint is that** the orbital angular momentum must always be less than the principal quantum number.

Требования, налагаемые на
To meet **the** diverse **requirements imposed on** both the machines, ...

Требование, предъявляемое к [*см.* **Основное требование, предъявляемое к ...**].

Требовать
This amount of leakage **necessitates** (*or* **requires,** *or* **demands**) large volumes in reserve.
The design **calls for** precision instrument ball bearings.
Computer-integrated manufacturing systems **call for** the coordinated participation of computers in all phases of ...
The implementation of these applications of radiation pressure to atoms **calls for** laser sources of sufficient power and tunability.
The disadvantages of this system are the added equipment and maintenance costs it **entails** (*or* **involves**).

Требовать дальнейших исследований
The place of these mollusks in the food chain **invites further investigation.**
The origin of the carbon monoxide evolved by the pyrolysis of lunar fines **calls for further investigation.**

Требовать жертв
There is a price to be paid for the higher resolution of this spectrograph.

Требовать использования
This task often **involves the complete resources of** the engineer.

Требовать много времени
This job **is time consuming.**

Требовать наличия
This **necessitates** tracers with long half-lives.

Требовать, чтобы
Time resolution of compounds whose spectra overlap **requires that** the laser pulse width **be** less than ...

Требоваться [*см. тж.* **Для ... требуется, Когда это необходимо, Необходимо**]
Where self-priming qualities **are called for** (*or* **required,** *or* **needed,** *or* **necessary,** *or* **essential**), ...
It takes a very powerful magnetic field **to** control the path of ...
Additional information **must be called on to** describe the eigenfunctions in more detail.
It takes a second **to** form a wave.

Требуемый [*см. тж.* **Время, необходимое для; Необходимый для того, чтобы**]
The difficult geometry **required of** field reflecting optics makes it necessary to use ...

The degree of decontamination **required of** reprocessing ...
This is a primary factor that determines the thrust **required from** the propulsion system **to** fly a given airplane.
This enables the operator to tilt the work **at** any **requisite** angle.
The potentiometer offers the **wanted** performance characteristics.
In the synthesis of **desired** platinum (II) complexes ...
The time **occupied in** (*or* **required for**) ascent from the zero line ...

Требуется
The great accuracy which **is** now **required** (*or* **demanded**) **of** many machine tools necessitates ...

Требуется много времени для того, чтобы
It takes long to understand these forces.

Требуется не только
There is more to the development of agricultural water resources **than** building dams and delivering water to the fields.

Требующий большой затраты энергии
Sulphuric acid is an **energy-consuming** (*or* **-expensive**) commodity.

Требующийся [*см.* **Время, необходимое для**].

Трение [*см.* **Тереться друг о друга**].

Трение друг о друга
The rubbing together of the two fault surfaces generates the elastic waves.

Трение стали о сталь
Chromium has a low coefficient of **friction,** being one-half that of **steel-on-steel.**

Третьестепенный
Secondary or **tertiary** supporting tasks ...

Трещина [*см.* **Без трещин, Изобилующий трещинами, Проверять на трещиноватость**].

Трёхкомпонентная смесь
A ternary mixture.

Трёхмерный [*см.* **Объёмный**].

Тропический вариант
A tropicalized radio set.

Труба [*см.* **По трубе**].

Трудная задача
This is **a challenging task** (*or* **a challenge**) which often involves the complete resources of the engineer.

Трудно
Bubbles of gas **have great difficulty in** getting out of the magma.
Driving forces **are difficult** (*or* **hard**) **to** measure accurately.
Such suspended droplets **are hard to** remove from the gas stream.
Even experienced economists **may be hard pressed to** guess the impact of new sources of a chemical.

Трудно возражать против такой оценки
If you look at this photograph you will find that **such a judgment is hard to argue with.**

Трудно или даже невозможно
Matched filters **are difficult if not impossible to** realize.

Трудно обеспечить
The uniform distribution of air through the cooling tower **is difficult to attain** in such units.

Трудно определить
Sometimes **it is an open question whether or not** a contaminant is having any biological effects.

Трудно переоценить
The importance of good health to old people **is difficult to overestimate.**

Трудно себе представить
The nature of the swivel **is difficult to imagine** (*or* **perceive**).
The extent of the application of electricity **can hardly be conceived.**

Трудно сказать
It is hard to tell whether such a jet is identical with ...

Труднодоступность
The inaccessibility of the hub section requires special tooling.

Труднодоступный
To measure air velocities in parts **not easily accessible** is a difficult task.

The new device saves time in **hard-to-reach** (*or* **hard-to-get-at,** *or* **inaccessible**) spots.
The part **is hard to get at** (*or* **difficult to reach**).

Труднообрабатываемый
The Table lists most **difficult-to-machine** alloys.

Трудноразрешимый
Stubborn mathematical problems ...

Трудности на пути к достижению этой цели
The main **difficulties encountered in reaching this goal were** energy loss processes involving ...

Трудность [*см. тж.* **Более серьёзные трудности, чем; Возникают трудности, Вызывать затруднения, Выходить из затруднения, Испытывать затруднения, Не представлять затруднений, Представлять затруднения, Преодоление трудности, Создавать большие затруднения**]
Thus we avoid some of **the problems** (*or* **difficulties**) **associated with** bypassing.

Трудные условия [*см. тж.* **Тяжёлые условия**]
Severe (*or* **Arduous**) cutting **conditions ...**

Трудный [*см.* **Весьма трудный, Сложный**].

Трудный вопрос
The nervous system presents two of the most **challenging questions** of contemporary biology.

Трудоёмкий
Activation analysis can be very **time consuming** (*or* **labour consuming,** *or* **labour intensive,** *or* **arduous,** *or* **laborious**).
In general this is **a cumbersome** (*or* **tedious**) procedure, but simple expressions are available for ...

Трудосберегающее устройство
Labour-saving device.

Трущиеся поверхности
Friction (*or* **Rubbing**) surfaces.

Трущиеся части
All internal **parts,** except those actually **in rubbing contact, ...**
Rubbing components (*or* **Friction parts**).

Туго входить [*см.* **Входить туго в**].

Туго завинчивать
Screw the plug **in hard** to avoid leakage at high pressure.

Туго закрученная спираль
The cavity contains **a tightly wound helix** consisting of a complex containing RNA and the protein *N* (*biol.*).

Туго затягивать гайку
Screw up the nut strongly (*or* **tight**).

Туго намотанный на каркас
A large number of turns of insulated wire **wound close together on a form ...**

Туго поджимать винт
Firmly tighten the screw.
The screws should be securely tightened.

Тугоплавкий
A **high-melting** (*or* **refractory**) alloy ...

Тупиться [*см.* **Затупляться**].

Турбопривод [*см.* **С турбоприводом**].

Тусклый блеск
The surface was polished to **a dull lustre.**

Тускнеть
When lead is freshly cut it has a bright lustre, but soon **dulls** due to the formation of...
As the light of the phosphorescent material slowly **decays, ...**

Тушить дугу [*см. тж.* **Гасить дугу**]
At the end of the run the "stop" push button is pressed which **extinguishes** (*or* **puts out,** *or* **quenches**) **the arc.**

Тушить пожар
The foam is effective in **putting out** oil **fires.**

Тщательно I [*см. тж.* **Весьма тщательно, Детально**]
They examined the source more **closely** with the aid of the new telescope.
If we had worked more **exhaustively** (*or* **laboriously**) we would have succeeded in preparing ...
One enzyme that has been **thoroughly** explored is ...
The design of a tower frame must be worked out **with care.**
Rate of fuel flow must be **carefully** (*or* **closely**) controlled.

Тщательно II
Pulp particles and reagents are mixed much more **intimately** than is possible with open type agitators.

Тщательно дистиллированный
Carefully distilled water ...

Тщательно изучать [*см. тж.* **Более тщательно изучать**]
It became clear that **a detailed look at** the model was required before ...
The subject **has been studied extensively** (*or* **thoroughly**).
Physical chemistry **should be closely studied** at this point.

Тщательно изучаться
This problem **is (now) under active study.**
Molecular diffusion in stagnant media **has been the subject of much study** (*or* **has received much study**) for more than a century.

Тщательно изучен
The alkali metals **are the most thoroughly studied** of all the metals.
This possibility **has been given careful** (*or* **painstaking**) **study.**

Тщательно наблюдать за
Mount Baker **is being closely** (*or* **carefully**) **observed** because it has been recently showing signs of renewed eruptive activity.

Тщательно наблюдать за больным
Under these circumstances **the patient should be carefully followed up** (*or* **observed**).

Тщательно перемешанный
A **well-stirred** electrolyte ...

Тщательно перемешаны
The solute vapour species **are mixed thoroughly** (*or* **intimately**) **with** the diluent.

Тщательно подобранные по размеру
These gas producers require **carefully sized** lumps of coal.

Тщательно рассмотреть
We **should examine** this problem more **closely.**

Тщательно регулировать
The atmosphere **must be controlled closely** (*or* **carefully**); slight variations in carbon content of the gas have serious effects on ...

Тщательно следить за
In operating a wet cooling tower **one must pay close attention to** the condition of the water.
It is well **to keep a close watch on** the valve.
The refrigerating engineer **should keep a watchful** (*or* **sharp**) **eye on** the cargo being loaded.
Watch the manometer **carefully.**

Тщательно следить за тем, чтобы
Much care must be taken to avoid the accidental puncture of a blood vessel.
Great care must be exercised to prevent dirt from entering the pump.
Take good care that the shaft **should** run smoothly.

Тщательно составленный
Carefully worded specifications are required.

Тщательное изучение [*см. тж.* **При тщательном изучении**]
A close look at (*or* **A careful study of**) hail reveals that the stones differ in appearance.
The system **is** now **under intensive study.**
Approval is granted only after **exhaustive** (*or* **painstaking**) **study by** the Committee.
Close inspection of the nuclei has shown that ...

Тщательное наблюдение
These boilers do not require **exacting** (*or* **careful**) **supervision** as regards water level.

Тщательное рассмотрение [*см. тж.* **Более тщательное изучение**]
A close examination of Figure V shows a very important feature.
A close look at well-formed single crystals shows that ...

Тщательный I [*см. тж.* **Более внимательное рассмотрение, Всеобъемлющий**]
The compound needs **elaborate** (*or* **thorough**) purification.
Much more **ambitious** calculations are needed to follow these final stages in detail.
On **painstaking** examination, ...

Solid mixtures require more **sophisticated** investigation.
The machines are subject to **rigorous** testing before dispatch.
Careful maintenance is essential.
Very **close** furnace control is required.
Diligent spraying must defend the seedlings.
Meticulous scientific and medical work ...
Thorough greasing of the bearings is important.
The **careful** choice of the diameter is important.

Тщательный II
This assures perfect atomization of the oil and **intimate** mixing of the combustion air with ...

Тщательный анализ
Careful analysis of sunlight reveals ...

Тщательный контроль
This requires **close control over** the pressure drop.

Тысячами
Asteroids **by the thousands** are moving against the background of the stars.

Тяжелее воздуха
A **heavier-than-air** object ...

Тяжёлые условия [*см. тж.* **В тяжёлых условиях, Трудные условия**]
The motor has to be capable of long operation **under rugged** (*or* **arduous**, *or* **demanding**, *or* **rigorous**, *or* **severe**) **conditions.**

Тянуться вдоль всего
A line of fall-out is defined which **runs the length of** the continent.

Тянуться за
A comet's tail **streams out behind** the comet.

Тянуться на
Comet tails have been observed **to extend** 10^3 km **from** the nucleus.

У

У
The flexibility in capacity is not so great as **with** steam-driven pumps.
In man the large intestine is about 5 ft in length.

У берега [*см.* **Вблизи берега**].

У нас вышла вся бумага
Our paper has run out (*or* **We have run out of paper**).

У нас есть все основания полагать, что
We have good reason to believe that ...

У нас на глазах
The molten lava solidified **before our eyes.**

У него обнаружен
Any patient who has undergone previous thyroid surgery must be suspected of having hypoparathyroidism if **he** (*or* **she**) **presents with** a low calcium.

У ... появились крылья
These animals **developed wings.**

У ... создаётся впечатление, что
Students often **form the impression that** a workable theory is universally accepted by scientists.

Убедительно
The utility of these powerful electric and magnetic fields has been demonstrated **in a conclusive way** (*or* **conclusively**, *or* **convincingly**).

Убедительно подтверждать
This **makes an impressive case in favour of** the reality of continental drift.
The preceding evidence **strongly supports** the dipolarionic structure of ...

Убедительно подтверждённый документальными доказательствами
If these scientists were more open-minded, they would give immediate recognition to any **well-documented** propositions.

Убедительно показывать, что
The foregoing aims **to bring out clearly that** the temperature problem is a most complex one.

Убедительно продемонстрировать
The laboratory **has clearly demonstrated** the value of ...

Убедительно указывать на [*см.* **Указывать со всей определённостью на то, что**].

Убедительно указывать на то, что
These observations **strongly suggest** (*or* **intimate**) **that** vapour cavities were formed within the sample itself.

Убедительное доказательство
There is compelling (*or* **strong**) **evidence** against nonmetric theories.
This would be **a convincing proof of** A's theory.

Убедительное доказательство того, что
Accurate measurements **have given conclusive** (*or* **firm**) **evidence of ...**
This provides strong (*or* **impressive**) **evidence that** this portion of the protein is on the inner surface of ...
This is strong proof that the transform segments are active faults (*geol.*).
An increase in the size of the unknown peak **is good evidence for** it being the substance added.

Убеждаться [*см.* **Чтобы убедиться в том, что**].

Убеждаться в том, что
The scientist **must assure himself that** the errors are stated on a reasonable basis.
Check that the liquid is of the correct specific gravity.
Fuel injectors should be (carefully) tested **to determine that** they are functioning properly.
Ensure that the mains supply is switched off.
Make (*or* **Be**) **sure that** the voltage selector is set correctly.
See (to it) that the face against which the leather fits is quite clean.
In order **to make certain that** a parent tree will produce offspring with ...
Thus Kepler **satisfied himself that** the orbit was oval.
By recalculating $\sqrt{\overline{u^2}}$ we were able **to verify** (*or* **ascertain**) **that** the approach of this section is consistent with ...
To convince yourself that this is correct, use appropriate unity factors.

Увеличение I [*см. тж.* **В порядке увеличения, Выигрыш, Повышение, При увеличении, Приводить к увеличению**]
The greater electron resistance rate results in **a build up of** net positive charge.
The enhancement of velocity ...
Ribs may be made a part of the moulded piece **for added** strength.
No **gain in** resolution is obtained.
The moisture was calculated from the weight **gain of** the carbonate.
This causes **an increase in** the size of the plant.
There is no **increase of** counting rate after injection.
This leads **to increased** (*or* **to a rise in**) production.
Increasing the irradiation dose decreases the rate of ...
A small **buildup of** liquid concentration has a big effect on ...

Увеличение II [*см. тж.* **Большое увеличение, С малым увеличением, С увеличением**]
36x magnification ...
Magnifying power 6x ...
A **6-x power magnifying** glass.
A **six-power magni**glass.

Увеличение в ... раз
A tenfold **increase of** (*or* **in**) ...

Увеличение на
An increase of 10 percent accompanies a change of coordination number from 4 to 8.

Увеличенный
An **enlarged** (*or* **magnified**) view of a crack (×750) ...

Увеличенный масштаб [*см.* **В увеличенном масштабе**].

Увеличивать I [*см. тж.* **Вносить вклад в, Значительно увеличивать, Обострять, Повышать, Углублять, Усиливать**]
The advantages of computing technology **could be multiplied** many times if ...

Увеличивать II [*см. тж.* **Повышать**]
The vortexes **contribute** significantly **to** the lift of the aircraft.
Curves and fillets **add** strength.
The formation of dust **adds to** the explosion hazard.
The coating considerably **extends** (*or* **prolongs**) the life of these alloys.
With binoculars, this range **can be (greatly) extended.**

This **magnifies** (*or* **enhances,** *or* **augments**) the aerodynamic moment.
Production **could be stepped up** (*or* **increased,** *or* **raised**) quickly.
The high light intensities available from laser sources **can contribute to** the homogeneous line width.
The increased speed of operation **ups** (*sl.*) the production.
The lense **enlarges** (*or* **magnifies**) the image two-fold.
The figure **is scaled up.**

Увеличивать III
This factor **contributes to** the confusion.

Увеличивать вдвое (втрое)
The output **will be doubled (trebled).**

Увеличивать до максимума
The preferred arrangement is that which **maximizes** the distance between the electron pairs.

Увеличивать дозу
It is important to start with **the** smallest possible **dose** and slowly **work up.**

Увеличивать до размеров
If an atom **were magnified to the size of** the Los Angeles Coliseum, ...

Увеличивать на
The amount of heat needed **to increase** (*or* **raise**) the temperature of one pound of water **(by)** one degree Fahrenheit ...

Увеличивать срок
This will enable them to offer a wider range of products without **extending the (delivery) time.**

Увеличивать срок службы
The bronze wear plates **extend the service life of** the cranes.

Увеличиваться [*см. тж.* **Нарастать**]
The amplitude of this frequency component **will be enhanced** markedly.
The difference between the two periods **tends to widen.**
The particles must cover greater distances, which means that the period of revolution **mounts.**
The supply of water **has been augmented** in many parts of ...
Resolution **is maximized** (*anton.* **minimized**) **by** applying ...
The proportion of volatiles **undergoes** (*or* **shows**) **a rise from** lignite **to** bituminous coal.
This term **rises** as the intermolecular distance decreases.
The importance of the laser **will continue to escalate.**
This pressure **can build up** (*or* **grow,** *or* **rise,** *or* **increase**) **to** high values.
Acceleration is expected **to climb to** four or more times the present 50 *g*.
Cleaners used in metal finishing **are growing in** complexity and number.
The vapour **increases in** transparency.
Domestic oil consumption **will soar** (*or* **rise**) **to ...**
The reaction **increases** (*or* **shows an increase**) **in** velocity.

Увеличиваться благодаря
The pressure **was augmented by** the centrifugal force.

Увеличиваться в несколько раз в размере и весе
The beetle **increased several times in size and weight.**

Увеличиваться в ... раз
Over the range of a_1 from 0 to 0.8, D **increased five- to ten-fold** (*or* **five to ten times,** *or* **by a factor of five to ten,** *or* **by five to ten times**).

Увеличиваться с
This difference **increases with** temperature (*or* **with increasing** temperature, *or* **as** the temperature **increases**).

Увеличиваться с расстоянием от
The depth to bedrock seafloor **increases away from** the axis.

Уверенно
Then you can predict **with confidence** the products formed.

Уверенность [*см.* **В полной уверенности, что; С уверенностью**].

Уверенность в том, что
It has been possible to reduce the section thickness of castings because of **the assurance that** porosity will not occur.

Увидеть
No man **will** ever **lay eyes on** these planets.

Угловой момент относительно Солнца
The angular momentum of each planet **taken about the Sun** can be calculated from ...

Углублять знания [*см.* **Безгранично расширять знания о**].

Углублять понимание [*см. тж.* **Улучшать**]
Chemists **have been refining their understanding of ...**

Углубляться в существо вопроса
The researcher **went to the heart of the matter.**

Угол [*см. тж.* **Видеть под ... углом, На углах, Направлен под углом, Повернуть на угол**]
An angle of 60° ...

Угол вылета снаряда
The shells were fired at low **angles of departure.**

Угол между
The angle between the centre line **and** the trace ... (*or* **The angle** the centre line **makes with** the trace ...).

Угол падения пластов составляет
The strata were dipping sixty degrees.

Угрожать [*см.* **Представлять собой угрозу для**].

Угрожать безопасности [*см.* **Когда это не угрожает безопасности населения**].

Угроза [*см.* **Ставить под угрозу**].

Удаваться [*см. тж.* **Нам повезло**]
Niels Bohr **was able to** explain its spectrum.
They **managed to** distinguish the particles.
It has been possible to calculate ...
We **succeeded in** separating ...

Удаление ... из
The elimination (*or* **removal**) **of** H_2O **from** the compound ...

Удаление отходов
We have used streams as natural **waste-disposal** (*or* **- removal**) systems.

Удаление покрытия
This is done by **stripping the coating from** a known area.

Удаление скоплений
The method is particularly effective for **dislodging accumulations of** soil **from** castings.

Удалён на значительное расстояние от [*см. тж.* **На значительном расстоянии от**]
The older volcanic islands **are well off** the Mid-Atlantic Ridge.

Удалён на ... сантиметров от [*см.* **Отстоять на ... сантиметров от**].

Удалённые друг от друга [*см. тж.* **Находящиеся на расстоянии ... друг от друга**]
The holes **are (spaced)** 15 ft **apart** (*or* **are spaced at** 15 ft, *or* **are separated by** 15 ft).

Удалённый
The ends of the flames **away from** the atomizers will be golden in colour.
Electrons **far removed from** the atom must be ...
The pawl engages the groove on the side **remote from** the shank.

Удалось получить некоторое представление о
Some insight into the actual configuration of the large bacterial subunit RNA **has been gained** (*biol.*).

Удалять [*см. тж.* **Устранять**]
The large amount of material that **has to be removed** in laser drilling ...
Foul gases **should be cleared out of** the furnace.
Much ash **has to be disposed of from** power stations.
The furnace **should be drained of** oil.
An exhaust fan **to draw off** the dry dust ...
Moisture may collect in the sumps, from which it **can be expelled** when necessary.
These lines **cannot be got rid of** by any form of heat treatment.
The fire side **should be kept clean of** soot and unburned carbon.
When the water **was removed from** the pit, ...
The bolts **may be** then **withdrawn.**
The scrap **is difficult to handle** because it is made up of punchings.

Удалять за пределы
The arm swings down, thus **bringing** the

casting **clear of** (*or* **away from**) the working area.

Удалять заусенцы [*см.* **Снимать заусенцы**].

Удалять из
The condenser **removes** (*or* **withdraws**) water **from** nitrogen.
The cloth must be vibrated periodically **to dislodge** the dust.
The alkoxy group **is eliminated from** the original ester.

Удалять отходы
Wastes may be dumped into the environment at a rate ...

Удалять с объекта
Such volumes of waste **should be shipped off-site.**

Удалять стружку
The drill should be backed from the work frequently to allow **removal of chips** and passage of coolant.

Удаляться в бесконечность
One focus of the ellipse **has moved off** (*or* **receded**) **to infinity.**

Удаляться друг от друга
The particles **are moving farther apart.**
Continents **are moving** (*or* **drifting**) **apart** at a very low rate.

Удаляться на большое расстояние от
When the comet **has moved to great distances from** the Sun, ...

Удаляться от [*см. тж.* **Отступать от**]
The water ring **recedes from** and reapproaches the rotor boss.
After the collision the molecule **moves away from** the wall.
As the ring of planet-forming gas **moved outward from** the solar nebula, ...

Удаляясь от
Lava continued to flow from the volcano to the sea **in a direction away from** the town.

Удар
Each **impact of** a molecule **with** (*or* **on**) a wall of the container ...
The impact of the fluid may either tend to close or open the valve.
Meteoric **impacts** (*or* **hits**) **upon** the skin of a rocket ...
Radioactive dust particles ... collected by **impaction against** the adhesive surface ...
Leaky valves often result from **pounding of** valves **against** their seats.
A hammer **blow on** hard rock ...

Удар молнии в провод
Lightning strokes to wire do not damage the wire itself.

Ударять [*см.* **Подвергать удару**].

Ударять с большой силой
Safety glass does not splinter if **struck forcibly.**

Ударяться о [*см. тж.* **Падать на**]
When water waves **strike** (*or* **hit**) a row of posts, new wave patterns are formed.
Rock particles carried in the current **strike against** the exposed bedrock of the channel surfaces.
The photograph depicts a jet of acetylene gas **impinging on** (*or* **striking**) a flat plate.
The shock wave **strikes** (*or* **impinges on**) the contact surface.

Удачно [*см. тж.* **Успешно**]
The mathematical force of attraction **works well in** explaining the observed phenomena.

Удачно назван
The cloud **is aptly called** a giant molecular-cloud complex.
The variable arm **is well named,** for it shows few consistencies and scarcely any trend (*biol.*).

Удачный
This term **is appropriate** because ...

Удваивать [*см.* **Увеличивать вдвое**].

Удвоенное произведение
This acceleration is equal to **twice the product of ...**

Удвоенный [*см. тж.* **Двойной**]
This distance must be multiplied by **twice** “pi”.

Уделено мало (*антон.* **много**) **внимания**
Multicomponent diffusion in porous materials **has received little** (*anton.* **much**) **attention.**

Уделено много внимания
The role of the orifice in determining bubble size **is treated at some length** [*or* **is given much space** (*or* **attention**)] in the book.

Уделять большое внимание
These aspects of chemical analysis **are a major preoccupation of** the analyst.

Уделять внимание
At present, more **emphasis is placed** [*or* **attention is focused** (*or* **centred**)] **on** performance.
Considerable **attention has been given to** the study of ...
Other organisms also **have** now **received** some **attention.**

Уделять главное внимание
Engines for combat-type aircraft **receive primary emphasis** (*or* **consideration,** *or* **attention**).
Our **main concern** in the first six chapters **was with** the behaviour of bound rays.
This problem **received the bulk of attention.**
The forging engineer's **primary consideration is** the force that the forging machine can deliver.

Уделять должное внимание
When the matter **receives proper** (*or* **due**) **attention** (*or* **the attention it needs**), ...

Уделять достаточно внимания
This subject **has received sufficient** (*or* **a fair amount of**) **attention** in the literature.

Уделять много внимания
The perfect heater chamber has not yet been developed, and **much thought** (*or* **consideration,** *or* **attention**) **is being given to** new designs.
Few polymerases from other eukaryotes **have received much** (*or* **detailed**) **attention** (*biol.*).
Considerable study has been given to electrolytes in ...

Уделять основное внимание [*см. тж.* **Особое внимание уделено**]
Prominence is given to the small-scale techniques.
Recently **most attention has been concentrated on** the use of ...

Уделять особое внимание
This paper will describe the research program in this area **with special emphasis on** nonlinear optical processing.

Уделяющий много внимания точности
Precision-minded engineers ...

Удержание плазмы
The confinement of a plasma by the magnetic field.
This provides perfect **containment.**
Magnetic fields provide possible means for **containing** gas **plasmas.**

Удерживаемые вместе
The virion molecule consists of a number of small units **held together by** noncovalent bonds.

Удерживаемый
Objects **held by** springs, atoms **held by** chemical bonds ...

Удерживать
To confine the beam **to** the interaction space, ...
The electrons **are confined to** the ring-shaped region by a magnetic guidefield.
The plasma **is held in place** (*or* **confined,** *or* **contained**) **with** a magnetic field.
Large diameter studs effectively **secure** the column in position.
Both the electrons and the light **can be confined to** a small volume in the single-heterostructure laser.

Удерживать в нужном положении
The ties **hold** the elements **in position.**

Удерживать вместе [*см. тж.* **Не давать распадаться**]
Strong forces among the unit particles of the solute material **tend to hold** these **together.**
The compressive stress **tends to hold** the particles **together.**

Удерживать во взвешенном состоянии
When particles **are held in suspension, ...**

Удерживать на месте
The sleeve **is held in place** (*or* **position**) **by** a tension spring.
A washer **holds** the entire assembly **in place.**

Удерживать на минимальном уровне

The oxidation of cellulose **must be kept** (*or* **held**) **at a minimum.**

Удерживать на низком уровне
The current **is kept low.**
With the proper transformer design the errors **may be kept low.**

Удерживать на орбите
The magnets **maintain** the particles **in orbit.**

Удерживать на постоянном уровне
The bandwidth **is held constant** (*or* **fixed**).

Удерживать на приемлемом уровне
The voltage drop **must be kept at an acceptable value.**

Удерживать на ... траектории
Bending and focussing magnets **confine** the particles **to a** circular **path.**

Удерживать на уровне
It is necessary **to keep the** SO_2 **level at** or below 0.01 mole percent.
To keep (*or* **hold**) the temperature **down to** about 70°F, ...

Удерживать от распада
These chemical bonds **hold** the atoms **together.**

Удерживаться в
The ion **is confined in** a trap.

Удерживаться вместе
Atoms of metals in liquid or solid metals **are held together by** the metallic bond.

Удерживаться на постоянном уровне
If the temperature and pressure **are held** (*or* **kept,** *or* **maintained**) **constant, ...**

Удерживаться на уровне
The downstream pressure **was held** (*or* **kept**) near zero.

Удерживаться от
The particles **are kept from** settling.

Удерживающий
It is recommended that, periodically, the nuts or screws **securing** (*or* **fixing,** *or* **fastening**) the clamping plate should be checked.

Удивительно, что
The surprising thing is that chemists have succeeded in ...

Удивляться [*см.* **Едва ли следует удивляться тому, что**].

Удлинён на одно звено
The original carbon chain **was extended by one link.**

Удлинять [*см. тж.* **Насаживать на**]
The delay period **may be lengthened** (*or* **extended**) **by** reducing ...

Удлиняться на ... процентов
A single (crystal) whisker **may elongate** five **percent** of its original length.

Удобная форма [*см.* **В удобной для использования форме**].

Удобнее всего
This vector sum is **most conveniently constructed** geometrically by ...

Удобно [*см. тж.* **Нам удобно**]
Study of the Schrödinger equation **is conveniently begun with** problems which ...
Jaundice **is conveniently divided into** three major types.

Удобно выражать
The relation between ... **is conveniently expressed by: ...**

Удобно измерять
The coefficients **are conveniently measured by** the use of the tube.

Удобно пользоваться
Paper **is convenient to use** for this purpose.

Удобно разделить на
The transit time mechanism **is conveniently split into** two parts.

Удобное расположение
Accessibility of controls is important.

Удобный
The scheme **was** particularly **handy for** making high-speed photographs.
Handy remote controls ...
These compasses **are** particularly **well suited as** azimuth-reference devices.
The compounds **are amenable to** [*or* **convenient** (*or* **suitable**) **for**] shock tube study.

Удобный в эксплуатации
These devices **are convenient in service** (*or* **operation**).

Удобный способ
This gives you **a handy** (*or* **convenient**) **way of** remembering the composition of ...

Удобство [*см.* **Для удобства**].

Удовлетворительная оценка
A reasonable estimate may be made by averaging ...

Удовлетворительно [*см. тж.* **Должным образом**]
The electrical equipment is **adequately** (*or* **well**) protected.

Удовлетворительно описывать
The single dimension d_p cannot be expected **to describe** the flow channel **adequately.**

Удовлетворительно согласовываться с
In the case of the Earth Kepler's hypothesis **rhymed** (*or* **agreed**) **satisfactorily with** Tycho's theory.

Удовлетворительный [*см. тж.* **Вполне удовлетворительный, Достаточный, Относительно высокая точность**]
Drilling was discontinued because of lack of **adequate** (*or* **satisfactory**) equipment.
The original modulation wave will be recovered with **fair** accuracy.
The total radiation can be determined with **reasonable** accuracy.
There was a **workable** theory.

Удовлетворять
The identification tapes **will comply with** the requirements.
The pickup **fills** the requirements.
The rate data **fit** Eq. (6) satisfactorily.
Samples **will fit** your requirements.
The set of curves **fits** the theory.
The heaters **match** our requirements.
The rate of production **must meet** demands.
The tube **meets** the specifications (*or* standards).
The current **obeys** this equation.
This condition **will be satisfied.**
The following equation **must be satisfied.**
To satisfy the need for ...
The controls have special features **to suit** our requirements.

Удовлетворять жёстким требованиям
Tight (*or* **Stringent,** *or* **Strict**) ultrasonic test **requirements must be met.**

Удовлетворять жизненные потребности
The coconut tree and fruit **supply** most of **the needs of life** for natives of tropical islands.

Удовлетворять потребности
Geothermal plants cannot **contribute** much more than 10 percent **of** the nation's future **requirements.**
Carbon and its simple compounds **provide** much **of** the world's energy **requirements.**
Today's chemists are attempting **to satisfy the** current **demand for** new chemicals.
These **demands will be met by** solar energy production.
The human brain can probably begin to utilize ketone bodies **for meeting** its energy **needs** as soon as ...

Удовлетворять потребностям [*см. тж.* **Отвечать потребностям**]
This approximation **will serve** our **needs** until we can develop some more sophisticated concepts.
Each furnace **handles** almost any heat treating **need.**
To meet this **demand** new processes were developed.

Удовлетворять принципу
To satisfy the Pauli exclusion **principle, ...**

Удовлетворять просьбу
More than 200 **requests for** observing time **were accommodated** in the first year of the telescope's operation.

Удовлетворять требованиям
Laser technology **can meet the requirements for** a reliable source of ...
The alloy does not quite **match** our **requirements.**
The composition will be made **to conform to** your **needs.**
The instruments **have become equal** (*or* **adequate**) **to the job**.
To fulfil (*or* **comply with,** *or* **meet,** *or* **satisfy**) **the** design **requirements, ...**

Удовлетворять уравнению
The change in the partial molal free energies **must obey** (*or* **satisfy**) this **equation.**

Удовлетворять условиям
v^2 **must satisfy** (*or* **meet**) **the conditions for** fast waves.

Удовлетворяться
You **will have to rest content with** the scant information available.
We **can content ourselves with** the results achieved.

Уже кратко упоминалось о
Brief mention has already been made of this procedure.

Уже не [*см.* **Больше не**].

Уже не за горами
A method to nickel plate this steel **is just around the corner.**

Уже не равен [*см.* **Более не равен**].

Уже по одной этой причине
For this reason alone the daylight period is lengthened by 7 min at the equator.

Уже при обычной температуре
The oxide explodes violently **even at ordinary temperatures.**

Узел [*см.* **Атомы, расположенные в узлах**].

Узкие пределы [*см.* **В узких пределах**].

Узкое место
The bottleneck is bound to be the energy.

Узнавать [*см. тж.* **Выяснять**]
I first **became aware of** the thermal lens effect in 1972.
To determine whether neoplastic tissues can be recognized from their nuclear magnetic resonance signals, ...

Уйти далеко вперёд
The nuclear power industry **has come a long way** since the first demonstration station went into operation.

Указан
The laser wavelength **is indicated by** the line on the far right of the figure.
The diameter of the jet **was** not **stated** (*or* **specified,** *or* **indicated**).
The physical properties of ... **are listed in** Table 2.
The chart **states** the mean variation for ...
As **pointed out in** the paper, ...

Указан в литературе
An experimental value of 0.694 cm^2/s **is reported in the literature.**

Указан в таблице
The table lists the diameters of Jupiter's satellites.

Указание I [*см. тж.* **Без указания, Выполнять указания, Данные, указывающие на; Есть признаки того, что; Есть указания на то, что; Имеется всё больше указаний на то, что; Имеются указания на то, что; Косвенное указание на то, что; Критерий, Признак, Согласно инструкции**]
An indication of the best method is given in the table.
This is **a** significant **indication that** the results of analysis are satisfactory.
This relationship **is evidence that** the universe is expanding.

Указание II [*см. тж.* **Выполнять указания, Согласно инструкции**]
Instructions for annealing are given below.

Указание на
The external form of clouds gives only indirect **clues to** the physical properties which determine their evolution.
Evidence for this depletion process was deduced from consideration of ...
This is further **evidence of** major changes in ...
Specification of the stereochemical relationship of the groups is always necessary.

Указание на присутствие
This is interpreted as **evidence for** unpaired electrons in the oxygen molecule.
We found **evidence of** the highly ionized atoms CIV and SiIV ...

Указанный [*см. тж.* **В указанном порядке, В указанных пределах, Приведённый, Приводиться**]
All parts larger than **indicated** should be made from ...
With the assumptions **outlined** (*or* **intimated,** *or* **listed,** *or* **mentioned**) **(above)** the required area can be calculated.
A bushing is placed on the end in the manner **shown.**

The power outputs **specified** (*or* **cited,** *or* **given**) **(above)** are those obtained at sea level.
μ_B is the viscosity of water at the temperature **in question.**
The gas is in equilibrium with liquid of the **stated** (*or* **indicated**) composition.
The bottles could be opened at a **prescribed** depth.
The study **cited** was of special interest.

Указанный в таблице
The values **indicated** (*or* **listed,** *or* **included,** *or* **contained**) **in the Table ...**

Указывать I [*см. тж.* **Если не указано иначе, Как указано, Показывать, Следует отметить, что**]
Increased second-stage pressure **denotes that** the third-stage valves require attention.
This near constancy **is evidence that** nucleons interact only with near neighbours.
No one has seen this body, but its presence **is evidenced by** observed fluctuations of ...
Deficient air supply **is indicated by** black smoke coming from ...
Figure 4 **indicates that** the yield of lactic acid decreases with ...
This **is an indication of** the ease with which the slurry can be mixed.
Any drastic changes **are indicative of** improper operation.
The use of auxiliary fans **points the way to** a method of ...
This **points to** a predominant terrestrial mode of deposition.
The experimental evidence **points to** the fact that ...
Recent researchers **point toward** the probability of ...
The figure **points up** some improvements which can be made in ...
Comparison with the available test results **reveals** good agreement with the computed values.
These investigations **suggest that** the magnetic mechanism may apply also to ...
When referring to electronic absorptions, we **cite** the wavelength of maximum absorption.

Указывать II [*см. тж.* **Доказывать, Показывать**]
These structure factors **will pinpoint** the atomic positions so that the crystal structure can be described.
Blueprints **specify** materials by specification numbers.
Thickness **must be specified** separately.
The values **must be marked with** the name of the manufacturer.

Указывать местонахождение дефектов
The instrument **pinpoints the defects.**

Указывать на I [*см. тж.* **Позволять делать вывод**]
The high heat flow **pointed to** some kind of thermal peculiarity.
The intensity of an ion signal **is indicative** (*or* **suggestive**) **of** the stability of the ion.
The Precambrian development of the blue-green algae **is attested by** the massive calcium-rich rock formations they left behind.
The name **implies** (*or* **suggests**) complete absence of ...
Equation (2.22) **suggests that** D_{AB} should be inversely proportional to total pressure.
This **suggests that** other nonvector mesons may participate.
That there was an appreciable liquid resistance **is suggested** (*or* **indicated**) **by** recent tests of ...
The irregularities observed ... **are evidence for** (*or* **of**) the existence of ...
This **points up** (*or* **to**) the significance of thunderstorms as a major source of ...
The diverse uses of these compounds **testify to** the commercial value of fluoroalkanes.
Four such relationships **can be pointed out.**
This clearly **shows** the need for an atom reservoir with ...
The term porosity **gives an indication of** the capacity of a rock to hold a fluid in storage.
He **has pointed to** the probable existence of ...
The lack of sediment **attested to** the youth of the mid-ocean ridges.
The rotation curves **imply** (*or* **intimate**) the presence of...

Указывать на II
A compass needle **will point at** (*or* **to,** *or* **toward**) the magnetic poles.

Указывать на существование
This type of faulting **is indicative of** tensional forces (*geol.*).

Указывать на то, что
The name halogen **alludes** (*or* **points**) **to the fact that** all the halogen elements form compounds with ...
The occasional scattering at wide angles **was evidence that** there is something hard in the atom.
The variability of the isotopic compositions in oceanic basalts **bears witness to the fact that ...**
The features **testify to the fact that** the river often wandered far to the west of its present course.

Указывать на широкие возможности применения
The intrinsic analogue nature of the charge packet in a charge-coupled device **suggests broad potentials for application to** sampled-signal processing.

Указывать название [*см.* **Название которого не указано**].

Указывать пути развития
These ideas **have guided the development of** other sensitive detection schemes.

Указывать пути усовершенствования
A detailed understanding of the effect **has guided the way to improvements in** the design of experiments.

Указывать путь к
Mendeleev's predictions **pointed the way for** future research.

Указывать со всей определённостью на то, что
All this evidence **indicates conclusively** (*or* **convincingly**) **that ...**
The location of the burst **strongly suggests** (*or* **intimates**) **that ...**

Указываться
The report **points out that ...**

Указываться в таблицах (в единицах)
The enthalpy **is** usually **tabulated in** cal/gm **or** cal/mol.

Указывающий на
Experimental results **indicative** (*or* **suggestive**) **of** the potential of this device are discussed.

Укладка бетона
Casting (*or* **Placing,** *or* **Laying**) **of concrete.**
Deposition (*or* **Pouring**) **of concrete.**

Укладывать
The machine has an unloader which **stacks** the components.
Paper capacitors are constructed by **stacking** alternate layers of foil and the dielectric.

Укладываться в [*см. тж.* **Вполне укладываться в допустимые пределы, Вписываться в**]
Not all multistep mechanisms **fit in** the above classification.

Укладываться в производственный план
The parts **are meeting the schedule.**

Укладываться в сжатые сроки
The designers had **to meet a tight schedule.**

Уклоняться (*напр.* **от снаряда**)
Even if the plane **takes evasive action,** the missile will change course to intercept.

Укомплектован
Each unit **comes** (*or* **is supplied**) **with** a vaporizer and control system.
The analyzer **is complete** (*or* **provided**) **with** a timer, count and cycle totalizers and an internal calibration program.
The set **comprises** a noise generator and a receiver.

Укреплять
The salt water binds the particles together, **giving** the clay layer **strength.**

Укреплять веру в
These facts **gave added credence to** the theory of continental drift.

Укреплять веру в то, что
This fact **strengthened the belief that** magnetic-dipole radiation was indeed responsible for the energy loss from the pulsars.

Укреплять позицию
His work greatly **strengthened** the plutonists' **case.**

Улавливать
To trap the solar energy, ...

Улавливаться
The finely divided carbon black **is recovered by** cyclones and bag filters.
Dirt and metal particles **are trapped by** the filter.

Улов
The annual **harvest of** codfish usually exceeds ...

Уложенные вплотную друг к другу
It would take 10^{41} protons **laid side by side** to stretch across the known universe.

Улучшать [*см. тж.* **Значительно улучшать** (*или* **повышать**)]
Such approaches are required **to perfect** separation schemes.
The discoveries scientists have made in **bettering** the flavour and texture of margarine ...
This further **enhances** the appearance of the apparatus.
The equipment should **gain in** performance through the application of ...
Efforts **to improve (upon)** the characteristics ...
This **makes for good** circulation.
Glass and mica **will upgrade** organic materials.

Улучшение [*см. тж.* **Вносить усовершенствование, Усовершенствование**]
The upper section is cooled for **better** absorption effeciency.
Betterment or deterioration **of** vision ...
No **gain in** resolution is obtained.
Future **improvements in** silicon diodes ...
Efforts are directed towards **refining** present techniques.
Upgrading of fastener quality will become increasingly urgent.

Улучшение по сравнению с
Improvement in sensitivity **over** (*or* **compared to**) conventional spectrofluorometry has led to ...

Улучшенные свойства
This vacuum plate has **enhanced** (*or* **improved**) physical **properties.**

Умалять значение
We do not mean **to minimize the importance of** other deep-earth gases.

Умение обращаться с
Some **facility with using** an electronic calculator is desirable.

Уменьшать [*см. тж.* **Понижать, Снижать, Сокращать**]
The figure **is scaled down.**
Each additional ring **lowers** the number of hydrogens in the general formula by two.
The diameter of the suction pipe **should be curtailed.**
The number of the burners in operation **must be cut down.**
Inhibitors **diminish** corrosion.
Increase in pressure **lowered** (*or* **reduced**) the combined yield.
This **trims** (*or* **reduces,** *or* **decreases**) the size of the generator to 1 cu ft.
To demagnify the picture, ...

Уменьшать вдвое
Redesigning **cut** the number of operations **in half** (*or* **halved** the number of operations).
This **reduced** residence time **by one half** (*or* **by 50 percent**).
The aeration can be expected **to reduce** this figure **by half** (*or* **to halve** the figure).

Уменьшать до минимума [*см.* **Сводить к минимуму**].

Уменьшать на
Electrified lubrication **lowered** (*or* **reduced**) the required driving force **by** 4.6%.

Уменьшать наполовину [*см.* **Уменьшать вдвое**].

Уменьшать опасность
Efforts were made **to alleviate** (*or* **to lessen,** *or* **to reduce**) **the** vortex **hazard.**

Уменьшаться [*см. тж.* **Ослабляться, Падать, Сокращаться**]
The yearly motion of a star, resulting from the Earth's motion, **grows smaller** as the distance of a star increases.
The approximation **decreases in** accuracy **with** increasing molecular density.
Metals **decrease** (*or* **show a decrease**) **in** conductivity when heated.
The intensity of change **is diminished.**

When a positive ion is formed from an atom, **there is a decrease in** size.
Detector noise **tends to diminish** (*or* **decrease**) **with** frequency.
The corrosion of aluminium alloys in boiling carbon tetrachloride **dropped** rapidly **as** the magnesium content increased.
The yield **falls to** 80% at 1000°.
The equilibrium constant **will fall** (*or* **decline**) **with** a rise in temperature.
This current gain **should fall off with** increasing emitter current.
Specific weight **goes down** (*or* **drops**) **as** the engine diameter is reduced.
In this atmosphere oxygen **is reduced to** 100 ppm.
The rate of reaction ultimately **tapers off.**
Under anaerobic conditions, free hydrogen production **is lowered** for the first three bacteria.

Уменьшаться в число раз, равное
The electric field **is** then **lowered by a factor equal to** the dielectric constant $\varepsilon/\varepsilon_0$.

Уменьшаться наполовину
Thus the resistance **is halved.**

Уменьшение I [*см. тж.* **Резкое уменьшение, С уменьшением, Снижение**]
A 53% **reduction in** wear was achieved.
A curtailment of the diameter ...
The cut in prices ...
A decline in the variety of such materials occurs when ...
Decline of head ...
A decrease in efficiency ...
Further **decrease of** the hole diameter causes ...
In addition to **the deterioration of** ductility, the strength **is** also **affected.**
A fall in friction ...
This would result in **decreased** (*or* **reduced**) buoyancy.
There is little **diminution of** volume in the oxidation of ammonia.

Уменьшение II
The demagnification of images employed is ...

Уменьшение в ... раз
A tenfold decrease of (*or* **in**) ...

Уменьшенный масштаб [*см.* **В уменьшенном масштабе**].

Умеренные широты
Showers in **temperate latitudes** may be initiated by ...

Умеренный
The process has proved successful for the production of grains of **moderate** size but is not suitable for very large grains.

Уместно отметить, что
It is pertinent to note that such reactions are totally nonspecific.

Уместный
Those results are discussed in Chapter 5, where they are more **appropriate.**

Умножать на
The value of the cross section **should be multiplied by** the fraction of ...

Умножение на
This element is obtained **by multiplying** the n elements in the ith row of A **into** (*or* **by**) the n elements in the jth column of B.
The probability function is obtained **by taking the product of ...**

Умноженный на
The rate of flow in weight units is the volume of flow **multiplied by** the density of the fluid.
Force equals mass **times** acceleration.
The output of the control potentiometer is represented as its output voltage **times** the factor θ/θ_F.

Умозрительная картина
Quantum electrodynamics offers no consistent **mental picture.**

Универсальность
The versatility of the machines ...

Универсальный
This is a **general-purpose** (*or* **all-purpose**) machine for butt welding both ferrous and nonferrous wires.
This is a **multi-purpose** instrumentation system which is suitable for operating a variety of machines or processes.
A **universal** lathe.
The equipment **is** sufficiently **versatile** to meet the many needs of the various users.
A **general-purpose** computer program ...

Уникальный в том смысле, что
The transfer RNAs **are unique in** having both a relatively constant molecular size and configuration (*biol.*).

Унифицирован
The nomenclature of nitrogen derivatives **is** not **unified** like that of oxygen derivatives.

Уничтожать [*см. тж.* **Аннулировать, Взаимно уничтожаться**]
All life **had been wiped out by** such floods.
When an electron and a positron meet, they **annihilate** each other.

Уничтожаться [*см.* **Взаимно уничтожаться**].

Уничтожен
Here, rocks **have been removed by** erosion.

Уничтожение окружающей среды человеком
Man's destruction of the environment ...

Уносимый вверх
The most likely source of atmospheric ice nuclei is provided by soil and mineral-dust particles **carried aloft by** the wind.

Уносить
The photon **carries away** some of the atom's intrinsic angular momentum.

Уносить от
A hyperbolic orbit **would drive** (*or* **carry**) this planetoid **away from** the Sun.

Уноситься
The products of disintegration **are swept away by** wind or water.

Уноситься в воздух
Some nitrogen **escapes into the air.**

Упакованы (*об атомах*) [*см.* **Плотно упакованы**].

Упаривать досуха
The ether solution **was evaporated to dryness.**

Упасть [*см.* **Падать**].

Упираться в [*см. тж.* **Опираться на**]
The Emperor Sea-mounts chain **meets** the Aleutian Trench at the northern end.
Place the valves in position, and push them up into the valve bodies until the guide spiders **are against** the shoulders at the upper end of the valve bodies.
The lockpin is screwed in through the valve body and normally **bears up against** the adjusting ring.
The shaft sleeve **is butted up against** a shoulder or the shaft.
When the program pin **is seated against** its stop button, ...

Уплотнение
A gas-tight **seal against** hydrogen ...
Excellent gas **sealing** is assured.

Уподоблять
The moving particle **can be likened to** a marble that rolls along ...

Упоминаемый
The three most commonly **referred to** analytical figures of merit for spectroscopic systems are ...

Упоминание [*см.* **Достоин упоминания**].

Упоминать [*см. тж.* **Был(о) упомянут(о), Ничего не упомянуто о том, что; Следует упомянуть**]
I **have** already **touched (up)on** (*or* **mentioned**) pumping, but the subject merits closer attention.
We **have** already **referred to** these features in Chap. 4.

Упоминаться
The amino acid arm **has received mention** (*or* **has been mentioned**) **as** being active in this function.

Упоминаться отдельно
Only where these bacteriophages are known to differ do they **receive individual mention.**

Упомянем лишь несколько из них
Interest is maintained by frequent cross-references to the other subjects of the curriculum. **To mention just a few:** hygrometry is related to ...

Упомянут
In that paper, **mention is made of (the fact that) ...**

Упомянут выше [*см.* **Вышеупомянутый**].

Упомянутый
The **cited** report failed to indicate ...

Упомянутый источник (*литературный*)
As **the cited source** points out, ...

Упор I [*см. тж.* **До упора**]
A stop is provided to limit the upward movement to the minimum for the job being welded.

Упор II [*см.* **Делать основной упор на, Особое внимание уделено**].

Упор делается на
In this chapter, **emphasis is given to** the more recent applications.

Упорный труд
Many years of **painstaking work ...**

Упорядоченный
The vectors λ are **ordered** sets of numbers.
Crystalline ice consists of a very **orderly** pattern of H_2O molecules.

Упорядоченным образом
The purpose of the forms is to gather information for a project **in an orderly fashion.**

Упорядочивать [*см.* **Приводить в порядок**].

Употребительный [*см. тж.* **Входить в употребление, Наиболее распространённый**]
Other **commonly encountered** (*or* **widely used,** *or* **widespread,** *or* **frequently used**) terms are ...

Употребление [*см.* **Входить в употребление, Выходить из употребления**].

Употребляемый в пищу
Some of the water is formed within the body as a product of oxidation of certain chemicals **taken in as food.**

Употреблять [*см. тж.* **Использовать**]
The polyethylene sheet **serves** (*or* **is used**) **as** in insulation.

Употреблять в пищу
The plant **is** often **used for food.**

Употребляться [*см.* **Обычно применяться**].

Употребляться в смысле
The term "red beds facies" **may be used to designate** any sequence of red sandstones and ...

Управление [*см.* **Дистанционно управляемый, С кнопочным управлением, С ручным управлением, С электронным управлением**].

Управление при помощи перфоленты
Punched-tape control.

Управляемый I
A microprocessor-**controlled** optical inspection system ...
A student-**run** organization ...

Управляемый II
The electrical inductivity of the material **must be controllable.**

Управляемый вручную [*см.* **С ручным управлением**].

Управляемый дистанционно
The clutch **is remote(ly) controlled.**

Управляемый компьютером
A **computer-controlled** motor ...

Управляемый по радио
Radio-controlled switches ...

Управляемый при помощи перфоленты
A **punched-tape controlled** machine ...

Управлять [*см.* **Осуществлять управление**].

Управляться
The chlorinator **is operated from** a program-controlled panel.
The robot **is supervised by** one operator.

Управляться на расстоянии
Substations **may be remotely controlled.**

Управляться человеком
The equipment **is operator controlled.**

Упразднение
This led to **the abandonment of** the grooved-plate process.

Упразднять
Once this step was taken, the old two-unit system **could be dispensed with.**

Упрочнён
The instrument **is ruggedized** to travel over the roughest terrain.

Упрощать
This **facilitates** structural correlations.
Each atom **may be simplified to** a fixed, positively charged nucleus.

Упрощать дело
Now mathematicians **simplify matters** by setting values equal to unity whenever they can.

Упрощение [*см.* **Для простоты**].

Упругость
Then the ring will regain its **spring** (*or* **springiness**).
The ring will be given sufficient **spring** to ensure freedom from leakage.

Упругость паров
The vapour pressure is 2.5 bar.

Упускать из виду
This fact **is** often **overlooked.**

Уравнение [*см.* **В левой (правой) части уравнения, Входить в уравнение, Вывод уравнения, По уравнению, С помощью уравнения, Соотношение**].

Уравнение говорит о том, что
Equation (2.43) **states that** the flux is proportional to ...

Уравнение относительно z
An equation in z.

Уравнение реакции горения
The equation for the combustion process.

Уравнение с одним неизвестным
An equation in one unknown.

Уравнение с ... переменными
An equation in two (three, etc.) **variables.**

Уравнение типа
Equations of the type (1.5.8).

Уравновешен [*см. тж.* **Сбалансированы**]
The vibrational temperature **may** not **be** completely **equilibrated** (*or* **brought to equilibrium**) close to the shock front.

Уравновешивать
The attractive forces of the two electrons for the two nuclei exactly **balance** the electron-electron and proton-proton repulsions.
Usually the pressure force **is balanced out by** an opposing force.
Any increase in rate produced during the swing to dead centre **would be** exactly **cancelled by** an equal decrease in rate after dead centre.
The barrier serves **to counterbalance** these forces.

Уравновешиваться
The cohesive force **is balanced by** an equal repulsive force.
Stagnant liquid elements **equilibrate with** the flowing gas and no mass transfer occurs.
The spindle head **is counterbalanced by** a weight which is suspended from a chain.
The potential energy curve has a maximum where the two forces **balance.**

Уровень [*см. тж.* **Высота, До такого уровня, что; Доводить до уровня, На уровне, Находиться на одном уровне с, Поддерживать на высоком уровне, Поднимать до уровня, Расход устанавливается на таком уровне, при котором**]
Water contained in the locks is used to raise or lower vessels from one **elevation** to another.
Eventually the speed rises to **the point** at which the resistance equals the gravitational force.

Усваивать [*см.* **Поглощать**].

Усвоение материала (*учебного и т.п.*)
The presentation is designed to aid rapid **assimilation.**

Усердно
Pluto (*the planet*) proved very difficult to discover, even though it was searched for **painstakingly.**

Усеян [*см.* **Усыпан**].

Усиление [*см.* **Выигрыш**].

Усиление звука I
Sound amplification systems.

Усиление звука II
The rate of **growth** and decay **of sound** in a room ...

Усиление поля

Speed is regulated by **strengthening the field of** the motor.

Усилен
Petroleum oils and greases **have been fortified by** chemical additives.

Усилен(ный)
The shell **has to be reinforced by** an extra plate.
The resin **is reinforced with** glass cloth.
Fibreglass-**reinforced** phenolic.
The aircraft features a **strengthened** wing.

Усиленный лазером
Laser-enhanced ionization ...

Усиливать I [*см. тж.* **Обострять**]
Various optical devices can be used **to enhance** the intensity of the laser beam.
The sample solvent **will** further **augment** background radiation.
A preamplifier is needed **to boost** the signal from the photomultiplier.
To intensify the milk flavour, ...
Water waves cancel or **reinforce** each other.
The designer **strengthened** the wing of the aircraft.

Усиливать II
There are many potential neurological abnormalities which **can aggravate** a tendency toward immobility (*med.*).

Усиливаться [*см. тж.* **Затухать и усиливаться**]
This effect **is** further **enhanced by** the tendency of ...
The coupling **may be strengthened by** magnetic fields.
These distortions **may be amplified by** carelessness.
Mixing **is enhanced by** high flow rates.

Усиливаться, ослабляться
The polarization **builds up** or **decays** slowly when ...

Усилие, прилагаемое к
The force (*or* **effort**) **exerted by** the shaft **on** the piston ...

Усилия [*см.* **Объединять свои усилия, Предпринимать усилия в области**].

Усилия направлены на
A parallel **effort went into** the control of contamination.

Ускользать от
This feature usually **eludes** (*or* **escapes**) the designer.

Ускоренный метод
The correct average is 3.14 compared with 3.37 ft by **the shortcut method.**
Shortcuts may be tempting since they speed up the process.

Ускоренными темпами
Oceanographic research has been going on **at a quickened** (*or* **an accelerated**) **pace.**

Ускорять
The appearance of molten rock at the surface **was precipitated by** the puncturing effect of ...
This stimulates the cortex of the adrenal gland **to step** (*or* **speed**) **up** (*or* **accelerate,** *or* **quicken**) its synthesis.
The particles **were accelerated to** maximum velocities.

Ускорять наступление (*болезни и т.п.*)
Thiazides **can precipitate** diabetes.

Ускорять распространение волны
The introduction of ... **accelerates the** combustion **wave.**

Ускорять реакцию
A chemical that **hastens** (*or* **accelerates,** *or* **speeds up**) **reactions ...**

Ускорять темп
He **accelerated the rate of** his work.

Ускоряться
The ring **picks up speed.**
The reaction **may be speeded up by** addition of ...
The combustion process **speeds up** (*or* **is accelerated**) to explosive proportions.

Ускоряться на
The electron volt is the energy gained by an electron when it **accelerates through** a potential difference of one volt.

Условившись, что
We shall omit subscripts of "system" on thermodynamic terms, **with the understanding that** all such terms refer to system characteristics.

Условие [*см. тж.* **В данных условиях, В других условиях, В жёстких условиях, В полевых условиях, В рабочих условиях, В тяжёлых условиях, В условиях, В цеховых условиях, В этих условиях, Выполнять условие, Если позволяют условия, Налагать условие, Неблагоприятные условия, При равных прочих условиях, При условиях, Режим, Соблюдать условие**]
The condition for symmetry **is ...**

Условие для
A prerequisite to the formation of the colour centre **is** the presence of aluminium impurities.

Условие заключается в том, что
The boundary **condition** on the wave function of this state **is that** it be flat.

Условия
The paper tells you how to compare various microprocessors in different application **scenarios.**

Условия наблюдения
Under **the** best **observing conditions ...**

Условия окружающей среды
Depending on **the environmental conditions, ...**

Условия эксперимента [*см.* **При условиях эксперимента**].

Условия эксплуатации
This ensures ease of welding under all **service** (*or* **operating**) **conditions.**

Условно I
This arrangement of the groups is **arbitrarily** called the *D* configuration.

Условно II
By convention the largest variance is taken as numerator.

Условно считается, что
By convention the pressure is positive if it tends to expand the gel.

Условный
Any choice of such a coordinate system **is a matter of convention.**
The **conventional** symbol of each particle is given.

Усложнённый
A measure of ... **complicated by** the effect of ...

Усложнять
This **adds complexity to** (*or* **complicates**) the paradox mentioned previously.
This **makes** the interpretation of experimental data **more difficult** (*or* **complicated**).

Усложнять дело (*или* **положение**)
An increase in sensitivity to nitrazepam **complicates the issue.**

Усложняться
The alignment of the magnets **is complicated by** thermal contraction.
The expression ... **becomes more involved** (*or* **complicated**) because ...

Усовершенствование [*см. тж.* **Вносить усовершенствование, Улучшение**]
Teams are working on **the advancement of** the technology of gas-cooled reactors.
Refinements (*or* **Improvements**) **in** observational procedure (*or* **in** apparatus) ...
Efforts are directed towards **refining** (*or* **perfecting**) present techniques.

Усовершенствование по сравнению с
The steering-gear **was a great advance on** the previous type.
The telemotor **is a great improvement on** (*or* **over**) the rods and bevel wheels usually employed to ...

Усовершенствованный
To consider **a more elaborate** (*or* **advanced**) machine ...
The **more refined** instruments (*or* methods) are ...
More sophisticated sensing elements are needed.
Modern kinetic theory leads to a **more sophisticated** form of Eq. (6).

Усовершенствованный вариант
The diode laser is **a refinement of** the electroluminescence diode.

Усовершенствовать
Original design **can** sometimes **be improved (upon)** (*or* **refined**).

Усомниться в [*см. тж.* **Сомневаться**]
The perturbation has never been large enough **to put in doubt** the nature of an event (*seism.*).

One **may question** the need for such great precision.

Успевать [*см. тж.* **Не успевать**]
Unless we remove the low-energy boundary layer before it **has a chance to** become turbulent, ...
Oil sprays onto the brickwork before the oil **has had an opportunity to** become atomized and mixed with air.
Adsorption occurs only after the adsorbate **has had time** (*or* **has managed**) **to** diffuse through ...

Успевать за
The instruments would never be able **to keep pace with** the reactions.

Успех [*см. тж.* **Большое достижение, Весьма успешно, Достигать успехов, С большим успехом, С успехом**]
Advances (*or* **Progress**) **in** electronics ...
Gains in automatic manufacturing ...

Успех в области
Much **progress toward** an understanding of the origins of life has been achieved.

Успешно [*см. тж.* **Весьма успешно, С большим успехом**]
There are many applications where multihead spot welders have been used **to** (*or* **with**) **advantage** (*or* **advantageously**).
The method was applied **with profit** to conventional interferometry.

Успешно выдерживать сравнение с
This material **compares favourably with** the best finishes.

Успешно использовать [*см. тж.* **Можно успешно использовать в качестве**]
A knowledge of these properties **is profitably employed** (*or* **used to advantage**) **in** manipulating ...
Physicists **have made good use of** this theory to explain ...
Good use is made of the plasma phenomena ...

Успешно использоваться
This procedure **is usefully** (*or* **successfully**) **employed** [*or* **is employed to** (*or* **with**) **advantage**].

Успешно применяться
Miniature mercury cells **can be used to advantage** (*or* **successfully**).

Успешно работать
The machine **has been in successful operation** (*or* **has been operating successfully**) for six years.

Успешный
Aluminium's resistance to sulphur permits its **advantageous** use for structural parts.

Усреднение
Averaging of readings gives a truer indication of ...

Усреднение по
The coefficient is found **by averaging** *T* **over** the ray half-period.

Усреднённый
Averaged data for 30 gases were used.

Усреднённый за
Averaged through the year (*or* **over a period of years**) ...

Усреднённый по времени
The **time-average** rate of absorption is ...

Усреднённый по массе
A **mass-average** value ...

Усреднять
Average the wavelength and calculate ...
The effects **are averaged (out).**

Усреднять по
This loss **is averaged over** frequency.
The axis of the earth's magnetic field **is averaged over** a substantial period.

Устанавливать I [*см. тж.* **На котором устанавливается, На станке можно установить**]
The laser generator **should be mounted** vertically.
Conveyors **have been erected** (*or* **installed,** *or* **set up**) to convey coal to ...
The valve **should be fitted on** the discharge side of the pipe.
The cabinet **may be located** (*or* **sited**) near the mill.
A workpiece **is set upon** the table.
A series of coils **is arranged along** the plasma duct.

Устанавливать II [*см. тж.* **Выяснять, Заранее устанавливать, Найдено, что; Необходимо выяснить, Обнаруживать, что; Определять, Расход устанавливается на таком уровне, при котором**]
Using this method we **can arrive at** the molecular formula of a compound.
The fundamental geological principles **were established** in the eighteenth century.
The method **for working out** the relative ages of rocks ...
The mass velocities of the streams **are fixed** (*or* **established,** *or* **assigned**) when the cross section is selected.
The accuracy of the plots **has** not **been** fully **ascertained.**
The specification **stipulates** for each class of cement a maximum viscosity ...

Устанавливать III
The conveyor **may be adjusted to** the proper discharge height.
This enables the table **to be positioned** automatically.
The thermostat control **can be set at** the degree of warming desired.
The amplifier **is set for** stable operation.
The monochromator **is set to** the same wavelength.
The propeller blades **may be set to** any desired pitch.

Устанавливать IV
The existence of this restriction **can be recognized from** the nature of the spectra.
Arrhenius **recognized that** this temperature dependence indicates an exponential increase in ...

Устанавливать в нужное положение
To bring the next hole **into position, ...**
The mechanism **positions** the indicator as shown in the illustration.

Устанавливать в ... положение
When the disk **is set in** any **position, ...**

Устанавливать в центрах станка
When the shaft **has to be put on centres in a lathe, ...**

Устанавливать взаимосвязь между
The Rydberg formula **correlates** the frequencies of all the observed ...
The curve **relates** impulses per minute **to** density.

Устанавливать деталь на станке
We **load** as many **parts** as possible **onto the worktables.**

Устанавливать допуск на
They **place a** close **tolerance on** the thickness of the material.

Устанавливать на
The value of t **is set to** unity.
The calibrated variable capacitor C **is** first **adjusted to** the value C_1 ...
Gain of the transducer **is set for** best stability.

Устанавливать на место
To place the machinery **into position, ...**

Устанавливать на нужную длину
When the stop pins **are set to the appropriate length, ...**

Устанавливать на нуль
The digital readout **is zeroed by** a pushbutton switch.
Set the pointer **to zero.**

Устанавливать однозначное соответствие между
The function **establishes a one-to-one correspondence between** the two sets.

Устанавливать параллельно
It is easier **to place** the ties **parallel to** the tunnel axis.

Устанавливать по
Align the base of the plotter **with** a parallel of latitude.

Устанавливать по высоте
An outside micrometer is used for **setting ... for height.**

Устанавливать под углом
The workpiece **may be set at** various **angles.**
The tool **can be set to** any required **angle** relative to the machine table.

Устанавливать предел
The requirement for a certain maximum unambiguous range **sets an upper limit on** the pulse repetition frequency in long-range research radars.
The effects of collimator thickness **place** (*or* **set**) **a lower limit on** the sensitive energy range.

Устанавливать против
If pressure altitude zero **is set opposite** a temperature of +15°C ...

Устанавливать резец
The cutter can be set for different jobs.

Устанавливать рекорд
That team of scientists **has set a** new **record for** accuracy.

Устанавливать рессоры
Front wheels **may be** independently **sprung.**

Устанавливать связь между
This theory **establishes a link between** electromagnetism **and** the weak force.
No attempt was made **to relate** the rock of one locality **to** those of another.

Устанавливать соответствие между
The map of transformation **sets up** (*or* **establishes**) **a correspondence between ...**

Устанавливать соотношение между
The guide number **relates** film speed, distance **and** aperture.

Устанавливать стандарт
These **standards have been laid down** (*or* **set up,** *or* **established**) **by ...**

Устанавливать требования
The standards **set forth the** minimum **requirements ...**

Устанавливать, что
The average value **was found to be** 16±3.
It can be easily **verified that** the Π-cascade is a stable structure.

Устанавливаться по размеру
In use, the unit **is set for a given size** and the reading of the micrometer is noted.

Установка I [*см. тж.* **Время установки, За одну установку детали, При одной установке**]
For **positioning** the work prior to drilling, the end face can be brought into contact with ...
The installation (*or* **erection,** *or* **mounting**) of the pillar ...

Установка II [*см. тж.* **Стоимость с установкой**]
Figure 1 shows **a setup** that uses the refraction effects ...

Установка детали на станке
Machining time per piece, including **loading** and unloading, is 2.39 hr.

Установка для
In Fig. 7 is shown **the setup for** lapping the bore of ...

Установка на нуль
This is accomplished by **setting** f_1 **to zero.**
The next step **is resetting the needle (to zero).**

Установлен I [*см. тж.* **Расположен**]
As soon as the workpiece **arrives at** the correct position, ...
The platform **was set in place** by derrick barges.
The apparatus **was set up** in a basement room.

Установлен II
It was determined (*or* **established,** *or* **found**) **that** the width of this band is ...
The presence of double-stranded loops **has been determined** in globin mRNA.

Установлен в вертикальной плоскости
The joint **is positioned in a vertical plane.**

Установлен на [*см.* **На ... имеется** (*или* **находится,** *или* **смонтирован,** *или* **установлен**)].

Установлена связь между
Lead salts from automobiles using leaded gasoline **have been linked to** brain damage in children living near heavily travelled roads.

Установление равновесия
The establishment of equilibrium between ...

Установленные правила
Under **regulations set up by** the Commission ...

Установленный I [*см. тж.* **Заранее установленный**]
The workpieces **mounted on** special fixtures ...
The thermocouple **positioned** (*or* **installed,** *or* **mounted**) **in** the outflow pipe ...

Установленный II
The clock **resting on** the stone base ...

Установленный III [*см. тж.* **Заранее установленный**]
If wear exceeds **prescribed** (*or* **stipulated,** *or* **assigned,** *or* **predetermined**) limits, the camshaft should be replaced.
All dimensions and clearances should be kept within the limits **set up** (*or* **established,** *or* **dictated**) **by** the manufacturer.
The conveyor feeds a **specified** amount of coal into ...

Установленный IV
According to rules **set up by** the Committee ...

Установленный V
This symmetry as **deduced from** experiments can be an important factor in ...

Установленный в промышленности
Hardness has been held within **industry-prescribed** limits.

Установленный между [*см.* **Находящийся между ... и**].

Установленный на колёсах
The **wheel-mounted** machines ...

Установленный на космическом корабле
A **space-borne** TV camera ...

Установленный на месте I
Field-erected compressor stations ...

Установленный на месте II
A beam of light is passed through the apparatus, first without the specimen cell and then with the specimen cell **in place.**

Установленный на ракете
A **rocket-borne** telescope ...

Установленный на салазках
A **skid-mounted** unit ...

Установленный на столе
To grind **table-mounted** work, ...

Установленный последовательно
This was accomplished by passing the vapour through two traps **(placed) in series** (*or* **in tandem**).

Установленный сзади
A bus with a **rear-mounted** engine.

Установлено, что
It is (*or* **was,** *or* **has been**) **found that** the stored energy is released in a stepwise manner.

Установочная погрешность
A positioning error.

Устаревать
Science essays tend **to get out of date.**
The former use of kieselguhr in ... **is** now **out of date.**

Устаревший
The company has introduced a press modernization scheme designed to bring **outdated** equipment up to modern standards.

Устарел
Magnesium powder **is** now **out of date** as a photographic flash-powder.

Устойчив [*см. тж.* **Погодоустойчивый**]
The units **are** moisture **resistant.**
All connections in the relay **are resistant** (*or* **immune**) **to** heat and vibration.
Acridine **is stable to** heat, alkali and acid.
Noise **resistant,** Wind **resisting ...**

Устойчивость к
Different compounds have different degrees of **tolerance for** such contaminants.

Устойчивый [*см. тж.* **Высокоустойчивый к, Наименее устойчивый к**]
Collards **are** more **tolerant of** (*or* **to**) high temperatures.

Устранение
Elimination of alkoxy-magnesium halide to form an aldehyde or ketone ...

Устранение вибрации [*см.* **Для устранения вибрации**].

Устранение люфта
There are facilities **for taking up** any **play** which may result from wear.

Устранение недостатков [*см. тж.* **Метод устранения неполадки**]
The procedure eliminates the possibility of untold hours of **debugging** when starting the machines.
The clearing of the trouble ...

Устранение трудностей
This can be used as a means of **remedying the problems** of today.

Removal (*or* **Elimination**) **of difficulties** [*or* **Surmounting** (*or* **Obviating**) **the difficulties**].

Устранён [*см. тж.* **В ... устранён**]
This limitation **is obviated in** the ball-and-disk integrator.
The noise **may be obviated by the use of** materials that ...
The cause of the overload **has been removed** (*or* **eliminated**).

Устранять [*см. тж.* **Аннулировать**]
Two photomultipliers operate in coincidence **to reject** spurious noise.
To ameliorate the unfavourable effects of ...
If a molecule of water **is eliminated** between two hydroxyl groups ...
How **to banish** noise and hum in high-fidelity sets.
Bend the lens **to cancel** the spherical aberration .
We should **clear away** this difficulty.
Determine whether these faults **can be corrected.**
This feature **does away with** the need for costly servocontrols.
The installation of a waste-heat boiler **eliminates** the need of some other equipment.
Standard forms of boiler and heating surface may be used, thus **obviating** the need for expensive special plants.
Some of the bad effects of copper in the steel **can be overcome by** the addition of nickel.
Such icing **is dealt with by** heating the intake air.
The part is polished **to remove** the blemishes acquired during ...
To place the magnets properly so as **to remove** part of the deviation, ...

Устранять аварию
These measures ensure that any **breakdown can be dealt with** quickly.

Устранять дефект
To correct (*or* **eliminate,** *or* **remedy**) **the trouble, ...**
Sandpaper **will cure the trouble.**
In steel casting this defect **is** not easily **rectified.**
The fault **should be remedied.**
It is best to use the finest sandpaper that **will remove the** surface **imperfections.**
In an attempt **to fix the defects of** the theory he used ...

Устранять затруднение
The use of thionyl chloride **eliminates this problem.**
This problem is remedied by prescribing the appropriate vitamin supplements.
To circumvent (*or* **obviate**) **a difficulty,** one has to ...
This problem has been countered (*or* **rectified**) **by** the addition of ...
The difficulty is easily **solved by the use of ...**
To get around this difficulty, many plants have ...
To overcome (*or* **deal with**) **the difficulty,** you have to...

Устранять затруднение, связанное с
To alleviate the problem of background light, ...

Устранять недостатки
During this stage the aircraft **is debugged** (*sl.*).
There are still some **bugs** (*sl.*) **to be worked out of** continuous casting.
This **flaw can be remedied by ...**
To clear (up) the trouble, ...

Устранять неисправность
After **the fault has been cleared** (*or* **remedied,** *or* **eliminated**) the carriage re-starts.

Устранять необходимость в
The technique **eliminates the need to** design ...
The development of the high-speed wind tunnel **obviated the need for** these techniques.
The method **obviates the necessity for** (*or* **dispenses with**) a second light source.
The new material **will save** costly grinding and finishing.
This **makes** shaft lining **unnecessary** in hard massive rocks.
The float process **does away with** the polishing operations.
Thus **the need to** store substantial quantities of spares **will be avoided.**
This **eliminates the necessity for** manual adjustments.

The new device **eliminates the need for** (*or* **of**) the coupling capacitor.
They **have done away with the need for** lenses.
This approximation **dispenses with the need for** complex computer calculations.

Устранять неопределённость
To control these uncertainties, ...

Устранять неполадки
The computer **trouble has been cleared up** (*or* **remedied,** *or* **eliminated**).

Устранять потерю
The loss of air **must be taken care of.**

Устранять разрыв [*см. тж.* **Сближать**]
To bridge the gap between the design procedures and the published data, ...
Ligase **repairs breaks in** DNA molecules.

Устранять слабину [*см.* **Забирать слабину**].

Устранять со своего пути
The body **moves** the fluid **out of its way.**

Устранять трудность [*см.* **Устранять затруднение**].

Устранять "узкие места"
Bottlenecks may be cleared (*or* **resolved**) **by** using additional operators.

Устранять утечку
To stop a leak, ...

Устраняться
Expansion **is counteracted** (*or* **eliminated,** *or* **precluded,** *or* **prevented**) **by** using two metals of different expansion coefficients.

Устроен так, что
The DNA molecule **is so structured that** it effectively guides ...
Low-reactance feeder busways **are so constructed that** the conductors of different phases are in close proximity.

Устройство [*см. тж.* **Общее устройство, Средство**]
All shear connectors must have some **provision** (*or* **arrangement,** *or* **contraption**) **to** prevent the lifting of the beam.
The cylinder has **a means for** cooling the mechanical parts.
The instrument incorporates **an** integration **facility.**
The arrangement consists of a small bell and hopper.
This control **means** (*or* **device**) is operated from the same regulator.

Уступать место [*см. тж.* **Переходить в**]
Atlantic water, when chilled, can sink to the sea floor, **making room for** more tropical water.
With depth the basaltic dikes **give way to** gabbroic rocks.
In satellite-communication terminals the maser amplifier **has given way to** the cooled parametric amplifier.

Уступать по важности только
The importance of good health to old people **is second only to** 'good neighbours and friends'.

Уступать по распространённости
Among household scientific instruments the aneroid barometer **is outnumbered only by** the clock and the thermometer.
Aluminium **is exceeded in abundance** only **by** oxygen and silicon.

Уступать по твёрдости
Boron carbide **ranks below** boron nitride **in hardness.**

Уступать только
Aluminium is making great inroads on many materials of construction, and today **it is second only to** steel.

Усугублять сложность
This **adds to the complexity of ...**

Усугубляться
This difficulty **is compounded** (*or* **aggravated**) **by** the fact that ...
These problems **were dramatized by** the inability ...

Усыпан
The surface of Deimos (*Martian satellite*) **is littered** (*or* **strewn**) **with** large boulders.

Утапливать в землю
Coaxial cables **are** installed in underground conduit, or simply **buried.**

Утверждать, что [*см. тж.* **Иногда утверждают, что**]
They **advocated that** continents had drifted apart.

This is equivalent to **the statement that** all gases deviate from ...
The scientists **argue** (*or* **reason**) **that** this difference rules out ...
The proponents of nuclear power **contend** (*or* **hold**) **that** these installations are accident proof.
The firm **maintains** (*or* **states,** *or* **asserts**) it has techniques for improving ...
This hypothesis **holds that** the universe has always looked exactly the way it does today.

Утверждение о том, что
This supports our **contention** (*or* **assertion,** *or* **statement**) **that** superconductivity is ...

Утечка [*см. тж.* **Давать течь, Испытание на течь, Плотный**]
Naphtha vapours **were leaking out** at a temperature of ...
Spillage of mercury from broken instruments ...

Утилизация отходов
New processes for **recovery of wastes** are being developed.

Утоление боли
This medicine is used for the **relief of pain.**

Утомительный
This is a **tedious** (*or* **cumbersome**) process.

Утоньшаться
The crust could **have been reduced in thickness** [*or* **thinned (down)**] **by** erosion.

Утоплен
The batteries of light **are recessed in** the factory ceiling.
The thermometer **is fitted flush with** the wall.
The field windings **are** completely **embedded** (*or* **buried**) **in** iron.

Уточнение
Numerous **refinements of** the terminology have been introduced.
This value may be subject to **refinement** (*or* **improvement**) when analyses are complete.

Уточнённый
Some years later a **(more) refined** version appeared.

Уточним:
To be precise, we observe that each point t belonging to the set T can be thought of as ...

Уточнять
The temperature values **have been refined** (*or* **improved,** *or* **adjusted**) **by** the application of instrumental corrections.
What kind of substance would be encoded by such a crystal **was** not **made clear.**

Ухватить
Only selected chapters need be read **to grasp** the essential concepts.

Уход
The valves need no **attention** (*or* **attendance,** *or* **maintenance**).
With minimum **care** these parts last indefinitely.
Minimum **care of** piping is needed.

Уход и эксплуатация
Care and Maintenance of Measuring Instruments (*heading*).

Уходить в бесконечность
The curve **goes to infinity.**

Уходящий (*антон.* **Приходящий**)
Outgoing (*anton.* **Incoming**) waves ...

Ухудшать [*см. тж.* **Неблагоприятно влиять на**]
Measurement errors **will deteriorate** the quality of data.
General attack destroys structural features and **impairs** (*or* **affects**) the reflectivity of the polished surface.
The accuracy of the machine **is** not **impaired by** wear on moving parts.
The greater weight of a larger dry engine **would have degraded** overall engine performance.

Ухудшаться
The performance of these devices **is adversely affected** if they are operated at a significantly lower voltage.
As a result the temperature of the entering air is increased and the performance of the cooling tower **is impaired.**

Ухудшение
To determine whether **the degradation of** human performance is additive, ...

In addition to **the deterioration of** ductility, strength properties are also affected.
Some **sacrifice of** scale sensitivity will accompany this added load.

Ухудшение памяти
Impairment of memory.

Участвовать в [*см. тж.* **Активно участвовать в, В котором участвует, Принимать участие в**]
Our investigations reveal that the pituitary-adrenal system **comes into play in** the regulation of behaviour based on "appetite" responses.
The ligases **have been implicated** (*or* **involved**) **in** influencing the biosynthesis of ...

Участвовать в реакции
The following compounds **are involved in the reaction: ...**

Участвующий в
The valences of the carbon atoms not **involved in** ring formation are situated ...
Species **participating** (*or* **involved**) **in** a chemical change ...

Участие I
The biologists established **the involvement** (*or* **participation**) **of** such compounds **in** cell division.

Участие II
Starting a new filtration cycle without **the attention of** an operator ...

Участок I
The high-energy orbit will cross and recross the target orbit on the outbound and inbound **legs of** the flight.
The portion of the curve from *A* to *B* ...
The orifice plate should be installed at a point where the longest possible straight **run of** the pipe will exist ...
The new **section of** the pipeline ...
Twenty-four superconducting magnets have been installed in one **segment of** the tunnel.

Участок II [*см. тж.* **Опытный участок**]
When plants (*заводы*) are completed **at** these **localities ...**
A construction **site ...**
At **sites** where the film was close to the radioactive substance ...
A bog is **a tract of** wet, spongy ground.

Участок III
The affected **areas of** the skin ...

Участок организма
There are potential differences between **body regions.**

Участок с большим движением
Best manoeuvrability in **traffic-congested areas ...**

Учебник по
A textbook of quantitative analysis.
As demonstrated in **texts** (*or* **text-books**) **on** quantum electronics, ...

Ученик
According to Blondlot and his **disciples ...**

Учёные теряются в догадках
It has been a matter of conjecture for years **whether** this radiation is truly diffuse, or ...

Учёный [*см.* **Исследователь**].

Учёт [*см. тж.* **Без учёта, Вести учёт, Для учёта, При учёте, С учётом**]
The inclusion of material dispersion leads to simple modifications of the expression for ...
The magnitude of $Q(t)$ is modified **to account for** the dependence of ...
The analysis of these waves involves **taking account of** (*or* **taking into account**) their amplitudes.
This theory evaluates the resolving power of the instrument **by considering** not only the diffraction caused by ..., but also that caused by the object itself.
A more rigorous treatment of molecular orbitals requires **a consideration of** algebraic sign of the associated wave functions.
The section is devoted to methods of **allowing for** axial dispersion.
Use is made of a photoelectric scanning system **to keep track of** buses as they pass check points.
Taking into account (*or* **consideration**) each defect is essential.

Учитывать [*см. тж.* **Если не учитывать, Если принять во внимание, что; Если учесть, что; Исправленный на активность, Не учитывать, Необходимо учесть, Принимать во внимание, Следует учитывать**]

The nonuniform spatial distribution of the laser beam **has to be taken into account.**
If the written equation **accounts for** all reactants and products, ...
It is necessary **to allow for** import of heat and moisture.
Account must be taken of the high optical losses ...
Allowances are made for this fact in the design of equipment.
Effects of gravity **must be allowed for.**
The expansion **should be allowed** (*or* **accounted) for** in the die design.
When employing this formula, **it should be considered that** C_1 and C_2 are ion concentrations of ...
In antenna design the effect of the earth **must be considered.**
Give due consideration, when measuring, **for** expansion of the workpiece by heat.
The plots **include** the frequency response.
Equation 8 **incorporates** the normal losses.
The effect of firing temperatures **must be kept in mind.**
The method does not **make** any **allowance for** the sulphur content of the feedstock.
Such a theory must **take account of** the experimental results.
The formula does not **take into consideration** (*or* **account**) cutter wear and ...
These terms **allow for** the dissipation of energy by ...
To account for the influence of a chemical reaction on, ...
Allowance for the wall "reflection" is included in the analysis.

Учитывать должным образом
All this **must be given proper weight in** designing ...
If one **were to take proper account of** these developments, ...
This **should be taken properly into account.**

Учитываться в [*см. тж.* **Не учитываться**]
Wave effects **must be built into** the ray treatment.
The volume of the preheat zone **was** not **considered** [*or* **taken into account** (*or* **consideration**), *or* **allowed for**] **in** the computation of reaction time.
The effect of geometry **is** not **included** (*or* **incorporated**) **in** the figure.
The movements of the magnetic poles are not important to the navigator, as its consequences **are taken care of in** suitable notes on maps and charts.

Учитывая
The stability of the equilibrium size was better than expected **having regard to** variations in the temperature of the environment.
Considering [*or* **Taking into consideration** (*or* **account**)] trunks, operator lines and meet-me conference lines, there are in all 130 lines which ...
With this result Graham's law becomes: ...

Учитывая большое внимание, уделяемое
With the spotlight fixed on the damaging effects of noise, it's not surprising to find leading companies setting up new departments and developing new protective devices.

Учитывая все обстоятельства
All things considered, drilling by laser is a costly process.
All things considered, the craters on that planet resemble those on Mars.

Учитывая сказанное [*см. тж.* **Исходя из этого**]
On this basis, it is not surprising that molecules such as CCl_4 are more stable than $C^{4+} + 4Cl^{-}$.

Учтён должным образом
The principle of additivity of resistances cannot be used unless all resistances **are properly accounted** (*or* **allowed**) **for** [*or* **taken into account** (*or* **consideration**)].

Ущерб [*см.* **Без ущерба для, Наносить ущерб**].

Уязвимое место
The machine has moisture detection devices in all **critical** (*or* **vulnerable**) **areas** where the saline electrolyte might intrude.

Уяснив это
With this point clear, we can continue with a discussion of ...

Ф

Фаза [*см.* **На ... градусов не в фазе с, Не в фазе с, Сдвинут по фазе, Совпадать по фазе**].

Фазовый состав
The phase constitution of hot tinned coatings has been investigated.

Факт
One **point** appears clearly established — none of the proteins is of host origin.

Фактически [*см. тж.* **По сути дела, По существу**]
Many of these supposed distinctions have now been shown to be erroneous; **in (point of) fact,** a number were known to be false several years prior to ...
We see that this partial molal volume is **in (actual) fact** (*or* **actually,** *or* **in effect,** *or* **in actuality**) the volume contributed by ...
In a runner of this type **virtually** all control of metal flow is lost.
The compound sugars are **in reality** (*or* **in fact**) sugar-like polysaccharides.
The discussion of pseudovectors belongs **properly** to the domain of the tensor calculus.
Conveyor-elevators are sometimes called simply elevators but they **are not true** elevators because ...
In effect these internal variations in the chemical process mean that the optimum behaviour of ...

Фактически нам нужно знать
What we really need (to know) is the length of the orbit.

Фактические данные
Factual evidence (*or* **data**).

Фактический
Only the response produced in animals provides a realistic measurement of the **true** (*or* **actual**) effects of these products.

Фактическое положение
This conclusion describes **the true state (of the affairs)**.

Факультативный
The second chapter is for **optional** use; it may be omitted entirely.

Фаска [*см.* **Иметь фаску, Снимать фаску**].

Фигура
Simple **geometries,** such as concentric spheres, parallel circular plates, and coaxial circular cylinders, ...

Фигурировать
Notice that the Fermi level does not **appear** in this expression.

Фигурирующий под названием
Forces, often **treated** (*or* **featured**) **under the name** van der Waals forces, provide ...

Физическая (Химическая) лаборатория (институт)
A physics (chemical) lab(oratory) (institute).

Физически допустимый
The **physically admissible** curves of Eq. 5 point to ...

Физически значимый
Only this part is **physically meaningful.**

Физически неосуществимый
Such a case is **physically unrealizable** (*or* **unfeasible**).

Физически осуществимый
This behaviour will be true for all **physically realizable** (*or* **feasible**) systems.

Физическое значение [*см.* **Иметь физическое значение**].

Фиксировать I
A shot bolt **locates** the cradle relative to the fixture.

Фиксировать II
When the temperature conditions are steady, **note** the thermometer reading.

Финансовая поддержка [*см.* **Получать финансовую поддержку**].

Флюс [*см.* **Покрывать флюсом**].

Фокусировать в одну точку
The device **focusses** a cluster of parallel lasers **on the same spot.**

Фокусировать в точку
A magnetic field **focusses** the photoelectrons **at a point.**
The secondary reflector **focusses** the laser beam **to a** fine **spot.**

Фокусироваться на I [*см. тж.* **Сфокусирован(ный) на**]
The laser beam **was focus(s)ed (up)on** the workpiece.
Pulsed laser radiation **is focus(s)ed on(to)** a small fuel pellet of solid deuterium-tritium.

Фокусироваться на II
The eye cannot **focus on** an object much closer to it than ...

Фокусировка на
By **focussing** a laser **into** the sample ...

Фон [*см.* **На фоне**].

Фоновый
The **background** fluorescence remained high.

Форма [*см.* **В виде, В краткой форме, В удобной для использования форме, Восстанавливать свою первоначальную форму, Доводить до заданных размера и формы, Иметь вид, Иметь форму, Неправильная форма, Обычной формы, Правильной формы, Приводить к форме, Придавать форму, Принимать форму**].

Форма Земли
The Earth's figure (*or* **shape**).

Форма ... искажается
A negative ion approaching ... **will be distorted in shape** as electrons are pulled toward the positive field.

Форма капли отклоняется от сферической
An oscillating **drop is distorted** (*or* **deviates**) **from the spherical shape.**

Форма молекулы
The molecular shape (*or* **The shape of the molecule**).

Форма поперечного сечения
The needle crystal has **a** circular **cross-sectional shape.**

Формировать [*см. тж.* **Придавать форму**]
Chemical evolution **has shaped** the molecules ...
The gravitational field of the satellite does much **to sculpture** (*or* **shape**) the outer edge of its ring.

Формула [*см. тж.* **С формулой**]
The formula for table salt **is** NaCl.

Формула образования
The equation for the formation of the tetra compound is ...

Формула реакции следующая
The reaction is formulated as (*or* **The reaction formula is**) $CH_4 + ...$

Формулировать
We now **can state** the conservation-of-energy principle.
This rule **is stated** as follows: ...

Формулировать таким образом, что
This expression **has been arranged so that** the function goes to zero at ...

Формулироваться
The question **is phrased** (*or* **formulated,** *or* **stated**) in the following way ...

Формулировка [*см.* **Постановка ...**].

Формы [*см. тж.* **-образный**]
An equation **of the form** $A + B = C$ ...
The end supports **are of** ring **form.**

Фото крупным планом
Then **a close-up photograph** can be made.

Фотографировать [*см. тж.* **Делать фотоснимок**]
The photographer **can shoot** objects between 2 and 23 feet away without ...
To take pictures (*or* **photos**).
To photograph such objects, ...
The Jupiter-facing hemisphere of Callisto **was imaged** at high resolution.

Фотография со "вспышкой"
Many cameras have provision for **flash photography.**

Функции станка не ограничиваются
The machine is not restricted to drilling.

Функционирование
The normal **operation** [*or* **function(ing)**] **of** the system ...

Функционировать
The right eye **was** normal and **functional.**

Функционировать в качестве
The pickup **acts** (*or* **functions**) **as** a miniature generator.

Функция [*см. тж.* **В функции, Выполнять функцию, Как функция**]
This distance **is a function of** the phase angle.

Функция ... состоит в
Hemoglobin **has the function of** distributing oxygen round the human body.
Acid-insoluble proteins of chromatin **are responsible for** regulating gene expression.

Футерованный
The furnace **is lined with** refractory material.

X

Хаотически [*см.* **Беспорядочно**].

Хаотический [*см.* **Беспорядочное движение**].

Характер [*см.* **Аналогичного характера, По своей природе, Природа**].

Характе́рен для
Such problems **are inherent in** (*or* **characteristic of,** *or* **typical for**) high-altitude, hypersonic flights.
A simple behaviour **is shown by** systems for which ...
The infrared spectrum **is characteristic of** the entire molecule.
The use of a colour change to indicate ... **is common to** a wide variety of titrimetric methods.
The DNA transcriptive properties **are intrinsic to** the enzyme.
This enzyme **is specific to** liver disease.

Характе́рен не только для
The economic role of ions **is not unique to** the twentieth century.

Характе́рен только для
Such asymmetry **is unique** (*or* **peculiar**) **to** events mediated by the weak force.

Характеризовать [*см.* **Классифицировать, Охарактеризовывать**].

Характеризовать как практически непроницаемый
Clay and shale **can be described as impermeable** rocks **for all practical purposes.**

Характеризовать по
Coke **is** also **classified by** (*or* **according to**) the temperature at which it is made.

Характеризоваться
The carburettors **incorporate** the following advantages: ...
The pentode **offers** 34 watt maximum plate dissipation and ...
The electrolyte recording medium employed **is characterized by** a low internal impedance.
The capacitor **features** (*or* **exhibits,** *or* **shows**) extraordinary stability.
The period since World War II **has been marked by** a steady advance of ...
The first stages **are exemplified by** a scarcity of known forms.

Характеризующийся [*см.* **Для которого характе́рно**].

Характеристика
The mechanical **behaviour** (*or* **characteristics,** *or* **properties**) of polymeric materials ...
Operational **features ...**
The first-rate **performance** of this electrode ...
For **the characterization of** complex samples, ...

Характе́рная особенность [*см. тж.* **Отличительная черта**]
The semi-permeability **is the characteristic property** (*or* **feature**) **of ...**
The distinctive characteristics (*or* **features**) **of** solid as opposed to liquid fuels ...
The distinguishing features of the machine **are ...**
To illustrate **the salient features of** the observed spectra, ...
A characteristic of the behaviour of composite volcanoes **is** their highly explosive eruption.
A distinguishing characteristic (*or* **feature**) **of** ordinary freezing **is** that for pure substances it takes place discontinuously.
It is **the hallmark of** such personnel that their training has conditioned them to decide how to do their work.

Характе́рно [*см.* **Для которого характе́рно**].

Характе́рный для [*см. тж.* **Присущий, Свойственный**]
The high spectral purity **characteristic of** laser light permits reduction of ...
The wet, salty soil **common to** the western states ...
The difficulty **innate to** all concepts of chemical regulation ...
This form of distortion is an **inherent** feature of all amplifiers.
This is one of the difficulties **accompanying** the development of high-energy solid propellants.
The spectrum indicates a chromophoric centre **characteristic for** conjugated ...
Characteristic of a fluidized process **is** the large pressure drop of ...
There are some dozens of lipids, each with this **distinctive** chemical pattern.
Each of these different hydrates has its own **distinctive** X-ray diffraction pattern.
The disadvantage **inherent in** these systems ...
Accidents **peculiar to** an explosives plant occur ...
Materials **peculiar to** this type of machine are used as ...

Характе́рный только для
Problems **unique to** such systems arise ...

Химическим путём
This effect may be produced **by chemical means** (*e.g. fermentation*).

Химическое соединение с
Crystalline solids in which boron occurs in **chemical combination with** oxygen ...

Ход I [*см. тж.* **Замедлять ход, Идти своим ходом, На ходу́, Обратный ход, Следить за ходом**]
The general **trend** (*or* **behaviour**) **of** the curve is as shown in Fig. 2.
This knowledge is helpful in defining **the course of** the overall reaction.
Progress of the flight test ...

Ход II [*см. тж.* **На гусеничном ходу**]
A piston **stroke ...**

Ход III [*см.* **Работать на холостом ходу**].

Ход IV [*см.* **В ходе выполнения программы, В ходе реакции**].

Ход вверх (*поршня*)
On the upstroke the contents are compressed from ...

Ход вниз (*поршня*)
On the downstroke, the piston ...

Ход кривой
The peak is about a factor of 10^4 above **the** general **run of** the abundance **curve.**

Ход развития
The time history of such a spectroscopic event ...

Ход рассуждений
The existence of this new satellite does not affect **the chain** (*or* **line**) **of argument** (*or* **reasoning**) here.

Ход реакции [*см. тж.* **Наблюдать за ходом реакции**]
Description of **the progress** (*or* **course**) **of a reaction ...**

Ходить с точностью, превышающей
Atomic clocks **keep time to better than** 0.01 second a year.

Холодная гибка
There is a supplementary device **to cold bend** architectural sections.

Холодная обработка
Tube drawing is **a cold-working process.**

Холодный [*см.* **Обрабатываться в холодном состоянии, Прокатывать в холодном состоянии**].

Холостой ход [*см.* **Работать на холостом ходу**].

Хорошая видимость
The operator has **a clear view** standing or sitting.
Clear vision is essential to an efficient derrick crane.
Good visibility was helpful in the search.

Хорошее приближение [*см. тж.* **В весьма хорошем приближении, В хорошем приближении**]
This force **can be closely approximated by** using the above formula.
This will enable you to get **a close approximation of** your altitude.

Хорошее соответствие [*см.* **Находиться в хорошем соответствии с**].

Хорошее состояние [*см.* **Содержать в хорошем состоянии**].

Хорошее сцепление с
The alloy coatings **have good adhesion to** steel.

Хорошо
The electrical equipment is **adequately** (*or* **well**) protected.
It is essential that the body of the machine is **effectively** earthed.
Aqueous solutions of ionic crystals **readily** conduct electricity.

Хорошо знаком с [*см. тж.* **Близко знаком с**]
Analysts **are well aware of** these difficulties.

Хорошо известно, что [*см. тж.* **Известно, что**]
It is common knowledge that relatively few offsprings survive to reproduce.

Хорошо известный
The **familiar** chemical term ligand ...

Хорошо изучен
Organic bromides **have been much studied.**
The detailed mechanisms of homogeneous catalytic processes **are well understood.**

Хорошо изученный
No completely satisfactory model of phage DNA replication has thus far been presented, not even for the **much-** (*or* **well-** *or* **thoroughly**) **studied** T4 (*biol.*).

Хорошо наблюдаться
The solar corona **is easily observable** at an eclipse.

Хорошо обозначенный [*см. тж.* **Чётко обозначен(ный)**]
The berm usually has a **well-defined** edge.

Хорошо оборудованный
A **fully equipped** laboratory.

Хорошо обрабатываться [*см.* **Легко поддающийся обработке**].

Хорошо оснащённый приборами
A **heavily** (*or* **well**) **instrumented** Earth satellite ...

Хорошо отполированный
A **highly** (*or* **well**) **polished** specimen ...

Хорошо отражать
These representations **adequately depict** the actual molecular structure.

Хорошо отражать действительность
Good agreement suggests that the model **is realistic** (*or* **adequate**).

Хорошо перемешанный
A **thoroughly mixed** liquid ...
A film separates two **well-stirred** masses of fluid.

Хорошо поддаваться
The system **is quite amenable to** theoretical analysis.

Хорошо поддаваться обработке
These materials **readily lend themselves to machining.**

Хорошо подогнанные друг к другу
Close-fitted parts are required for brazing.

Хорошо подогнаны (друг к другу) [*см.* **Быть хорошо** (*или* **плотно**) **подогнанными (друг к другу)**].

Хорошо подходить для
This scheme **is well suited to** the correction of ...

Хорошо подчиняться закону
Most gases **obey** (*or* **follow**) **this law closely.**

Хорошо понимать [*см. тж.* **Полностью понять**]
It is important **to fully appreciate** the behaviour of individual rays.
In order **to effectively grasp** (*or* **gain an insight into**) the principles of ...
To gain an appreciation of the way in which ...

Хорошо приспособлен для
These glasses **are attractive for** the direct analysis of water to PAH contamination.

Хорошо проветривать помещение
Keep the premises well ventilated (*or* **aired**).

Хорошо растворяться в
This compound **has considerable** (*or* **great,** *or* **high**) **solubility in** water.
Sodium nitrate **is very** (*or* **freely,** *or* **quite,** *or* **highly,** *or* **readily**) **soluble in** water.

Хорошо сконструированный
Well-engineered (*or* **-designed**) controlled systems ...

Хорошо согласовываться с [*см. тж.* **Близко совпадать**]
This result **accords** (*or* **agrees**) **well with** observed speeds for massive stars.
Thus a structure is devised that **fits** the experimental data **well.**
This value **agrees** (*or* **checks**) **nicely** (*or* **well,** *or* **closely,** *or* **satisfactorily**) **with** the data on ...

Хорошо соответствовать
Bohr's model **corresponded closely to** the idea of ...

Хорошо сохраняться
In the absence of impurities, even very concentrated solutions of hydrogen peroxide **keep quite well.**

Хорошо сочетаться
Nuclear energy **and** thermionic conversion **go well together** (*or* **are a good combination**).

Хорошо справляться с
A smaller computer **could do that job adequately.**

Хорошо укладываться в
Some of the ancient tools **fit neatly into** established categories.

Хорошо укладываться между
A silicon ion **fits nicely between** four oxygen ions.

Хотелось бы [*см.* **Нам хотелось бы**].

Хотя [*см. тж.* **Несмотря на то, что; Хотя и**]
Although this series is endless, the total can only be half as great as ...
Useful **though** the two minerals are, there is evidence that they may cause cancer.
As numerous **as are** the inorganic bromides that have found industrial use, the organic bromides have even wider application.

Хотя бы для
Radio position markers, guide-path directors ... all use amplitude modulation, **if only for** coded identification of a facility.

Хотя бы для того, чтобы
One might hope that ... **if only to** simplify the task of ...

Хотя бы из-за
The growth of the sophistication of machine-tool controls could not proceed faster than the development of the integrated-circuit chip solid-state controls, **if for no other reason than** the sheer size of the controls.

Хотя бы только для того, чтобы сохранить окружающую среду
If for no other reason than environmental concern, removal of the uranium would be desirable.

Хотя и [*см. тж.* **Как бы ни был**]
This model contains an implicit suggestion that photons have normal, **even if** very small, masses.
Though sensitive enough for high-quality organic spectroscopy, MPI does not approach the sensitivity of RIS.
This method, **while** expensive, is particularly advantageous when ...
Whilst (*or* **While**) such a description is not strictly accurate, it **(nevertheless)** provides qualitative insight.
Cocaine, valuable **as it is** as a local anaesthetic, has several clinical and commercial disadvantages.
Important **as** visual examinations of the data **are,** the question of how quasars are distributed ultimately calls for statistical analysis.

Хотя и не
These steps are similar in principle **if not** identical in many applications.

Хотя и существует
Notwithstanding all these difficulties, there is no other method.

Хотя и удалось многое узнать
However much has been learned in the past 50 years, it would be misleading to suggest that ...

Хотя их и мало
He has strong supporters, **few as they are.**

Хотя он и
The solar day, uneven **as it is,** carries one important advantage.

Хотя они и
Although similar in design to irrigation canals, power and drainage canals have special requirements.

Хотя они и хороши
Good as they are, even new machine-tools are not perfect.

Хранение [*см.* **Период хранения, При хранении, Срок хранения**].

Хранить в себе
Porosity determines in large part the ability of a given rock formation **to hold in storage** liquid petroleum or natural gas.

Храниться
The fundamental standard of mass **is kept on deposit** at the Bureau of Standards.
The goods **are stored at** the warehouse.
The machines **were warehoused** for three years.
The blueprints **are stowed in** an indexed file.

Храниться в холодном виде
The diazo component **must be kept cold** to prevent decomposition.

Хуже
Iron **is inferior to** (*or* **worse than**) copper as a conductor.

Ц

Царапать ножом
Pyrite **cannot be scratched by the knife.**

Царапина [*см.* **Без царапин**].

Царапина от ножа [*см.* **На котором нож оставляет царапину**].

Цвет [*см. тж.* **Выкрашенный в ... цвет, Расцвечен**]
The pH values at which the indicators change **colour** are marked on the curve.
The brown coloration of the snow ...
Pure gallium **is bluish white in colour.**
A drop of iodine **turns a dark blue** in the presence of starch.
The colour of the light **is** usually **a blue-green.**
Dark, brilliant hues ...
A **black-coloured** pigment ...
Magnesium **is silvery-white in appearance.**

Цве́та кожи *и т.п.*
A leather-**coloured** material ...

Цветная маркировка
In many cases, **colour coding** can be an aid in properly identifying the various functions.

Целевое назначение
The end use of the part should be indicated.

Целевой продукт
If a terminal alkane is **the target** (*or* **desired**) **product, ...**

Целесообразен
Sometimes barium contrast studies **are appropriate** (*or* **worthwhile**).

Целесообразно [*см. тж.* **Когда это целесообразно, Полезно, Рекомендуется**]
It is appropriate to consider this topic in more detail.
It makes sense to classify rocks according to ...
A patient with haemolytic anaemia **is best** admitted to hospital.
There is good reason to consider the weathering of ...
It is profitable (*or* **well**) **to** consider the ways in which points can be arranged to give a repeating array.
Some of these features **merit** close examination.
It is worthwhile investigating the behaviour of a gas.
It is sometimes **worthwhile to** dehumidify the inlet gas by ...
It is advantageous to use ...
It is more **expeditious to** make use of ...
Here **it is wise** (*or* **advisable,** *or* **expedient,** *or* **good practice**) **to** build a wooden platform a few inches from the floor.
The new technique has a wider field of application and **deserves** (*or* **is deserving of**) closer study.
This area **is worthy of** further investigation.

Целесообразно использовать

The controller **would be appropriate for use** in such a system.

Целесообразность
The utility of this shape **is** most apparent in nonlinear effects where a tightly focussed beam is utilized.
The advisability (*or* **wisdom**) **of** pursuing research into ...

Целесообразный [*см. тж.* **Эффективный**]
This is a **worthwhile** investment.
Hospital referral for further investigation **is indicated.**
Because of the high neutron output associated with deuterium-tritium fuel, a heat-cycle conversion system **would be appropriate.**
Suitable (*or* **Advisable,** *or* **Expedient,** *or* **Efficient**) methods for other vitamins **are** referred to in Table 1.

Целиком [*см. тж.* **Весь, Выполненный целиком из алюминия, Полностью**]
A lithospheric plate is a fragment of a spherical shell that moves **as a unit** over a complete spherical surface (*geol.*).
It was necessary to replace **the entire** (*or* **whole**) bottom of the tank.
These elements are made of uniform material **throughout** (*or* **completely**).
This coordinate system is made up **entirely of** straight lines melting at right angles.

Целиком автоматический [*см.* **Полностью автоматизированный**].

Целиком зависеть от
We **live with complete dependence on** two kinds of solutions. One is gaseous — the atmosphere, and the other is aqueous.

Целиком из стекла
All-glass vacuum apparatus.

Целое число
The wavelengths of the sound produced are related to the length of the vibrating strings by **integers** (*or* **integral numbers,** *or* **whole numbers**), n ($n = 1, 2, 3, \ldots$).

Целочисленный [*см. тж.* **Целый I**]
The principal quantum number can have any **integer** (*or* **integral,** *or* **whole-number**) value (1, 2, 3, ...).

Цель [*см. тж.* **В этих целях, Для достижения этой цели, Для наших целей, Достигать цели, Использовать для разных целей, Преследовать цель, С этой целью**]
The main **objective is to** determine ...
The intent of his method **was ...**
Our main **concern** at first **was** to reproduce such ...
In laser fusion **the object** (*or* **aim,** *or* **purpose**) **is to** compress fuels to extreme densities.
The accurate prediction of ... **is** primary **goal of** boundary-layer theory.

Цель достигнута
The above **objective has been met** (*or* **attained,** *or* **achieved**).

Цель ... состоит в
The aim of this book **is to** characterize ...
The goal (*or* **purpose,** *or* **objective**) **is to** show how ...
The intention in this chapter **is to** reveal ...

Цель состоит в том, чтобы
The objective in designing a packing **is to** provide a large surface and yet ...

Цельная конструкция
The unitized construction combines the body and frame into a single welded unit.

Цельнометаллический
The unit **is of all-metal construction** (*or* **is all metal**).

Цельносварный
All-welded metal specimens ...

Целью является
Here **the object** (*or* **purpose**) **is** to obtain information about ...

Целью ... является разработка
The program seeks techniques for locating ...

Целый I
Photons have **integer** spin.

Целый II
Vertical members, such as towers, poles or **entire** buildings, are often considered as ...

Целый ряд
In any problem of major importance it is good to have **a diversity of** approaches.

A variety (*or* **A number**) **of** techniques are used.
During the past half-century physicists have built **a succession of** particle accelerators.
With solution chromatography, **a large** (*or* **great,** *or* **wide**) **variety of** detection techniques have been employed.
The instrument will serve **a broad range of** astronomical purposes.

Целым рядом способов
Generalized drift can be derived **in a number of ways.**

Целых
The Moon is tilted to the plane of the primary's equator **by a good** 18°.

Цена
Typical ground terminals are expected **to be priced from** about $1 million **to** $5 million.

Цена снизится
The price will come down [*or* **will be reduced** (*or* **cut**)] as technology develops and demand grows.

Цениться за
The *ormer* **is valued for** its beautiful shell.
Butter **is prized for** the flavour that comes from ...

Центр [*см.* **В центре, По центру, Помещённый в центре, С центром в**].

Централизованно
Power may be supplied **centrally,** from a central office battery.

Центрально расположенный [*см.* **Помещённый в центре**].

Центрировать
Pins project from the tools **to centralize** the workpiece bore in relation to the electrodes.
It is essential that the spindle **is centralized** (*or* **centred**) while adjusting the alignment.
The centralizer serves **to align** the gauge within the bore.
The frame of the sight **is aligned with** the fore and aft axis of the airplane.

Центром которого является
The pointer indicates the proper degree of the arc, which **has for its centre** the pivot of the upper mirror.

Цепной привод [*см.* **С цепным приводом**].

Цепь замыкается
The strip makes momentary contact with the upper bar; as a result, **a circuit is completed** (*or* **closed**) and the machine is started.

Цикл [*см.* **Замыкать цикл, По циклу**].

Циркулировать по
The air **circulates through** the coil.

Циркуляционный поток
A circulatory flow.

Ч

Часовая стрелка [*см.* **По часовой стрелке, Против часовой стрелки**].

... частей на ... частей
A mixture of 8 **parts** sulphuric acid **to** 3 **parts** water ...

Частица более высокой энергии
More energetic particles may escape from the liquid surface into the gas phase.

Частица с бóльшим зарядом
The current is due to a few **heavily charged particles.**

Частичная природа (*от слова "частица"*)
Light, in addition to being a wave phenomenon, is known to have **a particulate nature.**
The particle nature of matter ...

Частично
The structure we have written is only **partially** correct.
This process consists **in part** of general oxidation.
A shock wave is reflected **in part** by boundaries between ...
Catabolic processes may degrade a substance **(only) part way.**
These errors **partially** (*or* **partly**) account for the deviation of ...
This goes **part way** toward reducing ...

Частично изучен
Many of the steps in amino acid metabolism **are (still only) partially understood.**

Частично ионизирован
Some molecular compounds are **partially ionized.**

Частично объяснять
This **is part of the reason for** the small body size of many people in improverished countries.

Частично потерявший зрение
Partially sighted people ...

Частично проталкивать через
The air expands, **moving** the piston **part way through** the cylinder.

Частный случай
The definition for **the special case of** the rectangular wing ...
Aeromechanics **is a special** (*or* **particular**) **case of** the more general field of fluid mechanics.
In **the specific case of** 25% dehydration ...

Часто [*см. тж.* **Более или менее часто, Довольно часто**]
Every so often there comes a revision of thinking.

Часто встречаться [*см. тж.* **Нередко встречаться, Широко распространён**]
Uridine **is frequent** among ...
Basaltic volcanics **are abundant** (*or* **frequently occur**) in some areas.
Such viruses **are of frequent occurrence.**
Brown fat **occurs extensively** in species which hibernate.
This phenomenon **is common(place)** (*or* **widespread,** *or* **usual**) along the English and French coasts.
This problem **is widely met** (*or* **encountered**) in practice.

Часто встречающийся [*см. тж.* **Наиболее распространённый**]
The metallurgy of the **commonly occurring** (*or* **encountered**) metals ...

Часто использоваться
Such substances are **of frequent use in** experiments.

Часто находят у
Hypocalcaemia **is** not **a common finding in** the elderly.

Часто приводимый пример
One **frequently cited instance of** symbiosis **is ...**

Часто применяемый
An **often-** (*or* **much-**)**used** (*or* **A frequently used**) analytical relation ...

Часто приходится иметь дело с
Circles of unit diameter **are frequently dealt with.**

Частота [*см.* **На частоте**].

Частотность
Seismic studies reveal **a** high **incidence of** earthquakes in this zone.

Часть I [*см. тж.* **Делить на части, Добавлять частями, Доля, Значительная часть, На ... частей, Неотъемлемая часть, Основная часть; ... частей на ... частей**]
A mixture consists of three **parts** acetic acid, two **parts** water.
The Yellowstone Park **is part of** a larger area ...
Part of the surface was corroded.
Remove **a portion of** the metal in the vicinity of ...

Часть II [*см. тж.* **Деталь, Обрабатываемая деталь, Составная часть**]
The machine is built of standardized **components** (*or* **parts**).

Часть III [*см.* **Внутренняя часть, Наружная часть**].

Часть IV [*см. тж.* **В левой (правой) части уравнения**]
Electrochemistry is **that part of** physical chemistry **which** includes phenomena occurring ...

Часть кривой
Consider now **the** lower **portion of the curve ...**

Часть спектра
This **portion** (*or* **region,** *or* **stretch**) **of the** electromagnetic **spectrum ...**

Частью которого является
Distortion of the connecting members of frame **of which the column forms** (*or* **is**) **a part ...**

Частые случаи
The high incidence of failure on start-up can usually be attributed to ...

Частями
380 g of $KMnO_4$ was added **portionwise** to a solution of ...

Чаще
It is more common to measure a freezing range.
The symbols of chemical elements consist of one, or **more commonly** (*or* **often**), two letters.

Чаще всего
Such operating instructions **more often than not,** lead to unsatisfactory results.
This is **most commonly** done using acetyl chloride.
Scotch-boiler shells are **most often** riveted, although they may also be welded.

Чаще всего используется
(By far) the most frequently used type of gas-liquid mass transfer equipment **is** the multiple tray column.
Almost any polar solid can be used, **the most common choices being** silica gel or alumina.

Чаще встречаться в
"Giant cells" **are more frequent in** malignant tissue than in normal tissue.

Чего и следовало ожидать
This **would** (*or* **is to**) **be expected** if ...

Чего можно достигнуть
What would be gained by improving the resolution of the scanning microscope to equal the resolution of ...?
An example of **what** laser welding **can accomplish** is provided by ...

Человек
Humans have no enzymes capable of breaking ...

Человеческая деятельность
Science, like any other area of **human endeavour** (*or* **activity**), has its illusions.
Pollution may result from **man's activities.**

Чем (это было)
Industry is now paying much more attention to ... **than was the case** (*or* **than it did**) a few years ago.

Чем больше, тем
The greater (is) the thermal energy of the carrier, **the less** it is affected by ...

Чем бы это ни было вызвано
Whatever is the cause, the net result is similar to ...

Чем в ином случае
The grid is swung further off **than would otherwise be the case.**

Чем думали раньше [*см.* **Чем считалось раньше**].

Чем и объясняется
The structure has a single heterojunction, **hence** the name single-heterojunction laser.

Чем меньше ... , тем больше ...
The smaller (is) the region of available space, **the greater (is)** the kinetic energy corresponding to a given wave function [*or* The kinetic energy ... **is (the) greater, the smaller (is)** the region].

Чем можно предположить исходя из
The O_2 molecule is more complex **than** a simple electron-dot formula **suggests.**

Чем обычно считают
This may occur more frequently **than is generally appreciated.**

Чем похожи и чем отличаются
How are the two forces **alike and how do they differ?**

Чем предполагалось
The phenomena are much more complicated **than had been suspected.**

Чем принято считать
These minerals are much more abundant **than is considered to be the case.**

Чем считалось раньше
These species may play a more significant role **than formerly recognized** (*or* **than considered before**).

Чем ..., тем
The lower (is) the temperature, **the longer (is)** the storage life.

Чем это необходимо в случае
Steel of smaller diameter can be used for reinforcements **than is required for** normal steel bolts.

Чередоваться [*см. тж.* **Перемежаться с**]
The signs of outputs of successive integrators **alternate.**

Times of plate collisions **alternate with** periods of continental rifting (*geol.*).

Чередующиеся [*см. тж.* **Перемежающиеся**]
Alternate blocking **and** passing of the constant flux ...
Alternating sequences of glycine **and** *L*-alanine ...
mRNA contains repetitive sequences **interspersed with** nonrepetitive (*biol.*).

Через I [*см. тж.* **Всего лишь через, Выражать через, Линия, проходящая через; Проходить через**]
We convert the transmission term into a length dependent absorption **via** Eq. (28).
The sporoplasm reaches the specific site of infection **by way of** the blood stream.
All ray power is transmitted **across** the interface.
Signals are transmitted from an external source **by way of** (*or* **through**) a transducer.
The biosynthesis of arginine starts with glutamic acid, and proceeds **by way of** ornithine and citruline.
The outputs of these cells are fed, **via** potentiometer circuits, to a galvanometer.
The cables enter the amplifier **via** a radio frequency filter unit.
The fan supplies air to the mine **via** the downcast manway.

Через II [*см. тж.* **Всего лишь через**]
This causes the expansion of the chamber **within** a few milliseconds **of** (*or* **after**) the passage of the particle.
This, 2 sec **later,** gives rise to ...
After one second the speed will have increased to 2.7 centimetres per second.
The characteristics of the boundaries are usually expressed **in terms of** impedances.
Many definite integrals can be expressed **in terms of** Bessel functions.

Через верх
The material to be crushed is fed in **at the top.**
Excess air is released **from the top of** the tank.

Через весь
This pair of electrons is free to move **throughout** the molecule.

Через каждые ... градусов
The degrees of direction of the compass rose are engraved **in** 30 **degree intervals.**
The intervals between these numbers are graduated **in** five **degree increments.**

Через каждые полчаса
At half-hourly intervals (*or* **Every half-hour**).

Через каждые шесть месяцев [*см.* **Раз в шесть месяцев**].

Через каждые 24 часа
Every 24 hours, hot oil is diverted to the second coke drum.

Через каждый час
At hourly intervals (*or* **Every hour**).

Через какую-то долю секунды после
A split second (*or* **A fraction of a second**) **after** detonation, an automatic air gun jolts the unit into detection position.

Через ... лет [*см. тж.* **По прошествии ... лет**]
Within a few years the first radio maps were available.

Через микроскоп [*см.* **В микроскоп**].

Через некоторое время [*см. тж.* **По истечении некоторого времени, Со временем**]
In due course they found that this component was the cell membrane.
After a time, one will have equipartition of energy.

Через некоторые промежутки времени
The pressure in the gas space is measured **at intervals.**

Через несколько минут [*см. тж.* **За какие-то секунды**]
Epinephrine must be administered **within minutes of** (*or* **after**) the onset of the "shock" reaction.

Через один
Alternate plates of the capacitors are connected together.

Через ... после
Within a few weeks of (*or* **after**) Roentgen's discovery physicians had begun to investigate ...

Через посредство
The heavier ions "feel" the effect of the laser beam **through the mediation of** the oscillating electrons.

Через произвольные промежутки времени
We applied the prod **at random intervals** while the muscle was in tremor.

Через промежутки в ... минут
The readings are taken **at intervals of** ten **minutes.**

Через равные промежутки времени
Samples of boiler water are drawn **at regular intervals.**

Чересчур мал [*см. тж.* **Слишком**]
This quantity of mass **is (far) too small to** see in an optical microscope.

Черта [*см. тж.* **В общих чертах, Иметь общие черты с, Особенность, Отличительная черта**]
The principal characteristic **feature** (*or* **property,** *or* **trait**) **of** such molecules is that ...

Чертёж [*см. тж.* **Масштабный чертёж**]
A drawing for a pump shaft sleeve.

Чертить
The shape of the cam **is** first **mapped out** (*or* **drawn,** *or* **traced**) on paper.

Чертить в масштабе
The diagram **is drawn to scale.**

Чертить линию на детали
To draw (*or* **scribe**) **a line on the workpiece, ...**

Чертить на схеме
The spectral transitions **must be drawn** vertically **in diagrams.**

Чёрно-белое изображение
A black and white image.

Чёрного цвета
Samples of boron having the highest purity **are black in colour.**

Чёткая линия раздела между
There is no **clear dividing line between** strong acids and weak acids.

Чёткий
There is no **clear-cut** distinction between ionic and covalent bonds.
More **clear-cut** results have been obtained with ...
Hypofunction of the adrenal medulla is not known to produce any **clear-cut** clinical syndrome.
This area has **a clearly** (*or* **well**) **defined** (*or* **clear**) boundary.

Чёткий отпечаток
The hemihydrate reforms the dihydrate, evolving considerable heat and expanding in the process, so **a sharp imprint of** the mould is formed.

Чётко
Newton's law of gravitation **neatly** explained the planetary movements.

Чётко выраженное различие
The structure is similar to that of ... but with several **distinct differences.**

Чётко выраженный
There are several **distinct** annealing stages.
Elemental carbon exists in two **well-defined** crystalline allotropic forms.
These compounds have **clearly** (*or* **sharply**) **defined** thermodynamic properties.
These copolymers have a less **pronounced** (*or* **marked**) block structure.
He has observed **clear-cut** changes of crystal habit.
The excited state-producing step occurs in a separate, **well-defined** reaction.
Well-marked differences have been discovered between ...

Чётко выявлять
In solution chemistry, one of the principal goals of research is that of **clearly recognizing** the factors that are involved.

Чётко обозначен(ный) [*см. тж.* **Хорошо обозначенный**]
Zones may be vague or **sharply defined** (*or* **clear cut**).
There is a **well-defined** inverse function.

Чётко определённый
The design engineer is usually required to determine the type of the equipment to be installed for some **well-defined** purpose.

Чётко очерчен(ный)

Well-defined lunar induction fields were observed.
We have seen the Earth from space, with its land, water, and air masses **clearly delineated.**

Чётко представлять себе
Before prescribing a hypnotic it is important **to be clear in one's mind** why it is required.

Чётко различимые
There are two **distinct** phases to the fusion process.

Чёткое изображение
Lenses must produce **a sharp** (*or* **clear-cut) image.**

Чёткое объяснение
No theory offers a satisfactory, **coherent** (*or* **clear-cut**) **explanation of** this fact.

Чёткое различие между [*см. тж.* **Не существует чёткого различия**]
There is **a clear-cut distinction between** physical changes and chemical changes.

Чёткость изображения
For **the best definition,** the lenses must be sharply focused.
Maximum **sharpness** over the whole negative is necessary.

Чётные (нечётные) зубья
Even- (odd)-numbered teeth.

Численно превосходить
Whenever molecules in the ground state **outnumber** molecules in excited states — absorption predominates.
In yeast, the 5 *S* cistrons were linked to those of the larger rRNA species, but they **outnumbered** the latter **by** a ratio of 2:1.

Численно равен
If the circuit is of low resistance, the current **will be numerically equal to** the rate of excitation of ...

Численно управляемый
Numerically controlled equipment ...

Численное значение
The numerical values of these quantities are given by ...

Число [*см. тж.* **Значительное количество**]
The dependence of the United States upon foreign sources is heavy indeed for **a** long **list of** metals.

Число Маха
The airplane will cruise at **Mach 2.7** (*or* **M2.7**).

Число ... ограничено
The possible electronic rearrangements **are limited in number.**

Число уменьшилось
These species **had declined in number.**

Чистая условность
This representation of *D* and *L* forms **is merely a convention.**

Чисто отполированный
A **clean polished** platinum electrode ...

Чисто случайно
He hit on a solution **by pure accident.**

Чистовая обработка [*см.* **Окончательная обработка**].

Чистота [*см.* **Следить за чистотой, Содержать в чистоте**].

Чистота поверхности
Surface finish is 20 to 30 microinches.

Чистоты́ [*см. тж.* **Высокой чистоты́**]
London "standard" silver **is** 92.5% **pure.**

Чистый
Uncombined iron ...

"Чистый" [*см.* **Не загрязняющий окружающую среду**].

Член
The highest-degree **term of** a polynomial forms ...
Higher **members of** the Balmer series ...
A six-**membered** ring (*chem.*).

Чреват серьёзными последствиями
Use of γ-rays as a condensing agent **is open to many hazards.**

Чрезвычайная мера [*см.* **Принимать чрезвычайные меры**].

Чрезмерная смазка
It is essential to avoid **over-** (*or* **excessive**) **lubrication of** any of the mechanical components.

Чрезмерно

Such deposits yield **badly** broadened spectra.

Materials that **excessively** load (*забивают*) grinding wheels ...

See that no portion of the casing has worn **too** thin.

The errors so obtained are apt to be **unduly** pessimistic.

This will cause the threads to wear **unduly.**

A **prohibitively** long exposure ...

Чрезмерно большой и тяжёлый

The engine **is oversize and overweight.**

Чрезмерно высокая стоимость

The cost of the machine **is prohibitive** (*or* **exuberant**).

Prohibitively (*or* **Unduly,** *or* **Excessively**) **high cost.**

Чрезмерно высокий

The vapour pressure of the dissolved hydrocarbons over the exit oil **may become excessive** (*or* **inappropriately,** *or* **excessively high**).

Чрезмерно дорого

Purchasing a separate coupler for each line **would be prohibitively expensive.**

Чрезмерно крупный

Reusable material is dropped on a vibrating screen to remove **oversize** debris.

Чрезмерно суживаться

Holes tend **to become undersized** after drilling and reaming because of stress relaxation.

Чрезмерно упрощённый

The relationships are based on **overly simplified** (*or* **oversimplified**) models.

Чрезмерное употребление

Abuse of analgesics containing *phenacetin* leads to papillary necrosis of the kidney.

Чрезмерное упрощение

Such a proposal **is an oversimplification.**

Чрезмерные расходы на

Lubrication **costs may become prohibitive** with inadequate engine maintenance.

Чрезмерный

This "shell" shields us from **excess** ultraviolet radiation.

Over-lubrication of the shaft.

That would give rise to **prohibitively large** loss of carbon.

This permits expansion without **undue** (*or* **excessive,** *or* **too much**) strain.

Что более важно

Many topics are presented here for the first time, but, **more importantly** (*or* **what is more important**), the material is brought together to give ...

Что, в действительности, так и есть

The atoms possess only one valence electron, so that these metals should be good conductors, **which is the case.**

Что важнее [*см.* **Что более важно**].

Что видно, например, из

The molecular spectra of ... are relatively featureless, **as exemplified by** the solution spectrum of ...

Что даёт

The two compounds combine **to form ...**

We multiply this expression by T **to give: ...**

Что ещё важнее [*см.* **Что более важно**].

Что ещё хуже [*см. тж.* **Хуже**]

Unfortunately, this phosphor emits less light and, **even worse,** the spectral distribution is peaked at 3800 °A.

Что заставит нас искать

The old deposits will become exhausted, **sending us in search of** new deposits.

Что и требовалось доказать

... which proves the statement.

Hence the supposition is impossible A must be zero, **as we wished** (*or* **set out to**) **prove.**

Thus $e = 0$, **which is the required result** (*or* **which is what we set out to prove,** *or* **which proves the theorem**).

Что касается

As for (*or* **to**) all flame spectroscopic methods, the flame provides an imperfect atom reservoir.

In terms of (*or* **As regards,** *or* **In regard to**) yields, one of the most successful attempts was that of ...

With gases, there are many cases in which we ...

Что на 8% больше, чем
Metalworking manufacturers invested $2 billion in plants and equipment in 1965, **8% more than** in 1964.

Что нас ожидает?
What is ahead in space research?

Что нужно сделать для того, чтобы
How can (*or* **does**) **one go about** determining that the loci of the genes ...
What needs to be done to achieve the best possible performance ...

Что обнаружено
The deposit is rough, **as revealed** microscopically.

Что означает
What is meant by the statement that ...?

Что означает, что
Thus, $E = 1$, **which is to say that** for every n, nf is less than u.

Что остаётся делать?
What is left for organic chemists **to do?**

Что отнюдь не так [*см. тж.* **Далеко не**]
If broken lumps of rock were the essential characteristic of the lunar surface, the same would be true for radio signals, **which emphatically it is not.**

Что приводит к
The stiffness of the bond is lessened **resulting in** a lowering of ...
The water table has often been pumped below sea level, **with a consequent** intrusion of sea water into the ground-water basin.

Что приводит к возникновению
These sublevels are thermally broadened in solution, **resulting in** broad and continuous absorption and emission spectra.

Что приводит к выражению [*см.* **Что даёт**].

Что приводит к образованию [*см.* **Что даёт**].

Что приводит к сокращению *и т.п.*.
Decreasing the size of the devices reduces the distance between gates, **resulting in a shorter** propagation delay.

Что произошло с ... ?
What became of the original atmosphere of ...?

Что сделано в области ...?
What has been accomplished toward creating ...?

Что следует, например, из
The instrument can also serve as a state-selective detector, **as exemplified by** the I_2 study of Ref. 14.

Что то же самое
An ace will be among the first nine cards at the top of a shuffled deck or, **what amounts to the same thing** (*or* **what is the same**) — among the first nine cards picked at random without replacement.

Что указывает на то, что
Test animals injected with bee venom can withstand otherwise lethal doses of radiation, **suggesting that** the venom might prove useful as a radioprotective drug.

Что установлено
The oil did not foam, **as determined by** simply shaking samples in ...

Чтобы [*см. тж.* **Для того, чтобы; С тем, чтобы**]
The sensitive element should be thin, **so (that)** it will be heated rapidly.

Чтобы избежать [*см.* **Во избежание**].

Чтобы исправить этот недостаток
To remedy this, the engineers designed ...

Чтобы лучше понять
To gain greater insight into why the above statement is valid, ...

Чтобы не
The error must be corrected sooner **lest** the discrepancy **be** discovered.
It is essential that the reactor core not be uncovered, **lest** the temperature in the core **rise** quickly.

Чтобы объяснить
The meteorites do not contain enough uranium or thorium **to account for** either the xenon or the fission tracks.

Чтобы понять значение сказанного
To appreciate the significance of this statement we must take a closer look at ...

Чтобы предотвратить [*см. тж.* **Во избежание**]
White phosphorus is usually stored under water **as a precautionary measure against** ignition.

Чтобы убедиться в том, что
Injectors are checked **to be certain** (*or* **to make sure**) **that** the nozzle valves are seating properly.

Что-либо другое
Then there will be competition for this resource, be it nestling sites, food **or whatever.**

Чувствителен к
The interlock **is sensitive to** downward pressure if ...

Чувствительность к радиации
The lethal dosage level depends on **the radiation sensitivity of** the organism.

Чувствительный к
This type of boiler **is** more **responsive** (*or* **sensitive**) **to** changes in pressure.

Чувствительный к гамма-лучам
A **gamma-ray-sensitive** instrument ...

Чувствительный к свету
Light-sensitive (*or* **Sensitive to light,** *or* **Photosensitive**) materials ...

Чувствительный к инфракрасному излучению
An **infrared-sensitive** instrument.

Чувствительный к ... цвету
The **green-** (**red-** etc.) **sensitive** retina ...

Чувство ориентации
Man is not gifted with **a directional sense** as some of the lower animals seem to be.

Чувствовать себя хорошо
A number of patients **do well** for years with very little therapy.

Чудеса инженерного гения
These **marvels of mechanical ingenuity ...**

Чуждый
The idea of quantum jumps **was alien to** traditional physics.

Чужеродный
Waterdrops containing **foreign** particles ...

Чуть выше
The hot body is at a temperature **just (barely) higher than ...**

Чуть меньше
If the regeneration **is just** (*or* **slightly,** *or* **somewhat**) **less than** the amount necessary to cause oscillations, ...
The half-life of thoron **is just under** a minute.

Чуть меньше, чем за
Such an astronaut would complete his circuit **in just under** ninety minutes.

Чуть ниже
The image is formed **just** (*or* **slightly,** *or* **somewhat**) **below** the centre of the objective, ...

Чуть превышен
Add solvent to the crude mixture until the solubility of the desired compound **is just exceeded.**

Чуть-чуть
If the body moves **ever so slightly** (*or* **a trifle**) off position, ...

Ш

Шаг вперёд [*см. тж.* **Большой шаг вперёд**]
A step forward in this direction was made by ...

Шаг за шагом
The reader is urged to examine each proof carefully, **step by step** (*or* **stepwise**).
It is best to adopt a practical **step-by-step** approach.

Шаг на пути к
Steps on the road to continuous operation are made ...

Шагнуть далеко вперёд
Optical computing **has evolved dramatically** in the years since ...

Шарнирно закреплённый на
An aileron is an auxiliary surface usually **hinged** (*or* **pivoted**) **to** the trailing edge of a wing.

Шарнирный [*см. тж.* **На шарнирах**]
The work head **is articulated,** and the part

carrying the drill holder oscillates about a horizontal axis.
A **swivel-mounted** wheel head ...

Шейка капли
Flow separation occurs near **the drop waist.**

Шероховатость I
Surface **irregularities** (*or* **roughness**) ...

Шероховатость II
Many errors and **roughnesses** remain in the book under review.

Шестерня [*см.* **Соединён шестерней с**].

Ширина ... составляет от ... до
The valley **ranges in width from** 30 **to** 60 km.

Шириной [*см. тж.* **Длиной**]
A slit 1 mm **wide** (*or* **of width** 1 mm) ...

Широкая публика
Making its initial appearance to **the general public** at the exhibition was the hydraulic ...

Широкие исследования
Extended (*or* **Extensive**) **studies.**
Widespread investigation.

Широкий [*см* . **В широком диапазоне**].

Широкий ассортимент
A broad spectrum of mechanisms ...
High production rates can be obtained for **a wide range** (*or* **variety**) **of** plastics.
Chamfering tools come **in a wide range of** sizes and configurations.
A broad assortment of wrenches ...

Широкий интерес к
This **widespread interest in** chemical lasers ...

Широко дискутироваться
The nature of this bond **is the subject of considerable discussion** (*or* **controversy**).

Широко известен как
The *W*-like part of the constellation **is popularly** (*or* **widely**) **known as** Cassiopeia's chair.

Широко изучаться
This phenomenon **has been much investigated.**
Gas absorption by liquid jets **has been studied extensively** in recent years.

Широко использовать
The metallurgical industry **makes wide use of** lime.
This radar system **makes good use of** silicon chips.
The metal industry **uses** silicon carbide **extensively.**
He **drew heavily on** alchemical notions.
For this purpose, geologists **widely accept** a system known as ...
We **lean heavily on** this technique.

Широко использовать опыт
The firm **is leaning heavily on the experience from** the program.

Широко использоваться
The compound **is in considerable use as** a catalyst.
In the field of organic chemistry the combustion reactions **are of great utility.**
Some of these solutions **are commonly** (*or* **widely,** *or* **extensively**) **used,** others are used very infrequently.
Extensive use is made of electric cables manufactured by ...
Carbon steel **is extensively** (*or* **heavily**) **used** (*or* **enjoys wide use**) **in ...**
Because of the widespread availability of ac power, ac motors **are in common use.**
This indicator **is in general use.**
Hard chrome plating **is used extensively** (*or* **has found wide use**) **in** engine repair work.
There are other abrasive materials whose **use is widespread.**
Ample (*or* **Great,** *or* **Much**) **use is made of** the laboratories at the mine.
There is wide use of Type 347 stainless steel.
Glass wool **is widely used** (*or* **employed**) **as** a filtering material.
The hack watch **has a wide use in** navigation.
Miniature cameras **are much used** (*or* **are in wide use**).

Широко использоваться в области
Satellite communications over the last quarter of a century **have gained widespread acceptance in** long-distance telephony.

Широко использоваться при
Reconstruction of Precambrian geologic history **relies heavily on** radiometric dating (*при воспроизведении ... широко используется ....*)

Широко используемый
A **much used** equation ...
Two such electrodes having these properties and **in common use** are based on ...

Широко используется в настоящее время
Several rotary drilling techniques **are of considerable current use.**

Широко обсуждаться
The possible existence of such matter **is the subject of wide speculation.**

Широко освещается в литературе
This effect **is the subject of a considerable literature** (*or* **is widely covered in the literature**).

Широко освещать данную область
As a survey paper, it **covers the field broadly.**

Широко открыт
When the valves **are wide open, ...**

Широко практиковаться
Both types of tests **are in common practice.**

Широко применяемый в
The pure crystals **required for much of** the modern solid state technology are prepared by ...

Широко применяться [*см. тж.* **Широко использоваться**]
This method **enjoys wide application.**
These solutions **are used widely** (*or* **extensively**).
The method **is practised** (*or* **employed,** *or* **applied**) **widely.**
Power cranes, shovels and scoops **are actively engaged in** earth-moving operations.

Широко распространено мнение о том, что
It is widely believed that the supplies of fuel ...

Широко распространён [*см. тж.* **Часто встречаться**]
The term orogeny **was in general use.**
Rhabdoviruses **are of widespread occurrence** throughout the Metazoa.
Chitin **occurs widely** (*or* **is common**) in nature.
Carbon **is extensively distributed** [*or* **is abundant** (*or* **widespread**)] in nature.
This vitamin **is widely distributed** (*or* **present**) in foods.

Широко распространённый среди
One type of plotter, **in wide use** among air navigators, is shown in Fig. 2.

Широко расставленные
Widely spaced rails ...

Широкое применение [*см. тж.* **Находить широкое применение**]
This has led to **widespread use of** road-making machines.

Широкое разнообразие [*см. тж.* **Ввиду широкого разнообразия ...**]
Such **wide diversity** in the structure of these crystals ...
The wide range (*or* **variety**) **of** drilling methods ...

Широкораспространённое мнение
Until 1956, **it was widely believed** [*or* **it was a widespread opinion** (*or* **belief**)] **that** such molecules enter cells passively.

Широкораспространённый
Bornite is a **widely occurring** mineral.
Induction heating is **a widely accepted** (*or* **used**) method.
Ordinary luminous bacteria of the *saprophytic* type **are widely distributed** (*or* **widespread**) sea organisms.
This is a practical and **often used** pump source for rhodamine 6G (*lasers*).
A more **widely held** hypothesis is that ...

Шкала [*см.* **На шкале, Наносить шкалу, По всей шкале, По шкале**].

Школа (*учёных*)
There are at present two major **schools of thought** concerning the nature of the ageing process.

Шлифовать [*см.* **Зашлифовывать**].

Шлифовать на станке
Spiral points **are machine ground.**

Шлифовать начисто
After annealing these surfaces **have to be ground smooth.**

Шлифовать с высокой степенью точности
The drill **is precision ground.**

Шлифовать стеклянной бумагой
After allowing the undercoating to dry hard and **glass-papering** it, ...

Шпонка [*см.* **Закреплять на шпонках**].

Штат [*см.* **Иметь штат**].

Штрих [*см.* **Со штрихом** (*антон.* **Без штриха**)].

Штриховать [*см.* **Заштрихованный**].

Шум взрыва [*см.* **Гул взрыва**].

Щ

Щелочные условия
Basic conditions.

Э

ЭВМ [*см.* **Закладывать в компьютер, Управляемый компьютером**].

Эквивалент
The engine's relatively open flow path allows it to "breathe" far more easily than its piston-engine **counterpart.**
This is **the** laser **equivalent to** (*or* **of**) the cascade emission observed in several rare earths.

Эквивалентный [*см.* **На равных основаниях** (*или* **правах**)].

Эквивалентный объём
The system can handle up to 960 voice channels or **the equivalent** in other forms of information.

Экономить
The method **offers savings in** (*or* **saves**) production time.

Экономить время
The system is **a** real **time saver.**

Экономить время и деньги
Assembly with adhesives **can be a time and money saver.**

Экономически осуществимый
Only the ready regenerability of the catalyst makes it **economically feasible** to use the process for ...

Экономически целесообразный
The proposed laser-initiated fusion-power plant **would be economically attractive** even if the capital cost were twice as high.

Экономически эффективный
The engineer can plan an **economic(al)** process for large-scale production of new substances.

Экономичное производство
In order to make possible **the economic manufacture of** the cam, ...

Экономичность
Decisions must be made on **the economic feasibility of** each proposed chemical process.

Экономия
The economy (*or* **saving**) **in** the material used ...
Further **savings in** costs of administration and equipment are accomplished.

Экономия материала
The new process enables **savings in material** to be made by comparison with the earlier techniques.

Экономия места [*см.* **Для экономии места**].

Экономия на
Savings in computer time ...

Экономия рабочей силы
Labour saving through mechanization ...

Экономящий время и деньги
This is but one example of the **time- and cost-saving** facilities.

Экран [*см.* **Демонстрироваться на экране**].

Экранироваться
The area surrounding the portion being welded **is shielded by** the inert gas.

Экскурс в [*см.* **Делать экскурс в историю**].

Эксперимент [*см.* **В условиях эксперимента, Методика эксперимента, Опыт, Проведение эксперимента, Ставить опыт**].

Экспериментальная партия
The machines are turning out 10-piece **pilot lots** for prototypes.

Экспериментальная установка
The experimental arrangement (*or* **set-up**) is shown in Fig. 21.

Экспериментально доступный
The **experimentally accessible** molar quantities ...

Экспериментально обнаружено, что
It has been found experimentally that ...

Экспериментальное устройство [*см.* **Экспериментальная установка**].

Экспериментальные данные
The experimental evidence (*or* **data**) provided by this plot is reassuring.

Экспериментальный
Pilot programmes are needed to develop ...

Экспериментальным путём
It is also possible to learn much about ... **by an experimental approach** [*or* **experiment(ation)**].
Experimentally, we find that the boiling point of ... is higher than ...

Эксплуатация [*см. тж.* **В условиях эксплуатации, Вступать в эксплуатацию, Вывод из эксплуатации, Выводить из эксплуатации, Находиться в эксплуатации, Пускать в эксплуатацию, Работа, Условия эксплуатации**]
After five years of **service** (*or* **operation**) the unit shows little wear.

Экстраполировать
It is possible **to extrapolate** heat-capacity data **to** absolute zero.

Экстремальный
In **extreme** cases over 30 tons of water have to be removed for each ton of coal mined.
Under **extreme** conditions of temperature and pressure ...

Эксцентрично по отношению к
The water-ring revolves **eccentric to** the blades.

Эксцентричный по отношению к
The inner rotor **is eccentric to** the outer rotor.

Эластичный
The entire mechanism is mounted on **resilient** rubber cushions.
Stretch hosiery.

Электрический привод [*см.* **Работать от электропривода, С электрическим приводом**].

Электроизоляционные свойства
This polymer has useful **electrical insulation properties.**

Электронное управление [*см.* **С электронным управлением**].

Электропокрытие серебром
A complex *dicyanosilver* (I) ion is used in **electroplating with silver.**

Электростанция на ископаемом топливе
A fossil-fuelled power plant.

Электростанция на угле
A coal-fired power station.

Элементарная ячейка (*крист.*)
The unit cell.

Элементарные знания
Anyone with **a rudimentary knowledge of** algebra could ...

Элементарный углерод, сера *и т.п.*
Elemental carbon, sulphur, etc.

Эллипс [*см.* **По эллипсу**].

Эмбриональное состояние [*см.* **Находиться в эмбриональном состоянии**].

Эмпирическое правило
The machine-tool relay is a relatively slow-operating device and thus **a** good **rule of thumb would be to** allow one and a half cycles of electrical time for energizing and deenergizing of the device.
A good **rule of thumb is** 2 hp per square inch per minute cutting rate.
Empirical guidelines to follow ...

Энергетика

An analysis of **the energetics of** fragment ion formation shows that ...

Энергетические запасы организма
The principal **energy stores of the body** are in the form of fat.

Энергетические ресурсы
The mineral and **energy resources of ...**

Энергично
The gold leaf responds quickly and **vigorously** (*or* **energetically**) to small electrostatic forces.

Энергия [*см.* **Выделяемая энергия, Высокой энергии, Запасённая энергия, Обладать меньшей энергией, чем; Освобождать энергию, Подводить энергию к, Расход энергии**].

Энергия луча повышается
The electron **beam is raised to a** maximum **energy of** 21 GeV.

Энергия не появляется и не исчезает
Energy cannot be created or destroyed.

Энергия передаётся
Energy is transferred from the laser photons **to ...**

Энергия разрыва связи
Bond dissociation, or rupture, energies are referred to as **bond strengths.**

Энергия ... увеличивается
The radiation **becomes more energetic.**

Эпохальный
The induction coil played a central role in three **epoch-making** discoveries.

Эрудирован
Practicing chemists **have to be well versed in** their areas of specialization.
Researchers **must be knowledgeable in** two diverse fields.

Эталон
In scientific work, **the reference is** usually water at 4°C.
This exposure is **a standard** to which similar sequences may be compared when correlations are made (*geol.*).
This criterion is still in general use as **a** convenient **yardstick for** measuring the extent to which losses must be controlled in order to ...

Эталон давления
The reference pressure is usually taken as 0.0002 dynes/cm^2, or 0.0002 microbar.

Этап [*см.* **В несколько этапов, В ... приёмов, На этой стадии, Стадия**].

Этапами
The specimen was warmed **by stages.**

Этим не исчерпывается
The similarity of the two substances **extends further.**

Этим ограничивается сходство
The new projectors look like other projectors, and **right there the similarity ends.**

Это I
The boiling point of a pure liquid **is defined as** the temperature at which ...

Это II
Sinusoidally varying quantities can be represented by complex rotating vectors. **Doing so** greatly simplifies ...

Это, в общем, согласуется с
This is in general agreement with the existence of ...

Это важно учесть при выборе
This has an important bearing on the method of ventilation.

Это видно (*или* **явствует**) **из**
This is apparent (*or* **evident**) **from** Fig. 9.10.
This is evidenced by the absence of hot bands in the spectrum.

Это возможно
This is a possibility (*or* **is possible**).

Это впечатление обманчиво
This impression is wrong.

Это – всё равно, что сказать
This is the same as saying there is a set that ...
This is another way of stating that ...
This is tantamount to stating that the chain elongation was adversely influenced.

Это – все, что мы можем сделать в области
This is as far as we can go with a thermodynamic treatment.

Это вызвано тем, что
This is due to the fact that ...

Это выражается в том, что
This is reflected in the fact that ...

Это далеко не всегда так
The mechanism proved satisfactory over a wide range of temperatures, but **this is by no means always the case.**

Это действительно так
A close look at the map will show that **this is the case** (*or* **this is so indeed,** *or* **this is true**).

Это достигается за счёт (*или* **ценой**) **потери** [*см. тж.* **За счёт**]
One can increase the resolution, but **a price must be paid in** a loss of light intensity.

Это ещё надо доказать
This has yet to be proved.

Это ещё не всё
However, **the story is not complete,** because the ability to ignore loads can be increased by ...
This is not the whole story, however.

Это имеет место
Actually **this is true** only when the electrons remain confined to ...

Это к делу не относится
The surface area of ... is equal to ..., but **that is irrelevant.**

Это как раз (и есть) тот
This is just the condition under which a convective flow can be established.

Это – лишь несколько примеров
Our industry has achieved many successes in such fields as aerospace, nuclear energy and electronics **to name only a few.**
This just starts the list.

Это маловероятно
Either ion would require a four-electron change and **this is unlikely.**

Это можно осуществить путём
This can be arranged by boiling ...
One way to do this is to use ...

Это можно осуществить с помощью
The way to do this is through an interference effect.
A pumping unit **will do the trick.**

Это название объясняется тем, что
This name arose (*or* **comes,** *or* **is derived**) **from the fact that ...**

Это не всегда так
This is not always the case.
This is not true in all cases.

Это не имеет места
This is not the case when the mutant gene is dominant.

Это не обязательно означает, что
This does not necessarily mean that diffusion is slower in liquids.

Это не обязательно так
This is not necessarily so (*or* **the case**).

Это не означает, что
Presumably the human species is no exception. **This is not to say that** our present gene pool is an optimum one.

Это не относится к
Such is not the case for all fluid logic elements.

Это – не просто совпадение
It is no coincidence that those planets all have rings.

Это не так [*см. тж.* **А на самом деле это не так**]
In quantum mechanics, however, **such** (*or* **this**) **is not the case.**

Это не так уж удивительно [*см. тж.* **Этому едва ли следует удивляться**]
This is not particularly surprising.

Это не удивительно
This is no surprise (*or* **not surprising**), since the first step of the two-step interaction is rather improbable.

Это объясняется тем, что [*см.* **Причина состоит в том, что**].

Это означает, что
In this case the reaction is exothermic; **that is (to say that)** energy is released.
What this means is (*or* **By this is meant that**) classical broad-band excitation of the S_1 state results in ...

Это особенно относится к
People with poor eyesight tend to show an unusually large amount of finger tremor. **This is particularly true of** (*or* **for**) far-sighted individuals.
This is especially true in regard to the RNA molecules.

Это особенно относится к случаям, когда
This is especially true where the area is a few square miles.

Это, по–видимому, действительно так
This appears to be the case.

Это происходит потому, что
The reason is that such a solid is made up of ...

Это так
That **such is the case** is suggested by ...

Это также не
Nor does it prove that heating due to radioactivity is the cause of the circulation.

Это также относится к
The two rotations have the same character, **so also do** (*or* **and so do**) the reflections through each of the three planes.
A similar statement is true for (*or* **of**) double-stranded DNA.
The screw characteristic will modify the cylinder length required, **this** (*or* **the same**) **is also true of** (*or* **for**) the operation temperatures in ...

Это указывает на целесообразность
This suggests the use of supersonic nozzle beams.

Это явно указывает на
This clearly demonstrates the essentially statistical character of the pressure.

Это явствует из
This is evident from the equilibrium relation.

Этого нельзя сказать о
Essentially similar events seem to characterize the muscle-cell potential, but **this is not true of** (*or* **for**) all cells.
The same cannot be said of certain other particles.

Этому едва ли следует удивляться
This is scarcely surprising.

Этот вопрос ещё окончательно не решён
Recognition of the tRNA by the ligase may or may not involve the anticodon — **this point has not been finally established** (*biol.*).

Эффект [*см.* **Давать наибольший эффект, Давать необходимый эффект**].

Эффективен [*см. тж.* **Весьма эффективен**]
The method **performs well.**
The human kidney **is** very **competent at** conserving sodium.

Эффективен для
This procedure **is** particularly **advantageous for** determinations at low levels.
The method **works for** all the patients alike.

Эффективен с точки зрения
The lens **is efficient at** increasing source efficiency.

Эффективнее [*см.* **Более эффективный**].

Эффективнее в 4 раза
The unit **outproduces** a conventional machine **up to 4:1.**

Эффективнее в ... раз
The 200-inch Palomar telescope **outperforms** Galileo's telescope **by a factor of** 40,000.

Эффективно
Magnetic separators **do a good job of** removing metallic material from ...
These components **will be adequately** cooled by the fluid flow.
The unique characteristics of lasers can be applied **validly** (*or* **profitably**) to analytical *MI* fluorimetry.
Nonvolatile fuels are burned **to advantage** in these engines.

Эффективно использовать
New efforts are needed **to turn** collective effects **to good advantage.**
To make good use of the new machines, ...

Эффективность
The performance of the telescope (engine, etc.) is limited by ...
The proof of **the validity of** this design lies in ...

The only way to attain **proficiency** (*or* **efficiency**) in the use of this computer is through practice.

Эффективность повышается с опытом
Proficiency (*or* **Efficiency**) in this skill **improves with practice** (*or* **experience**).

Эффективный [*см. тж.* **Высокоэффективный, Давать хорошие результаты, Целесообразный**]
Profitable operation of high-speed machine-tools ...
Hydrogen **is attractive as** a fuel.
This practice **is** more **appropriate** than changing the course of rivers.
Before **adequate** methods had been developed, ...
This theory does not always **work.**

Эффективный метод
A powerful (*or* **efficient,** *or* **proficient**) **method.**

Ю

Южный конец стрелки компаса [*см.* **Северный конец стрелки компаса**].

Юпитер
Exploration of the **Jovian** (*or* **of Jupiter's**) surface ...

Я

Явление
Liberation of chemical energy by combustion is **an** everyday **occurrence** (*or* **event**) of great importance in ...
The phenomenon of osmosis depends on such ...

Являться [*см. тж.* **Если он является, Представлять собой**]
The numbers 235 and 238 **represent** (*or* **are**) the mass numbers of the two isotopes of uranium.
The electron **makes** a better probe of the structure of matter.
The existence of a predicted isomerism **provides** (*or* **furnishes,** *or* **offers**) one of the most important confirmations of ...
The shock wave method **constitutes** a useful addition to the present techniques.

Являться вполне достаточным
Two different isoacceptors for a given amino acid **could well suffice.**

Являться главной причиной
This component **is primarily responsible for** the properties of the compound.

Являться доказательством того, что
The presence of porphyrins **is proof that** all the oil was derived from ...

Являться загадкой для
The structure of benzene **presented a puzzle for** chemists of the 19th century.

Являться заслугой
Credit for this **goes to** the computer.

Являться значительным препятствием
The nonuniformity of whiskers **presents a major obstacle.**

Являться инициатором
He **pioneered** the development of ...

Являться исключением из правила
This is the only reactor **exempted from the** indicated **rule.**

Являться исключением в том смысле (*или* **отношении**), **что**
The step-index profile **is exceptional in that** we can solve ...

Являться конкурентом
At one time the zeppelins **offered** serious **competition to** ocean liners.

Являться наиболее перспективным
For meeting the transmission needs of the more distant future the superconducting cable **offers** (*or* **holds**) **the greatest promise.**

Являться началом (**концом** *и т.п.*)
These developments **marked the beginning** (**end**, etc.) **of ...**

Являться неожиданностью для
The general adult deficiency in lactose **has come as a surprise to** physiologists.

Являться общим для
A number of features of DNA replication **are shared by both** prokaryotes **and** eukaryotes (*biol.*).
The two central carbon atoms are held together by a double bond, which means that the electron pairs **are shared by** these carbons.

Являться объектом исследования
Molecular diffusion in binary gas systems **has been the subject of investigation** for nearly a century.

Являться одним из
Glycine **ranked among** the most abundant products of experimental prebiotic syntheses.

Являться одной из основных причин
Systemic sclerosis does not **feature prominently among** the causes of disphagia.

Являться основной причиной
This **is mainly responsible for** the initial loss of weight.

Являться основой для
The maps **provided a basis for** the correlation of the rock units.

Являться предметом исследований
This **has been the subject of** some mathematical **studies.**

Являться предметом особого внимания
Copper **has been the object of much** concentrated **attention.**

Являться примером
The carbohydrates **exemplify** these stereochemical concepts.
The isolation and purification of the ergot alkaloids **exemplify** the methods used.
These projects **exemplify** the planning ability of the civil engineer.
This **provides an example of** an entropy discontinuity.
These minerals **serve as examples of** structural types.

Являться примером универсальности
A battery of machines built recently by ... **provides an example of the versatility of** the basic equipment.

Являться причиной [*см. тж.* **Быть причиной, Вызывать**]
Nucleic acids **are responsible for** protein synthesis.
Such diseases **are responsible for** (*or* **are the cause of**) much illness and death.
Information of this kind **has given rise to** fears that ...
The diffusion drag forces **may account for** the interactions between cells.

Являться прямой противоположностью
The formation of a compound from its elements **is (just) the opposite of** the decomposition of the compound to the component elements.

Являться результатом (*или* **следствием**) [*см. тж.* **Вызван, Вытекать из**]
The first term **is due to** the repulsion between molecules.
The wealth of structural information **arises from** differences in band position, shape and intensity.
This shape of the ray path **is a consequence** (*or* **result**) **of** the invariance ...
The small droplets **stem from** the condensation of vapours.
The discovery of beryllium **resulted from** the observation that ...

Являться свидетельством этого
The world tends towards order, not disorder; every snowflake **bears witness to** the fact.
This **constitutes** (*or* **is**) **evidence that** the ring remains intact.

Являться символом
The familiar pattern of electrons orbiting a nucleus **stands for** scientific knowledge and progress.

Являться средством
The clutch **provides** (*or* **offers**) **the means for** disconnecting the engine from ...
Micelles **provide an** additional **means of** creating droplets with ...

Являться типичным представителем
Cane or beet sugar, starch **may be cited as typical representatives of** this group.

Являться убедительным доказательством
This **proves conclusively** the advantage of ...
Infrared spectra of amino acids **furnish convincing proof that** the structures are best represented by ...
The project **provided a convincing demonstration** (*or* **proof**) **of ...**

Являться указанием на то, что
The angular unconformity **is evidence of** a vast erosion period (*geol.*).

Являться хорошим примером этого
The mosquito vectors of malaria **provide a good example.**

Являться частью [*см.* **Составлять часть**].

Являться шагом вперёд в области
The most recent system **takes** the overhead stacker crane feeding concept **a step further.**

Явно
The activities of ... are not **explicitly** included.
Where data are missing or **obviously** unreliable, ...
The maps show that such craters are **distinctly** fewer in number than was predicted.

Явно указывать на
This behaviour **points clearly to** the presence of ...

Явное доказательство [*см.* **Имеются явные доказательства того, что**].

Явный [*см.* **В явном виде**].

Явный абсурд
The argument that the electron mass is infinite **is a manifest absurdity.**

Явствовать из [*см. тж.* **Из ... видно, что; Из ... явствует, что**]
This **is apparent** (*or* **evident**) **from** the linear property of Eq. (15).
The strong tendency of water and ammonia to combine **is evidenced by** (*or* **is obvious from**) the very high solubility of ammonia in water.

Явствовать непосредственно из
An important property of tensors **is immediately evident from** Eq. (2.3).

Ядовит для [*см.* **Весьма ядовит для**].

Ядовит для человека
This insecticide **is toxic to man** (*or* **humans**).

Яркий I
Evidently many quasars are up to 100 times more **luminous** than ordinary galaxies.

Яркий II
A **dramatic** (*or* **brilliant,** *or* **spectacular**) proof is provided by ...

Яркий пример
The pocket electronic calculator **is** perhaps the most **dramatic** (*or* **prominent**) **example of** a new electronic instrument requiring a digital display.
One **glowing example of** good computer operation is ...

Ярко выделяться на фоне
Noctilucent clouds **stand out sharply against** the twilight sky.

Ярко выражен [*см. тж.* **Чётко выраженный**]
Changes in the band intensities **are** usually very much more **pronounced** (*or* **marked,** *or* **clear cut,** *or* **clearly defined**).

Ярко выражен у
Electronegativity is more **pronounced with** small atoms.

Ярко гореть
Clean magnesium **burns brilliantly** (*or* **with great brilliancy**) if heated in steam.

Ярко демонстрировать
The effectiveness of such systems **has been demonstrated** most **clearly** at ...

Ярко освещён
The cars **are brilliantly lighted.**

Ярко светиться
The centromeric regions of mammalian chromosomes **fluoresce** (*or* **glow**) **brightly** when thus stained.

Яркость звезды [*см. тж.* **В период наибольшей яркости**]
The luminosity (*or* **brightness**) **of a star.**

Яркость звезды возрастает в ... раз
The star flares up to hundreds of millions **of times** its former brightness.

Яркость кометы
Cometary brightness (*or* **The brightness of a comet**).

Яркость освещения
Lighting brilliancy is adjustable.

Ясно [*см.* **Абсолютно ясно, Чётко**].

Ясно виден
The foliation bands **are clearly visible.**

Intermediate gas distributions **are readily apparent** in observatory pictures.

Ясно отдавать себе отчёт в [*см.* **Остро сознавать**].

Ясно показывать, что
This record **makes it clear that** the difference ...

Ясно представлять себе [*см.* **Чётко представлять себе**].

Ясно сознавать [*см.* **Чётко представлять себе**].

Ясно, что [*см. тж.* **Совершенно ясно, что**]
It is apparent that these effects are ...
It was obvious that the particle has mass.

Ясное представление о [*см. тж.* **Иметь ясное представление о том**]
We have **a clear knowledge** (*or* **idea**) **of ...**

Ясность изложения
The clarity of presentation.

Ящик для запчастей и принадлежностей
A spares and accessories kit.